THE OFFICIAL® PRICE GUIDE TO

POTTERY
AND
PORCELAIN

THE OFFICIAL® PRICE GUIDE TO

POTTERY
AND
PORCELAIN

HARVEY DUKE

EIGHTH EDITION

HOUSE OF COLLECTIBLES • NEW YORK

Important Notice. All of the information, including valuations, in this book has been compiled from the most reliable sources, and every effort has been made to eliminate errors and questionable data. Nevertheless, the possibility of error, in a work of such immense scope, always exists. The publisher will not be held responsible for losses that may occur in the purchase, sale, or other transaction of items because of information contained herein. Readers who feel they have discovered errors are invited to *write* and inform us, so they may be corrected in subsequent editions. Those seeking further information on the topics covered in this book are advised to refer to the complete line of *Official Price Guides* published by the House of Collectibles.

To M. J. "Gus" Gustafson

for his friendship, support,
and just plain common sense

I've never regretted any of my purchases,
I've only regretted the things I didn't buy.
—BILL STERN

*This postcard reads: "A View of the Pottery District, Trenton, N.J." Someone
has written: "The most miserable place in Trenton. How would you like to
have to live in this district?"*

CONTENTS

ACKNOWLEDGMENTS

This book is more than just a price guide to me; it represents the pottery community, which is why I include clubs, newsletters, and books. This book represents input from all types of people—advanced collectors, in-depth dealers, club leadership, newsletter editors, and many authors—who have come together to make it as valuable as it is. It is their love of pottery and their generosity that give this book its depth and breadth.

I ask more of my consultants than many price guide editors, and I believe their hard work shows. I thank them all. They are all listed in the Consultants section which follows.

In addition, there were people and organizations who gave valuable assistance in many other ways:

Abingdon Collectors Club; Al Alberts; Robert and Edith Andrews; Glenn Appleman; Archives Center of the Museum of American History of the Smithsonian Institute; Paul Beedenbender; Dale Blann; Jay Blumenfeld and Mark Taylor, aficionados of Metlox produce; Ed Carson of Homer Laughlin, retired, for his help and his playfulness; Jack Chipman, whose excellent research enhances the histories of the California potteries included in this book, for his unflagging support; Paul Cuba; Sydney and Gary Darwin, of Cardinal China; Mr. Tom Dillard and the University of Central Arkansas Archives and Special Collections for giving me access to the Arkansas Art Pottery Research Materials; Judy Doyle; Jeff Eling of the Zanesville Library; Don Feldmeyer; Steve Finer; Lois Finnerty, 9167 Pekin Road, Novelty, Ohio 44072, one of my favorite dealers who always manages to find something I want; Dan Fortney; Betty Franks; Doris Frizzell; Bill Gates of the Ohio Historical Society; Linda and Richard Guffey; Norman Haas; the Hall China Company; Burdell and Doris Hall, always ready to lend a hand; Virginia Heiss who, with her husband Willard, did the original research on the Ransburg Pottery; Gordon Hoppe; Paul Isbell; Paul Jeromack; Doreen Johnson; Larry Jones; Allan Kaufman of Boro Photo for his professional guidance; Nicol Knappen, for his support and help; the Homer Laughlin China Company; Lois Lehner, for sharing her vast research; Rose Lindner; Susan Moore; Paul Moore; Esther Meyers, gracious and knowledgeable; the New York Public Library; the Ohio Historical Society; James and Shirley Parks; Diane Petipas of Mood Indigo in NYC; the Pfaltzgraff Pottery Company; Stan Pawlewski; Judy Posner, expert on all things figural—if it has a face, ask Judy; Ray Reiss; Brenda Roberts; Luke Ruepp; Ed Rutkowski; the Scio Pottery Company; Elizabeth Scott; Karen Silvermintz; Fran and Carl Stone; Ed Stump; Harvey Takasugi; Terry Telford, his keen eye and sharp mind have added immensely to this book; Jeff Thomas, at the OHS Archives; Tom Uebelhor; Uhl Collectors Society; Dave Walsh, Archivist, The Pfaltzgraff Pottery Company; and Rick Wisecarver.

Most important, I want to thank my friends, whose love is a life preserver on the stormy seas of life: Dave Caouette, Gus Gustafson, Pat Lyons, Gene and Mickey Meier, Jeff "JW" Nesler, Bob and Nancy Perzel, Todd Rinehart, and Alfred Zaher and Tom Buckley.

CONSULTANTS

Pottery people are special. And my consultants particularly so. Most of them were strangers to me when I first contacted them, but they didn't hesitate to say yes when I asked them to help.

And they do a lot more than most consultants. They might help create the chapters, correct my errors, add insight and wisdom from their own experience and research, and, as if that isn't enough, they help price. Whew! Which is why I list them with pride at the front of this book. Many of them are authors and I highly recommend their books (see Bibliography).

If you have any questions concerning the potteries and categories listed below, please write to my consultants. I will only be passing on your letters to them, so this will save you time. For potteries not listed here, or if you have any items that should be added to the listings, please write to me at the address below.

When writing to any of us, please type or clearly print your letter and be as *brief* as possible (do not exceed one page). Please keep questions to a minimum—one or two at the most, and make them specific. Any questions requiring a long answer—such as "Tell me all you know about such and such"—is unfair. Remember, the consultants and I answer questions as a courtesy to you, please be courteous to us.

We do not price unlisted items.

Most important, enclose a self-addressed, stamped envelope if you wish a reply.

Keep in mind, a sketch is better than a description, and a photo is better than a sketch. Please do not ask anyone to price unlisted items. I have indicated with a (C) or a (D) in the list below which consultants are collectors and/or dealers. Please do not ask collectors where to get pottery or if we have anything for sale; it is not appropriate.

Finally, many of these consultants have become good friends and that is the best part of doing this book.

My Address: Harvey Duke, 115 Montague Street, Brooklyn, New York 11201.

Abingdon

Robert Rush (C), 210 North Main Street, Abingdon, IL 61410.
Elaine Westover (C), Rt. 1, Box 145, Abingdon, IL 61410.

American Bisque

Joyce Roerig (C/D), Rt. 2, Box 504, Walterboro, SC 29488.

Bauer

Jack Chipman (C/D), PO Box 1079, Venice, CA 90291.

Buffalo

Phillip M. Sullivan (C), PO Box 69, South Orleans, MA 02662.

California Pottery

Jack Chipman (C/D), PO Box 1429, Redono Beach, CA 90278.

Camark

David Edwin Gifford (D), 12 Normandy Road, Little Rock, AR 72207.
Burdell and Doris Hall (C/D), PO Box 1501, Fairfield Bay, AR 72088.

Cardinal

Trish Claar (C), 2621 Manor Court, Owings, MD 20736.

Ceramic Art Studios

Jim Petzold (C), PO Box 46, Madison, WI 53701.

Cliftwood / Midwest

Burdell and Doris Hall (C/D), PO Box 1501, Fairfield Bay, AR 72088.

Cookie Jars

Joyce Roerig (C/D), Rt. 2, Box 504, Walterboro, SC 29488.

Coors

Robert Schneider and Margo Reheis (C), 3808 Carr Place North,
    Seattle, WA 98103.

Enesco

Steve Johnson (C), 4003 Jefferson Street, Sioux City, IA 51108.
Juarine Woolrich (C), RR 1, Box 13904, Cassville, MO 65625.

Figural Shakers

Larry Carey (C/D), PO Box 329, Mechanicsburg, PA 17055.

Florence

Jeanne Fredericks (C), 12364 Downey Avenue, Downey, CA 90242.
Sue and Jerry Kline (C/D), 913 East End Court, Gatlinburg, TN 37738.

Frankoma

Phyllis and Tom Bess (C/D), 14535 East 13th Street, Tulsa, OK 74108.

Gladding-McBean

James Elliott (C/D), 7345 35th Avenue NE, Seattle, WA 98115.
Marv Fogleman (C/D), 1914 West Carriage Drive, Santa Ana, CA 92704.

Gonder

John and Marilyn McCormick (C), 6400 Payne Street, Shawnee, KS 66226.

Hall

Elizabeth Boyce (C/D), 38 Carlotia Drive, Jeffersonville, IN 47130.
Jane and Don Warner-Smith (C/D), RR 1, Box 94B, Farmersville, IL 62533.

AUTUMN LEAF
Shirley Easley (C/D), 120 West Dowell Road, McHenry, IL 60050.

Homer Laughlin

Gus Gustafson (D), Buttzville Center, Box 106, Buttzville, NJ 07829.
Michael Haas (C/D), Buttzville Center, Box 106, Buttzville, NJ 07829.
Joanne Jasper (C/D), 28005 Balkins Drive, Agoura Hills, CA 91301.

FIESTA / HARLEQUIN / RIVIERA
Dennis Bialek (D), RD 4, Box 43, Hudson, NY 12534.

Hull

Barbara Burke (C), 4213 Sandhurst Drive, Orlando, FL 32813.
Joan Gray Hull (C), 1376 Nevada SW, Huron, SD 57350.
Brenda Roberts (C), Rt. 2, Highway 65 S, Marshall, MO 65340.

RED RIDING HOOD
The Twins Antiques & Collectables (C/D), Highway 242, Wayne City, IL 62895.

Iroquois

Paul Beedenbender (C), 1203 East Paris Street, Tampa, FL 33604.

McCoy

Jean Bushnell (C), 3081 Rock Creek Drive, Broomfield, CO 80020.
Joanne Lindberg (C/D), 79 Lexington Drive, Metuchen, NJ 08840.
Chiquita Prestwood (C/D), 120 Echo Drive, Lenoir, NC 28645.

Metlox

Carl Gibbs (C/D), 5513 Chenevert #1, Houston, TX 77004.
Marv Fogleman (C/D), 1914 West Carriage Drive, Santa Ana, CA 92704.

Morton

Burdell and Doris Hall (C/D), PO Box 1501, Fairfield Bay, AR 72088.

Niloak

David Gifford (C/D), 12 Normandy Road, Little Rock, AR 72207.
Burdell and Doris Hall (C/D), PO Box 1501, Fairfield Bay, AR 72088.

Parkcraft

Larry Carey (C/D), PO Box 329, Mechanicsburg, PA 17055.

Pennsbury

Joe Simone (C/D), 6 Duchess Lane, Dayton, NJ 08810.

Pfaltzgraff

Dave Walsh (C/D), The Pfaltzgraff Co., 140 East Market, York, PA 17401.
Dave Ziegler (C/D), RD 3, Box 3317, Spring Grove, PA 17362.

Ransburg

Jo Lauderdale (C), 2014 Richmond Road, Decatur, IL 62521.

Red Wing

Ron Linde (C), 11770 Falk Trail, Northfield, MN 55057.
Ray Reiss (C), 2144 North Leavitt, Chicago, IL 60647.

HAND-PAINTED DINNERWARE
Mary Bang (C/D), 5200 Duggan Plaza, Edina, MN 55439.
Monna Erickson (C/D), 1712 Harrison Court, Northfield, MN 55057.

Regal

Judy and Jeff Posner (C/D), RD 1, Box 273, Effort, PA 18330.

Rosemeade

Irene J. Harms (C), 2316 West 18th Street, Sioux Falls, SD 57104.

Roseville

Gordon Hoppe (C/D), 10120 32nd Avenue N., Plymouth, MN 55441
Tom Rago (D), 716 Silver Court, Hamilton Square, NJ 08690.

Royal

CURRIER & IVES
Betsey Edmondson (D), Betsey's Collectibles, 1404 Sylan Drive, Plano, TX 75074.

Rumrill

Mike Zaeske (C), 1796 North 9th Street, Kalamazoo, MI 49009.
Ron Linde (C), 11770 Falk Trail, Northfield, MN 55057.

Shawnee

Pam Curran (C), c/o Shawnee Club, PO Box 713, New Smyrna Beach, FL 32170.
Bev and Jim Mangus (C), 5147 Broadway NE, Louisville, OH 44641.
Duane and Janice Vanderbilt (C), 4040 Westover Drive, Indianapolis, IN 46268.

Southern Potteries

Don and Susan Burkett (C), 233 E. Wesley Road NE, Atlanta, GA 30305.
Susan Moore (C), 107 Yorkshire Circle, Lafayette, LA 70508.

Spaulding

Joe Devine (C/D), 1411 3rd Street, Council Bluffs, IA 51503.

Stanford

Kathy Kimball (C), Box 297-HCR-1, Grand Marais, MN 55604.

Stangl

Bob and Nancy Perzel (C/D), c/o Popkorn, 4 Mine Street, Flemington, NJ 08822.

Tamac

Phyllis and Tom Bess (C/D), 14535 East 13th Street, Tulsa, OK 74108.

Taylor, Smith & Taylor

LURAY
Ed Nenstiel, 4327 Ravensworth Road #125, Annandale, VA 22003.

Treasure Craft

Joyce Roerig (C/D), Rt. 2, Box 504, Walterboro, SC 29488.

Twin Winton

Joyce Roerig (C/D), Rt. 2, Box 504, Walterboro, SC 29488.

Uhl

Tim Hodges (C), 1378 West Andrew Lane, Jasper, IN 47546.

Van Briggle

Scott Nelson (C), PO Box 6081, Santa Fe, NM 87502.

Vernon Kilns

Bess Christensen (C), 1313 East Locust Avenue, Lompoc, CA 93436.
Harold Mathews (C), 24 Church Street, Honeoye, NY 14471.
Maxine Feek Nelson (C/D), 873 Marigold Court, Carlsbad, CA 92008.
Bill Stern (C), 361 North Orange Drive, Los Angeles, CA 90036.
Judi and Dave Thompson (C/D), 1668 Melissa Way, Anaheim, CA 92802.

Wallace

Marv Fogleman (C/D), 1914 West Carriage Drive, Santa Ana, CA 92704.

Watt

Dennis Thompson (C), Box 26067, Fairview Park, OH 44126.

Willow

Connie Rogers (C), 1733 Chase Street, Cincinnati, OH 45223.

BUFFALO
Phillip M. Sullivan (C), PO Box 69, South Orleans, MA 02662.

PREFACE

This book is an ongoing project, constantly evolving. Though this is the eighth edition of the book, it is my second time in charge, and there's been a number of changes.

I've added some thirty new potteries to the listings, and almost every chapter from the last edition has been expanded, some minimally, many in a major way, making this the most comprehensive pottery guide in print. I've tried to make the book even more useful by introducing innovative pricing charts and special price lists where appropriate. In a number of instances, the listings are as complete as I can make them because I believe information on what is available is as valuable as the pricing information. And I've added the "Chapter at a Glance" feature to help you find your way more easily.

I've polished up the glossary, which I think is one of the most comprehensive and useful of any price guide, and I've expanded the bibliography and traveler's directory. The extensive club and newsletter listings reflect the vitality of the hobby. And I've added repair and replacement services, as well as an overview of reproductions.

This edition is "built" on the previous one. Most of the text and listings from the last edition have been retained (except those errors that crept in). And while I've added more photos and drawings and reshot some of the pottery from the last edition to make identification more comprehensive, much of the identification material has been kept so that this edition is self-contained; you should not need to refer to the previous edition for anything.

Most general price guides give you long lists of prices and not much more. Sometimes you have to know quite a bit to be able to use the prices accurately: what's popular, what's rare, for example. While there's no substitute for collecting experience—and even with this book, the more you know, the more useful the book will be—I try to mitigate the situation by including as much useful information as I have room for. And while a price guide is no substitute for visiting an extensive collection and being given a thorough tour, I try to approximate that to the extent that I can.

No general price guide is a substitute for a book devoted to one pottery, so I refer you to the bibliography. Because I cannot include the amount of information and photos that a book devoted to one specific pottery or subject can, it is important that you have these books. Indeed, a number of chapters in this book can be used as companions to a good book.

As many changes as I've made, there is still more I want to do. As Harry Rinker, the noted expert on antiques and collectibles, once said to me: "The third edition is what you would have done the first time if you could." I think he's right, so I hope to see you here for my third.

INTRODUCTION: HOW TO USE THIS BOOK

CHAPTER AT A GLANCE

I hope you read this section carefully. It gives you a framework for evaluating the information in the book.

Devices I Have Used

To save space and avoid repeating certain explanations, here is a list of various ways I have included information.

1. Gold trim is indicated as "w/gold." Pieces that are covered with gold are referred to as "allover gold."

2. An asterisk (*) after a size indicates that the size is approximate.

3. A slash (/) in the listings means "or" as in the following example:

Jug, ball, blue/green/yellow, 1-quart . . . . $35 – $45

This means that the price is the same for all three colors. If each color needs to be priced differently, the listing is as follows:

Jug, ball, 1-quart
  Blue . . . . $45 – $55
  Green . . . . 35 – 45
  Yellow . . . . 30 – 40

4. Sometimes cookie jars or other kitchen pieces will have words printed or embossed on the body. These follow the entry in quotes to aid in identification.

Cookie jar, Monk, "Thou Shalt Not Steal Cookies"
Scissor Nest w/bird on top, "Scissor Nest"

5. There is no standard way of listing, naming, or describing cookie jars. Sometimes we have names from catalog sheets, but not always. If the jar is just a dog, say, or a dinosaur, that's no problem. But if it's a woodpecker on an acorn, should it be listed as "Woodpecker on acorn" or "Acorn w/woodpecker finial"? I opt for the second in my listings.

6. If a cookie jar or other piece has a matching shaker, bank, or other items, it is listed with a small indent as follows:

Monk, "Thou Shall Not Steal"
  Bank
  Canister
  Shaker
Owl, w/glasses
  Bank
  Shakers

7. Color variations are listed with a larger indent:

Owl, w/glasses
    Brown
    Multicolored
  Bank
    Multicolored
  Shakers

8. Some figural items were made as matching left-facing and right-facing pieces. These usually have the same value and are listed as follows:

Bird, robin, left/right, 3"

Shape Numbers

Where shape numbers (sometimes called stock numbers) are known, they follow a slash in the listing. For example:

Vase, scalloped, 10"   /445

I have tried to list shape numbers wherever possible. Some manufacturers marked numbers fairly often; others never did. In the latter case, some authors have discovered old shape lists and published the information. I have discovered other lists myself. I have included these numbers as an aid to buying and selling.

Pricing

With every book I write, I find myself making stronger and stronger statements about pricing. How many more books I will write and where it will all end, I don't know. Here is my current thinking.

Pricing is the most difficult part of doing a book. The collecting is exciting, and there's a lot I've learned just from being a collector. Research can be tedious but has an excitement of its own, turning up information bit by bit and piecing it into a whole. Finally, putting the book together is a creative challenge, trying to organize lots of information in a cohesive manner. But I would avoid pricing if I could.

However, publishers, for the most part, won't touch a book without prices. They feel it won't sell, and I can't say they are wrong. I know there are many collectors who want information and would buy a book for that reason alone. But how many of them there are, no one can say, and publishers are not willing to take a chance when price guides are a proven success.

So what am I up against when I sit down to price a book? Several things.

HOW LONG HAS IT BEEN COLLECTED   Hall China, popularly collected for almost twenty years now, has fairly consistent national pricing. The gap in the price range is small, sometimes nonexistent. In contrast, when I did my first edition of this book, Florence Ceramics was up-and-coming and did not have consistent national pricing. The price range was wide.

GEOGRAPHICAL CONSIDERATIONS What kind of national sales and distribution did a pottery have? That is, is it found all over the country because it was originally available nationally? If it is, then I need to get a representative sampling of national prices.

What about potteries that had national distribution but most of their products are found in certain regions and states. California, where Bauer is in abundance, is far more representational than New York, where very little shows up. I cannot let odd New York prices affect the overall picture.

UNREALISTIC PRICES I ignore prices that are too low. We've all heard of great finds, but these aren't a valid consideration. Likewise, high inflated prices are also ignored. This is a difficult situation for me because there are those who will compare my prices with another's and determine mine are not valid because they are low. So I am stating here for the record that I stand by my prices. And I appreciate all the positive remarks about them that I have received.

A word about auction prices: In general, auction prices are considered wholesale prices. The occasional bidding war does not have validity in terms of the national market. An exception is the rare item—Roseville's Della Robbia, for example—that only turns up at auction. This is where the market is, so these are accurate retail prices.

RANGES Since I want my prices to reflect the market, there might be instances of wide ranges from the lower to the higher price. If a particular piece has been seen, say, at $50, at $70, at $80, and at $100, then the range is $50–$100. Pricing it at $70–$80 or at $75 is not accurate because it does not reflect the range.

DESIRABILITY Does an item's scarcity mean it is worth a lot of money? No. There are many pieces of Hall China, for example, that I have never seen or heard of being in a collection. A lot of these pieces are, at best, nondescript, certainly not exciting to most collectors. Their scarcity does not indicate great value.

I have asked my consultants to keep this in mind when pricing and to use their experience and intuition to correctly place things in the price spectrum.

BOOK PRODUCTION SCHEDULES Remember, too, that due to the production time of a book, prices are at least six months old when the book is published. It might be nice if I could raise every price, say, 5 percent, to compensate for that, but some prices will go up more than 5 percent, some will stay the same, and some even might go down. Since I will not anticipate price fluctuations, all I can say is that prices are valid when these lists were compiled.

After the intense work that pricing entails, it is still a guide and only that. There is no way it could be anything more. It is a compass, to help you find your way through; it is not a topographical map.

Yet what happens?

Well, a lot of sensible people, who know a price guide is just that, use it in the way it was intended. But there are some dealers and collectors who react differently.

Collectors who don't like information being made publicly available make unhappy noises. Fortunately, most advanced collectors will always know more than what's in a book, and many are happy to share what they know; they reasonably understand that nothing stays a secret forever.

Most dealers will welcome the information because it gives them a better idea of how to buy than they might have had. But a few will automatically charge the high price in a range, no matter what region they are in. And there are those who will automatically double the high price, or worse, trying to push the limit; and unfortunately, there always seems to be a fool willing to pay those prices. Thankfully, these dealers and collectors are in the minority.

So when I see or read about people railing against price guides, I think: If a price guide is just that, and not a bible, what are these people angry about?

Okay, some price guides are bad, inaccurate due either to ignorance or avarice. But I think that I could disagree with every price in a *good* price guide and still get value from it. There's a lot of information to be gained just from seeing what's high and what's low and from the relationship between certain prices.

SYMBOLS   A single price followed by a plus (+) means that it is a seller's market. The price reflects a minimum, to give you some idea of value; pieces could go for a little more or a lot more.

"ND" means "Not Determined." Even though I am not pricing these pieces, I list them because I want you to know they exist; they are out there. Please remember, it is a measure of scarcity, *not* necessarily of value.

FINAL NOTE   All pricing is based on selling prices, not asking prices. My consultants and I do not take our prices from trade papers or shows.

Measurements and Sizes

You will find small variations in measurements between your pieces and the listings because there were variations in the pieces themselves. Pottery shrinks when fired. Shrinkage is not always uniform, though the potteries try to control it. Sometimes the body formula changes, and that affects shrinkage. Also, when new production molds are made from the master mold, slight size changes can occur. Therefore, a 6" plate can vary from an eighth to a quarter of an inch, and a 13" platter can vary up to half an inch. An 11"-tall cookie jar might be smaller.

Where possible, I have given the pottery's own measurement. If I didn't have that information, the measurement comes from (1) my own collection, (2) someone else's collection, and (3) measurements taken at collectors' shows and flea markets. What makes this even more difficult is that the measurement of a particular piece could vary between listings in a pottery's literature. I have tried to be consistent, but you will find quarter-inch and half-inch differences in my listings.

Measurements of lug-handled pieces could be confusing. A 10" plate with ½" lug handles could be measured across the lug handles for an 11" measurement or across the plate for a 10" measurement. For myself, I think I have measured them both ways over the years, but I have finally come to this conclusion: a 10" plate with ½" lug handles is still a 10" plate, so that's how I now measure these pieces. The exception is oval platters, which are easier to measure across the lug handle.

I want to say a few words about the difficulty of liquid measure. First, how can we tell how many ounces something holds when we're at a flea market or show? It's not practical to carry around a measuring cup and water. Second, how close to the top should we fill a piece when measuring? Surely it was not intended to be filled all the way to the rim. Third, I can tell you from my own experiments that every 6-cup teapot does not contain the same amount of ounces.

Fortunately, this is usually not a problem. If a line has only a 1-quart jug, when we find the jug, we know that's it. If a line has a 1-pint and a 1-quart jug, we can usually tell the difference by sight. But if a line has three or more sizes of jug, teapot, or whatever, things get more confusing. What I have tried to do in this situation, where I can, is give height measurements, though I still have a long way to go on this. So if you carry this book and a measuring device, you should be okay.

Lastly, a word about the 36s bowl and other measurements, such as 24s, 48s, etc. I have stated here before that these numbers were based on how many pieces were packed in a barrel, information I got from *The Second Oldest Profession* by Floyd McKee. Upon further investigation, I found this information to be wrong.

From what I now understand (and I still have some investigating to do), these measurements reflect the fact that pottery workers were paid by the piece. What the standard was originally based on and, more important, what the time frame was I have yet to determine. What I *can* say is that a 36s bowl means that thirty-six could be made in a certain period of time. An hour might seem likely, but I do not want to assume anything. For a bowl of a larger size, fewer could be made in the same period, say twenty-four, so these were called 24s. Therefore, the lower the number, the larger the item.

As I said, how these evolved is not known to me, but at some point standardization needed to be established so that wages could be set. A 36s bowl was always 1 pint and a 24s bowl was always 2 pints, and so on. That these sizes are fractions or multiples of 12 makes sense when you take into account that this system arose in an England that was using the duodecimal system (they went to decimals about 15 years ago). And all pottery orders are in dozens (i.e., 50 dozen, 100 dozen, etc.).

Of course, there are always those who will produce more or less than the standard, which is what piecework is all about.

Much of this terminology had disappeared from catalogs by the early 1930s, but the 36s bowl persisted for a longer time.

Dinnerware Listings

TERMINOLOGY There is some variation in terminology among potteries. What one calls a Batter Set, another calls a Waffle Set. Where I could, I have used consistent terminology, and I have also grouped similar items (see sample list below) so that looking up the same piece in different listings is easier. In some cases, a piece is so strongly identified with a particular name, I have left it rather than confuse anyone.

I have tried to standardize terminology as follows:

1. Bookend, candle holder, and shaker prices are for a single, unless "pair" is indicated.

2. Small bowls, such as **cereal and fruit bowls**, are listed as dishes.

3. I have not used **baker** and **nappy** (although they are the correct industry terminology), as they might confuse; they indicate oval and round serving bowls, respectively. My impression, from various listings, is that the oval bowl was generally considered a vegetable bowl, and the round one was considered a salad bowl. However, there are round vegetable bowls as well, and I have

tried to keep these distinctions in my listings. **Covered vegetable** or **covered dish** is a term for **casserole** that I have found in various potteries' listings. I have used "casserole" to be consistent.

4. Both ¼-pound and 1-pound **butters** are generally rectangular, though shapes can vary. A butter *dish* is round. All have lids unless otherwise noted by use of the word "open."

5. In refrigerator ware, the difference between a **butter** and a **leftover** is that the butter has a flat base and deep lid, and the leftover has a deep base and flat lid.

6. A **candlestick** has a stem; a **candle holder** does not.

7. **Canisters, casseroles, drip jars**, and **sugars** should be considered covered unless the word "open" is used.

8. **Compotes** are high-footed unless otherwise indicated.

9. **Cream soup saucers** are wider than regular saucers, as cream soups are wider than teacups.

10. **Eggcup** can be single or double; these are differentiated in the listings.

11. The plate under a gravy boat is variously called a **tray, underliner,** or **liner**. It is usually oval and did double duty as a pickle dish. For consistency, I am listing it as a liner.

12. In general, I have used **jug** for pitcher. Some potteries used one word, some the other. Ball jugs do not take lids; all other jugs should be considered covered unless the word "open" is used. If a jug has a stopper, that will be indicated in the listings.

13. There are three kinds of **stacking/leftover sets** (single leftovers come in a variety of shapes). The first kind is the square stacking set; it has straight sides, two or three sections, and a lid. The second kind is the round stacking set; it has straight sides, two or three sections, and a lid. Therefore, a three-piece stacking set is two sections and a lid, a four-piece stacking set is three sections and a lid.

The sections in these first two are shallow, a couple of inches deep. These are also called refrigerator sets because they are designed to take up minimal space in a refrigerator.

The third kind is the round stacking/nesting set. It has sloping sides with (usually) three sections and three lids. Each covered piece can nest inside the next larger, or they can stack, with their lids on—the larger on the bottom, the smaller on the top. This last arrangement can be a little precarious; I assume they were intended to be used separately and nested when not in use.

14. **Mug** means the piece has a handle; **tumbler** means the piece does not have a handle. A number of potteries used the word "mug" for tumblers, especially, it seems to me, ones that were low. However, I think it would be confusing to follow that usage.

15. **Soup** means rimmed, unless followed by the word **coupe**.

See the Glossary for other definitions.

SAMPLE LISTING The following list is included here to familiarize you with the style of dinnerware listings in this book. I have tried to be consistent so that it will be easy for you to look up any item, no matter what the pottery. Different classes of items have been grouped together, for example, the bowls. This way, if you buy a bowl and need to find it in the list, you have them all together for easy comparison.

Ashtray
Bowl, compote, oval, 12"
Bowl, fruit, footed, 11"
Bowl, mixing, 5"
Bowl, mixing, 6"
Bowl, mixing, 7"
Bowl, mixing, 8"
Bowl, salad, round, 9"
Bowl, soup, coupe, 8"
Bowl, soup, rimmed, 8½"
Bowl, vegetable, oval, 9"
Bowl, vegetable, divided, oval, 10"
Butter, ¼-pound
Butter, 1-pound
Butter dish
Candle holder
Canister, small
  Blank
  Cinnamon
  Mustard
Canister, large
  Blank
  Coffee
  Flour
  Sugar
Carafe
Casserole, 9"
Casserole, individual, 4"
Coffee pot
Coffee pot, AD
Compote
Creamer
Creamer, AD
Cup
Cup, AD
Cup, cream soup
Cup, jumbo
Custard
Dish, fruit, 5¼"
Dish, cereal, 6¼"
Dish, lug, 7¼"
Drip jar
Eggcup, single
Eggcup, double
Gravy
Gravy faststand

Gravy liner/pickle
Jug, ball
Jug, batter
Jug, milk
Jug, syrup
Jug, water, small
Jug, water, medium
Jug, water, large
Leftover, round, 4"
Leftover, round, 5"
Leftover, round, 6"
Leftover, square, 8"
Mug
Plate, 6"
Plate, 7¼"
Plate, 9"
Plate, cake, lug, 11"
Plate, chop, 12"
Plate, chop, 14"
Plate, grill, 10"
Plate, party, 10"
Plate, square, 8"
Platter, 11"
Platter, 13"
Platter, 15"
Platter, lug, 12"
Refrigerator set, 3-piece
Relish, 3-section
Saucer
Saucer, AD
Saucer, cream soup
Saucer, jumbo
Shaker, short
Shaker, tall
Sugar
Sugar, AD, open
Teapot
Tray, for batter set, round, 11"
Tray, celery, 10"
Tumbler, 12-ounce
Tureen
Utensil, cake server
Utensil, fork
Utensil, spoon
Vase
Vase, bud, 7" tall

DINNERWARE SETS   Many pieces were intended to be used in a variety of ways. Where appropriate, I have indicated different kinds of sets that could be made up. For example, Shawnee made the following boxed set: Corn-King Popcorn Set (four 6" bowls, one 12-ounce creamer/jug, and one large shaker). Now, I don't know how many of these sets were sold, but if you were finding more 6" bowls than you thought you might, or more creamers than sugars, this could be the answer.

DECORATING VARIATIONS   I have tried to squeeze in as much information as I could about variation in treatments (see "Background on Dinnerware" for more information on this and other dinnerware practices), but when buying sight-unseen, it is always best to inquire into all elements of a decoration—the color of a line or band, the style of a gold stamp, and the placement of these elements.

Marks

The seminal work on American marks was done by Barber in his 1903 *Marks of American Potters*. It was the basic reference for decades, and many books that followed merely repeated his listings without adding anything new.

This changed in 1982 with the publication of *Marks of the East Liverpool Pottery District* by William R. Gates and Dana Ormond. You will understand the magnitude of such an enterprise when I tell you that, even with so specific a focus, Gates and Ormond came up with over two thousand marks, and more have turned up since.

Imagine, then, doing such a book for the entire United States pottery industry. "Daunting" would be an entirely inadequate word. Yet Lois Lehner did that in her incredible *U.S. Marks on Pottery, Porcelain and Clay*, published in 1988. Advertising copy for the book stated that it covered over eight thousand potteries and fifteen thousand marks.

I cannot duplicate that kind of work (nor would I wish to try). What I have tried to do is show marks for those potteries and shapes that are listed in this guide.

General marks that were used on a variety of shapes will be found at the beginning of each chapter. These are of two types. The first is usually the company name, sometimes with the name of the city in which it was located. The second is the name of a body color, both with or without the company name. These marks generally date to the late 1920s, when variations in body color were being introduced. In the 1930s these color references, when used, were more incorporated into the mark.

If there is a particular mark for a shape, it is shown at the shape entry. Sometimes there is no way of knowing if a shape had its own mark. It might exist even if it has not shown up.

Here's an example of what kind of situation we mark hunters face. On those pieces of Homer Laughlin's Trellis that I find, there is usually the general stamped Homer Laughlin mark. However, on occasion, a stamped Trellis mark, with no mention of Homer Laughlin, will be found.

While there are exceptions to the rule, in general, items with small bases such as shakers and cups were not marked.

Sometimes you will find the same mark with or without the words "Made in the USA." I do not consider these two marks but rather a mark variation. Other variations are a date or other numerical manufacturing code and the words "Patented" or "Patent Pending." For the purposes of my coverage, I ignore these variations. Depending on which mark I reproduced for this book, these variations may or may not be included. They are useful if you are trying to date an individual piece or reconstruct a precise history of a pottery, but for this book I am interested only in the basic mark. If you want to know more about these variations, I highly recommend Lois Lehner's book (see Bibliography); she is very scrupulous about these details.

Marks have been reproduced from photocopies of the mark itself, from photocopies of the marks in trade publications, and from photographs, except where otherwise credited.

See also "Background on Marks."

Photos

When possible, I have tried to show a piece of flatware, as the outline of these pieces is important for identification, as well as a piece of hollowware so you can see the handle and lid treatment. Also shakers because sometimes you can't tell which shape they belong to just by looking at them.

Dating

The date in parenthesis following the name of a shape, line or decoration is the year of introduction. A "<" before a date, as in "<1933," means that it might have been introduced a year or two earlier but 1933 is the firmest date we have. When I am less sure, I use "ca."

Many lines were introduced at the annual Pittsburgh trade shows in January and July. A line introduced in January might be advertised a month earlier, sometimes as early as November, but full-time production did not start until sales were made at the trade show; therefore, I use the January date as the year of introduction.

Determining what year a line was discontinued is more difficult. I have included these only on the rare occasion when I have a date. At times I will use ">" after a date. I do this when I want you to have some idea of how short or long the period of manufacture was although I don't have an exact date of discontinuance.

Sources and Verification

A lot of the information in this book is based on original research, taken primarily from trade journals as well as from catalogs and other advertising material issued by the potteries themselves. Therefore, though mistakes can always crop up, I stand by my information, even when it contradicts information in other books.

One important thing to remember about using catalogs and similar material is that no listing should be accepted as complete. Some probably are, but we have no way of being sure. Even when we have catalog listings, they reflect production only for the year in which they are issued. Items might have been dropped prior to the issuance of the catalog or introduced afterward.

So while I have tried to make some of my lists as complete as possible, I am under no illusion that I have achieved that. In a number of cases I probably have, but there is no way of knowing what odd piece might turn up.

Sources I am wary of are department store ads, mail order catalogs (Sears, Montgomery Ward), and interviews with pottery workers. In the first two instances, the companies sometimes made up their own names. As to interviews, time dims memory, and no one can be expected to remember everything.

I have tried to use the pottery's names for shapes and decals/decorations wherever possible. When I have had to make up my own or have used names made up by other authors or collectors, I have employed Hazel Marie Weatherman's device of putting them in quotation marks. Where a pottery named a particular color, I have used capitals (Powder Blue); otherwise, lowercase letters (blue).

I am reluctant to make up shape names. Shapes were generally named by potteries. If I do not know a shape name, I give it a descriptive name, like "Square" or "Thin Swirl," so there will be less confusion if and when the proper name shows up.

As to decal names, some decals in the photos are not named because they are obscure and do not warrant the effort. Others that I feel are of interest I describe in parentheses.

In Closing

Many of these chapters are meant to be used in conjunction with a particular book; I don't have the space to include the number of photographs or the kind of identification that a more specialized book can. Please check the Bibliography.

If I have not covered a pottery that you would like included, or if I have left out a line from a particular pottery, or even if I have not listed a particular piece you know about, write to me (115 Montague Street, Brooklyn, NY 11201) and let me know what you would like to see. Many additions to this edition came about thanks to input from readers.

BACKGROUND ON ART POTTERY

There are some things to keep in mind if you are beginning a collection. Remember that these are generalizations; there is always an exception. When you know those, you are an advanced collector.

Artist

Certain artists, though the quality of their work can vary, are more desirable than others.

Manufacturer

Certain potteries are more desirable than others. Currently, Rookwood and Grueby are among the most popular. But be aware that while Roseville is more popular than Weller, an early Weller piece has more value than a middle-period Roseville. When evaluating one pottery against another, make sure you are speaking of comparable lines and periods.

Subject Matter

People, animals, and scenic decorations are more desirable than florals. But to give you an idea about exceptions, a beautiful, elaborate floral by a more desirable artist can bring a higher price than a poor scenic by a lesser artist.

Size

Larger pieces are more valuable than smaller pieces—the taller the vase the better. Pieces with fragile details that have survived intact—handles, delicate ewer lips—are more desirable. But size alone is not enough, the piece has to have a good line. If it is clunky, that detracts from price.

Condition

Americans are used to having everything cleanly packaged, preferably in clear plastic and untouched by human hands. Damage will have a negative effect on price. But a small chip on the bottom of a vase that does not interfere with the beauty of the decoration is a world apart from the crack that runs through a decoration.

Aesthetics

Finally, remember the old cliché "Beauty is in the eye of the beholder." What is clunky to one person is well proportioned to another. What is a poor color scheme to one is a bold approach to color for another. Good luck.

BACKGROUND ON DINNERWARE

Here are some useful things to know about industry practices that will help you understand what you are finding and avoid confusion.

SHAPES

There is often a strong similarity of style between potteries. In the late nineteenth century, every pottery had at least one plain round shape, one shape with an embossed rim, and an octagonal shape. The larger potteries, with stronger sales forces, could market more lines than their smaller competitors, but the shapes were still variations on these themes.

In the late 1920s many potteries began hiring designers to create original shapes. They also kept an eye on their competitor's lines and often urged their designers to create something similar.

Composition of Dinnerware Sets

From the Victorian era to the early twentieth century, dinnerware lines had a multiplicity of pieces: there might be ten sizes of platters alone. It was not unusual to have seventy-five or more different items in one line. By the 1930s the number of items in a set was drastically reduced, and certain pieces had multiple uses: the demitasse set could also be a breakfast set or a children's set, and the pickle tray served as the underplate for the gravy.

A basic set in the 1930s consisted of a cup and saucer, dinner plate, luncheon plate, salad plate, bread and butter plate, fruit and cereal dishes, soup bowl, round and oval vegetable bowls, covered casserole, gravy boat and underplate, teapot, sugar, and creamer.

Other pieces that can be found are shakers, eggcups, square underplates for round casseroles, coffee pots (sometimes when a line has a coffee pot, there is no teapot), gravy faststands, demitasse sets, batter sets, jugs, cream soups and saucers, large coffee cups and saucers. The more popular and long-lived a line, the more items that were made for it.

What is interesting are the different practices at different potteries. For example, W. S. George seems to have only one shaker shape. It was plain enough to use with several different dinnerware shapes. Yet Homer Laughlin, which designed a shaker for a number of their shapes, did not introduce one for Virginia Rose, one of their most popular shapes, until the 1950s, twenty years after the line was first brought out. If you are collecting a Virginia Rose decal from the 1930s, you need to know that the shaker was brought out in the 1950s or you'll search in vain for a shaker with your decal.

Pick-up Pieces

Shape lines could be fleshed out in two ways. One was with interchangeable pieces (pie plates, cake plates, etc.) that are not designed to go with one particular shape. Luray has a number of these pieces. Another way was to use pieces from other shapes even if there wasn't a particularly good match. Homer Laughlin's use of the plain rectangular Jade butter with the embossed round Virginia Rose line is a good example of that. Either way, these are called pick-up pieces.

Restyling

It was not unusual for a pottery to redesign an item, either because there were problems in manufacturing or to respond to changing public taste.

Reusing

It was easy and economical for a company to bring out a new shape using the flatware from a previous shape—plain flatware was definitely interchangeable—though in the case of Paden City's Shellcrest, they kept the hollowware from Elite and changed the flatware.

Shape Names

Different potteries sometimes used the same name for a shape or decoration. Cronin, French-Saxon, and Harker all had a Zephyr shape.

DECORATIONS

Decals

Decals were first used in the United States ca. 1890 but reached the peak of their popularity in the 1930s. Most were printed by stone lithography, which was replaced by photo lithography in the 1940s.

If you were to collect as many different examples of decal as you could find, you could have thousands in your collection and still have a long way to go.

Tens of thousands were designed. The decal manufacturers had designers on staff; they would custom-design a decal if requested, but many of their designs were done so that the company would have samples for customers to choose from. Many of these were never put into production.

Many potteries chose decals from sample books. Often a pottery got exclusive rights to a decal, but sometimes they used a decal that was in the public domain; or they gave up exclusivity and other potteries picked it up afterward, which explains why you might find one pottery's shape with another's decal.

Certain subject matter was very common; every pottery had a Mexican or southwestern decal, sometimes several petitpoint decals, cottage decals, and bird decals, plus hundreds of floral decals ranging from the realistic to the fantastic.

When you collect a particular decal, especially one of the less popular ones, you have no guarantee that every piece made in a particular shape will be found with that decal. If the shape was in production for many years, your decal might have been used early on and been retired before certain items were added to the shape. Or the orders for your decal may never have included a cream soup, for example, or some other piece.

Finally, only the most popular decals were given names by the potteries; most just had a number.

Underglaze versus Overglaze

There is an easy way to differentiate between the two. Run your finger over the surface of the ware, starting on an undecorated section and moving over a decorated section. If you feel a change in texture, it is overglaze; otherwise, it is underglaze.

Glazes

Some shapes were decorated in solid colors only, some with decals only, usually but not always on an Ivory or White background, and some shapes were decorated with both solid colors and decals. For the latter, where Ivory was not one of the solid colors, if you find a plain Ivory piece, it is probably an undecorated second.

Conversely, a piece in a shape that is usually decal-decorated might be found in a solid color. This is unusual but makes for a happy find, certainly more desirable than an undecorated second.

Treatment

Treatment refers to the interplay between the various decorative elements. For example, the same decal might have different treatments—it might have a colored line or a gold stamping. One of the well-known examples of this is Homer Laughlin's Mexicana; it is usually found trimmed with a red line but has also been found with blue, green, or yellow lines. Be especially aware of this when buying or selling by mail.

Trade Show Samples

Prospective new decals were shown to buyers at two annual shows, in January and July. The pieces that met with little interest were not put into production, yet often these samples made their way out into the world. There is no way to differentiate them from items that were produced.

Decorating Companies

There were (and still are) a number of companies that bought pottery from the factories and decorated it themselves. In general, these companies bought plain, white- or ivory-glazed pieces and added decorations, usually decals. Sometimes they bought decal-decorated pieces and added elaborate gold decoration to the rim and/or well. You can identify these pieces by (1) their sometimes garish overdecoration and (2) the decorator's mark overprinting the manufacturer's mark, sometimes obliterating it. Not all of these will be easy to identify, as some of the pieces will just have the decorating company's mark, and others are unmarked.

Gypsy Ware

These were items made by pottery workers for their own use (also called "lunch-hour pieces" or "end-of-day pieces"). They could be made either in the factory (hence the names in parentheses above) or in backyard kilns using odd pieces of pottery and decal brought home from the factory. This practice was especially common during the Depression. Some of these pieces were kept for personal use, and some were sold along the roadside (hence the name "Gypsy Ware").

BACKGROUND ON WILLOW
by Connie Rogers

Willow-pattern china has been produced by more companies for the past two hundred years than any other pattern.

Some of the earliest reproductions of Chinese landscapes were done on porcelain, but the Willow pattern as we know it was first produced by Spode on pearlware. This was an ivory earthenware with a glaze that was tinted pale blue to give it a whiter appearance so as to resemble porcelain. Other companies followed, producing Willow on all types of earthenware and stoneware. It became a pattern available to the masses who demanded it. Well over two hundred potteries in England alone manufactured Willow pattern in the nineteenth century.

The main components of the Willow pattern are the pagoda, willow tree, bridge with three figures, boat, island on the far shore, and two birds. There is also a large "apple" tree near the pagoda; the information that you can determine the manufacturer by the number of "apples" on the tree is erroneous. Another myth is that the piece is old if the birds are kissing.

The pattern came into being at a time when the transfer print method of decorating was first developed. This method enabled the Staffordshire potteries to produce blue-and-white Oriental patterns quickly and cheaply.

What is most important to understand is that not all Willow pattern is equal in quality or value. There is something in almost every price range. Most American Willow (with the exception of Buffalo pottery) is at the lower end of the scale. The three largest U.S. producers of Willow are Royal, Homer Laughlin, and Buffalo.

The Royal China Company (Sebring, Ohio) made hundreds of thousands of pieces of Willow dinnerware from the 1930s through the 1980s, mostly in blue but also in pink, green, and brown. It is best suited for everyday use and should not carry a high price tag.

Some early pieces of Royal (mostly plates) from the 1930s have been found with a simple rubber-stamp pattern underglaze. At least three different border designs have been documented.

In the 1940s, Royal began turning out thousands of pieces of Blue Willow, using the underglaze transfer-print process. An ad from that period states: "The demand is terrific. Delivery at once from our stockpile." The hollowware shapes are not marked, but they are easily recognized; they are simple and low with straight sides. Cup handles were round in the early years; an ad from the 70s shows the cups with pointed handles.

Scio Pottery Company (Scio, Ohio) Willow, which is a poorer-quality unmarked imitation of Royal, was made until a few years ago. Scio is not quality dinnerware and should not be sold for high prices just because it is decorated with the Willow pattern. The ware is coarser and the ink quality can range from very faint to muddy in the pattern.

Homer Laughlin (East Liverpool, Ohio, and Newell, West Virginia) also made a vast quantity of Willow from the 1920s to the 1960s, and most collectors consider it "everyday dishes" although a cut above Royal.

The early ware consisted of a small decal overglaze placed in the center of the piece. Occasionally, there was a simple line border in blue; other pieces are found with a more ornate stamped gold border. Many different shapes were used.

Homer Laughlin began using the underglaze transfer-printed traditional Willow pattern in the late 1930s, making complete dinner sets with additional serving pieces. The flat pieces, such as plates and platters, are marked and dated (see Homer Laughlin chapter for clarification of dating code). Most hollowware is unmarked. Identifying Homer Laughlin Willow is a matter of comparing the elements of the pattern with marked pieces and noting the similarity of the clay body in weight and color. Also, the shapes are documented in catalog reprints.

Many dealers will mistake the Laughlin hollowware for English pieces because of the high quality of the design as well as the shape. However, it is important to remember that after the McKinley Tariff Act was passed, all pieces imported into the United States, beginning in 1891, are marked with country of origin, and most have the name of the maker as well. Homer Laughlin pieces are *unmarked*.

Buffalo Pottery's semivitreous Blue Willow dinnerware, introduced in the early 1900s, was not made to be sold; it was given exclusively as premiums by the Larkin Soap Company. By buying soap and other products directly from the Larkin factory, the customer earned certificates that could be used to purchase premiums from the company catalog. Early pottery premiums were purchased by Larkin from other manufacturers, but in 1902–1903 they built the largest fireproof pottery in the world, in order to produce their own premiums.

All pieces were marked with a buffalo and a date. The first dated Blue Willow is 1905. The mark further states: "FIRST OLD WILLOW WARE MANUFACTURED IN THE UNITED STATES." An ad in the 1906 Larkin catalog reads: "This is the first old Willow Ware made in America; it is an exact reproduction of the famous English Ware in rich, dark blue under glaze; it is not only extremely serviceable, but these quaint-shaped pieces are largely sought by collectors of old china." Buffalo's "Chicago Jug" is a direct copy of one made by Doulton & Co., Burslem, England. Some of the other pieces, such as the covered vegetable and the gravy boat, are of the same shape as those made by Charles Allerton & Sons, Longton, England.

Collectors enjoy the hunt for Buffalo Willow. The pattern is well done, and there are many interesting shapes to find, including a number of different pitcher shapes in a variety of sizes. Of additional interest is Gaudy Willow. The underglaze pattern is done in brown. Overglaze hand painting is done in green, rust, brown, and navy blue. There is gold trim lining each of the "apples" on the tree, the fence posts, the medallions in the border, and other pattern elements.

Buffalo continued to manufacture date-marked semivitreous Blue Willow until 1915, when they began concentrating on vitrified china. After World

War I, Buffalo continued to produce the Willow pattern in institutional ware and expanded to green, red, and brown in addition to blue.

Along with Buffalo, other American-made restaurant ware provides a lower-priced Willow that is well suited for everyday family use. Many collectors concentrate on Shenango, as it seems to be the easiest to find, although it is quite common to mix and match the various makers of restaurant ware such as Bailey-Walker, Carr, Hall, Jackson, Mayer, and Sterling. Grill plates are handy for serving patio- or buffet-style because the dividers separate the hot and cold food. Easy to find and low in price ($15–$20), the chief disadvantage in collecting grill plates is that they are heavy and bulky to store.

People who like Willow pattern are not necessarily antique collectors. Many prefer and buy the new Willow, which is being made by many English companies today. And there are those collectors who use it all, the old and the new.

And you don't have to be interested in china to be a Willow collector. There is graniteware decorated in Willow, as well as tinware of all kinds: trays, tea tins, canisters, and many types of containers made in Japan, England, and the United States. Linen and paper products are also found in abundance.

Those interested in crafts and needlework find instructions for Willow-patterned items in needlepoint, embroidery, filet crochet, knitting, and counted cross-stitch. Many collectors have papered their walls, upholstered their furniture, and decorated lamp shades with the Willow pattern. A back issue of *Old House Journal* even showed a refinished bathtub with the Willow pattern all around the edge.

KNOWN UNITED STATES MANUFACTURERS OF WILLOW

The following list was compiled by Connie Rogers. It is a list of every U.S. pottery manufacturer (it does not include decorators) for whom a piece of Willow has been found. If you know of others, please write to her (see Consultants).

Semivitreous

Note: A plate shape that was made by both Mt. Clemens Pottery, Mt. Clemens, MI, and Stetson China Co., Lincoln, IL (Stetson called this shape Oxford) has been found with a Blue Willow decoration but no mark, so the manufacturer cannot be identified at this time.

This Blue Willow toaster is marked: "Toastrite, Pan Electric Co., Cleveland, Ohio."

American Chinaware Corporation (offices in Cleveland, OH)
Edwin Bennett Pottery Co., Baltimore, MD
Buffalo Pottery Co., Buffalo, NY
Canonsburg Pottery Co., Canonsburg, PA
Cleveland China Co., Cleveland, OH
Colonial Pottery Co., East Liverpool, OH
Cronin China Co., Minerva, OH
Crooksville China Co., Crooksville, OH
W. S. George Pottery Co., East Palestine, OH
Hopewell (previously Ostrow) China Co., Hopewell, VA
Illinois China Company, Lincoln, IL
James River Potteries, Hopewell, VA
E. M. Knowles China Co., Newell, WV
Homer Laughlin China Co., Newell, WV
Limoges China Co., Sebring, OH
McCoy Pottery Co., Roseville, OH
Mercer Pottery Co., Trenton, NJ
National China Co., East Liverpool and Salineville, OH
Paden City Pottery, Paden City, WV
Royal China Co., Sebring, OH
Salem China Co., Salem, OH
Scio Pottery Co., Scio, OH
E. H. Sebring Co., Sebring, OH
Sebring Pottery Co., Sebring, OH
Southern Potteries, Erwin, TN
Taylor, Smith & Taylor, Chester, WV
C. C. Thompson Pottery Co., East Liverpool, OH

Vitrified China

Pieces have also been found marked Knickerbocker and USA Ideal; makers for these are unknown. An unglazed Warwick China grill plate has been found; this may indicate production, but no finished pieces have been seen.
Bailey-Walker China Co., Bedford, OH
Buffalo China Co., Buffalo, NY
Carr China Co., Grafton, WV
Greenwood China Co., Trenton, NJ
Hall China Co., East Liverpool, OH
Jackson China Co., Falls Creek, PA
Mayer China Co., Beaver Falls, PA
D. E. McNicol China Co., Clarksburg, WV
Scammell China Co., Trenton, NJ
Shenango China Co., Newcastle, PA
Sterling China Co. (Caribe), Wellsville, OH
Syracuse China Co., Syracuse, NY
Van China Co., Trenton, NJ
Walker China Co., Bedford, OH
Wallace China Co., Huntington Park, CA
Wellsville China Co., Wellsville, OH

BACKGROUND ON MARKS

A mark could be stamped, embossed, impressed, incised, or a decal. Stamped marks (backstamps) were usually applied with a rubber stamp in black or colored ink, platinum, or gold. Impressed marks were either in the mold or a branding-iron type device was used. Incised marks were done by hand. Some marks, especially four-color ones, were decals.

A number of different elements can be part of a mark. Custom varied among manufacturers as to which elements were used, and often a pottery wasn't consistent even on its own wares. And since the stamping was done by hand, there is the human error factor. Here are the basic elements you will find.

Artist's Signature

Most often found on art pottery; usually just initials, sometimes the name. Sometimes a name or initials are incorporated into a decal; don't let this fool you into thinking a piece is hand-painted.

Body Composition

The majority of collectible U.S. ceramics is made of pottery, not porcelain or china. Some potteries produced one or the other body; some produced both. This can get confusing. For example, most of the collectible Homer Laughlin lines are pottery, yet the company name is Homer Laughlin *China* Company.

Sometimes body information is included in the mark. "S-V" for semivitreous and "S-P" for semiporcelain will be found in pre-1930 marks. See Glossary for further information.

Body Glaze / Color

In the late 1920s colored dinnerware became very popular. There was brightly colored dinnerware such as Bauer and solid-color bodies such as pink, ivory, yellow, green, and blue, which were used by a number of potteries. Of these last five colors, the first three were often used as backgrounds for decals. These colors were sometimes given their own name or incorporated into the mark or the shape name. Look for words such as "dawn," "rose," or "blush" to signify pink, "creme" or "ivo-" for ivory, and "golden" for yellow. For example, E. M. Knowles's shape Alice Anne will be found as Alice Annecreme, an ivory shade, and Alice Anneglow, a pink shade.

Rarely, just the color name was marked.

Decorating Firm Name

If you find a piece with more gold on it than good taste would dictate, it is likely from a decorating firm. Sometimes these appear stamped along with the manufacturer's name.

Decoration

Sometimes the name of the decoration appears as part of the mark. Some potteries were more consistent about this than others. Many of the Sebring family potteries, especially American Limoges, marked decoration names. Others almost never did.

Gold / Silver

Some pieces with gold decoration are so marked ("14-carat gold"). The amount of gold is negligible, and the mark is more of a sales device. What looks like silver decoration is really platinum and, rarely, you will find a piece marked as such.

Good Housekeeping Seal of Approval

Yes, Virginia, there was such a thing, and it (or an equivalent institute's name) will be found on some pottery. With rare exceptions, it does not increase the value of a piece.

Graphic Element

Some marks were given special treatment, often created by the shape designer, and could range from elegant use of type to a small drawing.

Hand Painted

Hand painting runs the gamut from an elaborate painting to a few strokes to give expression to a face on a cookie jar. There was a vogue for hand painting starting in the late 1930s, and these words in a mark could boost sales.

Made For . . .

When a line was exclusive for a distributor or department store, the name was usually included in the mark.

Made in USA

In 1898, Congress required all ware made for export to be so marked.

Manufacturer's Name

Whether the full name or the initials, this is the element found most often. Surprisingly, it is not present in every mark. Sometimes a company marked only the shape name or the body color.

Numbers

Can mean several things: (1) Impressed numbers often reflect a pottery's system of shape numbering; (2) stamped numbers could reflect (a) the shape number, (b) the month and date of manufacture, or (c) quality control information; some dates are obvious, some are coded; (3) some numbers that seem to have been written by hand in gold or ink reflect a glaze or decal.

Patent Pending / Patented

Some shapes or processes (such as Cameoware) were patented. Occasionally, a mark will contain the words "Patent Pending," "Patent Applied For," or "Patented."

Second Selection

Ware that did not pass quality control was either (1) sent to a reclaim department; (2) given an inexpensive decal decoration, marked "Second Selection," and sold cheaply; (3) sent to an outlet shop; (4) discarded; or (5) sold to a decorating shop.

Some potteries began marking their seconds when they found that customers would buy these at reduced prices, take them to a dealer who was selling first selections, claim they were sold less than perfect pieces, and get a good replacement.

Shape / Line Name

Sometimes the shape name was just lettered below the manufacturer's name; sometimes a special stamp was designed.

Symbolism

During the nineteenth century many American potteries employed familiar British symbols, such as the lion and the unicorn, in combination with a coat of arms, shield, or heraldic escutcheon to deceive consumers into believing their product was British. Only a few American firms were bold enough to challenge British domination of the market and employ straightforward names and American symbolism. The most famous of these was Homer Laughlin's stamp with the American eagle vanquishing the British lion.

Union Mark

Found on some dinnerware. The Brotherhood of Operative Potters campaigned to have ware marked to indicate it was made in a union shop. Not all potteries complied.

TIPS

This is a compilation of general thoughts and specific ideas based on my experience that will make collecting a little smoother and more enjoyable for you.

Buying

1. If you collect a particular dinnerware pattern, don't pass up a set, complete or incomplete. Some beginning collectors want a challenge, want to put a set together piece by piece, so they pass up a bunch of pieces or maybe buy an item or two if they can. I believe this is a mistake as most dinnerware (other than popular lines such as Fiesta, Luray, Russel Wright) is difficult to assemble in a set, and you should buy everything you see.

2. Buy expensive pieces first. It is very common to see new collectors buying the inexpensive, common items for a collection and passing up the rarer, more costly pieces. I understand that this can be a matter of economics, but wherever possible, buy the better piece as soon as you can. For one thing, you might not see it again so fast. And more important, the price might go up more dramatically than for the common pieces.

In the Field

1. Measure your finger span so that you can measure a piece "in the field" if you don't have a ruler or measuring tape handy. It is 9 inches from the tip of my thumb to the tip of my little finger when my hand is fully extended. This knowledge has come in very (pardon the pun) handy when I wanted a rough measurement and didn't have a ruler with me.

2. When checking for damage, your fingers can be more discerning than your eyes. Run your fingers around rims, bases, spouts, and lids—in other words, any edges and even over the surface. You might feel some chips or roughness that your eyes missed.

3. Beware marriages: mismatched tops and bottoms. Sometimes they're immediately apparent; other times they're not. It is not always possible to tell a marriage just from the shape, especially if you are not familiar with the piece. If you're buying via mail order, you can return it; if you buy a marriage at a flea market and discover it when you get home, you're out of luck.

The decoration can provide useful clues. In solid-color pieces, the colors must match of course. Yes, colors can vary slightly from batch to batch, but lids and bottoms are usually glazed and fired at the same time, so batch differences should not apply here. (To complicate things a little, don't forget that sometimes lids and bottoms have deliberately contrasting colors.)

In pieces decorated with decals and lines, remember that a lid might not have a piece of decal, especially small pieces such as sugars and AD pots. However, lids and bottoms always had the same lining. If a bottom has, say, a gold line and the lid a silver line or no line, or if the lid has a blue line and the bottom a black line, or whatever, then it *is* a marriage.

A related tip: in the 1940s we begin to see pairs of dinnerware shakers where one is tall and one is short. You need to know if the shakers in your set were made that way or if, as on rare occasion, a set was made with two sets of shakers, one tall and one short (Salem's Victory shape is an example of this).

And don't forget to count the holes in your shakers. There are no rules about how many holes a salt or pepper should have, but if your pair of shakers each has the same number of holes, you have two salts or two peppers.

4. A word about center-handled serving pieces, either one-, two-, or three-tier. You will find that the holes in the plates, through which the handles and stems are inserted, have been either molded or drilled.

If they have been molded (identifiable by the smooth, glazed edges around the hole), this was done deliberately at the pottery, with the intention of producing a center-handled serving piece. Chances are these were assembled at the pottery, though this work might have been farmed out.

If the hole has been drilled (identifiable by rough edges and minor chipping around the hole), this was probably done out of the pottery, by a firm with or without permission to do so. Though these are nice pieces to have, it is important to know that they were not intended to be part of the original line.

Condition

Be careful buying an item that has the price in marker or ink right on the piece. If the piece is crazed (and sometimes it is not easy to see the crazing), the ink can leach into the body and will be difficult if not impossible to remove. And if you pass up such an item, you might tell the dealer why. A little education can't hurt.

Cleaning

Here are some basic rules for cleaning pottery. People will tell you they've done otherwise successfully, and I'm sure they have, but I can't cover every situation, so these are general rules to save you grief.

1. Clean pottery with liquid soap and a soft sponge. Do not put them in the dishwasher. You can help the cleaning process with a liquid cleaner such as Fantastik, as well as a soft brush for corners and crevices. In general, do *not* use steel wool or other abrasive pads, and do *not* use abrasive powders. Even if your piece is protected by a clear glaze, remember that, while glazes are durable, they are not impervious. Decals, which are usually overglaze, are vulnerable, and gold or silver trim will very quickly wear off—as I have discovered to my chagrin.

2. If you buy an item that is crazed and has brown staining around the craze marks, or some marker residue, you might try soaking it in a solution of baking soda and water, either overnight or for a few days. I have tried this, and it seems promising, but I have not done it enough to make any specific recommendations. I have also heard that soaking in a bleach and water solution can help. When trying anything for the first time, test the process with a disposable piece of pottery.

3. Some labels will wash off easily in warm water. Other labels, and especially the residue of the gum on the back of labels, can be difficult to remove. The same applies to Scotch tape and masking tape, especially if it is old and dry. This is easy to remedy. First, take a small sharp knife or one-sided razor, and scrape off as much of the label or tape as you can. Next apply some solvent with a rag or paper towel to the residue; rub firmly and reapply as needed. Some residue will come right off; some will need a little work. With some of these products, make sure you are in a well-ventilated space.

The solvent I prefer is nail-polish remover. Others I have seen mentioned are lighter fluid and cooking oil (which will then require soap and water, an extra step).

Mailing Pottery

1. I don't think I am exaggerating when I say that we have *all* heard of those instances where a dealer has sent out a perfect piece of pottery, only to be called by the buyer and told that it was "as is" in some way, asking for a refund. When it is returned, it is indeed "as is," and it is also *not* the piece the dealer sent out originally.

To remedy this, some dealers note that their label must be intact if a piece is returned. I like that idea but would be concerned about unscrupulous people playing around with the label. A better idea is a rubber stamp with the dealer's name and address (or whatever). Using a regular ink pad, stamp this on all items shipped, lids as well as bottoms in the case of covered pieces. Let buyers know that the stamp must be intact on returned items. The idea is basically tamper-proof, and the ink rubs off easily if the buyer keeps the piece.

2. A lady wrote me from the Midwest saying that she had had her mother's Autumn Leaf shipped to her from California and was now looking for a way to sell it. Though there were some nice serving pieces, most of the flatware was chipped. What saddened me was the fact that she had paid $175 to a professional packer/shipper in California. She was willing to ship it on to a buyer, and I had to tell her that most dealers don't want chipped pieces, but more important,

they certainly don't want to pay shipping costs for them. Even if she could sell the flatware locally, she had already paid too much just to have it shipped to her. Please don't fall into this trap.

Packing

1. I think bubble wrap should be reusable, which is why I find it a nuisance to struggle with exhuming something in bubble wrap that has been encircled several times with thick tape. My solution to this, and I have been putting this request in with my orders, is to put a few rubber bands around the bubble wrap rather than tape. They hold just as well, make unpacking quick and easy, and the wrap is available for reuse.

2. I dislike Styrofoam peanuts, so here's a new idea: wood shavings. They come from scrap wood of trees that had been cut for other purposes and would be a fine addition to a mulch pile if not an inoffensive addition to a landfill. I don't know how easy it is to get these shavings, though I believe they have begun to appear in packing material catalogs. Over all, I still prefer wadded newspaper.

Finally, if you talk to some collectors, every dealer is bad news. And if you talk to some dealers, every collector is a pain in the neck. These are stereotypes. A good dealer-collector relationship adds an important dimension to both areas. For dealers, yes, it enhances business, but there is satisfaction in educating collectors and helping people build collections. Many dealers feel good knowing they are guiding a beginner down the right path or have added to an important collection.

And for collectors, an experienced dealer can provide access to pieces they might not otherwise have gotten and information that is not in any book. Knowledgeable collectors and dealers help educate each other. And learning is an important part of collecting.

MARKET SURVEY

It is difficult in a short overview to be entirely accurate; there are always exceptions. Please keep this in mind as you read.

Some general phenomena to consider:

The publication of a first book on a pottery will have a positive effect on prices. For example, Metlox prices are rising since the announcement of Carl Gibbs' book (see Bibliography/Coming Attractions).

Potteries that seldom or never marked their ware are potential sleepers. Every dealer cannot know every pottery.

Some pottery gets so high-priced that it has an adverse effect on its own collectibility. Hull is a good example. Prices are at a standstill and new collectors are scarce.

ART POTTERY

This market is very strong. Demand seems to be outstripping supply, which means that collectors are paying more for well-repaired pieces, and some damage is acceptable on larger or artist-signed pieces, which wasn't true a few years ago.

COWAN   Strong art deco designs and unusual shapes or glazes are doing well, as are artist pieces.

NEWCOMB COLLEGE   Super strong.

ROOKWOOD   The only possible weakness here are standard glaze pieces with floral decorations, other decorations are strong. Production ware is bringing more money, and artist-signed pieces are breaking records.

ROSEVILLE   Very strong.

VAN BRIGGLE   Dated pieces are still the most desirable, especially figurals and unusual glazes. It's important to be careful of the new, especially since many Van Briggle items have been in continuous production since they were introduced. Longlived glazes are especially tough to date.

WELLER   Coppertone, certain rare lines, and unusual figurals are doing very well, common and later lines are not.

There are a number of underestimated smaller art potteries that still have a lot of growth potential. And there is a very strong interest in matte-green glazes, whether from popular potteries such as Grueby and Teco, or less-noticed Hampshire and Wheatley, or even unmarked.

ART WARE

With art pottery prices still rising, many collectors have turned to industrial or cast art ware, especially potteries such as Abingdon, Haeger, and McCoy, all of which are seeing rising prices.

DINNERWARE / KITCHENWARE

This is a market that is slowly and steadily growing in some areas and settled in others. Right now, the most noticeable growth is in the California potteries, especially what might be termed the second rank, such as Pacific, Santa Anita, and Winfield. First rank, such as Bauer, Gladding-McBean (Franciscan), Metlox, and Vernon Kilns are still growing as well.

Of the eastern potteries, there is still growth potential in designs from Ben Seibel, Eva Zeisel, and others. Other lines, such as Fiesta, Harlequin, and a few other Homer Laughlin shapes, as well as Russel Wright, Harker's Cameoware, and Taylor, Smith & Taylor's Luray have matured, and very little if anything will join them; if any other line was going to be successful, it would be up there already. The exceptions are Hall China and Stangl Pottery, both of which are still experiencing strong growth in their most popular patterns, and some Pfaltzgraff lines due to their quantity.

HAND-PAINTED   As prices rise for Watt, collectors are turning to Purinton, Red Wing, and Blair among others.

NOVELTIES

COOKIE JARS   Reproductions are hurting the market in general, and especially those potteries where reproductions are known to have been made. The rare jars are still selling well, but the new jars are selling extremely well. This is undoubtedly due to the affordable prices and the fact that collectors feel safe buying new jars.

FIGURES　Keep an eye on the California potteries here.

FIGURAL PLANTERS / VASES　For a long time, it was hard to know who made many of these attractive pieces. As books continue to be published identifying manufacturers, popularity and prices are growing.

FIGURAL SHAKERS　This market continues strong. Even new shakers seem to quickly find their way into collections. Country of origin is usually not important. Many collectors seem to prefer shaker sets where the individual pieces are related but not identical. There have been some reproductions but this does not seem to have had a negative effect.

ABINGDON POTTERIES, INC.

Abingdon, Illinois

CHAPTER AT A GLANCE

BOOKENDS
COOKIE JARS
DINNERWARE
FIGURES
  Animals
  Chessmen
  People
KITCHENWARE
  Daisy
  Refrigerator Set

MISCELLANY
PLANTERS
SHORT LINES
  Asters
  Fern Leaf
  Sunflower
  Tri-Fern
VASES
WALL POCKETS

In 1908 the Abingdon Sanitary Manufacturing Company began making bathroom fixtures. In 1934 they introduced a line of art pottery made in a vitreous body. This line was manufactured until 1950.

Over 1,000 shapes were made and, over the years, almost 150 colors were used, most of them high-gloss. The most desirable colors are Bronze Black, renamed Gunmetal Black (lustrous black with metallic sheen); Copper Brown (semimatte, mottled, metallic copper brown with iridescent sheen); Fire Red, renamed Dubonnet (brilliant glaze with crystalline sparkle); Riviera Blue (semigloss dark blue); Royal Red, renamed Dubonnet (semigloss purplish red); and Sudan Red (matte reddish-tan).

See Roerig in Bibliography and see Clubs/Newsletters.

MARKS The shape number will usually be impressed in the bottom of a piece.

IMPRESSED The three impressed marks shown here will sometimes be found.

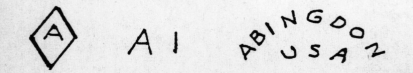

26

STAMPED   Of the four stamped marks shown, the most common is "Abingdon, USA" in a rectangular box.

ABINGDON

ASINGDON
U. S. A.

PRICING   Use the upper end of the price range for the desirable colors listed above.

BOOKENDS

Cactus, 6" /370	$50 – $75
Cactus (planter), 6½" /374	50 – 75
Colt, 6" /363	
Black	ND
Other colors	ND
Dolphin (planter), 5½" /444	
Decorated	35
Solid colors	15 – 25
Horsehead, 7" /441	
Black	75 – 85
Other colors	35 – 50
Quill, 8¼" /595	
Black base, white quill	75 – 100
Russian Dancer, 8½" /321	
Black	75 – 100
Other colors	50 – 75
Scotty, 7½" /650	
Black	100 – 125
Other colors	50 – 75
Sea Gull, 6" /305	
Solid colors	50 – 75

COOKIE JARS

The Plaid and Floral jars are the same shape. All cookie jars are decorated; some also were made in solid colors, as noted below.

Note: When Abingdon closed, molds were sold to other companies. These molds had the shape number impressed, so non-Abingdon jars will have them also. To distinguish between the two, remember that Abingdon jars had a stamped mark and were not cold-painted, as some of the reproductions are.

See also Daisy, below.

Baby, 11" /561	
Decorated	$350–$400
Solid colors	400 – 425
Choo Choo, 7½" /651	150 – 175

Clock, "Cookie Time," 9"   /653 .... *$80 – $90*
Fat Boy, 8¼"   /495
   Decorated. .... *375 – 400*
   Solid colors .... *300 – 325*
Floral, 8½"   /697DF .... *75 – 100*
(Happy) Hippo, 8"   /549
   "Bar Jar". .... *350 +*
   Black. .... *250 +*
   Decorated. .... *250 +*
   Solid color, green/pink. .... *200 – 225*
   Solid color, white. .... *175 – 200*
Hobby Horse, 10½"   /602. .... *190 – 200*
Humpty-Dumpty, 10½"   /663 .... *250*
Jack-in-the-Box, "ABC" and "Cookies," 11"   /611 .... *250 – 275*
Little Bo Peep, w/sheep, 12"   /694 .... *300 – 325*
Little Girl, "Cooky," 9½"   /693 .... *90 – 100*
Little Miss Muffet, 11"   /662 .... *225*
Little Ol' Lady, 7½"   /471
   Solid color, Blue/Chartreuse/Pink .... *200 – 225*
   Solid color, Black. .... *375 – 400*
   Decorated .... *200 – 225*
   Decorated Black Lady/Mammy /R. .... *550 +*
Money Bag, "$c,ook,ies," 7"   /588 .... *60 – 75*
Mother Goose, 12"   /695 .... *300 +*
Pineapple, 10½"   /664. .... *60 – 80*
Plaid, 8½"   /697DP. .... *75 – 100*
Pumpkin (Jack-o'-Lantern), 8"   /674 .... *300 +*

Wigwam cookie jar

Three Bears, 8³/₄" /696D . . . . *$100 – $125*
Wigwam, 11" /665 . . . . *500 +*
Windmill, 10¹/₂" /678 . . . . *200 – 225*
Witch, w/cat finial, 11¹/₂" /692 . . . . *400 +*

DINNERWARE

Bowl, soup, round, 5¹/₂" /341 . . . . *$20 – $25*
Dish, square, 5" /337 . . . . *20 – 25*
Plate, square, 7¹/₂" /339 . . . . *20 – 25*
Plate, round, 7¹/₂" /342. . . . . *20 – 25*
Plate, round, 12" /343 . . . . *45 – 50*
Plate, square, 10¹/₂" /340 . . . . *45 – 50*
Soup, covered, square, 4³/₄" /338 . . . . *35 – 45*

FIGURES

Animals

Goose, 5" /571
  Black . . . . *$30 – $40*
  Other colors . . . . *25 – 30*
Goose, leaning, 5" /98 . . . . *25 – 30*
Goose, upright, 2¹/₂" /99. . . . . *25 – 30*
Gull, 5" /562
  Black . . . . *50 – 60*
  Other colors . . . . *40 – 50*
Heron, 5¹/₂" /574
  Decorated . . . . *30 – 35*
  Solid colors . . . . *25 – 30*
Kangaroo, 7" /605
  Decorated . . . . *75 – 100*
  Solid colors . . . . *60 – 70*
Peacock, 7" /416 . . . . *75 – 100*
Pelican, 5" /572
  Decorated . . . . *30 – 35*
  Solid colors . . . . *25 – 30*
Penguin, 5¹/₂" /573
  Black . . . . *40 – 50*
  Decorated . . . . *30 – 35*
  Other colors . . . . *25 – 30*
Pouter Pigeon, 4¹/₂" /388. . . . . *30 – 40*
Swan, 3³/₄" /661
  Decorated . . . . *50 – 55*
  Solid colors . . . . *40 – 50*
Swordfish, 4¹/₂" /657
  Decorated . . . . *30 – 35*
  Solid colors . . . . *25 – 30*

Chessmen

Too rare to price, this listing is for information only.

Bishop, 4¹/₂"   /3905B..*ND*
Castle, 4"   /3905C..*ND*
King, 5¹/₂"   /3905K ....*ND*
Knight, 5"   /3905N ....*ND*
Pawn, 3¹/₂"   /3905P ....*ND*
Queen, 5"   /3905Q ....*ND*

People

Most of these were produced in white, blonde, or black only. Known exceptions are noted below.

Blackamoor, 7¹/₂"   /497
  Black ....*$60 – $70*
  Chartreuse ....*40 – 50*
  Decorated ....*50 – 60*
Fruit Girl, 10"   /3904.......................................*100 – 125*
Kneeling (Seated) **Nude**, 7"   /3903
  Black ....*300 – 350*
Nescia, 16"   /3901
  Black ....*ND*
Scarf Dancer, 13"   /3902
  Black ....*300 – 350*
  Gunmetal..*300 – 350*
  White...*300*
Shepherdess and Faun, 11¹/₂"   /3906
  Black ....*200 – 225*
  White...*150*

KITCHENWARE

Daisy

The jam jars and the tray make a set.

Each bottom was Ivory with lids either Blue daisies with yellow center or Jonquil yellow daises with brown center, with the exception of the jam jars, which were made in Jonquil yellow bodies with Ivory lids and fruit centers. The tray has a green line around the rim to match the leaves of the jam jars.

Cookie Jar, 8" high   /677D ....*$40 – $50*
Creamer ....*10 – 15*
Jar, grease, 4¹/₂" high, "G" ....*10 – 15*
Jar, jam
  Grape lid..*20*
  Plum lid..*20*
  Strawberry lid *20*
Shaker, range, "S" or "P", pair ....*20 – 25*

Sugar . . . . *$10 – $15*
Teapot . . . . *40 – 50*
Tray, 8" . . . . *10 – 15*

Refrigerator Set

The jugs were made in solid colors (either Dusty Blue, April Green, Sudan Red, Eggshell, or Golden Yellow) and the covered pieces in two color combinations (yellow with black covers or ivory with blue covers).

Butter, 1-pound   /RE4 . . . . *$15 – $20*
Casserole, 8"   /RE5 . . . . *15 – 20*
Jug, 1-pint   /202 . . . . *30 – 35*
Jug, 1-quart   /201 . . . . *40 – 45*
Jug, ice lip, 2-quart   /200 . . . . *50 – 55*
Jug, water, w/lid, 2-quart   /RE1 . . . . *35 – 45*
Leftover, oblong   /RE2. . . . . *15 – 20*
Leftover, round, 4"   /RE8. . . . . *15 – 20*
Leftover, round, 5"   /RE7. . . . . *15 – 20*
Leftover, round, 6"   /RE6. . . . . *15 – 20*
Leftover, square   /RE3 . . . . *15 – 20*

MISCELLANY

The masks were intended to hang on a wall.

Ashtray, Donkey, 5½"   /510 . . . . *$75 – $95*
Ashtray, Duo, 6¾" × 3½"   /356 . . . . *20 – 25*
Ashtray, Elephant, 5½"   /509. . . . . *75 – 95*
Ashtray, Greek, 4¼" × 3"   /326 . . . . *20 – 25*
Ashtray, Guard, square, 5"   /369 . . . . *20 – 25*
Ashtray, Trojan, 5" × 3½"   /316 . . . . *20 – 25*
Ashtray, Utility, round, 5½"   /317 . . . . *20 – 25*
Bowl, Morning Glory, 7"   /393. . . . . *35 – 45*
Bowl, Pineapple, 14¾" long   /700D . . . . *75 – 100*
Box, Butterfly, 4¾"   /580 . . . . *50 – 60*
Box, Candy Cane, 4½"   /607 . . . . *50 – 60*
Box, Lily Tray, 9½" long   /612. . . . . *50 – 60*
Candle Holder, Bamboo, 3½" square   /716D . . . . *15 – 20*
Candle Holder, Reflector, 6½"   /614. *25 – 35*
Cigarette Box, Elephant, 6"   /608 . . . . *50 – 75*
Console plate, Bamboo, 10½" diameter   /715D . . . . *30 – 40*
Jar, Elephant, 9¾"   /606. . . . . *125 – 150*
Jar, Pelican   /609D. . . . . *45 – 55*
Mask, female, 4"   /378 . . . . *ND*
Mask, female, 7½"   /376F. . . . . *ND*
Mask, male, 4"   /378 . . . . *ND*
Mask, male, 7½"   /376M . . . . *ND*
String holder, Chinese Face, 5½"   /702D . . . . *100 – 125*
String holder, Mouse, 8½"   /712D . . . . *100 – 125*

PLANTERS

Planter bookends are listed under Bookends.

Burro, 4½"   /673 .... $25 – $35
Daffodil   /668 .... 35 – 50
Donkey, 7½"   /669 .... 35 – 50
Dutch Shoe, 5" long
   Decorated .... 50 – 55
   Solid colors .... 35 – 45
Fawn, 5"   /672 .... 20 – 35
Gourd, 5½"   /667 .... 20 – 35
Pooch, 5½"   /670 .... 20 – 35
Puppy, 6¾" long   /652
   Decorated .... 35 – 50
   Solid colors .... 20 – 35
Ram, 4"   /671 .... 35 – 45

SHORT LINES

These lines have a variety of pieces, but rather than list each of them under their separate categories, I am putting them together here so that you can see how extensive each line is.

Asters

Bowl, flare, oval, 11½" × 8"   /450 .... $45 – $55
Bowl, oval, 15" × 9"   /452 .... 55 – 60
Bowl/Vase, 7"   /454 .... 45 – 55
Candle Holder, double, 4½"   /451 .... 25 – 35
Vase, 8"   /453 .... 30 – 35
Vase, 12"   /455 .... 55 – 60

Daisy

(Also called Sunflower) Came in Dawn Blue, Celadon Green, Royal Red, Antique White, Blonde, and Yellow Chartreuse as well as White with Yellow center and Yellow with Brown center.

Ashtray, 4½"   /386 .... $15 – $20
Bowl, 6½"   /399 .... 30 – 35
Bowl, 9½"   /383 .... 35 – 40
Bowl, 12"   382 .... 40 – 50
Candle Holder, 4½" diameter   /384 .... 15 – 20
Nut Cup, 3½"   /385 .... 15 – 20
Plate, salad, 7½"   /387 .... 15 – 20
Wall Pocket, 9"   /379 .... 45 – 70

Fern Leaf   (1937)

Described as a modern interpretation of the classic feather motif of the Empire period.

Bookend, 5½"   /428 .... $35 – $50

Bowl, 7¹/₄"   /423 .... *$30 – $35*
Bowl, 8¹/₂"   /424 .... *40 – 45*
Bowl, 10¹/₂"   /425 .... *50 – 55*
Bowl, Flower Boat, 13" × 4"   /426 .... *50 – 60*
Bowl, Fruit Boat, 15" × 6¹/₂"   /432.............................. *60 – 70*
Candle Boat, 3" × 5¹/₂" long   /434............................... *25 – 30*
Candle Holder/Bud Vase, 8"   /429............................... *20 – 30*
Candle Holder/Bud Vase, 5¹/₂"   /427 .... *15 – 20*
Jug, 1-quart, 8"   /430 .... *50 – 60*
Vase, 7¹/₄"   /420... *30 – 35*
Vase, 8³/₄"   /421... *35 – 40*
Vase, 10¹/₄"   /422.. *40 – 50*
Vase, 15"   /433 .... *125 – 150*
Wall Pocket, 7¹/₂"   /431 .... *35 – 50*

Morning Glory

Bowl, 7"   /393... *$35 – $45*
Vase, 5¹/₂"   /392... *25 – 30*
Vase, 7³/₄"   /391... *35 – 45*
Vase, 10"   /390 .... *40 – 50*

Shell   (1940)

Bowl, 6" diameter, 5¹/₂" high   /506 .... *$15 – $20*
Bowl, 7"   /502... *15 – 20*
Bowl, 10¹/₂"   /501 .... *20 – 25*
Bowl, 12"   /533 .... *30 – 35*
Bowl, 15"   /500 .... *35 – 40*
Bowl, deep, 9"   /610 .... *20 – 25*
Candle Holder/Ashtray, single, 4"   /503 .... *12 – 15*
Candle Holder, double, 4"   /505 .... *15 – 20*
Vase, oval, 7¹/₂"   /507 .... *15 – 25*
Vase, Planting, 7¹/₄"   /504 .... *25 – 30*
Wall Pocket, 7"   /508... *40 – 50*

Star

Bowl, console, 10"   /713... *$30 – $40*
Candle Holder, pair, 4¹/₄"   /714 .... *15 – 20*

Tri-Fern

Candle Holder, pair, 8"   /436 .... *$35 – $45*
Wall Pocket, 8" wide   /435 .... *125 – 150*

VASES

The Egret Sand Jar is the Egret Floor Vase with a dish fitted on top. There is a
small Head Vase that is too rare to price.

Acanthus, oval, 8"   /485... *$15 – $20*

Cactus vase

Slant Top, 9¹/₂"   /703 . . . . *$40 – $50*
Square Leaf, 9"   /708D . . . . *60 – 70*
Star, 7"   /463. . . . . *10 – 15*
Taper, 6"   /626 . . . . *30 – 35*
Trojan Head, 7¹/₂"   /499
   Black . . . . *75 – 100*
   Other colors . . . . *50 – 60*
Tulip, 6¹/₂"   /654 . . . . ·. *25 – 30*
Tulip   /604D . . . . *25 – 30*
Wheel Handle, 8"   /466 . . . . *25 – 30*
Wreath, 8"   /467. . . . . *30 – 35*

WALL POCKETS

Some of these were referred to as wall vases in company literature.

Acanthus bracket, 7"   /589 . . . . *$40 – $50*
Acanthus bracket, 8³/₄"   /649 . . . . *40 – 50*
Acanthus wall vase, 8³/₄"   /648 . . . . *40 – 50*
Apron, 6"   /699 . . . . *40 – 50*
Book, 6¹/₂"   /676D. . . . . *40 – 50*
Butterfly, 8¹/₂"   /601D. . . . . *50 – 75*
Calla, 9"   /586D . . . . *40 – 50*
Cherub bracket, 7¹/₂"   /587 . . . . *50 – 60*
Carriage Lamp, 10"   /711 . . . . *50 – 50*
Daisy, 7³/₄"   /379 . . . . *50 – 70*
Dutch Boy, 10"   /489 . . . . *80 – 100*
Dutch Girl, 10"   /490 . . . . *80 – 100*
Horn shape, double, 8¹/₂"   /493 . . . . *35 – 50*
Ionic, 9"   /457 . . . . *35 – 50*
Ivy Hanging Basket, 7"   /590D . . . . *50 – 70*
Leaf   /724 . . . . *35 – 40*
Match Box, 5¹/₂"   /675D . . . . *40 – 50*
Morning Glory (Lily), 9"   /377 . . . . *15 – 20*
Morning Glory (Lily), double, 7³/₄"   /375 . . . . *20 – 25*
Triad, 5¹/₂"   /640 . . . . *30 – 45*

AMERICAN BISQUE COMPANY

Williamstown, West Virginia

CHAPTER AT A GLANCE

COOKIE JARS
  Cartoons
  Disney

Flashers
Flintstones

Founded in 1919, the company produced cookie jars, florist ware, and kitchenware in an earthenware body. The figural cookie jars are the most collectible items. Closed in 1982.

See Roerig in Bibliography.

MARKS Most cookie jars will be found either unmarked or with "USA" impressed. Some early jars have a star-shaped design.

COOKIE JARS

A "corner" jar is designed with a 90-degree back so that it can fit comfortably in a corner. The **Brownie, Captain, Cop, Fire Chief** and **Pirate** jars, with hands on stomach, have the same bottom but different lids. **Flashers** are the collectors' name for a series of jars in which one of the elements of the design will change as you turn it (sort of a holographic effect but a more primitive technology). **Turnabouts** were not made by American Bisque but rather by the American Pottery Company, which had ties to American Bisque, per Joyce Roerig's research. See also Cardinal China.

Acorn, w/oak leaves (corner) .... $170 – $190
Alice in Wonderland .... 225 – 250
Animal Crackers, w/embossed animals .... 30 – 40
Ball of Yarn w/Kittens, small .... 60 – 70
Ball of Yarn w/Kittens, large .... 120 – 130
  Pitcher .... 150 – 175
Barrel, wooden, "Cookie Barrel" .... 30 – 35
Basket w/cat and handle lid .... 45 – 50
Basket w/cookies and handle lid (Basket O' Cookies) .... 50 – 60
Basket w/dog and handle lid .... 45 – 50
Basket w/rabbit and handle lid .... 45 – 50
Basket w/tray lid, "Cookie Tray" .... 300 – 325
Bear, sitting, eyes closed, w/bow (Bow Bear) .... 80 – 90

Bear, sitting, eyes open (Boy Bear) .... *$70 – $80*
Bear, w/bib and cookie (Baby Bear) .... *70 – 80*
Bear, w/hat and bow tie .... *80 – 90*
Beehive w/kitten finial .... *50 – 60*
Bell, Liberty, "Liberty" .... *100 – 125*
Bell (Ringing Bell), "Ring for Cookies" .... *40 – 45*
Blackboard (Chalkboard) **Boy** .... *350 – 375*
Blackboard (Chalkboard) **Clown** .... *275 – 300*
Blackboard (Chalkboard) **Girl** .... *350 – 375*
Blackboard (Chalkboard) **Hobo** .... *300 – 325*
Blackboard (Chalkboard) **Saddle** .... *275 – 300*
Boots, cowboy .... *200 – 225*
Box, quilted, w/kitten finial .... *120 – 140*
Box, quilted, w/dog finial .... *120 – 140*
Box, w/ribbon finial (Gift Box) .... *150 – 175*
Boy, Amish (Pennsylvania Dutch) .... *425 – 450*
Boy w/Churn .... *225 – 250*
Brownie, hands on stomach .... *100 – 125*
Bucket, Oaken, dipper finial .... *110 – 125*
Bull, hands in pockets, small .... *90 – 110*
Bull, hands in pockets, large .... *125 – 150*
Captain, hands on stomach .... *100 – 125*
Carousel, knob finial .... *50 – 60*
Carousel, pointed finial .... *100 – 125*
Cat, hands in pockets, large .... *125 – 145*
Cat, w/indented dots (Polka Dot Kitty) .... *75 – 85*
Chef, arms at side (star mark) .... *70 – 80*
Chef, head, w/tray lid, "Cookie Tray" .... *350 +*
Chef w/spoon, small .... *125 – 135*
Chef w/spoon, large .... *125 – 135*
Chick, w/tam and jacket .... *65 – 75*
Chiffonnier (corner) .... *165 – 185*
Churn, w/floral decoration .... *25 – 35*
Clock (Rudolph) .... *350 – 375*
Clock, w/face, "Cookie Time" .... *60 – 80*
Clown, full figure, hands on stomach .... *50 – 60*
Clown, full figure, arms raised (Happy)/CM .... *100 – 110*
Clown, w/indented dots .... *50 – 60*
Coach Lamp .... *125 – 150*
Coffee Pot, metal handle .... *35 – 45*
Coffee Pot, ceramic handle, w/pinecones .... *35 – 45*
Coffee Pot, cup and cookies .... *35 – 45*
Cookie Jar w/puppy finial, "Cookies" .... *65 – 75*
Cop, hands on stomach .... *100 – 125*
Cylinder, w/apple (Pippin) .... *25 – 35*
Cylinder, w/Bluebirds .... *30 – 35*
Cylinder, w/Daisies .... *30 – 35*
Davy Crockett, Boy, rifle in left hand .... *350 +*

Jack-in-the-Box, Spaceship, and Davy Crockett cookie jars.

Davy Crockett, Man, rifle in right hand . . . . *$700 +*
Dog, French Poodle . . . . *125 – 145*
Dog, w/scarf around head (Toothache Dog). . . . . *500 +*
Drum Majorette, head. . . . . *275 – 300*
Dutch Boy (cold paint). . . . . *35 – 45*
Dutch Boy (underglaze). . . . . *100 – 125*
Dutch Girl (cold paint) . . . . *35 – 45*
Dutch Girl (underglaze). . . . . *100 – 125*
Dutch Shoe . . . . *ND*
Elephant, Baby, w/bib. . . . . *150 – 175*
   w/gold. . . . . *250 – 275*
Elephant, Girl, dancing . . . . *150 – 175*
Elephant, hands in pockets (bank in lid) . . . . *150 – 175*
Elephant, in overalls w/ball cap /CM . . . . *130 – 160*
Elephant, in beanie (Sailor Elephant) . . . . *100 – 110*
Engine, ... *150 – 175*
Engine, long, "Cookie R.R." . . . . *80 – 90*
Feed Bag . . . . *90 – 100*
Fire Chief. . . . . *100 – 125*
Flower Jar . . . . *50 – 60*
Girl, Amish (Pennsylvania Dutch). . . . . *375 +*
Girl, Peasant. . . . . *400 +*
Granny. . . . . *150 – 175*
Hen w/chick on back
   Airbrushed colors. . . . . *125 – 150*
   White . . . . *100 – 125*
Horse, sitting, spotted /R . . . . *1000 +*
Igloo w/seal finial. . . . . *275 – 300*
Jack-in-the-Box. . . . . *125 – 150*

Lamb, Little Girl . . . . *$80 – $90*
Lamb in hat, w/collar . . . . *135 – 145*
Milk Can, bell in lid. . . . . *45 – 55*
Milk Wagon w/donkey, white/yellow, "Cookies & Milk" . . . . *100 – 110*
Mohawk Indian . . . . *2500 +*
Mug, marshmallows on lid (Hot Chocolate) . . . . *60 – 70*
Owl, w/glasses and mortarboard (Collegiate Owl) . . . . *70 – 90*
Paddlewheeler . . . . *225 – 235*
Pedestal Jar . . . . *30 – 35*
Pig, Boy, w/scarf . . . . *80 – 90*
Pig, Dancer, in tutu . . . . *130 – 160*
　w/polka dots. . . . . *115 – 135*
　Shakers, pair . . . . *20 – 25*
Pig, Farmer, w/straw hat and scarf /CM . . . . *130 – 150*
Pig, Girl, w/apron, flowers in hair . . . . *80 – 90*
Pig, Lady. . . . . *80 – 90*
Pig, w/indented dots . . . . *115 – 130*
Pirate, arms at side (star mark) . . . . *70 – 80*
Pirate, hands on stomach . . . . *125 – 150*
Potbellied Stove. . . . . *35 – 45*
Rabbit, farmer hat w/patch (Goofy Rabbit) . . . . *300 – 325*
Rabbit, hands in pockets . . . . *75 – 85*
　Bank . . . . *35 – 45*
Rabbit, in dress w/glasses (Mrs. Rabbit) . . . . *300 – 325*
Recipe Jar . . . . *100 – 110*
Ring Jar . . . . *20 – 25*
Rooster, Yellow w/gold . . . . *125 – 135*
Sack, w/cookies lid, "Cookies" . . . . *50 – 60*
Sack, w/pig lid (Pig-in-Poke). . . . . *70 – 80*
Saddle (no blackboard) . . . . *250 – 275*
　Lamp . . . . *250 +*
Sadiron. . . . . *125 – 150*
Santa, head, winking . . . . *375 +*
Schoolhouse w/bell in lid, "After School Cookies" . . . . *40 – 50*
Sea Bag. . . . . *150 +*
Sentry (not marked Disney). . . . . *75 – 95*
Snowman Bank . . . . *35 – 45*
Spaceship (Moon Rocket), "Cookies Out of the World". . . . . *275 – 300*
Spaceship w/Spaceman, "Cookies Out of the World" . . . . *700 +*
Spool of thread w/embossed needle. . . . . *125 – 140*
Strawberry (Sears) . . . . *30 – 35*
　Shakers, small, pair . . . . *10 – 15*
　Shakers, range, pair . . . . *20 – 25*
Tea Kettle. . . . . *40 – 50*
Top Hat w/bunny lid (Magic Bunny). . . . . *80 – 90*
Treasure Chest, open . . . . *125 – 135*
Treasure Chest, closed . . . . *150 – 175*

Truck, "Cookie Truck," 11½" .... $80 – $95
Truck, "Cookie Truck," 13" .... 80 – 95
Umbrella Kids (Sweethearts) .... 300 +
Yarn Doll, w/braids .... 110 – 125
   w/gold .... 210 – 225
   Bank .... 20 – 25

Cartoons

Baby Huey /R .... $2000 +
Casper /R .... 1000 +
   Bank .... 400 – 450
   Candy Jar .... 1500 +
Herman and Katnip .... ND
Little Audrey .... 3000 +
   Bank .... 600 – 700
Olive Oyl /R .... 2000 +
Popeye /R .... 800 +
Swee' Pea /R .... 3000 +
   Bank .... 600 +
Yogi Bear .... 375 – 450

Disney

Donald Duck, sitting .... $225 – $250
   Matching shakers, pair .... 35 – 45
Professor Ludwig Von Drake, head. .... 900 +
Toy Soldier in kiosk/Babes in Toyland .... 275 – 325

Flashers

(These are called Pan-Eye-Matic Cookie Jars in the catalog.)

Bear & Beehive (corner) .... $350 – $375
Cheerleaders (corner) .... 325 – 350
Clown .... 250 – 275
Cow and Moon .... 1000 +
Sandman, 2 kids watching TV (TV Bedtime). .... 275 – 325
Tortoise and Hare (Rabbit & Log). .... 700 +

Flintstones

The four jars have been reproduced.

Dino .... $950 – $1000
   Bank .... 450 – 500
Fred .... 1000 +
Fred and Wilma bank .... 400 – 425
Rubble's House .... 900 +
Wilma on telephone .... 1000 +

AMERICAN CHINAWARE CORPORATION

Chicago, Illinois

CHAPTER AT A GLANCE

BRIAR ROSE
NOUVELLE

PLAZA
PRIMROSE

There had been talk of mergers among Ohio potteries several times in the late nineteenth and early twentieth centuries. A few attempts had been made. But with the announcement in 1929 of the formation of the American Chinaware Corporation, spearheaded by Chicago businessman Louis H. Porter, the largest merger to that date had been accomplished.

There were nine Ohio general ware potteries with a total of 102 kilns in the new company. Carrollton Pottery Co., Carrollton; E. H. Sebring Co., Sebring; French China Co., Sebring; Knowles, Taylor & Knowles Co., East Liverpool; National China Co., Salineville; Pope-Gosser China Company, Coshocton; Saxon China Co., Sebring; and Smith-Phillips, East Liverpool, as well as the Strong Manufacturing Co. of Sebring, which made enamel ware. Sales offices and operating headquarters were in Chicago. The purpose of the consolidation was greater economies in purchasing and manufacturing.

ACC had no better success than its predecessors, and it declared bankruptcy in mid 1931. The tragedy of this failure was the number of potteries that did not survive this debacle. Only Carrollton and Pope-Gosser managed to reorganize and continue. Others just closed or were bought by other interests.

J. Palin Thorley came to the United States from England to work for the American Chinaware Corporation in 1929. Of their four known shapes, I have confirmed that he designed three; it is likely he designed Plaza as well.

Marks

There is evidence that "Amerce" was used as a sort of brand name, but I have never seen it marked on the pieces I have found. The backstamp here was used on several shapes.

41

BRIAR ROSE

Designed by J. Palin Thorley. Produced in an ivory body. After ACC's bankruptcy, this shape was bought by Salem China. I have found reference to an ashtray with snuffer, candle holder, and rose bowl made by ACC but no reference to these pieces made by Salem.

Some decals to look for are Festival of the Vintage (five or six underglaze patterns inspired by the eighteenth century in black, blue, fawn, maroon, and pink), and Godey's Ladies Book.

Ashtray w/snuffer	*$8 – $10*
Bowl, rose	*18 – 20*
Bowl, soup, coupe, 7"	*10 – 12*
Bowl, vegetable, round, 8"	*15 – 18*
Bowl, vegetable, oval, 9"	*15 – 18*
Butter dish, open	*15 – 20*
Candle holder	*12 – 15*
Casserole	*20 – 25*
Creamer	*4 – 6*
Cup	*4 – 6*
Dish, fruit	*2 – 3*
Dish, cereal	*3 – 4*
Gravy	*12 – 15*
Gravy liner/pickle	*6 – 8*
Plate, 6¼"	*1 – 2*
Plate, 7"	*4 – 5*
Plate, 9¼"	*7 – 9*
Plate, bread, 10"	*10 – 12*
Plate, cake, 10"	*10 – 12*
Platter, 11"	*10 – 12*
Platter, 13"	*12 – 15*
Platter, 22" × 18"	*30 – 35*
Saucer	*1 – 2*
Sugar	*8 – 10*

NOUVELLE   (1930)

Designed by J. Palin Thorley. Pieces of this shape have turned up marked Harker, which suggests that Harker bought the molds after ACC's bankruptcy.

Bowl, soup, 8"*	*$10 – $12*
Bowl, vegetable, oval, 9"*	*10 – 12*
Casserole	*20 – 25*
Creamer	*4 – 6*
Cup	*4 – 6*
Dish, 5½"*	*2 – 3*
Gravy	*12 – 15*
Gravy liner	*6 – 8*
Plate, 6"*	*1 – 2*
Plate, 9"*	*7 – 9*
Plate, square, tab handle	*10 – 12*

Primrose sugar, Nouvelle tab-handle plate, green lustre Plaza creamer and Nouvelle sugar. The Nouvelle sugar is backstamped "KTK," which would seem to indicate that not all the potteries in this merger switched their backstamps to the new name right away.

Platter, 11"* . . . . *$10 – $12*
Saucer . . . . *1 – 2*
Sugar . . . . *8 – 10*

PLAZA   (1931)

A gadroon shape.

Bowl, soup, 8"* . . . . *$10 – $12*
Bowl, vegetable, oval, 9"* . . . . *10 – 12*
Casserole . . . . *20 – 25*
Creamer . . . . *4 – 6*
Cup . . . . *4 – 6*
Dish, 5½"* . . . . *2 – 3*
Gravy . . . . *12 – 15*
Gravy liner . . . . *6 – 8*
Plate, 6"* . . . . *1 – 2*
Plate, 9"* . . . . *7 – 9*
Platter, 11"* . . . . *10 – 12*
Saucer . . . . *1 – 2*
Sugar . . . . *8 – 10*

PRIMROSE   (1930)

Designed by J. Palin Thorley.

Bowl, soup, 8"* . . . . *$10 – $12*
Bowl, vegetable, oval, 9"* . . . . *10 – 12*

Casserole . . . . *$20 – $25*
Creamer . . . . *4 – 6*
Cup . . . . *4 – 6*
Dish, 5½"* . . . . *2 – 3*
Gravy . . . . *12 – 15*
Gravy liner . . . . *6 – 8*
Plate, 6"* . . . . *1 – 2*
Plate, 9"* . . . . *7 – 9*
Platter, 11"* . . . . *10 – 12*
Saucer . . . . *1 – 2*
Sugar . . . . *8 – 10*

APPLEMAN AUTOWORKS, INC.

New York, New York, and Union City, New Jersey

Glenn Appleman was born in New York in 1949 and graduated with a Fine Arts degree in 1971 from the City University. He established his own studio and, according to a company brochure, produced "distinctive sculpture encompassing subjects ranging from Mao Tse Tung and Richard Nixon to armadillos and gorillas."

The car cookie jars which Appleman created were manufactured from 1977 to 1987, at first in Manhattan and, after 1982, in Union City. All the hand work that went into making each jar was expensive. Prices rose. Orders fell. The company closed its doors.

Buick Convertible
    Black/brown/green/red/white .... *$750 +*
    Black w/"Dewey Defeats Truman" .... *2500 +*
    Red w/Ten Cats .... *2500 +*
Buick Sedan
    Black/brown/green/red/white .... *700 +*
Corvette
    Black body w/white scoop .... *1000 +*
    Red body w/white scoop .... *1000 +*
    White body w/red scoop .... *1000 +*
Great American Trucks
    Gotham Trucking .... *1500 +*
    Moosehead Beer .... *1500 +*
    Stroh's Beer .... *1500 +*
    Vito's Veggies w/driver .... *1600 +*
Humperbump Police Car .... *700 +*
Humperbump Sedan
    Blue/green/red/white .... *650 +*
Mercedes-Benz Convertible
    Top down lid .... *900 +*
    Top raised lid .... *900 +*
Packard Convertible .... *750 +*
Packard Police Car
    Black and white .... *700 +*
    Blue and white .... *700 +*

Packard Sedan
   Blue/green/red/white . . . . *$850 +*
Phanta-Zoom
   Black w/red . . . . *700 +*
   Gray w/pink . . . . *700 +*
   Pink w/gray . . . . *700 +*
   Turquoise w/white . . . . *700 +*
Rolls-Royce
   Baby blue and black . . . . *ND*
   Black & crimson . . . . *1100 +*
   Black & pearl gray . . . . *1100 +*
   Black & yellow . . . . *1100 +*
   Brown & tan . . . . *1100 +*
   Maroon & cream . . . . *1100 +*
Sid's Taxi . . . . *700 +*
Skyway Cab . . . . *800 +*

ATLAS-GLOBE CHINA COMPANY

Cambridge, Ohio

Atlas-Globe was incorporated in November 1926, merging the Atlas China Company of Niles, Ohio, with the Globe China Company of Cambridge, Ohio. In mid 1932 it was reorganized again and became the Oxford Pottery Company. See Universal for further history.

BROADWAY

The flatware was made in both round and square shapes. This shape is the precursor of Universal's Mt. Vernon shape.

MARKS The word "Rose" in the backstamp shown here refers to the color of the body, not any decoration.

Bowl, vegetable, 9"* .... *$10 – $12*
Casserole .... *20 – 25*
Creamer .... *4 – 6*
Cup .... *4 – 6*
Dish, 5½"* .... *2 – 3*

Broadway: Hollyhock creamer (this decal is also found on Universal pieces), and "Daffodil" sugar.

Plate, round, 6¼" . . . . *$1 – $2*
Plate, round, 9"* . . . . *7 – 9*
Platter, 11½" . . . . *10 – 12*
Saucer . . . . *1 – 2*
Sugar . . . . *8 – 10*

OLD HOLLAND   (1931)

An embossed design incorporating windmills and people.

Made in an ivory body, Old Holland was available plain, decorated with decals, or with ivory centers and colored rims in either Delft Blue, Jade Green, or Canary Yellow.

PRICING   This line was continued by Universal when they bought Oxford. See that listing for values.

J. A. BAUER POTTERY COMPANY

Los Angeles, California

J. A. Bauer, who had run a family pottery in Paducah, Kentucky, moved to California for his health and established a new pottery in 1909. Red clay flowerpots were the first major item produced, but stoneware soon followed, with many utilitarian items made. Art pottery was added ca. 1915. The colored dinnerware was introduced in 1930, and artwares were added a little later in the decade. The firm closed in 1962.

There is some argument about who produced the first colored dinnerware but no doubt about who popularized it—Bauer. In 1936, Homer Laughlin would introduce its own colored line, Fiesta, and dominate the market with its superior sales force, but Bauer led the way. It made a number of colored dinnerware lines, but Ring is the most popular among collectors. Oil jars rate high interest also.

See Chipman in Bibliography.

MARKS Most items have an impressed mark with either the name "Bauer" or with some combination of the words Bauer, Los Angeles, Pottery, and USA. Many items will be found unmarked or stamped "Made in USA." (Marks courtesy Jack Chipman.)

BAUER
USA

BAUER
LOS ANGELES

BAUER
LOS MADE IN U.S.A. ANGELES

BAUER

DINNERWARE / KITCHENWARE

LA LINDA   (1939–1959)

Hard-to-find pieces are the plain ball jug, cookie jar, and oblong, plain (no band) butter dish.

Matte colors of green, blue, ivory, and dusty pink. Gloss colors of Burgundy, Chartreuse, Dark Brown, Gray, Green, Ivory, Light Brown, Olive Green, Pink, Turquoise, and Yellow.

PRICING   Burgundy and Dark Brown are at the high end of the range.

Bowl, soup, 7" .... *$18 – $24*
Bowl, vegetable, oval, 8" .... *18 – 24*
Bowl, vegetable, oval, 10" .... *25 – 30*
Bowl, vegetable, round, 9½" .... *25 – 30*
Butter dish, oblong plain .... *45 – 60*
Cookie jar, plain .... *60 – 75*
Creamer, old .... *7 – 10*
Creamer, new .... *7 – 10*
Cup .... *10 – 15*
Cup, Jumbo .... *25 – 30*
Custard .... *6 – 8*

La Linda place setting: 9" dinner, 7½" salad, 6" bread & butter; 6" soup/cereal; cup & saucer; "old" salt & pepper; "old" creamer & sugar; 13" chop plate.

Dish, 5" .... $6 – $8
Dish, 6" .... 10 – 15
Gravy .... 15 – 20
Jug, ball .... 35 – 45
Plate, 6" .... 4 – 6
Plate, 7½" .... 7 – 10
Plate, 9" .... 10 – 15
Plate, chop, 13" .... 25 – 30
Platter, oblong, 10" .... 12 – 16
Platter, oblong, 12" .... 15 – 20
Ramekin .... 6 – 8
Saucer .... 3 – 4
Saucer, Jumbo .... 3 – 4
Shaker, short, old .... 4 – 6
Shaker, tall, new .... 4 – 6
Sugar, old .... 12 – 16
Sugar, new .... 12 – 16
Teapot, plain, 6-cup .... 30 – 40
Tumbler, 8-ounce .... 12 – 16

MONTEREY   (1936–1945)

Hard-to-find pieces are the beverage server, cake plate, candlestick, midget set, sauce boat, 10½" plate, and relish. Rare pieces are console set and ashtray.

Colors: Burgundy, California Orange Red, Canary Yellow, Green, Ivory, Monterey Blue, Red Brown, Turquoise Blue, and White.

PRICING   Burgundy and Orange Red are at the high end of the range. Add 25% for White if it is uncrazed.

Beverage server w/cover .... $100 – $125
Bowl, fruit, footed, 8" .... 25 – 30
Bowl, fruit, footed, 9" .... 40 – 55
Bowl, fruit, footed, 12" .... 45 – 60
Bowl, salad/fruit, 11½" .... 40 – 55
Bowl, soup, 7" .... 25 – 30
Bowl, vegetable, oval, 10½" .... 40 – 55
Bowl, vegetable, round, 9½" .... 35 – 45
Bowl, vegetable, oval, divided .... 45 – 60
Butter, ¼-pound .... 60 – 75
Candlestick .... 35 – 45
Coffee server, w/wood handle, 8-cup .... 30 – 40
Console set, 3-piece .... 200 – 250
Creamer .... 10 – 12
Creamer, midget .... 20 – 25
Cup .... 18 – 24
Dish, 6" .... 10 – 15
Gravy .... 30 – 40
Jug, ice lip, 2-quart .... 60 – 75
Plate, 6" .... 8 – 10

Monterey: Clockwise from top: 13" chop plate, cup & saucer; gravy boat; shakers; oval vegetable; coffee server w/lid; 9" dinner plates.

Plate, 7¹/₂" .... *$10 – $12*
Plate, 9" .... *12 – 16*
Plate, 10¹/₂" .... *25 – 30*
Plate, cake, pedestal .... *100 – 150*
Plate, chop, 13" .... *35 – 45*
Platter, oval, 12" .... *30 – 40*
Platter, oval, 17" .... *40 – 45*
Relish, 3-part, 10¹/₂" .... *40 – 45*
Sauce boat .... *35 – 45*
Saucer .... *6 – 8*
Shaker .... *6 – 8*
Sugar .... *18 – 24*
Sugar, midget .... *20 – 25*
Teapot, old, 6-cup .... *60 – 75*
Teapot, new, 6-cup .... *60 – 75*

Tray (for midget cream and sugar) .... *$30 – $40*
Tumbler, 8-ounce .... *15 – 20*

PASTEL KITCHENWARE

This is the shape with the wide ribs. It was made in the same colors as La Linda. The Aladdin teapots are getting scarce.

Bowl, batter, 1-quart .... *$25 – $30*
Bowl, batter, 2-quart .... *45 – 60*
Bowl, mixing, 1-pint .... *10 – 12*
Bowl, mixing, 1½-pint.. *12 – 16*
Bowl, mixing, 1-quart .... *15 – 20*
Bowl, mixing, 1½-quart... *18 – 24*
Bowl, mixing, ½-gallon... *25 – 30*
Casserole, metal holder, 1½-pint .... *28 – 35*
Casserole, metal holder, 1-quart .... *35 – 45*
Cookie jar .... *75 – 100*
Jug, 1½-pint.. *20 – 25*
Jug, 1-quart .... *30 – 40*
Teapot, Aladdin, 4-cup .... *65 – 85*
Teapot, Aladdin, 8-cup .... *100 – 150*

RING (ca. 1931)

This is the line of dinnerware that prompted Homer Laughlin to create Fiesta. Rare pieces are the AD cup and saucer, ball jug, barrel-shaped and beer items, 5½" casserole, cigarette jar, coffee pot, eggcup, goblet, honey jar, jumbo cup, mustard, sugar shaker, the lids for the water bottle and beating bowl pitcher, and these bowls: pedestal, punch, salad/punch, and soufflé.

The basic colors you will find are Black, Burgundy, Orange Red, Chartreuse, Chinese Yellow, Dark Blue, Gray, Ivory, Jade Green, Light Blue, Light Brown, Olive Green, Red Brown, Turquoise, and White.

PRICING   Burgundy, Dark Blue, Ivory, Orange Red, and White are at the high end of the price range. Add 50% for Black.

Ashtray, 2" .... *$35 – $40*
Bowl, batter, 1-quart .... *75 – 100*
Bowl, batter, 2-quart .... *60 – 80*
Bowl, beating, 1-quart .... *45 – 60*
Bowl, beating pitcher, 1-quart .... *40 – 55*
Bowl, mixing, 1-pint .... *25 – 30*
Bowl, mixing, 1½-pint... *20 – 25*
Bowl, mixing, 1-quart .... *25 – 30*
Bowl, mixing, 1½-quart... *30 – 40*
Bowl, mixing, ½-gallon.. *40 – 55*
Bowl, mixing, 1-gallon .... *55 – 75*
Bowl, mixing, 1¼-gallon... *100 – 150*
Bowl, nesting, 6" .... *20 – 25*
Bowl, nesting, 7" .... *25 – 30*

Ring Ware: 14" chop plate; dealer sign ($200–250); Sombrero ashtray ($45–60); 12 oz tumbler w/handle; 6 oz tumbler w/handle; barrel tumbler w/handle; 1 qt pitcher and round butter dish.

Bowl, nesting, 8"	$30 – $40
Bowl, nesting, 9"	40 – 55
Bowl, pedestal, 14"	250 – 300
Bowl, punch 14".	250 – 300
Bowl, salad, low, 9"	30 – 40
Bowl, salad, low, 12"	65 – 85
Bowl, salad, low, 14"	100 – 150
Bowl, salad/punch, 9"	150 – 200
Bowl, salad/punch, 11"	200 – 300
Bowl, soup, 7½".	35 – 45
Bowl, soup, lug, 6".	35 – 45
Lid for above	ND
Bowl, soup, lug, 7" (restyled)	35 – 45
Bowl, vegetable, oval, 8".	35 – 45
Bowl, vegetable, oval, 10".	45 – 60
Bowl, vegetable, oval, divided.	65 – 85
Butter, ¼-pound	100 – 150
Butter dish, round.	100 – 150
Candlestick, spool.	75 – 100
Canister, 4½".	60 – 80
Canister, 6".	75 – 100
Canister, 6¾".	100 – 150
Carafe, metal handle.	50 – 65
Casserole, individual, 5½".	60 – 85
Casserole, metal holder, 6½".	45 – 60
Casserole, metal holder, 7½".	55 – 70
Casserole, metal holder, 8½".	60 – 80
Casserole, metal holder, 9½".	75 – 100
Cigarette jar.	150 – 200
Coffee pot, 8-cup.	150 – 200
Coffee server, wood handle, 6-cup.	45 – 60

Coffee server, wood handle, 8-cup .... *$60 – $80*
Cookie jar .... *200 – 300*
Creamer .... *15 – 20*
Creamer, AD. .... *15 – 20*
Cup, AD. .... *65 – 85*
Cup, coffee .... *20 – 25*
Cup, Jumbo .... *65 – 85*
Cup, punch. .... *20 – 25*
Cup, tea .... *20 – 25*
Custard .... *15 – 20*
Dish, dessert, 4" .... *15 – 20*
Dish, baking, w/lid, 4" .... *35 – 45*
Dish, cereal, 4¹/₂" .... *35 – 45*
Dish, fruit, 5" .... *20 – 25*
Eggcup .... *65 – 85*
Goblet .... *65 – 85*
Gravy bowl .... *60 – 80*
Jug, 1¹/₂-pint .... *30 – 40*
Jug, 1-quart. .... *40 – 55*
Jug, 2-quart .... *65 – 85*
Jug, 3-quart .... *75 – 100*
Jug, ball .... *100 – 150*
Jug, barrel .... *200 – 300*
Jug, beer. .... *200 – 300*
Jug, cream, 1-pint .... *35 – 45*
Jug, ice lip, w/metal handle, 2-quart .... *75 – 100*
Mug, barrel, 12-ounce .... *50 – 65*
Mustard. .... *150 – 200*
Pickle dish .... *20 – 25*
Pie baker, no holder, 9" .... *20 – 25*
Plate, 5" .... *20 – 25*
Plate, 6" .... *15 – 20*
Plate, 7¹/₂" .... *20 – 25*
Plate, 9" .... *25 – 30*
Plate, 10¹/₂" .... *50 – 65*
Plate, chop, 12" .... *40 – 55*
Plate, chop, 14" .... *50 – 65*
Plate, chop, 17" .... *75 – 100*
Platter, oval, 9" .... *25 – 30*
Platter, oval, 12" .... *35 – 45*
Ramekin, 4" .... *15 – 20*
Refrigerator jar, open .... *20 – 25*
Refrigerator set, 4 pieces .... *200 – 300*
Relish, 5 part .... *75 – 100*
Saucer, coffee/tea .... *10 – 15*
Saucer, AD .... *45 – 60*
Shaker, barrel shape .... *25 – 30*
Shaker, low .... *10 – 15*

Shaker, sugar. . . . . $100 – $150
Sherbet . . . . 50 – 65
Soufflé dish . . . . 150 – 200
Stein, beer . . . . 75 – 100
Sugar . . . . 35 – 45
Sugar, AD . . . . 30 – 40
Teapot, 2-cup. . . . . 75 – 100
Teapot, 6-cup. . . . . 75 – 100
Teapot, wood handle, 6-cup . . . . 75 – 100
Tumbler, 3-ounce . . . . 20 – 25
Tumbler, 6-ounce . . . . 15 – 20
Tumbler, 12-ounce . . . . 25 – 30
Tumbler, barrel shape, w/metal handle. . . . . 45 – 60
Vase, cylinder, 6". . . . . 45 – 60
Vase, cylinder, 8". . . . . 65 – 85
Vase, cylinder, 10". . . . . 75 – 100
Water bottle . . . . 75 – 100
  w/cover . . . . 200 – 300

MISCELLANY

ANIMALS / MINIATURE

Designed by Tracy Irwin. Part of the Cal-Art Pottery line. The Hippo and Scottie are hard to find.

Figures were made in a satin-matte white, less frequently in a satin-matte blue. High-gloss turquoise, orange-red, or other colors are hard to find, and a spatter effect is rare.

Dog, Collie. . . . . $150 – $200
Dog, Scottie, 4" high × 4½" long . . . . 150 – 200
Duck, head up . . . . 20 – 25
Duck, head down. . . . . 20 – 25
Duck, head under wing . . . . 25 – 30
Hippo, 3¼" high × 4½" long . . . . 150 – 200
Pony, on base. . . . . 150 – 200

OIL JARS

These seem to have been made in all colors. The 16" jar is the size seen most often.

  PRICING   Add 50% for black.

12" . . . . $800 – $1000
16" . . . . 800 – 1000
22" . . . . 1000 – 1500
24" . . . . 2000+

EDWIN BENNETT POTTERY

Baltimore, Maryland

CHAPTER AT A GLANCE

DINNERWARE   KITCHENWARE
Cameo

In 1841, Edwin Bennett came to America from Derbyshire, England, with his brothers Daniel and William to join his brother James at the pottery the latter had built in East Liverpool, Ohio. Dissatisfied with local transportation, they moved to Birmingham, south of Pittsburgh, in 1844. Two years later, Edwin moved to Baltimore and established his pottery for the manufacture of Cane and Rockingham ware.

Bennett ran the pottery individually until 1890 and, upon incorporation that year, as president until his death in 1908. He was succeeded as president by his son, Edwin H. Bennett. Through the years a variety of products were made, including parian, white granite, majolica, and semiporcelain. The firm closed in 1936.

MARKS   Most Bennett is backstamped with a variety of marks: "Bennett Bakeware," and "Bennett, S-V, Baltimore." "I1 Duce" will also appear on their kitchenware.

DINNERWARE

The majority of pieces found will be on a tan body; yellow and white bodies were also used. Bennett produced a variety of shapes. Of greatest interest to collectors is their Cameo line, which follows.

PRICING   Very little dinnerware is found; therefore, this list is generic. It represents pricing for Athena (<1925, White Granite, similar to Havilland's Ranson shape), Clytie (<1925, White Granite, plain round), Dryad (<1898, embossed), Pyramid (round flatware with square or rectangular serving pieces), Thetis (1921, plain round with loop finials), and Vesta (<1898, embossed).

Bowl, soup, 7½"..	*$10 – $12*
Bowl, vegetable, rectangular	*10 – 12*
Butter dish	*20 – 25*
Casserole..	*20 – 25*
Creamer	*4 – 6*
Cup	*4 – 6*
Dish, 5½"..	*2 – 3*
Eggcup..	*10 – 12*
Gravy...	*12 – 15*
Gravy faststand	*12 – 15*
Plate, 6"..	*1 – 2*
Plate, 8"..	*4 – 5*
Plate, 9"..	*7 – 9*
Plate, 10"...	*10 – 12*
Platter, 11"*	*10 – 12*
Saucer	*1 – 2*
Sugar...	*8 – 10*

Cameo   (1932)

The process was brought to Bennett by a German immigrant, George Bauer, who later brought it to Harker (which see) when Bennett closed.

Some of these pieces are from the Pyramid shape and are so marked. I haven't seen every piece on this list, so I don't know how many were original to Cameo (if any) and how many were taken from other shapes.

At least two patterns were made: Lily of the Valley and "Flower Tree" (leaves and flowers hanging from a branch). Cameo was made in at least four colors: Apricot, Sky Blue, pink, and Summer Yellow. A dark brown may show up.

Bowl, mixing, small..	*$10 – $12*
Bowl, mixing, medium..	*15 – 18*
Bowl, mixing, large...	*20 – 25*
Cake plate...	*12 – 15*
Casserole..	*25 – 30*
Creamer (Pyramid)..	*6 – 8*
Cup	*6 – 8*
Drip jar	*15 – 18*
Gravy...	*15 – 18*

Cameoware: Pyramid creamer, sugar, and tray, and barrel jug.

Plate, 6¼"* .... *$2 – $3*
Plate, 9" .... *10 – 12*
Saucer .... *2 – 3*
Shaker, range, pair .... *20 – 25*
Sugar (Pyramid) .... *10 – 15*
Tray (Pyramid) .... *15 – 18*
Utensil, cake server .... *15 – 18*

KITCHENWARE   (<1932)

The lemon reamer sits on the measuring cup; the waffle cover and dish are a set.
   You will find a variety of silk-screen and decal decorations that include
plaids (green and red, green and yellow, black and red, or black and yellow),
polka-dots (red, green, or blue), Willow (blue, green, or pink), and stylized
poppies (Green and Red, Black and Red, Green and Blue, or Green and Gold;
the first turn up most often). A French Provincial couple (a stock decal) on a
tan background is common also.

Bean Pot .... *$15 – $20*
Bowl, 6" .... *6 – 8*
Bowl, 7¼" .... *8 – 10*
Bowl, mixing, small .... *10 – 12*
Bowl, mixing, medium .... *12 – 15*
Bowl, mixing, large .... *15 – 20*
Bowl, mixing, lipped w/tab handle and spout .... *20 – 25*
Bowl, salad, square .... *15 – 18*
Canister, small, round (spice jar) .... *20 – 25*
Canister, small, square .... *20 – 25*
Canister, large, square .... *25 – 30*
Casserole, 7¼" .... *15 – 20*
Casserole .... *20 – 25*
Cookie jar, reed handle .... *30 – 35*
Cookie server, oval, reed handle .... *15 – 20*

Custard, 4"	*$4 – $6*
Drip Jar	*12 – 15*
Jug, barrel	*20 – 25*
Jug, batter	*25 – 30*

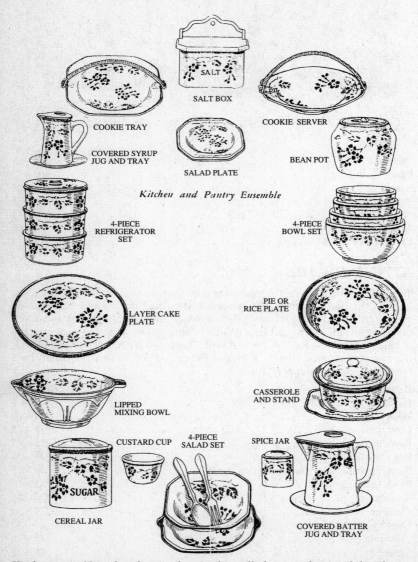

Kitchen and Pantry Ensemble

SALT BOX

COOKIE TRAY

COOKIE SERVER

COVERED SYRUP
JUG AND TRAY

SALAD PLATE

BEAN POT

4-PIECE
REFRIGERATOR
SET

4-PIECE
BOWL SET

LAYER CAKE
PLATE

PIE OR
RICE PLATE

LIPPED
MIXING BOWL

CASSEROLE
AND STAND

CUSTARD CUP

4-PIECE
SALAD SET

SPICE JAR

SUGAR

CEREAL JAR

COVERED BATTER
JUG AND TRAY

Kitchenware: Note that the pie plate is also called a rice plate, and that the casserole tray is called a stand.

Jug, covered. . . . . *$25 – $30*
Jug, ice lip . . . . *20 – 25*
Jug, syrup. . . . . *20 – 25*
Lemon reamer. . . . . *ND*
Mug, barrel . . . . *12 – 15*
Pie baker . . . . *10 – 12*
Plate, cake, 11" . . . . *10 – 12*
Pretzel jar . . . . *30 – 35*
Salt box . . . . *ND*
Shaker, range, pair . . . . *15 – 20*
Stack set, round, 4-piece . . . . *40 – 45*
Stack set, square, 3-piece . . . . *30 – 35*
Tray, Batter Set . . . . *10 – 12*
Tray, cookie. . . . . *10 – 12*
Underplate, casserole, 9" . . . . *10 – 12*
Underplate, salad bowl . . . . *10 – 12*
Utensil, cake server . . . . *12 – 15*
Utensil, fork. . . . . *20 – 25*
Utensil, spoon . . . . *15 – 20*
Waffle cover . . . . *15 – 20*
Waffle dish . . . . *5 – 7*

BLAIR CERAMICS, INC.

Ozark, Missouri

William Blair, related to the Purintons, started his company in 1946. It was listed in the trade journals as being in operation in 1954 but closed some years after. All ware seen so far is hand-painted semiporcelain.

Some of the patterns known are Autumn Leaf, Bamboo, Bird, Gay Plaid, Grey Glaze, Highland Plaid (I believe this is yellow bands with broad gray bands and lines of green and reddish brown), New Leaf, and Tropical Vine.

PRICING   Values below are for all patterns.

SQUARE DINNERWARE   Round dinnerware will also be found, but square is more common.

Bowl, 9"	$15 – $18
Bowl, soup, covered onion w/stick handle	8 – 12
Bowl, vegetable, handled, 10"	12 – 15
Bowl, vegetable, divided	12 – 15
Casserole	20 – 25
Coffee server	35 – 40
Coffee server, individual	30 – 40
Creamer	4 – 6
Cup, open handle	4 – 6
Cup, cream soup, closed handle	12 – 16
Dish, 4"	2 – 3
Gravy, w/stick handle	12 – 15
Jug, small	12 – 15
Jug, w/ice lip	15 – 18
Mug	12 – 15
Plate, 6"	1 – 2
Plate, 7"	4 – 5
Plate, 10"	10 –12
Platter, lug, 14"	12 – 15
Saucer	1 – 2
Saucer, cream soup	6 – 8
Shaker, pair	8 – 10
Sugar, w/stick handle	8 – 10
Tray, rectangular	12 – 15

Gay Plaid: Small jug, mug, jug w/ice lip, and 4" dish. Note the twisted handle on the larger pieces, perhaps to afford a firmer grasp, and the smooth handle on the mug.

Tray, relish, 3-part. . . . . *$12 – $15*
Tumbler. . . . . *18 – 20*

KITCHENWARE   The dispenser has a wooden lid with a pottery finial.

Dispenser, w/metal spigot, 4-gallon, 13" . . . . *$50 – $60*

BRAYTON-LAGUNA POTTERY

Laguna Beach, California

CHAPTER AT A GLANCE

BLACKAMOORS   Pairs
COOKIE JARS   Sets
FIGURES   MISCELLANY
  Animals   PEASANT WOMAN
  Individuals   SHAKERS

Begun in 1927 by Durlin Brayton, the company made dinnerware and novelty ware, including figures, cookie jars, and vases. Durlin Brayton died in 1951, and the company continued until 1968.

See Chipman and see Roerig in Bibliography.

MARKS   Early mark is an incised "Laguna Pottery." Later mark is "Brayton Laguna Pottery" either incised or ink-stamped. Some Disney pieces are ink-stamped "Gepetto Pottery."

64

BLACKAMOORS

Candleholder, black/burgundy/green, each $75,
Candleholder, pillow, black/burgundy/green, each 75
Figure w/bowl, black/burgundy/green/white, 8" .... 100 – 125
Head... $45 – $55
Wall Plaque, w/bowl, long coat, black/burgundy/green, 22".............. 90 – 100
Wall Plaque, w/bowl, pantaloons, black/burgundy/green .... 90 – 100

COOKIE JARS

See also Peasant Woman. See also Shakers.
   PRICING The wide price spread on the Mammy reflects rarity of color and design. Burgundy is the rarest skirt color; plaid design is rarer than zigzag.

Circus Tent .... $250 – $300
Gingham Dog .... 450 – 500
Grandma .... 350 – 400
Grandma, Wedding Ring .... 450 – 500
Lady w/Goose .... 700 – 800
Lady w/concertina... ND
Maid, black, w/pie .... 2000 +
Mammy, arms akimbo .... 750 – 1500
Ringmaster (Disney)....................................... 1500 +
Swedish Woman .... 500 – 600

FIGURES

Animals

Giraffes, necks intertwined, 18", pair .... $150 – $200
Horse, "Ma"... 70 – 80
Horse, "Pa" .... 70 – 80
Hound dog.. 45 – 50
Purple bull 100
Purple calf.. 55
Purple cow 75
Swan 65
Toucans, male/female, pair... 100 – 125
Zebra, small (1940).. 65
Zebra, large, head up, 11" (1940)..................................... 65
Zebra, large, head down (1940) 65

CALICO / GINGHAM   See also Cookie Jars.

Creamer, Calico Cat $50
Fireside, Calico Cat, 15" .... 90 – 95
Fireside, Gingham Dog, 15" .... 90 – 95
Shaker, Calico Cat/Gingham Dog, pair 55
Sugar, Gingham Dog... 50

Butch, Arthur, and Sambo.

Individuals

The listing indicates which of these are flower holders.

CHILDREN / BOYS

Arthur, w/elephant (1940) .... $75 – $85
Butch, w/boxes under his arms .... 75 – 85
Eugene, w/hanky on T-shirt .... 75 – 85
Jon, w/megaphone... 75 – 85
Peanuts, Oriental.. 80 – 90
Sambo, black w/chicken under arm .... 100 – 125

CHILDREN / GIRLS

Dorothy, sitting, legs sticking out in front .... $70 – $80
Ellen, feet pointed in, pigtail sticking out .... 70 – 80

Girl on stomach, Julia Ray, Weezy, Ellen, Emily, Pat, and Dorothy.

Emily, w/purse and knitting (1940).. *$70 – $80*
Frances, flower holder.. *20 – 25*
Girl with bird on basket, flower holder
    Decorated skirt.. *30 – 35*
    Solid-color skirt... *30 – 35*
Girl on stomach, one leg up.. *80 – 90*
Julia Ray, holding doll in front of her...................................... *70 – 80*
Marg, w/accordion.. *80 – 90*
Miranda, w/cape coat, holding flowers, 6½"................................ *65 – 75*
Pat, w/hat tied under chin, holding doll behind her......................... *70 – 80*
Sally, flower holder, Blue/Green/Pink/Yellow .... *20 – 25*
Weezy, w/jump rope .... *70 – 80*

OTHERS

Lady with Wolfhounds, Flower Holder... *$35 – $45*
Man w/cart, small... *35 – 45*
Man w/cart, medium.. *45 – 55*
Man w/cart, large .... *65 – 75*

Pairs

NATIONALITIES

Chinese Boy .... *$50 – $55*
Chinese Girl, w/bare-bottom baby .... *50 – 55*
Dutch Boy .... *40 – 45*
Dutch Girl.. *40 – 45*
Mexican Boy, Pedro, serape over shoulder.................................... *50 – 55*
Mexican Girl, Rosita, w/basket of flowers, fruits, and vegetables........... *50 – 55*
Russian Boy, Ivan, w/concertina... *40 – 45*
Russian Girl, Olga, w/babushka, basket on right arm .... *40 – 45*
Swedish Boy, Eric .... *40 – 45*
Swedish Girl, Inga .... *40 – 45*

Sets

CIRCUS   See also Cookie Jars and Shakers.

Circus Horses, 3 poses .... *$30 – $35*
Clown, sitting... *35 – 45*
Junior Elephant, planter... *35*
Mr. Elephant, planter *35*
Ring Master .... *45 – 55*

GAY NINETIES

Bar, 3 men and beer mug (1940).. *$75 – $85*
Bar, 3 men and spittoon (1940).. *75 – 85*
Matrimony (I have seen a promotional photo of Bride and Groom as an oval-framed wall plaque.)
    Bride and Groom .... *75 – 80*
    Seashore Honeymoon.. *75 – 80*

Matrimony: Bride & Groom, Seashore Honeymoon, Bedtime, and One Year Later.

Bedtime . . . . $75 – $80
One Year Later . . . . 75 – 80

MISCELLANY

Clothes

Bonnet . . . . $15 – $25
Corset . . . . 15 – 25
Hat . . . . 15 – 25
Shoes . . . . 15 – 25

PEASANT WOMAN

Cookie Jar . . . . $750 +
Flower holder, one basket . . . . 75 – 85
Flower holder, two baskets, left arm at waist . . . . 75 – 85
Flower holder, two baskets, left arm hanging down . . . . 75 – 85
Teapot . . . . 600 – 750

SHAKERS

For matching items, see also Animals, Calico/Gingham

Blacks, Butler/Maid $250
Blacks, Chef/Jemima . . . . 90 – 100
Calico Cat . . . . 45 – 50
Gingham Dog . . . . 45 – 50

BRUSH POTTERY (BRUSH-McCOY)

Roseville, Ohio

In 1899, James McCoy founded the J. W. McCoy Pottery. He produced utility ware and, soon after the turn of the century, art ware. In 1909, George S. Brush joined the firm as manager and, in 1911, the name of the pottery was changed to the Brush-McCoy Pottery Company.

James McCoy died in 1914, and in 1925 the name was changed again, to the Brush Pottery Company. (This is not to be confused with the earlier Brush Pottery that George Brush ran from 1907 to 1908.) Brush made a variety of wares, including cookie jars, figures, planters, florist ware, and other items. The pottery closed in 1982.

See Roerig and see Sanford in Bibliography.

MARKS   Pieces will be found unmarked or with "USA" or a shape number impressed.

COOKIE JARS

Many of these jars were designed by Don Winton when he and his brother were freelancing (see Twin Winton).

Angel w/wings (Little Angel), "For Little Angels Only"   /W17/R. . . . . *$750 +*
Auto, touring, old-fashioned . . . . *500 +*
Basket, hen lid . . . . *100 – 125*
Bear w/blanket, feet apart (Teddy)   /W14 . . . . *225 – 235*
Bear w/blanket, feet together (Teddy)   /014 . . . . *125 – 150*
Bear w/bow (Panda)   /W21
    Black & white /R. . . . . *225 – 250*
    Blue & white /R. . . . . *300 +*
Bear w/collar and cap, hands together (Smiling Bear)   /W46/R. . . . . *400 – 450*
Boy w/balloons, right hand in pocket . . . . *1000 +*
Cat, stylized (Siamese)   /W41. . . . . *500 +*
Chick & Nest   /W38/R. . . . . *450 – 475*
Clock, mantel, w/smiling face . . . . *175 – 200*
Clown, full figure   /W22
    Blue pants . . . . *250 – 275*
    Brown pants . . . . *150 – 175*
    Pink pants . . . . *200 – 225*
    Yellow pants . . . . *175 – 200*
Clown, head, hat lid . . . . *350 – 375*
Covered Wagon w/puppy finial   /W30/R. . . . . *600 – 650*
Cow w/cat finial   /W10
    Black /R. . . . . *1200 +*

Blue /R . . . . $1500+
Brown /R . . . . 100 – 125
Purple /R . . . . 1000+
Davy Crockett, "Davy Crockett" . . . . 275 – 300
   w/gold . . . . 550 – 650
   Mug . . . . 50 – 60
Dog, puppy in uniform w/nightstick (Puppy Police) /W39/R . . . . 550 – 600
Dog and basket /W54 . . . . 275 – 325
Donkey w/cart, ears out /W33
   Brown /R . . . . 350 – 375
   Decorated . . . . 450 – 475
Elephant, sitting, in baby bonnet w/ice cream cone /W8
   Gray /R . . . . 500+
   White /R . . . . 400+
Elephant w/monkey finial . . . . ND
Fish . . . . 475+
Frog in peaked hat (Hillbilly Frog) /43D /R . . . . 1500+
Girl, patched skirt, eating cookie (Little Girl) /017 . . . . 375 – 400
Granny w/rolling pin /019
   Green skirt /R . . . . 375 – 400
   White w/polka dot skirt /R . . . . 325 – 350
Hippo, sitting. w/derby hat /W45 . . . . 450 – 475
Hippo, standing w/monkey finial (Laughing Hippo) /W27/R . . . . 700+
Horse, Circus Horse, dog finial /W9/R . . . . 750+

Humpty Dumpty cookie jar w/peaked hat finial.

Horse, Hobby Horse, wooden barrel body w/saddle lid /W55 .... *$1000 +*
House w/chimney finial (Cookie House) .... *100 – 125*
Humpty Dumpty w/peaked hat finial
    White w/black trim.. *200 – 225*
    White w/brown trim..................................... *175 – 200*
Humpty Dumpty w/beanie & bow tie /W18/R .... *250 – 275*
Jar, canister, tulip decoration............................. *35 – 45*
Jar, cherry decoration..................................... *35 – 45*
Jar, cylinder, Three Bears, w/tree stump finial .... *75 – 95*
Jar, cylinder, wood grain, w/cat finial .... *50 – 60*
Jar, cylinder, wood grain, w/duck finial .... *50 – 60*
Jar, cylinder, wood grain, w/girl praying finial .... *50 – 60*
Lamp, Coach w/eagle finial .... *50 – 60*
Little Boy Blue w/staff & straw hat, small .... *650 – 700*
    w/gold.. *725 +*
Little Boy Blue w/staff & straw hat, large/R................. *700 – 750*
    w/gold.. *800 +*
    Mug .... *75 – 85*
Little Red Riding Hood, small .... *425 – 475*
    w/gold.. *700 +*
Little Red Riding Hood, large/R....................... *475 – 525*
    w/gold.. *750 +*
    Mug .... *80 – 90*
Log w/squirrel & axe finial .... *90 – 110*
Owl (Nite Owl)... *100 – 125*
    Yellow.. *175 – 200*
Owl, stylized /W42...................................... *400 +*
Peter Pan, elbows on knees, small/R........................ *425 – 500*
    w/gold /R... *750 +*
Peter Pan, elbows on knees, large/R .... *500 – 600*
    w/gold.. *850 +*
    Mug .... *75 – 85*
    w/gold.. *90 – 100*
Pig in top hat & tails (Formal Pig) /W7
    Black coat /R .... *200 – 225*
    Black coat w/gold /R .... *500 – 550*
    Green coat /R.. *225 – 250*
    Green coat w/gold /R................................. *475 – 525*
    Yellow coat /R .... *275 – 300*
    Yellow coat w/gold /R .... *475 – 525*
Pig, sitting, w/bow tie & cookie (Sitting Piggy) /W37/R............... *475 – 525*
    Bank... *350 – 375*
Pumpkin Coach w/two mice finial /R (Cinderella Pumpkin) *175 – 225*
Pumpkin w/two kids & locked door /W24 .... *300 – 325*
Rabbit w/chef's hat & bowl (Happy Rabbit) /W25
    Gray .... *225 – 250*
    White .... *200 – 225*
Raggedy Ann, arms out /W16 .... *400 – 450*

Brown. . . . . *$450 – $500*

Pink & yellow . . . . *375 – 400*

White w/patches . . . . *75 – 95*

Shoe (house) w/roof lid and chimney finial   /R. . . . . *75 – 95*

Squirrel in top hat & tails   /W15 . . . . *250 – 275*

Treasure Chest w/shell finial   /W28 . . . . *125 – 150*

BUFFALO POTTERY COMPANY

Buffalo, New York

Chartered in 1901 by John D. Larkin, the Buffalo Pottery began manufacturing at the end of 1903. First products were semiporcelain, intended both for premiums for the Larkin Soap Company, which had founded the pottery, and for retail sales. In 1915, Buffalo began making a china body; semiporcelain production seems to have ended around the time of World War I. By the late 1920s, Larkin found it cheaper to import most of its premiums, and manufacturing at Buffalo concentrated on china for the institutional market, with a lot of custom work being done. Automation in the 1940s resulted in a lower grade of china and a consolidation that eliminated the custom designs. Buffalo, now owned by Oneida, is still in business producing basic institutional lines.

DELDARE

Plate, Calendar, 1910. . . . . *$2200*
Plate, Salesman's Sample, 1908 . . . . *1200*

Fallowfield Hunt

Bowl, punch, footed, 14³/₄" *$6500*
Bowl, round, 9" *500*
Bowl, round, 12" *850*
Bowl, soup, 9" *275*
Cup *125*
Dish, 5" *150*
Jug, octagon, 8" *650*
Jug, octagon, 10" *750*
Jug, tankard, 12¹/₂" *1000*

Mug, 2½"... *$450*
Mug, 3½"... *400*
Mug, 4½"... *350*
Plaque, 12½"... *650*
Plate, 6½".. *125*
Plate, 8½".. *150*
Plate, 9¼".. *200*
Plate, 10".. *250*
Plate, chop, 14"... *650*
Relish, 12" × 6½".. *450*
Saucer... *75*
Sugar, hexagon, open... *300*
Tray, calling card, tab, 7¾"... *350*

THE FALLOWFIELD HUNT SCENES

The Fallowfield Hunt, Breakfast at the Three Pigeons
The Fallowfield Hunt, the Start
The Fallowfield Hunt, Breaking Cover
The Fallowfield Hunt, the Dash
The Fallowfield Hunt, the Death
The Fallowfield Hunt, the Return

Ye Olden Days

Ashtray/matchbox holder... *$500*
Bowl, fern, 8"... *550*
Bowl, nut, 8".. *500*
Bowl, salad, 9".. *500*
Bowl, vegetable, 8½" × 6½".. *450*
Candle holder, shield back, 7"...................................... *1200*
Candle holder/matchbox holder, w/finger ring, 5½".................. *600*
Candlestick, 9½".. *750*
Chocolate cup... *100*
Chocolate pot... *2500*
Chocolate saucer.. *100*
Creamer... *200*
Cup... *150*
Dish, 6½"... *225*
Humidor, 7"... *850*
Jardiniere, 8".. *750*
Jug, octagon, 6".. *450*
Jug, octagon, 7".. *500*
Jug, octagon, 8".. *525*
Jug, octagon, 9".. *600*
Jug, octagon, 10"... *725*

Jug, tankard, 12¹/₂"...$1000
Mug, 3¹/₂"..400
Mug, 4¹/₄"..350
Mug, tankard, 6³/₄..800
Plaque, wall, 12"...575
Plate, 6¹/₄"...125
Plate, 7¹/₄"...150
Plate, 8¹/₅₄"..175
Plate, 9¹/₂"...200
Plate, 10"...225
Plate, cake, pierced tab handles, 10".........................475
Plate, chop, 14"...650
Relish dish, 12" × 6¹/₂".....................................450
Saucer...75
Sugar..250
Tea tile, 6"...300
Teapot, 2 cup..350
Teapot, 4 cup..450
Tray, Heirlooms, 12" × 10¹/₂"................................750
Tray, calling card, round, tab handles, 7³/₄"................350
Vase, broad bottom, 8¹/₂"....................................1000
Vase, pinched waist, 9"......................................375
Vase, urn shape, 8"..1200

DRESSER SET

Dresser Tray, 12" × 9"..$650
Hair Receiver..375
Pin Tray, 6¹/₄" × 3¹/₂".......................................225
Powder Jar...350

YE OLDEN DAYS SCENES

Scenes of Village Life in Ye Olden Days
Traveling in Ye Olden Days
Heirlooms
Ye Village Gossips
Dancing Ye Minuet
Ye Village Street
Ye Olden Days

Ye Olden Times
Ye Town Crier
Ye Village Tavern
Ye Village Parson
An Evening at Ye Lion Inn
Vicar of Wakefield

Emerald

Ashtray w/match box holder...................................$750
Basket, 13" tall...1500+
Bowl, fern, 8"...700
Bowl, salad, 9"...950

Bowl, fruit, footed, octagon, 10" .... *$5000+*
Bowl, fruit, 12¼" *2000*
Candle holder, shield back, 7" *1250*
Candlestick, 9" *550*
Creamer *375*
Cup *200*
Humidor, 7" tall .... *1200+*
Jardiniere, 12" .... *2250+*
Jug, octagon, 6" *650*
Jug, octagon, 8" *750*
Jug, octagon, 9" *900*
Jug, octagon, 10" *1000*
Jug, tankard, 10½" .... *1200+*
Jug, tankard, 12" *1200*
Mug, 2¼" *500*
Mug, 4¼" *475*
Plate, 7¼" *500*
Plate, 8½" *650*
Plate, 9¼" *750*
Plate, 10" *900*
Plate, chop, 13½" *1400*
Saucer *150*
Shaker, 3" *350*
Sugar *400*
Tea tile, 6" *600*
Teapot *625*
Toothpick holder, 2¼" *400*
Tray, calling card, round, lug, 7" *500*
Tray, 13¾" × 10¼" *1200*
Tray/fruit bowl, 14" .... *5500+*
Vase, broad bottom, 8" *1200*
Vase, urn, 8" *1200*
Vase, 22½" .... *6000+*
Vase, cylinder, 13½" .... *1500+*
Wall plaque, Dr. Syntax, 12" *1500*
Wall plaque, Peacock, 12" *2000*
Wall plaque, Penn's Treaty, 13½" .... *2250+*
Wall plaque, Lost, 13½" *2250*
Wall plaque, 16½" *6000*

INKWELL SET

Inkwell, square *$1000*
Tray, 9" × 6½" *4000*
Complete set *6000*

EMERALD SCENES

A noble hunting party
The garden trio
Misfortune at Tulip Hall
Dr. Syntax stopt by highway men
Dr. Syntax sketching the lake
Dr. Syntax soliloquising
Dr. Syntax setting out to the lakes
Dr. Syntax entertained at college
Dr. Syntax mistakes a gentleman's house for an inn
Dr. Syntax robbed of his property
Dr. Syntax made free of the cellar
Dr. Syntax in the wrong lodging house
Dr. Syntax with the maid
Dr. Syntax copying the wit of the window
Dr. Syntax reading his tour
Dr. Syntax taking possession of his living
Dr. Syntax at Liverpool
Dr. Syntax and the bookseller
Dr. Syntax returned home
Dr. Syntax bound to a tree by highwaymen
Dr. Syntax making a discovery
Dr. Syntax sells Grizzle
Dr. Syntax star gazing

JUGS / PITCHERS

Neveau, not Nouveau, is the spelling on the bottom of the Art Neveau jug. The Poppies jug is the same shape as the Orchid Spray and has been found with a lid.

Art Neveau w/gold, 1908, 8½" *$850*
Blue Birds, 1917, 7" *300*
Buffalo Hunt w/gold trim, 6" *400*
Cinderella, 1907, 6" *600*
Dutch (Windmill), 6½" *475*
Fox Hunt/Whirl of the Town, 1907, 7" *550*
George Washington/Mount Vernon, w/gold, 7½" *550*
Geranium, 6½"
   Monochrome blue *350*
   Multicolor *400*
Geranium, tall, 7"
   Blue and salmon *400*
Gloriana, 9¼"
   Monochrome Blue, 1907 . . . . *650*
   Multicolor w/gold *700*
Gunner w/gold trim, 1907, 6" *400*
Holland (Dutch Children), 1907, 6" *500*
Hounds and Stag (Deer Hunt), 1907, 6½" *550*
Imperial, 6¾" *250*
John Paul Jones/Bon Homme Richard, 1908, 9¼" *900*
Landing of Roger Williams/Betsey Williams' Cottage, 1907, 6" *600*

Marbleized panels w/gold trim, 8" *$1000*
Mason, Beige/Green, 1907, 8¼" *950*
Melon shape, 1909, 8¾" *800*
New Bedford (Sperm Whales/Whaling Ship "The Niger"), 6" *750*
Old Mill, 6" *650*
Orchid Spray, 6" *300*
Pilgrim (Miles Standish/John Alden and Priscilla), 1908, 9" *950*
Poppies w/lid, blue monochrome, 6" *350*
Rip Van Winkle/Joseph Jefferson, 1906, 6½" *750*
Robin Hood, 1906, 8¼" *475*
Roosevelt Bears, 8" *2600*
Sailing Ships/Lightship (Nautical Jug), 1906, 9¼" *750*
Sailors/Lighthouse (Marine Jug), 1906/07, 9¼"
   Blue monochrome *700*
   Brown monochrome *700*
Triumph (blue poppies), 7" *500*
USSB (US Shipping Board), china body, 1928 .... *175*
Vienna, 6¾" *250*
Wild Duck/Dog "Major", 6" *400*

PLATES

These pieces were produced between 1905 and 1915. There is also a cup and saucer to match the HFCC Pelicans plate.

Most of the 7½" plates were decorated in a monochrome dark turquoise; many were also decorated in multicolor, noted below. All plates are on a green background except the Wolfe and Montcalm, which is on a white background. Some had gold trim.

Some 10½" plates are on a white backgrund.

Advertising

Burtt Bros. (The Locks), Lockport, NY, 1910, 7½" *$165*
Bing & Nathan Store, Buffalo, NY, 7½" *95*
George Krug (Buffalo), Buffalo, NY, 7½" *95*
George Krug, Jack Knife Bridge, Buffalo, NY, 7½" *150*
Home Furniture and Carpet Company (Pelicans), Indianapolis, IN, 7½" *150*
Home Furniture and Carpet Company, Toledo, OH (Stork), 7½" *100*
Katzman's Store, Independence Hall, Philadelphia, PA, 7½" *75*
L. L. Millring (Advance), Buffalo, NY, 7½" *85*
Sweeney Company, Main Street, Buffalo, NY, 7½" *125*
Wanamaker Store, Chicago, IL, 4¼" *60*
W. Price, Gates Circle, Buffalo, NY, 7½" *135*

Historical

These six plates were made in a 7½" size with either a monochrome dark turquoise or a multicolor decoration and in a 10" size in either Canton Blue or green. These could be bought three or six at a time.

Faneuil Hall, Boston, 10" *$55*
   Monochrome, 7½" *75*
   Multicolor, 7½" *125*

Niagara Falls, 7¹/₂" monochrome

Independence Hall, Philadelphia, 10" *$55*
   Monochrome, 7¹/₂" *75*
   Multicolor, 7¹/₂" *125*
Mount Vernon, 10". *55*
   Monochrome, 7¹/₂" *75*
   Multicolor, 7¹/₂" *125*
Niagara Falls, New York, 10" *55*
   Monochrome, 7¹/₂" *75*
   Multicolor, 7¹/₂" *125*
U.S. Capitol, Washington, 10" *55*
   Monochrome, 7¹/₂" *75*
   Multicolor, 7¹/₂" *125*
White House, Washington, 10". *55*
   Monochrome, 7¹/₂" *75*
   Multicolor, 7¹/₂" *125*

Commemorative / Geographical

Buffalo, NY (Buffalo), 7¹/₂". *$100*
Buffalo, NY (Buffalo), Bonrea pattern border, 7¹/₂" *150*
Buffalo, NY (Jack Knife Bridge), gold trim, 7¹/₄" *150*
Buffalo, NY (Lafayette Square), 7¹/₂" *95*
Buffalo, NY (McKinley Monument), 7/₂" *95*
Buffalo, NY (St. Mary Magdalen Church), 1907, 7¹/₂" *75*
Butte, MT (Richest Hill in the World), 7¹/₂" *175*
Cambridgeport, MA (Odd Fellows Hall), 1910, 7¹/₂" *100*
Cooperstown, NY (Indian Hunter), 7¹/₂". *100*
Great Falls, MT (B & M Smelter), 7¹/₂" *125*
Helena, MT (State Capitol), 1909, 7¹/₂". *175*
Montevideo, MN (Chippewa Bridge), 7¹/₂". *175*
New Bedford, MA (various scenes), 10¹/₂"
   Monochrome blue, white background *150*

Monchrome brown, white background *$150*
Monochrome green, white background *150*
New York City (Statue of Liberty), 7½" *200*
New York City (Trinity Church), 7½". *85*
New York City (Hudson Terminal Buildings), 7½". *95*

Commemorative / Organizations

Benevolent and Protective Order of Elks, 7½" *$85*
Improved Order of Red Men, Buffalo Tribe, 1909, 7½"
   Monochrome. *100*
   Multicolor *125*
Improved Order of Red Men, Erie Tribe, 7½" *100*
Modern Woodmen of America, Buffalo, NY, 1911, 7½
   Monochrome. *95*
   Multicolor *125*
UDC, Gen. A. P. Stewart Chapter, 10½". *250*
Woman's Christian Temperance Union, 9". *275*

Commemorative / People

The Roosevelt plate has gold trim.

Theodore Roosevelt, 8" *$250*
George Washington, 7½". *275*
Martha Washington, 7½" *275*
Wolfe and Montcalm, Quebec, white background, 1908 . . . . *125*

WILLOW, BLUE   (1905)

Company literature stated that Buffalo was the first pottery to make Blue Willow in the United States. Most of the items produced in 1905 had "First Old Willow Ware Manufactured in America, 1905" imprinted under the glaze on the base. The ware produced between 1905 and 1908 usually had scalloped edges. Since 1916, Buffalo has continued to produce Blue Willow in its vitrified ware; with some exceptions, this is generally not as valuable as the semivitreous line. See below.

   PRICING   The early scalloped pieces are generally priced one-third higher than the later production priced below. Marked 1905 pieces are generally priced 150% higher than those below.

Semivitreous

Production of this line continued until 1917.

Ashtray w/match safe. *$100*
Baker, 5½" *60*
Baker, 6¼" *65*
Baker, 7¾" *70*
Baker, 8½" *75*
Baker, 9½" *85*
Baker, 10¼" *125*
Baker, 11¾" *150*

Bone Dish, crescent, $3\frac{1}{2}" \times 6\frac{1}{2}"$ *$60*
Bowl, 1-pint *50*
Bowl, $1\frac{1}{2}$-pint *60*
Bowl, 2-pint *70*
Bowl, Oyster, footed, 1-pint *65*
Bowl, Oyster, footed, $1\frac{1}{2}$-pint *75*
Bowl, salad, square, 9" *275*
Bowl, coupe, $7\frac{1}{2}"$ *25*
Bowl, coupe, $8\frac{3}{4}"$ *30*
Bowl, soup, $7\frac{1}{4}"$ *25*
Bowl, soup, $8\frac{1}{2}"$ *30*
Bowl, soup, $9\frac{1}{2}"$ *35*
Butter, covered *170*
Butter, individual, $3\frac{1}{2}"$ *22*
Cake Cover *60*
Cake Plate, tab, 10" *135*
Candle Holder w/finger ring *175*
Casserole, round, $8\frac{1}{4}"$ *175*
Casserole, square, $7\frac{1}{2}" \times 9"$ *150*
Casserole, square, $8\frac{3}{4}" \times 11"$ *175*
Coaster, $3\frac{1}{2}"$ *35*
Compote *40*
Creamer, individual double lip, $2\frac{1}{2}$-ounce *40*
Creamer, Macen, $8\frac{1}{2}$-ounce *70*
Creamer, round, 8-ounce *70*
Creamer, round, 18-ounce *90*
Creamer, square, 15-ounce *90*
Creamer, Tankard #1, $2\frac{3}{4}$-ounce *45*
Creamer, Toy, 2-ounce *45*
Cup, bouillon *60*
Cup, coffee, AD (two different shapes) *25*
Cup, coffee, Amoy *25*
Cup, coffee, Jumbo *150*
Cup, coffee, Ovide *25*
Cup, tea, Amoy *25*
Cup, tea, Ovide *25*
Custard, handled, 7 ounce *40*
Dish, fruit, 5" *21*
Dish, fruit, $5\frac{3}{4}"$ *25*
Dish, cereal, $6\frac{1}{4}"$ *30*
Eggcup, Boston *60*
Eggcup, single *60*
Eggcup, double *60*
Gravy, square *55*
Gravy faststand, oval *100*
Jug, Buffalo, $\frac{3}{4}$-pint *125*
Jug, Buffalo, $1\frac{1}{4}$-pint *150*
Jug, Buffalo, 2-pint *150*

Jug, Buffalo, 3-pint *$150*
Jug, Buffalo, 4-pint *200*
Jug, Chicago, ⁷/₈-pint *125*
Jug, Chicago, 1¹/₂-pint *150*
Jug, Chicago, 2¹/₄-pint *160*
Jug, Chicago, 3¹/₄-pint *180*
Jug, Chicago, 4¹/₂-pint *200*
Jug, Hall Boy, 3¹/₂-pint *250*
Jug, covered, 1-pint *225*
Jug, covered, 1¹/₂-pint *250*
Jug, covered, 2¹/₄-pint *275*
Jug, covered, 3¹/₂-pint *300*
Mug, 11-ounce *65*
Mustard, covered *60*
Pickle, 8¹/₄" × 4¹/₂" *45*
Plate, 5¹/₄" *30*
Plate, 6¹/₄" *27*
Plate, 7¹/₂" *21*
Plate, 8¹/₄" *27*
Plate, 9¹/₄" *30*
Plate, 10" *38*
Plate, 10¹/₂" *40*
Plate, chop, 11" *100*
Plate, chop, 13" *150*
Platter, 7¹/₄" *160*
Platter, 8³/₄" *120*
Platter, 9³/₄" *110*
Platter, 10³/₄" *100*
Platter, 12" *110*
Platter, 14" *120*
Platter, 16" *160*
Platter, 18" *200*
Ramekin, 3¹/₂-ounce *25*
Sauce tureen, 6¹/₂" × 4¹/₂" *275*
Sauce tureen tray, 8¹/₂" × 6" *50*
Saucer *15*
Soup, rim, 7¹/₄" *25*
Soup, rim, 8¹/₂" *30*
Soup, rim, 9¹/₂" *35*
Stein mug, 13-ounce *100*
Sugar, Macen, individual *90*
Sugar, round *90*
Sugar, round, individual *90*
Sugar, square *90*
Tea tile, round, 6¹/₄" *125*
Teapot, individual, 14-ounce *250*
Teapot, Macen, 1-pint *225*
Teapot, round, 3¹/₄-pint *295*

Teapot, square, 2¼-pint... $295
Tureen, round, 9½"... 475

TOILET SET

Brush vase... $125
Chamber pot w/lid.. 300
Pitcher, small... 350
Pitcher, large... 700
Shaving mug.. 125
Slop jar w/lid... 200
Soap dish w/lid.. 250
Wash bowl.. 350

Vitrified

Jug, scalloped rim, 2¾"... $45
Jug, scalloped rim, 3¾"... 45
Jug, scalloped rim, 5"... 50
Jug, scalloped rim, 6"... 60
Jug, scalloped rim, 8½"... 70
Jug, scalloped rim, 10"... 100
Teapot, teaball, 15-ounce.. 275
Teapot, teaball, 3-pint.. 300

WILLOW, GAUDY

Buffalo was the only U.S. pottery to make Gaudy Willow. Gaudy Willow is
Blue Willow that has been hand-painted both over and under the glaze with additional colors of rust, green, blue, brown, and gold.

PRICING   All pieces are the same molds and sizes as Blue Willow. In
general, prices for Gaudy Willow run from three to six times those for Blue
Willow, as follows: high-priced Blue Willow is generally three times higher in
Gaudy Willow, and low-priced Blue Willow is generally six times higher.

CALIFORNIA ORIGINALS

Torrence, California

CHAPTER AT A GLANCE

COOKIE JARS
  Cartoons/Movies

Disney
Sesame Street

Bill Bailey started the company as Heirlooms of Tomorrow in 1944, making Dresden lace figurines. In 1955 he changed the name to California Originals and changed the product to cookie jars, shakers, ashtrays, figures, planters, and other items.

In the late 1950s, for about two years, the company produced ware for Gilner, which had lost its production facilities in a fire. Eventually, California Originals bought their molds for lazy Susans, animals, ashtrays, bowls, and vases. The company also bought the molds for three sizes of Brad Keeler's Swan planters.

At one time, the company employed 645 people, had contracts with Disney and Sesame Street, and sold to K-Mart, Montgomery Ward, J. C. Penny, and Sears. In 1979, Bailey sold the company to Harold Roman of Roman Ceramics. California Originals closed in 1982.

An interesting note: California Originals' molds and equipment were bought by Treasure Craft. They have no plans to use the molds, but California Originals was such a strong competitor, Treasure Craft didn't want anyone else to have the molds.

See Roerig in Bibliography.

COOKIE JARS

The shakers that go with the stumps match the finials. Disney and Muppet jars are at the end of the list.

MARKS   Some jars will have a "C—W" mark, representing Cumberland Ware, a subsidiary of Roman Ceramics. Since some of these jars were first made for California Originals, and others made just for Roman, I have listed them all together.

Airplane, pilot finial   /2629 . . . . $300+
Apple, 11" /8214 . . . . 25 – 30
Bakery, cookies on roof, "Cookie Bakery" /863 . . . . 35 – 45
Basket of carrots, rabbit finial   /703 . . . . 50 – 60

Beaver, wearing tie, w/coolie, 11¼"   /2625 .... $30 – $35
Bear, Brown, hands on tummy, 12"   /405............................ 30 – 35
Bear, in ranger hat, 13½"   /882...................................... 40 – 50
Bear, in sweater, tie and pants, 10½"   /2648........................ 30 – 40
Bear, Koala, 10"   /885.. 225 – 275
   Bank... 50 – 60
   Planter.. 20 – 25
   Shakers.. 30 – 40
Bear, Panda, 11"   /889... 175 – 200
Boy, w/baseball bat, 12"   /875...................................... 30 – 40
Bull (Ferdinand)   /870
   Brown stain.. 30 – 40
   Red... 40 – 50
Cat, embossed flowers, 12" long   /884............................... 30 – 40
Caterpillar w/hat and tie, butterfly finial, 10¼"   /583 .... 40 – 50
Christmas Tree   /873.. 225 – 250
Circus Wagon   /2631... 35 – 45
Clock, Alarm, smiling face, "Cookie Time," 13½"   /860............... 25 – 35
Clock, Cuckoo, 9½"   /840... 70 – 80
Clown, full figure, arms up, 12¼"   /862........................... 35 – 45
Clown, full figure, hand to hat .... 30 – 40
Clown, full figure, juggling three balls   /876 .... 35 – 45
Clown, head, 12½"   /859... 50 – 60
Clown, head and torso, hands in pockets .... 60 – 75
Coffee Grinder, 11½"   /861....................................... 20 – 30
Crocodile w/jar, "I Am a Cookie Crock," 12½"   /862................. 40 – 50
Cupcake, cherry finial, 9"   /886 .... 25 – 30
Dog, Cocker Spaniel, sitting, tongue out, 11¾"   /458................ 25 – 35
   Shakers.. 10 – 12
Dog, Schnauzer   /905.. 150 – 175
Dog, Yorkshire Terrier   /937...................................... 100 – 125
Duck   /857.. 25 – 35
Duckbill Platypus   /790... 100 – 125
Elephant w/clown on lid, 14¼"   /896
   Glazed... 35 – 40
   Stained.. 25 – 30
Elephant w/cap and tie, 11¾"   /881 .... 65 – 75
Elephant w/hat and suspenders, 10"   /2643......................... 20 – 30
Elf, head .... 100 – 125
Elf's School House, "School House"................................. 55 – 65
Engine   /2628... 45 – 55
Fire truck, "Fire," 11½" long   /841 .... 125 – 150
Flowerpot, w/flower, 12½"   /885 .... 35 – 45
Frog, reclining, hand under chin   /704 .... 40 – 45
   Bank.. 15 – 20
Frog, sitting   /884... 50 – 60
Frog, sitting, w/bow tie, 10½"   /2645
   Green... 35 – 45

Stain . . . . *$30 – $40*
Frog, w/bow tie, leaning on stone wall, 12½" L /877
 Green . . . . *50 – 60*
 Stain . . . . *40 – 50*
Ginger Bread House, 11½" /857 . . . . *30 – 40*
Girl, holding bowl of cookies. . . . . *125 – 150*
Gramophone, 11½" /891. . . . . *65 – 75*
Grinder, "Cookie," 11½" /861 . . . . *30 – 35*
Gumball Machine, glazed red/green, "1 cent each," 12" /890 . . . . *50 – 60*
Hen, 8½" /1127 . . . . *25 – 35*
Hippopotamus, w/embossed flowers, 14" L /883
 Green/Red glaze . . . . *30 – 40*
 Stain . . . . *25 – 35*
House, smiley face /741 . . . . *35 – 45*
Humpty Dumpty, on wall, 13" /882 . . . . *100 – 125*
Indian, licking lollipop, 12½" /738 . . . . *35 – 45*
Jack-in-the-Box, 11½" /865 . . . . *60 – 80*
Jeans, double-seamed denim, 10¼" /502. . . . . *25 – 35*
Lemon, 11" /8497-S . . . . *25 – 35*
Liberty Bell, "Liberty Throughout All the Land, 1776 – 1976," 10" /889 . . *25 – 35*
Lion w/gold mane . . . . *35 – 45*
Lion w/lollipop, crouching, bow on head /866 . . . . *35 – 45*
Lioness, yawning, w/cub, 12" /739 . . . . *275 – 325*
Little Red Riding Hood, /320 . . . . *300 – 350*
Man in barrel, "Down to the Last Cookie," 12½" /873 . . . . *35 – 45*
Milk Carton, "It's Milk and Cookies Time," 11½" /400 . . . . *25 – 30*
Monkey, sitting, w/banana, 13" /884 . . . . *50 – 60*
Mouse, 12½" /2630 . . . . *25 – 35*
Mouse in sailor hat (Sailor Mouse) /888 . . . . *40 – 50*
Noah's Ark, 12¼" L /881 . . . . *50 – 60*
Orange, 11" /8218 . . . . *25 – 35*
Owl, winking, 10" /2751 . . . . *25 – 35*
 Shakers, each . . . . *8 – 10*
Owl, wing raised, in overalls, winking, 12¼" /856 . . . . *35 – 45*
Pack Mule /2653 . . . . *125 – 150*
Pear, 11" /8217. . . . . *25 – 30*
Pelican, pelican finial . . . . *25 – 30*
Penguin, in vest and pants, wing up, 12" /839 . . . . *25 – 35*
Pepper, green, 8½" /8220 . . . . *25 – 30*
Pineapple, 12½" /8219. . . . . *25 – 30*
Rabbit, Buster Brown suit, 12" /724 . . . . *25 – 35*
Rabbit, eating cookie. . . . . *25 – 35*
Radio, old-fashioned, "Tune in a Cookie," 12" /888 . . . . *40 – 50*
Raggedy Ann, sitting on barrel, 13½" /859. . . . . *50 – 60*
Raggedy Ann, sitting on barrel, 13½" /860. . . . . *60 – 70*
Riverboat, "Southern Belle Cookie Jar," 14½" L /868 . . . . *100 – 125*
Roly Poly, turnabout, scarecrow, embossed flowers . . . . *40 – 50*
Rooster, 8½" /1127. . . . . *25 – 35*

Safe, money bag finial, "Thou Shall Not Steal"...................... *$25 – $35*
Safe, "Cookie Safe"
    Bulldog finial .... *25 – 35*
    Cat, sitting, finial .... *25 – 35*
    Cat, standing, finial .... *25 – 35*
    Rabbit w/cookie finial   /2630............................. *25 – 35*
    Sheriff finial .... *25 – 35*
Santa Claus   /871 .... *225 – 250*
Scarecrow w/pumpkins   /871 .... *150 – 175*
School House, "Lil Old School House," 11¼"   /869 .... *50 – 60*
Sheriff w/hole in hat, 12"   /726 .... *35 – 45*
Shakers.. *8 – 10*
Shoe House, tile roof, 12¼"   /2637................................ *35 – 45*
Shoe House, shingle roof, 12¾"   /874 .... *40 – 50*
Shop, Smiley Face cookies on roof, "Cookie Shoppe"   /2756 .... *35 – 45*
Smokey Bear .... *45 – 55*
Snowman   /872 .... *175 – 200*
Snail, 13"   /854 .... *30 – 40*
Store, "Cookie Bakery," 11¾"   /863
    Green roof/red roof... *35 – 45*
Stove, pot-bellied   /743 .... *30 – 40*
Strawberry, 8¾"   /8413-C .... *20 – 30*
Strawberry, 11"   /8215.. *30 – 40*
Stump
    Bear w/beehive finial, 15"   /2622.......................... *25 – 30*
      Shakers, each... *8 – 10*
    Mouse finial   /891 – 892..................................... *25 – 30*
    Mushroom finial .... *25 – 30*
    Owl, winking, finial, 14"   /2624............................ *25 – 30*
    Pheasant finial .... *30 – 40*
    Puppy w/cookie finial, 14"   /2623
      Stained .... *25 – 30*
      Glazed .... *30 – 40*
    Rabbit eating carrot finial, 14"   /2621 .... *25 – 30*
      Shakers, each... *8 – 10*
    Squirrel w/acorn finial   /2620 .... *25 – 30*
      Shakers, each... *8 – 10*
Stump, low
    Squirrel holding acorn finial, 12"   /863 .... *25 – 30*
Stump w/window and door, rabbits-in-loveseat finial .... *50 – 60*
Taxicab, yellow, 10¾" long   /501................................ *125 – 150*
Teapot w/embossed flowers, brass handle   /737 .... *25 – 30*
Toaster, silver, 11½"   /879 .... *65 – 75*
Treasure Chest w/octopus on lid, 11"   /878 .... *50 – 60*
Turtle, on back   /2627.. *25 – 30*
Turtle, Rabbit w/carrot on lid, 12½" L   /728 .... *25 – 30*
Turtle, rabbit w/cookies on lid   /2728............................. *25 – 30*
Turtle, sitting, feet out, 12¼"   /2635............................ *$25 – $30*

Shakers, each . . . . *8 – 10*
Turtle, sitting, w/flowers, 11½"   /842 . . . . *25 – 30*
Turtle w/top hat, hare finial   /2640 . . . . *75 – 90*
Van, red, 10" long   /843 . . . . *75 – 95*
Volkswagen Bug w/windup key, 7"   /2632 . . . . *75 – 95*

Cartoons / Movies

CARTOONS

Superman in telephone booth   /846/CM
  Monochrome . . . . *$250 – $275*
  Multicolor
    Brown booth *325*
    Silver booth   /R . . . . *400 – 425*
Wonder Woman, roping bank and robber   /847/R. . . . . *1000 +*
Woody Woodpecker   /980
  Monochrome . . . . *275 – 300*
  Multicolor . . . . *500 +*

MOVIES

Oliver Hardy . . . . *$750 +*
Stan Laurel . . . . *750 +*
W. C. Fields . . . . *750 +*

Disney

Eeyore, Tigger, and Winnie were sold through Sears.

Birthday Cake (Mickey's 50th), "Happy Birthday" w/Mickey finial. . . . . *$350 +*

Snow White w/bluebird cookie jar.

Cylinder, Donald Duck on train. . . . . $65 – $75
Cylinder, Dumbo . . . . 65 – 75
Donald Duck resting on pumpkin . . . . 150 +
Dumbo on pedestal, "Dumbo's Greatest Cookies on Earth" . . . . 500 +
Eeyore . . . . 325 – 350
Goofy holding barrel, "Goofy's Cookie Co" . . . . 500 +
Mickey Mouse in car, "Cookies" . . . . 300 – 325
Mickey Mouse resting on drum 150
Pinocchio, full figure, arms folded across chest. . . . . 500 +
Pinocchio w/fishbowl . . . . 500 +
Snow White w/bluebird . . . . 750 +
Tigger . . . . 125 – 175
Tree Stump w/Bambi, Thumper finial
    Glazed 350
    Stained 450
Winnie the Pooh hugging large honey pot, "Hunny" . . . . 85 – 95
Winnie the Pooh w/honey pot between legs . . . . 100 – 125

Sesame Street

Big Bird w/cookie jar, "Cookies"   /976 . . . . $75 – $95
Big Bird on nest   /971/R . . . . 50 – 60
Cookie Monster   /970/R . . . . 45 – 55
Count   /975/R . . . . 500 +
Ernie, hands clasped   /973/R . . . . 50 – 60
Ernie and Bert, "Ernie & Bert Fine Cookies"   /977/R . . . . 350 +
Oscar the Grouch in garbage can   /972/R . . . . 65 – 75

CAMARK POTTERY, INC.

Camden, Arkansas

CHAPTER AT A GLANCE

AQUARIA	MISCELLANY
FIGURES	VASES

Camark (the name comes from the first three letters of the city and the state) began as Camark Art and Tile Pottery in 1926, producing a wheel-thrown, hand-decorated line of art pottery, one of which was Le-Camark. (This was designed by John Lessel and based on the Lasa line he had developed while at Weller Pottery.) The founder, Jack Carnes, married into an oil-wealth-rich family, and according to Burdell Hall, it is believed that his in-laws financed the operation as a tax write-off. Carnes hired well-known European and American ceramic artists, but the market for handmade art wares was not good in the late 1920s, and the company was sold in 1928.

The new owners renamed it Camark Art Pottery and began production of molded industrial art wares, including novelty items and products for the florist and gift shop market. Japanese competition in the late 1950s led to the sale of the pottery to W. A. Daniel and his wife Mary in 1962; they renamed it Camark Pottery, Inc. The Daniels did not prosper. W. A. died in 1965, and Mary continued the business but had to institute many cutbacks. By 1968 sales were from an overstocked warehouse inventory with little or no manufacturing being done. This continued until Mary died in 1982.

In 1986 the remaining stock (thousands of pieces) and all other assets were purchased by brothers Gary and Mark Ashcroft, who attempted to bring the pottery back to life. It is no longer in operation.

The most collectible items are Le-Camark pieces, animal figures, and pitchers with figural handles.

COLORS Camark's color numbering system indicates the possibility of at least ninety different glazes. I have seen no attempt to identify them, but some of the names are Delphinium Blue, Dubonnet, Ivory, Light Mat Yellow, Lupin Blue, Peach, Seafoam Green, and Turquoise.

MARKS The most common is an impressed "CAMARK."

AQUARIA

These pieces were designed to hold glass globes suitable for flowers or for growing water plants, as well as for fish. Of course, the fun of these pieces, especially Wistful Kitten and Pensive Bird, are brought out when used with fish. The bowls are seldom found with figures other than the cats. The seal bowl came with a special clip to attach it to the figure. Blown-glass globes imported from Mexico were included in the purchase price.

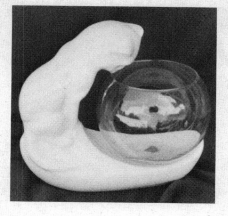

Aquaria: Cat w/bowl.

Balancing Seal, 13½" /552 . . . . *$40 – $50*
Bear on his back, 10" /870 . . . . *40 – 50*
Pensive Bird, 7½" /901 . . . . *40 – 50*
Seal (three), large, 16¾" /802 . . . . *50 – 60*
Tropical Fish, 8½" /200 . . . . *40 – 50*
Wistful Kitten, 8½" /900 . . . . *30 – 40*

FIGURES

Climbing cats came with hooks for hanging from the wall. Some of these were hand-decorated.

Cat, sitting, 10" /62 . . . . *$40 – $50*
Cat, tail up, 12" /085 . . . . *50 – 60*
Cat, climbing, head left, 15" /058 . . . . *35 – 45*
Cat, climbing, head right, 15" /058 . . . . *35 – 45*
Cat, climbing, head right, 11½" /N138 . . . . *30 – 35*
Cat, climbing, head right, 9½" /N155 . . . . *25 – 35*

MISCELLANY

Most of the Swan bowl/planters were hand-decorated. (HD)

Ashtray, Leaf, 5¾" /235 . . . . *$8 – $10*
Ashtray, Sunburst /D31 . . . . *10 – 12*
Ashtray, Texas shape /038 . . . . *12 – 16*
Bowl, Cabbage Leaf /051 . . . . *12 – 16*
Bowl, Pumpkin, small /R59 . . . . *10 – 15*
Bowl, Pumpkin, large /R58 . . . . *15 – 20*
Bowl/planter, Swans /521-HD . . . . *20 – 25*
Casserole, chicken lid . . . . *30 – 40*
Cotton dispenser, Bunny, 4" high . . . . *12 – 18*
Flower Frog, Bird /898 . . . . *18 – 20*
Flower Frog, Female Dancer . . . . *24 – 30*

Parrot-handled pitcher.

Flower Frog, Swans   /318 . . . . *$20 – $25*
Novelty, Dog, Miniature   /693   /694
   Pointer (leg lifted) . . . . *8 – 12*
   Setter (squatting) . . . . *8 – 12*
Novelty, Football, hog on top   /N130–15. . . . . *15 – 20*
Novelty, Lion, marked "Camden, Ark. Lions Club" . . . . *15 – 20*
Pitcher, bulbous, w/cat handle, 8½"   /088 . . . . *30 – 50*
Pitcher, Cat shape, 8"   /N145 . . . . *50 – 60*
Pitcher, pinch spout w/parrot handle . . . . *40 – 60*
Planter, Basket w/bird on handle . . . . *25 – 30*
Planter, Duck   /N74 – 15 . . . . *15 – 20*
Planter, Rooster   /501 . . . . *15 – 20*
Planter, Rolling Pin   /N1 – 51 . . . . *10 – 15*
Shakers, Letters "S" and "P," pair   /690 . . . . *10 – 15*
Shakers, bulbous, "S" and "P" handles, 2½", pair . . . . *10 – 15*
Shelf sitter, Humpty Dumpty   /R33 . . . . *25 – 30*
Sugar/Creamer on single base   /830 . . . . *10 – 15*
Wall Pocket, Scoop w/embossed flowers   /N45 . . . . *10 – 15*

VASES

Some of these shapes were made in different sizes.

Vase, 5", two handles   /304 . . . . *$10 – $15*
Vase, 7", five-finger   /132 . . . . *18 – 20*
Vase, 7", fluted   /974 . . . . *20 – 30*
Vase, 7½", Leaf   /597 . . . . *18 – 20*
Vase, 8¼" urn, two handles   /870 . . . . *18 – 22*
Vase, 10" fan   /288 . . . . *30 – 35*
Vase, 11", Morning Glory   /801M . . . . *40 – 50*
Vase, 11", Old World Pitcher   /268 . . . . *20 – 25*
Vase, 13½", Iris pitcher   /800R. . . . . *50 – 75*
Vase, 14", large fluted   /953 . . . . *25 – 30*

CANONSBURG POTTERY COMPANY

Canonsburg, Pennsylvania

CHAPTER AT A GLANCE

GEORGELYN
KEYSTONE
MISCELLANY
PRISCILLA/
   WASHINGTON COLONIAL

ROSEPOINT
SPARTAN
WESTCHESTER

Founded in 1901, the company manufactured semiporcelain dinnerware and toilet ware. Manufacturing ceased after a fire in 1975.

MARKS Canonsburg used a variety of backstamps, often incorporating a picture of a cannon.

GEORGELYN

A round shape with a scalloped edge and an indented line about ⅛" in from the rim, which repeats the edge.

Bowl, vegetable, oval, 9"*	$10 – $12
Casserole	20 – 25
Creamer	4 – 6
Cup	4 – 6
Dish, 5½"*	2 – 3
Plate, 6¼"*	1 – 2
Plate, 9"	7 – 9
Saucer	1 – 2
Sugar	8 – 10

KEYSTONE   (1934)

Distinguished by a variegated edge line, which is repeated on the lids as well as the openings into which the lids fit.

MARKS   I have found the two marks pictured here. Do not be confused by a mark you might find that is a keystone with the word "Keystone" across it and "C.P.Co." below. This is most likely a Chester Pottery mark.

Butter dish	*$20 – $25*
Casserole, w/embossed lug handles, 9".	*20 – 25*
Creamer	*4 – 6*
Cup	*4 – 6*
Plate, 6¼"*	*1 – 2*
Plate, 7¼"	*4 – 5*
Plate, 9"*	*7 – 9*
Platter, 11"*	*10 – 12*
Saucer	*1 – 2*
Sugar	*8 – 10*

MISCELLANY

Measurements for the Ohio jugs are height without lid.

Ohio jug, 4³⁄₈"	*$20 – $25*
Ohio jug, 5³⁄₄"	*20 – 25*
Ohio jug, 6³⁄₄"	*25 – 30*

PRISCILLA / WASHINGTON COLONIAL   (mid 1931)

Originally introduced as Priscilla, by April 1932 the name was changed to Washington Colonial and the finials were restyled. Distinguished by a heavily embossed band on the rim and around the hollowware.

I have only seen an ivory body, though pink, green, and yellow glazes were also advertised. This shape is usually found with decal decorations, but some undecorated pieces will show up.

The Ebenezer Cut Glass Company made matching stemware.

MARKS   Later pieces will be found with the American Tradition backstamp.

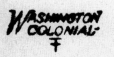

Priscilla Plate and teapot.

Casserole	*$20 – $25*
Creamer	*4 – 6*
Cup	*4 – 6*
Gravy	*12 – 15*
Gravy faststand	*12 – 15*
Plate, 6"	*1 – 2*
Plate, 7"	*4 – 5*
Plate, 9"	*5 – 7*
Plate, square, 7³/₄"	*5 – 6*
Saucer	*1 – 2*
Sugar	*8 – 10*
Teapot	*20 – 25*

ROSEPOINT

Canonsburg bought Steubenville in 1959 and acquired, among other things, the Rosepoint molds that Steubenville had bought from the defunct Pope-Gosser. Use Pope-Gosser pricing.

SPARTAN (1930)

(This shape was originally introduced as Georgelyn, but a December 1931 trade ad shows that the name had been changed to Spartan and a new round shape given the Georgelyn name.) A square shape with scalloped corners. This was made in an ivory body and a Sunset (yellow) glaze.

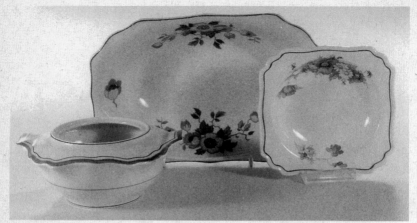

Spartan: Sugar (missing lid), vegetable bowl, and bread & butter plate.

Bowl, vegetable, 9¼"... *$10 – $12*
Creamer .... *4 – 6*
Cup .... *4 – 6*
Dish, 5¼"... *2 – 3*
Dish, 6½"*.. *3 – 4*
Plate, 6¼"*.. *1 – 2*
Plate, 8½"*.. *5 – 7*
Plate, 9¼"*.. *5 – 7*
Plate, square, 8"*.. *5 – 7*
Platter, oval, w/lid... *20 – 25*
Platter, rectangular, 13"* .... *12 – 15*
Saucer .... *1 – 2*
Sugar .... *8 – 10*
Teapot .... *25 – 30*

WESTCHESTER   (1935)

An Art Deco shape. The AD pieces were used for a child's tea set and a Mary and Her Lamb decal will be found.

Butter dish .... *$20 – $25*
Casserole... *20 – 25*
Coffee pot, AD .... *30 – 40*
Creamer .... *4 – 6*
Creamer, AD... *6 – 8*
Cup .... *4 – 6*

Westchester: Teapot, platter, and AD coffee pot.

Cup, AD. . . . . *$10 – $12*
Plate, 6". . . . . *1 – 2*
Plate, 7". . . . . *4 – 5*
Plate, 9". . . . . *5 – 7*
Platter, oval, lug, 11¾". . . . . *10 – 12*
Saucer . . . . *1 – 2*
Saucer, AD . . . . *3 – 5*
Sugar . . . . *8 – 10*
Sugar, AD, open . . . . *10 – 12*
Teapot . . . . *30 – 35*

CARDINAL CHINA COMPANY

Carteret, New Jersey

CHAPTER AT A GLANCE

COOKIE JARS
KITCHEN COMPANIONS

MISCELLANY
Utensils

Cardinal began manufacturing in 1946 as the Carteret China Company doing contract work in the lamp and gift business. As they started selling their own products, they used the name Cardinal China so they wouldn't be in competition with their clients. This business grew and the name Cardinal supplanted Carteret.

Business was so good that two lines had to be farmed out for manufacturing, the cookie jars (see below) and the shrimp boats which were made in Ohio. In 1960, Cardinal ceased its own manufacturing and started producing their lines abroad, first in Japan, later Hong Kong, Taiwan, and currently in the Philippines. They are still in business.

Cardinal used a white talc body. Designs were originated by Sidney Darwin, president, who worked closely with modeler Ralph Fiorentini and Ceramic Engineer Sam Kronman to develop the final product.

Cardinal was the first company in the United States to make a spoon rest—the double Daisy. Until then, saucers were used. People thought Cardinal was crazy, but they sold over one million.

See Roerig in Bibliography.

MARKS "Cardinal China" impressed on bottoms.

COOKIE JARS

Joyce Roerig was the first to discover that Cardinal's cookie jars were made by American Bisque to Cardinal's designs. They date from the late fifties to the early sixties.

Boy, head w/mortar board (Professor) /303 . . . . *$75 – $85*
Bus, "Cookie Bus" /308 . . . . *100 – 125*
Castle /307 . . . . *100 – 125*
Clown, full figure /315 . . . . *100 – 110*
Clown, head (Crying Clown), "I Want Some Cookies" /302 . . . . *75 – 85*
Elephant w/sailor hat "S.S. Kookie" /313 . . . . *165 – 185*
French Chef, head, "Petite Gateaux, Cookies" /305 . . . . *100 – 125*

Garage, "Free Parking for Cookies" /306 . . . . *$65 – $75*
Girl, head (Cookie Kate), "Cookies" /301 . . . . *75 – 85*
Pig, head (Porky Pig), "Go ahead. Make a pig of yourself" /304 . . . . *75 – 85*
Rooster /314
   Decorated . . . . *45 – 55*
   White . . . . *35 – 45*
Sack, "Cookies" /310 . . . . *40 – 50*
Safe, "Cookie Safe" /309 . . . . *50 – 60*
Soldier, full figure /312 . . . . *85 – 95*
   w/Bank in lid . . . . *100 – 125*
Telephone, old-fashioned /311 . . . . *50 – 60*

KITCHEN COMPANIONS (early 50s)

All of these items are green and yellow. The original sample was made in green and white and shown to a buyer from Woolworth's. He said white was not a good kitchen color, try yellow. The combination was a huge success, especially the Measuring Spoon Plant which sold over three million pieces, and established Cardinal's success. The Flower Pot spoon holder and the sprinkling bottle are the most easily found pieces.

The **coaster/ashtray** was called a "Coastray" and came with either a chartreuse or rose flower as well as yellow. The two-way **gravy ladle**, solid green, was designed to separate the fat from the gravy. The **Flower Pot and Planter measuring spoon holders** had yellow bottoms with green leaves, and often came with colorful plastic measuring spoons that suggested flowers when in place. The **Measuring Boy spoon holder** came with a coffee measuring cup as

Kitchen Companions: Top Row: *Chick egg cup, measuring spoon holder (planter shape), measuring spoon plant (plain), measuring spoon plant (basket).* Middle Row: *string nest, scissor nest, sprinkler, measuring spoon holder, and shakers.* Bottom Row: *Shaker holder (tree trunk), toothpick/shaker holder, shaker holder (leaf) and flower in pot shakers.*

Kitchen Companions: Top Row: *Single spoon rest, double spoon rest, single spoon rest (this one says "Spoon Rest" on leaf).* Middle Row: *Tea bag holders w/original box.* Bottom Row: *Apple wall pocket and wall lamp.*

well. The **shaker holders** (called "Versatrays") held plastic Daisy-shape shakers: Daisy (white w/yellow center) and Black-Eyed Susan (yellow w/brown center). Other color combinations found are: brown (yellow center), green (yellow center), and red (brown center). The **teabag holder** (two sold as a Tea-for-Two) has a small drainage hole in the center. There may be a mailbox-shape string holder.

   PRICING   For the price of a three-piece shaker set (holder plus two shakers) add the three prices together.

Coaster/ashtray, Flower shape	$6 – $8
Eggcup, Chick shape	12 – 14
Gravy Ladle, two spout	6 – 8
Measuring Spoon Plant (holder), Flower Pot (basket) shape	8 – 10
Measuring Spoon Plant (holder), Flower Pot (plain) shape	6 – 8
Measuring Spoon holder, Planter shape	10 – 12
Measuring Spoon holder, Oriental Man, "#1 Measure Boy"	15 – 18
Scissor Nest w/bird on top, "Scissor Nest"	10 – 12
Shaker, Flower, each	
Black-Eyed Susan	3 – 4
Daisy	3 – 4
Other colors	4 – 5
Shaker, Flower in Pot shape, each	6 – 8
Shaker, Oriental Boy, "Salt," each	10 – 12
Shaker, Oriental Girl, "Pepper," each	10 – 12
Shaker, shelf	12 – 15
Shaker Holder, Leaf shape	5 – 7
Shaker Holder, Tree Trunk shape	7 – 9
Shakers, Oriental Boy & Girl, set	22 – 25
Spoon Rest, Daisy shape, double, "Spoon Rest"	8 – 10
Spoon Rest, four-petal flower shape, single, "Spoon Rest"	6 – 8
Spoon Rest, Tulip shape, single, "Spoon Rest" /1132	6 – 8
Sprinkler Bottle, Oriental Man, "Sprinkle Plenty" /1131	25 – 30

String Nest w/bird on top, "String Nest" . . . . *$12 – $15*
Teabag holder/ashtray, Flower shape, yellow w/red center   /1107 . . . . *6 – 8*
Toothpick Holder, Bird shape, on leaf-shape shaker holder. . . . . *8 – 10*
Wall Lamp, Two Flowerpots on Shelf . . . . *35 +*

MISCELLANY

The **cheese tray** has the names of cheeses printed all over. Cheese plates and trays came with a stainless steel cheese knife with a ceramic "Swiss cheese" handle. The **letter holder** has a pottery head and upper torso of a mailman with a wire letter holder. The **dip plate** holds dip in the radish and vegetables on the leaf. The **Measure Mammy** is a ceramic torso that sits on three measuring cups and holds three spoons. The **shrimp boats** came in sets of four with a wooden mast and a white plastic sail which could be used as a place card. The **spoon rests** were advertised as usable for nuts, candy, or as an ash tray. The **wall pockets** are done in natural colors.

Butter pat, cup shape, "I'm a little Butter Cup" . . . . *$5 – $6*
Cheese plate w/mouse in cheese knife holder . . . . *25 – 30*
Cheese shaker, Tony. . . . . *35 – 40*
Cheese tray, 3³/₄" × 4³/₄". . . . .*6 – 8*
Condiment Set
　　Chester Cheezy. . . . . *20 – 25*
　　Garlic Gladys . . . . *20 – 25*
　　Jam Jar Janie . . . . *20 – 25*
　　Mustard Mario. . . . . *20 – 25*
　　Oscar Onion . . . . *20 – 25*
　　Roger Relish . . . . *20 – 25*
Jam dish w/matching spoon
　　Peach. . . . . *10 – 12*
　　Pineapple. . . . . *10 – 12*
　　Strawberry . . . . *10 – 12*
Letter Holder, Mailman, "Mail" on cap, gray and black   /1108 . . . . *12 – 15*
Measure Mammy . . . . *60 – 75*
Pincushion, Poodle w/thimble on tail . . . . *15 – 20*
Plate, dip, radish shape . . . . *10 – 15*
Ring holder, elephant . . . . *15 – 18*
Serving pieces
　　Carrot . . . . *8 – 10*
　　Celery . . . . *10 – 12*
　　Eggplant . . . . *8 – 10*
Shrimp Boat, set, cobalt/green/rose/yellow, w/mast & sail . . . . *22 – 25*
Spoon rest
　　Fish . . . . *6 – 8*
　　Peach . . . . *6 – 8*
　　Pineapple. . . . . *6 – 8*
Spoon rest, double, elephant head. . . . . *12 – 15*
Spoon rest, double, whale. . . . . *12 – 15*
Sprinkler, elephant . . . . *45 – 50*
Sprinkler, flatiron, Ivy decoration . . . . *45 – 50*

Teabag rest, teapot shape, "I'll hold the bag" .... *$5 – $6*
Toothpick holder, fish .... *8 – 10*
Toothpick holder, flatiron .... *8 – 10*
Toothpick holder, umbrella .... *8 – 10*
Wall Pocket, Banana.. *20 – 25*
Wall Pocket, Grape... *20 – 25*
Wall Pocket, Pepper .... *20 – 25*
Wall Pocket, Strawberry.. *20 – 25*

Utensils

These are stainless steel forks, knives and spreaders with figural ceramic handles.

   PRICING   Each utensil is $4.00. Complete sets would be slightly higher than the sum of all pieces.

FORKS, SEAFOOD   Handles have three-dimensional seafood at the end.

Clam	**Fish**	**Oyster**
Crab	**Lobster**	**Shrimp**

KNIVES, FRUIT   Wood-grain handles with three-dimensional fruit at the end.

Apple	**Berry**	**Pear**
Banana	**Peach**	**Pineapple**

SPREADERS, VEGETABLE   The entire handle is the vegetable.

Asparagus	**Corn**	**Radish**
Carrot	**Eggplant**	**Squash**
Celery	**Peas**	

CERAMIC ARTS STUDIO

Madison, Wisconsin

CHAPTER AT A GLANCE

Ceramic Arts Studio was begun in 1941 for the manufacture of hand-thrown flower pots and vases. The demand for novelties created by the banning of Japanese imports turned their attention to molded art pieces, primarily figures and shakers, in a semiporcelain body with underglaze and overglaze decoration. Betty Harrington began designing many of the items that are now collectible. Due to declining sales, the company closed in 1955.

See Holthaus in Bibliography and see Clubs/Newsletters.

MARKS Items are marked about 85% of the time with the words "Ceramic Arts Studio" stamped on a line or with the addition of "Madison, Wisconsin," stamped in a semicircle. If there is room, the name of a piece might appear. If there is no room, a piece will be unmarked.

In addition, most of the pieces have decorator touch marks. These are colored dots that identify the person who did the decorating.

DECORATIONS Most pieces were hand-painted, with the exception of the few one-color pieces you will find. These were dipped in the glaze.

Ceramic Arts pieces are generally found in one, two, or three different color schemes. For example, the Parrots, Pete and Polly, come in two different color schemes, green and yellow or red and yellow. In each scheme, one, two, or three colors usually predominate. For those pairs and sets done in more than one scheme, some people collect them in matching colors, others like to mix colors.

Some figures were elaborately decorated, with stripes, plaids, and floral designs on their clothes and varying hair color. For example, I have seen four Pioneer Susies. One is blond, one brunette, and two are redheads. One has a floral design on her apron, another has floral and stripes, and the other two have different plaid patterns. Other details vary as well. Obviously, you need to be fairly precise when mail ordering.

Red and gold overglaze is very desirable. Red, white, and black figures, as well as pink and black are among the popular color combinations, as is maroon on some of the tall figures. Chartreuse is easy to find.

DESIGNERS Most of these figures were designed by Betty Harrington, and hers are the most desirable. But other designers were involved. For example, Betty Harrington told Dan Fortney that a Japanese designer, we don't have his name, created the stylized Fox.

NOTE I have tried to include a lot of information in these listings. Here are some tips on how to read them:

1. Besides the size (taken from catalogs which are not always precise) and the shape number, figures that are also shakers are indicated with "/S" after the shape number.

2. Although most pairs are obvious, for convenience sake they are indicated with "AND" at the end of the first entry, and an indentation for the second.

3. A number of these pieces are in a sitting position but not all of them are shelf-sitters (pieces which perch on the edge of a shelf with legs or tails dangling over the side). Shelf-sitters are designated with (s/s).

4. Accessories for specific figures are indicated in parentheses as (Acc:).

PRICING For shaker versions of figures, add 50% to the figure price.

Each figure is priced separately. When buying a pair, everyone, myself included, likes to pay less than the price of the two figures separately. But this is really the dealer's decision and not the business of a price guide.

DISPLAYING YOUR CERAMIC ARTS FIGURES Here are some suggestions from the catalogs:

A ribbon bow around the neck of the curly lamb. A red ribbon around the necks of Fifi and Fufu, or attached by ribbons to Promenade Woman. And Summer and Winter Bell can be strung with ribbon.

As to pairings, the Shepherd or Shepherdess can be used individually with either the curly lamb or the goat with the paper flower. Other pairings are Daisy Donkey and Elsie Elephant, Little Boy Blue and Little Bo Peep and Miss Muffet #1 and Jack Horner #1.

There is some question as to which sheep went with Little Bo Peep. In the catalogs, the curly lamb is shown by itself, but when Little Bo Peep is shown, both the curly lamb and the lamb with wreath are on the same page. This combination is also supported by photos of old trade shows.

Looking at old catalogs and trade-show photographs, I can't help but feel that the idea was to have fun and do whatever you wanted, and not be bound by rules. So if you want to give Little Bo Peep twelve sheep, go ahead. Enjoy yourself!

ANIMALS

Bird, "Budgie" (s/s), 5" AND $30
    "Pudgie" (s/s), 5" 30
Bird, Canary, left (s/s) AND 40
    Canary, right (s/s) 40
Bird, Lovebirds, one piece, 2³/₄"   /138 30
Bird, Parakeets on branch, "Chip" facing right, 4" AND
    "Chirp" facing left, 4"   /S 30
Bird, Parrot, "Pete" (s/s), 7¹/₂" AND 40
    "Polly" (s/s), 7¹/₂" 40
Calico Cat, 3"   /A34   /S AND 20
    Gingham Dog, 2³/₄"   /A35   /S 20
Camel, stylized, 5¹/₂"   /337/S 75
Cat, Persian, Tomcat, tail up, 4³/₄"   /208 50
    (This is an alternate Father to go with Fluffy)

Cat, Persian, Tomcat (Father), "Tuffy" (s/s), 5¼"   /208N AND
   Cat, Persian, Mother, "Fluffy" (s/s), 4¼"   /109 .... *$50*
Cat, Persian, Kittens
   Playing, 2"   /112N *20*
   Scratching, 2"   /112 .... *20*
   Sleeping, #1, 1"   /110 .... *20*
   Sleeping, #2, 2"   /110N *20*
   Washing, #1, 2"   /111 .... *20*
   Washing, #2, 2"   /111N
   (Although there are six kittens, only three were sold with a set;
   which three variedfrom catalog to catalog.). *20*
Cat, "Puff," tail up AND *30*
   "Muff" *30*
Cat, Siamese, large, 4¼"   /A48   /S AND *30*
   Kitten, 3¼"   /A49   /S *30*
Cat, Siamese, stylized, "Thai," 4½"   /A70   /S AND
   "Thai-Thai," 5½"   /A71   /S *30*
Cat, w/bow, sitting, "Bright Eyes," 3" *25*
Deer, 3¾" AND Doe, stylized *40*
Dog, Boxer, "Billy," 2"   /A90   /S AND *20*
   "Butch," 3"   /A89   /S *20*
Dog, Cocker Spaniel, lying (s/s) *50*
Dog, Cocker Spaniel, sitting, 2½"   /183 AND
   Dog, Cocker Spaniel, standing, 2¾"   /184 .... *30*
Dog, Cocker Spaniel, 5¾"
   Black, "Sonny," eyes open   /336 .... *75*
   Light tan, "Honey," eyes closed   /335 .... *75*
Dog, Collie, Mother (s/s), 5"   /152 AND
   Dog, Collie, pups
   Playing, 2½"   /154 .... *20*
   Sitting, 2"   /155 .... *20*
   Sleeping, 2¼"   /153 .... *20*
Dog, Dachshund, standing, 3½" long   /206 .... *30*
Dog, Dachshund, "Sassy," 2¼" long   /A92   /S AND *40*
   Dachshund, "Waldo," 3¼" long   /A91   /S *40*
Dog, Pekingese, sitting up, 3"   /207 .... *40*
Dog, Pomeranian, sitting, 2¼"   /323 AND *30*
   Pomeranian, standing, 2¾"   /322 .... *30*
Dog, Poodle, "Fifi," 3"   /359/S AND *30*
   Poodle, "Fufu," 2½"   /360/S *30*
Dog, Scotty (one piece), 2¾" *40*
Dog, Scotty, "Sooty", black, 3"   /A55   /S AND *25*
   Scotty, "Taffy", white, 3"   /A54   /S *25*
Dog, stylized, 5" long *95*
Donkey, "Daisy," beflowered, 4¾"   /189 .... *50*
Donkey, "Dem," 4½" AND *75*
   Elephant "Rep," 4½" *75*
Duck, Mother *50*
Duck, Baby *30*
Elephant, Baby, sitting, trunk down *40*

Elephant, Baby, sitting, in diapers, trunk up, "Benny," 3¼"   /142 AND *$40*
    Elephant, Mother, trunk up, "Annie," 3¾"   /141 . . . . *40*
Elephant, "Elsie," beflowered, trunk up, 5"   /190 . . . . *75*
Elephant, large, trunk down *75*
Elephant, "Rep" (see Donkey "Dem")
Elephants, Wee, Boy, in shorts, "P"-shaped trunk, # ½"   /A31 AND *25*
    Wee, Girl, in skirt, "S"-shaped trunk, 3¼"   /A30   /S *25*
Ewe, small   /S AND *30*
    Ram, small   /S *30*
Fish, on tail, 4" Salt   /A5   /S AND *20*
    Fish, on tail, Pepper   /A6   /S *20*
Fish, Straight-tail, on stomach, "Swirl," 3"   /147 AND *20*
    Fish, Twist-tail, on stomach, "Swish," 2½"   /146. . . . . *20*
Fish, on wave, head up, 3½"   /A56   /S AND. *30*
    Fish, on wave, head down, 3½"   /A57   /S *30*
Fox   /A66   /S AND *30*
    Goose, startled   /A67   /S *30*
Fox, stylized. *75*
Giraffe, Large, 6½"   /324 AND *30*
    Giraffe, Young, 5½"   /325 . . . . *30*
Goat w/beard, "Ralph" (Acc: Paper sweet pea blossom) 4"   /283 . . . . *50*
Goose (see Fox)
Hen, tail up, stylized AND *40*
    Rooster, tail down, stylized *40*
Hippo (see Miscellany/Ashtray)
Horse, Colt, "Balky," 3¾"   /293 AND. *50*
    Colt, "Frisky," 3¾"   /292 . . . . *50*
Horse, Fighting stallion, "Lightning,"   /377 AND. *60*
    Fighting stallion, "Thunder," 5¾"   /378 . . . . *60*
Horse, Modern Colt. *75*
Horse, Mother, 4¼"   /379 AND *75*
    Spring colt, 3½"   /380. . . . . *75*
Horse, Palomino Colt, 5¾"   /209 . . . . *75*
Horse, head down, "Toby," 2¾"   /143 . . . . *50*
Horse head, head up, 3¼"   /A50   /S AND. *20*
    Horse head, head down, 3¼"   /A51   /S *20*
Jaguar, stylized. *75*
Lamb, Baby, "Frisky," with wreath, 3"   /194. . . . . *15*
Lamb w/bow *20*
Lamb, curly, 3¾"   /186 . . . . *20*
Leopard, head up, 3½"   /357 AND *50*
    Leopard, head down, 6¼" long   /358 . . . . *50*
Monkey, "Mr. Monk," bug on back, 4"   /170 . . . . *50*
Monkey, "Mrs. Monk," w/bow in hair, 3½"   /171 . . . . *50*
Monkey, "Baby Monk," bug on back, 2"   /172 . . . . *20*
Ox, 3" long   /A85   /S AND *20*
    Covered Wagon, 3" long   /A86   /S *20*
Panda w/hat, 2½" *50*
Panther, stylized *75*
Penguin, Mr. (top hat), 3¾"   /A13   /S AND *20*

Cinderella and Prince Charming.

CHILDHOOD FAVORITES

(See also Plaques) St. George could be paired with either Lady Rowena or the Dragon. Chargers could be bought separately. Green figures went with amber and black charger, chartreuse figure with copper green and black charger. Peter Pan and Wendy can be used as bookends.

Little Black Sambo w/umbrella /S AND $75
   Tiger /S.. 75
Little Boy Blue, asleep, 4½" long /163 40
Little Jack Horner, #1, displaying plum, (s/s), 4½" /137 50
Little Jack Horner, #2, hands on bowl, 4½" 40
Little Jack Horner, #3, pulling out plum, 4½" 30
Mary (Had a Little Lamb), bonnet in hand, 6¼" /185 30
Mary (Quite Contrary) w/watering can, 5" 60
Miss Muffet, #1, stirring food, 4½" /136 50
Miss Muffet, #2, all-over ruffled skirt, 4½" 40
Miss Muffet, #3, arm extended, 4½"................................... 30
Paul Bunyon, 4¼" AND 30
   Tree, 2½" /S... 30
Peter Pan, on separate leaf base, 5¼" /213 AND 60
   Wendy, on separate leaf base, 5¼" /214 60
Peter Rabbit, head in hands, elbows on knees, 3¾" /145................. 40
Pied Piper, 6¼" /105... 50
Pied Piper children,
   Boy, running, 3½" /106 20
   Girl, praying, 3" /108....................................... 20
   Girl, running, 3¼" /107 20
Santa Claus /S AND.. 30
   Evergreen Tree /S... 30

ST. GEORGE GROUP

Archibald the Dragon, 8" /369 .... $175
Charger, facing left, 5½" 95
Charger, facing right, 5½" 95
Lady Rowena, 8¼" /371.. 175
St. George (Acc: Lance), 8½" /370................................. 175

COUPLES / TRIOS

The Bedtime Boy and Girl were made to hold little candles.

Bashful, 4¾" AND $50
   Lover (Valentine) Boy, right arm out, 4¾" AND/OR 50
   Willing, girl leaning forward, 4¾"................................ 50
Bedtime Boy, 4¾" /156 AND 50
   Bedtime Girl, 4¾" /157 50
Berty, black, sitting w/ball, one leg up (s/s) AND 75
   Billy, black w/ball, (s/s)... 75
Betty, black AND 75
   Bobby, black, sitting, legs crossed, hand to face 75
Boy, "Jim," whistling, hands in pocket, 4¾" /125 AND.................... 20
   Girl, "June," hands behind, 4½" /126 20
Boy, "Nip," in overalls, sitting w/one leg under (s/s), 4" /119 AND............. 20
   Girl, "Tuck," sitting w/legs crossed (s/s), 4" /120 20
Boy w/Dog, sitting (s/s), 4¼" /223 AND............................. 50
   Girl w/Cat, sitting (s/s), 4¼" /224 50
Boy w/towel, pink and white 75

Bride, w/veil & bouquet, 4³/₄"   /201 AND $50
   Groom, left hand at waist, 5"   /202 50
Colonial Boy, dancing, 5¹/₂"   /217 AND 40
   Colonial Girl, dancing, left arm out, right holding skirt, 5"   /218 40
Colonial Boy, sitting, (s/s), 5"   /315 AND 40
   Colonial Girl, sitting, (s/s), 5"   /316 40
Colonial Man, 6³/₄"   /215 AND 50
   Colonial Woman, 6¹/₂"   /216 50
Cowboy, sitting, (s/s), 4³/₄" AND 50
   Cowgirl, sitting, (s/s), 4³/₄" 50
Cupid on flower, 5" 75
Dawn, stylized woman, kneeling, 6¹/₂" 75
Farmer Boy (Acc: Fishing pole) (s/s), 4³/₄"   /284 AND 50
   Farmer Girl (s/s), 4³/₄"   /285 50
Gay 90s Man "Harry," w/hat in right hand, dog at feet, 9¹/₂"   /103 AND 40
   Gay 90s Woman "Lillibeth," hand on face, 9"   /104 40
Gay 90s Man w/hat in left hand, dog at feet, 6³/₄"   /279 AND 60
   Gay 90s Woman, holding bag, 6¹/₂"   /280 60
Gremlin, sitting, 2¹/₂" AND 50
   Gremlin, standing, 4" 50
Hunter "Al" w/rifle, 6¹/₄" AND 20
   Cocker Spaniel "Kirby" hunting dog, 2" 20
Imps
   Devil w/spear, 5" 100
   Lying, 3¹/₂" long 100
   Sitting, 3¹/₂" 100
Mermaid, Baby, sitting, 3" AND 60
   Baby, lying, 2¹/₂" AND 60
   Mermaid, Mother, on rock, 4" 60
Nineteenth Century (Victorian) Man wearing cape, 6³/₄"   /211 AND 60
   Nineteenth Century (Victorian) Woman w/parasol, 6¹/₂"   /212 60
Pioneer Sam, w/pig and sack of grain, 5¹/₂"   /115 AND 40

Vases: Lu-Tang and Wing-Sang.

Pioneer Susie, sweeping (Acc: Broom), 5"   /116 . . . . $40
Promenade Man, holding cloak, 7³/₄"   /367 AND 75
  Promenade Woman, 7³/₄"   /368. 75
Shepherd, hat at feet, 8¹/₂" (Acc: Staff)   /365 AND 75
  Shepherdess, 8" (Acc: Staff)   /366 75
Southern Belle, "Lucindy," 7"   /159 AND 50
  Southern Gentleman, "Col. Jackson," 7¹/₄"   /158 50
Square Dance Boy, w/kerchief, 6¹/₂"   /290 AND. 50
  Square Dance Girl, w/kerchief, holding skirt, 6"   /291. 50
Wally, ball up, (s/s), 4¹/₂" AND. 75
  Willy, sitting (s/s), rubbing eye, ball in hand, 4 ¹/₂". 75
Winnie, lying, head on hands, 5¹/₂ " AND. 75
  Woody, 3¹/₄". 75
Young Love (Kissing) Boy, (s/s) 4¹/₂"   /286 AND 40
  Young Love (Kissing) Girl, (s/s) 4¹/₂"   /287 40

COUPLES-FOREIGN NATIONALITIES

Two of these sets fit together: The Swedish couple (her hand on his shoulder, his hand on her waist) and the Dutch Dancing couple (hands meet, his leg under her leg). The Dutch Love couple can be placed so that they are on the verge of a kiss, and Hans and Katrinka should be facing each other.

Balinese Dance Man, 9¹/₂"   /326 AND $75
  Balinese Dance Woman, 9¹/₂"   /327 75
Burmese Chinthe, 5³/₄". 50
Burmese Man, 5" AND 50
  Burmese Woman, 5" 50
Chinese Boy, hands in sleeves, 4¹/₄"   /A9   /S AND. 20
  Chinese Girl, hands in front, 4"   /A10   /S 20
Chinese Boy, sitting, one foot on shelf (s/s), 4"   /234 AND 20
  Chinese Girl, sitting, one foot on shelf (s/s), 4"   /235. 20
Chinese Boy, sitting, quilted jacket, "Sun-Li," (s/s), 5¹/₂"   /294 AND. 40
  Chinese Girl, sitting, quilted jacket, "Su-Lin," (s/s), 5¹/₂"   /295 40
Chinese Boy, smiling, arms folded, "Smi-Li," 6"   /296 AND. 40
  Chinese Girl, frowning, hands behind, "Mo-Pi," 6"   /297 40
Chinese Boy, standing, arms behind, "Ting a Ling," 5¹/₂"   /134 AND 30
  Chinese Girl, kneeling w/fan, "Sung Tu," 4"   /135. 30
Chinese Man, "Wing-Sang," w/gong, 6¹/₄" AND. 30
  Chinese Woman, "Lu-Tang," w/mandolin, 6¹/₄" 30
Cuban Girl, w/water jug, "Carmelita," 4¹/₄"   /133 AND 50
  Cuban Woman, fruit basket on head, "Carmen," 7¹/₄"   /132. 50
Dutch Boy, dancing, arms out, foot up, "Hans," 5¹/₂"   /167 AND 60
  Dutch Girl, dancing, arms out, foot up, "Katrinka," 5¹/₄"   /168 60
Dutch Boy, hands in pockets, 4"   /A3   /S AND 20
  Dutch Girl, hands clasped over apron, 4"   /A4   /S. 20
Dutch Boy, hand in pocket, arm behind, "Hans," 6¹/₂"   /304 AND 60
  Dutch Girl, hands clasped over chest, "Katrinka," 6¹/₄"   /305 60
Dutch Boy, sitting, hands on shelf, (s/s), 4¹/₂"   /239 AND. 30
  Dutch Girl, sitting, hands on shelf, (s/s), 4¹/₂"   /240 30
Dutch Love Boy, holding bouquet   /221 AND 50

Head vases: Manchu, Mei-Ling, Svea, and Sven.

Wee Swedish Boy, 3¼"   /A26   /S AND *$20*
   Wee Swedish Girl, 3"   /A27   /S *20*
Zulu Man, kneeling, 5½" AND *175*
   Zulu Woman, standing, 7" *175*

MINIATURES

Flowerpot, triangular. *$10*
Flowerpot, round. *10*
Flowerpot, square *10*
Gravy, Horse *40*
Pitcher, Aladdin's Lamp *40*
Pitcher, Buddha. *40*
Pitcher, Diana *40*
Pitcher, George Washington *40*
Toby Mug *50*
Vase, Chinese. *10*
Vase w/birds *15*
Vase w/ducks, round, 2" *15*

MISCELLANY

Some of the planter heads are also plaques. Skunky Bank is "also useful as a figurine or planter." Barber Head is for a shelf or wall and can be used for razors, combs, or money.

Ashtray, Hippo Ullie, 3½"   /352 . . . . *$110*
Ashtray, Pixie Boy clutching Toadstool, 5"   /210 . . . . *50*
Ashtray, Pixie Boy on Toadstool, 5"   /210 . . . . *50*
Ashtray, Pixie Boy on Snail, 5"   /210 . . . . *50*
Ashtray, Pixie Girl, waving, on Lilypad, 5"   /210 . . . . *50*
Ashtray, Pixie Girl, kneeling w/ Toadstool, 5"   /210. . . . . *50*
(All five "Pixies" are hand painted in blue, green and rose)
Bank, Barber Head "Tony," 4¼"   /319 . . . . *60*
Bank, Mr. Blankety Blank, 4½"   /339 . . . . *60*
Bank, Mrs. Blankety Blank, 4½"   /340 . . . . *60*
Bank, Paisley Pig, 3"   /343. . . . . *95*
Bank, Skunky, 4"   /198. . . . . *75*
Bell, Lillibelle, 6½"   /205 . . . . *75*
Bell, Summer Bell, 5¼"   /219 AND *60*
   Winter Bell, 5¼"   /220 . . . . *60*
Candle holder, Triad woman, each, 5" *75*
Candle holder/Vase, "Hear No Evil," AND *75*
   "Speak No Evil" AND "See No Evil" *75*
Honey Pot, beehive w/bee on lid. *30*
Planter, heads, African Man, 8" AND *100*
   African Woman, 8" *100*
Planter, head, "Barbie," 7" *95*
Planter, head, "Becky," 5¼"   /H306 . . . . *75*
Planter, head, "Bonnie," 7". *95*
Planter, head, Mei-Ling, 5". *75*
Planter, heads, Manchu, 7½" AND *120*

Lotus, 7³/₄" *$120*
Planter, heads, Svea, 6" AND 75
Sven, 6¹/₂" *75*
Planter, Lorelei w/Harp, on Seashell *150*
Vase, Lu-Tang/Wing-Sang *40*

PERFORMING

(See also Plaques)

Adam/Eve, on Serpent base, one piece, 12" (only three) *$2000*
Adonis, 9" AND *200*
Aphrodite, 7³/₄" *200*
Beth, 5"   /356 AND *40*
Bruce, 6¹/₂"   /355 .... *40*
Blythe, 6¹/₂" AND *100*
Pensive, 6" *100*
Comedy w/mask, 10"   /308 AND *125*
Tragedy w/mask, 10"   /309 .... *125*
Danse Macabre Man, 7³/₄" AND *600*
Danse Macabre Woman, 9" *600*
Dance Moderne, Man, one arm up, other down, 9¹/₂"   /341 AND
Dance Moderne Woman, one arm up, other down, 9¹/₂"   /342 .... *100*
Encore Man, 8¹/₄" AND *100*
Encore Woman, 8³/₄" *100*
Fire Man, 11¹/₄"   /328 AND *200*
Fire Woman, 11¹/₄"   /329 .... *200*
King's Jester, Flutist, 12" AND *150*
King's Jester, Lutist, 12" *150*
Maurice, (s/s) 7"   /350 AND *50*
Michele, (s/s), 7"   /351 .... *50*
Pierrette, (s/s), 6¹/₂"   /349 AND *75*
Pierrot, (s/s) 6¹/₂"   /348 .... *75*
Water Man, 11¹/₂"   /330 .... *175*
Water Woman, 11¹/₂"   /331 .... *175*

PLAQUES

Made to hang on a wall. Those which were also head planters are indicated in the listings. The hands of the dancing Dutch couple interlock. The lanterns of the Lantern Man and Woman hang loosely from a metal ring.

African Man, 8" AND *$125*
African Woman, 8" (head planters) *125*
Attitude, ballerina, leg forward, 9¹/₂"   /320 AND *50*
Arabesque, ballerina, leg back, 9¹/₂"   /321 .... *50*
Chinese Lantern Man, 8" AND *60*
Chinese Lantern Woman, 8" *60*
Cockatoo A AND *40*
Cockatoo B, 8" long *40*
Columbine AND *75*
Harlequin, 8" *75*

Comedy AND *$50*
    Tragedy (Masks), 5¹/₄" *50*
Dutch Boy, dancing, 8" AND *75*
    Dutch Girl, dancing, 8" *75*
Goosey Gander w/hat, one leg raised, 4³/₄" *60*
Grace, Ballet Dancer, 9"   /345 AND *50*
    Greg, Ballet Dancer, 9¹/₂"   /344 . . . . *50*
Hamlet, 8¹/₄" AND *125*
    Ophelia, 8¹/₄" (w/masks). *125*
Jack (Beanstalk), 6¹/₂" *60*
Jack Be Nimble, 5" *60*
Lotus, 8¹/₂" AND *120*
    Manchu, 8¹/₂" (head planters). *120*
Neptune w/Triton, 6" /374 . . . . *150*
    Mermaid, 6" /373 . . . . *150*
    Sprite, tail up, 4¹/₂" /375 . . . . *80*
    Sprite, tail down, 4¹/₂" /376 . . . . *80*
Shadow Dancer, Woman (A), 7" *75*
    Woman, 7" *75*
Zor, 9"   /353 AND *50*
    Zorina, 9"   /354 . . . . *50*

RELIGIOUS

Angel, arm down, "Blessing," 5³/₄"   /204 AND $50
    Angel, arm up, "Praise," 6¹/₄"   /203 . . . . $50
Angel, Baby, kneeling, Boy w/hands in lap, 4¹/₄" AND *40*
    Girl w/hands to face, 4¹/₄" *40*
Angel, praying, (s/s), 2³/₄" AND *40*
    Angel, sleeping (s/s), 2³/₄" *40*
Angel, w/candle, 5" *40*
Angel Group
    Praying (kneeling), 4¹/₂" *50*
    Singing, 3¹/₂" *50*
    Standing w/star, 5¹/₂" *50*
Isaac, bearded, 12"   /464 AND. *75*
    Rebecca, w/jug, 12"   /465 . . . . *75*
Madonna, modern w/bible, 9¹/₂" *75*
Madonna w/child, kneeling, 6¹/₂" *75*
Madonna w/gold halo, 9¹/₂" *75*
Our Lady of Fatima, 9¹/₄" *75*
St. Agnes w/lamb in arms, 6¹/₄" *75*
St. Francis, arms out, 2 birds, 7"
    Hand painted w/brown robe   /231 . . . . *75*
    White   /232. . . . . *75*
St. Francis, 2 birds, 9¹/₂" *95*
    Birdbath, for either of above St. Francis *20*

SETS

Balinese Dancers (See also Couples/Foreign Nationalities)

Bali Gong, 5½" $50
Bali Hai, 8" 75
   Bare torso 150
Bali Kris, 7½" 75
Bali Lao, 8½" 75
   Bare Torso 150
Ballet (See also Plaques)
   Ballet En Pose, (s/s) 4¾" /273 AND................................... 50
   Ballet En Repose, (s/s) 4¾" /274........................ 50
   Daisy, holding tutu, 5¼" 60
   Grace, (s/s), 6" AND..................................... 50
   Gregg, (s/s), 6" 50
   Pansy, hands on head, 5¾" 60
   Rose, tying laces, 4¾" 60
   Violet, sitting, 3" 60
Four Seasons
   Autumn Andy, w/books over shoulder, 5" /150........................ 50
   Spring Sue, w/shawl, 5" /148 50
   Summer Sally, sitting, w/pail, 3½" /149.......................... 50
   Winter Willy, sitting, w/snowball, 4" /151......................... 50
Harem Group ("Excellent gift for bachelors.")
   Harem Girl, reclining, 6" long /334 .... $50
   Harem Girl, sitting, 4½" /333....................................... 50
   Pillow... 20
   Sultan on pillow, 4½" /332...................................... 50
   Sultan, no pillow... 50
Legend of Hiawatha
   Birchbark Canoe (planter), 8" 75
   Bunny, 1¾" /267... 30
   Chipmunk, 2" /266 20
   Fawn, standing, 4¼" /265 75
   Hiawatha, 3½" 50
   Minnehaha, 6½".. 50
   Seagull, sits on canoe, 1¼" across.............................. 200
   Wee Indian Boy /S, 3" /A19 AND 20
   Wee Indian Girl /S, 3¼" /A20 20
Orchestra/Adults
   Accordian Lady, standing 200
   Cellist Man, sitting (Acc: Bow) 200
   Flute Lady, standing 200
   French Horn Man, sitting 200
   Guitar Man, sitting 200
   Violin Lady, standing 200
Orchestra/Kids
   Accordion Boy, 5" /191 50
   Banjo Girl, (s/s), 4" /192..................................... 50
   Bass Viol Boy, 4¾" /182.. 50
   Drummer Girl, 4¼" /179 50
   Flute Girl, 4¾" /178 50
   Guitar Boy, 5" /181... 50

Harmonica Boy, (s/s), 4"   /193 . . . . *50*
Saxophone Boy, 5¼"   /180 . . . . *50*
(Initially, Accordian and Harmonica Boys and Banjo Girl were sold
as a "Musical Trio" and the others were "The All Childrens Orchestra.")
Woodland Fantasy (See also Ash Trays)
Pixie Boy, "Peek-A-Boo," under Toadstool, 2½"   /197 . . . . *40*
Pixie Boy riding Snail, 2¾"   /195 . . . . *40*
Pixie Boy on Toadstool, 4"   /196 . . . . *40*
Pixie Girl, kneeling w/ Toadstool, 2½"   /199 . . . . *40*
Pixie Girl, waving, on Lilypad, 2¼"   /200 . . . . *40*
(The following seem to be related to the above but are not a part of it.
The Toadstool makes a pair with either the Elf or Frog.)
Elf, arms around legs, 2½"   /A22   /S *15*
Frog, serenading, 2"   /A23   /S *15*
Toadstool, 3"   /A21   /S *15*

SNUGGLES / LAP-SITTERS

These items fit together in various ways, whether one figure sits on another's
lap or back, or a dog in a doghouse. The large are for salt and the small are for
pepper. The Boy and Girl are pepper shakers that sit on the Chairs which are
salts. Kangaroo mother and baby can be matched or contrasted in color.

Baby Chick AND *$30*
Nest   /S, 2¾" *30*
Bear, Mother, 4¼"   /A36   /S AND
Bear, Baby in lap, 2¼"   /A37   /S *20*
Boy, 2¼" /A82 ON *30*
Chair, 3" overall /A83 . . . . *20*
Bunny, Mother, 4½"   /A40   /S AND *20*
Bunny, Baby, 2½"   /A41   /S *20*
Cats, Siamese, Peek AND *30*
Boo   /S, 3" *30*
Clown, 3¾"   /A52   /S AND *25*
Clown Dog in lap, 2½"   /A53   /S *25*
Cow, Mother, 5¼"   /A38 AND *50*
Calf, 2½"   /A39   /S *50*
Crocodile, 4½" long   /A64 AND *75*
(Native) Boy, 3"   /A65   /S *75*
Dog AND *20*
Doghouse   /S, 1¾" *20*
Elephant, 5"   /A60   /S, AND *75*
(Sabu) Boy, 2¾"   /A61   /S, on trunk *75*
Girl, 2¼" /A84 ON *30*
Chair, 3" overall /A83 . . . . *20*
Kangaroo, Mother, 4¾"   /A42   /S AND *30*
Baby, 2½"   /A43 . . . . *30*
Kitten   /S AND *30*
Cream Pitcher, 2½"   /S *30*
Monkey, Mother, 4"   /A46   /S AND *40*
Baby, 2½"   /A47   /S, on lap, 4" *40*

Mouse, 2"   /A58   /S AND *$15*
   Cheese, 3" long   /A59   /S *15*
Oak Sprite "Dokie" sitting ON *75*
   Fall Leaf/S, 3" *20*
Oak Sprite "Oakie" straddling . . . . . \ *75*
   Spring Leaf   /S 3" *20*
Seahorse, 3½"   /A62   /S AND *20*
   Coral, 3"   /A63   /S *20*
Skunk, Mother, 3½"   /A44   /S AND *20*
   Baby, 2"   /A45   /S . . . . : . *20*
Suzette (Poodle) ON
   Pillow   /S, 3" *15*

CLIFTWOOD ART POTTERIES, INC. / MIDWEST POTTERIES, INC.

Morton, Illinois

CHAPTER AT A GLANCE

CLIFTWOOD	MIDWEST
FIGURES	FIGURES
MISCELLANY	Miniatures
	MISCELLANY

One of six interrelated potteries in Morton, Cliftwood was begun in 1920 for the manufacture of miniature animals and toys. In 1925 art ware—vases, lamps, figurines—was added to the line. The company was sold in 1940 and re-named the Midwest Pottery Company. Midwest made items similar to those of Cliftwood, and the two are usually considered together. Midwest closed in 1944.

See Hall in Bibliography.

MARKS "Cliftwood Potteries" incised in script and a paper label with "Cliftwood, Pride of any Home." Midwest used a paper label only.

COLORS Some of the colors used by both of these potteries will be similar; some will not be because of different chemical formulations for the glazes.

PRICING If an item was made in one or two colors only, those colors are listed and priced specifically. The other items were made in a range of colors; use the following for price range information.

CLIFTWOOD

PRICING/COLORS Low end of range: all solid colors except cobalt. High end of range: cobalt and all drip combinations.

LOW END OF RANGE:

Blue	White	Matt turquoise
Green	Yellow	Matt white
Mulberry	Matt blue	Matt yellow

HIGH END OF RANGE:

Cobalt ("a deep blue black in semilustre finish")	Blue-mulberry drip	Green-pink drip
	Blue-white drip	Navy-yellow drip
	Brown drip	Red-blue drip
Blue-gray drip	Gray drip	Yellow-green drip

FIGURES

Bald Eagle, natural, 8½" $85
Billikin doll, 7½"
    Cobalt 75
    Rockingham 55
Billikin doll, 11"
    Cobalt 100
    Rockingham 85
Buffalo, natural, 6¼ × 10" 200
Bull Dog, sitting, "Nero" or "Barking dog" on base, 11" 80
Cat, reclining, 4½ × 1½" . . . . 15 – 25
Cat, reclining, 6" × 2" . . . . 20 – 35
Cat, reclining, 8½" × 3" . . . . 25 – 45
Cat, sitting, 5¾" . . . . 30 – 40
Crane, 6" . . . . 25 – 45
Elephant, trumpeting, 4" × 7" . . . . 25 – 45
Elephant, trumpeting, 7½" × 9" . . . . 35 – 60
Elephant, trumpeting w/top carrier, 5½" × 8" 60
Elephant, trunk down w/side carrier, 6" × 4" 60
Lion, 8" × 14" 90
Lioness, 7" × 12" 80
Police dog, reclining, 5" × 8½" . . . . 35 – 75
Police dog, reclining, 8" × 12" . . . . 65 – 125
Police dog, reclining, 11" × 18" . . . . 75 – 150

MISCELLANY

Beer mug, barrel shape . . . . $15 – $20
Beer pitcher, barrel shape . . . . 30 – 60
Bookend, Tree trunk w/woodpeckers, drip brown, 6" × 6", each 45
Bookend, Elephants, 6" × 5" × 3½", each 60
Bookend, Lion, natural colors, each 50
Bookend, Lioness, natural colors, each 50
Clock, octagonal, w/inkwells, 7" 150
Compote w/dolphin base, 8½" × 6" high . . . . 65 – 85
Console bowl w/dolphin base, 12" × 6" high . . . . 75 – 95

Desk lamp, Lion, natural colors, 10½" *$65*
Desk lamp, Lioness, natural colors, 10½". *65*
Flower frog, Frog, 6½" .... *20 – 25*
Flower frog, Lorelei on rocks, 7" .... *45 – 55*
Flower frog, Lily pad, 6". .... *18 – 35*
Flower frog, Tree stump, 3½". .... *16 – 25*
Flower frog, Turtle, 4" .... *12 – 20*
Flower frog, Turtle, 5½". .... *16 – 25*
Lamp w/embossed lovebirds, w/harp, 20". .... *50 – 100*
Matchbox holder, 5". .... *25 – 45*
Vase, handled, bust of Lincoln embossed on front, 10" *100*
Vase, #113, 14½". *40*
Vase, #132 (handles are snakes swallowing fish), 18¼". *80*

MIDWEST

PRICING / COLORS *Low end of range:* matte colors, solid colors. *Middle of range:* Hand-applied (brushed) glazes and air-brushed glazes. *High end:* items w/gold or platinum decoration and items with hand-painted underglaze.

LOW END OF RANGE:

Black	Green	Matte blue
Blue	Pink	Matte turquoise
Brown	Tan	Matte white
Cobalt	White	Matte yellow
Gray	Yellow	

MIDDLE OF RANGE:

Blue-mauve	Gray-green	Yellow-green drip
Brown-green		

FIGURES

Bird, Blue Bird, on stump, natural colors, 4½". .... *$10 – $12*
Bird, Blue Heron, 11" .... *25 – 35*
Bird, Blue Jay, on stump, 6½" .... *12 – 15*
Bird, Canaries, on stump, pair, 4½" .... *20 – 30*
Bird, Cockatoo, on pedestal, 6". .... *12 – 15*
Bird, Crane, 6". .... *14 – 18*
Bird, Egret, ... *10 – 12*
Bird, Parrot, on stump, 4½"
  Blue, yellow and green .... *10 – 12*
  White .... *10 – 12*
Bird, Pouter Pigeon, 8" .... *16 – 20*
Bird, Sea gull in flight, 12" .... *30 – 35*
Camel, tan, 8½". *20*
Cowboy on bronco, 7½". .... *20 – 30*

Deer, leaping, 8" .... *$14 – $18*

Deer, stylized, 12" .... *18 – 25*

Deer w/antlers, 12" .... *20 – 30*

Dog, Irish Setter, natural colors, 4½" *35*

Dog, Spaniel, 6" × 4"

   Black *25*

   White *18*

Ducks, mother and two babies (one piece), white w/yellow .... *10 – 18*

Elephant, 9" .... *15 – 20*

   GOP emblem in gold .... *18 – 25*

Fawn, leaping, 11½" *35*

Fighting Cock, 6½" .... *10 – 12*

Gazelle, 12" *35*

Goose, long-necked, white w/yellow, 5¾" *6*

Goose, long-necked, white w/yellow, 6¾" *8*

Hen, Leghorn, white w/yellow legs and cold-painted red comb, 7" *25*

Polar Bear, white, 8½" × 12" *30*

Pony, white/brown spots, 3½" × 4½" *12*

Race Horse on base, mahogany w/black, 7¼" *50*

Race Horse on white base, brown w/black mane, 10" *60*

Road Runner, stylized, 8" *12*

Rooster, Leghorn, 8" *25*

Squirrel, brown w/white drip, 9" *35*

Stallion, rearing, 6" *12*

Stallion, rearing, 10¾" *24*

Swan, 4½" *22*

Tiger, natural, 7" × 12" *40*

Wild Turkey, on stump, natural colors, 11½" *35*

Woman, bust, Art Deco,

   Pastels *40*

Top: *Polar bear, rabbit, duck.* Middle: *Squirrel.* Bottom: *Frog, rooster, turtle.*

White w/gold/platinum hair *$75*
Woman, dancing, Art Deco, white w/gold, 8½" *25*
Woman, nude, holding seaweed garland (September Morn), 11½"
   White *50*
   White w/gold *75*
   Solid 14K gold *100*
Woman w/Russian wolfhound, 11"
   Pastels *65*
   White w/gold/platinum dog *125*

MINIATURES   Note in the illustration that there are four different geese.

Bird, 1¾" *$6*
Boat, yellow and blue sails, 2" *8*
Camel, 2½" *8*
Duck, 2" *6*
Frog, 1" *8*
Goose, 1¾" *7*
Goose, 2¼" *8*
Hen, 1½" *8*
Polar Bear, 1¾" *8*
Rabbit, white w/pink ears, 1¾" *8*
Rabbits, kissing, 2½" *25*
Rooster, white/brown, 2" *8*
Squirrel, 2"
   Brown *10*
   White w/gold *12*
Swan, matte white, 2" *6*
Turtle, green, ¾" *8*

Top: *Bird, rabbits
kissing, boat.*
Middle: *Geese.*
Bottom: *Hen,
geese, rooster.*

MISCELLANY

The shelf-sitters are very similar to the ones made by Ceramic Arts Studios; be careful not to confuse them.

Candle Holder, w/finger ring, 7" $15
Candle Holder, Liberty arm w/torch, 7"................................... 25
Creamer, Cow, brown and white, 4³/₄"................................... 20
Honey jug, solid gold w/platinum lining, 5"............................. 22
Pitcher, Duck, cattail handle, 10" 36
Pitcher, Fish, green, 9¹/₂"... 34
Planter, Clown, white w/blue/green/yellow cap........................... 10
Planter, Cornucopia, Dolphin base, 6¹/₂" .... 18 – 25
Planter, Cornucopia, 5¹/₂" .... 15 – 20
Planter, Dog w/bow tie... 10
Planter, Elephant... 8
Planter, Fox.. 8
Planter, Mr. Duck w/blue/green hat, 5³/₄"............................... 12
Planter, Mrs. Duck w/blue/green bonnet, 5³/₄".......................... 12
Planter, Rabbit, white w/pink ears, 4" × 6"............................ 15
Planter, Swan, 5¹/₂" .... 12 – 25
Shaker, Scotty Dog, pair.. 10
Shelf-sitter, Oriental man/woman, black and white w/gold, 3¹/₂"........ 25
Wall mask, classical Greek god, 5³/₄".................................. 22
Wall mask, man, 18th century English w/beard, 5³/₄".................... 22
Wall mask, man w/curly hair, smiling, 5" 20
Wall mask, man w/mustache, pouting, 5" 20
Wall mask, African man, black, 9" × 4"................................. 30
   w/gold 40
Wall mask, African woman, black, 9" × 4".............................. 30
   w/gold 40

CONTINENTAL KILNS

Chester, West Virginia

In 1944, Vincent Broomhall, who had been art director at E. M. Knowles, and others formed Continental Kilns, which began production in 1945. According to Lehner, they intended to make a Belleek-type body, but all that has been found is hand-painted underglaze semiporcelain. Continental Kilns closed in 1957.

Besides the decorations listed below, other patterns I have found reference to are American Beauty Rose (<1952), Bermuda Rose (<1952), Cat-Tail (<1952), Charmaine (<1952), Golden Crocus (<1952), Golden Rose, Puritan, and Stardust.

MARKS A common backstamp is the pattern name followed by "by Continental Kilns, Underglaze, Hand Painted, U.S.A."

Bali - Hai
by
CONTINENTAL KILNS
Underglaze
Hand Painted
U. S. A.

"SQUARE"

Square or oblong pieces with a scallop in each corner.

Usually found with a hand-painted decoration. Three of the most common are Bali Hai (gray with red flower and green leaves), Tahiti (chartreuse with green and brown palm trees), and Woodleaf (<1952) (white with green leaves and brown stem).

Bowl, oblong, 10½" × 9¼"	$15 – $18
Bowl, square, 10¼"	15 – 18
Creamer	4 – 6
Cup	4 – 6
Dish, 5¼"	2 – 3
Dish, oblong, 6½" × 7¼"	6 – 8
Gravy faststand	12 – 15
Jug, tall	20 – 25
Plate, 6½"	1 – 2
Plate, 8¼"	4 – 5
Plate, 9½"	7 – 9
Platter, oblong, 11½"	10 – 12
Platter, oblong, 13½"	12 – 15
Saucer	1 – 2

Bali Hai shakers, dinner plate, and gravy faststand.

Left: *Tahiti.* Right: *Woodleaf.*

Shaker, square, each .... *$4 – $5*
Sugar .... *8 – 10*
Tumbler, square .... *12 – 15*

COORS
PORCELAIN COMPANY

Golden, Colorado

CHAPTER AT A GLANCE

ROCK-MOUNT / MELLO-TONE   THERMO-PORCELAIN
ROSEBUD

John J. Herold, an experienced pottery designer and manager (Owens, Weller and Roseville), went to Golden and interested Adolph Coors in his experimental use of local clays. Coors offered him an abandoned glass works, and in 1910 the Herold Pottery and China Company began making cooking utensils. In 1914 chemical products were added. By 1920, John Herold had left, and the company became the Coors Porcelain Company.

Hotelware was added to the line in the 1920s and dinnerware in the early 1930s. Coors produced many other products but today produces only chemical ware and industrial items.

NOTE Do not confuse the Coors Porcelain Company with H. F. Coors, Inglewood, California, founded in 1925 by Herman Coors, son of Adolph Coors. H. F. Coors produced ware, mostly kitchenware, marked Coorsite, Chefsware, and Alox.

See Schneider in Bibliography.

ROCK-MOUNT / MELLO-TONE

These are both solid-color lines. Rock-Mount: high gloss colors of Blue, Green, Ivory, Orange, Rose, and Yellow. Mello-Tone: pastel colors of Azure Blue, Spring Green, Coral Pink, and Canary Yellow.

PRICING Use 50% of Rosebud prices except for water jug which is full price. List below is for reference only.

Bowl, soup, 7¼"	**Custard**	**Platter**, oval, 12"
Bowl, vegetable, oval, 8"	**Dish**, fruit, 5½"	**Platter**, oval, 15"
Bowl, vegetable, round, 9"	**Dish**, cereal, 6¼"	**Saucer**
Casserole, oval, 1⅔-pint	**Gravy faststand**	**Shaker**
Casserole, round, 2¾-pint, 8"	**Jug**, water, 2-quart	**Sugar**
Creamer	**Plate**, 6¼"	**Teapot**, 6-cup
Cup	**Plate**, 7¼"	**Tumbler**, 10-ounce
	Plate, 9½"	

ROSEBUD   (1934–1942)

The two jugs were not intended as a **batter set**, but most collectors identify them that way, so that's how I've listed them. The **bean pots** resemble what other potteries would call utility jars, and the utility jar resembles a bean pot! The triple service **casseroles** are pudding bowls with lids. The **cream soup** is the sugar without a lid. The **eggcup** can be used as a juice tumbler. The **handled mixing bowls** resemble batter bowls. The lids are the same as those for the triple-service casseroles. The **muffin cover** sits on the 8¼" plate. The 10¼" **plate** doubled as an underliner for the casseroles and pie baker, the 9¼" for the medium straight casserole, and the 7¼" for the small straight casserole, the bean pots, and the utility jar. The handled **tumbler** looks like a chocolate mug; the footed tumbler resembles a goblet.

There are six basic colors, though some vary a great deal. The four original colors are green (ranges from turquoise to ash green), rose (ranges from light pink to burgundy), yellow, and blue. Ivory and orange were added later.

NOTE:

1. Lug-handled pieces always have the Rosebud decoration on the handle only.

2. Some covered pieces have the decoration on the lid only. These are noted in the listing below as (LDO) for lid decoration only.

3. Several items without the Rosebud decoration were included in the Rosebud line. These are listed at the bottom under "Undecorated."

4. Examine the rosebuds on each piece. High-end prices are for rosebuds with clear detail and good painting. Do not pay high prices for poor execution of these details.

MARKS Most Rosebud pieces are backstamped with the words "Coors Rosebud USA." Some pieces are unmarked.

COORS
ROSEBUD
U.S.A.

PRICING Ivory is the hardest color to find, especially in the baking dishes. Ivory and yellow are at the high end of the range.

Apple baker, open, 14-ounce, 4¾"	$25 – $30
Apple baker, w/lid, 12-ounce, 4¾"	35 – 40
Ashtray, round, 2 rests, 3½"	200 – 250
Bake Pan, 10¾" × 6¾" × 2"	35 – 40
Bake Pan, 12¼" × 8¼" × 2¼"	35 – 40
Baker, oval, 9¼"	35 – 40
Baker, oval, 11¼"	35 – 40
Baker, oval, deep, 6"	30 – 35
Bean pot w/lid, 1-pint	35 – 40
Bean pot w/lid, 1¾-pint	45 – 50
Bowl, mixing, handled, 1¾-pint	60 – 65
Bowl, mixing, handled, 3½-pint	55 – 60
Bowl, mixing, handled, 7-pint	70 – 75

Bowl, onion soup, w/lid (LDO) . . . . *$200 – $250*
Bowl, pudding, 2-pint, 5". . . . . *25 – 30*
Bowl, pudding, 3¹/₂-pint . . . . *30 – 35*
Bowl, pudding, 7-pint . . . . *50 – 60*
Bowl, soup, 8" . . . . *25 – 30*
Bowl, vegetable, lug, 8¹/₄" . . . . *20 – 25*
Casserole, Dutch, 1³/₄-pint. . . . . *60 – 70*
Casserole, Dutch, 3³/₄-pint. . . . . *70 – 80*
Casserole, French, 3³/₄-pint, 7¹/₂". . . . . *50 – 60*
Casserole, straight (LDO), 1-pint . . . . *50 – 60*
Casserole, straight (LDO), 2-pint . . . . *40 – 50*
Casserole, straight (LDO), 2³/₄-pint. . . . . *50 – 60*
Casserole, triple-service, 2-pint . . . . *40 – 50*
Casserole, triple-service, 3¹/₂-pint . . . . *50 – 60*
Casserole, triple-service, 7-pint. . . . . *60 – 75*
Creamer . . . . *30 – 40*
Cup . . . . *25 – 30*
Cup, cream soup, lug, 10-ounce, 4" . . . . *20 – 25*
Custard, 4" diameter. . . . . *10 – 20*
Dish, fruit, lug, 5" . . . . *8 – 12*
Dish, cereal, lug, 6". . . . . *12 – 16*
Eggcup, single, 3" diameter. . . . . *25 – 30*
Honey pot w/lid, 3 feet . . . . *90 – 100*
Honey pot spoon (undecorated) . . . . *150 – 200*
Jug, batter, 14-ounce . . . . *90 – 100*
Jug, syrup, 3-pint. . . . . *100 – 110*
Jug, water server, 3-pint . . . . *70 – 80*
    w/china/cork stopper . . . . *ND*
Loaf pan, 9" × 5" × 2¹/₂" . . . . *35 – 40*
Muffin cover, 5¹/₂". . . . . *50 – 60*
Pie baker, lug, 10¹/₄" . . . . *25 – 30*
Plate, 6" . . . . *10 – 15*
Plate, 7¹/₄" . . . . *10 – 15*
Plate, 8¹/₄" . . . . *25 – 30*
Plate, 9¹/₄" . . . . *15 – 20*
Plate, 10¹/₄" . . . . *20 – 25*
Plate, cake/Batter set tray, 11". . . . . *35 – 40*
Platter, oval, lug, 12" . . . . *20 – 25*
Ramekin, stick handle, 9-ounce, 4¹/₄" . . . . *20 – 30*
Refrigerator set, 3-piece (LDO), 5" square . . . . *50 – 60*
Saucer . . . . *6 – 10*
Shaker, 2¹/₂" high, each . . . . *12 – 16*
Shaker, sugar, handled, 5¹/₂" high, each . . . . *35 – 40*
Shaker, straight, 4¹/₂" high, each. . . . . *15 – 20*
Shaker, tapered, 4¹/₂" high, each. . . . . *15 – 20*
Shirred egg, lug, 6¹/₂" . . . . *20 – 25*
Sugar . . . . *30 – 35*
Teapot, 2-cup. . . . . *75 – 100*

Teapot, 6-cup. . . . . *$100 – $125*
Tumbler, handled, 8¹/₂-ounce, 4" high . . . . *35 – 40*
Tumbler, footed, 12-ounce, 5¹/₂" high. . . . . *45 – 50*
Utensil, cake server, 10" . . . . *60 – 75*
Utility/cookie jar, braided-rope handle, w/lid, 2¹/₂-pint . . . . *35 – 40*

Undecorated

All of the items listed here, with the exception of the thumb-print jug, were
sold as part of the Rosebud line.

Bean pot, individual . . . . *$15 – $20*
Bowl, pudding, 2-pint . . . . *25 – 30*
Bowl, pudding, 3¹/₂-pint. . . . . *30 – 35*
Bowl, pudding, 7-pint . . . . *50 – 60*
Bowl, mixing, 5" . . . . *20 – 25*
Bowl, mixing, 6" . . . . *20 – 25*
Bowl, mixing, 7" . . . . *20 – 25*
Bowl, mixing, 8" . . . . *20 – 25*
Bowl, mixing, 9" . . . . *30 – 35*
Bowl, mixing, 10" . . . . *35 – 40*
Cookie jar, braided-rope handle, 8-pint . . . . *35 – 40*
　　w/hand-painted decoration . . . . *45 – 50*
Cookie jar, stepped bands, 8-pint . . . . *50 – 60*
　　w/hand-painted decoration . . . . *60 – 70*
Jug, thumbprint, 4-pint . . . . *40 – 45*

THERMO-PORCELAIN (1932)

The tray and two covered jugs made a batter set. The straight casseroles came
with either a flat or a knob-handled lid. The two jugs were sold both with and
without lids. The handled mug resembles a chocolate mug.

These items were available in solid colors of ivory, deep green, and dark
brown, as well as hand painted or with decal decorations with gold or silver
trim on ivory or white bodies. Decals included Chrysanthemum, Floree, Garden (Open Window), Hawthorn, and Tulip.

PRICING Add $50 to the price of the coffee pots below if you find
them with the spreader and drip section.

Bowl, pudding, 2-pint . . . . *$35 – $40*
Bowl, pudding, 3¹/₂-pint. . . . . *35 – 40*
Bowl, pudding, 7-pint . . . . *65 – 70*
Bowl, Sunbeam, 3¹/₂-quart . . . . *35 – 40*
Cake/pie server, 10" . . . . *75 – 80*
Casserole, French, 3³/₄-pint, 7¹/₂". . . . . *55 – 60*
Casserole, straight, 7" . . . . *45 – 50*
Casserole, straight, 8" . . . . *45 – 50*
Casserole, triple-service, 2-pint. . . . . *45 – 50*
Casserole, triple-service, 3¹/₂-pint . . . . *55 – 60*
Casserole, triple-service, 7-pint. . . . . *75 – 80*
Coffee pot, low, 8-cup. . . . . *125 – 150*

Thermo Porcelain: Shakers and 8-cup low coffee.

Coffee pot, tall, 5-cup. . . . . $125 – $150
Coffee pot, tall, 8-cup. . . . . 150 – 175
Coffee pot, tall, 9-cup. . . . . 175 – 200
Custard . . . . 15 – 20
Jug, ³/₄-pint . . . . 100 – 125
  w/lid (syrup) . . . . 150 +
Jug, 3¹/₄-pint . . . . 125 – 150
  w/lid (batter) . . . . 175 +
Jug, water server, 3-pint . . . . 80 – 90
Mug, handled, 8-ounce, 4¹/₄" high . . . . 40 – 50
Pie baker, 9³/₄" . . . . 35 – 40
Refrigerator set, 3-piece, 5¹/₂" square . . . . 65 – 70
Shaker, 4¹/₄" high, each . . . . 25 – 30
Shaker, sugar, handled, 5" high, each . . . . 40 – 45
Tea for Two hot water pot . . . . 30 – 35
Tea for Two teapot . . . . 30 – 35
Tea for Two tray . . . . 15 – 20
Tea for Two set . . . . 75 – 90
Tray, 11¹/₄" . . . . 40 – 45

CHINA AND GLASS DISTRIBUTORS, INC.

New York, New York

Pantry Parade was an imprint of China and Glass Distributors. The line seen most often is the Red Tomato. There are a number of other items in Pantry Parade that I do not list. According to Lois Lehner, Stanford Pottery was a producer of Pantry Parade. But I have not been able to discover any other manufacturers nor if it was all made in the United States.

PANTRY PARADE

Red Tomato   (ca. 1949)

All the items listed here will be found in red. Other glazes reported are burgundy, green, turquoise, and iridescent green with gold stem. The cookie jar, ball jug, teapot, sugar, and creamer will be found in some of these other colors; I don't know about the other pieces.

Cookie Jar . . . . $30 – $40
Creamer . . . . 6 – 8
Drip . . . . 15 – 18

Red Tomato (Clockwise from top): Jug, drip jar, range shakers, table shakers, mustard, and marmalade.

131

Jug, ball . . . . *$20 – $25*
Marmalade, notched lid . . . . *20 – 25*
Mustard, notched lid . . . . *20 – 25*
Shaker, small, pair . . . . *10 – 12*
Shaker, range, pair . . . . *18 – 20*
Sugar . . . . *10 – 12*
Teapot . . . . *25 – 30*

Shakers

Strawberry, pair . . . . *$10 – $12*

CRONIN CHINA COMPANY

Minerva, Ohio

CHAPTER AT A GLANCE

DINNERWARE   Pottery Guild
SCROLL EDGE   Tulip
ZEPHYR   WORLD'S FAIR
KITCHENWARE

Cronin began operating in New Cumberland, West Virginia, ca. 1928. In 1934, Cronin bought and modernized the Owens China Company plant in Minerva, where they manufactured semiporcelain dinnerware and kitchenware until they closed in 1956.

MARKS Dinnerware had a variety of backstamps, the most common of which is a circular Union mark. Kitchenware usually had the raised mark "Bake Oven" in a rectangular box.

DINNERWARE

Cronin made a variety of shapes; Zephyr and kitchenware turn up most often.

"SCROLL EDGE"

Bowl, vegetable, oval, 9"* .... $10 – $12
Casserole .... 20 – 25
Cup .... 4 – 6

"Scroll Edge" custard, plate (green-sprayed edge), and cup.

Custard, 3¹/₂"	$4 – $6
Dish, 5¹/₂"*	2 – 3
Jug, batter, covered	25 – 30
Plate, 6¹/₄"	1 – 2
Plate, 7¹/₂"	5 – 7
Plate, 9¹/₄"	7 – 9
Plate, cake, lug, 11¹/₂"	10 – 12
Saucer, 6"	1 – 2
Shirred egg, 6¹/₄"	8 – 10

ZEPHYR   (1938)

A lightly banded, angular-handled shape. It was decorated in decals and solid colors including Mango red, Maroon, Medium blue, Medium green, Turquoise, and Yellow. I have found a trade card advertising "The new Mardi Gras line in red, green, blue and yellow," but I cannot tell if this was Cronin's designation or a retailer's.

Dinnerware

Bowl, soup, 7³/₄"	$10 – $12
Bowl, salad, round, 9¹/₂"	15 – 18
Creamer	4 – 6
Cup	4 – 6
Custard, 3¹/₂"	4 – 6
Dish, 5¹/₄"	2 – 3
Dish, shirred egg, lug, 6¹/₂"	8 – 10
Plate, 6¹/₄"	1 – 2
Plate, 9"	7 – 9
Plate, chop, lug, 10"	10 – 12
Plate, chop, lug, 11¹/₂"	12 – 15
Plate, chop, 14"	15 – 18
Platter, 11¹/₂"	10 – 12

Zephyr Dinnerware: Cup, plate (water lily decal), shaker, creamer & sugar (black flower with red center and red leaves), and old-style sugar (handles resemble cup).

Platter, 13¼" .... $12 – $15
Saucer .... 1 – 2
Shaker, each .... 4 – 5
Sugar .... 8 – 10
Teapot .... 20 – 25

Kitchenware
Some of the disk jugs come with the pattern name in the backstamp.

Bowl, mixing, 4" .... $6 – $8
Bowl, mixing, 5" .... 8 – 10
Bowl, mixing, 6¼" .... 10 – 12
Bowl, mixing, 7½" .... 12 – 15
Bowl, mixing, 9" .... 15 – 20
Bowl, salad, 9" .... 15 – 18
Casserole, 7½" .... 20 – 25
Casserole, individual, 4½" .... 8 – 12

Zephyr Kitchenware: Two drip jars with different finials, ball jug, and Apple Festival disk jug.

Jug, ball . . . . *$15 – $18*
Jug, disk, refrigerator. . . . . *18 – 20*
Pie baker, 9" . . . . *10 – 12*
Pie baker, 9³/₄" . . . . *10 – 12*

KITCHENWARE

You will probably find more kitchenware than dinnerware.

Bowl, mixing, 9" . . . . *$15 – $20*
Bowl, salad, 9" . . . . *15 – 18*
Casserole, 2-quart . . . . *20 – 25*
Casserole, lug, 1¹/₂-quart, 8" . . . . *20 – 25*
Cookie jar . . . . *40 – 45*
Custard . . . . *4 – 6*
Drip jar . . . . *12 – 15*
Jug, ball, ice lip . . . . *15 – 18*
Plate, grill . . . . *10 – 12*
Utensil, cake server . . . . *12 – 15*
Utensil, spoon . . . . *15 – 20*
Utensil, fork . . . . *20 – 25*

POTTERY GUILD

Pottery Guild is an imprint of Block China, a distributor. Cronin made a variety of items for them. There is evidence that other potteries manufactured for Block as well; do not assume everything marked Pottery Guild was made by Cronin. In addition to many Zephyr pieces marked Pottery Guild, you will also find the items listed below.

MARKS Pottery Guild has one of the few full-color marks.

Jug, batter	$25 – $30
Jug, syrup	20 – 25
Teapot	30 – 35
Tray, Batter Set	15 – 18

Pottery Guild Teapot (Teapot decal): Note the finial, most common on Pottery Guild items, but will also be found on other Cronin pieces.

SPECIAL PRICE LIST

"TULIP"

I have been told this was made for the A & P but have no confirmation. Some pieces will have the raised "Bake-Oven" mark.

DECORATION The easiest color to find is the light blue with dark blue tulips; next is the yellow with brown tulips. A teapot, sugar, and creamer in pink with blue tulips has been confirmed. My thanks to Jim Schaeffer for his contributions to this list.

Tulip: Teapot.

Bean pot, 7" diameter. . . . . *$15 – $20*
Bean pot, individual, 10-ounce, 3³/₄" diameter . . . . *12 – 15*
Casserole, French, w/spout, 4¹/₄" . . . . *8 – 12*
Casserole, French, w/spout, 6¹/₂" . . . . *15 – 20*
Casserole, lug, oval, 11" × 6¹/₂" . . . . *20 – 25*
Casserole, lug, round, 7¹/₂". . . . . *20 – 25*
Cookie jar . . . . *40 – 50*
Creamer . . . . *4 – 6*
Cruet, handled, 7¹/₂" high, each . . . . *10 – 12*
Custard, 4". . . . . *4 – 6*
Jug, 7" high . . . . *15 – 18*
Jug, ball . . . . *15 – 18*
Relish, 3-section, oval w/handle, 13". . . . . *12 – 15*
Sugar . . . . *8 – 10*
Teapot . . . . *20 – 25*
Tray, square, stick-handle, 7¹/₂". . . . . *8 – 10*

WORLD'S FAIR

Cronin was one of the potteries at the World's Fair of 1939–1940. The following two items were for sale.

Cake plate . . . . *$90 – $95*
Cake server . . . . *20 – 25*

CROOKSVILLE CHINA COMPANY

Crooksville, Ohio

CHAPTER AT A GLANCE

DINNERWARE
DARTMOUTH
DAWN
EUCLID
HARMONY
IVORA

PROVINCIAL WARE
QUADRO
  Silhouette
KITCHENWARE
PANTRY BAK-IN WARE

Founded in 1902, Crooksville manufactured semiporcelain dinnerware and kitchenware. Closed in 1959.

MARKS The first backstamp is an early mark that dates from at least the late 1920s through the 1930s. The second stamp was used in the 1940s. The third refers to body color, ca. late twenties.

DINNERWARE

DARTMOUTH (1939)

Bowl, 7³/₈"	$10 – $12
Bowl, mixing, 4"	6 – 8
Bowl, mixing, 6"	8 – 10
Bowl, mixing, 8"	10 – 12
Bowl, mixing, 9"	12 – 15
Casserole, 7¹/₂"	20 – 25
Cookie jar	45 – 50
Creamer	6 – 8
Cup	4 – 6
Gravy	15 – 18

Dartmouth: Sugar and creamer (Petitpoint Leaf), cookie jar (Nursery Rhyme), Carnival gravy and jug (Mexican decal).

Jug, syrup. . . . . *$25 – $30*
Plate, 6". . . . . *1 – 2*
Plate, 9"*. . . . . *7 – 9*
Plate, 10". . . . . *10 – 12*
Saucer . . . . *1 – 2*
Shaker, pair. . . . . *8 – 10*
Sugar . . . . *10 – 15*
Teapot . . . . *45 – 60*

DAWN   (1934)

An embossed dart-and-dot narrow border near the edge of the rim and the top of the hollowware and a ropelike embossing on the verge of the flatware and around the middle of the hollowware.

Bowl, vegetable, oval, 9". . . . . *$10 – $12*
Casserole. . . . . *20 – 25*
Cup . . . . *4 – 6*
Cup, AD. . . . . *10 – 12*
Cup, jumbo . . . . *15 – 20*
Dish, 5¼". . . . . *2 – 3*
Gravy. . . . . *12 – 15*
Plate, 6". . . . . *1 – 2*
Plate, 7". . . . . *4 – 5*

Plate, 9¼" .... *$7 – $9*
Plate, 10¼" .... *10 – 12*
Saucer .... *1 – 2*
Saucer, AD .... *2 – 5*
Saucer, jumbo .... *5 – 10*

EUCLID   (1935)

An embossed fruit and leaf design. Some items in the Pantry Bak-In Ware line were adapted to Euclid by redesigning the piece to include the embossing. These pieces are listed here.

Easily found decals are Autumn (sepia flowers and leaves) and "Vegetable Medley."

Bowl, mixing, 8½" .... *$8 – $10*
Bowl, mixing, 10½" .... *10 – 12*
Bowl, vegetable, rectangular, 9¼" .... *10 – 12*
Casserole, 4" .... *12 – 15*
Casserole, 8" .... *20 – 25*
Coaster, 4" .... *8 – 12*
Coffee pot .... *40 – 45*
Creamer .... *4 – 6*
Cup .... *4 – 6*
Custard .... *4 – 6*
Jug, batter .... *35 – 40*
Jug, syrup .... *30 – 35*
Pie baker, 9" .... *10 – 12*
Pie baker, 10" .... *12 – 15*
Plate, 6¾" .... *1 – 2*

Euclid: Autumn plate, coffeepot (Vegetable Medley), and batter set (Flower Shop).

Plate, 7¾" .... $4 – $5
Plate, 9" (casserole tray) .... 7 – 9
Plate, 9¾" .... 8 – 10
Platter, rectangular, 11½" .... 10 – 12
Platter, rectangular, 15½" .... 20 – 25
Saucer, 5¾" .... 1 – 2
Sugar .... 8 – 10
Tea tile .... 18 – 20
Tray, batter set. .... 12 – 15

HARMONY   (1936)

An embossed border of lovebirds surrounded by foliage. Very little Harmony is found.

Casserole .... $20 – $25
Creamer .... 4 – 6
Cup .... 4 – 6
Dish, 5½"* .... 2 – 3
Dish, 6¼"* .... 3 – 4
Plate, 6¼"* .... 1 – 2
Plate, 9"* .... 7 – 9
Saucer .... 1 – 2
Sugar .... 8 – 10

IVORA   (<1929)

This shape was restyled sometime in the 1930s.

Bowl, soup, 8¼" .... $10 – $12
Bowl, 36s .... 7 – 10
Bowl, vegetable, oval, 9" .... 10 – 12
Butter dish .... 20 – 25
Casserole, old style .... 20 – 25
Casserole, restyled, 9" .... 20 – 25
Creamer, old style. .... 4 – 6
Creamer, restyled .... 4 – 6
Cup, old style (same as Quadro) .... 4 – 6
Cup, restyled .... 4 – 6
Dish .... 2 – 3
Gravy .... 12 – 15

Pickle	*$6 – $8*
Plate, 6"	*1 – 2*
Plate, 9¼"	*7 – 9*
Saucer, 6"	*1 – 2*
Sugar, old style	*8 – 10*
Sugar, restyled	*8 – 10*
Teapot	*25 – 30*

PROVINCIAL WARE   (1930)

Embossed sprays of wheat and leaves decorate the shoulders of this shape.

Solid glazes of yellow or Emerald green were part of the original introduction in 1930. Other decorations included six Early American scenes: Bowls, Covered Wagon, Gold, Pilgrims, Pocahontas, and Valley Forge (these were green on yellow), as well as Eglantine, Portrait of a Rose (large central rose), Silhouette (two men at a table with a dog at their feet; see Special Price List following), Triloba, and Trinidad.

Provincial Ware

Bowl, vegetable, oval, 6"	*$10 – $12*
Casserole	*20 – 25*
Creamer	*4 – 6*
Cup	*4 – 6*
Dish, 5"	*2 – 3*
Gravy	*12 – 15*
Plate, 6"	*1 – 2*

Provincial Ware: Platter (emerald green) and creamer (house decal).

Plate, 6³/₄" .... *$3 – $4*
Platter, 11¹/₂" .... *10 – 12*
Saucer .... *1 – 2*
Sugar .... *8 – 10*
Teapot .... *25 – 30*

QUADRO   (1930)

A square shape with rounded corners.

Bowl, vegetable .... *$10 – $12*
Casserole .... *20 – 25*
Creamer .... *4 – 6*
Cup (same as Ivora) .... *4 – 6*
Dish, 5¹/₄" .... *2 – 3*
Eggcup .... *10 – 12*
Gravy .... *12 – 15*
Gravy liner .... *6 – 8*
Plate, 5³/₄" .... *1 – 2*
Plate, 8" .... *4 – 5*
Plate, 9¹/₂" .... *5 – 7*
Platter .... *10 – 12*
Saucer .... *1 – 2*
Sugar .... *8 – 10*

Quadro: Silhouette cup, Sweet Pea plate, and egg cup (floral).

SPECIAL PRICE LIST

SILHOUETTE

This decal is very similar to Hall China's Taverne decal, except that along with the two men at the table there is a dog. The **utility bowls** take lids with sunken knobs. See "Kitchenware," following, for composition of sets.

Silhouette was used on a variety of dinnerware shapes; these are indicated in parentheses. The kitchenware pieces will be found marked "Pantry Bak-In Ware." I have heard rumors of: (1) silhouette on a pink body and (2) a coaster, possibly Euclid. My thanks to Ed Rutkowski for alerting me to many of the rare pieces on this list.

Silhouette: Pantry Bak-In Ware cookie jar (with attachments for rattan handle), teapot, canister, "Pelican" syrup and batter jugs.

Bowl, mixing, 8" . . . . $15 – $18
Bowl, mixing, 9³/₄" . . . . 20 – 25
Bowl, mixing, lipped, 6" . . . . 12 – 15
Bowl, mixing, lipped, 8" . . . . 15 – 18
Bowl, mixing, lipped, 10" . . . . 20 – 25
Bowl, mixing, swag and tassel, 6" . . . . 12 – 15
Bowl, mixing, swag and tassel, 8" . . . . 15 – 18
Bowl, mixing, swag and tassel, 10" . . . . 20 – 25
Bowl, mixing, swag and tassel, 11" . . . . 25 – 30
Bowl, mixing, swag and tassel, 12" . . . . 30 – 40
Bowl, salad round, 9¹/₂" (has embossed petal effect) . . . . 30 – 35
Bowl, soup, 7¹/₄" . . . . 15 – 18
Bowl, utility, 4¹/₂" high . . . . ND

w/lid .... *ND*
Bowl, utility, 7½" × 6¼" high .... *ND*
   w/lid .... *ND*
Canister, cereal, 6¾" high
   Blank .... *$35 – $40*
   Oatmeal .... *45 – 50*
   Rice .... *45 – 50*
   Tea .... *45 – 50*
Canister, spice, 3½" high
   Blank .... *30 – 35*
   w/o lid (tumbler), 3½" .... *25 – 30*
Casserole, round, 4" .... *40 – 45*
Casserole, round, 6" .... *40 – 45*
Casserole, round, 8" .... *30 – 35*
Casserole (Euclid), 4" .... *40 – 45*
Coffee pot, metal drip .... *65 – 75*
   w/china drip .... *100 – 125*
Cookie jar, flat lid,
   w/rattan handle .... *45 – 50*
Cracker, tab handles
   Blank .... *ND*
   "Crackers" .... *ND*
Creamer (Arethusa) .... *8 – 10*
Creamer (Ivora, old style) .... *8 – 10*
Cup (Ivora) .... *8 – 10*
Cup (Provincial Ware) .... *8 – 10*
Dish (Ivora), 5¼" .... *4 – 5*
Dish, candy/relish, w/chrome frame
and handle (Provincial Ware), 6¾" .... *20 – 25*
Jug, basic, 4½" high .... *20 – 25*
Jug, basic, 7½" high (takes reamer) .... *30 – 35*
Jug, batter, "Pelican" .... *50 – 65*
Jug, batter, big bottom .... *35 – 40*
Jug, batter, bulbous .... *35 – 40*
Jug, syrup, big bottom .... *25 – 30*
Jug, syrup, bulbous .... *25 – 30*
Jug, syrup, "Pelican" .... *40 – 50*
Leftover, round, 4" .... *12 – 15*
Leftover, round, 6" .... *18 – 20*
Leftover, round, 8" .... *25 – 30*
Mug, tankard-style .... *40 – 45*
Pickle tray .... *10 – 12*
Pie baker, 10" .... *15 – 18*
Plate (Ivora), 9" .... *10 – 12*
Plate (Provincial Ware), 9" .... *10 – 12*
Plate (Quadro), 7" .... *7 – 9*
Plate (Quadro), 8" .... *7 – 9*
Plate (Quadro), 9½" .... *10 – 12*
Platter, oval, 11½" .... *15 – 18*

Reamer . . . . *ND*
Saucer (Ivora). . . . . *$3 – $4*
Saucer (Provincial Ware). . . . . *3 – 4*
Sugar (Arethusa) . . . . *12 – 15*
Sugar (Ivora, old style) . . . . *12 – 15*
Teapot, footed . . . . *50 – 65*
Tray, bread/sandwich, w/chrome frame
 and handle (Provincial Ware), 11¼" . . . . *30 – 35*
Tray, oval, 11½" . . . . *25 – 30*
Tray, round, pierced lug handles . . . . *20 – 25*

GLASSWARE

Tumbler, 4¾" high . . . . *$25 – $30*

METAL

Tray, oval, 18" . . . . *$35 – $40*

KITCHENWARE

PANTRY BAK-IN WARE   (1931)

Crooksville was one of the first potteries to venture heavily into decorated kitchenware. By the end of 1932, it had one of the most extensive lines of its kind. In 1934 it was given the Good Housekeeping Seal of Approval.

There are three **batter sets**: the "Pelican" batter and syrup on the round tray, the bulbous-bottom batter and syrup jugs on the oval tray, and the big-bottom batter and syrup on the oval tray. A **fruit juice set** consisted of the large jug, reamer, four juice tumblers (which are the spice jars without lids), and the round tray. The **leftover**, or refrigerator, set has flat lids with a slight depression so that the pieces can be nested or stacked. The **cereal jars** and **spice jars** came in sets of four, either blank or marked. Quadro plates were used as stands for the three round casseroles; and an oval platter was used for the oval casserole. See also Euclid.

Items I have seen reference to but have not confirmed are another cookie jar, another teapot, another refrigerator set, and a nappy set.

Kitchenware pieces were made in a pink body, ivory body, or yellow glaze.

Bean pot, 2 loop handles . . . . *$20 – $25*
Bowl, mixing, lipped, 6" . . . . *6 – 8*
Bowl, mixing, lipped, 8" . . . . *8 – 10*
Bowl, mixing, lipped, 10" . . . . *10 – 12*

Bowl, mixing, lipped, 11" .... *$12 – $15*
Bowl, mixing, lipped, 12" .... *15 – 20*
Canister, small (spice jar)... *25 – 30*
    w/o lid (tumbler) .... *20 – 25*
Canister, large (cereal jar).. *25 – 30*
Casserole, octagonal .... *20 – 25*
Casserole, oval .... *20 – 25*
Casserole, round, 4" .... *15 – 20*
Casserole, round, 6" .... *15 – 20*
Casserole, round, 8" .... *20 – 25*
Coffee pot, china drip .... *85 – 90*
Coffee pot, bulbous, metal drip...................................... *35 – 40*
Coffee pot, tall... *35 – 40*
Cookie jar, w/rattan handle.. *30 – 35*
Custard .... *4 – 6*
Jug, basic, small, 4½" high .... *15 – 20*
Jug, basic, medium, 7½" high.. *20 – 25*
Jug, basic, large.. *25 – 30*
Jug, basic, big-bottom .... *25 – 30*
Jug, batter, bulbous .... *25 – 30*
Jug, batter, "Pelican"... *35 – 40*
Jug, refrigerator, flat top, ice lip .... *30 – 35*
Jug, syrup, big-bottom... *20 – 25*
Jug, syrup, bulbous .... *20 – 25*
Jug, syrup, "Pelican".. *30 – 35*
Leftover, round, 4" .... *8 – 10*
Leftover, round, 6" .... *10 – 15*
Leftover, round, 8" .... *15 – 20*
Leftover, split oval (2 parts) .... *20 – 25*
Pie baker, 10" .... *10 – 12*
Reamer (for large jug)... *ND*
Teapot, footed.. *30 – 35*
Tray, oval, 11½" .... *10 – 12*
Tray, round, pierced lug handles..................................... *12 – 15*

*Pantry Bak-In Ware: Flat-top refrigerator jug w/ice lip (Petitpoint House),
big bottom syrup jug (floral), and bulbous batter jug (house and fence).*

ENESCO CORPORATION

Elk Grove Village, Illinois

Enesco is a distributor, one of the giants of the new collectibles market (Precious Moments and others). Most of its products are made overseas, particularly in Japan and, lately, China and Indonesia.

MOTHER IN THE KITCHEN

(Also called Prayer Lady; made approximately from the late 1950s to the late 1960s.) The canisters graduate down in size as follows: Flour, Sugar, Coffee, and Tea.

This line was made in pink, blue, and white with blue trim. A pair of shakers in a light blue with short puffy sleeves on the figure is also part of this line.

There is a yellow look-alike line made by Marco Pottery of Zanesville, Ohio, but this is *not* Mother in the Kitchen and was not made for Enesco.

PRICING Prices below are for pink. For blue, add 15%, for white with blue trim, add 25%. The shakers with puffed sleeves are $100.

Air freshener holder	*$100 – $125*
Bank, "Mother's Pin Money"	*125 – 150*
Bell	*75 – 90*
Bud vase	*125 – 150*
Butter dish	*200 – 250*
Candle holders, tapered, pair	*100 – 150*
Canister, Coffee	*200 – 250*
Canister, Flour	*200 – 250*
Canister, Sugar	*200 – 250*
Canister, Tea	*200 – 250*
Cookie Jar	*300 – 350*
Creamer	*50 – 75*
Crumb Tray w/broom	*150 – 200*
Egg timer w/timer, 6½"	*40 – 60*
Instant coffee w/spoon	*100 – 125*
Jug, milk	*150 – 200*
Mug	*125 – 175*
Napkin holder	*25 – 35*
Photo frame	*125 – 150*
Planter, 6½"	*100 – 150*
Ring holder	*75 – 100*
Scissors holder (wall hanging)	*150 – 200*
Scouring pad/Soap holder	*50 – 60*
Shakers, pair	*20 – 30*
Spoon rest	*40 – 50*
Spoon storage stand (holder)	*50 – 60*
Sprinkler	*150 – 200*

Prayer Lady: Wall plaque.

String holder	$200 – $225
Sugar w/spoon	60 – 90
Teapot	150 – 200
Toothpick holder	25 – 35
Wall plaque	75 – 100

KAY FINCH CERAMICS

Corona Del Mar, California

CHAPTER AT A GLANCE

FIGURES
  Animals
  People
MISCELLANY
  Banks
  Cookie Jars

Dog Items
Powder Jars
SEASONAL ITEMS
  Christmas
  Easter

Kay Finch came to California in 1926, at the age of twenty-two, with her husband, who had gotten a job there. She had had some formal instruction in clay modeling and continued classes in California. In 1937, William Manker, her teacher in the ceramics department at Scripps College, impressed by her work, encouraged her to do more with her skills. The support of her husband, Braden Finch, and a round-the-world trip during which she studied native ceramics convinced her that she should go into commercial production. Her husband quit his job to handle the administrative side of the business.

Kay Finch Ceramics officially began in 1939 in a studio next to their home in Corona del Mar, and with their first success in 1940, they moved to a studio and retail showroom on the Pacific Coast Highway. Animals were a specialty, especially dogs, thanks to an interest in champion dog breeding that Finch developed in the 1940s.

The quality of her work helped her company face the tide of Japanese imports that inundated other firms after World War II. She closed the company in 1963 upon the death of her husband and devoted herself to the full-time breeding of show dogs.

See Chipman and see Webb in Bibliography.

MARKS You will find marks that are either impressed, hand painted, or stamped.

KAY FINCH
CALIFORNIA

Kay Finch
Calif

FIGURES

Animals

The small duck was sold at no extra charge only with the Chinese Boy and Girl. Many of the dogs could be ordered with a base added. The pigs were dec-

Chanticleer, 10¹/₂", polychrome hand decoration.

orated with California flowers, and all except Grandpa could be had as a bank as well as a figure. For more Dog items, see Miscellany.

Bird, Mrs. Bird, 3" /454		$25
Bird, Mr. Bird, 4¹/₂" /453		25
Burro w/Saddlebags		45
Cat, Muff, sleeping kitten, 3¹/₄" /182		35
Cat, Puff, playing kitten, 3¹/₄" /183		35
Cat, Jezebel, contented, 6" /179		125
Cat, Mehitabel, playful, 8¹/₂" /181		135
Cat, Hannibal, angry, 10¹/₄" /180		145
Cat, Ambrosia, Persian, 10³/₄" /155		175
Chicken, Hen, Biddy, 8¹/₄" /176		75
Chicken, Rooster, Butch, 8¹/₄" /177		75
Chicken, Rooster, Chanticleer, 10³/₄" /129		175
Dog, Afghan /5016		85
Dog, Afghan (Best in Show), 18" /5490		650
Dog, Airedale /4832		75
Dog, Boxer, /5025		75
Dog, Bull Dog /5830		75

Dog, Cocker, 4"   /5260 .... *$65*
Dog, Cocker, 8"   /5201 .... *175*
Dog, Cocker (Vicki), sitting, 11"   /455 .... *250*
Dog, Cocker, standing   /5003 .... *50*
Dog, Dachshund   /5831 .... *75*
Dog, Dalmation/Coach Dog, 17"   /159 .... *550*
Dog, Foo Dog, 7"   /5601 .... *75*
Dog, Little Angels, each   /4911–63–64 .... *65*
Dog, Maltese   /5833 .... *55*
Dog, Pekingese (Peke), 14" long   /154 .... *300*
Dog, Playful Poodles, each   /5203   /5204 .... *250*
Dog, Playful Pups
  Lying   /5557 .... *50*
  Playing   /5555 .... *50*
  Romping   /5554 .... *50*
  Sitting   /5553 .... *50*
  Standing   /5016 .... *60*
Dog, Pom   /5832 .... *50*
Dog, Pom (Mitzi), 10"   /465 .... *225*
Dog, Poodle   /5024 .... *75*
Dog, Poodle (Beggar), 8"   /5262 .... *150*
Dog, Poodle (Beggar), 12"   /5261 .... *275*
Dog, Poodle (Perky), 16"   /5419 .... *500*
Dog, Pup, 8"   /5320 .... *100*
Dog, Scotty   /4831 .... *65*
Dog, Shepherd, head, 15"   /478 .... *375*
Dog, Show Dog, 13"   /5082 .... *450*
Dog, Westie   /4833 .... *60*
Dog, Wind Blown   /5757 .... *75*
Dog, Yorkshire   /4851 .... *55*
Dog, Yorky, 11"   /158 .... *275*
Dog, Yorky Pups, each   /170   /171 .... *100*
Doves, 8" × 5," each   /5101   /5102 .... *75*
Duck, small   /4631 .... *20*
Elephant, 5"   /4626 solid color/floral ears *65*
Elephant, Popcorn, trunk down, 6¾"   /192 .... *65*
Elephant, Peanuts, trunk up, 8¾"   /191 .... *85*
Elephant, Violet (Queen of the Circus), 17"   /190 .... *450*
Lamb, kneeling, 2¼"   /136 .... *20*
Lamb, prancing, w/floral collar, 10½"   /168 .... *175*
Lamb, life size, w/floral collar, 20"   /167 .... *750*
Owl, Tootsie, 3¾"   /189 .... *25*
Owl, Toot, 5¾"   /188 .... *75*
Owl, Hoot, 8¾"   /187 .... *125*
Penguin, Pee Wee, 3¼" *45*
Penguin, Polly, 4¼"   /467 .... *75*
Penguin, Pete, 7½"   /466 .... *150*
Pig, Sassy, 3½"   /166 .... *55*

Pig, Winkie, 3³/₄"   /185 . . . . $55
Pig, Grumpy, 6"   /165 85
Pig, Smiley, 6³/₄"   /164 75
Pig, Grandpa, 10¹/₂" × 16"   /163 175

People

Most of these items were decorated in pastels that were variously described as "soft" or "rich."

Angels, 3 styles, 4¹/₄," each $35
Bride, 6¹/₂"   /201 75
Cherub head, w/wings, 2³/₄"   /212 20
Chinese boy, 7¹/₂"   /4629 75
Chinese court lady, arm raised, 10¹/₂"   /401 175
Chinese court lady, arms folded, 10¹/₂"   /400 175
Chinese girl, 7¹/₂"   /4630 75
Chinese prince, 11¹/₄"   /451 200
Choir boy, kneeling, 5¹/₂"   /211 55
Choir boy, standing, 7¹/₂"   /210 65
Godey lady, w/muff, 7¹/₂"   /160 75
Godey man, 7¹/₂"   /160 75
Godey lady, 9¹/₂"   /122 125
Godey man, 9¹/₂"   /122, w/cape and hats   /122C, each 125
Groom, 6¹/₂"   /204 75
Peasant boy, 6³/₄"   /113 55
Peasant girl, 6³/₄"   /117 55
Scandie boy, 5¹/₄"   /127 50
Scandie girl, 5¹/₄"   /126 50

MISCELLANY

Powder jars will be found in the following decorations: Briar Rose, Cherry Blossom, Shaggy Daisy, and Zinnia.

Bank, Church, 6³/₄"   /4610 . . . . $100 – $200
Bank, English village, 5¹/₂"   /4611 . . . . 100 – 200
Bank, Russian barn, 4"   /4627 . . . . 100 – 200
Bank, Swiss chalet, 6"   /4628 . . . . 100 – 200
Bank, Victorian house, 5¹/₂"   /4612 . . . . 100 – 200
Cookie Jar, Cookie Pup, 12³/₄"   /4615 . . . . 300 +
    Shaker, 6"   /4617 35
Cookie Jar, Cookie Puss, 11³/₄"   /4614 . . . . 300 +
    Shaker, 6"   /4616 35
Dog, ashtray plaque, 7³/₄"   /5332 45
Dog, ashtray plaque,   /5331 35
Dog, bank, Doggie   /5301 50
Dog, cigarette box   /5333 45
Dog, head 12"   /476 250
Dog, head, ashtrays, various breeds, each 35
Dog, pin/tie slide   /5081 25

Dog, saucer plaque, 4³/₄" square   /4955 . . . . $35
Dog, stein   /5458 Afghan/Cocker/Doxie/Poodle/Scotty 45
Dog, Wall Plaque (Afghan), 27" long   /5525 300
Powder Jar, small, 2" × 3¹/₂"   /4632 25
Powder Jar, large, 3" × 3¹/₂"   /4633 25

SEASONAL ITEMS

Christmas
The reindeer and sleigh were decorated in gold and pearl lustre.

Candle Tower, 13"   /5564 . . . . ND
Candle Tower, 25"   /5562 . . . . ND
Cookie jar, cylinder, embossed Santa face . . . . $100 – $125
Reindeer, 11¹/₂"   /5475 150
Santa Claus, 18" × 18"   /6050 375
Santa plate, 16"   /5680 150
Santa sack holder, 10" × 10"   /5975 100
Sleigh, 12" × 6"   /5479 75
Vase, Santa Claus 50

NATIVITY SET   Decorated with gold and pearl lustre.

Babe in cradle   /4900A $50
Camel   /464 45
Lamb, kneeling   /136 20
Madonna, 6"   /5594 75
St. Joseph, 10"   /6054 75
Three Wisemen, set, 10"   /5590–1–2 250

Easter

Bunny, Bunnykin   /5303 . . . . $50
Bunny, Carrots   /473 100
Bunny, Cottontail, crouching   /152 50
Bunny, Listener   /452 125
Bunny in jacket   /5005 55
Bunny in jacket w/egg   /5005E 65
Egg, broken, small   /5543 20
Egg, broken, medium   /6010 35
Egg, broken, large   /5542 50

FLORENCE CERAMICS COMPANY

Pasadena, California

CHAPTER AT A GLANCE

BUSTS
FASHIONS IN BROCADE
FIGURES
  Birds
  People
  Groups
FLOWER HOLDERS
FRAMES
LAMPS
MISCELLANY
PLAQUES
SHADOW BOXES

In 1942, Florence Ward, a ceramic hobbyist, began commercial production of her designs. Operations began in a garage, expanded and moved several times, and by 1949 became one of the most modern plants in California. The ware was semiporcelain, with the glazes fired with the body. Overglaze decoration completed the pieces. The company was sold in 1964.

Most of the production was figures; picture frames, plaques, flower holders, bowls, and other accessories were also made.

MARKS Names of the figures are usually embossed on the bottom, though some are unnamed. In addition, a backstamp, usually in ink, sometimes in gold, will be found. Six backstamps are known, and all contain some combination of "Florence" "Florence Ceramics" "Pasadena, California," and "Copyrighted" in a circle or on a line.

BUSTS

Modern busts done in Satin White, traditional busts done in iridescent.

Boy, Modern, 9 3/4" *$180*
Boy, Traditional *175*
Girl, Modern, 9 1/2" *180*
Girl, Traditional *175*
La Petite, 8 1/4" . . . . *ND*
Madonna w/Child, 5 1/4" × 4 1/2" *90*
Mme. DuBarry, 8 1/2" *85*

FASHIONS IN BROCADE

Hand-fashioned in metallic brocade, these were top-of-the-line items with carefully detailed faces and hands and genuine feather hair ornaments. An old catalog lists four dress combinations: metallic gold with either Green, Vermouth, Mint, or Strawberry Vermouth.

Anita, 10" .... $700 +
Amelia, 12" .... 700 +
Caroline, 15" .... 700 +
Georgia, 12" .... 700 +
Lillian Russell, 15" .... 900 +
Marleen, 10" .... 700 +
Virginia, 15" .... 700 +

FIGURES

Birds

Several birds have turned up in the regular Florence style, listed below. There is also a later line of stylized birds and animals.

Baltimore Orioles (3), on branches .... $200 – $225
Cardinal, Red, 6" .... 200 – 250
Mocking Bird, baby, 5" .... 95 – 125
Mocking Birds (3), on branches .... 200 – 225
Pouter pigeon, white, satin finish .... 250 – 275
Pouter pigeon, white, gloss finish .... 250 – 275

People

These figures were glazed in a large variety of colors. They were then hand painted in rich colors to represent features and clothing detail and were fired a second time. Some had elaborate decorations that included applied flowers (usually roses), bow, lace, ringlets, and tresses, as well as gold trim.

In addition, a number of figures have articulated fingers. Note that some figures have never been found with these separated fingers, some only found with them and some both ways. There was also an economy line with none of these decorations.

The colors included gray, beige, maroon, aqua, pink, royal red, royal purple, rose, yellow, white, blue, and several shades of green. The first four colors, often touched with green or maroon, are the colors usually found on the economy figures. Yellow is hard to find. The Mermaids will be found in an iridescent mother-of-pearl finish. A figure can come in more than one color of dress or hair.

Alternate name spellings are indicated in parentheses. Some names were used for two different figures. These are indicated with (2). /Y after a name indicates a Young figure; /G after a name indicates authentic Godey costume.

GROUPS

For those who want to group their pieces, the following figures are made to go with each other: John Alden and Priscilla, Blue Boy and Pinkie, Blynken and Wynken, Companion and Spring Revelry, Douglas and the smaller Godey girls, Edward with Elizabeth and Victoria, Leading Man and Prima Donna, Mme Pompadour and Louis XV, Marie Antoinette and Louis XVI, and Scarlett, Rhett, Melanie, and Sue Ellen (there may be an Ashley); also the boy with life preserver and the girl with pail.

Yulen, Shen, She-Ti, Kiu, Chinese Girl and Boy, Blossom Girl and Lantern Boy are the Chinese figures group. The two Madonnas, the Madonna Bust, the three Choir Boys, and the Angel are the religious figures. The three Mermaids, called Merrymaids in the catalog, go with the Shell bowls. Cinderella and Prince Charming are one piece.

PRICING A range is given where appropriate; the more special the decoration, the higher the price. Some figures come in two versions, either plain or with articulated fingers and/or lavish decoration. These latter are listed as "fancy" and priced separately. For figures in yellow, add 30% to 40%.

Abigail, 8" /G	$115
Adeline, 9"	145
Alden, John, 9¼"	155
Amber/Parasol, 9¼"	300 – 350
Amelia, 8¼" /G	115
White w/roses and lace	145
Angel, 7"	75
Ann, 6"	55 – 60
Annabel, 8¼"	245
w/card in hand	275
Annette	195
Ballerina Child 1, 7"	135 – 145
Ballerina Child 2, 9½"	135 – 145
Ballerina Wood Nymph	135 – 165

Amber, Carol, and Lady Diane.

Martin, Fair Lady, and Vivian.

Claudia, 8¹/₄" *$115*
  Yellow, w/card in hand... *300+*
Coleen, 8".. *90 – 100*
  Fancy .... *135 – 150*
Companion, w/small bird in hand, moss green, 12" .... *500+*
Cynthia, 9¹/₄".. *250 – 300*
Darlene... *200 – 225*
David, 7¹/₂"   /Y .... *75 – 95*
Dear Ruth, 7³/₄" .... *ND*
Deborah, 9¹/₂"... *275*
Delia, 7³/₄"... *75*
  Fancy .... *110 – 125*
Denise, 10" .... *300+*
Diane, 8"... *175 – 200*
Dolores, 8¹/₂".. *130*
Doralee, white, 9¹/₂".. *275 – 300*
Douglas, 8¹/₄"   /G.. *110 – 120*
Edith, 7¹/₂".. *110*
Edward, 7"... *150 – 175*
Elaine, 6"   /G... *65*
Elizabeth, 8¹/₄" × 7" .... *275 – 300*
Ellen, 7" *120*
Ethel, 7" *95*
  Fancy *140*
Eugenia (Eugenie), 9"   /G *225*
Evangeline, 8¹/₄".. *ND*
Eve, 8¹/₂"... *140 – 150*
Fair Lady, 11¹/₂" .... *700+*
Fall, 6¹/₄"   /Y *85*
Gary, 8¹/₂".. *160 – 170*

Lisa, Dear Ruth, and Karla.

Genevieve, 8" . . . . *$95 – $110*
  Fancy . . . . *140 – 150*
Georgette, 10" . . . . *300 – 350*
Girl in pinafore, 7" . . . . *160 – 175*
Girl w/pail, 7¹/₂" . . . . *160 – 175*
Grace, 7³/₄" . . . . *80 – 90*
  Fancy . . . . *135 – 140*
Grandmother and I, 9" × 7" . . . . *500 +*
Haru, 11¹/₄" . . . . *300 +*
Her Majesty, 7" . . . . *125 – 155*
Irene, 6"   /G *55*
Jane (Merrymaid), 7" high *110*
Jeanette, 7³/₄" (2) *105*
  Fancy . . . . *135 – 150*
Jennifer, 8" *150*
Jim, 6¹/₄" . . . . *65 – 75*
Josephine, 9" *155*
Joy, 6"   /Y . . . . *55* ·
Joyce, 8¹/₂" . . . . *195 – 200*
Julie, 7¹/₄" *115*
Juliette . . . . *400 +*
Karen . . . . *250 +*
Karla (Ballerina), 9³/₄" *175*
Kay, 6³/₄" *55*
Kiu, 10¹/₄" . . . . *110 – 125*
Lady Diana, 10" . . . . *300 +*
Lantern Boy, 8¹/₄" . . . . *75 – 100*
Laura, 7¹/₂" *110*
Lavon, 8¹/₂" . . . . *225 +*
Leading Man, 10¹/₄" *285*
Lillian, 7"   /G *90*
Lillian Russell, 13¹/₄" . . . . *750 +*
Linda Lou, 7³/₄"   /Y . . . . *165 +*
Lisa (Ballerina), 9³/₄" *165*
Lisa, 7¹/₄" *120*
Lorry, 8"   /Y . . . . *175 – 200*
Louis XV, 12¹/₂" . . . . *250 – 300*
Louis XVI, 10" . . . . *175 – 225*
Louise, 7¹/₄"   /G *95*
Madeline, 9"
  Gray . . . . *125 – 130*
  Yellow *190*
Madonna Plain, 10" *85*
Madonna w/child, 10¹/₂" . . . . *125 +*
Margaret, 9³/₄" . . . . *300 +*
Margot, 8¹/₂" . . . . *150 – 175*
Marie Antoinette, 10" . . . . *195 – 225*
Marilynn . . . . *250 +*

Catherine, Elizabeth, and Edward.

Marsie, 8"	$175 – $190
Martha	275 +
Martin, 10½"	175 +
Mary, 7½"	250 +
Masquerade, holding black mask	325 – 350
Master David, 8"	175
Matilda, 8½" /G	105
Meg, 7¾"	110 – 150
Melanie, 7½"	100
Fancy	125 – 140
Memories, 5¼" × 6½"	450 +
Mikado, 13½"	ND
Mike, 6¼"	65 – 75
Mimi	60
Ming	175 – 200
Misha, 11¼"	325 – 375
Mmeo Pompadour, 12½"	295 – 395
Musette, 8¾"	190
Nancy, 6¾"	90
Fancy (peacock blue)	135
Nell Gwynn, 12"	650 +
Nita, 8"	ND
Oriental Girl /F–63	55
Our Lady of Grace, matte, ¾"	125
Pamela, 7¼" /Y	115
w/basket	125
Pat, 6"	60
Patrice	105 – 110
Patricia, 7"	105
Peasant Girl /2 baskets, 8¾"	75
Peter (?)	95 – 100
Pinkie, 12"	300 – 350

Children: Boy with life preserver, girl with pail, girl in pinafore, and boy with cone.

Prima Donna, 10" *$250*
Princess, 10¹/₄" .... *400+*
Priscilla, 7³/₄" *155*
Prom Boy, 9"   /Y *155*
Prom Girl, 9"   /Y .... *200 – 250*
Rebecca, 7" *120*
Rhett, 9" .... *125 – 150*
   Fancy .... *150 – 175*
Richard, white w/cape, 8¹/₄" .... *175+*
Roberta, 8¹/₂" *125*
Rosalie, 9¹/₂" .... *375+*
Rose Marie, 9¹/₂" .... *285+*
Rose Marie, 6¹/₄"/7"   /Y .... *135 – 140*
Rosie (Merrymaid), 7" long *110*
Sally, 6³/₄" .... *80 – 90*
Sarah, 7¹/₂" *85*
Sarah Bernhardt, 13¹/₄" .... *ND*
Scarlett, 8³/₄" .... *130 – 150*
   Fancy .... *175 – 200*
Shen, 7¹/₂" .... *90 – 100*
Sherri, 8¹/₂" .... *175 – 200*
She-Ti, 10¹/₄" .... *110 – 125*
Shirley, 8" *125*
   w/card in hand .... *150 – 175*
Spring Revelry, holding bird's nest, 12" .... *500+*
Stephen, 8³/₄" .... *150+*
Story Hour w/Boy & Girl, 8" × 6³/₄" .... *600+*
Story Hour w/Girl, 8" × 6³/₄" .... *500+*
Sue, 6" *55*

Mme. Pompadour, Blue Boy, Pinky, and Louis XV.

Sue Ellen, 8¼" *$110*
  Yellow *250*
Susan (Susann), 9" . . . . *225 – 300*
Suzanna /F–92 . . . . *180 – 225*
Tess, 7" . . . . *100 – 120*
Toy, 8½" . . . . *110 – 125*
Victor, 9¼" . . . . *150 – 175 +*
Victoria, seated, 8¼" × 7" . . . . *275 – 300*
Vivian, 9¾" /G . . . . *180 – 200*
Wynken, 5½" *95*
Yulan, 7½" . . . . *100 – 125*
Yvonne, 8¾" . . . . *100 – 120*
  Fancy . . . . *175 – 200*

FLOWER HOLDERS

Also called Flower Containers in old catalogs. Many of these were designed to
look like figures only, when not in use.

Ava, 10½" . . . . *$125 – $140*
Bea *35*
Beth, 7½" *35*
Blossom Girl, 8¼" . . . . *40 – 50*
Chinese Boy, 7¾" . . . . *40 – 45*
Chinese Girl, 7¾" . . . . *40 – 45*
Dutch Girl, small *45*
Dutch Girl, large *55*
Emily, 8" *35*

Fern, bust, 7" . . . . *$110 – $120*
June, 6" *35*
Kay, 7" *35*
Lantern Boy, 8¹/₄" . . . . *40 – 50*
Lea, 6" *35*
Lyn, 6" *35*
May, 5¹/₂" *35*
Mimi, 6" *35*
Molly, 6¹/₂" *35*
Patsy, 6" *35*
Peasant Man, large, w/flower cart . . . . *125 – 175*
Peg, 7¹/₂" *35*
Polly, 6" *35*
Sally, 6" *35*
Suzette, 7" . . . . *40 – 50*
Violet, bust, 7" . . . . *110 – 120*

FRAMES

Decorated frames came in the following sizes: 2 × 3, 3 × 4, 4 × 5, and 5 × 7.

PRICING Not many frames show up. A few have been priced to give you some idea of value.

	2" × 3"	3" × 4"	4" × 5"	5" × 7"
Apple Blossom				100
Lace				100
Nosegay	60		100	100
Provincial Rose				
Rose	100			

LAMPS

Shades were made of ninon (oval and round with lace trim), taffeta (skirted or ruffled), and pleated chiffon with velvet trim to match the figures. Bases were hardwood or polished brass.

PRICING The list below is from catalog sheets. I've included it to let you know what you can look for. Only Dear Ruth turns up enough to price.

Camille . . . . *ND*
Clarissa . . . . *ND*
Claudia . . . . *ND*
Dear Ruth (TV) . . . . *$500 +*
Delia . . . . *ND*
Elizabeth . . . . *ND*
Genevieve . . . . *ND*
Marie Antoinette . . . . *ND*
Musette . . . . *ND*
Scarlett . . . . *ND*
Vivian . . . . *ND*

MISCELLANY

The clocks are electric with Sessions movements. The lapel pins are small versions of the plaques. The shell pieces accessorized the Merrymaids. In addition to the pieces listed below, Florence made a line of artware that included bonbons, cigarette sets, trays, and bowls.

Ashtray, 2" × 3"	$20
Bonbon dish	60
Cigarette box	70 – 100
Clock, small	400 +
Clock, large	500 +
Diana powder box, 6" × 6¼"	225 – 250
Diana soap box	225 – 250
Figure, Cockatoo, matte white, 10"	200
Lapel pin, brown/gray/green	125 +
Lipstick holder	300 +
Pin box, small	50
Planter, Boy w/bass fiddle, 8¼"	125
Planter, Girl w/harp, 8¼"	125
Planter, Swan, matte white, 12" long	250 +
Shell ashtray, 7¼" × 10¾"	50 – 60
Shell bowl, 11½"	75 +
Shell bowl, 15½"	100 +
Shell wall vase, 6" × 6½"	55
Tray, 2 handles, w/roses	75 – 80
Vase, bud, small /A–18	65
Vase, cornucopia, pink	75
Vase, cottage	75

PLAQUES

Cameo, w/scarf, oval	$95 – $100
Cameo, w/bow, oval	95 – 100
Figure, w/fan, rectangular	95 – 100
Figure, w/muff, rectangular	95 – 100
Figure, w/parasol, rectangular	95 – 100
Figure, w/side muff, rectangular	95 – 100

SHADOW BOXES

One of the higher-priced lines, the boxes were backed in velvet, and the hats were made with fabrics, feathers, and trimmings.

Bernice (Poke Bonnet)	ND
Jacqueline (Pill Box Hat)	ND

FRANKOMA POTTERY

Sapulpa, Oklahoma

CHAPTER AT A GLANCE

DINNERWARE	**KITCHENWARE**
LAZY BONES	**NOVELTIES**
MAYAN-AZTEC	BOOKENDS
MISCELLANY	FIGURES
ORBIT	Animals
PLAINSMAN	Animals / Miniature
WAGON WHEELS	People
WESTWIND	SHAKERS

In 1927, John Frank moved to Norman, Oklahoma to establish the new ceramics department for the University of Oklahoma. In 1933, while still working at the university, he established Frank Potteries in Norman, using a light clay he had found near the town of Ada. In 1934, the name was changed to Frankoma Potteries, and he left the university to work at the pottery full time in 1936. The business was moved to Sapulpa in 1938 and renamed Frankoma Pottery. In 1953, a new, desirable brick red clay was found nearby and by 1954 the transition to its use was complete. Frankoma is still in business; see Travelers Directory.

See Bess in Bibliography and Coming Attractions.

MARKS Most pieces will have the name Frankoma impressed in the bottom of the piece; some early pieces will have the name stamped in black. From 1936 to 1938 an impressed panther in front of a vase was placed over the name.

PRICING Double the price for pieces made from Ada clay.

DINNERWARE

All of Frankoma's collectible dinnerware lines were designed by John Frank. The Lazybones and Westwind butter are the same shape. The corn

167

dish, crescent salad, taco holder and warmer are the same in all lines and are priced under "Miscellany." Frankoma uses "baker" for casserole. The Lazy Susettes had ball bearing bases.

All lines were made in Prairie Green and Desert Gold. You will find certain pieces in a variety of other colors as well, including Autumn Yellow, Black, Brown Satin, Flame (priced fifty percent higher than the other colors), Peach Glow, Robin Egg Blue, White Sand, and Woodland Moss. Because colors and pieces were added and dropped over the years, a complete set in any of these colors will be very difficult to assemble.

CURRENT PRODUCTION   Current production items have a /C in the lists below and show current retail prices. New colors have been added and are used on the dinnerware lines as well as the gift lines. These include Black, Black/Terra Cotta, Brown, Cabernet, Country Blue (sponge), Forest, Navy, Navy/Terra Cotta, Teal, Teal/Terra Cotta, White, and White/Terra Cotta.

LAZYBONES   (1953)

This line has been discontinued, and is no longer being made. A couple of items are still in the general catalog.

Bean pot, individual/custard, 6-ounce. *$5*
Bowl, divided, 11" *15*
Bowl, round, 8" *12*
Bowl, service, footed (flower bowl   214), 12" . . . . *15 – 18*
Bowl, single serving, 3-ounce *4*
Bowl, soup, 6" . . . . *9 – 10*
Bowl, tab handle, 9" *12*
Bowl, vegetable, 24-ounce. *12*
Butter, ¼-pound   /C *13*
Casserole, 1½-quart. . . . . *12 – 15*
Casserole, 2-quart *25*
Casserole, 3-quart *25*
Casserole, restyled, 3-quart *25*
Casserole, 5-quart . . . . *40 – 50*
Creamer. *9*
Cup, 7-ounce *8*
Cup, soup, 11-ounce *9*
Cup, tea, 5-ounce *8*
Dish, cereal, 14-ounce *7*
Dish, salad/gumbo, 24-ounce *6– 7*
Jug, 2-quart *20*
Lazy Suzette, 5-section, 12"   /C. *40*
Mug, 18-ounce. *12*
Plate, 7" . . . . *8 – 10*
Plate, 10" . . . . *12 – 15*

Platter, 13" . . . . *$15 – $20*
Saucer, 5" . . . . *2 – 3*
Shaker, each . . . . *5 – 8*
Spoon holder *6*
Stein, 18-ounce /C *10*
Sugar *11*
Trivet . . . . *40 – 50*
Tumbler, juice, 6-ounce . . . . *4 – 5*
Tumbler, 12-ounce . . . . *8 – 10*

MAYAN-AZTEC (1945)

This line is still in production. The casseroles are called Baker/Bean pots in company literature. The individual and 5-quart casserole are hard to find.

Available in Prairie Green, Desert Gold, and White Sand. The coffee mug, crescent salad, and corn dish were available in 8 colors, including Flame.

Bowl, 8-ounce /C *$6*
Bowl, 14-ounce /C *7*
Bowl, 20-ounce *10*
Bowl, vegetable, 1-quart /C *10*
Butter, ¼-pound /C *15*
Casserole, individual *30*
Casserole, 2-quart /C *24*
Casserole, 3-quart /C *29*
Casserole, 5-quart /C . . . . *40 – 50*
Creamer *9*
Creamer, restyled /C *9*
Cup /C *8*
Jug, 2-quart /C *20*
Mug, 8-ounce *10*
Mug, 14-ounce /C *10*
Mug, coffee, 12-ounce *10*
Plate, 7" /C *7*
Plate, 9" *10*
Plate, 10" /C *13*
Plate, chop, footed, 15" *40*
Platter, oval, deep, 13" *20*
Platter, oval, deep, 17" *20*
Platter, oval, deep, lug, 13" /C *20*
Platter, oval, shallow, 17" /C *20*
Platter, steak, rectangular, shallow, 13" /C *15*
Saucer /C *5*
Shaker, short, pair /C *12*
Sugar /C *11*

Mayan-Aztec:
Two-cup teapot.

Teapot, round, 2-cup   /C *$12*
Teapot, round, 6-cup   /C *19*
Teapot, tall, 2-cup . . . . *25 – 35*
Teapot, tall, 6-cup . . . . *45 – 50*
Tray, rectangular, 9"   /C *8*

MISCELLANY

These are generic items that were available for all the Frankoma dinner-ware lines.

Corn dish   /C *$6*
Salad, crescent/bone dish, 6½" . . . . *5 – 10*
Taco holder   /C *7.50*
Warmer   /C *10*

ORBIT   (1959–1962)

In 1958 John Frank bought Synar Ceramics near Muskogee, Oklahoma, and in 1959 renamed it Gracetone Pottery, after his wife Grace. In 1962 he sold it to J. C. Taylor who operated it until 1967.

Orbit was available in three colors: Aqua, Cinnamon, and Pink Champagne.

Ashtray/Nut dish *$15– $25*
Bowl, pedestal, 6" *15*
Butter, ¼-pound . . . . *25 – 30*
Casserole, 1-quart . . . . *30 – 35*
Compote, 8" *20*
Creamer *10*
Cup *10*

Orbit: Footed gravy and teapot on hotplate/warmer.

Dish, cereal, 14-ounce *$14*
Gravy boat, 25-ounce . . . . *28 – 30*
Hot plate warmer *15*
Lazy Susan, 7-section, w/center cover, 15" . . . . *45 – 50*
Lazy Susan, 7-section, w/medium covers, 15" . . . . *45 – 50*
Marmalade *20*
Plate, 7" *8*
Plate, 10" . . . . *12 – 15*
Platter, breakfast, 10" . . . . *15 – 18*
Platter, 17" *20*
Saucer . . . . *2 – 3*
Shaker . . . . *8 – 10*
Spoon rest *25*
Sugar *15*
Susanette, 5-piece (3 sections in bowl on stand), 10" . . . . *50 – 60*
Teapot, 8-cup . . . . *50 – 60*
Tumbler, 4 . . . . *8 – 10*

PLAINSMAN   (1948)

Originally named Oklahoma. This line is still in production. The individual and 5-quart baker are hard to find.

Available in Prairie Green, Desert Gold, Brown Satin, Woodland Moss, and Autumn Yellow (not all pieces in each color). In addition, many pieces were available in 8 standard colors, including Flame.

Bowl, 9-ounce *$3– $4*
Bowl, 14-ounce   /C *7*
Bowl, 20-ounce *10*

Bowl, 4 ½-quart   /C.. *$36*
Bowl, rectangular, divided, handled, 13"   /C *20*
Bowl, vegetable, oval, 12".................................... *15*
Bowl, vegetable, square, 9"   /C.............................. *10*
Casserole, individual....................................... *30*
Casserole, 2-quart   /C...................................... *24*
Casserole, 3-quart   /C...................................... *29*
Casserole, 5-quart   /C...................................... *50*
Cheese dip.. *20 – 25*
Creamer, small.. *4– 5*
Creamer, large   /C.. *9*
Cup, 5-ounce   /C.. *6*
Cup, 8-ounce   /C.. *8*
Cup, AD... *10*
Gravy, 2-spout.. *15*
Gravy boat *15*
Jug, 3-quart *30*
Mug, 12-ounce... *10*
Mug, 16-ounce   /C.. *12*
Plate, 6½".. *5*
Plate, 7"   /C.. *7*
Plate, 9"... *9*
Plate, 10"   /C.. *13*
Plate, chop, footed, 15".................................... *25*
Platter, rectangular, deep, 13"............................... *25*
Platter, rectangular, deep, 17"............................... *20*
Platter, rectangular, deep, handled, 13"   /C.................... *20*
Platter, rectangular, deep, handled, 17"   /C.................... *35*
Platter, rectangular, shallow, 9"   /C.......................... *8*
Platter, rectangular, shallow, 11"............................ *15*
Platter, rectangular, shallow, 13"   /C......................... *15*
Saucer   /C... *5*
Saucer, AD... *5*
Shaker, pair   /C.. *12*
Sugar, small.. *10*
Sugar, large   /C.. *11*
Teapot, round, 6-cup *18– 25*
Teapot, tall, 6-cup... *25– 30*
Teapot, 12-cup.. *30 – 35*
Tumbler, juice, 6-ounce *5*
Tumbler, 12-ounce *10*

WAGON WHEELS (1941–1983)

This line basically has been discontinued, except for the few pieces indicated following. The candle holder is the ashtray/candle holder restyled

Wagon Wheel: Creamer, sugar, shakers, and ashtray/candle holder.

without the finger ring or cigarette rests. The individual and 5-quart baker are hard to find.

Available in Prairie Green and Desert Gold. The horseshoe came in 8 standard colors.

Ashtray/Candle holder, 6" *$30*
Bowl, 20-ounce *10*
Bowl, divided, rectangular, 13" *20*
Bowl, vegetable, 1-quart *15*
Candle holder, 6" *20*
Casserole, individual *30*
Casserole, 2-quart *25*
Casserole, 3-quart *35*
Casserole, 5-quart *50*
Creamer   /C *8*
Creamer, AD *8*
Cup   /C *9*
Dish, 6-ounce *8*
Dish, 14-ounce *10*
Horseshoe, miniature *8*
Jug, 1½-quart *20*
Jug, 2-quart   /C *24*
Lazy Susan, 7-section, 15" *50*
Mug, 16-ounce   /C *15*
Plate, 7" *7*
Plate, 9" *9*
Plate, 10" *13*
Plate, chop, footed, 15" *30*
Platter, rectangular, 13" *25*
Platter, rectangular, handled, 13" *30*
Platter, rectangular, 17" *20*

Saucer, 5" *$3*
Shaker, pair   /C *14*
Sugar,   /C *12*
Sugar, AD *8*
Teapot, 2-cup   /C *15*
Teapot, 6-cup *50*
Trivet *55*
Tumbler *15*
Vase, 3½" *35*
Vase, 7" *25*

WESTWIND

This line is still being produced.

Baking dish, 10" *$15*
Bean pot, individual/custard, 6-ounce *5*
Bowl, chili/soup, 14-ounce   /C *7*
Bowl, 1-quart   /C *10*
Bowl, single serving, 3-ounce *4*
Bowl, divided, rectangular, 13" *20*
Butter, ¼-pound   /C *13*
Casserole, 1½-quart *20*
Casserole, 2½-quart   /C *29*
Casserole/candy dish, 18-ounce .... *12 – 15*
Creamer   /C *9*
Cup   /C *8*
Dish, fruit, 10-ounce .... *4 – 5*
Gravy, 2 spout   /C *15*
Jug, 1-quart *15*
Jug, 2-quart *20*
Mug, double coffee *12*
Plate, 7"   /C *7*
Plate, 10"   /C *13*
Platter, deep, rectangular, 13" *25*
Platter, deep, rectangular, 17" *20*
Platter, steak, shallow, rectangular, 11" *15*
Platter, steak, shallow, rectangular, 13" *18*
Saucer   /C *5*
Shaker, pair   /C *12*
Sugar   /C *11*
Teapot, 2-cup   /C *12*
Teapot, 6-cup   /C *19*
Tray, 9" *10*
Tumbler, juice, 6-ounce *5*
Tumbler, 12-ounce *10*

KITCHENWARE

Batter set, complete. *$125*
    Batter, 4¹/₂"   /87 . . . . *45*
    Creamer   /87A *12*
    Sugar   /87B. *12*
    Syrup   /87D *35*
Decanter, fingerprint, 1-quart, 7"   /84 . . . . *40*
Decanter, fingerprint, 2-quart, 8¹/₂"   /83. . . . . *35*
Guernsey
    Creamer, 2"   /550. . . . . *10 – 15*
    Creamer, 3¹/₂"   /93A. *20*
    Milk pitcher, 25-ounce   /93 . . . . *25 – 35*
    Shaker, pair *25*
Jug, ¹/₂-gallon   /86. . . . . *35 – 45*
Jug, swirled honey   /833 . . . . *15*
Modern
    Grease pot   /46. . . . . *24*
    Shaker, range   /45H . . . . *12 – 15*

NOVELTIES

John Frank's skill is most clearly evident in the figures he created.
    PRICING   Double values for Ada clay.

BOOKENDS

Bucking Bronco . . . . *$125 – $150*
Charger Horse . . . . *75 – 100*
Dreamer Girl *150– 200*
Mallard Head . . . . *200 – 250*
Mountain Girl. . . . . *125 – 175*
Ocelot (Puma on Rocks) . . . . *150 – 250*
Rearing Clydesdale *250*
Red Irish Setter. . . . . *90 – 100*
Seahorse. . . . . *350 – 400*

FIGURES
Animals

Bucking Bronco *$250*
Circus Horse. . . . . *85 – 200*
Cocker Spaniel . . . . *175 – 200*
Coyote Pup *450*
English Setter, 5¹/₄". *150*
Gannet. *600*
Pacing Leopard. *250*

Pekingese . . . . *$350 – $400*
Prancing Colt . . . . *600 – 650*
Prancing Percheron . . . . *350 – 400*
Puma w/Prey . . . . *300 – 350*
Rearing Clydesdale . . . . *175 – 350*
Reclining Puma . . . . *15 – 150*
Seated Puma . . . . *15 – 200*
Terrier, 5¼" . . . . *185 – 200*
Walking Ocelot *350*

Animals/Miniature

Bull *$50*
Donkey *100*
Elephant *50*
Elephant, walking *100*
English Setter, 2⅞" *50*
Flower Holders
   Duck *165*
   Elephant *165*
   Fish *165*
   Hobby Horse *165*
Puma . . . . *45 – 50*
Swan . . . . *45 – 50*
Terrier, 2⅞" *100*
Trojan Horse *50*

People

Cowboy *$400*
Dreamer Girl *150– 200*
Fan Dancer . . . . *150 – 350*
Flower Girl . . . . *75 – 90*
Gardener Boy, w/overalls . . . . *90 – 115*
Gardener Boy, w/pants . . . . *90 – 115*
Gardener Girl . . . . *80 – 100*
Harlem Hoofer . . . . *1000 – 1200*
Indian Chief . . . . *40 – 150*
Indian Bowl Maker . . . . *40 – 150*
Monk w/Basket . . . . *150 – 200*
Torch Singer . . . . *1000 – 1200*

SHAKERS

Barrel *$15*
Bull *75*
Dutch Shoes . . . . *25 – 35*
Elephant *75*
Jug . . . . *15 – 20*

Cowboy figure.

Torch Singer figure.

Oil Derrick . . . . *$15 – $20*
Puma *65*
Tepee *20*
Wheat Shock . . . . *15 – 20*

FRENCH-SAXON CHINA COMPANY

Sebring, Ohio

CHAPTER AT A GLANCE

ALOHA   ROSLYN
HERMOSA   ZEPHYR

The Saxon China Company began in 1911 and over the years had close ties to the French China Company, as both were owned by the Sebring family. Both companies were part of the American Chinaware Company merger of 1929 and ceased to exist when that company declared bankruptcy in 1932. W. V. Oliver purchased the old Saxon plant, named his company French-Saxon and, at the end of 1934, began making semiporcelain dinnerware and kitchenware. He died in 1963, and Royal China bought the company in 1964.

MARKS French-Saxon used a knight and shield graphic backstamp, which was a variant of an old Saxon mark, as well as a circular Union mark.

ALOHA

A plain coupe shape.

There were two solid-color lines. The regular line, which is marked Aloha Dinnerware, included chartreuse, dark green, maroon, and rust. The other line, Aloha Pastels, included light blue and pink.

Bowl, vegetable, oval, 9"	*$10 – $12*
Casserole	*20 – 25*
Creamer	*4 – 6*
Cup	*4 – 6*
Dish, 5½"*	*2 – 3*
Plate, 6¼"*	*1 – 2*
Plate, 9"	*7 – 9*
Plate, lug, 10¼"	*10 – 12*
Platter, 11"*	*10 – 12*
Saucer	*1 – 2*
Sugar	*8 – 10*

HERMOSA   (<1936)

Alternating large and small scallops with an indented line just inside the rim.

Bowl, soup	*$10 – $12*
Bowl, vegetable, oval, 9"*	*10 – 12*

Aloha: Plate, creamer, sugar (note single handle), and cup.

Casserole . . . . *$20 – $25*
Creamer . . . . *4 – 6*
Cup . . . . *4 – 6*
Dish, 5½"* . . . . *2 – 3*
Plate, 7½" . . . . *4 – 5*
Plate, 9¼" . . . . *7 – 9*
Plate, lug, round, 10¼" . . . . *10 – 12*
Platter, oval, 11¼" . . . . *10 – 12*
Saucer . . . . *1 – 2*
Sugar . . . . *8 – 10*

ROSLYN (1937)

An embossed design of picket fence with roses placed on flatware rims and around the tops of hollowware pieces.

Bowl, soup, 8"* . . . . *$10 – $12*
Bowl, vegetable, 9"* . . . . *10 – 12*
Casserole . . . . *20 – 25*
Creamer . . . . *4 – 6*
Cup . . . . *4 – 6*
Dish, 5½"* . . . . *2 – 3*
Plate, 6¼"* . . . . *1 – 2*
Plate, 9⅜" . . . . *7 – 9*
Plate, lug, 6¾" . . . . *2 – 3*
Platter, 11"* . . . . *10 – 12*
Saucer . . . . *1 – 2*
Shaker, tall, pair . . . . *8 – 10*
Sugar . . . . *8 – 10*

Roslyn: Tall shaker, plate (floral with pink Astilbe), cup, and creamer.

ZEPHYR (1938)

The easiest pieces to find are the shaker, sugar, creamer, and plates. Hardest are the teapot and casserole.

Zephyr was decorated with decals and in solid colors. There are two solid-color lines: Romany (called "Grenada" by some collectors) and Rancho. Romany colors are red, yellow, dark blue, and green. Black was used as a contrasting color on lids, odd pieces, and service items. Pastel shades will also be found. Rancho comes in standard 1940s colors: maroon, gray, chartreuse, and dark green.

MARKS   Romany and Rancho will be found with only their names stamped, though not on every piece.

PRICING   Use the low end of the range for decal-decorated pieces and

ROMANY
F. S. C. CO.
Sebring, Ohio
U. S. A.
Union Made

Rancho colors, the high end for Romany colors.

Bowl, soup, 7¾"	$10 – $15
Bowl, 36s	7 – 12
Bowl, vegetable, round, 8½"	12 – 18
Casserole	20 – 30
Coffee pot	35 – 45
Creamer, open handle	4 – 8
Creamer	4 – 8
Cup	4 – 8
Dish, 5¼"	2 – 4
Dish, 6"	3 – 5
Gravy boat	12 – 18
Plate, 6"	1 – 3
Plate, 7"	4 – 7
Plate, 9"	7 – 10
Plate, 10"	10 – 15
Plate, chop, 13"	15 – 22
Plate, lug, 6½"	2 – 4
Plate, lug, 10"	10 – 15
Saucer	1 – 3
Shaker, short, pair	8 – 12

Zephyr (Clockwise from top): Plate, gravy, cup, sugar, tall shaker, short shaker, and restyled creamer. I don't have absolute proof that the tall shaker is Zephyr; I include it because of its resemblance to Roslyn in concept and because its colors match.

Shaker, tall, pair . . . . *$10 – $15*
Sugar . . . . *8 – 12*

W. S. GEORGE POTTERY COMPANY

East Palestine, Ohio

CHAPTER AT A GLANCE

DINNERWARE
ARGOSY
ASTOR
BASKETWEAVE
BOLERO
CAPE COD
DEL RIO
ELMHURST
FLEURETTE

GEOMETRIC
GEORGETTE
LIDO
RADISSON
RAINBOW
   Petitpoint Rainbow
RANCHERO
KITCHENWARE

In 1898 William S. George leased the East Palestine Pottery Company from the Sebring brothers. He bought the pottery, ca. 1903, and renamed it. Early in its history, W. S. George produced hotel ware and semivitreous toilet ware, as well as the semiporcelain dinnerware that was produced until the company closed, ca. 1960.

MARKS   The three backstamps in capital letters I date to ca. 1930 and earlier. The same for the backstamp with the entwined "WSG." Cavitt-Shaw is a selling division set up in the late 1930s.

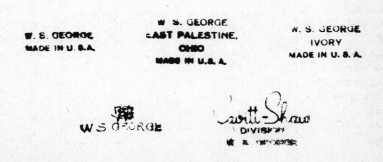

W. S. GEORGE
MADE IN U. S. A.

W. S. GEORGE
EAST PALESTINE,
OHIO
MADE IN U. S. A.

W. S. GEORGE
IVORY
MADE IN U. S. A.

W. S. GEORGE

Cavitt-Shaw
DIVISION

DINNERWARE

In my mind, W. S. George is distinctive for a number of reasons. First, it is one of the few Ohio potteries that included compotes in its dinnerware lines. Also, many of its eggcups were shape-specific rather than generic. It was almost unique in having sugar lids that would also fit the creamer. And finally, it seems that W. S. George made a shaker in only one shape, Ranchero, but used it with a number of lines, including Bolero, Elmhurst, and Georgette.

ARGOSY (<1929)

Argosy flatware is both round (slightly scalloped) and square (rounded corners) with an embossed line dividing the rim into panels. There is a distinctive handle on the paneled hollowware.

Argosy was made in three glazes, Ivory, Pink, and Yelo-tint (yellow), which were decal-decorated. It was also made in a solid gray-blue called Rhapsody Blue (a nod to Gershwin).

Bowl, vegetable, rectangular, 9"* .... *$10 – $12*

Casserole	*20 – 25*
Creamer	*4 – 6*
Cup	*4 – 6*
Dish, 5"	*2 – 3*
Gravy	*12 – 15*
Gravy liner	*6 – 8*
Plate, 6⅛"	*1 – 2*
Plate, 7"	*4 – 5*
Plate, 9"	*5 – 7*
Plate, square, 7"	*4 – 5*
Plate, square, 9"*	*5 – 7*
Platter, rectangular, 11"*	*10 – 12*
Saucer	*1 – 2*
Sugar	*8 – 10*
Teapot	*20 – 25*

Argosy: Sugar and creamer (Parrot Tulips), round dinner plate, and Breakfast Nook square 7" plate.

ASTOR (1926)

There is fluting on the rim of the flatware and the shoulder of the hollowware.

A number of decals were used, including Blue Willow.

ASTOR
W. S. GEORGE

Bowl, 36s . . . . *$7 – $10*
Bowl, vegetable, round, 8³/₄" . . . . *10 – 12*
Casserole . . . . *20 – 25*

Astor: Plate (bird on branch), sugar, and creamer.

Creamer... *$4 – $6*
Cup .... *4 – 6*
Plate, 6¼"* .... *1 – 2*
Plate, 7¼" .... *4 – 5*
Plate, 9¼"* .... *5 – 7*
Platter, 11"* .... *10 – 12*
Saucer .... *1 – 2*
Sugar .... *8 – 10*

BASKETWEAVE   (1930–1938>)

The Ohio jug has the Basketweave pattern in a broad band around the top and bottom. The party plate, with its off-center cup ring, is the smallest I have ever seen.

Decorated in decals and solid colors of blue, brown, green, and maple bisque. Most decals are on a yellow glaze, though I have seen an occasional piece of green with a decal. Pastels Plus, patterns with colored rims, were introduced in 1938. They include Dallas (bluebonnets make up a five-pointed star), Fresno (a Willow-style design), Lancaster (Godey-type ladies), Omaha (stylized wheat in gold and brown/red rim), and Taos (basket of primarily yellow flowers/yellow rim).

Casserole, lug .... *$20 – $25*
Creamer.. *4 – 6*
Cup .... *4 – 6*
Dish, 5¼" .... *2 – 3*
Eggcup... *10 – 12*
Gravy.. *12 – 15*

Basketweave: Plate, Green Pine Cone creamer, eggcup (green), and gravy (green). Although curious, Pine Cone is the correct name for the geometric decoration on the creamer.

Jug, Ohio, batter. . . . . *$25 – $30*
Jug, Ohio, syrup. . . . . *20 – 25*
Plate, 6¼". . . . . *1 – 2*
Plate, 9⅛". . . . . *7 – 9*
Plate, grill, 10". . . . . *8 – 10*
Platter, oval, 11". . . . . *10 – 12*
Saucer (off-center cup ring), 6⅛". . . . . *3 – 4*
Sugar . . . . *8 – 10*
Teapot. *30– 35*

BOLERO   (mid 1933)

A fluted coupe shape. Originally, Bolero had an oval teapot, casserole, sugar, and creamer. These were later restyled, perhaps as late as 1939, into the round shape that is more commonly found. Hard-to-find pieces are the old-style items.

The covered cream soup doubled as an individual casserole. The old-style creamer was unusual in that it came with a lid. Several shell relishes could be arranged in a fanlike design to make a centerpiece.

Three colors, called Bolero Faience, were introduced in 1934: alabaster, lemon yellow, and turquoise (with and without decal). These colors are rare. In addition I have found pieces in brown and cobalt blue, for which I have no information.

Many decal decorations were used, including Calico (flowers and leaves in calico patterns), Flight (geese on the wing), Pals (two subtly colored fish), and Cherry Blossom (pink and green) from the late 1930s and early 1940s, which are the most easily found. Gracia was also used; see Elmhurst, following.

Bowl, salad, lug, 10"* . . . . *$15 – $18*
Bowl, soup, lug, 6"*. . . . . *10 – 12*
Bowl, vegetable, oval, 9"* . . . . *10 – 12*
Bowl, vegetable, round, 9". . . . . *10 – 12*
Casserole. . . . . *20 – 25*
Casserole, straight side . . . . *20 – 25*
Compote . . . . *20 – 25*
Creamer. . . . . *4 – 6*
Creamer, old style, w/lid. . . . . *8 – 10*
Cup . . . . *4 – 6*

Bolero: Old-style Cherry Blossom oval teapot, Calico oval sugar, and oval creamer with an indented handle.

Bolero: Back: *Old-style oval creamer on left, oval creamer with restyled handle on right.* Front: *Covered onion soup, Calico relish and double-spouted gravy.*

Bolero: Gracia plate, Gracia restyled round creamer and sugar.

Cup, cream soup, w/lid .... *$16 – $20*
Custard cup... *4 – 6*
Dish, lug, 6½" .... *3 – 4*
Gravy, double lip, round, handled............................... *12 – 15*
Pickle.. *6 – 8*
Plate, 6¾" .... *1 – 2*
Plate, 8" .... *4 – 5*
Plate, 9¼" .... *7 – 9*
Platter, oval, 11¾" .... *10 – 12*
Platter, round, lug, 12" .... *12 – 15*
Relish, shell shape .... *12 – 15*
Saucer .... *1 – 2*
Shaker (generic), pair .... *8 – 10*
Sugar .... *8 – 10*
Sugar, old style .... *8 – 10*
Teapot, oval... *30 – 35*
Teapot, round.. *30 – 35*

CAPE COD (1937)

A plain round coupe shape with raised "dots" encircling each piece.
Some decals used are Netherlands (windmill landscape) and Tulip Row (tulips).

Bowl, vegetable, oval, 9"* .... *$10 – $12*
Casserole .... *20 – 25*
Compote .... *20 – 25*
Creamer... *4 – 6*
Cup .... *4 – 6*
Dish, 5½"* .... *2 – 3*
Plate, 6¼"* .... *1 – 2*
Plate, 9" .... *7 – 9*
Platter, 11"* .... *10 – 12*
Saucer .... *1 – 2*
Sugar .... *8 – 10*

DEL RIO (1935)

A periodic embossed crosshatch on the flatware rims and around the shoulder of the hollowware. The flatware is very similar to Paden City's Sally Paden shape.

Del Rio: Granada gravy liner/pickle, Polka Dot creamer, and Ochre plate.

Some of the decals you will find are Granada (1935, diamond grillwork on the panel in either black, blue, green, or rose), Hobnail, Polka Dot (1935, red dots with silver cross trim on the embossing, Ochre body, or light blue dots and silver and White body), and Sylvan (1935, silhouette border of trees in black, blue, green, or rose).

Bowl, soup, 7⁵/₈"... *$10 – $12*
Casserole.. *20 – 25*
Creamer.. *4 – 6*
Cup .... *4 – 6*
Dish, 5¹/₄"... *2 – 3*
Gravy.. *12 – 15*
Gravy liner/pickle... *6 – 8*
Plate, 6¹/₄"*.. *1 – 2*
Plate, 8¹/₈"... *4 – 5*
Plate, 9"*.. *7 – 9*
Platter, oval, 13¹/₈"....................................... *12 – 15*
Saucer.. *1 – 2*
Sugar... *8 – 10*

ELMHURST   (1938)

A paneled shape with a slightly scalloped rim and a winglike design on the tops of the handles and on the finials. Not much Elmhurst is found.

Decorated in decals and solid colors. Decals: Pergola (a flower-bedecked doorway), Gracia (Mexican: pottery and flowers on a serape; larger pieces show a tile-roofed doorway), Harvest (stylized wheat), Tasket (a basket of flowers, predominately red), and Wing (birds on flower trellis). Pastels introduced in 1939: apple green, blue, maple sugar, pink, turquoise, and yellow.

Bowl, lug soup .... *$10 – $12*
Bowl, 36s .... *7 – 10*
Bowl, soup, coupe, 8"* .... *10 – 12*
Bowl, vegetable, oval, 9"* .... *10 – 12*
Bowl, vegetable, round, 9"*..................................... *15 – 18*
Bowl, vegetable, round, w/lid .... *20 – 25*
Casserole, footed, w/handles, 8" .... *20 – 25*
Creamer.. *4 – 6*
Cup .... *4 – 6*
Cup, AD.. *10 – 12*
Dish, 5" .... *2 – 3*
Dish, 6" .... *3 – 4*
Eggcup.. *10 – 12*
Gravy... *12 – 15*
Gravy faststand .... *12 – 15*
Gravy liner .... *6 – 8*
Plate, 6" .... *1 – 2*
Plate, 7" .... *4 – 5*
Plate, 8¼" .... *4 – 5*
Plate, 9" .... *7 – 9*
Plate, 10" .... *10 – 12*
Platter, 11" .... *10 – 12*
Platter, 13" .... *12 – 15*

Elmhurst: Plate and egg cup.

Platter, 15½"	*$15 – $18*
Saucer	*1 – 2*
Saucer, AD	*3 – 5*
Sugar	*8 – 10*
Teapot	*20 – 25*

FLEURETTE   (1936)

A round shape with an embossed floral design around the flatware rims and the hollowware shoulders and embossed flower on the handles and knobs. The sugar lid also fits the creamer.

Decals include Cross-Stitch (a petitpoint bouquet).

Bowl, vegetable, oval, 9"*	*$10 – $12*
Casserole	*20 – 25*
Creamer	*4 – 6*
Cup	*4 – 6*
Dish, 5¼"*	*2 – 3*
Gravy	*12 – 15*
Plate, 6¼"*	*1 – 2*
Plate, 9"*	*7 – 9*
Saucer	*1 – 2*
Sugar	*8 – 10*

GEOMETRIC   (1931)

Deeply embossed overlapping circles on the rims of the flatware and over the hollowware bodies.

Offered in a blue glaze and a bright white called La Blanche, as well as white with decals.

GEOMETRIC
. S GEORGE
..ADE IN U. S. A

Casserole	*$20 – $25*
Creamer	*4 – 6*
Cup	*4 – 6*
Plate, 8⅛"	*4 – 5*

Geometric: Plate (silhouette) and cup. Note that because of the outer surface having an embossed design, any decal will be placed on the inside of the hollowware.

Saucer . . . . *$1 – $2*
Sugar . . . . *8 – 10*
Teapot . . . . *20 – 25*

GEORGETTE   (1933)

Called "Petal" by some collectors. A round, paneled shape.

Decorated originally in decals; the solid colors, which are more easily found than the decals, were added in 1947. Colors are aqua, chartreuse, dark green, gray, light green, maroon, medium blue, pink, and yellow. Many decals were used, but few are found: Federal (eagle and stars), Jolly Roger (ships in black silhouette sailing around the various pieces; this decal was called Nantucket on the Cape Cod shape), and Peasant are among the more interesting.

Bowl, 36s . . . . *$7 – $10*
Bowl, vegetable, oval, 9" . . . . *10 – 12*
Casserole . . . . *20 – 25*
Creamer . . . . *4 – 6*
Cup . . . . *4 – 6*
Cup, AD . . . . *10 – 12*
Cup, jumbo . . . . *15 – 18*
Custard . . . . *4 – 6*

Georgette: Peasant plate, creamer, AD cup, and sugar.

Dish, 5½"	*$2 – $3*
Dish, 6½"	*3 – 4*
Gravy	*12 – 15*
Plate, 6½"	*1 – 2*
Plate, 8½"	*4 – 5*
Plate, 9¼"	*7 – 9*
Plate, 10¼"	*10 – 12*
Platter, 13"	*12 – 15*
Saucer	*1 – 2*
Saucer, AD	*3 – 5*
Saucer, jumbo	*6 – 8*
Sugar	*8 – 10*

LIDO (1932)

A square shape with scalloped corners on the flatware. Candlesticks are rare. Note the two styles of sugar. An experiment with horizontal cup handles, called Streamline (also Nes-Teas), was tried. I have not seen one.

Decal decorations on either a white or Canary-Tone (yellow) glaze include Breakfast Nook (flowers entwine a picket fence below an open window w/birdcage and flowerpot), Cherry Blossom, Dalrymple (a scattering of red flowers), Gaylea (yellow and red/purple flowers against a fence), and Prim (pot of primroses next to a window). The ashtray was often used for both advertising and souvenirs.

<table>
<tr><td>LIDO
W. S. GEORGE
WHITE
MADE IN U.S.A.</td><td>LIDO
W. S. GEORGE
CANARY TONE
MADE IN U.S.A.</td></tr>
</table>

Lido: Gaylea plate, Breakfast Nook sugar (no handles), cup (Mexican decal that is not Gracia), and Dalrymple teapot.

Ashtray, hexagonal, 3 rests, 4½"..................................... $4 – $5
Bowl, soup, 7¾".. *10 – 12*
Bowl, 36s.. *7 – 10*
Bowl, vegetable, 9" .... *10 – 12*

Lido Breakfast Nook plate, Picasso dish, eggcup (floral), and Cherry Blossom candlestick.

Butter dish.	$20 – $25
Candlesticks, pair.	25– 30
Casserole, 9¹/₂".	20 – 25
Casserole, lug	20 – 25
Creamer.	4 – 6
Cup	4 – 6
Cup, AD.	10 – 12
Cup, cream soup	12 – 16
Dish, 5¹/₂".	2 – 3
Dish, 6³/₈".	3 – 4
Eggcup.	10 – 12
Gravy.	12 – 15
Gravy faststand	12 – 15
Gravy liner, 7¹/₂".	6 – 8
Plate, 6¹/₂".	1 – 2
Plate, 7¹/₂".	4 – 5
Plate, 9¹/₄".	7 – 9
Plate, 10¹/₄".	10 – 12
Plate, lug, 6¹/₄".	2 – 3
Platter, 11³/₄".	10 – 12
Platter, 13¹/₄".	12 – 15
Saucer	1 – 2
Saucer, AD	3 – 5
Saucer, cream soup	6 – 8
Shaker (generic), pair	8 – 10
Sugar	8 – 10
Sugar, no handle	8 – 10
Teapot	30 – 35

RADISSON   (ca. 1920s–1940>)

RADISSON
W. S. GEORGE
MADE IN U. S. A.

This is W. S. George's version of Havilland's Ranson pattern. Many pieces were made in this line; I have priced just a sampling.

Bowl, soup, 8¹/₄".	$10 – $12
Bowl, soup, coupe, 8"	10 – 12
Bowl, 36s, 1¹/₃-pint.	7 – 10
Bowl, vegetable, oval, 9"*	10 – 12
Bowl, vegetable, round, 9"*	15 – 18
Butter dish.	20 – 25

Butter pat, 3³/₈" . . . . *$4 – $6*
Casserole . . . . *20 – 25*
Creamer. . . . . *4 – 6*
Cup, AD. . . . . *10 – 12*
Cup, bouillon . . . . *12 – 16*
Cup, tea . . . . *4 – 6*
Custard, handled (chocolate cup) . . . . *ND*
Dish, 5³/₈". . . . . *2 – 3*
Eggcup. . . . . *10 – 12*
Gravy. . . . . *12 – 15*
Gravy faststand . . . . *12 – 15*
Gravy liner/pickle, 9". . . . . *6 – 8*
Plate, 6¹/₄"* . . . . *1 – 2*
Plate, 9"** . . . . *7 – 9*
Platter, 11"* . . . . *10 – 12*
Saucer, AD . . . . *3 – 5*
Saucer, bouillon. . . . . *1 – 2*
Saucer, tea . . . . *1 – 2*
Sugar . . . . *8 – 10*
Teapot . . . . *25 – 30*

RAINBOW   (1934)

The casserole, candle holder, handled custard, compote, and round gravy
are hard to find. The sugar lid can be used on the creamer as well.

Glazed in solid colors of blue, green, pink, tan, and yellow. Decals on
ivory or yellow body: Celestial (a lacy doily in the center of the well),
Cross Stitch (Colonial motifs in black w/red), Fantasy (a circle of six blue
bowls with maize poppies), Hollyhock (six groups of orchid, blue, yellow,
and green), Iceland Poppy, Reflection (a willow and its reflection in two
tones of mulberry), and Santa Rosa (a floral bouquet with a tulip project-
ing). See also Petitpoint Rainbow, following.

W. S. George
Rainbow

Bowl, 36s . . . . *$7 – $10*
Bowl, vegetable, oval, 8³/₄" . . . . *10 – 12*
Candle holder, pair . . . . *20 – 25*
Casserole . . . . *20 – 25*
Compote, 10" . . . . *20 – 25*
Creamer. . . . . *4 – 6*
Cup . . . . *4 – 6*

Rainbow: Back: *Cross Stitch handled custard and compote.* Front: *Old-style gravy, Breakfast Nook candle holder, and relish. These are hard-to-find pieces.*

Custard, handled . . . . *$12 – $15*
Dish, 5¼" . . . . *2 – 3*
Eggcup . . . . *10 – 12*
Gravy, oval . . . . *12 – 15*

Rainbow: Iceland Poppy plate, eggcup, cup, and restyled gravy.

Gravy, round . . . . *$12 – $15*
Plate, 6¹/₄" . . . . *1 – 2*
Plate, 7¹/₄" . . . . *4 – 5*
Plate, 8¹/₄" . . . . *4 – 5*
Plate, 9¹/₄" . . . . *7 – 9*
Platter, oval, 10" . . . . *10 – 12*
Platter, oval, 11¹/₄" . . . . *10 – 12*
Platter, oval, 13" . . . . *12 – 15*
Relish . . . . *12 – 15*
Saucer . . . . *1 – 2*
Sugar . . . . *8 – 10*

PETITPOINT RAINBOW

In mid 1935, Petit Point, an embossed needlecraft effect, was introduced on the Rainbow shape in the following colors: cobalt blue, light green, yellow, and chocolate brown (the hardest color to find). It does not seem to be an extensive line. The only pieces missing from this list are probably a smaller plate and a dish.

Rainbow Petitpoint: Plate and covered creamer.

Creamer .... *$4 – $6*
Cup .... *4 – 6*
Plate, 9¼" .... *7 – 9*
Saucer .... *1 – 2*
Sugar .... *8 – 10*

RANCHERO   (1938)

Designed by Simon Slobodkin. A plain round coupe shape. The eggcup and teapot are hard to find.

The following decals on a golden glaze background are most easily found: Fruit Fantasy (fruit in pink, blue, yellow, orange, and red with green and black leaves), Indian Corn (an ear of corn; this is so precise it almost looks like a photograph), Rosita (clusters of pink roses), Shortcake (strawberries with a shadow), Tom Tom (drum and stick motif), and Wampum (three versions in predominant shades of Iroquois red, Cherokee blue, or Navajo brown).

Some retail stores, such as Carole Stupell in New York, offered personalization of Ranchero in either ivory or pink glaze.

Bowl, vegetable, round.................................. *$15 – $18*
Butter, ¼-pound .... *20 – 25*
Casserole .... *20 – 25*
Coffee pot .... *35 – 40*
Creamer.. *4 – 6*

Ranchero: Indian Corn coffeepot, Fruit Fantasy teapot, Shortcake coffeepot, and butter with initials.

Cup . . . . *$4 – $6*
Cup, AD. . . . . *10 – 12*
Dish, 5¹/₂" . . . . *2 – 3*
Eggcup . . . . *ND*
Gravy, 2-spout. . . . . *12 – 15*
Plate, 6¹/₄" . . . . *1 – 2*
Plate, 9" . . . . *7 – 9*
Platter . . . . *10 – 12*
Saucer . . . . *1 – 2*
Saucer, AD . . . . *3 – 5*
Shaker (generic), pair . . . . *8 – 10*
Sugar . . . . *8 – 10*
Sugar, no handle . . . . *8 – 10*
Teapot . . . . *ND*

KITCHENWARE

For the longest time, I thought that W. S. George, unlike its competitors, produced no kitchenware. Recently, these bowls were found. There should be at least one more. The Georgex teapot was advertised as having an extra hard and heat-resisting body and came in a choice of four colors: blue, pink, turquoise, or yellow. It is basically the Ranchero shape, but there are slightly engraved lines around the lid finial and around the shoulder and foot of the bottom.

Bowl, mixing, 8¹/₄" . . . . *$12 – $15*
Bowl, mixing, 9¹/₂" . . . . *15 – 20*
Teapot, Georgex, 6-cup. . . . . *20 – 25*

Kitchenware: This mixing bowl uis decorated with decals of ships with fantastical designs on the sails. The pointed projections around the rim would seem to make this bowl prone to chipping.

Shakers: **Back:** *Solid color, Gracia, and initials.* **Front:** *Cherry Blossom, Shortcake, Fruit Fantasy, and Dalrymple. This is WSG's "generic" shaker. I suspect that it was designed to be part of the Ranchero shape, but I've seen it on catalog sheets for Bolero, Georgette, Lido, and Radisson as well. One reason for my assumption, aside from similarity of shape, is that Ranchero was introduced in 1938, and the shakers are found only with decorations active from the late thirties through the forties and fifties.*

GLADDING, McBEAN & COMPANY

Los Angeles, California

CHAPTER AT A GLANCE

ART WARE
  Ox-Blood
DINNERWARE / SOLID-COLOR
CORONADO (SWIRL)
METROPOLITAN / TIEMPO
MONTECITO / DEL ORO
PALOMAR
RANCHO-WARE / DUO-TONE
DINNERWARE / DECALED

STARBURST (DUET/OASIS)
DINNERWARE / EMBOSSED /
  HAND-PAINTED
APPLE
DESERT ROSE
IVY
WILD FLOWER
MISCELLANY

The company began in 1875, producing sewer pipe. Architectural terra cotta was added in 1884; tile and other building materials followed. In 1923 the company purchased Tropico Potteries in Glendale, a tile and faience manufacturer, and in 1933 bought the West Coast properties of the American Encaustic Tiling Company, making Gladding one of the top-ranked tile producers of its time.

The Franciscan line, an earthenware body for art ware and dinnerware, was introduced in 1934; initially bright and pastel colored dinnerware, it grew to include decal decorations and the embossed, hand-painted underglaze line that is still popular. Catalina Clay Products was bought in 1937. The purchase included the ware in stock, the molds, and the rights to the name. Gladding went on to produce several lines under the name "Catalina Pottery."

In 1942 fine china was first produced at the Glendale plant. It was marketed under the name Franciscan China until 1947, when the name was changed to Franciscan Fine China.

In 1962, Gladding merged with the Lock Joint Company to become the International Pipe & Ceramic Corporation, which incorporated in April 1963 as the Interpace Corporation. It was sold to Wedgwood (England) in 1979, which continued to manufacture in America until 1984, at which time the Glendale plant was closed and all Franciscan production transferred to England, where it is still made today.

See Chipman in Bibliography and see Clubs/Newsletters..

BODY The earthenware body is made from a substance called "malinite," which was developed by GMB chemists and is covered by several patents. Company literature states:

Malinite is the most important technical achievement in the pottery industry in the past century. Instead of wares being made from clay, the basic material of the Malinite body is talc rock, the same material from which talcum powder is produced. Combined with the talc is an amorphous flux which in the heat of the kiln so binds together the molecules of talc that an extremely tough and durable body is formed, highly resistant to thermal shock and free from internal flaws. The most important feature of Malinite is the fact that glazes become so fused with the body that they cannot craze.

MARKS/CATALINA
The first group of marks shown here was incised.

Later, impressions were made in the molds, as shown in the second group of marks. Also, a cactus holder in the shape of a cat, with "LINA" printed on the side, was used.

CATALINA
CATALINA   ISLAND   CATALINA
                624   C 60 ?

The third group shows impressions made in 1937. Note the first use of the word "Pottery."

CATALINA
C 806   CATALINA
POTTERY   RANCHO

The fourth group shows backstamps used from 1937 to 1942.

CATALINA   CATALINA
MADE IN   REG. U. S.
U.S.A.   PAT. OFF.
POTTERY   RANCHO

MARKS/GLADDING McBEAN

The backstamps in group 1 were used on ware made from 1934. There are two sizes of the GMB in an oval; they were used with and without the additional "Made in USA," which came in three sizes and often was stamped without other marks. The largest of the three was used experimentally for acid imprints on dark glazes from 1937 to 1938 but was determined to be impractical.

The first stamp to use the Franciscan name was this capital F in a box done in two sizes. Made to replace the GMB in an oval, it was used from September 1938 to February 1939.

Replacing the big F were two stamps used in 1939, the word "Pottery" changing to "Ware" because it was thought to be more prestigious. Also, the "2nd," "*x*" (sometimes written in a loopy style) and "RK" (run of kiln) marks were used to protect dealers (see "Background on Marks" in Introduction). These were etched with acid. They were quickly discontinued when it was discovered that the acid fumes left marks on the face of the ware when stacked for storage.

From 1939 to 1949 these round stamps were used. The stamps in ¾" and 1" sizes were used from February 1939 to August 1940. The ⅞" size was made July 1940 and used with or without "Hand Decorated" until 1947, at which time the numbers below the stamps were added to identify workers.

This stamp was used from 1949 to February 1953.

This stamp, the first to use the phrase "Oven-Safe," was used from February 1953 to July 1958.

This stamp, with the phrase "Color-Seal," was used from February 1954 to July 1958.

ART WARE

OX-BLOOD (1935–1942)

"A magnificent red, produced from copper under unusual firing conditions. No two pieces are exactly alike and the color varies through a wide range." Company records date Ox-Blood as a line from 1938, but it was available as a glaze as early as 1935. You will also find candlesticks, ashtrays, and a box with a white lid.

Bird, French Pheasant /C806 . . . . *$350*
Bowl, small /16 . . . . *125*
Bowl, square, low, 7¹/₂" /282 . . . . *225*
Bowl, round /79 . . . . *225*
Bowl, round, 10" /C283 . . . . *275*
Bowl, round, 16" /C287 . . . . *275 +*
Vase /288 . . . . *250 +*
Vase, low /140 . . . . *175 – 225*
Vase, small /104 . . . . *225*
Vase, low, 4¹/₂" /C277 . . . . *275*
Vase, round, 4¹/₂" /132 . . . . *75 – 125*

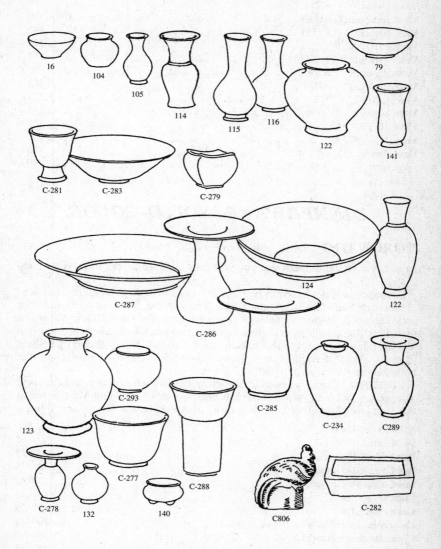

16
104
105
114
115
116
122
79
141
C-281
C-283
C-279
C-287
C-286
124
122
123
C-293
C-285
C-234
C289
C-278
132
C-277
140
C-288
C806
C-282

Ox-blood

Vase, square, 4½"   /C279 .... *$225*
Vase, small, 5"   /C300 .... *ND*
Vase, round, 5½"   /C293 .... *225*
Vase, bottle, 6"   /105 .... *175*
Vase, footed, 6"   /C281 .... *175*
Vase, Japanese (flaring), 6"   /C278 .... *250 – 350*
Vase, beaker, 7½"   /141 .... *145*
Vase, 8¼"   /C284 .... *275*
Vase, flare top, 8¾"   /114 .... *250*
Vase, flaring, 9"   /C285 .... *350+*
Vase, flaring, 9"   /C289 .... *275*
Vase, ball, 9½"   /122 .... *350*
Vase, bottle, 9½"   /116 .... *250*
Vase, 10½"   /115 .... *250*
Vase, 11"   /C290 .... *250*
Vase, flaring, 11"   /C286 .... *350+*
Vase, large, 11"   /123 .... *350+*

DINNERWARE / SOLID-COLOR

CORONADO   (Also called Swirl) (1934–1954>)

In addition to the dinnerware, you will find art ware pieces in the Coronado shape.

Coronado was decorated in both satin matte and high-gloss glazes. Initially, Satin Ivory, Satin Green, and Satin Blue were offered, followed by Satin White and Turquoise (gloss). This was followed by Satin Gray, Satin Turquoise (celadon), Satin Yellow, and gloss colors of Copper, Coral, Maroon, and Light Yellow (almost indistinguishable from Satin Yellow). You will also find pieces in gloss colors of Apple Green, Ruby, and White. These were special-order colors and are very hard to find.

PRICING   Coral is about 25% below the low end of the range. Ivory, Turquoise, and Yellow are at the low end; Copper, Gray, and Maroon are at the high end. Add 50% for gloss colors of Apple Green, Ruby, and White.

Ashtray, oval, 4½" .... *$8 – $10*
Bowl, salad, 10" .... *50 – 60*
Bowl, soup, 8" .... *12 – 15*
Bowl, vegetable, oval, 10" .... *30 – 35*
Bowl, vegetable, round, 9" .... *12 – 15*
Butter, ¼-pound .... *30 – 40*
Casserole, 10½" .... *45 – 50*
Casserole, individual w/lid (onion soup), 5½" .... *40 – 45*
Cigarette box, rectangular .... *80 – 95*
Coffee pot, AD .... *35 – 45*
Coffee pot, 8-cup .... *100 – 125*
Creamer, flat .... *8 – 10*
Creamer, footed .... *25 – 35*

Coronado

Cup	$4 – $6
Cup, AD.	12 – 15
Cup, cream soup	20 – 25
Cup, jumbo	45
Custard/sherbet, 5" × 2" high	15 – 18
Dish, 6"	6 – 8
Gravy, faststand.	15 – 20
Jug, 2½-quart.	65
Nut cup, footed, 2¼" × 1⅞" high.	20 – 25
Plate, 6½"	4 – 5
Plate, 7¼"	6 – 7
Plate, 8"	7 – 8
Plate, 9¼"	8 – 10
Plate, 10½"	10 – 12
Plate, chop, 12½"	20 – 25
Plate, chop, 14"	30 – 35
Plate, party, crescent	40
Plate, salad, crescent	15 – 20
Platter, oval, 10"	15 – 20
Platter, oval, 13"	20 – 25

Platter, oval, 15½" .... $25 – $30
Relish, oval, 9½" .... 15 – 18
Saucer .... 1 – 2
Saucer, AD .... 4 – 5
Saucer, cream soup .... 10 – 12
Saucer, jumbo .... 10 – 15
Shaker, each .... 7 – 9
Sugar, flat .... 10 – 12
Sugar, footed .... 25 – 35
Teapot, flat, 6-cup .... 30 – 35
Teapot, footed, 6-cup .... 100 – 125
Tumbler .... 25 – 35

METROPOLITAN   (1940)

Designed by Morris Sanders for an exhibit of industrial design at the Metropolitan Museum of Art in New York, hence the name. All shapes are square or rectangular.

Originally produced in satin finish colors of Ivory, Ivory and Coral, Ivory and Turquoise, and Ivory and Gray. In the combinations, Ivory was used as a liner and for the lid and handles. Chocolate Brown and Plum, both lined with Ivory, were also made.

There is evidence of early decal decoration but no indication that these were produced. Trio, a 1950s decal decoration of three stylized leaves, *was* produced from 1954 to 1957.

PRICING   Solid Ivory and Plum are at the high end of the range.

Ashtray/coaster .... $10 – $12
Bowl, salad, rectangular, 10" .... 30 – 40
Bowl, vegetable, divided .... 25 – 35
Bowl, vegetable, rectangular .... 25 – 35
Butter, ¼-pound 45
Casserole/covered vegetable 65
Casserole, individual 35
Coffee pot, 6-cup 75
Creamer .... 12 – 15
Cup .... 6 – 8
Dish, berry .... 5 – 7
Dish, soup/cereal .... 15 – 20
Gravy .... 20 – 22
Gravy liner/relish .... 12 – 15
Jug, 1½-quart .... 45 – 55
Plate, 6" .... 4 – 6
Plate, 8" .... 6 – 8
Plate, 10" .... 10 – 12
Plate, cake/chop, 13" .... 35 – 45
Platter, rectangular, 14" .... 35 – 45
Saucer .... 2 – 4
Shaker .... 10 – 12
Sugar .... 18 – 20

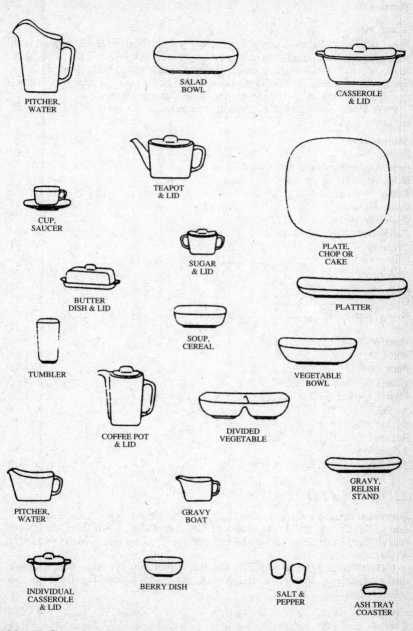

PITCHER,
WATER

SALAD
BOWL

CASSEROLE
& LID

TEAPOT
& LID

CUP,
SAUCER

SUGAR
& LID

PLATE,
CHOP OR
CAKE

BUTTER
DISH & LID

PLATTER

TUMBLER

SOUP,
CEREAL

VEGETABLE
BOWL

COFFEE POT
& LID

DIVIDED
VEGETABLE

PITCHER,
WATER

GRAVY
BOAT

GRAVY,
RELISH
STAND

INDIVIDUAL
CASSEROLE
& LID

BERRY DISH

SALT &
PEPPER

ASH TRAY
COASTER

Metropolitan

Teapot, 6-cup. . . . . *$45 – $50*
Tumbler. . . . . *20 – 25*

Tiempo

From 1949 to 1954, the Metropolitan shape was the basis of the Tiempo line in solid gloss colors, some of which are Copper (reddish-brown), Hot Chocolate (dark brown), Leaf (dark green), Mustard (yellow), Pebble (light brown), Sprout (light green), Stone (light gray), White, and a pink. Copper was discontinued in 1951. Some of these were House & Garden colors.

PRICING Sprout is at the bottom of the range; Copper, White, and pink are at the high end.

Ashtray/coaster. . . . . *$10 – $12*
Bowl, salad, 10". . . . . *30 – 40*
Bowl, vegetable, rectangular, 1-quart . . . . *18 – 20*
Bowl, vegetable, divided . . . . *20 – 25*
Butter, ¼-pound *35*
Casserole. . . . . *45 – 55*
Casserole, individual. . . . . *22 – 25*
Coffee pot, 6-cup. . . . . *50 – 60*
Creamer, ... *10 – 12*
Cup . . . . *6 – 8*
Dish, berry . . . . *5 – 7*
Dish, soup/cereal . . . . *10 – 12*
Gravy. . . . . *20 – 22*
Gravy liner/relish. . . . . *12 – 15*
Jug, 1½-quart. . . . . *45 – 55*
Plate, 6". . . . . *4 – 6*
Plate, 8". . . . . *6 – 8*
Plate, 10". . . . . *10 – 12*
Plate, cake/chop, 13". . . . . *25 – 30*
Platter, rectangular, 14" . . . . *25 – 30*
Saucer . . . . *2 – 4*
Shaker . . . . *10 – 12*
Sugar . . . . *18 – 20*
Teapot, 6-cup. . . . . *45 – 50*
Tumbler. . . . . *20 – 25*

MONTECITO (1937)

Decorated in gloss colors of Coral, Eggplant (purple/maroon), Ruby, Turquoise, and Light Yellow and matte colors of Celadon, Coral, Satin Gray, and Satin Ivory. The Montecito shape is the basis of the Del Oro line, which is Chinese Yellow and white.

PRICING Eggplant: add 20% and Ruby: multiply by four. There is also a duo-tone style of Montecito; add 20% to the values below. For Del Oro, use prices below.

Creamer . . . . *$18 – $20*
Cup . . . . *8 – 10*
Cup, cream soup . . . . *15 – 18*

Eggcup	$15 – $18
Gravy faststand	20 – 25
Plate, 7½"	5 – 7
Plate, 8½"	6 – 8
Plate, 9½"	7 – 9
Plate, 10½"	10 – 12
Platter, octagonal	25 – 45
Saucer	2 – 4
Saucer, cream soup	5 – 7
Shaker	10 – 12
Sugar	18 – 20
Teapot	55 – 65
Teapot, individual	65 – 75

PALOMAR

A fine china. Made in solid colors of Jasper Green, Primrose Yellow, Cameo Pink, Robin Egg Blue, Jade Green, Dove Grey and white.

Coffee pot	$80 – $100
Creamer	30 – 40
Cup	15 – 19
Saucer	4 – 6
Sugar	35 – 40
Teapot	80 – 100

RANCHO-WARE (1937)

Commonly found in solid satin colors of coral, matte green, ivory, and turquoise, as well as Old California colors that include Flame Orange and Turquoise (Glacial) blue. These were made from Catalina Island dinnerware molds.

Bowl, chowder, w/lid, shell shape	$75 – $85
Bowl, salad, fluted	40 – 50
Bowl, utility	18 – 24
Bowl, vegetable, round, small	25 – 30

CUP & SAUCER

CUP & SAUCER

CREAM SOUP CUP & SAUCER

FRUIT

CREAMER

SUGAR

TEAPOT

HANDLED TALL TUMBLER

CEREAL

VEGETABLE

VEGETABLE, OVAL

JUG

VEGETABLE, LARGE

TALL TUMBLER

HANDLE FOR TUMBLER

JUG, INSET HANDLE

JUG, ICE LIP

COFFEE CARAFE

JUG, FLAT BOTTOM

SMALL TUMBLER

Rancho: Note the two styles of casserole and cup.

**HANDLED
SMALL TUMBLER**

CHOWDER

RAMEKIN

COASTER

**INDIVIDUAL
CASSEROLE**

CASSEROLE

UTILITY BOWL

AD SUGAR

AD CREAMER

**CASSEROLE WITH
UNDERPLATE**

GOURD SHAKERS

FLUTED SALAD

TULIP SHAKERS

**VINEGAR
CRUET**

**GOURD
MUSTARD**

**VEGETABLE,
SMALL**

FLUTED CEREAL

Rancho: Note the two styles of casserole and cup.

Bowl, vegetable, round, large .... *$35 – $45*
Bowl, vegetable, round, lug .... *18 – 24*
Bowl, vegetable, oval.. *25 – 30*
Casserole, individual (covered ramekin)............................... *35 – 45*
Casserole, medium .... *35 – 45*
Casserole, large.. *45 – 65*
Coaster .... *12 – 15*
Coffee carafe w/wood handle .... *45 – 65*
Creamer .... *12 – 15*
Creamer, AD... *12 – 15*
Cup .... *15 – 20*
Cup, cream soup, lug... *25 – 30*
Dish, cereal, lug... *18 – 24*
Dish, cereal, fluted.. *25 – 30*
Dish, fruit, lug.. *18 – 24*
Jug... *45 – 65*
Jug, ice lip .... *45 – 65*
Jug, flat bottom .... *45 – 65*
Jug, insert handle, w/lid.. *75 – 100*
Mustard, Gourd shape .... *45 – 65*
Plate, B & B... *8 – 10*
Plate, dessert .... *10 – 12*
Plate, salad... *12 – 15*
Plate, salad, fluted .... *25 – 30*
Plate, dinner.. *20 – 25*
Plate, dinner, fluted .... *25 – 30*
Plate, service .... *25 – 30*
Plate, chop, 13" .... *35 – 45*
Plate, chop, 14" .... *35 – 45*
Plate, chop, 16" .... *35 – 45*
Platter, oval... *20 – 25*
Ramekin .... *8 – 10*
Relish... *12 – 15*
Saucer .... *8 – 10*
Shaker, Gourd shape, each .... *8 – 10*
Shaker, Tulip shape, each .... *8 – 10*
Sugar .... *18 – 24*
Sugar, AD, open .... *18 – 24*
Teapot .... *65 – 85*
Tumbler, small .... *8 – 10*
Tumbler, small, handled .... *8 – 10*
Tumbler, tall, handled.. *18 – 24*
Tumbler, tall .... *18 – 24*
    w/metal and wood handle .... *25 – 30*
Vinegar w/spout .... *45 – 65*

Duo-Tone

In mid 1939, Duo-Tone colors were added to the Ranchero shape: satin ivory
on the outside with linings of satin matte colors of coral, blue, green, or yellow.

This treatment seems to have been used on a few pieces only, though more may turn up. The cup was restyled for this line.

Bowl, salad... *$40 – $50*
Bowl, vegetable .... *30 – 35*
Creamer .... *15 – 20*
Cup .... *25 – 30*
Cup, bouillon... *30 – 35*
Dish, salad, leaf .... *30 – 35*
Dish, soup/cereal .... *25 – 30*
Jug.. *55 – 80*
Plate, B & B.. *10 – 12*
Plate, dessert .... *12 – 15*
Plate, salad.. *15 – 18*
Plate, dinner... *25 – 30*
Plate, chop .... *40 – 50*
Platter .... *25 – 30*
Saucer .... *10 – 12*
Saucer, bouillon.. *12 – 15*
Sugar .... *25 – 30*
Tumbler... *25 – 30*

DINNERWARE / DECALED

Gladding-McBean produced a number of transfer-printed lines from the late 1930s and early 1940s through to the 1980s, but the most popular with collectors is Starburst.

STARBURST (1954)

Eclipse shape designed by George James. The condiment tray holds the mustard and two cruets.

PRICING Duet (1956) and Oasis (1955), as well as a pure white glaze, were produced on the same shape. For Duet, subtract 25% from the prices below; for Oasis, subtract 10%.

Ashtray, individual, 1 rest, 4".. *$15*
Ashtray, large, oval, 4 rests, 7¹/₂"................................... *40*
Bowl, salad.. *95*
Bowl, vegetable, divided, round, 8¹/₂"................................. *24*
Bowl, vegetable, large, oval.. *65*
Butter, ¹/₄-pound *50*
Candle holder *60*
Canister, Coffee *125*
Canister, Flour (Cookie).. *150*
Canister, Sugar *100*
Canister, Tea... *75*
Casserole, individual, 5³/₄".. *125*
Casserole, medium, 8¹/₂".. *70*
Casserole, large, 9³/₄"... *100*

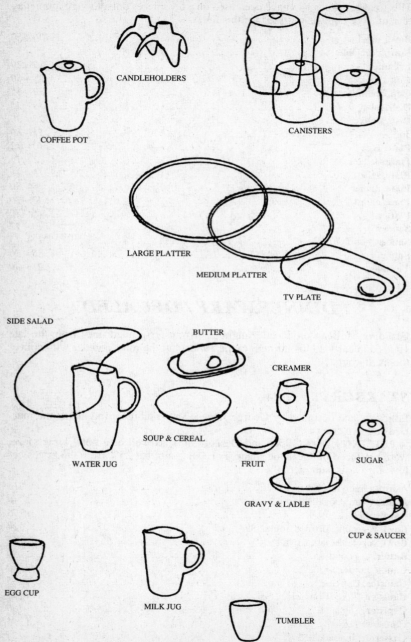

CANDLEHOLDERS

CANISTERS

COFFEE POT

LARGE PLATTER

MEDIUM PLATTER

TV PLATE

SIDE SALAD

BUTTER

CREAMER

WATER JUG

SOUP & CEREAL

FRUIT

SUGAR

GRAVY & LADLE

CUP & SAUCER

EGG CUP

MILK JUG

TUMBLER

Eclipse

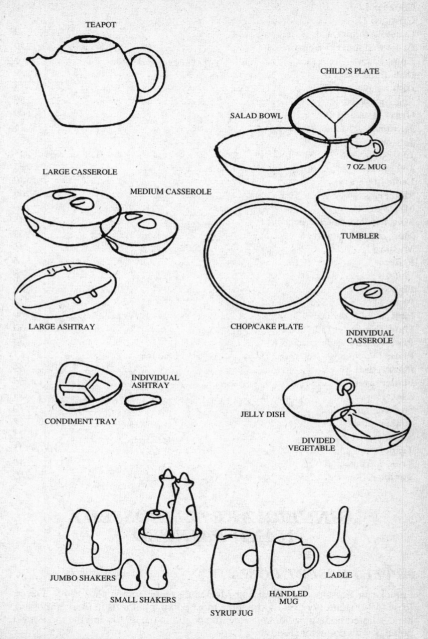

TEAPOT

CHILD'S PLATE

SALAD BOWL

7 OZ. MUG

LARGE CASSEROLE

MEDIUM CASSEROLE

TUMBLER

LARGE ASHTRAY

CHOP/CAKE PLATE

INDIVIDUAL CASSEROLE

INDIVIDUAL ASHTRAY

CONDIMENT TRAY

JELLY DISH

DIVIDED VEGETABLE

JUMBO SHAKERS

SMALL SHAKERS

SYRUP JUG

HANDLED MUG

LADLE

Eclipse

Coffee pot *$90*
Creamer *15*
Cruet w/stopper, Oil. *50*
Cruet w/stopper, Vinegar. *50*
Cup *6*
Dish, fruit, 5³/₄" *9*
Dish, soup/cereal, 7" *13*
Eggcup, footed. *50*
Gravy faststand *40*
Jelly dish, w/handle, 7¹/₄" *25*
Jug, milk *75*
Jug, syrup. *55*
Jug, water. *95*
Ladle (for gravy) *30*
Mill, Pepper *100*
Mill, Salt *100*
Mug, handled, small, 7-ounce *45*
Mug, handled, large *60*
Mustard. *45*
Plate, 6" *6*
Plate, 8" *8*
Plate, 9¹/₂" *20*
Plate, 11" *12*
Plate, child's, divided, 9". *60*
Plate, chop/cake, 13¹/₄" *80*
Plate, crescent (side salad), 9¹/₂" *30*
Plate, TV, oblong w/cup ring *65*
Platter, oval, 13" *60*
Platter, oval, 15" *80*
Saucer *3*
Shaker, small. *12*
Shaker, jumbo. *22*
Sugar *15*
Teapot . . . . *100 – 125*
Tray, condiment, 6¹/₂" *40*
Tumbler, 6-ounce . . . . *ND*

DINNERWARE / EMBOSSED / HAND-PAINTED

APPLE / DESERT ROSE / IVY

Franciscan Classics was Gladding-McBean's name for Apple (1940), Desert
Rose (1941), and Ivy (1948), the three most popular patterns in their embossed,
hand-painted underglaze dinnerware line begun in the 1940s and the three most
popular with collectors today.

   Although all Franciscan Classics are microwave-safe (per the company),

Franciscan Classics: Ivy teapot, Apple pitcher, and Desert Rose coffeepot.

three pieces were made as a microwave set; these are marked /M in the listing below. Gladding also made 6" square tiles. Matching glassware was made by Imperial Glass, and there were matching metal tea kettles as well; see listing following Desert Rose.

NOTE Apple and Desert Rose have been in continuous production since their introduction, though some items were made for a limited time.

APPLE

This line is based on Weller Pottery's Zona line Apple design. However, a comparison of pieces will show that Gladding-McBean did not use Weller's molds but redesigned and modified the pattern. The lidded pieces have Apple finials.

Baker, 1-quart, 9½" × 8¾" /M .... $120 – $130
Baker, 1½-quart, 14" × 9" /M .... 140 – 150
Baker, Apple shape, 5¼" .... 125 – 135
Bowl, batter, 7" long .... 250 – 275
Bowl, long and narrow, 15½" .... 250 – 275
Bowl, mixing, 6" .... 90 – 100
Bowl, mixing, 7½" .... 120 – 130
Bowl, mixing, 9" .... 140 – 150
Bowl, porringer, 6" .... 50 – 60
Bowl, salad, scalloped, 10" .... 90 – 100
Bowl, soup, flat, 8½" .... 14 – 18
Bowl, soup, footed, 5½" .... 18 – 20
Bowl, vegetable, 7¾" .... 20 – 25
Bowl, vegetable, 8½" .... 25 – 30
Bowl, vegetable, 9" .... 30 – 35
Bowl, vegetable, divided, 10¾" .... 35 – 40
Bowl, vegetable, scalloped, 8¼" .... 25 – 30

Butter, 1/4-pound . . . . *$40 – $50*
Casserole, 1 1/2-quart . . . . *60 – 75*
Casserole, 2 1/2-quart . . . . *240 – 260*
Casserole, individual, stick handle . . . . *45 – 55*
Casserole, in metal frame w/lid . . . . *240 – 260*
Coaster, 3 3/4" . . . . *20 – 25*
Coffee pot, 8-cup, old style . . . . *60 – 70*
Coffee pot, redesigned . . . . *60 – 70*
Compote, 8" . . . . *70 – 80*
Cookie jar . . . . *180 – 200*
Creamer . . . . *20 – 25*
Creamer, AD . . . . *15 – 20*
Cup, AD . . . . *18 – 20*
Cup, jumbo . . . . *25 – 30*
Cup, tea . . . . *10 – 12*
Dish, fruit, 5 1/4" . . . . *8 – 10*
Dish, soup/cereal, 6" . . . . *9 – 11*
Eggcup . . . . *18 – 20*
Gravy faststand . . . . *35 – 40*
Jam jar, old style . . . . *80 – 100*
Jam jar, Apple shape . . . . *110 – 120*
Jug, small . . . . *100 – 125*
Jug, syrup, 1-pint . . . . *70 – 80*
Jug, 1-quart . . . . *70 – 80*
Jug, 2-quart . . . . *90 – 100*
Ladle (for tureen), plain, 10" . . . . *120 – 130*
Mug, 7-ounce . . . . *15 – 20*
Mug, 10-ounce . . . . *40 – 50*
Mug, round bottom, 12-ounce . . . . *35 – 40*
Plate, 6 1/2" . . . . *4 – 8*
Plate, 8 1/2" . . . . *6 – 10*
Plate, 9 1/2" . . . . *8 – 12*
Plate, 10 1/2" . . . . *10 – 14*
Plate, buffet/grill, round, divided, 11" . . . . *50 – 60*
Plate, chop, 12" . . . . *90 – 95*
Plate, chop, 14" . . . . *175 – 185*
Plate, coupe/dessert, 7 1/2" . . . . *30 – 35*
Plate, coupe/steak, oval, 11" . . . . *100 – 125*
Plate, crescent (side salad), 8" . . . . *30 – 35*
Plate, party, 10 1/2" . . . . *100 +*
Plate, snack, square, 8"   /M . . . . *90 – 100*
Plate, 3-part (child's), 9" × 7 1/4" . . . . *70 – 80*
Plate, TV, oval w/cup well, 14" . . . . *90 – 100*
Platter, 12 3/4" . . . . *50 – 60*
Platter, 14" . . . . *60 – 70*
Platter, 17"–19" . . . . *175 – 185*
Relish, oval, 10" × 4 1/2" . . . . *40 – 50*
Relish, 3-part, 11 3/4" × 9 1/2" . . . . *60 – 70*

Salt/Pepper Mill, bulbous base . . . . *$90 – $100*
Salt/Pepper Mill, cylindrical . . . . *125 – 130*
Salt/Pepper Mill, wood top and base . . . . *125 – 130*
Saucer, 5³/₄" . . . . *4 – 6*
Saucer, AD, 4¹/₂" . . . . *4 – 5*
Saucer, jumbo, 7" . . . . *4 – 8*
Shaker, small . . . . *15 – 18*
Shaker, tall . . . . *25 – 28*
Sherbet . . . . *18 – 20*
Sugar . . . . *20 – 25*
Sugar, AD . . . . *18 – 20*
Teapot, 6-cup, old style . . . . *70 – 80*
Teapot, 6-cup, redesigned . . . . *70 – 80*
Trivet, round, fluted, 6" . . . . *40 – 50*
Tumbler, 6-ounce . . . . *50 – 60*
Tumbler, 10-ounce . . . . *25 – 30*
Tureen, footed, small . . . . *300 – 325*
Tureen, pedestal base . . . . *ND*
Tureen, 3 feet, large . . . . *400 – 450*
Two-tier tidbit . . . . *80 – 85*

ARTWARE / GIFTWARE

Ashtray, oval, 9" . . . . *$50 – $60*
Ashtray, square . . . . *55 – 65*
Ashtray, individual, Apple shape . . . . *15 – 20*
Box, cigarette, 4¹/₂" × 3¹/₄" . . . . *100 – 125*
Box, round, 4³/₄" *150*
Candle holder, 3" . . . . *50 – 60*
Ginger jar . . . . *250 +*
Napkin ring . . . . *30 – 35*
Piggy bank . . . . *120 – 130*
Tea canister . . . . *250 +*
Thimble . . . . *60 – 70*
Tile, square, 6" . . . . *40 – 50*
Tile, round, 6" . . . . *70 – 80*

DESERT ROSE

Lidded pieces have Rose Bud finials. The lining was dropped in 1947. At three different times, child's sets were marketed from existing items. One consisted of the 9" three-part plate and 7-ounce mug. Another consisted of the coupe dessert plate, the 7-ounce mug, and a porringer. The third was the three-part plate and the tall 10-ounce mug.

Baker, 1-quart, 9¹/₂" × 8³/₄" /M . . . . *$120 – $130*
Baker, 1¹/₂-quart, 14" × 9" /M . . . . *140 – 150*
Bowl, bouillon, w/lid, rosebud finial, 4¹/₂" . . . . *150 +*
Bowl, long and narrow, 15¹/₂" . . . . *300 +*
Bowl, mixing, 6" . . . . *90 – 100*
Bowl, mixing, 7¹/₂" . . . . *120 – 130*

Bowl, mixing, 9".. $140 – $150
Bowl, porringer, 6"... 50 – 60
Bowl, salad, scalloped, 10"................................... 90 – 100
Bowl, soup, flat, 8½".. 14 – 18
Bowl, soup, footed, 5½".................................... 18 – 20
Bowl, vegetable, 8".. 25 – 30
Bowl, vegetable, 9".. 30 – 35
Bowl, vegetable, divided, 10¾"............................. 35 – 40
Butter, ¼-pound.. 40 – 50
Candle holder .... 40 – 50
Casserole, 1½-quart... 50 – 60
Casserole, 2½-quart.. 200 – 250
Coffee pot, AD... 170 – 190
Coffee pot, 8-cup .... 80 – 90
Compote, 8".. 70 – 80
Compote, low, 6"... 100 – 125
Cookie jar .... 180 – 200
Creamer... 20 – 25
Creamer, AD, 3½".. 40 – 45
Cup, AD.. 18 – 20
Cup, coffee.. 40 – 50
Cup, jumbo.. 25 – 30
Cup, tea .... 10 – 12
Cup, tall, 10-ounce... 15 – 20
Dish, fruit, 5¼".. 8 – 10
Dish, soup/cereal, 6"....................................... 9 – 11
Eggcup .... 18 – 20
Goblet, 6½"... 100 – 125
Gravy faststand.. 35 – 40
Jam jar... 80 – 100
Jug, small, 4" .... 100 – 125
Jug, syrup, 1-pint .... 70 – 80
Jug, 1-quart... 70 – 80
Jug, 2½-quart .... 90 – 100
Ladle (for tureen), plain, 10½"............................. 120 – 130
Mug, 7-ounce .... 15 – 20
Mug, 10-ounce .... 22 – 25
Mug, tall, 10-ounce 125
Mug, round bottom, 12-ounce .... 35 – 40
Pickle/Relish, 11"... 40 – 50
Plate, 6½".. 4 – 8
Plate, 8½".. 6 – 10
Plate, 9½".. 8 – 12
Plate, 10½".. 10 – 14
Plate, buffet/grill, round, divided, 11" .... 50 – 60
Plate, chop, 12" .... 90 – 95
Plate, chop, 14" .... 175 – 185
Plate, coupe/steak, oval, 11" .... 30 – 35

Plate, crescent (side salad), 8" . . . . *$30 – $35*
Plate, dessert (coupe) . . . . *50 – 60*
Plate, heart, 5³/₄" × 5¹/₂" . . . . *70 – 80*
Plate, party, 10 12" . . . . *80 – 90*
Plate, snack, square, 8"   /M . . . . *90 – 100*
Plate, 3-part (child's), 9" × 7¹/₄" . . . . *70 – 80*
Plate, TV, w/cup well, oval, 14" . . . . *90 – 100*
Platter, 12" . . . . *50 – 60*
Platter, 14" . . . . *60 – 70*
Platter, 17" . . . . *175 – 185*
Relish, 3-part, 12" × 9¹/₂" . . . . *70 – 80*
Salt/Pepper Mill, bulbous base, 6" . . . . *90 – 100*
Salt/Pepper Mill, cylindrical, 6" . . . . *125 – 130*
Saucer, AD, 4³/₄" . . . . *4 – 5*
Saucer, coffee/tea, 5³/₄" . . . . *4 – 6*
Saucer, jumbo, 7" . . . . *4 – 8*
Shaker, small . . . . *15 – 17*
Shaker, tall . . . . *24 – 28*
Sherbet, footed, 4" . . . . *18 – 20*
Sugar . . . . *20 – 25*
Sugar, AD . . . . *40 – 50*
Teapot, individual . . . . *175 – 200*
Teapot, 6-cup . . . . *70 – 80*
Toast cover, rosebud finial, 5¹/₂" . . . . *90 – 100*
Trivet, round, fluted, 6" . . . . *70 – 80*
Tumbler, 6-ounce . . . . *40 – 50*
Tumbler, 10-ounce . . . . *20 – 25*
Tureen, flat bottom . . . . *450 – 500*
Tureen, footed . . . . *450 – 500*
Tureen, 3 feet . . . . *400 – 450*
Two-tier tidbit . . . . *80 – 85*

ARTWARE / GIFTWARE

Ashtray, square, 4³/₄" . . . . *$50 – $60*
Ashtray, Rose, individual, 3¹/₂" . . . . *55 – 60*
Bell, Danbury, 4¹/₄" . . . . *45 – 55*
Bell, dinner, 6" . . . . *100 – 110*
Box, cigarette, 4¹/₂" × 3¹/₂" . . . . *100 – 125*
Box, heart, 4¹/₂" . . . . *150 +*
Box, oval . . . . *200 +*
Box, round, 4³/₄" . . . . *100 – 110*
Bud vase, 6" . . . . *90 – 100*
Candy dish, oval, 7" . . . . *100 – 120*
Ginger jar . . . . *100 – 110*
Hurricane lamp . . . . *125 – 135*
Napkin ring . . . . *30 – 35*
Piggy bank . . . . *120 – 130*
Tea canister . . . . *100 – 110*

Thimble . . . . *$60 – $70*
Tile, square, 6" . . . . *40 – 50*
Tile, round, 6" . . . . *70 – 80*

METAL
Available in Apple and Desert Rose only.

Tea kettle . . . . *$90 – $100*

IVY

The cup was redesigned. The green line was dropped from a number of pieces in 1955, especially hollowware items.

Bowl, salad, 11¼" . . . . *$140 – $150*
Bowl, soup, flat, 8½" . . . . *25 – 30*
Bowl, soup, footed, 5½" . . . . *35 – 40*
Bowl, vegetable, 7¼" . . . . *50 – 65*
Bowl, vegetable, 8¼" . . . . *65 – 75*
Bowl, vegetable, divided, 12¼" . . . . *75 – 85*
Butter, ¼-pound . . . . *75 – 95*
Casserole, 1½-quart . . . . *125 – 145*
Coffee pot, 8-cup . . . . *175 – 200*
Compote, 8" . . . . *75 – 95*
Creamer . . . . *30 – 35*
Cup . . . . *18 – 20*
Cup, jumbo . . . . *45 – 50*
Dish, fruit, 5¼" . . . . *18 – 20*
Dish, soup/cereal, 6" . . . . *22 – 24*
Gravy faststand . . . . *70 – 80*
Jug, 2½-quart . . . . *125 – 135*
Ladle, plain . . . . *120 – 130*
Mug, round bottom, 12-ounce . . . . *50 – 60*
Pickle/Relish, 10½" . . . . *60 – 70*
Plate, 6½" . . . . *8 – 10*
Plate, 8½" . . . . *18 – 20*
Plate, 9½" . . . . *22 – 24*
Plate, 10½" . . . . *24 – 26*
Plate, buffet, 11" . . . . *80 – 90*
Plate, cake, 13" . . . . *180 – 190*
Plate, chop, 12" . . . . *100 – 110*
Plate, chop, 14" . . . . *180 – 190*
Plate, crescent (side salad) . . . . *40 – 50*
Plate, TV, oval, w/cup well, 14" . . . . *100 – 125*
Platter, 11¼" . . . . *70 – 80*
Platter, 13" . . . . *100 – 110*
Platter, 19" . . . . *200 – 220*
Relish, divided, 12" . . . . *70 – 80*
Saucer . . . . *4 – 6*
Saucer, jumbo . . . . *4 – 8*

Shaker	$20 – $25
Sherbet, footed, 4"	30 – 35
Sugar	40 – 45
Teapot, 6-cup	150 – 175
Tumbler, 10-ounce	35 – 40
Tureen, 8³⁄₄"	350 – 450
Two-tier tidbit	100 – 120

GIFTWARE

Ashtray, Leaf (individual), 4¹⁄₂"	$20 – $25
Dark green	20 – 25
Light green	45
Tile, square, 6"	50 – 60

WILDFLOWER   (1942)

". . . the colorful wildflowers that make the slopes and valleys of California one of the world's most spectacular sights each spring . . . the dramatic yellow gold of the Poppy and the brilliant blue of the Lupin join gaily with the more subtle colors of the Shooting Star and the Mariposa Lily." Don't confuse the shakers with Meadow Rose. The green and yellow of these are different; they match Wildflower colors.

Ashtray, Mariposa Lily, 3¹⁄₂"	$50 – $65
Ashtray, Poppy, 3¹⁄₂"	50 – 65
Bowl, salad, round, 10"	200 – 250
Bowl, vegetable, round, 9"	150 – 175
Casserole, 1¹⁄₂-quart	250 – 300
Coffee pot	250 – 300
Creamer	70 – 85
Cup	35 – 40
Cup, AD	90 – 100
Cup, jumbo	90 – 100
Dish, 5¹⁄₂"	30 – 35
Dish, 6"	45 – 50
Gravy faststand	150 – 175
Jam jar	200 – 225
Jug, water	250 – 300
Pickle/Relish, 12"	100 – 125
Plate, 6¹⁄₂"	20 – 25
Plate, 8¹⁄₂"	35 – 40
Plate, 9¹⁄₂"	45 – 55
Plate, 10¹⁄₂"	60 – 75
Plate, chop, 12"	150 – 175
Plate, chop, 14"	250 – 300
Platter, 14"	150 – 175
Saucer	10 – 15
Saucer, AD	20 – 25
Saucer, jumbo	20 – 25

Shakers, Rose, pair . . . . $75 – $125
Sherbet, footed . . . . 85 – 125
Sugar . . . . 100 – 110
Teapot . . . . 250 – 300
Tumbler, 10-ounce . . . . 250 – 300

MISCELLANY

These items were produced in white. They were also part of the Terra Cotta Specialties line produced from 1937 to 1940. This was a special stain applied to the Malinite body. All are vases except the Mermaid and the two Samoan pieces, which are figures.

		White	*Terra Cotta*
Bird /C802	. . . .	$125 – $150	$150 – $200
Bird on base /C806	. . . .	150 – 175	175 – 225

C-807

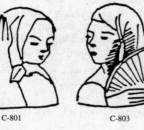

C-801   C-803

C-808

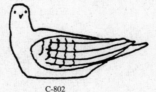

C-802

C-805

C-806

C-804

Miscellany

	White	Terra Cotta
Girl, head, large /C804	$125 – $150	$150 – $200
Girl w/fan /C803	125 – 150	150 – 200
Lady w/corsage, bust /C814	125 – 150	150 – 200
Lady w/hat /C805	125 – 150	150 – 200
Malayan Woman, turbaned head /C809	125 – 150	150 – 200
Mermaid /C813	250	
Samoan Girl, reclining /C808	125 – 150	150 – 200
Samoan Mother and Child /C807	150 – 225	225 – 250
Table ornament, Grape /C810	75 – 125	
Table ornament, Fruit and Nut /C812	75 – 125	
Vase, Bust, Peasant Girl /C801	45 – 75	100 – 145

GONDER CERAMIC ARTS, INC.

Zanesville, Ohio

CHAPTER AT A GLANCE

CONSOLE SETS
COOKIE JARS
DINNERWARE
  La Gonda
  Miscellany
FIGURES

Animals
People
MISCELLANY
PLANTERS
VASES

Gonder Ceramic Arts was founded in late 1941 at the old Zane Pottery (formerly Peters and Reed) by Lawton Gonder, who had previously worked at American Encaustic Tile and at Florence Pottery (which produced RumRill). Despite the market for inexpensive ware for the chain stores, Gonder decided to manufacture a higher yet reasonably priced art pottery.

In 1946, demand was so great that he built an addition to his plant and opened another plant at a lumber mill in Zanesville for the manufacture of lamps. This was named Elgee Pottery (Lawton Gonder's initials) and operated until it was destroyed by fire in 1954. To continue this production, he again added onto the original building.

Business began to be affected adversely by foreign imports, so in 1955 Gonder began training his employees in the manufacture of tile, the business he had grown up in. In February 1957, all production was changed over to other ceramic products.

GLAZES Among the artistic innovations that Gonder can take credit for is the development of commercial Flambe glazes (flame red color with streaks of yellow; I've also heard this described as a candy-apple burgundy) and gold crackle, which had never been achieved successfully.

Here are known glaze names:

24	Mother of Pearl Lustre	Celadon
25	Coral Lustre	Ming yellow
26	White Chinese Crackle	Ming blue
27	Turquoise Chinese Crackle	Gold lustre
28	Ebony Green	Gold Antique/brown background
29	Royal Purple	Yellow Chinese Crackle
30	Wine Brown	

Very rarely you may find a metallic glaze.

PRICING Values below are for common colors. Add 50% for Gold Crackle. Add 25% for the three Chinese crackles: turquoise, white, and yellow as well as for Flambe and Ming blue or Ming yellow.

CONSOLE SETS

The first number is the bowl; the second is the candle holder.

PRICING The first value is for the bowl; the second is for a pair of candle holders.

Crescent Moon /J-55 /J-56 .... *$25 / 15*
Shell, 16½" × 6½" /505 /517 .... *30 – 35 / 15*
Star Fish /500 /501 .... *ND*
E-12 /E-14 .... *20 / set*
K-14 /H-14 .... *30 – 35 / 15*

COOKIE JARS

Bucket, rope handle, "Ye Olde Oaken Bucket" /974 .... *$100 – $125*
Pirate w/pistol/R .... *1800 – 2000*
  Bank .... *ND*
Round w/swirls, plain lid /P24 .... *40 – 50*
Round w/swirls, sleeping dog on lid /924 .... *50 – 60*
Sheriff, reaching for guns /950/R
  Flesh-tone face .... *1800 – 2000*
  Yellow w/green trim .... *1500 – 1600*
  Bank .... *250 – 300*

DINNERWARE

La Gonda (1947)

Square shape. When the jug is full, the weight may be too much for the handle to bear. I am not sure whether the stacked sugar and creamer was intended to be a part of this line.

Often found in drip glazes; blue, brown, gray, green, pink, and yellow have been reported.

Casserole, individual, stick handle /952 .... *$10 – $15*
Coffee pot .... *55 – 60*
Creamer /923 .... *6 – 8*
Creamer/sugar, stack, no handles /740 .... *12 – 15*
Cup, round .... *6 – 8*
Cup, cream soup, lug .... *10 – 12*
Jug, ice lip /917 .... *20 – 25*
Mug /909 .... *8 – 10*
Plate, 8½" .... *12 – 15*
Saucer .... *5 – 7*
Saucer, cream soup .... *6 – 8*

La Gonda 8¹/₂" plate and sugar.

Shaker, pair . . . . *$15 – $20*
Sugar   /923 . . . . *8 – 10*
Teapot, 2-cup . . . . *25 – 30*
Teapot, 6-cup   /914 . . . . *45 – 50*

Miscellany

Carafe, w/stopper, 8"   /994 . . . . *$18 – $24*
Driftwood mug *10*
Relish, 6-part, 18" × 11" . . . . *15 – 18*
Ribbed creamer   /P33 . . . . *6*
Ribbed sugar   /P33 . . . . *8*
Ribbed teapot   /P31 . . . . *25*
Striated creamer . . . . *8 – 10*
Striated jug . . . . *18 – 24*

FIGURES

Animals

Cat, Modern, 15"   /521 . . . . *$250 – $300*
Deer (2), 11" long   /690 . . . . *25 – 30*
Deer, head, vase, 10¹/₂"   /518 . . . . *25 – 30*
Elephant, stylized, 7¹/₂" × 10"   /108 . . . . *250 – 300*
Elephant   /207 . . . . *45 – 50*
Game Cock, 11"   /525 . . . . *35 – 40*
Game Hen, 7" . . . . *35 – 40*
Goose, head up   /B-15 . . . . *10 – 15*
Goose, head down   /B-14 . . . . *10 – 15*
Horse head, 13" long   /576 . . . . *75 – 85*
Panther, resting, 15" long   /217 . . . . *75 – 80*
Panther, resting, 19" long   /210 . . . . *150 – 175*

People

The **Chinese peasant with basket** is often found with chips on nose and tip of hat brim because it is poorly balanced and falls forward easily. Gonder called the **madonnas** "Lady Fatima." You can hang a rosary from the clasped hands of #772. The **porters** came as a pair with a wooden rod held on their shoulders (one stood behind the other) and with a basket that hung from the rod. A catalog illustration shows ivy in the basket. None have been found with these accoutrements. The **water bearers** (which came as a male and female pair) had two vessels each hanging from strings attached to their shoulder braces.

PRICING All water bearers are priced *with* water vessels. The Balinese woman is ND because she is usually found with the bowl missing, being sold as a candle holder!

Balinese porter, man /764. . . . . *$40 – $50*
Balinese water bearer, man, flower on base, 14" /763 . . . . *35 – 40*
Balinese water bearer, woman, flower on base, 14" /763 . . . . *35 – 40*
Balinese woman, bowl on head, leaf base, 14" /762. . . . . *ND*
Chinese peasant, head, 11" /541. . . . . *200 – 225*
Chinese peasant, kneeling, 6" /547 . . . . *15 – 20*
Chinese peasant, standing, 8" /545. . . . . *15 – 20*
Chinese peasant w/basket, vase, 9" /519. . . . . *25 – 30*
Chinese water bearer, man /777 . . . . *35 – 40*
Chinese water bearer, woman /777. . . . . *35 – 40*
Chinese water bearer, man, bending left, 12" . . . . *35 – 40*
Chinese woman, hands on hips, 13" /763. . . . . *25 – 30*
Gay Nineties water bearer, man . . . . *80 – 100*
Gay Nineties water bearer, woman. . . . . *80 – 100*
Madonna, full figure /549 . . . . *15 – 20*
Madonna, full figure, hands clasped /772. . . . . *15 – 20*
Madonna, upper torso /E-303 . . . . *12 – 15*

MISCELLANY

I have heard the sampans called junks, but a junk has a high poop deck and sails, whereas sampans are just skiffs.

Ashtray, Horse head /548 . . . . *$15 – $18*
Basket /H-39 . . . . *12 – 15*
Basket, 9" tall × 13" long /L-19 . . . . *30 – 35*
Bookends, Horse head, pair /582. . . . . *40 – 50*
Bowl /H-29. . . . . *15 – 20*
Bowl, shell, 13" long /J-71. . . . . *30 – 35*
Bowl, shell, 13" × 6" (same shape as Shell console) . . . . *25 – 30*
Cornucopia /521. . . . . *20 – 25*
Ginger jar, round /529 . . . . *30*
Ginger jar, square, w/lid and base, 10" /530 . . . . *35 – 40*
Jar, round, engraved dragons, w/lid and base, 7" /533 . . . . *50*
Sampan, 15½" long /520. . . . . *25 – 30*
Sampan, 10" long /550 . . . . *15 – 18*

PLANTERS

Cornucopia   /J-66 .... $25 – $35
Swan   /E-44 .... 10 – 12
Swan   /J-31 .... 25 – 30

VASES

Vase, 5¹/₂" /H-83 .... $15 – $18
Vase, 6"   /H-80 .... 15 – 18
Vase, 6"   /H-82 .... 15 – 18
Vase, 7"   /216 .... 18 – 20
Vase, 7"   /360 .... 12 – 15
Vase, 7"   /382 .... 12 – 15
Vase, 7"   /389 .... 12 – 15
Vase, 7¹/₂" /H-42 .... 18 – 20
Vase, Pinecone, 7¹/₂"   /507 .... 18 – 20
Vase, 8"   /402 .... 18 – 20
Vase, 8"   /410 .... 18 – 20
Vase, 8"   /419 .... 18 – 20
Vase, 2 swans on base, 8"   /H-47 .... 18 – 20
Vase, embossed stork, 8"   /H-76................................ 18 – 20
Vase, 8"   /H-79 .... 15 – 18
Vase, 8"   /H-84 .... 18 – 20
Vase, 8"   /H-86 .... 18 – 20
Vase, Chinese, 8"   /537 .... 15 – 18
Vase, cornucopia, 8"   /691 .... 18 – 20
Vase, ewer, 8"   /H-73 .... 15 – 18
Vase, 8¹/₂" /H-52 .... 15 – 18
Vase, 8¹/₂" /H-56 .... 15 – 18
Vase, 8¹/₂" /H-62 .... 15 – 18
Vase, 8¹/₂" /H-68 .... 15 – 18
Vase, 8¹/₂" /H-69 .... 15 – 18
Vase, 8¹/₂" /H-74 .... 12 – 15
Vase, 8¹/₂" /H-75 .... 15 – 18
Vase, leaves, 8¹/₂"   /H-67 .... 18 – 20
Vase, 9"   /H-5 .... 15 – 18
Vase, 9"   /H-7 .... 15 – 18
Vase, 9"   /H-10 .... 15 – 18
Vase, 9"   /H-33 .... 18 – 20
Vase, 9"   /H-36 .... 15 – 18
Vase, 9"   /H-77 .... 15 – 18
Vase, 9"   /H-78 .... 15 – 18
Vase, 9"   /H-81 .... 15 – 18
Vase, w/fish, 9"   /H-85 .... 20 – 25
Vase, 9"   /H-87 .... 15 – 18
Vase, 9"   /J-61.. 25 – 28
Vase, 9"   /J-70.. 25 – 30
Vase, embossed butterfly, 9" .... 30 – 35

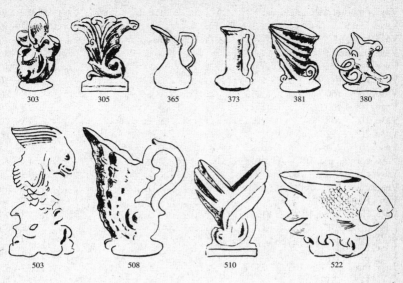

303   305   365   373   381   380

503   508   510   522

540   604   605   606   607

674   674   E-1   E-3   E-4   E-5

E-6   E-44   E-49   E-60   E-64   E-79

Vase, embossed leaping deer, 9"   /215 . . . . *$25 – $30*
Vase, fan, 9"   /J-60 . . . . *25 – 30*
Vase, harp, 9"   /J-57 . . . . *25 – 30*
Vase, pinched, 9"   /607 . . . . *30 – 35*
Vase, Scarla Fish, 9" × 11¹/₂"   /522 . . . . *40 – 50*
Vase, Butterfly, 9¹/₂"   /523 . . . . *40 – 50*
Vase, 10"   /601 . . . . *18 – 20*
Vase, 10"   /603 . . . . *18 – 20*
Vase, 10"   /683 . . . . *18 – 20*
Vase, 10"   /720 . . . . *15 – 18*
Vase, 10"   /J-64 . . . . *30 – 35*
Vase, cornucopia, 10"   /H-14 . . . . *15 – 18*
Vase, curtain, 10"   /605 . . . . *18 – 20*
Vase, ewer, 10"   /606 . . . . *25 – 30*
Vase, Feather, 10"   /539 . . . . *25 – 30*
Vase, Horse head, 10"   /540 . . . . *35 – 40*
Vase, Swan, 10"   /802 . . . . *25 – 30*
Vase, 2-handled, 10"   /604 . . . . *30 – 35*
Vase, Javanese, 10¹/₂"   /513 . . . . *30 – 35*
Vase, three-leaf fan, 10³/₄"   /504 . . . . *30 – 35*
Vase, 11"   /517 . . . . *25 – 30*
Vase, 11"   /J-35 . . . . *25 – 30*
Vase, 11"   /J-69 . . . . *20 – 25*
Vase, 11"   /J-773 . . . . *25 – 30*
Vase, ewer, 11"   /J-25 . . . . *30 – 35*
Vase, ewer, 11"   /J-54 . . . . *25 – 30*
Vase, Swan, 11"   /530 . . . . *35 – 40*
Vase, Trumpet Lily, 11"   /876 . . . . *35 – 40*
Vase, 11¹/₂"   /598 . . . . *30 – 35*
Vase, Flame, 11¹/₂"   /510 . . . . *25 – 30*
Vase, Gull and Pile, 11¹/₂"   /514 . . . . *45 – 50*
Vase, Sea Horse, 11³/₄"   /524 . . . . *35 – 40*
Vase, 12"   /K-26 . . . . *25 – 30*
Vase, 12"   /M-4 . . . . *30 – 35*
Vase, 12"   /M-8 . . . . *35 – 40*
Vase, Peacock, 12"   /K-15 . . . . *30 – 35*
Vase, embossed flowers, 13"   /868 . . . . *25 – 30*
Vase, ewer, 13"   /M-9 . . . . *35 – 40*
Vase, Shell tankard, 13"   /508 . . . . *35 – 40*
Vase, Shell tankard w/starfish on base, 13"   /508 . . . . *35 – 40*
Vase, embossed storks, 13"   /640 . . . . *55 – 60*
Vase, Dolphin, 15"   /503 . . . . *55 – 60*
Vase, thin neck, 17"   /531 . . . . *60 – 65*

HAEGER POTTERIES

Dundee and Macomb, Illinois

CHAPTER AT A GLANCE

ASHTRAYS	LEAVES
BOOKENDS	MISCELLANY
BOWLS	PLANTERS
CANDLE HOLDERS	TABLE LAMPS
CANDY DISHES	TV LAMPS
FIGURES	VASES
FLOWER FROGS	

Haeger began in 1871 as a brickyard. In 1914 art pottery was introduced under the guidance of Martin Stangl. In 1938 the Royal Haeger line, designed by Royal Hickman, was introduced. It is still in production today.

Haeger made many lines, including dinnerware and florist ware, but it is the Royal Haeger line, specifically the hundreds of designs by Royal Hickman, that is most collectible today.

NOTE All pieces listed are from the Royal Haeger line. Many items came in several sizes. In these cases, prices are given for the smallest and largest, so you can extrapolate the intermediate prices.

PRICING As Haeger becomes more collectible, certain colors will gain greater popularity with collectors than others. For now, the bright red and glossy black introduced in the mid 1940s are certainly of interest and are at the high end of the price range. In addition, be alert for two hard-to-find finishes: Boko (or Boco), which looks like the glaze has been bubbled over the surface of the piece, and D'Este, which resembles rough, horizontal grooving. Add 50% to the prices for these finishes.

ASHTRAYS

Some ashtrays are also figurines; these are noted in parentheses.

Cat, Leopard, 8½" /R-632		$25 – $30
Cog Wheel /R-230		7 – 9
Deer, Fawn, 8½" /R-1283		25 – 30
Diamond, 9" /R-1215		7 – 9
Dog, Boxer (figurine), 13" /R-1399		35 – 45
Dog, Cocker, standing, 12" /R-1443		35 – 45

Dog, Poodle, 12"   /R-1441 .... *$35 – $45*
Elephant, 4"   /R-668 .... *15 – 20*
Heart, 7¹/₂"   /R-1184.. *7 – 9*
Heart, double, 9"   /R-1363...................................... *7 – 9*
Leaf, 5"   /R-449 .... *7 – 9*
Leaf, 6"   /R-597 .... *7 – 9*
Leaf, 8"   /R-567 .... *8 – 10*
Palette, 9¹/₂"   /R-811 .... *7 – 9*

BOOKENDS

Some bookends are also planters. These are noted in parentheses.
   PRICING   All values are per pair.

Calla Lily   /R-475.. *$18 – $20*
Cat, Leopard (planter), 15"   /R-638 .... *45 – 50*
Cat, Lion Head, 7¹/₂"   /R-700 .... *25 – 30*
Horse, Stallion (planter), 8¹/₂"   /R-641 .... *25 – 30*
Horse Head (figurine), 7"   /R-1365 .... *25 – 30*
Indian (planter)   /R-741 .... *45 – 50*
Ram, 9"   /R-132 .... *30 – 35*
Ram's Head, 5¹/₂"   /R-718 .... *20 – 25*
Water Lily, 5"   /R-1144 .... *18 – 20*

BOWLS

Oyster Shell, 15"   /R-985... *$15 – $18*
Petunia   /R-737 .... *10 – 12*
Sailfish planter bowl, 11"   /1191................................. *35 – 40*
Star Fish, 14"   /R-967 .... *20 – 22*
Swan, 11"   /R-955... *18 – 20*
Swan flower, 12"   /R-1218 .... *30 – 35*
Violin, 17"   /R-293 .... *25 – 30*

CANDLE HOLDERS

Prices are per pair.

Apple, 2¹/₂"   /R-1206... *$10 – $12*
Butterfly, 6¹/₂"   /R-1208 .... *15 – 18*
Chinese figures, 5"   /R-622 .... *12 – 15*
Cornucopia   /R-312... *8 – 10*
Fish, 5"   /R-183... *20 – 25*
Fish, (2) (R-203 .... *25 – 30*
Leaf, 5"   /R-437 .... *8 – 10*
Plume   /R-295.. *8 – 10*
Star Fish, 6"   /R-968 .... *10 – 12*
Swan, 8"   /R-516... *15 – 18*

CANDY DISHES

Calla Lilly, 7¹/₂"   /R-431.. *$18 – $20*
Cat, Leopard, 7"   /R-631 .... *25 – 30*

Dolphin, 7¹/₂" /R-512 . . . . *$25 – $30*
Elephant (3), 8¹/₄" /R-625 . . . . *25 – 30*
Horse Head, 7" /R-685 . . . . *25 – 30*
Polar Bear, 7¹/₂ /R-664 . . . . *25 – 30*
Turtle, 9¹/₄" /R-684 . . . . *25 – 30*

FIGURES

Bird, Parrot/Macaw, 14" /R-180 . . . . *$35 – $45*
Bird, Pouter Pigeon, 7" /R-233 . . . . *20 – 25*
Bird, Pouter Pigeon, 7¹/₂" /R-108 . . . . *20 – 25*
Buddha, 10¹/₂" /R-694 . . . . *35 – 40*
Cat, Black Panther, 18" /R-683 . . . . *50 – 60*
Cat, Black Panther, 24" /R-495 . . . . *85 – 95*
Cat, Egyptian, tall /R-758 . . . . *85 – 95*
Cat, Egyptian, head down, 6¹/₂" /R-493 . . . . *15 – 18*
Cat, Egyptian, head up, 7¹/₂" /R-494 . . . . *18 – 22*
Cat, sitting, 6" /R-898 . . . . *20 – 25*
Cat, sleeping, 7" /R-896 . . . . *20 – 25*
Cat, standing, 7" /R-897 . . . . *20 – 25*
Cat, Tiger, 11" /R-314 . . . . *30 – 35*
Cat, Tigress, 8" /R-313 . . . . *25 – 30*
Cowboy on Bucking Horse, 13" /R-424 . . . . *90 – 110*
Deer, Does (2), bust, 14¹/₂" /R-624 . . . . *25 – 30*
Deer, Fawn, kneeling, 7¹/₂" /R-413 . . . . *12 – 15*

Giraffe and young figure /1301.

Deer, Fawn, standing, 11½"   /R-412 .... *$15 – $18*
Deer, Stag, resting, 14½"   /R-880.................................. *35 – 40*
Dog, Cocker Pup, begging, 4"   /R-779 .... *12 – 15*
Dog, Cocker Pup, rolling, 6"   /R-778 .... *12 – 15*
Dog, Cocker Pup, sleeping, 6"   /R-776............................... *12 – 15*
Dog, Cocker Pup, standing, 4¾"   /R-777 .... *12 – 15*
Dog, Collie   /R-734.. *50 – 60*
Dog, Dachshund, 14½"   /R-736 .... *50 – 60*
Dog, Miss Peke   /R-781 .... *22 – 25*
Dog, Mister Scot   /R-780 .... *22 – 25*
Dog, Russian Wolfhound, head down, 7"   /R-318 .... *22 – 25*
Dog, Russian Wolfhound, head up, 7"   /R-319...................... *22 – 25*
Dog, Shetland Puppies (3)   /R-782 .... *25 – 30*
Ducks (3), wings down, 11"   /R-237 .... *25 – 30*
Elephant, 5"   /R-785 .... *25 – 30*
Elephant, 9"   /R-539 .... *50 – 60*
Fish (3), noses down, 10"   /R-157A................................. *45 – 55*
Garden Girl, 14"   /R-1179 .... *40 – 45*
Giraffe (2), 15"   /R-218 .... *85 – 95*
Giraffe and Young (bust)   /R-740.................................. *30 – 35*
Giraffe and Young, 13½"   /R-1301................................. *70 – 80*
Girl, Gypsy, 17½"   /R-1224.. *50 – 60*
Girl w/2 bowls, 13"   /R-1225 .... *40 – 45*
Hen, 4"   /R-401... *15 – 18*
Horse, dappled, 6"   /R-402.. *18 – 20*
Horse, 7"   /R-103 .... *18 – 20*
Horse, 13"   /R-415 .... *45 – 55*
Horse, racing, 9"   /R-1130 .... *30 – 35*
Horse, racing (2), 10"   /R-408 .... *55 – 65*
Horse, Mare and Foal, standing, 13½"   /R-451 .... *50 – 55*
Horse and Colt (bust)   /R-739.................................... *25 – 30*
Indian on Horse   /R-721 .... *60 – 70*
Little Brother, 11½"   /R-1254..................................... *25 – 30*
Little Sister, 11½"   /R-1253...................................... *25 – 30*
Man, Chinese Musician, 11"   /R-711 .... *22 – 25*
Man, Peasant, 17"   /R-382 .... *40 – 50*
Mermaid on Sailfish, 20"   /R-1178................................. *125 – 145*
Neptune on Sailfish, 20"   /R-1177................................. *125 – 145*
Nude, 14"   /R-181... *40 – 45*
Pheasant Cock, 6"   /R-165 .... *18 – 22*
Pheasant Hen, 6"   /R-164 .... *12 – 15*
Polar Bear, standing, 5½"   /R-376B .... *22 – 25*
Polar Bear, 7"   /R-375B... *25 – 30*
Polar Bear, 16"   /R-702... *55 – 65*
Polar Bear Cub, sitting, 3"   /R-375A.............................. *12 – 15*
Polar Bear Cub, standing, 2½"   /R-376A........................... *12 – 15*
Prospector, large   /R-722.. *40 – 50*
Prospector w/Burros, 11½"   /R-479 .... *50 – 60*
Rooster, 5"   /R-400... *15 – 18*

FLOWER FROGS

Bird, 7"   /R-820 .... *$18 – $22*
Bird, flying, 17½"   /R-125 .... *65 – 75*
Birds (2), 11"   /R-359.. *20 – 25*
Birds (3), on branch, 7"   /R-361................................... *18 – 20*
Deer, standing, 11½"   /R-104...................................... *18 – 22*
Deer, Stag   /R-772 .... *18 – 20*
Fish, Tropical (2), 11"   /R-360 .... *30 – 35*
Fish, Trout, leaping, 7"   /R-169B .... *20 – 25*
Fish (3), noses down, 12½"   /R-157B .... *40 – 45*
Jockey   /R-788 .... *35 – 40*
Nude, sitting, 6"   /R-189... *18 – 22*
Nude on Fish, 10"   /R-363... *45 – 50*
Nude w/Seal, 13"   /R-364.. *40 – 45*

LEAVES

Banana, 13"   /R-909... *$12 – $15*
Banana, 18"   /R-910... *18 – 20*
Elephant Ear, 11"   /R-916... *10 – 12*
Elephant Ear, 13"   /R-915... *12 – 15*
Lily, 11"   /R-908... *10 – 12*
Tropical, 10"   /R-914... *10 – 12*
Tropical, 14"   /R-913... *12 – 15*
Wine, 10"   /R-911... *10 – 12*
Wine, 15"   /R-912... *12 – 15*

MISCELLANY

Birdhouse, w/2 birds, 9½"   /R-287 .... *$18 – $22*
Fish bowl stand, Mermaid, 11½"   /R-656............................ *25 – 30*
Pitcher, Fish, 9"   /R-595... *30 – 35*
Wall Pocket, Grape Vine   /R-745 .... *20 – 25*
Wall Pocket, Rocking Horse   /724.................................. *20 – 25*

PLANTERS

Cat, Leopard   /R-760 .... *$25 – $30*
Deer, Fawn, 17"   /R-1351.. *20 – 25*
Donkey Cart, 11¼"   /R-754... *12 – 15*
Elephant, 10½"   /R-563.. *25 – 30*
Fish, 8½"   /R-752 .... *18 – 20*
Fish, large   /R-719 .... *25 – 30*
Gazelle, 14"   /R-869.. *25 – 30*
Gondolier, 19½"   /R-657... *25 – 30*
Horse, racing (2), 18"   /R-883 .... *30 – 35*
Horse, Colt, 14"   /R-875.. *25 – 30*
Turtle, 11"   /R-834... *15 – 18*

TABLE LAMPS

Some lamps are also planters; these are noted in parentheses. Expect to pay about 30% more for lamps with original shades.

Acanthus Leaf /5349... *$32 – $35*
Bison, bird finial /5171 .... *70 – 80*
Cabbage Rose, 24" .... *28 – 32*
Cat, Leopard on rock... *70 – 80*
Cowboy on horse .... *90 – 100*
Deer, Fawns (2) /5195.. *35 – 38*
Deer, Fawn (planter), 18½"....................................... *12 – 15*
Deer, running.. *50 – 60*
Duck, flying... *50 – 60*
Fighting cock .... *50 – 55*
Fish, Flying /5351 .... *55 – 65*
Fish on Wave .... *60 – 65*
Horse Head, horse head finial.................................... *55 – 60*
Horses, racing (2) .... *70 – 80*
Horses, mare and foal .... *55 – 60*
Indian on horse... *90 – 100*
Mermaid /5398... *55 – 60*
Plume (3) /5292... *32 – 35*
Plume, square base /5024 .... *32 – 35*

TV LAMPS

Bronco... *$25 – $30*
Comedy and Tragedy.. *25 – 30*
Dog, Cocker... *25 – 30*
Fish, angel (2) .... *30 – 35*
Gazelle, 10½" .... *25 – 30*
Gazelle, leaping.. *25 – 30*
Greyhound (planter), 13" /6202 .... *25 – 30*
Horse, colt... *25 – 30*
Horses, racing (2) .... *30 – 35*
Panther .... *25 – 30*
Peacock .... *25 – 30*

VASES

Angel, 7" /R-1141 .... *$20 – $22*
Ballet, female, 13½" /R-1216 .... *18 – 20*
Ballet, male, 13½" /R-1215..................................... *18 – 20*
Bird, Peacock, 10" /R-453 .... *25 – 28*
Bird, Peacock, all styles /R-31 .... *25 – 28*
Bird, Sea Gulls (3), wings up, 16" /R-208 .... *60 – 70*
Bird of Paradise, 12¾" /R-186.................................. *25 – 28*
Butterfly, 7½" /R-1221 .... *15 – 18*
Cornucopia, double, 16" /R-246................................. *15 – 18*

Cornucopia, double shell, 7¹/₂"   /R-322 . . . . *$18 – $20*
Cornucopia w/nude, 8"   /R-426 . . . . *15 – 18*
Deer, running, 15"   /R-706 . . . . *15 – 18*
Deer, standing, 15"   /R-707 . . . . *15 – 18*
Duck, flying, 9"   /R-903 . . . . *20 – 22*
Duck, flying, 14"   /R-1465 . . . . *22 – 25*
Duck, setting, 9"   /R-904 . . . . *20 – 22*
Fan, 9¹/₂"   /R-714 . . . . *12 – 15*
Feather, 8¹/₂"   /R-723 . . . . *12 – 15*
Fish, 6¹/₂"   /R-1136 . . . . *18 – 20*
Fish, Sailfish, 9"   /R-271 . . . . *18 – 20*
Fish, Swordfish, 6"   /R-901 . . . . *18 – 20*
Fish, Trout, 7"   /R-284 . . . . *25 – 28*
Fish/Waves   /R-742 . . . . *20 – 22*
Gazelle, 13"   /R-115 . . . . *15 – 18*
Goose Quills, 17¹/₂"   /R-888 . . . . *15 – 18*
Leaf, single, 12¹/₂"   /R-138 . . . . *15 – 18*
Leaf, Elm, 12"   /R-320 . . . . *15 – 18*
Pegasus, bust, 11¹/₄"   /R-393 . . . . *45 – 50*
Peter Pan, 10"   /R-917 . . . . *20 – 22*
Pinecone, 9"   /R-1189 . . . . *12 – 15*
Pinecone, 12"   /R-1190 . . . . *15 – 18*
Seashell, 11"   /R-701 . . . . *18 – 20*
Shell, Conch, 8"   /R-321 . . . . *18 – 20*

Pegasus vase /393.

Swan, 8" /R-430.. *$15 – $18*
Swan, 13" /R-856.. *25 – 28*
Swan, both styles, 16" /R-36 .... *35 – 40*
Tulip, 8" /R-646... *12 – 15*

HALL CHINA COMPANY

East Liverpool, Ohio

Robert Hall had been a director of the East Liverpool Pottery Company. In 1901 that company and four others attempted a merger that did not succeed. In 1903 he bought the pottery, renamed it the Hall China Company, and continued making the semiporcelain dinnerware and toilet ware the old company had produced.

He died in 1904, and his son began a search for a one-fire process (body and glaze fired at the same time) for making vitrified china. Long experimentation paid off in 1911, and Hall still makes one-fire vitrified hotel and restaurant ware.

In 1920 the first gold-decorated teapots were introduced for retail sale and are now almost synonymous with the Hall name. In 1931 decal-decorated kitchenware and dinnerware, both for premium sales and retail, were introduced. Refrigerator ware, especially the items given away with a new refrigerator, date to the late 1930s and early 1940s. Hall is still going strong today.

Hall is unique among the potteries that made semiporcelain or vitreous ware in that almost all its lines are collectible: teapots, decal-decorated ware (especially Autumn Leaf), refrigerator ware, and kitchenware.

NOTE Hall reissued many of its pieces, including some classic designs, in its Americana line, which was made for several years in the 1980s. They were all decorated in solid colors (none of the decals or gold decorations were used) and were generally marked with the H/4 mark. Beside the mark, another way to identify them are the colors and color combinations that were new to this line. Now that Americana has been discontinued, some of these pieces are becoming collectible.

See Duke and see Easley in Bibliography.

MARKS   Mark 1 (H/2) was used in the 1920s. Mark 2 (H/3) was used from ca. 1930. Mark 3 (H/4) has been supplanting Mark 2 since 1972; both are still in use. Mark 4 (HSQK) dates to 1932 and was used on kitchenware only. Mark 5 (HD) or a variant is found on dinnerware. Abbreviations after each one are the codes collectors use in mail-order advertisements.

Mark 1 (H/2)

Mark 2 (H/3)

Mark 3 (H/4)

Mark 4 (HSQK)

Mark 5 (HD)

BEER SETS

Barrel mug, solid-color	$8 – $10
Flagon mug, decal	45 – 50
Flagon mug, solid-color	10 – 12
Pretzel jar, decal	175 – 200
Tankard jug, decal	125 – 150
Tankard jug, solid-color	50 – 75

CHILDREN'S WARE

Creamer, Philadelphia, Bo-Peep	$45 – $50
Divided dish, round, w/chick stopper, Bo-Peep, 8"	150 – 175
Divided dish, square, Children's Zoo	150 – 175
Mug, Little Hunter, 5-ounce	65 – 75

DINNERWARE / KITCHENWARE: DECAL-DECORATED

These decal-decorated lines are among the most popular of Hall China's products. They were available retail as well as premiums for companies such as Best Tea, Cook Coffee, Great American Tea, Standard Coffee, and the best known, Jewel Tea, for which Hall made Autumn Leaf, one of the best-selling U.S. dinnerware lines of all time.

AUTUMN LEAF

Although production of Autumn Leaf for the Jewel Tea Company ceased around 1978, the Hall China Company continues to manufacture special items for the National Autumn Leaf Collectors Club (see Clubs); these are becoming collectible in their own right, and some pieces are listed below.

Aladdin teapot, 7-cup	*$45 – $55*
Ball jug, #3	*40 – 45*
Bud vase	*175 – 195*
Butter, ¼-pound	*175 – 225*
Butter, MJ, ¼-pound	*400 – 600*
Butter, Hallcraft, ¼-pound	*1200 +*
Butter, 1-pound	*400*
Cake plate	*18*
Candy dish on metal base	*400 – 425*
Casper shakers, pair	*18 – 25*
Clock, battery	*200 – 300*
Clock, electric	*400 – 500*
Conic mug	*50 – 60*
Flute French baker, 10-ounce, 4½"	*8 – 10*
Flute French baker, 10-ounce, 4¾"	*35 – 40*
Flute French baker, 2-pint	*125 – 150*
Flute French baker, 3-pint	*18 – 22*
Ft. Pitt baker	*125 – 150*
Irish coffee mug	*90 – 100*
Jordan drip coffee, 5-cup	*225 – 275*
J-Sunshine coffee pot, 8-cup	*35 – 40*
J-Sunshine coffee pot, 9-cup	*40 – 50*
J-Sunshine creamer	*35*
J-Sunshine jug	*20 – 24*
J-Sunshine sugar	*35 – 45*
J-Sunshine teapot	*45 – 55*
Marmalade, 3-piece	*60 – 75*
MaryLou stack set	*70 – 75*
MJ electric coffee maker	*295*
Mustard, 3-piece	*60 – 75*
New England bean pot, 1 handle	*900 +*

Ruffled-D
cream soup

Jewel candy dish

Clock

Fort Pitt baker

Jordan
drip coffee

MaryLou
stack set

St. Denis
cup & saucer

Tootsie
covered drip

M. J.
electric percolator

Round warmer

Tootsie
casserole

Zeisel bean pot
(cookie jar)

Ruffled-D
pickle dish

Irish coffee mug

Conic mug

Ruffled-D gravy

Ruffled-D covered
oval vegetable

Ruffled-D
three-tier tidbit

Autumn Leaf patterns

New England bean pot, 2 handles .... *$150 – $175*
Newport teapot, old, 7-cup .... *175 – 195*
Newport teapot, new, 7-cup *175*
Pie baker .... *22 – 24*
Range shaker, pair... *20 – 25*
Ruffled-D line
   Bowl, soup, 8¹/₂..................................... *12 – 16*
   Bowl, vegetable, divided .... *65 – 75*
   Bowl, vegetable, oval, covered...................... *40 – 50*
   Bowl, vegetable, round.............................. *70 – 80*
   Bowl, vegetable, oval .... *18 – 24*
   Cream soup .... *24 – 30*
   Creamer... *15 – 18*
   Cup... *5 – 8*
   Dish, 5¹/₂" *4*
   Dish, 6¹/₂" .... *8 – 10*
   Gravy .... *18 – 24*
   Pickle dish .... *20 – 25*
   Plate, 6" .... *4 – 6*
   Plate, 7¹/₄".. *4 – 6*
   Plate, 8" .... *9 – 12*
   Plate, 9" .... *7 – 12*
   Plate, 10" .... *10 – 15*
   Platter, oval, 11¹/₂".............................. *18 – 22*
   Platter, oval, 13¹/₂".............................. *18 – 25*
   Saucer... *2 – 3*
   Sugar .... *15 – 18*
   Tidbit, 3-tier..................................... *95 – 115*
Salad bowl.. *20 – 24*
St. Denis cup .... *20 – 25*
St. Denis saucer... *4 – 6*
Sunshine bowl, #1 (custard) .... *5 – 8*
Sunshine bowl, #3 .... *10*
Sunshine bowl, #4 .... *15*
Sunshine bowl, #5 .... *20*
Tootsie casserole .... *38 – 45*
Tootsie cookie jar .... *175 – 195*
Tootsie covered drip... *20 – 25*
Warmer base, oval *125*
Warmer base, round *100*
Zeisel "cookie jar" .... *150 – 175*

One of a Kind or Nearly

Bingo butter... *$2500 +*
Boston teapot, 2-cup .... *ND*
Butter, bud-ray lid, 1-pound .... *2700 +*
Cake server .... *500 +*
Candle holder, ball shape .... *ND*

Candle holder, ruffled base . . . . $225 +
Candy dish, covered. . . . . ND
Colonial shaker . . . . ND
Fork . . . . ND
Morning Set creamer . . . . ND
Morning Set sugar. . . . . ND
Morning Set teapot . . . . ND
Saf-handle batter bowl . . . . 2000 +
Sunshine Cereal Set canister, Tea . . . . ND
Sunshine Cereal Set canister, Sugar. . . . . ND
Teapot, Sunshine/1978 (106 made) . . . . ND
Vase, square . . . . ND
Vase, round . . . . ND

Cloth

Curt-towel . . . . $40 – $45
Dish towel, cotton, 16" × 33" 40
Tablecloth, plastic, 54" × 54" . . . . 100 – 150
Tablecloth, plastic, 54" × 72" . . . . 100 – 150
Tablecloth, sailcloth, 54" × 54" . . . . 60 – 75
Tablecloth, sailcloth, 54" × 72" . . . . 60 – 75
Tablecloth/napkin set, 56" × 81" . . . . 200 +

Glass

Douglas
  Hurricane lamp. . . . . $200 +
  Percolator/Carafe w/warmer base . . . . 150 – 200
  Serving sauce dish. 150
Dripper . . . . ND
Goblet, footed, 10½-ounce. . . . . 45 – 55
Royal Glass-Bake Ovenware
  Bowl set, 4-piece . . . . 75 – 100
  Casserole, oval, 1-quart 35
  Casserole, round, 2-quart 35
  Vegetable, divided 35
Sherbet, footed, 6½-ounce. . . . . 40 – 45
Tumbler, clear, 15-ounce. . . . . 30 – 35
Tumbler, frosted, 9-ounce . . . . 20 – 24
Tumbler, frosted, 14-ounce . . . . 12 – 14

Metal

Bread box. . . . . $100 – $200
Cake safe, allover decoration. . . . . 40 – 50
Cake safe, side decoration . . . . 30 – 45
Canister, round, 6" . . . . 10 – 30
Canister, round, 7" . . . . 10 – 30
Canister, round, 8¼" . . . . 10 – 30
Canister, square, set of 4 . . . . 90 +

Canister, round, white plastic lid................................. *$12 – $15*
Canister set, round w/coppertone lid................................. *150 +*
Cleanser can .... *1000 +*
Coffee dispenser .... *150 – 200*
Flour sifter................................. *200 +*
Fruitcake tin, 7" diameter
    Tan................................. *3 – 8*
    White .... *5 – 10*
Goldentone base .... *20 – 30*
Kitchen chair................................. *ND*
Silverplate flatware
    Eating pieces, each................................. *25*
    Serving pieces, each................................. *35*
Stainless steel flatware
    Eating pieces, each................................. *15 – 20*
    Serving pieces, each................................. *25 – 35*
Thermos................................. *150 +*
Tray, oval................................. *40 – 75*
Tray, rectangular .... *90 – 110*
Wastebasket................................. *300 +*

Plastic

Plastic covers
    Bowls, set................................. *$45 – $55*
    Food mixer .... *30 – 40*
    Toaster................................. *30 – 40*

Melmac (1959–1962) The cup, sugar, creamer, soup and vegetable bowl were not decorated.

    Creamer *$10*
    Cup *6*
    Dinner, 10"................................. *8 – 10*
    Platter, 14"................................. *35 – 40*
    Salad, 7"................................. *7 – 8*
    Saucer, 6"................................. *1 – 2*
    Sugar *10*
Shelf lining, 25-ft roll .... *50 – 75*

Miscellany

Coaster .... *$5 – $8*
Fatigue mat, 18" × 30"................................. *ND*
Hot pad, oval................................. *8 – 15*
Hot pad, round .... *8 – 15*
Pinochle deck .... *125 – 140*
Place mat................................. *15 – 25*
Tray, rectangular, wood and glass................................. *100 – 150*

National Autumn Leaf Collector's Club

These pieces are clearly marked as club issues. Prices have begun to rise shortly after each issue.

Ball jug, #1 (1992) . . . . *$100 – $125*
Candle holder, ring handle (1991) . . . . *90 – 100*
Candle holders, pair (1989). *225*
Casserole, large (1991) *150*
Chocolate tumbler, set of four (1992) . . . . *80 – 110*
Donut jug (1991) . . . . *70 – 80*
Donut teapot (1993) . . . . *150 – 175*
Edgewater vase (1987) . . . . *225 – 250*
French teapot (1992). . . . . *100 – 125*
New York teapot (1984) . . . . *500 +*
Oyster cup (1992) . . . . *175 – 200*
Packet sugar, rectangular (1990). . . . . *60 – 70*
Philadelphia teapot, sugar and creamer (1990) . . . . *175 – 225*
Punch bowl set (bowl and 12 cups) (1993) . . . . *300 – 400*
Solo teapot (1991) . . . . *70 – 80*
Tea-for-Two, 3-piece set (1990) . . . . *175 – 200*

BLUE BLOSSOM / BLUE GARDEN   (1939)

Silk-screened decal on Cobalt blue glaze. According to Hall, this was the first
time that cobalt blue had been successfully introduced in vitrified cooking
ware. No piece is easy to find, though the Saf-handle casserole #4 turns up with
a little more frequency than the other pieces.

PRICING   Prices are still rising strongly on this very popular line. The "B"
and/or "G" that follows each entry indicates the decoration the piece has been
found in. Price given is for either decoration.

Airflow teapot (B/G) . . . . *$375 +*
Aladdin teapot (G) . . . . *375 +*
Automobile teapot (G)] . . . . *ND*
Ball jug, #1 (B/G). . . . . *150 – 175*

*Blue Blossom Streamline teapot, Autumn Leaf bud vase, and Crocus
Bingo water bottle.*

Ball jug, #2 (B/G). . . . . *$150 – $175*
Ball jug, #3 (B/G). . . . . *125 – 135*
Ball jug, #4 (B/G). . . . . *125 – 135*
Banded batter bowl (B) . . . . *150 – 160*
Banded casserole (B). . . . . *85 – 95*
Banded cookie jar (B/G). . . . . *225 – 250*
Banded jug, 1¹/₂-pint (B/G) . . . . *65 – 75*
Banded jug, 2-quart (B/G). . . . . *85 – 95*
Banded shaker, each (B). . . . . *45 – 50*
Banded syrup (B) . . . . *150 – 165*
Big Lip bowl, 6" (B/G) . . . . *30 – 35*
Big Lip bowl, 7¹/₂" (B/G) . . . . *40 – 45*
Big Lip bowl, 8⁵/₈" (B/G) . . . . *50 – 55*
Big Lip casserole, knob handle, 2-quart (B/G) . . . . *75 – 85*
Big Lip casserole, knob handle, 2¹/₂-quart (B). . . . . *80 – 90*
Big Lip covered drip (B/G). . . . . *60 – 70*
Big Lip custard (B/G). . . . . *25 – 30*
Bingo butter (B/G) . . . . *300 +*
Bingo leftover (B/G) . . . . *200 – 225*
Bingo water bottle (B/G). . . . . *750 +*
Cereal Set canister (B/G) . . . . *175 – 200*
Cereal Set shaker, each (B/G). . . . . *60 – 75*
Doughnut jug (B/G) . . . . *300 +*
1188 drip (B/G) . . . . *45 – 60*
French stirred egg dish (B) . . . . *50 – 60*
Handled shaker, salt/pepper, each (B/G) . . . . *40 – 50*
Handled shaker, sugar/flour, each. . . . . *60 – 75*
Hook Cover teapot (B) . . . . *275 – 300*
Loop-handle jug (B/G) . . . . *140 – 160*
Loop-handle leftover (B/G) . . . . *120 – 135*
Morning Set creamer (B/G) . . . . *35 – 50*
Morning Set sugar (B/G) . . . . *50 – 65*
Morning Set teapot (B/G). . . . . *250 – 275*
New England bean pot, #4 (B/G) . . . . *150 – 175*
New York creamer (B/G) . . . . *60 – 75*
New York sugar (B/G) . . . . *75 – 85*
New York teapot, 6-cup (G) . . . . *275 – 300*
New York, 10- or 12-cup (B). . . . . *285 – 325*
100 casserole, oval, w/handle (B) . . . . *75 – 85*
103 casserole, oval, w/handle (B) . . . . *100 – 125*
Saf-handle batter bowl (B/G). . . . . *225 – 250*
Saf-handle casserole, #1 (B/G) . . . . *65 – 75*
Saf-handle casserole, #4 (B/G)
    w/decorated lid . . . . *45 – 50*
    w/plain lid . . . . *45 – 50*
Saf-handle coffee server (B/G). . . . . *300 – 350*
Saf-handle cookie jar (B/G). . . . . *250 – 300*
Saf-handle syrup (B/G). . . . . *150 – 175*

Saf-handle teapot, 6-cup (B/G).. $300 – $350
68 casserole, round, no handle (G).. 65 – 75
76 casserole, round, no handle (B).. 65 – 75
77 casserole, round, no handle (B).. 65 – 75
691 drip coffee pot (B) .... 350 – 375
Streamline teapot, 6-cup (B/G).. 300 – 350
Sunshine bowl, #2 (G).. 35 – 40
Sunshine bowl, #3 (G).. 40 – 45
Sunshine bowl, #4 (G).. 45 – 50
Sunshine bowl, #5 (G).. 50 – 60
Sunshine bowl, #6 (G).. 60 – 75

BLUE BOUQUET

In general, add 10% to Taverne prices.

CROCUS

Of all the decals on an ivory background, this is the most popular.

Aladdin teapot, 6-cup .... $350 +
Art Deco creamer .... 30 – 35
Art Deco sugar .... 40 – 45
Ball jug, #3.. 135 – 150
Banded coffee pot .... 50 – 65
Banded shaker, each .... 45 – 50
Beverage mug .... 75 – 85
Big Lip soup tureen .... 350 +
Bingo butter.. 500 +
Bingo leftover .... 250 – 300
Bingo water bottle, 7".. 750 +
Boston teapot, 6-cup .... 200 – 275
Cake plate .... 30 – 35
Classic jug .... 150 – 175
Clover soup tureen .... 350 +
Colonial casserole .... 50 – 55
Colonial creamer.. 25 – 30
Colonial sugar .... 40 – 45
Colonial teapot, 6-cup .... 60 – 70
Crest Drip-o-lator .... 60 – 70
Dinnerware, D-line
   Bowl, soup, 8½" .... 30 – 35
   Bowl, vegetable, round, 9⅛" .... 35 – 40
   Bowl, vegetable, oval, 10¼".. 30 – 35
   Cup.. 20 – 22
   Dish, 5⅝ .... 7 – 8
   Dish, 6" .... 20 – 22
   Gravy .... 30 – 40
   Plate, 6⅛" .... 10 – 12

Plate, 7¼" . . . . *$8 – $10*
Plate, 8¼" . . . . *10 – 12*
Plate, 9⅛" . . . . *16 – 18*
Plate, 10¼" . . . . *45 – 50*
Platter, small, 11¼" . . . . *25 – 30*
Platter, large, 13¼" . . . . *30 – 35*
Saucer . . . . *4 – 5*
Tidbit server . . . . *90 – 110*
Doughnut teapot . . . . *ND*
Egg drop shaker, each . . . . *25 – 30*
1188 open drip . . . . *45 – 50*
Flagon mug, 10-ounce . . . . *75 – 80*
Flute French baker . . . . *25 – 35*
Handled shaker, salt/pepper . . . . *30 – 35*
Handled shaker, sugar/flour . . . . *50 – 55*
Jordan drip coffee pot . . . . *350 +*
J-Sunshine jug . . . . *65 – 75*
Kadota drip coffee pot . . . . *300 – 350*
MaryLou creamer . . . . *25 – 30*
MaryLou leftover, rectangular . . . . *55 – 60*
MaryLou leftover, square . . . . *60 – 75*
MaryLou sugar . . . . *35 – 40*
Melody teapot . . . . *ND*
Meltdown coffee pot . . . . *65 – 75*
  w/aluminum drip, embossed Crocus . . . . *80 – 95*
Meltdown creamer . . . . *35 – 45*
Meltdown sugar . . . . *50 – 55*
New England bean pot, #4 . . . . *150 – 165*
New England bean pot, #5 . . . . *150 – 165*
New York creamer . . . . *35 – 40*
New York sugar . . . . *45 – 50*
New York teapot, 2-cup . . . . *150 – 165*
New York teapot, 6-cup . . . . *140 – 150*
New York teapot, 8-cup . . . . *165 – 175*
New York teapot, 12-cup . . . . *175 – 185*
Pie baker . . . . *30 – 40*
Pretzel jar . . . . *110 – 150*
Salad bowl . . . . *25 – 30*
St. Denis cup . . . . *35 – 45*
St. Denis saucer . . . . *15 – 25*
Step-down coffee pot, small . . . . *55 – 65*
  w/decal-decorated china drip . . . . *ND*
  w/metal drip . . . . *60 – 70*
  w/metal drip embossed w/Crocus . . . . *75 – 85*
Step-down coffee pot, large . . . . *60 – 70*
Streamline teapot . . . . *375 +*
Sunshine bowl, #1 . . . . *50*
Sunshine bowl, #2 . . . . *25 – 35*

Sunshine bowl, #3	$15 – $20
Sunshine bowl, #4	20 – 22
Sunshine bowl, #5	22 – 25
Sunshine casserole	40 – 55
Sunshine cereal set canister	ND
Sunshine covered drip	35 – 40
Sunshine jug, #4, w/lid	120 – 135
Sunshine jug, #5, w/lid	120 – 135

FANTASY

In general, use Blue Blossom prices.

#488

In general, use Crocus prices.

HALLCRAFT

Both of these lines were designed by Eva Zeisel ca. late 1940s or early 1950s and distributed by Midhurst China.

Century

Ashtray	$5 – $7
Bowl, salad	12 – 15
Bowl, soup/cereal, 8"	6 – 8

Meadow Flower Banded cookie jar, Fantasy Sunshine casserole, and #488 Sunshine teapot.

Bowl, vegetable, 10½"..*$12 – $15*
Bowl, vegetable dish, double...................................*15 – 20*
Butter dish ....*25 – 30*
Casserole (covered dish), 2-quart ....*20 – 25*
Creamer ....*8 – 10*
Cup ....*4 – 5*
Dish, fruit, 5¾" ....*4 – 5*
Gravy..*12 – 14*
Jug, 1¼-quart..*10 – 15*
Ladle ....*15 – 25*
Plate, 6"...*2 – 3*
Plate, 8"...*4 – 5*
Plate, 10¼"...*6 – 8*
Platter, 13¾"...*12 – 15*
Platter, 15" ....*15 – 20*
Relish..*18 – 20*
Saucer ....*1 – 2*
Shaker ....*8 – 10*
Sugar ....*12 – 15*
Teapot, 6-cup..*125 – 150*

Tomorrow's Classic

Prices are for Bouquet, less for other patterns.

Ashtray ....*$10 – $12*
Baker, 11½-ounce...*12 – 15*
Bowl, coupe soup, 9"...*10 – 12*
Bowl, fruit, footed ....*45 – 55*
Bowl, onion soup, covered....................................*35 – 45*
Bowl, salad, 14½" ....*30 – 35*
Bowl, vegetable dish, 8¾" ....*15 – 20*
Butter dish ....*75 – 90*
Candlestick, short, ½" high....................................*25 – 35*
Candlestick, tall, 8" high.......................................*35 – 45*
Casserole (covered dish), 1¼-quart.........................*55 – 65*
Casserole (covered dish), 2-quart ....*65 – 75*
Celery dish ....*18 – 20*
Coffee pot, 6-cup...*90 – 110*
Creamer ....*8 – 10*
Creamer, AD..*8 – 10*
Cruet, 1-pint ....*25 – 35*
Cup ....*8 – 10*
Cup, AD..*10 – 12*
Dish, cereal, 6"..*4 – 5*
Dish, fruit, 5¾" ....*4 – 5*
Eggcup, double ....*15 – 18*
Gravy..*35 – 45*
Jug, small, 1¼-quart ....*25 – 35*
Jug, large, 3-quart ....*35 – 45*

Ladle (for gravy) . . . . *$20 – $25*
Marmite, 12-ounce . . . . *30 – 35*
Plate, 6" . . . . *3 – 4*
Plate, 8" . . . . *7 – 9*
Plate, 11" . . . . *12 – 15*
Platter, 12¼" . . . . *25 – 30*
Platter, 15" . . . . *30 – 35*
Platter, 17" . . . . *35 – 45*
Saucer . . . . *2 – 3*
Saucer,   AD . . . . *2 – 3*
Shaker, each . . . . *8 – 10*
Sugar . . . . *12 – 15*
Sugar,   AD . . . . *8 – 10*
Teapot, 6-cup. . . . . *125 – 150*
Vase, 8¾" high. . . . . *35 – 45*

MEADOW FLOWER

In general, use Blue Blossom prices.

PINK MORNING GLORY

In general, add 25% to Taverne prices.

POPPY   (1933)

(Called Orange Poppy by some collectors to distinguish it from Red Poppy.)
Available through the 1950s from the Great American Tea Company.

Ball jug, #3 . . . . *$85 – $100*
Bellevue coffee pot . . . . *400 +*
Bellevue teapot . . . . *400 +*
Boston teapot . . . . *225 – 250*
Cake plate . . . . *18 – 20*
Cake server . . . . *ND*
Dinnerware, C-line
   Bowl, soup, 8½" . . . . *30 – 35*
   Bowl, vegetable, round, 9⅛" . . . . *35 – 40*
   Cup . . . . *30 – 35*
   Dish, 5⅝" . . . . *8 – 10*
   Dish, 6" . . . . *15 – 18*
   Plate, 6⅛" . . . . *8 – 10*
   Plate, 7¼" . . . . *10 – 12*
   Plate, 9⅛" . . . . *20 – 22*
   Platter, oval, 11¼" . . . . *25 – 30*
   Platter, oval, 13¼" . . . . *30 – 35*
   Saucer . . . . *4 – 5*
Doughnut teapot . . . . *400 +*
Flute French baker . . . . *15 – 20*
Fork . . . . *ND*

Golden Key coffee pot. . . . . *$60 – $70*
Golden Key creamer. . . . . *25 – 30*
Golden Key sugar . . . . *25 – 30*
Handled shaker, each . . . . *15 – 20*
Loop-handle leftover. . . . . *65 – 75*
Melody teapot . . . . *325 – 350*
Mustard, 3-piece . . . . *70 – 75*
New England bean pot, #4 . . . . *100 – 110*
100 oval casserole . . . . *55 – 65*
101 oval casserole . . . . *75 – 80*
103 oval casserole . . . . *100 – 150*
Pie Baker . . . . *35 – 40*
Pretzel jar . . . . *75 – 100*
Salad bowl . . . . *18 – 20*
76 round casserole. . . . . *50 – 60*
S-Lid coffee pot . . . . *50 – 60*
Spoon . . . . *100 – 135*
Streamline teapot . . . . *275 – 300*
Sunshine bowl, #1 . . . . *8 – 10*
Sunshine bowl, #3 . . . . *10 – 15*
Sunshine bowl, #4 . . . . *15 – 20*
Sunshine bowl, #5 . . . . *20 – 25*
Sunshine bowl, #6 . . . . *30 – 40*
Sunshine bulge shaker, each. . . . . *45 – 50*
Sunshine casserole . . . . *45 – 55*
Sunshine Cereal Set canister . . . . *175 – 195*
Sunshine Cereal Set shaker . . . . *55 – 65*
Sunshine covered drip . . . . *20 – 25*
Sunshine jug, #4 . . . . *45 – 50*
Sunshine jug, #5 . . . . *20 – 25*
Windshield teapot . . . . *350 +*

POPPY AND WHEAT

In general, use Crocus prices.

RED POPPY

Available from the mid 1930s to the mid 1950s from the Grand Union Company. Note that the Aladdin teapot has a white background; all other pieces have an ivory background.

Aladdin teapot . . . . *$125 – $150*
Ball jug, #4 . . . . *75 – 80*
Cake Plate. . . . . *15 – 20*
Dinnerware, D-line
   Bowl, soup, 8½". . . . . *20 – 25*
   Bowl, vegetable, oval, 10½" . . . . *25 – 35*
   Bowl, vegetable, round, 9⅛ . . . . *25 – 35*

Cup	*$12 – $15*
Dish, 5⅝"	*4 – 5*
Dish, 6"	*10 – 12*
Gravy	*65 – 75*
Plate, 6¼"	*3 – 5*
Plate, 7¼"	*4 – 6*
Plate, 8¼"	*5 – 8*
Plate, 9⅛"	*10 – 12*
Plate, 10"	*55 – 70*
Platter, 11¼"	*20 – 25*
Platter, 13¼"	*25 – 30*
Saucer	*2 – 3*
Egg Drop shaker, each	*20 – 25*
1188 open drip	*35 – 45*
Flute French baker	*15 – 20*
Handled shaker, each	*10 – 15*
Marylou creamer	*10 – 15*
Marylou leftover, rectangular	*55 – 75*
Marylou leftover, square	*65 – 85*
Marylou sugar	*15 – 20*
New York teapot	*75 – 90*
Pie baker	*20 – 30*
Pretzel jar	*ND*
Rickson coffee	*40 – 50*
Rickson creamer	*10 – 15*
Rickson milk jug	*45 – 55*
Rickson sugar	*15 – 20*
Salad bowl	*12 – 15*
Sunshine bowl, #1 (custard)	*16*
Sunshine bowl, #3	*12 – 15*
Sunshine bowl, #4	*15 – 18*
Sunshine bowl, #5	*18 – 22*
Sunshine casserole	*25 – 30*
Sunshine covered drip	*15 – 20*
Sunshine jug, #5	*15 – 20*

ROSE PARADE

Usually has a pink flower decal; occasionally you'll find a blue or a pink and yellow flower decal.

PRICING   Add 10% for hard-to-find decals.

Flute French baker	*$60 – $70*
Jordan drip coffee pot	*200 – 250*
Salad bowl	*30 – 40*
Sani-Grid bowl, 6⅛"	*12 – 15*
Sani-Grid bowl, 7½"	*15 – 18*
Sani-Grid bowl, 8⅞"	*22 – 25*
Sani-Grid creamer	*18 – 20*

Sani-Grid jug, small . . . . *$22 – $25*
Sani-Grid jug, medium . . . . *30 – 35*
Sani-Grid jug, large . . . . *35 – 40*
Sani-Grid shaker, each . . . . *15 – 18*
Sani-Grid sugar . . . . *18 – 20*
Sani-Grid teapot, 3-cup . . . . *50 – 60*
Sani-Grid teapot, 6-cup . . . . *50 – 60*
Straight-side bowl, #1 . . . . *20 – 22*
Straight-side bowl, #3 . . . . *12 – 15*
Straight-side bowl, #4 . . . . *18 – 20*
Straight-side bowl, #5 . . . . *22 – 25*
Tab-handle bean pot . . . . *60 – 70*
Tab-handle casserole . . . . *30 – 35*
Tab-handle covered drip . . . . *35 – 40*

TAVERNE

Taverne was a very popular pattern, some of it used as a premium for Hellick's Coffee in Pennsylvania. In addition to Hall China pieces, there is dinnerware made by Taylor, Smith & Taylor (which see) and a rolling pin made by Harker (see following). Matching glass and metal items are also available. Note: Do not confuse this with Crooksville's Silhouette pattern, which has a small dog at the foot of the table.

Ball jug, #3 . . . . *$150 – $160*
Banded Coffee pot, 9-cup . . . . *60 – 70*
Banded shaker, each . . . . *30 – 35*
Beverage mug . . . . *75 – 85*
Bobby berry . . . . *18 – 20*
Bobby nappy . . . . *25 – 35*
Classic jug . . . . *135 – 155*

Poppy & Wheat New England bean pot #3, Taverne coffeepot, and Poppy Doughnut teapot.

Colonial bowl, #1 (custard) .... *$15 – $22*
Colonial bowl, #3 .... *12 – 15*
Colonial bowl, #4 .... *15 – 20*
Colonial bowl, #5 .... *20 – 25*
Colonial casserole .... *40 – 60*
Colonial coffee pot, 9-cup .... *75 – 90*
Colonial covered drip .... *25 – 28*
Colonial creamer .... *20 – 22*
Colonial drip coffee .... *250 – 275*
Colonial jug, #2 .... *30 – 35*
Colonial jug, #3 .... *40 – 45*
Colonial shaker .... *20 – 25*
Colonial sugar .... *25 – 30*
Colonial teapot, 6-cup .... *75 – 95*
Dinnerware, D-line
   Bowl, soup, 8½" .... *20 – 25*
   Bowl, vegetable, oval, 10½" .... *30 – 35*
   Cup .... *15 – 20*
   Dish, 5⅝" .... *8 – 10*
   Dish, 6" .... *9 – 12*
   Plate, 6⅛" .... *5 – 7*
   Plate, 7¼" .... *8 – 10*
   Plate, 8¼" .... *12 – 15*
   Plate, 9⅛" .... *15 – 25*
   Plate, 10" .... *40 – 45*
   Platter, 11¼" .... *25 – 30*
   Platter, 13¼" .... *30 – 35*
   Saucer .... *3 – 4*
Egg drop shaker, each .... *18 – 20*
Flute French baker .... *15 – 20*
Handled shaker, each .... *45 – 50*
Kadota drip coffee pot .... *225 – 250*
MaryLou creamer .... *20 – 25*
MaryLou leftover, rectangular .... *50 – 55*
MaryLou leftover, square .... *65 – 75*
MaryLou sugar .... *25 – 30*
New England bean pot, #4 .... *125 – 150*
New York teapot, 6-cup .... *175 – 250*
Pie baker .... *40 – 50*
Pretzel jar .... *135 – 145*
Salad bowl .... *20 – 25*
St. Denis cup .... *35 – 45*
St. Denis saucer .... *15 – 20*
Streamline teapot, 6-cup .... *275 +*
Sunshine bowl, #3 .... *20 – 25*
Sunshine bowl, #4 .... *25 – 30*
Sunshine bowl, #5 .... *30 – 35*
Sunshine casserole .... *55 – 65*

Sunshine covered drip .... *$45 – $55*
Tea tile, round, 6" .... *100 +*

HARKER POTTERY

Rolling Pin .... *$155 – $175*

WILDFIRE

A premium for the Great American Tea Company, the body is white rather than the usual ivory.

Aladdin teapot	*$100 – $125*
Big Lip bowl, 6"	*12 – 15*
Big Lip bowl, 7½"	*15 – 20*
Big Lip bowl, 8⅝"	*20 – 25*
Big Lip casserole, sunken knob	*30 – 40*
Big Lip covered drip	*35 – 40*
Boston teapot, 6-cup	*150 – 175*
Cake plate	*20 – 22*
Dinnerware, D-line	
Bowl, soup, 8½"	*15 – 20*
Bowl, vegetable, oval, 10½"	*20 – 22*
Bowl, vegetable, round, 9⅛"	*25 – 28*
Cup	*15 – 20*
Dish, fruit, 5⅝"	*5 – 6*
Dish, cereal, 6"	*8 – 10*
Gravy	*20 – 25*
Plate, B & B, 6⅛"	*4 – 5*
Plate, salad, 7¼"	*6 – 8*
Plate, breakfast, 9⅛"	*9 – 10*
Plate, dinner, 10"	*20 – 25*
Platter, oval, 11¼"	*25 – 30*
Platter, oval, 13¼"	*20 – 25*
Saucer	*2 – 3*
Tidbit, 3-tier	*75 – 90*
Egg Drop shaker, each	*15 – 18*
Flute French baker	*15 – 20*
Handled shaker, each	*22 – 25*
MaryLou creamer	*20 – 25*
MaryLou sugar	*25 – 30*
Pie baker	*22 – 25*
Salad bowl	*18 – 20*
Sani-Grid creamer	*20 – 22*
Sani-Grid jug, small	*50 – 60*
Sani-Grid jug, medium	*60 – 75*
Sani-Grid jug, large	*70 – 85*
Sani-Grid shaker	*20 – 22*
Sani-Grid sugar	*20 – 25*
Sani-Grid teapot, 6-cup	*175 – 200*

S-Lid coffee pot, 9-cup . . . . *$60 – $75*
Straight-side bowl, #1 . . . . *20 – 22*
Straight-side bowl, #3 . . . . *10 – 15*
Straight-side bowl, #4 . . . . *15 – 20*
Straight-side bowl, #5 . . . . *20 – 25*
Sunshine covered drip . . . . *30 – 40*
Sunshine jug, #5 . . . . *45 – 55*
Tab-handle casserole . . . . *30 – 35*
Tab-handle covered drip . . . . *20 – 25*

WILDFIRE BLUE   These items are blue outside with the Wildfire decal inside. Covered pieces are blue-bottomed with decal on white lids.

Big Lip bowl, 6" . . . . *$15 – $18*
Big Lip bowl, 7¹/₂". . . . . *18 – 20*
Big Lip bowl, 8⁵/₈". . . . . *20 – 25*
Big Lip casserole, sunken knob . . . . *40 – 50*
Straight-side bowl, #1 . . . . *15 – 18*
Straight-side bowl, #3 . . . . *20 – 25*
Straight-side bowl, #4 . . . . *25 – 30*
Straight-side bowl, #5 . . . . *30 – 35*

DINNERWARE / KITCHENWARE: SOLID COLORS

BANDED

This line was made in a wide variety of colors but is most often found in Chinese Red.

PRICING   Prices for Chinese Red, Indian Red, Cobalt Blue, and Art Glaze Yellow (called Screaming Yellow by collectors) are at the high end of the range. Other colors are at the low end.

Batter bowl . . . . *$70 – $85*
Bowl, 6" . . . . *20 – 25*
Bowl, 7³/₈". . . . . *25 – 30*
Bowl, 8³/₄". . . . . *30 – 35*
Carafe. . . . . *300+*
Casserole . . . . *45 – 55*
Cookie jar . . . . *90 – 110*
Jug, 1¹/₂-pint . . . . *20 – 25*
Jug, 2-quart. . . . . *40 – 50*
Shaker . . . . *20 – 25*
Syrup . . . . *75 – 85*

SAF-HANDLE

Comes in a wide variety of colors, but Chinese Red is the easiest to find.

PRICING   Prices for Chinese Red, Indian Red, and Cobalt Blue are at the high end of the range. Other colors are at the low end.

Cookie jar

Coffee server

Batter bowl	$100 – $125
Casserole, #1, 4⅞"	50 – 60
Casserole, #2, 5¼"	45 – 55
Casserole, #4, 8⅛"	30 – 35
Coffee server	275 – 325
Cookie jar	275 – 325
Creamer	20 – 30
Sugar	35 – 45
Syrup	75 – 95
Teapot, 8-ounce, 3"	75 – 85
Teapot, 10-ounce, 3⅜"	75 – 85
Teapot, 6-cup	*See Teapot Chart*

REFRIGERATOR WARE

ARISTOCRAT

Butter	$20 – $25
Butter, blue–green	25 – 30
Leftover	
Blue–green	20 – 25
Chinese Red	35 – 50
Delphinium	25 – 30
Ivory or tan	15 – 20
Sunset/Garden	15 – 20
Water server, Cobalt	100 – 125
Tan	90 – 110
Water server, tilt top, blue–green	125 +

BINGO

Most easily found in Chinese Red.

Butter	
Chinese Red/Art Glaze Yellow	$125 – $150
Delphinium/Lettuce	85 – 100
Leftover	
Chinese Red/Art Glaze Yellow	110 – 125

Delphinium/Lettuce .... $65 – $85
Water bottle, 27-ounce, 7" .... 175 – 200
Water bottle, 48-ounce, 7⅝" .... 175 – 200

EMPEROR

Butter
  Delphinium .... $20 – $25
  Other colors .... 15 – 20
Leftover .... 15 – 20
Water server, Delphinium .... 60 – 85
Water server, green .... 75 – 95

HOTPOINT

Leftovers
  Rectangular, Sandust .... $20 – $25
  #1 round, Green Lustre .... 20 – 25
  #2 round, Maroon .... 25 – 30
  #3 round, Warm Yellow .... 30 – 35
  #1 square
    Chinese Red .... 20 – 25
    Indian Red .... 20 – 25
  #2 square, Addison Gray... 20 – 25
  #3 square, Green Lustre .... 20 – 25
  #4 square
    Daffodil .... 30 – 35
    Maroon .... 30 – 35
  #5 square, Daffodil .... 35 – 45
Water server .... 60 – 75
  w/china cork .... 100 – 125

L to R: *Emperor, Patrician, and Aristocrat water servers.*

KING

Covered roaster	*$15 – $20*
Open roaster	*10 – 15*

MONTGOMERY WARD

Bowl, small	*$20 – $25*
Bowl, medium	*20 – 25*
Bowl, large	*20 – 25*
Butter	*20 – 25*
Leftover	*15 – 20*
Water server	*50 – 60*

NORRIS

Water server, w/o lid	*$15 – $20*
Water server, w/lid	*ND*

PATRICIAN

Butter	*$25 – $30*
Leftover	*15 – 20*
Water server, Cobalt	*150 – 175*
Water server, Delphinium	*45 – 60*
Water server, Garden	*65 – 75*
Water server, odd green	*75 – 85*

PRINCE (G.E.)

Casserole	*$20 – $25*
Leftover, rectangular	*15 – 20*
Leftover, round, small	*6 – 12*
Leftover, round, large	*20 – 25*
Water server	*50 – 55*

PRINCE (Westinghouse)

Leftover, rectangular	*$15 – $20*
Leftover, round	*6 – 12*
Water server	*50 – 55*

QUEEN

Covered roaster	*$15 – $20*
Open roaster	*10 – 15*

SEARS

Three-part leftover, complete	*$100 – $125*
Center section	*50 – 55*
End section	*25 – 35*

TEAPOT CHART

Hall manufactured more teapots, both in quantity and variety, than any other U.S. pottery. Considering the variety in shapes, sizes, and decorations, including solid-color, gold-stamped, and decal-decorated, you could have over two thousand teapots without a duplication.

PRICING

1. The prices here are for six-cup teapots only. Two-cup teapots are very desirable and worth about 25% more. Four-cup pots are not as desirable but are hard to find, so are worth as much. Eight-, ten-, and twelve-cup pots are not worth much more than the six-cup teapot.

2. Prices are for gold-decorated teapots only (not Gold Label), with the obvious exception of Chinese Red, and with the exception of the Doughnuts, which are generally found without gold decoration and are priced accordingly. Add 25%–50% if gold-decorated.

3. Prices for the Aladdin and French are without infusers. For the standard white infuser with gold band for the Aladdin, add 10%; for a color-matched infuser, add 25%. For the French, add 20% for the infuser.

4. Prices are for old teapots only.

5. For teapot in Art Glaze Yellow and Indian Red, use Cobalt prices.

For gold-decorated sugars and creamers, Boston, New York, and Philadelphia creamers: $20–$30, sugars: $25–$35. Hollywood creamer and sugar is ND.

	Airflow	Aladdin	Albany	Automobile	Baltimore
Black............	$55 – $65	$30 – $40	$55 – $70	$650 – $750	$60 – $70
Cadet.............	45 – 55	45 – 55	50 – 70	650 – 750	40 – 50
Camellia..........	55 – 65	50 – 60	55 – 65	650 – 750	55 – 65
Canary	40 – 50	30 – 35	50 – 60	600 – 650	45 – 50
Chinese Red	110 – 125	125 – 150	200 – 250	750+	200 – 250
Cobalt............	50 – 60	50 – 60	75 – 85	750+	65 – 75
Delphinium........	45 – 55	50 – 55	55 – 65	600 – 700	45 – 55
Dresden...........	50 – 60	50 – 60	55 – 65	600 – 700	45 – 50
Emerald	50 – 60	75 – 85	50 – 60	650 – 700	45 – 55
Green Lustre.......	50 – 60	50 – 55	55 – 65	600 – 650	45 – 55
Ivory.............	60 – 70	40 – 50	55 – 65	650 – 700	50 – 60
Mahogany..........	55 – 65	55 – 65	50 – 60	650 – 700	45 – 55
Marine	50 – 60	55 – 65	55 – 65	700 – 750	50 – 60
Maroon...........	55 – 65	35 – 45	60 – 70	600 – 650	40 – 45
Orchid	450+	350+	300+	750+	300+
Pink.............	55 – 65	45 – 55	50 – 70	650 – 750	60 – 75
Rose	65 – 75	60 – 65	55 – 65	650 – 750	60 – 75
Stock Brown.......	55 – 65	55 – 65	55 – 65	600 – 650	55 – 60
Stock Green	55 – 65	55 – 65	55 – 65	600 – 650	55 – 60
Turquoise	45 – 55	45 – 55	55 – 65	600 – 650	45 – 50
Warm Yellow......	45 – 55	50 – 60	55 – 65	600 – 650	45 – 55

	Basket	Basketball	Bird Cage	Boston	Cleveland
Black..........	$150 – $200	$600 – $700	$350 – $450	$35 – $45	$75 – $80
Cadet...........	125 – 150	600 – 700	400 – 450	35 – 45	65 – 75

	Basket	Basketball	Bird Cage	Boston	Cleveland
Camellia.........	$150 – $175	$600 – $700	$400 – $450	$45 – $50	$65 – $75
Canary..............	75 – 95	600 – 650	300 – 350	35 – 45	60 – 70
Chinese Red	275 – 300	800+	600 – 700	200 – 225	225 – 250
Cobalt	225 – 275	800+	600 – 700	65 – 75	75 – 90
Delphinium........	125 – 150	600 – 700	400 – 450	35 – 45	65 – 75
Dresden...........	125 – 150	600 – 700	400 – 450	30 – 40	65 – 75
Emerald...........	125 – 175	600 – 700	400 – 450	40 – 50	60 – 70
Green Lustre	125 – 150	600 – 700	400 – 450	35 – 45	50 – 60
Ivory	150 – 175	600 – 700	400 – 450	40 – 50	65 – 75
Mahogany.........	125 – 150	600 – 700	400 – 450	35 – 45	60 – 70
Marine............	150 – 175	600 – 700	400 – 450	35 – 45	65 – 75
Maroon	150 – 175	600 – 700	300 – 350	35 – 40	70 – 80
Orchid	500+	750+	650+	300+	400+
Pink..............	150 – 175	600 – 700	400 – 450	35 – 45	75 – 85
Rose	150 – 175	600 – 700	400 – 450	40 – 50	75 – 85
Stock Brown	140 – 160	550 – 650	400 – 450	30 – 35	55 – 65
Stock Green	140 – 160	550 – 650	400 – 450	30 – 35	55 – 65
Turquoise	150 – 175	500 – 600	400 – 450	35 – 45	60 – 70
Warm Yellow	150 – 175	600 – 700	400 – 450	30 – 35	50 – 60

	Doughnut	Football	French	Globe	Hollywood
Black...........	$350 – $400	$600 – $700	$25 – $35	$80 – $100	$55 – $65
Cadet.............	350 – 400	600 – 700	25 – 35	75 – 85	50 – 60
Camellia	350 – 400	600 – 700	25 – 35	85 – 95	50 – 55
Canary............	350 – 400	600 – 700	25 – 35	75 – 90	45 – 55
Chinese Red	400 – 450	750+	200 – 250	250 – 300	150 – 175
Cobalt	400 – 450	750+	40 – 50	80 – 90	60 – 75
Delphinium........	350 – 400	600 – 700	25 – 30	75 – 85	50 – 60
Dresden...........	350 – 400	600 – 700	25 – 30	75 – 80	50 – 60
Emerald...........	350 – 400	600 – 700	35 – 45	80 – 90	50 – 60
Green Lustre	350 – 400	600 – 700	30 – 35	75 – 85	50 – 60
Ivory	300 – 325	600 – 700	25 – 35	80 – 90	45 – 55
Mahogany.........	300 – 325	600 – 700	25 – 30	80 – 90	60 – 75
Marine............	325 – 375	600 – 700	30 – 35	80 – 90	55 – 65
Maroon	325 – 375	600 – 700	25 – 30	80 – 90	35 – 40
Orchid	700+	750+	350+	300+	400+
Pink..............	325 – 350	600 – 700	25 – 30	80 – 90	35 – 45
Rose	350 – 400	600 – 700	35 – 45	80 – 90	50 – 60
Stock Brown	275 – 300	500 – 600	20 – 25	75 – 85	35 – 45
Stock green	275 – 300	500 – 600	20 – 25	75 – 85	35 – 45
Turquoise	325 – 350	600 – 700	25 – 30	75 – 85	50 – 60
Warm Yellow	325 – 350	500 – 600	20 – 30	75 – 85	45 – 55

	Hook Cover	Illinois	Indiana	Kansas	Los Angeles
Black	$50 – $60	$200 – $225	$220 – $225	$250 – $300	$45 – $55
Cadet..............	20 – 25	200 – 225	225 – 250	250 – 300	40 – 50
Camellia	45 – 55	200 – 225	225 – 250	250 – 300	40 – 50
Canary.............	35 – 45	200 – 225	225 – 250	250 – 300	30 – 40

	Hook Cover	Illinois	Indiana	Kansas	Los Angeles
Chinese Red. . .	$150 – $175	$350 – $400	$350 – $400	$350 – $400	$150 – $175
Cobalt.	65 – 75	200 – 225	275 – 300	300 – 350	50 – 60
Delphinium	25 – 35	200 – 225	225 – 250	250 – 300	50 – 60
Dresden	25 – 35	200 – 225	225 – 250	250 – 300	35 – 45
Emerald	50 – 60	200 – 225	225 – 250	250 – 300	45 – 55
Green Lustre	40 – 50	200 – 225	225 – 250	250 – 300	40 – 50
Ivory.	35 – 45	200 – 225	225 – 250	250 – 300	35 – 45
Mahogany	45 – 55	200 – 225	225 – 250	250 – 300	35 – 45
Marine	50 – 60	200 – 225	225 – 250	250 – 300	35 – 45
Maroon.	50 – 60	200 – 225	200 – 225	250 – 300	35 – 45
Orchid	400+	600+	600+	600+	400+
Pink	45 – 55	200 – 225	225 – 250	250 – 300	40 – 50
Rose	45 – 55	200 – 225	225 – 250	250 – 300	45 – 55
Stock Brown	35 – 45	100 – 125	125 – 150	225 – 275	30 – 40
Stock Green	35 – 45	100 – 125	125 – 150	225 – 275	30 – 40
Turquoise.	40 – 50	200 – 225	225 – 250	250 – 300	40 – 50
Warm Yellow	35 – 45	200 – 225	225 – 250	250 – 300	30 – 40

	Melody	Moderne	Nautilus	New York
Black	$200 – $225	$40 – $60	$225 – $250	$30 – $35
Cadet	200 – 225	30 – 35	225 – 250	25 – 30
Camellia.	200 – 225	40 – 45	225 – 250	35 – 45
Canary	175 – 200	25 – 30	175 – 200	25 – 30
Chinese Red.	200 – 225	250 – 275	325 – 350	250 – 275
Cobalt.	200 – 225	50 – 60	275 – 325	35 – 45
Delphinium	200 – 225	25 – 35	225 – 250	25 – 30
Dresden	200 – 225	25 – 35	225 – 250	25 – 30
Emerald	200 – 225	40 – 50	225 – 250	20 – 25
Green Lustre	200 – 225	40 – 45	175 – 200	25 – 30
Ivory.	150 – 175	20 – 25	200 – 225	25 – 30
Mahogany	200 – 225	40 – 45	225 – 250	25 – 30
Marine	200 – 225	35 – 45	225 – 250	25 – 35
Maroon.	200 – 225	35 – 45	225 – 250	25 – 30
Orchid	400+	400+	600+	400+
Pink	200 – 225	35 – 45	225 – 250	25 – 35
Rose.	200 – 225	40 – 45	225 – 250	35 – 45
Stock Brown	125 – 150	30 – 35	125 – 150	20 – 25
Stock Green	125 – 150	30 – 35	125 – 150	20 – 25
Turquoise.	200 – 225	45 – 50	225 – 250	30 – 40
Warm Yellow	200 – 225	45 – 50	225 – 250	25 – 30

	Ohio	Parade	Philadelphia	Rhythm	Saf-handle
Black	$175 – $200	$40 – $50	$40 – $50	$150 – $175	$135 –$150
Cadet	200 – 225	35 – 45	30 – 40	150 – 175	125 – 150
Camellia	200 – 225	35 – 45	30 – 40	150 – 175	125 – 150
Canary	200 – 225	20 – 25	30 – 40	75 – 90	65 – 75
Chinese Red	350 – 400	150 – 175	150 – 175	250 – 300	250 – 300
Cobalt	175 – 200	60 – 80	35 – 45	175 – 200	75 – 100

	Ohio	Parade	Philadelphia	Rhythm	Saf-handle
Delphinium	$200 – $225	$35 – $45	$35 – $45	$150 – $175	$125 – $150
Dresden	200 – 225	30 – 40	30 – 40	150 – 175	125 – 150
Emerald	175 – 200	35 – 45	35 – 45	150 – 175	125 – 135
Green Lustre	200 – 225	30 – 40	25 – 30	150 – 175	125 – 135
Ivory	200 – 225	35 – 45	35 – 45	150 – 175	125 – 150
Mahogany	200 – 225	30 – 40	35 – 40	150 – 175	125 – 150
Marine	200 – 225	35 – 45	35 – 45	150 – 175	125 – 150
Maroon	200 – 225	30 – 40	30 – 40	150 – 175	125 – 135
Orchid	500+	400+	400+	500+	500+
Pink	200 – 225	35 – 45	30 – 40	150 – 175	125 – 150
Rose	200 – 225	35 – 45	30 – 35	175 – 200	125 – 150
Stock Brown	125 – 150	25 – 35	25 – 30	125 – 150	125 – 135
Stock Green	125 – 150	25 – 35	25 – 30	125 – 150	125 – 135
Turquoise	200 – 225	30 – 40	25 – 30	150 – 175	125 – 135
Warm Yellow	200 – 225	30 – 40	30 – 40	150 – 175	100 – 125

	Sani-Grid	Star	Streamline	Surfside	Windshield
Black	$65 – $75	$85 – $100	$60 – $70	$125 –$150	$75 – $90
Cadet	30 – 40	75 – 90	45 – 60	125 – 150	65 – 75
Camellia	50 – 65	80 – 90	55 – 65	125 – 150	30 – 40
Canary	35 – 45	65 – 75	40 – 50	90 – 100	50 – 70
Chinese Red	50 – 65	300 – 350	100 – 150	250 – 300	250 – 300
Cobalt	65 – 75	90 – 125	75 – 90	150 – 175	100 – 125
Delphinium	30 – 40	65 – 75	50 – 60	125 – 150	65 – 85
Dresden	30 – 40	65 – 75	50 – 60	125 – 150	65 – 85
Emerald	45 – 60	70 – 80	60 – 70	90 – 100	65 – 75
Green Lustre	50 – 65	65 – 75	50 – 60	90 – 100	65 – 75
Ivory	40 – 50	70 – 80	50 – 60	125 – 150	50 – 60
Mahogany	50 – 65	70 – 80	50 – 60	125 – 150	65 – 75
Marine	55 – 70	75 – 90	65 – 75	125 – 150	65 – 75
Maroon	60 – 75	65 – 75	50 – 65	100 – 125	30 – 40
Orchid	400+	500+	500+	600+	400+
Pink	50 – 65	70 – 80	60 – 70	125 – 150	65 – 75
Rose	50 – 65	70 – 80	70 – 80	125 – 150	65 – 75
Stock Brown	55 – 60	65 – 75	45 – 55	90 – 100	45 – 55
Stock Green	55 – 60	65 – 75	45 – 55	90 – 100	45 – 55
Turquoise	50 – 75	30 – 40	40 – 50	90 – 100	45 – 55
Warm Yellow	50 – 65	60 – 70	45 – 55	90 – 100	65 – 75

HARKER POTTERY COMPANY

East Liverpool, Ohio, and Chester, West Virginia

CHAPTER AT A GLANCE

The Harker Pottery Company incorporated in July 1889, but various Harkers had been in the pottery business since before 1850, producing yellow and Rockingham ware and, after 1879, whiteware. Harker produced semiporcelain dinnerware, toilet ware, hotelware, kitchenware, and advertising pieces.

In 1931, faced with the choice of remodeling its old plant in East Liverpool, where there was the threat of floods, or moving, it bought the old E. M. Knowles plant in Chester and abandoned its East Liverpool operations. The company closed in 1972.

Of greatest interest to collectors is the Cameoware line and the Hotoven kitchenware.

MARKS This arrow was used in a number of backstamps dating from the turn of the century and possibly earlier to the 1940s. "Stone China" (and a "Semi-Porcelain" variation) are early marks. "Harker 1840" was used through the 1920s. The dinnerware mark, used in the 1930s, was stamped in black, green, gold, and red. I was told it was stamped in black until 1945. The rectangular mark seems to have replaced the arrow mark in the 1940s.

The Columbia full-color decal mark is a distribution device. Some stores had exclusive rights to Harker ware in their "territory," so to be able to sell to other stores in the same area, Columbia China was created. It probably didn't fool anyone.

Harker Pottery Co.
East Liverpool, Ohio

ADVERTISING, COMMEMORATIVES, AND SOUVENIRS

Of all the Ohio dinnerware manufacturers, Harker seems to have been the most prolific when it came to special-order items, especially souvenir pieces. Pictured are a sampling of pieces from the 1930s and 1940s.

Advertising/Commemoratives/Souvenirs: Back: *Plate ("Wolf Robe—Cheyenne Chief"), plate ("Voices of the Night"), Gargoyle jug ("Saratoga Battle Monument, Schuylerville, NY"). Front: Early Gadroon Gem creamer (head of George Washington with view of Mt. Vernon on one side, and "200th anniversary of the birth of George Washington, 1732–1932, Kriebel's Dairy, Hereford, Pa." on reverse, jug ("Sunrise" on one side and "Sunset" on the other). It is my impression that Harker made more of this type of ware than most potteries. Four of the five pieces here are stock items that can be "personalized." For instance, the plate with the Indian head is stamped "Souvenir of Hudson, NY." Only the Saratoga Monument has a customized decal.*

DINNERWARE

Records are sparse on some of Harker's dinnerware lines, especially those from the 1930s. I know two names, Puritan and Windsor, that I have not been able to apply to a particular shape. Maybe one of these is Embossed Rim.

BARBECUE WARE

Barbecue Ware was so named because the glaze resembled a mix of mustard and ketchup. The reddish ketchup coloring can range from very heavy to almost nonexistent.

Barbecue
OUTDOOR-WARE
by
HARKER POTTERY CO.
U.S.A.

SWIRL DINNERWARE

Creamer	$4 – $6
Cup	4 – 6
Dish, 6¼"	1 – 2
Plate, 9½"	7 – 9
Platter, 13¾"	12 – 15
Saucer	1 – 2
Sugar	8 – 10

KITCHENWARE

Jug, refrigerator, round	$25 – $30
Pie baker, 9"	10 – 12
Shaker, range, round, pair	15 – 20
Teapot, Zephyr, 5-cup	30 – 35
Utensil, fork	20 – 25
Utensil, spoon	15 – 20

SPECIAL PRICE LIST

CAMEO WARE   (1940)

The Cameo Ware process was brought to the United States by George Bauer. It was first made here at the Edwin Bennett Pottery in Baltimore in the early 1930s. When that company closed, Bauer moved the process to Harker. They introduced the process in kitchenware and specialty items; dinnerware was added in 1941. Bauer owned the rights to the process and received a royalty.

Cameo Ware was made in Blue and Pink. Some pieces, mostly Zephyr, have turned up in yellow; these are marked with a "/Y" in the listing below. Black has been rumored but not substantiated; a Harker employee told me that green and apricot were tried, but I have never seen any.

Harker called the common decoration Dainty Flower. You will also find White Rose, Wild Rice Intaglio, and some miscellaneous items, including a salad set.

Delft Ware is a short line in either solid blue bottoms with white interiors and white lids or white bottoms and blue lids.

PRICING   This is one of those lines for which I want to emphasize that prices are for pieces in very good condition. I have seen too much poor-quality Cameo Ware. Price Delft Ware 20% below Cameo Ware.

Dainty Flower

Some company literature calls this decoration White Blossom, and the color is called Dainty Blue. This seems to be the most plentifully found of the different decorations. It will be found on Kitchenware, Miscellany, Plain Round, Swirl, Virginia, and Zephyr shapes, as listed below.

KITCHENWARE   A **pastry set** consisted of a 9" baker and a rolling pin. The 9¼"-tall **refrigerator jug** is the same shape as the GC, but without the embossed vertical lines. The **utensils** were made in solid blue or pink with white handles, no other decoration.

Bowl, MA baking, 4" . . . . *$6 – $8*
Bowl, MA baking, 5" . . . . *8 – 10*
Bowl, MA baking, 6" . . . . *10 – 12*
Bowl, mixing/baking, 9" *15*
Bowl, mixing/baking, 10" *20*
Bowl, mixing/baking, 11" *25*
Bowl, mixing/baking, 12" *30*
Custard, 6-ounce . . . . *5 – 6*
Drip jar, round . . . . *15 – 18*
Drip Jar, Skyscraper . . . . *15 – 18*
Jug, Ohio, ½-pint, syrup . . . . *15 – 20*

Jug, Ohio, 1-pint. . . . . *ND*
Jug, Ohio, 1¹/₂-pint . . . . *ND*
Jug, Ohio, 2¹/₂-pint . . . . *ND*
Jug, Ohio, 3¹/₂-pint, batter . . . . *$35 – $45*
Jug, refrigerator, round, 2-quart   /Y . . . . *30 – 35*
Jug, refrigerator, square, 2-quart . . . . *30 – 35*
Jug, refrigerator, square, 9¹/₄". . . . . *35 – 45*
Pie Baker, 9" . . . . *15 – 20*
Pie Baker, 10" . . . . *15 – 20*
Rolling Pin. *65*
Shaker, range, round, pair   /Y. . . . . *15 – 20*
Shaker, range, skyscraper, pair . . . . *15 – 20*
Utensil, cake server   /Y. . . . . *12 – 15*
Utensil, fork   /Y. . . . . *20 – 25*
Utensil, spoon   /Y . . . . *15 – 20*

MISCELLANY At first glance, the square salads resemble Virginia, but they are not that shape. The shakers are the Modern Age style but without the embossing.

Ashtray. . . . . *$20 – $25*
Bowl, salad, square, 6¹/₂" *15*
Bowl, salad, square, 7¹/₂" *15*
Bowl, salad, square, 8¹/₂" *15*
Casserole, square . . . . *35 – 40*
Creamer, Gem. . . . . *15 – 20*
Creamer, square. . . . . *12 – 15*
Shaker, pair (Modern Age style) . . . . *8 – 10*

Cameo Ware: Dainty Flower miscellany: Square salad bowls, square casserole, Gem open sugar, and square creamer and sugar. The square salad bowls are based on an Early Gadroon shape, not the Virginia shape.

Sugar, Gem, open .... $15 – $20
Sugar, square .... *15 – 18*
Tea tile, octagonal, 6½" .... *15 – 20*

SHELL WARE (1948)

Bowl, salad, 9" .... $20 – $25
Creamer .... *8 – 10*
Cup .... *5 – 8*
Cup, AD .... *10 – 12*
Dish, 5½" .... *4 – 6*
Dish, lug, 6¼" .... *5 – 7*
Plate, square, 7¾" .... *5 – 6*
Plate, 6½" .... *2 – 3*
Plate, 7½" .... *5 – 7*
Plate, 9½" .... *7 – 9*
Platter, 11¼" .... *12 – 15*
Platter, 13½" .... *15 – 18*
Saucer .... *2 – 3*
Saucer, AD .... *4 – 6*
Sugar .... *12 – 15*

VIRGINIA The flatware in this line is basically square. Some Plain round pieces were mixed with it to round out the set. A metal handle for the 12¾" cake plate converted it into a carrier. A set included the cake plate, six 7¾" plates and an optional cake server.

Ashtray .... $10 – $15
Bowl, soup, 7¾" .... *12 – 15*
Bowl, 36s, 1-pint .... *8 – 10*
Bowl, vegetable, 9" .... *12 – 15*
Casserole (Plain round) .... *25 – 30*
Creamer (Plain round) .... *6 – 8*
Cup (Plain round) .... *5 – 8*
Cup, AD (Plain round) .... *10 – 12*
Dish, cereal .... *5 – 7*
Dish, fruit .... *4 – 6*
Plate, 6¾" .... *2 – 3*
Plate, 7¾" .... *4 – 5*
Plate, 8¾" .... *5 – 6*
Plate, 9¾" .... *7 – 9*
Plate, 10¾" .... *10 – 12*
Plate, cake, 12¾" .... *12 – 15*
Platter, 10½" .... *10 – 12*
Platter, 12½" .... *12 – 15*
Saucer .... *1 – 2*
Saucer, AD (Plain round) .... *3 – 5*
Sugar (Plain round) .... *8 – 10*

ZEPHYR Covered pieces have knob finials, with the exception of the **bowls**, which came open or with deep Glas-Bake lids with lug handles.

The **au gratin casserole** came with an 8¼" round underplate. The **1½-quart casserole** came with a 9¼" round underplate, and the **2-quart casserole** came with a 10¼" round underplate. The **cheese box** was made in solid blue. **Coffee pots** were sold with or without metal drip sections. A **salad set** consisted of either the 8" or 9" bowl and a solid blue fork and spoon.

Bowl, 6"	/Y	$8 – $10
Bowl, 7"	/Y	10 – 12
Bowl, 8"	/Y	10 – 12
Bowl, 9"	/Y	12 – 15
Casserole, 1½-quart, 7½".		30 – 35
Casserole, 2-quart, 8½"		30 – 35
Casserole, au gratin, 1½-quart		30 – 35
Cheese box, round, 4¾".		20 – 25
Coffee pot, 4-cup		35 – 40
Coffee pot, 6-cup		35 – 40
Coffee pot, 8-cup		35 – 40
Cookie jar		65 – 75
Refrigerator stack set, 3-piece		30 – 35
Refrigerator stack set, 4-piece		35 – 40
Teapot, 5-cup	/Y	35 – 40
Tray, cheese, round, 11"		20 – 25

Miscellany   This category encompasses items that do not have the standard decorations. The **baby feeders** came in Blue or Pink; decorations include two ducks and three rabbits. I have seen the round one-part only in a photo; it appears to be the Kiddo bowl. The **Jumbo cup** came in Blue with "Dad" or Pink with "Mother" on the side. The **Kiddo Set** came in Blue or Pink: decorations include bear with balloon, cat, dog wheeled toy, duck, duck with umbrella, and toy soldier.

Cameo Ware Children's Ware: Back: *Child's feeding dish (two ducks).* Front: *Bowl (dog), plate (hobby horse), mug (elephant), bowl (doll w/balloon?), and plate (duck).*

Baby feeder, round, 1-part, metal bottom $25
Baby feeder, round, 3-part, metal bottom 25
Baby feeder, hexagonal, all ceramic 25
Jumbo cup .... *10 – 12*
Jumbo saucer, 7" .... *3 – 5*
Kiddo Set
   Bowl .... *15 – 18*
   Mug .... *18 – 20*
   Plate .... *15 – 18*

SALAD SET   (1944)
On the Swirl shape, four decorations were made in Blue or Pink: apple, maple leaf, pear, or tulip.

Bowl, 9" .... $25 – $30
Plate, salad .... *12 – 15*

White Rose

A rose decoration, made exclusively for Montgomery Ward. Dinnerware was made in Blue or Pink, though blue is more common. According to literature, kitchenware was made in blue only.

   A rolling pin and a cake server rounded out the kitchenware line.

WHITE ROSE
carv-kraft
◆ ◆ ◆ **BY HARKER**

KITCHENWARE

Drip jar, round... $12 – $15
Drip jar, Skyscraper...................................... *12 – 15*
Jug, refrigerator, square, 2-quart .... *30 – 35*

Cameo Ware: White Rose Skyscraper range set.

Pie baker, 9" .... *$12 – $15*
Pie baker, 10" .... *12 – 15*
Refrigerator jar (MA), 4" *10*
Refrigerator jar (MA), 5" *12*
Refrigerator jar (MA), 6" *15*
Rolling pin, solid-color .... *45 – 50*
Shaker, Skyscraper .... *15 – 20*
Tea tile, octagonal, 6½" .... *18 – 20*

PLAIN ROUND   The Montgomery Ward catalog refers to a cream soup
cup that I have not seen.

Bowl, soup, 7½" .... *$12 – $15*
Bowl, vegetable, oval, 9" .... *12 – 15*
Bowl, vegetable, round, 9" .... *18 – 20*
Casserole .... *20 – 25*
Creamer .... *6 – 8*
Cup .... *6 – 8*
Dish, 5½" .... *3 – 4*
Dish, lug, 6¼" .... *4 – 6*
Gravy .... *15 – 18*
Gravy liner .... *8 – 10*
Plate, 6¼" .... *2 – 3*
Plate, 7⅛" .... *5 – 7*
Plate, 9" .... *7 – 9*
Plate, 9¾" .... *10 – 12*
Plate, cake, 11" .... *12 – 15*
Platter, oval, 11" .... *12 – 15*
Platter, oval, 13" .... *15 – 20*
Platter, oval, 15¼" .... *20 – 25*
Saucer .... *2 – 3*
Sugar .... *10 – 15*

VIRGINIA

Plate, salad, square, 7¼" .... *$6 – $7*
Platter, 12¾" .... *15 – 18*

Cameo Ware: Wild Rice jug.

ZEPHYR

Bowl, 6"	$10 – $12
Bowl, 7"	12 – 15
Bowl, 8"	12 – 15
Bowl, 9"	15 – 18
Casserole, 1½-quart, 8½"	25 – 30
Teapot, 5-cup, 30-ounce	35 – 40

Wild Rice Intaglio   (ca. 1950)

A blue and white decoration. Very little shows up.

Wild Rice
INTAGLIO
by
HARKER POTTERY CO
U.S.A.

Cup	ND
Jug	ND
Saucer	ND

EMBASSY   (1937)

The flatware for this line is a plain round shape.

Bowl, vegetable, oval, 9"*	$10 – $12
Casserole	20 – 25
Creamer	4 – 6

Embassy: Petitpoint teapot and creamer (floral).

Cup . . . . *$4 – $6*
Dish, 5¹/₂" . . . . *2 – 3*
Plate, 9"* . . . . *7 – 9*
Saucer . . . . *1 – 2*
Sugar . . . . *8 – 10*
Teapot . . . . *25 – 30*

"EMBOSSED RIM"

I have not discovered a name for this shape, but it seems to date to the early 1930s.

Ashtray . . . . *$6 – $8*
Bowl, vegetable, oval, 9"* . . . . *10 – 12*
Casserole . . . . *20 – 25*
Creamer . . . . *4 – 6*
Cup . . . . *4 – 6*
Dish, 5¹/₂" . . . . *2 – 3*
Plate, 6¹/₄" . . . . *1 – 2*
Plate, 9" . . . . *7 – 9*
Platter, oval, 11¹/₂" . . . . *10 – 12*
Saucer . . . . *1 – 2*
Sugar . . . . *8 – 10*

ENGRAVED

This line was produced by the same process as Cameo Ware, but Harker called these Engraved patterns. These pieces look as though they were introduced in the 1950s, and I suspect that Harker didn't call them Cameo because sales of that line had run their course and the company wanted something that seemed new.

Background colors were Butter Yellow, Celadon Green, Celeste Blue, Coral, and Pink Cocoa. Some of the patterns were Bamboo, Brown-Eyed Susan

Embossed Rim: Early American Silhouette plate and cup.

(white daisies with brown center on yellow background), Cock O'Morn (rooster), Coronet (leaves), Country Cousins (two birds on flowering branch), Dogwood, Ivy Wreath, Petit Fleurs (a band of five-petal flowers), Provincial (a Pennsylvania Dutch pattern), and Star-Lite (stars).

Creamer . . . . *$4 – $6*
Cup . . . . *4 – 6*
Dish, 5¹/₂"* . . . . *2 – 3*
Plate, 6¹/₄" . . . . *1 – 2*
Plate, 7" . . . . *4 – 5*
Plate, 10" . . . . *10 – 12*
Plate, party, 8¹/₄" . . . . *6 – 7*
Platter, 11¹/₄" × 9³/₄" . . . . *10 – 12*
Saucer . . . . *1 – 2*
Sugar . . . . *8 – 10*
Tray, cake, round, 10" . . . . *12 – 15*
Utensil, cake server . . . . *12 – 15*

"GADROON"/EARLY

This line seems to date to the late 1920s if not earlier. I have found both round and square flatware. Early company literature refers to Melrose but it is not clear if that is a shape or decoration name.

Creamer . . . . *$4 – $6*
Cup . . . . *4 – 6*
Dish, lug, 5¹/₂" . . . . *2 – 3*
Plate, 6¹/₄" . . . . *1 – 2*
Plate, lug, round, 6¹/₂" . . . . *2 – 3*
Plate, 8³/₄" . . . . *7 – 9*
Plate, round, 8³/₄" . . . . *7 – 9*

Gadroon/early: Divided plate and cup.

Plate, lug, 9¾"	$10 – $12
Plate, divided, lug, 9¾"	12 – 15
Platter, Tree-in-Well	30 – 40
Saucer	1 – 2
Sugar	8 – 10

HOSTESS   (1935)

Floral and scroll periodic embossing around the edge of a slightly scalloped rim. Tab handles on casserole and creamer.

Bowl, vegetable, oval, 9"*	$10 – $12
Casserole	20 – 25
Creamer	4 – 6
Cup	4 – 6
Dish, 5½"*	2 – 3
Plate, 6¼"*	1 – 2
Plate, 9"*	7 – 9
Platter, 11"*	10 – 12
Saucer	1 – 2
Sugar	8 – 10

MISCELLANY

These are pieces you will find in familiar decals, but they are not part of a particular shape. The Gem creamer has a gadroon edge around the top. The jumbo saucer has a slight embossing around the inside of the rim.

Ashtray	$6 – $8
Creamer, Gem	8 – 10
Cup, jumbo	15 – 18

Miscellany: Jumbo cups: Father (Corinthian), Mother (Cameo pink), Dad (Cameo blue), and Petitpoint. Ashtray (red flower). The "Father" mug is an unusual shape; you will find the other shape more readily. Saucers will be found either plain or with a light embossing around the rim.

Saucer, jumbo . . . . *$6 – $8*
Sugar, Gem . . . . *8 – 10*

MODERN AGE   (1940)

Modern Age is characterized by a faintly impressed zigzag design on all pieces. It has a narrow, often oval body with a lifesaver finial on the lid. In order to expand the Modern Age line, Harker put this finial on lids from other shapes, Zephyr for one, but these pieces seldom show up. The teapot, creamer, sugar, and cookie jar are usually found. Items from other lines, such as Zephyr bowls and casseroles, and MA bowls, were used as pickup pieces. They will be found with the Modern Age mark but will not have the impressed design.

The two **refrigerator jugs** were used with the tray as a batter set.

Colorful Fruit, Petit Point, and Modern Tulip are the common decals. Flower Basket and English Ivy are also found.

MARKS   A red and black decal was used as a mark.

Bowl, mixing, 11" . . . . *$20 – $25*
Cake tray, lug, 11½" . . . . *15 – 20*
Casserole, 6" . . . . *15 – 20*
Casserole, 8¾" . . . . *20 – 25*
Cookie jar, oval . . . . *30 – 35*
Creamer, oval . . . . *4 – 6*

*Modern Age:
Petitpoint teapot,
Modern Tulip
sugar and
creamer.*

Custard	$4 – $6
Drip jar	12 – 15
Jug, refrigerator, oval, 1-quart	20 – 25
Jug, refrigerator, oval, 2-quart	25 – 30
Platter, round, 11½"	15 – 20
Shaker, small, oval, pair	8 – 10
Sugar, oval	8 – 10
Teapot, oval, 6-cup	30 – 35
Tray, cake, 11½"	12 – 15
Utensil, cake server	12 – 15
Utensil, fork	20 – 25
Utensil, spoon	15 – 20

NEWPORT

Three narrow embossed lines around the outside of the rim on the flatware and around the foot of the hollowware.

Decals seen on this are Farmer and Petitpoint Bouquet.

Bowl, soup, 7⅞"	$10 – $12
Bowl, vegetable, oval, 9"*	10 – 12
Casserole	20 – 25
Creamer	4 – 6
Cup	4 – 6
Dish, 5½"*	2 – 3
Gravy	12 – 15
Plate, 6¼"	1 – 2
Plate, 9½"	7 – 9
Saucer	1 – 2
Sugar	8 – 10

Newport: Petitpoint shaker, plate (farmer's wife feeding chickens), and creamer (teapot and fruit). Note the resemblance of Newport's flatware to E. M. Knowles' Deanna shape flatware.

Nouvelle: Silhouette butter, shirred egg dish (fruit and flower basket), Triflower cup, and Silhouette gravy. Compare the butter finial and the gravy handle to the Nouvelle sugar in the American China Corporation chapter.

"NOUVELLE" (1932)

This is the Nouvelle shape of the American China Corporation, so I have used the same name. ACC sold its Briar Rose shape to Salem, and I assume that is how Harker acquired Nouvelle. I have dated it to 1932, the year ACC went bankrupt. Harker might have changed the name.

Bowl, soup, 8"* .... *$10 – $12*
Bowl, vegetable, oval, 9"* .... *10 – 12*
Butter dish .... *20 – 25*
Casserole .... *20 – 25*
Creamer .... *4 – 6*
Cup .... *4 – 6*
Cup, cream soup .... *12 – 16*
Dish, 5½"* .... *2 – 3*
Dish, shirred egg, lug, 7" .... *8 – 10*
Gravy .... *12 – 15*
Gravy liner .... *6 – 8*
Plate, 6"* .... *1 – 2*
Plate, 9"* .... *7 – 9*
Platter, 11"* .... *10 – 12*
Saucer .... *1 – 2*
Sugar .... *8 – 10*

PÂTÉ-SUR-PÂTÉ

By definition pâté-sur-pâté is a paste-on-paste technique that is as different from Harker's Pâté-Sur-Pâté as is Cameo Ware, which it superficially resembles. Unlike Cameo Ware, the raised patterns for this line were in the mold. Each piece is glazed in white and fired. Then it is glazed a second time in the contrasting color, which is wiped from the surface, revealing the white on the pattern below and leaving the second color in the depressed portion of the design. It is then fired a second time.

Pâté-sur-Pâté: L to R: *Floral Band and Laurelton plates.*

Two common patterns are "Flower Border" (this will also be found in white with decal decoration) and Laurelton.

PRICING   Use Plain round values below for both patterns.

"PLAIN ROUND"

This is the shape usually found in Cameo Ware.

Bowl, soup, coupe, 7½" . . . . *$10 – $12*
Bowl, vegetable, round, 8¾" . . . . *15 – 18*
Creamer . . . . *4 – 6*
Cup . . . . *4 – 6*
Cup, AD. . . . . *10 – 12*
Dish, 5½" . . . . *2 – 3*
Dish, 6" . . . . *3 – 4*
Dish, lug, 6" . . . . *4 – 5*
Plate, 6¼" . . . . *1 – 2*
Plate, 9¼" . . . . *7 – 9*
Platter, oval, 11¾" . . . . *10 – 12*
Platter, oval, 13½" . . . . *12 – 15*
Saucer, 6" . . . . *1 – 2*

Saucer, AD . . . . *$3 – $5*
Sugar . . . . *8 – 10*

QUAKER MAID / ROCKINGHAM

Harker reintroduced its Rockingham Ware in the 1950s with a number of historical-type items (listed separately below). They came in three colors: Dark Brown, Honey Brown, and Bottle Green. Dark Brown is the most common color.

This was followed by the Quaker Maid dinnerware line in Dark Brown (also referred to as Brown Drip in company literature).

There were two styles of sugar and creamer, one with a "pinched neck."

NOTE Despite Harker's literature, this was not an exact reproduction of the Rockingham glaze. It did not have the mottled or sponged look of Rockingham, which probably would have been too expensive to reproduce. Rather, it seems to have what is known as a "breaking glaze," which means the glaze shows lighter on the raised embossing. Also, it has a drip glaze on the rims and lips, which was not characteristic of Rockingham.

Other potteries manufactured a brown drip, including Hull, McCoy, Pfaltzgraff, and Scio, but once you see Harker's version—with a more complex coloration in the drip than those of the others—you will always be able to recognize it.

genuine
Quaker Maid
COOK
WARE
HARKER CHINA CO.
East Liverpool,
Ohio, USA

PRICING Values are the same for all three glazes.

Ashtray, square, 6³/₄" . . . . *$4 – $6*
Bowl, salad, round, 11" . . . . *15 – 18*
Bowl, soup/cereal . . . . *5 – 6*
Bowl, soup, coupe, large . . . . *10 – 12*
Bowl, vegetable, divided . . . . *12 – 15*
Bowl, vegetable, oval, 1¹/₂-pint . . . . *10 – 12*
Bowl, vegetable, round, 9" . . . . *12 – 15*
Butter, ¹/₄-pound . . . . *15 – 20*
Casserole, 1-quart . . . . *15 – 20*
Casserole, 2-quart . . . . *15 – 20*
Coffee pot, 8-cup . . . . *30 – 35*
Creamer . . . . *4 – 6*
Creamer, pinched . . . . *4 – 6*
Cup . . . . *4 – 6*
Dish, fruit . . . . *2 – 3*
Gravy bowl, 1¹/₂-pint . . . . *10 – 12*

Jug, 1-pint . . . . *$10 – $12*
Jug, 2-pint . . . . *12 – 15*
Jug, beverage serve, 8-cup . . . . *30 – 35*
Ladle (for gravy bowl). . . . . *ND*
Mug, 10-ounce. . . . . *10 – 12*
Pie baker, individual, 6¾" . . . . *8 – 10*
Plate, 6¼" . . . . *1 – 2*
Plate, 7¼" . . . . *5 – 6*
Plate, 10¼" . . . . *8 – 10*
Platter, 11¼" . . . . *10 – 12*
Platter, 13½" . . . . *12 – 15*
Saucer . . . . *1 – 2*
Saucer, Walnut wood (for mug) . . . . *ND*
Server, center handle, 10¼" . . . . *8 – 10*
Shaker, pair. . . . . *8 – 10*
Shaker, range, pair . . . . *15 – 18*
Sugar . . . . *8 – 10*
Sugar, pinched. . . . . *8 – 10*
Tidbit, 3-tier . . . . *10 – 12*

Historical Items

The American Eagle plates were sold as a serving set of one 10¼" plate and six 7¼" plates. I have seen Daniel Boone and Jolly Roger referred to as mugs; they

HOUND-HANDLED
MUG

AMERICAN EAGLE
TRIVET

JOLLY ROGER
JUG

DANIEL BOONE
JUG

SOAP DISH

Rockingham

have spouts, and Harker literature calls them jugs. An insert was made for the hound-handled mug that could convert it into a candle holder. The Rebekah at the Well teapot does not have the drip glaze; it is solid-color. Some of these items were included in the Quaker Maid line.

Ashtray, American Eagle, 8¼" diameter .... *$10 – $12*
Ashtray, tobacco-leaf shape, 9¼" × 5" .... *10 – 12*
Bread Tray, "Give Us This Day Our Daily Bread," 12" × 10" .... *15 – 18*
Jug, Daniel Boone, ¾-pint... *20*
Jug, Hound-handled, 2-quart.. *55 – 60*
Jug, Jolly Roger, ½-pint *20*
Mug, Hound-handled, 18-ounce .... *30 – 35*
   w/candle insert .... *40 – 45*
Plate, American Eagle, 7¼" .... *8 – 10*
   Above as Wall Plate .... *8 – 10*
Plate, American Eagle, 10¼" .... *12 – 15*
   Above as Wall Plate .... *12 – 15*
Soap Dish, "Soap," 6" × 4¾" .... *10 – 12*
Teapot, Rebekah at the Well, 6-cup .... *55 – 60*
Tidbit, American Eagle, 2-tier .... *20 – 25*
Trivet, American Eagle, 7" .... *18 – 20*

ROSEMERE (1936)

A band of floral embossing around the rim of the flatware and the shoulder of the hollowware, with the flower repeated on the handles.

Bowl, vegetable, oval, 9"* .... *$10 – $12*
Casserole .... *20 – 25*
Creamer .... *4 – 6*
Cup .... *4 – 6*
Dish, 5½" .... *2 – 3*
Plate, 6¼" .... *1 – 2*
Plate, 9"* .... *7 – 9*
Platter, 11" .... *10 – 12*
Saucer .... *1 – 2*
Sugar .... *8 – 10*

Rosemere: Petitpoint creamer.

ROYAL GADROON   (1947)

A gadroon-edge shape; many solid colors and decorations were used over its long life.

Known solid colors are Celadon (Chinese gray green), Celeste (sky blue), Charcoal (gray black), Chesterton (silver mist gray), Corinthian (teal green), Pink Cocoa (beige), Sun Valley (chartreuse), and Chocolate Brown. Harker must have liked the Chesterton name, because they created the Chesterton Series in Avocado, Wedgewood Blue, Pumpkin, and Golden Harvest. This explains why you will find the Chesterton name stamped on colors other than gray. You will also find pieces in some of these colors with decorations on them.

Of the decals, Ivy is the most readily found. Others include Bermuda (bands of leaves), Bouquet (a Nove Rose–type decoration), Bridal Rose, Magnolia, and Sweetheart Rose (sprays of small roses).

Cake Sets: There were many decorations used on cake sets (10¼" tray, cake server, and either four or six 6¼" plates). These include four different Currier & Ives scenes, four different Fruit arrangements, Game Birds, Godey Ladies, Old-Fashioned Autos, and more. The likelihood is that these decorations were not used on complete dinnerware sets.

Royal Gadroon seems to be the shape most often found with the special-order decorations.

MARKS You will find some Gadroon stamped with the Pâté-sur-Pâté mark. This process was used to create the contrasting white edge on the colored pieces.

Ashtray, 4¾"	$6 – $8
Ashtray, 5¼"	6 – 8
Bowl, salad, 10½"	15 – 18
Bowl, soup, 8½"	10 – 12
Bowl, onion soup, lug	8 – 10
Bowl, vegetable, oval, 9"	10 – 12
Bowl, vegetable, round, 7¾"	10 – 12
Bowl, vegetable, round, 9"	15 – 18
Casserole	20 – 25
Creamer	4 – 6
Cup	4 – 6
Cup, AD	10 – 12
Dish, 6"	3 – 4
Eggcup	10 – 12
Gravy	12 – 15
Gravy liner/pickle	6 – 8

Royal Gadroon: Square pink plate with overglaze "Thistle" decoration and teapot (violets).

Plate, 6¼" .... *$1 – $2*
Plate, 7¼" .... *4 – 5*
Plate, 9¼" .... *7 – 9*
Plate, 10¼" .... *10 – 12*
Plate, chop, 11" .... *12 – 15*
Plate, party, square, 8½" .... *6 – 7*
Plate, square, 8¼" .... *6 – 7*
Platter, embossed handle, 11" .... *10 – 12*
Platter, embossed handle, 13½" .... *12 – 15*
Platter, embossed handle, 15½" .... *15 – 18*
Saucer .... *1 – 2*
Saucer, AD .... *3 – 5*
Shaker, pair .... *8 – 10*
Sugar .... *8 – 10*
Teapot .... *30 – 35*
Tidbit, 3-tier .... *15 – 20*

SHELL WARE / SWIRL

Harker used both names for this shape. This shape was used primarily for Cameo, but other decorations, such as French Provincial, will be found.

PRICING Values are for all decorations except Cameo, which is priced above.

Bowl, salad, round, 9" .... *$15 – $18*
Creamer .... *4 – 6*
Cup .... *4 – 6*
Cup, AD .... *10 – 12*

Shell Ware/Swirl: Barbecue Outdoor Ware plate, Silhouette sugar (missing lid), and creamer (fruit and flower basket).

Dish, lug, cereal/soup, 6¼" .... *$5 – $6*
Dish, fruit .... *2 – 3*
Plate, saucer (no cup ring), 6" .... *1 – 2*
Plate, 6½" .... *1 – 2*
Plate, 7½" .... *5 – 7*
Plate, 9½" .... *7 – 9*
Platter, 11¼" .... *10 – 12*
Platter, 13½" .... *12 – 15*
Saucer, AD .... *3 – 5*
Sugar .... *8 – 10*

STONEWARE

A 1950s line. The individual casserole seems to have been used as the covered drip. A pair of table shakers is one short and one tall.

Solid colors of Blue Mist, Golden Dawn, Shell Pink, and White Cap. Patterns: Peacock Alley (peacocks and leaves) and Seafare (abstract fish).

Ashtray, 5¼" .... *$5 – $7*
Ashtray, 8¼" .... *6 – 8*
Bean pot, 2-quart .... *15 – 20*
Bowl, salad, round, 10" .... *15 – 18*
Bowl, vegetable, round, 9" .... *10 – 12*
Bowl, vegetable, divided .... *12 – 15*
Butter, ¼-pound .... *15 – 20*
Carafe, 8-cup, w/warmer .... *30 – 35*
Casserole, individual, 13-ounce .... *10 – 12*
Casserole, flat cover, 2-quart .... *15 – 20*
Casserole, foil-covered, 1½-quart .... *15 – 20*
Casserole, foil-covered, 2½-quart .... *15 – 20*
Casserole, foil-covered, 4-quart .... *20 – 25*
Casserole, knob cover, 2-quart .... *15 – 20*
Coffee pot, 6-cup .... *25 – 30*

Cookie jar, 3-quart .... $25 – $30
Creamer .... 4 – 6
Cruet .... 12 – 15
Cup .... 4 – 6
Dish, fruit .... 2 – 3
Dish, soup/cereal .... 3 – 4
Drip jar .... 10 – 12
Gravy .... 10 – 12
Gravy ladle .... ND
Jug, 1-pint .... 10 – 12
Pie baker, 9" .... 10 – 12
Plate, 5⁷/₈" .... 1 – 2
Plate, 7¹/₈" .... 4 – 5
Plate, 7³/₄" .... 5 – 6
Plate, 10¹/₈" .... 8 – 10
Platter, 11¹/₄" .... 10 – 12
Platter, 13¹/₄" .... 12 – 15
Rolling pin .... ND
Saucer .... 1 – 2
Shaker, range, pair .... 15 – 18
Shaker, short, each .... 4 – 5
Shaker, tall, each .... 4 – 5
Sugar .... 8 – 10

VIRGINIA

A square shape with scalloped corners. The Plain round casserole, cup, creamer, and sugar seem to have been used with this shape, certainly in the Cameo Ware line.

The lug-handle platter will be found unsigned with many decorations unfamiliar to Harker; these are attributed to the Stetson China Company, which

Virginia: Cottage platter, Mallow plate, Silhouette creamer and sugar. Be careful: Harker sold blanks to Stetson, and I have seen many of the platters with no backstamp and decals that may not be Harker.

decorated blanks they bought from other potteries. When I find one of these without a backstamp, I assume it was not made by Harker.

Decals founds on this shape include Cameo, Mallow, Monterey, Silhouette/Early American, Tulip, and Yellow Rose.

Bowl, soup, 7¾".	$10 – $12
Bowl, vegetable, 8¼".	10 – 12
Casserole.	20 – 25
Creamer	4 – 6
Cup	6 – 8
Dish, 5".	2 – 3
Dish, lug, 6⅝".	5 – 6
Plate, 6½".	2 – 3
Plate, 8".	6 – 7
Plate, 8¾".	7 – 8
Plate, 9¾".	10 – 12
Platter, lug, rectangular, 11¼".	10 – 12
Platter, rectangular, 13¾".	12 – 15
Platter, lug, square, 10¾".	10 – 12
Platter, lug, square, 12¾".	15 – 18
Saucer	1 – 2
Sugar	8 – 10

WHITE CLOVER   (1951)

Designed by Russel Wright. Good Design winner, Museum of Modern Art, New York. The ashtray and divided vegetable were later additions to the line.

Made in four colors: Golden Spice, Coral Sand, Meadow Green, and Charcoal. The Cloverleaf decoration will be found on items followed by /C in the listing below. The other items are solid color only.

Ashtray /C.	$45 – $50
Bowl, vegetable, 7¼".	20 – 25
Bowl, vegetable, covered, 8¼".	30 – 35
Bowl, vegetable, divided, 11¾" /C.	30 – 35
Casserole, covered, 2-quart /C.	45 – 50
Clock, GE.	70 – 80
Creamer /C.	12 – 15
Cup /C.	10 – 12
Dish, cereal/soup, 5" /C.	6 – 8
Dish, fruit /C.	4 – 6
Gravy /C.	20 – 25
Jug, covered, 2-quart /C.	50 – 55
Plate, 6".	5 – 6
Plate, 7⅝".	6 – 7
Plate, 9¼".	8 – 10
Plate, 10" /C.	10 – 12
Plate, 11".	18 – 20
Plate, chop, 9¼".	10 – 12
Plate, chop, 10".	12 – 15

*Wood Song:
Teapot.*

Plate, chop, 11"   /C . . . . *$20 – $25*
Platter, 13¹/₄"   /C . . . . *20 – 25*
Saucer . . . . *2 – 3*
Shaker, either size, each   /C . . . . *12 – 15*
Sugar . . . . *15 – 18*

WOOD SONG

A lightly engraved maple leaf pattern with twig handles and finials on most of the hollowware.

Butter, ¹/₄-pound . . . . *$20 – $25*
Creamer . . . . *4 – 6*
Cup . . . . *4 – 6*
Dish, 5¹/₂"* . . . . *2 – 3*
Mug . . . . *12 – 15*
Plate, 6¹/₄"* . . . . *1 – 2*
Plate, 9"* . . . . *7 – 9*
Saucer . . . . *1 – 2*
Sugar . . . . *8 – 10*
Teapot . . . . *25 – 30*

KITCHENWARE

"GC"

I call this GC because the shape originated with the Gem Clay Forming Company. I have found several of the squat refrigerator jugs marked with the Gem Clay backstamp, both with the Kelvinator decal and undecorated. I have been told that Gem Clay made refrigerator ware only in the early part of the 1930s, so I assume that Kelvinator took the shape to Harker when Gem Clay said they could no longer fill orders. It's possible that Gem also made the leftover and the tureen and that Harker added the other items, but this is only a guess on my part. The glass lids on the Kelvinator pieces were made by Federal Glass.

GC (Clockwise from top): Coffeepot (red and black hearthside decal), Gingham Tulip tall refrigerator jug, Mallow relish, Doll House large custard, Navajo small custard, and Kelvinator squat refrigerator jug.

Raised vertical lines descend partway down the sides of these kitchenware pieces.

PRICING   Add 50% for Kelvinator decal.

Bowl, mixing, 9" × 4¹/₄" high . . . . *$15 – $18*
Bowl, mixing, square foot, 9³/₄" × 3³/₄" high . . . . *18 – 20*
Bowl, utility, 5³/₈" × 3³/₄" high . . . . *7 – 10*
Custard, 6-ounce, 2" high . . . . *4 – 6*
Custard, 8-ounce, 2¹/₂" high . . . . *5 – 7*
Jug, refrigerator, squat . . . . *20 – 25*
Jug, refrigerator, tall, 9¹/₄" . . . . *25 – 30*
Leftover, glass lid . . . . *10 – 12*
Teapot . . . . *30 – 35*
Tureen, 7¹/₂" . . . . *25 – 30*

HOTOVEN   (1926)

Harker claimed this was the first decal-decorated line of ovenware made. Along with the general pieces listed here, you will find kitchenware from other shapes with the Hotoven mark (see GC and Zephyr).

The **batter set** consisted of two Ohio jugs, the ¹/₂-pint and the 3¹/₂-pint on the square Virginia 12³/₄" tray. The **cake set** could be had with either a round 11" plate and the cake server or the square 12³/₄" plate and server. **Custards** were sold individually or as a set of six in a metal frame. The **Handy Style bowls** look like large custards. The **MA bowls** came with flat glass lids; they were called baking bowls without the lids and refrigerator jars with the lids. The

Ohio jugs were sold with and without lids and came in five sizes, which I have listed. However, only the ¹/₂-pint syrup and the 3¹/₂-pint batter turn up with any regularity. You will find the 2¹/₂-pint jugs, but I have never seen the other two. A **pastry set** consisted of the rolling pin and the 9" pie baker. The **refrigerator stack sets** were available with either two or three bottoms and a lid.

The **rolling pin** dates back to Prohibition, and the story is told that it was used for holding liquor. It's your choice as to whether to believe that or not. According to Harker literature, it was intended to be filled with ice water, which would help keep dough firm, hence the rubber stopper at one end. The square and rectangular **shakers** with paper lids probably date back to the late 1920s.

Several of these pieces are found paneled as well as plain; the paneled versions are listed separately below.

MARKS There are several variations of the Hot-Oven marked. Some are stamped in black; the full-color mark is a decal and was used until 1940.

Don't be puzzled by the Hot-Oven marks you find on square plates. These were used as casserole undertrays.

PRICING Double values for Monterey decal.

Bake dish, open, 6¹/₄"	*$4 – $5*
Bake dish, open, 7¹/₂"	*5 – 6*
Bake dish, open, 8¹/₂"	*6 – 7*
Bean pot, individual	*5 – 6*
Bowl, 7¹/₂"	*10 – 12*
Bowl, 8¹/₂"	*12 – 15*
Bowl, batter, paneled, 9³/₄"	*18 – 20*
Bowl, footed, 1-pint, 5"	*6 – 8*
Bowl, footed, 1¹/₂-pint, 6"	*8 – 10*
Bowl, footed, 2-pint, 7"	*8 – 10*
Bowl, Handy Style, 12-ounce	*ND*
Bowl, Handy Style, 16-ounce	*ND*
Bowl, Handy Style, 20-ounce	*ND*
Bowl, MA baking, 4"	*4 – 6*
w/glass lid	*5 – 7*
Bowl, MA baking, 5"	*6 – 8*
w/glass lid	*7 – 9*
Bowl, MA baking, 6"	*8 – 10*
w/glass lid	*10 – 12*
Bowl, mixing, 9"	*15 – 18*

Kitchenware: Top: *Mixing bowl (tulips with a Mallow-like touch of black).*
Bottom: *Carnivale footed bowl, Silhouette MA bowl, and Oriental Poppy bake
dish. These are Harker's names for these bowls. I do not know what MA
stands for.*

Bowl, mixing, 10" .... *$18 – $20*
Bowl, mixing, 11" .... *20 – 25*
Bowl, mixing, 12" .... *25 – 30*
Bowl, ribbed, 10½" .... *20 – 25*
Butter, 1-pound .... *35 – 45*

*Kitchenware: Tulip Rope and Arch bowl, Oriental Poppy Rope and Arch
batter bowl with lip and tab handle, Pastel Tulip ribbed bowl, and Silhouette
Arch batter bowl with lip.*

Casserole, plain, 7½" .... *$20 – $25*
Casserole, plain, 8½" .... *20 – 25*
Cup, jumbo .... *10 – 12*
Custard, 6-ounce, 2" high....................................... *4 – 6*
Custard, 8-ounce, 2½" high .... *6 – 7*
Drip jar, Skyscraper .... *12 – 15*
Flour scoop .... *35 – 40*
Jug, Gargoyle handle, small .... *15 – 20*
Jug, Gargoyle handle, medium .... *15 – 20*
Jug, Gargoyle handle, large..................................... *20 – 25*
Jug, Ohio, ½-pint, syrup .... *25 – 30*
Jug, Ohio, 1-pint .... *ND*
Jug, Ohio, 1½-pint .... *ND*
Jug, Ohio, 2½-pint .... *ND*
Jug, Ohio, 3½-pint, batter .... *35 – 40*
Jug, refrigerator, round .... *20 – 25*
Jug, refrigerator, square....................................... *20 – 25*
Pie baker, 9" .... *10 – 12*
Pie baker, 10" .... *10 – 12*
Platter, round, 11"... *12 – 15*
Platter, square, 12¾".. *15 – 20*
Refrigerator stack set, 3-piece................................. *30 – 35*
Refrigerator stack set, 4-piece................................. *40 – 45*
Rolling pin
  Decal *65*
  Kelvinator *75*
Saucer, jumbo, 7" .... *3 – 5*
Shaker, rectangular, paper lid .... *ND*
Shaker, Skyscraper, pair.. *15 – 20*
Shaker, square, paper lid .... *ND*
Tea tile, octagonal, 6½".. *18 – 20*
Teapot .... *30 – 35*
Tray, round, 11" .... *15 – 20*
Utensil, cake server, all styles .... *12 – 15*
Utensil, fork, all styles....................................... *20 – 25*
Utensil, spoon, all styles .... *15 – 20*

ARCH   Some of these pieces have an embossed rope effect just below the rim.

Bowl, w/spout, 9½" .... *$18 – $20*
Bowl, w/rope, 8¾"... *15 – 18*
Bowl, w/rope, spout, and tab handle, 8¾"....................... *18 – 20*
Jug, w/lid .... *25 – 30*

PANELED

Casserole, 7½" .... *$15 – $20*
Jug, Ohio, batter, ½-pint .... *25 – 30*
Jug, Ohio, syrup, 3½-pint .... *20 – 25*

Kitchenware: Back: *Carnivale Arches jug, Oriental Poppy ribbed collar jug and Tulip Gargoyle jug.* Front: *Cameo Pink Ohio syrup jug, Navajo Ohio syrup jug, and "Wild Poppies" Ohio syrup jug. Note the differences in the three lids.*

Leftover, tall . . . . $15 – $20
Stack set, 3-piece . . . . 30 – 35

Kitchenware: Deco Dahlia teapot, Silhouette coffeepot (this is the same shape as GC without the embossed ribs), and Monterey 1-pound butter.

Kitchenware: Mallow rectangular shaker, Triflower scoop, Silhouette drip jar, and Tulip square shaker. The shakers have paper or foil lids, and probably date to the late twenties. Early drip jars said "Lard" while later ones said "Drips."

ZEPHYR

The bases of these pieces have a cut-in effect. Covered pieces will be found with three different finials: a sunken knob (this seems to be the early version), a ball knob, and a Deco-like fin.

The **au gratin** is deeper than the standard casserole. It came with an 8³/₄" undertray. The basic difference in the coffee pot and teapot is the style of spout.

Though there are some pieces that bear a passing resemblance to Zephyr, the pieces below are the only ones listed in company literature.

PRICING   Double values for Monterey decal.

Bowl, serving, 6" . . . . *$8 – $10*
Bowl, serving, 7" . . . . *10 – 12*
Bowl, serving, 8" . . . . *10 – 12*
Bowl, serving, 9" . . . . *12 – 15*
Casserole, 1¹/₂-quart, 7¹/₂" . . . . *20 – 25*
Casserole, 2-quart, 8¹/₂" . . . . *20 – 25*
Casserole, au gratin . . . . *20 – 25*
Casserole tray, 8¹/₄" . . . . *5 – 6*
Casserole tray, 10¹/₄" . . . . *10 – 12*
Cheese box, covered . . . . *12 – 15*
Cheese tray, round, 11" . . . . *12 – 15*
Coffee pot, 4-cup . . . . *30 – 35*
Coffee pot, 6-cup . . . . *30 – 35*
Coffee pot, 8-cup . . . . *30 – 35*
Cookie jar, 7³/₄" . . . . *35 – 40*

Zephyr: Barbecue Outdoor Ware teapot (note darker ketchup coloring on bottom, lighter mustard coloring on top), Monterey cheese tray, Petitpoint cheese box (sits in the center of the cheese tray), and Petitpoint coffeepot. The basic difference between the coffeepot and teapot is the style of spout and how the lid sits on the bottom.

Custard . . . . *$4 – $6*
Refrigerator stack set, round, 4-piece . . . . *40 – 45*
Teapot, 5-cup. . . . . *30 – 35*

Modern Vase creamer, sugar (red and black line treatment), and Whistling Teakettle creamer. This sugar and creamer shape, the most easily found among Harker shapes, puzzles me. I know it goes with the plain round shape found with the Cameo decoration (I've seen plates, cups, saucers, and casseroles that match), but I can't help thinking that they were used in the late thirties to replace the more elaborate Virginia pieces when they began to look old fashioned.

HOPEWELL CHINA COMPANY

Hopewell, Virginia

Sol Ostrow founded Hopewell in the early 1920s, making a standard grade of semiporcelain dinnerware. The name changed to the James River Potteries in the mid 1930s.

MARKS The ship mark seems to date to the 1920s. By 1930 it was replaced with the Ostrow China mark.

ENGLISH BRAMBLEBERRY

An embossed decoration.

Bowl, vegetable, oval, 9"*	*$10 – $12*
Casserole	*20 – 25*
Creamer	*4 – 6*
Cup	*4 – 6*
Dish, 5½"*	*2 – 3*
Plate, 6½"	*1 – 2*
Plate, 9"*	*7 – 9*
Platter, 11"*	*10 – 12*
Saucer	*1 – 2*
Sugar	*8 – 10*

PRINCESS ANNE

A plain round shape.

Bowl, vegetable, oval, 9½"	*$10 – $12*
Butter dish	*20 – 25*

Princess Anne: Creamer, butter dish, and sugar.

Casserole	$20 – $25
Creamer	4 – 6
Cup	4 – 6
Dish, 5½"*	2 – 3
Plate, 6¼"*	1 – 2
Plate, 9"*	7 – 9
Platter, 11"*	10 – 12
Saucer	1 – 2
Sugar	8 – 10

A. E. HULL
POTTERY COMPANY

Crooksville, Ohio

CHAPTER AT A GLANCE

ART WARE
ART WARE/EARLY
BLOSSOM FLITE
BOW-KNOT
BUTTERFLY
CALLA LILY
  (JACK-IN-THE-PULPIT)
CAMELLIA (OPEN ROSE)
CONTINENTAL
DOGWOOD (WILD ROSE)
EBBTIDE
IRIS (NARCISSUS)
MAGNOLIA (MATTE)
MAGNOLIA (GLOSSY)
MARDI GRAS (GRANADA)
ORCHID
PARCHMENT AND PINE
POPPY
ROSELLA
SERENADE
SUNGLOW
THISTLE
TOKAY (TUSCANY)
TROPICANA
TULIP (SUENO TULIP)

WATER LILY
WILD FLOWER (NUMBERED)
WILDFLOWER (REGULAR)
WOODLAND MATTE / GLOSSY
DINNERWARE
HOUSE 'N GARDEN SERVING WARE
  Mirror Brown
  Rainbow
KITCHENWARE
CINDERELLA
CRESCENT
JUST RIGHT
  Floral
  Vegetable
LITTLE RED RIDING HOOD
MARCREST
NULINE BAK-SERVE
UTILITY WARE / EARLY
  Wheat
NOVELTIES
COOKIE JARS
FIGURES
MISCELLANY
PLANTERS
VASES

The company was begun in 1905 for the manufacture of stoneware. In 1907, Hull purchased the Acme Pottery Company which made semiporcelain dinnerware. Art ware, florists ware, kitchenware, and tile were added to the lines, and in the late thirties Hull began introducing the matte finish pastel art pottery for which it is best known. Production of this ware continued through the fifties. Hull ceased production in 1985.

When known, the shape numbers have been included in the listings. Note that for some lines every shape and size has a separate number, and in others the same shape in different sizes will have the same number.

See Burke, see Hull, and see Roberts in Bibliography.

MARKS   Early marks include a capital "H" in either a circle or a diamond, impressed. Later marks include the words "Hull," "Hull Art" or "Hull Ware" with "USA" in block letters or script, as well as the shape number and size, either raised or impressed.

ART WARE

When using these listings, please remember that a number of vases were pitcher-shaped, so are listed under vase, not pitcher.

ART WARE / EARLY

Most of these pieces consist of multicolored banded vases and jardinieres predominantly in high gloss red, blue, and green. Most have the circle "H" mark. Literally hundreds of pieces are known.

Flowerpot/attached saucer, 6"...	*$50*
Jardiniere, 3" /546	*35*
Jardiniere, 4" /546	*35*
Jardiniere, 5" /536	*55*
Jardiniere, 7" /546	*80*
Jardiniere, 7" /550	*85*
Jardiniere, 7" /551	*85*
Jardiniere, 8" /536	*85*
Jardiniere, 9" /536	*100*
Vase, 5¹/₂" /25..	*55*
Vase, 7" /40	*65*
Vase, 8" /26	*70*
Vase, 8" /32	*70*
Vase, 8" /39	*70*

BLOSSOM FLITE   (1955)

Multicolored embossed flowers and leaves over a basketweave background of high gloss pink with blue lattice decor and Metallic green interior, or Charcoal gray decor with pink interior.
    The long-spouted pitcher could be used for watering plants.
    PRICING   Add 10% for gold trim.

Basket, 6" /T2	*$50*
Basket, low, 8" × 9" /T8..	*115*
Bowl, console, w/ring handles, 16¹/₂" × 6³/₄" T10..........................	*95*
Bowl, low, 4-sided, handled, 10" /T9	*125*
Candle holder, w/finger ring, pair /T11	*50*
Cornucopia, 10¹/₂" /T6	*85*
Creamer /T15	*40*
Honey Jug, 6" /T1..	*50*
Pitcher, long spout, 8¹/₂" /T3...	*100*
Planter/Flower bowl, handled, 10¹/₂" /T12..............................	*75*
Sugar /T16...	*40*

Teapot /T14 . . . . *$85*
Vase, basket, ruffled, 8¹/₂" /T4 . . . . *100*
Vase, handled, square pedestal, 10¹/₂" /T7 . . . . *85*
Vase, pitcher, 13¹/₂" /T13 . . . . *135*

BOW-KNOT (1949)

Embossed multi-colored flowers and bows in matte finish on a background of either pink with blue, or blue with blue or turquoise. Many pieces had embossed bows.

Hull was reaching perfection in detail and creativity with this most collectible of lines. Unfortunately, the 1950 fire destroyed the molds. The large basket, ewer, jardiniere, and vase are rare.

Basket, 6¹/₂" /B25 . . . . *$225*
Basket, 10¹/₂" /B12 . . . . *650*
Basket, 12" rare /B29 . . . . *1800*
Bowl, console, 13¹/₂" /B16 . . . . *300*
Candle holders, cornucopia, pair /B17 . . . . *175*
Cornucopia, 7¹/₂" /B5 . . . . *145*
Cornucopia, double, 13" /B13 . . . . *225*
Creamer /B21 . . . . *150*
Ewer, 5¹/₂" /B1 . . . . *165*
Ewer, 13¹/₂" B15 . . . . *1300*
Flowerpot, w/attached saucer, 6¹/₂" /B6 . . . . *165*
Jardiniere, w/handles, 5³/₄" /B18 . . . . *165*
Jardiniere, w/handles, 9³/₈" /B19 . . . . *900*
Sugar /B22 . . . . *150*
Teapot /B20 . . . . *400*
Vase, footed, 5" /B2 . . . . *145*
Vase, 6¹/₂" /B3 . . . . *145*
Vase, 6¹/₂" /B4 . . . . *145*
Vase, 8¹/₂" /B7 . . . . *185*
Vase, 8¹/₂" /B8 . . . . *185*
Vase, 8¹/₂" /B9 . . . . *185*
Vase, 10¹/₂" /B10 . . . . *325*
Vase, 10¹/₂" /B11 . . . . *335*
Vase, 12¹/₂" /B14 . . . . *1200*
Wall Plaque/Plate /B28 . . . . *1200*
Wall Pocket, Cup/Saucer /B24 . . . . *195*
Wall Pocket, Sad Iron, no mark *195*
Wall Pocket, Pitcher /B26 . . . . *195*
Wall Pocket, Broom (whisk) /B27 . . . . *195*

BUTTERFLY (1956)

Pink and blue flowers and butterflies with black decorate either cream-colored matte with turquoise interiors or glossy, all-white pieces.

PRICING Glossy pieces are not as popular as matte; subtract 10% to 20%.

Ashtray, heart shape   /B3 .... *$50*
Basket, 8"   /B13 .... *125*
Basket, 3 handles, 10½"   /B17 .... *300*
Bowl, console, 3 feet   /B21 .... *100*
Bowl, fruit, pinched, 10½" × 4¾"   /B16 .... *100*
Candle holder, 3 feet, pair   /B22 .... *35*
Candy dish, bonbon, round, open   /B4 .... *35*
Candy dish, urn shape, square, open   /B6 .... *45*
Cornucopia, 6½"   /B2 .... *35*
Cornucopia (vase), 10½"   /B12 .... *75*
Creamer   /B19 .... *50*
Flower dish, rectangular, 9¾" × 6¾   /B7 .... *45*
Jardiniere, 6"   /B5 .... *45*
Lavabo Font   /B24 .... *100*
Lavabo Bowl   /B25 .... *100*
Lavabo Set, 16"   /B24/B25 .... *200*
Sugar   /B20 .... *50*
Teapot   /B18 .... *135*
Tray, 3 part, 11½"   /B23 .... *100*
Vase, bud, footed, pitcher, 6"   /B1 .... *40*
Vase, 3 feet, 7"   /B10 .... *50*
Vase, 3 feet, 9"   /B9 .... *50*
Vase, 3 feet, 10½"   /B14 .... *75*
Vase/pitcher, 8¾"   /B11 .... *95*
Vase/pitcher, 13½"   /B15 .... *160*
Window box, 12¾" × 4¾"   /B8 .... *45*

CALLA LILY   (Also called Jack-in-the-Pulpit) (1938)

Embossed flowers with arrowhead-shaped green leaves in solid matte colors of cream, blue, green, purple, or turquoise, and matte-color combinations of blue/pink, cinnamon/green, cinnamon/turquoise, rose/green, and rose/turquoise.

PRICING Solid purple is the most desirable; add 10% to the prices below.

Bowl, 8"   /500-32 .... *$125*
Bowl, 10"   /500-32 .... *160*
Bowl, console, w/handle, 13"   /590-32(33?) *275*
Candle holder, finger ring, pair   /580-39 .... *150*
Cornucopia, 8"   /570-33 .... *100*
Ewer, 10"   /506 .... *275*
Flowerpot w/attached saucer, 6"   /592 .... *125*
Jardiniere, 7"   /591 .... *275*
Vase, 5"   /530-33 .... *80*
Vase, 6"   /500-33 .... *95*
Vase, 6"   /502-33 .... *95*
Vase, 6"   /503-33 .... *95*
Vase, 6"   /504-33 .... *95*
Vase, 6"   /505 .... *95*

Vase, 6"   /520-33 .... *$95*
Vase, 6"   /540-33 .... *95*
Vase, 6¹/₂"   /501-33 .... *95*
Vase, 7"   /510-33 .... *125*
Vase, 7"   /530-33 .... *110*
Vase, 7¹/₂"   /550-33 .... *125*
Vase, 8"   /500-33 .... *125*
Vase, 8"   /520-33 .... *125*
Vase, 9¹/₂"   /530-33 .... *300*
Vase, 10"   /520-33 .... *300*
Vase, 10"   /560-33 .... *300*

CAMELLIA   (Also called Open Rose) (1943)

A diverse, matte glazed line of pink and/or yellow open roses on matte pastel backgrounds of pink and blue or all white. Colored backgrounds are more desirable, but prices are the same as white. The 12" vase is hard to find, and the Mermaid planter is rare.

Basket, 6¹/₄"   /142 .... *$300*
Basket, 8"   /107 .... *275*
Basket, 10¹/₂"   /140 .... *800 – 1000*
Basket, hanging, 7"   /132 .... *200*
Bowl, console, dove head handles, 12"   /116 .... *275*
Bowl, low, 7"   /113 .... *95*
Candle holders, Dove shape, pair, 6¹/₂"   /117 .... *250*
Cornucopia, 8¹/₂"   /101 .... *110*
Cornucopia, 8¹/₂"   /141 .... *135*
Creamer, 5"   /111 .... *85*
Ewer, 4³/₄"   /128 .... *65*
Ewer, 7"   /105 .... *195*
Ewer, 8¹/₂"   /115 .... *225*
Ewer, 13¹/₄"   /106 .... *550*
Jardiniere, ram's head handles, 8¹/₄"   /114 .... *350*
Planter, Mermaid w/shell, 10¹/₂"   /104 .... *ND*
Sugar, open, 5"   /112 .... *85*
Teapot, 8¹/₂"   /110 .... *325*
Vase, 4³/₄"   /127 .... *45*
Vase, 4³/₄"   /128 .... *65*
Vase, 4³/₄"   /130 .... *55*
Vase, 4³/₄"   /131 .... *55*
Vase, 6¹/₄"   /120 .... *85*
Vase, 6¹/₄"   /121 .... *85*
Vase, 6¹/₄"   /122 .... *85*
Vase, 6¹/₄"   /133 .... *85*
Vase, 6¹/₄"   /134 .... *85*
Vase, 6¹/₄"   /135 .... *85*
Vase, 6¹/₄"   /136 .... *85*
Vase, 6¹/₄"   /137 .... *85*
Vase, 6¹/₄"   /138 .... *85*

Vase, Swan, 6½" /118 .... $110
Vase, 6½" /123. 85
Vase, bud, 7" /129 95
Vase, 8½" /102. 125
Vase, 8½" /103. 110
Vase, 8½" /108. 175
Vase, 8½" /119. 110
Vase, hand, 8½" /126. 225
Vase, 8½" /141. 135
Vase, 8½" /143. 150
Vase, 12" /124 275
Vase, Lamp (hurricane), 10½" /139. 400
Wall Pocket, 8½" /125 275

CONTINENTAL (1959)

"Sophisticated modern shapes" in colors of Evergreen, Persimmon, and Mountain Blue with contrasting vertical stripes.

The candy dish is the compote with a lid. The consolette bowl has candle holders at each end. The two-purpose vase can be turned over and used as a candle holder. The square candle holder/planter and the rectangular footed planter make a console set.

Ashtray, 8" /A1 .... $35
Ashtray, 10" /C52 55
Ashtray, pinched, rectangular, 12" /A3. 60
Ashtray w/pen, free form, 10" /A20. 50
Basket, 12¾" /C55. 125
Bowl, Caladium Leaf, 14" × 10½" /C63. 75
Bowl, consolette, 13¼" /C70 75
Candle holder/planter, footed, square, 4½" /C67 25
Candy dish, 8½" /C62C 50
Compote, footed/planter, 5½" × 6¾" /C62 40
Flower bowl, open footed, square, 9¼" /C69 50
Flower dish, 15½" × 4¾" /C51 55
Planter, footed, rectangular, 8½" × 4½" /C68. 25
Vase, 8½" /C53 45
Vase, bud, 9½" /C66 40
Vase, rose, 9¾" /C28 50
Vase, two purpose, 10" /C61 55
Vase, rose, 12" /C29 75
Vase, free form, 12½" /C54 60
Vase, pitcher, 12½" /C56. 135
Vase, 13¾" /C58 95
Vase, open front, 14½" /C57. 95
Vase, slender neck, 15" /C59. 100
Vase, pedestal, 15" /C60 100

DOGWOOD (Also called Wild Rose) (1942)

One or two embossed dogwood flowers on matte backgrounds of blue/peach, all peach, or turquoise/peach. Dogwood's popularity has been rapidly increasing. The tall ewer is rare.

NOTE   The teapot without a lid is sometimes sold as a watering can.

Basket, 7½" /501 . . . . *$265*
Bowl, console, cornucopia, 11½" /511 . . . . *200*
Bowl, low, 7" /521 . . . . *100*
Candle holders, cornucopia, pair, 4" /512 . . . . *150*
Cornucopia, 4" /522 . . . .*55*
Ewer, 4¾" /520 . . . .*95*
Ewer, 8½" (marked as 6½") /505 . . . . *225*
Ewer, 11½" /506 . . . . *300*
Ewer, 13½" /519 . . . . *700*
Jardiniere, 4" /514 . . . .*75*
Teapot, 6½" /507 . . . . *300*
Vase, 4¾" /516 . . . . *55*
Vase, 4¾" /517 . . . . *55*
Vase, suspended, 6½" /502 . . . . *150*
Vase, 6½" /509 . . . . *85*
Vase, 6½" /513 . . . . *100*
Vase, 8½" /503 . . . . *95*
Vase, 8½" /504 . . . . *95*
Vase, 8½" /515 . . . . *50*
Vase, 10½" /510 . . . . *200*
Window box, rectangular, 10½" /508 . . . . *150*

EBBTIDE   (1955)

Fish and seashell designs (as well as snails, mermaids, coral and plants) in glossy colors of Shrimp (rose) and Turquoise or Wine and Seaweed (chartreuse).

Ebbtide: Pitcher /E10.

PRICING   With gold trim, add 10%.

Ashtray w/Mermaid /E8	*$150*
Basket, 9¹/₈" /E5	*95*
Basket, 16¹/₂" × 8³/₄" /E11	*200*
Bowl, console w/snail, 15³/₄" × 9" /E12	*150*
Candle holder, pair, 2¹/₂" /E13	*75*
Cornucopia, 11³/₄" /E9	*125*
Cornucopia w/Mermaid, 7¹/₂" /E3	*175*
Creamer /E15	*45*
Sugar /E16	*45*
Teapot /E14	*165*
Vase, bud, 7" /E1	*55*
Vase, twin fish, 7" /E2	*75*
Vase, Angel Fish, 9¹/₄" /E6	*95*
Vase, fish, 11" /E7	*125*
Vase/pitcher, 8¹/₄" /E4	*95*
Vase/pitcher, 14" /E10	*175*

IRIS   (Narcissus) (1940)

One or two embossed irises decorate this line on matte finish bodies of blue and rose, all peach, or rose and peach combinations. The solid peach pieces do not seem to be as sought after as the multi-colored pieces, but values are similar.

The small advertising plaque is hard to find and the large one is rare. Both are ND.

Basket, 7" /408	*$275*
Bowl, console, 12" /409	*200*
Bowl, Rose, 4" /412	*65*
Bowl, Rose, 7" /412	*125*
Candle holders, pair, 5" /411	*125*
Ewer, 5" /401	*75*
Ewer, 8" /401	*200*
Ewer, 13¹/₂" /401	*450*
Jardiniere, 5¹/₂" /413	*95*
Jardiniere, 9" /413	*300*
Vase, 4³/₄" /402	*50*
Vase, 4³/₄" /403	*50*
Vase, 4³/₄" /404	*50*
Vase, 4³/₄" /405	*50*
Vase, 4³/₄" /406	*50*
Vase, 4³/₄" /407	*50*
Vase, 7" /402	*95*
Vase, 7" /403	*95*
Vase, 7" /404	*95*
Vase, 7" /405	*95*
Vase, 7" /406	*95*
Vase, 7" /407	*95*
Vase, bud, 7¹/₂" /410	*115*
Vase, 8¹/₂" /402	*125*

Vase, 8½" /403. . . . . *$125*
Vase, 8½" /404. . . . . *125*
Vase, 8½" /405. . . . . *125*
Vase, 8½" /406. . . . . *125*
Vase, 8½" /407. . . . . *125*
Vase, 10½" /403. . . . . *300*
Vase, 10½" /404. . . . . *300*
Vase, 10½" /405. . . . . *300*
Vase, 10½" /414. . . . . *300*
Vase, 16" /414 . . . . *500*

MAGNOLIA (Matte) (1946)

Embossed Magnolia flowers on backgrounds of either pink or blue or rose (often resembles brown) and yellow. Prices are usually identical though some collectors seem to prefer pink/blue.

Basket, 10½" /10 . . . . *$300*
Bowl, console, 12½" /26. . . . . *150*
Candle holders, pair, 4½" /27. . . . . *100*
Cornucopia, 8½" /19. . . . . *95*
Cornucopia, double, 12½" /6 . . . . *125*
Creamer /24 . . . . *50*
Ewer, 4¾" /14 . . . . *45*
Ewer, 7" /5. . . . . *95*
Ewer, 13½" /18 . . . . *300*
Sugar, open /25 . . . . *50*
Teapot /23 . . . . *150*
Vase, 4¾" /13. . . . . *40*
Vase, 6¼" /4. . . . . *45*
Vase, 6¼" /11. . . . . *45*
Vase, 6¼" /12. . . . . *45*
Vase, 6¼" /15. . . . . *45*
Vase, 8½" /1. . . . . *95*
Vase, 8½" /2. . . . . *95*
Vase, 8½" /3. . . . . *95*
Vase, 8½" /7. . . . . *95*
Vase, 10½" /8. . . . . *125*
Vase, 10½" /9. . . . . *125*
Vase, w/winged handles, 12¼" /17 . . . . *225*
Vase, 12½" /22. . . . . *225*
Vase, w/tassle, open handles, 12½" /21. . . . . *225*
Vase, w/tassle, closed handles, 12½" /21 . . . . *225*
Vase, floor vase, 15" /16 . . . . *400*
Vase, floor vase, 15" /20 . . . . *400*

MAGNOLIA (Glossy) (1947)

(Also called New Magnolia) Most of the shapes in the glossy line are the same as the matte; they consist of hand-painted pink or blue embossed Magnolias on a solid pink glossy background.

PRICING   Add 10% for gold trim.

Basket, 10½" /H14	$225
Bowl, console, 13" /H23	75
Candle holder, pair, 4" /H24	75
Cornucopia, 8½" /H10	65
Cornucopia, double, 12" /H15	75
Creamer /H21	50
Ewer, 8½" /H11	75
Ewer, 13½" /H19	250
Sugar /H22	50
Teapot /H20	125
Vase, 5½" /H1	30
Vase, 5½" /H2	30
Vase, ewer, 5½" /H3	40
Vase, 6½" /H4	30
Vase, 6½" /H5	30
Vase, 6½" /H6	30
Vase, 6½" /H7	30
Vase, 8½" /H8	65
Vase, 8½" /H9	65
Vase, 10½" /H12	75
Vase, 10½" /H13	75
Vase, w/winged handles, 12½" H16	150
Vase, w/tassle, closed handles, 12½" /H17	150
Vase, 12½" /H18	150

MARDI GRAS   (Also called Granada)

A matte line that encompasses a variety of shapes—some plain and some with undecorated embossed flowers. Colors are: white, pink top/blue bottom, or peach/rose (on the floral pieces). Many of the vases and planters come in solid colors of pink and yellow. See also Kitchenware.

Basket, 8" /32	$125
Basket, 8" /65	125
Basket, Morning Glory, 8" /62	400
Ewer, 10" /31	115
Ewer, Morning Glory, 11" /66	400
Teapot, 5½" /33	200
Vase, 9" /47	45
Vase, 9" /48	45
Vase, 9" /49	45
Vase, 9" /215	45
Vase, 9" /216	45
Vase, 9" /217	45

Vase, 9" /218 .... *$45*
Vase, 9" /219 .... *45*
Vase, Morning Glory, 9" /61 .... *200*

ORCHID (1939)

Hand-painted embossed Orchids decorate rose pink/ivory, blue/rose pink, or all blue matte finish backgrounds. Pieces in this very collectible line have been increasingly difficult to locate lately, especially larger items such as the 9¹/₂" jardiniere.

Basket, 7" /305 .... *$500*
Bookends, pair, 7" /316 .... *800 – 1200*
Bowl, console, 13" /314 .... *300*
Bowl, low, 7" /312 .... *100*
Candle holders, 4", pair /315 .... *200*
Ewer, 13" /311 .... *600*
Jardiniere, 4³/₄" /317 .... *75*
Jardiniere, 4³/₄" /310 .... *95*
Jardiniere, 6" /310 .... *175*
Jardiniere, 9¹/₂" /310 .... *400*
Vase, 4¹/₂" /304 .... *75*
Vase, 4³/₄" /301 .... *75*
Vase, 4³/₄" /302 .... *75*
Vase, 4³/₄" /303 .... *75*
Vase, 4³/₄" /307 .... *75*
Vase, 4³/₄" /308 .... *75*
Vase, 6" /301 .... *125*
Vase, 6" /302 .... *125*
Vase, 6" /303 .... *125*
Vase, 6" /304 .... *125*
Vase, 6¹/₂" /300 .... *125*
Vase, 6¹/₂" /307 .... *125*
Vase, 6¹/₂" /308 .... *125*
Vase, bud, 6³/₄" /306 .... *125*
Vase, 8" /301 .... *175*
Vase, 8" /302 .... *175*
Vase, 8" /303 .... *175*
Vase, 8" /307 .... *175*
Vase, 8" /308 .... *175*
Vase, 8" /309 .... *175*
Vase, 8¹/₂" /304 .... *175*
Vase, 10" /301 .... *300*
Vase, 10" /302 .... *300*
Vase, 10" /303 .... *300*
Vase, 10" /307 .... *300*
Vase, 10¹/₄" /304 .... *300*
Vase, 10¹/₂" /308 .... *300*

PARCHMENT AND PINE   (1951)

Pine cone sprays on glossy backgrounds of Pearl gray with brown trim or Turquoise with black trim. The cornucopias were made in a left facing and right facing version; they are marked with an "L" or an "R" suffix. Larger pieces are getting scarce; cornucopias seem to be commonplace.

Ashtray/center bowl   /S14 .... *$110*
Basket, 6"   /S3 .... *75*
Basket, 16"   /S8 .... *160*
Bowl, console, 16"   /S9 .... *95*
Candle holder, pair, 2³/₄"   /S10 .... *50*
Coffee pot, 8"   /S15 .... *125*
Cornucopia, left/right, 8"   /S2 .... *50*
Cornucopia, left/right, 12"   /S6 .... *90*
Creamer   /S12 .... *35*
Ewer, 13¹/₂"   /S7 .... *185*
Planter/window box   /S5 .... *85*
Sugar   /S13 .... *35*
Teapot   /S11 .... *100*
Vase, 6"   /S1 .... *50*
Vase, 10"   /S4 .... *75*

POPPY   (1943)

A matte line with yellow and pink hand-painted embossed Poppies on pink and blue, pink and cream or allover cream backgrounds. Poppy has been getting more difficult to find and seems to be as popular as Bow-Knot. The large basket and ewer are rare.

Basket, 9"   /601 .... *$600*
Basket, 12"   /601 .... *1200*
Cornucopia, 8"   /604 .... *225*
Ewer, 4³/₄"   /610 .... *100*
Ewer, 13¹/₂"   /610 .... *700*
Jardiniere, 4³/₄"   /603 .... *65*
Jardiniere, 4³/₄"   /608 .... *75*
Planter/bowl, 6¹/₂"   /602 .... *150*
Vase, 4³/₄"   /605 .... *65*
Vase, 4³/₄"   /606 .... *65*
Vase, 4³/₄"   /607 .... *65*
Vase, 4³/₄"   /611 .... *65*
Vase, 4³/₄"   /612 .... *65*
Vase, 6¹/₂"   /605 .... *95*
Vase, 6¹/₂"   /606 .... *95*
Vase, 6¹/₂"   /607 .... *95*
Vase, 6¹/₂"   /611 .... *95*
Vase, 6¹/₂"   /612 .... *95*
Vase, 8¹/₂"   /605 .... *150*

Vase, 8½"   /606. . . . . *$150*
Vase, 8½"   /607. . . . . *150*
Vase, 8½"   /611. . . . . *150*
Vase, 8½"   /611. . . . . *150*
Vase, 10½" /605. . . . . *300*
Vase, 10½" /606. . . . . *300*
Vase, 10½" /607. . . . . *300*
Vase, 10½" /611. . . . . *300*
Vase, 10½" /612. . . . . *300*
Wall Pocket, 9" /609 . . . . *350*

ROSELLA (1946)

Glossy wild rose designs on either coral or ivory backgrounds. Flowers are found in either pink or white, with or without green painted leaves. One piece of R1 has been found in a matte finish. There are both left- and right-handed versions of R9, R11, and R13, with "L" and "R" suffixes after each number in the mark; values are the same.

Basket, 7" /R12 . . . . *$185*
Cornucopia, left/right, 8½"   /R13 . . . . *75*
Creamer, 5½" /R3. . . . . *50*
Ewer, 6½" /R7
    Dimpled *100*
    Smooth *45*
Ewer, left/right, 6½" /R9 . . . . *75*
Ewer, left/right, 7" /R11 . . . . *85*
Sugar, open, 5½" /R4 . . . . *50*
    w/lid *60*
Vase, 5" /R1 . . . . *35*
Vase, 5" /R2 . . . . *35*
Vase, 6½" /R5 . . . . *45*
Vase, 6½" /R6 . . . . *45*
Vase, 6½" /R7 . . . . *45*
Vase, heart shape, 6½"   /R8 . . . . *75*
Vase, 8½" /R14 . . . . *75*
Vase, 8½" /R15 . . . . *75*
Wall Pocket, heart shape, 6½"   /R10 . . . . *85*
Window box, ... *ND*

SERENADE (1957)

Embossed birds on branches. Pieces are either Regency (pastel) blue with Sunlight yellow interior, Shell pink with Pearl gray interior, or Jonquil yellow with Willow green interior.

The candy jar is the urn with the addition of a lid. The casserole came with a metal warmer stand. The footed fruit bowl and the candlesticks made a console set. The window box looks like an elongated bowl.

PRICING Some pieces will be found in a solid color with undecorated birds; subtract 25% for these pieces. Add 10% for gold trim.

Ashtray, 3-sided, 13" × 10½"   /S23 .... $95
Basket, bonbon, 6¾"   /S5 95
Basket, 12" × 11½"   /S14 350
Bowl, footed fruit, 11½"   /S15 110
Candlestick, pair, 6½"   /S16 70
Casserole, 9"   /S20 125
Cornucopia (vase), 11"   /S10 95
Creamer   /S18 45
Mug, 8-ounce   /S22 55
Pitcher, beverage, 1½-quart   /S21 125
Sugar   /S19 45
Teapot, 6-cup   /S17 175
Urn, no cover, 5¾"   S3 50
    w/cover (candy dish)   /S3C 95
Vase, 14"   /S12 100
Vase, bud, 6½"   /S1 50
Vase, flared, 8½"   /S6 55
Vase, pedestal, 8½"   /S7 55
Vase, pitcher, 6½"   /S2 60
Vase, pitcher, 8½"   /S8 85
Vase, pitcher, 13¼"   /S13 350
Vase, Puritan (hat), 7¼"   /S4 55
Vase, rectangular, 10½"   /S11 95
Window box, 12½"   /S9 95

SUNGLOW (1948)

Hand-painted embossed flowers, either five-petaled or pansies, in glossy colors of pink on yellow background or yellow on pink background. Sometimes butterflies and bows are part of the decoration. Some Bow-Knot molds were used for Sunglow pieces.

One of the unusual aspects of this line are the kitchenware pieces.

PRICING Add 10% for gold trim.

Basket, 6½"   /84 .... $65
Bell, pottery handle, no mark, 6½"   /87 75
Bell, rope handle, no mark, 6¼"   /86 75
Bowl, mixing, 5½"   /50 20
Bowl, mixing, 7½"   /50 30
Bowl, mixing, 9½"   /50 40
Casserole, 7½"   /51 50
Cornucopia, 8½"   /96 50
Drip jar, 5¼"   /53 35
Ewer, 5½"   /90 40
Flowerpot, 5½"   /97 35
Flowerpot, 7½"   /98 45
Pitcher, 24-ounce   /52 35

Pitcher, ice lip, 7¹/₂"   /55. .... $85
Planter, hanging, 7"   /99 65
Shaker, pair, 2³/₄"   /54 20
Vase, 5¹/₂"   /88. 35
Vase, 5¹/₂"   /89. 35
Vase, 6¹/₂"   /91. 40
Vase, 6¹/₂"   /92. 40
Vase, 6¹/₂"   /93. 40
Vase, 6¹/₂"   /100. 40
Vase, 8"   /94 45
Vase, 8¹/₂"   /95. 45
Vase, embossed flamingo, 8³/₄"   /85 45
Wall Pocket, Cup/saucer, 6¹/₄"   /80 65
Wall Pocket, Iron, unmarked, 6"   /83. 65
Wall Pocket, Pitcher, 5¹/₂"   /81. 65
Wall Pocket, Whisk broom, 8¹/₂"   /82 65

THISTLE   (1938)

Hand-painted embossed thistle flowers on solid matte backgrounds of blue, pink, or turquoise.

Vase, 6¹/₂"   /51. .... $150
Vase, 6¹/₂"   /52. 150
Vase, 6¹/₂"   /53. 150
Vase, 6¹/₂"   /54. 150

TOKAY   (Also called Tuscany) (1958)

Names are used interchangeably.

Decoration is embossed grapes and leaves with twig handles. Tokay is pink grapes and green leaves on cream background with Light Green bottom and Sweet Pink top. Tuscany is either Gray-Green grapes on Sweet Pink background or Forest Green grapes on Milk White background. All are high gloss.

The candy dish is the planter with a lid. The consolette is a footed bowl with two candle holders at either end. The floor vase, slender neck vase, and leaf bowl may have been made in Tuscany colors only.

PRICING   Prices are the same for all colors though pink and green seem to be more popular.

Basket, 8"   /6 .... $75
Basket, Moon, 10¹/₂"   /11 95
Basket, pedestaled, 12"   /15 175
Bowl, flower, leaf shape, 14" × 10¹/₂"   /19. 55
Bowl, fruit, 9¹/₂"   /7 125
Candy dish, covered, 8¹/₂"   /9C 95
Consolette, 15³/₄"   /14. 145
Cornucopia, 6¹/₂"   /1. 35
Cornucopia, 11"   /10 55

Creamer, /17 .... $35
Planter, 5½" × 6½" /9 50
Sugar /18 35
Teapot, 6-cup /16 125
Urn, 5½" /5 55
Vase, 6" /2 35
Vase, 8¼" /4 75
Vase, 10" /8 95
Vase, floor, 15" /20 200
Vase, spool, 12" /12 85
Vase/pitcher, 8" /3 80
Vase/pitcher, 12" /13 175
Vase/pitcher, slender neck, 14" /21 175

TROPICANA   (1959)

This very rare high gloss line consists of Caribbean figures on a pure white background with a Tropic Green edge. Molds from the Continental line were used.

The scarceness is partly due to Tropicana's issue in 1959–1960 during the Cuban crisis. It simply was not popular during this era, and there is speculation that a lot of the product was destroyed because of the international situation.

Ashtray, 10" × 7½" /T52 .... $400
Basket, fancy, 12¾" /T55 700
Flower bowl, 15½" × 4¾" /T51 400
Planter vase, 14½" /T57 600
Vase, flat sided, 8½" /T53 400
Vase, slender, 12½" /T54 500
Vase/pitcher, 12½" /T56 600

TULIP   (Also called Sueno Tulip) (1938)

Hand-painted tulips are featured on this popular matte finish line in cream/blue, pink/blue, or all blue coloration.

Basket, 6" /102–33 .... $225
Flowerpot w/saucer, 4¾" /116–33 95
Flowerpot w/saucer, 6" /116–33 165
Jardiniere, 5" /117–30 95
Jardiniere, 7" /115–33 300
Vase, 4" /100–33 65

Tropicana:
Flower bowl /T51.

Vase, suspended, 6"   /103–33 .... *$175*
Vase, bud, 6"   /104–33 .... *95*
Vase, 6"   /106–33 .... *95*
Vase, 6"   /107–33 .... *95*
Vase, 6"   /108–33 .... *95*
Vase, 6"   /110–33 .... *95*
Vase, 6"   /111–33 .... *95*
Vase, 6¹/₂"   /100–33 .... *95*
Vase, 6¹/₂"   /101–33 .... *95*
Vase, 6¹/₂"   /106–33 .... *95*
Vase, 8"   /100–33 .... *150*
Vase, 8"   /105–33 .... *150*
Vase, 8"   /107–33 .... *150*
Vase, ewer, 8"   /109–33 .... *195*
Vase, 9"   /101–33 .... *175*
Vase, 10"   /100–33 .... *250*
Vase, 10"   /101–33 .... *300*
Vase, ewer, 13"   /109–33 .... *375*

TUSCANY   See Tokay

WATER LILY   (Matte) (1948)

Raised, hand-painted Water Lilies on pastel backgrounds of either Walnut (brown) and Apricot (white flower) or Turquoise and Sweet Pink (yellow flower) with an embossed, rippling water effect. Turquoise and Sweet Pink is more popular.

PRICING   Add 10% for gold trim.

Basket, 10¹/₂"   /L14 .... *$300*
Bowl, console, 13¹/₂"   L21 .... *150*
Candle holder, pair, 4¹/₂"   /L22 .... *100*
Cornucopia, 6¹/₂"   /L7 .... *70*
Cornucopia, double, 12"   /L27 .... *165*
Creamer   /L19 .... *50*
Ewer, 5¹/₂"   /L3 .... *55*
Ewer, 13¹/₂"   /L17 .... *350*
Flowerpot/saucer, 5¹/₂"   /L25 .... *125*
Jardiniere, 5¹/₂"   /L23 .... *95*
Jardiniere, 8¹/₂"   /L24 .... *250*
Sugar   /L20 .... *50*
Teapot   /L18 .... *175*
Vase, 5¹/₂"   /L1 .... *45*
Vase, 5¹/₂"   /L2 .... *45*
Vase, ewer, 5¹/₂"   /L3 .... *55*
Vase, 6¹/₂"   /L4 .... *55*
Vase, 6¹/₂"   /L5 .... *55*
Vase, 6¹/₂"   /L6 .... *55*
Vase, 8¹/₂"   /LA *150*

Vase, 8½"   /L8 .... $125
Vase, 8½"   /L9 125
Vase, 9½"   /L10 125
Vase, 9½"   /L11 125
Vase, 10½"   /L12 165
Vase, 10½"   /L13 165
Vase, 12½"   /L15 300
Vase, 12½"   /L16 300

WILD FLOWER   (Numbered, old series) (1942)

Hand-painted, embossed wildflower sprays featuring Trillium, on pastel backgrounds of blue and pink, pink and brown, or solid cream. There are also a lot of cream and blue pieces with gold trim. Larger items are quite scarce since their very ornate design renders them quite fragile. /I in the list below identifies pieces that are identical to regular Wildflower.

   PRICING   Add 10% for gold trim.

Basket, low, 7"   /65 .... $700
Basket, 10½"   /66 1500
Basket, 10½"   /79 2000
Bowl, console, 12"   /70 325
Candle holder, double, pair, 4"   /69 200
Cornucopia, 6¼"   /58 125
Creamer   /73 250
Ewer, 4½"   /57 95
Ewer, 7¼"   /63 300
Ewer, 13½"   /55   /I 1000
Jardiniere, 4"   /64 75
Sugar, open   /74 250
Teapot, butterfly finial   /72 1000
Vase, 4½"   /56 95
Vase, 5¼"   /52 125
Vase, 6¼"   /54 125
Vase, 6¼"   /60 135
Vase, 6¼"   /61 135
Vase, 6¼"   /62 135
Vase, ewer, 7¼"   /63 300
Vase, cornucopia, 7½"   /68 115
Vase, 8½"   /51 250
Vase, 8½"   /53   /I 250
Vase, 8½"   /67 275
Vase, 8½"   /75 275
Vase, butterfly handles, 8½"   /76 275
Vase, 8½"   /78 275
Vase, 10½"   /59 250
Vase, 10½"   /77 300
Vase, 12"   /71 300

WILDFLOWER   (Regular) (1946)

Hand-decorated embossed wildflowers (identified in company literature as Trillium, Mission, and Bluebell) on backgrounds of pink and blue or yellow and rose decorate this matte finish line. Flowers are often brighter than in the old series.

Basket, 10½" /W16	*$350*
Bowl, console, 12" /W21	*125*
Candle holders, pair, no mark, 2½" /W22	*100*
Cornucopia, 7½" /W7	*75*
Cornucopia, 8½" /W10	*95*
Ewer, 5½" /W2	*65*
Ewer, 8½" /W11	*150*
Ewer, 13½" /W19	*450*
Vase, 5½" /W1	*45*
Vase, 5½" /W3	*45*
Vase, 6½" /W4	*65*
Vase, 6½" /W5	*65*
Vase, 7½" /W6	*75*
Vase, 7½" /W8	*75*
Vase, 8½" /W9	*125*
Vase, 9½" /W12	*135*
Vase, 9½" /W13	*135*
Vase, 10½" /W14	*150*
Vase, fan, 10½" /W15	*150*
Vase, 12½" /W17	*200*
Vase, 12½" /W18	*200*
Vase, floor, 15" /W20	*425*

WOODLAND

Matte   (1949 / Pre-Fire)

Matte-finish items have multi-colored floral designs featuring pink flowers with yellow centers on *both* sides of the pieces. Backgrounds are pastels of Harvest Yellow and green or Dawn Rose and peach. A number of gloss-finish pieces in solid colors of white, ivory, or light pink exist, some with gold trim; values are the same as the other pieces as these do not appeal to all collectors.

Matte   (1950 / Post-Fire)

Not every item in the original line was remade. Similar in colors to the previous line except for a poorer quality finish and lack of fine detail. There is only a pink flower on the front side and leaves on the reverse. Post-fire pieces are more difficult to find than the earlier ones, but are not as desirable.

Glossy   (1950)

Same as 1950 matte line but in glossy colors of peach/pink, chartreuse/rose, or blue/dark green. Easily found with gold trim.

PRICING If you find white with gold, add 10%.

	Pre-Fire	Post-Fire	Glossy
Basket, hanging, 7½" /W12	$500	—	$35
Basket, 8¾" /W9	185	125	110
Basket, 10½" /W22	750	350	215
Bowl, console, 14" /W29	275	175	100
Candle holder, pair, 3½" /W30	130	100	70
Cornucopia, 5½" /W2	55	45	40
Cornucopia, 6¼" /W5	65	—	—
Cornucopia, 11" /W10	130	75	65
Cornucopia, double, 14" /W23	450	—	—
Creamer /W27	75	50	35
Ewer, 5½" /W3	65	50	45
Ewer, 6½" /W6	85	75	65
Ewer, 13½" /W24	550	250	200
Flowerpot/saucer, 5¾" /W11	150	100	75
Jardiniere, 5½" /W7	125	75	65
Jardiniere, 9½" /W21	650	500	250
Planter, hanging, 5¾" /W31	125	—	—
Sugar /W28	75	50	35
Teapot /W26	325	175	125
Vase, 5½" /W1	55	—	35
Vase, 6½" /W4	65	50	45
Vase, 7½" /W8	95	65	60
Vase, suspended, 7½" /W17	225	—	—
Vase, 8½" /W16	125	100	80
Vase, bud, double horn, 8½" /W15	125	125	65
Vase, 10½" /W18	165	125	95
Vase, 12½" /W25	350	—	—
Wall Pocket, Shell, 7½" /W13	150	100	75
Window box, 10" /W14	100	100	55
Window box, 10½" /W19	125	—	95

DINNERWARE

HOUSE 'N GARDEN SERVING WARE (1960)

This is a general name for a variety of lines, the most popular of which is Mirror Brown. Other colors were used on these lines and many shapes were shared between them. None were in continuous manufacture as long as Mirror Brown.

NOTE Some shape numbers were reused when molds were retired.

Mirror Brown (1960–1985)

Glazed in Mirror Brown with Ivory Foam edges.

The **Chicken server** is decorated with an engraved chicken in the well. The **Coffee carafe** was made to fit in the 7-ounce coffee cup. The **Dutch oven** is two square bakers. The **hexagonal sauce dish** and the **four-compartment tray** make a Chip 'n Dip set. The **jam/mustard** is the same piece as the individual bean pot except that it has a cutout in the lid for a spoon. The **oval tray** was part of three two-piece sets: **Soup 'n Sandwich** (w/soup mug), **Snack Set** (w/coffee mug), and **Toast 'n Cereal** (w/12-ounce cereal bowl). The **salad bowl** came with two non-ceramic utensils. The **Warmer** (no number) went under the 3-pint French handle casserole (the set number is 579).

The bottoms of some of the covered pieces were sold separately as bakers or open casseroles. In the list below, these are marked "Open" following the appropriate listing.

Ashtray, heart shape, 7"   /18 .... $25
Ashtray, ruffled, 8"   /563 25
Bank, piggy, Corky   /195 40
   w/Blue/Pink trim 40
Bank, piggy, Corky (jumbo)   /197 100
   w/Turquoise & yellow trim 100
Bank, piggy, sitting   /196 40
   w/Turquoise & yellow trim 40
Bean pot, individual, 12-ounce   /524 5
Bean pot, 2-quart   /510 20
Bowl, Bake & Serve, tab handle, 6½" diameter   /589 6
Bowl, mixing, 6"   /536 6
Bowl, mixing, 7"   /537 9
Bowl, mixing, w/pouring spout, 8"   /538 12
Bowl, mixing, 5¼"   /505 10
Bowl, mixing, 6¾"   /506 12
Bowl, mixing, 8¼"   /507 15
Bowl, onion soup, lug, w/lid, 12-ounce   /535 7
   Open   /534 5
Bowl, salad/spaghetti, 10¼"   /545 25
Bowl, salad, low, oval, 6½" × 5¼"   /508 18
Bowl, salad server, rectangular, 11" × 6½"   /583 18
Bowl, serving, divided, 14½" × 8½"   /577 50
Bowl, serving dish, lug, oval, 10" × 5"   /574 8
Bowl, soup/salad, 6½"   /569 6
Bowl, vegetable, divided, 10¾" × 7¼"   /542 12
Bud vase, 9"   /535 22
Butter, ¼-pound   /561 6
Canister, ball shape, "Tea," 6" 60
Canister, ball shape, "Coffee," 7" 60
Canister, ball shape, "Sugar," 8" 60
Canister, ball shape, "Flour," 9" 60
Canister, Train Set
   Caboose 500
   Coal Car 500
   Engine 500
   Passenger Car 500
Carafe, w/lid, 2-cup   /505 25

Casserole, Chicken lid, 1-quart   /5840 . . . . *$60*
Casserole, Chicken lid, 2-quart   /5850 . . . . *60*
Casserole, Duck lid, 1-quart   /5280 . . . . *60*
Casserole, Duck lid, 1-quart   /5770 . . . . *60*
Casserole, French handle, 5¼"   /527 . . . . *7*
   Open   /513 . . . . *5*
Casserole, French handle, 3-pint   /562 . . . . *7*
   Open   /567 . . . . *5*
Casserole, Hen on Nest   /592 . . . . *75*
Casserole, oval, 2-pint, 10" × 7¼"   /544 . . . . *18*
   Open   /543 . . . . *12*
Casserole, oval, 2-quart, 10" × 7¼"   /548 . . . . *20*
Casserole, round, 32-ounce   /507 . . . . *15*
   Open (Baker)   /506 . . . . *10*
Casserole, restyled, 32-ounce   /314 . . . . *15*
Chicken baker, w/Chicken lid, 13⅜" × 11" high   /560 . . . . *125*
Chicken baker, no lid, 13⅜" × 10½" × 3"   /558 . . . . *60*
Chicken server, w/Chicken lid, 13⅜" × 10" high   /559 . . . . *125*
Chicken server, no lid, 13⅜" × 10½" × 2"   /557 . . . . *60*
Chip 'n Dip, leaf shape, 11½" × 8¾"   /583 . . . . *18*
Chip 'n Dip, leaf shape, 12¼" × 9"   /591 . . . . *18*
Chip 'n Dip, leaf shape, 15" × 10½"   /521 . . . . *20*
Coaster/Spoon rest, Gingerbread Boy, 5"   /399 . . . . *25*
Coffee carafe, w/lid, 2-cup *25*
Coffee pot, lock lid, 60-ounce, 8-cup   /522 . . . . *25*
Cookie jar, "Cookies," 94-ounce   /523 . . . . *25*
Cookie jar, Ginger Bread Boy   /323 . . . . *150*
Corn serving dish, 9¼" × 3⅜"   573 . . . . *25*
Creamer/jug, 8-ounce   /518 . . . . *4*
Cruet, "Oil," 12-ounce   /584 . . . . *20*
Cruet, "Vinegar," 12-ounce   /585 . . . . *20*
Cup, tea, 6-ounce   /529 . . . . *5*
Cup, coffee, 7-ounce   /597 . . . . *5*
Custard, 6-ounce   /576 . . . . *8*
Dish, cereal/fruit, 12-ounce, 5¼"   /503 . . . . *3*
Dish, fruit, 6"   /533 . . . . *5*
Dish, individual, leaf shape, 7¼" × 4¾"   /590 . . . . *8*
Dutch oven, 3-pint   /565 . . . . *30*
   Open (square baker)   /568 . . . . *15*
Egg plate, w/engraved chickens, 9¼"   /591 . . . . *22*
Gravy boat, 16-ounce   /511 . . . . *14*
Gravy liner, oval, 10¼" × 6"   /512 . . . . *8*
Jam/Mustard jar, w/spoon, 12-ounce   /551 . . . . *6*
Jug, 2-pint   /525 . . . . *15*
Jug, 5-pint   /509 . . . . *25*
Jug, ball, ice lip, 2-quart   /514 . . . . *20*
Mug, coffee, 9-ounce   /502 . . . . *4*
Mug, continental, footed, 10-ounce   /571 . . . . *10*

Mug, soup, 11-ounce   /553 .... $5
Pie baker, 9¼"   /566 25
Plate, 6½"   /501 3
Plate, 8½"   /531 9
Plate, 9⅜"   /599 9
Plate, 10¼"   /500 5
Plate, spaghetti, ind., oval, 10¾" × 8¼"   /581 11
Platter, fish shape, individual, with engraved fish, 11¼" × 7¾"   /596 35
Platter, steak, oval, individual, 11¾" × 9"   /541 9
Platter, steak, oval, Well 'n Tree, 14" × 10"   /593 40
Ramekin, 2½-ounce   /600 6
Roaster, 7-pint   /534 125
  Open   /536 60
Sauce bowl, hexagonal, 5½" diameter   /584 10
Saucer, tea, 5½"   /530 3
Saucer, coffee, 5⅞"   /598 3
Shaker, grated cheese, "Cheese," 12-ounce   /582 20
Shaker, salt, jug shape, w/cork, 3¾" high   /515 4
Shaker, pepper, jug shape, w/cork, 3¾" high   /516 4
Shaker, salt, jug shape, w/o cork, 2¼"* high   /594 4
Shaker, pepper, jug shape, w/o cork, 2¼"* high   /595 4
Shaker, salt, mushroom shape, 3¾" high   /587 10
Shaker, pepper, mushroom shape, 3¾" high   /588 10
Skillet server, 11½" × 7¾"   /595 15
Spoon rest, "Spoon Rest," 6¾"   /594 25
Stein, beer, 16-ounce   /526 6
Stein, jumbo, 32-ounce   /572 40
Sugar, 12-ounce   /519 5
Teapot, 5-cup   /549 20
Tid-bit tray, 2-tier   /592 28
Tray, 4-compartment, 6-sided, 12" × 11"   /585 50
Tray, Gingerbread Man, 10" × 10"   /198 30
Tray, oval, cup well at side   /554 7
Tray, Serv-All, leaf shape, 12" × 7½"   /540 50
Warmer 40

Rainbow

Rainbow was made in fewer items than Mirror Brown.

The four colors were Avocado, Butterscotch, Mirror Brown, and Tangerine, all with Ivory Foam edge. The mixing bowls and Serv-All tray were available in Mirror Brown and Tangerine only. In addition, a Rainbow flyer indicates that all House 'n Garden pieces were made in Mirror Brown and Tangerine.

	Avocado	Butterscotch	Tangerine
Bowl, mixing, 6"	$10	$15	$12
Bowl, mixing, 7"	12	17	14
Bowl, mixing, w/pouring spout, 8"	25	35	35
Bowl, vegetable, divided, 10¾" × 7¼" /942	12	22	20

	Avocado	*Butterscotch*	*Tangerine*
Bowl, soup/salad, 6½"	*$5*	*$6*	*$6*
Chip 'n Dip set, leaf shape, 12¼" × 9" /591	22	25	25
Cup, 6-ounce	*4*	*5*	*5*
Dish, individual, leaf shape, 7¼" × 4¾" /590.	*8*	*12*	*10*
Jug, ball, ice lip, 2-quart /514	*35*	*35*	*35*
Mug, coffee, 9-ounce.	*4*	*5*	*5*
Plate, 8½"	*8*	*8*	*8*
Plate, 10½"	*6*	*8*	*8*
Saucer, 5½"	*4*	*5*	*5*
Tid-bit tray, 2-tier /592.	*40*	*40*	*40*
Tray, oval, cup well at side /554	*12*	*12*	*12*
Vase, bud, 9" /935	*25*	*25*	*25*

KITCHENWARE

Not all of Hull's very early or late kitchenware is collectible. Some of the early ware, when unmarked, is not distinguishable from similar products made at the same time. See also Sunglow in the Art Ware section.

CINDERELLA   (1948)

The bakers are the casseroles minus lids.
    This line consists of two hand-painted, underglaze decorations on yellow or white backgrounds: 1. "Blossom" (a large pink or yellow flower) or 2. "Bouquet" (three flowers, yellow, blue and pink).

Baker, 7½" /21	*$35*
Baker, lug, 8½" /21	*45*
Bowl, mixing, 5½" /20.	*20*
Bowl, mixing, 7½" /20.	*40*
Bowl, mixing, 9½" /20.	*60*
Casserole, 7½" /21	*70*
Casserole, lug, 8½" /21	*80*
Cookie jar, 10" /30	*100*
Creamer /28	*30*
Grease jar, 32-ounce /24.	*40*
Pitcher, 16-ounce /29	*45*
Pitcher, 32-ounce /29	*55*
Pitcher, ice lip, 64-ounce /22	*85*
Serving dish, square, 9½".	*15*
Shaker, range, pair /25	*45*
Sugar /27.	*40*
Teapot /26	*95*

CRESCENT   (1952)

Named for the crescent-shape finials on the lids. The small mixing bowl doubled as a cereal bowl.

Rose w/maroon handles and lids, or yellow w/dark green handles and lids.

Bowl, mixing, 5½"..$10
Bowl, mixing, 7½"..15
Bowl, mixing, 9½"..20
Casserole, lug, 6¼"..25
Casserole, lug, 10"...40
Cookie jar..65
Creamer...20
Jug, w/ice lip..35
Mug, 12-ounce...15
Shaker, pair..20
Sugar...25
Teapot, 6-cup...65

JUST RIGHT

The shapes are the same for these two lines.

Floral

An embossed yellow flower with a brown center on an ivory background that is reminiscent of Abingdon's Daisy pattern.

Bowl, cereal, 6"..$12
Bowl, mixing, 5"...10
Bowl, mixing, 6"...15
Bowl, mixing, 7"...20
Bowl, mixing, 8"...25
Bowl, mixing, 9"...30
Bowl, mixing, lipped, 9"...40
Bowl, salad, 10½"..45
Casserole, 7½"...40
Casserole, French, open, 5"..15
  w/lid..25
Cookie jar, "Cookies"..50
Grease jar, "G"..35
Jug, 1-quart...40
Shaker, range, "S" or "P," pair..25

Vegetable

An embossed pattern in solid colors of coral, green, or yellow.

Bowl, cereal, 6"...$15
Bowl, mixing, 5"...12
Bowl, mixing, 6"...18
Bowl, mixing, 7"...25
Bowl, mixing, 8"...30
Bowl, mixing, 9"...35
Bowl, mixing, lipped, 9"...50
Bowl, salad, 10½...50
Casserole, 7½"...45

Casserole, French, open, 5"... *$20*
   w/lid.. *30*
Cookie jar, "Cookies"... *60*
Grease jar, "G".. *40*
Jug, 1 quart... *50*
Shaker, range, "S" or "P".. *30*

LITTLE RED RIDING HOOD   (1943)

Designed by Louise Bauer. While these items were credited to Hull, and sold by them, Joyce Roerig discovered that most of the production was done by Regal China.

A figural line featuring Red Riding Hood and the Wolf with hand-painted detail and floral decals (usually Poppy) on a gloss white background with or without gold and red trim. Gold trim is fairly common. Some all-white pieces will be found; these are less popular.

The planter and the water pitcher with the ruffled skirt may be one of a kind. The advertising plaque and baby dish are extremely rare, as are two other pieces that have turned up since the last edition of this book: one is a basket utilizing the wolf jar bottom and a flowered lid with tab handle, the other is a stick-handled casserole with a Red Riding Hood lid and bows around the bottom. Several types of mustard spoons exist, with and without floral decals.

This line is not only popular among Hull collectors, but is sought by many others as well.

NOTE   Beware of Mexican cookie jars that closely resemble Hull's. Identification: they are slightly smaller in height and overall size. Also, gold decals are being added to pieces and refired. See Pam Curran's remarks under Shawnee in the Reproduction section of the appendices for advice that also applies to Red Riding Hood.

PRICING   You will note that some of the prices reflect a "downward market correction" as they say on Wall Street.

Advertising plaque, "Featuring Little Red Riding Hood, Covered by Pat. Des. No.135889"... *ND*
Baby dish, three-compartment.. *$5000+*
Bank, standing, 7".. *650*
Bank, Wall, slot in basket, 9".. *2200+*
Butter dish... *395*
Canister, blank.. *650*
Canister, Cereal... *1000*
Canister, Coffee... *650*
Canister, Flour.. *650*
Canister, Popcorn.. *2200+*
Canister, Potato chips... *2200+*
Canister, Pretzels... *2200+*
Canister, Salt... *1000*
Canister, Sugar.. *650*
Canister, Tea.. *650*
Canister, Tidbits.. *2200+*
Casserole dish, red handle, w/lid.. *ND*

*Red Riding
Hood: Rare
casserole.
Value: ND*

Cookie jar, w/apron, open end basket (dozens of floral variations) *$350*
Cookie jar, w/apron, round basket. *350*
Cookie jar, no apron, round basket (Poinsettias). . . . . *900+*
Creamer, side open *150*
Creamer, spout on top of head, tab handle *250*
Creamer, ruffled skirt, ring handle *375*
Grease jar, Wolf lid, ears up *900*
Grease jar, Wolf lid, ears down. . . . . *975+*
Jar, Cracker, basket in front, 8½" *575*
Jar, Dresser, bow in front, basket on side, 9" *625*
Jar, Spice, Allspice *700*
Jar, Spice, Cinnamon. *700*
Jar, Spice, Cloves. *700*
Jar, Spice, Ginger. *700*
Jar, Spice, Nutmeg. *700*
Jar, Spice, Pepper. *700*
Jars, Spice, set of six *4200*
Jug, batter, 6⅞" *400*
Jug, milk, 8". *300*
Jug, water, ruffled skirt, 8" . . . . *ND*
Lamp . . . . *2300+*
Match box, 5¼" (2 styles) *750*
Mug, hot chocolate. . . . . *2000+*
Mustard jar, w/spoon, 5½". *375*
     without spoon, 5½" *325*
Planter, basket on side . . . . *ND*
Shaker, pair, 3½" *60*
Shaker, pair, 4½" *850*
Shaker, pair, 5½" *150*
Shaker, kneeling, pair. . . . . *ND*
String holder, wall hanging, 9" *2500*
Sugar, side, open *150*
Sugar, "creeping," open. . . . . *250 – 275*

Sugar, ruffled skirt, covered *$400*
Teapot *325*
Wall Bank . . . . *2200+*
Wall Pocket/planter *475*

MARCREST

This line was a mystery for a while. Now we know that some of it was made by Hull. As Brenda Roberts reports, it was made for Marshall Burns, a Chicago distributor. Hull made a dinnerware line in pastel colors of coral, mint green, pink, yellow, and white. The brown dinnerware was made by Western Stoneware.

Ashtray 7½" *$10*
Bowl, mixing, small *15*
Bowl, mixing, medium *25*
Bowl, mixing, large *35*
Cocoa pot, 11" *65*
Jug, 7½" *40*
Mug, 9-ounce *15*

NULINE BAK-SERVE   (1937)

Items in this line were available in three embossed designs: diamond quilt (B prefix on numbers), drape and panel (D prefix on numbers), and fish scale (C prefix on numbers).

Colors are blue, cream, maroon, pink, turquoise, and yellow.

Bean pot, 5½"   /19 . . . . *$35*
Bowl, mixing, 5"   /1 . . . . *20*
Bowl, mixing, 6"   /1 . . . . *25*
Bowl, mixing, 7"   /1 . . . . *30*
Bowl, mixing, 8"   /1 . . . . *35*
Bowl, mixing, 9"   /1 . . . . *40*
Casserole, 7½"   /13 . . . . *50*
Casserole, stick handle, 4½"   /15 . . . . *25*
Cookie jar, 8"   /20 . . . . *100*
Custard, 2¾"   /14 . . . . *10*
Jug, batter   /7 . . . . *65*
Jug, tilt, ice lip, 7"   /29 . . . . *70*
Jug, tilt, ice lip, 2-quart, 8½"   /29 . . . . *85*
Jug, syrup   /7 . . . . *55*
Mug, 3½"   /25 . . . . *15*
Teapot, 6-cup   /5 . . . . *75*

UTILITY WARE / EARLY

Issued in the 1920s, most pieces are either green or yellow, or have colored bands on solid colored bodies, though many variations exist.

Bowl, green, 7"   /421 . . . . *$40*
Bowl, fluted, 5"   /106 . . . . *30*

Casserole, 7½"   /113 . . . . *$65*
Mug, "Happy Days," 5"   /497. . . . . *45*
Salt box, fluted, 6"   /111 . . . . *125*
Stein, 6½"   /496 . . . . *70*
Tankard, 9½"   /492 . . . . *225*

Wheat   This line was made in blue, green, tan, and yellow, though green is the most easily found color. Shades of green will vary.

Wheat: Sugar canister.

Canister, 6½"
    Coffee. *$80*
    Rice *80*
    Sugar *80*
    Tea *80*
Cruet, oil, 6½" . . . . *ND*
Cruet, vinegar, 6½" . . . . *ND*
Salt, wooden lid *100*
Spice jar, 3½"
    Cinnamon *65*
    Ginger *65*
    Mustard *65*
    Nutmeg *65*
    Pepper *65*
    Spice *65*

NOVELTIES

While some of these items will have a Hull mark, many will be marked with a line name only, such as Imperial, which Hull made in prodigious quantity from 1960 to 1980.

COOKIE JARS

See also Kitchenware/Cinderella, Crescent, Heritageware, House 'n Garden, Just Right, and Little Red Riding Hood.

Barefoot Boy .... *$375 – $400*
Duck   /966, 11½" .... *60 – 75*
Hen and Chick, 11½"   /968 .... *275 – 300*
Little Boy Blue, 12½"   /971 .... *1000 +*

FIGURES

The swing band was matte ivory with a little hand decoration (facial features, buttons) and gold trim.

Band, Swing
  Accordian Player, 6" .... *$100 – $150*
  Band Leader, 6½" .... *100 – 150*
  Clarinet Player, 6" .... *100 – 150*
  Drummer, 5½" .... *100 – 150*
  Tuba Player, 5¾" .... *100 – 150*
Love birds   /93 .... *40*
Swan 8½"   /69 .... *40*

MISCELLANY

Both the #197 Pig and the Corky Pig banks have a cork with an attached metal ring in the snout for emptying coins.

Bank, pig, sitting, 6"   /196 .... *$50*
Candle holder, Bandanna Duck, pair, 3½" *60*
Wall Pocket, Chinese Sage Mask, 8"   /120
  Gloss Black *25*
  Gold *25*
Wall Pocket, Flying Goose, 6"   /67 .... *35*
Wall Pocket, Mandolin, 7"   /84 .... *35*
Wall Pocket, Violin, 7"   /85 .... *35*

PLANTERS

Many of these came in more than one decorative treatment. Some of these doubled as either ashtrays, centerpieces, or vases; these are noted in parenthesis. Wall Pocket/Planters are listed as Wall Pockets in Miscellany above.

Baby w/Pillow, 5½"   /92 .... *$25*
Bandanna Duck, 3½"   /76 .... *20*
Bandanna Duck, 7"   /75 .... *30*
Bandanna Duck, 9"   /74 .... *45*
Basket girl, 8"   /954 .... *40*
Cherub, head, 7¼"   /90 .... *25*
Chickadee, tail down, 5¼"   /474 .... *20*
Chickadee, tail up, 6"   /F473 .... *20*
Clown, 6½" × 8½"   /82 .... *35*
Dancing girl, 7"   /955 .... *50*
Ducks (pair), large   /94 .... *25*
Geese (pair), heads up, 6½"   /95 .... *45*

Girl, head, 6¹/₂"   /62   /159 .... $25
Goose, long-neck, "The Duchess," 12¹/₄"   /411 .... *50*
Knight on Horse, 8"   /55 .... *65*
Lamb, 7¹/₂"   /965 .... *45*
Madonna, bust, hands clasped (vase), 7"   /24 .... *25*
Madonna, bust, hands clasped, 9¹/₂"   /417 .... *50*
Madonna, kneeling (vase), 7¹/₄"   /25 .... *30*
Madonna, standing, 8" × 7"   /81 .... *35*
Madonna, standing w/urns, 11¹/₂"   /27 .... *45*
Madonna w/child (vase), 7"   /26 .... *30*
Parrot pulling cart, 9¹/₂" long   /60 .... *30*
Pheasant   /61 .... *30*
Pig, bust, 6¹/₂"   /39   /159 .... *25*
Poodle, bust, 6¹/₂"   /38   /159 .... *25*
Poodle, 8"   /114 .... *40*
Rooster, 5³/₄"   /53 .... *20*
St. Francis, 11¹/₂"   /89 .... *55*
Swan, head up, 6"   /80 .... *30*
Swan (pair), 10¹/₂"   /81 .... *65*

VASES

Bird, 9" $50
Hand w/Cornucopia, 7³/₄"   /83 .... *35*
Peacock, embossed, 10¹/₂"   /73 .... *35*
Shell, 9"   /415 .... *35*
Suspended   /108 .... *35*
Triple bulb, 7"   /107 .... *25*
Unicorn, 9¹/₂"   /98 .... *35*
Unicorn, 11¹/₂"   /99 .... *45*

IROQUOIS CHINA COMPANY

Syracuse, New York

Begun in 1905. Closed in 1969. Produced hotel ware. Best known to collectors today for its Russel Wright and Ben Seibel lines. Of the five Seibel lines, Impromptu and Informal are the easiest to find, Inheritance and Intaglio are difficult, and Interplay is rare.

MARKS All of the lines listed here have marks specific to their shapes.

CARRARA MODERN (<1955)

A marbled effect on either dark gray or white background.

Au gratin, oval, 9½"	$12 – $15
Bowl, vegetable, divided w/lid, oval	40 – 50
Bowl, vegetable, round, 9⅛"	15 – 18
Bowl, vegetable, round, 10"	18 – 20
Casserole, oval, 9½"	40 – 50
Coffee pot w/locklid	50 – 60
Creamer	10 – 12
Cup	6 – 8
Dish, 6¼"	4 – 6
Dish, 6⅝"	4 – 6
Gravy	15 – 18
Gravy liner	10 – 12
Jug, covered, 7½" high	40 – 45
Plate, 6½"	5 – 7

Carrera Modern:
Platter and cup.

Plate, 7½" .... *$8 – $10*
Plate, 9½"* .... *12 – 15*
Plate, chop, 13½" .... *25 – 30*
Platter, oval, 12½" .... *20 – 25*
Platter w/indented well and tree .... *30 – 40*
Saucer .... *2 – 3*
Shaker, pair .... *12 – 15*
Sugar .... *12 – 15*

CASUAL CHINA (1946)

Designed by Russel Wright. Several pieces were restyled, including cup/saucer, gravy, teapot, sugar, creamer, butter dish, mug, water pitcher, and several dishes. The old teapot is sometimes called a coffee pot. Hard-to-find pieces include AD cup/saucer, butters, carafe, new gravy, mug, and party plate. You will find many more stack creamers, both sizes, than stack sugars. In the restyled line, the fruit dish is the sugar bowl minus the lid.

Colors found are Aqua, Avocado Yellow, Brick Red, Canteloupe, Charcoal Grey, Ice Blue, Lemon Yellow, Lettuce Green, Nutmeg Brown, Oyster Gray, Parsley Green (dark green), Pink Sherbet (1955), Ripe Apricot, and Sugar White. Mustard Gold (brownish yellow) replaced Avocado. Around 1953–1954, Iroquois added a mottled glaze effect to the line that it called Raindrop. Decorations, mostly floral, were added in 1959.

PRICING For items that were restyled, price is the same for old and new unless otherwise stated. Add 40% for Aqua, Brick Red, and Canteloupe.

Dinnerware

Bowl, gumbo, 8¼" × 7¾" .... $30 – $35
Bowl, salad, 10" .... 25 – 30
Bowl, soup, 5". .... 18 – 20
   Lid for above .... 15 – 20
Bowl, vegetable, 8". .... 20 – 22
Bowl, vegetable, 10". .... 26 – 28
Bowl, vegetable, w/lid, 10". .... 45 – 50
Butter, old .... 75 – 90
Butter, restyled. .... 100 – 125
Carafe. .... 90 – 125
Casserole, 2-quart .... 50 – 60
Casserole, 4-quart .... 70 – 80
Coffee pot. .... 80 – 90
Coffee pot, AD. .... 60 – 65
Creamer, new .... 15 – 18
Creamer, stack, regular .... 8 – 10
Creamer, stack, family .... 20 – 25
Cup. .... 8 – 10
Cup, AD. .... 80 – 90
Cup, coffee, tall, 9-ounce. .... 20 – 25
Dish, fruit, 9-ounce. .... 7 – 8
Dish, cereal, 11½-ounce. .... 7 – 8
Gravy, w/lid/stand, restyled. .... 80 – 90
Gravy, w/lid, old .... 25 – 28

Casual China: Butter, old-style creamer (bird decoration), carafe, restyled sugar and creamer.

Gravy stand, old .... *$10 – $12*
Mug, old .... *45 – 50*
Mug, restyled .... *65 – 75*
Pitcher, w/lid, old... *65 – 70*
Pitcher, restyled .... *125 +*
Plate, 6¹/₂"... *5 – 6*
Plate, 7³/₈".. *7 – 8*
Plate, 9¹/₂".. *8 – 9*
Plate, 10" .... *9 – 10*
Plate, chop, 14" .... *30 – 35*
Plate, party .... *40 – 45*
Platter, 12³/₄" .... *16 – 18*
Platter, 14¹/₂" .... *18 – 24*
Saucer.. *2 – 3*
Saucer, AD.. *20 – 25*
Saucer, coffee.. *5 – 7*
Shaker, stacking.. *10 – 12*
Sugar, stack, regular... *15 – 20*
Sugar, stack, family size .... *25 – 30*
Sugar, restyled .... *15 – 18*
Teapot, old (coffee pot) .... *60 – 75*
Teapot, restyled .... *100 – 125*

Cookware

Casserole, 3-quart .... *$60 – $65*
Casserole, 4-quart .... *60 – 65*
Casserole, 6-quart .... *90 – 100*
Dutch oven, 6-quart... *90 – 100*
Fry pan, w/lid, 10¹/₄".. *150*
Percolator .... *ND*
Sauce pan, w/lid, 3¹/₂-pint..................................... *100 – 125*
Serving tray, electric, 17¹/₂" × 12¹/₄" .... *ND*

IMPROMPTU   (1956)

Designed by Ben Seibel. The candelabra is officially called a centerpiece insert and sits on the centerpiece dish. A condiment set is the condiment dish with two cruets, two shakers, and the mustard. Several pieces came with metal warmers.

Known decorations are Aztec, Beige Rose, Blue Doves, Blue Vineyard, Bridal White (all white), Colonial Blue/Pink, Country Garden, El Camino, Fjord, Frolic, Garland, Georgetown, Grapes, Harvest Time, House of Flowers, Jardinieres, Lazy Daisy, Luau, Old Orchard, Parasols, Pins and Beads, Pompon, Pyramids, Sleepy Hollow, Spring Flowers, Stellar, Tiara, Vision, and Wild Rose.

Ashtray/butter pat/coaster, 4⅛" .... *$8 – $10*
Bowl, salad .... *15 – 18*
Bowl, soup, coupe, 7¼" .... *10 – 12*
Bowl, soup, lug, 14-ounce .... *10 – 12*
Bowl, vegetable, 8½" .... *10 – 12*
Bowl, vegetable, divided, 12½" .... *12 – 15*
Bowl, vegetable, oval, 10" .... *10 – 12*
Butter, ¼-pound .... *15 – 20*
Candelabra, cone-shaped ceramic base w/5 metal arms .... *ND*
Casserole, 2-quart .... *20 – 25*
   w/warmer .... *30 – 35*
Celery, 15" .... *15 – 20*
Centerpiece dish, 14½" .... *ND*
Cheese dish, round, covered .... *20 – 25*
Coffee pot, 7-cup .... *50 – 60*
   w/warmer .... *60 – 70*
Compote, fruit, 5¼" .... *15 – 20*
Condiment dish, w/metal handle .... *20 – 25*

Impromptu

Creamer .... *$4 – $6*
Cruet w/stopper .... *20 – 25*
Cup, low, 2¹/₄" .... *4 – 6*
Cup, tall, 3" .... *4 – 6*
Gravy faststand .... *12 – 15*
Jug, water, 11¹/₂" high .... *35 – 45*
Mug, 11-ounce... *12 – 15*
Mustard... *15 – 18*
Plate, 6¹/₂" .... *1 – 2*
Plate, 8" .... *4 – 5*
Plate, 10" .... *10 – 12*
Platter, 11" .... *10 – 12*
Platter, 13" .... *12 – 15*
Relish tray/individual platter, 11³/₄" .... *10 – 12*
Saucer, low cup .... *1 – 2*
Saucer, tall cup .... *1 – 2*
Shaker, either size.. *6 – 8*
Sugar .... *8 – 10*

INFORMAL

Designed by Ben Seibel. The following lids are interchangeable: casserole/dutch oven/fry pan, gumbo soup/saucepan, and samovar/sugar.

All informal decorations have reverse solid colors. These are used on the undersides of flatware, the outsides of hollowware, and the insides of cups. Some pieces don't have the pattern, just a solid color; these are indicated with "/S" in the list below. Decorations include Blue Diamonds, Blue Vineyard, Bombay Blue/Green, Georgetown, Harvest Time, Lazy Daisy, Old Orchard, Rosemary, Sleepy Hollow, and Teuton/Thane.

Ashtray/butter pat/coaster .... *$8 – $10*
Bowl, soup, coupe, 8"   /S .... *10 – 12*
Bowl, soup, gumbo, open, 18-ounce .... *10 – 12*
      w/lid .... *12 – 15*
Bowl, soup, lug, 13-ounce, 7¹/₂"............................... *10 – 12*
Bowl, vegetable, oval, divided, 11"   /S....................... *10 – 12*
Bowl, vegetable, oval, 10¹/₂" .... *10 – 12*
Butter, ¹/₄-pound, rectangular .... *15 – 20*
Casserole, 2-quart, 9¹/₄"....................................... *20 – 25*
Cheese dish, round, covered .... *20 – 25*
Coffee pot, 9-cup.. *50 – 60*

Informal

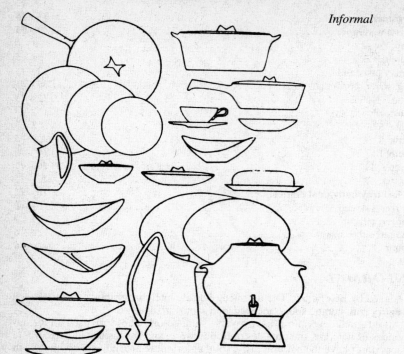

Creamer	$4 – $6
Cup /S	4 – 6
Dish, fruit /S	2 – 3
Gravy faststand	12 – 15
Jug, milk, 40-ounce, 9" high	35 – 40
Lazy Susan (Buffet Server), 1 section	6 – 8
6 sections on revolving metal stand	50 – 60
Mug, 11-ounce	12 – 15
Plate, 6½"	1 – 2
Plate, 8" /S	5 – 7
Plate, 10¼"	10 – 12
Platter, 12"	10 – 12
Platter, 15½"	15 – 18
Samovar, metal spout, 24-cup	80 – 90
Saucer /S	1 – 2
Shaker, either size	6 – 8
Sugar	8 – 10

COOKING ITEMS Per company literature, you could fry, bake, broil, roast, and then serve in these items.

Dutch oven, w/lid, 4-quart	$40 – $45

Fry pan, w/lid, 10" .... $40 – $45
Saucepan, w/lid, 1-quart .... 40 – 45

INHERITANCE

Designed by Ben Seibel. Many of the serving pieces were "elegantly pedestaled on black lacquer" stands. Items that came with these stands have /S after the listing below. There was also a black lacquer serving tray.

DECORATIONS Baroque, Beige Rose, Cotillion, Dynasty, Grecian Gold, Knollwood, Medallion, Pyramids, Sheer White (undecorated or with a gold or platinum band), Su-Shi, and Teuton/Thane.

Bowl, salad, 10"   /S .... $15 – $18
Bowl, soup, 9" .... 10 – 12
Bowl, vegetable, divided, rectangular .... 12 – 15
Bowl, vegetable, oval, 9¾" .... 10 – 12
Casserole, 1½-quart   /S .... 20 – 25
Creamer .... 4 – 6
Cup .... 4 – 6
Dish, footed, 4½" .... 2 – 3
Dish, 6" .... 3 – 4
Gravy faststand .... 12 – 15
Plate, 6¼" .... 1 – 2
Plate, 8" .... 4 – 5
Plate, 10½" .... 10 – 12
Platter, 12½" .... 12 – 15
Platter, 16"   /S .... 15 – 18
Saucer .... 1 – 2
Sugar .... 8 – 10
Teapot   /S .... 30 – 40

INTAGLIO

Designed by Ben Seibel. An embossed band with a light-and-shadow effect. The trivet did multiple duty, as a tile for the teapot, a trivet for the casserole, a chip 'n' dip with the fruit dish, and a canape server with the soup/cereal.

DECORATIONS Blue Dahlia, Old English (Blue/Pink), Painted Daisy, Rosette (Jade/Sun), Diamond White, and Woodale.

Beverage Server, w/lid, 8-cup .... $25 – $35
Bowl, vegetable .... 10 – 12
Casserole, 2½-quart.. 20 – 25
Creamer .... 4 – 6

Cup . . . . *$4 – $6*
Dish, fruit. . . . . *2 – 3*
Dish, soup/cereal . . . . *2 – 3*
Plate, 6⅝" . . . . *1 – 2*
Plate, 8½" . . . . *4 – 5*
Plate, 10⅝" . . . . *10 – 12*
Platter, small . . . . *10 – 12*
Platter, 15¼" . . . . *15 – 18*
Saucer . . . . *1 – 2*
Sugar . . . . *8 – 10*
Trivet Server . . . . *10 – 15*

INTERPLAY   (<1954>)

This line is rare; I have no information on it. I would appreciate hearing from collectors who have company brochures and buying experience.

PATTERN LIBRARY

Aztec, Fjord, and Pyramids are the same design, repeating triangles but in different colors.

AZTEC   A geometric pattern in sun-toned gold and burnt orange.

BAROQUE   A border of taupe scroll work with accents of saffron gold.

BEIGE ROSE   A perfect rose in softest pink and beige.

BLUE DIAMONDS   Three floral diamonds in Bristol blue and charcoal gray are lightly accented with yellow on a translucent white background. Reverse side color repeats Bristol blue.

BLUE DOVES   A bower of delicate green branches encircles two pale blue doves. Fragile little flower shapes in unusual pastels add a unique color accent.

BLUE VINEYARD   A border design of berries and flowers in blue and brown with reverse blue color.

BOMBAY BLUE/GREEN   Shapes within shapes. Blue: Burnt ochre/blue/black combine with Bristol blue. Green: Lime/blue-green/black contrasted with gray-green.

COLONIAL BLUE/PINK   Old-fashioned rose bouquet in varying shades of blue or pink.

COTILLION   A tiny, jewel-like banded pattern of coin gold scrolls and turquoise squares.

COUNTRY GARDEN   A raised enamel border treatment. Meadow flowers in a muted gray and a gray-green highlighted by pink and deep orange.

DAHLIA   Golden Dahlia: gossamer blossoms applied as if by hand in warm orange/gold and two-tone pink with brown and ochre accents; or Blue Dahlia: cool turquoise blue and lavender/mauve with green line work.

AZTEC/FJORD/PYRAMIDS

BEIGE ROSE

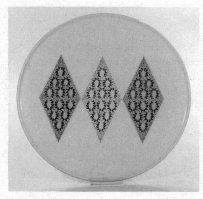

BLUE DIAMONDS

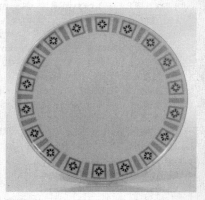

BOMBAY

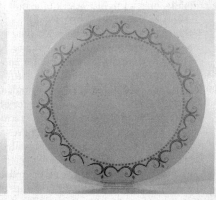

COLONIAL BLUE/PINK

COTILLION

Pattern Library

DYNASTY   A band of burnt red-orange inscribed with mystic Oriental characters in golden ochre.

EL CAMINO   Burnt orange accents on a brown and white geometric band.

FJORD   A geometric pattern in blue and green.

FROLIC   Abstract forms in pink, deep orange, and delicate tropic green.

GARLAND   A modern floral in blue and white.

GEORGETOWN   A floral band in green and brown.

GRAPES   Lavender/pink grapes with brown and green leaves.

GRECIAN GOLD   A modified Grecian key motif in coin gold and silvery gray.

HARVEST TIME   Autumn foliage in a silhouette pattern and color scheme; three leaves—one orange, one yellow, one pale gray—displayed against white. Reverse side color is burnt orange.

HOUSE OF FLOWERS   A semiformal border arrangement of floral and leaf designs in seven colors ranging from violet to soft pinks and greens.

JARDINIERES   Hanging baskets in charcoal gray, coral, and pink.

KNOLLWOOD   Airy sprays of green leaves with light, medium, and dark blue flowers.

LAZY DAISY   Five breeze-touched daises—blue, field green, and citron yellow—are gracefully arrayed in a dell of translucent white china. Reverse side color repeats the citron yellow.

LUAU   Red tropical flowers with mustard accents.

MEDALLION   Reminiscent of a regal seal done in tones of golden buff and gray-green.

OLD ORCHARD   Fruits and grapes in blue and brown with brown leaves, reverse brown color.

PAINTED DAISY   Warm soft pink with yellow, ochre, and brown details, or cool light-to-dark blue and turquoise with shades of green for accent.

PARASOLS   Star shapes of pale blue and lavender with flashes of gleaming gold in an Oriental manner.

PINS AND BEADS   Turquoise and birch brown.

POMPON   A Far Eastern motif of chrysanthemum blossoms. A bright orange center accents the sandstone petals.

PYRAMIDS   A geometric border of muted blue and gray.

ROSEMARY   Three roses in warm tones of pink with dainty green leaves on translucent white, with a reverse delicate gray-green color.

ROSETTE   Petal upon petal shaded from solid tone to delicate tint in warm, sunny apricot with soft beige-to-brown centers, stems, and leaves, or cool turquoise with lime green and avocado detailing.

SLEEPY HOLLOW   Flowers in hues of blue, gold, and green on translucent white with citron yellow backing.

SPRING FLOWERS   Splashes of burnt orange, spring green, yellow, turquoise, soft brown.

GARLAND

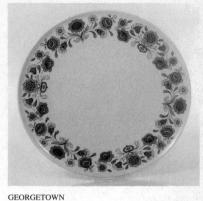

GEORGETOWN

GRAPES

GRECIAN GOLD

HARVEST TIME

JARDINIERES

Pattern Library

KNOLLWOOD

LAZY DAISY

OLD ORCHARD

PAINTED DAISY

ROSEMARY

ROSETTE

Pattern Library

SLEEPY HOLLOW

STELLAR

TEUTON/THANE

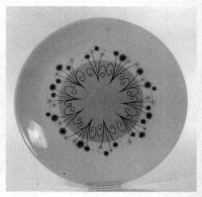

VISION

WILD ROSE

WOODALE

Pattern Library

STELLAR　Starlike shapes in dove green, golden apricot, soft gray.

SU-SHI　Stylized daisies in orange and pink.

TEUTON/THANE　A contemporary motif suggesting heraldic symbols. Thane: sky blue and lettuce-leaf green set off by Bristol blue. Teuton: sand and russet with burnt orange.

TIARA　Spanish influence shows in this border design of loops and lines set off by burnt orange and black.

VISION　Jewel-like accents of pink and sapphire blue with pinpoints and lines of subtle gray in an off-center pattern.

WILD ROSE　Lovely roses amid a graceful swirl of leaves.

WILD VIOLET　A border design similar to Georgetown in shades from blue to purple.

WOODALE　A band of blue and purple five-petaled flowers and buds with green leaves.

JAMES RIVER POTTERIES

Hopewell, Virginia

Originally begun as the Hopewell China Company, the name was changed ca. 1935, possibly as the result of a reorganization.

MARKS Most pieces are marked. Usually pieces have one of the three marks shown. The conjoint "JR," either impressed or stamped in blue, is the most common. Some pieces will be found with either the script backstamp in red or a black block letter backstamp.

VIRGINIA

CASCADE (1935)

Designed by Simon Slobodkin.

Bowl, vegetable, round, 8½"	*$9 – $10*
Cookie jar	*30 – 35*
Creamer	*4 – 6*
Cup	*4 – 6*
Dish, 6"	*2 – 3*
Dish, lug, 6¼"	*3 – 4*
Pickle, 10¾"	*6 – 8*

Cascade Relish, sugar, creamer, and teapot.

Plate, 6¼" .... *$1 – $2*
Plate, 9½" .... *5 – 7*
Platter, 13½" .... *12 – 15*
Relish .... *10 – 12*
Saucer .... *1 – 2*
Sugar .... *8 – 10*
Teapot .... *20 – 25*

EDWIN M. KNOWLES CHINA COMPANY

Chester and Newell, West Virginia

CHAPTER AT A GLANCE

DINNERWARE	MARION
ALADDIN	POTOMAC/AMERICAN TRADITION
ALICE ANN	REGENT
ARCADIA / SYLVAN	ROSLYN
BEVERLY	SYLVAN
CREME FLUTE	WILLIAMSBURG
DEANNA	YORKTOWN
DIANA	**KITCHENWARE**
ESQUIRE	OHIO JUGS
HOSTESS	UTILITY WARE

In 1900, six months after the announcement that Taylor, Smith and Lee were building a pottery in Chester, Edwin M. Knowles, son of the founder of Knowles, Taylor, Knowles, announced a second pottery for that town: the Knowles China Company. Ware was on the market in 1901. Production was semiporcelain: toilet ware, dinnerware, kitchenware, and specialties. In 1913 the company built additional facilities in Newell, West Virginia. The Chester plant was sold to Harker in 1931, and the Newell plant ceased manufacturing in 1963. Don't be confused by the fact that Knowles used an East Liverpool, Ohio, mailing address.

E. M. Knowles did not have an outstanding sales success with any one line, as did some of its competitors, but collectors today are drawn to Deanna, a solid-color ware with both bright and pastel colors (as well as decals), Yorktown dinnerware for its art deco shape, the Utility Ware kitchen line, and Russel Wright's Esquire.

MARKS The first four backstamps refer to body color. "The Edwin M. Knowles Ivory" dates to 1925, when Knowles followed Sebring's lead being the second general ware pottery to manufacture an ivory body. Nile (green), Roma (yellow), and Old Rose (pink) all date to the late 1920s, when these colors were popular.

The next backstamp, the vase, dates to the 1920s and perhaps earlier. It seems to have been taken out of use around 1929–1930 and then brought back

THE EDWIN M. KNOWLES IVORY

ROMA

OLD ROSE

NILE

EDWIN M KNOWLES CHINA CO.

EDWIN M. KNOWLES CHINA CO. MADE IN U. S. A.

THE EDWIN M. KNOWLES CHINA CO. UNION MADE IN U.S.A.

in 1939 for a few years. It had either "Vitreous" (white-bodied institutional ware) or "Semi-Vitreous" across it, though the latter is most often found.

The ship backstamp was introduced ca. 1930–1931. It was sometimes used by itself, more often in combination with a shape name in either script or block letters beneath it.

The *K* in an oval backstamp replaced the ship ca. 1940.

Knowles was better than many potteries at dating its pieces. The first two digits of the number found under many backstamps indicate the year of manufacture.

DINNERWARE

E. M. Knowles had a distinctive way of naming some of their shapes. For certain shapes, the name would change depending on the body color. For example, Alice Ann is an ivory body, but on a pink body it is called Alice Annglow.

ALADDIN

A round shape. From what I can tell, this shape seems to be Deanna-shape pieces with a new casserole, teapot, sugar, creamer, gravy, cup, AD cup, and cream soup cup. The sherbet did double duty as a single eggcup.

Bowl, oval, 8"*	$10 – $12
Bowl, oval, 9"*	10 – 12
Bowl, round, 8"*	15 – 18
Bowl, round, 9"*	15 – 18
Bowl, round, 10"*	18 – 20
Bowl, soup, coupe, 8"*	10 – 12
Bowl, 36s	7 – 10
Butter dish, open	15 – 20
Casserole	20 – 25
Coaster	8 – 12
Creamer	4 – 6
Cup	4 – 6
Cup, AD	10 – 12

Aladdin: Creamer and sugar (Currier & Ives), and teapot.

Cup, cream soup .... *$12 – $16*
Dish, 5¹/₂"* .... *2 – 3*
Dish, 6¹/₄"* .... *3 – 4*
Eggcup, double .... *10 – 12*
Gravy .... *12 – 15*
Gravy liner .... *6 – 8*
Plate, 6"* .... *1 – 2*
Plate, 7"* .... *4 – 5*
Plate, 8"* .... *5 – 6*
Plate, 9"* .... *7 – 9*
Plate, 10"* .... *10 – 12*
Plate, chop .... *15 – 20*
Plate, square, 7"* .... *5 – 6*
Platter, 8"* .... *8 – 10*
Platter, 11"* .... *10 – 12*
Platter, 13"* .... *12 – 15*
Platter, 15"* .... *15 – 18*
Saucer .... *1 – 2*
Saucer, AD .... *3 – 5*
Saucer, cream soup .... *5 – 8*
Sherbet .... *10 – 12*
Shaker, pair .... *8 – 10*
Sugar .... *8 – 10*
Teapot .... *25 – 30*

ALICE ANN (1931)

An octagonal shape with an embossed decoration inside the rim of the flatware and around the shoulder of the hollowware. There are two styles of casserole.

Alice Ann Creme (ivory) and Alice Annglow (pink). Decals: Pansy.

Bowl, oval, 8"* .... *$10 – $12*
Bowl, oval, 9"* .... *10 – 12*

Alice Ann: Plate (decal with a touch of black similar to Harker's Mallow), and gravy.

Bowl, round, 8¹/₂"..$15 – $18
Bowl, soup, 7¹/₂"..10 – 12
Bowl, 36s...7 – 10
Butter dish..20 – 25
Casserole..20 – 25
Creamer...4 – 6
Cup..4 – 6
Cup, AD..10 – 12
Cup, cream soup..12 – 16
Dish, 5¹/₂"*...2 – 3
Dish, 6¹/₄"*...3 – 4
Gravy..12 – 15
Gravy faststand...12 – 15
Jug...15 – 20
Plate, 6¹/₄"*...1 – 2
Plate, 7"*...4 – 5
Plate, 8"*...5 – 6
Plate, 9"*...7 – 9
Plate, 10"..10 – 12
Platter, 8"*...8 – 10
Platter, 10"*...10 – 12
Platter, 11"*...10 – 12
Platter, 13"*...12 – 15
Platter, 15"*...15 – 18
Saucer...1 – 2
Saucer, AD..3 – 5
Saucer, cream soup...5 – 8
Sugar..8 – 10

ARCADIA (1934)

Periodic embossing around the rim of the flatware and the shoulder of the hollowware. This is the Sylvan flatware with redesigned hollowware.

Arcadia/Sylvan: Plate (underglaze green), sugar, and creamer (silver stamp and line).

You will find underglaze green on the embossed medallion.

Bowl, oval, 9"*	*$10 – $12*
Casserole	*20 – 25*
Creamer	*4 – 6*
Cup	*4 – 6*
Dish, 5½"*	*2 – 3*
Plate, 6"*	*1 – 2*
Plate, 9¼"	*7 – 9*
Platter, 11"	*10 – 12*
Saucer	*1 – 2*
Sugar	*8 – 10*

BEVERLY   (Originally called Regent) (1941)

Like Aladdin, Beverly used flatware, shakers, and eggcup from Deanna. The casserole, teapot, sugar, cream, cup, AD cup, and cream soup cup were new. Again, the sherbet did double duty as a single eggcup.

Bowl, oval, 9½"	*$10 – $12*
Bowl, round, oval, 8¾"	*15 – 18*
Bowl, round, 9½"	*15 – 18*
Bowl, soup, coupe, 8"	*10 – 12*
Bowl, soup, lug, 6¾"	*8 – 10*
Bowl, 36s	*7 – 10*
Butter dish, open	*15 – 20*
Casserole	*20 – 25*
Coaster	*8 – 12*
Creamer	*4 – 6*
Cup	*4 – 6*
Cup, AD	*10 – 12*
Cup, cream soup	*12 – 16*
Dish, 5¼"	*2 – 3*

Beverly: Creamer (Strawberry), plate (Italian hilltop village), and sugar (Rosebud).

Dish, 6¼" . . . . *$3 – $4*
Eggcup, double . . . . *10 – 12*
Gravy . . . . *12 – 15*
Gravy faststand . . . . *12 – 15*
Gravy liner . . . . *6 – 8*
Plate, 6½" . . . . *1 – 2*
Plate, 7½" . . . . *4 – 5*
Plate, 8½" . . . . *5 – 6*
Plate, 9¼" . . . . *7 – 9*
Plate, 10" . . . . *10 – 12*
Plate, chop, 12¼" . . . . *12 – 15*
Plate, square, 7"* . . . . *5 – 6*
Platter, 11½" . . . . *10 – 12*
Platter, 13½" . . . . *12 – 15*
Platter, 15¼" . . . . *15 – 18*
Saucer . . . . *1 – 2*
Saucer, AD . . . . *3 – 5*
Saucer, cream soup . . . . *5 – 8*
Sherbet . . . . *10 – 12*
Shaker, pair . . . . *8 – 10*
Sugar . . . . *8 – 10*
Teapot . . . . *25 – 30*

CREME FLUTE

A round shape with fluted rim on the flatware and fluted body on the hol-lowware.

Bowl, oval, 9" . . . . *$10 – $12*
Bowl, round, 9"* . . . . *15 – 18*
Bowl, soup, coupe, 8"* . . . . *10 – 12*
Bowl, 36s . . . . *7 – 10*

Casserole	*$20 – $25*
Creamer	*4 – 6*
Cup	*4 – 6*
Dish, 5½"	*2 – 3*
Dish, 6¼"*	*3 – 4*
Dish, lug, 6½"	*4 – 5*
Eggcup, single	*10 – 12*
Gravy	*12 – 15*
Plate, 6"	*1 – 2*
Plate, 7"	*4 – 5*
Plate, 9"*	*7 – 9*
Plate, 10"*	*10 – 12*
Platter, 11½"	*10 – 12*
Platter, 13"	*12 – 15*
Platter, 15"*	*15 – 18*
Saucer	*1 – 2*
Sugar	*8 – 10*

DEANNA   (1938)

The easiest pieces to find are the sugar, creamer, and shakers. Casserole, butter, eggcup, and teapot are difficult.

Deanna was decorated in solid colors and decals, the latter on either a Creme (ivory) or a Terra-Tan body.

There were two lines of solid colors. One had bright colors that Knowles called "Festive" though this was not an official name: green, red, blue, and yellow. The other was a pastel line, officially called Caribbean: Peach, Turquoise, Lemon Yellow, and Powder Blue. Pieces have also been found in the burgundy, pink, and russet colors used on the Yorktown shape.

Decals: Gayla, Valencia (various fruits), "Palmtree," and Tia Juana (Mexican).

PRICING   Solid colors are at the high end of the range.

Bowl, salad, round, 9"	*$15 – $18*
Bowl, round, 10"	*18 – 20*
Bowl, soup, coupe	*10 – 12*
Bowl, soup, lug, 6"	*8 – 10*
Bowl, 36s	*7 – 10*
Bowl, vegetable, oval, 9½"	*10 – 12*
Bowl, vegetable, round, 7"	*8 – 10*
Butter, open	*15 – 20*
Casserole	*20 – 25*
Coaster	*8 – 12*
Creamer	*4 – 6*
Cup	*4 – 6*
Cup, AD	*10 – 12*
Dish, 5¼"	*2 – 3*
Dish, 6¼"	*3 – 4*
Eggcup, double	*10 – 12*
Gravy	*12 – 15*
Gravy liner/pickle/relish	*6 – 8*

Deanna: Tia Juana eggcup, Tia Juana shaker, Tia Juana plate, Valencia plate, coaster, and teapot.

Plate, 6¼" .... *$1 – $2*
Plate, 7½" .... *4 – 5*
Plate, 8" .... *5 – 6*
Plate, 9¼" .... *7 – 9*
Plate, 10" .... *10 – 12*
Plate, cake, lug, 11" .... *10 – 12*
Plate, chop .... *15 – 20*
Platter, 11½" .... *10 – 12*
Platter, 13½" .... *12 – 15*
Platter, 15"* .... *15 – 18*
Saucer .... *1 – 2*
Saucer, AD .... *3 – 5*
Shaker, pair .... *8 – 10*
Sugar .... *8 – 10*
Teapot .... *30 – 35*

DIANA (1933)

A hexagonal shape with an embossed crisscross design on the rim of the flat-ware and around the body of the hollowware.

Bowl, soup, 8"* .... *$10 – $12*
Bowl, vegetable, 9"* .... *10 – 12*
Casserole .... *20 – 25*
Creamer .... *4 – 6*
Cup .... *4 – 6*
Dish, 5"* .... *2 – 3*
Dish, 6"* .... *3 – 4*
Gravy .... *12 – 15*

Diana: Gravy.

Plate, 6"* . . . . *$1 – $2*
Plate, 7"* . . . . *. 4 – 5*
Plate, 9"* . . . . *. 7 – 9*
Platter, 11"* . . . . *10 – 12*
Platter, 13"* . . . . *12 – 15*
Saucer . . . . *. 1 – 2*
Sugar . . . . *8 – 10*

ESQUIRE (1956–1962)

Designed by Russel Wright.

There are six basic decorations (background colors in parentheses): Botanica (brown), Grass (blue), Seeds (yellow), Solar (white), Snow Flower (pink), and Queen Anne's Lace (white), as well an Antique White (a matte glaze), which is rarely found. Mayfair, a rose decal on a high-gloss white background, has also been found.

Bowl, vegetable, divided, 13¼" *$45*
Bowl, vegetable, round, w/lid, 9¼" *35*
Bowl, vegetable, oval, 12¼" *35*
Compote, 12½" wide × 7½" high . . . . *125 +*
Creamer . . . . *8 – 10*
Cup . . . . *10 – 12*
Dish, footed, dessert/fruit, 5½" . . . . *6 – 8*
Dish, footed, cereal/soup, 6¼" . . . . *10 – 12*
Gravy, 6¼" wide × 4¼" high . . . . *35 – 45*
Jug, 2-quart . . . . *85 – 100*
Plate, 6¼" . . . . *4 – 6*
Plate, 8¼" . . . . *8 – 10*
Plate, 10¼" . . . . *10 – 12*
Platter, oval, 13" . . . . *25 – 30*
Platter, oval, 14¼" . . . . *30 – 35*
Platter, 16" . . . . *65 – 75*
Saucer . . . . *3 – 5*
Server, centerpiece, 22" . . . . *125 +*
Shaker, pair . . . . *30 – 40*
Sugar . . . . *30 – 40*
Teapot . . . . *125 – 150*

HOSTESS   (1935)

A plain round shape. The hollowware has angular handles and a terraced effect on the finials.

Bowl, soup, 8¼"... $10 – $12
Casserole.. 20 – 25
Creamer .... 4 – 6
Cup .... 4 – 6
Dish, lug, 6½" .... 4 – 5
Plate, 6"*.. 1 – 2
Plate, 9¼" .... 7 – 9
Plate, square, 7"... 5 – 6
Platter, 11"*... 10 – 12
Saucer .... 1 – 2
Sugar .... 8 – 10

MARION   (1930)

A ribbed shape.

THE
EDWIN M. KNOWLES
MARION

Bowl, vegetable, 8¼".. $10 – $12
Creamer .... 4 – 6
Cup .... 4 – 6

Marion: Back: *Plate (floral with Wisteria) and plate (Tulip floral).* Front: *Narrow open sugar (Tulip floral), wide open sugar (green), and creamer (green).*

Dish, 5¼" . . . . *$2 – $3*
Plate, 7" . . . . *4 – 5*
Plate, 9" . . . . *7 – 9*
Plate, 10" . . . . *10 – 12*
Platter, 13¾" . . . . *12 – 15*
Saucer . . . . *1 – 2*
Sugar . . . . *8 – 10*

POTOMAC (1939)

A round shape.

The most heavily promoted decoration was American Tradition: "Reviving early American beauty in dinnerware of today." See box for a listing of known patterns.

AMERICAN TRADITION

Acoma   Indian motif.
Apple Pickers   Based on a Currier & Ives print (brown tint).
Colonial Curtsey   Woman curtseying, in flower wreath.
Concord   Fruit basket center w/trim available in any of the predominant colors of the center decoration.
Flower Patch   Reproduction of an early American hooked rug.
Goose Girl   Girl w/geese in front of house.
Governor's Lady   Tulips and foliage in an orchid shade.
Nantucket   A sailing vessel above a floral semiwreath.
Penelope's Flower Basket
Revere   A stencil pattern.
The Southern Homestead   Old Southern home with children in center, floral semiborder.
Spirit of '76   Red, white, and blue bands enclose the three figures from the painting by Willard.
Winter Scene   Based on a Currier & Ives print.

Bowl, oval, 8½" . . . . *$10 – $12*
Bowl, oval, 9½" . . . . *10 – 12*
Bowl, round, 8" . . . . *12 – 15*
Bowl, round, 9" . . . . *15 – 18*
Bowl, round, 10" . . . . *18 – 20*
Bowl, soup, coupe, 8¼" . . . . *10 – 12*
Bowl, soup, lug, 6¾" . . . . *8 – 10*
Bowl, 36s . . . . *7 – 10*
Butter, open, 7½" . . . . *15 – 20*
Casserole, 8" . . . . *20 – 25*
Creamer . . . . *4 – 6*
Cup . . . . *4 – 6*

Potomac: Spirit of '76 creamer and sugar.

Cup, AD... *$10 – $12*
Cup, cream soup .... *12 – 16*
Dish, 5½" .... *2 – 3*
Dish, 6¼" .... *3 – 4*
Eggcup, double (Deanna) .... *10 – 12*
Gravy .... *12 – 15*
Gravy liner, 9¼" .... *6 – 8*
Plate, 6¼" .... *1 – 2*
Plate, 7¼" .... *4 – 5*
Plate, 8¼" .... *5 – 6*
Plate, 9¼" .... *7 – 9*
Plate, 10¼" .... *10 – 12*
Plate, chop, 12¼" .... *12 – 15*
Plate, square, 7¾" .... *5 – 6*
Platter, 8½" .... *8 – 10*
Platter, 11½" .... *10 – 12*
Platter, 13¼" .... *12 – 15*
Platter, 15¼" .... *15 – 18*
Saucer .... *1 – 2*
Saucer, AD .... *3 – 5*
Saucer, cream soup .... *5 – 8*
Shaker, pair .... *8 – 10*
Sugar .... *8 – 10*
Teapot, 6-cup.. *25 – 30*

REGENT   See Beverly.

ROSLYN   (1929)

A gadroon-edge shape.

Bowl, oval, 9"* .... *$10 – $12*
Casserole .... *20 – 25*
Creamer .... *4 – 6*
Cup .... *4 – 6*
Dish, 5½"* .... *2 – 3*

Roslyn: Plate and gravy.

Gravy	$12 – $15
Plate, 7"	5 – 7
Plate, 9⅛"	7 – 9
Platter, 11"*	10 – 12
Platter, 13"	12 – 15
Saucer	1 – 2
Sugar	8 – 10

SYLVAN (1934)

A periodic embossed edge. See also Arcadia.

Casserole	$20 – $25
Creamer	4 – 6
Cup	4 – 6
Plate, 9"	7 – 9
Saucer	1 – 2
Sugar	8 – 10

WILLIAMSBURG (mid 1941)

Casserole	$20 – $25
Creamer	4 – 6
Cup	4 – 6
Dish, 5¼"	2 – 3
Dish, lug, 5¾"	3 – 4
Plate, 6"	1 – 2
Plate, 9¼"	7 – 9
Plate, 10¼"	10 – 12
Plate, cake, lug, 10"	10 – 12
Platter, 11½"	10 – 12
Saucer	1 – 2

Williamsburg: Coffeepot, sugar, and creamer.

Sugar	*$8 – $10*
Teapot	*25 – 30*

YORKTOWN   (1936)

A round shape; deliberately there are no ovals—no oval bowls or platters, as are usually found in round shapes. I have seen it suggested that this was named Yorktown because that was the scene of a great American victory, which was the intent for this dinnerware line.

Sugar, creamer, and shakers are easy to find, candle holders are hard to find, and the cookie jar and two-handle gravy are rare.

Introduced in an ivory body, four solid colors were available by mid 1936: Cadet Blue, Russet, Yellow, and Burgundy. Other colors that have been found are Chinese Red, green, red (orange), and pink.

By mid 1936 decals had been added as well. Perhaps the most readily found is Penthouse (flowerpots on shelves); others include Arbor (trellis with rose clusters), Bar Harbor (sailboats), "Flower Basket" (two versions), "Flower Pots" (same idea as Penthouse but different execution), Golden Wheat, Green Wheat, Pantry Shelf, Pink Lady (border design of roses), Surrey Village (an English scene), Topsy (sprays of stylized leaves and flowers in red and black), and Water Lily.

PRICING   Solid colors are at the high end of the range.

Bowl, fruit, console	*$25 – $30*
Bowl, round, 8"	*15 – 18*
Bowl, round, 9"	*18 – 20*
Bowl, round, 10"	*20 – 25*
Bowl, soup, coupe, 8"	*12 – 15*
Bowl, soup, lug	*10 – 12*
Bowl, 36s	*10 – 12*
Butter, open	*20 – 25*
Candle holders, pair	*25 – 30*
Casserole	*25 – 30*

Yorktown (Clockwise from top): *Penthouse teapot, Water Lily gravy, candle holder (red band and silver lines), Penthouse shaker, and coaster ("Flower Pots").*

Coaster	$12 – $15
Cookie jar	ND
Creamer	6 – 8
Cup	6 – 8
Cup, AD	12 – 15
Custard	8 – 10
Dish, 6"	4 – 5
Dish, 6½"	5 – 6
Gravy, round	15 – 18
Gravy, 2-handle	ND

BAR HARBOR   "COUNTRY HOUSE"

Yorktown Decal Library

PANTRY SHELF

TOPSY

Yorktown Decal Library

Gravy liner	*$8 – $10*
Plate, 6½"	*2 – 3*
Plate, 7"	*5 – 6*
Plate, 8"	*6 – 8*
Plate, 9¼"	*8 – 10*
Plate, 10"	*12 – 15*
Plate, chop	*20 – 25*
Platter, 11"	*12 – 15*
Platter, 13"	*15 – 20*
Platter, 15"	*20 – 25*
Saucer	*2 – 3*
Saucer, AD	*5 – 7*
Shaker, pair	*10 – 12*
Sugar	*10 – 15*
Teapot	*45 – 50*

KITCHENWARE

OHIO JUGS

½-pint	*$20 – $22*
2½-pint	*25 – 28*
3½-pint	*28 – 30*

UTILITY WARE   (mid 1938)

Horizontally ribbed bottoms form a sort of foot on this shape. The hardest-to-find pieces are the teapot and coffee pot, which are listed in Knowles catalogs but not pictured; I have never seen either of these. The 4" **leftover** doubled as a

Utility Ware: Syrup jug (chefs bearing food), water jug (red), and refrigerator jug (yellow floral decal). The refrigerator jug was sold with and without a lid, and is the model for Hall China's Prince water jug.

drip. The lid of the **serving jug** can be swung to one side for pouring without having to remove it. The **refrigerator jug** could be purchased with or without

Utility Ware: Shaker (red base and white body), Fruits cookie jar, butter (red tab handles and white body), and Fruits small leftover.

a lid. The **refrigerator set** can stack or nest. The serving **utensils** were made by Harker and decorated by Knowles.

Utility Ware will be found in (1) solid colors of blue, green, red or yellow; (2) white with bands of red, green, or blue around the bottom ribs; (3) red and yellow combination; and (4) with decal decoration. Of the decals, the most readily found is Fruits (pear, apple, and grapes). Note that the Valencia decal was also used. This, too, is a combination of fruits which Knowles also called Fruit (singular) in its literature, and Montgomery Ward called Sequoia in its catalog.

Bowl, mixing, 6" .... *$6 – $8*
Bowl, mixing, 8" .... *10 – 12*
Bowl, mixing, 10" .... *15 – 20*
Bowl, salad, 9" .... *15 – 18*
Butter, 1-pound.. *25 – 30*
Casserole, 7½" .... *20 – 25*
Casserole, 8½" .... *20 – 25*
Casserole tray, 10" .... *10 – 12*
Coffee pot (metal drip), 6-cup..................................... *ND*
Cookie jar, 1-gallon .... *30 – 35*
Custard, 5-ounce... *4 – 6*
Jug, batter, 2½-pint... *35 – 40*
Jug, refrigerator, 3-pint .... *35 – 40*
Jug, serving/water, icelip w/lid, 4½-pint.......................... *20 – 25*
Jug, syrup, 1½-pint .... *30 – 35*
Leftover, 4" .... *6 – 10*
Leftover, 5" .... *10 – 15*
Leftover, 6" .... *15 – 20*
Mug (tumbler), 9-ounce... *15 – 20*
Pie baker, 9½"... *10 – 12*
Shaker, range, pair .... *15 – 20*
Shirred egg, lug, 6¼" .... *8 – 10*
Teapot, 6-cup.. *ND*
Tray, Batter Set, lug, 11"... *10 – 12*
Utensil, cake server .... *12 – 15*
Utensil, fork.. *20 – 25*
Utensil, spoon .... *15 – 20*

KNOWLES, TAYLOR AND KNOWLES

East Liverpool, Ohio

In 1854, Isaac Knowles, a carpenter and cabinetmaker, and Isaac Harvey began producing Rockingham and yellowware, the mainstays of the potteries in East Liverpool. In the mid 1860s, Harvey withdrew, and in 1870, Isaac Knowles's son, Homer S. Knowles, and son-in-law, John N. Taylor, joined the firm. In 1872 white ware production began; it was so successful it quickly replaced Rockingham and yellowware.

In 1887 the company announced its intention to build a china factory. Production of Belleek and art goods began early in 1889, but the plant was destroyed by fire in November 1890. It was rebuilt, and a fine bone china body, but not Belleek, was made and soon named Lotusware. By the end of 1897, KTK's interest in Lotusware was waning; it is likely that it stopped production at this time. It was too expensive to produce, and the company was more interested in the semiporcelain wares it had begun manufacturing several years earlier. Hotel china was added around the turn of the century.

Business slumped in the 1920s, and in 1929 the managers, mostly third-generation family members, decided to join the American China Corporation, but they did not survive the dissolution of that ill-fated venture. KTK had been the largest dinnerware manufacturer in the United States.

CORONADO   (<1926)

A band of thin ribs between the verge and the well on the flatware and on the lower body and lid of the hollowware.

Bowl, oval, 9"	*$10 – $12*
Bowl, soup, 7½".	*12 – 15*
Butter dish	*20 – 25*
Casserole	*20 – 25*
Creamer	*4 – 6*
Cup	*4 – 6*
Dish, 5½"*	*2 – 3*
Gravy	*12 – 15*
Gravy liner	*6 – 8*
Plate, 6"*	*1 – 2*
Plate, 7"	*5 – 7*

Coronado: Teapot, creamer, 9" plate, and sugar.

Plate, 9"* .... *$7 – $9*
Platter, 11"* .... *10 – 12*
Platter, 13" .... *12 – 15*
Platter, 15" .... *18 – 20*
Saucer .... *1 – 2*
Sugar .... *8 – 10*

"LOTUS" (late 1920s)

The shape was used in KTK's Lotus Ware line. Here, in a semiporcelain body, it's used for dinnerware. I do not know how extensive this line is.

I have seen this shape in solid colors only: Blue, Green, Rose, and Rust.

Creamer .... *$4 – $6*
Cup .... *4 – 6*
Jug w/lid .... *25 – 30*

"Lotus": Cup, dinner plate, and covered jug.

Plate, 9¼" . . . . *$7 – $9*
Platter, 11" . . . . *10 – 12*
Saucer . . . . *1 – 2*
Sugar . . . . *8 – 10*

HOMER LAUGHLIN CHINA COMPANY

East Liverpool, Ohio, and Newell, West Virginia

CHAPTER AT A GLANCE

Incorporated in 1896 as the Homer Laughlin China Company, the pottery began production in East Liverpool, Ohio, in 1874 as the Laughlin Brothers Pottery, but Homer's brother Shakespeare withdrew in 1877, the same year it was announced that the pottery had won the medal and highest diploma for Best White Granite at the Centennial Exposition of 1876.

In 1905 a plant was built in Newell, and operations there grew until, in 1929, the East Liverpool facilities were closed. Despite its name, Homer Laughlin has produced semiporcelain dinnerware, kitchenware, and novelties. China was produced for a short time only, around the turn of the century, and in 1959 vitreous dinnerware and institutional ware lines were introduced. The company, one of the largest in the world, is still manufacturing today.

Thanks to its Fiesta line and related products, Homer Laughlin's name is synonymous with brightly colored dinnerware. Though not an originator in this field, Laughlin's superior sales organization enabled it to become a leader. Many other lines are of interest to collectors, including dinnerware designed by Frederick Hurten Rhead, head designer from 1928 to 1942, and by Don Schreckengost, head designer from 1945 to 1960.

See Jasper in Bibliography and see Clubs/Newsletters.

MARKS A variety of backstamps were used, many specific to a particular shape. The one below is a general one used on a variety of shapes, including those that had their own stamp.

ART POTTERY

ART CHINA

Although Homer Laughlin produced a porcelain body for a very limited time at the end of the 19th century, the ware with the Art China mark is actually the basic semiporcelain body used for dinnerware. It is decorated with decals (some of which are intentionally designed to look hand painted) and a sprayed brown background in imitation of the products of Rookwood, Weller, and the other major art potteries of the time.

Laughlin produced a wide variety of items, including berry bowls and saucers, bonbons (both footed and covered), compotes, jumbo and mustache

Art China: Stein w/thumb rest handle (Elks), Currant punch cup, and stein w/thumb rest ("Compliments of The Berger Manufacturing Company, Canton, Ohio, Everything in Sheet Metal").

cups, cracker jars, ice cream plates, jelly jars, loving cups, molasses cans, covered muffins, plaques, rose bowls, a variety of salad bowls, spoon trays, shaving mugs, whiskey jugs, and a three-piece cereal set that seems to be a child's set.

The most common decoration is Currant (twigs of berries and leaves). Other classic turn-of-the-century decorations such as animals, monks, and Gibson girls were made, as well as special-order decorations for groups and organizations.

Bowl, orange . . . . *$125 – $150*
Bowl, ruffled . . . . *100 – 125*
Chocolate pot . . . . *200 – 225*
Creamer, Danube . . . . *40 – 50*
Jug, Dutch . . . . *100 – 125*
Jug, Geisha . . . . *100 – 125*
Plate, 9" . . . . *50 – 60*
Punch cups . . . . *40 – 45*
Spittoon, Grant . . . . *125 – 150*
Stein, thumb rest handle
   Elks . . . . *160 – 180*
   Promotional . . . . *160 – 180*
Sugar, Danube . . . . *60 – 75*
Teapot, Danube . . . . *125 – 150*
Tobacco jar . . . . *175 – 200*
Tray, bread, Fedora . . . . *75 – 90*
Tray, celery . . . . *60 – 75*
Tray, comb and brush . . . . *90 – 100*
Tumbler, Lemonade . . . . *40 – 50*
Tumbler, Lemonade, w/handle . . . . *50 – 60*
Vase, slim, 12" . . . . *100 – 125*
Vase, slim, 16" . . . . *175 – 200*

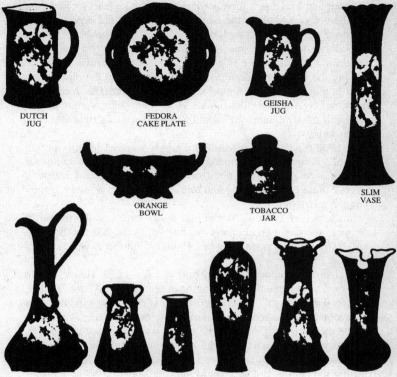

DUTCH
JUG

FEDORA
CAKE PLATE

GEISHA
JUG

ORANGE
BOWL

TOBACCO
JAR

SLIM
VASE

OTHER VASE SHAPES

Art China

DINNERWARE

PRE-1930 DINNERWARE LINES

American Beauty, Angelus, Colonial, Empress, Genesee, Golden Gate, Hudson, Niagara, and Seneca are some of the shapes Laughlin produced in the early part of the century.

PRICING Use Newell values on pages 413–414.

HOMER LAUGHLIN DATING CODES

The following explanation of dating codes is from Homer Laughlin.

The original trademark merely identifying the product as Laughlin Brothers appeared from the beginning in 1871 until around 1890. Unfortunately reproductions are unavailable. [Authors Note: This is reproduced in Lehner; see Bibliography.] The second trademark featuring the American Eagle astride the prostrate British Lion signifying the end of the domination of the British in the dinnerware field in this country was in use until around 1900. The third trademark merely featuring the initials HLC with slight variations has appeared on all dinnerware manufactured since that time and continues today.

In 1900 the trademark featured a single numeral identifying the month, a second single numeral identifying the year and a numeral 1, 2, or 3 designating the point of manufacture as East Liverpool, Ohio. *[These referred to the first three plants constructed by Homer Laughlin.]*

In the period 1910–1920, the first figure indicated the month of the year, the next two numbers indicated the year, and the third figure designated the plant. Number 4 was N, number 5 was N5, and the East End plant was L.

A change was made for the period of 1921–1930. The first letter was used to indicate the month of the year, such as "A" for January, "B" for February, "C" for March. The next single digit number was used to indicate the year and the last figure for the plant.

For the period 1931–1940 the month was expressed as a letter, but the years was indicated with two digits. Plant No. 4 was "N," No. 5 was "R," No. 6 and 7 were "C," and No. 8 was listed as "P." During the period, E-44R5 would indicate May of 1944 and manufactured by plant No. 5. The current trademark has been in use for approximately 70 years, and the numbers are the only indication of the year that items were produced.

AMERICANA (1949–1956)

Made exclusively for Montgomery Ward. This line is a hybrid in terms of shape. The AD cup and saucer were designed specifically for Americana, and the eggcup is the Cable shape; the other pieces are taken from the Brittany, Empress, and Willow shapes and are marked, when known, /B, /E, and /W, respectively, in the list below.

Decorated in a series of pink (maroon) underglaze American scenes based on Currier & Ives prints, with a leaf border. The line was possibly inspired by Vernon Kilns's Our America.

NOTE In general, I have used a Homer Laughlin list that provides the names of the decorations on the different items. Names verified from the ware itself are in quotes.

The Montgomery Ward catalog lists a cream soup and saucer that is not in Laughlin's listings.

MARK The mark contains the name of the individual decoration.

Bowl, soup, coupe, 9"   /E   /"Fox Hunting. Full Cry" . . . . *$12 – $15*
Bowl vegetable, covered, 9"   /B   /Body: Husking, Lid: Partridge Shooting . . *50 – 60*
Bowl, vegetable, oval, 8"   /E   /Maple Sugaring . . . . *18 – 22*
Bowl, vegetable, round, 8"   /E   /"The Road Winter" . . . . *18 – 22*
Creamer   /W   /"Surrender of Burgoyne, 1777/Declaration of Independence". *10 – 12*
Cup   /W   /"View of New York" . . . . *8 – 10*
Cup, AD   /View of San Francisco . . . . *18 – 20*
Dish, fruit, 5"   /E   /"On the Mississippi" . . . . *5 – 7*
Eggcup   /Across the Continent . . . . *16 – 18*
Gravy   /W   /"Preparing for Market and Harvest" . . . . *18 – 22*
Gravy liner/pickle   /B   /Winter in the Country . . . . *12 – 15*
Plate, 6"   /B   /"Hudson River—Crow Nest" . . . . *4 – 5*
Plate, 7"   /B   /"Clipper Ship Great Republic" . . . . *5 – 7*
Plate, 9"   /B   /Western Farmer Home . . . . *10 – 12*
Plate, 10"   /B   /"Home Sweet Home" . . . . *15 – 20*
Plate, chop, 13"   /The Rocky Mountains . . . . *20 – 25*
Plate, square, 8"   /"Landing of the Pilgrims, 1620" . . . . *12 – 15*

Americana: Eggcup (Across the Continent), sugar (Birthplace of Washington/Franklin's Experiment), creamer (Surrender of Burgoyne, 1777/Declaration of Independence), plate (Home Sweet Home), and teapot (Washington Family at Mt. Vernon).

Platter, 11¾"   /B   /"View of Harper's Ferry, Va" .... $12 – $15
Platter, 13"   /B   /"Suspension Bridge. Niagara Falls" .... 20 – 25
Platter, 15"   /B   /Home for Thanksgiving .... 35 – 45
Saucer   /E   /"View of New York" .... 2 – 4
Saucer, AD   /View of San Francisco .... 7 – 10
Sugar   /W   /"Birthplace of Washington/Franklin's Experiment" .... 15 – 20
Teapot   /W   /Washington Family at Mt. Vernon .... 65 – 75

BRITTANY   (1936–1954>)

The casserole is the round vegetable with a lid. The bouillon cup took a lid.
The sugar, creamer, gravy, and possibly other pieces were restyled.

Decals (underglaze silk screen): Constellation ("dynamic concentric bands
pleasingly interrupted with groups of stars") and Plaids (B1201, rose and blue;
B1202, green and blue; B1203, yellow and blue; and B1205, yellow and
black). A series of border treatments, including Laurel Leaf, were done in Blue,
Green, Ocher, and Pink.

Bowl, salad, round, 9"* .... $15 – $18
Bowl, salad, round, 10"* .... 18 – 20
Bowl, soup, 8"* .... 10 – 12
Bowl, soup, 9"* .... 12 – 15
Bowl, 36s .... 7 – 10
Bowl, vegetable, oval .... 10 – 12
Casserole .... 20 – 25
Creamer .... 4 – 6
Cup .... 4 – 6

*Brittany: Platter (Laurel Leaf), creamer, and sugar (identified as
Hemlock by Joanne Jasper from a Wards catalog), and AD cup.
The Laurel and Hemlock patterns are the two most common
underglaze decorations found on Brittany.*

Cup, AD.	$10 – $12
Cup, cream soup (Willow)	12 – 16
Dish, 5½"*	2 – 3
Dish, 6¼"*	3 – 4
Gravy	12 – 15
Gravy liner	6 – 8
Plate, 6¼"	1 – 2
Plate, 7¼"	4 – 5
Plate, 8"*	5 – 6
Plate, 9"*	7 – 9
Plate, 10"	10 – 12
Plate, chop, 10"*	12 – 15
Plate, chop, 12"*	15 – 20
Platter, oval, 11½"	10 – 12
Platter, 13"*	12 – 15
Platter 15"*	15 – 20
Saucer	1 – 2
Saucer, AD	3 – 5
Sugar	8 – 10

CENTURY (1931)

Designed by Frederick Hurten Rhead. A square shape with scalloped corners. Some pieces will be found with either square or oval wells; this results in some size differences in the platters. The square butter dish with round lid is an early piece, so far found only with decal decoration, that was replaced by the ½-pound butter from the Jade shape, called oblong in company records. Century is the basis of the Riviera line, which is priced separately just below. See also Century Vellum.

PRICING The most popular decorations are Mexicana (mid 1937), Maxicana (Max is the sleeping Mexican), Hacienda, and Conchita; these Mexican decals are priced separately.

	Mexican Decals	Other Decorations
Bowl, soup, 7¾"	$18 – $22	$10 – $12
Bowl, vegetable, oval, 9"	25 – 30	15 – 18
Bowl, salad, round, 9"	25 – 30	15 – 18
Butter, oblong (Jade)	ND	45 – 55
Butter dish, square, 1-pound	150+	60 – 75
Casserole	125 – 140	35 – 45
Creamer	18 – 22	4 – 6
Cup	12 – 15	4 – 6
Cup, AD	ND	ND
Cup, cream soup	65+	12 – 16
Dish, 5½"	10 – 12	5 – 6
Dish, 6"	30 – 40	12 – 15
Gravy	25 – 30	12 – 15
Gravy faststand, square	ND	ND

	Mexican Decals	Other Decorations
Gravy liner/pickle	$45 – $50	$12 – $15
Jug, batter	150+	50 – 60
Jug, syrup	150+	50 – 60
Plate, 6½"	10 – 12	1 – 2
Plate, 7"	12 – 15	4 – 5
Plate, 9"	18 – 20	5 – 7
Plate, 10"	45+	12 – 15
Platter, 11"	20 – 22	10 – 12
Platter, 13"	22 – 25	12 – 15
Platter, 15"	25 – 30	15 – 18
Platter, lug, square, 10"	ND	ND
Saucer	7 – 9	1 – 2
Saucer, AD	ND	ND
Saucer, cream soup, 7"	ND	ND
Sugar	20 – 25	10 – 12
Teapot	175+	55 – 70

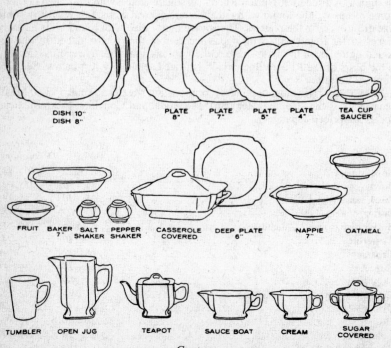

DISH 10"
DISH 8"　　PLATE 8"　　PLATE 7"　　PLATE 5"　　PLATE 4"　　TEA CUP SAUCER

FRUIT　　BAKER 7"　　SALT SHAKER　　PEPPER SHAKER　　CASSEROLE COVERED　　DEEP PLATE 6"　　NAPPIE 7"　　OATMEAL

TUMBLER　　OPEN JUG　　TEAPOT　　SAUCE BOAT　　CREAM　　SUGAR COVERED

Century

Century (Clockwise from top): *English Garden plate, Hacienda teapot, English Garden faststand gravy, butter dish, and syrup jug.*

CENTURY VELLUM

Homer Laughlin introduced its Vellum glaze on the Century shape in 1931. Do not make the mistake of confusing this with any floral decal.

"The demand for colored tableware has already resulted in the production of a wide range of colored bodies and glazes. But the majority of these wares were made in obvious tones of yellow, green, pink and blue, so it was felt by Homer Laughlin that any pronounced color was limited in its appeal to those interested only in a dominant color. What was needed was a color value possessing a universal appeal, which would meet the demand for a tableware of color and serve, as well, as a harmonious background, but which would not consciously suggest any pronounced tone.

"In the search for this ideal background it was recognized that the surface texture was just as important as the choice of color. Then the experiments as to glaze and color went hand in hand until the research revealed that the desired quality lay in a nonreflecting surface. In short, the sheen and glow of this ivory tone must be emphasized by the nonreflecting qualities of the glaze. Months of experiments finally resulted in the achievement of the concern's objective.

"The color and texture of Vellum suggest old polished ivory or alabaster rather than a glazed veneer. It is beautifully smooth and makes a ware of perfect fitness for any setting. The deep ivory satisfied all color requirements and provides a rich but restful harmony in any household interior.

"It was obvious that a glaze of this color and texture would require a more modern treatment than the old-fashioned white and ivory tableware. Hence ornate and historical adaptations were eliminated from the Vellum decorative program and the architectural influence decided upon for the motive of the shape. The Century shape is structural in effect. It is free from all ornamentation and produces an ideal background for decoration."

SPECIAL PRICE LIST

Riviera When the Riviera line was created in the late 1930s, it was based on the Century shape, with the addition of the disk jug, handled tumbler (mug), juice tumbler, and ¼-pound butter that were designed for this line and the shakers taken from the Tango shape. The disk jug (yellow is common; other colors are rare) and six juice tumblers made up a juice set. You will find more cups than saucers.

Decorated in solid colors: green, mauve blue, red, and yellow. The Ivory pieces you will find are, technically, undecorated Century. AD cups and saucers and cream soup cups and saucers have been found but are too rare to price. Cobalt blue and rust brown (similar to Wells's Art Glaze brown) pieces have turned up.

PRICING Red is at high end of range; add 20% for Ivory.

Bowl, salad, round, 9"	$20 – $25
Bowl, soup, 8½"	20 – 24
Bowl, 36s, Ivory	35 – 45
Bowl, vegetable, oval, 9"	25 – 28
Butter, ¼-pound	140+
Butter, oblong (Jade)	90 – 100
Casserole	100 – 125
Creamer	9 – 12
Cup	14 – 16
Cup, AD, Ivory	ND
Cup, cream soup, Ivory	ND
Dish, 5½"	10 – 14

Dish, 6" . . . . *$35 – $40*
Gravy . . . . *20 – 25*
Jug, batter
    Green . . . . *145 +*
    Other colors . . . . *175 +*
Jug, disk
    Mauve blue . . . . *175 +*
    Red . . . . *ND*
    Yellow . . . . *135 – 150*
Jug, syrup
    Red . . . . *145 +*
    Other colors . . . . *175 +*
Plate, 6" . . . . *7 – 10* ✗
Plate, 7" . . . . *12 – 15*
Plate, 9" . . . . *18 – 22* ✗
Plate, 10" . . . . *45 +*
Platter, 11½" . . . . *20 – 25*
Platter, lug, 11½" . . . . *20 – 25*
Platter, lug, 12" . . . . *20 – 25*
Platter, lug, 13½" . . . . *25 – 28*
Platter, 16" . . . . *40 – 45*
Saucer . . . . *3 – 5* ✗
Saucer, AD, Ivory . . . . *ND*
Saucer, cream soup, Ivory . . . . *ND*
Shaker (Tango), each . . . . *10 – 12*
Sugar . . . . *16 – 20*
Teapot . . . . *110 +*
Tumbler, handled . . . . *75 – 90*
Tumbler, juice
    Green . . . . *35 +*
    Ivory . . . . *45 +*
    Mauve blue . . . . *35 +*
    Red . . . . *35 +*
    Turquoise . . . . *45 +*
    Yellow . . . . *35 +*

CORONET   (1935)

Looking at old trade magazines, one finds that Homer Laughlin did an advertising blitz for this shape. Ironically, very little is found today. A round shape with embossed panels on the rim and a thin band of embossed flowers on the verge; the panels and flowers are repeated around the hollowware.

Glazed in solid colors of Ming Yellow, Old Ivory, and Sea Green. Decal decorations are most commonly found, including the one that resembles Hall China's #488.

There are many decals, including a Nasturtium with a gold edge and Co. 100: a group of cosmos as a center decoration in gray, rose, pink, and blue. And there's a stamped decoration that has the floral sprays on the verge traced in platinum.

Bowl, lug, soup	*$8 – $10*
Bowl, salad, 9"*	*15 – 18*
Bowl, soup	*10 – 12*
Bowl, vegetable, oval, 9½"	*10 – 12*
Casserole	*20 – 25*
Creamer	*4 – 6*
Cup	*4 – 6*
Dish, 5¼"	*2 – 3*
Dish, lug	*3 – 4*
Gravy	*12 – 15*
Gravy liner	*6 – 8*
Plate, 6"	*1 – 2*
Plate, 7¼"	*4 – 5*
Plate, 8"	*4 – 5*
Plate, 9"	*7 – 9*
Plate, 10"	*10 – 12*
Platter, 11"	*10 – 12*
Platter, 13"	*12 – 15*
Platter, 15"	*15 – 18*
Saucer	*1 – 2*
Sugar	*8 – 10*

Coronet: Cup (floral embossing overstamped in silver), oval vegetable, and creamer.

EPICURE (<1953)

Designed by Don Schreckengost. Characterized by a very thin, angled rim.

Decorated in solid colors: Charcoal, Pink, Turquoise, and White. Company records indicate that the ladle was made in White only, but a black ladle has been found.

Epicure: Ashtray with a lug handle on one side and cigarette rests opposite.

Ashtray	$35 – $45
Bowl, salad, round, 9"	20 – 25
Bowl, soup, coupe	15 – 18
Casserole (covered vegetable)	55 – 65
Casserole, individual, round	40 – 50
Coffee pot	100 – 125
Creamer	12 – 15
Cup, coffee	18 – 20
Cup	15 – 18
Dish, cereal	15 – 18
Dish, fruit	10 – 12

Epicure: Casserole, plate, nut dish, and coffee pot.

Dish, nut, 4½" x 1" high . . . . *$15 – $20*
Gravy. . . . . *20 – 25*
Gravy liner . . . . *18 – 22*
Ladle . . . . *ND*
Plate, 6½" . . . . *7 – 9*
Plate, 8½" . . . . *12 – 15*
Plate, 10" . . . . *15 – 18*
Platter, 9" . . . . *18 – 20*
Platter, 11" . . . . *20 – 25*
Saucer . . . . *3 – 5*
Shaker, pair. . . . . *20 – 25*
Sugar . . . . *20 – 25*
Tidbit, 2-tier . . . . *50 – 60*

FIESTA   (1936)

Designed by Frederick Hurten Rhead. Some pieces were restyled in the late 1960s.

Decorated in solid colors: Introduced in Blue, Green, Ivory, Red, and Yellow. Turquoise was added in 1937. Chartreuse, Forest Green, Gray, and Rose were added after the war and Medium Green in the late 1950s.

PRICING   If an item is not priced in the chart below, it is not known to exist in that color.

	Red	Blue	Green	Ivory	Yellow
Ashtray.	$55	$55	$48	$55	$48
Bowl, mixing, #1	145	145	125	145	125
Bowl, mixing, #2	95	95	80	95	80
Bowl, mixing, #3	110	110	95	110	95
Bowl, mixing, #4	120	120	105	120	105
Bowl, mixing, #5	140	140	125	140	125
Bowl, mixing, #6	175	175	150	175	150
Bowl, mixing, #7	225	225	200	225	200
Bowl, mixing, lids, each.	600 – 700	600 – 700	600 – 700	600 – 700	600 – 700
Bowl, salad, footed, 11½"	285	285	250	285	250
Bowl, salad, individual, 7½"	75	—	—	—	65
Bowl, salad (unlisted), 9½"	ND	ND	ND	ND	95

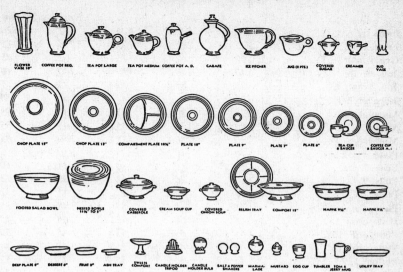

Fiesta

	Red	Blue	Green	Ivory	Yellow
Bowl, serving, 8½"	$50	$50	$38	$50	$38
Bowl, serving, 9½"	60	60	50	60	50
Bowl, soup, 8¾"	50	50	40	50	40
Cake plate, flat	750+	750+	675	750+	675
Candle holder, bulb, each	55	55	45	55	45
Candle holder, tripod, pair	450	450	395	450	395
Carafe	250	250	215	275	215
Casserole	200	200	165	200	165
Casserole, French	—	—	—	—	265
Coffee pot	225	225	185	225	185
Coffee pot, AD	295	295	250	295	250
Compote, 12"	175	175	145	175	145
Compote, sweets	80	80	65	80	65
Covered onion soup	550	550	450	550	450
Creamer	28	28	24	28	24
Creamer, stick handle	48	48	40	48	40
Creamer, individual (specialty)	185	—	—	—	65
Cup	35	35	26	40	26
Cup, AD	65	65	55	65	55
Cup, cream soup	60	60	45	60	45
Dish, dessert, 6"	55	55	45	55	45
Disk water pitcher	145	145	110	145	110
Eggcup	65	65	55	65	55
Fruit, 4¾"	32	32	26	32	26

	Red	Blue	Green	Ivory	Yellow
Fruit, 5½"	$32	$32	$26	$32	$26
Fruit, 11¾"	225	225	175	225	175
Gravy boat	62	62	45	62	45
Jug, ice lip	140	140	110	140	110
Jug, 2-pint	85	85	75	85	75
Juice pitcher	325	—	—	—	50
Marmalade	230	230	185	230	185
Mug	80	80	55	95	55
Mustard	230	230	185	230	185
Plate, 6"	10	10	6	10	6
Plate, 7"	14	14	10	14	10
Plate, 9"	20	20	12	20	12
Plate, 10"	40	40	32	45	32
Plate, chop, 13"	48	48	35	48	35
Plate, chop, 15"	65	65	45	65	45
Plate, grill, 10½	65	65	55	65	55
Plate, grill, 12"	45	45	35	45	35
Platter, 12½"	45	45	35	45	35
Relish tray (lazy susan), 5-part	195**	195**	195**	195**	195**
Saucer	5	5	3	5	3
Saucer, AD	18	18	15	18	15
Shaker, each	15	15	12	15	12
Sugar	55	55	45	55	45
Sugar, individual (specialty)	—	—	—	—	85
Syrup	285	285	245	300	245
Teapot, medium	175	175	145	175	145
Teapot, large	185	185	155	185	155
Tray, for individual cream/sugar	—	75	—	—	275
Tray, utility	45	45	38	45	38
Tumbler, juice	45	45	38	45	38
Tumbler, water	65	65	55	65	55
Vase, 8"	625	625	550	625	550
Vase, 10"	725	725	650	725	650
Vase, 12"	825	825	750	825	750
Vase, bud, 6¼"	75	75	65	75	65

**Add 15% for each red, blue, or ivory section.

	Turquoise	Chartreuse	Forest Green	Rose/ Gray	Medium Green
Ashtray	$48	$85	$85	$85	$165
Bowl, mixing, #1	125	—	—	—	—
Bowl, mixing, #2	80	—	—	—	—
Bowl, mixing, #3	95	—	—	—	—
Bowl, mixing, #4	105	—	—	—	—
Bowl, mixing, #5	125	—	—	—	—
Bowl, mixing, #6	150	—	—	—	—
Bowl, mixing, #7	200	—	—	—	—

	Turquoise	Chartreuse	Forest Green	Rose/ Gray	Medium Green
Bowl, mixing, lids, each . . . . $600–$700	—	—	—	—
Bowl, salad, footed, 11½" 250	—	—	—	—
Bowl, salad, individual, 7½" 65	—	—	—	$95
Bowl, salad (unlisted), 9½" . . . . —	—	—	—	—
Bowl, serving, 8½" 38	$60	$60	$60	125
Bowl, serving, 9½" 50	—	—	—	—
Bowl, soup, 8¾" 40	65	65	65	125
Cake plate, flat 675	—	—	—	—
Candle holder, bulb, each 45	—	—	—	—
Candle holder, tripod, pair . . . 400	—	—	—	—
Carafe. 215	—	—	—	—
Casserole 165	250	250	250	500
Casserole, French . . . . —	—	—	—	—
Coffee pot 185	285	285	285	—
Coffee pot, AD 265	—	—	—	—
Compote, 12" 145	—	—	—	—
Compote, sweets 70	—	—	—	—
Covered onion soup . . . . . . 2500+	—	—	—	—
Creamer 24	36	36	36	65
Creamer, stick handle 45	—	—	—	—
Creamer, individual (specialty) . . . . —	—	—	—	—
Cup 26	47	42	42	60
Cup, AD 55	275	275	275	—
Cup, cream soup 45	75	75	75	3500+
Dish, dessert, 6" 45	65	65	65	300+
Disk water pitcher 110	275	275	275	650
Eggcup 55	150	150	150	—
Fruit, 4¾" 26	36	36	36	300+
Fruit, 5½" 26	36	36	36	75
Fruit, 11¾" 200	—	—	—	—
Gravy boat 45	75	75	75	150
Jug, ice lip 110	—	—	—	—
Jug, 2-pint 75	150	150	150	—
Juice pitcher . . . . —	—	—	1400+*	—
Marmalade 185	—	—	—	—
Mug 55	95	95	95	125
Mustard 185	—	—	—	—
Plate, 6" 6	12	12	12	20
Plate, 7" 10	16	16	16	35
Plate, 9" 12	22	22	22	48
Plate, 10" 32	55	55	55	100

	Turquoise	Chartreuse	Forest Green	Rose/ Gray	Medium Green
Plate, chop, 13"	$35	$80	$80	$80	$165
Plate, chop, 15"	45	110	110	110	—
Plate, grill, 10½"	35	65	65	65	—
Plate, grill, 12"	—	—	—	—	—
Platter, 12½"	35	75	75	75	125
Relish tray (lazy susan), 5-part................	195**	—	—	—	—
Saucer.....................	3	6	6	6	10
Saucer, AD................	15	85	85	85	—
Shaker, each...............	12	20	20	20	45
Sugar	45	75	75	75	150
Sugar, individual (specialty)	—	—	—	—	—
Syrup	260	—	—	—	—
Teapot, medium...........	145	255	255	255	525+
Teapot, large	155	—	—	—	—
Tray, for individual cream/sugar.............	235	—	—	—	—
Tray, utility	38	—	—	—	—
Tumbler, juice	38	325	325	55***	—
Tumbler, water	55	—	—	—	—
Vase, 8"....................	550	—	—	—	—
Vase, 10"...................	650	—	—	—	—
Vase, 12"..................	750	—	—	—	—
Vase, bud, 6¼"	65	—	—	—	—

*Gray only.
**Add 15% for each red, blue, or ivory section.
***Rose only.

FIESTA HARMONY SERVICE

Introduced in June 1936. The Harmony Service is ensembles of Fiesta and Nautilus. "In each ensemble, the Nautilus items are decorated with patterns which harmonize with the Fiesta color selected for that particular set." The Nautilus patterns and the color they coordinate with are N 258 (yellow), an orchid; N 259 (green), a spray of tulips; N 260 (red), leaves and lines in red and black; and N 261 (blue), a flower basket.

The composition of the 76-piece Harmony set was as follows (sugar lid counts as a separate piece):

NAUTILUS
Eight 7" plates
Eight 4" plates
Eight teacups
Eight saucers
Eight 4" fruits

FIESTA
Eight 10" plates (reg. 8")
Eight 7" plates (reg. 5")
Eight 6" desserts (soup/cereals)
One 15" chop plate
One 12" compote

One 10" dish	Two bulb candle holders
One 7" baker	One salt and pepper
One 7" nappy	One sugar and creamer

The 76-piece service sold for $19.50 ($23.50 with Red Fiesta).

Ironstone

Fiesta was restyled in 1969 and called Fiesta Ironstone. All the standard colors were dropped except red (renamed Mango Red). Two colors were added: Antique Gold and Turf Green. The Fiesta line was finally discontinued at the end of 1972.

PRICING   Add 20% for red.

Ashtray	*$20 – $25*
Bowl, salad, 10"	*35 – 40*
Bowl, soup	*10 – 12*
Casserole	*40 – 45*
Coffee pot	*50 – 60*
Creamer	*6 – 8*
Cup	*7 – 8*
Dish, fruit	*5 – 6*
Dish, soup/cereal	*8 – 10*
Gravy	*20 – 25*
Gravy liner/pickle	*25 – 30*
Red	*85 – 95*
Jug, disk	*45 – 50*
Marmalade	*35 – 45*
Mug	*20 – 25*
Plate, 7"	*3 – 4*
Plate, 10"	*10 – 12*
Platter, 13"	*15 – 20*
Saucer	*1 – 2*
Shaker, pair	*10 – 12*
Sugar	*12 – 15*
Teapot	*40 – 50*

Reissue

Fiesta was reissued in 1986. The cup, mug, and creamer were restyled from the original. The standard coffee pot was originally used, but production problems led to its restyling. New pieces include a 12" rimmed bowl, ¼-pound butter, custard, napkin ring (this is the handle to the 2-pint jug), 9½" and 11½" platters, 9" rimmed soup, and serving tray.

The reissue will be found in ten colors: Apricot, Black, Cobalt, Green, Lilac (introduced 1/94, to be discontinued 12/95), Periwinkle (blue), Rose (bright pink), Turquoise, White, and Yellow (pale). Every piece was not made in every color. Special orders are being filled, such as Looney Tunes decorations sold at Warner Bros. stores, so there's no telling what may turn up. Pieces with blue and yellow bands have been seen.

The "new Fiesta" as it is sometimes called is still available as of this writing and selling well. A number of collectors are mixing the old with the new.

PRICING   The list below is for reference purposes only. It is not within my purview to reflect current retail prices, which can vary. *NOTE:* I have seen Black and Cobalt advertised as "discontinued." Not true; beware price gougers.

Bowl, serving, 8¹/₄"
Bowl, soup, rimmed, 9"
Bowl, soup, rimmed, 12"
Butter, ¹/₄-pound
Candle holder, bulb
Candle holder, tripod
Casserole
Coffee pot
Creamer
Cup
Cup, AD
Cup, bouillon, 4"
Dish, fruit, 5¹/₄"
Dish, cereal, 5¹/₂"
Dish, soup/cereal, 6³/₄"
Gravy boat, 16-ounce
Jug, disk, miniature, 4-ounce
Jug, disk, 28-ounce
Jug, disk, 67-ounce
Mug, 8¹/₂-ounce

Napkin ring
Plate, 6¹/₂"
Plate, 7"
Plate, 9"
Plate, 10¹/₄"
Plate, chop, 12"
Platter, oval, 9³/₈"
Platter, oval, 11¹/₂"
Platter, oval, 13¹/₄"
Platter, round, 11¹/₂"
Saucer
Saucer, AD
Shaker
Sugar
Sugar/Creamer/Figure 8 Tray Set
  (Specialty)
Teapot, 36-ounce
Tray, serving, round, 12"
Vase, 9¹/₂"
Vase, bud, 6¹/₄"

GEORGIAN   (1934)

A round shape with a lightly embossed dot and dash design around the outer rim of the flatware and the tops of the hollowware. This is a traditional shape that "compares favorably both in quality and beauty with fine English and Continental wares" and was decorated in "typically eighteenth century patterns."

   CRAFTSMAN   Craftsman is a line of decorations. Georgian's first appearance in the trade ads indicated it was decorated in Craftsman patterns of Chartreuse, Mauvette, Primuline, and Rosolane.

PRICING Values below are for all decorations, including Craftsman.

Bowl, salad, 9"	*$15 – $18*
Bowl, salad, 10"	*18 – 20*
Bowl, soup, 8"	*10 – 12*
Bowl, soup, lug	*8 – 10*
Bowl, vegetable, oval, 9"	*10 – 12*
Casserole	*20 – 25*
Creamer	*4 – 6*
Cup	*4 – 6*
Cup, AD	*10 – 12*
Cup, cream soup	*12 – 16*
Dish, 5¼"*	*2 – 3*
Dish, 6"*	*2 – 3*
Gravy	*12 – 15*
Gravy faststand	*12 – 15*
Gravy liner/pickle, 9"	*6 – 8*
Plate, 6¼"	*1 – 2*
Plate, 7"*	*4 – 5*
Plate, 8"*	*5 – 6*
Plate, 9"*	*7 – 9*
Plate, 9¾"	*7 – 9*
Plate, cake	*12 – 15*
Plate, chop, 13½"	*20 – 25*
Plate, square, 8"	*5 – 6*
Platter, 11"	*10 – 12*
Platter, 13"	*12 – 15*
Saucer	*1 – 2*
Saucer, AD	*3 – 5*
Saucer, cream soup	*6 – 8*
Shaker, pair	*8 – 10*
Sugar	*8 – 10*
Teapot	*30 – 35*

GEORGIAN / EGGSHELL (1940)

AD cup and saucer, square plate, and teapot were added in 1941.

MARKS If you are unsure of differentiating between the regular and Eggshell Georgian just by body, note that Eggshell Georgian had its own mark. The regular Georgian usually had the generic HL mark, sometimes the stamp shown on page 396.

Bowl, salad, 9" .... $15 – $18
Bowl, salad, 10" .... 18 – 20
Bowl, soup .... 10 – 12
Bowl, soup, lug .... 8 – 10
Bowl, 36s .... 7 – 10
Bowl, vegetable, oval, 9" .... 10 – 12
Bowl, vegetable, oval, 10" .... 12 – 15
Casserole .... 25 – 30
Creamer .... 4 – 6
Cup .... 4 – 6
Cup, AD .... 10 – 12
Cup, cream soup .... 12 – 16
Dish, 5¼"* .... 2 – 3
Dish, 6" .... 3 – 4
Gravy .... 12 – 15
Gravy faststand .... 12 – 15
Gravy liner, 8"* .... 12 – 15
Plate, 6¼" .... 1 – 2
Plate, 7" .... 4 – 5
Plate, 8" .... 5 – 6
Plate, 9" .... 7 – 9
Plate, 10" .... 10 – 12
Plate, square, 8" .... 7 – 9
Plate, chop, 14" .... 20 – 25
Platter, 11" .... 10 – 12
Platter, 13" .... 12 – 15
Platter, 15" .... 15 – 18
Saucer .... 1 – 2
Saucer, AD .... 3 – 5
Saucer, cream soup .... 6 – 8
Shakers, pair .... 8 – 10
Sugar .... 8 – 10
Teapot .... 30 – 35

*Georgian:
Teapot, shaker,
plate, and cup.*

HOMER LAUGHLIN GOES TO WAR

In July 1942 it was announced that Homer Laughlin "recently started making vitrified ware for Army and Navy use. The factory has been making semivitreous ware for some time as a part of the lease-lend act, the ware going to the British maritime commission. This has now been superseded by the production of vitrified ware for the American armed forces."

HARLEQUIN

Harlequin was sold as an inexpensive alternative to Fiesta exclusively through Woolworth's. The handle is reminiscent of Salem's Tricorne shape. The butter dish is the Jade shape. Saucers are scarcer than cups.

Decorated in solid colors (which changed over the years): chartreuse, dark green, gray, light green, maroon, mauve blue, medium green, red, rose, spruce green, turquoise, and yellow.

PRICING Add 10% for light green, maroon, and red; add 20% for chartreuse, gray, dark green, mauve blue, and spruce green; and double prices for medium green. Note that some butters are discolored due to butter absorption; do not pay full price for these.

Ashtray, regular	$45 – $50
Ashtray, "Basketweave"	40 – 45
Ashtray/saucer	65 +
Bowl, 36s	35
Bowl, soup, 8"	15 – 20
Bowl, vegetable, oval, 9"	18 – 20
Bowl, vegetable, round, 9"	20 – 25
Butter, ½-pound (Jade)	100 – 125
Candle holders, pair	150 – 175
Casserole	85 – 95
Creamer	10 – 12
Creamer, "high lip"	85 – 95
Creamer, individual	12 – 15
Creamer, "novelty"	25 – 30
Cup	10 – 12
Cup, AD	35 – 40
Cup, cream soup	20 – 25
Cup, large, tankard	85 +
Dish, 5½"	8 – 10
Dish, 6½"	18 – 22
Eggcup, double	20 – 25
Eggcup, individual	30 – 35
Gravy	22 – 25
Jug, ball	55 – 70
Jug, milk, 22-ounce	30 – 35

Jug, syrup . . . . *$225 – $250*
Marmalade . . . . *100 +*
Nut dish, individual . . . . *12 – 15*
Plate, 6" . . . . *3 – 5*
Plate, 7" . . . . *7 – 9*
Plate, 9" . . . . *10 – 15*
Plate, 10" . . . . *20 – 25*
Platter, 10" . . . . *15 – 18*
Platter, 13" . . . . *18 – 22*
Relish tray, 4-section . . . . *275 +*
Saucer . . . . *3 – 5*
Saucer, AD . . . . *15 – 20*
Shaker, each . . . . *8 – 12*
Sugar . . . . *18 – 22*
Teapot . . . . *75 – 90*
Tumbler . . . . *40 – 50*

Animals

Cat	Donkey	Duck
Fish	Lamb	Penguin

PRICING Animals in maroon, mauve, spruce green, or yellow: $140+. Animals in cobalt, red, or turquoise: $200+.

Reissue

Harlequin was reissued for a few years beginning in 1979 on the occasion of Woolworth's 100th anniversary; it was called Harlequin Ironstone. Some pieces were restyled. The sugar bowl had solid handles and finial; the oval platter was dropped and replaced by a round chop plate. There was no teapot.

Colors were the original medium green, rose, turquoise, and yellow. The turquoise and yellow are very close to the original colors; you might be able to tell them apart if they were next to each other. The medium green and rose (called Coral in the reissue) are identifiably different.

The cup, saucer, and cereal bowl in turquoise and yellow can easily be confused with the old pieces. The dinner and salad plates in these colors have an "HLC" mark, which the originals did not, so this will help with their identification.

JADE (1932)

A square shape with a slightly rounded effect.

Homer Laughlin introduced its Clair de Lune glaze, "the pale, soft alluring color of moonlight," on this shape. Clair de Lune is a pale greenish-ivory color and seems to have been exclusive to this short-lived, little-produced shape. A variety of floral decals were used.

Bowl, salad, round . . . . *$18 – $20*
Bowl, soup . . . . *10 – 12*
Bowl, vegetable, oval . . . . *12 – 15*
Butter, oblong . . . . *45 – 55*
Casserole . . . . *35 – 45*
Creamer . . . . *10 – 12*

Jade: Plate and casserole.

Cup	*$6 – $8*
Cup, AD	*12 – 15*
Dish, cereal	*6 – 8*
Gravy	*15 – 18*
Gravy faststand	*20 – 25*
Gravy liner	*8 – 10*
Jug, batter	*ND*
Jug, syrup	*ND*
Plate, 6"	*2 – 4*
Plate, 7"	*4 – 6*
Plate, 8"	*6 – 8*
Plate, 9"	*10 – 12*
Plate, 10"	*12 – 15*
Platter, 11"	*12 – 15*
Platter, 13"	*15 – 20*
Platter, 15"	*20 – 25*
Saucer	*2 – 3*
Saucer, AD	*3 – 5*
Sugar	*12 – 15*
Teapot, tall	*75 +*

JUBILEE

Issued in 1948 to celebrate Homer Laughlin's 75th anniversary. Designed by Don Schreckengost. The lug soup, 7½" vegetable bowl, and 15" platter seem not to have been made for the solid-color line.

Jubilee was glazed in solid colors of Celadon Green, Cream Beige, Mist Grey, and Shell Pink. In 1952, **Suntone** (brown with white finials and handles; the eggcup foot and the gravy faststand liner are also white) and **Skytone** (like Suntone but blue instead of brown) were introduced. Skytone will be found decorated with Star Dust (green leaves and white flowers). Kitchen Kraft bowls and the Fiesta disk jug and tumblers have been found in Jubilee colors.

Flame Flower is perhaps the most common decal.

PRICING   Use the low end of the range for decal-decorated pieces. Use the high end of the range for the colors and for Skytone and Suntone.

Bowl, lug, soup, 6"*	$10 – $12
Bowl, mixing, 6" (Kitchen Kraft)	125 +
Bowl, mixing, 8" (Kitchen Kraft)	125 +
Bowl, mixing, 10" (Kitchen Kraft)	125 +
Bowl, soup, coupe, 7³/₄"	12 – 15
Bowl, vegetable, round, 7¹/₂"	15 – 18
Bowl, vegetable, round, 8¹/₂"	15 – 18
Casserole	30 – 35
Coffee pot	40 – 45
Creamer	8 – 10
Cup	6 – 8
Cup, AD	12 – 15
Dish, 5¹/₂"	5 – 7
Dish, lug, 6"	7 – 9
Eggcup	12 – 15
Gravy faststand	15 – 18
Jug, disk (Fiesta)	250 +
Plate, 6¹/₄"	2 – 3
Plate 7"	4 – 5

Jubilee: Flame Flower teapot and coffee pot.

TEAPOT

CREAMER

AD CUP

TEA CUP

COUPE SOUP

SUGAR

FRUIT DISH

PEPPER

LUG SOUP

COFFEE POT

SALT

GRAVY FASTSTAND

ROUND VEGETABLE

CASSEROLE

PLATTER, 15"

PLATTER, 13"

PLATTER, 11"

EGGCUP

Jubilee

Plate, 9"	*$7 – $9*
Plate, 10"	*10 – 12*
Plate, chop, 15"	*20 – 25*
Platter, 11"	*10 – 12*
Platter, 13"	*12 – 15*
Platter, 15"	*15 – 18*
Saucer	*2 – 3*
Saucer, AD	*3 – 5*
Shaker, pair	*10 – 12*
Sugar	*10 – 12*
Teapot	*45 – 55*
Tumbler, juice (Fiesta)	*80 – 90*

KRAFT BLUE / PINK   (1938)

There is an embossed ropelike border on most pieces; cup and small jug are exceptions. This was not a very extensive line.

Generally found in blue with the handles in contrasting white; pink (Kraft Pink) was also made. This shape was later manufactured in a tan body with hand-painted decorations.

Hand Painted
HOMER LAUGHLIN
MADE IN U.S.A.

Bowl, soup, coupe	*$10 – $12*
Creamer	*4 – 6*
Cup	*4 – 6*
Cup, cream soup	*12 – 16*
Eggcup	*10 – 12*
Jug, ball, small	*8 – 10*
Plate, 6½"	*1 – 2*
Plate, 7⅛"	*4 – 5*
Plate, 9"*	*7 – 9*
Plate, 10¼"	*10 – 12*
Platter, 10"*	*10 – 12*
Platter, 12"*	*12 – 15*
Saucer	*1 – 2*

Kraft Blue: Plate (hand-painted house), creamer (white floral silk-screen decoration), cream soup, small ball jug/novelty creamer, cup (hand-painted windmill), and teapot.

Sugar . . . . *$8 – $10*
Teapot . . . . *20 – 25*

KWAKER

This shape is most easily identified by the top of the handle, which is squared. Flatware is a plain round shape.

Bowl, salad, 9"* . . . . *$15 – $18*
Bowl, salad, handled . . . . *18 – 20*
Bowl, soup, 9" . . . . *12 – 15*
Bowl, soup, coupe, 8" . . . . *10 – 12*
Bowl, 36s . . . . *7 – 10*
Bowl, vegetable, oval, 9" . . . . *10 – 12*
Bowl, vegetable, oval, 11" . . . . *12 – 15*
Butter dish . . . . *20 – 25*
Casserole, 9"* . . . . *20 – 25*
Creamer . . . . *4 – 6*
Cup . . . . *4 – 6*
Cup, AD. . . . . *10 – 12*
Cup, coffee . . . . *6 – 8*
Dish, 5¹/₈" . . . . *2 – 3*
Gravy . . . . *12 – 15*
Gravy liner . . . . *6 – 8*
Jug, 8-ounce. . . . . *10 – 15*
Jug, 3¹/₂-pint. . . . . *20 – 25*
Plate, 6" . . . . *1 – 2*
Plate, 8⁷/₈" . . . . *5 – 6*
Plate, 9¹/₂" . . . . *7 – 9*

Kwaker: Teapot, plate, and large jug. Banded decorations, as on the teapot and plate, are more commonly found on Kwaker.

Plate, cake, lug, 10¼" .... *$12 – $15*
Platter, 7¼" .... *10 – 12*
Platter, 9⅛" .... *10 – 12*
Platter, 11" .... *10 – 12*
Platter, 13" .... *12 – 15*
Platter, 15¼" .... *15 – 18*
Platter, 17¼" .... *20 – 25*
Saucer .... *1 – 2*
Saucer, AD .... *3 – 5*
Saucer, coffee .... *2 – 3*
Sugar .... *8 – 10*
Teapot .... *30 – 35*

LIBERTY   (1942)

A gadroon-edged shape with a slight scallop.

One of the interesting decals on this shape is Old Master paintings with a gold-stamped border.

Bowl, salad, round, 8¼" .... *$15 – $18*
Bowl, soup, 8¼" .... *10 – 12*
Bowl, vegetable, oval, 9½" .... *10 – 12*
Casserole .... *20 – 25*
Creamer .... *4 – 6*
Cup .... *4 – 6*
Dish, 5" .... *2 – 3*
Dish, 6¼" .... *3 – 4*
Gravy .... *12 – 15*
Gravy liner/pickle .... *6 – 8*

Liberty: Blue Heaven teapot (Currier & Ives–type decal), plate (The Cornfield, Amsterdam, Holland by Constable in well), and Historical America sugar.

Plate, 6¼" .... *$1 – $2*
Plate, 7¼" .... *4 – 5*
Plate, 8¼" .... *4 – 5*
Plate, 9¼" .... *7 – 9*
Plate, 10⅛" .... *10 – 12*
Platter, oval, 11½" .... *10 – 12*
Platter, oval, 13½" .... *12 – 15*
Platter, oval, 15½" .... *15 – 18*
Saucer .... *1 – 2*
Sugar .... *8 – 10*
Teapot .... *25 – 30*

SPECIAL PRICE LIST

CURRIER & IVES

These Currier & Ives decals came with two different treatments. Sun Gold has a gold-stamped filigree border, and Blue Heaven has a wide blue border with a gold line.

Bowl, soup, 8¼" .... *$12 – $15*
Bowl, vegetable, oval, 9½" .... *12 – 15*
Casserole .... *25 – 30*
Creamer .... *6 – 8*
Cup .... *6 – 8*
Dish, 5" .... *3 – 4*
Gravy .... *15 – 18*
Gravy liner/pickle .... *8 – 10*
Plate, 6¼" .... *2 – 3*
Plate, 8¼" .... *6 – 8*
Plate, 10¼" .... *12 – 15*
Platter, 11½" .... *12 – 15*
Platter, 13½" .... *15 – 18*
Platter, 15½" .... *20 – 25*
Saucer .... *2 – 3*
Sugar .... *10 – 15*
Teapot .... *35 – 45*

SPECIAL PRICE LIST

HISTORICAL AMERICA   (1939–1958)

The shape used for this decoration is Liberty. The scenes pictured are based on the art of Joseph Boggs Beale. There is a floral border. Maroon is the common color; blue will be found.

NOTE   In general, I have used a Homer Laughlin list that provides the names of the decorations on the different items. Names verified from the ware itself are in quotes.

MARK   The mark shown was used on the larger pieces; the top portion only was used for the smaller pieces.

Bowl, soup, 8¼"   /"Ponce de Leon Discovers Florida, 1512" . . . *$12 – $15*
Bowl, vegetable, oval, 9½"   /"Lincoln's Gettysburg Address, 1863" . . . *18 – 22*
Bowl, vegetable, round   /Pony Express . . . . *18 – 22*
Casserole   /Ben Franklin. . . . . *50 – 60*
Creamer   /Star Spangled Banner . . . . *10 – 12*
Cup   /"Franklin's Experiment, 1752" . . . . *8 – 10*
Dish, fruit   /"Lincoln As a Rail Splitter, 1834" . . . . *5 – 7*
Dish, soup/cereal   /"Traveling By Old Stage Coach, 1847" . . . . *8 – 10*
Gravy   /"Lincoln's Gettysburg Address, 1863" . . . . *18 – 22*
Plate, 6¼"   /"Paul Revere Crossing Bridge into Medford Town, 1775" . . *4 – 5*
Plate, 7"   /"The First Tone From the Liberty Bell, 1753". . . . . *5 – 7*
Plate, 8"   /Purchase of Manhattan Island . . . . *10 – 12*
Plate, 9"   /"Betsy Ross Showing the First Flag". . . . . *12 – 15*
Plate, 10"   /"George Washington Taking Command of the Army, 1775" *15 – 20*
Platter, 11"   /"The First Steamboat, The Clermont, 1807". . . . . *12 – 15*
Platter, 13"   /First Thanksgiving. . . . . *20 – 25*
Saucer   /"Arrival of the Mayflower, 1607". . . . . *2 – 4*
Sugar   /"Barbara Fritchie, 1863" . . . . *15 – 20*
Teapot   /Pony Express . . . . *65 – 75*

MARIGOLD   (1934)

This shape has periodic embossed elements. I have seen the odd piece glazed in solid dark green, but this shape basically has decal decorations or underglaze hand painting on the embossed elements.

MARIGOLD
UNDERGLAZE
HANDPAINTED
U. S. A.

Bowl, salad, 9"	$15 – $18
Bowl, soup, 8"*	10 – 12
Bowl, soup, coupe, 8"*	10 – 12
Bowl, vegetable, oval, 9"	10 – 12
Bowl, 36s	7 – 10
Casserole	20 – 25
Creamer	4 – 6
Cup	4 – 6
Dish, 5¹/₂"*	2 – 3
Dish, 6"*	3 – 4
Gravy	12 – 15
Gravy liner	6 – 8
Plate, 6¹/₂"	1 – 2
Plate, 7¹/₈"	4 – 5
Plate, 8"*	5 – 6
Plate, 9"*	7 – 9
Plate, 10"*	10 – 12
Plate, square, 8¹/₄"	6 – 8
Platter, 10¹/₂"	10 – 12
Platter, 11³/₄"	10 – 12
Platter, 13"*	12 – 15
Platter, 15"*	15 – 18
Saucer	1 – 2
Sugar	8 – 10

Marigold: Creamer (red and black underglaze decoration), oval vegetable (green underglaze decoration), and sugar (floral).

NAUTILUS   (1936)

Shell-like embossing on the finials and feet of the sugar, creamer, gravy, and casserole and on the slight lug of the gravy liner/pickle and the platters.

One of many decals is Early America (a variety of scenes, such as a three-masted ship, steamboat, and covered wagon at western fort, all with smoke rising). See also Fiesta Harmony Service.

NAUTILUS
MADE IN U.S.A

Bowl, salad, 9"	*$15 – $18*
Bowl, soup	*10 – 12*
Bowl, soup, coupe	*10 – 12*
Bowl, 36s	*7 – 10*
Bowl, vegetable, 9"	*10 – 12*
Casserole	*25 – 30*
Creamer	*4 – 6*
Cup	*4 – 6*
Cup, AD.	*10 – 12*
Dish, 5¼"	*2 – 3*
Dish, 6"	*3 – 4*
Dish, lug, 5½"	*3 – 4*
Gravy	*12 – 15*
Gravy liner/pickle	*6 – 8*
Plate, 6¼"	*1 – 2*
Plate, 7¼"	*4 – 5*
Plate, 8¼"	*5 – 6*

Nautilus: Old Curiosity Shop platter, AD cup, creamer, and restyled Eggshell creamer (suspension bridge decal). The shell lug handles were retained when Nautilus was restyled for the Eggshell version.

Plate, 9¼" .... $7 – $9
Plate, 10" .... *10 – 12*
Plate, square, 8" .... *5 – 6*
Platter, 11"* .... *10 – 12*
Platter, lug, 13½" .... *12 – 15*
Saucer .... *1 – 2*
Saucer, AD .... *3 – 5*
Sugar .... *8 – 10*

Pastels   Made in a talc body. You will find Nautilus glazed in the four colors used for Serenade: blue, green, pink, and yellow.

Bowl, salad, round, 9"* .... $18 – $20
Bowl, soup, 8"* .... *12 – 15*
Bowl, soup, lug .... *10 – 12*
Bowl, vegetable, oval, 9"* .... *12 – 15*
Casserole .... *40 – 45*
Creamer .... *6 – 8*
Cup .... *6 – 8*
Cup, AD. .... *12 – 15*
Cup, cream soup .... *15 – 20*
Dish, 5" .... *3 – 4*
Dish, 6"* .... *4 – 5*
Eggcup, double .... *12 – 15*
Gravy .... *15 – 18*
Gravy liner .... *10 – 12*
Plate, 6" .... *2 – 3*
Plate, 7" .... *5 – 6*
Plate, 8" .... *6 – 7*
Plate, 9" .... *8 – 10*
Plate, 10" .... *12 – 15*
Platter, 11" .... *12 – 15*
Platter, 13" .... *15 – 18*
Saucer .... *2 – 3*
Saucer, AD .... *3 – 5*
Sugar .... *10 – 15*

NAUTILUS / EGGSHELL   (1937)

The first line to be introduced in the Eggshell weight. Some pieces were restyled.

Some of the decals used are "Adobe" (N–1406, adobe house with cactus), Daisy Field, Delphinium, "Flamingos" (N–1401), Mexicana, and Starflower (N–1471, bright red flowers and green leaves).

Bowl, oval, 9"* .... $10 – $12
Bowl, oval, 10"* .... 12 – 15
Bowl, round, 9"* .... 15 – 18
Bowl, round, 10"* .... 18 – 20
Bowl, soup, 8"* .... 10 – 12
Casserole .... 20 – 25
Creamer .... 4 – 6
Cup .... 4 – 6
Cup, cream soup .... 12 – 16
Dish, 5½"* .... 2 – 3
Dish, 6¼"* .... 3 – 4
Gravy .... 12 – 15
Gravy faststand .... 12 – 15
Gravy liner .... 6 – 8
Plate, 6"* .... 1 – 2
Plate, 7"* .... 4 – 5
Plate, 8"* .... 5 – 6
Plate, 9"* .... 7 – 9
Plate, 10"* .... 10 – 12
Plate, chop, 14"* .... 15 – 20
Plate, square, 8"* .... 6 – 7
Platter, 11"* .... 10 – 12
Platter, 13"* .... 12 – 15
Platter, 15"* .... 15 – 18
Saucer .... 1 – 2
Saucer, cream soup .... 5 – 8
Sugar .... 8 – 10
Teapot .... 30 – 35

EGGSHELL

Introduced in 1937. A lightweight ware. "Before this new light-weight ware could become a reality, concentrated research and laboratory experiments over a long period were necessary. New precision machines and tools had to be developed . . . The resulting ware has extraordinary advantages due to its light weight and the rigid control exercised throughout every stage of its manufacture. Each piece is far more uniform in quality that has heretofore been possible. The edges of the pieces are thin and delicate. The texture is exceptionally beautiful and the glaze is unusually rich, uniform and satisfying." The first shape to be made in Eggshell was Nautilus, which had originally been made in a regular body. This was followed by Eggshell Swing in 1938 and Eggshell Theme and Eggshell Georgian (restyled from the original Georgian) in 1940.

Please be clear about this; Georgian and Nautilus are found in two bodies, regular and Eggshell, while Swing and Theme were made only in the Eggshell body.

NEWELL

Designed by Frederick Rhead. A gadroon edge on a scalloped shape. There were at least 56 items in this shape. I have listed them all to give you an idea of how complete pre-1930 lines could be, though even earlier lines could have upward of 80 items.

Newell was decal-decorated on a white or yellow body. I have seen a decal decoration on a green body. Decals on green bodies for any shape are rare.

Bowl, 30s	$7 – $10
Bowl, 36s	7 – 10
Bowl, oval, 5½"	8 – 10
Bowl, oval, 7⅛"	8 – 10
Bowl, oval, 8⅛"	10 – 12
Bowl, oval, 9¼"	10 – 12
Bowl, oval, 10¼"	12 – 15
Bowl, oyster, ¾-pint	7 – 10
Bowl, oyster, 1¼-pint	10 – 12
Bowl, round, 6⅛"	10 – 12
Bowl, round, 7¼"	12 – 15
Bowl, round, 8¼"	15 – 18
Bowl, round, 9⅛"	15 – 18
Bowl, soup, 9⅛"	10 – 12
Bowl, soup, coupe, 7¼"	10 – 12
Bowl, soup, coupe, 8"	10 – 12
Butter dish	20 – 25
Butter pat, 3"	4 – 6
Casserole, 10"	20 – 25

Newell: Creamer, sugar, plate (green with decals; this is unusual), small open sugar and creamer, and #2023 tall jug. The small sugar and creamer have unglazed bottoms and are unmarked. However, the decal is identical to one found on the Trellis shape, so I am including them as possible *Newell pieces.*

Creamer .... *$4 – $6*
Cup .... *4 – 6*
Cup, AD. .... *10 – 12*
Cup, bouillon .... *12 – 16*
Cup, coffee .... *6 – 8*
Dish, 5" .... *2 – 3*
Dish, 5¹/₂" .... *2 – 3*
Dish, 5³/₄" .... *3 – 4*
Dish, 6¹/₄" .... *3 – 4*
Gravy .... *12 – 15*
Gravy faststand .... *12 – 15*
Gravy liner/pickle, 8" .... *6 – 8*
Jug, ¹/₂-pint. .... *6 – 8*
Jug, 1-pint .... *8 – 10*
Jug, 1¹/₂-pint. .... *10 – 12*
Jug, 2¹/₂-pint. .... *12 – 15*
Jug, 4-pint .... *15 – 20*
Plate, 6¹/₄" .... *1 – 2*
Plate, 7¹/₄" .... *4 – 5*
Plate, 8¹/₂" .... *4 – 5*
Plate, 9¹/₈" .... *7 – 9*
Plate, 10" .... *10 – 12*
Plate, lug, cake. .... *10 – 12*
Platter, oval, 8³/₈" .... *6 – 8*
Platter, oval, 9¹/₄" .... *6 – 8*
Platter, oval, 10¹/₂" .... *10 – 12*
Platter, oval, 11¹/₂" .... *10 – 12*
Platter, oval, 12¹/₂" .... *12 – 15*
Platter, oval, 13¹/₄" .... *12 – 15*
Platter, oval, 15¹/₄" .... *15 – 18*
Platter, oval, 17¹/₄" .... *20 – 25*
Saucer, 5³/₄" .... *1 – 2*
Saucer, AD, 4¹/₂" .... *3 – 5*
Saucer, bouillon, 5³/₄" (same as tea) .... *1 – 2*
Saucer, coffee, 6" .... *2 – 3*
Sugar .... *8 – 10*
Teapot .... *30 – 35*

OLD ROMAN   (ca. 1932)

An obscure shape with an embossed rim. It will be found in a rich Ming Yellow glaze with decals and a Sea Green solid glaze.

Old Roman

Bowl, soup, 8"* .... *$10 – $12*
Bowl, vegetable, 9"* .... *15 – 18*
Creamer .... *4 – 6*
Cup .... *4 – 6*
Dish, 5¹/₂"* .... *2 – 3*

Old Roman: Plate. What is unusual about this plate is that it is green with a Wells Art Glaze mark.

Plate, 6¼" . . . . *$1 – $2*
Plate, 9" . . . . *7 – 9*
Plate, square, 8" . . . . *7 – 9*
Platter, 12"* . . . . *10 – 12*
Saucer . . . . *1 – 2*
Sugar, open . . . . *8 – 10*

ORLEANS   (ca. 1932–1941>)

An OvenServe lookalike. See OvenServe for a shape comparison. Some company records show an open sugar, but others confirm that a lid was manufactured. Very little Orleans turns up. The gravy and liner are especially hard to find.

MARK   The few pieces I have seen have been unmarked.

Bowl, salad, round, 8¾" . . . . *$15 – $18*
Bowl, soup, 8" . . . . *10 – 12*

Orleans: Creamer, platter, and syrup jug.

Bowl, 36s . . . . *$7 – $10*
Bowl, vegetable, oval, 8¼" . . . . *10 – 12*
Creamer . . . . *4 – 6*
Cup . . . . *4 – 6*
Dish, 5½"* . . . . *2 – 3*
Gravy . . . . *12 – 15*
Gravy liner/pickle . . . . *6 – 8*
Jug . . . . *15 – 20*
Plate, 6½" . . . . *1 – 2*
Plate, 7"* . . . . *4 – 5*
Plate, 8"* . . . . *4 – 5*
Plate, 9" . . . . *7 – 9*
Plate, 10¼" . . . . *10 – 12*
Platter, 11⅜" . . . . *10 – 12*
Saucer . . . . *1 – 2*
Sugar . . . . *8 – 10*

PICCADILLY

The hollowware has straight sides and was intended to go with the plain round flatware of the Brittany shape.

PRICING   Use Brittany values.

Piccadilly: Creamer and sugar.

DISTRIBUTORS

Over the years, Homer Laughlin has manufactured ware for a large number of distributors. Sometimes standard Laughlin patterns were used; sometimes patterns were exclusive to the distributor. These pieces were usually backstamped with the distributor's name and often the pattern name. Occasionally, a Homer Laughlin mark will be found alongside. Some of the many distributors were Alliance China Company, Cunningham & Pickett (1938–1969), Lifetime China Co., J. J. Newberry, A. E. Salone (West Coast), Sears, Montgomery Ward, and F. W. Woolworth.

QUAKER OATS

A number of lines were produced as premiums for the Quaker Oats Company. The following six seem to be the most popular or readily found. Pieces of OvenServe and Pastoral will be found marked both Homer Laughlin and Taylor, Smith & Taylor because Quaker Oats had both companies manufacturing them. The smaller pieces came in the box; there was a coupon for ordering the larger pieces to complete a set. It is the smaller pieces that generally are found.

Carnival   This is basically a solid-color line. A rare decal decoration will be found.

   PRICING   Gray, light green, dark green, turquoise, and yellow are at the low end of the range; cobalt, ivory, and red are at the high end.

Cup	*$5 – $7*
Dish, cereal	*8 – 10*
Dish, fruit	*7 – 9*
Plate, 6½"	*3 – 4*
Plate, 9"	*ND*
Saucer	*2 – 3*

Harvest

Cup	*$4 – $6*
Dish	*2 – 3*
Saucer	*1 – 2*

OvenServe   Solid colors: dark brown, dark green, pink, and turquoise. I have not seen any confirmation that Melon Yellow and Orange were used by Quaker Oats.

Quaker Oats: Tea Rose plate and Carnival cup (unusual to find a piece of Carnival with a decal). Be careful not to confuse Tea Rose shape with Tango shape; they are similar.

Baker, oval, 6¼" .... $4 – $6
Bowl, round, 3¾" .... 3 – 5
Bowl, round, 5½" .... 4 – 6
Custard .... 4 – 6

Pastoral

Cup .... $4 – $6
Dish .... 2 – 3
Saucer .... 1 – 2

Tea Rose   (1937)

Cup .... $4 – $6
Dish, fruit .... 2 – 3
Dish, oatmeal .... 3 – 4
Plate, 6¾" .... 1 – 2
Plate, 9½" .... 7 – 9
Saucer .... 1 – 2

Tudor Rose   There should be other pieces.

Cup .... $4 – $6
Plate .... 3 – 4
Saucer .... 1 – 2

Wild Rose

Cup .... $4 – $6
Dish .... 2 – 3
Saucer .... 1 – 2

RAVENNA   (ca. 1932)

Like Orleans, an OvenServe lookalike. See OvenServe for comparison.

Ravenna

Ravenna: Cup, plate, and sugar (missing lid).

Casserole	*$20 – $25*
Creamer	*4 – 6*
Cup	*4 – 6*
Dish, 5¼"	*2 – 3*
Dish, 6"	*3 – 4*
Plate, 6"*	*1 – 2*
Plate, 7"	*4 – 5*
Plate, 10"*	*10 – 12*
Platter, 11"	*10 – 12*
Saucer	*1 – 2*
Sugar	*8 – 10*

REPUBLIC

Homer Laughlin's version of Havilland's Ranson. Made in both an Ivory and White body.

Bowl, salad, 9"	*$15 – $18*
Bowl, soup, 9"*	*12 – 15*
Bowl, soup, coupe, 8"*	*10 – 12*
Bowl, soup, coupe, 9"*	*12 – 15*
Bowl, vegetable, oval, 9"*	*10 – 12*
Bowl, 36s	*7 – 10*
Butter dish	*20 – 25*
Butter pat	*4 – 6*
Casserole	*20 – 25*
Creamer	*4 – 6*
Cup	*4 – 6*
Cup, AD.	*10 – 12*
Cup, coffee	*6 – 8*
Dish, 5½"*	*2 – 3*
Dish, 6¼"*	*3 – 4*
Gravy	*12 – 15*
Gravy faststand	*12 – 15*
Gravy liner/pickle, 8¾"	*6 – 8*
Plate, 6"*	*1 – 2*
Plate, 7"*	*4 – 5*

Republic: Plate (gold trim) and teapot.

Plate, 8"* .... $5 – $6
Plate, 9"* .... 7 – 9
Plate, 10"* .... 10 – 12
Platter, 11" .... 10 – 12
Platter, 13" .... 12 – 15
Platter, 15" .... 15 – 18
Platter, 17" .... 20 – 25
Saucer .... 1 – 2
Saucer, AD .... 3 – 5
Saucer, coffee .... 2 – 3
Sugar .... 8 – 10
Sugar, AD .... 10 – 12
Teapot .... 30 – 35

RHYTHM

Designed by Don Schreckengost. The covered vegetable bottom is the same as the open vegetable. The Swing-shape shaker was used with Rhythm. The jug and the 15" platter seem to have been made for the decal-decorated lines only.

Rhythm was decorated in solid-color glazes of Burgundy, Chartreuse, Gray, Green (dark green), and Harlequin Yellow. The spoon holder in Turquoise is presumed to have been sold with Harlequin.

Decals: American Provincial (a Pennsylvania Dutch design by Don Schreckengost; the first silk-screened decal used at Homer Laughlin), Golden Wheat, Rhythm Rose (a large rose), and White Flower (white dogwood with yellow centers and green leaves, made for J. J. Newberry). American Provincial and Rhythm Rose are easily found.

See Charm House following.

Bowl, mixing, Green, 6" (Kitchen Kraft) . . . . *$90 – $100*
Bowl, mixing, Yellow, 8" (Kitchen Kraft) . . . . *100 – 110*
Bowl, mixing, Chartreuse, 10" (Kitchen Kraft) . . . . *110 – 125*
Bowl, soup, 8" . . . . *12 – 15*
Bowl, vegetable, round, 8½" . . . . *15 – 18*
Casserole . . . . *45 – 55*

DINNER PLATE, 10"

LUNCHEON PLATE, 9"

SALAD PLATE, 8"

PIE PLATE, 7"

TEA SAUCER

TEA CUP

BREAD & BUTTER PLATE, 6"

COVERED TEA POT -

CREAM PITCHER

COV'D. SUGAR

CEREAL SOUP, 5½"

SAUCE BOAT

ROUND VEGETABLE, 8½"

COUPE SOUP, 8"

WATER JUG, 2 qts.

COVERED CASSEROLE

FRUIT, 5¼"

SALT

PEPPER

OVAL PLATTER, 15½"

OVAL PLATTER, 13½"

OVAL PLATTER, 11½"

SAUCEBOAT STAND, or PICKLE, 9"

Rhythm

Rhythm: American Provincial plate, shaker (Swing shape), shaker (Charm House shape), and teapot.

Creamer/both sizes	$7 – $9
Cup	6 – 8
Dish, 5½"	5 – 7
Dish, footed, 5½" (Charm House)	10 – 12
Gravy	15 – 18
Cobalt/Turquoise	35 +
Gravy liner/pickle, 9"	10 – 12
Jug, 2-quart	60 +
Plate, 6"	5 – 6
Plate, 7¼"	6 – 8
Plate, 8"	15 – 18
Plate, 9"	8 – 10
Plate, 10"	15 – 18
Plate, divided	50 – 60
Platter, oval, 11½"	14 – 16
Platter, oval, 13½"	16 – 18
Platter, oval, 15½"	20 – 25

Rhythm: Low creamer (windmill decal), tall creamer, and sugar. The creamer and sugar on the right have an unusual decal; the creamer with a rubber stamp, and the sugar with a flower and bee.

Saucer. . . . . *$2 – $3*
Shaker, pair (Swing) . . . . *12 – 15*
Spoon Rest
  Turquoise/Yellow . . . . *175 – 200*
  Dark Green . . . . *225 – 250*
  Decal-decorated. . . . . *125 – 150*
Sugar . . . . *15 – 18*
Teapot . . . . *45 – 55*
Tid-bit, 3-tier . . . . *35 – 40*

CHARM HOUSE

Charm House used the Rhythm line with some pieces of the hollowware restyled. This restyled shape was used for Highland Plaid and other decorations in the Dura-Print line: patterned flatware accented by hollowware in solid colors of black, blue, brown, chartreuse, green, white, and Harlequin Yellow. (Do not confuse Dura-Print with Dura-Tone, another Laughlin line.) Known pieces that were restyled are the cup, sugar, creamer, fruit dish, and shaker.

Now, here's where it can get confusing. There are two points to keep in mind:

1. *Some Charm House pieces were used in the Rhythm line.* The fruit dish is found in Rhythm colors stamped with the Rhythm mark, and the photo shows the Charm House shaker with the American Provincial decal.

2. *The Rhythm gravy was used in the Charm House line.* This explains the odd colors found on the gravy.

PRICING Charm House values should not be much different from

Charm House: Dura-Print Highland Plaid pattern on plate and saucer with contrasting solid color cup, sugar, and creamer in the Charm House shape.

Charm House: Dura-Print Dundee Plaid (green and brown plaid with green hollowware). Note difference in striping from Highland Plaid.

Rhythm's but, as you can see in the previous gravy prices, that is not always true. The list below is of pieces known to have been used in Charm House lines; it is for reference only.

Bowl, cereal/soup	**Plate**, 7¹/₄"
Bowl, salad, round, 8³/₄"	**Plate**, 9¹/₄"
Bowl, soup, coupe	**Plate**, 10³/₄"
Casserole	**Platter**, oval, 11³/₄"
Creamer	**Platter**, oval, 13¹/₂"
Cup	**Saucer**
Dish, fruit, 5¹/₄"	**Shaker**
Gravy	**Sugar**
Gravy liner/pickle	**Teapot**
Plate, 6¹/₄"	

SERENADE   (1939)

A lightly embossed wheat sheaf decorates the shoulders and rims of this shape.

Solid pastel colors: "a soft, rich, faintly dull glaze" of blue, green, pink, and yellow. A Kitchen Kraft casserole in Serenade colors with the Serenade backstamp is very rare. Company records show that fewer lids than bottoms were made. See also Nautilus/Pastels.

Serenade

HOMER LAUGHLIN

MADE IN U.S.A.

Serenade:
Creamer, shaker,
and coffee pot.

Bowl, soup, 8"	*$20 – $25*
Bowl, vegetable, round, 9"	*20 – 25*
Casserole	*85 – 95*
Casserole (Kitchen Kraft)	*ND*
Creamer	*12 – 15*
Cup	*12 – 15*
Dish, 6"	*8 – 10*
Dish, cereal, lug	*20 – 25*
Gravy	*15 – 20*
Gravy liner/pickle, 9"	*12 – 15*
Plate, 6¼"	*4 – 6*
Plate, 7"	*8 – 10*
Plate, 9"	*12 – 15*
Plate, 10"	*20 – 25*
Plate, chop, 15"	*30 – 35*
Platter, oval, 12½"	*18 – 20*
Saucer	*2 – 3*
Shaker, pair	*15 – 18*
Sugar	*15 – 18*
Teapot	*75 – 85*

SWING   (1938)

One of the Eggshell weight lines. Swing has delicate round handles and finials that are easily broken. Company records indicate the existence of a 10" oval vegetable. The shakers, designed to go with this shape, were also used with the Rhythm shape, so you will find them in Rhythm solid colors and decals.

Decals: Prima Donna (S-105-C), a rhythmic spray pattern, and Green Goddess, an Oriental arrangement.

NOTE   Homer Laughlin did something different for Swing; the handles and finials were colored Mist Blue or Salmon/Coral (both names were used), the color being in the body, not in the glaze. There are also white handles.

Bowl, soup, 8"	$12 – $15
Bowl, vegetable, oval, 9"	12 – 15
Casserole	45 – 55

Swing: Cream soup, platter (an abstract vase and flower decal), and Briar Rose teapot.

Swing: Breakfast set pieces: covered toast, eggcup, AD sugar, AD cup, AD creamer, and AD coffee pot. All are Briar Rose except for Chinese Princess cup.

Celery tray, 11½" × 5½" .... *ND*
Coffee pot, AD .... *$40 – $50*
Creamer .... *6 – 8*
Creamer, AD. .... *8 – 10*
Cup .... *6 – 8*
Cup, AD. .... *12 – 15*
Cup, cream soup .... *20 – 25*
Eggcup. .... *12 – 15*
Muffin cover .... *35 – 45*
Plate, 6" .... *2 – 3*
Plate, 7" .... *5 – 6*
Plate, 8" .... *8 – 10*
Plate, 9" .... *8 – 10*
Plate, 10" .... *12 – 15*
Platter, 11" .... *12 – 15*
Platter, 13" .... *15 – 18*
Platter, 15" .... *20 – 25*
Saucer .... *2 – 3*
Saucer, AD .... *4 – 6*
Saucer, cream soup .... *8 – 10*
Shaker, pair. .... *12 – 15*
Sugar .... *12 – 15*
Sugar, AD, open .... *8 – 10*
Teapot .... *40 – 45*

TANGO (1937–1941>)

A solid-color line. There is not a lot out there, but it is popular with collectors. Company records indicate that the AD cups and saucers, of which very few were made, may have been the Republic shape.

Solid colors: burgundy, green, mauve blue, red, and yellow.

Bowl, salad, round, 8¾" .... *$20 – $25*
Bowl, soup, 8½" .... *12 – 15*
Bowl, vegetable, oval, 9" .... *20 – 25*
Casserole .... *85 +*
Creamer. .... *10 – 12*
Cup. .... *10 – 12*
Cup, AD .... *ND*
Dish, 6". .... *7 – 9*
Eggcup .... *ND*
Plate, 6" .... *4 – 6*
Plate, 7" .... *5 – 7*
Plate, 9" .... *12 – 15*
Plate, 10" .... *15 – 20*
Platter, oval, 11½". .... *12 – 15*
Saucer. .... *3 – 5*
Saucer, AD. .... *ND*

Tango: Shaker, plate, eggcup, and cup.

Shaker, each .... $10 – $12
Sugar .... 12 – 15

THEME (1940)

A band of embossed fruit around the rim of the flatware and the shoulder of the hollowware. Although Homer Laughlin did not do special-order commemoratives and souvenir plates, outside decorating shops used Laughlin blanks, and Theme plates are perhaps the most common of the Laughlin shapes to be used in this fashion.

Bowl, salad, 9" .... $15 – $18
Bowl, soup, 8"* .... 10 – 12
Bowl, 36s .... 7 – 10
Bowl, vegetable, oval, 9" .... 10 – 12
Casserole .... 20 – 25
Creamer .... 4 – 6
Cup .... 4 – 6
Cup, AD .... 4 – 6
Cup, cream soup .... 12 – 16

Theme: Platter (distinctive decal of colored window panes behind vase of flowers on table), shaker, and sugar.

Dish, lug, 5½"	*$3 – $4*
Gravy	*12 – 15*
Gravy faststand	*12 – 15*
Gravy liner	*6 – 8*
Plate, 6"	*1 – 2*
Plate, 7"	*4 – 5*
Plate, 8"	*5 – 6*
Plate, 9"	*7 – 9*
Plate, 10"	*10 – 12*
Plate, chop, 14"	*15 – 20*
Plate, square, 8"	*7 – 9*
Platter, 11"*	*10 – 12*
Platter, 13"	*12 – 15*
Platter, 15"*	*15 – 18*
Saucer	*1 – 2*
Saucer, AD	*3 – 5*
Saucer, cream soup	*6 – 8*
Shaker, pair	*8 – 10*
Sugar	*8 – 10*
Teapot	*30 – 35*

TRELLIS   (ca. 1929)

Designed by Frederick Rhead. This is basically the same shape as Newell but with alternating areas of either cross-hatch or scallop embossed on the rims and shoulders.

I have seen a few pieces glazed in green or blue, but this is basically a decal-decorated line, on either yellow or white body.

Trellis: Sugar, creamer, small jug, plate (blue), and casserole (silver lines).

Bowl, vegetable, oval, 7¼" .... *$10 – $12*
Casserole .... *20 – 25*
Creamer .... *4 – 6*
Cup .... *4 – 6*
Dish, fruit, 5¼" .... *2 – 3*
Dish, cereal, 6" .... *3 – 4*
Jug, small .... *8 – 10*
Plate, 7" .... *4 – 5*
Plate, 8" .... *4 – 5*
Plate, 9" .... *7 – 9*
Plate, 10" .... *10 – 12*
Platter, small .... *10 – 12*
Saucer .... *1 – 2*
Sugar .... *8 – 10*

VIRGINIA ROSE   (1933)

The batter and syrup jugs (made only for J. J. Newberry), cream soup cup/saucer, and shaker (made only in the 1950s) are hard to find. The Jade oblong butter is often found in sets of Virginia Rose, as is the Cable-shape eggcup, which was often mixed with other shapes. Be careful: Many collectors refer to Virginia Rose butter or shakers when they mean the Jade butter and the Kitchen Kraft or Swing shakers with the standard decal.

Virginia Rose was produced for over 20 years and was decorated with over 450 treatments. See "What's in a Name: Virginia Rose" below for specifics about the two most popular ones: JJ 59 and VR 128. The Dresden decoration, from the 1950s, was made for a supermarket chain.

PRICING A number of Kitchen Kraft prices will be found with the JJ 59 and VR 128 decals, so I've included them in the pricing.

VIRGINIA ROSE
MADE IN U.S.A.

	JJ 59 & VR 128	Other Decals
Bowl, mixing, 6" (Kitchen Kraft)	$25 – $30	—
Bowl, mixing, 8" (Kitchen Kraft)	25 – 30	—
Bowl, mixing, 10" (Kitchen Kraft)	30 – 35	—
Bowl, 36s	15 – 18	$7 – $10
Bowl, soup, coupe, 8½"	15 – 18	10 – 12
Bowl, soup, rimmed, 8½"	15 – 18	10 – 12
Bowl, vegetable, oval, 8"	20 – 25	10 – 12
Bowl, vegetable, oval, 9⅜"	15 – 18	10 – 12
Bowl, vegetable, oval, 10"	15 – 18	12 – 15
Bowl, vegetable, round, 9½"	20 – 25	15 – 18
Butter dish, oblong (Jade).............................	75 – 85	40 – 45
Casserole..	75 – 85	25 – 30
Casserole (Kitchen Kraft/both styles)	40 – 50	—
Creamer	10 – 12	4 – 6
Cup	6 – 8	4 – 6
Cup, cream soup	ND	15 – 20
Dish, 6"	5 – 7	3 – 4
Eggcup (Cable)	35 – 40	—
Gravy..	20 – 25	12 – 15

Virginia Rose: #VR 128 cream soup, plate (Tulips in a Basket), Dresden shaker, #JJ59 syrup, and batter jug.

	JJ 59 & VR 128	Other Decals
Gravy faststand . . . . *ND*		*$12 – $15*
Gravy liner/pickle, 9" . . . . *$12 – $15*		*6 – 8*
Jug, batter, open . . . . *125+*		—
w/lid . . . . *ND*		—
Jug, syrup, open . . . . *125+*		—
w/lid . . . . *ND*		—
Mug (Cable) . . . . *35 – 40*		—
Pie baker, 9½" (Kitchen Kraft) . . . . *20 – 25*		—
Plate, 6¼" . . . . *3 – 4*		*1 – 2*
Plate, 7" . . . . *5 – 8*		*4 – 5*
Plate, 8" . . . . *12 – 15*		*4 – 5*
Plate, 9" . . . . *7 – 9*		*7 – 9*
Plate, 10" . . . . *10 – 12*		*10 – 12*
Plate, cake (Kitchen Kraft) . . . . *40 – 50*		—
Plate, lug, 11" . . . . *18 – 20*		*10 – 12*
Platter, 11½" . . . . *15 – 18*		*10 – 12*
Platter, 13½" . . . . *20 – 25*		*12 – 15*
Platter, 15½" . . . . *30 – 35*		*15 – 18*
Saucer . . . . *2 – 3*		*1 – 2*
Saucer, cream soup, 7" . . . . *ND*		*ND*
Shaker, each . . . . —		*8 – 10*
Shaker (Kitchen Kraft) . . . . *40 – 50*		—
Shaker (Swing) . . . . *40 – 50*		—
Sugar . . . . *15 – 18*		*8 – 10*
Utensil, cake server (OvenServe) . . . . *30 – 35*		—

WHAT'S IN A NAME: VIRGINIA ROSE

Virginia Rose is a shape name, but collectors are misled into thinking it the decoration name because of the Wild Rose–style decal most often found on this shape. Actually there are two related decals.

JJ 59 (the prefix on the number indicates that this was made exclusively for the J. J. Newberry stores) has small pink and white flowers of equal size, and green, gray, and brown leaves.

VR 128 has large and small flowers, both pink, white, and purple with a touch of yellow, and green leaves. This was sold through Woolworth's, which could explain its plentitude (a retired employee remembers it being shipped by the railroad-car load).

WELLS (1930–1940>)

Designed by Frederick Hurten Rhead; distinguished by a thin rim and openwork handles. The **ashtray**, with its embossed design on the rim, is not part of the

Wells shape; it will also be found in the OvenServe Pumpkin glaze. Alternative lids to the **batter and syrup jugs**, which are round and leave the spout exposed, have been reported. The **cake tray** was probably used as the tray to the batter set. Company records indicate two other sizes of oval vegetable, probably 8" and 10", as well as at least one other dish and one other platter size.

Solid colors, known as Wells Art Glazes (see "Marks" below), include blue, Leaf Green (1930), Peach (1930), Rust Brown (1930), Vellum Ivory, and Melon Yellow (used on OvenServe and may have originally come out on that line). Colors will vary somewhat. A red glaze and a blue glaze have been found, but they were not production colors and are very rare.

Decals (which are a little less commonly found) were put on a standard ivory body. They include Flowers of the Dell (sprays of blue and purple flowers with yellow centers and green leaves), Hollyhock, Tulip (Wells 5623), Palm Tree, "Pink Clover," and "Rain Tree." There is also a decal strongly resembling Hall China's #488.

MARKS Despite the mark and despite the fact that there was an Arthur Wells, the colored line is correctly called Wells Art Glazes, not Art Wells Glazes as I have seen used. The Peacock mark in either black or multicolor will also be found on pieces of Century and Jade.

PRICING Green and Pink are at the low end of the range; Peach, Rust, and yellow are at the high end. Blue and red are too rare to value. Use the high end of the range for attractive decals.

Ashtray, 4½"	$15 – $20
Bowl, 36s	12 – 15
Bowl, round, 7¼"	12 – 15
Bowl, round, 8¼"	15 – 18
Bowl, round, 9¼"	18 – 20
Bowl, soup, 8"	15 – 18
Bowl, vegetable, 9"	15 – 18
Butter dish	60 – 75
Butter pat	12 – 15
Casserole, 8"	50 – 60
Coffee pot, AD	85 – 95
Covered toast	60 – 75
Creamer	12 – 15
Creamer, AD.	15 – 20
Cup	12 – 15
Cup, AD.	15 – 20
Cup, bouillon	ND
Cup, coffee	18 – 20
Cup, cream soup	20 – 25

Dish, 5¼"	*$8 – $10*
Dish, 6"	*10 – 12*
Eggcup, double	*18 – 20*
Gravy	*20 – 25*
Gravy faststand, round, no spout	*25 – 30*
Gravy liner/pickle, 9"	*12 – 15*
Jug, batter	*65 – 75*
Jug, syrup	*75 – 85*
Plate, 6¼"	*5 – 6*
Plate, 7"	*6 – 8*
Plate, 8"	*10 – 12*
Plate, 9"	*10 – 12*
Plate, 10"	*12 – 15*
Plate, cake, open lug, 10"	*20 – 25*
Plate, square, 8"	*10 – 12*
Platter, 11½"	*15 – 20*
Platter, 13½"	*18 – 22*
Platter, 15½"	*25 – 28*
Platter, 17½"	*35 – 40*
Saucer	*2 – 3*
Saucer, AD	*4 – 6*
Saucer, cream soup	*8 – 12*
Sugar	*16 – 20*
Sugar, flat handles	*16 – 20*
Sugar, AD	*16 – 20*
Teapot	*60 – 75*

WHAT'S IN A NAME: WELLS

Homer Laughlin used Wells as both a shape name and a line name. This explains why you will find the Wells Peacock backstamp on the Century and Jade shapes. When Jade came out in 1932, it was advertised as part of the Wells line. It was not unusual for a pottery to bank on the name of a successful line by extending it to other pieces; this is likely the case here.

SPECIAL PRICE LIST

WILLOW

Laughlin put its Willow pattern on a variety of shapes over the years. I have noted some shape names in the lists below as a start to sorting this out. Remember that a lot of flatware and some hollowware were used interchangeably between shapes, so some pieces will be difficult to identify.

Laughlin made Willow in two basic styles, decal-decorated and transfer-printed. Most of the decal-decorated pieces date from the 1920s, possibly earlier, to the early 1930s. There is not much around. Most of what you will find is the allover transfer-printed traditional design. This seems to date from the mid 1930s; it was made until at least 1964.

Both styles utilized a semivitreous body. Laughlin did put its transfer-printed design on hotelware, but too little has turned up for me to make a list at this time.

Decal-Decorated   This is usually a small decal of the basic Willow design in blue on a white background, with either a blue line, a gold line, or some gold treatment, often a repeating stamp.

There can be lots of variation. For example, a 17½" platter with an elaborate stamped gold border and four small pieces of Blue Willow decal has been seen. Also, two Yellowstone platters, one with a gold-stamped rim, the other with a pumpkin-colored luster encircling the rim.

There should be a cup, saucer, creamer, and sugar, but none have been reported.

Bowl, 36s (Republic)...................................$10 – $12
Casserole ....*ND*
Cup, AD (Jade)...*10 – 12*

Willow: Decal-decorated platter.

Jug (Empress), 8-ounce, 4" .... *$12 – $15*
Jug, 24-ounce, 5" .... *ND*
Plate, 9" (Empress).. *6 – 8*
Plate, 10" .... *8 – 10*
Platter, 11³/₄" (Eggshell Georgian) .... *15 – 18*
Platter, 13¹/₂" .... *18 – 20*
Platter, 15" (Yellowstone)..................................... *20 – 25*
Platter, 17¹/₂" .... *25 – 30*
Saucer, AD (Jade) .... *3 – 5*

Transfer Printed   (<1936)   Several pieces, known as the Willow shape, were made for this line; these are identified in the list below. This transfer print has the traditional border and will be found in both Blue and Pink. Note that the teapot bottom is the Wells shape. Rather than the Wells lid, this lid has a finial with eight "petals" around a central mound; the sugar finial is the same. This teapot will be found with other decorations. There is a Willow-shape teapot—see Americana—but no one has reported finding it with the Willow pattern. Odd. The single eggcup is sometimes referred to as a Chinese teacup.

PRICING   Values below are for both blue and pink.

Bowl, lug, soup (Willow)..................................... *ND*
Bowl, soup, rim, 8¹/₄" .... *$10 – $12*
Bowl, soup, coupe, 8¹/₄" .... *10 – 12*
Bowl, 36s (Empress)... *7 – 10*
Bowl, vegetable, oval, 9" .... *10 – 12*
Bowl, vegetable, round, 9".................................... *10 – 12*
Casserole, round (Empress)................................... *30 – 35*
Creamer (Willow) .... *10 – 12*
Cup, 2¹/₄" high (Willow)...................................... *6 – 8*
Cup (Epicure).. *12 – 15*

Willow: Transfer printed plate, Willow shape creamer, sugar, and jug.

Cup, cream soup (Willow) . . . . *ND*
Cup, jumbo, 4" (Willow) . . . . *$20 – $25*
Dish, 5¼" . . . . *3 – 4*
Dish, 6" . . . . *3 – 4*
Eggcup, single (Cable) . . . . *10 – 12*
Gravy (Willow), 7¼" . . . . *18 – 22*
Gravy liner/pickle . . . . *ND*
Jug . . . . *18 – 20*
Plate, 6¼" . . . . *2 – 3*
Plate, 7⅛" . . . . *5 – 5*
Plate, 9¼" . . . . *6 – 8*
Plate, 10" . . . . *8 – 10*
Platter, 11" . . . . *12 – 15*
Platter, 13" . . . . *15 – 18*
Platter, 15½" . . . . *18 – 20*
Saucer, 5¾" . . . . *2 – 3*
Saucer, jumbo, 7" (Willow) . . . . *4 – 5*
Sugar (Willow) . . . . *12 – 15*
Teapot (Wells bottom) . . . . *45 – 50*

YELLOWSTONE   (late 1920s)

An octagonal shape made first in an Ivory body and later in the Century Vellum glaze. There are six sizes of jugs. Some lids were made, probably early on, but these are extremely rare.

   PRICING   Double values for Mexican decals.

Bowl, 30s . . . . *$7 – $10*
Bowl, 36s . . . . *7 – 10*
Bowl, round, 9⅜" . . . . *15 – 18*
Bowl, soup, 9" . . . . *12 – 15*
Bowl, soup, coupe, 8⅛" . . . . *10 – 12*

Yellowstone: Syrup jug, plate (sailing ships), eggcup, and teapot. The other decal is a pale rose.

Bowl, vegetable, oval, 9" .... *$10 – $12*
Bowl, vegetable, round, 9½" .... *15 – 18*
Butter dish .... *20 – 25*
Butter pat, 3" .... *4 – 6*
Casserole, 8" .... *25 – 30*
Creamer .... *4 – 6*
Creamer, AD. .... *6 – 8*
Cup .... *4 – 6*
Cup, AD. .... *10 – 12*
Cup, coffee .... *6 – 8*
Dish, cereal, 6¼" .... *3 – 4*
Dish, fruit, 5⅝" .... *2 – 3*
Gravy .... *12 – 15*
Gravy faststand .... *12 – 15*
Gravy liner/pickle, 8½" .... *6 – 8*
Jug, 1-pint .... *12 – 15*
Plate, 6⅛" .... *1 – 2*
Plate, 7" .... *4 – 5*
Plate, 8" .... *5 – 6*
Plate, 8⅞" .... *7 – 9*
Plate, 9¾" .... *10 – 12*
Plate, cake, lug, 9½" .... *10 – 12*
Plate, lug, 10¼" .... *12 – 15*
Platter, 11¼" .... *10 – 12*
Platter, 13⅜" .... *12 – 15*
Platter, 15" .... *15 – 18*
Platter, 17¼" .... *20 – 25*
Saucer, AD, 4⅞" .... *3 – 5*
Saucer, coffee, 6¼" .... *2 – 3*
Saucer, tea, 5⅞" .... *1 – 2*
Sugar .... *8 – 10*
Sugar, AD .... *10 – 12*
Teapot .... *30 – 35*

KITCHENWARE

APPLETREE

Called Orange Tree by some, Laughlin's records refer to these as Appletree.

These were made in three solid colors: green, and OvenServe's Orange (pumpkin) and Melon Yellow. A bowl in white with a red band has been reported.

PRICING   Do not overpay for these bowls.

Bowl, 5" .... *$10 – $15*
Bowl, 6" .... *20 – 25*
Bowl, 7" .... *25 – 30*
Bowl, 8" .... *30 – 35*
Bowl, 9" .... *35 – 40*

KITCHEN KRAFT   (mid 1937)

Designed by Frederick Hurten Rhead. Officially called Kitchen Kraft OvenServe, probably to take advantage of OvenServe's good reputation. The fork, spoon, and cake server are from the embossed OvenServe line. The jug was sold both open and lidded. There is a reference in company records to a Salad Nappy (bowl).

Kitchen Kraft will be found in solid Fiesta colors (introduced in January 1938) of blue, green, red, and yellow. A Serenade casserole in pastel colors was made, but only a few lids have been found—not surprising since company records indicate maybe one lid was made for every hundred bottoms.

The mixing bowls were also glazed in Chartreuse, Forest Green, and Harlequin Yellow as an exclusive for J. C. Penney. And they were glazed as well in the Jubilee colors of Celadon, Gray, and Pink.

Decals: Mexicana (mid 1937) and Sunporch (a striped umbrella over a patio table set with dinnerware in Fiesta colors).

PRICING For Kitchen Bouquet, price halfway between the first and second price columns. For Sun Porch, the Chinese decals, and other special decorations, use the same values as for the Mexican decals. For prices on the odd color mixing bowls, see Rhythm for the J. C. Penney colors, and see Jubilee.

	Decals	Mexican Decals	Solid Colors
Bowl, mixing, 6"	$20 – $22	$30 – $35	$60 – $70
Bowl, mixing, 8"	22 – 25	35 – 45	70 – 80
Bowl, mixing, 10"	25 – 30	45 – 55	80 – 90
Cake plate	20 – 25	30 – 35	45 – 55
Casserole, individual	55 – 65	85 – 95	125 – 150
Casserole, 7½"	30 – 35	50 – 60	75 – 85
Casserole, 8½"	30 – 35	60 – 70	85 – 95
Coffee pot	40 – 50	—	—
Covered jar, small	50 – 60	110 – 125	225 – 250
Covered jar, medium	60 – 70	100 – 110	200 – 225
Covered jar, large	70 – 80	125 – 140	250 – 275
Jug w/lid	60 – 70	100 – 125	165 – 185
Pie baker, 9"	18 – 22	35 – 45	40 – 50
Pie baker, 10"	20 – 25	45 – 50	50 – 60
Platter, oval, 13"	30 – 35	55 – 65	75 – 85
Refrigerator stack set, 4-piece	80 – 90	125 – 150	165 – 185
Shaker, pair	30 – 35	45 – 50	85 – 95
Utensil, cake server	25 – 30	40 – 50	80 – 90

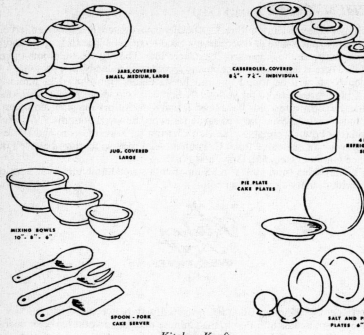

JARS, COVERED
SMALL, MEDIUM, LARGE

CASSEROLES, COVERED
8¼" - 7¼" - INDIVIDUAL

JUG, COVERED
LARGE

4 PC.
REFRIGERATOR
SET

MIXING BOWLS
10" - 8" - 6"

PIE PLATE
CAKE PLATES

SPOON - FORK
CAKE SERVER

SALT AND PEPPER
PLATES 6" - 9"

Kitchen Kraft

	Decals	Mexican Decals	Solid Colors
Utensil, fork............................	$35 – $40	$60 – $70	$100 – $110
Utensil, spoon	30 – 35	50 – 60	90 – 100

Kitchen Kraft: Coffee pot.

OVENSERVE   (1933)

(Note that the correct spelling, per Laughlin's trade advertising, is one word with a cap *S* in the middle.) Homer Laughlin's first kitchenware line; dinnerware was made as well but is more difficult to find. The long spoon, which doesn't turn up very often, was made especially for Woolworth's. The bean pot could double as a leftover.

OvenServe was decorated in solid colors and decals, as well as with handpainted and stamped decorations. **Solid colors**: Melon Yellow and Orange (pumpkin). See also Quaker Oats. **Decals**: OS-81 (1935) is bright green, orange, red, and yellow and fits over the embossing. There is another multicolor decal in softer hues that also fits the embossing. **Hand painted**: The most common decoration is an underglaze green hand painted over the raised decoration (blue is occasionally found). You will also find Polychrome, a pastel four-color underglaze decoration hand painted directly over the embossed design. **Stamped**: "Stars" (silver stars, sometimes with a red line).

PRICING   Decals that fit over the embossing are at the high end of the range.

Bean pot, 6½"*	*$15 – $20*
Bean pot, 7½"*	*15 – 20*
Bean pot, individual	*5 – 7*
Bowl, mixing, 6¼"	*6 – 8*
Bowl, mixing, 8"*	*8 – 10*
Bowl, mixing, 9"*	*10 – 12*
Bowl, mixing, 10"*	*12 – 15*

OvenServe Dinnerware: Cup (Orange/pumpkin), #OS-81 plate, and creamer (green underglaze decoration).

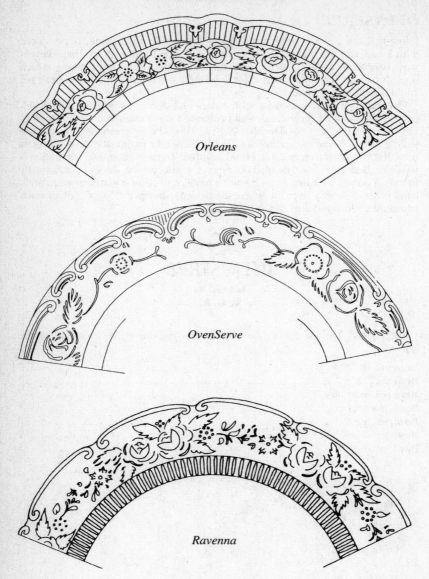

Orleans

OvenServe

Ravenna

This drawing will give you a closeup of the essential differences between the embossing on these three closely related lines. If you have difficulty telling them apart, note that OvenServe has no verge decoration, Ravenna has narrow ribs, and Orleans has more of a panel effect. Of all the potteries in the Ohio/West Virginia area, only Homer Laughlin had the sales staff and manufacturing capability to market such similar lines.

Bowl, mixing, 11"* .... *$15 – $20*
Bowl, mixing, 12"* .... *20 – 25*
Casserole, 8½" .... *20 – 25*
Casserole, stick handle, open, 4⅜" .... *6 – 8*
Casserole, stick handle, open, 5⅛" .... *6 – 8*
Creamer .... *15 – 20*
Cup .... *12 – 15*
Custard, 3½" .... *4 – 6*
Leftover, 4½" .... *6 – 10*
Leftover, 5¼" .... *10 – 15*
Pie baker, oval .... *12 – 15*
Pie baker, round, 9" .... *10 – 12*
Pie baker, round, 11" .... *12 – 15*
Plate, 7" .... *8 – 10*
Plate, 9¼" .... *12 – 15*
Saucer .... *3 – 5*
Shirred egg, lug, 6" .... *12 – 15*
Shirred egg, lug, 7" .... *12 – 15*
Sugar .... *25 – 30*
Utensil, cake server .... *25 – 30*
Utensil, fork .... *35 – 40*
Utensil, spoon .... *30 – 35*
Utensil, spoon, long, 12" .... *35 – 45*

Royal OvenServe   These pieces were made for the Royal Metal Manufacturing Company.

Bowl, mixing, w/lid .... *ND*
Casserole .... *$20 – $25*
Pie baker, oval, 13" .... *15 – 20*
Plate, cake .... *12 – 15*
Platter .... *12 – 15*

NOVELTIES

WORLD'S FAIR / EXPOSITIONS

Four Seasons plate	*$55 – $65*
George Washington pitcher, 2"	
Bisque	*35 – 40*
Ivory	*35 – 40*
George Washington pitcher, 5"	*40 – 45*
Golden Gate ashtray	*75 – 90*
Golden Gate plate	*100 – 125*
Martha Washington pitcher, 2"	
Bisque	*35 – 40*
Ivory	*35 – 40*
Martha Washington pitcher, 5"	*50 – 55*
New York World's Fair service plate	*115 – 125*
Potter's Plate	
Green/ivory	*40 – 50*
Tan/turquoise	*30 – 40*
Vase, 6"	*75 – 90*
Vase, 8"	*75 – 90*
Vase, 10"	*75 – 90*
Zodiac cup/saucer	*50 – 60*

LEIGH POTTERS, INC.

Alliance, Ohio

One of the Sebring family potteries, which began life as the Crescent China Company. Its history was bound up with that of the Sebring Pottery Company until 1943, when the joint company was bought by National Unit Distributors, which continued to manufacture pottery under the Leigh name.

MARKS   This Ohio outline backstamp is the most common of the general marks.

ARISTOCRAT

See Sebring.

ULTRA   (1929–1930)

Designed by Gale Turnbull. Ultra is a square Art Deco shape released in 1930. A round Art Deco shape was released in 1929. This probably has a different name, but until it is discovered I have combined the two in this listing as they are both popular with collectors.

Butter dish, round	$30 – $35
Casserole, round	30 – 35
Casserole, square	30 – 35
Creamer, round	6 – 8
Creamer, square	6 – 8
Cream soup, round	18 – 20
Cup, round	5 – 7
Cup, square	5 – 7
Cup, AD, round	12 – 15
Dish, 5"	4 – 5
Gravy, round	15 – 18
Gravy faststand, round	15 – 18

Ultra: French Tulip square creamer, "Hyacinth" square sugar, "Deco Tulip" tidbit, round AD cup/saucer, and Green Wheat round casserole.

Plate, 7" . . . . *$4 – $5*
Plate, 8¼" . . . . *4 – 5*
Plate, 9" . . . . *7 – 9*
Platter, lug, 11½" . . . . *12 – 15*
Saucer . . . . *1 – 2*
Saucer, AD . . . . *3 – 5*
Sugar, round . . . . *10 – 12*
Sugar, square . . . . *10 – 12*
Teapot, round . . . . *40 – 45*
Teapot, square . . . . *40 – 45*
Tidbit, center handle . . . . *15 – 20*

LIMOGES CHINA COMPANY

Sebring, Ohio

CHAPTER AT A GLANCE

DINNERWARE
CASINO
CORINTHIAN, TROJAN
"SQUARE"
"THIN SWIRL"

TRIUMPH
VICTORY
KITCHENWARE
JIFFY WARE

The Sebring family announced construction of its fourth pottery in Sebring in the spring of 1902, with the intention of manufacturing real china there. Construction was almost completed by the end of the year; production began even though the building was not finished till the end of 1903. By January 1904, the name Sterling China Company had been announced, but by July the name was changed to Limoges, and production had switched over to semiporcelain as china had proved to be unprofitable.

Kitchenware was added in the 1930s. In 1943, Limoges and its sister company, Sebring, were bought by National Unit Distributors. Around 1949, litigation brought by Limoges of France resulted in the official change of the company name to American Limoges, though those two words had been used in their advertisements since the mid 1930s. Operations ceased in 1955.

Very little Sterling china shows up. If you find a piece, hold it up to a strong light and look through it. If it is translucent, you have a hard-to-find piece of Sterling's real china.

Victor Schreckengost designed a number of interesting lines for Limoges but very little besides Triumph and Casino turns up today.

NOTE Despite its name, Limoges made the same quality dinnerware as its competitors. Beware the dealer who charges high prices because they don't know better.

MARKS The first three backstamps are pre-1930. The other six reflect glazes. These were used in the thirties.

DINNERWARE

CASINO   (ca. 1954)

A short line in the shape of card suits, with matching decal decoration.

Casino: Back: *Queen of Hearts heart-shaped plate, King of Hearts diamond-shaped platter.* Front: *Creamer, sugar, King of Hearts diamond-shaped ashtray with stamped advertising, King of Hearts heart-shaped dish, and spade-shaped cup. The cup, sugar, and creamer have a fan and axe decoration.*

Ashtray, diamond .... *$15 – $20*
Creamer, diamond .... *10 – 12*
Cup, club .... *10 – 12*
Dish, heart .... *15 – 20*
Plate, spade .... *16 – 18*
Platter, diamond .... *20 – 25*
Saucer, heart .... *4 – 5*
Sugar, diamond .... *15 – 18*

CORINTHIAN / TROJAN

These are Sebring Pottery shapes used by American Limoges. See that chapter for listing and pricing. Common decals found on Limoges' Corinthian and Trojan are Blue Willow, Old Dutch, and Toledo Delight.

Corinthian/Trojan: Old Dutch plate, Blue Willow plate, and Toledo Delight coffee pot.

Square: Butter dish, Iris plate, butter pat, and teapot.

"SQUARE"

A square shape with a double scallop at the corners. Distinguished by its arrowhead finial. You will find pieces of "Square" with a Royal China mark.

Butter dish	*$15 – $20*
Casserole	*15 – 20*
Creamer	*4 – 6*
Cup	*4 – 6*
Gravy	*8 – 10*
Plate, 6½"	*1 – 2*
Plate, 7"	*2 – 3*
Plate, 9"	*4 – 5*
Plate, lug, 11¼"	*10 – 12*
Saucer	*1 – 2*
Sugar	*8 – 10*
Teapot, 6-cup	*20 – 25*

"THIN SWIRL"

Bowl, salad, 9"	*$15 – $18*
Bowl, soup, 8"	*10 – 12*
Bowl, vegetable, oval, 9"*	*10 – 12*
Butter dish	*20 – 25*
Butter pat	*4 – 6*
Casserole	*20 – 25*
Creamer	*4 – 6*
Cup	*4 – 6*
Dish, 5½"*	*2 – 3*
Gravy	*12 – 15*
Plate, 6¼"*	*1 – 2*
Plate, 8"*	*5 – 6*
Plate, 9"*	*7 – 9*
Plate, square, 9½"	*7 – 9*

Thin Swirl: Gravy (ivory w/green-decorated handle), plate, butter pat (green w/stamped advertising), and teapot.

Platter, 11"* .... $10 – $12
Saucer .... 1 – 2
Sugar .... 8 – 10
Teapot .... 30 – 35

TRIUMPH   (1937)

Designed by Viktor Schreckengost. Triumph, with its horizontal fluting, is an interesting variation on Salem's Victory, with vertical fluting, also designed by Schreckengost.

Bowl, soup, 8¼" .... $10 – $12
Bowl, soup, lug .... 8 – 10
Bowl, utility .... 7 – 10
Bowl, vegetable, oval, 9" .... 10 – 12
Bowl, vegetable, round, 8¾" .... 15 – 18
Butter, open .... 15 – 20
Casserole .... 20 – 25
Coffee pot .... 40 – 45
Cream .... 4 – 6
Cup .... 4 – 6

Cup, AD. . . . . *$10 – $12*
Dish, 5½" . . . . *2 – 3*
Dish, cereal . . . . *3 – 4*
Eggcup . . . . *10 – 12*
Gravy . . . . *12 – 15*
Gravy faststand . . . . *12 – 15*
Plate, 6½" . . . . *1 – 2*
Plate, 7" . . . . *5 – 7*
Plate, 8" . . . . *5 – 7*
Plate, 9" . . . . *7 – 9*
Plate, 10" . . . . *10 – 12*
Plate, 11" . . . . *12 – 15*
Plate, chop, 11" . . . . *12 – 15*
Plate, chop, 13" . . . . *15 – 20*
Platter, 11" . . . . *10 – 12*
Platter, 13" . . . . *12 – 15*
Platter, 15" . . . . *15 – 18*
Platter, lug, 11" . . . . *10 – 12*
Saucer . . . . *1 – 2*
Saucer, AD . . . . *3 – 5*
Shaker . . . . *6 – 8*
Sugar . . . . *8 – 10*
Teapot . . . . *35 – 40*

VICTORY

You will find pieces of Victory, a Salem China shape, with the Limoges mark shown here. The explanation: both companies were owned by the Sebring interests, and when Salem couldn't produce enough Victory to fulfill orders, Limoges took on additional production. They would not or could not put another pottery's mark on their ware, so they adapted Salem's backstamp.

KITCHENWARE

JIFFY WARE   (1938)

The ashtray does extra duty as both lid and undertray for the custard.

Ashtray	*$6 – $8*
Custard	*4 – 6*
Drip jar, side handle	*12 – 15*
Eggcup	*10 – 12*
Jug, refrigerator, small	*15 – 20*
Jug, refrigerator, large	*20 – 25*
Leftover, small	*6 – 10*
Leftover, medium	*10 – 15*
Leftover, large	*15 – 20*
Platter, lug	*12 – 15*
Shaker, range, handled, pair	*15 – 20*

Jiffy Ware: Custard and Red Head Poppy refrigerator jug.

NELSON McCOY POTTERY

Roseville, Ohio

CHAPTER AT A GLANCE

Originally organized as the Nelson McCoy Sanitary & Stoneware Company in 1920. Nelson was the son of J. W. McCoy (see Brush/Brush-McCoy) who helped back his son's enterprise. At first, stoneware kitchen items were produced, but in 1926 industrial artware was introduced.

The name of the company changed to the Nelson McCoy Pottery in 1933, and cookie jar production began around 1940. In 1967, Nelson McCoy, Jr., sold the McCoy Pottery to the Mt. Clemens Pottery (which see).

See Clubs/Newsletters.

DINNERWARE / KITCHENWARE

BROWN DRIP

Baker, oval, 9¼" × 6¼" $15
Baker, oval, 10½" × 7¼" 15
Baker, oval, 12½" × 9½" 25
Baker, oval, 14¼" × 11¼" 35
Bean pot, individual, 12-ounce 5
Bean pot, 1½-quart 20

Bean pot, 3-quart.. *$30*
Bowl, 1-pint... *10*
Bowl, 1-quart... *12*
Bowl, 1¹/₂-quart.. *15*
Bowl, C. O.. *15*
Bowl, soup, coupe... *9*
Bowl, spaghetti, 12¹/₂"... *12*
Bowl, vegetable, divided.. *18*
Bowl, vegetable, round, 28-ounce, 9"................................ *15*
Butter dish, ¹/₄-pound... *15*
Candle holder.. *12*
Canister, coffee... *40*
Canister, flour.. *40*
Canister, sugar.. *40*
Canister, tea.. *40*
Casserole, 2-quart... *15*
Casserole, 3¹/₂-quart.. *18*
Casserole, French, 12-ounce.. *8*
Casserole, French, 14-ounce.. *9*
Casserole, hen on nest, 3-quart.................................... *50*
Cookie jar... *25*
Corn holder.. *20*
Creamer.. *5*
Cruet, oil/vinegar... *20*
Cup, 8-ounce... *5*
Cup, jumbo soup, 18-ounce.. *12*
Cup, Sr. coffee/Jr. soup, 12-ounce................................. *10*
Custard, 6-ounce... *5*
Dish, au gratin, lug, 7-ounce...................................... *8*
Dish, au gratin, lug, 14-ounce..................................... *9*
Dish, soufflé, 9-ounce... *8*
Dish, soufflé, 2-quart... *10*
Dish, soup/cereal, 6³/₄"... *6*
Dish, soup/ice cream, 12-ounce..................................... *6*
Gravy, oval, 21-ounce.. *15*
Jug, 16-ounce.. *12*
Jug, 32-ounce.. *25*
Jug, 80-ounce.. *35*
Margarine container.. *12*
Mug, 8-ounce... *5*
Mug, 12-ounce.. *7*
Mug, footed, 12-ounce.. *8*
Mug, pedestal, 6-ounce... *8*
Mug, pedestal, 8-ounce... *9*
Mug, pedestal, 10-ounce.. *10*
Mug, soup, double handle, 12-ounce................................. *10*
Pie baker, 9".. *18*
Pitcher and bowl set, small.. *25*

Pitcher and bowl set, large *$50*
Plate, 7¼" *7*
Plate, 10" *9*
Plate, sandwich (jumbo cup ring) *9*
Platter, fish shape, 12" *25*
Platter, fish shape, 18" *35*
Platter, oval, 13½" *15*
Saucer *3*
Shaker, regular, each *4*
Shaker, miniature, each *4*
Stein, 16-ounce *10*
Sugar *7*
Teapot, 6-cup, long spout *25*
Teapot, 6-cup, short spout *25*

EL RANCHO

Turn the tureen lid right side up and it doubles as a cracker server (serve-all).

Coffee server . . . . *$140 – $160*
Food warmer, covered (Chuck Wagon shape) . . . . *150 – 200*
Ice tea server (barrel w/spigot) . . . . *175 – 200*
Mug, coffee . . . . *30 – 40*
Soup tureen, 5-quart w/lid . . . . *275 – 350*
    Serve-All lid only *150*

SUBURBIA

Bean Pot . . . . *$20 – $25*
Mug . . . . *6 – 10*
Plate *10*

TEA SETS

A complete set should be worth about $10 more than the prices of the individual pieces combined.

Daisy creamer . . . . *$10 – $12*
Daisy sugar . . . . *10 – 12*
Daisy teapot . . . . *30 – 40*
Ivy creamer . . . . *10 – 12*
Ivy sugar . . . . *10 – 12*
Ivy teapot . . . . *40 – 50*
Pine Cone creamer . . . . *10 – 12*
Pine Cone sugar . . . . *10 – 12*
Pine Cone teapot . . . . *30 – 40*
Two Tone green creamer . . . . *10 – 12*
Two Tone green sugar . . . . *10 – 12*
Two Tone green teapot . . . . *30 – 40*

NOVELTIES

BOOKENDS

Some bookends doubled as planters; these are listed below.

Bird .... *$55 – $65*
Lily.. *40 – 50*
Swallow .... *125 – 150*

Planter Bookends

Bird Dog, pair .... *$125 – $175*
Violin, pair.. *50 – 60*

COOKIE JARS

The **Cabbage** jar is thought of as a drip jar by some collectors, making a range set with the shakers. The **Elephant** came two ways. The earlier had the trunk split between the lid and bottom; the later had the whole trunk on the lid. Except for canisters and cylinders, I have listed under **Jar** those jars that are not figural. The **"Pel-guin"** name indicates that this was called Penguin in catalogs but, erroneously, Pelican by collectors. The **W. C. Fields** jar is a snack jar.

The **Mammy** cookie jar was used as the basis of a new jar with the addition of "Dem Cookies Shor Am Good" in embossed letters. This jar was clearly marked as new but there is a reproduction circulating, with a McCoy mark, that is intended to fool buyers. This is not authentic.

Note that some jars are listed with cold-painted "Cookies" or "Cookie Cabin." It is not known whether all these jars were made with the cold paint and some got washed off or if McCoy made them both with and without the cold paint.

There are a number of ND jars in this listing. Many of them are presumed to be one or two of a kind.

Aladdin's Lamp (see Teapot)
Animal Crackers (round jar, embossed animals), clown head finial
   No dots .... *$50 – $70*
   Raised dots... *50 – 70*
Apollo
   Black... *ND*
   Silver .... *1000 +*
Apple, flat leaves on lid
   Aqua... *45 – 60*
   Maroon... *45 – 60*
Apple, green leaf lid, red/white .... *25 – 35*
Apple, one-leaf finial
   Red w/green leaf .... *50 – 75*
   Red w/gold leaf .... *65 – 95*
   Green w/green leaf .... *30 – 45*
   Yellow w/green leaf...................................... *30 – 45*
Apple, one-leaf finial, serrated edge, yellow .... *ND*

Apple, two-leaf finial, three-dimensional, red .... *$35 – $45*
Asparagus, bunch .... *30 – 40*
Astronauts on space capsule
   Aqua.. *500 +*
   Blue.. *500 +*
Auto, old-fashioned (Touring Car)...................................... *70 – 85*
Bananas, bunch .... *90 – 110*
Bank, building (Cookie Bank)... *115 – 130*
Barn, "Dutch Treat".. *35 – 45*
Barn, red, cow in door .... *300 +*
Barrel, "Nabisco".. *50 – 65*
Barrel, no bands
   Dutch Boy .... *30 – 40*
   Dutch Girl and Boy... *ND*
   Roses, black, stylized.. *ND*
Barrel, two raised bands around top and bottom, w/"Cookie" sign finial ..... *35 – 40*
Barrel, two raised bands around top and bottom, w/"Cookie" sign on side
   Small.. *25 – 35*
   Large .... *30 – 40*
Barrel w/gingerbread boy .... *65 – 75*
Baseball w/boy finial (Baseball Boy) .... *225 – 300*
Basket, bushel, eggs lid .... *45 – 55*
Basket, bushel, potatoes lid .... *45 – 55*
Basket, bushell, strawberries .... *45 – 60*
Basket, bushel, tomatoes lid .... *45 – 60*
Basket, bushel, tall, fruit lid
   Natural colors .... *55 – 65*
   Pastel colors.. *55 – 65*
Basket, square, woodgrain, strawberries
   Dark .... *100 – 125*
   Light.. *90 – 100*
Basket, embossed eagle
   Dark brown .... *35 – 45*
   Light brown... *35 – 40*
Basket, low, w/2 kittens .... *500 +*
Basket, rope weave (Forbidden Fruit)
   Red apple finial .... *60 – 70*
   White apple finial .... *ND*
Basketweave bottom w/Apples lid..................................... *45 – 55*
Basketweave bottom w/Dog lid .... *45 – 55*
Basketweave bottom w/Duck lid .... *45 – 55*
Basketweave bottom w/Kitten lid .... *45 – 55*
Basketweave bottom w/Lamb lid....................................... *45 – 55*
Basketweave bottom w/Pears lid .... *45 – 55*
Basketweave bottom w/Pinecone lid .... *45 – 55*
Bean Pot, 6-pint
   Black w/hand-painted florals... *30 – 40*
   Green w/Garden Lady decal .... *65 – 75*

Orange w/Three Owls decal. . . . . *$65 – $75*
White w/hand-painted florals . . . . *40 – 50*
White w/Spice Delight decal. . . . . *35 – 45*
Bean Pot, 4-quart
    Black w/hand-painted florals. . . . . *30 – 40*
    White w/hand-painted florals . . . . *30 – 40*
    Reissue, black w/hand-painted flowers . . . . *35 – 45*
Bean Pot, red w/brass bail . . . . *30 – 40*
Bear, cookie in vest (also called Teddy Bear)
    Brown w/yellow clothes . . . . *225 – 300*
    Ivory w/cold paint, "Cookies" . . . . *70 – 80*
    Ivory w/cold paint, plain. . . . . *45 – 60*
    Red w/black trim. . . . . *ND*
Bear, Hamm's, w/polka dot tie . . . . *200 – 225*
Bear, Hillbilly   /R . . . . *ND*
Bear, Honey, next to tree trunk
    Rustic . . . . *60 – 75*
    White . . . . *ND*
    Yellow. . . . . *100 – 125*
    Yellow w/brown decoration . . . . *125 – 150*
Bear, Koala. . . . . *85 – 100*
Bear, Panda, holding lollipop (w/swirl). . . . . *225 – 250*
Bear, Panda, upside down . . . . *30 – 40*
    w/red "Avon" heart on foot . . . . *90 – 100*
Bear, Snow, holding flower . . . . *50 – 60*
Bear, Teddy w/bird on head (Teddy and Friend). . . . . *35 – 45*
Bear and barrel . . . . *65 – 75*
Bear and beehive. . . . . *35 – 40*
Bell, Liberty Bell . . . . *40 – 50*
Bell, ring finial, "Cookies" . . . . *30 – 40*
Betsy the Baker, arms folded
    Pillbox hat . . . . *150 – 225*
    Rounded cap . . . . *ND*
    Ruffled chef's hat . . . . *200 – 225*
Bird House (Wren House)
    Brown bird w/green trim . . . . *125 – 175*
    Pink bird w/black trim . . . . *125 – 175*
    "V"-topped lid . . . . *ND*
Bobby the Baker, in chef's hat w/spoon. . . . . *40 – 50*
Box, jewel
    "Cookie Box". . . . . *125 – 145*
    Plain . . . . *ND*
Box, Western w/belt around, rectangular . . . . *125 – 175*
Boy, bust, w/hat (Cookie Boy)
    Aqua. . . . . *125 – 150*
    White . . . . *125 – 150*
    Yellow. . . . . *125 – 150*
Boy, bust, bareheaded, yellow (Bareheaded Cookie Boy) . . . . *ND*
Burlap Bag, small . . . . *30 – 40*

Burlap Bag, large
  Bird finial, red . . . . *$40 – $50*
  Handle finial . . . . *30 – 40*
Cabbage . . . . *125 – 150*
  Shakers, pair . . . . *45 – 55*
Cabin, log cabin
  Black . . . . *ND*
  w/"Cookie Cabin" in cold paint . . . . *ND*
  Brown . . . . *75 – 85*
  w/"Cookie Cabin" in cold paint . . . . *75 – 85*
Caboose, "Cookie Special"
  Red . . . . *ND*
  White . . . . *150 – 175*
  Yellow . . . . *ND*
Canister, big-bottom
  Almond w/caramel cover . . . . *25 – 35*
  Brown drip . . . . *25 – 35*
  Children (Crayola Kids) . . . . *40 – 50*
  Daisy Delight . . . . *35 – 45*
  Greystone . . . . *30 – 40*
  Indian design, orange w/cold paint . . . . *40 – 50*

Big-bottom canister.

  Pink and blue bands . . . . *35 – 45*
  Sahara . . . . *25 – 35*
  Sandstone . . . . *25 – 35*
  Stonecraft . . . . *25 – 35*
  Strawberry Country . . . . *30 – 40*
Canister, Children at Play . . . . *40 – 50*
Canister, low
  Floral decals . . . . *25 – 35*
  Gray and brown . . . . *25 – 35*
  White . . . . *25 – 35*
  Yellow w/"Cookies" in black . . . . *25 – 35*
Canister, straight sides (several styles)
  Flower Burst blue . . . . *35 – 45*
  Flower Burst orange . . . . *35 – 45*
  Fruit Festival . . . . *35 – 45*
  Gingham Patchwork . . . . *35 – 45*
  Madrid (brown and tan bands) . . . . *50 – 75*

Nostalgia, "No matter . . . kitchen best." .... *$45 – $55*
Spice Delight .... *30 – 40*
Violets. .... *35 – 45*
Cat, black w/decorated face (Coalby Cat) .... *300 +*
Chairman of the Board /R .... *500 +*
Chef, head, "Cookies" on hat
  Blue face .... *ND*
  White face .... *80 – 100*
Chest, Pirate
  Black .... *ND*
  Brown (bronze) .... *100 – 135*
  Silver .... *100 – 125*
Chiffonnier, Early American (Chest of Drawers) .... *45 – 55*
Chinese Lantern, "Fortune Cookie"
  Gold trim .... *100 – 125*
  Green trim .... *ND*
  Red trim .... *45 – 55*
Chipmunk .... *95 – 115*
Christmas Tree .... *500 +*
Churn, wooden, old, 3 bands .... *200 – 250*
Churn, wooden, new, 2 bands, "Cookie Churn" .... *25 – 35*
Circus wagon (Barnum's Animals), clown head finial .... *300 +*
Clock w/mouse finial, "Time for Cookies" .... *30 – 40*
Clown, full figure (Little Clown) .... *60 – 80*
Clown in Barrel, "Cookies"
  Blue. .... *90 – 110*
  Green .... *90 – 110*
  Pink .... *100 – 125*
  White .... *100 – 125*
  Yellow. .... *90 – 110*
Clown Bust /R .... *40 – 50*
Clown Head, sad .... *60 – 80*
Coal Scuttle w/kitten finial
  Black bucket w/brown cat .... *175 – 225*
  Yellow bucket w/white cat .... *200 – 250*
Coca-Cola can .... *55 – 65*
Coffee Grinder .... *30 – 40*
Coffee Pot (Chuck Wagon)
  Blue sponge .... *80 – 90*
  Brown and cream .... *55 – 65*
  Ivory w/pink and blue bands .... *55 – 65*
  Spice Delight .... *50 – 60*
Coffee Pot (Cookie Pot)
  Aqua w/fruit decal. .... *ND*
  Aqua w/Pennsylvania Dutch decal .... *35 – 45*
  Tan (cream) and brown. .... *ND*
  White w/flower decal .... *35 – 45*
  White w/Pennsylvania Dutch decal .... *35 – 45*

Cork Lid

  Brown.. $100 – $150

  Ivory and brown .... 150 – 225

Corn, embossed ears

  White .... 60 – 85

  Yellow... 60 – 85

Corn, whole ear

  White w/green leaves .... 125 – 150

  Yellow w/green leaves..................................... 120 – 130

Covered Wagon

  Gold .... ND

  Ivory w/brown... 60 – 75

Cow, reclining, "Cookies and Milk"

  Brown and green... ND

  White w/black spots and colored trim...................... ND

Cylinder #28, plain lid

  Amberware (brown), "Cookies" .... 35 – 40

  Any Time Is Cookie Time .... 60 – 70

  Black, pink flowers....................................... 50 – 60

  Blue flowers decal .... ND

  Brown sponge .... ND

Cylinder #28.

Chef .... 40 – 50

Cobalt blue .... 35 – 40

Cookie Express .... 65 – 75

Fruit.. 30 – 40

Green and yellow bands................................... 100 – 125

"Honest, Mom, I Didn't Snitch . . ." .... 65 – 75

Lost Glaze (purple and gold marbleized)................... 100 – 125

Mustard .... 30 – 40

Mustard w/green drip...................................... 35 – 45

Pink Roses .... 30 – 40

Red Apple .... 30 – 40

Red Poppy .... 30 – 40

Red Roses... 30 – 40

Vegetables .... 30 – 40

Wheat... 40 – 50

Yellow, Red Poppies .... 40 – 50

Cylinder, #28
    Cat lid. . . . . *$200 – $225*
    Lamb lid. . . . . *225 – 250*
    Puppies lid . . . . *175 – 225*
Cylinder, Bamboo . . . . *70 – 80*
Cylinder, basketweave
    Ivory. . . . . *30 – 40*
    Ivory w/brown lid . . . . *30 – 40*
Cylinder, cartoon
    Bugs Bunny . . . . *140 – 170*
    Popeye . . . . *125 – 150*
    Yosemite Sam . . . . *125 – 150*
Cylinder, Christmas scene . . . . *ND*
Cylinder, modern, paneled
    Black. . . . . *30 – 40*
    Brown. . . . . *30 – 40*
    Floral decals . . . . *30 – 40*
    Yellow. . . . . *30 – 40*
Davy Crockett, head   /R . . . . *500 +*
Dog, head (Clyde), white w/red cap . . . . *150 – 175*
Dog, Hound, rump in air, tail finial (Thinking Puppy)
    Solid brown . . . . *20 – 30*
    Tan w/hand-painted face details . . . . *20 – 30*
Dog, right arm over chest (Mac). . . . . *65 – 75*
Dog in Doghouse
    Blue bird finial. . . . . *200 – 225*
    Pink bird finial . . . . *200 – 225*
Dog, puppy, holding "Cookie" sign, unpainted . . . . *65 – 75*
    w/cold-painted sign . . . . *70 – 80*
Doghouse, "Snoopy" . . . . *225 – 250*
Drum . . . . *65 – 75*
Duck, leaf in bill. . . . . *55 – 65*
Elephant, split trunk . . . . *225 – 275*
Elephant, whole trunk . . . . *125 – 150*
Engine
    Black w/gold and red . . . . *100 – 125*
    Gold . . . . *ND*
    Orange . . . . *150 – 175*
    Silver . . . . *200 – 275*
    Yellow w/black and red . . . . *125 – 150*
    Yellow w/black and red, "Jupiter 60". . . . . *125 – 150*
Fireplace (Colonial Fireplace) . . . . *65 – 75*
Flowerpot w/tulip and flowerpot finial
    Red . . . . *200 – 225*
    Yellow. . . . . *200 – 225*
Flowerpot w/plastic flowers . . . . *500 +*
Football w/boy finial (Football Boy). . . . . *200 – 250*

Freddy the Gleep
    Green /R .... *ND*
    Multicolor. .... *ND*
    Yellow /R .... *$500 +*
Frontier Family, embossed Early American scenes
    Knob finial .... *45 – 55*
    Turkey finial, brass bail .... *ND*
Garbage Can .... *35 – 45*
Globe w/silver plane and gold trim .... *200 – 275*
Goose (Goodie Goose), white w/blue/pink/yellow scarf .... *30 – 40*
Grandfather Clock
    Brown. .... *60 – 80*
    Dark green. .... *100 – 125*
    Orange .... *75 – 100*
    Silver .... *100 – 125*
Grandma (Granny)
    Full color .... *75 – 95*
    White w/trim .... *100 – 125*
Grapes
    Bird finial .... *ND*
    Stem finial .... *ND*
Happy Face
    Black. .... *ND*
    White .... *ND*
    White eyes, plain .... *30 – 40*
    Yellow. .... *30 – 40*
    Yellow w/black eyes, "Have a Happy Day" .... *30 – 40*
Hen on basket
    Brown. .... *50 – 60*
    White .... *50 – 60*
Hen on Nest .... *65 – 85*
Horse, Circus
    Black. .... *175 – 225*
    White .... *ND*
Horse, Hobby (Rocking Horse)
    Brown and green. .... *100 – 150*
    White .... *125 – 175*
Hot Air Balloon
    Tan. .... *35 – 45*
    Tan w/red bands .... *35 – 45*
    Yellow. .... *35 – 45*
    Yellow w/red bands. .... *35 – 45*
House (Cookie House) .... *100 – 125*
House, 2-story
    Dark blue roof .... *ND*
    Maroon roof. .... *250 – 350*
Ice cream cone. .... *30 – 40*

Indian Head (Chief Pontiac) /R . . . . *$250 – $325*
  w/"No Cookies" . . . . *ND*
Jack-o'-Lantern
  Orange . . . . *450 – 550*
  Orange w/green lid . . . . *450 – 550*
Jar, ball shape, 2 handles, angled or square finial
  Black . . . . *25 – 35*
  Blue . . . . *25 – 35*
  Green . . . . *25 – 35*
  White w/Dutch girl . . . . *50 – 75*
  Yellow . . . . *25 – 35*
Jar, ball shape, 2 handles, hobnail

Ball-shape jar w/two handles and square finial.

  Blue/Green/Yellow . . . . *$65 – $95*
Jar, ball shape, 2 handles, honeycomb
  Brown/Maroon/Turquoise . . . . *25 – 35*
Jar, concave
  Black, w/hand-painted florals . . . . *35 – 40*
  Blue, w/hand-painted florals . . . . *35 – 40*
  Tan, w/hand-painted florals . . . . *35 – 40*
Jar, 2 handles, embossed "Cookie Jar" . . . . *30 – 40*
Jar, hexagon, "W" finial
  Decorated . . . . *35 – 45*
  Plain . . . . *30 – 40*
Jar, oval, hand-decorated
  White w/red flowers . . . . *45 – 55*
  Yellow w/blue flowers . . . . *45 – 55*
Jar, paneled (2 different lids), fruit decals . . . . *30 – 40*
Jar, round, ivory w/green ivy leaves . . . . *75 – 100*
Jar, round, low, yellow (New Yellow Cookie) . . . . *30 – 40*
Jar, round, plain, white w/gold . . . . *40 – 50*
Jar, round, straight sides, 2 handles, Blue Field stoneware-type decoration . . *40 – 50*
  Canyon . . . . *40 – 50*
Jar, round, white w/gold rooster finial . . . . *ND*
Jar, square, white (Country Kitchen) . . . . *65 – 75*
Jar, square, "V" finial
  Decorated . . . . *35 – 45*
  Plain . . . . *30 – 40*
Jar, straight sides, honeycomb . . . . *65 – 75*

Jar, straight sides, Mediterranean .... $65 – $75

Jar, tan w/brown brush strokes .... 80 – 100

Jar, tilt

   Fruit decal .... 30 – 35

   Strawberry Country decal .... 30 – 35

Jar, upside-down heart, hobnail Aqua/blue/lavender/white/yellow .... 350 – 400

Jug, 1 handle, Coca-Cola decal .... 55 – 65

Jug, small, 1 handle, ivory and brown, "Cookie Jug" .... 25 – 35

Jug, large, 1 handle, ivory and brown, "Cookie Jug" .... 25 – 35

Jug, large, 1 handle, ivory and brown, Eagle decal .... 25 – 35

Jug, engraved "Cookie Jug". .... 20 – 30

Jug, rope bottom, 2 handles, green. .... 30 – 35

Jug, rope bottom, 2 handles, embossed "Cookie Jug"

   Green .... 30 – 35

   Sahara .... 30 – 35

Kangaroo, old, tan and brown (Birchwood) .... 350 – 425

Kangaroo, new, blue .... 275 – 300

Keebler House, tree shape .... 50 – 60

Kettle, brass handle (Gypsy Kettle), "Cookie Kettle"

   Avocado .... 30 – 40

   Bronze .... 30 – 40

   White .... 30 – 40

Kettle, brass handle, "Nibble Kettle"

   Black. .... 50 – 60

   White .... 100 – 125

Kettle, Tea, brass handle

   Black. .... 30 – 40

   White w/rose .... 200 – 225

Kettle, Tea, jumbo, brass handle .... 45 – 50

Kettle, Tea, hammered finish, brass handle (3 different shapes) .... 35 – 45

Kettle, Tea, hammered finish, stationary bail

   Black. .... 25 – 35

   Black w/hand-painted flowers .... 30 – 40

   Bronze .... 30 – 40

   Bronze w/hand-painted flowers .... 30 – 40

Kissing Penguins (Love Birds)

   Black. .... 500 +

   Dark green .... ND

   Rustic (brown and green over ivory) .... ND

   White .... 50 – 60

Kittens (3) on Yarn Ball

   Green/Maroon/Yellow .... 65 – 85

Lantern (Lamp) .... 55 – 65

Lemon .... 45 – 55

Leprechaun

   Green /R .... 1000 +

   Multicolor /R. .... ND

   Red /R .... 1000 +

Lollipops, round w/lollipop finial .... 40 – 50

Lunch Box (Lunch Bucket)
Green lid. . . . . *ND*
Orange lid . . . . *$25 – $35*
White lid. . . . . *ND*
Majorette, sitting on drum . . . . *ND*
Mammy, hands on stomach, "Cookies"
Aqua /R . . . . *500 +*
Ivory /R
w/cold paint face . . . . *150 – 200*
w/checked apron . . . . *200 – 225*
Yellow /R . . . . *500 +*
w/cold-paint face . . . . *500 +*
Mammy, hands on stomach, "Dem Cookies Sho Got Dat Vitamin A" . . . . *ND*
Mammy w/Cauliflowers /R . . . . *1000 +*
Milk Can, w/2 side handles, embossed Liberty Bell and Seal (Bicentennial)
Black. . . . . *35 – 45*
Bronze . . . . *35 – 45*
Brown drip . . . . *35 – 45*
Silver, Early American . . . . *55 – 65*
Milk Can, w/2 shoulder handles
"Ask Grandma" . . . . *45 – 55*
Blue Willow . . . . *40 – 50*
Brown and white . . . . *25 – 35*
Cow. . . . . *40 – 50*
Eagle decal, "The Spirit of '76". . . . . *30 – 40*
Fruit Festival . . . . *30 – 40*
Gingham flowers . . . . *30 – 40*
Happy time decals . . . . *35 – 45*
Rooster decal (Yorkville) . . . . *30 – 40*
Windmill (Antique Dutchland) . . . . *40 – 50*
Milk Can, old
Black, w/hand-painted florals. . . . . *30 – 35*
Blue, w/hand-painted florals. . . . . *30 – 35*
Green, w/hand-painted florals . . . . *30 – 35*
Ivory, w/hand-painted florals . . . . *30 – 35*

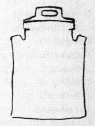

*Old
milk
can*

*Milk can
w/no
handles*

*Milk can
w/side
handles*

*Milk can
w/shoulder
handles*

Yellow, w/hand-painted florals. . . . . *$30 – $35*
Milk Can, no handles, tree decal (Laurel) . . . . *30 – 40*
Milk Can, no handles, pinched neck
    Blue fruit decal . . . . *30 – 40*
    Farm scene decal. . . . . *40 – 50*
    Fruit decals . . . . *30 – 40*
    Seagram's Benchmark . . . . *40 – 50*
Milk Can, old-fashioned (reissue of old milk can)
    Colonial decal . . . . *40 – 50*
    Floral decal . . . . *45 – 55*
Modern, angled lid w/wing finial. . . . . *35 – 45*
Monk, "Thou Shall Not Steal". . . . . *35 – 45*
Mother Goose
    Brown. . . . . *125 – 150*
    White . . . . *100 – 125*
Mouse, head, yellow. . . . . *30 – 40*
Mug w/engraved mugs . . . . *35 – 45*
Nursery Rhyme canisters, brass finial
    Baa Baa Black Sheep . . . . *55 – 65*
    Humpty Dumpty. . . . . *55 – 65*
    Little Bo Peep . . . . *55 – 65*
    Little Boy Blue. . . . . *55 – 65*
    Little Miss Muffet . . . . *55 – 65*
    Mary, Mary, Quite Contrary. . . . . *55 – 65*
Oaken Bucket
    Gray. . . . . *25 – 35*
    Green . . . . *25 – 35*
    Silver . . . . *50 – 60*
    Tan. . . . . *20 – 25*
Orange . . . . *40 – 50*
Owl, head . . . . *35 – 45*
Owl, Robin Hood costume, "Woodsy Owl"
    Green . . . . *ND*
    Green w/decoration. . . . . *125 – 150*
Owl, wing over chest
    Brown. . . . . *25 – 35*
    Yellow (Rattan). . . . . *25 – 35*
Owls, Mr. and Mrs.. . . . . *80 – 100*
    w/pinecone lid . . . . *ND*
Pagoda, hexagonal, brown/yellow lid
    Daisy decoration . . . . *35 – 45*
    Plain . . . . *30 – 40*
Peanut
    Brown. . . . . *30 – 40*
    Yellow. . . . . *30 – 40*
Peanut Bird, yellow. . . . . *100 – 150*
Pear, lightly embossed flat leaf on lid
    Aqua. . . . . *95 – 115*
    Yellow. . . . . *95 – 115*

Pear, leaf and stem finial
    Aqua w/pink blush . . . . *$65 – $75*
    Yellow w/pink blush . . . . *55 – 65*
Pel-guin
    Aqua . . . . *200 – 250*
    White w/decoration . . . . *75 – 125*
    Yellow . . . . *200 – 250*
Penguin w/hat and scarf (Chilly Willy)
    Blue scarf . . . . *35 – 45*
    Red scarf . . . . *35 – 45*
    Yellow scarf . . . . *35 – 45*
Pepper
    Brown . . . . *ND*
    Green, regular . . . . *30 – 40*
    Green, larger . . . . *30 – 40*
    Red . . . . *ND*
    Yellow . . . . *30 – 40*
Picnic Basket . . . . *55 – 65*
Pig, Harley-Davidson decal (Harley Hog) . . . . *350 +*
Pig, sitting up, pink (Bank) . . . . *90 – 100*
Pig, reclining, tail finial, white . . . . *35 – 45*
Pig, winking, dressed . . . . *275 – 300*
Pineapple
    Gold tint . . . . *125 – 175*
    Natural . . . . *70 – 90*
Pineapple, modern
    Green and brown . . . . *70 – 80*
    Yellow and brown . . . . *70 – 80*
Pitcher, fancy handle
    Blue Willow . . . . *30 – 40*
    Floral decal . . . . *30 – 40*
    Fruit Festival . . . . *30 – 40*
    Rooster and flowers decal (Yorkville) . . . . *30 – 40*
    Spice Delight . . . . *30 – 40*
Pitcher, plain, Gaytime, aqua w/white lid, Pennsylvania Dutch design
    Kneeling people . . . . *40 – 50*
    Standing people . . . . *45 – 55*
Pitcher, tilt
    Black, w/hand-painted florals . . . . *35 – 45*
    Blue, w/hand-painted florals . . . . *35 – 45*
    Green, w/hand-painted florals . . . . *35 – 45*
    Yellow, w/hand-painted florals . . . . *35 – 45*
Quaker Oats . . . . *450 +*
Rabbit, Hocus, ears standing up
    Blue w/decoration . . . . *35 – 45*
    Brown . . . . *45 – 50*
    Gray . . . . *35 – 45*
    White w/decoration . . . . *35 – 45*
Raggedy Ann (Rag Doll) . . . . *85 – 95*

Rocking Chair w/Dalmatians   /R . . . . *$350+*
Rooster
   White w/gray (Gray Rooster) . . . . *75 – 85*
   Yellow w/brown (Yellow Rooster) . . . . *70 – 80*
Rooster, White w/red comb . . . . *55 – 75*
Sack (Cookie Sack), white w/gold . . . . *55 – 65*
Safe (Cookie Safe), money bag finial . . . . *40 – 50*
Santa, head (bank) . . . . *175 – 225*
School Bus, old, kids in window . . . . *ND*
School Bus, new, "Bus" . . . . *45 – 55*
Soccer Ball w/whistle finial
   Black and white w/red whistle . . . . *500+*
   Black and white w/silver whistle . . . . *500+*
   Yellow . . . . *ND*
Spaceship (Friendship 7) . . . . *125 – 175*
Squirrel . . . . *500+*
Stagecoach
   Brown . . . . *800+*
   White   /R . . . . *900+*
Stove, old-fashioned (Cookstove)
   Black . . . . *25 – 35*
   White . . . . *25 – 35*
Stove, pot-bellied
   Black . . . . *25 – 35*
   White . . . . *25 – 35*
Strawberry, old, maroon . . . . *55 – 65*
   w/white drip . . . . *55 – 65*
Strawberry, new
   Red . . . . *30 – 40*
   White . . . . *30 – 40*
Stump, frog finial . . . . *60 – 80*
Stump, monkey finial . . . . *40 – 50*
Stump, mushroom finial . . . . *40 – 50*
Stump, rabbit (also called mouse) finial . . . . *40 – 50*
Stump, squirrel finial (Cookie Log) . . . . *35 – 45*
Teapot
   Green . . . . *50 – 60*
   Metallic black . . . . *50 – 60*
   White . . . . *50 – 60*
Teapot, Aladdin style . . . . *35 – 45*
Tepee
   Slant cover . . . . *225 – 275*
   Straight cover   /R . . . . *200 – 250*
Tomato . . . . *45 – 55*
Tony Veller . . . . *ND*
Top hat, Uncle Sam . . . . *500+*
Traffic Light . . . . *35 – 45*
Tugboat, old, "Cookie Tug" . . . . *ND*

Tugboat, new, w/anchor and life preserver, "USS Cookie" . . . . *$30 – $40*
Tureen . . . . *45 – 55*
Turkey, short, multicolor . . . . *150 – 200*
Turkey, tall
   Brown and green . . . . *250 – 300*
   White, decorated . . . . *300 – 375*
Turtle w/butterfly finial (Timmy Tortoise) . . . . *30 – 40*
Vase, black w/floral lid. . . . . *ND*
W. C. Fields. . . . . *125 – 175*
Wedding Jar w/gold trim . . . . *75 – 100*
Wine Press. . . . . *ND*
Wishing Well, "Wish I Had A Cookie"
   Brown and green . . . . *35 – 45*
   Pink . . . . *ND*

Designer Accents

Apple . . . . *$25 – $35*
Bear w/chocolate chip cookie . . . . *35 – 45*
Cat . . . . *40 – 50*
Cat, stuffed, (Kid's Stuff)
   Lime green. . . . . *ND*
   Peach . . . . *35 – 45*
   Pink . . . . *35 – 45*
Cow, Down on the Farm . . . . *55 – 65*
Cylinder
   "Cookies," blue/brown . . . . *30 – 35*
   "Cookies," black/blue/red grid . . . . *30 – 35*
   "Grandma's Cookie Jar"
      Blue . . . . *30 – 35*
      Brown . . . . *30 – 35*
   Simple Pleasures. . . . . *30 – 35*
   Wild Ducks . . . . *30 – 35*
Dog, sitting, stuffed
   Blue . . . . *35 – 45*
   Spotted. . . . . *ND*
   Tan. . . . . *35 – 45*
Duck. . . . . *30 – 40*
Goose w/scarf . . . . *30 – 35*
Panda. . . . . *45 – 60*
Penguin . . . . *45 – 60*
Pig . . . . *45 – 60*
Pillsbury Doughboy . . . . *30 – 40*
Rabbit . . . . *45 – 60*
Rooster, painted. . . . . *50 – 60*
Rooster, white . . . . *35 – 45*
Tilt Strawberry. . . . . *25 – 35*
Turkey . . . . *ND*

CARVED

Cat	$30 – $40
Dancing Bears, blue/chocolate	30 – 40
Duck Family, beige/blue	30 – 40
Farm House	30 – 40
Wild Flower, beige/blue	30 – 40

FIGURES

Made in the following colors unless otherwise indicated in the list below: aqua, brown, white, and yellow.

Bird of Paradise, white w/red topknot	$25 – $35
Calf	15 – 20
Cat, tall neck, black	30 – 40
Lion, sitting	30 – 40
Lion, stalking, brown/chartreuse/maroon	30 – 40
Panther, small, black	35 – 50
Panther, large, black	75 – 100
Rooster	18 – 22

Stretch

You will find solid colors of green (aqua), powder blue, white, yellow, and, occasionally, pink.

Dachshund	$100 – $125
Dog w/stubby tail	125 – 200
Goat	40 – 50
Horse	50 – 60
Lion	100 – 150
Ram	50 – 60

Stretch Animals: Dog w/stubby tail and lion.

FLOWERPOTS

These have attached saucers. You will find them in shades of aqua, green, dark green, pink, plum, rust, white, and yellow.

PRICING   Other shapes will be found; use the prices below.

Basketweave

Small	$8 – $10
Medium	12 – 15

Flowerpots: L to R. Top: *Beaded, Stonewall, and Flower Patch.* Bottom:
Greek Key, Basketweave, and Diamond Quilt.

Large	*$15 – $20*
Beaded	
Small	*8 – 10*
Medium	*12 – 15*
Large	*15 – 20*
Diamond Quilt	
Small	*8 – 10*
Medium	*12 – 15*
Large	*15 – 20*
Flower Patch	
Small	*8 – 10*
Medium	*12 – 15*
Large	*15 – 20*
Greek Key	
Small	*8 – 10*
Medium	*12 – 15*
Large	*15 – 20*
Stonewall	
Small	*6 – 8*
Medium	*8 – 10*
Large	*10 – 12*

JARDINIERES

See also Butterfly.
    PRICING   These prices are for medium-size jardinieres.

Acorns	*$35 – $45*
Basketweave and Berries	*40 – 60*

Flying Birds .... *$45 – $60*
Holly .... *35 – 45*
Lotus .... *30 – 40*

MINIATURES

Made in solid colors of (in descending order of frequency found) aqua, white, blue, yellow, and pink; some pieces were made in gold and in lavender.

NOTE There are other miniatures that are rare; the ones priced below you have some chance of finding.

Animals

Fish .... *$20 – $25*
Pouter pigeon .... *20 – 25*
Swan .... *20 – 25*

Other

Mini-Cornucopia .... *$20 – $25*
Mini-Pitcher .... *15 – 20*
Mini-Vase .... *15 – 20*

MISCELLANY

Banded bowl (pink w/blue bands), several sizes .... *$15 – $50*
Basket, Basketweave... *30 – 40*
Basket, Oak Leaf and Acorn .... *30 – 40*
Basket, Pine Cone .... *25 – 30*
Bird Bath.. *20 – 25*
Decanter, Pierce Arrow...................................... *65 – 80*
Decanter Set, Apollo Mission
   Astronaut .... *75 – 90*
   LEM... *ND*
   Missile .... *30 – 40*
Decanter Set, Train
   Caboose... *45 – 60*
   Coal Car .... *40 – 50*
   Engine .... *35 – 45*
   Passenger Car....................................... *50 – 60*
Drip Jar, Cabbage... *75 – 100*
Mug, Robin Hood .... *ND*
Mug, "Your Father's Mustache" .... *15 – 20*
Pencil Holder, Boot .... *20 – 25*
Pitcher, Parrot .... *125 – 150*
Reamer .... *40 – 60*
Shaker, Cabbage, each .... *25 – 30*
Shaker, Cucumber (salt)..................................... *25 – 30*
Shaker, Mango (pepper) .... *25 – 30*
Spoon Rest, Penguin.. *80 – 100*
Spoon Rest, Butterfly .... *80 – 100*

Stein, Boot . . . . *$25 – $30*
Stein w/hunt scene, metal lid . . . . *20 – 30*
Strawberry jar w/Birds . . . . *25 – 35*
TV Lamp, Panther . . . . *40 – 50*
Watering Can (Sprinkler, Turtle shape) . . . . *30 – 40*

PLANTERS

See also Bookends.

Figural

The Banana Boat and Barrel planters are considered the Calypso line.

Alligator . . . . *$25 – $35*
Anvil w/applied chain and hammer, 9"   /627 . . . . *18 – 22*
Automobile . . . . *15 – 20*
Baby Carriage and Dog, "What About Me?" . . . . *35 – 50*
Ball, 4¹/₂" . . . . *12 – 15*
Banana Boat planter . . . . *75 – 90*
Barrel planter . . . . *85 – 95*
Bathtub . . . . *12 – 15*
Bird . . . . *12 – 18*
Bird Dog and Fence . . . . *100 – 150*
Bird on Nest . . . . *15 – 20*
Canisters, 1 piece, "Coffee/Tea/Sugar/Salt" . . . . *ND*
Carriage w/umbrella . . . . *125 – 150*
Cat and Basket . . . . *20 – 25*
Cat and Well . . . . *60 – 70*
Cat w/basket on stool, 7" × 4¹/₂"   /743 . . . . *20 – 25*
Cat w/large bow . . . . *18 – 22*
Cobbler's Bench . . . . *18 – 20*
Conch Shell . . . . *35 – 45*
Convertible . . . . *15 – 20*
Convertible w/wire windshield . . . . *15 – 20*
Cowboy Boots, 7" × 6"   /780 . . . . *25 – 30*
Cradle . . . . *15 – 20*
Cradle w/embossed flowers . . . . *25 – 30*
Doe and Fawn . . . . *20 – 25*
Dog, Pointer . . . . *30 – 40*
Dog, Poodle w/bow, solid base . . . . *25 – 30*
Dog, Poodle w/leash, pierced base . . . . *45 – 50*
Dog and Cart . . . . *18 – 22*
Dog and Shirt . . . . *25 – 30*
Dog and Turtle . . . . *25 – 30*
Driftwood, 8¹/₂" × 3¹/₂"   /787 . . . . *12 – 15*
Duck, small . . . . *10 – 12*
Duck (2) and Eggs . . . . *15 – 20*
Duck w/leaves . . . . *15 – 18*
Duck w/umbrella and leaves . . . . *75 – 125*

Dutch Shoe .... *$12 – $15*
Dutch Shoe w/Flower, 7¹/₂"   /23 .... *15 – 20*
Fawn (2) .... *15 – 20*
Fawn (3) w/trees .... *125 – 175*
Fish, multicolor .... *250 – 300*
Flying Duck... *60 – 75*
Frog .... *18 – 22*
Frog, small.. *8 – 10*
Frog, large .... *15 – 18*
Frog and Leaf .... *10 – 12*
Frog and Lotus, 5" × 4"   /21....................................... *10 – 12*
Frog and Umbrella... *75 – 125*
Gondola, 11¹/₂" × 3¹/₂" .... *25 – 30*
Goose and Cart... *18 – 20*
Hand w/Harlequin cuff .... *25 – 35*
Hat, cowboy... *25 – 35*
Hat w/embossed stars (small Uncle Sam's hat)...................... *20 – 25*
Hillbilly .... *20 – 25*
Hobby Horse.. *35 – 45*
Humpty Dumpty .... *20 – 24*
Iron .... *15 – 20*
Lamb, curly w/large bow .... *25 – 35*
Lamb and Baby, "Baa Baa Black Sheep" .... *15 – 20*
Lamb and Flower... *15 – 18*
Lamb w/small bow .... *12 – 15*
Liberty Bell, 4th of July .... *200 – 350*
Liberty Bell, 8th of July .... *100 – 125*
Lion .... *35 – 45*
Log.. *12 – 15*
Log and Wheel .... *25 – 35*
Old Mill, "Down by the Old Mill Stream," 7¹/₂" × 6¹/₂"   /744.............. *20 – 25*
Orange.. *25 – 30*
Oriental Man w/basket .... *25 – 30*
Oriental Man and Wheelbarrow .... *25 – 30*
Parrot and Bowl.. *30 – 40*
Pelican.. *15 – 20*
Pheasant .... *35 – 45*
Piano .... *40 – 50*
Pig .... *12 – 15*
Plow Boy (cowboy on horse at trough)................................ *55 – 75*
Puppy... *20 – 30*
Quail, two, 9" × 7"   /765 .... *40 – 50*
Rabbit and Stump .... *30 – 40*
Rhinoceros.. *ND*
Robin Hood .... *ND*
Rocking Chair .... *25 – 30*
Rodeo Cowboy .... *75 – 100*
Rolling Pin w/Little Boy Blue, 7¹/₂"   /621........................... *60 – 75*

Rooster .... $20 – $25
Scoop and Mammy, 7½" /620 .... 125 – 150
Scotties (4).. 30 – 35
Shell.. 12 – 15
Shell (2), 8½" /617... 12 – 15
Shoe, bronze.. ND
Shoe, single .... 15 – 20
Shoes, two, w/bows, 4½" × 5½" /64................................. 12 – 15
Snow Man .... 20 – 25
Spinning Wheel w/dog and cat, 7¼" × 7¼" /737...................... 20 – 25
Squirrel, 5" × 4½" /34.. 15 – 20
Stork w/baby and basket.. 25 – 35
Stump .... 10 – 12
Swan .... 20 – 25
Swan, neck separate... 20 – 25
Swan, neck attached .... 20 – 25
Swans, 2, 8½" /618 .... 25 – 30
Turtle.. 35 – 40
Turtle w/embossed leaves .... 20 – 25
Uncle Sam (head and hat) .... 45 – 60
Uncle Sam and Eagle .... ND
Village Smithy, 7½" × 6½" /746..................................... 25 – 35
Wishing Well, 6¾" × 6" /725.. 18 – 22
Zebra w/baby .... 175 – 225

Regular

Cross w/leaves and pods .... $30 – $40
Dish w/Swan .... ND
Dish w/applied bud... 35 – 40
Oval w/leaves .... 15 – 20
Planter w/birds (4) .... ND
Planter w/birds (2) .... 20 – 25

SHORT LINES

Blossomtime

Urn... $20 – $25
Vase, square.. 20 – 25
Vase, 2 handles .... 20 – 25

Butterfly

Made in six colors, listed in descending order of availability: green, blue, white, yellow, lavender, and coral.

Bowl, irregular edge, small .... $10 – $15
Bowl, irregular edge, large... 15 – 25
Bowl, oval, large, w/handles .... 35 – 45
Cup .... 10 – 12

Fernery planter, small .... *$10 – $15*
Fernery planter, large .... *15 – 20*
Hanging pot .... *35 – 45*
Jardiniere, small .... *10 – 15*
Jardiniere, medium.. *20 – 25*
Jardiniere, large .... *35 – 40*
Jardiniere w/drainage plate, small .... *10 – 12*
Jardiniere w/drainage plate, medium .... *25 – 30*
Jardiniere w/drainage plate, large .... *35 – 45*
Jug .... *45 – 50*
Planting dish.. *25 – 35*
Plate, large... *75 – 100*
Vase, Butterfly shape... *25 – 35*
Vase, bulb shape .... *20 – 25*
Vase, double cylinder (binocular) .... *30 – 35*
Vase, large w/large handles....................................... *35 – 40*
Vase, "V" shape.. *20 – 30*
Vase, water glass, small.. *10 – 20*
Vase, water glass, large .... *20 – 30*
Wall pocket.. *100 – 150*
Window box .... *35 – 40*

VASES

Figural

Cat .... *$35 – $45*
Chrysanthemum... *85 – 100*
Cowboy Boots.. *25 – 30*
Fawn .... *30 – 40*
Feather .... *35 – 45*
Grape.. *30 – 40*
Hand and Cornucopia .... *25 – 30*
Hyacinth .... *85 – 100*
Lily.. *30 – 35*
Lily, triple .... *45 – 55*
Magnolia .... *85 – 100*
Poppy... *95 – 125*
Ram's Head .... *85 – 110*
Sunflower .... *45 – 50*
Tulip, double .... *30 – 40*
Wagon Wheel .... *25 – 30*

Regular

Early American .... *$20 – $25*
English Ivy .... *40 – 50*
Wheat .... *25 – 30*

WALL POCKETS

Basketweave	*$40 – $50*
Bellows	*45 – 50*
Birdbath	*50 – 60*
Blossomtime	*40 – 50*
Clock	*60 – 70*
Early American	*ND*
Fan	*50 – 60*
Iron and Trivet	*45 – 55*
Leaf	*35 – 40*
Leaves and Berries	*ND*
Lily, figural	*45 – 50*
Love Bird	*55 – 70*
Mailbox, "Letters"	*55 – 65*
Mexican	*30 – 40*
Owl and Trivet	*50 – 60*
Umbrella	*50 – 60*
Violin	*55 – 65*

FRUIT

Apple	*$40 – $50*
Banana	*55 – 65*
Grapes	
Purple	*55 – 75*
Purple-black	*ND*
Red	*50 – 60*
White (pale green)	*55 – 75*
Orange	*45 – 50*
Pear	*55 – 60*

WALL BRACKETS

Bird	*$150 – $250*

WALL POCKET / VASE

Flower (5 petal)	*$25 – $30*
Flower and Bird	*40 – 45*

STONEWARE

Bean Pot, Bean Pods	*$25 – $35*
Jug, Angel Fish	*30 – 35*
Jug, Barrel	*35 – 50*
Jug, Buccaneer	*40 – 60*
Jug, Grapes	*35 – 45*
Jug, Water Lily, fish handle, small	*35 – 50*

Jug, Water Lily, fish handle, large. . . . . *$55 – $60*
Mug, Barrel . . . . *15 – 18*
Mug, Buccaneer. . . . . *15 – 18*
Mug, Grapes . . . . *12 – 15*
Salt Box, horizontal ribs . . . . *50 – 75*

METLOX POTTERIES

Manhattan Beach, California

CHAPTER AT A GLANCE

Metlox (a contraction of metallic oxide) was established in 1927 by T. C. Prouty and his son Willis for the manufacture of ceramic outdoor signs. Business suffered during the Depression, and when T.C. died in 1931, his son reorganized the company for the manufacture of dinnerware.

The first colored set, California Pottery, came out in 1931. The Poppytrail name, after the state flower, was introduced in mid 1934 on a new set that included kitchenware. Other dinnerware lines of the 1930s included Mission Bell, a pastel line made for Sears; Pintoria (squared corners); and Yorkshire. It was in the 1930s that Carl Romanelli was hired. He designed the miniature animals and the Modern Masterpieces lines.

Production was limited during World War II; Metlox, like many other potteries, was manufacturing for the military. In 1946, Willis sold Metlox to Evan K. Shaw, whose American Pottery had burned. Shaw introduced the decorated lines beginning with California Ivy and brought out other lines throughout the 1950s (including the striking designs of Frank Irwin, such as California Contempora, Free Form, and Mobile) and the sculpted shapes by Bob Allen and Mel Shaw in the 1960s. In 1958, Metlox purchased the trade name and certain molds from Vernon Kilns and established its Vernonware division, which produced the Vernon patterns and new ones of its own.

Metlox's popular and extensive cookie jar line was produced from 1959 until the pottery closed in 1989.

See Chipman, see Fogleman, and see Roerig in Bibliography, and see Gibbs in Bibliography/Coming Attractions.

MARKS California Pottery is an early 1930s mark. Metlox used a variety of backstamps with the Poppytrail name.

DINNERWARE / SOLID-COLOR

PINTORIA (1936)

An unusual shape, the flatware is rectangular or square in outline with a round well. This was intended as a luncheon service.

Bright gloss colors: Canary Yellow, Delphinium Blue, Old Rose, Poppy Orange, Rust, Turquoise Blue, and White.

Bowl, Fruit /421 . . . . *$30 – 35*
Bowl, serving /415 . . . . *80 – 85*
Creamer /419 . . . . *70 – 75*
Cup /400 . . . . *40 – 45*
Plate, B & B /403 . . . . *22 – 25*
Plate, luncheon /405 . . . . *40 – 45*
Plate, serving /429 . . . . *70 – 75*
Saucer /402 . . . . *18 – 20*
Sugar /418 . . . . *70 – 75*

Pintoria

PLAIN

The **cookie jar** is the lidded Tom 'n' Jerry bowl without the lettering. The four **Range shakers** are Salt, Pepper, Flour, and Sugar.

Bowl, batter, handled /78	*$35 – $40*
Bowl, pudding, deep /225	*22 – 25*
Bowl, salad /232	*35 – 40*
Bowl, salad, individual /222	*15 – 18*
Bowl, soup, individual, 2 handle w/lid /209	*40 – 45*
Bowl, soup, rim /207	*25 – 28*
Bowl, soup/cereal, lug /212	*12 – 15*
Bowl, Tom 'n' Jerry w/lid	*90 – 100*
Bowl, vegetable, oval /214	*28 – 30*
Bowl, vegetable, oval /214¹/₂	*30 – 32*
Bowl, vegetable, round /215	*28 – 30*
Butter, ¹/₄ pound /213	*50 – 60*
Carafe, ball shape, wood handle /238	*30 – 35*
Carafe, ribbed /238-A	*35 – 40*
Celery /223C	*20 – 25*
Coaster /265	*10 – 12*
Coffee pot, footed /253	*50 – 55*
Coffee pot, swirl top, pedestal bottom	*60 – 65*
Cookie jar	*115 – 125*
Creamer /219	*18 – 20*
Creamer, AD /219¹/₂	*15 – 18*
Cup, AD /201-D	*22 – 28*
Cup, coffee /201	*15 – 18*
Cup, jumbo /200J	*22 – 25*
Cup, tea /200	*10 – 12*
Cup, Tom 'n' Jerry	*15 – 18*
Custard /224	*18 – 20*
Dish, fruit /221	*10 – 12*
Gravy /223	*22 – 25*
Grease jar /244	*40 – 45*
Jam jar w/lid /220	*45 – 50*
Jug, ball, ice lip	*60 – 65*
Jug, batter, w/lid /901C	*45 – 50*
Jug, footed, spout on top w/lid /245	*45 – 55*
Jug, horizontal ribs, ice lip /257	*60 – 65*
Jug, serving, small /251	*18 – 20*
Jug, serving, medium /250	*20 – 25*
Jug, serving, large /249	*25 – 30*
Jug, serving, x-large /248	*30 – 35*
Jug, syrup w/lid /902C	*30 – 35*
Jug, water, ice lip /237L	*45 – 50*
Mug /236M	*15 – 18*
w/attached handle	*20 – 25*
Mustard /224M	*45 – 50*

Plate, chop, 12"   /229½ .... $20 – $25
Plate, chop, 14"   /230 .... 25 – 30
Plate, chop, 17"   /231 .... 35 – 40
Plate, coupe, b & b   /228 .... 10 – 12
Plate, coupe, salad   /228 ½ .... 12 – 15
Plate, coupe, dinner   /229 .... 15 – 18
Plate, rim, b & b   /203 .... 8 – 10
Plate, rim, salad   /204 .... 10 – 12
Plate, rim, luncheon   /205 .... 12 – 15
Plate, rim, dinner   /206 .... 15 – 18
Plate, grill   /227 .... 20 – 22
Platter, oval, 11½"   /216 .... 25 – 30
Platter, oval, 13¾"   /217 .... 30 – 35
Relish, scalloped, small, one handle   /226 .... 25 – 30
Relish, scalloped, large, two handle   /226A .... 30 – 35
Saucer, AD   /202-D .... 6 – 8
Saucer, jumbo   /202J .... 6 – 8
Saucer, tea/coffee   /202 .... 3 – 4
Shaker, footed, each   /234 .... 10 – 12
Shaker, handled, each   /234A .... 10 – 12
Shaker, horizontal ribs, each   /234S .... 12 – 15
Shaker, range (four), each   /240 – 243 .... 25 – 35
Sherbet   /211 .... 20 – 22
Sugar   /218 .... 22 – 25
Sugar, AD, open   /218½ .... 15 – 20
Teapot, 2-cup   /11 .... 50 – 55
Teapot, 6-cup   /10 .... 40 – 45
Tea tile/hot plate   /266 .... 20 – 25
Tumbler   /235T .... 12 – 15
   w/attached handle .... 15 – 20

YORKSHIRE   (ca. 1936)

This is a swirl shape similar to Gladding-McBean's Coronado. Shaker sets are
either two smalls or two talls.

Decorated in solid colors. Bright gloss: Canary Yellow, Delphinium Blue,
Old Rose, Poppy Orange, Rust, and Turquoise Blue. Pastel satin glazes: Opal-
ine Green, Peach, Pastel Yellow, Petal Pink, Powder Blue, Satin Ivory, and
Satin Turquoise.

Ashtray   /551 .... $18 – $20
Bowl, console   /532 .... 40 – 45
Bowl, salad   /533 .... 45 – 50
Bowl, soup/cereal, lug   /512 .... 12 – 15
Bowl, vegetable, round, 8"*   /515 .... 28 – 30
Butter, ¼-pound   /513 .... 50 – 60
Candle holder   /581 .... 20 – 25
Carafe, wooden handle   /538 .... 35 – 40

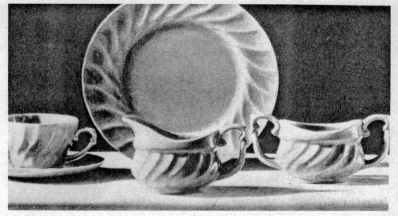

Yorkshire

Celery /524	....	*$20 – $25*
Coffee pot, small /539	....	*40 – 45*
Coffee pot, large /540	....	*50 – 55*
Creamer /519	....	*18 – 20*
Cup, AD /500D	....	*22 – 28*
Cup, tea /500	....	*10 – 12*
Cup, cream soup /509	....	*40 – 45*
Dish, fruit, 5¼"* /521	....	*10 – 12*
Eggcup, double, footed /520	....	*25 – 30*
Gravy /522	....	*20 – 25*
Gravy faststand /523	....	*30 – 35*
Jug, large /537	....	*40 – 45*
Plate, b & b /503	....	*8 – 10*
Plate, salad /504	....	*10 – 12*
Plate, luncheon /505	....	*12 – 15*
Plate, dinner /506	....	*15 – 18*
Plate, chop /530	....	*30 – 35*
Platter, oval, 11" /516	....	*25 – 30*
Platter, oval, 13¾" /517	....	*30 – 35*
Relish, 3-part, handled /527	....	*35 – 40*
Relish, 5-part, handled /526	....	*50 – 55*
Saucer /502	....	*3 – 4*
Saucer, AD /500D	....	*6 – 8*
Saucer, cream soup /510	....	*10 – 12*
Shaker, tall, handled, each /580	....	*15 – 18*
Shaker, small, handled, each /534	....	*10 – 12*
Sherbet, footed /511	....	*20 – 22*
Sugar, open /518	....	*20 – 22*
Teapot, small /569	....	*65 – 70*

Teapot, large   /570 .... $50 – $55
Tumbler, small   /535 .... 15 – 18
   w/attached handle .... 20 – 25
Tumbler, large   /536 .... 20 – 25

DINNERWARE / DECORATED

AZTEC / CONTEMPORA / FREE FORM / MOBILE

This is one of the most distinctive shapes in U.S. dinnerware. The lid on the **beverage server** is the juice cup. The **divided vegetable** has equal sections; the **twin vegetable** has one section larger than the other. The flatware and some bowls in Free Form and Mobile are different in shape than Aztec and Contempora.

California Contempora ("pink, black, and gray with black and white two tone hollowware in tune with the new trend toward textured finishes, with satin-flecked glaze"), California Free Form ("cocoa, chartreuse, and sharp yellow against a background of palest gray, 'textured' with tiny dots of color"), and California Mobile ("purple, yellow, turquoise, and pink on a pale gray flecked background") are the same pattern but with different colors.

PRICING   Creamers are easy to find; sugars with perfect lids are hard to find. Subtract 10% from values below for Aztec.

Ashtray, small   /87 .... $45
Ashtray, large   /89.. 55
Beverage server   /80... 225 – 250
Bowl, fruit   /21... 15 – 18
Bowl, salad   /10... 300 +
Bowl, soup   /07 .... 22 – 25
Bowl, soup/chowder, lug   /12 .... 30 – 35
Bowl, vegetable   /15 .... 50 – 55
Bowl, vegetable, divided   /29 .... 90 – 95
Bowl, vegetable, w/handle   /66 200
Bowl, vegetable, covered, w/handle   /26........................... 300 +
Bowl, vegetable, twin   /65 200
Butter, ¼-pound   /13... 95 – 100
Celery   /39... 50 – 55
Cigarette box   /69... 125
Coaster   /20.. 28 – 30
Coffee pot   /40... 225 – 250
Creamer   /19.. 25
Cup   /00.. 18
Mug, cocoa... 35 – 40
Flowerpot, 3"   /97.. 55 – 60
Flowerpot, 4"   /98.. 65 – 70
Flowerpot, 6"   /99.. 75 – 80
Gravy   /23.. 40 – 45
Jam & Jelly   /28.. 55 – 60
Pitcher, milk   /43.. 180 – 200

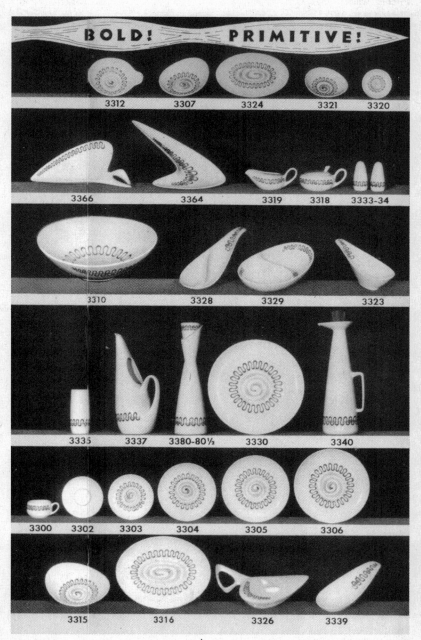

BOLD! PRIMITIVE!

3312 3307 3324 3321 3320

3366 3364 3319 3318 3333-34

3310 3328 3329 3323

3335 3337 3380-80½ 3330 3340

3300 3302 3303 3304 3305 3306

3315 3316 3326 3339

Aztec

Pitcher, water   /37 . . . . *$210 – $230*
Plate, b & b   /03 . . . . *11 – 12*
Plate, salad   /04 . . . . *15 – 18*
Plate, luncheon   /05 . . . . *32 – 35*
Plate, 10"   /06 . . . . *20 – 25*
Plate, chop   /30 . . . . *80 – 85*
Platter, 9"   /24 . . . . *45 – 50*
Platter, 11"   /16 . . . . *45 – 50*
Platter, 13"   /17 . . . . *55 – 60*
Relish, jawbone (boomerang)   /64 . . . . *115 – 125*
Saucer   /02 . . . . *5*
Shaker, each   /33   /34 . . . . *20 – 25*
Sugar   /18 . . . . *50 +*
Tumbler, juice cup   /80½ . . . . *40 – 45*
Tumbler, 6¼"   /35 . . . . *45 – 50*

CALIFORNIA IVY

Hollowware pieces have twig handles.

Bowl, salad bowl, 11¼" . . . . *$50 – $55*
Bowl, soup, lug, 6¾" . . . . *18 – 20*
Bowl, soup, individual, stick handle, 5" *17*
Bowl, vegetable, round, 9" *45*
Bowl, vegetable, round, 2-part, lug, 11" *45*
Butter, ¼-pound *55*
Coaster, 3¾" *10*
Coffee pot, tall, 7-cup *75*
Creamer . . . . *18 – 20*
Cup *13*
Dish, 5¼" *12*
Dish, 6¾" *14*
Gravy *30*
Jug, 2½-quart *40*
Mug, w/handle, 7-ounce *18*
Plate, 6⅜" *7*
Plate, 8" *9*
Plate, 9" *10*
Plate, 10⅛" *11*
Plate, chop, buffet server, 13⅛" *45*
Platter, oval (gravy liner), 9" *24*
Platter, oval, 11" *40*
Platter, oval, 13" *48*
Saucer *3*
Shaker *14*
Sugar . . . . *20 – 25*
Teapot, 6-cup *55*
Tumbler, tall, 13-ounce *22*

HOMESTEAD

Homestead, based on Early American folk art themes (various farm scenes), was decorated in three styles: Homestead Provincial (dark green and burgundy), Colonial Homestead (red and brown), and Provincial Blue (blue). Homestead uses many of the same shapes as Rooster.

Ashtray, square, 4½"... *$15*
Ashtray, square, 6⅜"... *20*
Ashtray, square, 8¼"... *25*
Bowl, salad, 11⅛"... *75*
Bowl, soup, 8"... *20*
Bowl, soup, individual, 5"... *20*
Bowl, vegetable, covered, 1-quart... *85*
Bowl, vegetable, round, 7⅛"... *55*
Bowl, vegetable, round, 10"... *55*
Bowl, vegetable, rectangular, divided, 12"... *65*
Bowl, vegetable, basket, 8⅛"... *65*
Bread server, rectangular, 9½"... *65*
Butter, rectangular... *75*
Candy, covered... *95*
Canister, Coffee... *60*
Canister, Flour... *80*
Canister, Sugar... *75*
Canister, Tea... *50*
Canister set (four)... *275*
Casserole, Hen lid, 1¼-quart... *95*
Casserole, kettle, 2½-quart... *95*
Coaster, 3¾"... *15*
Coffee carafe, 44-ounce... *95*
Coffee pot, 7-cup... *100*
Cookie jar... *65*
Creamer... *20*
Cruet... *40*
Cruet set, 2-piece... *95*
Cruet set, 5-piece... *150*
Cup... *12*
Dish, 6"... *15*
Dish, 7¼"... *19*
Eggcup... *22*
Flowerpot... *30*
Flowerpot... *40*
Gravy... *40*
Jug, 1½-pint... *60*
Jug, 1-quart... *75*
Jug, 2¼-quart... *95*
Lazy Susan set, 7-piece... *150*
Mug, 8-ounce... *20*

Mug, Tankard, 1-pint. . . . . . ./. *$30*
Mustard (cruet set) *45*
Planter, Clock *75*
Plate, 6³/₈" *9*
Plate, 7¹/₂" *11*
Plate, 10" . . . ./. *15*
Plate, chop/buffet server, 12¹/₄" *75*
Platter, oval, 11" *55*
Platter, oval, 13¹/₂" *75*
Platter, oval, 16" *150*
Saucer *4*
Shaker (cruet set) *15*
Shaker, w/handle. *10*
Shaker, Hen, salt *25*
Shaker, Rooster, pepper *25*
Sugar *35*
Teapot *125*
Tumbler, footed, 11-ounce *25*

ROOSTER

The shapes in this line are based on old toleware (lacquered or enameled metalware) pieces—down to the "rivets" on the hollowware pieces.

   Rooster was decorated in four styles: Red Rooster (red and brown trim), California Provincial (shades of deep red, straw yellow, and leaf green with a smoky effect on edges and handles), Bleu Rooster (pastel shades of blue and yellow), and a mostly yellow version. Some pieces of Red Rooster were decorated in solid red as well; these are indicated by an R following the item in the listing below.

   PRICING   Values below are for California Provincial; subtract 20% for the other patterns.

Ashtray, square, 4¹/₂"   /R *$20*
Ashtray, square, 6³/₈"   /R *25*
Ashtray, square, 8¹/₄"   /R *30*
Bowl, salad, 11¹/₈"   /R *75*
Bowl, soup, 8" *24*
Bowl, soup, individual, 5"   /R. *24*
Bowl, vegetable, covered, 1-quart *145*
Bowl, vegetable round, basket shape, 7¹/₈"   /R *65*
Bowl, vegetable, round, 10". *55*
Bowl, vegetable, round, divided, 7¹/₈"   /R. *65*
Bowl, vegetable, rectangular, divided, 12"   /R *60*
Bowl, vegetable, basket, 8¹/₈"   /R *60*
Bread server, rectangular, 9¹/₂"   /R *85*
Butter, rectangular   /R *95*
Canister, Coffee   /R. *60*
Canister, Flour   /R. *80*
Canister, Sugar   /R. *75*
Canister, Tea   /R *50*

Red Rooster rooster-decorated dinner plate, solid red cup, and rooster-decorated saucer.

Canister Set (four)   /R *$275*
Casserole, Hen lid, 1¼-quart *125*
Casserole, individual, Hen on lid. *55*
Casserole, kettle, 2½-quart   /R *125*
Coaster, 3¾"   /R *20*
Coffee carafe, 44-ounce   /R *110*
Coffee pot, 6-cup   /R. *115*
Cookie jar   /R *75*
Creamer   /R *28*
Cruet   /R *60*
Cruet set, 2-piece   /R *145*
Cruet set, 5-piece   /R *195*
Cup. *16*
Cup   /R *8*
Dish, 6". *18*
Dish, 7¼" *25*
Eggcup   /R. *25*
Gravy   /R. *50*
Jewelry box *75*
Jug, 1½-pint   /R. *80*

Jug, 1-quart   /R *$95*
Jug, 2¼-quart   /R. *125*
Lazy Susan set, 7-piece *195*
Marmalade *65*
Mug, 8-ounce   /R. *25*
Mug, Tankard, 1-pint   /R. *35*
Mustard (cruet set) *55*
Pepper Mill/Salt Shaker, pair. *75*
Plate, 6⅜". *9*
Plate, 7½". *12*
Plate, 9½". *19*
Plate, 10½". *16*
Plate, chop/buffet server, 12¼" *95*
Platter, oval, 9½" *35*
Platter, oval, 11" *40*
Platter, oval, 13½". *45*
Platter, oval, 16" *85*
Platter, turkey, 22 ½". *195*
Salt box w/wooden lid   /CP *150*
Saucer. *5*
Shaker, w/handle, small   /R *15*
Shaker, w/handle, large (cruet set)   /R *20*
Shaker, Pepper (Rooster). *30*
Shaker, Salt (Hen) *30*
Sugar   /R *40*
Teapot *145*
Tumbler, footed, 11-ounce   /R *35*
Tureen . . . . *350+*
Wall Pocket *75*
Wall Pocket (Match Box)   /CP. *75*
Watering Can *85*

CALIFORNIA PROVINCIAL   These sets are too rare to price; they are listed here for your information.

Measuring cup set
　⅓-**cup**　　　　　¼-**cup**　　　　　½-**cup**　　　　　**1-cup**
Utensil holder, ceramic, w/wooden rings
　Cake lifter　　　　**Fork**　　　　　**Funnel**　　　　　**Slotted spoon**

DINNERWARE / EMBOSSED

DELLA ROBBIA

An embossed border of "flowers, fruit and foliage . . . hand-painted in tones of green, yellow, brown and orange on off-white."

Baker, oval . . . . *$45 – $55*
Bowl, soup, 8" . . . . *18 – 20*

Bowl, vegetable, 9" .... *$35 – $40*
Bowl, vegetable, 9³/₄"... *40 – 45*
Bowl, vegetable, divided, 11¹/₄"............................ *55 – 60*
Butter, oval, ¹/₄-pound .... *55 – 60*
Casserole, 2-quart *95*
Coffee pot, 8–10-cup.. *90 – 100*
Creamer .... *22 – 25*
Cup *12*
Dish, fruit, 6" *12*
Dish, cereal, 7".. *14*
Gravy, 1-pint .... *30 – 35*
Plate, 6¹/₂" *8*
Plate, 8" .... *10 – 11*
Plate, 10¹/₄" .... *12 – 14*
Plate, chop, 12"* *75*
Platter, 12" *40*
Platter, 13³/₄"... *50*
Saucer *3*
Shaker, each *12*
Sugar *28*
Teapot, 6-cup... *110 – 120*

SCULPTURED GRAPE

Casseroles were called covered vegetables. The fork and spoon are wood with ceramic handles. The canisters are four different sizes.

This embossed pattern of grapes, leaves, and vines will be found in three decorations: Antique Grape (soft beige grapes and leaves on a warm white background), Sculptured Grape (blue grapes; also called Blue Vintage), and Vintage Pink (pink grapes, green leaves, and brown twigs on a white background).

Bowl, salad, round, 12" *$65*
Bowl, soup, 8" /VP.. *18 – 20*
Bowl, vegetable, oval, 10¹/₄" *50*
Bowl, vegetable, round, 8¹/₂" .... *35 – 40*
Bowl, vegetable, round, 9¹/₂" /VP .... *40 – 45*
Bowl, vegetable, divided, round, 8¹/₂"........................ *45 – 50*
Bowl, vegetable, divided, round, 9¹/₂" /VP .... *50 – 55*
Butter, ¹/₄-pound /VP.. *55 – 60*
Canister, Coffee .... *50 – 55*
Canister, Flour .... *70 – 75*
Canister, Sugar .... *60 – 65*
Canister, Tea.. *40 – 45*
Casserole, 1-quart .... *75 – 85*
Casserole, 2-quart *95*
Coffee pot, 10-cup /VP .... *90 – 100*
Compote, footed, 8¹/₂".. *65 – 70*
Creamer /VP.. *22 – 25*

Sculptured Grape

Cup   /VP *$12*
Dish, fruit, 6¼"   /VP *12*
Dish, cereal, 7¼"   /VP *14*
Gravy faststand   /VP . . . . *35 – 40*
Jug, 1½-pint *40*
Jug, 1¼-quart *55*
Jug, 2¼-quart *70*
Mug, cocoa, 8-ounce . . . . *22 – 25*
Plate, 6½"   /VP *8*
Plate, 7½"   /VP . . . . *10 – 11*
Plate, 9" *17*
Plate, 10½"   /VP . . . . *12 – 14*
Plate, chop, 12" *75*
Platter, oval, 9¾" *40*
Platter, oval, 12½" *40*
Platter, oval, 14"   /VP *50*
Relish, 2-part (Jam and Jelly) . . . . *50 – 55*
Sauce boat, 1-pint . . . . *40 – 45*
Saucer   /VP *3*
Shaker, salt, tall   /VP *12*
Shaker, pepper, short   /VP *12*
Sugar   /VP *28*
Teapot, 7-cup   /VP . . . . *110 – 120*
Tumbler, 10-ounce *25*
Utensil, Fork *35*
Utensil, Spoon *25*

NOVELTIES

COOKIE JARS

The **Broccoli, Corn, Eggplant,** and **Red Pepper** jars are a canister set, but I've listed them here. The **Easter Bunny** and the **Santa Claus** were made in allover brown color to resemble chocolate versions of these figures. The **Rag Doll Girl** will be found with red hair and a white and blue outfit; this matches the **Rag Doll Boy**. Both are Raggedy Ann/Andy types. She also comes with blond or red hair in outfits of other colors; Metlox named this one "Pretty Ann."

Acorn w/woodpecker finial . . . . *$375 – $385*
Apple
    Red . . . . *35 – 45*
    Yellow . . . . *125 +*
Automobile w/mouse family, luggage finial (Mouse Mobile)   /548 . . . . . *200 – 225*
Barn w/rooster finial (Mac's Barn) . . . . *350 +*
Barrel of apples . . . . *30 – 40*
Barrel of cookies, 11" . . . . *100 – 125*
Barrel of nuts, chipmunk finial, 11" . . . . *70 – 85*

Barrel of pretzels, 11"... *$100 – $125*
Bear, in sweater holding cookie, brown (Teddy)   /527.................... *40 – 45*
Bear, in sweater holding cookie, white (Teddy)   /538 .... *40 – 45*
Bear, in tutu (Bear Ballerina)...................................... *100 – 125*
Bear, on skates (Roller Bear)...................................... *125 – 150*
Bear, Panda, holding lollipop...................................... *100 – 125*
Bear, Panda, right arm across stomach .... *75 – 100*
Bear, Uncle Sam.. *950 +*
Bear, w/green leaves (Koala)   /549......................... *100 – 125*
Bear, w/large bow tie (Beau)...................................... *40 – 50*
    Shakers... *35 – 45*
Bear, w/sombrero (Pancho) .... *70 – 80*
    Shakers... *45 – 50*
    Sombrero chip-and-dip, small .... *20 – 25*
    Sombrero chip-and-dip, large .... *35 – 45*
Beaver w/flower bouquet .... *250 – 300*
Box w/Strawberries.. *50 – 60*
Boy, Cookie .... *300 – 350*
Boy, head, w/cap (Cub Scout) .... *900 +*
Broccoli, bunch .... *125 – 150*
Cabbage w/rabbit finial .... *100 – 125*
Calf (Ferdinand).. *750 +*
Calf, head (Calf-Says-Moo)... *275 – 300*
Canister, square, w/embossed flower .... *30 – 40*
Cat, stylized (Calico)   /556 .... *145 – 155*
    Green .... *200 – 225*
Cat, tail on left side (Ali) .... *200 – 225*
    Shakers... *95 – 100*
Cat, realistic, tail on right side (Katy) .... *95 – 105*
Cat, head, hat lid.. *100 – 125*
Chef, head... *300 +*
Chicken (Mother Hen).. *40 – 50*
Clown, full figure, 2 buttons   /524
    White w/black trim.. *175 – 225*
    Yellow w/green trim .... *125 – 150*
Clown, head (Happy) .... *900 +*
Corncobs .... *125 – 150*
Cow, w/bell around neck, butterfly finial   /526................ *300 +*
Cow, w/flowers and bell around neck, butterfly finial   /550 .... *225 – 250*
Cow, head, bow finial.. *275 – 300*
Daisy ball .... *50 – 60*
Debutante (made for T. M. James and Sons) .... *400 – 450*
Dinosaur, Monoclonius, blue/rose/yellow (Mona) .... *140 – 160*
Dinosaur, Stegasaurus, blue/rose/yellow (Dino)..................... *140 – 160*
Dinosaur, Tyrannosaurus Rex, blue/rose/yellow (Rex)................ *140 – 160*
    Cow-painted .... *350 +*
Dog, Basset... *400 +*
Dog, Fido .... *200 – 225*

Dog, Scottie
    Black. . . . . *$125 – $150*
    White . . . . *150 – 175*
Dog, stylized (Gingham)   /557 . . . . *145 – 155*
    Blue. . . . . *200 – 225*
Doll, boy, sitting, hands in pockets. . . . . *200 – 225*
Doll, girl, sitting, hands at sides . . . . *175 – 200*
    Other colors (Pretty Anne) . . . . *200 – 225*
Drum, children playing embossed on sides (Gingerbread)   /528
    Glazed . . . . *125 – 150*
    Stained . . . . *100 – 120*
Drum Major, head (Drummer Boy) . . . . *700 +*
Duck in rain gear, white w/yellow trim/yellow (Puddles) . . . . *50 – 60*
Duck w/hat (Francine). . . . . *250 – 275*
Duck (Sir Francis Drake) . . . . *50 – 55*
    Platter. . . . . *35 – 50*
    Shakers, pair . . . . *20 – 25*
    Tureen w/ladle. *75*
    Wall clock *100*
Dutch Boy, hands on suspenders . . . . *150 – 175*
Dutch Girl, w/bowl and spoon. . . . . *150 – 175*
Eggplant. . . . . *150 +*
Fish (Pescado) . . . . *150 – 175*
Frog in tie and collar, holding flower. . . . . *225 – 250*
Fruit basket
    Tan/White . . . . *40 – 50*
Girl, black, sitting (Topsy) w/polka dots (blue/red/yellow). . . . . *600 +*
Girl, Candy. . . . . *70 – 90*
Girl, head, w/cap (Brownie). . . . . *750 +*
Girl w/doll in pocket and bow finial (Cookie Girl)   /537 . . . . *75*
Goose w/hat and shawl (Mother Goose). . . . . *200 – 225*
Goose w/mobcap and shawl (Lucy) . . . . *50 – 60*
Grapefruit   /523 . . . . *125 +*
Grapes . . . . *300 – 350*
Hen, blue, closed beak . . . . *300 – 350*
Hippo (Bubbles) w/waterlily finial. . . . . *350 +*
House (Mushroom Cottage)   /550. . . . . *300 – 325*
Humpty-Dumpty. . . . . *125 – 150*
    Wall clock *100*
Kangaroo, in apron, joey finial, 11¼". . . . . *1300 +*
Lamb, head, hat lid . . . . *175 – 200*
Lamb, sitting, w/collar. . . . . *175 – 200*
Lamb, sitting, w/flower wreath around neck . . . . *175 – 200*
Lion, sitting, tail in front . . . . *150 – 175*
Little Red Riding Hood . . . . *1200 +*
Mammy, blue. . . . . *400 – 450*
    Red . . . . *700 +*
    Yellow trim (Cook) *350*

Shakers, blue, pair *$200*
    Red, pair *200*
    Yellow trim, pair *200*
Mouse Chef (Pierre). .... *100 – 125*
    Cheese shaker (Julius Cheeser). *20*
    Shakers, pair .... *40 – 50*
Noah's Ark /534 .... *100 – 125*
Nun, holding plate of cookies. .... *750 +*
Orange .... *60 – 65*
Owl, stylized. .... *40 – 45*
    White .... *125 – 150*
Parrot /555 .... *350 +*
Pear
    Green .... *100 – 125*
    Yellow. .... *125 – 150*
Pelican in sailor's cap (Salty), "US Diving Team" .... *175 – 200*
Penguin in hat and scarf (Frosty). .... *125 – 150*
Pig, Little, sitting, scarf around neck .... *200 +*
Pig w/scarf, standing (Little Piggy) /531
    Floral decoration. .... *150 +*
    Stained .... *120 – 140*
Pig in dress on scale (Slenderella). .... *150 – 175*
Pineapple .... *75 – 100*
Pinecone w/bluebird finial
    Glazed .... *200 – 225*
    Stained .... *150 +*
Pinecone, w/squirrel holding acorn finial, 11". .... *75 – 85*
Pinocchio, head /R .... *375 – 400*
Pot, daisy finial, green/yellow *50*
Pumpkin. .... *125 – 150*
Pumpkin w/boy finial .... *400 +*
Rabbit (Easter Bunny)
    Chocolate .... *ND*
    White .... *275 – 300*
Rabbit, in dress and apron w/carrot (Mrs. Bunny) .... *250 +*
Rabbit, lying, w/clover finial .... *200 – 225*
    Platter. .... *40 – 50*
    Shaker, pair .... *45 – 50*
Raccoon w/three apples (Cookie Bandit) /532 .... *100 – 125*
Rooster, blue, open beak .... *350 – 375*
Rose .... *400 +*
Santa Claus
    Black. .... *450 – 500*
    White .... *350 – 400*
    Candy/Planter
        Black. .... *125 – 150*
        White .... *100 – 125*
Seal, white (Sammy). .... *450 – 500*
    Shaker, pair .... *75 – 100*

Squash, green . . . . *$150+*
Strawberry *50*
Stump, owls (1 large, 1 small) finial   /535 . . . . *50 – 60*
Tulip, Yellow . . . . *450+*
Walrus w/sailor hat and kerchief   /552
    Brown . . . . *300 – 325*
    White . . . . *100 – 125*
Watermelon . . . . *350+*
Whale w/duck finial   /554 . . . . *300 – 350*
Wheat Shock   /522 . . . . *100 – 125*

FIGURES

Animals / Miniature   (<1939)

Designed by Carl Romanelli. The most common glaze is Satin White, then Satin Turquoise and Satin Green. There is also a high-gloss mottled brown and turquoise. Other colors may be found.

Alligator/Crocodile . . . . *$50 – $60*
Bear, on back . . . . *50 – 60*
Dog, cubistic . . . . *50 – 60*
Dog, Scotty . . . . *50 – 60*
Donkey . . . . *50 – 60*
Duck . . . . *50 – 60*
Elephant, trunk back . . . . *50 – 60*
Fish, three, 4" . . . . *50 – 60*
Hippo . . . . *50 – 60*
Horse front left leg up . . . . *50 – 60*
Horse, rearing . . . . *50 – 60*
Horse . . . . *50 – 60*
Lizard . . . . *50 – 60*
Monkey, on all fours . . . . *50 – 60*
Otter . . . . *50 – 60*
Seal . . . . *50 – 60*
Turtle, standing . . . . *50 – 60*

Animals: Monkey and badger.

MORTON POTTERY COMPANY

Morton, Illinois

CHAPTER AT A GLANCE

KITCHENWARE   COOKIE JARS
AMISH PANTRY WARE   FIGURINES
PILGRIM   Miniatures
ROCKINGHAM   MISCELLANY
WOODLAND   PLANTERS
NOVELTIES   TV LAMPS
BANKS

One of the six interrelated potteries in Morton. Begun in 1922 for the manufacture of utility items, the company began expanding into novelties in the late 1930s based on the successful marketing of political items. It closed in 1971.
 See Hall in Bibliography.
 MARKS An incised mark with "Morton" and "USA" or the shape number.
 PRICING / COLORS The Pilgrim kitchenware colors will be found on other objects. If an item was made in one or two colors only, those colors are listed and priced specifically. The other items were made in a range of colors; use the following for price range information. When a single price is given, it is the middle of the range.

LOW END OF RANGE:
Burgundy   Gray   Pastel yellow
Chartreuse   Pastel blue   White
Golden brown   Pastel green

MIDDLE OF RANGE:
Black
Brown
Majolica (a brushed multicolor of blue, dark rose, green, and yellow on white)
Pilgrim apple green
Pink
Red (an automobile lacquer was used)

HIGH END OF RANGE:
Cobalt   Pilgrim canary yellow Pilgrim blue

KITCHENWARE

Morton's advertising claimed "originators of colored kitchen pottery." The lines below are primarily kitchenware, though there is an occasional cup, plate, and flowerpot. I always thought flowerpots were strange items to have in a kitchenware list until I pictured them on a kitchen windowsill with their matching colors.

The beater bowl pitcher was a set with an egg beater. Despite its name, it is a straight-sided pitcher shape, not a bowl. Some of the casseroles and pie bakers came in nickel-plated steel frames. Different-size coasters were made and are listed under the items they were intended to go with. See also Rockingham for additional kitchenware.

PRICING For the Amish and Pilgrim kitchenware, blue and green are at the low end of the range and yellow is at the high end. Steel frames for the casseroles w/o handles and the pie bakers are included in the prices.

AMISH PANTRY WARE (1929)

Solid colors of blue, green, or yellow (see Pilgrim). Hand-painted cold-paint decorations were also done but are hard to find and are not in great condition when they are found.

Baker, round, 1¼-pint, 5"	*$15 – $50*
Baker, round, 1½-pint, 6"	*20 – 60*
Baker, round, 2½-pint, 7"	*25 – 70*
Baker, round, 3-pint, 8"	*30 – 80*
Bean pot, 1 handle, sunken knob, 3-quart	*45 – 100*
Beater bowl pitcher, w/beater, 1-quart	*40 – 90*
Bowl, baking dish, 5"	*15 – 50*
Bowl, baking dish, 6"	*20 – 60*
Bowl, baking dish, 7"	*25 – 70*
Bowl, baking dish, 8"	*30 – 80*
Bowl, cook/serve, 2½-pint, 7"	*25 – 70*
Bowl, cook/serve, 2-quart, 8"	*30 – 80*
Bowl, cook/serve, 3-quart, 9"	*35 – 90*
Bowl, mixing, 1-pint, 5"	*15 – 50*
Bowl, mixing, 2-pint, 6"	*20 – 60*
Bowl, mixing, 3-pint, 7"	*25 – 70*
Bowl, mixing, 4-pint, 8"	*30 – 80*
Bowl, mixing, 5-pint, 9"	*40 – 100*
Bowl, porridge, 11-ounce	*15 – 50*
Canister, tea and coffee, 1½-quart	*35 – 90*
Canister, cereal, 3-quart	*45 – 100*
Canister, pantry, 5-quart	*55 – 110*
Canister, cookie, 9-quart	*65 – 120*
Casserole, sectioned lid, 2¾-pint, 8"	*40 – 90*
Casserole, (pudding dish), lug, 3½-pint, 9"	*35 – 85*
Creamer, 12-ounce	*15 – 50*

Cup . . . . *ND*
Custard, 10-ounce . . . . *$15 – $50*
Jug, batter . . . . *40 – 100*
　　Coaster . . . . *10 – 40*
Jug, ice box, 1¹/₂-pint, 3³/₄" high . . . . *30 – 80*
Jug, ice tea, 3¹/₄-quart, 8" high . . . . *50 – 105*
　　Coaster . . . . *15 – 50*
Jug, milk, 4¹/₂-pint, 5¹/₂" high . . . . *30 – 80*
Jug, syrup . . . . *20 – 60*
　　Coaster . . . . *5 – 20*
Jug, water, 2¹/₂-quart, 7" high . . . . *40 – 100*
Leftover (ice box jar), 1-quart, round, 5¹/₂" . . . . *45 – 85*
Match box . . . . *40 – 100*
Pie baker, 9" . . . . *35 – 85*
Plate, 8" . . . . *ND*
Salt box . . . . *50 – 105*
Saucer . . . . *ND*
Saucer, porridge . . . . *10 – 40*
Shaker (spice), 5" high . . . . *15 – 50*
Sugar . . . . *35 – 85*
Teapot, 48-ounce . . . . *ND*
Tile (tea), round, 5¹/₄" . . . . *ND*
Tumbler (ice tea beaker), 16-ounce, 6" high . . . . *15 – 50*
　　Coaster . . . . *5 – 20*

PILGRIM

The pie baker doubled as an undertray for the casserole. A beverage set was the Colonial jug and six mugs.

　　Glazed in a soft blue, apple green, and canary yellow.

Baker/nappy, 4" *$15*
Baker/nappy, 5" *20*
Baker/nappy, 6" *25*
Baker/nappy, 7" *30*
Baker/nappy, 8" *35*
Baker/nappy, 9" *40*
Beater bowl pitcher, w/beater *40*
Bowl, mixing, 5" *10*
Bowl, mixing, 6" *12*
Bowl, mixing, 7" *14*
Bowl, mixing, 8" *18*
Bowl, mixing, 9" *22*
Bowl, mixing, 10" *26*
Bowl, mixing, 11" *32*
Bowl, mixing, 12" *42*
Bowl, vegetable, w/lid, oval . . . . *ND*
Butter, 1-pound *50*
Casserole *45*

Casserole, handled. *$35*
Custard, 48s, 5-ounce* *6*
Custard, 30s, 7-ounce* *8*
Custard, 24s, 10-ounce* *10*
Flowerpot/saucer, 4" *12*
Flowerpot/saucer, 5" *12*
Flowerpot/saucer, 6" *12*
Flowerpot/saucer, 7" *22*
Flowerpot/saucer, 8" *24*
Jug, 42s *15*
Jug, 36s *16*
Jug, 30s *20*
Jug, 24s *22*
Jug, 12s *24*
Jug, ice-box *30*
Jug, batter *40*
    Coaster *10*
Jug, Colonial, beverage *40*
Jug, syrup. *20*
    Coaster *5*
Match box *40*
Mug, Colonial *10*
Pie baker *35*
Salt box *50*
Shaker, range. *15*
Tea-for-Two hot water pot *30*
Tea-for-Two teapot *30*
Tea-for-Two tray *15*
Teapot, 1-cup. *20*
Teapot, 2-cup. *23*
Teapot, 3-cup. *25*
Teapot, 4-cup. *29*
Teapot, 5-cup. *33*
Teapot, 7-cup. *40*

ROCKINGHAM

Baker, round, 5¹/₂" *$10*
Baker, round, 6¹/₂" *15*
Baker, round, 7¹/₂" *20*
Baker, round, 8¹/₂" *25*
Batter jar and beater *50*
Bowl, utility, 7" *20*
Casserole, 3-quart, 8" *40*
Custard, 5-ounce. *6*
Incense burner, Church *25*
Incense burner, Oriental figure *35*
Mold, heart shape *40*
Mug, Barrel, plain *10*

Blatz... *$18*
"Happy Days Are Here Again"................................ *22*
Old Heidelberg.. *20*
Sweeney.. *18*
Pie baker, 9"... *30*
Pitcher, Barrel, 90-ounce *35*
Teapot, stacking, 1-cup *12*

WOODLAND

Brown and green spatter on yellowware. The flower bowl and frog are usually found together; the price is for both pieces.

Beater bowl pitcher, w/beater *$80*
Bowl, mixing, paneled, 5" *40*
Bowl, mixing, paneled, 6" *50*
Bowl, mixing, paneled, 7" *60*
Bowl, mixing, paneled, 8" *70*
Bowl, mixing, paneled, 9" *80*
Bowl, utility, 7" *60*
Casserole, 8" *75*
Coffee server, 8-cup *90*
Custard *20*
Flower bowl, log shape, embossed oak leaves, w/flower frog, yellowware, rectangular................................... *60*
Grease jar, 4" *45*
Grease pitcher, 2³/₄" *40*
Jug, barrel, ¹/₂-pint *70*
Jug, barrel, 1-pint....................................... *80*
Jug, barrel, 1-quart...................................... *90*
Jug, barrel, 1¹/₂-quart *100*
Jug, barrel, ¹/₂-gallon *110*
Jug, ice box, 1¹/₂-pint *90*
Jug, refrigerator, flat, w/lid, 4" *105*
Jug, milk, w/advertising *85*
Jug, milk, double spout *70*
Jug, water, w/ice lip, 7".................................. *110*
Pie baker, 9" *120*
Shaker, pair... *110*
Teapot, 3-cup.. *65*
Teapot, 3¹/₂-cup *75*
Teapot, 4-cup.. *85*
Teapot, 5-cup.. *95*
Vase, bulbous, 10³/₄" *225*

NOVELTIES

There are some novelties made in the Rockingham glaze; these are listed in the previous Rockingham section.

BANKS

Skedaddle and Skedoodle had a hole in the back, for both removal of coins and for hanging on a wall. The slot was on top. The other pig bank is freestanding.

Acorn. . . . . *$25 – $30*
Bulldog, 3³/₄" × 3". . . . . *20 – 25*
Cat, reclining, 4" × 6". . . . .`. . . . . *20 – 25*
Hen, 4"× 3". . . . . *25 – 30*
Pig, 5¹/₂" × 7" . . . . *35 – 40*
Pig, Skedaddle, legs out. *20*
Pig, Skedoodle, legs crossed *20*
Scottie Dog, 7". . . . . *30 – 35*
Shoe House, 9" . . . . *20 – 25*
Uncle Sam, 4" × 2". . . . . *15 – 18*

COOKIE JARS

Basket of Fruit . . . . *$30 – $35*
Blue Bird, 9" . . . . *35 – 40*
Coffee pot, "Cookies". . . . . *20 – 25*
Cylinder, circus animals decals and tent-top lid. . . . . *20 – 25*
French Poodle, head, white w/cold-painted bow at neck. . . . . *35 – 40*
Hen w/chick finial on lid . . . . *100 – 125*
Hillbilly head w/straw hat. . . . . *35 – 40*
Milk can, "Cookies" . . . . *20 – 25*
Owl, chartreuse/dark green, cold-paint eyes . . . . *25 – 30*
Panda. . . . . *35 – 40*
Pineapple, 14". *22*
Turkey w/chick finial on lid
  Brown w/red wattle *125*
  White. *150*

French Poodle cookie jar.

*Panda and Blue
Bird cookie jars.*

FIGURINES

The man and woman make a pair.

Cat, reclining, 6" long *$12*
Cat, reclining, 9" long *16*
Davy Crockett, lamp base, 7¹/₂" *75*
John Kennedy, Jr., saluting, age 3 . . . . *30*
Man, in knickers, holding bouquet, 7¹/₂" *18*
Oxen w/yoke, pair, 3¹/₄" *30*
Stork, 7¹/₂" *14*
Woman in sunbonnet w/baskets of flowers, 7³/₄" *18*

Miniatures

ANIMALS

Bear, knee crossed, 2¹/₄" *$10*
Blue Jay, 2¹/₂" *7*
Blue Jay on stump, 4" /596 . . . . *9*
Deer, on base, 4¹/₂" /595 . . . . *9*
Deer, on base, looking back /627 . . . . *8*
Deer, on four legs /645 . . . . *9*
Dog, nose in air /583 . . . . *12*
Dog, sniffing ground /576 . . . . *12*
Dog, squatting /506 . . . . *12*
Donkey, "Kennedy," 2" *30*
Duck *8*
Elephant, trunk rolled back over head,
"GOP/candidate's name" on side /606 . . . . *15 – 20*
Elephant, trunk extended forward, trumpeting, 2¹/₂" *7*
Fawn, 2¹/₂" /542 . . . . *7*
Horse, 2³/₄" /593 . . . . *7*
Horse, 2³/₄" /599 . . . . *7*

Miniature Animals: Top: *Horse /593, Wild Horse /604, Horse /599.* Middle: *Bear, leg crossed.* Bottom: *Turkey, elephant, trunk forward, elephant, trunk rolled back /606, bird /596, squirrel, lamb /594, kangaroo and fawn /542.*

Horse, Wild, 2³/₄" /604 . . . . $7
Kangaroo, 2³/₄" /602 7
Lamb, 2¹/₂" /594 7
Rabbit, 3" 8
Squirrel, 2¹/₄" 10
Stork, 4" /597 9
Swordfish, 4" /598 9
Turkey, 2¹/₂" 12

OTHER

Bean pot, "Bloomingtom Eastern Star" $8
Ewer, solid color, 2¹/₄" /546 6
   Decorated 8
Ewer and basin, 1 piece, 1³/₄" 8
Jug, ribbed 7
Lamp, Aladdin, 2" 6
   Cobalt 8
Lamp, hurricane, 2¹/₄" /544 7
Teapot, ribbed, 2" 6
Vase, 2" 8
Vase, 2¹/₄" 8

MISCELLANY

The grass growers are white bisque. The hen sugar and rooster creamer are a set.

Bookend, Atlas on book, globe on shoulders, 5" $30
Bookend, Eagles, 6" 30

Miniatures: Top: *Teapot, hurricane lamp, Aladdin's lamp, ewer (hand decorated), ewer (solid color).* Middle: *Ewer and basin (one piece).* Bottom: *Vase, 2",* *Vase, 2¹/₄".*

Bookend/planter, Parrots, Majolica, 6" *$30*
Creamer, Rooster *11*
Dresser Tray, man's collar w/tie *14*
Dresser Tray, woman's collar, hand-painted brooch *12*
Grass grower, Christmas tree *12*
Grass grower, Pig *15*
Lamp, Horse and Colt, 9¹/₂" *50*
Lamp, Irish Setter and Pheasant *55*
Lapel pin, stein, "We Want Beer"/"Repeal the 18th" *35*
  As above, Donkey handle *45*
Lollypop Tree, 9¹/₄" *25*
Pie Bird, Bird, 5" *30*
Pie Bird, Duckling, 5" *32*
Pie Bird, Rooster, 5" *37*
Plate, Santa Claus face, 8" *30*
Plate, Santa Claus face, 12" *45*
Punch bowl, Santa Claus head .... *ND*
  Mug *15*
Shakers, loaves of bread, pair *15*
Spoon rest, fish *12*
Spoon rest, pansy *12*
Spoon rest, pears *10*
Spoon rest, skillet *12*
Sugar, Hen *14*
Vase, hand *10*
Wall pocket, bird in flight *20*
Wall pocket, harp *15*

Wall pocket, lady gardener w/hoe *$12*
Wall pocket, lady gardener w/watering can *12*
Wall pocket, Owl on crescent moon.. *18*
Wall pocket, Parrot w/grapes *20*
Wall pocket/planter, Cockatoo, small *18*
Wall pocket/vase, Cockatoo, large *24*

PLANTERS

The oxen figures (see Figurines) are intended to be used with the covered wagon.

Cat *$16*
Covered Wagon, natural colors *18*
Cowboy and Cactus, natural colors, 7" *12*
Duck.. *8*
Fawn, 8¹/₂"   /645 .... *8*
Fish *8*
Lady, dancing, Deco, 8" *18*
Lamb *14*
Mrs. Claus, 9¹/₂" *25*
Rooster *8*
Santa Claus, 9¹/₂" *30*
Santa next to chimney w/gold bell *20*
Santa on Chimney, 7" *18*
Sleigh, small
    Red... *15*
    White... *12*
Sleigh, large, red *25*
Sleigh, large, open runners, white w/holly decal........................ *18*
Snowman, white w/black hat and red/green scarf, 9³/₄" *20*
Turkey, brown only, 5"... *12*
Turkey, brown only, 7¹/₂" *40*

TV LAMPS

The Panther was designed for Morton by Royal Hickman. There is also a figure version.

Black Panther, 28" *$30*
Buffalo on rocky cliff, natural colors, 11" *75*
Horse's head, 18" *35*
Leopard, natural colors, 14" *35*
Lioness on log, black/brown, 10" *35*

MT. CLEMENS POTTERY COMPANY

Mt. Clemens, Michigan

CHAPTER AT A GLANCE

OXFORD   VOGUE
PETAL

Begun in 1915 for the manufacture of semiporcelain dinnerware. Manufactured for S. S. Kresge. Closed in 1987.

MARKS Much is unmarked or has a raised "USA" on it. One backstamp that will be found is an intertwined "M. C. P. Co."

OXFORD (<1932)

Although this is a Mt. Clemens shape, Stetson used it for decorating, and Oxford is Stetson's name for it. I don't know the Mt. Clemens name.

Bowl, salad, 9"*	$15 – $18
Bowl, soup, 8"*	10 – 12
Bowl, vegetable, oval, 9"*	10 – 12
Casserole	20 – 25
Creamer	4 – 6
Cup	4 – 6
Dish, 6"	3 – 4
Gravy	12 – 15
Plate, 7¼"	4 – 5
Plate, 10"	7 – 9
Platter, 11¼"	10 – 12
Saucer	1 – 2
Sugar	8 – 10

PETAL

Most readily found in solid colors of burgundy, dark blue, medium green (most common), and yellow. Decals will also be found.

"Petal" and Vogue bread and butter plates.

Bowl, soup, 8" .... *$10 – $12*
Bowl, 36s .... *7 – 10*
Bowl, vegetable, round, 7¹/₂" .... *10 – 12*
Bowl, vegetable, round, 8¹/₂" .... *10 – 12*
Butter dish .... *20 – 25*
Creamer .... *4 – 6*
Cup .... *4 – 6*
Cup, cream soup .... *12 – 16*
Dish, 5¹/₄" .... *2 – 3*
Dish, 6" .... *3 – 4*
Gravy .... *12 – 15*
Plate, 6" .... *1 – 2*
Plate, 7¹/₂" .... *5 – 7*
Plate, 9¹/₄" .... *7 – 9*
Platter, 11¹/₄" .... *10 – 12*
Platter, 13¹/₂" .... *12 – 15*
Platter, lug, 15" .... *15 – 18*
Saucer .... *1 – 2*
Sugar .... *8 – 10*
Sugar, lug .... *8 – 10*

VOGUE

Has an embossed rim with birds, flowers, and urns. Decorated in solid colors and decals.

Bowl, vegetable, oval, 9¹/₄" .... *$10 – $12*
Butter dish .... *20 – 25*
Creamer .... *4 – 6*
Cup .... *4 – 6*
Dish, 5¹/₈" .... *2 – 3*
Dish, 6" .... *3 – 4*
Plate, 6¹/₄" .... *1 – 2*

Plate, 7" .... *$5 – $7*
Plate, 9¹/₄" .... *7 – 9*
Platter, 11¹/₄" .... *10 – 12*
Saucer .... *1 – 2*
Sugar .... *8 – 10*

NILOAK POTTERY COMPANY

Benton, Arkansas

CHAPTER AT A GLANCE

ART POTTERY   Flower Frogs
MISSION WARE (Swirl)   Planters
CASTWARE   Planters, Cold-Paint
FIGURES   Shakers
FIGURALS   **KITCHENWARE**

Niloak (kaolin, a type of clay, spelled backward) pottery, an unglazed swirl ware manufactured by the Eagle Pottery Company of Benton, came to market in early 1910. In 1911, the company was incorporated as the Niloak Pottery Company, with Charles Hyten, who had been owner of Eagle, as a director and general manager. Company fortunes waxed and waned in the next two decades. Financial difficulties led to the introduction of Hywood Art Pottery, a glazed ware, in late 1931, as well as industrial castware, pottery that was made in a mold rather than being hand-thrown like the art pottery lines.

The Hywood name stayed in use until 1937, and swirl was made sporadically into the 1940s, but it was the castware that carried the company through the hard times and began to improve its fortunes. The company was reorganized in 1934 with ownership going to Hardy Winburn III. Charles Hyten left the company in 1941.

With the coming of World War II, Niloak converted to war production. After the war, the pottery concentrated on filling large back orders, but new sales were minimal, and in 1947 it became the Winburn Tile Company, which still exists today, manufacturing porcelain mosaic tile.

See Gifford in the Bibliography.

MARKS Niloak used a variety of marks. Some you will find are "NILOAK" in capital letters either incised in the mold, impressed die stamp, or slightly embossed.

ART POTTERY

MISSION WARE (SWIRL)

Glazed on the inside so that the appropriate pieces would hold water. Many of the vase shapes came in a wide range of sizes.

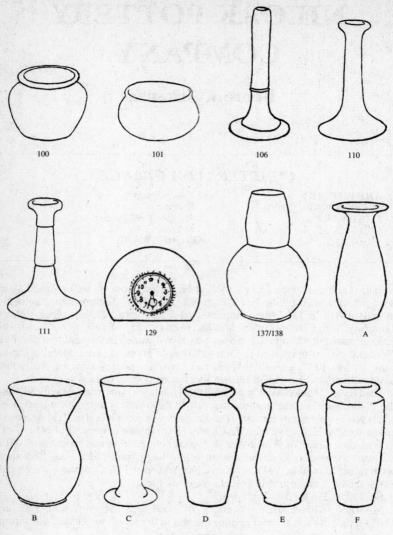

100   101   106   110

111   129   137/138   A

B   C   D   E   F

Mission Ware

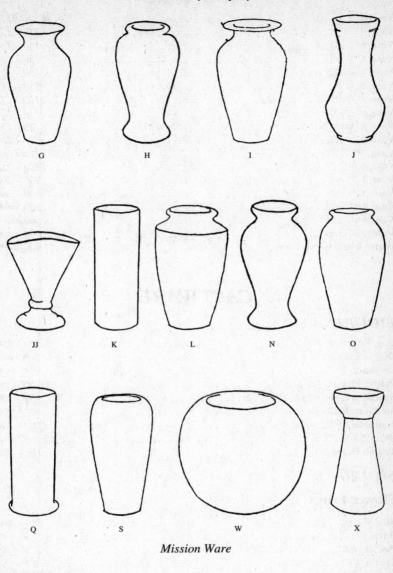

Mission Ware

Tumbler (drinking cup), 4" × 3"	/127	....	*$90 – $110*
Vase, 3¹/₂"	/I	....	*70 – 80*
Vase, 3¹/₂"	/J	....	*70 – 80*
Vase, 3¹/₂"	/S	....	*70 – 80*
Vase, 5"	/B	....	*80 – 90*
Vase, 5"	/D	....	*80 – 90*
Vase, 5"	/F	....	*80 – 90*

Vase, 5" fan   /JJ .... *$150 – $175*
Vase, 6"   /A. .... *110 – 130*
Vase, 6"   /Q. .... *110 – 130*
Vase, 8"   /G. .... *150 – 175*
Vase, 8"   /K. .... *150 – 175*
Vase, 8"   /L. .... *150 – 175*
Vase, 8"   /N. .... *150 – 175*
Vase, 8"   /X. .... *150 – 175*
Vase, 8" bud   /106. .... *125 – 150*
Vase, 9"   /C. .... *175 – 200*
Vase, 9"   /E. .... *175 – 200*
Vase, 10"   /N. .... *200 – 250*
Vase, 12"   /N. .... *250 – 300*
Vase, 14"   /N. .... *400 – 500*
Vase, 16"   /H. .... *500 – 600*
Vase, 16"   /N. .... *500 – 600*
Vase, 18"   /O. .... *600 – 800*
Water bottle w/cup cover, 8"   /137   /138 .... *300 – 400*

CASTWARE

FIGURES

Dog, Retreiver, 4½" .... *$40 – $50*
Dog, Scottie .... *30 – 40*
Elephant, 2¼" .... *40 – 60*
Pouter Pigeon, 4¾" .... *60 – 80*
Southern Belle, w/hat, 7¼" .... *80 – 100*
Southern Belle, 10" .... *100 – 120*
Southern Belle, sitting, 4¼" .... *80 – 100*
Swan, 2¾" .... *30 – 40*
Trojan Horse, 8¾" .... *100 – 120*

FIGURALS

Flower Frogs

Bird, 7¼" .... *$40 – $50*
Duck, 6" .... *30 – 40*
Pelican, 6¾" .... *25 – 35*
Turtle, 4¾" .... *25 – 35*

Planters

Airplane, 2" .... *$80 – $100*
Bird, several styles, 2½" × 3½" .... *35 – 45*
Camel, 3¾" .... *30 – 40*
Cannon, 2" .... *40 – 50*
Canoe, 5½" long .... *$40 – $50*

Canoe, 11" long . . . . *$30 – $40*
Cart, 4¹/₂" . . . . *30 – 40*
Clown and Drum, 7¹/₂" . . . . *35 – 45*
Cornucopia, 3¹/₄" . . . . *15 – 20*
Cradle, 6" . . . . *40 – 60*
Deer, freestanding, 5¹/₄" . . . . *30 – 40*
Deer, freestanding, 10" . . . . *80 – 100*
Deer, two, 7¹/₂" . . . . *35 – 45*
Deer in grass, facing left, 5" . . . . *20 – 30*
Deer in grass, facing right, 5" . . . . *20 – 30*
Deer in grass, 7" . . . . *30 – 40*
Deer in grass, 8" . . . . *30 – 40*
Dog, 3³/₄" . . . . *40 – 50*
Dog, Bulldog, 2" × 5³/₄" . . . . *40 – 50*
Dog, Poodle, 3¹/₂" . . . . *60 – 80*
Dog, Scottie, 3¹/₂" . . . . *30 – 40*
Duck, head down, 3³/₄" . . . . *20 – 30*
Duck, head up, 4¹/₂" . . . . *15 – 25*
Duck, open beak, wings up, 4¹/₂" . . . . *20 – 30*
Elephant, leaning forward, 7" . . . . *30 – 40*
Elephant, trunk out, 3¹/₂" × 6¹/₂" . . . . *60 – 80*
Elephant, trunk over head, w/howdah, 3¹/₄" . . . . *60 – 80*
Elephant, trunk over head, w/howdah, 4¹/₄" . . . . *40 – 50*
Elephant on Drum, 6¹/₄" . . . . *10 – 20*
Elephant on Drum, "N", 6" . . . . *20 – 30*
Fish, 9" long . . . . *30 – 40*
Fox, facing left/right, 4¹/₂" . . . . *35 – 45*
Frog, 3¹/₄" . . . . *20 – 30*
Frog, 5" . . . . *25 – 35*
Frog on Lily Pad, 4" . . . . *25 – 35*
Frog in Water Lily, 4¹/₄" . . . . *25 – 35*
Goat, 4¹/₄" . . . . *80 – 100*
Keystone Cop and Donkey, 7" . . . . *30 – 40*
Polar Bear, 3¹/₄" . . . . *35 – 45*
Pouter Pigeon, 9" . . . . *60 – 80*
Rabbit, 3¹/₂" . . . . *20 – 30*
Rabbits (two), 4³/₄" . . . . *30 – 40*
Rocking Horse, 6¹/₄" . . . . *80 – 100*
Rooster, 6¹/₄" . . . . *20 – 40*
Rooster, 8¹/₂" . . . . *25 – 35*
Shoe, high heel, w/strap, 2³/₄" . . . . *20 – 30*
Squirrel, left/right, 6" . . . . *20 – 30*
Squirrel, opening between arms, 5" . . . . *20 – 30*
Tank, 2¹/₂" . . . . *50 – 60*
Turtle, 8¹/₂" long . . . . *35 – 45*
Wishing Well, covered, 8" . . . . *30 – 40*
Wishing Well, open, 8¹/₂" . . . . *40 – 50*
Wooden Shoe, 5" long . . . . *10 – 15*

PLANTERS W / EMBOSSED FIGURES

Cat and Basket, 4¹/₄".. *$15 – $25*
Monkey and Basket, 4"... *15 – 25*
Peter Pan on bowl, 7¹/₂"... *15 – 25*
Rabbit and Log, 4¹/₄"... *15 – 25*

PLANTERS W / COLD PAINT These are an untypical brown/tan color with cold-painted details such as eyes and beaks.

Camel, 3¹/₄"... *$35 – $45*
Kangaroo w/boxing gloves, 5"..................................... *35 – 45*
Parrot, 4¹/₂"... *35 – 45*
Pelican, 5¹/₂".. *35 – 45*
Polar bear, 3¹/₂".. *35 – 45*
Seal, 4³/₄".. *35 – 45*

Shakers

Birds, pair, 2¹/₂".. *$30 – $40*
Bullets, pair, 2³/₄".. *50 – 60*
Geese, pair, 2".. *40 – 50*
Penguins, pair, 2³/₄".. *40 – 60*

KITCHENWARE

Aladdin creamer.. *$20 – $30*
Aladdin sugar.. *20 – 30*
Aladdin teapot .... *40 – 50*
Creamer, cow, 4¹/₂"... *60 – 80*
Creamer, high spout, 5" .... *12 – 15*
Creamer, side handle, 2".. *10 – 15*
Creamer, side handle, 4".. *15 – 20*
Jug, ball... *30 – 40*
Jug, petal, 8¹/₄".. *65 – 80*
Shaker, salt, "S" handle .... *10 – 15*
Shaker, pepper, "P" handle.. *10 – 15*

PADEN CITY POTTERY COMPANY

Paden City, West Virginia

CHAPTER AT A GLANCE

DINNERWARE
BLUE WILLOW
ELITE
HIGHLIGHT
MANHATTAN
NEW VIRGINIA
PAPOCO
REGINA
SALLY PADEN

SHELL CREST
Caliente
SHENANDOAH
VIRGINIA
KITCHENWARE
BAK-SERV
WORLD'S FAIR

Paden began operations in 1914, manufacturing semiporcelain dinnerware. Kitchenware was added in the 1930s. The company closed in 1963.

Paden was one of the potteries that exhibited at the 1938–1939 World's Fair. It manufactured a souvenir salad bowl.

MARKS Paden used a number of backstamps. The first two are pre-1930. The third is one of the best known, a graphic with a kiln. It is usually found in black but was done as a color decal for the World's Fair salad bowl. The Grecian ivory seems to be a little-used glaze stamp.

DINNERWARE

BLUE WILLOW   (1937)

An interesting variation on a theme. Paden took certain pieces from its Elite shape and embossed the Blue Willow design into the body of this short set (only seven different items were made) and glazed it in a deep blue in such a

Patio Shell Crest plate, Blue Willow plate, Morning Glory Shenandoah Ware AD cup/saucer, and Paden Village Shell Crest teapot.

way that the design shows through. "The design is etched into the molds by a new photographic process."

It was available as a breakfast or luncheon set and packed complete in a carton, as follows: six each of the cup, saucer, dinner, salad, and cereal, with one each of the bowl and platter.

Bowl, salad, 9"* . . . . *$12 – $15*
Cup . . . . *4 – 6*
Dish, cereal, lug . . . . *4 – 5*
Plate, 7" . . . . *5 – 6*
Plate, 9" . . . . *10 – 12*
Platter, 10"* . . . . *12 – 15*
Saucer . . . . *2 – 3*

ELITE   (1936)

This shape evolved into the Shell Crest shape (which see). The hollowware had the shell finials and feet, but the flatware was plain round.

Decal decorations include Hollyhock (red, blue, and yellow hollyhocks next to a yellow picket fence), Iris (one large iris), Paden Garden (rows of red, blue, and yellow flowers with green and black leaves in gray pots on pink and black shelves), Sun Ray (flowers and leaves in a red and black cross-stitch), and Wisteria.

Caliente (see special price list following) was first introduced on the Elite shape and was sold by Montgomery Ward, but very little Elite flatware in Caliente colors is found.

PRICING   Prices below are for decal-decorated pieces. See Shell Crest for special Caliente price list.

Bowl, soup, 8" . . . . *$10 – $12*
Cup . . . . *4 – 6*
Creamer . . . . *4 – 6*
Dish, 5⅛" . . . . *2 – 3*
Gravy . . . . *12 – 15*

Plate, 6½" .... *$1 – $2*
Plate, 7⅜" .... *4 – 5*
Plate, 9¼" .... *7 – 9*
Plate, chop, round, 12¾" .... *15 – 20*
Saucer .... *1 – 2*
Shaker, pair .... *8 – 10*
Sugar .... *8 – 10*

HIGHLIGHT (1951–1953)

Designed by Russel Wright. Made for a very short time, there is some question as to whether a listed AD cup/saucer, butter, divided vegetable, jug w/lid, mug, relish, and teapot were ever made.

Several pieces were made in Snow Glass: salad plate, saucer, sugar lid, round vegetable bowl, lid for oval pottery bowl, water pitcher, tumblers in three sizes, and fruit dish. These are extremely rare; it is a seller's market.

Made in six colors: Blueberry, Citron, Green, Nutmeg, Pepper, and White. White was introduced to replace Snow Glass.

MARKS   The mark bears the name of the distributor, Justin Tharaud.

Bowl, vegetable, oval .... *$35 – $40*
Bowl, vegetable, round .... *40 – 45*
   w/pottery lid .... *60 – 70*
Creamer .... *18 – 20*
Cup .... *18 – 20*
Dish, small, all sizes *15*
Plate, B & B. .... *8 – 10*
Plate, salad .... *18 – 20*
Plate, dinner .... *20 – 25*
Plate, chop .... *40 – 50*
Platter, oval .... *35 – 45*
Saucer .... *8 – 10*
Sugar .... *32 – 35*

MANHATTAN   (1933)

As best I can tell, Manhattan uses the Regina hollowware. The change is in the flatware, which is round with a slight scallop.

Bowl, vegetable, oval, 9" .... *$10 – $12*
Casserole .... *20 – 25*
Creamer .... *4 – 6*
Cup .... *4 – 6*
Dish, 5"* .... *2 – 3*
Dish, 6"* .... *3 – 4*
Gravy .... *12 – 15*

Plate, 6"* . . . . *$1 – $2*
Plate, 7"* . . . . *4 – 5*
Plate, 9"* . . . . *7 – 9*
Platter, 12¹/₂" . . . . *12 – 15*
Saucer . . . . *1 – 2*
Sugar . . . . *8 – 10*

NEW VIRGINIA   (1940)

Originally named American, the name was changed to New Virginia within a couple of months. I have no evidence, but this name change could indicate that the Virginia shape, introduced the year before, was discontinued. New Virginia utilized the same thin-rimmed flatware as did Virginia.

Bowl, salad, round . . . . *$15 – $18*
Bowl, vegetable, oval. . . . . *10 – 12*
Bowl, soup, 8"* . . . . *10 – 12*
Casserole . . . . *20 – 25*
Creamer . . . . *4 – 6*
Cup . . . . *4 – 6*
Dish, 5¹/₂"* . . . . *2 – 3*
Gravy. . . . . *12 – 15*
Gravy liner/pickle . . . . *6 – 8*
Plate, 6¹/₄"* . . . . *1 – 2*
Plate, salad. . . . . *4 – 5*
Plate, dinner. . . . . *10 – 12*
Platter, 11"* . . . . *10 – 12*
Platter, 13"* . . . . *12 – 15*
Saucer . . . . *1 – 2*
Shaker, pair . . . . *8 – 10*
Sugar . . . . *8 – 10*
Teapot . . . . *25 – 30*

PAPOCO

A square shape with an embossed rim.

Bowl, vegetable, rectangular, 9" . . . . *$10 – $12*
Casserole. . . . . *20 – 25*
Creamer . . . . *4 – 6*
Cup . . . . *4 – 6*
Dish, 5¹/₂"* . . . . *2 – 3*
Plate, 7" . . . . *4 – 5*
Plate, 8³/₄" . . . . *5 – 6*
Plate, 9³/₄" . . . . *7 – 9*
Platter, rectangular, 13¹/₂" . . . . *12 – 15*

Saucer . . . . *$1 – $2*
Sugar . . . . *8 – 10*

REGINA   (1932)

Square flatware with scalloped corners.
    This is a decal-decorated line, but some pieces in Caliente colors have turned up.

Bowl, salad, 9"* . . . . *$15 – $18*
Bowl, soup, 8" . . . . *10 – 12*
Bowl, vegetable, oval, 9" . . . . *10 – 12*
Casserole . . . . *20 – 25*
Creamer . . . . *4 – 6*
Cup . . . . *4 – 6*
Dish, 5½" . . . . *2 – 3*
Gravy . . . . *12 – 15*
Plate, 7" . . . . *4 – 5*
Plate, 9" . . . . *7 – 9*
Plate, 10" . . . . *10 – 12*
Platter, 11½" . . . . *10 – 12*
Platter, 12½" . . . . *12 – 15*
Platter, 13½" . . . . *15 – 18*
Saucer . . . . *1 – 2*
Sugar . . . . *8 – 10*

SALLY PADEN   (1934)

Periodic squares of embossed crosshatching band the rim and encircle the body. Be careful; this shape is extremely similar to W. S. George's Del Rio shape.

Bowl, salad, 9"* . . . . *$15 – $18*
Bowl, vegetable, oval, 9"* . . . . *10 – 12*
Casserole . . . . *20 – 25*
Creamer . . . . *4 – 6*
Cup . . . . *4 – 6*
Dish, 6" . . . . *3 – 4*
Plate, 6¼"* . . . . *1 – 2*
Plate, 9¼" . . . . *7 – 9*
Platter, oval, 11½" . . . . *10 – 12*

Saucer . . . . *$1 – $2*
Sugar . . . .*8 – 10*

SHELL CREST   (mid 1937)

(Also spelled Shellcrest in some old ads.) The Elite shape had plain, round flat-ware and hollowware with shell-like handles, finials, and feet. In mid 1937, Paden took the Elite hollowware, added flatware with the same shell-like embossing, slightly lug, at opposing edges and called it their Shellcrest shape. The candle holders seem to have been made in Caliente colors only. Although there is no reason they weren't decorated with decals, I haven't seen any.

Decorated in bright solid colors (see Caliente below) and pastel solid colors ("a playmate to Caliente") of Azure, Celadon, Cream, and Rose; shakers are the most easily found pastel pieces.

Decals you will find include Cornflower (a spray of cornflowers), Cottage Shelf (bric-a-brac on shelves), Good Earth (farmer plowing), Nasturtium, Patio (1938; pottery and a single red flower next to a doorway or under an awning), Petit Point (a rose bouquet), Rosetta (a rose amid other flowers), Spinning Wheel (woman at wheel), Studio (pottery and flowers; similar to Patio but with more flowers and no doorway), Thistledown (a spray of thistles), and Village (houses and trees).

MARKS   This backstamp with a variant spelling, which I cannot explain, is the only one I have seen.

Bowl, salad, round, 9" . . . .*$18 – $20*
Bowl, soup . . . .*12 – 15*
Bowl, vegetable, oval, 10" . . . .*12 – 15*
Candle holder . . . .*ND*
Casserole, no feet . . . .*25 – 30*
Casserole, footed . . . .*30 – 35*
Creamer . . . .*6 – 8*
Cup . . . .*6 – 8*
Cup, cream soup . . . .*14 – 16*
Dish, 5¹/₄" . . . .*3 – 4*
Dish, 6¹/₄" . . . .*4 – 5*
Gravy . . . .*15 – 18*
Plate, 6¹/₄" . . . .*2 – 3*
Plate, 7¹/₂" . . . .*5 – 6*
Plate, 8¹/₂" . . . .*6 – 7*
Plate, 9¹/₂" . . . .*8 – 10*
Plate, 10¹/₂" . . . .*12 – 15*

Plate, chop, 12½"	$20 – $25
Platter, oval, 12"	15 – 18
Platter, oval, 14½"	20 – 25
Platter, oval, 16½"	25 – 30
Saucer	2 – 3
Saucer, cream soup	8 – 10
Shaker, pair	12 – 15
Sugar	10 – 15
Teapot	40 – 45

SPECIAL PRICE LIST

Caliente The Caliente line was introduced on the Elite shape in mid 1936. In 1938, half a year after the introduction of Shell Crest, it was brought out on that shape as well as on the Bak-Serv ware. Elite seems to have been phased out at this time, as Elite flatware is not easily found.

The handled casserole seems to be the Rhythm bottom with a restyled lid. The lug casserole has lug handles on both the bottom and the lid, which can be used as a pie baker. Odd pieces from other shapes will turn up in Caliente colors.

Solid colors: Tangerine Red, Turquoise Green, Sapphire Blue, and Lemon Yellow.

Caliente
MADE IN U S A

BAK-SERV There is a fourth size of mixing bowl.

Bowl, mixing, 7½"	$12 – $15
Bowl, mixing, 8¼"	15 – 18
Bowl, mixing, 9⅛"	18 – 20
Bowl, salad, 10"	20 – 25
Carafe	35 – 40
Casserole, curl finial, 1½-quart, 8"	30 – 35
Casserole, lug, 1½-quart, 7"	30 – 35
Casserole, w/handle	30 – 35
Jug, ball	25 – 30
Under tray, w/handles	20 – 25

ELITE

Bowl, soup, 7"	$15 – $18
Plate, 6¼"	3 – 4
Plate, 7⅛"	5 – 7
Plate, 9"	10 – 12
Plate, 9¾"	12 – 15

NEW VIRGINIA

Teapot, 6-cup	$40 – $50

SHELL CREST The standard Shell Crest casserole was made in a version with no feet, in the usual solid colors and in two mixed-color versions: red with yellow lid and blue with yellow lid.

Bowl, soup	*$15 – $18*
Bowl, vegetable, oval, 10"	*15 – 18*
Candle holders, pair	*25 – 30*
Casserole, footed	*30 – 35*
Casserole, no feet	*30 – 35*
Creamer	*6 – 8*
Cup	*6 – 8*
Cup, cream soup	*18 – 22*
Dish, 5¹/₄"	*4 – 5*
Gravy	*18 – 20*
Gravy liner/pickle	*8 – 10*
Plate, 6¹/₂"	*3 – 4*
Plate, 7¹/₂"	*5 – 7*
Plate, 9¹/₂"	*8 – 10*
Plate, 10¹/₂"	*12 – 15*
Platter, 14¹/₄"	*25 – 30*
Saucer	*2 – 3*
Saucer, cream soup	*8 – 10*
Shaker, pair	*10 – 12*
Sugar	*10 – 15*
Teapot	*50 – 60*

SHENANDOAH   (1944)

As best I can tell, the New Virginia flatware and shakers were used with this shape.

The most frequently found decorations are underglaze decals that are intended to resemble hand painting. Novice collectors sometimes mistake these for Blue Ridge. Seven of these are known: Cosmos, Jonquil, Miniver Rose, Morning Glory, Nasturtium, Poppy, and Strawberry. Regular overglaze decals will also be found.

MARKS Sometimes the pattern name will be present.

Casserole, lug, 9¹/₂"	*$20 – $25*
Creamer	*4 – 6*
Cup	*4 – 6*
Cup, AD	*10 – 12*
Gravy	*12 – 15*

Gravy liner, 9" .... *$6 – $8*
Plate, 6¼" .... *1 – 2*
Plate, 9" .... *7 – 9*
Platter, oval, 13½" .... *12 – 15*
Platter, oval, 16" .... *20 – 25*
Saucer .... *1 – 2*
Saucer, AD .... *3 – 5*
Shaker, pair .... *8 – 10*
Sugar .... *8 – 10*
Teapot .... *30 – 35*

VIRGINIA   (1939)

Originally named Bilmer, the name was changed to Virginia within a couple of
months. The flatware has a very thin rim, almost reminiscent of Laughlin's
Epicure. See New Virginia.

Solid pastel colors (called Anita Glazes) of Powder Blue, Celadon Green,
Dusty Rose, and Straw Yellow. These seem to be the same pastel glazes found
on Shell Crest.

Bowl, soup, lug .... *$8 – $10*
Casserole .... *20 – 25*
Creamer .... *4 – 6*
Cup .... *4 – 6*
Dish, 5¹/"* .... *2 – 3*
Plate, 6¼"* .... *1 – 2*
Plate, 9"* .... *7 – 9*
Platter, 11"* .... *10 – 12*
Saucer .... *1 – 2*
Sugar .... *8 – 10*

KITCHENWARE

BAK-SERV   (1931)

Distributed exclusively by the Great Northern Products Company of Chicago.
Not much of this kitchenware line is found, and there doesn't seem to be any
overall shape similarity; rather it seems to be an amalgam of different items. I've
seen mixing bowls in two different shapes, and there might be additional ones.

There is a fourth size of mixing bowl, and there should be at least one other
size of leftover. The lug casserole has lug handles on both the bottom and the
lid, which can be used as a pie baker.

PADEN BAKSERV

OVEN PROOF
BAK-SERV

P. C. P. CO.
MADE IN U.S.A.

BAK-SERV
GUARANTEED
OVEN-PROOF
P. C. P. Co.

Bak-Serv: Coffee pot (two styles) and Rose Marie (shape name) teapot. The coffee pot on the right is slightly larger with a thicker handle, but the big difference, which I couldn't pick up in this photo, is a slightly impressed geometric pattern on the body.

Bak-Serv: Patio ball jug, Spinning Wheel carafe and Dresden (Nove Rose variation) jug.

Bak-Serv: Footed fruit bowl.

Bak-Serv is a decal-decorated line. Solid Caliente colors were added in 1938 (see page 525). Besides the decal decorations, the Rose Marie teapot (1930) was decorated in marbleized iridescent colors of green or yellow.

Bowl, fruit, footed, 10"	*$20 – $25*
Bowl, lipped, 6"	*8 – 10*
Bowl, mixing, 5"	*6 – 8*
Bowl, mixing, 6"	*8 – 10*
Bowl, mixing, 7"	*10 – 12*
Bowl (Sally Paden), 8"	*10 – 12*
Carafe, ceramic lid, wooden handle	*25 – 30*
Casserole, curl finial, 1½-quart, 8"	*20 – 25*
Casserole, curl finial, ribbed bottom, 1½-quart, 8"	*20 – 25*
Casserole, ribbed bottom, sunken knob, 8¼"	*20 – 25*
Casserole underplate, square (Regina)	*5 – 6*
Coffee pot	*30 – 35*
Custard	*4 – 6*
Jug, ball	*15 – 20*
Jug, footed	*15 – 20*
Leftover, 3½"	*6 – 10*
Leftover, 5¼"	*10 – 12*
Pie baker, 9"	*10 – 12*
Pie baker, 10"	*10 – 12*
Teapot, "Rose Marie"	*25 – 30*
Iridescent green/yellow	*30 – 35*

WORLD'S FAIR

Salad Bowl, 10"	*$100 – $125*

PARKCRAFT

Burlington, Iowa

CHAPTER AT A GLANCE

DAYS OF THE WEEK   MONTHS OF THE YEAR
FAMOUS CITIES   NURSERY RHYMES
FAMOUS PEOPLE   STATES

Parkcraft was a distribution company that contracted out its manufacturing. It sold to the retail trade through its Heather House News mail-order catalog and to wholesalers through a company called Flint Hills Specialty Co. It had items manufactured either in the U.S. or abroad. Most of the shakers have pottery bodies. It is most collected for its series of shakers.

See Carey in Bibliography and see Clubs/Newsletters.

DAYS OF THE WEEK   Made in Japan.

PRICING $50 to $60 per set. Complete set: $375.

Monday (Wash Day)	Cake of soap / Washtub
Tuesday (Ironing Day)	Iron / Basket of laundry
Wednesday (Mending Day)	Sewing basket / Spool of thread
Thursday (Visiting Day)	Front door / Lady in good clothes
Friday (Cleaning Day)	Dust pan / Feather duster .
Saturday (Baking Day)	Loaf of bread / Two slices of bread on plate
Sunday (Church Day)	Holy Bible / Pipe organ

FAMOUS CITIES

In this series of eighteen sets, the salt shaker is a book open flat, with the name of the city, its nickname, and a drawing on each page of either famous buildings or places in the city or products it's known for. The theme-related peppers are listed below.

PRICING $30 to $35 per set.

CITIES ABROAD

Agra, India	Taj Mahal
Amsterdam, Holland	Wooden shoe
Cairo, Egypt	Pyramid
Capetown, So. Africa	Diamond
Havana, Cuba	Cigar w/wrapper

Killarney, Ireland	Shamrock
London, England	Crown
Paris, France	Eiffel Tower
Rio de Janeiro, Brazil	Sack of sugar, "Produzido no Brazil"
Tokyo, Japan	Pagoda
Toronto, Canada	Maple leaf
Venice, Italy	Gondola

CITIES IN THE UNITED STATES

Chicago, IL	Wrigley Building
Hannibal, MO	Figure of Tom Sawyer
Honolulu, HA	Ukelele
Philadelphia, PA	Liberty Bell
Springfield, IL	Bust of Abe Lincoln
Washington, DC	Washington Monument

FAMOUS PEOPLE

In this series of seven sets, the salt shaker is an open scroll with the person's name, accomplishment, dates of birth and death. The pepper shaker is a bust of the person.

PRICING $30 to $35 per set.

Buffalo Bill
Christopher Columbus
Benjamin Franklin
Charles Lindbergh
Will Rogers
Betsy Ross
George Washington

MONTHS OF THE YEAR

In this series, the salt shaker is a tall column with the name of the month, the flower and birthstone of the month, the astrological sign and its name, and two illustrations typical of the month. Each salt is decorated in one of four colors representing the seasons: spring, green; summer, yellow; fall, russet; and winter, blue. The theme-related peppers are listed below.

PRICING $30 to $35 per set.

January	Snowman w/broom
February	Red heart
March	Irish clay pipe w/metal shamrock
April	Blue Easter egg
May	Flower basket
June	Three-tiered wedding cake
July	Firecracker with string wick
August	Bathing beauty
September	Schoolbooks tied with a belt
October	Jack-o'-lantern
November	Pilgrim's hat
December	Christmas present (gift box)

NURSERY RHYMES   (Also called Mother Goose) (1962)

These are bone china miniatures that were made in Japan.

PRICING $85 to $100 per set.

Cat and Fiddle	Cow Jumping Over Moon
Humpty Dumpty on a wall	Humpty Dumpty fallen
Jack at well	Jill w/bucket
Little Bo Peep	Sheep
Little Boy Blue w/horn	Cow
Little Jack Horner	Pumpkin pie w/cherry on top
Little Miss Muffet	Tuffet
Little Red Riding Hood w/basket	Wolf in disguise
Mary Had a Little Lamb	Lamb w/red bow
Old King Cole w/pipe and bowl	Fiddlers Three
Old Woman Who Lived in a Shoe	Shoe House
Peter, Peter, Pumpkin Eater	Pumpkin w/girl's face

STATES

The salt shakers are in the shape of the state (though not to scale), with the name of the state in raised letters, and major lakes and rivers painted in blue. The peppers are theme related.

This series was made in two different sets. The first set was introduced in 1957. As Alaska and Hawaii were admitted into the Union in 1959, they are missing from this set. For reasons of economy, a number of matching pieces were repeated; for example, there are two states with a lump of coal, two with bathing beauties, oil rigs, and sheaves of wheat. There are three with light-houses and ears of corn and four (!) with cotton bolls.

The second set was introduced in 1968. All fifty states are represented, and there are no repeats in the matching pieces.

Original production was done at the Taneycomo Ceramic Company in Hollister, Missouri. On these sets, the embossing of the state name is sharp, and the blue is dark. Bottoms are flat, with remnants of the Scotch tape used in place of corks sometimes found; they are most often marked Parkcraft, although sometimes the original mark may have been light or may have been obliterated.

Some time after the second set was brought out, Taneycomo ownership changed; these sets can be identified by embossing that is not as sharp and a lighter blue. These generally do not have a Parkcraft mark, and there is a slight sheen to the bisque bottoms.

Ownership changed again, but quality got even poorer, sales fell off, and the line was discontinued.

NOTE   In the list below, two matching pieces are listed if there was a change from the first to the second set. Some, as you can see, remained the same.

PRICING $30 to $35 per set.

Alaska	Igloo
Alabama	Cotton boll / Slice of watermelon
Arizona	Cactus
Arkansas	Razorback hog
California	Bathing beauty / Orange
Colorado	Pack mule

Connecticut	Graduation cap (mortar board), "Yale"
Delaware	Lighthouse
Florida	Bathing beauty / Fish
Georgia	Rebel hat
Hawaii	Hawaiian girl
Idaho	Potato
Illinois	Ear of corn / Bust of Abe Lincoln
Indiana	Racing car and driver
Iowa	Ear of corn
Kansas	Sheaf of wheat
Kentucky	Whiskey jug
Louisiana	Cotton boll / Sack of sugar
Maine	Lighthouse / Pine tree
Maryland	Oyster
Massachusetts	Bean pot, "Beans"
Michigan	Automobile
Minnesota	Canoe
Mississippi	Cotton boll / Steamboat
Missouri	Mule
Montana	Gun
Nebraska	Ear of corn / Cowboy boots
Nevada	Card, Ace of Spades
New Hampshire	Snowman
New Jersey	Miss America
New Mexico	Pueblo
New York	Statue of Liberty
No. Carolina	Pack of cigarettes
No. Dakota	Sheaf of wheat / Oil rig
Ohio	Rubber tire
Oklahoma	Oil rig / Bust of Native American
Oregon	Duck
Pennsylvania	Lump of coal / Liberty Bell
Rhode Island	Rooster, Rhode Island Red

Ohio salt shaker and rubber tire pepper shaker.

So. Carolina	Lighthouse / Cotton boll
So. Dakota	Pheasant
Tennessee	Cotton boll / Horse head
Texas	Oil rig / Cowboy hat
Utah	Covered wagon
Vermont	Maple syrup bucket, "Vermont Maple Syrup"
Virginia	Ham
Washington	Apple
West Virginia	Lump of coal
Wisconsin	Wedge of Swiss cheese
Wyoming	Bucking bronco

PENNSBURY POTTERY

Morrisville, Pennsylvania

CHAPTER AT A GLANCE

BIRDS
DINNERWARE / KITCHENWARE
MISCELLANY

PLAQUES, TILES, AND TRAYS
RAILROAD AND SHIP ITEMS

The Pennsbury Pottery was founded in 1950 by Henry Below (rhymes with Jell-O). He had been the general manager at Stangl Pottery, Trenton, New Jersey, which explains some of the similarity in ware, especially the carved, hand-painted designs. Below died in 1959, and his wife, Lee, carried on the business. She died in 1968 and the eldest son, Ernst, continued the business until 1970, when the pottery went into bankruptcy. A fire in 1971 destroyed the entire structure.

Pennsbury can usually be distinguished by its light tan to brown background and by the carved and hand-painted decorations, similar to those done at the Stangl Pottery. An exception are two blue and white patterns. Blue Dowry (same pattern as Folkart) and Toleware (fruit and leaves).

See Henske in Bibliography.

MARKS "Pennsbury Pottery" or "Pennsbury Pottery, Morrisville, Pa" will be found, either hand painted, hand incised, or impressed in the mold, on most pieces. "Anna" will be found on some pieces. This is not an artist's signature but a local way of abbreviating Pennsylvania.

BIRDS

Several of these birds have both left- and right-facing versions. The earlier birds have the hand-painted mark; later birds, of lesser quality (not as elaborately decorated), have the incised mark. Some mold variations will be found. All-white or all-ivory birds are rare.

Audubon's Warbler, 4" /122 .... *$200 – $225*
Barn Swallow, 6¼" /123 .... *250 – 275*
Bird of Paradise, 10" /121 .... *ND*
Blue Bird, 4" /103
    Pink Chest/White chest .... *150 – 175*
Blue Jay, 10½" /108
    w/o leaf .... *400 – 450*
    w/ leaf .... *450 – 500*
Cardinal, left/right, 6½" /120 .... *200 – 225*
Chickadee, 3½" /111 .... *150*

Crested Chickadee, left/right, 4"   /101 . . . . *$150 – $175*
Duckling, sitting/standing, 6½" . . . . *ND*
Eagle, 6½"   /215 . . . . : . . . . *ND*
Gnat Catcher (two versions), 6½"   /107 . . . . *225 – 250*
Gold Finch, left/right, 4"   /102 . . . . *150*
Hawk. . . . . *ND*
Hen, 10½"   /P201
   Delft blue *200*
   Multicolor *250*
   Pink w/brown *200*
   Tan w/brown *200*
   White . . . . : *200*
   White w/cobalt. *200*
   White w/dark brown. *200*
   White w/green *200*
   White w/light brown *200*
   White w/red comb. *225*
   Yellow w/brown *200*
Hummingbird, 3½"   /119. . . . . *225 – 250*
Hummingbird, double. *350*
Magnolia Warbler, left/right   /112 . . . . *175 – 200*
Nut Hatch, left/right 3½"   /110. . . . . *125 – 150*
Quail . . . . *ND*
Red Start, 3"   /113 . . . . *175 – 200*
Ring-necked Pheasant . . . . *600 +*
Rooster, 11½"   /P202
   Delft blue *200*
   Multicolor *250*
   Pink w/brown *200*
   Tan w/brown *200*
   White *200*
   White w/cobalt. *200*
   White w/dark brown. *200*
   White w/green *200*
   White w/light brown *200*
   White w/red comb. *225*
   Yellow w/brown *200*
Scarlet Tanager, early/late, 5½"   /105. . . . . *250 – 275*
Western Tanager, left/right, 5½"   /104 . . . . *250 – 275*
Wood Duck, 10"   /114 . . . . *600*
Wren, two versions, 3"   /109
   Brown. . . . . *100 – 125*
   w/detail. . . . . *125 – 150*
Wren (Marsh), 6½"   /106 . . . . *225 – 250*

DINNERWARE / KITCHENWARE

The cheese-and-cracker (also called chip-and-dip) is the 5" compote on the 11"
plate. The cylinder casseroles are straight-sided; the small casserole is shaped
like a powder box and is considered as such by some collectors.

Major patterns: Black Rooster, Folkart, Hex, Pennsylvania Hex, and Red Rooster. Hex has small hearts between the teardrop-like design elements; Pennsylvania Hex does not.

PRICING　Prices below are for Red Rooster.

Dinnerware

Bowl, cereal　/1169 . . . . $20 – $25
Bowl, deep soup　/1193 . . . . 25 – 30
Bowl, pretzel, 12" × 8"　/1077 35
Bowl, round, 9"　/1192 . . . . 30 – 35
Bowl, round, 11"　/1310 . . . . 40 – 45
Bowl, vegetable, divided　/1049 . . . . 45 – 50
Butter dish, square　/1234 45
Cake stand, 11"　/1030 . . . . 65 – 75
Candle holder, Rooster/Hen figural, pair　/131 . . . . 75 – 80
Cheese-and-cracker (Chip-and-Dip)　/1031 75
Coffee pot, 2-cup　/1145 75
Coffee pot, 6-cup　/1113 85
Creamer　/1076 20
Creamer, small　/1222S 20
Cruet, jug shape, Amish or Rooster stopper, pair　/1236 . . . . 85 – 95
Cup　/1164 . . . . 15 – 26
Eggcup　/1224 25
Jug, miniature　/1115 . . . . 15 – 18
Jug, ½-pint　/1116 . . . . 20 – 25
Jug, 1-pint　/1118 . . . . 25 – 30
Jug, 1-quart　/1119 . . . . 65 – 70
Jug, 2-quart　/1120 . . . . 80 – 90
Jug, 3-quart　/1121 . . . . 100 – 125
Mug, coffee　/1167 25
Pepper mill, black metal top and base w/handle . . . . ND
Plate, 8"　/1068 . . . . 25 – 30
Plate, 10" . . . . 25 – 30

Rooster: Plate.

Plate, 11" /1029 .... *$30 – $35*
Platter, oval, 8" × 11" /1200 .... *30 – 35*
Platter, oval, 11" × 14" /1277 .... *40 – 45*
Relish Tree, 5-part, triangular, 11¹/²" × 14¹/²" /1289 .... *65*
Salt mill, black metal top and base .... *ND*
Saucer /1164 .... *6 – 8*
Shaker, Amish, pair /1237–8 .... *40*
Shaker, pitcher shape, pair /1114 .... *25 – 30*
Snack set (cup and saucer) /1165 .... *20 – 25*
Sugar /1076 .... *20 – 25*
Sugar, small /1222S .... *20 – 25*
Teapot, 4-cup /1153 .... *50 – 60*
Tray, 7¹/²" × 5" *25*
Tray, round, 14/15" .... *ND*
Tumbler, 3³/₄" .... *30 – 35*
Tureen w/ladle /1163 .... *85*
      w/metal stand .... *125 – 150*

Kitchenware

The canisters have rooster finials.

Canister, coffee, 8" /1293 .... *$100*
Canister, flour, 9" /1294 .... *125*
Canister, sugar, 9" /1295 .... *125*
Canister, tea, 8" /1292 .... *100*
Cookie jar, 8" /1226 .... *125 – 150*
Pie baker, individual, crimped, 6¹/²" .... *ND*
Pie baker, 9" .... *75 – 80*
Spice jar, square, 3³/₄" .... *40 – 45*

MISCELLANY

Ashtray, 3 rests, 5" /1300
      Amish couple .... *$15 – $20*
      Advertising .... *15 – 20*
Cigarette box, 5" × 4" /1004 .... *45 – 50*
Desk basket, 5" /2013
      Rooster .... *45 – 50*
      Rotary .... *25 – 30*
Mug, beer
      Amish scenes *50*
      Barbershop/Eagle *25*
Plate, bread, round, 8" /1280 .... *35*
Plate, bread, rectangular, 9" × 6" /1279 .... *45*
Slick-Bunny *65*
Slick-Chick, blue *65*
      Brown .... *25 – 35*
      Yellow .... *25 – 35*

Wall pocket, square, 6¹/₂"
    Easy-to-find decorations . . . . *$70 – $80*
    Hard-to-find decorations . . . . *85 – 95*

PLAQUES, TILES, AND TRAYS

The plaques and tiles are the same shape except that the plaques have a hole going through the piece so that it can be hung from a wall; the tiles do not.

A great variety of decorations, especially sayings, will be found on these pieces. Some of theses are pieces made as commemoratives, advertising items, or public relations giveaways. Plaques with dinnerware patterns are listed as trays in the dinnerware section.

Ashtray, octagonal, 5" × 3" . . . . *$15 – $20*
Ashtray, round, 5"
    Doylestown National Bank . . . . *15 – 20*
    Solebury National Bank. . . . . *15 – 20*
    Summerseat, 1804–1954 . . . . *15 – 20*
Ashtray, round, 8"
    Pennsbury Inn . . . . *25 – 30*
Ashtray, 8¹/₂" × 5¹/₄"
    Laurel Ridge. . . . . *45 – 50*
Coaster, 5"
    Doylestown Trust Company . . . . *20 – 25*
Desk basket
    National Exchange Club . . . . *35 – 40*
Rectangular, 7¹/₂" × 5¹/₂"
    Red/Black Rooster . . . . *40 – 50*
    Commemorative. . . . . *40 – 50*
Round, crimped edge, 4"   /1186
    Black/Red Rooster . . . . *35 – 40*
    Sayings (easy to find) . . . . *25 – 30*
    Sayings (hard to find) . . . . *35 – 40*
Plaque, round, 5"
    Groundhog Lodge #9 . . . . *35 – 40*
    Washington Crossing. . . . . *15 – 20*
Plaque, round, 6"   /1055
    Pennsylvania Dutch scenes . . . . *40 – 50*
    Skunk. . . . . *60 – 70*
    Two men drinking . . . . *60 – 70*
Plaque, round, 8"
    Greater Lower Bucks County Week . . . . *25 – 30*
Plate, 8"
    Bristol, PA 1966 . . . . *40 – 50*
    Fidelity-Mutual. . . . . *25 – 30*
    Rotary International Golden Anniversary . . . . *25 – 30*
Tile, square, 6"   /1288. . . . . *30 – 35*
Tray, 7¹/₄" × 5¹/₄"
    Iron Horse Ramble. . . . . *35 – 40*
    National Education Association . . . . *25 – 30*

RAILROAD AND SHIP ITEMS

The ashtrays are sometimes referred to as plaques. These pieces have the embossed design molded in the item.

Railroad

Ashtray, 7½" × 5½"   /2103
   C. P. Huntington   /Central Pacific RR .... *$55 – $60*
   Cambelback   /Reading RR .... *55 – 60*
   General   /Western & Atlantic RR .... *55 – 60*
   John Bull   /Camden & Amboy RR .... *55 – 60*
   Lafayette   /Baltimore & Ohio RR .... *55 – 60*
   999   /New York Central & Hudson RR .... *60 – 65*
   Star   /Central RR of NJ .... *55 – 60*
   Stourbridge Lion   /Delaware & Hudson RR......................... *50 – 55*
   Tiger   /Pennsylvania RR. .... *55 – 60*
Desk basket, Lafayette .... *60 – 70*

Ship

Ashtray, 7½" × 5½"   /2103
   Barkentine 1880 .... *$85 – $95*
   Dreadnought.. *85 – 95*
   Schooner .... *85 – 95*
Ashtray, 9½" × 7"   /2113
   Flying Cloud .... *90 – 100*
   Lightning... *90 – 100*
   Raleigh... *90 – 100*
Ashtray, 11" × 8"   /2114
   Charles W. Morgan .... *100 – 110*
   Constitution .... *100 – 110*
Ashtray, 13½" × 10¼"   /2115
   Flying Cloud .... *110 – 125*
   River Steamboat.. *125 – 150*

PFALTZGRAFF POTTERY COMPANY

York, Pennsylvania

CHAPTER AT A GLANCE

DINNERWARE   CERAMEX
COUNTRY-TIME   MISCELLANY
GOURMET   **NOVELTIES**
YORKTOWNE   COOKIE JARS
KITCHENWARE   MUGGSY

Pfaltzgraff, the oldest family-owned pottery in continuous operation in America, is believed to have begun in 1811 for the manufacture of redware. A number of different potteries in various locations were operated by family members. The name changed to the Pfaltzgraff Pottery Company in 1896. Art pottery was manufactured from 1931 to 1937. Kitchenware was introduced in the 30s. The pottery is still in operation today producing both earthenware and china.

MARKS The Keystone and the Castle marks are the most commonly found. They are usually engraved but can be stamped as well.

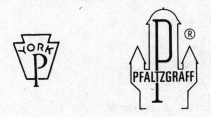

DINNERWARE

COUNTRY-TIME   (ca. 1952)

Designed by Ben Seibel. Advertised as "America's most complete line of serving accessories . . . complete with place settings."

Platters could be hung from the wall. Metal stands, with ceramic warmers, were available in copper, nickel, or brass plating for the butter warmer, tureen, coffee pot, coffee samovar, gravy boat, and 2-quart and 3-part casserole.

Cups were made with both closed handles (same shape as Roseville's Raymor) and open handles. Platters had cutouts in the handles so they could be hung from the wall.

Pieces were made in solid colors of Aztec Blue or Teal Blue, or underglaze decorated with either a Sunburst or Fruit/Leaf design as follows: blue design with Saffron Yellow or Smoke Gray glaze, and brown design with white glaze.

Bowl, salad, individual, 6"   /135 . . . . *$10 – $12*
Bowl, salad, 10½"   /134 . . . . *25 – 30*
Butter warmer   /101 . . . . *35 – 45*
Casserole, individual, 12-ounce   /162 . . . . *30 – 35*
Casserole, 2-quart   /165 . . . . *40 – 45*
Casserole, divided, w/2 lids   /185 . . . . *85 – 95*
Casserole, 3-part, rectangular w/three lids, 21" × 6½"   /190 . . . . *90 – 100*
Coffee pot, 10-cup   /187. . . . . *50 – 55*
Coffee samovar, 28 cups   /197 . . . . *75 – 85*
Creamer   /157 . . . . *10 – 12*
Cruet, oil   /132 . . . . *25 – 30*
Cruet, vinegar   /132 . . . . *25 – 30*
Cup, both styles   /180. . . . . *7 – 9*
Gravy, stick handle   /102 . . . . *30 – 35*
Jug, 2-quart   /186 . . . . *30 – 35*
Meat board and platter   /126 . . . . *30 – 35*
Plate, 8½"   /177 . . . . *8 – 10*
Plate, 10"   /199. . . . . *12 – 15*
Plate, Bar-B-Q (divided), 11¼". . . . . *15 – 18*
Platter, 11"   /128 . . . . *15 – 18*
Platter, 12"   /129 . . . . *18 – 20*
Platter, 13"   /130 . . . . *20 – 25*
Saucer   /189 . . . . *3 – 5*
Shaker, pair   /117   /118 . . . . *25 – 30*
Sugar   /156. . . . . *12 – 15*
Tray, Relish & Cheese, 16" × 6½"   /114. . . . . *30 – 35*
Tureen, 6-quart   /167 . . . . *65 – 75*
Utensil, fork, wood handle   /134 . . . . *25 – 30*
Utensil, spoon, wood handle   /135 . . . . *25 – 30*

GOURMET (1950)

The original Gourmet line, **Gourmet Oven Ware**, also called **Provincial Gourmet**, made up of various baking and serving pieces (casseroles, shirred eggs, and stewpots) was brought out in 1940. It was unglazed on the outside with French Brown glaze on the inside and on the lids.

In 1948 the Gourmet line was expanded to include: **Gourmet Copenhagen** (Copenhagen Stone Blue and Danish Stone, a light color; most pieces were blue, some the lighter color, lidded pieces had blue lids and light bottoms), **Gourmet a la Francaise** (Algerian Charcoal Brown and Tangier Tan; most pieces were brown, a few tan, lidded pieces had brown lids and tan bottoms) and **Gourmet Snowflake** (blue snowflakes on a light body).

The Brown Drip version, introduced in 1950, was originally marketed as "Gourmet Royale." Eventually it was called **Gourmet**. Glazed in "rich brown (Albany slip) with glacial white drip."

A wide variety of **ashtrays** were available; I have listed a few. Some of these could be personalized with a bronze initial. A few came with gold-plated lighters. The **bean pots** may have been redesigned as alternate company listings show 2½-quart , 3½-quart, and 5-quart sizes. The individual **casserole** was intended to sit on the 7" plate. Both the **gravy faststand** and **stick handle gravy** have a "fat" and a "lean" spout.

The **lazy susans** are on wooden revolving bases. The **pie baker** came with a recipe label. A **punch set** was made from the straight-side salad bowl with the addition of punch cups and the large ladle. The **shirred egg** could also be used for candy and nuts. The **tureens** were the bean pots with notched lids and ladles. The small sat on the 10" plate, and the large on a 12" plate that some collectors refer to as a chop plate, though it was only intended as an underplate for the tureen.

SETS All stands had walnut legs with brass fittings. Double Casserole: two 2-quart casseroles on warmer stand. Triple Casserole: three 1-quart casseroles on stand. Salad Master: Straight-side salad bowl, two cruets, two shakers, wooden servers on stand.

Chip & Dip, two piece w/stand /0306 .... *$22*
Coffee pot, 10-cup /0303 .... *35*
Coffee samovar, 20-cup /312 .... *75+*
Condiment *21*
Creamer /382 .... *7*
Cruet, oil/vinegar, handled w/cork stopper /315 .... *13*
Cruet, Casino, ceramic lid /7231 .... *17*
Cup /80R *2*
Cup, punch .... *ND*
Dish, 4½" /936R *5*
Gravy, double spout, stick handle *22*
   Loop handle *18*
Gravy saucer *6*
Jug, 6-ounce /381* *12*
Jug, 10-ounce /382* *14*
Jug, 14-ounce /383 .... *24*
Jug, 32-ounce /384* *32*
Jug, 48-ounce /385 .... *36*
Jug, 60-ounce, ice lip /386* *42*
Lazy Susan, one piece, 5-part , 11" /220 .... *28*
Lazy Susan, 3 dishes and center bowl, 14" /308 .... *32*
Lazy Susan, 3 dishes and center bowl, 16" /309 .... *45*
Lazy Susan, 4 dishes and 2-quart casserole /313 .... *65*
Mug, 12-ounce /391 .... *6*
Mug, beer, 16-ounce /392 .... *8*
Pie baker, 9½" /7016 .... *18*
   w/box *28*
Plate, 7" /85R *4*
Plate, 10" /88R *6*
Plate, barbecue, 3-part, 11" /87 .... *18*
Plate, steak, 12" *18*
Platter, 14" /320 .... *24*
Platter, 16" /337 .... *29*
Rarebit, oval, lug, 8" *8*
Rarebit, oval, lug, 9½" /328 .... *12*
Rarebit, oval, lug, 11" /330 .... *17*
Roaster, oval, 14" /325 .... *33*
Roaster, oval, 16" /326 .... *38*
   w/warmer stand *53*
Saucer /89R *3*
Server, 3-part, center handle (Jam & Relish) /350 .... *27*
Shaker, 4½" high, pair /317 /318 .... *19*
Shaker, Liberty Bell, pair *35*
Shaker, Owl, pair *35*
Shirred egg dish, 6" /360 .... *12*
Souffle dish, 5-ounce, petite *8*
Souffle dish, 1-quart, 8" /398 .... *11*
Souffle dish, 2-quart *18*
Sugar /381 .... *11*
Teapot, 6-cup /0381 .... *18*

w/warmer stand	$28
Tile, round, 9" /7281	18
on wrought iron stand	28
Tray, cheese & relish, w/carving board, 16" /314	35 +
Tray, sandwich, lug, w/cup ring, 11"	16
Tray, serving, 4-part, center handle, 15" long	20
Tray, 2-tier	18
Tureen, 2½-quart /310	35
Ladle, small	15
Tureen, 5-quart /393	45
Ladle, large	18
Plate, 12"	8

Other

Ashtray, Palette, 11" /AT33	$12
Ashtray, Palette w/lighter, 112" /SS4	18
Ashtray, round, 4"	12
Ashtray, round, w/lighter, 9"	18
Ashtray, Shell, 7" /7943	10
Ashtray, Skillet, 9" /AT32	15
Candle holder, finger ring, 6" /333	18
Planter, Donkey, 10" high /P666	18
Planter, Elephant	30 +
Planter, Jug, 3 pockets, 8½" /P100	12

YORKTOWNE   (1967)

Designed by Maury Mountain. "A collection of authentic nineteenth-century reproductions." Still in production, this is one of the best-selling U.S. oven-to-table lines of all time.

The **au gratin** is also called a rarebit. The oval **bakers** were also called roasters. The wooden **cheeseboards** all have molded sections to hold crackers. A **ewer and basin** set consisted of the 8" pitcher and 12" bowl. The **measurers** came in two styles. The early style had the measurement stamped in the bowl; the later style had the measurement embossed in the bowl. A **punch set** consisted of the dough bowl, twelve punch cups (handles broke easily), and the ladle.

The blue flower decorations on a gray-blue matte glaze background is based on Pfaltzgraff's nineteenth-century salt-glazed stoneware. There are two basic decorations. The early one was a Pennsylvania Dutch–type tulip. The second and current one is two blossoms arching out of several leaves. Depending on the size of the piece, there might be only one blossom or just the leaves. Certain pieces have special decorations of their own.

NOTE   Items marked with a "/C" in the list below are in the current (Fall '94) catalog and are priced accordingly. Items which have been discontinued are sometimes reissued for a short run. You can obtain a catalog by calling 1-800-999-2811.

PRICING   Some collectors have very definite preferences for either the early or current decoration, but this has not affected values.

Ashtray /611	$15
Au gratin, 8" /260	15

Au gratin, 9½" /265 /C *$13.50*
Au gratin, 11" /270 .... *19*
Baker, oval, 7" /240 .... *15*
Baker, oval, 1-quart, 9½" /241 /C *14.50*
Baker, oval, 14" /247 .... *35*
Baker, rectangular, 2-quart /236 /C *29*
Baker, square, 8" /237 .... *35*
Bean pot, old, 2½-quart /070 .... *35*
Bean pot, new, 2½-quart /072 .... *35*
Bell ornament /365 .... *12*
Bowl, batter, handle & spout, 2½-quart /464 .... *35*
Bowl, dough/punch, 8-quart /462 .... *65*
Bowl, mixing, 1-pint, 6" /456 /C *8.50*
Bowl, mixing, 1½-quart, 8" /458 /C *13*
Bowl, mixing, 3-quart, 10" /460 /C *21.50*
Bowl, salad /220 .... *28*
Bowl, salad /224 .... *28*
Bowl, serving, 7" /010 /C *12.50*
Bowl, soup, rim, 8½" /012 /C *10*
Bowl, vegetable, 9" /011 /C *17*
Bread tray /528 .... *25*
Butter, ¼-pound /028 /C *17*
Butter tub, "Butter," 8-ounce /065 .... *20*
Cake stand, pedestal /530 .... *28*
Candle holder, 3" /568 .... *18*
Candle holder, 5¼" /574 .... *15*
Candle snuffer /582 .... *15*
Candlestick, finger ring, pair, 3½" /564 /C *16*
    [Canisters below are straight-sided]
Canister, "Tea," 4¾" /509 /C *11.25*
Canister, "Coffee," 5¼" /508 /C *16.50*
Canister, "Sugar," 6" /507 /C *21.25*
Canister, "Flour," 7" /506 /C *26*
    [Canisters below are straight-sided w/lug handles]
Canister, "Tea," 5" high *15*
Canister, "Coffee," 6" high *20*
Canister, "Sugar," 7" high *25*
Canister, "Flour," 8" high *30*
    [Canisters below are beehive shape]
Canister, "Tea" *20*
Canister, "Coffee" *25*
Canister, "Sugar" *30*
Canister, "Flour" *35*
Casserole, individual, 12-ounce /305 .... *20*
Casserole, 2-quart /315 /C *36*
Casserole, 3½-quart /325 .... *45*
Cheese & Cracker w/dome, oval /702 .... *30*
Cheese crock (used for 977) /920 .... *8*
Cheese keeper w/dome, round /970 .... *20*
Cheese plate, round /971 .... *10*

Cheeseboard, wood, rectangular w/two crocks   /977 .... $25
Cheeseboard, wood, round w/cheese keeper & dome   /975 .... *35*
Cheeseboard, wood, oval w/cheese keeper & dome   /976 .... *30*
Chip 'N Dip w/bowl, 12"   /180 .... *25*
Chip Server   /181 .... *18*
Clock   /925 .... *45*
Coaster, embossed center design *8*
Coffee pot/server, 8-cup   /492 .... *45*
Cookie jar, "Cookies"   /540   /C *27*
Corn dish   /047 .... *10*
Creamer   /024   /C *12.50*
Crock, "Ice"   /650 .... *35*
Crock, open, 8¹/₂" high   /567 .... *30*
Crock, "Coffee," wood lid   /497 .... *12*
Crock, "Instant Coffee," wood lid   /496 .... *12*
Crock, "Non-dairy Creamer," wood lid   /494 .... *10*
Crock, "Sweetener," wood lid   /491 .... *10*
Crock, "Utensils," 6¹/₄"   /500   /C *15*
Crock, onion soup w/stick handle, open, 12-ounce   /295   /C *12*
Cruet, oil/vinegar, each   /441   /442 .... *15*
Cup, 9-ounce   /001   /C *5.50*
Cup, punch, open handle *4*
Custard, 5¹/₂-ounce   /577 .... *7*
Demi-mug   /284 .... *12*
Demi-mug saucer   /285 .... *3*
Dish, fruit, 4¹/₂"   /008   /C *7*
Dish, soup/cereal, 6"   /009   /C *5.50*
Drippings jar *15*
Eggcup, chicken shape *18*
Flowerpot w/saucer, 4" *8*
Flowerpot w/saucer, 4¹/₂" *10*
Flowerpot w/saucer, 5" *12*
Gravy boat, 23-ounce   /433   /C *22*
Gravy liner   /C *3*
Honey pot, "Honey," 16-ounce   /480 .... *15*
Jam/relish server, 3-part   /043 .... *30*
Jug, cork stopper, 25-ounce   /563 .... *20*
Jug, cork stopper, 40-ounce   /564 .... *25*
Jug, cork stopper, 1-gallon   /565 .... *35*
Jug, Toby, 18-ounce   /418 .... *25*
Ladle, large   /155   /C *14*
Lazy Susan, 4-part, plastic base   /130 .... *40*
Loaf pan, lug, 2-quart   /235 .... *20*
    [Prices below are for both styles]
Measurer, ¹/₄-cup   /106 .... *6*
Measurer, ¹/₃-cup   /107 .... *8*
Measurer, ¹/₂-cup   /108 .... *10*
Measurer, 1-cup   /109 .... *12*
    Rack for above *15*

Mug, 12-ounce   /288. . . . . *$9*
Mug, coffee, 10-ounce   /289   /C *8*
Mug, pedestal, 10-ounce   /290   /C. *10*
Mug, souper, 14-ounce   /280 . . . . *12*
Napkin holder   /C *12*
Napkin ring   /018. . . . . *4*
Pie baker, 9"   /576   /C. *15*
Pitcher, mini   /413 . . . . *10*
Pitcher, 16-ounce   /414 . . . . *12*
Pitcher, 1-quart   /446 . . . . *18*
Pitcher, 2½-quart   /416   /C *29*
Plate, 7"   /003   /C. *4.50*
Plate, 8½"   /005   /C *7.50*
Plate, 10"   /004   /C *6.50*
Plate, steak, oval, 12"   /007   /C *16.50*
Plate, super (chop), round, 12" *20*
Platter, 14"   /016   /C. *21*
Platter, 16"   /017 . . . . *30*
Porringer, 6"   /569 . . . . *18*
Quiche, 9"   /233 . . . . *25*
Salt box, 5½" × 6"   /560 . . . . *35*
Saucer   /002   /C. *3*
Scoop, small   /101. . . . . *6*
Scoop, medium   /102 . . . . *8*
Scoop, large   /103 . . . . *10*
    Rack for above *12*
Shaker, Liberty Bell, pair *35*
Shaker, Owl, pair *35*
Shaker, spice, handled, each   /056 . . . . *16*
Shaker, sugar, handled, each. *16*
Shaker, sugar, pear shape (Muffineer), each   /055. . . . . *25*
Shaker, pair   /026   /027 . . . . *16*
Snack tray   /039. . . . . *16*
Souffle, petit   /405. . . . . *12*
Souffle, 1-quart   /406 . . . . *18*
Souffle, 2½-quart   /408. . . . . *25*
Spoon rest, owl   /512 . . . . *25*
Spoon rest, spoon   /515   /C. *9*
Sugar   /022   /C *13.25*
Table Lite (Hurricane Lamp) w/glass   /620. . . . . *18*
Tankard, 19-ounce, Eagle decoration   /286. . . . . *20*
Teapot (Petit), 19-ounce   /555 . . . . *24*
Teapot, 42-ounce   /550. . . . . *36*
Tid-bit, two-tier, wood handle *18*
Tray, 2 segments & board, rectangular, 17"   /717 . . . . *25*
Tray, 4 segments, rectangular, 17"   /716 . . . . *30*
Tray, wine & cheese w/dome & carafe   /718. *35*
Tray, metal w/tile & 2 bowls, 17"   /920. . . . . *30*

Trivet, round, lug /518 .... $22
Trivet, square, 7¹/²" /615 /C.. *11*
Tureen, 3¹/₂-quart w/ladle & plate /160 /C *70*
Utensil, fork, wood *3*
Utensil, spoon, wood... *3*
Vase, bud /800 .... *15*
Vase, bud, boot shape /801 .... *18*

KITCHENWARE

Pfaltzgraff began manufacturing kitchenware in the late thirties with a variety of pieces. Its Ceramex line, identifiable by the incised lines that encircle each item, was introduced in the early forties.

CERAMEX

Ceramex was originally introduced in gloss glazes of aqua, blue, green, wine, and yellow. Later colors added were pastel blue, colonial blue, chartreuse, gray, forest green, and peach. Many of these colors were used on other kitchenware items. Red will also be found.

Bowl, batter, w/handle & lip $35
Bowl, mixing, 6" *10*
Bowl, mixing, 7" *12*
Bowl, mixing, 8" *15*

BATTER BOWL

CANISTER (COOKIE JAR)

REFRIGERATOR JUG

TALL WATER JUG

Kitchenware

ORIENTAL TEAPOT   QUEEN TEAPOT   REGENT TEAPOT

Kitchenware

Bowl, mixing, 9" *$18*
Bowl, mixing, 10" *20*
Canister (cookie jar), tilt lid *45*
Jug, water, ball. *35*
Jug, water, tall, 7" *30*

MISCELLANY

Jug, ball, 2-quart *$25*
Jug, refrigerator *25*
Jug, refrigerator, scalloped foot. *25*
Teapot, Boston *25*
Teapot, Oriental. . . . . *35 – 45*
Teapot, Queen . . . . *55 – 65*
Teapot, Regent . . . . *45 – 55*

NOVELTIES

COOKIE JARS

Some of these jars are in the Muggsy style, with the same range of colors, but have not been attributed to the Jessops. See Kitchenware/Ceramex and Muggsy for additional cookie jars.

Apple   /670 . . . . *ND*
Clown, head . . . . *ND*
Clown, w/drum   /662. . . . . *$175 – $200*
Cookie Bag, "Cookies"   /658 . . . . *100 – 125*
Cookie Clock   /657 . . . . *150 – 175*
Cookie Cop   /655 . . . . *400 +*
Cookie House   /660. . . . . *175 – 200*
Cylinder, floral, "Cookies"   /656 . . . . *100 – 125*
Cylinder, w/fish decal . . . . *125 – 150*
Engine (Cookie Flyer)   /659 . . . . *175 – 200*
French Chef   /664. . . . . *250 – 275*
Merry-Go-Round   /663 . . . . *400 +*
Old Lady in Shoe   /661 . . . . *150 – 175*
Pear   /672. . . . . *ND*

Pineapple /673 . . . .*ND*
Strawberry /671 . . . .*ND*

MUGGSY

The Muggsy line was introduced ca. 1954, but there is some evidence to suggest there was at least one piece in the early forties. Designed by Dorothy and Norman Jessop. "New as gossip and just as sure to start a conversation." Made until 1960.

In an old catalog, the **child's bowl** shows Ho Ho the Elephant, but the actual bowl has Jo Jo on it. The **Cookie clock** and **Cookie cop** are in the Muggsy style but have not been attributed to the Jessops. **Decanters** are listed in a 1959 price list but are very rare. A black-faced **sprinkler** has been reported but not confirmed. Some design sketches have been found, but there is no information if the items pictured, such as a lamp with a nose that lights up, were put into production. Prototypes of Christmas ornaments were also made.

Seven colors were used on the hand-painted mugs.

Ashtray, Burnie. . . . . *$125 – $150*
Ashtray, white w/red polka dots . . . . *100 – 125*
Canape Carri, w/lid . . . . *200 – 250*
Child's Circus Set
   Bowl /Jo Jo the Elephant . . . . *35 – 45*
   Mug /Ko Ko the Clown . . . . *45 – 55*
   Plate, 7" /Yo Yo the Giraffe . . . . *45 – 55*
Cookie jar, Derby Dan (1941) . . . . *250 – 275*
Decanters, one fifth
   Bourbon, Man in top hat. . . . . *ND*
   Gin, Man, hands clasped . . . . *ND*
   Rye, Farmer . . . . *ND*
   Scotch, Scotsman . . . . *ND*
Jar, Handy Harry w/lid . . . . *175 – 200*
Jar, Pretzel Pete . . . . *ND*
Mugs, Regular Set, 16-ounce, 5"
   Cock-eyed Charlie *35*
   Flirty Gertie *35*
   Handsome Herman *35*
   Jerry the Jerk *35*
   Pickled Pete. *35*

JO JO THE ELEPHANT

KO KO THE CLOWN

YO YO THE GIRAFFE

Child's Circus Set

Muggsy: Myrtle the Sprinkler

Sleepy Sam $35
Mugs, Sporting Set, 16-ounce, 5"
    Brawny Bertram . . . . *55 – 75*
    Diamond Dick . . . . *55 – 75*
    Fairway Freddie . . . . *55 – 75*
    Muscles Moe . . . . *75 – 95*
    Pigskin Pete . . . . *65 – 85*
    Rodney Reel . . . . *55 – 75*
Mugs, Miniature (Cigarette holders). The last is unmarked.
    Comb-shaped eyebrows, center part in hair . . . . *80 +*
    Jigger . . . . *65 – 75*
    Nick . . . . *65 – 75*
Sprinkler, Myrtle . . . . *165 – 185*
Stopper, each . . . . *35 – 55*
    Set of four in original box . . . . *175 – 200*
Tumbler
    Cockeyed Charlie . . . . *65 – 85*
    Handsome Herman . . . . *65 – 85*
    Jerry the Jerk . . . . *65 – 85*
    Pickled Pete . . . . *65 – 85*
    Rugged Richard . . . . *65 – 85*
    Sleepy Sam . . . . *65 – 85*

POPE-GOSSER
CHINA COMPANY

Coshocton, Ohio

CHAPTER AT A GLANCE

BRIAR ROSE   MODERNE
CANDLEWICK   ROSE POINT

Founded in 1902, Pope-Gosser was one of the potteries to join the ill-fated American China Corporation, which went bankrupt in 1932. Pope-Gosser was reorganized by Frank Judge and produced semiporcelain dinnerware until 1958.

MARKS The Pegasus mark (not shown) is the earliest, followed by the arc mark from the 1920s, the Aladdin's Lamp mark, and then the wreath mark from the 1940s and 1950s. Be careful; sometimes shape names in capital letters were used under the last three, more often decoration names. Typographically, there is no way to differentiate.

BRIAR ROSE

Pope-Gosser apparently bought this shape from Salem China. Use that listing for values.

Briar Rose
by
Pope-Gosser

CANDLEWICK

Matching stemware by the Seneca Glass Company of Morgantown, West Virginia, was available in all-crystal or crystal with a colored base of Amber, Cobalt Blue, Green, or Ruby.

Bowl, vegetable, oval, 9"* . . . . *$10 – $12*
Casserole . . . . *20 – 25*
Creamer . . . . *4 – 6*
Cup . . . . *4 – 6*
Dish, 5½" . . . . *2 – 3*
Plate, 6¼" . . . . *1 – 2*
Plate, 9"* . . . . *7 – 9*
Platter, 11" . . . . *10 – 12*
Saucer . . . . *1 – 2*
Sugar . . . . *8 – 10*

MODERNE   (1929)

A plain round shape with squared handles.

Bowl, vegetable, 9" . . . . *$10 – $12*
Casserole . . . . *20 – 25*
Creamer . . . . *4 – 6*
Cup . . . . *4 – 6*
Dish, 5½"* . . . . *2 – 3*

Moderne: Plate (fish) and cup (checkerboard).

Plate, 7³/₄" .... *$5 – $7*
Plate, 9"* .... *7 – 9*
Platter, 11"* .... *10 – 12*
Saucer .... *1 – 2*
Sugar .... *8 – 10*

ROSEPOINT (1934)

Distinguished by a raised design of trailing roses with a rose finial on the covered pieces. Introduced in plain white with no decoration. Decals were added in 1935.

One of the more popular patterns in American tableware, there is also matching silverware and glassware.

Bowl, oval, 9"* .... *$10 – $12*
Casserole .... *20 – 25*
Creamer .... *4 – 6*
Creamer, AD. .... *6 – 8*
Cup .... *4 – 6*

Rosepoint: AD coffee pot

Cup, cream soup .... *$12 – $16*
Plate, 6" .... *1 – 2*
Plate, 9" .... *7 – 9*
Plate, 10" .... *10 – 12*
Saucer .... *1 – 2*
Saucer, cream soup .... *6 – 8*
Sugar .... *8 – 10*
Sugar, AD .... *10 – 12*
Teapot .... *30 – 35*
Teapot, AD .... *30 – 35*

PORCELIER MANUFACTURING COMPANY

South Greensburg, Pennsylvania

CHAPTER AT A GLANCE

APPLIANCES
KITCHENWARE

LIGHT FIXTURES

Porcelier began in East Liverpool in 1927, founded by Emanual and Jack Dim and Harry and Hymie Tauber. In the spring of 1930 they moved the company to South Greensburg, PA, purchasing the old American China Company building; they took with them several employees. At first Porcelier manufactured lighting fixtures, both wall and ceiling, then expanded to coffee drip-o-lator pots and electric percolators.

Other products included teapots, sugars, creamers, shakers, mugs, jugs, ashtrays, canisters, and electrified items such as toasters, waffle irons, and lamps. In 1954 the company closed and sold off its equipment. The building was bought by Pittsburgh Plate Glass.

Many Porcelier items have embossed designs which are hand painted under the glaze. Colors can vary on the hand-painted pieces. For example, I have seen Flamingo pieces in pale pink and deep pink. Be careful of this if you do mail order. Some decals were used as well.

NOTE   I have seen little literature on Porcelier, so the names below are either ones that collectors use or ones I have made up.

See Clubs/Newsletters.

Porcelier

TRADE MARK
VITRIFIED
CHINA

APPLIANCES

Coffee pot, electric, tall	*$50 – $55*
Creamer	*6 – 8*
Sugar	*8 – 10*

Toaster . . . . *$500 +*
Waffle Iron . . . . *100 – 150*

KITCHENWARE

Many teapots were transformed into drip coffees by the addition of an aluminum drip. Ceramic drip sections were used but are harder to find.

PRICING   Add $25 for pots found with a plain ceramic drip.

Asian (Korean) Letters
    Double boiler insert . . . . *$20 – $25*
    Teapot . . . . *30 – 35*
Bluebird teapot . . . . *35 – 40*
Cactus
    Ball jug . . . . *40 – 45*
    Coffee pot, 2-cup . . . . *45 – 50*
    Coffee pot, 4-cup . . . . *45 – 50*
    Coffee pot, 6-cup . . . . *45 – 50*
    Coffee pot, 8-cup . . . . *45 – 50*
    Creamer . . . . *8 – 10*
    Sugar . . . . *10 – 12*
Canary (Yellow Birds) teapot . . . . *35 – 40*
Cattail teapot . . . . *35 – 40*
Cottage
    Creamer . . . . *6 – 8*
    Sugar . . . . *8 – 10*
    Teapot, 6-cup . . . . *25 – 30*
Deer teapot, 8-cup . . . . *40 – 45*
Dolls (Dutch/Swedish)
    Creamer . . . . *6 – 8*
    Sugar . . . . *8 – 10*
    Teapot, 6-cup . . . . *30 – 35*
    Teapot, 8-cup . . . . *30 – 35*
        w/gold . . . . *35 – 40*

Tomato, Deer, and Cattail teapots. The Deer teapot is not confirmed as Porcelier but is collected as such.

Double Floral
Creamer .... *$4 – $6*
Sugar .... *6 – 8*
Teapot, 6-cup. .... *20 – 25*

Flamingo
Creamer .... *8 – 10*
Sugar .... *10 – 12*
Teapot .... *40 – 45*

Flight
Creamer .... *6 – 8*
Disk pitcher. .... *40 – 45*
Sugar .... *8 – 10*
Teapot, 6-cup. .... *30 – 35*
Teapot, 8-cup. .... *30 – 35*

Floral Spray
Ball jug .... *30 – 35*
Creamer .... *4 – 6*
Double boiler insert .... *20 – 25*
Sugar .... *6 – 8*
Teapot, 2-cup. .... *20 – 25*
Teapot, 4-cup. .... *20 – 25*
Teapot, 6-cup. .... *20 – 25*

Fruit (Pears)
Teapot, 2-cup. .... *30 – 35*
Teapot, 4-cup. .... *30 – 35*
Teapot, 6-cup. .... *30 – 35*
Teapot, 8-cup. .... *30 – 35*

Hearth
Creamer .... *6 – 8*
Disk pitcher. .... *40 – 45*
Sugar .... *8 – 10*

Double Floral creamer, Paneled Rose sugar, Floral Spray double boiler insert, Cottage sugar, and Floral Spray teapot.

Teapot . . . . *$30 – $35*

Log Cabin
  Creamer . . . . *6 – 8*
  Sugar . . . . *8 – 10*
  Teapot, 6-cup. . . . . *30 – 35*

Paneled Rose
  Creamer . . . . *4 – 6*
  Sugar . . . . *6 – 8*
  Teapot, 6-cup. . . . . *20 – 25*

Rose and Wheat teapot . . . . *35 – 40*

Sack (Rope Bow)
  Creamer . . . . *6 – 8*
  Double boiler insert . . . . *20 – 25*
  Sugar . . . . *8 – 10*
  Teapot, 4-cup. . . . . *25 – 30*
  Teapot, 6-cup. . . . . *25 – 30*

Sailboats
  Creamer . . . . *6 – 8*
  Sugar . . . . *8 – 10*
  Teapot . . . . *30 – 35*

Tomato
  Creamer . . . . *8 – 10*
  Sugar . . . . *12 – 15*
  Teapot, 6-cup. . . . . *40 – 45*

Tree Stump
  Creamer . . . . *6 – 8*
  Sugar . . . . *8 – 10*
  Teapot, 4-cup. . . . . *30 – 35*
  Teapot, 6-cup. . . . . *30 – 35*

World's Fair (internal dimensions on the teapots)
  Creamer . . . . *25 – 30*
  Disk pitcher, 5" high. . . . . *100 – 125*
  Disk pitcher, 7" high. . . . . *100 – 125*
  Sugar . . . . *30 – 40*
  Teapot, 4-cup (4½") . . . . *200 – 225*
  Teapot, 6-cup (5"). . . . . *200 – 225*
  Teapot, 8-cup (5½") . . . . *200 – 225*
  Teapot, 10-cup (6") . . . . *200 – 225*

LIGHT FIXTURES

Ceiling, single *$15*
Ceiling, double. *20*
Wall, each *15*

POTTERY GUILD

New York, New York

Pottery Guild is an imprint of Block China, a distributor. Though most if not all of the kitchenware with this mark was made by the Cronin China Company, there is no confirmation of where the cookie jars were made. For that reason, I am listing them separately.

See Roerig in Bibliography.

COOKIE JARS

Balloon Lady, Rose bottom, decorated lid $125
Chef, w/tray of cookies, decorated 175
Dutch Boy
    Blue .... 50 – 60
    Brown bottom, decorated lid .... 60 – 75
    Yellow .... 50 – 60
Dutch Girl
    Blue .... 50 – 60
    Blue bottom, decorated lid .... 60 – 75
Elsie the Cow, in barrel, "Elsie, Handle with Care" .... 275 – 325
Little Girl, Blue bottom, decorated lid .... 60 – 75
Little Red Riding Hood, Blue bottom, decorated lid......................... 150
Old King Cole .... 225 – 275
Rooster, decorated.. 50 – 60

PURINTON POTTERY

Wellsville, Ohio, and Shippenville, Pennsylvania

CHAPTER AT A GLANCE

Bernard Purinton founded the company in 1936 with the purchase of the East Liverpool Potteries Company in Wellsville. Needing better, more modern facilities, he built a new plant in Shippenville which began production at the end of 1941. Dinnerware, kitchenware, and novelties were made. The primary product had a hand-painted slip decoration under the glaze. Some solid color ware was made as well. The plant closed in 1959.

See Morris in Bibliography.

MARKS Pieces are backstamped with the name "Purinton" in script, and sometimes with the words "Slip Ware" in block letters. Many pieces are not marked.

DECORATIONS Besides the decorations listed below, some others you will find are: Blue Starflower, Cactus Flower, Chartreuse, Crescent, Harmony, Ivy Red, Ivy Yellow, Red Half-flower, Saraband, Tea Rose, and Mountain Rose.

COOKIE JARS / FIGURAL

Farmer Pig w/hat, scarf, suspenders, holding ear of corn, 7½" high × 10" long $600 +

Howdy-Doody, head only, 8½" . . . . 750 +

    Bank, head and shoulders, 8½" . . . . 750 +

Humpty-Dumpty, 10" . . . . 450 +

Rooster, 11½" . . . . 350 +

Cookie jars: Howdy-Doody, Humpty Dumpty, and Rooster.

DINNERWARE / KITCHENWARE / OTHERS

Purinton is one of those potteries best listed by decoration rather than shape so as to reflect collecting patterns.

Dinnerware The lid for the **sugar** and **marmalade** is the same. The Kent jug was intended as a sauce pitcher. The mug jug is a mug with a pouring lip. The three-part **relishes** will be found with ceramic, metal, or wooden handles, or with no handles. The two-part relishes are extremely rare, especially with seahorse handles. The party plate and cup was called a **Tea & Toast**. There are two two-cup **teapots**: one is the creamer with the sugar/marmalade lid (there is a matching six-cup teapot), and the other is called "round body"; the bottom of its handle comes to a point.

Kitchenware An old ad shows a **batter set** made up of the coffee pot and a matching two-cup pot on a tray; none have been reported. The **Apartment canister** is rectangular; the heights given are with lid. Four wedge-shape **canisters** were sold on a lazy Susan. The **coffee drip section** was made only during WWII when metal was not available. It has an open bottom and is used with cheese cloth. It is *not* decorated. After the war, a ceramic bottom and a lid were added and was sold as a round **drip jar**. This drip jar is also the bottom piece of the **stacking refrigerator/vegetable** set. The half oval drip jar sometimes has "Fats" on the lid. The **lazy Susan** is comprised of four wedge-shaped canisters on a wooden tray.

Other Purinton made a number of items not generally associated with the kitchen or dining room. Occasionally, these will be found in a dinnerware pattern; these are listed under Other. For prices for non-dinnerware decorations on these items, see Miscellany. The **divided ashtray** is the jam and jelly without a ceramic handle. The **rectangular vases** are the Apartment canisters without lids.

APPLE

An apple outlined with a thick red band, brown and yellow brush strokes over ivory in the center, with lots of green leaves and brown twigs around it. Do not confuse this with Fruit.

Dinnerware

Baker, 7" /140	$22
Bean pot, w/lid, individual /131	35
Bowl, fruit, footed, 12" /118	65
Bowl, salad, 11" /134	75
Bowl, spaghetti, rectangular, 14½" /141	ND
Bowl, vegetable, 8" /137	30
Bowl, vegetable, divided, 10" × 8¼"	55
Butter, open, ¼-pound	100
Casserole, 9" /135	75
Coffee pot, 8-cup /60	75
Creamer /102	20
Creamer, individual /113	20
Cruet, oil/vinegar, bottle shape, 1 pint, set /122/123	100
Cruet, oil/vinegar, jug shape, round, handled, set	150
Cruet, oil/vinegar, jug shape, square, handled, set	75
Cup /128	10
Dish, cereal, 5¼" /126	15
Dish, dessert, 4" /133	10
Dish, jam/jelly, 5½" × 4¾"	50
Jug, beverage, ice lip, 2-pint /105	75
Jug, Dutch, 2-pint, 5½" /109	35
Jug, Dutch, 5-pint, 7¾" /110	75
Jug, Kent, 1-pint /107	30
Marmalade jar /108	50

Jugs: Maywood Kent jug, Apple beverage jug, and Petals Dutch jug.

Teapots: Rose two-cup round body, Intaglio two-cup (creamer with lid), and matching Apple six-cup teapot.

Mug, beer, barrel shape, 16-ounce, 5" high   /146 . . . . *$60*
Mug, coffee, 8-ounce, 4" high   /145 . . . . *50*
Mug jug, 8-ounce   /104 . . . . *50*
Pickle, oblong, 6"   /139 . . . . *20*
Plate, 6³/₄"   /136 . . . . *15*
Plate, 8¹/₂"   /127 . . . . *20*
Plate, 9³/₄"   /130 . . . . *25*
Plate, chop, 12"   /117 . . . . *65*
Plate, party/lap, 8¹/₂"   /138 . . . . *20*
Platter, oblong, 11" *50*
Platter, oblong, 12"   /142 . . . . *50*
Platter, divided, oblong, 12¹/₄" *75*
Relish, three-part   /116 . . . . *45*
Saucer *3*
Shaker, jug shape, pair   /114 . . . . *25*
Shaker, stack, pair *75*
Sugar   /101 . . . . *25*
Sugar, individual   /113 . . . . *20*

Apple: Dinner plate.

Canisters: Chartreuse half-oval, Fruit narrow oval, and Apple wide oval.

Teapot, 2-cup (creamer w/lid)　/103 . . . . *$25*
Teapot, 2-cup, round body, 4" high . . . . *ND*
Teapot, 6-cup (same shape as creamer w/lid)　/100 . . . . *65*
Tray, roll, oblong, 11" *50*
Tumbler, juice, 6-ounce, 2¾" high　/115 . . . . *25*
Tumbler, 12-ounce, 4¾" high　/111 . . . . *30*

Kitchenware

Canister, half-oval　/119 . . . . *$65*
Canister, narrow oval　/121 . . . . *75*
Canister, Apartment, 5½" high *75*
Canister, Apartment, 7½" high　/132 . . . . *75*
Canister, square, small *150*
Canister, square, large *150*
Cookie jar, narrow oval　/124 . . . . *80*
Cookie jar, wide oval *125*
Cookie jar, square, blade lid *175*
Cookie jar, square, wooden lid *150*
Drip, half oval *50*
Drip, Shake & Pour shape *50*
Lazy Susan, complete
　Apple & three-fruit *130–160*

Canisters: Apple Apartment canisters, small and large, and Pennsylvania Dutch square canister/cookie jar.

All Apple . . . . *ND*
Shaker, range, oval   /120 . . . . *$50*
Shaker, Shake & Pour
   Salt & Pepper, pair *50*
   Cinnamon & Sugar/Flour/Spice/Sugar, each. *80*

Other

Ashtray, divided, metal cigarette holder *$100*
Candle holder, Star shape, two piece *100*
Candy dish, double   /106 . . . . *45*
Night bottle/vase, w/tumbler, 1-quart   /112. . . . . *125*
Planter, ivy/Honey pot, 6½"   /604 . . . . *100*
Planter, ivy (jug shape)   /610 . . . . *45*
Wall pocket   /106 . . . . *75*

FRUIT

There are several variations on Fruit. One of the basic patterns is an apple, solid red (as opposed to the outlined apple of the Apple decoration) with a brown stem and one green leaf. Another is a solid-color red apple overlapping a yellow pear. Some larger pieces will show an apple, grapes, pear, and pineapple. And some pieces will be found with only a pear.

The four-fruit version was generally done on early production in Wellsville. When the company moved to Shippenville, the apple and pear predominated. Later, in response to an order from Esmond, a distributor, the four fruits reappeared in a more refined version. This explains why certain pieces made only in Shippenville will not be found with the early four-fruit decoration.

Four items have been found with blue trim; these are priced in the list below. The square cruets are found with either blue or green grapes; price is the same for both.

Dinnerware

Bowl, fruit, footed, 12"   /118. . . . . *$60*
Coffee pot, 8-cup   /60 . . . . *45*
   w/drip. *85*
Creamer   /102. . . . . *15*
Creamer, individual   /113. . . . . *20*
Cruet, oil/vinegar, plain. *75*
Cruet, oil/vinegar, bottle shape, 1-pint   /122/123 . . . . *75*
Cruet, oil/vinegar, jug shape, square, handled. *40*
   w/blue trim. *85*
Cup   /128. . . . . *12*
Jug, Dutch, 2-pint, 5½"   /109 . . . . *30*
Jug, Dutch, 5-pint, 7¾"   /110 . . . . *65*
Jug, Kent, 1-pint   /107. . . . . *25*
Jug, Oasis, leather handle. . . . . *750 +*
Plate, 9¾"   /130. . . . . *50*
Plate, chop, 12"   /117 . . . . *65*

Fruit: Dinner plate.

Plate, party/lap, 8½"   /138 .... $50
Relish, two-part, seahorse handle .... 75 – 100
Relish, three-part   /116 40
Saucer 5
Shaker, jug shape, pair   /114 20
Shaker, round, pair 50
Sugar   /101 20
Sugar, individual   /113 20
Teapot, 2-cup, round body, 4" high 20
Tumbler, juice, 6-ounce, 2¾" high   /115 25
Tumbler, 12-ounce, 4¾" high   /111 30

Kitchenware

Canister, half-oval   /119 .... $50
  w/blue trim 60
Canister, narrow oval   /121 60
  w/blue trim 85
Canister, round, wood lid, 5" × 6½" high 65
Cookie jar, narrow oval   /124 70
Cookie jar, round, wood lid, 5" × 6½" high 75
Drip, half oval 40
  w/grapes 50
Lazy Susan, complete, solid apple & fruit 100–125
Lazy Susan, miniature, complete 200
Shaker, range, cone 40
Shaker, range, oval   /120 40
  w/blue trim 60
Stack refrigerator set 95–125

Other

Night bottle/vase, w/tumbler, 1-quart   /112 .... $95

HEATHER PLAID / NORMANDY PLAID

Heather Plaid is broad bands of Turquoise with lines of burgundy and yellow.
Normandy Plaid is broad bands of burgundy with chartreuse and forest green
lines.

PRICING Pricing below is for Normandy Plaid. Add 15 to 20% for Heather Plaid.

Dinnerware

Baker, 7" /140 .... $22
Bean pot, w/lid, individual /131 .... *35*
Bowl, fruit, footed, 12" /118 .... *65*
Bowl, salad, 11" /134 .... *ND*
Bowl, spaghetti, rectangular, 14½" /141 .... *ND*
Bowl, vegetable, 8" /137 .... *30*
Bowl, vegetable, divided, 10" × 8¼" *45*
Butter, open, ¼-pound *80*
Casserole, 9" /135 .... *70*
Coffee pot, 8-cup /60 .... *ND*
Creamer /102 .... *20*
Creamer, individual /113 .... *20*
Cruet, oil/vinegar, jug shape, round, handled .... *ND*
Cruet, oil/vinegar, jug shape, square, handled *75*
Cup /128 .... *10*
Dish, cereal, 5¼" /126 .... *15*
Dish, dessert, 4" /133 .... *10*
Dish, jam/jelly, 5½" × 4¾" *50*
Jug, beverage, ice lip, 2-pint /105 .... *75*
Jug, Dutch, 2-pint, 5½" /109 .... *35*
Jug, Dutch, 5-pint, 7¾" /110 .... *75*
Jug, Kent, 1-pint /107 .... *30*
Marmalade jar /108 .... *50*
Mug, beer, barrel shape, 16-ounce, 5" high /146 .... *60*
Mug, coffee, 8-ounce, 4" high /145 .... *50*
Mug jug, 8-ounce /104 .... *50*
Pickle, oblong, 6" /139 .... *20*
Plate, 6¾" /136 .... *10*
Plate, 8½" /127 .... *15*
Plate, 9¾" /130 .... *20*

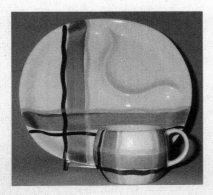

Heather/Normandy Plaid: Party plate and cup (tea and toast).

Plate, chop, 12"   /117 . . . . *$50*
Plate, party/lap, 8½"   /138 . . . . *15*
Platter, oblong, 11" *50*
Platter, oblong, 12"   /142 . . . . *50*
Platter, divided, oblong, 12¼" . . . . *ND*
Relish, three-part   /116 . . . . *40*
Saucer *3*
Shaker, jug shape, pair   /114 . . . . *25*
Shaker, stack, pair *75*
Sugar   /101 . . . . *25*
Sugar, individual   /113 . . . . *20*
Teapot, 2-cup (creamer w/lid)   /103 . . . . *25*
Tray, roll, oblong, 11" *35*
Tumbler, juice, 6-ounce, 2¼" high   /115 . . . . *25*
Tumbler, 12-ounce, 4¾" high   /111 . . . . *30*

Kitchenware

Canister, Apartment, 5½" high *$75*
Canister, Apartment, 7½" high   /132 . . . . *75*
Cookie jar, wide oval *125*
Drip, half oval *50*
Drip, Shake & Pour shape *45*
Shaker, range, oval   /120 . . . . *40*
Shaker, Shake & Pour
   Cinnamon & Sugar/Flour *75*
   Salt/Pepper *45*

Other

Ashtray, divided, metal cigarette holder *$50*
Candle holder, Star shape, two-piece . . . . *ND*
Candy dish, double   /106 . . . . *45*
Planter, ivy (jug shape)   /610 . . . . *45*
Wall pocket   /106 . . . . *ND*

INTAGLIO

Intaglio was made in six colors: Brown, which is the most common, Turquoise, which is a little scarcer, and Baby Blue, Caramel, Coral, and Sapphire, which are hard to find. This pattern has broad vertical columns of color, usually with a flower and leaf decoration etched over the color. Other decorations, such as a palm tree, will be found.

    PRICING   Prices below are for Brown. Add 20% for Turquoise. Add 50% for Baby Blue, Caramel, Coral, and Sapphire. Three items are found with a Palm Tree etching; these are priced in the list below.

Dinnerware

Baker, 7"   /140 . . . . *$20*
Bean pot, w/lid, individual   /131 . . . . *35*

Bowl, fruit, footed, 12"   /118 .... *$60*
Bowl, salad, 11"   /134.. *65*
Bowl, spaghetti, rectangular, 14¹/₂"   /141 .... *ND*
Bowl, vegetable, 8"   /137 .... *25*
Bowl, vegetable, divided, 10" × 8¹/₄" *40*
Butter, open, ¹/₄-pound *75*
Casserole, 9"   /135... *55*
Coffee pot, 8-cup   /60.. *75*
Creamer   /102 .... *18*
   w/Palm Tree *70*
Creamer, individual   /113 .... *ND*
Cruet, oil/vinegar, jug shape, square, handled, set *60*
Cup   /128 .... *8*
Dish, cereal, 5¹/₄"   /126... *12*
Dish, dessert, 4"   /133... *8*
Dish, jam/jelly, 5¹/₂" × 4³/₄"... *40*
Jug, beverage, ice lip, 2-pint   /105 .... *75*
Jug, Dutch, 2-pint, 5¹/₂"   /109 .... *35*
Jug, Dutch, 5-pint, 7³/₄"   /110... *75*
Jug, Kent, 1-pint   /107 .... *40*
Marmalade jar   /108 .... *50*
Mug, beer, barrel shape, 16-ounce, 5" high   /146.......................... *60*
   w/Palm Tree *150*
Mug, coffee, 8-ounce, 4" high   /145...................................... *50*
Mug jug, 8-ounce   /104 .... *50*
Pickle, oblong, 6"   /139 .... *15*
Plate, 6³/₄"   /136 .... *10*
Plate, 8¹/₂"   /127 .... *15*
   w/Palm Tree *150*
Plate, 9³/₄"   /130 .... *20*
Plate, chop, 12"   /117.. *55*
Plate, party/lap, 8¹/₂"   /138 .... *15*
Platter, oblong, 11"... *40*
Platter, oblong, 12"   /142.. *40*

Intaglio: Dinner plate.

Platter, divided, oblong, 12¼" $75
Relish, three-part /116 40
Saucer 3
Shaker, jug shape, pair /114 25
Shaker, stack, pair 75
Sugar /101 25
  w/Palm Tree 85
Sugar, individual /113 .... ND
Teapot, 2-cup (creamer w/lid) /103 25
Teapot, 2-cup, round body, 4" high 40
Teapot, 6-cup (same shape as creamer w/lid) /100 75
Tray, roll, oblong, 11" 35
Tumbler, juice, 6-ounce, 2¾" high /115 25
Tumbler, 12-ounce, 4¾" high /111 30

Kitchenware

Canister, Apartment, 5½" high $75
Canister, Apartment, 7½" high /132 75
Cookie jar, wide oval 100
Cookie jar, square, wooden lid 100
Drip, half oval 50
Drip, Shake & Pour shape 50
Lazy Susan, complete .... ND
Shaker, range, oval /120 65
Shaker, Shake & Pour 45

Other

Ashtray, divided, metal cigarette holder $85
Candle holder, Star shape, two-piece 80
Candy dish, double /106 40
Planter, ivy/Honey pot, 6½" /604 .... ND
  w/Palm Tree 125
Planter, Violet /600 75
Wall pocket /106

MAYWOOD

A white, four-petaled flower, outlined in brown, with a yellow and green center, on a gray/green slip.

Dinnerware

Baker, 7" /140 .... $20
Bowl, fruit, footed, 12" /118 60
Bowl, salad, 11" /134 65
Bowl, vegetable, 8" /137 25
Bowl, vegetable, divided, 10" × 8¼" 40
Casserole, 9" /135 55
Creamer /102 18

Maywood: Dinner plate.

Cruet, oil/vinegar, jug shape, square, handled, set . . . . *ND*
Cup /128 . . . . *$8*
Dish, cereal, 5¼" /126 . . . . *12*
Dish, dessert, 4" /133 . . . . *8*
Dish, jam/jelly, 5½" × 4¾" *40*
Jug, beverage, ice lip, 2-pint /105 . . . . *ND*
Jug, Dutch, 2-pint, 5½" /109 . . . . *ND*
Jug, Dutch, 5-pint, 7¾" /110 . . . . *ND*
Jug, Kent, 1-pint /107 . . . . *40*
Marmalade jar /108 . . . . *50*
Mug, beer, barrel shape, 16-ounce, 5" high /146 . . . . *60*
Mug, coffee, 8-ounce, 4" high /145 . . . . *50*
Mug jug, 8-ounce /104 . . . . *50*
Pickle, oblong, 6" /139 . . . . *15*
Plate, 6¾" /136 . . . . *10*
Plate, 8½" /127 . . . . *15*
Plate, 9¾" /130 . . . . *20*
Plate, chop, 12" /117 . . . . *55*
Plate, party/lap, 8½" /138 . . . . *15*
Platter, oblong, 11" *40*
Platter, oblong, 12" /142 . . . . *40*
Platter, divided, oblong, 12¼" *75*
Relish, three-part /116 . . . . *ND*
Saucer *3*
Shaker, jug shape, pair /114 . . . . *35*
Sugar /101 . . . . *25*
Teapot, 2-cup (creamer w/lid) /103 . . . . *25*
Teapot, 6-cup (same shape as creamer w/lid) /100 . . . . *75*
Tray, roll, oblong, 11" *35*
Tumbler, juice, 6-ounce, 2¾" high /115 . . . . *ND*
Tumbler, 12-ounce, 4¾" high /111 . . . . *ND*

Kitchenware

Canister, Apartment, 5½" high . . . . *ND*

Canister, Apartment, 7½" high   /132 . . . . *ND*
Cookie jar, wide oval . . . . *ND*
Shaker, range, oval   /120 . . . . *ND*
Shaker, Shake & Pour . . . . *ND*

Other

Ashtray, divided, metal cigarette holder *$85*
Candy dish, double   /106 . . . . *ND*
Vase, rectangular, 4½"   /100 . . . . *50*
Vase, rectangular, 6½"   /200 . . . . *50*
Wall pocket   /106 . . . . *75*

MING TREE

An Oriental-style tree with brown leaves and black trunk and branches. Some
pieces will have a small pagoda in the background.

Dinnerware

Dish, cereal, 5¼"   /126 . . . . *$18*
Dish, dessert, 4"   /133 . . . . *15*
Plate, 9¾"   /130 . . . . *40*
Plate, chop, 12"   /117 . . . . *95*
Shaker, jug shape, pair   /114 . . . . *50*
Teapot, 2-cup (creamer w/lid)   /103 . . . . *45*
Teapot, 6-cup (same shape as creamer w/lid)   /100 . . . . *95*

Other

Flowerpot/jardiniere, 6" *$50*
Sprinkler (watering can) *125*
Vase, rectangular, 4½"   /100 . . . . *50*
Vase, rectangular, 6½"   /200 . . . . *50*

Ming Tree: Dinner plate.

Palm Tree: Dinner plate.

PALM TREE

Palm Trees with brown trunks and turquoise leaves; some brown birds fly overhead.

Dinnerware

Jug, beverage, ice lip, 2-pint   /105 . . . . *ND*
Jug, Dutch, 2-pint, 5¹/₂"   /109 . . . . *ND*
Mug, beer, barrel shape, 16-ounce, 5" high   /146. . . . . *$180*
Mug jug, 8-ounce   /104 . . . . *150*
Plate, 9³/₄"   /130 . . . . *100–300*
Shaker, jug shape, pair   /114 . . . . *100*

Kitchenware

Cookie jar, wide oval *$375*
Shaker, range, oval, pair   /120 . . . . *175*
Shaker, Shake & Pour, pair. *175*

Other

Planter, basket, 6¹/₂" high   /606 . . . . *ND*
Planter, ivy/Honey pot   /604 . . . . *$200*
Sprinkler (watering can) . . . . *ND*

PEASANT GARDEN

This is the decoration on the Peasant candle holders, hence its name. Thick bands of red alternate with a Laurel leaf motif on the rims of flatware and the bottoms of hollowware. Red and yellow flowers with green leaves decorate the wells of the flatware and the lids of the hollowware.

Dinnerware

Bowl, fruit, footed, 12"   /118 . . . . *$260*
Bowl, vegetable, 8"   /137 . . . . *120*
Casserole, 9"   /135 . . . . *ND*

Peasant Garden: Party plate and cup (tea and toast).

Creamer /102 .... *$80*
Cup /128 .... *40*
Dish, cereal, 5¼" /126 .... *60*
Dish, dessert, 4" /133 .... *40*
Marmalade jar /108 .... *200*
Plate, 6¾" /136 .... *60*
Plate, 8½" /127 .... *80*
Plate, 9¾" /130 .... *100*
Plate, chop, 12" /117 .... *260*
Plate, party/lap, 8½" /138 .... *80*
Saucer *15*
Shaker, jug shape, pair /114 .... *100*
Sugar /101 .... *100*
Teapot, 2-cup (creamer w/lid) /103 .... *100*
Tray, roll, oblong, 11" *200*

PENNSYLVANIA DUTCH

Traditional "folk art" heart and tulip decoration in pink and teal.

Dinnerware

Baker, 7" /140 .... *$40*
Bowl, fruit, footed, 12" /118 .... *130*
Bowl, vegetable, 8" /137 .... *60*
Butter, open, ¼-pound *200*
Casserole, 9" /135 .... *ND*
Creamer /102 .... *40*
Creamer, individual /113 .... *ND*
Cruet, oil/vinegar, bottle shape, 1-pint /122/123, set *200*
Cruet, oil/vinegar, jug shape, square, handled, set *150*
Cup /128 .... *20*
Dish, cereal, 5¼" /126 .... *30*
Dish, dessert, 4" /133 .... *20*
Dish, jam/jelly, 5½" × 4¾" *100*

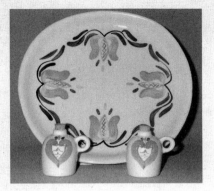

Pennsylvania Dutch: Dinner plate with Tulip motif and Jug shakers with heart motif.

Jug, beverage, ice lip, 2-pint   /105 .... *ND*
Jug, Dutch, 2-pint, 5½"   /109 .... *80*
Jug, Dutch, 5-pint, 7¾"   /110 .... *ND*
Jug, Kent, 1-pint   /107 .... *60*
Marmalade jar   /108 .... *100*
Mug, beer, barrel shape, 16-ounce, 5" high   /146 .... *120*
Mug, coffee, 8-ounce, 4" high   /145 .... *100*
Mug jug, 8-ounce   /104 .... *100*
Pickle, oblong, 6"   /139 .... *40*
Plate, 6¾"   /136 .... *30*
Plate, 8½"   /127 .... *40*
Plate, 9¾"   /130 .... *50*
Plate, chop, 12"   /117 .... *130*
Plate, party/lap, 8½"   /138 .... *40*
Platter, oblong, 11" *100*
Platter, oblong, 12"   /142 .... *100*
Platter, divided, oblong, 12¼" *150*
Relish, three-part   /116 .... *90*
Saucer *6*
Shaker, jug shape, pair   /114 .... *50*
Shaker, stack, pair *150*
Sugar   /101 .... *50*
Sugar, individual   /113 .... *ND*
Teapot, 2-cup (creamer w/lid)   /103 .... *50*
Teapot, 6-cup (same shape as creamer w/lid)   /100 .... *130*
Tray, roll, oblong, 11" *100*
Tumbler, juice, 6-ounce, 2¾" high   /115 .... *40*
Tumbler, 12-ounce, 4¾" high   /111 .... *50*

Kitchenware

Canister, Apartment, 5½" high *$150*
Canister, Apartment, 7½" high   /132 .... *150*
Canister, square, small .... *ND*
Canister, square, large .... *ND*

Cookie jar, wide oval *$250*
Cookie jar, square, blade lid *350*
Cookie jar, square, wooden lid *300*
Drip, half oval . . . . *ND*
Drip, Shake & Pour shape *100*
Lazy Susan, complete . . . . *ND*
Shaker, range, oval   /120 . . . . *ND*
Shaker, Shake & Pour *100*

Other

Ashtray, divided, metal cigarette holder *$200*
Candle holder, Star shape, two-piece *200*
Candy dish, double   /106 . . . . *90*
Night bottle/vase, w/tumbler, 1-quart   /112 . . . . *ND*
Planter, ivy/Honey pot, 6½"   /604 . . . . *150*
Vase, bud (Rebecca jug), 7¾"   /605 . . . . *ND*
Vase, rectangular, 4½"   /100 . . . . *ND*
Vase, rectangular, 6½"   /200 . . . . *ND*
Wall pocket   /106 . . . . *150*

PETALS

Two three-petaled flowers, one in blue and one in red, with green leaves.
   NOTE: No one has yet reported a saucer.

Dinnerware

Baker, 7"   /140 . . . . *$30*
Bowl, fruit, footed, 12"   /118 . . . . *75*
Casserole, 9"   /135 . . . . *85*
Coffee pot, 8-cup   /60 . . . . *110*
Creamer   /102 . . . . *25*
Cup   /128 . . . . *12*
Dish, cereal, 5¼"   /126 . . . . *18*
Dish, dessert, 4"   /133 . . . . *12*
Jug, beverage, ice lip, 2-pint   /105 . . . . *90*
Jug, Dutch, 5-pint, 7¾"   /110 . . . . *75*
Pickle, oblong, 6"   /139 . . . . *24*

Petals: Dinner plate.

Plate, 9³/₄" /130 .... $40
Plate, chop, 12" /117 .... *ND*
Relish, three-part /116 .... *ND*
Shaker, jug shape, pair /114 .... *40*
Sugar /101 .... *ND*
Tumbler, juice, 6-ounce, 2³/₄" high /115...................... *35*
Tumbler, 12-ounce, 4³/₄" high /111 .... *ND*

Kitchenware

Cookie jar, narrow oval /124 .... *$100*

Other

Planter, ivy/Honey pot, 6¹/₂" /604 .... *$35*

SEAFORM

Seaform was Purinton's shape name, but collectors use it for the pattern. Half flowers in pink with yellow centers alternate with green leaves around these pieces.

There are fewer pieces in Seaform than in the standard dinnerware line, and many of them are different shapes.

Bowl, soup /326 .... $15
Bowl, vegetable, divided /344 55
Bowl, vegetable, footed /312 45
Butter, open... 100
Coffee server /360 .... *ND*
Creamer /302.. *ND*
Cup /328 10
Dish, dessert /333.. 10
Plate, round, 7" /336 20
Plate, round, 10¹/₄" /330... 36
Platter, 12¹/₂" /342 .... *ND*
Saucer /329 3

Seaform: Dinner plate.

Shaker, pair   /314 . . . . *$50*
Sugar, open   /301 . . . . *ND*
Teapot   /300 . . . . *ND*
Tray (for sugar & creamer), 9" × 5"   /303 . . . . *ND*

MISCELLANY

The **child's pieces** were made in three-piece sets consisting of the breakfast plate, the beer or coffee mug, and the cereal bowl. They have been found with a cat, deer, dog, duck, or elephant decorations. The book-shaped **decanters** (three "books" to a set in a wire rack) came either plain or with paper labels that said "Three Musketeers" across the top and "Scotch," "Bourbon," and Whiskey" below. The **honey pot** is also an **ivy planter**. The **jug-shaped ivy planter** has been seen only with dinnerware patterns, so it is not listed below.

You may find a Tom and Jerry bowl and mugs, and small animals. These are rare. It is common to find many of the pieces listed here in hard-to-find decorations.

PRICING   The prices here are for the variety of non-dinnerware decorations that can be found on these items. For dinnerware decorations, see the specific listing.

Ashtray, square . . . . *ND*
Ashtray, divided, metal cigarette holder, Souvenir pieces . . . . *ND*
Bank, pig, small *$65*
Bank, Uncle Sam *100*
Candle holder, Peasant Lady, pair . . . . *750 +*
Candle holder, Star shape, two-piece *150*
Child's bowl *100*
Child's mug *145*
Child's plate *130*
Decanter, book shape, three in wire rack . . . . *125 – 135*
  w/paper labels . . . . *150 +*
Flowerpot/jardiniere, small *20*
Flowerpot/jardiniere, large *25*
Planter, basket   /606 . . . . *35*
Planter, ivy/Honey pot   /604
  Souvenir . . . . *85 – 100*
  Various decorations *30*
Planter, ivy (jug shape)   /610
Planter, pig, small *65*
Planter, Violet   /600 . . . . *50*
Shaker, "Old Salt" *100*
Shaker, "Pepper, His Wife" *100*
Sprinkler (watering can) *125*
Teapot, 6-cup (angled handle) . . . . *150 – 175*
Teapot, Tea-Guard, 2-cup
  Blue/green/yellow *35*
Vase, bud (Rebecca jug)   /605 . . . . *35*
Vase, cornucopia   /603 . . . . *25*

Vase, rectangular /100 .... *425 – $40*
Vase, rectangular /200 .... *25 – 40*
Wall pocket *75*

DOROTHY PURINTON PLATES

These were hand painted on a variety of plates; the ones known are listed after each decoration. It is a seller's market on these hard-to-find pieces.

Amish School Kids, dinner .... *$250 +*
Apple, "Too Soon Old, Too Late Schmart," dinner....................... *250 +*
Autumn Leaf Festival, breakfast/dinner/salad .... *250 +*
Fruit, "Some ha meat ... Be Thankit," chop............................ *250 +*
Intaglio, Log Cabin, "Pennsylvania," dinner............................ *250 +*
Pennsylvania Dutch, "Bless This House . . .," chop .... *250 +*
Wedding Plate, chop .... *250 +*

HARPER J. RANSBURG

Indianapolis, Indiana

Harper J. Ransburg had decorated glass and made wax candles prior to entering the field of pottery. It was while experimenting with decorating glass cookie jars that he visited a friend at the Louisville Pottery Company in Louisville, Kentucky. A vase caught his eye and he asked if it could be made into a cookie jar. A sample was thrown on a wheel, and Ransburg's first cookie jar, the #207, was created. The year was ca. 1930.

Eventually, Ransburg was buying ware from Louisville and from the Uhl Pottery in Huntingburg, Indiana. When Uhl closed, ware was bought from Western Stoneware. These pieces came to the factory glazed on the inside and bisque on the outside. The lids on the early jars were unglazed on the underside at first; complete glazing of lids began in the mid 1930s. Ransburg sprayed the bisque with a solid color, and the piece then went down a production line, where several people cold-painted the decoration.

Eventually, hand-painted metal items, mostly kitchenware, were added to the line. Note that at no time in its history did the plant do its own manufacturing. The company was sold to Hamilton Cosco in 1967.

MARKS "Ransburg Genuine Hand Painted Indianapolis USA" in script in an artist's palette engraved on the bottom of the larger pieces, and "Ransburg" in caps engraved on the bottom of smaller pieces.

COLORS The first six colors that Ransburg used on the body of their ware were Black, Blue, Cream, White, Green, and Yellow. The Blue, Green, and Yellow were bright, primary colors. An employee suggested Red, which Ransburg reluctantly tried, and it became the most popular of all.

KITCHENWARE

The footed bowl is the lower half of the #700 cookie jar. The munch jar resembles a casserole.

A wide variety of painted decorations were used, including flowers and nursery rhymes. Of the flowers, Aster and Hollyhock are the most common. Other patterns include Cosmos and Iris.

PRICING Values below are for Aster or Hollyhock decoration. Other decorations will be higher or lower depending on desirability.

Bowl, batter, small	*$10 – $12*
Bowl, batter, medium	*12 – 15*
Bowl, batter, large	*15 – 20*
Bowl, salad, 3 feet	*30 – 40*
Bowl, salad, pedestal, small	*20 – 25*
Bowl, salad, pedestal, large	*20 – 25*
Cookie jar, ball /700	*30 – 40*
Cookie jar, cylinder	*30 – 40*
Cookie jar /207	
Aster/Hollyhock	*25 – 35*

Aster handled shaker, footed ball sugar and cream; the latter set a shape made by Uhl. The set of three jugs are the same shape.

Davy Crockett. . . . . *$120 – $140*
Humpty Dumpty . . . . *65 – 75*
Mary Had a Little Lamb . . . . *65 – 75*
Creamer, ball shape *15*
Drip jar, flat . . . . *25 – 30*
Drip jar, footed *20*
Jug, ball shape, small. . . . . *10 – 12*
Jug, ball shape, medium . . . . *15 – 18*
Jug, ball shape, large . . . . *20 – 25*
Jug, tilt, ice lip . . . . *25 – 30*
Munch jar . . . . *35 – 40*
Shaker, ball, 3 feet, pair . . . . *15 – 20*
Shaker, handled, pair. . . . . *15 – 20*
Sugar, ball shape *15*
Teapot, ball shape . . . . *35 – 45*

RED WING POTTERIES, INC.

Red Wing, Minnesota

CHAPTER AT A GLANCE

DINNERWARE/HAND-PAINTED
CASUAL
  Bob White
  Round-Up
  Smart Set
FUTURA
  Tampico
DINNERWARE /
  KITCHENWARE/SOLID-COLOR
FRUIT SERVICE
GYPSY TRAIL HOSTESS WARE
  Chevron

Fondoso
Reed
LABRIEGO
TOWN AND COUNTRY
VILLAGE GREEN / BROWN
NOVELTIES
ASH RECEIVERS
COOKIE JARS / FIGURAL
FIGURES / PEOPLE
MISCELLANY
PLANTERS

The company began in 1877 as the Red Wing Stoneware Company making crocks, jugs, and the other utilitarian ware needed at the time. In 1894 it joined with its neighbors, Minnesota Stoneware and North Star Stoneware, to form the Union Stoneware Company, a marketing organization. Each pottery was still separate. North Star closed in 1896. The remaining two potteries merged with the Union company in 1906, and the name was changed to Red Wing Union Stoneware Company.

In 1933, Red Wing began producing artware for George Rumrill and in 1935 introduced the first of its dinnerware lines. As stoneware was no longer the only product, it changed its name to the Red Wing Potteries, Inc., in 1936. The pottery closed in 1967.

Early Red Wing stoneware is very collectible, as is the artware and dinnerware manufactured from the 1930s through 1967.

See Bougie and Newkirk, see DePasquale, see Tefft and see Viehl in Bibliography, and see Reiss in Biliography/Coming Attractions. See Clubs/Newsletters.

MARKS Most of the dinnerware is backstamped. A wing, first used on stoneware ca. 1912, features prominently in many of the marks.

DINNERWARE / HAND-PAINTED

CASUAL SHAPE

Bob White (1955)

Designed by Charles Murphy. The coffee mug, cruet, and Lazy Susan are uncommon. The beverage server and large water pitcher are rare. The pepper mill, trivet, tumbler, and 2-gallon water jar are very rare.

NOTE A few experimental Bob White plates have been found with all-white backgrounds rather than speckling. These are priced below.

Beverage server, w/stopper	$95
Stand for above	20
Bowl, salad, 12"	85
Bowl, soup	20 – 25
Bowl, vegetable	28 – 32
Bowl, vegetable, divided	25 – 35
Butter, ¼-pound	75
Butter Warmer, stick handle, w/lid	90
Stand for above	20
Casserole, 1-quart	40
Stand for above	15 – 20
Casserole, 2-quart	40
Stand for above	15 – 20
Double stand (for two)	35 – 45
Casserole, 4-quart	50
Stand for above	15 – 20
Cookie jar	60 – 70
Creamer	35

Bobwhite: Tall shakers, butter, and creamer.

Cruet, w/stopper, pair .... $200 – $225
    Stand for above. .... 25 – 35
Cup, coffee 5
Dish, cereal 25
Dish, fruit. .... 14 – 16
Gravy, stick handle, w/lid .... 45 – 55
    Stand for above. .... 15 – 20
Hors d'oeuvres holder .... 50 – 65
Jug, water, small, 60-ounce. .... 50 – 60
Jug, water, large, 112-ounce .... 90 – 110
Lazy Susan w/stand 100
Marmite, handled, w/lid 65
Mug .... 75 – 95
Nut bowl, 5-part. .... ND
Pepper mill, tall. 250
Plate, 6½" 5
    Experimental white .... 40 – 50
Plate, 7½" .... 7 – 8
    Experimental white .... 40 – 50
Plate, 10½" .... 10 – 12
    Experimental white .... 100 – 125
Platter, 13" .... 90 – 100
Platter, 20" .... 90 – 110
    Stand for above. .... 15 – 20
Relish dish, 3-section .... 45 – 55
Saucer 4
Shaker, bird, pair. .... 40 – 50
Shaker, tall, pair .... 25 – 35
Sugar .... 30 – 35
Teapot 125
    Stand for above. 15
Tray, Bread, rectangular, 24" .... 90 – 100
Tray, Cocktail, rectangular .... 30 – 40
Trivet. .... 100 – 125
Tumbler. .... 100 – 125
Water jar, w/base, 2-gallon 525
    w/solid base, 2-gallon 600

Round-Up

A Western-theme decoration, with cowboys predominating.

Beverage server w/stopper .... $350 +
Bowl, salad, 10½". .... 90 – 100
Bowl, soup .... 55 – 65
Bowl, vegetable, divided .... 70 – 80
Butter, ¼-pound. .... 150 – 175
Casserole, 1-quart .... 125 – 150
Casserole, 2-quart .... 150 – 175
Casserole, 4-quart .... 200 – 225

Cookie Jar . . . . *$400 +*
Creamer . . . . *45 – 50*
Cruet (pair) w/stopper . . . . *350 +*
   Stand for above . . . . *100 – 125*
Cup, coffee . . . . *35 – 45*
Dish, cereal/salad, 6" . . . . *35 – 45*
Dish, fruit/sauce . . . . *35 – 45*
Gravy, stick handle, w/lid . . . . *100 – 125*
Jug, 60-ounce . . . . *125 – 150*
Jug, 112-ounce . . . . *200 – 225*
Mug, coffee . . . . *90 – 100*
Plate, 6½" . . . . *15 – 20*
Plate, 7½" . . . . *25 – 35*
Plate, 10½"
   Chuckwagon . . . . *65 – 75*
   Cowboys around fire . . . . *100 – 125*
Platter, 13" . . . . *50 – 75*
Platter, 20" . . . . *300 +*
Relish, 3-part . . . . *100 – 125*
Saucer . . . . *10 – 12*
Shaker, tall, each . . . . *75 – 85*
Sugar . . . . *65 – 75*
Teapot . . . . *200 – 225*
Tray, Bread, rectangular, 24" . . . . *200 – 250*
Water cooler, 2-gallon . . . . *ND*

Smart Set   (1955)

The iron stands with double warmer for the 2-quart casserole and the 20" platter both had decorated pottery handles.

Beverage server w/stopper . . . . *$175 – $195*
Bowl, salad, 10½" . . . . *95 – 110*
Bowl, salad, individual, 5½" . . . . *15 – 18*
Bowl, soup . . . . *18 – 20*
Bowl, vegetable, divided . . . . *55 – 65*
Butter Warmer, stick handle, w/lid . . . . *40 – 50*
Butter, ¼-pound . . . . *95 – 110*
Casserole, 1-quart . . . . *55 – 65*
Casserole, 2-quart . . . . *60 – 70*
Casserole, 4-quart . . . . *75 – 95*
Creamer . . . . *18 – 20*
Cruets (pair) w/stopper and stand . . . . *175 – 200*
Cup . . . . *15 – 18*
Gravy, stick handle, w/lid . . . . *75 – 85*
Jug, 60-ounce . . . . *85 – 95*
Jug, 112-ounce . . . . *100 – 125*
Lazy Susan (5 dishes) w/carrier and tray . . . . *150 – 160*
Marmite, stick handle, w/lid . . . . *40 – 50*
Pepper mill . . . . *100 – 125*

Plate, 6½" .... *$8 – $10*
Plate, 7½" .... *12 – 15*
Plate, 10½" .... *20 – 25*
Platter, 13" .... *50 – 60*
Platter, 20" .... *125 – 150*
Relish, 3-part .... *65 – 75*
Sauce dish .... *10 – 12*
Saucer .... *3 – 4*
Shaker, each .... *30 – 35*
Sugar .... *18 – 20*
Teapot .... *200 – 225*
Tray, Bread, 24" .... *75 – 95*
Tray, Cocktail .... *35 – 45*

FUTURA SHAPE

Tampico   (1955)

A "South of the Border look . . . in rich browns, greens and vivacious melon accents, lightly flecked with brown overall."

Beverage server, w/lid .... *$85 – $95*
Bowl, round .... *25 – 30*
Bowl, salad, 12" *85*
Bowl, soup .... *18 – 22*
Bowl, vegetable, divided .... *35 – 45*
Butter, ¼-pound *35*
Cake plate, ruffled edge, stemmed foot *45*
Casserole *85*
Creamer .... *20 – 25*
Cup .... *8 – 10*
Dish, cereal .... *12 – 15*
Dish, sauce/fruit .... *8 – 10*
Gravy faststand .... *50 – 60*
Jug, 1-quart .... *95 – 110*
Jug, 2-quart .... *85 – 95*
Jug, ball .... *ND*
Mug .... *55 – 60*
Nut bowl, 5-part *85*
Plate, 6½" .... *5 – 7*
Plate, 8½" .... *10 – 12*
Plate, 10½" .... *11 – 13*
Platter, 13" .... *25 – 35*
Platter, 15" .... *35 – 45*
Relish dish .... *25 – 35*
Saucer .... *4 – 6*
Shaker, pair *35*
Sugar *22*
Teapot .... *100 – 125*

Trivit, 6¾" . . . . *$75 – $95*
Water jar, 2-gallon, w/stand. *500*

DINNERWARE / KITCHENWARE / SOLID-COLOR

FRUIT SERVICE   (1939)

Designed by Belle Kogan. An old ad refers to this line as the Terrace Fruit Service Group. A flyer I was sent shows six cookie jars under the Gypsy Trail Hostess Ware name, not surprising since the colors match; I assume the other pieces in this group were also a part of the Gypsy Trail Hostess Ware line.

Though I have not handled enough of these pieces to be sure, I suspect that the large casseroles are the large salad bowls with a lid added, and the individual casseroles are the individual salads with a lid added. Known shapes are apple, bananas, cherries, grapes, orange, pear, pineapple, and, despite the name, pepper and cabbage.

Royal blue, green, orange, pink, turquoise, white, and yellow are the colors I have identified.

PRICING   Add 20% to 25% for Royal blue.

Casserole, large
    Apple . . . . *$45 – $55*
    Pear . . . . *45 – 55*
    Pineapple . . . . *45 – 55*
Casserole, individual, 5"
    Apple . . . . *25 – 35*
    Orange . . . . *25 – 35*
    Pineapple . . . . *25 – 35*
Cookie jar
    Apple, 8"   /193 . . . . *110 – 125*
    Bananas, 9"   /231 . . . . *110 – 125*
    Cabbage, 8½"   /233 . . . . *250 +*
    Grapes, 9½"   /232. . . . . *110 – 125*
    Pear, 9"   /194. . . . . *110 – 125*
    Pineapple, 8½"   /205. . . . . *110 – 125*
Marmalade
    Apple . . . . *30 – 35*
    Pear . . . . *30 – 35*
    Pineapple . . . . *30 – 35*
Salad bowl, individual
    Apple . . . . *15 – 20*
    Pear . . . . *15 – 20*
    Pineapple . . . . *15 – 20*
Salad bowl, large
    Apple . . . . *30 – 35*
    Pear . . . . *30 – 35*
    Pineapple . . . . *30 – 35*

GYPSY TRAIL HOSTESS WARE

Gypsy Trail Hostess Ware was a collection of four lines (Chevron, Fondoso, Plain, and Reed) designed by Belle Kogan.

Chevron

Decorated in Ivory, Orange, Royal Blue, Turquoise, and Yellow.

PRICING   Add 25% for Royal Blue.

Ashtray, 4" /160	$15 – $20
Bowl, vegetable, 9" /156	30
Candlestick, Kettle, 3", each /158	15 – 18
Coffee pot, AD /167	60 – 65
Creamer /154	15 – 18
Cup /152	20 – 25
Cup, AD /165	25 – 30
Custard, footed /170	18 – 20
Dish, cereal (soup pot) /171	15 – 18
Drip jar /161	35 – 40
Jug, 19-ounce /168	25
Jug, 32-ounce /168	35
Jug, 70-ounce, w/ice lip /164	60
Jug, Rooster handle, 11½"	100 – 125
Plate, 6" /151	6
Plate, 7" /151	7
Plate, 8" /151	8
Plate, 10" /151	10 – 12
Plate, 12" /151	12 – 15
Plate, grill, 11" /159	20
Platter, oval, 12" /163	20

Chevron: Rooster-handled jug.

Platter, oval, 14"   /163 . . . . *$25*
Platter, round, sandwich tray, 15"   /166. . . . . *30*
Saucer,   /152. . . . . *4 – 5*
Saucer, AD   /165 . . . . *7 – 10*
Shaker, range, pair   /162 . . . . *20 – 25*
Sugar   /153 . . . . *25*
Teapot, 6-cup   /150 . . . . *55 – 60*
Vase, Kettle, 3"   /157 . . . . *20 – 25*

Fondoso   (1939)

Decorated in Orange, Powder Blue, Turquoise, and Yellow; also in pastel shades of Blue, Green, Pink, and Yellow. Mixing bowls were made in Russet and Ivory.

Bowl, mixing, 5"   /F137 . . . . *$30*
Bowl, mixing, 6"   /F137 . . . . *30*
Bowl, mixing, 7"   /F137 . . . . *30*
Bowl, mixing, 8"   /F137 . . . . *30*
Bowl, mixing, 9"   /F137 . . . . *30*
Bowl, salad, 11"   /F121 . . . . *25 – 30*
Bowl, soup, coupe, 7¹/₂"   /F125 . . . . *15 – 20*
Bowl, vegetable, round, 8" *30*
Butter, 1-pound   /F128 . . . . *35 – 45*
Canister, coffee, 2-pound capacity, 8¹/₂"   /F135 . . . . *ND*
Canister, flour, 3¹/₂-pound capacity, 8¹/₂"   /F134. . . . . *ND*
Canister, sugar, 5-pound capacity, 8¹/₂"   /F133. . . . . *ND*
Casserole, 8¹/₂"   /F127 . . . . *35*
Coffee pot   /F112 . . . . *50 – 60*
Coffee server, wood handle   /F111. . . . . *50 – 60*
Cookie jar, 8¹/₂"   /F132 . . . . *ND*
Creamer, small   /F106 . . . . *12 – 15*
Creamer, large   /F108. . . . . *15 – 18*
Cup   /F104. . . . . *16 – 18*
Cup, dessert, no handle, footed, 4"   /F118 . . . . *18 – 20*
Custard   /F119 . . . . *15*
Dish, lug, cereal/soup   /F124. . . . . *15 – 18*
Jug, batter   /F129. . . . . *65 – 75*
Jug, straight, 18-ounce   /F117. . . . . *25*
Jug, straight, 32-ounce   /F117. . . . . *30*
Jug, straight, 76-ounce   /F117. . . . . *60*
Jug, syrup   /F130. . . . . *35 – 45*
Jug, tilt, 70-ounce   /F116 . . . . *60*
Marmite, French, w/lid, 4¹/₂"   /F123. . . . . *20 – 25*
Marmite, low, w/lid, 4¹/₂"   /F122 . . . . *20 – 25*
Mug, no handle (tumbler), 7-ounce   /F114 . . . . *18 – 20*
Mug, no handle (tumbler), 10-ounce   /F115 . . . . *18 – 20*
Plate, 6¹/₂"   /F101. . . . . *6*
Plate, 8¹/₂"   /F101. . . . . *8*
Plate, 9¹/₂"   /F101. . . . . *10*

Fondoso and Reed: L to R: *Reed cup and saucer, Reed creamer, Fondoso sugar canister, Fondoso small and range shakers, and Reed tumbler.*

Plate, 12"   /F101 . . . . $12 – $15
Plate, chop, 14"   /F102 . . . . *15 – 20*
Platter, oval, 12"   /F103 . . . . *15 – 18*
Relish dish   /F138 . . . . *15 – 18*
Sauce dish, 5½"   /F120 . . . . *12 – 15*
Saucer   /F104 . . . . *4 – 5*
Shaker, small, pair   /F109 . . . . *10 – 15*
Shaker, large, pair   /F136 . . . . *20 – 25*
Shirred egg dish   /F126 . . . . *15 – 20*
Sugar, small   /F105 . . . . *15 – 20*
Sugar, large   /F107 . . . . *20 – 25*
Teapot, 3-cup   /F113 . . . . *45*
Teapot, 6-cup   /F113 . . . . *60*
Tray, Batter Set, rectangular   /F131 . . . . *25 +*

Reed

Decorated in Ivory, Orange, Royal Blue, Turquoise, and Yellow. Mixing bowls were also made in Russet.

   PRICING   Add 25% for Royal Blue.

Bowl, mixing, 5"   /127 . . . . $25
Bowl, mixing, 6"   /127 . . . . *25*
Bowl, mixing, 7"   /127 . . . . *25*
Bowl, mixing, 8"   /127 . . . . *25*
Bowl, mixing, 9"   /127 . . . . *25*

LABRIEGO

Blue, green, and yellow.

Casserole, French, oval, small		*$40 – $60*
Casserole, French, oval, medium		*40 – 60*
Casserole, French, oval, large		*40 – 60*
Coffee server		*60 – 75*
Creamer		*20 – 25*
Jug, water		*35 – 40*
Mug		*25 – 30*
Shaker, pair		*30 – 35*
Sugar		*30 – 35*
Teapot		*50 – 60*

TOWN AND COUNTRY (1947)

Designed by Eva Zeisel.

An informal, slightly eccentric design; plates are coupe shape, a little higher on one side. The **Lazy Susan** consists of seven 7" × 5" relish dishes with the mustard/condiment in the center. The **mustard** has a ball-shaped stopper with an attached spoon and a small hole on top with a tiny lid, for filling the stopper with hot water, ostensibly so that mustard will apply easily.

Glazes are glossy or half-matte: Chalk White, Chartreuse, Coral, Dusk Blue, Forest Green, Gray, Metallic Brown, Peach, Rust, and Sand. In addition, some pieces have turned up in colors that were used in other lines: Jade Green and Lime Green (Quartette), Light Blue (Tweedtex), and Plum (Iris).

Bean pot		*$150 – $200*
Bowl, mixing, 9"		*60 – 75*
Bowl, salad, 8½"		*40 – 50*
Bowl, salad, 13"		*45 – 60*
Bowl, salad/cereal, 5¼"		*8 – 12*
Bowl, vegetable, oval, 8"		*25 – 30*
Casserole, individual (marmite)		*25 – 35*
Casserole		*40 – 55*
Coaster/ashtray		*12 – 15*
Creamer		*10 – 15*
Cruet w/stopper		*60 – 75*
Cup		*12 – 15*
Jug, small		*30 – 40*
Jug, medium, 2-pint		*40 – 50*
Jug, large, 3-pint		*55 – 75*
Jug, syrup		*45 – 60*
Ladle/wood handle (for tureen)		*ND*
Lazy Susan (7 relish trays on wood ring)		*150 – 175*
Mug		*30 – 40*
Mustard (condiment) jar		*40 – 55*
Plate, 6½"		*10 – 12*
Plate, 8"		*15 – 18*

Plate, 10¹/₂" .... $20 – $25
Platter, 9" .... 20 – 25
Platter, 10⁵/₈" .... 25 – 30
Platter, 15" × 11¹/₂" .... 40 – 50
Relish, 7" × 5" .... 18 – 20
Relish, 9" × 6" .... 20 – 25
Salad spoon, wood handle, left and right hand .... ND
Sauce dish, 7" × 5" .... 6 – 10
Saucer .... 4 – 5
Shaker, small, each .... 12 – 15
Shaker, large, each .... 15 – 20
Soup tureen .... ND
Sugar .... 18 – 20
Teapot .... 125 – 150

VILLAGE GREEN / BROWN (1953 / 1955)

Introduced in 1953, Village Green had green flatware. The hollowware was brown outside and green inside, with green lids on the covered pieces. Village Brown pieces, brought out in 1955, were glazed in solid brown.

The handled trivets were intended for use with the casseroles.

Baking dish, 6" .... $10 – $12
Baking dish, 12" .... 12 – 15
   w/lid .... 20 – 25
Bean pot, 2-quart .... 25 – 35
Bean pot, 4-quart .... 20 – 25
Beverage server, 8-cup .... 65 – 75
Bowl, salad, small .... 15 – 18
Bowl, salad, 9" .... 30 – 35
Bowl, salad, 12" .... 45 – 55
Bowl, soup .... 15 – 18
Bowl, vegetable .... 20 – 25
Bowl, vegetable, divided .... 15 – 20
Butter, ¹/₄-pound .... 50 – 60
Casserole, 1-quart .... 20 – 25
Casserole, 2-quart .... 30 – 35
Casserole, 4-quart .... 40 – 45
Creamer .... 5 – 7
Cup .... 7 – 8
Dish, cereal .... 10 – 12
Dish, sauce .... 8 – 10
Gravy, w/tray .... 45 – 55
Jug, 4-cup .... 30 – 35
Jug, 10-cup .... 45 – 50
Jug, syrup .... 15 – 20
Marmite .... 6 – 8
Marmite, handled .... 10 – 12
Mug, beverage .... 15 – 18

Mug, coffee . . . . *$25 – $30*
Plate, 6" . . . . *4 – 6*
Plate, 8" . . . . *10 – 12*
Plate, 10" . . . . *8 – 10*
Plate, chop, 14" . . . . *35 – 45*
Platter, Tree-in-Well, 13" . . . . *15 – 18*
Platter, Tree-in-Well, 15" . . . . *18 – 20*
Saucer *5*
Shaker, pair . . . . *20 – 25*
Sugar . . . . *10 – 12*
Teapot, 6-cup. . . . . *65 – 75*
Trivet, handled, 8" . . . . *20 – 25*
Trivet, handled, 10" . . . . *20 – 25*
Trivet, handled, 12" . . . . *20 – 25*
Warmer . . . . *35 – 45*
Water jar, 2-gallon . . . . *250 – 300*
   w/stand . . . . *350 – 400*

NOVELTIES

ASH RECEIVERS

Cat . . . . *$95 – $105*
Dog . . . . *95 – 105*
Donkey . . . . *85 – 95*
Elephant . . . . *85 – 95*
Fish . . . . *85 – 95*
Pelican . . . . *85 – 95*

COOKIE JARS / FIGURAL

Commonly found in solid colors of blue, brown, green, pink, and yellow with hand-painted details in other colors. White is a rare color. See also Fruit Service.

Donkey ash receiver.

Carousel... $450 +
Chef (Pierre)
    Blue... *100 – 115*
    Brown.. *100 – 115*
    Green... *175 – 200*
    Pink w/black details................................ *225 – 250*
    Yellow.. *70 – 90*
Dutch Girl (Katrina)
    Blue/Brown... *100 – 115*
    Green... *175 – 200*
    Yellow.. *70 – 90*
Jack Frost w/palette, on pumpkin, short......................... *450 – 500*
Jack Frost w/palette, on pumpkin, tall........................... *450 – 500*
King of Hearts, w/bag of tarts, "Tarts"
    Chartreuse.. *325 – 375*
    Hand-painted.. *450 +*
    Pink w/black details................................ *325 – 375*
    White... *325 – 375*
Monk (Friar Tuck), "Thou Shalt Not Steal"
    Blue/Brown... *100 – 120*
    Green... *175 – 200*
    Yellow.. *70 – 90*
Peasants, dancing
    Munch jar.. *45 – 55*

FIGURES / PEOPLE

These will be found both hand-painted and in solid colors including coral, dark brown, gray, Woodland Green, maroon, white, and yellow. Not all figures have been seen in every color.

    The following are pairs: Boy with Apple and Girl with Flower, Cowboy and Cowgirl, Man with Accordion and Woman with Tambourine, and Oriental God and Goddess. The Oriental Woman is referred to as Chinese Mandarin by some.

    These will be found both hand painted and in solid colors: gray, maroon, and yellow are known.

Boy w/Apple, 8½" /1122
    Hand-painted $150
Cowboy /B1415
    Hand-painted *175*
    Solid-color.. *80 – 100*
Cowgirl /B1414
    Hand-painted *175*
    Solid-color.. *80 – 100*
Girl w/Flower, 8½" /1121
    Hand-painted *150*
Maiden w/lyre and deer (The Muse) /B2507
    Solid-color.. *80 – 100*
Maidens, 2 (The Nymphs), 16½" /B2500
    Solid-color.. *80 – 100*

Man w/Accordion   /B1417
   Hand-painted *$150*
   Solid-color. . . . . *60 – 75*
Man w/Bouquet, next to hydrant, 10³/₄"   /1350
   Solid-color. . . . . *80 – 85*
Oriental God   /1389
   Hand-painted *135*
   Solid-color. . . . . *50 – 70*
Oriental Goddess   /1308
   Hand-painted *135*
   Solid-color. . . . . *50 – 70*
Oriental Man w/jug   /1349
   Solid-color. . . . . *65 – 80*
Oriental Woman   /1365
   Solid-color. . . . . *65 – 80*
Satyr   /1310
   Solid-color. . . . . *60 – 80*
Woman w/Tambourine   /B1416
   Hand-painted *150*
   Solid-color. . . . . *60 – 75*

MISCELLANY

I have seen the large casseroles referred to as cookie jars, but we know from the Fruit line that Red Wing made large and individual casseroles, and I believe the same principle applies here.

Miscellany (Clockwise from top): *Saturn teapot, Rooster teapot, Fish individual casserole, and Rooster individual casserole.*

Casserole, Fish, individual *$60*
Casserole, Fish, large *95*
Casserole, Rooster, individual. *50*
Casserole, Rooster, large. *75*
Reamer, footed . . . . *100 – 150*
Teapot, Rooster /257. . . . . *60 – 75*
Teapot, Saturn . . . . *90 – 110*
  Royal Blue. . . . . *125 – 150*

PLANTERS

Note that the lid on the piano is often missing because it broke easily.

Banjo, 15" (white w/black detail) /908 . . . . *$40 – $50*
Canoe, Birchbark
  10" /734 . . . . *150*
  12" /735 . . . . *150*
  17" /733 . . . . *150*
Dachshund /1342 . . . . *60*
Flying Horse (Pegasus) /1340 . . . . *40 – 50*
Giraffe, 11" (brown w/tan fleck) /896. . . . . *150*
Guitar /M-1484. . . . . *40 – 50*
Piano, w/piano lid /M-1525. . . . . *150 – 225*
Rabbit /1339 . . . . *35 – 45*
Sheep /1343 . . . . *35 – 45*
Swan /259 . . . . *20 – 25*
Violin, 14¹/₂" (rust w/black detail) /907 . . . . *40 – 50*

REGAL CHINA CORPORATION

Antioch, Illinois

CHAPTER AT A GLANCE

ALICE IN WONDERLAND
COOKIE JARS
HUGGIES

OLD MACDONALD
PEEK-A-BOOS

Founded ca. 1938, Regal was bought by Royal China and Novelty Company (no relation to Royal China) in the 1940s and was afterward used as the manufacturing arm of their contract and premium business. Regal is best known as the manufacturer of the Jim Beam bottles. Due to declining interest in these bottles, the company closed in 1992.

See Roerig in Bibliography.

ALICE IN WONDERLAND

These are licensed Walt Disney items and are based on the Disney cartoon.

Cookie jar, Alice . . . . *$3000 +*
Creamer, White Rabbit, full figure w/watch . . . . *400 – 500*
Jug, milk, King of Hearts . . . . *600 +*
Shaker, Alice
    Decorated head and feet w/gold, pair . . . . *500 +*
    Fully decorated, pair . . . . *600 +*
    White w/gold, pair . . . . *500 +*
Shakers, Tweedledum and Tweedledee . . . . *800 +*
Sugar, White Rabbit, rabbit-head finial . . . . *450 – 550*
Teapot, Mad Hatter . . . . *2500 +*

COOKIE JARS

See also Alice in Wonderland, Old MacDonald, and Peek-a-Boos. Matching pieces are listed below each cookie jar.

Baby Pig in pinned diapers . . . . *$500 – $525*
Boy w/Butter Churn . . . . *325 – 375*
Cat (Puss n Boots)
    Peach/White . . . . *375 – 400*
    Gray . . . . *400 +*
    Creamer . . . . *100 – 125*

Shakers	$225– $250
Sugar	100 – 125
Clown, full figure, holding cookie	700 +
Shakers	250– 300
Davy Crockett, head	650 – 700
Dutch Girl	450 +
Shakers	200 – 225
Fisherman/Whaler	600 +
French Chef	400 +
Shakers	200 – 225
Goldilocks w/Baby Bear	350 – 400
Shakers	275 – 300
Humpty-Dumpty w/gold, red, or yellow base	300 – 350
Shakers	200 – 225
Kraft-T Bear	200 – 225
Lion, Hubert, w/glasses	1000
Bank (Made by Lefton/Japan)	40 – 50
Majorette (head)	450 – 500
Miss Muffet on tuffet w/spider	350 – 400
Oriental Lady w/baskets	450 – 550
Poodle, Fifi	500
Quaker Oats	125 – 150
Rocking Horse	275 – 325
Toby, "Toby Cookies"	600 – 700
Uncle Mistletoe	750 +

HUGGIES (1948)

These shakers were designed by Ruth Van Tellingen Bendel. Official name is "Snuggle Hugs." Bunnies and bears are the easiest to find; pigs are the most elusive, especially the Pig Bank.

Color variations are not uncommon. Where the word "colors" appears in a listing, it refers to patches of different colors that can appear on a piece.

MARKS "c Van Tellingen" is incised just below the tail or on the base of the item. Sometimes the name of the item or "Pat. Pend." is incised as well. Fire destroyed the molds ca. 1958, and the new molds were incised "Bendel."

NOTE Be aware of Occupied Japan imitations. They weigh less than the Regal pieces.

Bear Hug

Bear Hugs marked "Bendel" are worth $50–$60.

Brown w/black	$20 – $25
Brown w/pink	20 – 25
Cream	20 – 25
Green	20 – 25
Green w/black tail, colors	20 – 25
Pink	20 – 25
Pink w/black tail	20 – 25
Pink w/black tail, colors	20 – 25
Pink w/brown and black	20 – 25

Tan (beige) .... $20 – $25
Tan w/brown... 20 – 25
White w/pink and brown.. 20 – 25
Yellow .... 20 – 25
Yellow w/black tail... 20 – 25
Yellow w/black tail, colors.. 20 – 25
Yellow w/gold .... 30 – 35

Boy/Dog Hug

Boy's face can vary from light gray through dark gray to black and from pink
to tan. Variations in boy are listed. White dog w/brown goes with brown or
pink/tan face; white dog w/black goes with gray to black face.

White.. $75 – $85
White w/brown face.. 80 – 90
White w/gray to black face .... 90 – 100
White w/pink/tan face .... 80 – 90

Bunny Hug

Yellow or green bunnies with hand-painted underglaze clothes, and yellow
bunnies with hand-painted overglaze roses, marked J. L. Stieff Art Studio, have
also been found. Bunny Hugs marked "Bendel" are worth $85–$100.

Brown .... $20 – $25
Gray w/pink and dark gray... 20 – 25
Green... 20 – 25
Green w/black tail .... 20 – 25
Green w/black tail, colors .... 20 – 25
Green w/brown and black.. 20 – 25
Green w/painted clothes .... 50 – 75
White... 20 – 25
White w/black tail .... 20 – 25
White w/black tail and spots... 20 – 25
White w/black tail, colors.. 20 – 25
Yellow .... 20 – 25
Yellow w/black tail... 20 – 25
Yellow w/black tail, colors .... 20 – 25
Yellow w/painted clothes .... 50 – 75

Duck Hug

Yellow .... $30 – $35
Yellow w/black .... 40 – 50
Yellow w/red.. 40 – 50

Dutch Boy/Girl Hug

Boy is white with red hair, rosy cheeks, yellow shoes, and marks on trousers.
Girl is white with rosy cheeks and blue on cap and apron.

White... $35 – $45
White w/color .... 35 – 45

Love Bug Hug

SMALL   There is a wide variation in the grayish green coloring.

Grayish Green .... *$65 – $75*
Maroon .... *65 – 75*
Pink w/black spots .... *100 – 125*

LARGE

Maroon .... *$275 – $300*

Mary/Lamb Hug

Listings reflect variations in lamb only; Mary is white with red-brown hair, green on scarf, and orange on skirt.

Black lamb .... *$50 – $60*
Gray lamb .... *50 – 60*
Gray lamb w/black tail .... *50 – 60*
Gray lamb w/black tail and ears............................... *50 – 60*
White lamb .... *50 – 60*
White lamb w/black tail....................................... *50 – 60*
White lamb w/black tail and ears .... *50 – 60*
Yellow lamb .... *50 – 60*
Yellow lamb w/black tail .... *50 – 60*
Yellow lamb w/black tail and ears .... *50 – 60*

Mermaid/Sailor Hug

Mermaid is tan with red-brown hair and green tail. Sailor is white with rosy cheeks, black shoes, and blue trim.

Tan mermaid, White Sailor .... *$125 – $150*
Painted Mermaid and Sailor.................................... *250 – 275*

Pig Hug, small

Pink .... *ND*
Pink w/colors... *ND*
Yellow .... *ND*

Pig Hug, large

White w/black spots .... *$300 +*
White w/gray and black .... *300 +*
White w/gray and black, "BANK"................................ *300 +*

OLD MACDONALD

The canisters and spice jars all have red barrel bottoms with black hoops. The lids for the large canisters are either Grandma or Grandpa. The lids for the medium canisters and the spice jars are either Boy, Girl, Grandma, Grandpa, Horse, or Turkey.

Butter, ¼-pound, cow head on lid. .... *$200 – $225*
Canister, medium
   Cereal .... *225 – 250*
   Coffee.. *225 – 250*
   Flour .... *225 – 250*
   Salt.. *225 – 250*
   Sugar .... *225 – 250*
   Tea... *225 – 250*

Canister, large

    Cookies . . . . *$300 – $350*

    Peanuts . . . . *300 – 350*

    Popcorn . . . . *300 – 350*

    Potato Chips . . . . *300 – 350*

    Pretzels . . . . *300 – 350*

    Soap . . . . *300 – 350*

    Tid-Bit . . . . *300 – 350*

Cookie jar, Barn . . . . *325 – 350*

Creamer, Rooster . . . . *100 – 125*

Grease jar, pig head on lid . . . . *175 – 200*

Jar, spice

    Allspice . . . . *100 – 125*

    Cinnamon . . . . *100 – 125*

    Cloves . . . . *100 – 125*

    Ginger . . . . *100 – 125*

    Nutmeg . . . . *100 – 125*

    Pepper . . . . *100 – 125*

Jug, milk, embossed cow's head w/gold bell . . . . *450 – 500*

Shaker, boy and girl, pair . . . . *85 – 100*

Shaker, churn shape, pair . . . . *75 – 95*

Shaker, flour sack shape, embossed sheep, pair . . . . *150 – 200*

Sugar, roosting hen lid . . . . *100 – 125*

Teapot, duck head on lid . . . . *300 – 325*

PEEK-A-BOOS

These bears in pajamas were designed by Ruth Van Tellingen Bendel. A complete shaker set has each bear covering alternate eyes. There was limited production on the cookie jar.

Cookie jar   /R . . . . *$1400 +*

Shaker, small

    White w/red . . . . *275 – 300*

Peek-A-Boo cookie jar, large and small shakers.

White w/peach. . . . . *$275 – $300*
Shaker, large
    White w/red. . . . . *450 – 500*
    White w/gold. . . . . *450 – 500*

ROBINSON-RANSBOTTOM POTTERY COMPANY

Roseville, Ohio

CHAPTER AT A GLANCE

COOKIE JARS
KITCHENWARE
HOBNAIL

KITCHENETTE
SWIRL
ZEPHYRUS

In the fall of 1900, the four Ransbottom brothers acquired the Oval Ware and Brick Company in Beem City (one mile north of Roseville) and early in 1901 began producing stoneware jardinieres, cuspidors, and red flowerpots as the Ransbottom Brothers Pottery; they soon became the world's largest producer of stoneware jars. In 1908 they incorporated as the Ransbottom Brothers Pottery Company. In 1920, with the market for stoneware declining, they merged with the Robinson Clay Product Company, a manufacturer of tile and brick products. In the early 1920s, production shifted to gardenware: birdbaths, planting tubs, jardinieres with pedestals, large vases, urns, and strawberry jars. Kitchenware was added in the 1930s. The company is still in business.

According to Mr. Alfred Ransbottom, most of the hand-decorated items were made from 1947 to 1957.

MARKS Two impressed marks are generally found. One is a crown, and the other is the inscription "RRPCo, Roseville, Ohio" (sometimes just "RRPCo"). Note: some people mistake this mark for Roseville Pottery; don't be fooled.

COOKIE JARS

Apple, round, w/embossed apples .... $30 – $35
Chef .... 150 – 175
   w/gold .... 250 – 275

Cow over Moon (Hi Diddle Diddle) . . . . *$275 – $300*
    w/gold . . . . *375 – 400*
Dutch Boy . . . . *225 – 275*
Dutch Girl . . . . *225 – 275*
Monkey (Jocko) . . . . *300 – 325*
Ol' King Cole . . . . *400 – 450*
Oscar, head w/doughboy hat . . . . *150 – 175*
Owl w/glasses and book, "Cookie Stories" . . . . *70 – 90*
Peter, Peter, Pumpkin Eater
    w/gold . . . . *300 – 350*
    w/o gold . . . . *250 – 300*
Ringed jar w/tiger cubs on lid . . . . *50 – 60*
Sheriff Pig . . . . *125 – 135*
    w/gold . . . . *150 – 175*
Snow Man (Frosty) . . . . *500 +*
Whale w/beret . . . . *700 +*
World War II Soldier (Bud) . . . . *275 – 325*
World War II Sailor (Jack) . . . . *275 – 325*

KITCHENWARE

The important thing to remember about these lines is that every piece was not
made in every color.

HOBNAIL   (1937–ca. 1943)

The casserole and refrigerator jars seem to be the bakers with a lid.
    Manufactured in solid colors of Blue, Ivory, Pink, Turquoise, and Yellow.

Baker, 4¹/₂" . . . . *$3 – $4*
Baker, 5¹/₂" . . . . *4 – 5*
Baker, 6¹/₂" . . . . *5 – 6*
Baker, 7¹/₂" . . . . *6 – 8*
Bowl, 5" . . . . *3 – 5*
Bowl, 5³/₄" . . . . *5 – 7*
Bowl, 6³/₄" . . . . *7 – 9*
Bowl, 7³/₄" . . . . *10 – 12*
Bowl, 8³/₄" . . . . *12 – 15*
Casserole, 7¹/₂" . . . . *15 – 20*
Custard . . . . *2 – 3*
Pitcher, 1¹/₄-pint . . . . *6 – 8*
Pitcher, 2¹/₂-pint . . . . *8 – 10*
Pitcher, 3¹/₄-pint . . . . *10 – 12*
Pitcher, ice lip, 4-pint . . . . *10 – 12*
Refrigerator jar, 4¹/₂" . . . . *10 – 15*
Refrigerator jar, 5¹/₂" . . . . *15 – 20*
Refrigerator jar, 6¹/₂" . . . . *15 – 20*

KITCHENETTE   (1938–early 1950s)

Over the years, pieces were added and dropped, and colors were refined. It seems to have evolved into a line called Kitchen. The mustard seems to be the custard with a lid.

Kitchenette colors are Blue, Brown, Pink, Turquoise, and Yellow. Kitchen colors are Blue, Ivory, Jade, Peach, and Yellow.

Baker, 5" .... $3 – $5
Baker, 6" .... 5 – 6
Baker, 7" .... 6 – 8
Baker, 8" .... 8 – 10
Bowl, 5" .... 3 – 5
Bowl, 6" .... 5 – 7
Bowl, 7" .... 7 – 9
Bowl, 8" .... 10 – 12
Bowl, 9" .... 12 – 15
Casserole, 7¼" .... 15 – 20
Casserole, 8¼" .... 15 – 20
Custard, 5-ounce .... 2 – 3
Jug, ½-pint .... 5 – 6
Jug, 1-pint .... 6 – 7
Jug, 2-pint .... 7 – 8
Jug, 3-pint .... 8 – 10
Jug, 4-pint .... 10 – 12
Jug, ice lip, 3-pint .... 12 – 15
Jug, ice lip, 4-pint .... 12 – 15
Jug, w/lid, 2-pint .... 15 – 20
Jug, w/lid, 3-pint .... 15 – 20
Mustard, w/lid, 5-ounce .... 10 – 12
Pie plate, 9½" .... 8 – 10
Refrigerator jar, w/lid, 5½" .... 15 – 20

Zephyrus jug and Kitchenette jug.

Refrigerator jar, w/lid, 6½" .... *$15 – $20*
Sugar .... *8 – 10*

SWIRL   (ca. 1946)

Available in solid colors of Blue, Cocoa, Ivory, Jade, and Yellow.

Baker, 5½" .... *$3 – $5*
Baker, 6½" .... *5 – 6*
Baker, 7¼" .... *6 – 8*
Baker, 8¼" .... *8 – 10*
Bowl, 5" .... *3 – 5*
Bowl, 6" .... *5 – 7*
Bowl, 7" .... *7 – 9*
Bowl, 8" .... *10 – 12*
Bowl, 9" .... *12 – 15*
Casserole, 8¼" .... *15 – 20*
Pitcher, 1½-pint .... *5 – 6*
Pitcher, 2½-pint .... *8 – 10*

ZEPHYRUS   (1946 or 1947)

Decorated in solid colors of Corn Yellow, Ivory, Pink, Robin Egg Blue, and Turquoise; look for a hand-tinted version in turquoise, pink, and blue on an ivory body.

Baker, 5½" .... *$3 – $5*
Baker, 6½" .... *5 – 6*
Baker, 7¼" .... *6 – 8*
Baker, 8¼" .... *8 – 10*
Bowl, 5" .... *3 – 5*
Bowl, 6" .... *5 – 7*
Bowl, 7" .... *7 – 9*
Bowl, 8" .... *10 – 12*
Bowl, 9" .... *12 – 15*
Casserole, 8¼" .... *15 – 20*
Pitcher, 1½-pint .... *5 – 6*
Pitcher, 2½-pint .... *8 – 10*
Pitcher, ice lip, 3½-pint .... *12 – 15*

ROSEVILLE POTTERY COMPANY

Roseville and Zanesville, Ohio

CHAPTER AT A GLANCE

BANEDA	JUVENILE WARE
CARNELIAN II	MOSTIQUE
CORINTHIAN	PINECONE
DONATELLO	RAYMOR
FALLINE	ROSECRAFT HEXAGON
FERRELLA	ROSECRAFT VINTAGE
FLORENTINE	TUSCANY
FUTURA	ZEPHYR LILY

Organized in 1892, Roseville began manufacturing stoneware in a factory previously owned by the Owens Pottery Company in Roseville. A second location was bought in Roseville, but it was two facilities purchased in Zanesville that were to become the manufacturing center of the pottery. One of these was previously owned by the Mosaic Tile Company; here the company continued to produce utilitarian stoneware. The other location was used for the production of art ware, starting in 1900.

A number of top designers were hired due to the strong competition in the field, but the hand-decorated lines they created were phased out at the end of the second decade because of waning interest. From this point on, decoration was either in the mold with varying glazes or, to a lesser degree, decals.

Company fortunes began waning after World War II, and Roseville introduced Raymor in 1952 in what is said to be an attempt to stave off bankruptcy. It didn't work, and the company closed in 1954.

Roseville is possibly the most popular art pottery collected today and a large reason is the wide range and plenitude of product in a range of prices. As time progresses and prices rise, the later lines are becoming more desirable.

See Buxton in Bibliography. Although out of print, it is well worth seeking out. See Evans, see Huxford, and see Kovel.

PRICING   Size is definitely a factor. For a line such as Mostique, this can be a pretty straightforward matter. For a line such as Pinecone, with its more dramatic shapes, design becomes an additional element in gauging value. For pieces with molded detail, prices are for pieces with very good to excellent detail. For items made from worn molds or with weak color, deduct 20%.

A word about pricing jardiniere pedestals. Opinions can vary depending on who you ask. Many feel that if you find a jardiniere and pedestal, the pedestal should be equivalent in value to the jardiniere. But if a pedestal is found by itself, it is less than the value of the jardiniere because it cannot be displayed effectively. The other side of this, of course, is that pedestals are harder to find, but that factor does not seem to affect pricing.

Note A tip from Gordon Hoppe: The #197 footed bowl is being reproduced and is stamped "Made in Japan." However, some bowls have been seen with the stamp sanded off. Look for an unglazed area where the mark was located, as well as color variation.

BANEDA (ca. 1933)

A background of high-gloss rose or matte green with an embossed band of white or yellow flowers, orange pumpkin-like fruit, and green leaves.

Bowl, 12" /237 .... *$200 – $250*
Bowl, hexagonal, 10" /234 .... *175 – 225*
Bowl, round, 6" /232 .... *180 – 240*
Candlestick, 4", each /1088 .... *75 – 125*
Candlestick, 5", each /1087 .... *125 – 175*
Jardiniere, 4" /626 .... *160 – 200*
Jardiniere, 5" /626 .... *175 – 225*
Jardiniere, 6" /626 .... *200 – 250*
Jardiniere, 7" /626 .... *275 – 350*
Jardiniere, 8" /626 .... *350 – 500*
Jardiniere, 9" /626 .... *450 – 650*
Jardiniere, 10" /626 .... *650 – 850*
Vase, 4" /587 .... *150 – 200*
Vase, 4" /603 .... *160 – 220*
Vase, 5" /235 .... *225 – 275*
Vase, 5" /601 .... *175 – 225*
Vase, 6" /588 .... *200 – 250*
Vase, 6" /589 .... *225 – 275*
Vase, 6" /591 .... *250 – 300*
Vase, 6" /602 .... *225 – 275*
Vase, 6" /605 .... *300 – 350*
Vase, 7" /590 .... *275 – 350*
Vase, 7" /592 .... *275 – 350*
Vase, 7" /604 .... *275 – 350*
Vase, 7" /606 .... *300 – 400*
Vase, 7" /610 .... *300 – 400*
Vase, 8" /593 .... *350 – 450*
Vase, 8" /595 .... *350 – 450*
Vase, 9" /594 .... *375 – 475*
Vase, 9" /596 .... *425 – 500*
Vase, 10" /597 .... *500 – 650*
Vase, 12" /598 .... *600 – 750*
Vase, 12" /599 .... *650 – 800*

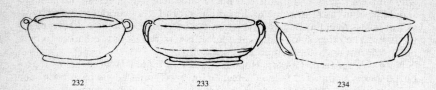

232   233   234

 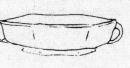

235   237   587   588

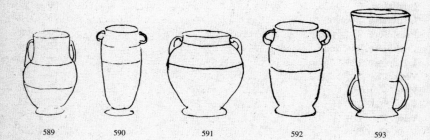

589   590   591   592   593

594   595   596   597

Baneda

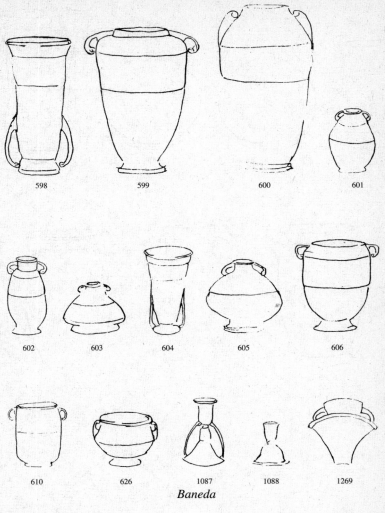

598 599 600 601

602 603 604 605 606

610 626 1087 1088 1269

Baneda

Vase, 15" /600 . . . . *$900 – $1100*
Wall box, 8" /233 . . . . *275 – 375*
Wall pocket, 8" /1269 . . . . *500 – 750*

CARNELIAN II (ca. 1915)

Thick mottled colors, several on one piece. Any number of color combinations may be found.

   PRICING Values reflect strong, thick mottled glazes with two or three colors minimum. Add 10% to 20% for four, five, or more color combinations. Subtract 10% to 20% for weak, uneven glazes with dull, uninspiring colors.

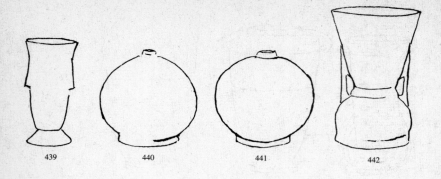

439   440   441   442

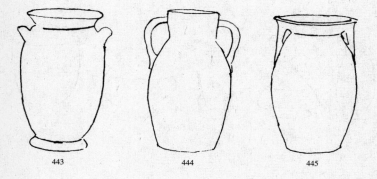

443   444   445

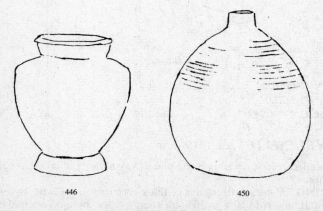

446   450

Carnelian II

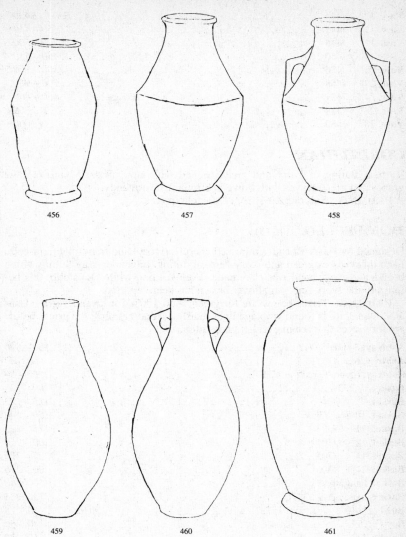

456   457   458

459   460   461

Carnelian II

Sand jar, 28"   /461 . . . . *$1200+*
Vase, 8"   /440 . . . . *225 – 275*
Vase, 8"   /441 . . . . *225 – 275*
Vase, 9"   /439 . . . . *175 – 225*
Vase, 12"   /442 . . . . *375 – 475*
Vase, 12"   /443 . . . . *300 – 400*

Vase, 12"	/444	$300 – $400
Vase, 12"	/445	350 – 450
Vase, 12"	/446	400 – 500
Vase, 14"	/450	450 – 550
Vase, 20"	/456	500 – 700
Vase, 24"	/458	700 – 900
Vase, 24"	/457	650 – 800
Vase, 28"	/459	800 +
Vase, 28"	/460	1000 +

CORINTHIAN

Vertical fluting of ivory and green topped with an embossed band of blue grapes and green leaves with flowers. Similar to Normandy.

PRICING Subtract 20% from Donatello prices.

DONATELLO (1915)

Designed by Harry Rhead. Embossed cherubs (ivory) and trees on a terra-cotta band that crosses green and ivory vertical fluting. Lavender-gray fluting with a brown and ivory band was also made. You will find white Donatello; this belongs to the Ivory line. An allover brown has been reported.

PRICING Prices below are for green. Add 100% for lavender-gray. Usually, Donatello is found with age lines, hairlines, and/or chips; the prices below are for pieces that are in excellent condition.

Ashtray, 3-sided /15		$60 – $90
Ashtray, round /16		60 – 80
Ashtray, round, flared top /17		60 – 80
Basket /233		100 – 125
Basket, 9" /301		125 – 175
Basket, 10½" /302		150 – 200
Basket, 11" /303		175 – 225
Basket, 12" /304		200 – 250
Basket, 14" /305		225 – 275
Basket, 14" /306		200 – 250
Basket, hanging, 6" /327		150 – 200
Basket, hanging, 8" /327		175 – 225
Bowl /88		50 – 75
Bowl /89		40 – 60
Bowl /90		60 – 80
Bowl /91		40 – 60
Bowl /92		70 – 90
Bowl, 4" /227		30 – 50
Bowl, 5" /227		40 – 60
Bowl, 5" /238		40 – 60
Bowl, 6" /53		40 – 60
Bowl, 6" /60		40 – 60
Bowl, 6" /227		40 – 60
Bowl, 6" /238		40 – 60

Bowl, 7"   /53 . . . . *$50 – $75*
Bowl, 7"   /238 . . . . *50 – 75*
Bowl, 8"   /54 . . . . *50 – 75*
Bowl, 8"   /60 . . . . *50 – 75*
Bowl, 10"   /55 . . . . *80 – 120*
Bowl, 10"   /60 . . . . *80 – 120*
Bowl, 12"   /60 . . . . *100 – 150*
Bowl, footed, 4"   /231 . . . . *50 – 60*
Bowl, footed, 5"   /231 . . . . *60 – 80*
Bowl, footed, 6"   /231 . . . . *80 – 100*
Candle holder, finger ring   /1011 . . . . *75 – 125*
Candlestick, finger ring   /10091 . . . . *75 – 125*
Candlestick, 7½"   /1008 . . . . *75 – 100*
Candlestick, 10"   /36 . . . . *90 – 125*
Candlestick, 10"   /1022 . . . . *90 – 125*
Compote   /232 . . . . *150 – 200*
Flower frog, 2½"   /14 . . . . *20 – 30*
Flower frog, 3½"   /14 . . . . *20 – 30*
Flowerpot w/saucer, 4"   /580 . . . . *50 – 60*
Flowerpot w/saucer, 5"   /580 . . . . *60 – 80*
Flowerpot w/saucer, 6"   /580 . . . . *80 – 100*
Incense burner . . . . *250 +*
Jardiniere, 4"   /575 . . . . *50 – 75*
Jardiniere, 5"   /575 . . . . *60 – 90*
Jardiniere, 6"   /579 . . . . *80 – 120*
Jardiniere, 8"   /579 . . . . *100 – 150*
Jardiniere, 10"   /579 . . . . *125 – 175*
Jardiniere, 12"   /579 . . . . *150 – 250*
Pitcher   /1307 . . . . *200 – 250*
Plate, 6"   /61 . . . . *100 – 150*
Plate, 8"   /61 . . . . *150 – 200*
Powder jar   /1 . . . . *200 – 250*
Powder jar   /2 . . . . *275 – 350*
Vase, bud, 6"   /116 . . . . *80 – 120*
Vase, 6"   /118 . . . . *50 – 65*
Vase, 6"   /184 . . . . *50 – 65*
Vase, 7"   /113 . . . . *50 – 65*
Vase, 8"   /101 . . . . *60 – 80*
Vase, 8"   /102 . . . . *60 – 80*
Vase, 8"   /103 . . . . *60 – 80*
Vase, 8"   /104 . . . . *60 – 80*
Vase, 8"   /113 . . . . *60 – 80*
Vase, 8"   /118 . . . . *60 – 80*
Vase, 8"   /184 . . . . *60 – 80*
Vase, 10"   /105 . . . . *90 – 120*
Vase, 10"   /106 . . . . *90 – 120*
Vase, 10"   /107 . . . . *90 – 120*
Vase, 10"   /108 . . . . *90 – 120*

Vase, 10" /113 .... *$90 – $120*
Vase, bud, 10" /115 .... *150 – 200*
Vase, 10" /184 .... *90 – 120*
Vase, 12" /109 .... *130 – 160*
Vase, 12" /110 .... *130 – 160*
Vase, 12" /111 .... *130 – 160*
Vase, 12" /112 .... *130 – 160*
Vase, 12" /113 .... *130 – 160*
Vase, 12" /184 .... *130 – 160*
Vase, 15" /113 .... *190 – 225*
Vase, bud, double /8 .... *75 – 100*
Vase, bud, double /9 .... *100 – 125*
Wall pocket, 10" /1202 .... *150 – 175*
Wall pocket, 12" /1212 .... *175 – 200*

FALLINE (ca. 1933)

Pea pod–like designs circle pieces on matte background of mottled terra cotta that shades into either chocolate brown, purple, or green/royal blue.

PRICING Prices are for green/royal blue. Subtract 10% to 20% for brown. Prices reflect strong mold definition and strong color. Subtract 10% to 20% for weak color or mold detail.

Bowl, 8" /244 .... *$225 – $275*
Candlestick, 3½" /1092. .... *200 – 250*
Vase, 6" /642 .... *300 – 375*
Vase, 6" /643 .... *300 – 350*
Vase, 6" /644 .... *325 – 375*
Vase, 6" /650 .... *350 – 400*
Vase, 6½" /645. .... *325 – 375*
Vase, 7" /647 .... *325 – 375*
Vase, 7" /648 .... *350 – 400*
Vase, 8" /646 .... *350 – 400*
Vase, 8" /649 .... *350 – 400*
Vase, 8" /651 .... *400 – 450*
Vase, 9" /652 .... *450 – 500*
Vase, 12" /653 .... *600 – 750*
Vase, 13½" /654. .... *800 – 900*
Vase, 15" /655 .... *1000 – 1200*

FERRELLA (ca. 1930)

Shapes have brown or rose mottled glaze with greenish-yellow shells embossed on rim or base emphasized with cutouts.

PRICING For strong mold definition and strong color, add 10% to 20%.

Bowl, 8" /211 .... *$300 – $350*
Bowl, footed, 4" /210. .... *200 – 250*
Bowl, footed, 12" × 7" /212 .... *350 – 400*
Bowl w/frog, 8" /87 .... *400 – 450*

Candlestick, each, 4" /1078		$200 – $225
Flower frog, 2½" /15		40 – 60
Flower frog, 3½" /15		40 – 60
Flowerpot, 5" /620		300 – 350
Vase, 4" /497		200 – 250
Vase, 4" /498		150 – 200
Vase, 5" /500		200 – 250
Vase, 5" /503		225 – 275
Vase, 5½" /504		225 – 275
Vase, 6" /499		250 – 300
Vase, 6" /501		250 – 300
Vase, 6" /502		225 – 275
Vase, 6" /505		250 – 325
Vase, 8" /506		350 – 400
Vase, 8" /508		350 – 400
Vase, 8" /509		350 – 400
Vase, 9" /507		400 – 450
Vase, 10" /511		450 – 550
Wall pocket, 6½" /1266		500 +

FLORENTINE   (ca. 1924)

Panels of textured sections alternate with vertical garlands.
   PRICING   Subtract 20% from Donatello values.

FUTURA   (ca. 1924)

Wide variety of styles: geometric, Art Deco, and floral. Large range of colors and glazes.

Bowl, 8" /188		$200 – $300
Bowl, 10" /195		150 – 250
Bowl, flower, rectangular, 12" × 5" × 3½" /196		300 – 400
Candlestick, 4" /1075		125 – 200
Candlestick, 4" /1073		100 – 150
Candlestick, 4" /1072		150 – 250
Planter, 6" /190-3½		150 – 250
Planter, 6" /189-4		175 – 300
Planter, 4" /85		200 – 250
Planter, square, footed, 5" /198		225 – 300
Vase, rectangular, 5" × 1½" × 5" /81		150 – 250
Vase, 5" /421		150 – 250
Vase, 6" /82		200 – 300
Vase, 6" /380		250 – 350
Vase, 6" /381		200 – 300
Vase, 6" /397		200 – 250
Vase, 6" /422		250 – 350
Vase, 6" /423		175 – 275
Vase, 7" /382		200 – 300

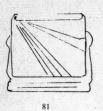

81

82

85

187

188

189

190

195

196

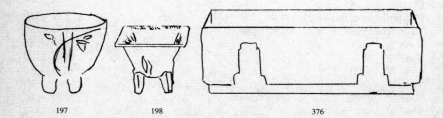

197   198   376

Futura

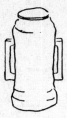

381

382

384

387

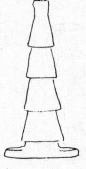

389

390

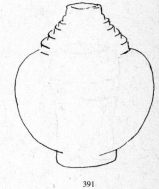

391

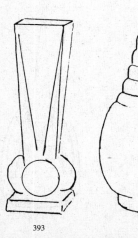

393

394

396

399

Futura

400

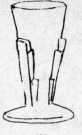

401

403

404

405

406

407

409

410

411

Futura

412

421

424

425

426

427

428

433

434

435

1072

1075

Futura

Vase, 7" /387 .... $450 – $650
Vase, 7" /399 .... 300 – 400
Vase, 7" /403 .... 350 – 500
Vase, 7" /424 .... 350 – 550
Vase, 7¹/₂" /405 .... 400 – 600
Vase, 8" /383 .... 300 – 450
Vase, 8" /384 .... 400 – 600
Vase, 8" /385 .... 400 – 550
Vase, 8" /386 .... 300 – 450
Vase, 8" /401 .... 350 – 450
Vase, 8" /402 .... 300 – 400
Vase, 8" /404
  Blue... 750 – 900
  Green .... 550 – 700
Vase, 8" /425 .... 375 – 500
Vase, 8" /426 .... 500 – 650
Vase, 8" /427 .... 450 – 600
Vase, 8" /428 .... 400 – 550
Vase, 9" /388 .... 300 – 400
Vase, 9" /389 .... 450 – 650
Vase, 9" /407 .... 400 – 600
Vase, 9" /409 .... 600 – 750
Vase, 9" /412 .... 1500 +
Vase, 9" /429 .... 350 – 450
Vase, 9" /430 .... 400 – 600
Vase, 10" /390 .... 800 +
Vase, 10" /391 .... 800 +
Vase, 10" /392 .... 400 – 550
Vase, 10" /395 .... ND
Vase, 10" /408 .... 400 – 500
Vase, 10" /431 .... 350 – 500
Vase, 10" /432 .... 300 – 500
Vase, 10" /433 .... 400 – 550
Vase, 10" /434 .... 800 +
Vase, 10" /435 .... 350 – 500
Vase, 12" /393 .... 800 – 1000
Vase, 12" /394 .... 800 +
Vase, 12" /410 .... 600 – 800
Vase, 12" /436 .... 500 – 700
Vase, 12" /437 .... 500 – 700
Vase, 14" /411 .... 600 – 900
Vase, 15" /438 .... 600 – 800
Window box, 15" × 4" × 6" /375 .... 350 – 450

JUVENILE WARE

Called Juvenile I (matte) and Juvenile II (high gloss) by collectors.

Hand-painted transfer designs (the nursery rhyme decorations are decals) with childhood motifs: chicks, ducks, rabbits, dogs, cats, nursery rhymes, Sunbonnet girls, Santa Claus, and more.

PRICING There are four patterns that are very desirable and hard to find. Although it is essentially a seller's market for these, a multiple follows each name to give you some indication of value: Cat with Umbrella (2X), Fat Puppy—*not* the skinny puppy (2X), Pig with Hat (2X), and Santa Claus (3X).

Roseville's catalog shows a variety of B & M sets (bowl and milk pitcher)—nine different ones. Prices below are "generic."

Bowl, 5"	$75 – $125
Bowl, 6"	90 – 150
Bowl, flared /13	ND
Creamer	60 – 100
Creamer, side handle	100 – 150
Creamer, angled handle	100 – 150
Cup and saucer, small /6	90 – 125
Cup and saucer, medium /7	100 – 140
Cup and saucer, large /8	120 – 150
Eggcup, stemmed /1	150 – 200
Feeding dish, 6¼" /8	80 – 120
Feeding dish, curled-over rim, 6" /6	80 – 120
Feeding dish, curled-over rim, 7½"	90 – 130
Mug, slightly bowed sides /7	75 – 125
Mug, straight sides /5	75 – 125
Mug, 2 handles /6	100 – 150
Plate, 5¾"	75 – 110
Plate, 6¾" /2	80 – 120
Plate, 7⅞" /7	100 – 150
Plate, divided, 9" /9	200 – 250

Tea Set

The creamer and sugar match the teapot in shape.

Creamer	$100 – $125
Sugar	100 – 125
Teapot	200 – 250

Toilet Set

Pieces in this set range from very hard to find to rare. This list is more to let you know what you can look for.

Basin	ND
Chamber pot, small	ND
Chamber pot, large	ND
Chamber vase	ND
Ewer	ND
Soap dish	ND

MOSTIQUE

Indian-like designs in bright colors incised on rough-textured background of gray or tan. Insides are brightly glazed, usually green.

Basket, hanging, 6" /334	$160 – $190
Basket, hanging, 8" /334	190 – 230

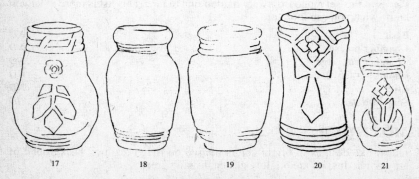

Mostique

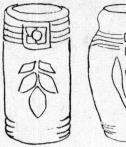

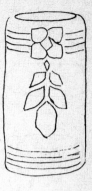

22   23   24   25

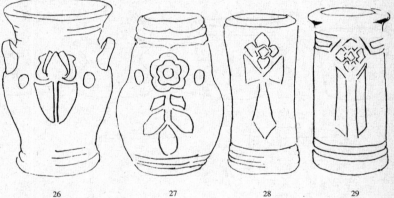

26   27   28   29

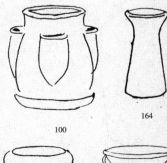

72

100

164

30   99   131   221

Mostique

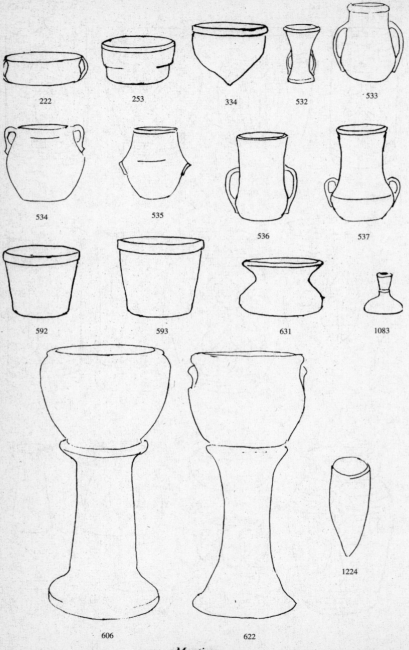

222   253   334   532   533

534   535   536   537

592   593   631   1083

606   622   1224

Mostique

Bowl, 4"	/131	$35 – $50
Bowl, 5"	/73	40 – 60
Bowl, 5"	/131	40 – 60
Bowl, 6"	/72	45 – 70
Bowl, 6"	/131	45 – 70
Bowl, 6"	/221	45 – 70
Bowl, 7"	/73	60 – 75
Bowl, 7"	/131	60 – 75
Bowl, 8"	/72	75 – 100
Bowl, 8"	/222	75 – 100
Candlestick, each, 4"	/1083	40 – 50
Frog, 2½"		15 – 20
Frog, 3½"		20 – 25
Jardiniere, low, 5"	/253	50 – 65
Jardiniere, low, 6"	/253	60 – 75
Jardiniere, 6"	/592	60 – 90
Jardiniere, 6"	/606	60 – 90
Jardiniere, 7"	/593	80 – 100
Jardiniere, 7"	/606	80 – 100
Jardiniere, 7"	/622	80 – 100
Jardiniere, 8"	/593	110 – 140
Jardiniere, 8"	/606	110 – 140
Jardiniere, 8"	/622	110 – 140
Jardiniere, 9"	/593	140 – 175
Jardiniere, 9"	/606	140 – 175
Jardiniere, 9"	/622	140 – 175
Jardiniere, 10"	/592	175 – 225
Jardiniere, 10"	/606 and pedestal	550 – 700
Jardiniere, 10"	/622 and pedestal	550 – 700
Jardiniere, 12"	/593	225 – 275
Spittoon	/631	250 +
Strawberry jar, 10"	/99	250 – 325
Strawberry jar, 10"	/100	325 – 400
Vase, 6"	/1	60 – 75
Vase, 6"	/2	60 – 75
Vase, 6"	/3	60 – 75
Vase, 6"	/4	60 – 75
Vase, 6"	/5	60 – 75
Vase, 6"	/6	60 – 75
Vase, 6"	/164	50 – 60
Vase, 6"	/532	60 – 75
Vase, 8"	/7	80 – 110
Vase, 8"	/8	80 – 110
Vase, 8"	/9	80 – 110
Vase, 8"	/10	80 – 110
Vase, 8"	/11	80 – 110
Vase, 8"	/12	100 – 125
Vase, 8"	/13	100 – 125

Vase, 8"	/14	$80 – $110
Vase, 8"	/164	60 – 80
Vase, 8"	/532	80 – 110
Vase, 8"	/533	120 – 150
Vase, 8"	/534	120 – 150
Vase, 8"	/535	80 – 110
Vase, 9"	/536	160 – 190
Vase, 10"	/15	160 – 190
Vase, 10"	/16	175 – 225
Vase, 10"	/17	175 – 225
Vase, 10"	/18	160 – 190
Vase, 10"	/19	160 – 190
Vase, 10"	/20	175 – 225
Vase, 10"	/21	160 – 190
Vase, 10"	/22	160 – 190
Vase, 10"	/23	175 – 225
Vase, 10"	/24	175 – 225
Vase, 10"	/164	100 – 125
Vase, 10"	/532	160 – 190
Vase, 10"	/537	190 – 220
Vase, 12"	/25	190 – 220
Vase, 12"	/26	225 – 260
Vase, 12"	/27	225 – 260
Vase, 12"	/28	175 – 225
Vase, 12"	/29	175 – 225
Vase, 12"	/30	225 – 260
Vase, 12"	/164	160 – 200
Vase, 12"	/532	190 – 220
Vase, 15"	/164	225 – 260
Wall pocket, 10"	/1224	125 – 160
Wall pocket, 12"	/1224	160 – 200

PINECONE

Designed by Frank Ferrell. Embossed brown pinecones with long green needles on background of green, blue lined with orange, or gold blended with brown and lined with green. Branch-like handles.

	Green	Blue	Gold
Ashtray, 3 rests /25	$50 – $75	$100 – $125	$75 – $100
Basket, 8" /352	150 – 175	250 – 375	200 – 300
Bowl, 5" /320	45 – 65	80 – 120	65 – 85
Bowl, 6" /354	50 – 75	100 – 125	75 – 100
Bowl, 8" /355	60 – 80	120 – 150	80 – 120
Bowl, 9" /321	75 – 125	150 – 200	100 – 150
Bowl, 12" /322	100 – 150	200 – 250	150 – 200
Bowl, 15" /323	150 – 200	250 – 300	200 – 250
Bowl, Rose, 4" /278	40 – 60	60 – 90	50 – 75

	Green	Blue	Gold
Bowl, Rose, 6" /261	$45 – $75	$75 – $125	$60 – $100
Bowl, Rose, 7" /288	75 – 90	125 – 160	100 – 125
Candlestick, single /1123	45 – 75	75 – 125	60 – 100
Candlestick, 4½" /1099C	40 – 60	80 – 100	60 – 80
Candelstick, double, 4½" /1124	100 – 125	200 – 250	150 – 200
Candlestick, triple, 5½" /1106	150 – 175	250 – 300	200 – 250
Centerpiece, two candle holders, 5" × 3½" × 2½" /356	175 – 200	275 – 350	200 – 250
Centerpiece, six candle holders, 6" /324	225 – 300	350 – 400	250 – 350
Cornucopia, 6" /126	45 – 60	75 – 100	60 – 80
Cornucopia, 8" /128	75 – 90	125 – 160	100 – 125
Ewer, 10" /909	190 – 225	300 – 375	250 – 300
Ewer, 15" /851	300 – 400	500 – 600	400 – 500
Flower frog /32	50 – 60	75 – 100	60 – 80
Flower frog /33	50 – 60	75 – 100	60 – 80
Flower frog, 4" /20	75 – 110	125 – 175	100 – 150
Flower frog, 5" /21	75 – 110	125 – 175	100 – 150
Flowerpot, 5" /633	75 – 110	130 – 180	100 – 150
Jardiniere, 3" /632	40 – 60	60 – 90	50 – 75
Jardiniere, 4" /632	50 – 80	75 – 110	60 – 100
Jardiniere, 5" /632	60 – 90	100 – 150	80 – 120
Jardiniere, 6" /632	75 – 110	125 – 175	100 – 150
Jardiniere, 7" /632	110 – 150	175 – 250	150 – 200
Jardiniere, 8" /632	150 – 200	250 – 325	200 – 275
Jardiniere, 9" /632	200 – 300	350 – 400	250 – 350
Jardiniere, 10" /632	250 – 350	400 – 500	300 – 400
Planter, 5" /124	50 – 75	100 – 125	75 – 100
Planter, 9" × 3" × 3½" /379	75 – 90	125 – 160	100 – 125
Umbrella stand, 20" /777	400 – 500	800 – 1000	600 – 800
Vase, 6" /748	60 – 75	90 – 125	75 – 100
Vase, 6" /838	60 – 75	90 – 125	75 – 100
Vase, 6" /839	60 – 75	90 – 125	75 – 100
Vase, 7" /841	75 – 90	125 – 160	100 – 125
Vase, urn, 7" /121	75 – 100	125 – 175	100 – 150
Vase, 8" /842	100 – 150	150 – 200	125 – 175
Vase, 8" /843	100 – 150	150 – 200	125 – 175
Vase, 8" /844	110 – 150	200 – 250	150 – 200
Vase, 8" /845	150 – 200	250 – 300	200 – 250
Vase, bud, 8" /113	100 – 125	150 – 200	125 – 150
Vase, urn, 8" /908	100 – 150	200 – 250	150 – 200
Vase, 9" /848	110 – 150	190 – 250	150 – 200
Vase, 10" /747	150 – 200	250 – 300	200 – 250
Vase, 10" /804	150 – 225	250 – 350	200 – 300
Vase, 10" /848	190 – 225	300 – 375	250 – 300
Vase, 10" /849	190 – 225	300 – 375	250 – 300

		Green	*Blue*	*Gold*
Vase, urn, 10" /910		$175 – $225	$300 – $350	$225 – $275
Vase, 12" /805		250 – 300	400 – 500	300 – 400
Vase, 12" /806		250 – 300	450 – 550	350 – 450
Vase, urn, 12" /911		190 – 250	325 – 425	250 – 340
Vase, 14" /850		300 – 400	500 – 600	400 – 500
Vase, 15" /807		350 – 450	600 – 750	450 – 550
Vase, urn, 15" /912		350 – 425	550 – 675	450 – 550
Vase, urn, 18" /913		400 – 500	650 – 800	500 – 650
Wall bracket, 5" × 8" /1		150 – 200	250 – 300	175 – 225
Wall flowerpot, 4" /1283		200 – 300	400 – 500	300 – 400
Wall pocket, double, 8" /1273		100 – 150	200 – 300	150 – 250
Window Box, 10" × 5½" /380		150 – 200	250 – 300	200 – 250

RAYMOR (1952)

Designed by Ben Seibel. This is the line that Roseville hoped would save it from bankruptcy; it didn't. Most pieces have the shape number in the 100 series on the bottom; restyled pieces, which include cup and saucer (from oval to round) and the plates (from indented bottoms to oval) are in the 200 series.

A **condiment set** consists of two cruets, shakers, and the jam/relish on the condiment stand. The **creamer** takes a lid; creamer and sugar lids, especially mint, are hard to find. The **jam/relish** is also called a mustard. The **mug** comes in short- and long-handled versions; the latter is preferred.

Raymor will be found in Contemporary White (ivory) as well as four colors that were made in two variations each: plain (which tends to be matte finish) or mottled (which tends to be gloss finish). The colors are Autumn Brown, Avocado Green, Terra Cotta, and Beach Gray. Some collectors refer to the plain version of Autumn Brown as chocolate brown and the plain version of Avocado Green as black because both are darker than the mottled versions. To further complicate things, the Avocado Green comes in a light mottling (possibly poor glazing) and a darker version; the latter is more common and is referred to as Frogskin by collectors. Later colors, mostly found on restyled pieces, are Chartreuse and Robin's Egg Blue.

In case this is a bit confusing, here it is in list form:

PLAIN (MATTE)	**MOTTLED (GLOSSY)**
Autumn Brown (chocolate)	Autumn Brown
Terra Cotta	Terra Cotta
Beach Gray	Beach Gray
Avacado Green (black)	Avocado Green (light)
	Avocado Green (dark/Frogskin)

Brown is the easiest color to find. Frogskin is the most desired.

Ashtray /203	
Bean pot, individual /195	$35 – $40
Bean pot, 2-quart, 7" /193	40 – 45
Bean pot, 3-quart, 5" /194	45 – 50
Bean pot, 4-quart, 8" /187	75 – 90
Bowl, fruit, w/handle (fruit basket) /166	ND

Bowl, salad   /161 . . . . *$75*
Bowl, soup, lug   /155 . . . . *15*
Bowl, vegetable, 9¹/₂" × 6"   /160 . . . . *20*
Bowl, vegetable, divided, 13" × 7"   /165 . . . . *135 – 145*
Bun warmer   /202 . . . . *250 – 300*
Butter dish   /181 . . . . *50 – 75*
Casserole, individual   /199 . . . . *40 – 45*
Casserole, medium, 10¹/₂" × 8¹/₂"   /183 . . . . *45 – 50*
Casserole, large   /185 . . . . *75 – 100*
Casserole, handled, 1¹/₂-quart   /198 . . . . *45 – 50*
Casserole, handled, 2¹/₂-quart   /197 . . . . *50 – 70*
Casserole, handled, 4-quart   /196 . . . . *70 – 100*
Celery/Olive, 15¹/₂" × 6¹/₄"   /177 . . . . *45 – 50*
Cheese/Relish Set   /180 . . . . *ND*
Coffee pot, large   /176 . . . . *175 – 225*
  Ceramic stand for above . . . . *75 – 100*
Condiment stand   /173 . . . . *30 – 35*
Corn server, 12¹/₂"   /162 . . . . *20 – 25*
Covered ramekin, 6¹/₂" × 4³/₄"   /156 . . . . *15 – 20*
Creamer, w/lid   /158 . . . . *20 – 25*
Cruet, oil/vinegar   /170   /171 . . . . *20 – 25*
Cup   /150 . . . . *9 – 12*
Dish, fruit, lug, 5"   /192 . . . . *15*
Gravy boat   /190 . . . . *20 – 25*
Jam/Relish   /172 . . . . *40 – 45*
  Spoon for above . . . . *ND*
Jug, water   /189 . . . . *75 – 90*
Mug   /179 . . . . *50 – 60*
Pickle dish, 9¹/₂"   /191 . . . . *15 – 20*
Plate, 8¹/₂"   /153 . . . . *12 – 15*
Plate   /154 . . . . *8 – 10*
Plate, 10¹/₂"   /152 . . . . *15 – 20*
Plate, chop, 15³/₄"   /164 . . . . *25 – 30*
Platter, 14"   /163 . . . . *20 – 25*
Platter, steak, w/well, 20"   /178 . . . . *75*
Relish/Sandwich tray   /182 . . . . *45 – 50*
Saucer   /151 . . . . *3 – 5*
Shaker, salt   /168 . . . . *15*
Shaker, pepper   /169 . . . . *15*
Shirred egg dish   /200 . . . . *60*
Sugar   /157 . . . . *15 – 20*
Teapot   /174 . . . . *100 – 125*
Tray for sugar/creamer   /159 . . . . *15 – 18*
Trivet, bean pot   /188 . . . . *45 – 50*
Trivet, casserole, medium   /184 . . . . *45 – 50*
Trivet, casserole, large   /186 . . . . *45 – 50*
Trivet, teapot   /175 . . . . *45 – 50*
Warmer, doubled stacked   /201 . . . . *ND*

135

134

136

47

8

137

266

268

269

138

267

271

270

272

1240

Rosecraft Hexagon

ROSECRAFT HEXAGON

Dark hexagonal bodies in brown, green, and blue with an impressed design that may repeat a lining color.

Bowl, 4"   /124 . . . . *$75 – $125*
Bowl, 4"   /135 . . . . *90 – 130*
Bowl, 5"   /136 . . . . *120 – 160*
Bowl, 6"   /137 . . . . *150 – 200*
Jardiniere, 4"   /138 . . . . *175 – 225*
Vase, 4"   /266 . . . . *100 – 140*
Vase, 5"   /267 . . . . *125 – 175*
Vase, 6"   /268 . . . . *150 – 200*
Vase, 6"   /269 . . . . *150 – 200*
Vase, 7"   /8 . . . . *225 – 275*
Vase, 8"   /270 . . . . *200 – 250*
Vase, 8"   /271 . . . . *200 – 250*
Vase, 10"   /272 . . . . *300 – 350*
Vase, bud, double, 5"   /47 . . . . *250 – 300*
Wall pocket, 8"   /1240 . . . . *200 – 250*

ROSECRAFT VINTAGE

Classic shapes with a banded design of vines, leaves, and berries in a light brown against a darker background, usually brown, though dark purple and charcoal black have also been found.

Bowl, 3"   /143 . . . . *$50 – $75*
Bowl, footed, 3"   /139 . . . . *50 – 75*
Bowl, footed, 4"   /140 . . . . *60 – 90*
Bowl, footed, 5"   /141 . . . . *75 – 100*
Bowl, footed, 6"   /142 . . . . *80 – 120*
Jardiniere, 5"   /607 . . . . *100 – 125*
Jardiniere, 6"   /607 . . . . *125 – 175*
Jardiniere, 6"   /144 . . . . *125 – 175*
Jardiniere, 7"   /607 . . . . *175 – 225*
Jardiniere, 8"   /607 . . . . *225 – 275*
Jardiniere, 9"   /607 . . . . *275 – 325*
Jardiniere, 10"   /607 . . . . *325 – 375*
Vase, 3"   /9 . . . . *60 – 90*
Vase, 4"   /273 . . . . *75 – 100*
Vase, bud, double, 4¹/₂"   /48 . . . . *175 – 225*
Vase, 5"   /274 . . . . *80 – 120*
Vase, 6"   /275 . . . . *100 – 150*
Vase, 6"   /276 . . . . *100 – 150*
Vase, 8"   /277 . . . . *125 – 175*
Vase, 8"   /278 . . . . *150 – 200*
Vase, 10"   /279 . . . . *250 – 300*
Vase, 12"   /280 . . . . *300 – 350*

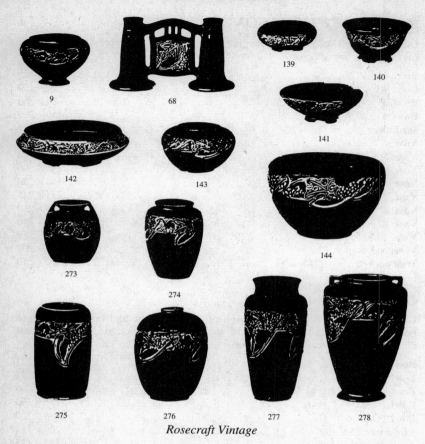

9   68   139   140

141

142   143

144

273

274

275   276   277   278

Rosecraft Vintage

Wall pocket, 8"   /1241 . . . . *$175 – $225*
Window box, 10"   /372 . . . . *200 – 250*

TUSCANY

Handles blend into lightly embossed grapes and leaves on lightly mottled backgrounds of pink, gray, or light green.

Bowl, 4"   /12
Bowl, 4"   /67 . . . . *$40 – $60*
Bowl, 4"   /68 . . . . *40 – 60*
Bowl, 6"   /171 . . . . *50 – 70*
Bowl, 9"   /172 . . . . *90 – 120*
Bowl, 10"   /173 . . . . *80 – 110*
Bowl, 12"   /174 . . . . *90 – 120*
Bowl, 14" × 6" × 3¹/₂"   /181 . . . . *100 – 125*

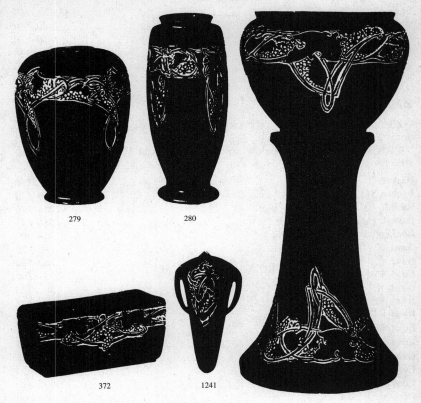

279 280

372 1241

607

Rosecraft Vintage

Bowl, 15" /112		*$100 – $125*
Candlestick, each, 3½" /1066		*25 – 40*
Candlestick, each, 4" /1067		*30 – 45*
Vase, 5" /70		*50 – 80*
Vase, 5" /341		*50 – 80*
Vase, 6" /615		*60 – 90*
Vase, 6" /71		*60 – 90*
Vase, 6" /342		*50 – 80*
Vase, 7" /343		*60 – 90*
Vase, 8" /80		*90 – 120*
Vase, 8" /344		*80 – 110*
Vase, 8" /345		*90 – 120*
Vase, 9" /346		*100 – 125*
Vase, 10" /347		*120 – 150*
Vase, 10" /348		*125 – 160*

Vase, 12"　/349 .... *$150 – $180*
Vase/flower arranger, 5"　/69 .... *60 – 80*
Vase/flower arranger, 5"　/66 .... *50 – 70*
Wall pocket, 7"　/1254 .... *120 – 150*
Wall pocket, 8"　/1255 .... *120 – 150*

ZEPHYR LILY

White and yellow day lilies on background of embossed swirls in blue, green, or terra cotta blending to green.

    PRICING　The prices below are for brown. Add 10% for blue; subtract 10% for green.

Basket, 7"　/393 .... *$90 – $130*
Basket, 8"　/394 .... *80 – 120*
Basket, 10"　/395 .... *125 – 175*
Basket, hanging, 5"　/472 .... *125 – 175*
Bookend, each　/16 .... *75 – 100*
Bowl, 5"　/470 .... *50 – 75*
Bowl, 6"　/472 .... *60 – 80*
Bowl, 8"　/474 .... *75 – 100*
Bowl, 10"　/476 .... *80 – 120*
Bowl, 12"　/478 .... *100 – 125*
Bowl, oval, 14"　/479 .... *125 – 175*
Bowl, footed, 6"　/473 .... *60 – 80*
Bowl, footed, 10"　/8 .... *100 – 125*
Candle holder, 2", each　/1162 .... *30 – 40*
Candlestick, 4½", each　/1163 .... *40 – 50*
Cookie jar,　/5 .... *200 – 250*
Creamer,　/7-C .... *40 – 60*
Ewer, 6"　/22 .... *80 – 120*
Ewer, 10"　/23 .... *150 – 200*
Ewer, 15"　/24 .... *225 – 275*
Flowerpot w/saucer, 5"　/672 .... *50 – 75*
Jardiniere, 4"　/671 .... *60 – 80*
Jardiniere, 6"　/471 .... *80 – 110*
Jardiniere, 6"　/671 .... *80 – 110*
Sugar　/7-S .... *40 – 60*
Teapot　/7-T .... *150 – 200*
Tray, console boat, 10"　475 .... *100 – 120*
Tray, leaf shape, 12"　/477 .... *100 – 125*
Vase, 6"　/130 .... *60 – 80*
Vase, cornucopia, 6"　/203 .... *60 – 80*
Vase, 6"　/205 .... *75 – 100*
Vase, 7"　/131 .... *75 – 100*
Vase, 7"　/132 .... *75 – 100*
Vase, bud, 7"　/201 .... *60 – 80*
Vase, 7"　/206 .... *80 – 120*
Vase, 8"　/133 .... *80 – 120*

Vase, 8" /134 .... *$80 – $120*
Vase, 8" /202 .... *90 – 130*
Vase, 8" /204 .... *75 – 100*
Vase, 9" /135 .... *100 – 125*
Vase, 9" /136 .... *100 – 125*
Vase, 10" /137 .... *125 – 160*
Vase, 10" /138 .... *125 – 160*
Vase, 12" /139 .... *175 – 225*
Vase, 12" /140 .... *175 – 225*
Vase, 15" /141 .... *250 – 325*
Vase, floor, 18"   /142 .... *325 – 400*
Wall pocket, 8"   /1297 .... *150 – 175*
Window box, 8"   /1393 .... *80 – 120*

ROYAL CHINA COMPANY

Sebring, Ohio

CHAPTER AT A GLANCE

DINNERWARE / EARLY	COLONIAL HOMESTEAD
REGAL	COUNTRY HEARTH
ROYALTY	FAIR OAKS
"SWIRL"	MEMORY LANE
"TAB TOP"	THE OLD CURIOSITY SHOP
WINDSOR	TRADITION
DINNERWARE / LATE	CURRIER & IVES
BUCK'S COUNTY	WILLOW

Royal moved their operation from Omaha, Nebraska, to the site of the old E. H. Sebring Pottery in 1933. In 1934 they drew the first kiln; they made semiporcelain dinnerware, as well as cookware and premiums. In 1969 the company was purchased by the Jeannette Glass Corporation and underwent several changes of ownership after that. Operations ceased in 1986.

MARKS   There are several general backstamps you will commonly find.

The following marks refer to body color.

These last two marks I am a little unsure of. I have found them on pieces of Royal as well as pottery that might be from other manufacturers.

DINNERWARE / EARLY

You will find pieces of American Limoges' "Square" shape with Royal's Shell Pink mark. For pricing, see the listing in the American Limoges chapter.

REGAL (1937)

This shape is distinguished by thin fluting. On the flatware pieces, the fluting extends from the rim over the verge and slightly into the well.

Bowl, round, 8¾"	$15 – $18
Bowl, oval, 9"	10 – 12
Butter dish	20 – 25
Casserole	20 – 25
Creamer	4 – 6
Cup	4 – 6
Gravy	12 – 15
Plate, 6¼"	1 – 2
Plate, 7¼"	4 – 5
Plate, lug, 10½"	10 – 12
Saucer	1 – 2
Shaker, tall, pair	8 – 10
Sugar	8 – 10
Teapot	20 – 25

Regal: Tall shaker, tab-handle plate, and teapot.

ROYALTY   (1936)

A band of spider-web embossing distinguishes this shape. So far only decal decorations have been seen; no solid colors.

Bowl, oval, 9"* .... *$10 – $12*
Casserole .... *20 – 25*
Creamer .... *4 – 6*

Royalty: Tall shaker, Pink Castle plate, Pink Castle creamer and sugar.

Cup	*$4 – $6*
Dish, 5"	*2 – 3*
Gravy	*12 – 15*
Gravy liner/pickle, 8¼"	*6 – 8*
Plate, 6¼"	*1 – 2*
Plate, 7¼"	*4 – 5*
Plate, 9¼"	*7 – 9*
Saucer	*1 – 2*
Shaker, tall, pair	*8 – 10*
Sugar	*8 – 10*
Teapot, 6 cup	*20 – 25*

"SWIRL"

Swirl is usually decorated with decals; Cherry Blossom seem to be the most common. I have also found Swirl in two solid colors: a blue glaze with a mustard yellow showing through, and a bright yellow. I would expect other colors.

Bowl, salad, 9"	*$10 – $15*
Bowl, soup, 8"	*10 – 12*
Casserole	*20 – 25*
Creamer	*4 – 6*
Cup	*4 – 6*
Cup, AD	*10 – 12*
Gravy	*12 – 15*
Plate, 6¼"	*1 – 2*
Plate, 10½"	*10 – 12*
Plate, lug, 10½"	*10 – 12*
Saucer	*1 – 2*
Saucer, AD	*5 – 8*
Shaker, pair	*8 – 10*

*Swirl: Shaker,
Cherry Blossom
plate, and teapot.*

Sugar . . . . *$8 – $10*
Teapot . . . . *25 – 30*

"TAB TOP"

A plain round shape with small tabs on the tops of the handles.

Bowl, oval, 9"* . . . . *$10 – $12*
Casserole . . . . *20 – 25*
Creamer . . . . *4 – 6*
Cup . . . . *4 – 6*
Dish, 5¹/₂"* . . . . *2 – 3*
Gravy . . . . *12 – 15*
Plate, 9¹/₄" . . . . *7 – 9*
Plate, lug, 10¹/₂" . . . . *10 – 12*
Saucer . . . . *1 – 2*
Shaker, pair . . . . *8 – 10*
Sugar . . . . *8 – 10*
Teapot, 2-cup . . . . *15 – 20*
Utensil, cake server . . . . *12 – 15*
Utensil, fork . . . . *20 – 25*
Utensil, spoon . . . . *15 – 20*
Utensil, spoon, 10¹/₂" . . . . *15 – 20*

"Tab Top": Orchid plate, two-cup teapot, Orchid shaker, cup, and gravy (blue band over ivory).

Windsor: Cup and saucer (note square well), shaker, and teapot.

WINDSOR

A square, Art Deco–like shape. The cup has a square foot and the saucer a square cup indent.

Bowl, soup, 7³/₄".	$10 – $12
Butter dish	20 – 25
Casserole	20 – 25
Casserole, round, 9¹/₂".	20 – 25
Casserole, square.	20 – 25
Coffee pot	35 – 40
Creamer	4 – 6
Cup	4 – 6
Dish, 5"	2 – 3
Dish, 6"	3 – 4
Gravy	12 – 15
Plate, 6¹/₄"	1 – 2
Plate, 7¹/₄"	4 – 5
Plate, 9¹/₄"	7 – 9
Plate, lug, 9³/₄".	10 – 12
Platter, oval, 8¹/₄"	8 – 10
Platter, oval, 11¹/₄"	10 – 12
Saucer	1 – 2
Shaker, pair	8 – 10
Sugar	8 – 10

DINNERWARE / LATE

These patterns seem to range from the forties to the sixties at least. I have not been able to discover names for these shapes, though Chippendale might be the name for one of them, so I am listing them by pattern and pricing generically.

BUCK'S COUNTY   Brown on yellow.

COLONIAL HOMESTEAD   Green on white.

COUNTRY HEARTH   Green on white.

FAIR OAKS   A brown on white print with touches of green, red, and yellow, all underglaze. Same as Memory Lane but with a different border.

*Currier & Ives mug, Currier & Ives handled shaker, and Old Curiosity Shop
teapot. Note the handle on the mug is different than the others. The teapot and
shaker is the shape you see most often.*

MEMORY LANE   Rose on white.

THE OLD CURIOSITY SHOP   Green on white.

TRADITION   Pink on white; other colors may be found.

Ashtray	*$6 – $8*
Bowl, 5½"	*5 – 7*
Bowl, soup, 8½"	*10 – 12*
Bowl, round, 9"	*15 – 18*
Casserole	*20 – 25*
Creamer	*4 – 6*
Cup	*4 – 6*
Dish, 5½"	*2 – 3*
Dish, 6¼"	*3 – 4*
Gravy	*12 – 15*
Plate, 6½"	*1 – 2*
Plate, 9"	*7 – 9*
Plate, 10"	*10 – 12*
Plate, cake, lug, 10"	*10 – 12*

Buck's County

Colonial Homestead

Fair Oaks

Memory Lane

Old Curiosity Shop

Tradition

Pattern Library: The images may vary in each pattern; the borders tell you which pattern it is.

Saucer	*$1 – $2*
Shaker, handled, pair...	*8 – 10*
Sugar	*8 – 10*
Teapot	*20 – 25*

CURRIER & IVES

Scarce pieces are the lug-handle cereal, the mug, the 9" and 11" plates, the wall plaque, and the center-handle sandwich server. Mixing bowls have been reported but not confirmed. The 11" lug platter, called serving platter by Royal, is referred to by collectors as a chop plate, cake plate, or vegetable bowl liner, so be careful when ordering by mail. My thanks to Betsey Edmondson for the depth of this listing.

The line came in two colors: blue and white, pink and white.

Ashtray, round, 5¼" /Couple on bench .... *$6 – $8*
Bowl, soup, 8½" /House & ice skaters .... *10 – 12*
Bowl, vegetable, round, 9" /Log Cabin, Maple Sugaring................ *15 – 18*
Bowl, vegetable, round, deep, 10" /House & family .... *8 – 10*
Butter, ¼-pound /Couple in horse-drawn sleigh .... *25 – 30*
Casserole, 7¾" /Bottom: Couple in buggy, Lid: Woman on horse,
Knob: Couple on bench *50*
Creamer /Train .... *6 – 8*
Cup /Lady w/buggy driving team of horses......................... *4 – 6*
Dish, 3¾" .... *3 – 4*
Dish, fruit, 5½" /House & children .... *5 – 6*
Dish, cereal/salad, 6¼" /Man pulling sleigh w/team of horses .... *6 – 8*
Dish, lug, 6¼" .... *8 – 10*
Gravy, oval, 6" /Horse w/couple in sleigh...................... *12 – 15*
Gravy liner, lug /Boy at well................................. *6 – 8*
Mug, 2⅝" high × 3¾" across /Horses and buggy .... *25 +*
Pie baker, 9⅞" /Old Grist Mill .... *18 – 20*
Plate, 6⅜" /Harvesting grain .... *2 – 3*
Plate, 7¼" /House, trees, sail boat on lake..................... *7 – 9*
Plate, 9" .... *9 – 11*
Plate, 10¼" /Old Grist Mill .... *6 – 8*
Plate, 11" .... *20 +*

Currier & Ives

Plate, chop, 12" /Horse-drawn sleigh, man chopping ice *$20*
Platter, oval, 13" × 10¼"   /House & bull . . . . *35 – 40*
Platter, serving, round, lug, 11"   /Wagon train & mountains . . . . *15 – 20*
Sandwich server, center handle, 13¼"   /Cow barn, man w/pitchfork,
house w/lady, Center handle: fork of hay . . . . *50 +*
Saucer   /Steamboat . . . . *1 – 2*
Shaker, pair   /Horse & buggy . . . . *15 – 18*
Sugar   /Steamboat . . . . *8 – 10*
Teapot   /Bottom: Sail boat, Lid: Light House. . . . . *50 – 60*
Tidbit, 3-tier *40*
  Bottom plate, 9¼"   /Old Grist Mill
  Middle plate, 6⅜"   /Harvesting Grain
  Top bowl, 5½"   /Children at fence
Wall Plaque, rectangular, 5¼" × 6¾"   /Wagon Train . . . . *50 +*

Tumblers

These coordinating glass tumblers will be found four ways:

WHITE ON BLUE
3¼"   /Woman driving horse team . . . . *$5 – $8*
3½"   /Steamboat . . . . *5 – 8*
4¾" . . . . *ND*
5½"   /Old Grist Mill . . . . *8 – 10*

BLUE ON WHITE
5½"   /The Roadside Mill . . . . *$8 – $10*

BLUE ON WHITE W/GOLD RIM
5½"   /Old Grist mill . . . . *$8 – $10*

BLUE ON WHITE FROSTED
8-ounce, 5½"   /Barn in trees . . . . *$10 – $12*

WILLOW

Royal produced two versions of Willow. A rubber-stamped underglaze decoration was used in the thirties, on a variety of shapes including Regal and Royalty. These were stamped in blue, red, or gold. At least three different border decorations have been documented.

The second version, the standard transfer-printed underglaze pattern, was produced from the forties until the company closed. Either of four colors was used: blue (the most common), pink, green, and (occasionally found) brown.

MARKS Royal used both general and specific backstamps for Willow.

The *rubber-stamp* pattern will be found with "Royal" in a box, with a crown on top, as well as unmarked. Some pieces were made for Hamilton Ross and will have that company's "Ming Red" backstamp on it.

The *transfer-printed* line will be found with the RC in palette, as well as the following: "Willow Ware by Royal" (tree mark), "Blue Willow by Royal," and Royal Ironstone. Later marks not shown are "Royal China Jeannette" and "Cavalier Ironstone" general marks with Blue Willow inserted as the pattern name.

PRICING This list is of transfer-printed pieces; subtract 20% for the rubber-stamped pieces. Values below are for blue; add 10% for green and pink.

Ashtray, 5½"	*$8 – $10*
Bowl, soup, 8½"	*10 – 12*
Bowl, vegetable, round, 9"	*12 – 15*
Bowl, vegetable, round, 10"	*12 – 15*
Casserole	*20 – 25*
Creamer	*8 – 10*
Cup	*5 – 6*
Dish, 5½"	*3 – 4*
Dish, 6½"	*3 – 4*
Gravy	*10 – 12*
Pie baker	*10 – 12*
Plate, 6¼"	*3 – 4*
Plate, 9"	*5 – 7*
Plate, 9¾"	*7 – 8*
Plate, chop, 12"	*12 – 15*
Plate, chop, 13½"	*15 – 18*
Plate, grill, 10½"	*10 – 12*
Plate, lug, 7"	*8 – 10*

Willow: Transfer-printed ashtray.

Plate, lug, 10½" . . . . *$12 – $15*
Plate, party, 9" . . . . *10 – 12*
Saucer . . . . *1 – 2*
Server, 2-tier . . . . *18 – 20*
Server, 3-tier . . . . *25 – 30*
Shaker, handled, each . . . . *8 – 10*
Sugar . . . . *10 – 12*
Teapot . . . . *30 – 35*

RUMRILL POTTERY COMPANY

Little Rock, Arkansas

CHAPTER AT A GLANCE

ARTWARE
Athenian Group
Classic Group
Coffee Table Ensemble
Continental Group
Empire Group
Fern Group
Florentine Group
Fluted Group
Garden Items
Georgia Rose Group
Grecian Group
Indian Group

Mandarin Group
Manhattan Group
Medieval Group
Miscellaneous Group
Miscellany
Neo-Classic Group
Novelties
Renaissance Group
Shell Group
Swan Group
Sylvan Group
Trumpet Flower Group
Vintage Group

George Rumrill founded a distribution firm called Arkansas Products Company ca. 1930. Early on, pottery was sold, but the only manufacturer identified so far is Camark. Whether it was made for him or he bought other's stock is not known.

In 1933, he introduced RumRill Art Pottery (to which he changed the company name), which was made for him at the Red Wing Potteries in Red Wing, MN; at first he used Red Wing shapes, later his own. Rumrill left Red Wing around January of 1938, and made an arrangement with the Florence Pottery in Mt. Gilead, OH, for production of his wares, which began around December of that year. The exact nature of the arrangement is unknown. Ads from the period proclaim "NOW! With our own factory established at Mt. Gilead, Ohio, we offer finer quality and service than ever before."

In October of 1941, the Florence Pottery burned to the ground. The production facilities, molds, and stock on hand were gone. RumRill was wiped out. He closed the business officially in late 1942 and, within a few months, died of tuberculosis at age fifty-two.

Pre-1939 production is referred to as RumRill by Red Wing. Post-1939 production is referred to as post-Red Wing, as manufacturers other than the Florence Pottery were involved. According to Ray Reiss (see Bibliography/Coming Attractions), Shawnee produced ware for RumRill in the year between leaving Red Wing and beginning production at Florence. Then, for about a year after the fire, Gonder produced ware for RumRill. This is understandable, as Lawton

Gonder managed the Florence Pottery from 1936 to 1941 and then opened his own pottery in Zanesville. He had to have known George Rumrill. This was probably the basis for the business arrangement.

RumRill produced what is generally referred to as industrial art ware rather than art pottery. Some dinnerware was made. Trade listings from the late thirties refer to "peasant tableware," though this has not been identified.

One thing that has puzzled collectors is the exact spelling of the company name. I have seen it spelled three ways in ads and other sources: Rumrill, Rum-Rill and Rum Rill. As company catalogs seem to consistently stick to the Rum-Rill spelling, I have done likewise.

GLAZES   RumRill by Red Wing can be found with exteriors of solid colors, blended colors, or stippled colors with some interiors lined in another color. Among the easily found glazes are matte colors of pink and turquoise, as well as Dutch Blue (blue w/white stippling), Eggshell (matte white), Pompeiian (Antique Ivory), Ripe Wheat (dark brown blending into tan), and Robin's Egg blue.

Less easy to find is Marigold (yellow) and Jade—Green Matte.

Among the harder to find glazes are Crocus (gray-green exterior with pink lining), Mermaid (green w/brown stippling), Gypsy Orange, Lotus (ivory exterior with yellow lining), Matte Black, Snowdrop (ivory and green), and Stippled Lavender

The most desirable glaze of all is Nokomis (from Longfellow's "Hiawatha"). It is a very flat olive gray that is more desirable when there is some green in it.

Post-Red Wing is usually found in single color finishes.

MARKS   RumRill by Red Wing is frequently marked "Rumrill" in block letters, and often the pieces are numbered with a three-digit shape number up to 731. Many pieces can have a number and no name. Post-Red Wing pieces often have the name "RumRill" embossed in large lettering. Most of these pieces are numbered. The number is almost always two digits preceded by a single letter. The more distant from the letter A, the larger the piece. Many of these numbers are illegible due to glaze coverage.

ARTWARE

All the artware listed here was made by Red Wing.

ATHENIAN GROUP

The design of most pieces incorporates the nude female figure. #572 is a base for either #573 or #574.

Bowl, 8¹/₂"   /567 . . . . $100 +
Bowl, 10"   /572/573 . . . . 350 +
Bowl, footed, 11"   /571 . . . . 250 +
Bowl, shallow, 11¹/₂"   /572/573 . . . . 350 +
Candle holder, 10"   /563 . . . . 100 +
Candle holder, double, 9"   /564 . . . . 100 +
Vase, nude on turtle, 9¹/₂"   /576 . . . . 150 +
Vase, footed, three nudes, 10"   /570 . . . . 250 +

Left, *Athenian Group: Shape # 568*. Center, *Classic Group: Shape # 495*. Right, *Continental Group: Shape # 240*.

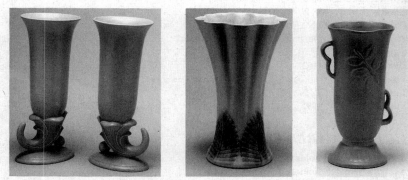

Left, *Empire Group: Shape # 678*. Center, *Fern Group: Shape # 383*. Right, *Florentine Group: Shape # 362*.

Left, *Fluted Group: Shape # 299*. Right, *Grecian Group: Shape # 183*.

Vase, footed, two nudes, 11¹/₂"　/568 . . . . *$200+*
Vase, footed, two nudes, 11¹/₂"　/569 . . . . *250+*

CLASSIC GROUP

Shapes are characterized by widespread vertical grooves. There is an earlier version of #271 that is similar, but with different handles.

Basket, footed, 8"　/285 . . . . *$60*
Bowl, 6"　/276 . . . . *25*
Bowl, tab handle, 8"　/273 . . . . *40*
Bowl, 9"　/278 . . . . *35*
Bowl, 9"　/342 . . . . *50*
Bowl, 12"　/233 . . . . *100*
Bowl, footed, 12"　/231 . . . . *100*
Bowl, 2-handle, footed, 12"　/316 . . . . *125*
Bowl, 2-handle, 13¹/₂"　/494 . . . . *120*
Bowl, 2-handle, footed, 14¹/₂"　/271 . . . . *125*
Candle holder, pair, 2¹/₂"　/357 . . . . *40*
Candle holder, double, pair, 7¹/₂"　/495 . . . . *75*
Candle holder, triple, pair, 6¹/₂"　/408 . . . . *50*
Candlestick, pair, 7"　/231 . . . . *50*
Urn w/lid, 8¹/₂"　/462 . . . . *60*
Vase, 5¹/₂"　/500 . . . . *40*
Vase, 6"　/344 . . . . *30*
Vase, ewer, 10"　/295 . . . . *60*

COFFEE TABLE ENSEMBLE

Ashtray w/match holder, 3¹/₂"　/659 . . . . *$15*
Ashtray w/match holder, 4³/₄"　/660 . . . . *20*
Ashtray w/match holder, 5¹/₂"　/658 . . . . *25*
Candy box w/lid, 8¹/₂"　/656 . . . . *60*
Cigarette box w/lid, 7"　/657 . . . . *50*

CONTINENTAL GROUP

Elegant designs and subtle embossed surface patterns.

Bowl, three feet, 6"　/335 . . . . *$40*
Bowl, 2-handle, 10¹/₂"　/410 . . . . *60*
Bowl, 11"　/392 . . . . *100*
Bowl, 2-handle, 13"　/338 . . . . *120*
Bowl, tab handle, 14¹/₂"　/393 . . . . *120*
Bowl w/attached candle holders, 19"　/419 . . . . *160*
Candle holder, ring, double, footed, 9"　/240 . . . . *60*
Candy dish w/lid, 6"　/339 . . . . *60*
Urn, footed w/lid, 14"　/252 . . . . *120*
Vase, footed, 2-handle, 8"　/337 . . . . *40*
Vase, ewer, dragon handle, 10"　/220 . . . . *75*

EMPIRE GROUP (1937)

Cornucopia shapes. Introduced in Flesh, Green Gray, Olive Green, Pink, and White.

Vase, 6½" /682. . . . . *$30*
Vase, 8" /679 . . . . *50*
Vase, globe top, 8" /680. . . . . *50*
Vase, double, 9½" wide /685. . . . . *60*
Vase, 10" /681 . . . . *60*
Vase, wide mouth, 10" wide /683 . . . . *75*
Vase, wide mouth, 11" wide /684 . . . . *60*
Vase, 14" /678 . . . . *85*

FERN GROUP

Embossed arrow-head-shaped fern fronds rising from the base.

Bowl, 3 feet, 7" /376 . . . . *$40*
Bowl, 3 feet, 9½" /378. . . . . *60*
Bowl, footed, 12" /377. . . . . *75*
Candlesticks, pair, 3" /409 . . . . *50*
Vase, 3 feet, 6" /385. . . . . *30*
Vase, fan, footed, 7" /517 . . . . *40*
Vase, 3 feet, 7½" /518 . . . . *50*
Vase, 9" /515 . . . . *60*
Vase, 3 feet, 9½" /382 . . . . *100*
Vase, 10" /516 . . . . *50*
Vase, 14" /383 . . . . *125*

FLORENTINE GROUP

Pieces have embossed floral treatments and/or embellished handles.

Basket, 7" /348 . . . . *$30*
Bowl, tab handles, 9" /232. . . . . *60*
Planter, rectangular, 10" × 4" × 3½" /237 . . . . *50*
Vase, 5" /365 . . . . *30*
Vase, 5½" /360. . . . . *30*
Vase, 6½" /427. . . . . *30*
Vase, tab handles, 7½" /369 . . . . *40*
Vase, footed, 2-handle, 9½" /362 . . . . *45*
Vase, footed, 2-handle, 9½" /247 . . . . *40*
Vase, 4 feet, 9½" /421 . . . . *50*
Vase, 3-handle, 9½" /420. . . . . *75*
Vase, 10" /308 . . . . *80*
Vase, 4 feet, 13" /423. . . . . *100*

FLUTED GROUP

Vertical grooves at about one-half-inch intervals create a "fluted" pattern.

Bowl, 7" /497 .... $40
Bowl, footed, oval, 8½" /300 45
Bowl, pedestal, 2-handle, 9½" /453 50
Bowl, 2-handle, 14" /395 75
Candlesticks, pair, 4½" /454 40
Vase, 5½", footed /294 30
Vase, 5½", 2-handle /320 40
Vase, 6", footed, 2-handle /256 30
Vase, 6½", 3-footed /390 20
Vase, 7", footed, 2-handle /356 25
Vase, 7", footed, 2-handle /299 40
Vase, 7½", footed, 2-handle /387 35
Vase, 8", 2-handle /296 35
Vase, 8½", 3-footed /258 50
Vase, 9", footed, 2-handle /267 60
Vase, 11" urn, footed, 2-handle /301 120

GARDEN ITEMS

Floor vase, 15" /145 .... $100
Floor vase, 2-handle, 15" /155 85
Floor vase, 2-handle, 15" /186 85
Floor vase, 17½" /166 135
Floor vase, scalloped rim, 20" /374 .... 150+
Sand jar, stag, 15" /107 125
Sand jar, flowered panels, 22" /104 125
Urn, Cupid, 12" /131 125
Urn, 24" /731 .... 350+
Urn, fluted, 24" /717 .... 350+

GEORGIA ROSE GROUP

(Medallion Line) A stylized flower is applied to each piece.

Bowl, 10" /219F $85
Vase, 7½" /170F 60
Vase, 8" /174F 60
Vase, 9" /195F 65
Vase, 2-handle, 10" /200F 185
Vase, 10½" /203F 125
Vase, 10½" /196F 85
Vase, footed, 11" /463F 125

GRECIAN GROUP

Smooth surfaces emphasizing flowing symmetry.

Bowl, tab handle, 5" /277 .... $30
Bowl, oval, 2-handle, 11½" /303 75
Vase, 6", 2-handle /302 30
Vase, 6" /305 20

Vase, 6", 2-handle   /287 . . . . $20
Vase, 7", 2-handle   /364 . . . . *30*
Vase, 7", 2-handle   /368 . . . . *30*
Vase, 7¹/₂" loving cup, footed, 2-handle   /506 . . . . *30*
Vase, 2-handle, 7¹/₂" diameter   /261 . . . . *60*
Vase, 8"   /183 . . . . *40*
Vase, 8¹/₂", 2-handle   /375. . . . . *70*
Vase, 8¹/₂", 2-handle   /288. . . . . *50*
Vase, 2-handle, 10" diameter   /200. . . . . *125*
Vase, 10¹/₂"   /196. . . . . *75*
Vase, 12"   /401 . . . . *60*

INDIAN GROUP

Smooth, flowing shapes emphasizing simplicity of design.

Bowl, 7¹/₂" diameter   /170. . . . . $40
Bowl, 2-handle, 7¹/₂" diameter   /262. . . . . *60*
Bowl, 8" diameter   /174 . . . . *30*
Bowl, 4¹/₂"   /315 . . . . *30*
Bowl, 10"   /219. . . . . *60*
Bowl, 2-handle, 9"   /198. . . . . *40*
Candlesticks, webbed, pair, 4¹/₂"   /546 . . . . *40*
Jug, water w/stopper, 8" diameter   /50. . . . . *50*
Vase, 5¹/₂"   /309. . . . . *25*
Vase, 5¹/₂"   /291. . . . . *30*
Vase, single handle, 5¹/₂"   /207 . . . . *30*
Vase, bud, 7"   /182 . . . . *25*
Vase, ewer, 7"   /184 . . . . *30*
Vase, 9" diameter   /268. . . . . *60*
Vase, 9"   /195 . . . . *65*
Vase, jug, single handle, 9"   /204 . . . . *85*

MANDARIN GROUP

Most pieces in this group are octagonal.

Bowl, 6"   /314 . . . . $50
Bowl, 7"   /310 . . . . *40*
Bowl, shallow, 11"   /331. . . . . *50*
Vase, 4"   /311 . . . . *20*
Vase, 5"   /297 . . . . *20*
Vase, 7"   /353 . . . . *30*
Vase, 9"   /312 . . . . *60*
Vase, 9"   /332 . . . . *50*
Vase, 11"   /313 . . . . *75*

MANHATTAN GROUP

Bowl, 12"   /537. . . . . $65
Candle holder, quadruple, 2-handle, 14¹/₂" wide   /539 . . . . *90*

Left, *Indian Group: Shape # 262*. Right, *Mandarin Group: Shape # 353*.

Left, *Manhattan Group: Shape # 501*. Right, *Medieval Group: Shape # 389*.

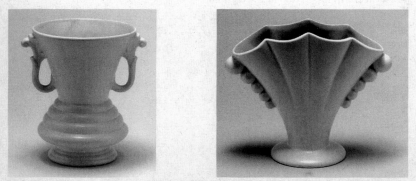

Left, *Miscellaneous Group: Shape # 631*. Right, *Neo-Classic Group: Shape # 668*.

Candlesticks, pair, 3³/₄" diameter /554 .... *$25*
Dish, 15¹/₂" diameter /534 .... *75*
Vase, 7¹/₂" /532. .... *50*
Vase, bud, fan, 7¹/₂" wide /541. .... *50*
Vase, footed, 8" wide /501. .... *30*
Vase, footed, 7¹/₂" /507 .... *30*
Vase, footed, 7¹/₂" /533 .... *50*
Vase, 3 cylinders, 7¹/₂" /543. .... *70*
Vase, 3 cylinders, 7¹/₂" /542. .... *70*
Vase, 3 feet, 8¹/₂" /538 .... *70*
Vase, footed, 9" /536 .... *50*
Vase, 10" /544 .... *60*
Vase, footed, 12¹/₂" /535 .... *80*

MEDIEVAL GROUP

Pieces have a distinctive flared top; all are footed.

Bowl, 9¹/₂" /398 .... *$40*
Candle holder, double, pair, 5¹/₄" /397 .... *50*
Vase, 5¹/₂" diameter /407 .... *20*
Vase, 7" /389 .... *40*
Vase, 8¹/₂" /406. .... *40*
Vase, 3 feet, 11" /422. .... *60*

MISCELLANEOUS GROUP

This is the official name for this group; do not confuse with Miscellany below.
Typical open-mouthed bowls and vases.

Bowl, footed, 4¹/₂" /354 .... *$30*
Bowl, 2-handle, 5" /281. .... *30*
Bowl, tab handles, 6¹/₂" /274 .... *30*
Bowl, 7" /341 .... *30*
Bowl, 7¹/₂" /372 .... *40*
Bowl, 7¹/₂" /304 .... *30*
Bowl, footed, 7¹/₂" /363 .... *40*
Vase, ribbed, 5¹/₂" /499 .... *30*
Vase, 2-handle, 5³/₄" /318. .... *30*
Vase, elephant handle, 6" /215. .... *50*
Vase, footed, 6" /355 .... *30*
Vase, swirl, 7" /451 .... *60*
Vase, 7" /370 .... *30*
Vase, 2-handle, footed, 7¹/₂" /502 .... *30*
Vase, 2-handle, 7¹/₂" /503. .... *30*
Vase, 2-handle, footed, 7¹/₂" /504 .... *30*
Vase, 2-handle, 7¹/₂" /505. .... *30*
Vase, 2-handle, 9¹/₂" /290. .... *40*
Vase, 10" /366 .... *75*
Vase, 2-handle, footed, 10¹/₂" /292 .... *75*

MISCELLANY

RumRill catalogs show many pieces that are not part of any group, though some might seem to belong to one or another. This is a small selection.

Candle holders, footed, pair, 6½" /597 .... *$50*
Centerpiece, Eagle /15½" /548 .... *125*
Cornucopia, double, 3" /650... *20*
Vase, 2½" /653... *30*
Vase, 4" /605 .... *20*
Vase, ball, 3 holes, 6" /600 .... *50*
Vase, ball, 3 holes, 8" /600 .... *80*
Vase, ball, 3 holes, 6" /601 .... *50*
Vase, ball, 3 holes, 8" /601 .... *80*
Vase, footed, fan, 8" /594 .... *50*
Vase, figural nude, 9" /595 .... *165*
Vase, footed w/birds, 9" /599 .... *70*
Wallpocket, 9" /647 .... *50*

NEO-CLASSIC GROUP   (1937)

Decorated with columns of balls.

Bowl, 10" /672... *$50*
Bowl, footed, 11" /676.. *75*
Candlesticks, pair, 4" /673 .... *40*
Vase, 3 feet, 8" /667... *60*
Vase, 8", footed /669 .... *60*
Vase, 8", footed /670 .... *60*
Vase, 8" /663 .... *50*
Vase, 8½", (3 feet) /671 .... *80*
Vase, 9" /675 .... *50*
Vase, 9" /664 .... *50*
Vase, 10", footed /665 .... *75*
Vase, 10", footed, fan /668 .... *60*
Vase, 12", footed /666 .... *100*
Vase, 15" /674 .... *125*

NOVELTIES

This is a general grouping of knick-knacks, bookends, ashtrays, and other pieces that are not design related. The carafe made a set with the tumblers.

Ashtray, 4" /54 .... *$20*
Ashtray, 4" /549 .... *25*
Ashtray, square, 6½" /550.. *20*
Ashtray, frog, 5" /428 .... *55*
Ashtray w/match holder, 6" wide /336 .... *20*
Bookends, Eagle, pair, 5½" /333....................................... *100*
Bookends, polar bear, pair, 7" wide /396 .... *125*
Bookends, shell, pair, 6" /391 .... *50*

Left, *Novelties: Shape # 555.* Center, *Renaissance Group: Shape # 528.* Right, *Shell Group: Shape # 432.*

Left, *Swan Group: Shape # 257.* Right, *Sylvan Group: Shape # 514.*

Left, *Trumpet Flower Group: Shape # 493.* Right, *Vintage Group: Shape # 624.*

Candle holder, 3 feet, 6" wide, each   /430. . . . . *$30*
Candy dish, swan, 6½" wide   /484 . . . . *65*
Carafe/wine jug w/stopper, 8¾"   /52 . . . . *60*
Cornucopia, 3"   /558 . . . . *20*
Jug, ball, 7½" diameter   /547 . . . . *30*
Planter, Fish, 6½" wide   /386 . . . . *30*
Seahorses and glass bowl, 11"   /555 . . . . *125*
Tray, curved reeds, 9" wide   /553 . . . . *40*
Tumbler, 2⅜" high   /53 . . . . *30*
Vase, 3"   /327 . . . . *20*
Vase, fan, 3"   /557. . . . . *20*
Vase, 4"   /324 . . . . *20*
Vase, 4"   /326 . . . . *20*
Vase, 4"   /323 . . . . *20*
Vase, bud, 4"   /325 . . . . *20*
Vase, bud, 6½"   /329. . . . . *15*
Vase, bud, 8"   /510 . . . . *20*

RENAISSANCE GROUP

Embossed vertical feathers in all pieces except deer inset which goes with the #526 bowl.

Bowl, footed, 8"   /520 . . . . *$70*
Bowl, 9½"   /524 . . . . *50*
Bowl, 10½"   /530 . . . . *40*
Bowl, low, 12"   /526 . . . . *20*
Candle holder/vase, 6"   /529 . . . . *20*
Inset, Deer, 10"   /531 . . . . *30*
Vase, 6"   /522 . . . . *30*
Vase, footed, 6½"   /496 . . . . *40*
Vase, 7"   /519 . . . . *30*
Vase, footed, 7"   /552 . . . . *40*
Vase, footed, 7½"   /523 . . . . *40*
Vase, 7¾"   /525. . . . . *50*
Vase, footed, 8"   /528 . . . . *40*
Vase, 3 feet, 10½"   /527 . . . . *75*
Vase, footed, 12½"   /521 . . . . *85*

SHELL GROUP

Shell shapes or shell-patterned surfaces.

Bowl, footed, 8"   /412. . . . . *$60*
Bowl, footed, 12"   /414. . . . . *75*
Bowl, 12½"   /415 . . . . *120*
Candle holder, triple, 8½"   /545 . . . . *50*
Candlesticks, pair, 3¾"   /417. . . . . *40*
Candy dish, three-part, 8¼"   /461 . . . . *40*
Cornucopia, double, 19" wide   /452 . . . . *150*

Creamer, small, 4½"   /460 . . . . *$20*
Sugar, small, 4½"   /459 . . . . *20*
Sugar, large, 6¼"   /429 . . . . *30*
Vase, short, 7¾" diameter   /432 . . . . *30*
Vase, cornucopia, footed, 7¼"   /413 . . . . *40*
Vase, footed, 8¼"   /431 . . . . *50*
Vase, cornucopia, double, 9½"   /416 . . . . *50*

SWAN GROUP

A swan is incorporated into the design of each piece.

Bowl, 8"   /282 . . . . *$40*
Bowl, 2-handle, 7½"   /279 . . . . *40*
Bowl, 2-handle, 8"   /444 . . . . *60*
Bowl, 2-handle, 10"   /440 . . . . *50*
Bowl, triple swan, 10½"   /284 . . . . *120*
Bowl, oval, 2-handle, 11"   /441 . . . . *60*
Candlesticks, pair, 5"   /418 . . . . *50*
Planter, 6"   /259 . . . . *25*
Planter, 9"   /260 . . . . *60*
Urn w/lid, 2-handle, 11"   /352 . . . . *85*
Vase, 6½"   /257 . . . . *60*
Vase, 2-handle, 8½"   /388 . . . . *75*
Vase, 2-handle, 9"   /298 . . . . *75*
Vase, 2-handle, 9"   /443 . . . . *75*
Vase, 2-handle, 10"   /442 . . . . *50*
Vase, 2-handle, 10"   /248 . . . . *85*
Vase, footed, 2-handle, 10"   /246 . . . . *85*

SYLVAN GROUP

Large, symmetrical leaves encircle each piece.

Basket, oval, 8½"   /438 . . . . *$60*
Bowl, 8"   /445 . . . . *40*
Bowl, footed, oval, 8"   /455 . . . . *20*
Bowl, crimped rim, oval, 9"   /436 . . . . *75*
Bowl, footed, 2-handle, 12½"   /435 . . . . *120*
Bowl, low, 2-handle, oval, 17"   /437 . . . . *100*
Candle holder, double, pair, 5¼"   /397 . . . . *60*
Candlestick, pair, 3½"   /433 . . . . *25*
Decanter, footed w/stopper, 11½"   /449 . . . . *70*
Vase, 2-handle, 5½"   /450 . . . . *30*
Vase, footed, 6"   /514 . . . . *30*
Vase, fan, footed, 7"   /439 . . . . *40*
Vase, 8"   /447 . . . . *50*
Vase, ewer, 9½"   /448 . . . . *60*
Vase, fluted, 11"   /446 . . . . *120*

TRUMPET FLOWER GROUP   (mid 1934)

Trumpet Flowers are incorporated into the design of each piece.

Bowl, shallow, 8"   /492 . . . . *$40*
Bowl, footed, 8½"   /489 . . . . *40*
Bowl, 9"   /493 . . . . *75*
Bowl, footed, 9"   /488 . . . . *90*
Bowl, elongated, 12½"   /487 . . . . *90*
Bowl, footed, 13"   /485 . . . . *120*
Candle holders, pair, 4½"   /490 . . . . *75*
Vase, 7"   /486 . . . . *60*
Vase, footed, 10"   /491 . . . . *100*

VINTAGE GROUP

Each piece has embossed grapes in the design.

Basket, 12½"   /615 . . . . *$100*
Bowl, footed, 10"   /625 . . . . *75*
Bowl, square, 10"   /623 . . . . *75*
Bowl, shallow, 10"   /621 . . . . *50*
Bowl, 2-handle, rectangular, 11½"   /619 . . . . *85*
Bowl, 12"   /614 . . . . *85*
Bowl, 12½"   /618 . . . . *75*
Bowl, 14½"   /626 . . . . *120*
Bowl, footed, 15"   /617 . . . . *150*
Bowl, "S" shape, 15"   /612 . . . . *120*
Candlesticks, pair, 5½" wide   /622 . . . . *40*
Grape cluster decoration, 7½"   /627 . . . . *30*
Urn, footed, w/lid, 9½"   /624 . . . . *100*
Vase, ewer, 11"   /616 . . . . *80*
Vase, 12"   /613 . . . . *100*
Vase, footed, 12"   /620 . . . . *75*

SALEM CHINA COMPANY

Salem, Ohio

CHAPTER AT A GLANCE

Ground was broken near the end of 1898 for the Salem China Company, founded by Pat and John McNichol, Dan Cronin, and William Smith, all of East Liverpool, Ohio. Production of ware began around November 1899, and the plant was in full operation by January 1900. The products were white granite and semiporcelain. The company also engaged in distribution.

Salem was purchased by the Sebrings in 1918. At this time Floyd McKee joined the firm; he retired in 1950 as general manager. McKee is the author of *The Second Oldest Profession*, a history of the pottery industry. Manufacturing ceased in 1960, and Salem is now operating solely as a distributor.

Most of the shapes and many of the decorations marketed in the 1930s and 1940s were designed by Viktor Schreckengost.

MARKS The first three marks were used prior to ca. 1930. While I have dated them to the 1920s, they may have been used as far back as the company's founding.

667

The circle mark seems to be transitional from the 1920s to the 1930s, but I have not been able to date it precisely.

Antique Ivory and Yukon Yellow (not shown) refer to body color and date to the late 1920s.

I have seen the Salem Maid stamp only on the Streamline shape. I believe Salem Maid was a promotional program, and this mark may be found on other shapes.

The rectangular mark was used from the late 1930s to the early 1940s, the cup and saucer from the early 1940s.

DINNERWARE

I have included a number of decal descriptions in this chapter because many were created by Viktor Schreckengost, the head of Salem's art department and an important 20th-century U.S. designer.

There's one important fact to keep in mind. Salem used the same decal on different shapes, a usual practice among the potteries. However, they often changed the name. So Petitpoint Basket on Victory is called Flower Basket and Sampler on other shapes.

BONJOUR

Sometimes the sugar bowl was sold as an open bowl.

Decorations

DUTCH PETITPOINT (80141) A petitpoint Dutch boy and girl (she is carrying two buckets) in colors of red, blue, and warm light brown. Border stamped with a lacy 22-karat gold design. Open sugar.

MORNING GLORY (80542) A semiborder of morning glories in blues, pinks, and yellows, with a cluster in the center of the well. The edge is trimmed with a blue line.

Bowl, soup . . . . $10 – $12
Bowl, oval, 9" . . . . 10 – 12

Bonjour: Dutch Petitpoint creamer.

Casserole	*$20 – $25*
Creamer	*4 – 6*
Cup	*4 – 6*
Dish, 5¹/₂"*	*2 – 3*
Gravy	*12 – 15*
Plate, 6"	*1 – 2*
Plate, 7"	*5 – 7*
Plate, 9"	*7 – 9*
Plate, 10"	*10 – 12*
Platter, 11"	*10 – 12*
Saucer	*1 – 2*
Sugar	*8 – 10*

BRIAR ROSE   (1932)

Designed by J. Palin Thorley for the American China Corporation, this was bought by Salem when ACC went bankrupt.

Decal decorations include Rosebud Chintz, Godey Print (called Godey Ladies on Victory), and Golden Pheasant. Also look for the monochrome blue Turkey Set: 22" platter and twelve 10¹/₂" plates.

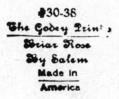

Bowl, soup, coupe, 7"	*$10 – $12*
Bowl, vegetable, round, 8"	*12 – 15*
Bowl, vegetable, oval, 9"	*10 – 12*

Briar Rose: Plate (Rose bouquet) and Godey Print soup bowl.

Butter dish, open. . . . . *$15 – $20*
Casserole . . . . *20 – 25*
Creamer . . . . *4 – 6*
Cup . . . . *4 – 6*
Dish, fruit. . . . . *2 – 3*
Dish, cereal . . . . *3 – 4*
Gravy. . . . . *12 – 15*
Gravy liner/pickle . . . . *6 – 6*
Plate, 6¼" . . . . *1 – 2*
Plate, 7". . . . . *4 – 5*
Plate, 9¼" . . . . *7 – 9*
Plate, 10½" . . . . *10 – 12*
Plate, bread, 10". . . . . *10 – 12*
Plate, cake, 10" . . . . *10 – 12*
Platter, 11" . . . . *10 – 12*
Platter, 13" . . . . *12 – 15*
Platter, 22" × 18" . . . . *40 – 50*
Saucer . . . . *1 – 2*
Sugar . . . . *8 – 10*

CENTURY

Solid Color

RANCH STYLE   Birch Gray, Cedar Coral, Lime Yellow, and Pine Green.

MADE IN U.S.A.
WARRANTED
22 CARAT GOLD

Decorations

BANQUET SERVICE WARE   Century was one of the shapes used for special orders available to churches, fraternal orders, etc. The group's name, initials or insignia were done in either gold or platinum (on the rim of the flatware and the outside of the hollowware), and a line on the edge and verge was available in gold, platinum, or colors.

SPRING TULIP   (70156-PE) Tulips in shades of yellow, pink, burnt orange, and blue-lavender with green leaves in a black and yellow wicker basket, placed slightly off the center of the well. A band of platinum encircles a band of blue-lavender on the rim.

ZEPHYR   (7005) Concentric circles of platinum-gold alloy bands and lines.

Century: Gravy (Petitpoint floral), Petitpoint Basket AD cup, cup (Bird of Paradise), and Sailing creamer.

Bowl, soup, coupe, 7" .... *$10 – $12*
Bowl, soup, lug .... *8 – 10*
Bowl, 36s .... *7 – 10*
Bowl, vegetable, oval, 9" .... *10 – 12*
Bowl, vegetable, round, 8" .... *12 – 15*
Butter, open, single lug .... *15 – 20*
Casserole .... *20 – 25*
Creamer .... *4 – 6*
Cup .... *4 – 6*
Dish, cereal .... *4 – 6*
Dish, fruit .... *2 – 3*
Gravy .... *12 – 15*
Pickle, lug (open butter) .... *6 – 8*
Plate, 6" .... *1 – 2*
Plate, 7" .... *4 – 5*
Plate, 8" .... *5 – 6*
Plate, 9" .... *7 – 9*
Plate, 10" .... *10 – 12*
Plate, chop, lug, 11" .... *12 – 15*
Plate, chop, lug, 13" .... *15 – 20*
Saucer .... *1 – 2*
Shaker, pair .... *8 – 10*
Sugar .... *8 – 10*
Teapot .... *25 – 30*

FREE-FORM   (1940s)

Designed by Viktor Schreckengost, who told me that the cup was the first to receive a design patent in 50 years. While this is not the first footed shape (Paden City's Shell Crest comes to mind), it is one of the most distinctive in design. Footed pieces are noted in the listing below. The cruet set consisted of two shakers, two cruets, and a tray.

The three more common decorations are Hopscotch (thick and thin lines form abstract star shapes), Primitive (resembling archaeologic cave paintings), and Southwind ("Autumnal beauty and motion expressed by the charcoal-shaded branch, tipped by wind swept leaves of soft turquoise, burnt orange, and delicate green/gold").

free • form
by
Salem
Pat. Pend.
primitive
✿ ☆ 5 5 U

Bowl, decorative, footed .... $15 – $20
Bowl, salad, square .... 15 – 18
Bowl, soup, coupe .... 10 – 12
Bowl, soup, onion .... 8 – 10
Bowl, vegetable .... 10 – 12
Bowl, vegetable, divided .... 12 – 15
Butter, ¼-pound .... 20 – 25
Casserole, 2-quart .... 20 – 25
Coaster, 3½" .... 8 – 12
Coffee server .... 35 – 30
Creamer, footed .... 6 – 8
Cruet, footed .... 15 – 20
Cup, footed .... 8 – 10
Dish, fruit .... 2 – 3
Gravy .... 12 – 15
Gravy liner/pickle .... 6 – 8
Jug, 12-ounce .... 12 – 15
Jug, 62-ounce .... 20 – 25
Plate, 6" .... 1 – 2
Plate, 7" .... 4 – 5
Plate, 10" .... 10 – 12
Plate, patio, 10½" .... 10 – 12
Platter, single lug, 13" .... 12 – 15

Free Form: Primitive plate, cup, and teapot.

Platter, square, 13" .... *$12 – $15*
Saucer .... *1 – 2*
Shaker (tall/short), footed, pair .... *10 – 12*
Sugar, footed .... *10 – 15*
Teapot, footed .... *35 – 40*
Tray (cruet set) .... *8 – 10*

HEIRLOOM

A square shape with scalloped corners and a gadroon edge.

Decal-decorated on a tan or white body. Look for Pink Chateau, an underglaze print.

MARKS The castle backstamp is found on most pieces of Heirloom. On some pieces you will find this Corot stamp. The decoration is a blue underglaze print, which I assume is after a Corot painting.

Bowl, salad, round, 9" .... *$15 – $18*
Bowl, soup, 7³/₄".. *10 – 12*
Butter dish .... *20 – 25*
Casserole... *20 – 25*
Creamer .... *4 – 6*
Cup .... *4 – 6*
Dish, 5¹/₂"*.. *2 – 3*
Gravy... *12 – 15*

Heirloom: Plate and gravy.

Gravy faststand . . . . *$12 – $15*
Plate, 6" . . . . *1 – 2*
Plate, 7" . . . . *4 – 5*
Plate, 9" . . . . *7 – 9*
Plate, square, 6½" . . . . *3 – 4*
Platter, 11"* . . . . *10 – 12*
Saucer . . . . *1 – 2*
Sugar . . . . *8 – 10*

LOTUS BUD

Designed by Viktor Schreckengost.
    Many decorations had a "Far Eastern" flavor.
    MARKS   From this backstamp, we can see that Farmer in the Dell was sold as part of Sears's Harmony House line.

Bowl, oval, 9"* . . . . *$10 – $12*
Bowl, soup, 8¼" . . . . *10 – 12*
Casserole . . . . *20 – 25*
Creamer . . . . *4 – 6*
Cup . . . . *4 – 6*

Lotus Bud: Farmer in the Dell plate, Petitpoint Sampler creamer and sugar.

Dish, 5½"*	*$2 – $3*
Plate, 6"	*1 – 2*
Plate, 9"*	*7 – 9*
Platter, 12"	*12 – 15*
Saucer	*1 – 2*
Sugar	*8 – 10*

NEW YORKER   (mid 1933)

An embossed band around the rim.

Decorations

GLENMORE   (28132) A cluster of tulips with green and rust colors predominating in front of a black lattice. It is trimmed with a golden brown line on the edge and the verge.

MONTROSE   (28852-PA) A border design with orchid flowers predominating. Trimmed with a platinum gold alloy.

MORNING GLORY   (28542) Border design of morning glory blossoms and other summer flowers with green leaves.

PINK CHATEAU   (2601) English-type underglaze print of a chateau with a boating scene in the foreground, done in a soft pink color.

Ashtray	*$6 – $8*
Bowl, oval, 9"*	*10 – 12*
Bowl, soup, 8"*	*10 – 12*
Casserole	*20 – 25*
Creamer	*4 – 6*
Cup	*4 – 6*
Dish, 5½"*	*2 – 3*
Plate, 6"	*1 – 2*
Plate, 7¼"	*5 – 7*
Plate, 9"*	*7 – 9*
Platter, 11½"	*10 – 12*
Saucer	*1 – 2*
Sugar	*8 – 10*

STREAMLINE

See Tricorne.

Decorations

ZEPHYR   (9005) Concentric circles of bands and lines done in a platinum gold alloy.

SYMPHONY   (1940)

Designed by Viktor Schreckengost. Embossed concentric circles around verge of flatware and bottom of hollowware.

Bowl, oval, 9"*	*$10 – $12*
Casserole	*20 – 25*
Creamer	*4 – 6*
Cup	*4 – 6*
Dish 5½"	*2 – 3*
Gravy	*12 – 15*
Plate, 6½"	*1 – 2*
Plate, 7"*	*4 – 5*
Plate, 9"*	*7 – 9*
Plate, 10"	*10 – 12*

Symphony: Sweet Sue plate, creamer and sugar (floral), and coffee pot. Note the two different finials.

Plate, lug, 7¼"	*$5 – $6*
Platter, lug, 11¾"	*10 – 12*
Saucer	*1 – 2*
Sugar, regular knob finial	*8 – 10*
Sugar, three-point finial	*8 – 10*

TRICORNE   (1934)

Distinguished by its triangular flatware and angular handles, Tricorne was designed to attract attention. It was introduced initially in Mandarin, a bright red art glaze on the rims of the flatware and the outside of the hollowware, the first brightly colored dinnerware made by an Ohio pottery. Later decorations are colored concentric bands on the verge—Coral Red, Royal Blue, and Platinum (called Artiste)—and decals: Dutch Petitpoint (boy and girl), Jonquil, Polo (pony and rider in black outlined in gray and coral red, designed by Margaret Blumenthal), Sailing (sailboats, designed by Margaret Blumenthal), and a Bridge Set with card suits. Mandarin is the most easily found.

SETS A 24-piece bridge set, service for four, consisted of party plates, cups, nut dishes, sandwich tray, creamer, covered sugar, and two items of glassware: a tumbler (that fit into the cup ring on the party plate) in alternating bands of red and black stripes, to harmonize, and sippers (straws).

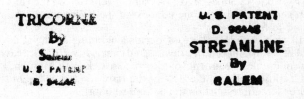

NOTE Tricorne was restyled with round flatware and named Streamline.

Candle holder	*ND*
Casserole	*$30 – $35*
Coffee pot	*50 – 60*
Creamer	*8 – 10*
Cup	*6 – 8*
Cup, AD	*12 – 15*
Dish, 5¼"	*5 – 6*
Nut dish, 3¾"	*12 – 15*
Plate, 5½"	*3 – 4*
Plate, 6¼"	*5 – 6*
Plate, 9"	*10 – 12*
Plate, party, 9"	*10 – 12*
Plate, sandwich, 11½"	*12 – 15*
Saucer	*3 – 4*
Saucer, AD	*5 – 8*
Sugar	*15 – 20*

Tricorne: Advertising nut dish and Sailing teapot. Victory: Mary Had a Little Lamb AD coffee pot and Petitpoint Basket coffee pot.

VICTORY   (1938)

Designed by Viktor Schreckengost. A band of thin ribs on the rims of the flatware, with vertical ribbing on the bottoms of the hollowware. The moustache cup is a hard-to-find novelty.

You will find a wide variety of decals, including Godey Ladies, Indian Tree, Basket Petitpoint, and Parkway (red berries and black leaves). There were also solid-color treatments of Green, Lipstick Red, Maroon, Periwinkle Blue, and Yellow: color on the rims of the flatware and on the outside of the hollowware (sometimes just on the bottom ribbing).

A fifteen-piece Little Lady Party Set for children consisted of four each of 6½" plates and AD cups and saucers, an AD open sugar and creamer, and an 8½" lug sandwich plate. It was decal-decorated with Basket Petitpoint or Mary Had a Little Lamb.

See also Limoges.

BASKET PETITPOINT   (60183-GV) Brown wicker basket of flowers in shades of old rose, yellow, orange, and lavender. Verge decorated with 22-karat gold band.

BLUE BASKET   (60159) Tulips and other yellow, green, and delicate pink flowers in a blue basket. A blue band with 22-karat gold verge line.

BOUNTIFUL (60171-HS) Five different fruits—peaches, grapes, apples, pears, and cherries—in natural tones in a hand-painted style.

COLONIAL FIRESIDE (60182 [1939]) Authentic Colonial scenes "adapted" by Viktor Schreckengost. There are four different scenes centered around the fireside and rendered in mellow browns, tans, and greens.

DENMARK (60190 [1939]) A "modern" design of a clear-toned bellflower in silver gray with burnt-orange-tipped petals. Small stylized button flowers in pale and darker blue dip above the bell flower. At the left, among green leaves, are two wide orange-colored blossoms with scalloped edges. There is a narrow blue line on the verge.

DOILY PETITPOINT (60179-NL) A petitpoint rendering of old-fashioned needlework with a rose center and floral border on a fawn background.

EMPIRE (P-60768) Inspired by French Empire style. Dresden patterns of small sprays of flowers enclosed by a pink pastel band.

GARDEN (60167) A bouquet with red and yellow tulips predominating. The verge is decorated with a fine coral line surrounded by a heavier gray band.

GODEY PRINTS (60-38 [also called Godey Fashions]) Based on designs in the "Lady's Book" by Louis Antoine Godey. There seem to be three different "poses" in authentic colors.

INDIAN TREE (60160-NL) After the design of Thomas Minton. The Indian Tree is surrounded by flowers in deep pinks, blues, and yellows with green foliage.

INTRINSIC (60042) A wide band of 23-karat gold on the verge encircles a 23-karat gold treatment of dots and circles with a scalloped design.

JANE ADAMS (60207-NL) A nest of yellow and orange flowers, rich green leaves, and a sprinkling of blue forget-me-nots.

MINUET {60147) Designed by Olivia Lord. An "olde tyme" lady and gentleman in pastel colors, surrounded by a wreath of pink roses and enclosed by a pastel blue band on the verge.

PARKWAY (60134) Sprays of leaves in black with red berries. Verge decorated with band of red.

PIONEER (B-60193) Five subjects: Pioneer Maid, Tilling the Soil, The Spinster, The Harvester, and At Ease. Trimmed with a deep blue band on the verge.

SEPTEMBER (60371-GV) A ring of large wide-open flowers and leaves in mellow fall foilage hues—sunshine yellow, acorn brown, and pumpkin orange—encircled by a narrow gold line on the verge.

SUMMER DAY (60E128) Red, black, and golden tan flowers and green leaves in a blue vase. The verge is lined in a 22-karat etched gold band with leaf design in it.

SUN VALLEY (60144-HS) Wild mountain flowers of the western ranges in yellow, rose, blue, and green in a hand-painted style.

TULIP (60101-NL) Tulips set off-center.

VIENNA (B-60178) A rose design surrounded by rose lace on a blue and ivory background. Broad ivory band on the verge with thin brown lines on either side.

Ashtray	*$6 – $8*
Bowl, 6¹/₄"	*6 – 8*
Bowl, lug, 6³/₄"	*8 – 10*
Bowl, soup, 8¹/₄"	*10 – 12*
Bowl, vegetable, round, 8"	*12 – 15*
Casserole	*25 – 30*
Candle holders, pair	*30 – 35*
Coffee pot	*45 – 50*
Coffee pot, AD	*30 – 40*
Creamer	*4 – 6*
Creamer, AD	*6 – 8*
Cup	*4 – 6*
Cup, AD	*10 – 12*
Cup, cream soup	*12 – 16*
Dish, 5¹/₂"	*2 – 3*
Dish, 7¹/₄"	*8 – 10*
Gravy	*12 – 15*
Mustache cup	*15 – 20*
Plate, 6"	*1 – 2*
Plate, 7"	*4 – 5*
Plate, 10"	*10 – 12*
Plate, cake, 10"	*10 – 12*
Plate, lug, 7¹/₄"	*4 – 5*
Platter, oval, 11"	*10 – 12*
Platter, oval, 13"	*12 – 15*
Saucer	*1 – 2*
Saucer, AD	*3 – 5*
Saucer, cream soup, 7¹/₈"	*6 – 8*
Shaker, small, pair	*8 – 10*
Shaker, tall, pair	*10 – 12*
Sugar	*8 – 10*
Sugar, AD	*10 – 12*

KITCHENWARE

HOTCO

Salem's only kitchenware line. The ashtray doubled as a lid to a small jar.

*Hotco: Mug (Johnston Hot Chocolate), Petitpoint Basket jug,
Pioneer ashtray and tab-handle custard (floral).*

Ashtray . . . . *$6 – $8*
Butter, 1-pound . . . . *25 – 30*
Casserole . . . . *25 – 30*
Custard . . . . *4 – 6*
Drip . . . . *12 – 15*
Jug, small. . . . . *10 – 15*
Jug, medium . . . . *15 – 20*
Jug, large . . . . *20 – 25*
Leftover, round, small. . . . . *6 – 10*
Leftover, round, medium. . . . . *10 – 15*
Leftover, round, large . . . . *15 – 20*
Mug . . . . *12 – 15*
Pie baker . . . . *10 – 12*
Plate, chop . . . . *15 – 20*
Shaker, handled, pair. . . . . *15 – 20*
Utensil, cake server . . . . *12 – 15*
Utensil, fork. . . . . *20 – 25*
Utensil, spoon . . . . *15 – 20*

NOVELTIES

FISH SET   (mid 1933)

All pieces are shaped like fish except the shell-shape dish.

Pieces were made in a plain yellow glaze or a white glaze with tones of pink,
green, or blue gray.

Bone dish, 9"	$12 – $15
Plate, 9" × 10"	12 – 15
Platter, long, 21" × 11"	35 – 40
Platter, round, 16" × 14"	25 – 30
Shell dish, 7" diameter	6 – 8

Fish

SCIO POTTERY COMPANY

Scio, Ohio

In the 1920s, the Carrollton China Company of Carrollton, Ohio, opened a production facility in Scio. It ran only a few years and was closed in 1927. The loss of jobs was disastrous to the town, whose population fell from 1,200 to 400 in five years.

In 1932, Lew Reese, who was employed at a pottery in New Cumberland, West Virginia, happened to pass by the abandoned plant while rabbit shooting with some friends he was visiting. He made some inquiries and decided that here was the opportunity to put into practice his idea that American manufacturers could compete with the cheap Japanese imports if they were properly mechanized.

He quit his job and, with the support of the town, reopened the pottery. Production began in 1933, and until 1950 only white ware was made. On January 1 of that year a decorating kiln began operations. Lew Reese died in 1952. The pottery is still in business.

Scio makes three basic dinnerware shapes: Donna, a coupe shape; Ranson, a periodic embossment; and Swirl.

MARKS   Scio is either unmarked or has a raised "USA."

CASUAL BROWN

This is a brown drip line similar to those made by Hull, McCoy, and others. Some pieces are from the Donna shape.

Bean Pot	$15 – $20
Bowl, soup/salad	8 – 10
Bowl, vegetable, 8½"	8 – 10
Butter, ¼-pound	10 – 15
Creamer	4 – 5
Cup	2 – 3
Dish, 6¾"	1 – 2
Jug, Cable, small, 11-ounce	6 – 8
Jug, Cable, medium	8 – 10
Jug, Cable, large	10 – 12
Mug, 10-ounce	4 – 6
Plate, 7½"	3 – 4
Plate, 10"	4 – 6
Platter, 13"	8 – 10
Saucer	1
Shaker, tall, each	3 – 5

Sugar . . . . *$6 – $8*
Tidbit, 3-tier . . . . *10 – 12*

DONNA

This is a coupe shape with straight sides, similar to a popular Royal China shape. Be careful not to confuse the two.

Blue Willow

Bowl, soup, 7³/₄" . . . . *$8 – $10*
Bowl, vegetable, 8¹/₂" . . . . *8 – 10*
Creamer . . . . *6 – 8*
Cup . . . . *4 – 5*
Dish, 5¹/₂" . . . . *2 – 3*
Dish, 6" . . . . *2 – 3*
Plate, 6" . . . . *2 – 3*
Plate, 7¹/₂" . . . . *3 – 4*
Plate, 9¹/₄" . . . . *4 – 6*
Plate, 10" . . . . *6 – 7*
Platter, 11¹/₂" . . . . *8 – 10*
Platter, 13" . . . . *10 – 12*
Saucer *1*
Sugar . . . . *8 – 10*

Currier & Ives

The cup in this decoration is more traditional in shape than that used in Blue Willow.

Bowl, soup, 8¹/₄" . . . . *$8 – $10*
Bowl, vegetable, 8¹/₂" . . . . *8 – 10*
Creamer . . . . *4 – 6*
Cup . . . . *4 – 5*

Donna shape: Blue Willow cup, saucer, and 9¹/₄" plate.

SEBRING
POTTERY COMPANY

Sebring, Ohio

CHAPTER AT A GLANCE

DINNERWARE	DORIC
ARISTOCRAT	GADROON
BARBARA JANE	PEGASUS
CORINTHIAN	TROJAN

The Sebring family established its first pottery in East Liverpool in 1887. In 1899, after having opened several other potteries, the Sebrings decided to consolidate their interests, bought land in Mahoning County, Ohio, and established the town of Sebring. The second pottery to be built there was named the Sebring Pottery. It produced semiporcelain dinnerware, toilet ware, and specialties. Some art ware and kitchenware was made in the 1930s. Sebring and its sister company Limoges (which see) were bought in 1943 by National Unit Distributors, and the name Sebring disappeared, only the Limoges name being used in advertisements.

NOTE   From the introduction of semiporcelain ca. 1890, dinnerware had been produced in a white body. In 1923, Sebring broke with convention and brought out its Ivory Porcelain, a semiporcelain dinnerware with an ivory body. E. M. Knowles followed in kind two years later, and by the end of the 1920s the white body had virtually disappeared from dinnerware production, not to be seen again until the late 1940s.

MARKS   The first backstamp is pre-1930. Of the other stamps, most from the 1930s, you can see that Sebring marked the glaze more often than the shape.

DINNERWARE

Collecting dinnerware made by the Sebring family potteries can be a confusing endeavor. Many shapes were shared by these potteries. I have tried to indicate some of these mutual endeavors throughout the text in the appropriate chapters. For Sebring, note that you will find pieces of American Limoges's Triumph with a Sebring mark.

Further confusion awaits in Sebring's three "Greek" lines, all of them fluted designs with scalloped edges. I have sorted it out as best I could from old trade ads and pieces I have found. Further refinement may be required, but for now, here's how I see it:

Doric is a square shape.

Corinthian is a round shape, rimmed, with a square sugar and creamer and perhaps other square pieces.

Trojan is a round shape, coupe, with round sugar and creamer, and, to further confuse matters, a square salad plate.

Some pieces may have been shared between these lines.

ARISTOCRAT (1932)

Introduced by Sebring, you will find a lot of Aristocrat also made by (and marked) Leigh. You will find a lot of solid colors with band treatments as well as decals.

Bowl, salad, 8³/₄" . . . . *$15 – $18*
Bowl, soup, 7³/₈" . . . . *10 – 12*
Casserole . . . . *20 – 25*
Coffee pot . . . . *35 – 40*
Creamer . . . . *4 – 6*
Cup . . . . *4 – 6*
Dish, 5¹/₂" . . . . *2 – 3*
Gravy . . . . *12 – 15*
Plate, 6¹/₄" . . . . *1 – 2*
Plate, 7¹/₄" . . . . *4 – 5*
Plate, 9" . . . . *5 – 7*

Platter, oval, 11½" .... $10 – $12
Platter, oval, 13" .... 12 – 15
Platter, oval, 15½" .... 15 – 18
Saucer .... 1 – 2
Shaker, pair .... 8 – 10
Sugar .... 8 – 10
Teapot .... 30 – 35

BARBARA JANE

This shape is distinguished by thin, vertical fluting on the hollowware items and a band of fluting that begins at the verge and goes into the well on the flatware items. The handles on the Barbara items are round; the Old English handles, pointed top, turn up.

There seem to be rimmed and coupe versions of this shape; perhaps some restyling was done.

Ashtray, 4" .... $4 – $5
Baker .... 10 – 12
Bowl, fruit/salad, footed. .... 15 – 18
Bowl, soup, 9" .... 10 – 12
Bowl, soup, coupe .... 10 – 12
Bowl, 36s .... 7 – 10
Bowl, vegetable, round .... 10 – 12
Butter dish .... 20 – 25
Candlestick, each .... 12 – 15
Casserole .... 20 – 25
Creamer .... 4 – 6
Cup, AD coffee, Barbara. .... 10 – 12
Cup, AD coffee, Old English .... 10 – 12
Cup, bouillon, Barbara .... 12 – 16
Cup, bouillon, Old English .... 12 – 16
Cup, cream soup .... 12 – 16

Barbara Jane:
Plate and teapot.

Cup, tea, Barbara. . . . . *$4 – $6*
Cup, tea, Old English . . . . *4 – 6*
Dish, 5¼". . . . . *2 – 3*
Dish, 5¾". . . . . *2 – 3*
Dish, 6¼". . . . . *3 – 4*
Eggcup. . . . . *10 – 12*
Gravy. . . . . *12 – 15*
Gravy faststand . . . . *12 – 15*
Gravy liner/pickle . . . . *6 – 8*
Jug . . . . *20 – 25*
Plate, 6¼" . . . . *1 – 2*
Plate, 7". . . . . *4 – 5*
Plate, 8". . . . . *4 – 5*
Plate, 9¼". . . . . *5 – 7*
Plate, chop, 14"* . . . . *15 – 20*
Plate, grill, 6 sections w/center well . . . . *15 – 20*
Plate, service . . . . *15 – 20*
Platter, 11"* . . . . *8 – 12*
Platter, 13"* . . . . *12 – 15*
Platter, 15"* . . . . *15 – 18*
Platter, 17½" × 13" . . . . *20 – 25*
Saucer, AD coffee. . . . . *3 – 5*
Saucer, cream soup . . . . *6 – 8*
Saucer, tea. . . . . *1 – 2*
Sugar . . . . *8 – 10*
Teapot, low . . . . *20 – 25*
Teapot, tall. . . . . *20 – 25*
Tray, bread/cake, lug, square w/square well. . . . . *15 – 20*
Vase . . . . *15 – 20*

CORINTHIAN   (<1933)

A round, fluted design with scalloped edges. The flatware is rimmed. The sugar and creamer are square. See also Trojan. The Corinthian shape was also used by American Limoges (which see).

Bowl, salad, round, 9"* . . . . *$15 – $18*
Bowl, soup, 8"* . . . . *10 – 12*
Bowl, vegetable, oval, 9"*. . . . . *10 – 12*
Casserole. . . . . *20 – 25*
Creamer . . . . *4 – 6*
Cup . . . . *4 – 6*
Cup, cream soup . . . . *12 – 15*
Dish, 5¼"*. . . . . *2 – 3*
Eggcup. . . . . *10 – 12*
Gravy. . . . . *12 – 15*
Plate, 6¼" . . . . *1 – 2*
Plate, 8" . . . . *4 – 5*
Plate, 9" . . . . *5 – 7*

Aristocrat coffee pot, Gadroon teapot, and Doric batter jug (green).

Saucer	*$1 – $2*
Sugar	*8 – 10*

DORIC (1930)

Designed by Gale Turnbull. A square shape that has wide ribs and scalloped edges and a shell finial. Cups have square bottoms.

Originally introduced in solid colors of ivory, rose, Jade (green), and Maize (yellow), as well as a number of decal decorations, including Gladiola, Egyptian Grass (papyrus), Love Tree (Indian Tree), and Magenta Rose.

Bowl, soup, 8"	*$10 – $12*
Bowl, soup, coupe, 7¹/₂"	*10 – 12*
Bowl, vegetable, 8"	*10 – 12*
Casserole	*20 – 25*
Creamer	*4 – 6*
Creamer, AD.	*6 – 8*
Cup	*4 – 6*
Cup, AD.	*10 – 12*
Dish, 5"	*2 – 3*
Dish, 5¹/₂"	*2 – 3*
Gravy	*12 – 15*
Jug, batter	*20 – 25*
Plate, 6"	*1 – 2*
Plate, 7"	*4 – 5*
Plate, 9"	*5 – 7*
Platter, rectangular, 11"	*10 – 12*
Platter, rectangular, 13"	*12 – 15*

Saucer	*$1 – $2*
Saucer, AD	*3 – 5*
Sugar	*8 – 10*
Sugar, AD	*10 – 12*
Teapot	*20 – 25*

GADROON (<1926)

A gadroon edge shape. Initially, many hollowware items such as the teapots were oval. At some point, the casserole, sugar, and creamer were redesigned as round. Sizes followed by an asterisk are approximations.

Gadroon is most often found with the Golden Maize body, but ivory was made as well. The most common decorations are decals; the Poppy and the Jasmine seem to be the most common. An interesting decoration is the Early American (underglaze monochrome scenes of early American life).

You will also find solid colors with line treatments such as Coral Gables (Golden Maize body with coral lines).

Bowl, fruit/salad, footed	*$15 – $18*
Bowl, soup, 8"	*10 – 12*
Bowl, soup, coupe	*10 – 12*
Bowl, 36s	*7 – 10*
Bowl, vegetable, round, 8"*	*10 – 12*
Bowl, vegetable, round, 9"*	*10 – 12*
Bowl, vegetable, oval, 9¼"	*10 – 12*
Bowl, vegetable, oval, 10"*	*12 – 15*
Butter dish	*20 – 25*
Casserole, oval	*20 – 25*
Casserole, round	*20 – 25*
Creamer	*4 – 6*
Creamer, round	*4 – 6*
Cup	*4 – 6*
Cup, AD	*10 – 12*
Cup, bouillon	*12 – 15*
Cup, cream soup	*12 – 15*
Dish, 5¼"	*2 – 3*
Dish, 6¼"	*3 – 4*
Domed cover, 8" diameter	*25 – 35*
Eggcup	*10 – 12*
Gravy	*12 – 15*
Gravy faststand	*12 – 15*
Gravy liner/pickle	*6 – 8*
Jug, 12s	*20 – 25*
Jug, 24s	*20 – 25*
Jug, 30s	*15 – 20*
Jug, 36s	*12 – 15*
Plate, 6¼"	*1 – 2*
Plate, 7"	*4 – 5*
Plate, 8"	*5 – 6*
Plate, 9"	*7 – 9*

Plate, 10" . . . . *$10 – $12*
Plate, embossed design, 9¼" . . . . *10 – 12*
Plate, lug, 7" . . . . *4 – 5*
Plate, lug, underplate for dome . . . . *10 – 12*
Plate, square, 9" . . . . *6 – 8*
Plate, service . . . . *10 – 12*
Platter, oval, 9"* . . . . *8 – 10*
Platter, oval, 11½" . . . . *10 – 12*
Platter, oval, 13"* . . . . *12 – 15*
Platter, oval, 15"* . . . . *15 – 18*
Saucer . . . . *1 – 2*
Saucer, AD . . . . *3 – 5*
Saucer, cream soup . . . . *6 – 8*
Sugar . . . . *8 – 10*
Sugar, round . . . . *8 – 10*
Teapot, 2-cup . . . . *25 – 30*
Teapot, 4-cup . . . . *25 – 30*
Teapot, 6-cup . . . . *30 – 35*
Tray, cake, lug, round, 10" . . . . *15 – 18*
Tray, cake, lug, square . . . . *15 – 18*

PEGASUS

RED HEAD POPPY

Casserole . . . . *$20 – $25*
Creamer . . . . *4 – 6*

Pegasus: Red Head Poppy plate and gravy.

Cup	$4 – $6
Dish, 5½"*	2 – 3
Gravy	12 – 15
Plate, 6¼"*	1 – 2
Plate, 10"	10 – 12
Platter, 11"	10 – 12
Saucer	1 – 2
Sugar	8 – 10

TROJAN   (1936)

An updated version of Corinthian but with no rim; shell finials. See also American Limoges.

This was decorated in both solid colors and decals. The solid colors included burgundy, cobalt blue, green, yellow, and possibly others and seems to have been called Rainbow Ware. Decals include Ceylon (Indian Tree) and Italian (a decal intended to look hand painted).

Bowl, vegetable, oval, 9"	$10 – $12
Casserole	20 – 25
Coffee pot	35 – 40
Creamer	4 – 6
Cup	4 – 6
Dish, 5¼"	2 – 3
Dish, lug, 6"	3 – 4
Gravy	12 – 15
Plate, 6"	1 – 2
Plate, 7"	4 – 5
Plate, 9"	5 – 7
Plate, lug, 10½"	7 – 9
Plate, square, 8"	5 – 6
Saucer	1 – 2
Sugar	8 – 10

SHAWNEE POTTERY COMPANY

Zanesville, Ohio

CHAPTER AT A GLANCE

Shawnee began operations in 1937, in the old buildings of the American Encaustic Tiling Company, stating their intentions to produce art pottery, brightly colored dinnerware, and kitchenware, among other products, in an earthenware body. An arrowhead found on the grounds prompted the company to name itself after the local Shawnee Indians.

Early pieces were manufactured to designs supplied by S. S. Kresge, S. H. Kress, Woolworth, and McCrory stores. Sears soon followed with orders for a dinnerware and kitchenware line. The company closed in 1961.

Shawnee is best known for (1) the Rudy Ganz designs of Smiley Pig, Puss 'n Boots, Muggsy, and other whimsical characters and (2) Corn-King and Corn-Queen, the most popular of the corn-style dinnerware.

KENWOOD CERAMICS This is a separate sales division set up by Shawnee to produce higher-priced lines for the department store, gift shop, and florist market. All items were manufactured at the Shawnee pottery. Throughout the text, I have indicated items that were made under the Kenwood name.

See Mangus and see Vanderbilt in Bibliography and see Curran in Bibliography/Coming Attractions. See Clubs/Newsletters.

MARKS Either an incised shape number, incised "USA," or embossed "Shawnee," or a combination of two or three of these, on the bottom of pieces.

Some of the character pieces will have names on them. Some pieces are unmarked. According to John Bonistall, the last president of Shawnee, there is no exact way to date pieces from the style of the mark. However, Pam Curran notes that "USA" generally indicates pre–World War II, "USA" with a number is generally 1945 to 1961, and "Shawnee, USA" with a number is generally 1946 to 1961.

Occasionally, paper or foil labels may be found. Some are Shawnee: Indian Head inside an arrow, "Shawnee" in oval or rectangle, Corn King or red, black, and white Sample label. Others are from distributors or decorating houses.

I have used spellings of names that are accurate, verified by spellings on the bottoms of the various pieces.

NOTE I have double-listed some items. For example, the Fernware cookie jar is listed under both Cookie Jars and Fernware. This way, if you are using either section, you don't have to flip back and forth, and you know you have a complete listing in both sections.

COOKIE JARS

All early figural jars (1942–1945) were originally cold-painted. The Smiley had a triangular opening on the rim of the jar and the bottom of the lid; this was later changed to a round opening.

The **Dutch Boy** and **Dutch Girl** with embossed patterns on the bottoms are marked "Great Northern" and are numbered 1025 and 1026, respectively. These have *not* been found with gold trim. The standard Dutch Boy with gold decoration has his name written on his pants.

There is a mold variation of **Puss 'n Boots;** the tail comes over the right foot. So far, there is very little differentiation in price between the two versions. Be aware of the Regal China cat cookie jar that strongly resembles Puss 'n Boots, except that it has a fish on the hat rather than a bird.

The gold-decorated **"Smiley"** Pig has his name written on his torso. The gold-trimmed yellow neckerchief Smiley has a pointier scarf than the others; these were decorated at an outside decorating house, not at Shawnee. The overglaze red collar on **"Winnie"** Pig covers a blue, green, or peach underglaze. A few Winnie banks with a gold-trimmed lid and a *forest green* bottom have been reported.

The **cookie jar banks** have the bank in the head (the base of the lid is sealed off; the bottoms can be used for cookies). The "Smiley" bank has vertical lines impressed on the overalls. The "Winnie" bank has a plaid design impressed on the coat.

The **Elephant** is an ice server, *not* a cookie jar. See Miscellany.

NOTE Where dates of introduction are not known, patent dates have been included. These are not absolute indicators of when production started.

PRICING Variations on some of these jars seem to be endless. The quality and elaborateness of hand-painted decoration can vary widely and will affect the value.

Some gold-trimmed jars will be found with flies, bugs, butterflies, hair, or other items painted on them. It is generally accepted that these are seconds that were touched up in a variety of ways to hide flaws. It is a seller's market on these very desirable pieces.

Clown, "JoJo," on back, w/seal finial   /12 . . . . *$350 – $400*

    w/gold . . . . *600 – 650*

Cottage /6. . . . . *$800 +*
Corn-King/Queen /66 . . . . *175 – 200*
Dog, "Muggsy" (Pat. 1944), bow around head. *400 – 450*
   White w/blue bow and hand-painted decoration. . . . . *400 – 450*
      w/gold . . . . *1200 +*
      w/gold and decals . . . . *850 – 900*
   White w/green bow and hand-painted decoration, gold and decals . . . . *ND*
Drum Major /10 (Pat. 1947) . . . . *400 – 450*
   w/gold . . . . *750 +*
Dutch Boy, "Happy" (Pat. 1942), hands in pockets
   Butterscotch and Yellow (Great Northern) *300*
   White w/blue scarf and brown buttons, (cold paint) tops on blue, white, or
   yellow bottoms *100*
      w/gold and decals . . . . *250 – 300*
      w/gold and patches *350*
   White w/striped pants, single stripe *175*
      w/gold and decals *350*
   White w/striped pants, double stripe *200*
Dutch Girl, "Cooky" (Pat. 1942), hands clasped in front
   White w/cold-paint lid and blue/white/yellow bottoms *100*
      w/gold . . . . *300 – 350*
      w/gold and decals . . . . *300 – 350*
   White w/underglaze tulip and trim *175*
      w/gold and decals . . . . *300 – 350*
   White w/red hair bows and cuffs (cold paint) *125*
   White w/hand-painted blue decoration (Great Northern). *275*
   White w/two-tone green decoration (Great Northern) *300*
Elephant "Lucky," (Pat. 1942), w/bow tie, trunk up
   Allover white *100*
   Red bow tie (cold paint). *100*
   White w/hand-painted decoration, gold and decals . . . . *700 – 900*
Fernware, octagon
   Blue/turquoise/yellow . . . . *75 – 100*
Four-sided canisters
   Blue/green/yellow . . . . *75 – 100*
Fruit /84 . . . . *125 – 150*
   w/gold . . . . *200 – 225*
Hexagon (Basketweave)
   Blue/Turquoise/yellow *100*
   w/gold and decals *125*
Jug /75
   Blue/green/yellow . . . . *100 – 125*
   Pennsylvania Dutch decoration *175*
Little Chef, hexagon w/embossed chef and gingerbread boy, "Cookies"
   Caramel/green/yellow (solid colors). . . . . *125 – 150*
   Caramel w/hand-painted decoration (cold paint). . . . . *125 – 150*
   Cream w/hand-painted decoration . . . . *125 – 150*
   White w/hand-painted decoration . . . . *125 – 150*
      w/gold . . . . *200 – 225*

Owl (Pat. 1944), winking
White w/hand-painted decoration..*$150*
  w/gold...*300 – 350*
Pig, "Smiley" (1942) 3-pint, 11½"
  Allover gold/platinum......................................*800 +*
  Bank in lid, butterscotch/chocolate bottom   /60......................*350*
    w/gold...*500 – 600*
  Blue/red neckerchief (cold paint)...................................*100*
  Blue neckerchief...*200 – 225*
    w/gold and decals...*325 – 350*
  Blue neckerchief w/black hooves................................*225 +*
    and buttons w/gold and decals...............................*350 – 400*
  Green neckerchief w/hand-painted Shamrock...................*200 – 225*
    w/gold..*400*
  Red neckerchief w/embossed Clover Blossom......................*400*
    w/gold...*600 – 800*
  Red neckerchief w/hand-painted apples/plums...................*350 – 375*
  Red neckerchief w/hand-painted chrysanthemum/tulip...........*300 – 350*
    w/gold...*400 – 450*
  Yellow neckerchief w/gold and decals............................*350*
  Yellow neckerchief w/hand-painted strawberries w/gold.................*400*
Pig, "Winnie" (1945), 3-pint, 12"
  Bank in lid, chocolate/butterscotch bottom   /61......................*350 +*
    w/gold...*500 – 600*
  Blue/peach collar, w/embossed flower..........................*250 – 275*
    w/gold...*450 – 500*
  Green collar w/embossed Clover Blossom..........................*450*
  Green collar w/embossed Shamrock................................*300*
  Green collar w/hand-painted apples w/gold.....................*800 – 1000*
  Red collar w/embossed flower and gold.........................*450 – 500 +*
Puss 'n Boots (Pat. 1945), w/hat and bow around neck
  Allover gold/platinum..*700 – 800*
  White w/hand-painted decoration.............................*150 – 175*
    w/gold and decals..*350 +*
Sailor Boy, "Jack Tar," w/kerchief and sailor hat
  Allover gold/platinum..*700 – 800*
  Allover white..*100*
  Black kerchief (cold paint)......................................*100*
  White w/hand-painted features, black/blond hair (1942)..............*125*
    w/gold ("USN" on hat)...*700 +*
    w/gold and decals ("USN" on hat)..............................*700 +*
Snowflake (beanpot shape), tab handles
  Blue/green/yellow..*75 – 100*
Valencia
  All colors..*100 +*

DINNERWARE

Of these three lines, Valencia is very much the traditional 1930s line, with an
extensive number of items, including the batter set, candle holders, and com-

pote. By contrast, the Corn lines and Lobster are much smaller, with a barbecue/casual flavor typical of the 1940s and 1950s. This is especially true of Lobster, which has a mug but no cup and only a compartment plate.

Corn-King / Corn-Queen / White Corn (ca. 1945–1961)

Here's how to tell the difference between these lines. White Corn has kernels of white with green husks. Gold-trimmed White Corn has kernels shaded in greens, yellows, and browns, with white sometimes showing through. All pieces are gold-trimmed. The interior of the hollowware pieces will be white (not yellow as in Corn-King/Corn-Queen). White Corn was the first Corn line and is not as extensive as the later lines.

Corn-King was introduced in 1946, using the original White Corn items plus additional pieces to make a complete dinnerware line. It has bright yellow kernels and light green husks. In 1954 or 1955 the colors were changed to lighter yellow kernels and darker green husks in order to boost sales, and the name was changed to Corn-Queen.

Pieces of Corn-King will be found with gold trim. Also, an Indian Corn–type decoration has been found on Corn-King shakers and may be found on other pieces. The gold trim on both Corn-King and White-Corn, as well as the Indian Corn treatment, are assumed to have been done by a decorating firm.

The utility jar doubled as a sugar (with the small jug as a creamer) or as a drip jar (making a range set with the larger shakers). The lid for the large teapot and the sugar are interchangeable. The sugar shaker is found only in White Corn; it was *not* made in Corn-King or Corn-Queen.

SETS Several boxed sets were available in Corn-King and Corn-Queen. Three interesting ones are: Pop Corn Set, #109 (four 6" bowls, one 12-ounce creamer/jug [for melted butter], and one large salt shaker); Snack Set, #101 (four 10" plates, four mugs); and Corn Roast Set, #108 (four corn holders, platter, butter dish, and small shakers).

REPRODUCTION WARNING Watch out for a Corn-King reproduction. So far, the shakers and a creamer and sugar have been reported. The shakers are a little shy of 4½" tall, and the kernels are in neat horizontal rows, rather than naturally staggered as in the real Shawnee. Also, the tops are more peaked than rounded. The creamer has an open, hooktype handle.

PRICING Corn-Queen is harder to find than Corn-King and not as sought after.

CORN-KING / CORN-QUEEN

Bowl, mixing, round, 5" /5	$22 – $25
Bowl, mixing, round, 6½" /6	25 – 30
Bowl, mixing, round, 8" /8	30 – 35
Bowl, soup/cereal, oval /94	45 – 50
Bowl, vegetable, oval, 9" /95	65 – 70
Butter, ¼-pound /72	45 – 50
Casserole, individual, 9-ounce /73	80 – 90
Casserole, 1½-quart /74	60 – 70
Cookie jar /66	175 – 200

Creamer/Jug, 12-ounce   /70 . . . . *$25*
   w/gold . . . . *90 – 110*
Cup   /90 . . . . *30 – 35*
Dish, oval, 6"   /92 . . . . *40*
Jug, 1-quart   /71 . . . . *75 – 80*
   w/gold *175*
Mug, 8-ounce   /69 . . . . *45 – 50*
Plate, oval, 8"   /93 . . . . *35*
Plate, oval, 10"   /68 . . . . *40*
Platter, oval, 12"   /96 . . . . *55*
Relish tray/Spoon holder   /79 . . . . *35*
Saucer   /91 . . . . *22 – 25*
Shaker, small, pair, 3¼",   /76 . . . . *22 – 25*
   w/gold *75*
Shaker, large, pair, 5¼"   /77 . . . . *30*
   w/gold *110*
Sugar/Utility jar, 14-ounce   /78 . . . . *30*
   w/gold . . . . *90 – 110*
Teapot, 10-ounce   /65 . . . . *175 – 200*
Teapot, 30-ounce   /75 . . . . *90*
   w/gold . . . . *175 – 200*

WHITE CORN   Mark Supnick reports White Corn was made as a premium for a soap company.

Creamer *$30*
Jug, 1-quart *90*
Shaker, small, pair *24*
Shaker, range, pair *30*
Shaker, sugar . . . . *60 – 70*
   w/gold . . . . *125 – 150*
Sugar *40*
Teapot, 30-ounce *100*

Lobster   (1954–1956, Kenwood)

Many pieces in this line were designed by Robert Heckman. Originally, bottoms were glazed in glossy Van Dyke Brown or satin Charcoal Gray. The Charcoal Gray was later changed to glossy Mirror Black. These colors are documented; other colors that have turned up are not. Lids were white with red lobsters. The claw shakers, laydown shakers, spoon holder, hors d'oeuvres holder, and pin are red. The mug is white with red lobster handle.

The bean pot/snack jar is sometimes referred to as a cookie jar. The mixing bowls doubled as open bakers. The pin was a 1954 promotional giveaway. A wooden fork and spoon were sold to go with the salad bowl.

Bean pot/snack jar, 40-ounce . . . . *$250 +*
Bowl, batter, handled, 8" . . . . *75 +*
Bowl, chili/salad/soup, 5¾" *25*
Bowl, mixing, 5" *35*
Bowl, mixing, 7" *40*

Bowl, mixing, 9"... $45
Bowl, salad/spaghetti, 14" .... 45 – 50
Butter, ¼-pound... 65 – 75
Casserole, French, individual, 10-ounce .... 12 – 15
Casserole, French, 16-ounce .... 25 – 30
Casserole, French, 2-quart .... 40 – 45
Creamer.. 50 +
Hors d'oeuvres holder .... 125 – 150
Mug, 8-ounce .... 100 – 125
Pin, red lobster 75
Plate, compartment, 11¾".. 25 – 30
Relish pot, 5½-ounce... 75
Shaker, claw, pair .... 30 – 35
Shaker, full laydown, pair .... 150 – 175
Spoon holder, double... 150 – 175
Sugar/Utility jar .... 25 – 30

Valencia   (1937)

Designed by Louise Bauer. Swirled ribbing on the flatware rims and on hollowware bodies. Made exclusively for Sears Roebuck & Co. Be careful not to
confuse this with other swirled shapes, such as Gladding-McBean's Coronado
or Metlox's Yorkshire. The array of items available, including the stack set, tripod candle holder, utensils, and vases, indicate the strong influence of Homer
Lauglin's Fiesta and Kitchen Kraft in creating this line.

The relish consists of a tray, four quarter-round inserts, and a round center
insert. An old catalog shows water jugs of a shape that differs from the ball jug;
these may have been restyled between design and production.

The four original colors were Blue (cobalt), Green (spruce), Tangerine, and
Yellow. A maroon and an ivory (pale yellow) also exist.

MARKS   Most Valencia is unmarked. Occasionally, you will find "USA"
or "Valencia" impressed.

PRICING   It should be noted that Valencia is essentially a poor-quality
ware with many pieces turning up as is. I mention this to emphasize that values
below are for pieces in very good condition.

The Valencia flyer contains sketches of every listed piece but a photo (not
shown) of only a few items. It is questionable whether every piece was put into
production. Therefore, I have listed Valencia in two parts. The first part are
pieces known to exist. The second are in the flyer but have not been reported.
My thanks to Pam Curran for this breakdown.

CONFIRMED

Bowl, mixing, 9"... $40 +
Bowl, round, 8½"... 20 – 25
Bowl, round, 9½"... 25 – 30
Bowl, soup, 8".. 15 – 20
Candle holder, bulb, pair... 35 +
Carafe w/lid... 45 +
Coaster.. 15 – 20
Coffee pot... 60 +

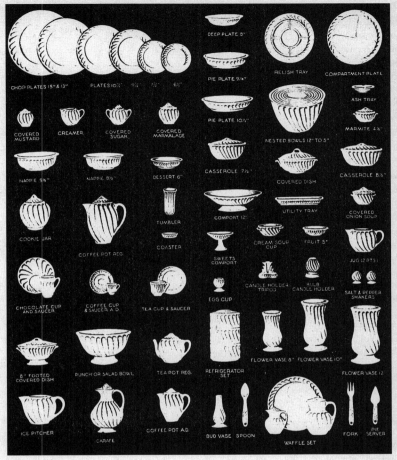

Valencia

Creamer	*$15 – $20*
Cup	*10 – 15*
Cup, AD	*15 – 20*
Dish, 5"	*10 – 15*
Dish, 6"	*15 – 18*
Eggcup	*15 – 20*
Jug, ball, ice lip, 64-ounce	*45 +*
Jug, batter	*50 +*
Jug, syrup	*50 +*
Plate, 6½"	*8 – 10*
Plate, 10¾"	*15 – 20*
Plate, chop, 13"	*25 +*

Relish, 6-piece . . . . *$125 +*
Saucer . . . . *5 – 8*
Saucer, AD . . . . *7 – 10*
Shaker, pair . . . . *18 – 20*
Sugar . . . . *15 – 20*
Teapot . . . . *50 +*
Tray/batter set, round, w/impressed rings for jugs . . . . *50 +*
Tumbler . . . . *25 +*
Vase, footed, bud . . . . *20 +*

UNCONFIRMED These prices have been based on similar solid-color lines of comparable desirability.

Ashtray . . . . *$15 – $20*
Bowl, footed, punch-salad . . . . *50 +*
Bowl, marmite, lug, w/lid, 4^1/$_2$ . . . . *30 +*
Bowl, mixing, 5" . . . . *20 +*
Bowl, mixing, 6" . . . . *25 +*
Bowl, mixing, 7" . . . . *30 +*
Bowl, mixing, 8" . . . . *35 +*
Bowl, mixing, 10" . . . . *ND*
Bowl, mixing, 11" . . . . *ND*
Bowl, mixing, 12" . . . . *ND*
Bowl, soup, onion, lug w/lid . . . . *30 +*
Candle holder, tripod, pair . . . . *45 +*
Casserole, 7^1/$_2$" . . . . *40 +*
Casserole, 8^1/$_2$" . . . . *50 +*
Casserole, footed, lug, 8" . . . . *60 +*
Casserole, lug (covered dish) . . . . *50 +*
Coffee pot, AD . . . . *60 +*
Compote, footed, 12" . . . . *50 +*
Compote, pedestal . . . . *50 +*
Cookie jar . . . . *75 – 100*
Cup, cream soup, lug . . . . *20 – 25*
Cup, tall, chocolate . . . . *20 – 25*
Jug, ball, ice lip, 32-ounce . . . . *35 +*
Marmalade . . . . *45 +*
Mustard . . . . *45 +*
Pie baker, 9^1/$_4$" . . . . *25 +*
Pie baker, 10^1/$_2$" . . . . *25 +*
Plate, 7^3/$_4$" . . . . *10 – 15*
Plate, 9^3/$_4$" . . . . *15 – 18*
Plate, chop, 15" . . . . *35 +*
Plate, grill . . . . *25 +*
Saucer, chocolate, off-center cup ring . . . . *7 – 10*
Stack set, round, 4-piece . . . . *65 +*
Utensil, fork . . . . *55 +*
Utensil, pie server . . . . *35 +*
Utensil, spoon . . . . *45 +*

Utility tray, rectangular . . . . *$30 +*
Vase, footed, 8" . . . . *25 +*
Vase, footed, 10" . . . . *35 +*
Vase, footed, 12" . . . . *45 +*

FIGURINES

These figurines are approximately 3" tall, except for the Dog, Gazelle, and Lamb.

Canary, head down . . . . *$8 – $12*
Crane . . . . *8 – 12*
Dog, Terrier, 6" *30*
Fawn, 4½" . . . . *8 – 12*
Gazelle, 10½" long   /614 . . . . *45 – 50*
Lamb, 6" *30*
Pekingese . . . . *45 – 50*
  w/gold and decals . . . . *100 – 110*
Puppy . . . . *45 – 50*
  w/gold and decals . . . . *100 – 110*
Rabbit . . . . *45 – 50*
  w/gold and decals . . . . *100 – 110*
Raccoon . . . . *45 – 50*
  w/gold and decals . . . . *100 – 110*
Reindeer, antlered . . . . *45 – 50*
  w/gold and decals . . . . *100 – 110*
Squirrel . . . . *45 – 50*
  w/gold and decals . . . . *100 – 110*
Tumbling bear . . . . *45 – 50*
  w/gold and decals . . . . *100 – 110*

Miniatures   (ca. 1941–1942)

Bear, Cub, 2⅜" . . . . *$10 – $15*
Bird, baby, sitting . . . . *10 – 15*
Bird, flying . . . . *10 – 15*
Circus Horse, 2⅝" . . . . *10 – 15*
Fish, Tropical . . . . *10 – 15*
Lamb, 2⅛" . . . . *10 – 15*
Pig, standing . . . . *10 – 15*
Rabbit, sitting . . . . *10 – 15*
Rooster, White Rock, 2⅛" . . . . *10 – 15*

FLOWERPOTS

Burlap surface . . . . *$5 – $15*
Diamond quilted w/crimped base . . . . *5 – 15*
Pot   /484 . . . . *5 – 15*
Pot w/5-petal flower around rim . . . . *5 – 15*
Pot w/scalloped rim   /436 . . . . *5 – 15*
Square   /410 . . . . *5 – 15*
Three-footed w/embossed flower . . . . *5 – 15*

KITCHENWARE (FIGURAL)

These listings cover kitchenware pieces in the shape of animals, people, and objects such as baskets, buckets, and jugs.

Creamers / Sugars

CREAMERS   A solid yellow Elephant has been reported but not confirmed as Shawnee. The yellow Smiley has the Clover Blossom embossing.

Elephant, white w/hand-painted decoration . . . . *$25 – $30*
    w/gold *175*
    w/gold and decals *175*
    Allover gold/platinum *225*
Puss 'n Boots, white w/hand-painted decoration (marked Puss 'n Boots) . . . . . . *35 – 40*
    w/gold *190*
    w/gold and decals *190*
    Allover gold/platinum *225*
    Green and yellow   /85 . . . . *45*
    w/gold . . . . *150 – 175*
Smiley the Pig, white w/peach flower (marked Smiley in script) . . . . *45 – 50*
    w/gold *175*
    Allover gold/platinum . . . . *225 – 250*
    Clover Blossom w/red neckerchief . . . . *75 – 80*
    w/gold *200*
    Yellow w/blue neckerchief   /86 . . . . *45 – 50*
    w/gold *175*

SUGARS   The bucket matches the Dutch Boy and Dutch Girl cookie jars. See my remarks about Baskets under Miscellany and about the sugar under Pennsylvania Dutch.

Bucket, blue and white . . . . *$45 – $55*
    w/gold and decals . . . . *90 – 110*
Jug, blue/green/yellow . . . . *35 – 40*

Jugs / Pitchers

So far Bo Peep has been found in white with bonnet decorated in colors of royal blue, light green, and lavender and coat in either blue, green, peach, and red. The red and yellow version is slightly smaller than the decorated white versions.

Chanticleer . . . . *$75 – $100*
    w/gold . . . . *250 +*
    w/gold and decals . . . . *250 +*
    Allover gold/platinum . . . . *400 – 500*
Little Bo Peep, white (marked Bo-Peep in script) *110*
    w/gold *225*
    w/gold and decals *225*
Little Bo Peep, small, red and blue   /47 . . . . *80 – 90*
    w/gold *175*

Smiley Pig pitcher and Tom Tom teapot.

Little Boy Blue, red and blue /46 . . . . *$90 – $100*
    w/gold *185*
Smiley Pig
    Allover gold/platinum . . . . *600 +*
    Apple *250*
    Clover Blossom (embossed) w/red bandanna *195*
    Peach and blue flower/Red and blue flower (embossed) *125*
    w/gold . . . . *250 +*

Shakers

Note: Reproductions of the Chef "S" and "P" marked "Made in Korea" have been found. Off-size Smiley and Winnie shakers have been found; they are not quite as tall as the large shakers.
    PRICING Priced each.

LARGE SHAKERS Most approximately 5" tall. The fat Dutch Boy and Dutch Girl match the cookie jar. Pairs of Smiley have four and five holes; there were no Winnie pairs. The Smiley (five holes) and Winnie (four holes) pairs are found in the red Heart and the Clover Blossom (see following) decoration only.

Chanticleer . . . . *$25 – $30*
    w/gold *45*
Dutch boy, fat *22*
    w/gold and decals *75*
Dutch boy, skinny, w/gold . . . . *15 – 17*
Dutch girl, fat *22*
    w/gold and decals *75*
Dutch girl, skinny, w/gold . . . . *15 – 17*

Fruit. *$15*
    w/gold *30*
Jug, blue/green/yellow. *15*
Muggsy *50*
    w/gold . . . . *100 – 110*
Smiley Pig, blue/green/peach/red neckerchief . . . . *45 – 55*
    w/gold *100*
    w/gold and decals *100*
    Clover Blossom. *80*
Swiss boy, w/gold *30*
Swiss girl, w/gold *30*
Winnie Pig, Heart *60*
    Clover Blossom. *80*

SMALL SHAKERS Most approximately 3¹/₄" tall. Be careful not to confuse Farmer Pig with Smiley Pig.

Bo-Peep (matches Sailor Boy) . . . . *$8 – $10*
    w/gold *20*
Chanticleer *15*
    w/gold *35*
Chef "S"/"P" . . . . *8 – 10*
    w/gold *20*
Cottage *125*
Duck. *15*
Farmer pig w/hat and shovel. . . . . *10 – 12*
    w/gold . . . . *25 – 30*
Flower Cluster . . . . *10 – 12*
    w/gold *20*
Flowerpot . . . . *8 – 10*
    w/gold *20*
Fruit. . . . . *10 – 12*
    w/gold *20*
Milk can . . . . *8 – 10*
    w/gold and decals *20*
Muggsy . . . . *25 – 30*
    w/gold *75*
Owl
    Gray eyes. . . . . *10 – 12*
    w/gold *30*
    Green eyes. . . . . *15 – 20*
    w/gold *30*
Puss 'n Boots. . . . . *12 – 15*
    w/gold *30*
Sailor Boy (matches Bo Peep). . . . . *8 – 10*
    w/gold *20*
Smiley Pig, blue/green/peach/red neckerchief . . . . *20 – 25*
    w/gold . . . . *35 – 40*
    Clover Blossom. *35*

Watering can .... *$8 – $10*
    w/gold *20*
Wheelbarrow .... *8 – 10*
    w/gold *20*
Winnie Pig, blue/green/red/peach collar .... *25 – 30*
    w/gold .... *35 – 40*
    Clover Blossom *35*

Teapots

All teapots, except the Corn Ware, were made prior to 1954.

Cottage .... *$350 +*
Elephant
    Blue/green/yellow .... *125 – 150*
        w/gold *250*
    Decorated .... *175 +*
        w/gold *250*
Granny Ann, lavender/peach apron *125*
    w/gold and decals .... *250 +*
    Green apron *150*
        w/gold and decals .... *250 +*
    Matte finish, w/gold .... *300 +*
Sunflower .... *40 – 50*
Tom Tom (Tom the Piper's Son)   /44
    Blue pants .... *90 – 100*
        w/gold .... *200 +*
    Red pants (matte) *250*
    White pants .... *90 – 100*
        w/gold .... *200 +*

KITCHENWARE LINES

These are a number of lines, both figural and nonfigural, that I am listing together for ease of reference.

Clover Blossom   (Also called Clover Bud or Clover Flower) (1946–1947)

The Clover Blossom is an embossed decoration. This is the only Smiley cookie jar with an embossed decoration, and these are the only Smiley creamer and jug with a bandanna. The sugar and teapot are the only nonfigural items in this line. Actually, what collectors call the sugar was listed as either a jam jar or a drip jar, making a range set with the large shakers.

    Note: Do not confuse these pieces with Smiley and Winnie items that have the green Shamrock (no flower) on them.

    PRICING   All pieces may be found with gold trim; add 100%.

Cookie jar, Smiley, 3-pint, 11½" *$400*
Cookie jar, Winnie, 3-pint, 12" *450*
Creamer, Smiley .... *75 – 80*
Jug, Smiley, 2-quart *195*

Shaker, Smiley, 3¹/₄" *$35*
Shaker, Winnie, 3¹/₄" *35*
Shaker, Smiley, 5" *80*
Shaker, Winnie, 5" *80*
Sugar/Jam Jar/Drip, Clover Blossom finial .... *50 – 60*
Teapot, Clover Blossom finial, 6-cup (42-ounce)........................ *85 – 90*

Cottage   (Official name; also called Cookie House or House)

The way to identify these house-shaped pieces is by the *rounded* red door on the front with a window on either side. The brown roof is the lid.

   PRICING   This line is so rare, it is basically a seller's market.

Cookie jar   /6 .... *$800 +*
Shaker, pair   /9 .... *250*
Sugar   /8 .... *175*
Teapot   /7 .... *350 +*

Decorative

An abstract flower done with three red brush strokes, a red dot, and green/red leaves.

Shaker, range, pair *$45*
Shaker, small, pair... *35*
Utility/drip jar .... *45 – 50*

Embossed   (pre–World War II)

An embossed design in a horizontal band around the bottom of each piece. Marked "USA." Decorated in solid colors of blue, green, and yellow.

Creamer *$20*
Jug, 7"   /60 .... *30*
Shakers, pair, 5" *20*
Sugar .... *20 – 25*
Teapot .... *30 – 40*

Fernware   (Also called Wheat) (pre–World War II)

Octagonal shape with a vertical fern-like strand on each panel. Marked "USA." Decorated in solid colors of powder blue, peach, turquoise, and yellow. Green has been reported, but that could be the turquoise.

Bowl, 5" .... *$15 – $30*
Bowl, 6" .... *15 – 30*
Bowl, 7" .... *15 – 30*
Bowl, 8" .... *15 – 30*
Bowl, 9" .... *15 – 30*
Bowl, batter *30*
Canister, 2¹/₂-quart, 7¹/₄" high   /412 .... *60*
Coffee pot, 5-cup .... *50 – 60*
   w/pottery drip... *75*
Cookie jar, octagonal, 4-quart, 8¹/₂" high   /424 .... *70 – 80*
Creamer .... *20 – 25*

Drip jar . . . . *$30 – $35*
Jug, 1¹/₂-pint . . . . *35 – 40*
Jug, ball, 2-quart . . . . *35 – 40*
Matchbox holder . . . . *75 +*
Salt box . . . . *60 +*
Shakers, octagonal, pair, 3¹/₂" *15*
Sugar . . . . *22 – 25*
Teapot, 2-cup . . . . *60 – 70*
Teapot, 6-cup . . . . *35 – 40*

Flower and Fern   (pre–World War II)

A daisy-like flower and a fern frond embossed on one side and a chrysanthe-mum-like flower and fern frond embossed on the other. Marked "USA." Decorated in solid colors of blue, green, turquoise, and yellow.

Coffee pot, 5-cup . . . . *$50 +*
   w/ceramic drip . . . . *75 +*
Creamer . . . . *12 – 15*
Creamer, Aladdin . . . . *18 – 20*
Creamer, ball jug *20*
Drip Jar . . . . *30 – 35*
Flowerpot w/tray, 3" . . . . *8 – 10*
Flowerpot w/tray, 4¹/₂" . . . . *8 – 10*
Jardiniere, 2¹/₄" . . . . *8 – 10*
Jardiniere, 4" . . . . *8 – 10*
Jardiniere, 7" . . . . *18 – 20*
Jug, ball, 4-cup . . . . *25 – 30*
Matchbox holder . . . . *50 +*
Salt box . . . . *50 +*
Shaker, round, small . . . . *8 – 10*
Shaker, square, large . . . . *6 – 8*
Sugar, covered, no handles *15*
Sugar, open, handles . . . . *12 – 15*
Sugar, Aladdin . . . . *18 – 20*
Teapot, 2-cup . . . . *25 – 30*
Teapot, 6-cup . . . . *20 – 25*

Fruit

Designed by Robert Heckman. A bright yellow basket with colorful fruit. Note that the ball jug only is white, not yellow. The large shaker hooks over the edge of the sugar, which forms a range set.

   PRICING   Add 100% for gold trim.

Casserole   /83 . . . . *$60*
Cookie jar   /84 . . . . *125 – 150*
Jug, ball   /80 . . . . *50*
Shaker, large, pair   /85 . . . . *30*
Shaker, small, pair   /82 . . . . *22*
Sugar/Utility jar   /81 . . . . *25 – 30*

Pennsylvania Dutch   (Was erroneously called Hearts and Flowers) (ca. 1948)

Designed by Robert Heckman. A white body with a large red and blue double heart, two red and yellow flowers, and green and brown leaves. Finials are red.

The coffee pot was also used as a covered jug. The jug-shaped jar is usually referred to as a sugar but was called a jar in patent records; it could have been intended as a jam or drip jar. A 34-ounce batter/beater jug is shown in patent records but has not yet been reported.

PRICING   Add 100% for gold trim.

Coffee pot, 52-ounce /52	$150
w/aluminum drip	175
Cookie jar, jug shape /75	175
Creamer, ball jug, 12½ ounce	35 – 40
Creamer, tilt	35 – 40
Jar, jug shape	40 – 50
Jug, ball, 64-ounce	80
Shaker, jug shape, pair, 5"	40
Sugar, open, tab handles	35 – 40
Teapot, Boston, 10-ounce /10	100 +
Teapot, Boston, 14-ounce /14	60 – 70
Teapot, Boston, 18-ounce /18	50 – 60
Teapot, Boston, 27-ounce /27	50 – 60
Teapot, round handle, 30-ounce	60 – 70

Snowflake   (pre–World War II)

Horizontal lines with an incised snowflake. The eight-cup teapot became the coffee maker with the addition of the aluminum dripper—which reduced the capacity to six cups. A Shawnee employee reports that the sugar and creamer were Proctor & Gamble giveaways. Marked "USA."

Listed colors are Dark Blue, Powder Blue, Burgundy, Dark Green, Old English Ivory, Turquoise, Bright White, and Yellow. Peach has also been seen. Not all pieces were made in every color.

Bowl, mixing, 5"	$10 – $20
Bowl, mixing, 6"	10 – 20
Bowl, mixing, 7"	10 – 20
Bowl, mixing, 8"	10 – 20
Bowl, mixing, 9"	10 – 20
Canister/cookie jar, beanpot shape, tab handles, 2-quart	100
Coffee maker, 8-cup	60 – 70
w/aluminum dripper	100
Creamer	25
Drip jar	30 – 35
Jug, ball, 24-ounce /P-157	45
Jug, utility, 1½-pint, 5" high	45 – 50
Shaker, 4"	8 – 10
Sugar, open	25
Teapot, 2-cup	30 – 40

Teapot, 5-cup. . . . . *$40 – $50*
Teapot, 8-cup. . . . . *60 – 70*

Sunflower   (Also called Daisy) (ca. 1947)

Solid white with an embossed Sunflower that is underglaze-decorated yellow with brown center, green leaves, and brown stem.
   The coffee pot doubled as a covered jug. Marked "USA."

Coffee pot/covered jug. *$125*
Creamer, ball shape *40*
Jug, ball *75*
Shaker, range, pair, 5". *30*
Shaker, small, pair, 3½". *25*
Sugar . . . . *35 – 40*
Teapot . . . . *40 – 50*
   w/gold . . . . *80 – 100*

Tulip

All have a hand-painted tulip, red outside and yellow center with green leaves.

Cookie jar, Smiley. . . . . *$300 – $350*
Creamer, ball, blue cord band . . . . *100 +*
Jug, ball, blue cord band . . . . *200 +*
Teapot *45*

LAMPS

The Polynesian Man and Woman are brown-skinned; a black-skinned version has been found that may be one of a kind.
   Lamps are rarely marked. Identifying factors: a glazed interior and a glazed "inner-strength ring" on base. All decoration is underglaze unless otherwise noted.

Clown w/Umbrella, cold paint *$45*
Deer . . . . *30 – 40*
Duck and Drum, cold paint *45*
Elephant w/one foot on ball, cold paint. *45*
Head, Black Man, gold trim
   Small *50*
   Large *75*
Head, Black Woman, gold trim
   Small *50*
   Large *75*
Mother Goose . . . . *50 – 75*
Oriental Man, w/cricket jar . . . . *15 – 20*
Oriental Man, playing mandolin
   Small . . . . *15 – 20*
   Large *20*
Oriental pair, man (cricket jar)/woman (fan). *20*
Oriental Woman, playing mandolin
   Small . . . . *15 – 20*
   Large *20*

Oriental Woman, w/fan	*$15 – $20*
Polynesian Man, kneeling, playing drum, gold trim	*75*
Polynesian Woman, kneeling, left hand on head, gold trim	*75*
Ribbed w/bows, blue/pink	*35 – 45*
Spanish Dancers	*25*
Victorian Man	*20*
Victorian Man and Woman	*35*
Victorian Woman	*20*

MISCELLANY

The **Bank, Howdy Doody**, was brought out in 1950 and was available for about a year. The **Baskets**, which are decorated in blue or green, are considered utility jars by some; others suspect they are sugars. They match Puss 'n Boots. (I seem to recall that illustrations for the fairy tale show Puss carrying a basket.) The **Bookends, Potter's Wheel**, originally designed in the late 1930s by Rudy Ganz for RumRill, were resurrected in 1960 as a limited-edition presentation piece. Only one **Child's Feeding Dish, Smiley Pig**, has been seen so far. The **Ice Server, Jumbo** (also marketed under the Kenwood line), has been mistaken for a cookie jar, but the plastic gasket around the lid shows its true function.

The coaster/ashtrays, Flight ashtrays, Panther ashtrays, and Sundial dishes are Kenwood items. The **coaster/ashtrays** have a club, diamond, heart, or spade embossed in the well and come in green, pink, turquoise, or yellow. **Flight** ashtrays are boomerang shape and done in black, pink, turquoise, or white, all with gold. A **Panther** set consists of one large ashtray for cigarettes (with black panther decoration) and two small ones for cigarettes, pipe, or fat cigar; all done in beige and black. The **Sundial** pieces have glossy black bottoms with either pink or turquoise lids; they came with brass stands and warmers.

Ashtray, Flight, 8½"	*$8 – $10*
Ashtray, Flight, 13"	*8 – 10*
Ashtray, Indian Arrowhead, brown	*150 – 200*
Ashtray, Panther, large	*20*
Ashtray, Panther paws, small	*15*
Ashtray, triangular w/3 geese	*20*
Ashtray, w/squirrel	*15*
Bank, Bull Dog, 4¾" high	*150 – 175*
Bank, Howdy Doody riding a pig	*350 – 400*
Bank, Tumbling Bear, 5¼" high	*150 – 175*
Basket, oval	*75 +*
w/gold and decals	*125 +*
Basket, round	*75 +*
w/gold and decals	*125 +*
Bookend/planter, flying geese, embossed /4000	*20*
Candle Holder, cornucopia shape	*12 – 15*
Candle Holder w/handle /3026	*10 – 12*
Child's Feeding Dish, Smiley Pig	*ND*
Clown pot holder /619	*14 – 16*
w/gold	*22 – 25*

Coaster/ashtray   /411 .... *$8 – $10*
Creamer, Quill, red feather in circle of blue dots   /12 .... *45 – 50*
Creamer, tilt, blue/yellow   /10 .... *25 – 30*
Creamer, tilt, single flower   /40 .... *25*
 w/gold *35*
Creamer, tilt, double flower   /52 .... *25*
 w/gold *35*
Darner (Darn-Aid), woman figural, pink/blue skirt, 5" *45*
Flower Frog, Bouquet .... *25 – 30*
Flower Frog, Dolphin .... *25 – 30*
Flower Frog, Sea Horse .... *25 – 30*
Flower Frog, Snail .... *30 – 35*
Flower Frog, Swan .... *25 – 30*
Flower Frog, Turtle .... *30 – 35*
Ice Server, "Jumbo" Elephant, pink w/black, pink, or white collar, 11"   /60 ..... *125*
Incense Burner, Oriental man .... *50 – 60*
Jug, diamond embossing around middle .... *20 – 25*
Magnolia Blossom, ashtray .... *12 – 15*
Magnolia Blossom, console set .... *25 – 35*
Magnolia Blossom, jardiniere *30*
Mug, bronze   /990 .... *25*
Pie Bird, blue/pink base, 5¼" *40*
Sundial casserole, 16-ounce *25*
Sundial casserole, 1-quart *30*
Sundial chafing dish, 2-quart .... *40 – 45*
Watering Can, embossed flowers on wicker background *15*

PLANTERS

Figural planters were discontinued in 1954. These are listed by the names that collectors use. Known Shawnee names, courtesy of Pam Curran and Bev and Jim Mangus, follow these in parentheses. Many of these planters were part of the Kenwood line.

The Elf shoe and Elf on Shoe are both shape #765. The Poodle (#725) and the Lamb (#724) were decorated in gold on black glaze. The Tractor Trailer Cab and the Tractor Trailer make up a set. Several four-piece Train Sets have been reported in white with hand-painted trim.

Basket   /640 .... *$16 – $18*
Basket, picnic   /J540P *25*
Basket Cradle, 8" long .... *18 – 20*
Basketweave   /44 .... *8 – 10*
Bear and Wagon (Cub Bear and Wagon), 7¼" long   /731 .... *45 – 50*
Bicycle Built for Two, 9¾" long   /735 .... *40 – 50*
Bird, Cockatiel   /523 .... *10 – 12*
 w/gold .... *18 – 20*
Bird, head and tail up .... *8 – 10*
Bird, head down, tail up .... *8 – 10*
Bird, Love Birds, figural .... *10 – 12*
Bird on rim of planter   /767 .... *18 – 20*

Birds (two) on Nest . . . . *$10 – $12*
Birds (four) on Driftwood, light brown bisque/gray glaze   /502 . . . . *40 – 45*
Bowl   /150. . . . . *5 – 6*
Bowl   /160. . . . . *5 – 6*
Bowl, Leaf   /439 . . . . *10 – 12*
Bowl, rectangular   /163. . . . . *8 – 10*
Bowl w/embossed flower   /181 . . . . *8 – 10*
Bowl w/embossed flower   /182 . . . . *8 – 10*
   w/gold . . . . *14 – 16*
Bowl w/embossed three-petal flower . . . . *6 – 8*
Boy and Chicken   /645 . . . . *18 – 20*
   w/gold . . . . *25 – 30*
Boy and Dog   /582 . . . . *8 – 10*
   w/gold . . . . *15 – 18*
Boy and Gate . . . . *8 – 10*
   w/gold . . . . *12 – 14*
Boy and Stump   /532. . . . . *10 – 12*
   w/gold . . . . *16 – 18*
Boy and Stump, leaning   /533 . . . . *10 – 12*
Boy and Wheelbarrow   /750. . . . . *16 – 18*
Bridge   /756 . . . . *16 – 18*
Buddha   /524 . . . . *16 – 18*
Bull   /668 . . . . *10 – 12*
Bull and Leaf *30*
Butterfly   /524 . . . . *10 – 12*
Canopy Bed, 8" long   /734. . . . . *75 – 100*
Cart   /775 . . . . *12 – 14*
Cat playing horn (Cat and Sax), 6¼" long   /729. . . . . *40 – 50*
Chick and Cart   /720. . . . . *20 – 22*
   w/gold *28*
Chick and Egg (Chic and Egg), 5¼" long   /730 . . . . *20 – 25*
Children and Shoe   /525 . . . . *16 – 18*
Circus Wagon . . . . *35 – 40*
Clock   /1262 . . . . *16 – 18*
Clown   /607 . . . . *20 – 22*
   w/gold *28*
Clown w/Boxes . . . . *45 – 50*
Coal Bucket, round, w/embossed flower   /J541P . . . . *16 – 18*
Coal Scuttle w/embossed flower . . . . *16 – 18*
Colt and Stump   /2028 . . . . *35 – 40*
Conch Shell   /241. . . . . *10 – 12*
Convertible   /506
   Four spokes. . . . . *10 – 12*
   Eight spokes . . . . *10 – 12*
Covered Wagon, small   /514 . . . . *10 – 12*
Covered Wagon (Prairie Schooner), large, 10¼" long   /733. . . . . *25 – 30*
   w/gold . . . . *45 – 50*
Cradle   /625 . . . . *18 – 20*

Cradle /J542P $25
Deer and Fawn (planting dish), figural   /669 .... 16 – 18
  w/gold 25
Doe and Fawn (two Fawns), 5½"   /721 .... 16 – 18
  w/gold 25
Dog, kneeling.. 8 – 10
Dog, pushing carriage   /704 .... 12 – 14
Dog, sitting
  Hand-painted .... 12 – 14
  Solid-color .... 12 – 14
Dog, Chihuahua and Doghouse, 8" long   /738 .... 20 – 22
Dog, Hound and Peke   /611 .... 12 – 14
  w/gold .... 16 – 18
Dog, Hound Dog .... 12 – 14
Dog, Hound Dog w/jug   /610 .... 12 – 14
  w/gold .... 18 – 20
Dog, Poodle, black w/gold   /725.................................. 16 – 18
Dog, Poodle on 3-wheel cart   /712 25
Dog, Puppy on Shoe
  Two-button style.. 8 – 10
  Three-button style .... 8 – 10
Dog, Spaniel and Doghouse, 8" long   /739........................ 20 – 22
Dog, Terrier and Doghouse, 8" long   /740 .... 20 – 22
Dog in Boat, 6½" long   /736 .... 18 – 20
Donkey, figural .... 12 – 14
Donkey and Basket, head up, 5¾"   /722......................... 16 – 18
Donkey and Cart, small   /538.................................... 8 – 10
  w/gold .... 12 – 14
Donkey and Wicker Basket, head down   /671...................... 16 – 18
Donkey and Wooden Cart, small   /455 .... 10 – 12
Donkey and Wooden Cart, large   /456............................ 12 – 14
Donkey in Hat w/cart, large   /709............................... 16 – 18
Dove and planting dish   /2025 .... 16 – 18
Duck, small .... 8 – 10
Duck pulling Cart   /752 .... 12 – 14
Duckling, 7½" long   /720.. 18 – 20
  w/gold 25
Elephant, small   /759... 10 – 12
Elephant and Howdah .... 16 – 18
Elephant and Leaf 35
Elf and Shoe, 6½" long   /765.................................... 16 – 18
  w/gold 25
Elf and Wheelbarrow, 5"... 12 – 15
Engine (19th-century Engine), 10¼" long   /732 .... 40 – 45
Fawn   /535 .... 6 – 8
  w/gold .... 16 – 18
Fawn and Fern, 6"   /737 .... 16 – 20
Fawn and Log, 7⅛" long   /766 .... 25 – 30

Fawn and Stump /624 . . . . *$16 – $18*
   w/gold *25*
Fish (Angel Fish), 9" high . . . . *45 – 55*
Fish, 10½" long (also a vase) /717 . . . . *40*
Fish, on waves, small /845 . . . . *10 – 12*
Fish, tail up, mouth open . . . . *10 – 12*
Fox and Bag /2029 . . . . *18 – 20*
Frog on Lily Pad, 6" long /726 . . . . *25*
Gazelle (Ibex) /613 . . . . *12 – 14*
   w/gold . . . . *20 – 22*
Gazelle, head w/baby /840
   Glossy . . . . *45 – 50*
   Matte . . . . *45 – 50*
Gazelle, figural, pink/white, with scalloped planter on mirror,
  black base /522 . . . . *40 – 45*
Gazelle, figural /614 . . . . *40 – 50*
Giraffe‾ /521 . . . . *22 – 25*
Girl, playing instrument, embossed /576 . . . . *18 – 20*
Girl and Basket /534 . . . . *10 – 12*
   w/gold . . . . *16 – 18*
Girl and Flower Basket (Colonial Lady) /616 . . . . *16 – 18*
   w/gold *25*
Girl and Gate /581 . . . . *8 – 10*
Girl and Parasol /560 . . . . *18 – 20*
Girl and Watering Can (Dutch Girl Sprinkling Flowers) . . . . *8 – 10*
Girl and Well . . . . *10 – 12*
Goose, small . . . . *5 – 7*
Goose, flying /707 . . . . *16 – 18*
Goose, flying, in relief /820 . . . . *20 – 25*
High Chair w/kitten, 6¼" /727 . . . . *45 – 50*
Hobby Horse /660 . . . . *12 – 16*
House /J543P *25*
Kitten, 4⅝" long /723 . . . . *16 – 18*
Kitten and Basket /2026 . . . . *22 – 25*
Lamb, upright, at trough . . . . *12 – 14*
Lamb w/Bow, black w/gold /724 . . . . *16 – 18*
Leaf, large /440 . . . . *12 – 14*
Leaf, 6½" /822 . . . . *14 – 16*
   w/gold . . . . *18 – 20*
Leather, stitched, square . . . . *12 – 14*
Man and Pushcart (Tony the Peddler) /621 . . . . *18 – 20*
   w/"Rum Carioca" *25*
Mexican Boy w/basket . . . . *18 – 20*
Mexican Girl w/basket . . . . *18 – 20*
Mill (Dutch Mill), 6½" long /715 . . . . *18 – 20*
   w/gold . . . . *25 – 30*
Mill (Old Mill), 7" long /769 . . . . *20*
   w/gold *25*

Tractor Trailer /681		*$25 – $30*
Tractor Trailer Cab /680		*25 – 30*
Train Set, complete		*125*
Train Set Box Car /552		*25 – 30*
Train Set Caboose /553		*25 – 30*
Train Set Coal Car /551		*25 – 30*
Train Set Locomotive /550		*25 – 30*
Trellis /517		*18 – 20*
Tulip Leaf /466		*8 – 12*
Water Trough (Pump and Trough), 9³/₈" long /716		*16 – 18*
Watering Can, wicker w/embossed flowers, large		*12 – 14*
Watering Can w/embossed flower		*12 – 14*
Wheelbarrow		*5 – 7*
Wheelbarrow w/embossed flower		*12 – 14*
Wishing Well w/Dutch Boy and Girl /710		*18 – 20*
World Globe /635		*12 – 14*

SUSAN SETS (1950s/Kenwood)

These sets were made in combinations of black, pink, turquoise, and white. Came with copper or brass frames and holders.

SALAD SUSAN A revolving salad set with two cruets, two shakers, and two bowls. Copper frame. Came with wooden fork and spoon. Cruets were black with white stoppers, shakers were white, and bowls were pink or turquoise with black lines around rim.

   PRICING Per set: $70–$90.

Bowl, salad, 9"	**Cruet**, vinegar
Cruet, oil	**Shaker**

SAUCY SUSAN A revolving eight-piece condiment set: two cruets, two shakers, and four covered sauce cups with notched lids. Black and white, pink and white, or turquoise and white. Copper or brass frame.

   PRICING Per set: $70–$80.

Cruet, oil	**Sauce cup w/server and lid**
Cruet, vinegar	**Shaker**

SUPPER SUSAN A one-quart chafing dish surrounded by six serving dishes, lazy susan–style, on a revolving brass stand with a ceramic warmer. Made in 16" and 18" sizes; the size of the servers will vary. The chafing dish was also sold as a separate item with a brass stand. Black and white or pink and white with black cover. The white had a black spatter decoration.

   PRICING Per set: $60–$70.

Chafing dish, 1-quart	**Server**, large	**Server**, small

TOASTEE SUSAN A revolving copper toast or napkin holder with two covered dishes, one for butter and the other divided for preserves. Black and white, pink and white, or turquoise and white.

PRICING Per set: $45–$50.

Butter dish w/lid **Preserve dish**, 2-part, w/lid

MISCELLANY Made in glossy black with white stopper and white warmer. Matches the cruets in shape. Brass stand.

Patio Carafe, 48-ounce . . . . *$45 – $50*

TEAPOTS (NONFIGURAL)

Conventional Style #1	*$30 – $35*
Conventional Style #2, w/pinky rest	*30 – 35*
Criss Cross	*30*
Elite	*30 – 35*
Embossed Rose	*30 – 35*
Horizontal Ribbed Base	*30 – 35*
Laurel Wreath	*25 – 35*
Paneled	*30 – 35*
Ribbed Collar	*45*
Rosette, blue/burgundy/green/yellow/white	*20 – 30*
Spiral	*25 – 30*
Vertical Ribbed Base	*30 – 35*

VASES

Bamboo vase w/Oriental Girl /702	*$10 – $12*
Boot	*10 – 12*
Bow Knot /819	*16 – 18*
Boy w/cornucopia	*14 – 16*
Bud /705	*8 – 10*
Bud /735	*8 – 10*
Bud /865	*8 – 10*
Bud /1125	*8 – 10*
Bud /1135	*8 – 10*
Bud /1203	*10 – 12*
Bud, Cornucopia	*10 – 12*
Bud, Leaf, 7¹/₂" /821	*12 – 14*
Bud, Swan /725	*10 – 12*
Bud, w/two handles /1178	*10 – 12*
w/gold	*14 – 16*
Burlap surface /890	*15 – 20*
Cornucopia /835	*15 – 20*
w/gold	*25 – 28*
Cornucopia /865	*5 – 7*
Doe in Shadowbox /850	*20 – 22*
Dolphin /828	*20*
Elf w/Flower	*12 – 15*
Embossed Feathers /1258	*20 – 25*
Embossed Flowers, small /875	*10 – 12*

CONVENTIONAL STYLE #1

CONVENTIONAL STYLE #2, W/PINKY REST

ELITE

HORIZONTAL RIBBED BASE

PANELED

RIBBED COLLAR

VERTICAL RIBBED BASE

Teapots

Fan /1264. . . . . *$12 – $14*
Flowered /1225 . . . . *14 – 18*
Frog and Guitar . . . . *14 – 16*
Gazelle and Baby   /841 . . . . *50 – 60*
Girl and Cornucopia . . . . *14 – 16*
Hand, large . . . . *18 – 20*
Iris, embossed . . . . *8 – 10*
Leaf, 9¹/₂"   /823 . . . . *20 – 22*
Leaves, Philodendron, embossed   /805 . . . . *16 – 18*
   Hand-painted w/gold . . . . *20 – 22*
Pineapple /839. . . . . *12 – 14*
   w/gold . . . . *18 – 20*
Pitcher /1168 . . . . *8 – 10*
Pouter Pigeons /829 . . . . *20 – 22*
   w/gold . . . . *24 – 28*
Ribbed, "V" shape, 9"   /809. . . . . *16 – 18*
   w/gold . . . . *20 – 22*
Swan /806 . . . . *16 – 18*
   w/gold . . . . *20 – 22*
Tulip /1115 . . . . *14 – 16*
   w/gold . . . . *18 – 20*
Wheat   /1267 . . . . *18 – 20*

WALL POCKETS

Bird on Cornucopia . . . . *$15 – $30*
Birdhouse /830 . . . . *15 – 30*
Bow /434 . . . . *15 – 30*
Daffodil (embossed) . . . . *15 – 30*
Feather, red . . . . *15 – 30*
Girl and Rag Doll   /810. . . . . *15 – 30*
Grandfather Clock /1261. . . . . *15 – 30*
Little Jack Horner /585 . . . . *15 – 30*
Mantel Clock /530 . . . . *15 – 30*
Mary and Her Lamb /586 . . . . *15 – 30*
Scotty Dog . . . . *50 – 75*
Star w/embossed moon, clouds, and stars . . . . *15 – 30*
Telephone /529 . . . . *15 – 30*
Wheat . . . . *15 – 30*

SMITH-PHILLIPS

East Liverpool, Ohio

In 1900, Josiah T. Smith and William R. Phillips purchased the French China Company from the Sebrings (known as "The Klondike" because of its distance from the pottery district in East Liverpool). They began manufacturing semi-porcelain dinnerware and toilet sets in 1901. In 1929 they merged with the American China Corporation. When that company declared bankruptcy, Smith-Phillips was reorganized as the Johnson Pottery. That company failed and went into receivership. The property was sold in 1937 to the Specialty Porcelain Works of Newell, Virginia, which manufactured electric refractories.

MARKS   Sometimes this general backstamp was used; other times a shape-specific backstamp was used.

PRINCESS

This is the Smith-Phillips shape you will find most often.

Bowl, soup, 7⅝"..	$10 – $12
Bowl, vegetable, oval, 9"*......................................	10 – 12
Casserole...	20 – 25

Princess: Orador plate and Nasturtium jug.

722

Creamer	*$4 – $6*
Cup	*4 – 6*
Dish, 5¼"*	*2 – 3*
Jug	*20 – 25*
Plate, 6¼"	*1 – 2*
Plate, 7⅛"	*5 – 7*
Platter, oval, 13¼"	*10 – 12*
Saucer, 5¾"	*1 – 2*
Sugar	*8 – 10*

SOUTHERN POTTERIES, INC.

Erwin, Tennessee

CHAPTER AT A GLANCE

Established in 1917 as Clinchfield Pottery (after the Carolina, Clinchfield and Ohio Railroad that sold them land), it was chartered on April 8, 1920, as Southern Potteries, Inc. In the early years, production was decal-decorated hotel ware and semivitreous dinnerware; collector interest in this period is primarily advertising pieces: plates, bowls, and ashtrays.

Underglaze hand painting gradually became the major type of decoration, and in the mid 1930s the name Blue Ridge was introduced for these wares. By the early 1950s they were averaging 24 million pieces of pottery per year and had produced over 4,100 patterns. In 1942 a line of china specialties was added. Hand painting is labor-intensive; escalating labor costs as well as cheap imports led to the closing of the pottery in 1957.

The most desirable decorations are people, animals, holiday themes, indoor scenes, outdoor structures, Victory edge trim (repeated border trim of three dots and a dash, which is Morse code for "V"), and anything else that isn't floral or fruit.

See Newbound in Bibliography and see Clubs/Newsletters.

MARKS Backstamps indicating "Underglaze, hand painted, Southern Potteries." The words "Blue Ridge," and a representation of a pine tree and mountains were added ca. 1935.

NOTE   Southern made ware for a number of distributors, also called jobbers, who bought from several different potteries. Finding one of these jobber's marks on a piece of pottery does not necessarily mean that it was made by Southern.

PRICING   A price range is given throughout. The low end is for the less pretty, less interesting patterns, and the high end is for the prettier, more interesting patterns. How do you differentiate? There are certain subtleties that cannot be described in a short text, but here are some general rules. The more colors in a pattern and, to a certain extent, the more intricate the pattern, the more popular it is. Colors such as the browns, chartreuse, and the yellows (sometimes called the 1950s colors) are the least popular. Colors such as the blues, pinks, purples, and reds are the most popular.

ARTIST-SIGNED PIECES / CHARACTER JUGS

All the jugs were made in china and the plates and platters in earthenware.

NOTE   Unauthorized reproductions of the jugs, plates, and platters are currently being made and are *sometimes* marked with a Blue Ridge stamp. Here's what you need to know to recognize these: (1) the new jugs are earthenware, not china; (2) jug handles are cast in the mold, not applied, as were the originals; (3) impressed names found on the original jugs (except Indian) are missing; and (4) scenes other than the ones listed below are used on the plates and platters.

Artist-Signed Pieces   Tom Turkey is also called "Turkey Gobbler," and Wild Turkey is also called "Turkey Hen." These pieces are based on Audubon's drawings.

Cup, Tom Turkey. . . . . *ND*
Plate, "Flower Cabin," 10½". . . . . *$425 – $525*
Plate, "Gold Cabin," 10½" . . . . *500 – 600*
Plate, "Green Mill," 10½". . . . . *425 – 525*
Plate, "Tom Turkey," 10½". . . . . *600 – 700*
Plate, "White Mill," 10½". . . . . *450 – 550*
Plate, "Quail," 11¾" . . . . *500 – 600*
Platter, "Black Ducks" . . . . *ND*
Platter, Tom Turkey, 17½". . . . . *700 – 800*
Platter, Wild Turkey, 17½". . . . . *750 – 900*
Saucer, Tom Turkey . . . . *ND*

Character Jugs

Daniel Boone. . . . . *$600 – $700*
Indian . . . . *575 – 675*
Paul Revere. . . . . *500 – 600*
Pioneer Woman . . . . *400 – 500*

CHINA / EARTHENWARE SPECIALTIES

Called Classic Specialties in some old ads, these pieces were introduced beginning in 1942. Most were made in the new china body. Many were decorated to match the dinnerware lines.

The hard-to-find pieces are the advertising plate, counter sign, chocolate tray, AD pot with matching flared sugar and creamer, Duck, Lily and Nude boxes, carafe, Watauga jug, and small jugs. If there is a specific Southern name, it is included in the listing.

In the **AD cups and saucers**, the china set comes in one shape, with a fancy handle and scalloped saucer. The earthenware sets come in a variety of shapes. In the **jugs**, Alice and Antique are the same shape but different sizes, hence the two names. The **Art Nouveau figure** is the type often called Scarf Dancer. These are marked with the old Clinchfield backstamp.

PRICING Most specialties were produced in china only, some in earthenware only, and some in either body. This is indicated by a C or E following the item. For items made in both bodies, there are two listings.

NOTE Some collectors feel that the gold-trimmed Betsy is overvalued as it is not hand painted and the gold was probably put on outside the Southern factory.

Advertising plate /E	$375 – $475
Ashtray	
round, 5" /E	25 – 40
round w/advertising, 5" /E	40 – 60
round w/railroad advertising, 5" /E	50 – 80
square /E	12 – 18
Ashtray w/rests, 6½" /E	12 – 18
Bonbon, 4-part, top-handle /C	65 – 85
Bonbon, deep shell (Shell Bonbon) /C	50 – 65
Bonbon, deep shell (Shell Bonbon) /E	40 – 55
Bonbon, flat shell (Dorothy) /C	50 – 75
Box, Duck (Mallard), 5¼" × 4" /C	500 – 700
Box, Lily, 7" × 5" /C	600 – 850
Box, Nude (Dancing Nude), 4" × 3½" /C	575 – 800
Box, Shell (Seaside), 4¼" × 3½" /C	90 – 130
Box, Tiered (Rose Step), 5½" × 4" /C	95 – 135
Box, Tiered (Rose Step), 5½" × 4" /E	45 – 75
Candy box, round scallop, 6" /C	90 – 120
Carafe, w/lid /E	85 – 105
w/o lid	70
Celery Leaf /C	40 – 55
Celery Leaf /E	30 – 45
Chocolate pot /C	130 – 200
Cigarette box, square, 4⅜" × 4¼" /E	55 – 75
Cigarette box w/4 ashtrays /E	105 – 150
Coffee pot, AD /C	ND
Coffee pot, AD /E	80 – 100
Coffee pot, tall	85 – 105
Counter Sign /E	350 – 450
Creamer, AD, flared /C	60 – 65
Creamer, pedestal /C	45 – 55
Cup, AD /C	30 – 40
Cup, AD (all shapes) /E	10 – 20
Figure, Art Nouveau, 6¼"	ND
Figure, Art Nouveau, 8½"	ND

Lazy Susan, complete, 15½". . . . . *$500 – $600*
   Center bowl. . . . . *80 – 100*
   Quarter section. . . . . *70 – 80*
Pitchers
   Abby /C . . . . *150 – 200*
   Abby /E . . . . *25 – 35*
   Alice /C . . . . *120 – 150*
   Alice /E . . . . *70 – 100*
   Antique, 3½" /C . . . . *85 – 100*
   Antique, 5" /C . . . . *65 – 85*
   Antique, 5" /E . . . . *45 – 50*
   Betsy /C . . . . *100 – 140*
      w/decals and gold . . . . *225 – 250*
   Betsy /E . . . . *75 – 95*
   Chick /C. . . . . *85 – 95*
   Chick /E. . . . . *40 – 55*
   Clara (paneled) /C . . . . *80 – 90*
   Grace /C . . . . *65 – 85*
   Grace /E. . . . . *40 – 55*
   Helen /C. . . . . *85 – 95*
   Jane /C. . . . . *95 – 120*
   Martha (Grace Scroll) /C . . . . *85 – 100*
   Martha (Grace Scroll) /E . . . . *35 – 50*
   Milady /C. . . . . *145 – 175*
   Milady /E . . . . *ND*
   Rebecca /C. . . . . *120 – 170*
   Sally /C . . . . *110 – 160*
   Sculptured Fruit (Petite), 6½" /C. . . . . *65 – 75*
   Sculptured Fruit, 7" /C . . . . *70 – 80*
   Sculptured Fruit (Deluxe), 7½" /C . . . . *85 – 95*
   Spiral, 4" /C. . . . . *85 – 100*
   Spiral, 7" /C. . . . . *65 – 85*
   Virginia, 3¾" /C . . . . *85 – 100*
   Virginia, 6½" /C . . . . *70 – 90*
   Watauga /C. . . . . *300 – 375*
   Watauga /E . . . . *85 – 100*
Powder box, round, 5" /C . . . . *95 – 135*
Relish, heart /C . . . . *70 – 125*
Relish, leaf, T-handle /C . . . . *65 – 80*
Relish, leaf, 3-part (Martha Snack Tray) /C . . . . *95 – 105*
Relish, loop handle /C . . . . *65 – 75*
Relish, Maple leaf (Cake Tray) /C. . . . . *45 – 65*
Relish, Maple leaf (Cake Tray) /E. . . . . *45 – 55*
Saucer, AD /C . . . . *10 – 20*
Saucer, AD (all shapes) /E . . . . *5 – 10*
Shaker, apple, small, pair /E . . . . *30 – 40*
Shaker, apple, large, pair /E . . . . *35 – 45*
Shaker, blossom top, pair /E . . . . *35 – 45*
Shaker, bud top, pair /E. . . . . *35 – 45*

Shaker, chicken, pair   /E .... $95 – $150
Shaker, duck, pair   /E .... 200 – 300
Shaker, tall, pair   /C .... 55 – 65
Shaker, tall, pair   /E .... 45 – 55
Sugar, AD, flared   /C .... 60 – 65
Sugar, pedestal   /C .... 45 – 55
Tea tile, round, 6"   /E .... 35 – 55
Tea tile, square, 6"   /E .... 35 – 55
Tea tile, square, 8"   /E .... 35 – 55
Teapots
  Ball   /E .... 75 – 100
  Chevron Handle   /C .... 100 – 125
  Fine Panel   /C .... 110 – 135
  Snub Nose   /C .... 120 – 145
  Square Round, small   /E .... 75 – 100
  Square Round, large   /E .... 85 – 105
Tray, chocolate pot, 15¼" × 8¾"   /C .... 350 – 450
Utensil, Cake server, 9"   /E. .... 25 – 40
Utensil, Fork, 8⅞"   /E. .... 30 – 45
Utensil, Spoon, 9¼"   /E .... 30 – 45
Vases
  Boot, 8"   /C .... 75 – 95
  Bud, bulbous, 5¼"   /C .... 85 – 100
  Bud, tapered, 5"   /C .... 85 – 100
  Handled, 8"   /C. .... 75 – 90
  Handled, 8"   /E. .... 30 – 40
  Round, 5"   /C .... 65 – 85
  Ruffled, 9"   /C. .... 75 – 95
  Ruffled, 9"   /E. .... 65 – 75
  Tapered, 7½"   /C .... 85 – 105

Charm House

Creamer   /C .... $45 – $60
Marmite, 7¼" × 5½"   /C .... 90 – 110
Pitcher   /C .... 150 – 200
Relish, small   /C .... 80 – 100
Relish, medium   /C .... 90 – 110
Relish, large, divided   /C .... 100 – 120
Shakers, pair   /C .... 75 – 90
Sugar   /C. .... 45 – 60
Teapot   /C .... 200 – 275

Good Housekeeping

Creamer   /C .... $25 – $35
Shakers, blossom top, pair   /C .... 65 – 85
Shakers, bud top, pair   /C .... 65 – 85
Sugar   /C. .... 25 – 35
Teapot   /C .... 120 – 170
Teapot, mini-Ball   /C .... 110 – 150

DINNERWARE

SHAPES   A number of official shape names have turned up. In addition to the ones listed here (unofficial names in quotes) with date of introduction, there are also the Bristol, Richmond, Dixie, and LeComte shapes, which were all introduced pre-1935. One of these is probably the official name for Trellis. Note that some Skyline hollowware was restyled in 1953 and 1955.

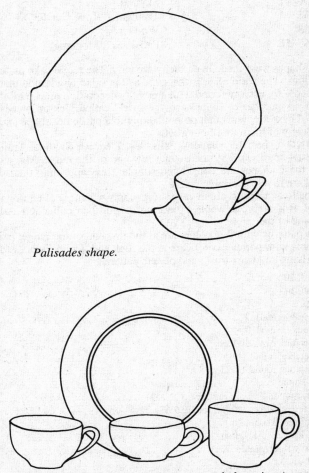

Palisades shape.

Skyline shape (original cup plus two restyled versions).

Known shapes: Astor (early 1940s?), Candlewick (1939), Clinchfield (pre-1935), Colonial (1939), Monticello ("Waffle") (pre-1939), Palisades ("Moderne") (1955/1956), Piecrust (1948), Skyline (1950), Trailway ("Rope Handle") (1953), "Trellis" (pre-1935), Woodcrest (1953).

pre-1935	"Trellis"
pre-1935	Clinchfield
pre-1939	Monticello ("Waffle")
1939	Candlewick
1939	Colonial
1940s (?)	Astor
1948	Piecrust
1950	Skyline
1953	Trailway ("Rope Handle")
1953	Woodcrest
1955–56	Palisades ("Moderne")

These shapes were made in earthenware only. The round cake plate comes in two versions. The chop plate is the same as the salad bowl underplate. The 6" square plates are usually found with a novelty decoration or as part of a set.

NOTE A number of shapes are "generic," called pick-up pieces by some potteries. These are items that do not belong to a particular shape and could be used with any of them to fill out a set.

PRICING The later shapes—Palisades, Piecrust, Skyline, Trailway, and Woodcrest—are about 25% below the low end of the range. Many of the designs on these shapes are considered simpler, less appealing than the earlier ones, and are in less desirable colors.

Monticello and Trellis are in very short supply. Chances of putting together a set are nil. But everyone wants a piece or two for their collection. Add 25% to the high end of the range.

Simple patterns with few colors are at the low end of the range; more elaborate patterns with popular colors are at the high end. Double prices for holiday (Thanksgiving and Christmas) and people patterns.

Bowl, salad, 10"	$35 – $45
Bowl, salad, 14"	45 – 55
Bowl, soup, 8"	12 – 14
Bowl, lug (tab cereal), 7"	10 – 12
Bowl, vegetable, oval, 9½"	15 – 25
Bowl, vegetable, oval, divided, 9½"	18 – 25
Bowl, vegetable, round, 9½"	15 – 25
Bowl, vegetable, round, divided, 8½"	18 – 25
Butter, ¼-pound	20 – 35
Butter pat, round, 4"	20 – 30
Casserole (covered vegetable), round, 9½"	60 – 75
Casserole, French (ramekin)	25 – 45
Casserole, French, individual	20 – 30
Celery/gravy liner/pickle, 7½"	15 – 25
Coffee pot	75 – 105
Covered toast	80 – 95
Lid only	60 – 80
Creamer	10 – 15
Creamer, square round	10 – 15
Cup	10 – 12

Cup, jumbo . . . . $25 – $30
Dish (berry), 5¼" . . . . 5 – 8
Dish (cereal), 6" . . . . 10 – 12
Eggcup . . . . 12 – 20
Gravy boat . . . . 12 – 25
Plate, 6" . . . . 5 – 7
Plate, 7" . . . . 6 – 9
Plate, 8" . . . . 8 – 14
Plate, 9" . . . . 8 – 16
Plate, 10" . . . . 10 – 20
Plate, cake, round, 10½" . . . . 25 – 35
Plate, cake, round, flat rim, 10½" . . . . 25 – 35
Plate, cake, square, 12" . . . . 30 – 40
Plate, chop, 11" to 12" . . . . 25 – 35
Plate, chop, 14" . . . . 35 – 45
Plate, grill . . . . 25 – 35
Plate, party, 8½" . . . . 20 – 30
Plate, square (Novelty), 6" . . . . 40 – 65
Plate, square (salad), 8" . . . . 12 – 18
Platter, oval, 9" . . . . 15 – 20
Platter, oval, 11" . . . . 18 – 23
Platter, oval, 13" . . . . 20 – 25
Platter, oval, 15" . . . . 22 – 28
Saucer . . . . 3 – 6
Saucer, jumbo . . . . 10 – 15
Shaker, pair . . . . 35 – 50
Sherbet . . . . 15 – 20
Sugar . . . . 15 – 20
Sugar, square round . . . . 15 – 20
Teapots
  Colonial . . . . 100 – 110
  Palisades . . . . ND
  Piecrust . . . . 85 – 95
  Skyline . . . . 75 – 85
  Trailway (rope handle) . . . . 85 – 95
  Woodcrest . . . . 95 – 110
Tidbit, 1-, 2-, or 3-tier . . . . 20 – 30

SPECIAL PRICE LIST

Children's Ware The bowl and the plate come in both Astor and Skyline shapes. These highly desirable earthenware pieces will be found with decorations of circus motifs and playful animals.

Bowl (Astor), 6¼" . . . . $50 – $60
Bowl (Skyline), 6¾" . . . . 50 – 60

French Peasant

French Peasant Variant

Still Life

Language of Flowers

Kitchen Shelf

Ham 'n' Eggs

Cock O' the Morn

Rooster

Cock O' the Walk

Thanksgiving Turkey

Weathervane

Christmas Tree (mistletoe variation)

Feeding dish, deep, 6¾" .... *$80 – $90*
Mug, 2¾" .... *45 – 65*
Plate, grill .... *85 – 100*
Plate .... *70 – 95*

SPECIAL PRICE LIST

French Peasant Reminiscent of French Quimper ware, this is one of Southern's most popular patterns.

NOTE The Man and the Woman alternate on the plates, so if you have a 10" plate with a woman, there will not be a 10" plate with a man. On other pieces you will find either the man or woman, and on the larger pieces you will find both.

Ashtray, square   /E .... *$20 – $30*
Bowl, salad, 10"   /E .... *125 – 175*
Bowl, tab cereal   /E .... *20 – 30*
Bowl, vegetable, oval   /E .... *50 – 70*
Bowl, vegetable, round   /E .... *50 – 70*
Box, candy   /C .... *150 – 200*
Box, cigarette   /E .... *120 – 150*
Butter pat, round, 4"   /E .... *25 – 35*
Chocolate pot, Pedestal   /C .... *250 – 300*
Coffee pot, tall   /E .... *ND*
Coffee pot, AD   /E .... *ND*
Covered toast   /E .... *150 – 250*
Creamer, AD   /E .... *80 – 90*
Creamer, Pedestal   /C .... *80 – 95*
Cup   /E .... *20 – 30*
Cup, AD .... *50 – 60*
Cup, jumbo .... *65 – 85*
Eggcup   /E .... *35 – 45*
Jug, Alice   /E .... *175 – 250*
Jug, Antique   /C .... *150 – 200*
Jug, Clara   /C .... *125 – 175*
Jug, Helen   /C .... *125 – 175*
Jub, Milady   /C .... *190 – 250*
Plate, 6"   /E .... *10 – 15*
Plate, 7"   /E .... *20 – 30*
Plate, 8"   /E .... *35 – 45*
Plate, 9"   /E .... *50 – 60*
Plate, 10"   /E .... *45 – 65*
Plate, 11"   /E .... *80 – 100*
Plate, grill   /E. .... *75 – 95*

Platter, 11"   /E .... $90 – $105
Platter, 13"   /E .... 100 – 120
Platter, 15"   /E .... 150 – 200
Relish, leaf celery   /C .... 60 – 80
Relish, deep shell   /C... 85 – 115
Relish, flat shell   /C... 85 – 115
Saucer   /E .... 15 – 20
Saucer, AD... 20 – 25
Saucer, jumbo .... 35 – 40
Shakers, tall   /C... 175 – 250
Sugar, AD   /E .... 80 – 90
Sugar, Pedestal   /C .... 85 – 95
Teapot, Colonial   /E .... 150 – 180
Tea tile, round, 6"   /E... ND
Tea tile, square, 8"   /E... ND
Tray, for AD set .... ND
Tray, for chocolate set   /C... 700 – 900
Tray, Maple Leaf (cake)   /C .... 80 – 110
Tray, Martha snack   /C .... 150 – 185
Vase, ruffled   /C... 150 – 200

SPECIAL SETS

Breakfast Sets

Five pieces from the Astor shape (cup, saucer, two plates and cereal) and eight generic shapes make up this thirteen-piece (including the coffee lid) set. The coffee pot is earthenware.

PRICING   Complete sets are priced below. Individual items are priced in the dinnerware section; the list below is for reference only.

Bowl, cereal, 6"	**Creamer**, AD	**Plate**, 8"
Butter pat, 4"	**Cup**	**Saucer**
Coffee pot, AD	**Eggcup**	**Sugar**, open, AD
Covered toast	**Plate**, 6"	

COMPLETE SETS

Everyday patterns .... $200 – $275
Fruit patterns .... 225 – 300
Interesting patterns .... 250 – 325
People/Desirable patterns .... 375 – 500

Child's Tea Set

The sixteen-piece Child's Tea Set consists of AD coffee pot/lid, AD open sugar and creamer, four AD cups and saucers, and four 6" plates. All these pieces are standard items from the Specialties line, and the only thing that makes them a "child's tea set" is putting them together as such. Therefore, the price below is for a set. For individual items, see Specialties pricing.

Flower or Fruit patterns . . . . *$275 – $350*
People patterns . . . . *375 – 500*

Salad Plate Sets

Traditional salad sets come with a large salad bowl, fork and spoon, and eight plates and sometimes an underplate for the salad bowl. Most of Southern's sets seem to comprise only the eight plates. There are additional items for some decorations; they are listed below the plates. Each plate has a different but related decoration (e.g., eight different birds on same shape with same border trim). The two exceptions to this are Flower Bowl and Still Life, which have the same decoration on all pieces.

NOTE Some sets are composed of six plates, most have eight; this information is given in parentheses in the list below. So far, only four plates have turned up in the Caribbean and Mandarin lines. Fruit Squares is the name given to the County Fair decoration when found on 6" square plates. Plates are round unless otherwise marked.

PRICING Prices are per plate.

Candied Fruit (8), 8" . . . . *$10 – $15*
Caribbean (4), 8" . . . . *ND*
County Fair (Avon) (8), 8" . . . . *10 – 18*
   Bowl, salad, 14" . . . . *45 – 55*
   Cup . . . . *12 – 15*
   Plate, square (Fruit Squares), 6" . . . . *15 – 20*
   Plate, chop, 14" . . . . *35 – 45*
   Saucer . . . . *8 – 10*
   Utensil, fork . . . . *30 – 45*
   Utensil, spoon . . . . *30 – 45*
Country Life (8), square, 6" . . . . *ND*
Duff (8), 8" . . . . *10 – 15*
Flower Bowl, 8" . . . . *15 – 20*
   Bowl, salad, 14" . . . . *45 – 55*
   Plate, chop, 14" . . . . *35 – 45*
Fruit Cocktail (8), 8" . . . . *10 – 15*
Fruit Fizz (8), 8" . . . . *10 – 15*
Garden Flowers (8), 8" . . . . *15 – 20*
Honolulu (6), 8" . . . . *10 – 18*
Language of Flowers (8), 8" . . . . *65 – 75*
Lavender Fruit (8), 8" . . . . *10 – 15*
Mandarin (4) . . . . *ND*
Mexico Lindo . . . . *ND*
Songbird, Astor (8), 8" . . . . *45 – 75*
Songbird, Colonial (8), 8" . . . . *50 – 75*
Songbird, Skyline (8), 8" . . . . *45 – 75*
Sowing Seeds (8), Square, 6" . . . . *45 – 65*
   Bowl, salad, 14" . . . . *75 – 125*
   Plate, chop, 14" . . . . *65 – 115*
Square Dance (8), square, 8" . . . . *60 – 75*
   Bowl, salad, 14" . . . . *125 – 200*
   Carafe . . . . *150 – 200*

Cup . . . . *$35 – $45*
Plate, chop, 14" . . . . *125 – 175*
Plate, party. . . . . *75 – 85*
Still Life, 8" . . . . *15 – 20*
Bowl, salad, 14". . . . . *45 – 55*
Plate, chop, 14" . . . . *35 – 45*

KITCHENWARE

Rare pieces are the batter set trays, the batter and syrup jug lids, and the leftovers.
Leaf decorations are the most common; anything else is considered desirable.
PRICES Leaves and Daisy Chain are the common decorations; use the low end of the range.

Baking dish, 8" × 13". . . . . *$25 – $35*
Baking dish, 5-part, 8" × 13". . . . . *25 – 35*
Bowl, mixing, 5" . . . . *15 – 20*
Bowl, mixing, 6" . . . . *15 – 20*
Bowl, mixing, 7½". . . . . *20 – 25*
Bowl, mixing, 8½". . . . . *20 – 25*
Bowl, mixing, 9½". . . . . *25 – 30*
Bowl, mixing, 10½". . . . . *25 – 30*
Bowl, mixing, 11¼". . . . . *30 – 35*
Bowl, utility, all sizes. . . . . *25 – 40*
Casserole, deep lid, 9". . . . . *35 – 45*
Casserole, knob lid, 8¼". . . . . *35 – 45*
Custard . . . . *8 – 12*
Jug, batter w/lid. . . . . *75 – 95*
Jug, syrup w/lid. . . . . *75 – 95*
Leftover, 4¼". . . . . *25 – 35*
Leftover, 5". . . . . *30 – 40*
Leftover, 6". . . . . *35 – 45*
Pie baker . . . . *25 – 35*
Shaker, range, pair . . . . *45 – 55*
Tray, Batter Set, 7½" × 11½". . . . . *150 – 200*
Tray, Batter Set, 9½" × 13½". . . . . *150 – 200*

SPAULDING CHINA COMPANY

Sebring, Ohio

Spaulding was begun by Morris Feinberg and Irving Miller in 1942 in a plant where they had been producing clock bodies. The advent of World War II meant that brass for the clock works was no longer available, so they turned to the production of giftwares. Major production was in the Royal Copley line, which was sold to chain stores such as Woolworth's and Kresge's. Leslie and Marjorie Wolfe, who did all the original research on Spaulding, estimate that 85 percent of production was in Royal Copley. In order to gain access to the more upscale florist and gift shop market, the Royal Windsor line was created and sold through distributors, as was the Spaulding line. In 1957, due to foreign competition and the changing business climate, Feinberg, the president of the company, decided to retire and sell the plant. He made arrangements with China Craft of Sebring to fulfill orders, which they did for almost two years.

See Wolfe in Bibliography and Devine in Coming Attractions.

MARKS Marks include "Royal Copley" stamped in either gold or green or embossed. According to the Wolfes, more Royal Copley was unmarked than marked. All production items had paper labels, including Royal Copley, Royal Windsor, and Spaulding, but few of these are found today.

NOTE 1. Some of the figurines and planters come as left- and right-facing pairs. These are noted as "left/right" in the listings below and are each valued at the price shown.

2. While the three lines were basically distinct, there was some overlap. For example, a Royal Copley piece may be found with a Spaulding or Royal Windsor label. This is not a problem for most collectors as they collect all of Spaulding's production, regardless of line.

738

BIRDS

Some bird planters were also made; see Planters following.

Bluebird, left/right, 5"	$22
Bunting (Seed Eater), 5"	18
Canary, 5½"	26
Cockatoo, 7¼"	28
Cockatoo, big, 8¼"	30
Dove, 5"	15
Finch, 5"	18
Flycatcher (Thrasher), 7¾"	26
Hunt's Swallow, female, head down, 8"	30
Hunt's Swallow, male, head up, 8"	30
Jay, 8" /S	30
Kingfisher, left/right, 5"	22
Kinglet, small, 3½"	20
Kinglet, 5"	15
Lark, baby, 3½"	20
Lark (Skylark), 5"	14
Lark (Skylark), 6½"	18
Long's Finch #2, 5"	35
Nuthatch, 4½"	15
Parakeets, 7⅜"	35
Parrot, 8"	28
Seagull (Gull), 8"	30
Sparrow w/open beak, 5"	15
Sparrow, Blue, 5½"	30
Swallow on double stump, left/right, 7¼"	26
Swallow w/extended wings, 7"	45
Swallow, left/right, 8"	20
Thrush, 6½"	18
Titmouse, 8"	22
Vireo, 4½"	15
Wren, little, 3½"	20
Wren, 6¼"	18
Wrens (double birds on stump)	35

Ducks

These are all Royal Windsor. See also Duck and Mallard planters.

Gadwell, Hen 6¾"	$65
Gadwell, Drake, 8½"	65
Green-Winged Teal, Hen, 7½"	65
Green-Winged Teal, Drake, 8½"	65
Mallard, Duck, 7"	25
Mallard, Drake, small	65
Mallard, Hen, small	65
Mallard, Drake, large, 8½"	65
Mallard, Hen, large, 6¼"	65
Mallard, baby, erect head, 6"	16

Mallard, baby, bending head, 5"...$16
Mallard, medium, erect head, 7¹/₂"..60
Mallard, medium, bending head, 7"..60
Mallard, large, erect head, 9¹/₄"...30
Mallard, large, bending head, 8³/₄"..30

Fowl

ROYAL COPLEY

Grouse, 4³/₄"   /S..$26
Hen, small, #1, 5¹/₂"...20
Hen, small, #2, 6"...24
  Black and white...48
Hen, large, 7"
  Black and white...48
  Other tail-feather colors.....................................28
Pheasant, small, 4"   /S...18
Pheasant, large, 5¹/₂"...34
Pheasant, large, tail up,   /S
  Natural colors..24
  White...24
Pheasant, large, tail back   /S
  Natural colors..24
  White...24
Rooster, small, #1, 6"..20
Rooster, small, #2, 6¹/₄"...24
  Black and white...48
Rooster, large, 8"
  Black and white...48
  Other tail-feather colors.....................................28

ROYAL WINDSOR

Hen, small, 6¹/₂"...$20
  w/gold..30
Hen, small, 6¹/₂"...22
Hen, medium, 7³/₄"...38
Hen, large, 10"...48
Rooster, small, 7"..20
Rooster, small, 7"..22
Rooster, medium, 8¹/₄"...38
Rooster, large, 10¹/₄"..48

DECAL-DECORATED ITEMS

These items will be found with either an ivory glaze or a darker butterscotch glaze. Preference for one or the other is a matter of individual taste. Add 25% to 50% for gold trim.

Child's Lamp, 8"..$35
Cornucopia, 6³/₈"...20

Cornucopia, 8¼" *$24*
Jug, plain, 6" *15*
Jug, beaded collar and handle, 6" *15*
Planter, Joyce, 4" *14*
Planter, Linley, 4" *14*
Plaque/Planter, Books of Remembrance, 5" *14*
Plaque/Planter, Dutch Scenes, 8"
   The Cornfield *36*
   Crossing the Brook. *36*
   The Mill. *36*
   Valley Farm *36*
Plaque/Planter, floral, 8" *35*
Vase, Lloyd, 6" *25*
Vase, floral handle, 6¼". *15*
Vase, 2 handles, 6¼" *15*
Vase, 2 handles, beaded collar, 6¼" *15*
Vase, King, 7" *16*
Vase, Betty, 8" *22*
Vase, cylinder, 8", Happy Birthday/Lord's Prayer/Thinking of You *35*
Vase, Rachel, 8" *30*
Vase, 2 handles, 8". *18*
Vase, Barbara, 8¼" *30*
Vase, Juarine, 10" *40*
Vase, Marjorie, 10" *40*
Vase, Shirley, 10" *40*

EMBOSSED LINES

Spaulding made several short lines that had abstract or floral designs embossed on the outside. For individual items with animals or florals embossed on them, see Planters, Embossed, and Vases, Embossed, below.

Bamboo

A lamp made from the wall pocket is in Wolfe; it is too rare to price.

Planter, oval, 5¾" *$14*
Planter/Vase, 4½" *10*
Vase, 8" *15*
Wall Pocket, 7". *34*
Window Box, 4" × 7½" *15*

Black Floral

Black Floral Leaf and Stem planter *$10*
Black Floral Leaf and Stem vase, 6½" *15*
Black Floral Leaf and Stem vase, 8". *14*
Black Floral Leaf and Stem window box, 3½" *16*

Harmony

Planter, small, 4½" *$10*
Planter, large, 6½" *14*

Vase, 7½"... *$14*
Window Box, 4½"... *15*

Ivy

Add 25% to 50% for gold trim.

Planter, footed, 4"... *$10*
Vase, footed, 7".. *12*
Vase, footed, 8".. *14*
Vase, Pillow, footed, 6¼".. *12*
Window Box, 4" × 7".. *12*

Philodendron

Planter, footed, 4¼".. *$12*
Planter, footed, 4" × 7¼"... *14*
Vase, footed, 7½"... *14*

Pink Dogwood

Planter, oval, 3½".. *$12*
Planter, oval, small, 4½"... *12*
Plaque/planter, 4½"... *16*
Vase, 8¼"... *18*

Riddle

Planter, round, little, 5".. *$15*
Planter, round, large, 7"... *18*
Planter, oval, 4"... *16*

FIGURES

The black and brown cats are the same figure.

Blackamoor Man w/drum, 8".. *$25*
Blackamoor Woman w/drum, 8".. *25*
Cat, Black, left/right, 8" (each)................................. *35*
Cat, Brown, left/right, 8" (each)................................. *40*
Dancing Lady, 8"... *68*
Deer and fawn, heads, 8½".. *28*
Dog, 6½".. *24*
Dog, looking up, 8"... *25*
Dog, head cocked, 8½"... *25*
Dog, Airedale, 6½".. *25*
Dog, Cocker Spaniel, 8"... *25*
Dog, Cocker Spaniel, head up, 6¼"................................. *24*
Dog, Spaniel w/collar, 6"... *24*
Dog, Spaniel, 6¼"... *24*
Kitten w/ball of yarn, 6½"
　　Pink ball... *38*
　　Yellow ball.. *28*
Mallard, 7"... *25*

Oriental Boy, 7¹/₂"...$18
Oriental Girl, 7¹/₂".. 18
Teddy Bear, 5¹/₂".. 48

MISCELLANY

All lamps are full figure.

Ashtray, Affectionate Birds, 5¹/₂".......................................$20
Ashtray, Bow and Ribbon, 5"... 26
Ashtray, freeform, 5¹/₂" × 8"... 16
Ashtray, freeform, 6" × 9"... 16
Ashtray, Leaf and Bird, 5¹/₂"... 12
Ashtray, Leafy, 5"... 10
Ashtray, Lily Pad and Bird, 5"... 12
Ashtray, oval, 5" × 6" w/horse head/rooster/salmon figure............. 35
Ashtray, oval, 5¹/₂" × 8¹/₂"... 16
Ashtray, Straw Hat w/Bow, 5".. 16
Ashtray, square, 4¹/₂" × 5³/₄"... 16
Ashtray, triangular, 4¹/₄" × 5¹/₂"..................................... 16
Bank, Farmer Pig, 5¹/₂"... 45
Bank, Pig, small, 4¹/₂"... 35
Bank, Pig, medium, 6"... 40
Bank, Pig, large, 7¹/₂"... 42
Bank, Pig w/bow tie, 6¹/₄".. 30
Bank, Rooster... 55
Bank, Teddy Bear, 7¹/₂"... 54
   Black and white..................................... 68
Barber Pole (for used razor blades), 6¹/₄"............................ 35
Boot, small, 5¹/₄" /S... 18
Boot, medium, 6" /S... 20
Boot, large... 35
Creamer, Chick, 4³/₄" /S.. 20
Creamer, Duck, 4¹/₂" /S... 20
Creamer, Leaf... 18
Creamer, Miss Piggie, 4¹/₄"... 45
Creamer, Pig, 4¹/₂" /S.. 20
Lamp, Birds in Bower, 8".. 40
Lamp, Child, 7³/₄".. 40
Lamp, Clown, 7¹/₂".. 65
Lamp, Cocker Spaniel, 10"
   Black and white..................................... 58
   Brown.. 50
Lamp, Dancing Girl Copley... 65
Lamp, Deer and Fawn on tree trunk, 11"................................ 50
Lamp, Flower on tree trunk, 10¹/₂".................................... 38
Lamp, Oriental Boy.. 35
Lamp, Oriental Girl... 35
Lamp, Pig, 6¹/₂".. 55

Lamp, Thorup's Rose, 8½". *$38*
Mug, Fish handle, "Baby". *45*
Pitcher, Daffodil, 8". *36*
Pitcher, Floral Beauty, 8". *36*
Pitcher, Pome Fruit, 8". *36*
Smoking Set, Mallard
    Ashtray *15*
    Cigarette Holder. *15*
Sugar, Leaf *18*

PLANTERS

Embossed

These pieces may be square, rectangular, or round, sometimes footed, and may have the decoration embossed on one or both sides. Some are open through the center. The plaque/planters can hang on a wall or stand on a table.

Big Blossom, 3". *$14*
Bird Tracks, 3¼". *15*
Bird Tracks, 4½". *15*
Deer and Doe, heads, 7½". *16*
Deer and Fawn, heads, footed, 6". *22*
Double Spray, 4½". *14*
Fall Arrangement, footed, 5¾". *15*
Fish, oval, 3¾". *18*
Floral Arrangement, 3½". *12*
Hildegard, 2½" × 7¼". *12*
Laura's Twig, 5". *18*
Leaf, half-circle, 4". *14*
Little Imagination, 4½". *14*
Open, Bird in flight, 7¼". *22*
Open, Deer, 7¼". *22*
Open, Fish, 5¾". *20*
Parallel Rays, 4½". *12*
Plaque/Planter, Fruit *18*
Plaque/Planter, Hen *35*
Plaque/Planter, Rooster *35*
Rex, 2½" × 7¼". *12*
Rib and Cornice, small. *10*
Rib and Cornice, medium *12*
Rib and Cornice, large *12*
Ribbed, little, 3½". *10*
Ribbed, big, 4⅛". *12*
Running Gazelle, 6". *16*
Running Horse, 6". *16*
Sectioned, 2½" × 6¼". *12*
Spooks, 4". *18*
Star w/Angel, 6¾". *30*
Strange Tracks, 3½". *14*

Trailing Leaf and Vine, 4" × 7½". *$18*
Triple Leaf, round, 4". *16*
Water Lily, 6¼". *14*
Wilder Leaf, 4". *16*

Figural

The planters with the white poodles came in black, green, or pink. The Stuffed Animal series (Dog, Duck, and Elephant) has slightly raised seams, as if sewn.

Angel, small, 6¼". *$25*
   w/gold *40*
Angel, small, variant, 6½". *35*
Angel, large, 8". *30*
Apple w/Finch, 6½". *22*
Baby Lamb, 4¼". *30*
Barefoot Boy, 7½". *26*
Barefoot Girl, 7½". *26*
Bear Cub on stump, 8¼". *30*
Bear in planter (Norma). *65*
Big Apple, 5½". *16*
Birdhouse w/bird, 8". *50*
Black Cat, 8". *35*
Black Cat and Cello, 7½". *54*
Black Cat and Tub, 5¼". *25*
Boat shape, 3½". *14*
Bowl w/bird on rim, 4". *14*
Boy leaning on barrel, 6". *20*
Bunting, 5". *20*
Cat, resting, 5¾". *60*
Cats, Siamese, 9". *75*
Clown, 8¼". *45*
Coach, 3¼" × 6". *18*
Cockatiel, 8½". *45*
Cocker Head, 5". *16*
Cocker Spaniel, head tilted, 7¾". *25*
Cocker Spaniel, head up, 8". *25*
Cocker Spaniel, sitting, 7". *24*
Cocker Spaniel and Basket, 5½". *16*
Deer and Fawn, heads, w/side planter, 3⅛". *32*
Deer and Fawn, heads, w/side planter, 5⅛". *34*
Deer and Fawn, heads, 8¼". *30*
Deer and Fawn, heads, 9". *28*
Deer and Stump, 8". *26*
Deer on Sled (Little Huck), 6". *35*
   Spotted, w/gold trim *45*
Deer on Sled, 6½". *36*
Dog, raised right paw, 7½". *38*
Dog, Stuffed Animal, 5½". *28*
Dog and Mailbox, 7¾". *25*
   Black and white *50*

Elephant, stuffed animal. Note the "seams" where the legs join the torso and down the middle of the head and trunk. These seams identify this as one of the stuffed animals.

Dog and String Bass, 7" $75
Dog and Wagon, 5³/₄" 25
Dog in Picnic Basket, 7³/₄" 60
Duck, eating grass, 5¹/₂" 16
Duck, Stuffed Animal, 6" 28
Duck, Wood Duck, 5¹/₂" 18
Duck, Wood Duck, mature, 7¹/₄" 25
Duck and Mailbox, 6³/₄" 50
Duck and Wheelbarrow, 3³/₄" 18
Dutch Boy and Bucket, 6" 20
Dutch Girl and Bucket, 6" 20
Elephant, Stuffed Animal, 6¹/₂" 36
Elephant and Ball, small, 6" 24
Elephant and Ball, large, 7¹/₂" 30
Elf and Shoe, 6" 26
Elf and Stump, 6" 26
Fancy Finch on tree stump, 7¹/₂" 45
Farm Boy, 6¹/₂" 24
Farm Girl, 6¹/₂" 24
Fighting Cock, 6¹/₂" 28
Girl and Barrel, 6¹/₄" 20
Girl and Wheelbarrow, 7" 24
Hat, small, 5¹/₂" 25
Hat, large, 7" 28
Hen, head up, 7³/₄" 30
Horse, grazing, 4³/₄" 32
Hummingbird on Flower, 5¹/₄" 26
Indian Boy and Drum, 6¹/₂" 20
    w/gold 30
Jumping Salmon, 6¹/₂" × 11¹/₂" 50
Kitten and Ball of Yarn, 8¹/₄"
    Pink Ball 35
    Yellow Ball 25
Kitten and Birdhouse, 8" 65

Kitten and Book, 6½"..$25
Kitten and Boot, 7½"...*40*
Kitten and Moccasin, 8"..*32*
Kitten in Cradle, 7½"..*55*
Kitten in Picnic Basket, 8"...*60*
Madonna, hands together, 6½".......................................*30*
Madonna w/side planter, 6¼".......................................*40*
Mallard, 7¾"..*18*
Mallard, sitting, 5"..*28*
Mallard, small, bending head, 7⅛"..................................*28*
Mallard, large, bending head, 9¼".................................*34*
Mallard, Split-Neck, 8"..*20*
Oriental Boy, basket on back, 8"...................................*35*
Oriental Boy, bamboo side planter, 7½"............................*35*
Oriental Boy leaning on urn, 5½"..................................*18*
Oriental Boy w/basket on ground (lantern boy), 7¾"................*20*
Oriental Child w/big vase (holding vase), 4¾".....................*15*
Oriental Child w/big vase (clasped hands), 4¾"....................*15*
Oriental Girl, basket on back, 8".................................*35*
Oriental Girl, bamboo side planter, 8"............................*35*
Oriental Girl leaning on urn, 5½".................................*18*
Oriental Girl w/basket on ground (pregnant lady), 7¾".............*20*
Peter Rabbit, 6½"..*35*
Pigtail Girl, 7"...*28*
Pony, 5¼"..*16*
Poodle, posing w/bow, 4¾"...*25*
Poodle, resting, 6½...*38*
Poodle, white, erect, 7"..*36*
Poodle, white, prancing, 6".......................................*32*
Poodle, white, sitting, 7⅛".......................................*32*
Pouter Pigeon, 5¾"..*20*
Pup and Suitcase, 7"..*35*
Pup in basket, 7"
  w/gold *25*
Ram, head, 6½"..*35*
Rooster, head down, high tail, 7¾"................................*26*
  Black and white *55*
Rooster, head down, low tail, 7¼"................................*26*
Rooster, head up, 8"..*35*
Rooster, walking, 5½"
  Black and white *35*
  Brown *25*
Rooster and Wheelbarrow, 8".......................................*65*
Salt Box, 5½"...*26*
Spice Box, 5½"..*36*
Star, ribbed, w/candle holder, 4¾"................................*18*
Star, ribbed, w/candle holder, 6¼"................................*20*
Tanager, 6¼"..*18*

Teddy Bear, sitting, 6¼". *$35*
Teddy Bear, 6¼". *35*
   Black and white *45*
Teddy Bear, 8". *45*
   Black and white *55*
Teddy Bear and Basket on back, 6¼" *48*
Teddy Bear and Concertina, 7½". *64*
Teddy Bear and Mandolin, 6¾" *45*
Teddy Bear and rear planter, 7½" *58*
Teddy Bear on stump, 5½" *26*
Warbler, 5" *16*
Woodpecker, 6¼" *20*

Head

Some of these were made to hang on the wall; these are indicated by /WP in the list below. The Blackamoor Prince is the same as the Blackamoor man but with a white turban.

Blackamoor Man, 8" *$35*
   w/gold *45*
Blackamoor Prince, 8". *40*
Blackamoor Woman, 8". *35*
   w/gold *45*
Chinese Boy w/big hat, small, 6¾" *35*
Chinese Boy w/big hat, large, 7½"   /WP. *25*
Chinese Girl w/big hat, small, 6¾" *35*
Chinese Girl w/big hat, large, 7½"   /WP *25*
Colonial Old Man, 8" *40*
Colonial Old Woman, 8" *40*
Island Lady, 8" *50*
Island Man   /WP. *50*
Lady, bare shoulder, 6" *30*
Lady, gloved, 6" *30*
Pirate, 8" *40*
"Tony," 8¼" *45*
Wide Brim Hat Boy, 7½"   /WP. *35*
Wide Brim Hat Girl, 7½"   /WP *35*

PLANTER / VASES

Embossed

Comma, 5¼" *$16*
Fish, half-circle, 5½" *20*
Fish, open, 5¼" *18*
Oriental Dragon, footed, 5½" *18*
Oriental Fish, footed, 5½" *18*

Figural

Deer, little, head, 7". *$24*
Duck on Stump, 8" *35*

Fish, 5¹/₂"
    Brown *$48*
    Yellow *38*
Gazelle, head, 9" *30*
Goldfinch on Stump, 6¹/₂" *46*
Horse, head, 6¹/₄" *22*
    Black *45*
    Palomino *25*
Kitten on Stump, 6¹/₂" *28*
Madonna, hands together, 9"   /RW *35*
Nuthatch *18*

VASES

Embossed

Bow and Ribbon, footed, 6¹/₂" *$18*
Carol's Corsage, 7" *20*
Fall Arrangement, round, 7¹/₂" *16*
Fish, round, 7" *16*
Fish, round, 8" *18*
Floral Elegance, 8" *25*
Hardy Stem and Leaf, 7¹/₄" *20*
Homma, oval, 8¹/₄" *18*
Stylized Leaf, 5¹/₂"... *12*
Stylized Leaf, 8¹/₂"... *15*
Trailing Leaf and Vine, 8¹/₂" *20*

Figural

Horse w/Mane, head, 8"
    Brown w/black mane *$45*
    Gray w/yellow mane... *35*
Mare and Foal, heads, 8¹/₂" *30*
Parrot, bud, 5".. *18*
Rooster, 7"... *28*
Wren on Stump *28*

STANFORD POTTERY

Sebring, Ohio

Begun in 1945 by George Stanford who had been a manager at Spaulding China in Sebring. Stanford made semiporcelain gift items and, according to Lehner, made items for National Silver (Nasco) and China and Glass Distributors (Pantry Parade). A fire closed the pottery in 1961.

Corn is Stanford's most collectible line.

CORN

Pieces of Corn are heavy and seem to be vitrified china rather than the semivitreous that has been reported for other Stanford items. The **individual casserole** is often called a butter, but butters have flat bottoms. The **spoon rest** resembles an ear of corn with an oval depression on top. It is rare.

MARKS You will find an occasional unmarked piece, but generally pieces are impressed with "Stanford" or "Stanfordware," often with a number, sometimes just a number alone. The party plate is impressed "Stanford, Sebring, Ohio 709."

Casserole, individual, 8¹/₂" long	$25 – $40
Cookie jar, 10" /512	75 – 100
Creamer /508	20 – 35
Cup	15 – 20
Drip jar /518	35 – 40
Jug, 7¹/₂" /513	35 – 50
Plate, party, oval, 9" /709	25 – 30
Relish, 9¹/₂" × 3³/₄"	25 – 35
Shaker, 2³/₄"	20 – 35

Corn: Individual casserole and teapot.

Shaker, range, pair, 4¼" . . . . *$15 – $20*
Spoon rest, 8½" × 5" . . . . *45 – 60*
Sugar   /507 . . . . *25 – 35*
Teapot   /511 . . . . *50 – 75*
Tumbler, 4½"   /601 . . . . *30 – 35*

STANGL POTTERY

Flemington and Trenton, New Jersey

John Martin Stangl joined the Fulper Pottery Company, Flemington, in 1910 as a chemist and plant superintendent. He left in 1914 to work for the Haeger Potteries and returned in 1919. He became president of Fulper in 1926, at which time he bought a share of the company. In the same year, the company bought the Anchor Pottery Company of Trenton and began manufacturing operations there.

The name Stangl Pottery came into use in the 1930s and was officially adopted in 1955. J. M. Stangl died in 1972, and his estate ran the company until it was bought in 1973 by the Wheaton Glass Company. It closed in 1978 when the Susquehanna Broadcasting Company bought it for its real estate, specifically the outlet shop in Flemington.

See Duke in Bibliography and see Clubs/Newsletters.

BIRDS OF AMERICA

In 1940, Stangl introduced a line of pottery birds, designed by Auguste Jacob, which they expanded greatly in 1942 when World War II cut off Japanese imports. The return of foreign competition in 1947 resulted in curtailed production, with sporadic reissues until 1977. Birds continued in production until 1978. These later birds are dated. Stangl did not number consistently; the gaps in numbers do *not* signify birds yet to be discovered.

There will be some variation in coloring and quality as these birds were painted by dozens of different decorators.

Be alert for repairs. Many have been restored with varying degrees of skill, some so well that even a scrupulous dealer can be fooled. Because of the intricacy of some of these figures, examine them very carefully.

If one measurement is given, it is for height; two measurements are for height and length. Most measurements are from catalog sheets; actual sizes may vary a little. All spellings are per Stangl's catalogs. Variations in names are indicated in parentheses.

MARKS Marks will vary. You will find the backstamp shown here or the name "Stangl" engraved. The number of the bird is often included, and this can be stamped or engraved.

NOTE Thanks to Rob Tonkin, we have a correction on the number for the European Finch. It is #3922, not #3722. Note that the lime-green flowers with yellow centers on the base match those of #3923, the Vermilion Fly-Catcher.

3250 A	**Standing Duck**, 3¹/₄"	$90 – $100
3250 B	**Preening Duck**, 2³/₄"	90 – 100
3250 C	**Feeding Duck**, 1³/₄"	90 – 100
3250 D	**Gazing Duck**, 3³/₄"	90 – 100
3250 E	**Drinking Duck**, 1¹/₂"	90 – 100
3250 F	**Quacking Duck**, 3¹/₄"	90 – 100
3273	**Rooster**, 5³/₄"	600 +
3274	**Penguin**, 6"	500 – 550
3275	**Turkey**, 3¹/₂"	500 – 550
3276 S	**Bluebird**, 5"	80 – 100
3276 D	**Bluebirds**, pair, 8¹/₂"	150 – 170
3285	**Rooster**, early, 4¹/₂"	70 – 85
3285	**Rooster**, late, 4¹/₂"	40 – 50
3285	**Rooster**, shaker, early	70 – 85
3285	**Rooster**, shaker, late	40 – 50
3286	**Hen**, early, 3¹/₄"	70 – 85
3286	**Hen**, late, 3¹/₄"	40 – 50
3286	**Hen**, shaker, early	70 – 85
3286	**Hen**, shaker, late	40 – 50
3400	**Love Bird**, single, 4"	80 – 100
3400	**Love Bird**, single, revised, 4"	50 – 60
3401 S	**Wren**, tan (light brown), 3¹/₂"	200 – 225
3401 S	**Wren**, revised, dark brown, 3¹/₂"	50 – 60
3401 D	**Wren**, pair, tan (light brown), 8"	250 – 300
3401 D	**Wren**, pair, revised, dark brown, 8"	85 – 100
3402 S	**Oriole**, beak down, 3¹/₄"	125 – 150
3402 S	**Oriole**, revised, 3¹/₄"	50 – 65

3402 D	**Oriole**, pair, 5¹/₂"	$225 – $250
3402 D	**Oriole**, pair, revised, w/leaves, 5¹/₂"	100 – 125
3404 D	**Love Birds**, pair, kissing, 4¹/₂"	450 – 500
3404 D	**Love Birds**, pair, revised, not kissing, 5¹/₂"	100 – 125
3405 S	**Cockatoo**, 6"	50 – 65
3405 D	**Cockatoo**, pair, 9¹/₂"	165 – 195
3405 D	**Cockatoo**, pair, revised, open base, 9¹/₂"	100 – 125
3406 S	**Kingfisher**, 3¹/₂"	60 – 75
3406 D	**Kingfisher**, pair, 5"	125 – 150
3407	**Owl**, 4"	350 – 400
3408	**Bird of Paradise**, 5¹/₂"	100 – 125
3430	**Duck**, 22"	ND
3431	**Duck, standing**, 8"	450 – 500
3432	**Duck**, running, 5" Brown/Grayish white w/black spots	450 – 500
3433	**Rooster**, 16"	1700 – 2000
3443	**Flying Duck** 9"	275 – 300
3444	**Cardinal** (female), pine cones, 6¹/₂"	125 – 150
3444	**Cardinal**, revised, 7"	
	Pink glossy	80 – 100
	Red matte	100 – 125
3445	**Rooster**, gray, 9"	200 – 225
3445	**Rooster**, yellow, 9"	150 – 175
3446	**Hen**, gray, 7"	175 – 200
3446	**Hen**, yellow, 7"	150 – 175
3447	**Yellow** (Prothonatary) **Warbler**, 5"	65 – 75
3448	**Blue-headed Vireo**, 4¹/₄"	60 – 70
3449	**Paroquet** (Parrot), 5¹/₂"	150 – 160
3450	**Passenger Pigeon**, 9" × 18"	1000 +
3451	**Willow Ptarmigan**, 11" × 11"	2000 +
3452	**Painted Bunting**, 5"	80 – 100
3453	**Mountain Bluebird**, 6¹/₈"	800 – 1000
3454	**Key West Quail Dove**, 9"	250 – 325
3454	**Key West Quail Dove**, wings spread	800 +
3455	**Shoveler**, 12¹/₄" × 14"	1200 +
3456	**Cerulean Warbler**, 4¹/₄"	55 – 65
3457	**Pheasant** (Walking), 7¹/₄" × 15"	1600 – 1800
3458	**Quail**, 7¹/₂"	1100 +
3459	**Fish Hawk** (Falcon/Osprey), 9¹/₂"	3000 +
3490 D	**Redstarts**, pair, 9"	225 – 250
3491	**Hen Pheasant**, 6¹/₄" × 11"	200 – 250
3492	**Cock Pheasant**, 6¹/₄" × 11"	200 – 250
3518 D	**White Headed Pigeon**, pair, 7¹/₂" × 12¹/₂"	550 – 600
3580	**Cockatoo**, medium, 8⁷/₈"	125 – 150
	Pastel	250 +
3581	**Chickadees**, group (three), 5¹/₂" × 8¹/₂"	200 – 225
3582	**Parrakeets**, pair, 7"	
	Blue	225 – 250
	Green	175 – 200

3583	**Parula Warbler**, 4¹/₄"	*$50 – $65*
3584	**Cockatoo**, large, 11³/₈"	*225 – 250*
	Signed "Jacob"	*275 – 300*
	Pastel	*600 +*
3585	**Rufous Humming Bird**, 3"	*55 – 65*
3586	**Pheasant** (Della Ware), 9" × 15¹/₂"	*600 – 650*
3589	**Indigo Bunting**, 3¹/₄"	*70 – 80*
3590	**Chat** (Carolina Wren), 4¹/₂"	*150 – 175*
3591	**Brewer's Blackbird**, 3¹/₂"	*100 – 125*
3592	**Titmouse**, 2¹/₂"	*50 – 60*
3593	**Nuthatch**, 2¹/₂"	*50 – 60*
3594	**Red-faced Warbler**, 3"	*60 – 75*
3595	**Bobolink**, 4³/₄"	*125 – 150*
3596	**Gray Cardinal** (Pyrrhuloxia), 4³/₄"	*70 – 80*
3597	**Wilson Warbler**, 3¹/₂"	*50 – 60*
3598	**Kentucky Warbler**, 3"	*50 – 60*
3599	**Humming Birds**, pair, 8" × 10¹/₂"	*250 – 300*
3625	**Bird of Paradise**, 13¹/₂"	*1600 +*
3626	**Broadtail Humming Bird**, blue flower, 6"	*100 – 125*
3627	**Rivoli Humming Bird**, pink flower, 6"	*100 – 125*
3628	**Rieffers Humming Bird**, 4¹/₂"	*100 – 125*
3629	**Broadbill Humming Bird**, 4¹/₂"	*100 – 125*
3634	**Allen Humming Bird**, 3¹/₂"	*75 – 85*
3635	**Goldfinches**, group (four), 4" × 11¹/₂"	*175 – 200*
3715	**Blue Jay** (peanut), 10¹/₄"	*650*
3716	**Blue Jay** (leaf), 10¹/₄"	*650*
3717	**Blue Jay**, pair, 12¹/₂"	*2200 +*
3746	**Canary right**, rose flower, 6¹/₄"	*200 – 225*
3747	**Canary left**, blue flower, 6¹/₄"	*200 – 225*
3749 S	**Scarlet Tanager**, pink body, 4³/₄"	*175 – 200*
3749 S	**Western Tanager**, red matte body, 4³/₄"	*200 – 225*
3750 D	**Scarlet Tanager**, pink body, pair, 8"	*325 – 350*
3750 D	**Western Tanager**, red matte body, pair, 8"	*350 – 400*
3751 S	**Red-Headed Woodpecker**, 6¹/₄"	
	Pink glossy	*125 – 150*
	Red matte	*150 – 175*
3752 D	**Red-Headed Woodpecker**, pair, 7³/₄"	
	Pink glossy	*225 – 250*
	Red matte	*275 – 300*
3754 S	**White Wing Crossbill**, 3¹/₂"	
	Pink glossy	*650 +*
3754 D	**White Wing Crossbill**, pair, 8³/₄"	
	Pink glossy	*325 – 350*
	Red matte	*350 – 375*
3755 S	**Audubon Warbler**, 4¹/₄"	*150 – 175*
3756 D	**Audubon Warbler**, pair, 7³/₄"	*350 – 375*
3757	**Scissor-Tailed Flycatcher**, 11"	*600 – 650*
3758	**Magpie-Jay**, 10³/₄"	*800 +*

3810	**Blackpoll Warbler**, 3½"	*$150 – $160*
3811	**Chestnut-backed Chickadee**, 5"	*100 – 125*
3812	**Chestnut-sided Warbler**, 4"	*90 – 100*
3813	**Evening Grosbeak**, 5"	*125 – 150*
3814	**Black-throated Green Warbler**, 3⅛"	*100 – 125*
3815	**Western Blue Bird**, 7"	*400 – 450*
3848	**Golden-crowned Kinglet**, 4⅛"	*90 – 100*
3849	**Goldfinch**, 4"	*80 – 100*
3850	**Yellow Warbler**, 4"	*80 – 100*
3851	**Red-breasted Nuthatch**, 3¾"	*70 – 80*
3852	**Cliff Swallow**, 3¾"	*100 – 125*
3853	**Golden-Crowned Kinglets**, group, 5½" × 5"	*550 – 600*
3868	**Summer Tanager**, 4"	*550 – 600*
3921	**Yellow-headed Verdin**, 4½"	*1200 +*
3922	**European Finch**, 4½"	*800 – 1000*
3923	**Vermillion Fly-Catcher**, 5¾" tall	*800 – 1000*
3924	**Yellow-throated Warbler**, 5½"	*425 – 450*
3925	**Magnolia Warbler**	*1900 +*

Miscellany

Bird on Gourd	*$175 – $200*
Deviled egg plate	*75 – 100*

CHILDREN'S WARE

Kiddie Sets   (Also called Kiddie Ware) (ca. 1942 to 1970s)

These were available as two-piece sets (a cup and a three-compartment dish) or three-piece sets (a 9" plate, a cup, and a bowl). Bowls are the hardest pieces to find.

All patterns were hand-painted; most were hand-carved. Those that never were are indicated as (nc) (for "never carved") in the list below.

DECORATIONS   There are distinct decorations for the two-piece sets and the three-piece sets, with one exception: The Cookie Twins divided dish has the Ginger Boy on the left and the Ginger Girl on the right. The cup that goes with each set is decorated differently. A new decoration, Bunny, has turned up. It is too rare to price.

PRICING   A few patterns were reissued on a white body; some carved, some not, even though the pattern had originally been carved. These were made in the mid 1970s, some perhaps in the late 1960s. Most had a straight-sided mug. I have listed these patterns with a   /W. Pieces should be priced 10% to 20% less than prices below. Note: Little Bo Peep and Little Boy Blue are the two easiest decorations to find; do not overpay for these.

TWO-PIECE SETS

ABC (1956)   /W

Cup	*$50*
Dish	*100*

Bunny Lunch (1958)

Cup	*125*
Dish	*175*

Cookie Twins (1957)
    Cup *$125*
    Dish *175*

Ducky Dinner (1958)
    Cup *75*
    Dish *125*

Five Little Pigs (1956)
    Cup *125*
    Dish *175*

Kitten Capers
    Cup *65*
    Dish *125*

Mealtime Special
    Cup *50*
    Dish *100*

Our Barnyard Friends
    Cup *75*
    Dish *125*

Playful Pups
    Cup *65*
    Dish *125*

THREE-PIECE SETS

Blue Elf (1958)
    Cup . . . . *$100+*
    Bowl *150*
    Plate *200*

Carousel, Blue border
    Cup *70*
    Bowl *125*
    Plate *175*

Carousel, Pink border
    Cup *70*
    Bowl *125*
    Plate *175*

Carousel, Gold border
    Cup *70*
    Bowl *125*
    Plate *175*

Cat and the Fiddle (1956)
    Cup *125*
    Bowl *150*
    Plate *225*

Circus Clown (1965) (nc)   /W
    Cup *60*
    Bowl *95*
    Plate *150*

Flying Saucer
    Cup . . . . *ND*

Bowl . . . . *ND*
Plate . . . . *ND*
Ginger Boy (1957)
   Cup *$100*
   Bowl *150*
   Plate *200*
Ginger Cat (1965) (nc)   /W
   Cup *70*
   Bowl *125*
   Plate *175*
Ginger Girl (1957)
   Cup *100*
   Bowl *150*
   Plate *200*
Goldilocks
   Cup *100*
   Bowl *150*
   Plate *200*
Humpty-Dumpty, Blue border
   Cup *60*
   Bowl *95*
   Plate *150*
Humpty-Dumpty, Pink border
   Cup *70*
   Bowl *80*
   Plate *160*
Humpty-Dumpty, Lime Green border
   Cup *60*
   Bowl *95*
   Plate *150*
Indian Campfire
   Cup *125*
   Bowl *175*
   Plate *225*
Jack in the Box
   Cup *60*
   Bowl *95*
   Plate *150*
Little Bo Peep
   Cup *50*
   Bowl *65*
   Plate *100*
Little Boy Blue   /W
   Cup *50*
   Bowl *65*
   Plate *100*
Little Quackers (1958)   /W
   Cup *70*

Bowl *$125*
Plate *175*
Mary Quite Contrary (1956)
   Cup *100*
   Bowl *150*
   Plate *200*
Mother Goose, Blue
   Cup *125*
   Bowl *150*
   Plate *225*
Mother Goose, Pink
   Cup *125*
   Bowl *150*
   Plate *225*
Mother Hubbard (nc)
   Cup *60*
   Bowl *95*
   Plate *150*
Peter Rabbit
   Cup *100*
   Bowl *150*
   Plate *200*
Pink Fairy (1958)
   Cup *100*
   Bowl *150*
   Plate *200*
Pony Trail
   Cup *125*
   Bowl *175*
   Plate *225*
Ranger Boy
   Cup *125*
   Bowl *175*
   Plate *225*
Wild Animals
   Cup *150*
   Bowl *175*
   Plate *250*
Wizard of Oz
   Cup . . . . *ND*
   Bowl . . . . *ND*
   Plate . . . . *ND*
Woman in the Shoe (early)
   Cup *125*
   Bowl *150*
   Plate *225*
Woman in the Shoe (1956)
   Cup *60*

Bowl	*$95*
Plate	*150*

Miscellany

A cup, red body, with a cartoon character (Hans or Fritz?), has been found. It is not known whether it was intended to be part of the Kiddie Ware line or was a separate item. The divided dish with the Bluebirds should be part of a set, but a cup has not yet been found. The baby's feeding dish has been found decorated with either a green lamb or a blue lamb. The pet feeding dish has either a cat (Ginger Cat) or dog on it. Only one tile has been found, and it has the Pink Carousel decoration on it. See color section.

Cup	*ND*
Divided dish, Bluebirds	*ND*
Feeding dish, baby, 8¼" × 1¾" deep	*$200 +*
Feeding dish, pet	*200 +*
Tile round, 5½"	*ND*
Warming dish, 3-part, ceramic-tip cork	*500 +*

Musical Mug   (Early 1940s)

Made for Lunning. A mug, 3" deep, on a hollow flared base, 2" deep, making it 5" tall overall, with a large handle. Lunning added the musical device, which was placed in the base.

Jack and Jill	*$250 +*
Mary Had a Little Lamb	*250 +*
Toy Soldiers	*250 +*

DINNERWARE / EARLY

#1388 / #2000

These were Stangl's most popular lines of dinnerware in the 1930s. Production was severely curtailed when the new hand-painted line was introduced in 1942, continuing for perhaps a year longer. Sets of various sizes in all four basic colors in both Colonial and Americana lines were called Rainbow Sets.

#1388

A fluted shape with alternating thick and thin ribs.

Of these two lines, #1388 was brought out first, but I have not been able to pinpoint the year of introduction.

The candy dish with bird finial seems to be the small mixing bowl with a special lid. This is a guess. The teacup is footed; the coffee cup is wider than the tea and is not footed.

Based on old catalog lists, a number of other pieces may show up.

Solid Colors / Colonial   (1932)

Colonial is the name for the #1388 solid-color line. Colonial Blue, Persian Yellow, and Silver Green were introduced in 1924. The 1935 listing includes Rust, Tangerine, and Surf White. In 1937, Aqua Blue was added, and Surf White became Satin White. All of these colors were still available in 1940.

The four basic colors are Colonial Blue, Persian Yellow, Silver Green, and Tangerine, which are the most easily found. Aqua Blue, Rust, Satin Brown, and Satin White are harder to find, especially the last two colors. Burgundy, Satin Blue, and a deep plum have been found, but there is no evidence that they were ever put into production.

NOTE Some of the hollowware decorated in Rust and in Tangerine will have a matte green interior rather than being an allover color. If this is important to you, keep it in mind when mail-ordering.

Ashtray, 3½"	$12
Baking shell	15
Bean pot, one handle, 7" high	45
Bean pot, individual	18
Bottle, refrigerator, w/ pottery stopper, 9"	ND
Bowl, console, oval, 12" × 8"	25
Bowl, mixing, 5"	ND
Bowl, mixing, 7½"	ND
Bowl, mixing, 9"	ND
Bowl, mixing, 14"	ND
Bowl, salad, round, lug, 8"	20
Bowl, salad, round, lug, 10"	25
Bowl, salad, round, lug, 14"	ND
Bowl, soup, lug, 4½"	8
Bowl, soup, lug, 5"	8
w/lid	16
Bowl, vegetable, oval, 10"	15
Butter chip, 2¼"	8
Candle holder, single, 3½" tall	12
Candle holder, triple	50
Candy jar w/bird finial	ND
Carafe, w/wood handle	35
w/pottery stopper,	45
Casserole, 5"	25
Casserole, 8"	35
Casserole, individual, stick handle	10
w/lid	15
Cigarette box, 4½" × 3½"	35
Coffee pot, AD, 6-cup	60
Compote, 7"	15
Creamer	10
Creamer, AD	10
Creamer, individual, 2½" high	8
Cup	8
Cup, AD	8
Cup, coffee	9
Custard cup, 3½"	6
Dish, 6"	8
Eggcup	8
Gravy faststand	20

Hors d'oeuvres, 5-part, 12" *$35*
Hors d'oeuvres, round, 3-part, 9" *25*
Hors d'oeuvres, oval, 11½" *25*
Hors d'oeuvres, oval, 18½" .... *ND*
Jelly mold, small .... *ND*
Jelly mold, large .... *ND*
Jug, 2½" high *12*
Jug, 3½" high *12*
Jug, 4½" high *18*
Jug, 5½" high *25*
Jug, 7½" high *35*
Jug, ball, ice lip *35*
Jug, syrup *30*
   w/lid *40*
Jug, waffle, 2-quart *35*
   w/lid *45*
Mug (tumbler) *20*
Pie baker, 11" *25*
Plate, 6" *3*
Plate, 7" *4*
Plate, 8" *6*
Plate, 9" *9*
Plate, 10" *12*
Plate, chop, 12" *25*
Plate, chop, 14" *30*
Plate, grill, 10" *16*
Plate, grill, 11½" *20*
Platter, oval, 12" *18*
Platter, oval, 14" *22*
Ramekin, 4" *8*
Relish, 2-part, 6½ × 7" *20*
Relish, 3-part, 12" × 7" *20*
Relish, oval, 6-part, 19" .... *ND*
Saucer *3*
Saucer, AD *5*
Server, center handle *10*
Shaker, pepper, 2-hole *8*
Shaker, salt, 4-hole *8*
Shirred egg, 8" × 6" *15*
Sugar *12*
Sugar, AD *12*
Sugar, individual 2½" high, open *8*
Teapot, 6-cup *50*
Teapot, individual *30*
Tray/shakers *18*
Tray/sugar and creamer, individual, 8" × 4" *15*
Tray/sugar and creamer, regular *15*

Newport (Pattern #3333) A sailboat done in shades of blue with white sails. Some pieces will have only sea gulls and waves.

Ashtray, 4 rests . . . . *ND*
Bowl, salad, deep, 10" *$60*
Bowl, salad, shallow, 10". *60*
Bowl, salad, 12" *75*
Bowl, soup, lug, 4½" *20*
Bowl, vegetable, oval, 10" *50*
Candle holder *35*
Carafe, w/wood handle *85*
  w/pottery stopper *100*
Creamer *20*
Cup *15*
Dish, fruit, 6" *20*
Plate, 6" *15*
Plate, 7" *15*
Plate, 8" *20*
Plate, 9" *25*
Plate, 10" *35*
Plate, chop, 12" *60*
Plate, chop, 14" *75*
Saucer *8*
Shaker, regular, each. *12*
Shaker, figural, each *150*
Sugar *25*
Teapot *100*

#2000   (1936)

A plain round shape. Its number, 2000, will be found inscribed on the bottom.
  The carafe was brought out in 1938; it's hard to find, as are the ashtray and butter pat. Old price lists indicate a 12" footed salad bowl that has not been seen; a 12" bowl with straight sides and no foot has been seen. The Gravy Fast-stand is the lug soup attached to a 6" plate.

Solid Colors / Americana

The #2000 solid-color line is called Americana. Made in four solid colors: Colonial Blue, Silver Green, Tangerine, and Persian Yellow.

Ashtray, 4" *$12*
Bowl, lug, 4" *7*
Bowl, salad, 7" *12*
Bowl, salad, 10". *30*
Bowl, salad, 11½" *35*
Bowl, soup, coupe, 7½" *10*
Bowl, soup, lug, 5". *10*
  w/lid *18*
Bowl, vegetable, oval, 8" *20*
Bowl, vegetable, oval 10" *20*
Butter pat . . . . *ND*
Carafe w/wooden handle. *35*
  w/pottery stopper *45*
Coffee pot, AD *50*
Creamer *6*

Creamer, individual *$10*
Cup *8*
Cup, AD. *9*
Cup, coffee *9*
Cup, cream soup, 2 open handles, 5" *10*
Dish, fruit, 5½" *7*
Gravy Faststand *15*
Jug, ball w/ice lip. *35*
Jug, ½-pint. *15*
Jug, 1-pint *20*
Jug, 1-quart *25*
Jug, 2-quart, ice lip w/handle wrapped *35*
    w/lid. *50*
Mug (tumbler) *12*
Plate, 6" *3*
Plate, 7" *4*
Plate, 8" *6*
Plate, 9" *7*
Plate, 10" *9*
Plate, chop, 12" *25*
Plate, chop, 14" *35*
Platter, oval, 12" *10*
Platter, oval, 14" *15*
Relish, 2-section *6*
Saucer *2*
Saucer, AD *4*
Saucer, coffee *3*
Saucer, cream soup *4*
Shakers, pair *16*
    w/metal holder *36*
Sugar *10*
    w/bird finial. *20*
Sugar, open, individual *10*
Teapot, 6-cup. *35*
Teapot, 8-cup. *40*
Tray, sugar/creamer, 4½" × 8¼" *8*

Ranger (Pattern #3304/Also called Cowboy and Cactus)

Attributed to Tony Sarg. A cowboy design in shades of blue, brown, and marigold yellow. Smaller pieces have the cactus only. The candle holders and regular shakers have the Ranger colors only, no design.

    PRICING I have priced only those pieces of Ranger known to exist. Please let me know if you find others.

Bowl, oval, 10" *$100*
Bowl, salad, 7". *100*
Bowl, salad, 10". *150*
Candle holder, each *35*
Carafe, w/wood handle *125*
    w/pottery stopper *150*

Creamer	*$40*
Cup	*35*
Cup, coffee	*35*
Dish, fruit, 5¹/₂"	*30*
Dish, lug, 5"	*30*
Plate, 6"	*50*
Plate, 8"	*85*
Plate, 9"	*100*
Plate, 10"	*125*
Plate, chop, 12"	*150*
Plate, chop, 14"	*175*
Platter, oval, 12"	*100*
Saucer	*15*
Shaker, regular, pair	*50*
Shaker, figural, pair	*400*
Sugar	*50*
Teapot	*150*

DINNERWARE / HAND-PAINTED

In 1942, Stangl introduced a line of dinnerware on a red clay body with new shapes and decorations. The unfired item would be brushed (sprayed as of ca. 1953) with white engobe, the pattern stenciled on and then carved in. It then went for the first firing, after which decorators hand painted the colors on within the carved outlines. It was then sprayed with a clear glaze and fired a second time.

A few pieces were not carved and are marked (nc) in the lists below.

MARKS "Stangl Pottery" in an oval, often with "Trenton, N.J." is the backstamp most often found, usually with the decoration name below.

PRICING It is condition that determines price. Many pieces marked as seconds were actually firsts, as these were often sent to Stangl's Flemington outlet when stock was needed.

AMBER GLO

Designed by Kay Hackett.

Bowl, salad, 10"	*$30*
Bowl, salad, 12"	*35*
Bowl, soup, coupe, 7¹/₂"	*10*
Bowl, soup, lug, 5¹/₂"	*9*
Bowl, vegetable, covered, 8"	*35*
Bowl, vegetable, divided	*30*
Bowl, vegetable, round, 8"	*20*
Butter dish	*30*
Casserole, 6"	*20*
Casserole, 8"	*40*
Casserole, individual, knob, 4"	*15*
Casserole, individual, stick, 6"	*15*

Apple Delight

Blueberry

Country Garden

Fruit

Fruit and Flowers

Golden Blossom

Thistle

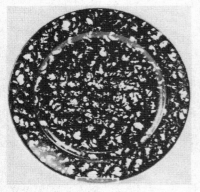

Town & Country

Tulip

Wild Rose

Casserole w/handle, 6" *$20*
Casserole w/handle, 8" *25*
Cigarette box, 3³/₄" × 4¹/₂" *30*
Coaster/Ashtray *8*
Coffee pot, individual *45*
Coffee pot, 4-cup *40*
Coffee pot, 8-cup *40*
Coffee server . . . . *45 – 50*
Coffee warmer *18*
Creamer *8*
Creamer, Casual *15*
Creamer, individual *12*
Cruet *25*
Cup *7*
Dish, cereal, 5¹/₂" *9*
Dish, fruit, 5¹/₂" *9*
Dish, pickle *15*
Dish, relish *20*
Eggcup *8*
Gravy boat *15*
Gravy boat stand *8*
Mug, coffee, low *15*
Pitcher, 6-ounce *15*
Pitcher, ¹/₂-pint *18*
Pitcher, 1-pint *20*
Pitcher, 1-quart *25*
Pitcher, 2-quart *35*
Plate, 6" *4*
Plate, 8" *9*
Plate, 9" *9*
Plate, 10" *10*
Plate, 11" *15*
Plate, chop 12¹/₂" *20*
Plate, chop 14¹/₂" *25*
Platter, Casual, 13³/₄" *35*
Saucer *2*
Server, center handle *6*
Shaker *8*
Sugar *12*
Sugar, Casual *15*
Sugar, individual *12*
Teapot *35*
Tray, bread *25*
Tray, condiment *20*

BLUEBERRY

Pat. #3770. Designed by Kay Hackett.

PRICING Seconds were decorated in shades of blue only; 25%–50% less for these items.

Ashtray, rectangular *$30*
Bowl, mixing, 4" (nc). *12*
Bowl, mixing, 5¹/₂" (nc) *20*
Bowl, mixing, 7" (nc). *25*
Bowl, mixing, 9" (nc). *35*
Bowl, salad, 10" *40*
Bowl, salad, 12" *60*
Bowl, soup, coupe, 7¹/₂" *20*
Bowl, soup, lug, 5¹/₂" *15*
Bowl, vegetable, covered, 8" *65*
Bowl, vegetable, divided, oval/rectangular *40*
Bowl, vegetable, round, 8". *35*
Butter dish *35*
Casserole, 6" *28*
Casserole, 8" *75*
Casserole, individual, knob, 4" *14*
Casserole w/handle, 6" *25*
Casserole w/handle, 8" *35*
Chip 'n' Dip (nc). *65*
Coaster/Ashtray *15*
Coffee, individual *50*
Coffee pot, 4-cup. *50*
Coffee pot, 8-cup. *60*
Coffee server. *65*
Coffee warmer *25*
Creamer *15*
Creamer, individual *15*
Cruet *35*
Cup *10*
Cup, jumbo *40*
Dish, cereal, 5¹/₂" *18*
Dish, fruit, 5¹/₂" *15*
Dish, pickle *20*
Dish, relish *25*
Eggcup. *12*
Gravy boat *20*
Gravy boat stand *12*
Mug, coffee, 2-cup. *35*
Pitcher, 6-ounce *15*
Pitcher, ¹/₂-pint. *20*
Pitcher, 1-pint *25*
Pitcher, 1-quart *35*
Pitcher, 2-quart *60*
Plate, 6" *8*
Plate, 8". *15*
Plate, 9". *15*
Plate, 10". *18*
Plate, 11". *25*

Plate, chop, 12½" $35
Plate, chop, 14½" 45
Platter, Casual, 13¾" 40
Platter, oval, 14¾" 45
Saucer 6
Saucer, jumbo 10
Server, center handle 12
Shaker 10
Sugar 15
Sugar, individual 15
Teapot 60
Tray, bread 40
Tray, condiment 30

CHICORY

Designed by Kay Hackett.

Bowl, salad, 10" $40
Bowl, salad, 12" 50
Bowl, soup, coupe, 7½" 18
Bowl, soup, lug, 5½" 15
Bowl, vegetable, divided 35
Bowl, vegetable, round, 8" 35
Butter dish 35
Casserole, 6" 28
Casserole, 8" 55
Casserole, individual, knob, 4" 16
Casserole w/handle, 6" 25
Casserole w/handle, 8" 35
Coaster/Ashtray 15
Coffee pot, 8-cup 50
Coffee warmer 20
Creamer, old style 10
Creamer, revised 10
Cruet 30
Cup 10
Dish, cereal, 5½" 15
Dish, fruit, 5½" 12
Dish, pickle 20
Dish, relish 25
Eggcup 12
Gravy boat 20
Gravy boat stand 12
Mug, coffee, 2-cup 35
Pitcher, 6-ounce 18
Pitcher, ½-pint 25
Pitcher, 1-pint 30
Pitcher, 1-quart 40

Pitcher, 2-quart *$50*
Plate, 6" *6*
Plate, 8" *12*
Plate, 9" *12*
Plate, 10" *15*
Plate, 11" *25*
Plate, chop, 12¹/₂" *30*
Plate, chop, 14¹/₂" *40*
Platter, Casual, 13³/₄" *45*
Saucer *5*
Server, center handle *10*
Shaker *10*
Sugar, old style *15*
Sugar, revised *15*
Teapot *50*
Tray, bread *35*

COUNTRY GARDEN

Designed by Kay Hackett. "Yellow jonquils, bluebells, buttercups make every piece setting a delight." "And different flowers on every piece make each place setting a perennial nosegay!"

Ashtray, fluted, 5" (nc) *$15*
Bowl, salad, 10" *45*
Bowl, salad, 12" *60*
Bowl, soup, coupe, 7¹/₂" *20*
Bowl, soup, lug, 5¹/₂" *15*
Bowl, vegetable, divided *35*
Bowl, vegetable, round, 8" *35*
Butter dish *35*
Cake stand *30*
Casserole, 8" *60*
Casserole, individual, stick *25*
Casserole w/handle, 6" *25*
Casserole w/handle, 8" *35*
Cigarette Box, 3³/₄" × 4¹/₂" *40*
Clock, plain *35*
Coaster/Ashtray, ruffled *12*
Coaster/Ashtray (nc) *10*
Coffee pot, 4-cup *50*
Coffee pot, 8-cup *55*
Coffee pot, filter *75*
Coffee warmer *22*
Creamer *12*
Creamer, individual *15*
Cruet *30*
Cup *13*
Dish, cereal, 5¹/₂" *15*

Dish, fruit, 5½" *$13*
Dish, pickle *20*
Dish, relish *25*
Eggcup *12*
Gravy boat *20*
Gravy boat stand *20*
Mug, coffee, low *20*
Mug, coffee, 2-cup *30*
Pitcher, 6-ounce *18*
Pitcher, ½-pint *25*
Pitcher, 1-pint *30*
Pitcher, 1-quart *40*
Pitcher, 2-quart *50*
Plate, 6" *6*
Plate, 7" *8*
Plate, 8" *15*
Plate, 9" *15*
Plate, 10" *18*
Plate, 11" *35*
Plate, chop, 12½" *40*
Plate, chop, 14½" *45*
Plate, grill (nc) *20*
Plate, party, 8" (nc) *6*
Plate, party, 10" (nc) *8*
Platter, Casual, 13¾" *45*
Platter, oval, 14¾" *45*
Sauce boat *20*
Saucer *5*
Saucer for mug *10*
Server, center handle *10*
Server, 2-tier *25*
Server, 3-tier *35*
Shaker *10*
Sugar *16*
Sugar, individual *15*
Teapot *50*
Tray, bread *40*
Tray, condiment *25*

COUNTRY LIFE

Designed by Kurt Weise, adapted by Kay Hackett.

Generally, each piece has a different decoration on it, though some are repeated (eggcup and shaker have the same duckling, creamer and cup have the same hen, and the salad and coupe soup have the same duck).

Some pieces have alternate decorations, as listed. It is thought that the original decorations on these items were not cost-effective and they were simplified. For example, the 1956 price list pictures the soup with the two ducks, the harder-to-find decoration. The one duck takes less labor to produce.

The 14¹/₂" chop could be customized with your farm's name.

Bowl, salad, round, 10"   /Pig at fence.................................... *$175*
Bowl, vegetable, divided   /Duck and ducklings *200*
Bowl, vegetable, round, 8"   /Mallard w/green head *150*
Bowl, vegetable, round, 8"   /Calf, chained, rearing hind legs *200*
Coaster   /Duckling... *45*
Creamer   /Hen *40*
Cup   /Hen *60*
Dish, fruit, 5¹/₂"   /Pony *75*
Dish, fruit, 5¹/₂"   /Rooster *35*
Eggcup   /Chick.. *45*
Plate, 6"   /Rooster.. *25*
Plate, 8"   /Pig at fence *100*
Plate, 8"   /Cow standing in grass *150*
Plate, 10"   /Farmer's wife harvesting carrots........................ *200*
Plate, 10"   /Rooster... *125*
Plate, 11"   /Farmer baling hay *225*
Plate, chop, 12¹/₂"   /Farmhouse................................... *300*
Plate, chop, 12¹/₂"   /Farmhouse w/vegetable garden *400*
Plate, chop, 14¹/₂"   /Barn.. *350*
   w/farm name... *425*
Platter, Casual   /Hen and ducklings................................ *250*
Saucer   /Three little eggs *15*
Shaker, each   /Duckling... *35*
Soup, coupe, 8"   /Mallard w/green head, centered...................... *100*
Soup, coupe, 8"   /Mallard w/green head, on right, facing duck's rear
sticking out of the water *200*
Sugar   /Rooster.. *60*
Tray, bread   /Hen with chicks *250*

FRUIT

Designed by Kay Hackett. Various combinations of apple, cherry, grape, peach, pear, and plum. "A natural freshness imparted by lovely fruits for dining pleasure." This began as a salad set and was expanded to a full dinnerware line around 1945. Initially, the yellow border stopped just short of the rim, showing a brown edge. Later, to simplify production, it became all yellow. There are two styles of cups.

Ashtray, fluted, 5" (nc) *$15*
Bean pot, 2 handles (nc) *85*
Bowl, mixing, 4" (nc).. *15*
Bowl, mixing, 5¹/₂" (nc) *20*
Bowl, mixing, 7" (nc).. *25*
Bowl, mixing, 9" (nc).. *35*
Bowl, mixing, 10" *45*
Bowl, salad, 11"... *55*
Bowl, salad, 12" (nc) *50*
Bowl, soup, coupe, 7¹/₂".. *20*

Bowl, soup, lug, 5½" *$15*

Bowl, vegetable, covered, 8" .... *65 – 70*

Bowl, vegetable, divided, oval, 8" *40*

Bowl, vegetable, divided, round, 10" *40*

Bowl, vegetable, round, 8" *35*

Butter dish *40*

Cake stand *25*

Casserole, 6" *25*

Casserole, 8" *65*

Casserole, individual, stick *25*

Casserole w/handle, 6" *25*

Casserole w/handle, 8" *35*

Cigarette box .... *65 – 75*

Clock *45*

Coaster/Ashtray (nc) *12*

Coffee pot, 4-cup *75*

Coffee pot, 8-cup *65*

Coffee server .... *ND*

Coffee warmer *25*

Creamer *12*

Creamer, individual *15*

Cruet *35*

Cup (leaf decoration) *10*

Cup (peach decoration) *12*

Cup, Jumbo *40*

Dish, cereal, 5½" *18*

Dish, fruit, 5½" *15*

Dish, pickle *20*

Dish, relish *35*

Eggcup *12*

Gravy boat *25*

Gravy boat stand *15*

Mug, coffee, low *20*

Mug, coffee, 2-cup *35*

Pitcher, 6-ounce *18*

Pitcher, ½-pint *25*

Pitcher, 1-pint *30*

Pitcher, 1-quart *35*

Pitcher, 2-quart *50*

Plate, 6" *6*

Plate, 7" *10*

Plate, 8" *18*

Plate, 9" *15*

Plate, 10" *20*

Plate, 11" *30*

Plate, chop, 12½" *35*

Plate, chop, 14½" *45*

Plate, party, 8" (nc) *6*

Platter, Casual, 13³/₄" *$45*
Platter, oval, 14³/₄" *45*
Sauce boat *25*
Saucer . . . . *. 5*
Saucer, Jumbo *10*
Saucer for mug *10*
Server, center handle *10*
Server, 2-tier *30*
Server, 3-tier *35*
Shaker *10*
Sherbet *20*
Sugar *15*
Sugar, individual *15*
Teapot *60*
Teapot, individual . . . . *35 – 40*
Tile, octagonal/square/round, 6" *20*
Tray, bread *40*
Tray, condiment *22*
Tray, square, 7¹/₂" (nc) *20*

FRUIT AND FLOWERS

Designed by Kay Hackett.
    The two-cup mug will be found with straight sides or tapered sides.

Ashtray, fluted, 5" (nc) *$15*
Bowl, salad, 10" *45*
Bowl, salad, 12" *65*
Bowl, soup, coupe, 7¹/₂" *20*
Bowl, soup, lug, 5¹/₂" *15*
Bowl, vegetable, divided *45*
Bowl, vegetable, round, 8" *35*
Butter dish *40*
Casserole, 8" *65*
Casserole, individual, stick *25*
Casserole w/handle, 6" *25*
Casserole w/handle, 8" *35*
Coaster/Ashtray *15*
Coffee pot, 4-cup *60*
Coffee pot, 8-cup *75*
Coffee warmer *25*
Creamer *15*
Cruet *35*
Cup *13*
Dish, cereal, 5¹/₂" *15*
Dish, fruit, 5¹/₂" *15*
Dish, pickle *25*
Dish, relish *35*
Eggcup *15*

Gravy boat	*$25*
Gravy boat stand	*15*
Mug, coffee, low	*25*
Mug, coffee, 2-cup	*35*
Pitcher, 6-ounce	*15*
Pitcher, ¹/₂-pint	*18*
Pitcher, 1-pint	*25*
Pitcher, 1-quart	*50*
Pitcher, 2-quart	*60*
Plate, 6"	*9*
Plate, 7"	*12*
Plate, 8"	*15*
Plate, 9"	*15*
Plate, 10"	*18*
Plate, 11"	*35*
Plate, chop, 12¹/₂"	*40*
Plate, chop, 14¹/₂"	*45*
Plate, grill (nc)	*25*
Plate, party, 8" (nc)	*7*
Platter, Casual, 13³/₄"	*45*
Platter, oval, 14³/₄"	*50*
Sauce boat	*25*
Saucer	*6*
Saucer for mug	*10*
Server, center handle	*15*
Server, 2-tier	*30*
Server, 3-tier	*40*
Shaker	*12*
Sugar	*18*
Sugar, individual	*15*
Teapot	*75*
Tile, octagonal/round, 6"	*20*
Tray, bread	*40*
Tray, condiment	*25*

GARDEN FLOWER

Designed by Kay Hackett.

The following flowers were used for the decoration: blue Balloon Flower, pink Bleeding Hearts, purple Campanula, yellow Calendula, blue Flax, blue Morning Glory, pink Phlox, pink Rose, yellow Sunflower, and yellow Tiger Lily.

Bowl, salad, round, 10" /Campanula	*$40*
Bowl, salad, round, 11" /Balloon Flower	*50*
Bowl, soup, lug, 5¹/₂" /Morning Glory	*15*
Bowl, vegetable, divided, round, 10" /Balloon Flower	*40*
Bowl, vegetable, round, 8" /Phlox	*35*
Casserole, 6" /Balloon Flower	*25*
Casserole, 8" /Balloon Flower	*55*

Casserole, w/handle, 6"   /Balloon Flower $25
Casserole, w/handle, 8"   /Tiger Lily. *30*
Cigarette Box   /Rose *40*
Coaster/Ashtray   /Rose *15*
Creamer   /Calendula and Morning Glory *10*
Creamer, individual   /Rose *15*
Cup   /Rose *10*
Dish, cereal, 5½"   /Morning Glory *15*
Dish, fruit, 5½"   /Calendula *12*
Eggcup   /Campanula *15*
Pitcher, ½-pint   /Campanula *25*
Pitcher, 1-pint   /Rose *30*
Pitcher, 1-quart   /Balloon Flower. *35*
Pitcher, 2-quart   /Sunflower. *45*
Plate, 6"   /Balloon Flower *6*
Plate, 8"   /Bleeding Heart. *12*
Plate, 9"   /Tiger Lily. *12*
Plate, 10"   /Rose *15*
Plate, 11"   /Sunflower. *25*
Plate, chop, 12½"   /Rose, Tiger Lily, and Balloon Flower *35*
Plate, chop, 14½"   /Morning Glory and Sunflower *40*
Saucer   /Leaves *5*
Server, center handle. *10*
Server, 2-tier *25*
Server, 3-tier *35*
Shaker, coupe or cylinder   /Flax *8*
Sherbet   /Flax. *20*
Sugar   /Calendula and Morning Glory. *12*
Sugar, individual   /Bleeding Hearts *12*
Teapot   /Sunflower. *50*
Teapot, individual   /Balloon Flower *35*

GOLDEN HARVEST / MAGNOLIA

Designed by Kay Hackett. "Striking tones of off-rose and white against a soft gray-green."

   PRICING   Use these prices for both Golden Harvest and Magnolia.

Ashtray, rectangular $20
Bowl, salad, 10" *40*
Bowl, salad, 12" *50*
Bowl, soup, coupe, 7½" *20*
Bowl, soup, lug, 5½" *12*
Bowl, vegetable, covered, 8" *45*
Bowl, vegetable, divided *35*
Bowl, vegetable, round, 8". *30*
Butter dish *35*
Carafe   /Vase . . . . *ND*
Casserole, 6" *20*

Casserole, 8" *$45*
Casserole, individual, knob *12*
Casserole w/handle, 6" *22*
Casserole w/handle, 8" *35*
Cigarette box, 3³/₄" × 4¹/₂" *40*
Coaster, Ashtray *12*
Coffee pot, individual *50*
Coffee pot, 8-cup *45*
Coffee server *75*
Coffee warmer *20*
Creamer *7*
Creamer, individual *15*
Cruet *32*
Cup *7*
Dish, cereal, 5¹/₂" *15*
Dish, fruit, 5¹/₂" *12*
Dish, pickle *15*
Dish, relish *18*
Eggcup *12*
Gravy boat *15*
Gravy boat stand *12*
Mug, coffee, 2-cup *30*
Mug, coffee, low *15*
Pitcher, 6-ounce *15*
Pitcher, ¹/₂-pint *20*
Pitcher, 1-pint *25*
Pitcher, 1-quart *30*
Pitcher, 2-quart *35*
Plate, 6" *6*
Plate, 8" *12*
Plate, 9" *10*
Plate, 10" *15*
Plate, 11" *25*
Plate, chop, 12¹/₂" *25*
Plate, chop, 14¹/₂" *35*
Platter, Casual, 13³/₄" *35*
Saucer *5*
Server, center handle *8*
Shaker *10*
Sugar *12*
Sugar, individual *15*
Teapot *50*
Tray, bread *25*
Tray, condiment *22*

LYRIC

Designed by Kay Hackett. "Black on white, laced with arabesques of mellow brown."

Bowl, salad, 10" *$40*
Bowl, soup, lug, 5¹/₂" *15*
Bowl, vegetable, divided *35*
Bowl, vegetable, round, 8" *40*
Casserole, individual, knob, 4" *18*
Cigarette Box, 3³/₄" × 4¹/₂" *50*
Coaster/Ashtray *20*
Coffee server *85*
Creamer *14*
Creamer, Casual *20*
Cup *12*
Mug, coffee, low *20*
Mug, coffee, 2-cup. *35*
Plate, 6" *7*
Plate, 8" *15*
Plate, 10" *20*
Plate, chop, 12¹/₂" *45*
Saucer *5*
Sugar *18*
Sugar, Casual. *20*

ROOSTER

The shakers are undecorated. The rooster is similar to the one on Country Life—don't confuse the two.

Bowl, salad, 10" *$50*
Bowl, soup, coupe, 7¹/₂" *30*
Bowl, soup, lug, 5¹/₂" *20*
Bowl, vegetable, round, 8" *40*
Cake stand *35*
Clock *55*
Creamer *15*
Cup *15*
Dish, fruit, 5¹/₂" *20*
Dish, cereal, 5¹/₂" *20*
Eggcup. *18*
Mug, coffee, 2-cup. *30*
Pitcher, 1-pint *25*
Pitcher, 1-quart *35*
Pitcher, 2-quart *45*
Plate, 6" *10*
Plate, 8" *18*
Plate, 10" *30*
Plate, chop, 12¹/₂" *45*
Saucer *8*
Server, center handle. *15*
Server, 2-tier *25*
Server, 3-tier *35*

Shaker *$8*
Sugar *20*

THISTLE

Designed by Kay Hackett. The 9" grill plate is plain, not #1388.
    NOTE A Japanese imitation, with a decal and no carving, was made. It is marked "Japan."

Ashtray, rectangular *$25*
Bowl, mixing, 4" (nc) *12*
Bowl, mixing, 5½" (nc) *20*
Bowl, mixing, 7" (nc) *25*
Bowl, mixing, 9" (nc) *35*
Bowl, salad, 10" *40*
Bowl, salad, 12" *50*
Bowl, soup, coupe, 7½" *20*
Bowl, soup, lug, 5½" *15*
Bowl, vegetable, covered, 8" *60*
Bowl, vegetable, divided *35*
Bowl, vegetable, round, 8" *35*
Butter dish *35*
Casserole, 6" *25*
Casserole, 8" *60*
Casserole, individual, knob *12*
Casserole, individual, stick *25*
Casserole w/handle, 6" *20*
Casserole w/handle, 8" *30*
Chip 'n' Dip (nc) *55*
Cigarette Box *40*
Coaster/Ashtray *15*
Coffee pot, individual *50*
Coffee pot, 4-cup *50*
Coffee pot, 8-cup *60*
Coffee server *75*
Coffee warmer *20*
Creamer *10*
Creamer, individual *15*
Cruet *30*
Cup *7*
Dish, cereal, 5½" *15*
Dish, fruit, 5½" *12*
Dish, pickle *20*
Dish, relish *22*
Eggcup *15*
Gravy boat *20*
Gravy boat stand *15*
Mug, coffee, low *20*
Mug, coffee, 2-cup *35*

Pitcher, 6-ounce	*$15*
Pitcher, ¹/₂-pint	*20*
Pitcher, 1-pint	*25*
Pitcher, 1-quart	*40*
Pitcher, 2-quart	*50*
Plate, 6"	*6*
Plate, 8"	*12*
Plate, 9"	*12*
Plate, 10"	*15*
Plate, 11"	*30*
Plate, chop, 12¹/₂"	*30*
Plate, chop, 14¹/₂"	*40*
Plate, grill (nc)	*25*
Plate, party, 8" (nc)	*6*
Platter, Casual, 13³/₄"	*40*
Platter, oval, 14³/₄"	*40*
Sauce boat	*20*
Saucer	*5*
Server, center handle	*10*
Shaker	*10*
Sugar	*15*
Sugar, individual	*15*
Teapot	*50*
Tray, bread	*35*
Tray, condiment	*25*

TOWN AND COUNTRY

"Recaptures the flavor of the popular enamelware of the last century."

The butter bottom, gravy underplate, and oval relish tray are all the same piece. The cake plate turns upside down to become the Chip and Dip. The coffee mug is taller and narrower than the soup mug; the latter is the same as the juicer stand. The relish and the vanity tray are the same piece and in some listings is also called an ashtray. The tureen was sold as a four-piece set (lid, bottom, ladle, and chop plate). The sponge holder is the same as the soup/cereal. The cheese-and-cracker is shaped like a dust pan.

Town and Country is one color sponged over white engobe so that some white shows through. It was made in black, blue, brown, green, honey (added in 1977), and yellow. Crimson is listed in a 1974 catalog but has not been reported.

PRICING Honey is about 10% less than the low price. Some items have been seen only in blue or yellow.

	Blue	Other Colors
Baking Dish, rectangular, tab handles, 1¹/₂-quart, 7" × 10"	*$60*	*$40*
Baking Dish, rectangular, tab handles, 2¹/₂-quart, 9" × 14"	*85*	*60*
Bean pot/cookie jar, 3-quart	*85*	*65*
Bowl, chowder/chili, 26-ounce, 6³/₄"	*35*	*25*
Bowl, fruit 2¹/₂-quart, 10"	*55*	*45*

	Blue	Other Colors
Bowl, pear shape, 8"	—	$25
Bowl, porridge, 26-ounce, 6^1/$_2$"	$40	25
Bowl, salad, round, 3-quart, 10"	55	40
Bowl, soup/cereal, 15-ounce, 5^3/$_4$"	30	20
Bowl, vegetable, round, 1^1/$_2$-quart, 8"	45	35
Butter, ^{1}/$_4$-pound	50	35
Cake platter/Chip and Dip, 12^1/$_2$"	85	60
Candle holder, flower shape, pair, 2^1/$_4$" high	50	—
Candle holder w/ finger ring (glass globe)	45	35
Candlestick, pair, 7^1/$_2$"	85	50
Candy, clover shape, 3-part	40	—
Canister, milk pail shape, 3-quart	85	60
Casserole, 1^1/$_2$-quart	70	45
Casserole, 2-quart	70	45
Casserole, 2^1/$_2$-quart	75	50
Casserole, 3-quart	75	50
Cheese and Cracker (dust pan shape)	75	60
Clock, plate, 10"	—	45
Clock, skillet shape (battery powered)	65	55
Coffee pot, 5-cup	75	50
Cornucopia, 10^1/$_2$"	—	55
Creamer	20	15
Cup	20	12
Dessert mold, fluted, 6"	40	35
Dessert mold, ribbed, 7^1/$_2$"	45	40
Gravy boat	35	25
Gravy boat stand	20	15
Jug, 1^1/$_2$-pint	40	35
Jug, 2^1/$_2$-pint	50	45
Juicer, citrus, on stand	60	50
Ladle	40	25
Lamp	150	—
Mug, coffee, 13-ounce	35	25
Mug, soup, 14-ounce	35	25
Napkin ring	25	15
Pan, bread/loaf, 2-quart, 4^3/$_4$" × 10"	50	35
Pie baker, 10^1/$_2$"	45	35
Plate, 6"	9	6
Plate, 8" (8^1/$_4$")	20	12
Plate, 10" (10^5/$_8$")	25	15
Plate, chop, 12^1/$_2$"	40	30
Platter, oval, 11"	50	25
Platter, oval, 15"	60	35
Relish tray, square, 7^1/$_2$"	25	20
Saucer	8	4

	Blue	Other Colors
Shaker, cylinder shape	$15	$10
Shaker, cylinder shape, handled	20	12
Snack server, skillet shape, 8½"	50	30
Spoon rest, 8¾"	35	25
Sugar	30	25
Teapot, 5-cup	75	50
Tidbit, single, 10"	30	15
Tile, square, 6"	20	15
Tray, snack, oval, 8¼"	20	15
Tureen, 3½-quart	250	150
Wall pocket, 7½" long × 4⅜" tall	50	—

Bath Accessories

	Blue	Other Colors
Ashtray, bathtub shape	$40	$25
Canister, corked	85	50
Chamber pot, handled	85	65
Flowerpot/planter, 3"	20	10
Flowerpot/planter, 4"	30	15
Flowerpot/planter, 5"	40	20
Flowerpot/planter, 7"	50	25
Ginger jar	85	50
Pitcher and bowl set, small	175	100
Pitcher and bowl set, large	225	150
Shaving mug	40	20
Soap dish, rectangular	40	35
Sponge bowl, round	30	20
Tissue box cover	50	35
Toothbrush holder	45	35
Tumbler, 9-ounce	25	20
Vanity tray, square	25	20

TULIP / BLUE / YELLOW

Designed by Kay Hackett. The Tulip in blue was made only for Marshall Field in Chicago.

Bean Pot, 2 handles (nc)	$75
Bowl, salad, 10"	40
Bowl, salad, 11"	50
Bowl, soup, coupe, 7½"	20
Bowl, soup, lug, 5½"	15
Bowl, vegetable, divided, oval, 8"	40
Bowl, vegetable, divided, round, 10"	40
Bowl, vegetable, round, 8"	35
Casserole, 6"	25
Casserole, 8"	45

Casserole w/handle, 6"..$20
Casserole w/handle, 8"...30
Cigarette Box 45
Coaster/Ashtray 12
Coffee pot, individual 35
Coffee pot, 8-cup...55
Creamer 10
Creamer, individual 15
Cup 10
Dish, cereal, 5½" 15
Dish, fruit, 5½" 12
Eggcup..15
Gravy boat 25
Mug, coffee, 2-cup..35
Pitcher, ½-pint...25
Pitcher, 1-pint 30
Pitcher, 1-quart 35
Pitcher, 2-quart 40
Plate, 6" 6
Plate, 8" 12
Plate, 9" 15
Plate, 10" 18
Plate, 11" 20
Plate, chop, 12½" 30
Plate, chop, 14½" 40
Saucer 5
Server, center handle...10
Shaker 8
Sherbet 20
Sugar...12
Sugar, individual...15
Teapot 50

WILD ROSE

Designed by Kay Hackett. "Wild Rose stays in full bloom, always!"

Bowl, soup, coupe, 7½"..$20
Bowl, soup, lug, 5½" 15
Bowl, salad, 10"..40
Bowl, salad, 12"...55
Bowl, vegetable, divided 40
Bowl, vegetable, round, 8"..35
Butter dish 35
Cake stand 25
Casserole, 8" 50
Casserole, individual, stick 25
Casserole w/handle, 6"..25
Casserole w/handle, 8"..30
Cigarette Box 40

Coaster/Ashtray *$15*
Coffee pot, 4-cup. *55*
Coffee pot, 8-cup. *55*
Coffee warmer *20*
Creamer *10*
Cruet *35*
Cup *7*
Dish, cereal, 5¹/₂" *15*
Dish, fruit, 5¹/₂" *15*
Dish, pickle *25*
Dish, relish *25*
Eggcup *12*
Gravy boat *25*
Gravy boat stand *12*
Mug, coffee, low *20*
Mug, coffee, 2-cup. *35*
Pepper mill . . . . *ND*
Pitcher, 6-ounce *15*
Pitcher, ¹/₂-pint. *20*
Pitcher, 1-pint *25*
Pitcher, 1-quart *40*
Pitcher, 2-quart *60*
Plate, 6" *6*
Plate, 8" *12*
Plate, 9" *12*
Plate, 10" *15*
Plate, 11" *25*
Plate, chop, 12¹/₂" *30*
Plate, chop, 14¹/₂" *40*
Platter, Casual, 13³/₄" *35*
Saucer *5*
Server, center handle. *10*
Server, 2-tier *25*
Server, 3-tier *35*
Shaker *10*
Sugar *15*
Sugar, individual *15*
Teapot *55*
Tray, bread *40*
Tray, condiment *25*

GENERIC LIST

DINNERWARE / GROUP LIST #1

Use this list for the following patterns: Apple Delight, Bachelor Button, Bella
Rosa, Bittersweet, Blue Daisy, Cranberry, Fairlawn, Festival, First Love, Flora,
Garland, Golden Blossom, Golden Grape, Grape, Jonquil, Mediterranean, Moun-

tain Laurel, Orchard Song, Prelude, Provincial, Sgraffito, Stardust, Starflower, Tiger Lily, Water Lilies, Windfall, and Yellow Tulip.

Ashtray, fluted.. *$12*
Bowl, salad, 10"... *35*
Bowl, salad, 12"... *45*
Bowl, soup, coupe, 7½".. *15*
Bowl, soup, flat, 8¼"... *15*
Bowl, soup, lug, 5½"... *12*
Bowl, vegetable, 8".. *30*
Bowl, vegetable, covered, 8".. *40*
Bowl, vegetable, divided.. *25 – 30*
Butter, ¼-pound... *35*
Cake stand *20*
Candle warmer... *15*
Casserole, 6".. *15*
Casserole, 8".. *40*
Casserole, individual, knob, 4"....................................... *10*
Casserole, individual, stick-handle, 6"............................... *15*
Casserole, skillet, 6"... *20*
Casserole, skillet, 8"... *25*
Cigarette Box *35*
Coaster/Ashtray *8*
Coffee pot, 8-cup... *40*
Creamer *8*
Cruet *30*
Cup *10*
Dish, cereal, 5½"... *12*
Dish, fruit, 5½".. *10*
Eggcup... *10*
Gravy.. *15*
Gravy liner *10*
Mug, low... *15*
Mug, 2-cup... *25*
Pitcher, 6-ounce... *15*
Pitcher, ½-pint.. *20*
Pitcher, 1-pint.. *25*
Pitcher, 1-quart... *35*
Pitcher, 2-quart... *40*
Plate, 6"... *5*
Plate, 8"... *10*
Plate, 9"... *12*
Plate, 10".. *15*
Plate, 11".. *15*
Plate, chop, 12¼".. *25*
Plate, chop, 14½".. *30*
Plate, grill (steak), 11" (nc)... *20*
Plate, picnic, 8" (nc)... *4*

Plate, picnic, 10" (nc) *$5*
Platter, Casual, 13³/₄" *35*
Platter, oval, 14³/₄" *35*
Sauce boat *20*
Saucer *3*
Server, center handle *7*
Server, 2-tier *20*
Server, 3-tier *25*
Shaker *8*
Sherbet *20*
Sugar *12*
Teapot, 6-cup *40*
Tile *15*
Tray, bread *30*
Tray, pickle *15*
Tray, relish *22*

DINNERWARE / GROUP LIST #2

Use this list for the following patterns: Aztec, Bamboo, Blue Melon, Colonial
Rose, Colonial Silver, Florette, Galaxy, Monterey, Morning Blue, Paisley, Pe-
tit Flowers, Piecrust, Pink Lily, Posies, Ringles, Rustic, Scandinavia, Spun
Gold, Sunshine, Terra Rose, Treasured, White Grape, and Yellow Flower.

Bowl, salad, 10" *$20*
Bowl, salad, 12" *25*
Bowl, soup, coupe, 7¹/₂" *10*
Bowl, soup, flat, 8¹/₄" *10*
Bowl, soup, lug, 5¹/₂" *8*
Bowl, vegetable, 8" *18*
Bowl, vegetable, covered, 8" *30*
Bowl, vegetable, divided *25*
Butter, ¹/₄-pound *25*
Cake stand *20*
Candle warmer *10*
Casserole, 4" *12*
Casserole, 6" *12*
Casserole, 8" *30*
Casserole, individual, knob, 4" *8*
Casserole, individual, stick-handle, 6" *12*
Casserole, skillet, 6" *12*
Casserole, skillet, 8" *15*
Cigarette Box *25*
Coaster/Ashtray *5*
Coffee pot, 8-cup *35*
Creamer *7*
Cruet *20*
Cup *7*

Dish, cereal, 5¹/₂" *$10*
Dish, fruit, 5¹/₂" *8*
Eggcup *8*
Gravy *10*
Gravy liner *6*
Mug, stack *15*
Mug, 2-cup *15*
Pitcher, 6-ounce *10*
Pitcher, ¹/₂-pint *15*
Pitcher, 1-pint *20*
Pitcher, 1-quart *25*
Pitcher, 2-quart *35*
Plate, 6" *5*
Plate, 8" *8*
Plate, 9" *10*
Plate, 10" *12*
Plate, chop, 12¹/₄" *15*
Plate, chop, 14¹/₂" *20*
Platter, Casual, 13³/₄" *25*
Platter, oval, 14³/₄" *25*
Saucer *3*
Server, center handle *5*
Server, 2-tier *15*
Server, 3-tier *20*
Shaker *5*
Sugar *8*
Teapot, 6-cup *35*
Tray, bread *20*
Tray, pickle *12*
Tray, relish *15*

STOBY MUGS   (1936)

Designed by Tony Sarg. The hat (lid) serves as an ashtray for six of the mugs. Batch and Grand have attached hats.

The Stobies were originally issued with hand-painted natural features. The six with separate lids were reissued in the 1970s in solid colors of brown (with black trim), chartreuse, or yellow. Depression's name was changed to Cry Baby. A seventh, rare mug named Smart Aleck has been found.

PRICING   Prices are for mugs with *correct* hat. Expect to pay less if it is a marriage. For the reissues, price the brown at $100–$125 and the chartreuse or yellow at $75–$100.

Archie, 6¹/₂"   /1681 .... *$200*
Batch, 5"   /1679 .... *250*
Chief, 6"   /1676 .... *250*
Depression (Cry Baby), 5"   /1677 .... *200*
Grand, 5"   /1673 .... *225*
Henpeck, 6¹/₄"   /1680 .... *225*

Stoby mugs. L to R. Top: Chief, Batch, Cry Baby, and Parson. Bottom: Sport, Grand, Henpeck, and Archie. (Photo courtesy of Lou Kovi, Jr.)

Parson, 6¹/₂" /1675..$200
Smart Aleck...ND
Sport, 5¹/₂" /1678..225

STERLING CHINA COMPANY

Sebring, Ohio

In the spring of 1902, announcement was made that the Sebrings planned to build a fourth pottery in the town that they had founded. It was named Sterling China. Its purpose was the manufacture of real china, "thin" china, not the semiporcelain being made in Sebring's other companies. The building was almost complete by the end of the year and manufacturing began around this time.

In the spring of 1904, Sterling announced it was changing its output to "mainly" semiporcelain, about three-fourths of production, with the rest for thin china "if warranted." By July, the name had been changed to the Limoges China Company and, from what I can tell, no china was being made.

It would be nice to call this a brief flowering in the history of U.S. porcelain manufacture, but actually it's more like a footnote. However, one line turns up enough that I wanted to include it in this book. I call it "Pilgrim."

MARKS This crown mark appears on both china and semiporcelain bodies. It is the only general mark I have seen. You will also find marks specific to various shapes.

"PILGRIM"

Pilgrim was put on more than one shape, the names of which I don't know, but most turn up on a shape with twelve-sided flatware and hexagonal hollowware. This is semivitreous, not china.

Bluish-gray decals of Pilgrim life with blue trim.

Butter pat, 3¼"	$4 – $6
Casserole	20 – 25
Coffee pot	35 – 40
Creamer	4 – 6
Cup	4 – 6
Cup, AD	10 – 12
Dish, 5½"*	2 – 3
Plate, 6"*	1 – 2
Plate, 8"	5 – 6
Plate, 10"*	10 – 12
Plate, chop, 12¼"	15 – 20
Saucer	1 – 2

Pilgrim: Cup, dinner plate, butter pat, creamer, AD cup, and sugar.

Saucer, AD .... *$3 – $5*
Sugar .... *8 – 10*

STERLING CHINA COMPANY

Wellsville, Ohio

Sterling was founded in 1917 by a group of pottery men who bought the Patterson Brothers yellow ware plant. They began to make basic vitreous hotel china, such as bowls, cups, and mugs. As business grew, the line expanded. During World War II, Sterling was one of the major suppliers of china for the armed services; the Navy "E" flew over the plant for many years.

In 1948, Sterling brought out the Russel Wright line, the first new hotel china shape in many years. Sterling bought the Scammell China Company of Trenton, New Jersey, in 1954, taking over the manufacture of Lamberton ware. For business purposes, the company uses an East Liverpool address. It is still in business.

There is much to interest hotel ware collectors in this company's lines, but for other collectors, only the Russel Wright line attracts.

MARKS The Russel Wright pieces will be found with "Sterling China by Russel Wright" either raised or impressed.

RUSSEL WRIGHT (1948)

This is a restaurant ware line designed for easy handling and to minimize breakage. For example, the underside of the plate is designed for an easy grip, and the sugar lid has a finger-grip depression. Most distinctive of a restaurant line are the four sizes of platters and the individual creamers; the one-ounce is for coffee or tea, the three-ounce is for cereal or dessert. The salad bowl is sized for individual salads that are served as a main course. The two-quart jug was restyled into the ball jug.

A mug has also been found in the later solid colors (see below) and decorations only. Whether it was designed by Wright or adapted by Sterling from his cup is not known.

Wright chose colors that would provide attractive backgrounds for food: Ivy green, Straw yellow, Suede gray, and Cedar brown. Sterling also glazed pieces of this line in Shell Pink. Note that some pieces of Shell Pink will have the stamped Shell Pink mark but *not* the Russel Wright mark; others will have the Russel Wright mark but *not* the Shell Pink backstamp. Decal and air-brushed decorations on beige, Shell Pink, and white will also be found.

A second line designed by Wright for Sterling was Polynesian, produced for Shun Lee Dynasty in New York. Very little turns up.

PRICING All colors are of equal value. Add 15%–20% for the Polynesian decoration. Others are not found in enough abundance to make them more desirable; use the prices below.

Ashtray, w/match holder . . . . *$60 – $70*
Bouillon . . . . *12 – 14*

Russel Wright: Polynesian teapot ($85–95), Palm Tree ashtray ($85), coffee bottle, and ball jug.

Bowl, onion soup, w/lid, 11-ounce .... *$18 – $20*
Bowl, salad, 7¹/₂" .... *6 – 7*
Bowl, soup, 6¹/₂". .... *10 – 12*
Celery, 11". .... *15 – 20*
Coffee bottle, 2-cup. .... *70 – 80*
Creamer .... *12 – 15*
Creamer, individual, 1-ounce. .... *10 – 12*
Creamer, individual, 3-ounce .... *10 – 12*
Cup .... *8 – 9*
Cup, AD, open handle. .... *15 – 20*
Fruit. .... *5 – 6*
Gravy/sauce boat, open handle .... *12 – 15*
Jug, ball (restyled). .... *80 – 90*
Jug, water, 2-quart. .... *80 – 90*
Mug .... *12 – 15*
Plate, 6¹/₄" .... *5 – 6*
Plate, 7¹/₂" .... *6 – 7*
Plate, 9". .... *7 – 8*
Plate, 10¹/₄" .... *8 – 9*
Plate, 11¹/₂". .... *12 – 15*
Platter, oval, 7¹/₈" .... *8 – 10*
Platter, oval, 10¹/₂" .... *10 – 12*
Platter, oval, 11³/₄" .... *12 – 14*
Platter, oval, 13⁵/₈" .... *16 – 18*
Relish, oval, 4-part, 16¹/₂" .... *50 – 60*
Saucer .... *3 – 4*
Saucer, AD .... *12 – 15*
Sugar .... *8 – 10*
Teapot, 10-ounce. .... *55 – 65*

STETSON CHINA COMPANY

Lincoln, Illinois

CHAPTER AT A GLANCE

AIRFLOW
ANNETTE

IONIC
OXFORD

Stetson began as a decorating firm. They bought a lot of ware from other potteries, especially Harker and Mt. Clemens. According to Lehner, they bought the Illinois China Company in 1946 to assure a steady source of pottery. They ceased operations in 1966.

MARKS   Stetson used a variety of backstamps, including the ones below. However, much of its output was unmarked.

AIRFLOW

I've seen other names for this shape, but this is the only one I can confirm.

Although it is usually decorated in decals, I've seen a rare piece glazed in solid red.

MARKS   Lois Lehner's book shows a wonderful backstamp that has a drawing of a plane in it.

PRICING   Add 50% for Mexican decal.

Bowl, salad, round, 8½"...	*$15 – $18*
Bowl, vegetable, oval 9"*...	*10 – 12*
Casserole...	*20 – 25*
Covered onion..	*12 – 15*
Creamer, small...	*4 – 6*
Creamer..	*4 – 6*
Cup..	*4 – 6*

Airflow: Solid color bread & butter and small creamer (Mexican decal).

Dish, 5¼"* .... $2 – $3
Plate, 6¼" .... 1 – 2
Plate, 7"* .... 4 – 5
Plate, 9"* .... 5 – 7
Platter, 11¼" .... 10 – 12
Saucer .... 1 – 2
Sugar .... 8 – 10
Sugar, small .... 8 – 10

ANNETTE   (mid 1933)

A rim of birds, flowers, and urns encircled by a gadroon-effect embossment. This is Mt. Clemens's Vogue shape.

Bowl, salad, 9"* .... $15 – $18
Bowl, soup, 8"* .... 10 – 12
Bowl, vegetable, oval, 9"* .... 10 – 12
Casserole .... 20 – 25
Creamer .... 4 – 6
Cup .... 4 – 6
Dish, 5¼"* .... 2 – 3
Plate, 6¼"* .... 1 – 2
Plate, 9"* .... 5 – 7
Platter, 11"* .... 10 – 12

Saucer . . . . *$1 – $2*
Sugar . . . . *8 – 10*

IONIC

I have seen hand-painted decorations on this shape confused with pieces made by Southern Potteries.

Bowl, salad, 9". . . . . *$15 – $18*
Bowl, vegetable, oval, 9"* . . . . *10 – 12*
Cake dome, finger hole, 9½" . . . . *25 – 30*
Casserole . . . . *20 – 25*
Creamer . . . . *4 – 6*
Cup . . . . *4 – 6*
Dish, 5½"* . . . . *2 – 3*
Plate, 6" . . . . *1 – 2*
Plate, 10¼" . . . . *10 – 12*
Platter, 11"* . . . . *10 – 12*
Saucer . . . . *1 – 2*
Sugar . . . . *8 – 10*

OXFORD   (<1932)

This is a Mt. Clemens shape.

Bowl, salad, 9"* . . . . *$15 – $18*
Bowl, soup, 8"* . . . . *10 – 12*
Bowl, vegetable, oval, 9"* . . . . *10 – 12*
Casserole . . . . *20 – 25*
Creamer . . . . *4 – 6*
Cup . . . . *4 – 6*
Dish, 6" . . . . *3 – 4*
Gravy . . . . *12 – 15*

Oxford: Plate (Acacia) and gravy (house with garden).

STEUBENVILLE POTTERY COMPANY

Steubenville, Ohio

CHAPTER AT A GLANCE

DINNERWARE
ADAM (ANTIQUE)
AMERICAN MODERN
  Glassware
  Tablecloths/Napkins
BETTY PEPPER
CONTEMPORA

MONTICELLO
OAKLEY
OLIVIA
ROSEPOINT
SHALIMAR
WOODFIELD

Begun in 1879, Steubenville made white granite and semivitreous wares typical of the period: dinnerware and toiletware. Its most famous product was American Modern dinnerware designed by Russel Wright. In its time it was the most popular dinnerware in America; by the mid 1950s over 125 million pieces had been sold. The company closed in 1959, but molds were bought by the Canonsburg Pottery, which continued to produce some pieces.

American Modern is by far the most popular Steubenville line, but Woodfield has a lot of interest because of the similarity of glazes.

MARKS Shown here are two general marks, the first of which is pre-1930, and four marks that refer to body color.

DINNERWARE

Most of the decal-decorated lines will be found on an ivory or white body, though pink and yellow bodies were also used. Steubenville's most popular line is Russel Wright's American Modern, then Woodfield and Adam Antique.

ADAM (ANTIQUE)   (1932)

An embossed design bands the hollowware and decorates the rims of the flatware with the addition of a gadroon edge. This is a traditional English style.
   Numerous floral decals were used.

Ashtray	*$6 – $8*
Candlestick, pair	*20 – 25*
Cereal, lug, 5½"	*2 – 3*
Coffee pot	*35 – 40*
Coffee pot, AD	*30 – 40*
Covered muffin	*20 – 25*
Creamer	*4 – 6*
Creamer, AD	*4 – 6*
Cup	*4 – 6*
Cup, AD	*10 – 12*
Cup, cream soup	*12 – 16*
Eggcup	*10 – 12*
Gravy	*12 – 15*
Gravy faststand	*12 – 15*
Hot water pot	*30 – 40*
Jug, 1-quart	*15 – 18*
Jug, 2-quart	*20 – 25*
Pickle	*6 – 8*
Plate, 6"	*1 – 2*
Plate, square, 6"	*2 – 3*
Plate, 7"	*4 – 5*

Adam: AD coffee pot, AD sugar, AD creamer (all with white floral decal), and teapot (red and silver lines).

Plate, 8" . . . . *$4 – $5*
Plate, 9" . . . . *5 – 7*
Plate, 10" . . . . *7 – 9*
Plate, 11" . . . . *10 – 12*
Plate, square, 8" . . . . *5 – 6*
Platter, 11" . . . . *10 – 12*
Saucer . . . . *1 – 2*
Saucer, AD . . . . *3 – 5*
Saucer, cream soup . . . . *6 – 8*
Shaker . . . . *4 – 5*
Sugar . . . . *8 – 10*
Sugar, AD . . . . *10 – 12*
Teapot . . . . *30 – 35*

AMERICAN MODERN   (1939–1959)

Designed by Russel Wright. Hard-to-find pieces include the butter, jug/carafe, handled divided relish, lidded jug, party plate, ramekin, refrigerator dish, relish rosette, stack set, and tumbler.

The **child's bowl** is the ramekin without a lid. Be careful distinguishing between the **sauce boat** and the **baker**. The size difference is the obvious clue; also the sauce boat is deeper and more oval, and its lug handles are thinner and wider than those of the baker. The **sugar** has only one handle; don't confuse it with anything else.

The **fork** and the **spoon** were made for the Woodfield shape but are collected as part of American Modern due to similarity of glaze. See Woodfield for prices.

Decorated in the following solid colors: Bean Brown, Chartreuse Curry, Coral, Granite Gray, Seafoam Blue (a deep turquoise), and White were the original colors; during World War II, Black Chutney replaced Bean Brown, and Cedar Green was added. Cantaloupe and Glacier Blue (powder blue speckled with darker blue) were added in the 1950s.

Steubenville Blue, also added in 1950s, is thought to be an attempt to return Seafoam to the line, but it couldn't be duplicated. Very little turns up.

Some decorations will turn up: Spencerian and Chutney Leaf are known.

PRICING   Coral and Gray are at the low end of the range, Chartreuse is in the middle, and Seafoam is at the high end. Add 25% for Cedar and Chutney. Add 100% for Bean Brown, Cantaloupe, Glacier Blue, Steubenville Blue, and White.

While decorated pieces are rare, they are priced the same as solid-color pieces.

Ashtray/coaster, 3½" . . . . *$12 – $15*
Bowl, vegetable, round, lug handles (baker), 9¾". . . . . *25 – 30*
Bowl, rectangular, vegetable, 9½" × 6¾" × 2¼" deep . . . . *15 – 18*
Bowl, rectangular, salad, 11" × 7½" × 4¾" deep . . . . *50 – 60*
Butter. . . . . *150 – 200*
Casserole, stick handle . . . . *45 – 50*
Celery . . . . *25 – 30*
Child's bowl *45*
Child's plate *65*

American Modern: Butter, relish rosette, and tall water jug.

American Modern: AD coffee pot, teapot, shakers, and coffee pot.

American Modern: This picture of the original cup and two restyled versions provide an interesting example of the basics of ergonomic design. The original cup (left) has a severely turned-in lip. To drain it you will have to hit your nose with the cup rim or tilt your head back at an extreme angle. And the handle is too small to accommodate even one finger. It is not comfortable to drink from. The first restyling (center) is an improvement with its larger handle, but the lip is still turned in. The second (right) is more successful.

Child's tumbler . . . . *$45 – $50*
Coffee pot . . . . *110 – 150*
Coffee pot, AD . . . . *45 – 60*
Creamer . . . . *12 – 15*

Cup . . . . *$12 – $15*
Cup, AD . . . . *20 – 25*
Cup cover . . . . *75 – 100*
Dish, lug, fruit, 5¼" . . . . *10 – 12*
Dish, lug, soup, 5¾" . . . . *12 – 14*
Gravy, 10½" . . . . *18 – 20*
Gravy liner/pickle, 11" . . . . *15 – 18*
Jug, water, tall . . . . *65 – 90*
Jug, w/lid . . . . *150 – 175*
Jug/carafe . . . . *125 – 140*
  w/stopper . . . . *ND*
Plate, 6¼" . . . . *5 – 7*
Plate, 8" . . . . *15 – 18*
Plate, 10" . . . . *10 – 12*
Plate, party, 11½" × 10" . . . . *45 – 50*
Platter, divided, 13" × 9½" . . . . *50 – 60*
Platter, rectangular, 9" × 13½" . . . . *20 – 25*
Platter, square, 13" . . . . *20 – 25*
Ramekin, individual w/lid, 5" . . . . *100 – 125*
Refrigerator dish, w/lid, 5¼" . . . . *100 – 125*
Relish, divided, w/handle . . . . *125 – 150*
Relish rosette, 11" . . . . *125 +*
Sauce boat, 7¾" . . . . *35 – 40*
Saucer . . . . *2 – 3*
Saucer, AD . . . . *10 – 12*
Shaker . . . . *8 – 10*
Stack set . . . . *165 – 200*
Sugar . . . . *12 – 14*
Teapot . . . . *65 – 75*
Tumbler/Mug . . . . *45 – 50*
Vegetable, round, w/lid, 12" . . . . *40 – 45*

Glassware

Came in colors of Chartreuse, Coral, Crystal, Smoke Gray, and Seafoam. The ice tea, juice, and water originally sold for $4.95 for a set of twelve. Stemmed pieces have an /S in the list below; these are easier to find than tumblers.

Chilling bowl w/liner . . . . *$75 +*
Cocktail   /S . . . . *18 – 20*
Cordial   /S . . . . *30 – 35*
Dish, dessert . . . . *30 – 35*
Double old-fashioned . . . . *75 +*
Goblet   /S . . . . *18 – 25*
Iced tea . . . . *30 – 35*
Juice . . . . *20 – 25*
Pilsner . . . . *65 – 75*
Sherbet   /S . . . . *15 – 18*
Water (luncheon) . . . . *25 – 30*
Wine   /S . . . . *18 – 20*

Tablecloths / Napkins

Abstract and Brush Stroke were made by Leacock; Plaid was made by Simtex Modern.

Napkins were 15" × 15" in solid colors of Gray, Seafoam, or Yellow. Cloths (original price) were 54" × 54" ($5.95), 54" × 72" ($8.95), and 63" × 80" ($10.95). They came in three patterns and varying color combinations, as follows.

PRICING Napkins: $15 to $20. Tablecloths: $65 to $75.

Brush Stroke	*Abstract*	*Plaid*
Coral on Gray	Coral on Gray	Coral on Gray
Chartreuse on Yellow	Chartreuse on Yellow	Chartreuse on Yellow
Gray on Gray	Gray on Gray	Seafoam on Yellow
Seafoam on Gray	Chartreuse on Gray	Black Chutney on Seafoam
Gray on Yellow		

BETTY PEPPER (1936)

A shape designed for the Associated Merchandising Corporation and sold exclusively through their member stores, such as Bloomingdale's in New York, Joseph Horne in Pittsburgh, and Hudson's in Detroit. The shape is a plain round with slightly rounded lug handles and finials on some pieces.

Betty Pepper was decal-decorated, mainly floral designs, with band treatments featured. Known decorations are Garden Gate (flowers on a picket fence), Somerset (unknown), and a water lily decal.

Bowl, vegetable, oval. . . . . *$10 – $12*
Casserole . . . . *20 – 25*

Betty Pepper: Teapot.

Creamer . . . . *$4 – $6*
Cup . . . . *4 – 6*
Dish, 5¹/₂" . . . . *2 – 3*
Gravy faststand . . . . *12 – 15*
Plate, 6¹/₄"* . . . . *1 – 2*
Plate, 9"* . . . . *5 – 7*
Platter, 13¹/₂" . . . . *12 – 15*
Saucer . . . . *1 – 2*
Sugar . . . . *8 – 10*
Teapot, 2-cup . . . . *15 – 20*

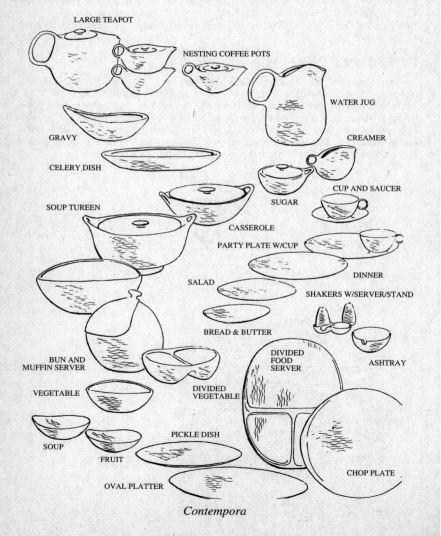

LARGE TEAPOT

NESTING COFFEE POTS

WATER JUG

GRAVY

CREAMER

CELERY DISH

SUGAR

CUP AND SAUCER

SOUP TUREEN

CASSEROLE

PARTY PLATE W/CUP

DINNER

SALAD

SHAKERS W/SERVER/STAND

BREAD & BUTTER

BUN AND
MUFFIN SERVER

DIVIDED
FOOD
SERVER

ASHTRAY

VEGETABLE

DIVIDED
VEGETABLE

SOUP

PICKLE DISH

FRUIT

CHOP PLATE

OVAL PLATTER

Contempora

CONTEMPORA

Designed for Raymor by Ben Seibel. "Rippling sgraffito texture harmonizes with new and exciting color." Colors are Charcoal, Fawn, Mist Gray, and Sand White.

Ashtray	*$15*
Bowl, salad, 11"	*50*
Bowl, soup, 6³/₄"	*12*
Bowl, vegetable, 9"	*20*
Bowl, vegetable, divided, 9"	*35*
Bun and Muffin server	*125 +*
Casserole	*45*
Celery dish, 13³/₄"	*35*
Coaster	*10*
Coffee pot, nesting	*65*
Creamer	*15*
Cup	*9*
Dish, fruit, 6"	*5*
Gravy	*25*
Jug	*90*
Pickle dish, 10¹/₂"	*10*
Plate, 7"	*4*
Plate, 8³/₄"	*6*
Plate, 10¹/₂"	*8*
Plate, chop, 14¹/₄"	*35*
Plate, party, 10¹/₂"	*25*
Platter, divided (food server), 3-section, 16¹/₄"	*45*
Platter, oval, 14¹/₂"	*15*
Saucer	*3*
Shaker	*10*
Shaker server w/handle	*15*
Sugar	*15*
Teapot	*65*
Tureen	*250 +*

MONTICELLO

Distributed by Herman Kupper. A round, gadroon-edged shape.

Look for two solid "pâté-sur-pâté" colors of coral and blue. There are a number of decals: "Shadowy gray fronds and blue berries" were used on two decorations: "Prince Charming" had a coral background, and "Cinderella" had a gray-blue background.

MARKS That is Jefferson's house pictured in the mark.

Bowl, vegetable, oval, 9"* . . . . *$10 – $12*
Bowl, soup, lug . . . . *10 – 12*
Casserole . . . . *20 – 25*
Creamer . . . . *4 – 6*
Cup . . . . *4 – 6*
Dish, 5¹/₂"* . . . . *2 – 3*
Plate, 6¹/₄"* . . . . *1 – 2*
Plate, 10¹/₂" . . . . *7 – 9*
Platter, 11"* . . . . *10 – 12*
Saucer . . . . *1 – 2*
Sugar . . . . *8 – 10*

OAKLEY

See Olivia.

OLIVIA   (1926)

A gadroon edge shape. Steubenville made a similar shape called Oakley. The difference seems to be that Oakley had acorn finials on the covered pieces and was a round shape. The bottoms of the batter set were used earlier; Steubenville designed new lids for Olivia.

Bowl, salad, 8¹/₂" . . . . *$15 – $18*
Bowl, soup, 8¹/₄" . . . . *10 – 12*
Bowl, vegetable, oval, 9" . . . . *10 – 12*
Butter dish . . . . *20 – 25*
Butter dish, square . . . . *25 – 30*
Casserole . . . . *20 – 25*

Olivia: Back: *AD coffee pot, plate (Bouquet of Tulips), and Cattail creamer (this is the decal commonly found on Universal pieces). Front: Breakfast set hot water pot (lavender), AD open sugar, teapot, eggcup, and AD creamer.*

Coffee pot, AD	*$30 – $40*
Covered toast	*20 – 25*
Creamer	*4 – 6*
Creamer, AD	*6 – 8*
Cup	*4 – 6*
Cup, AD	*10 – 12*
Dish, 5¼"	*2 – 3*
Dish, 6"	*3 – 4*
Eggcup	*10 – 12*
Gravy	*12 – 15*
Gravy faststand	*12 – 15*
Gravy liner	*6 – 8*
Hot water pot	*30 – 40*
Jug, batter	*25 – 30*
Jug, syrup	*20 – 25*
Plate, 6"	*1 – 2*
Plate, 9"	*5 – 7*
Plate, 9½"	*7 – 9*
Plate, cake, embossed lug, 10¾"	*10 – 12*
Platter, 11"	*10 – 12*
Platter, 13"	*12 – 15*
Platter, 15"	*15 – 18*
Platter, 16¾"	*18 – 20*
Saucer	*1 – 2*
Saucer, AD	*3 – 5*
Sugar	*8 – 10*
Sugar, AD, open	*6 – 8*
Teapot	*30 – 35*

ROSEPOINT

Steubenville bought the Rosepoint molds from Pope-Gosser when that company closed in 1958. Since Steubenville closed in 1959, they did not make it for very long. The only piece I've seen had the Pope-Gosser mark with "by Steubenville" added below. Use Pope-Gosser pricing.

SHALIMAR   (1938)

The surface has a lightly embossed pattern of flowers and fronds. Made in three colors: ivory, pink, and white.

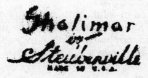

Bowl, vegetable, oval, 9"*	*$10 – $12*
Casserole	*20 – 25*

Shalimar: Coffee pot.

Coffee pot	$35 – $40
Creamer	4 – 6
Cup	4 – 6
Dish, 5½"	2 – 3
Plate, 6¼"*	1 – 2
Plate, 9"*	5 – 7
Platter, 11"*	10 – 12
Saucer	1 – 2
Sugar	8 – 10

WOODFIELD (1941)

Distinguished by the leaf pattern on the body and the leaf finials on the covered pieces. There are two styles of cup; one has more of a foot than the other. The small party plate paired with a cup was called a Tea-and-Toast Set, the large party plate with a cup was called a Video Set. While party plates can be hard to find in other shapes, it is probably the most common piece in Woodfield. The small bowl is about the size of the cereal/salad, only deeper, and was available with or without the lid. The fork and spoon, although made for this set, are collected with the American Modern line, which shares glazes with this line. These utensils were made by Universal and most likely shipped in the bisque stage to Steubenville, where they were glazed.

Woodfield was introduced in solid colors of Dove Gray, Golden Fawn (chartreuse), Jungle Green, and Salmon Pink. These were exactly the same glazes as were used on American Modern but with the names changed, as follows:

Chartreuse Curry = Golden Fawn
Coral = Salmon Pink
Granite Gray = Dove Gray
Seafoam Blue = Jungle Green

Rust and Tropic (dark green) were added in 1951; Tropic probably replaced Jungle Green at this time. Rust is not found as readily as the other colors.

I have seen a Golden Fawn teapot with gold outlining on the leaves. It is not an effective decoration; the gold does not show up well on chartreuse. I assume this was not done at the factory.

PRICING   Golden Fawn is at the low end of the range; Jungle Green, Rust, and Tropic are at the high end; and Gray and Pink are in the middle.

Woodfield
MFG BY
STEUBENVILLE

Ashtray, 4½"	*$12 – $15*
Bowl, salad, round, 11"	*15 – 18*
Bowl, vegetable, square, divided (diagonally)	*20 – 25*
Bowl, vegetable, oval, 10½"	*18 – 20*
Bowl, individual	*12 – 15*
w/lid	*20 – 25*
Butter, ¼-pound	*40 – 50*
Celery-Centerpiece, footed, 11½"	*20 – 25*
Creamer	*8 – 10*
Creamer, large	*8 – 10*
Cup, both styles	*8 – 10*
Dish, cereal/salad	*5 – 7*
Gravy, stick handle	*12 – 15*
Jug, 9½" tall	*35 – 45*
Mug, handled	*15 – 18*
Plate, 6¾"	*2 – 3*
Plate, 9"	*7 – 9*
Plate, 10½"	*10 – 12*
Plate, chop, 13½"	*15 – 18*

Woodfield: Small creamer and sugar, shakers, teapot, quarter-pound butter, and large creamer and sugar.

Plate, party (Tea-and-Toast), 9" .... *$6 – $8*
Plate, party (Video Set) .... *14 – 16*
Platter, oval, 13½" .... *12 – 15*
Relish, 2-part, 9½" .... *30 – 35*
Saucer .... *2 – 3*
Shaker, each .... *8 – 10*
Sugar .... *12 – 15*
Sugar, large .... *12 – 15*
Teapot .... *35 – 40*
Utensil, fork .... *45 – 60*
Utensil, spoon .... *45 – 60*
Utilitray, 10¼" .... *15 – 20*

TAMAC POTTERY

Perry, Oklahoma

The name Tamac is a joining of the first initials of the last names of the two couples who founded the pottery, Leonard and Marjorie *Ta*te and Allen and Betty *Mac*auley. The two couples met in New York, became good friends, and in September 1946 decided to start a pottery business. They chose Perry, Oklahoma, where Leonard Tate had been born and raised.

They built a small plant behind Leonard's father's garage and used a white-bodied clay from Georgia because of its ability to withstand high firing temperatures. The business grew rapidly, and in 1949, utilizing free land donated by the state as part of an industrial promotion, as well as money from stock sales, they built a new plant on a cross-country highway. This brought tourists, and daily tours were given. The business continued to expand.

The Macauleys, grown tired, sold their interest in Tamac to the Tates. There were cash flow problems because the wholesale accounts, a growing part of the business, did not pay until orders were completed. The local banks were not supportive, and the Tates were forced into bankruptcy and eventual sale of Tamac in 1952.

It was bought by Earl Bechtold and run by his son Raymond. They added additional pieces to the line but also ran into financial problems and sold Tamac in 1963. New freeways and turnpikes rerouted the flow of tourists, and the new owners, Robert and Lenita Moore, were forced to close in 1972.

See Bibliography for upcoming Oklahoma pottery book by Phyllis and Tom Bess.

GLAZES   The glazes in order of introduction are as follows: Butterscotch (yellow with brown trim), Avocado (yellow-green trimmed in darker green), Frosty Pine (pine green with a foam trim), Frosty Fudge (soft brown with foam), and Raspberry (pink with foam). Butterscotch was soon discontinued due to quality inconsistencies and firing problems. In later years, Honey was added (ivory beige).

Avocado, Frosty Fudge, and Frosty Pine are the more easily found colors. Raspberry is rare and was not used on every piece. It was mostly available on dinnerware.

MARKS   Two types of marks were used. The first was incised and the later was a black backstamp. They both read "TAMAC Perry, Oklahoma, U.S.A."

DINNERWARE

Tamac advertised its dinnerware as "free form," though this applies to almost all the pieces they made. "We do not let our own convenience rule our choice of designs. Instead, we form every piece to fit your hand, nestle for easy storage, and to hold plenty of food or drink. Tamac is made to be used. Our modern free-form shapes subtly change when viewed from different angles."

I have listed what collectors call the tall teapot as an AD coffee pot because it is not that big and relates in size to the AD cups and saucers. The fruit, soup, and serving bowls are basically the same shape, just different sizes.

AD coffee pot with AD cup and saucer seen from two different angles.

PRICING Double prices for Raspberry.

Bowl, cereal/soup, 16-ounce .... $7 – $8
Bowl, serving, 1-quart, 8" .... 8 – 9
Bowl, serving, 2-quart, 10" .... 12 – 15
Bowl, serving, 4-quart, 13" .... 15 – 18
Bowl, soup, 12-ounce, 6" .... 7 – 8
Butter, open .... 25 – 35
Casserole, 2-quart .... 45 – 50
Coffee pot, AD .... 70 – 75
Creamer, 8-ounce .... 6 – 8
Creamer, AD .... 9 – 10
Cup, AD, 2-ounce .... 12 – 15
Cup, barbecue, 10-ounce .... 6 – 8
Cup, coffee, 8-ounce .... 5 – 7
Cup, tea, 6-ounce, round .... 7 – 8
Decanter w/stopper, 1-quart .... 60 – 65
Dish, fruit, 8-ounce .... 6 – 8
Goblet, 6-ounce 15
Gravy, faststand, 16-ounce .... 15 – 20
Jug, juice, 24-ounce .... 20 – 25
Jug, w/ice guard, 2-quart .... 30 – 35
Jug, 4-quart (holds 3 quarts) .... 25 – 30
Mug, closed handle, 12-ounce .... 10 – 12
Mug, open handle, 12-ounce .... 15 – 18
Plate, 7" .... 7 – 8
Plate, 8¼" .... 8 – 9
Plate, 10" .... 9 – 10
Plate, barbecue, 15" .... 12 – 15
Plate, chop, 18" .... 25 – 35
Platter, 12" .... 12 – 15
Relish, divided .... 12 – 15
Saucer, 6" .... 3 – 4

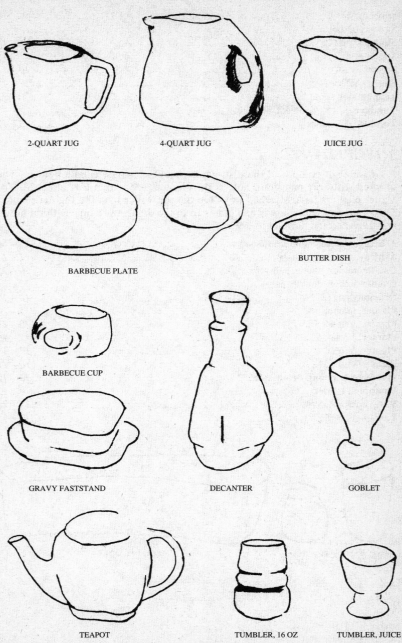

2-QUART JUG　　4-QUART JUG　　JUICE JUG

BARBECUE PLATE　　BUTTER DISH

BARBECUE CUP

GRAVY FASTSTAND　　DECANTER　　GOBLET

TEAPOT　　TUMBLER, 16 OZ　　TUMBLER, JUICE

Dinnerware

Saucer, AD .... *$8 – $10*
Saucer, barbecue, 7" .... *4 – 5*
Shakers, pair .... *8 – 10*
Spoon rest .... *12 – 15*
Sugar .... *10 – 12*
Sugar, AD, open .... *9 – 10*
Teapot, long spout, 3-pint .... *70 – 75*
Tumbler, juice, stemmed, 4-ounce .... *5 – 7*
Tumbler, 16-ounce .... *8 – 12*

MISCELLANY

A **console set** comprised the dish garden and two single candle holders. The **planter** with tray and drain hole is the planter/vase with a tray attached. The Violet planters have attached trays too but are wider than the regular planter. Tamac marketed the bowls and plates from the dinnerware line as floral bowls and trays and the tumbler as a vase.

Ashtray, club/diamond/heart/spade.. *$5 – $6*
Ashtray, Oklahoma shape... *12 – 15*
Candle holder, single, pair .... *20 – 25*
Candle holder, double, pair .... *30 – 35*
Dish garden, 12" .... *12 – 15*
Planter, mantel, 14" .... *15 – 20*
Planter, mantel, 18" .... *20 – 25*
Planter, Violet, 5" .... *12 – 15*
Planter, Violet, 6" .... *12 – 15*
Planter/Vase, 5" .... *10 – 12*
Planter w/tray and drain hole, 5"... *12 – 15*
Toothpick holder .... *10 – 12*
Vase, freeform, 5½".. *15 – 20*
Vase, wall, 5" high... *12 – 15*

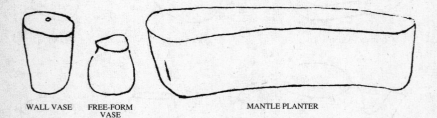

WALL VASE   FREE-FORM   MANTLE PLANTER
              VASE

Accessory Pieces

TAYLOR, SMITH & TAYLOR COMPANY

Chester, West Virginia

CHAPTER AT A GLANCE

DINNERWARE	
BEVERLY	Coral-Craft
DELPHIAN	MARVEL
EMPIRE	PARAMOUNT
FAIRWAY	PASTORAL
GARLAND	PEBBLEFORD
LAUREL	PLYMOUTH
Taverne	VISTOSA
LURAY	VOGUE

In 1899, John Taylor, Charles and William Smith, and Joseph Lee announced the formation of the Taylor, Smith and Lee Company to be located in Chester, West Virginia (an East Liverpool, Ohio postal address was used for business purposes). Construction began in January of 1900, and ware was on the market a year later.

In 1901, Joseph Lee left the company, and the name changed to Taylor, Smith & Taylor. White granite may have been manufactured in the early years, but most of the company's production was in semiporcelain: toilet ware, dinnerware, kitchenware, and specialties. In 1972 the company was sold to Anchor Hocking, which continued production until 1981.

Luray, the pastel solid-color dinnerware, has the most collector interest. Vistosa, the bright solid-color dinnerware, would have more interest if the line were more extensive.

MARKS   The Gryphon backstamp is probably the first mark used by the company. The TST crossed over the star dates from the 1910s to the 1920s. The Shield backstamp was used from at least the late 1920s to 1935. The Wreath backstamp was used from 1936 to at least 1953. The Premier backstamp was announced in March 1934 for use on the Vogue shape and on ware with better treatments. Madrid, a backstamp used by itself, refers to a deep yellow glaze and probably dates from the late 1920s to the mid 1930s.

With the exception of Luray, Vistosa, and Coral-Craft, TST seems to have abandoned specific shape marks in the 1930s.

DINNERWARE

A solid green glaze, sometimes decorated with silver trim, and Madrid, a solid deep yellow glaze, which will be found with decals, were both used on the Paramount shape. Rose-Mist, a pink body, was introduced around September of 1930 and used with the Capitol, Garland, and Paramount shapes, if not others.

EARLY DINNERWARE   A number of lines from the 1920s will be found, though not easily. These include Avona (TST's version of Havilland's Ranson shape), Belva, Capitol, Iona, Latona, Pennova, Regal (a square shape), and Verona (a plain round shape).

NOTE   The Luray line is based on two earlier shapes, Empire and Laurel. Some collectors think of these as "Luray shapes with decals." They are distinctive shapes in their own right.

BEVERLY   (1936)

An embossed band of three strips of alternating squares encircled the rims and the edges of the hollowware bodies, most of which have square, four-footed bases.

NOTE   Beverly uses the flatware introduced a few months earlier for the Delphian shape. Reusing flatware for different shapes is not unusual, except that generally plain round shapes were involved in this practice. I've never seen it done with as elaborate a design as Delphian/Beverly. I suspect that the Delphian hollowware was either too difficult to produce or too fragile because of that exuberant finial, so TS&T restyled the hollowware and named it Beverly.

Butter dish	$20 – $23
Casserole	20 – 25
Creamer	4 – 6
Cup	4 – 6
Gravy	12 – 15
Plate, 6¼"	1 – 2

Beverly: Sugar, creamer, plate (blades of grass and floating flowers), and casserole. In order to determine if a plate has a Beverly or Delphian decal (and it could be both), you need to find matching hollowware to confirm.

Plate, 9¼"	*$7 – $9*
Plate, 10¼"	*10 – 12*
Saucer	*1 – 2*
Sugar	*8 – 10*

DELPHIAN   (mid 1935)

An embossed band of three strips of alternating squares encircled the rims and the hollowware bodies. See Beverly, above.

Delphian: Sugar (Trumpet Flower), plate (Fence and Roses), cup (Petitpoint), and casserole (Trumpet Flower).

Decals: Look for the Rose, an underglaze print in either blue, green, or pink.

Casserole . . . . $20 – $25
Creamer . . . . 4 – 6
Cup . . . . 4 – 6
Plate, 6¼" . . . . 1 – 2
Plate, 9¼" . . . . 7 – 9
Plate, 10¼" . . . . 10 – 12
Saucer . . . . 1 – 2
Sugar . . . . 8 – 10

EMPIRE   (1936)

A plain round shape, with budlike finials on the lids. The hollowware in this shape was used for the Luray line, as well as for the flatware that it shared with Laurel. Any sighting of "Luray in Ivory with decals" is Empire.

Note: The sugar without handles seems to date from the 1940s. I am not positive that it's a sugar, but it's too small for a drip, and there are no range shakers, so sugar it is.

Bowl, soup, 7¾" . . . . $10 – $12
Bowl, 36s . . . . 7 – 10
Bowl, vegetable, oval, 9¼" . . . . 10 – 12
Bowl, vegetable, oval, 10¼" . . . . 10 – 12
Butter dish . . . . 20 – 25
Casserole . . . . 20 – 25
Creamer . . . . 4 – 6
Cup . . . . 4 – 6
Dish, 5⅜" . . . . 2 – 3
Dish, lug, 5⅞" . . . . 3 – 4
Gravy . . . . 12 – 15

Empire: Creamer (Lu-Ray Persian Yellow with brown sunflower/unmarked), teapot (Lu-Ray Persian Yellow with a sprayed-on band of rust brown; you will also find pieces with sprayed double bands of brown and blue), and sugar (Acacia).

Gravy liner/pickle, 9¹/₂" .... *$6 – $8*
Plate, 6¹/₄" .... *1 – 2*
Plate, 7¹/₄" .... *4 – 5*
Plate, 8¹/₄" .... *4 – 5*
Plate, 9¹/₄" .... *7 – 9*
Plate, 10" .... *10 – 12*
Platter, oval, 7¹/₈" .... *6 – 8*
Platter, oval, 11¹/₂" .... *10 – 12*
Platter, oval, 13¹/₂" .... *12 – 15*
Saucer .... *1 – 2*
Sugar .... *8 – 10*
Sugar, no handles .... *8 – 10*
Teapot .... *30 – 35*

FAIRWAY   (1934–1940>)

A scalloped rim with periodic groups of embossed roses dropping into the well of the flatware and encircling the hollowware. Offered originally in short sets, it was expanded to a complete service by mid 1934.

Bowl, lug soup, 6" .... *$10 – $12*
Casserole .... *20 – 25*
Creamer .... *4 – 6*
Cup .... *4 – 6*
Dish, 5¹/₈" .... *2 – 3*
Eggcup .... *10 – 12*
Gravy .... *12 – 15*
Plate, 6¹/₄" .... *1 – 2*
Plate, 7¹/₄" .... *4 – 5*
Plate, 9¹/₄" .... *7 – 9*
Plate, 10" .... *10 – 12*

Fairway: Flower Cart sugar, plate (Poppies), cup (floral), and creamer (flowerpots).

Platter, oval, 11½" .... *$10 – $12*
Saucer .... *1 – 2*
Sugar .... *8 – 10*

GARLAND   (1933–1942>)

Originally brought out as a short set, it was later expanded. Distinguished by a scalloped rim with embossed leaves that extend slightly into the well.

Available in green, yellow, or decal-decorated on Old Ivory. One of the more heavily promoted decorations is Castle, an underglaze print in either black, blue, green, or pink.

Bowl, lug soup, 6" .... *$10 – $12*
Bowl, soup, 7¾" .... *10 – 12*
Creamer .... *4 – 6*
Cup .... *4 – 6*
Cup, cream soup .... *12 – 16*
Dish, lug, 6" .... *3 – 4*
Plate, 6¼" .... *1 – 2*
Plate, 7" .... *4 – 5*
Plate, lug, 10¼" .... *10 – 12*
Platter, 11½" .... *10 – 12*
Saucer .... *1 – 2*
Sugar, open .... *4 – 6*
Teapot .... *20 – 25*

LAUREL   (1933)

Designed by J. Palin Thorley. This is TS&T's first thin-rim shape. The flatware had an embossed tab handle, and the lids had an embossed ray effect around the finials. It was used as the flatware in the Empire shape and the Luray line.

Decals: Look for Aster (a stylized center motif in two tones of either blue, gray, green, or red), "Chintz" (an allover pattern in gray and green with touches of yellow), and Pannier (a colorful fruit basket design). For Taverne, see below.

Garland: Cup, plate, Pink Castle cream soup, and teapot.

Laurel: Teapot (silver tassel).

Bowl, 36s	*$7 – $10*
Bowl, soup, 7½"	*10 – 12*
Bowl, vegetable, oval, 9¼"	*10 – 12*
Bowl, vegetable, oval, 10¼"	*12 – 15*
Butter dish	*20 – 25*
Casserole	*20 – 25*
Creamer	*4 – 6*
Cup	*4 – 6*
Cup, cream soup	*12 – 16*
Dish, 5¼"	*2 – 3*
Gravy	*12 – 15*
Gravy liner/pickle, 9½"	*6 – 8*
Plate, 6¼"	*1 – 2*
Plate, 7¼"	*4 – 5*
Plate, 8½"	*4 – 5*
Plate, 9¼"	*7 – 9*
Plate, 10"	*10 – 12*
Plate, cake, round, 10¾"	*10 – 12*
Platter, oval, 7" × 5"	*8 – 10*
Platter, oval, 11½"	*10 – 12*
Platter, oval, 13½"	*12 – 15*
Saucer	*1 – 2*
Saucer, cream soup	*6 – 8*
Sugar	*8 – 10*
Teapot	*30 – 35*

SPECIAL PRICE LIST

TAVERNE

This decal is most associated with Hall China, but Hall's Taverne dinnerware is hard to find; pieces of TS&T's Taverne dinnerware are only a

Taverne: Laurel butter dish, Vogue salad bowl, and Laurel cup w/Taverne decal on one side and You Are Drinking "Hellick's" Triple City Blend *on the reverse.*

little easier to find. Most pieces are the Laurel shape; the shape name follows the listing.

Bowl, salad   /Vogue . . . . *$30 – $35*
Bowl, soup, 7½"   /Laurel. . . . . *20 – 25*
Bowl, 36s . . . . *20 – 25*
Bowl, vegetable, 9¼"   /Laurel. . . . . *30 – 35*
Butter dish   /Laurel. . . . . *100 – 125*
Casserole   /Laurel . . . . *45 – 60*
Creamer   /Laurel. . . . . *20 – 22*
Cup   /Laurel . . . . *15 – 20*
Dish, 5½"   /Laurel . . . . *8 – 10*
Gravy   /Laurel. . . . . *20 – 25*
Gravy liner, 9½"   /Laurel. . . . . *10 – 15*
Plate, 6½"   /Laurel . . . . *5 – 7*
Plate, 9¼"   /Laurel . . . . *15 – 20*
Platter, small, 7" × 5"   /Laurel. . . . . *20 – 25*
Platter, 11½"   /Laurel. . . . . *25 – 30*
Platter, 13½"   /Laurel. . . . . *30 – 35*
Saucer   /Laurel . . . . *3 – 4*
St. Denis cup . . . . *35 – 45*
St. Denis saucer. . . . . *15 – 20*
Sugar   /Laurel. . . . . *25 – 30*

LURAY   (mid 1938)

Named after the Luray Caverns. Some TS&T ads refer to their "Luray shape," but actually Luray is an amalgam of two shapes and several pickup pieces. The hollowware is Empire (except for the Laurel cream soup), and the flatware is Laurel/Empire (see above). The teacup and the AD cup belong to neither line, having been designed specifically for Luray. In the listing below, I have marked E or L next to the hollowware to indicate the shape; unmarked items are pickup pieces (see "Background on Dinnerware").

Luray is a good example of how potteries added additional items to popular lines. For example, the juice pitches and tumblers, quarter-pound butter, and salad bowl were added in 1941.

Luray came in Windsor Blue, Surf Green, Persian Cream (yellow), and Sharon Pink. Chatham Grey was added in 1948. Decals were used on the colored pieces as early as 1938. These pieces are elusive. Decal-decorated ivory pieces marked Luray occasionally turn up; these seem to be from the late 1940s. Matching silverware and glass tumblers (three sizes) were also available.

NOTE   The coasters that some identify with Luray were brought out around 1943. They were *not* advertised as being part of Luray and came in sets of four colors: blue, green, ivory, and pink. However, I have included them here since three of the four colors belong to the Luray line.

MARKS   Luray bears the backstamp above or just "USA."

PRICING   No one color of the original four seems to be more desirable. Though gray is hard to find, not that many collectors are actively seeking it. For gray, add 20% to 50% for the easier-to-find pieces such as cups, saucers, 6" and 9" plates, and shakers; add 50% to 100% for such hard-to-find pieces as the butter dish, grill plates, 8" plate, and the AD pieces.

Some hard-to-find pieces such as the salad bowl and flat water jug turn up a lot more often in yellow than in the other colors. These are priced accordingly in the list below.

Luray: Chocolate set sugar, creamer, cup, and saucer.

Bowl, mixing, 5½" . . . . *$45 – $50*
Bowl, mixing, 6¾" . . . . *55 – 75*
Bowl, mixing, 8¾" . . . . *75 – 95*
Bowl, mixing, 10" . . . . *90 – 120*
Bowl, salad, 9¾" . . . . *35 – 45*
    Yellow . . . . *25 – 30*
Bowl, soup, 7¾" . . . . *10 – 12*
Bowl, 36s . . . . *30 – 40*
Bowl, vegetable, oval, 10½" . . . . *8 – 10*
Bowl, vegetable, round, 9" . . . . *10 – 12*
Bud urn . . . . *120 – 140*
Bud vase . . . . *120 – 140*
Butter, ¼-pound   /E . . . . *30 – 35*
Casserole, 8"   /E . . . . *85 – 95*
Chocolate set creamer . . . . *40 – 50*
Chocolate set cup . . . . *40 – 50*
Chocolate set pot . . . . *150 – 175*
Chocolate set saucer . . . . *15 – 20*
Chocolate set sugar . . . . *50 – 70*
Coaster, 3" . . . . *25 – 30*
Coffee pot, AD   /E . . . . *85 – 100*
Creamer   /E . . . . *3 – 5*
Creamer, AD   /E . . . . *18 – 25*
Cup . . . . *3 – 5*
Cup, AD . . . . *12 – 15*
Cup, cream soup   /L . . . . *40 – 50*
Dish, 5" . . . . *2 – 3*
Dish, lug, 6¼" . . . . *12 – 15*
Eggcup . . . . *12 – 15*

Luray: Bud vase, urn vase, and epergne.

Epergne . . . . *$90 – $100*
Gravy /E . . . . *15 – 18*
Gravy faststand /E . . . . *15 – 20*
Gravy liner/pickle, 9½" . . . . *15 – 18*
Jug, juice, 38-ounce /E . . . . *100 – 125*
Jug, water, flat, 76-ounce /E . . . . *35 – 45*
 Yellow . . . . *25 – 35*
Jug, water, footed, 76-ounce /E . . . . *40 – 50*
Muffin cover /E . . . . *85 – 100*
Nut dish, 4½" . . . . *40 – 50*
Plate, 6¼" . . . . *1 – 3*
Plate, 7¼" . . . . *4 – 6*
Plate, 8½" . . . . *10 – 15*
Plate, 9¼" . . . . *5 – 6*
Plate, 10" . . . . *10 – 12*
Plate, cake, lug, 11" . . . . *30 – 40*
Plate, chop, 14"–15" . . . . *20 – 25*
Plate, grill, 10" . . . . *15 – 18*
Platter, 11½" . . . . *10 – 12*
Platter, 13½" . . . . *12 – 14*
Relish, 4-section . . . . *75 – 85*
Saucer, 6" . . . . *1 – 2*
Saucer, AD . . . . *5 – 7*
Saucer, cream soup, 6½" . . . . *15 – 20*
Shaker /E . . . . *4 – 6*
Sugar /E . . . . *6 – 8*
Sugar, AD /E . . . . *25 – 35*
Teapot w/curved spout /E . . . . *50 – 70*
Teapot w/flat spout /E . . . . *70 – 90*
Tumbler, juice, 5-ounce . . . . *25 – 30*
Tumbler, water, 9-ounce . . . . *45 – 50*

CORAL-CRAFT

Introduced in 1939, this line is, essentially, pink Luray (though it is not re-fered to as Luray in TS&T's ads) with a white decoration. There were five decorations: Maple Leaf, Tulip, Floral Border, Laurel Wreath, and Chinese Temple. Use mid-range Luray prices for these pieces.

MARVEL   (1932)

Designed by J. Palin Thorley. An engraved line defines alternating wide and narrow panels with embossed groups of roses adorning the narrow panels. The lids have rosebud finials.

Bowl, salad, 9½" .... *$15 – $18*
Bowl, soup, 8" .... *10 – 12*
Bowl, vegetable, oval, 9¼" .... *10 – 12*
Bowl, vegetable, round, 8¾" .... *15 – 18*
Butter dish .... *20 – 25*
Casserole .... *20 – 25*
Creamer .... *4 – 6*
Cup .... *4 – 6*
Cup, cream soup .... *12 – 16*
Dish, 5⅛" .... *2 – 3*
Dish, 5¼" .... *2 – 3*
Dish, 6½" .... *3 – 4*
Eggcup .... *10 – 12*
Gravy .... *12 – 15*
Plate, 7" .... *4 – 5*
Plate, 9" .... *7 – 9*
Platter, 11½" .... *10 – 12*
Platter, 13½" .... *12 – 15*
Saucer .... *1 – 2*
Saucer, cream soup .... *6 – 8*
Sugar .... *8 – 10*
Teapot .... *20 – 25*

Marvelle: Sugar, plate, butter dish, gravy, and cup.

PARAMOUNT   (<1928)

A round shape with an irregular outline on the flatware, with octagonal wells, and a thin embossed line around the rim, and distinct pierced handles. There are a number of square pieces as well, including the teapot, sugar, and creamer. Some pieces will have two holes in a pierced lug handle; this is for placement of a rattan handle.

Bowl, soup, square, 7"	$10 – $12
Bowl, vegetable, rectangular, 9" × 6¾"	10 – 12
Bowl, vegetable, rectangular, 10" × 7¼"	12 – 15
Butter dish	20 – 25
Butter pat	6 – 8
Casserole, footed, rattan handle, 11" × 8¼"	20 – 25
Creamer	4 – 6
Cup	4 – 6
Dish, round, 5⅛"	2 – 3
Gravy	12 – 15
Gravy liner/pickle, 8½"	6 – 8
Jug, batter	35 – 40

Paramount: Back: *Grill plate.* Middle: *Square relish (note holes for rattan handle), batter set (green w/silver lines).* Front: *Creamer and sugar.*

Jug, syrup. . . . . *30 – 35*
Plate, 6¾". . . . . *$1 – $2*
Plate, 8". . . . . *4 – 5*
Plate, 9¾". . . . . *7 – 9*
Plate, grill, 11". . . . . *10 – 12*
Plate, square, 6". . . . . *1 – 2*
Plate, square, 9". . . . . *7 – 9*
Platter, rectangular, 13¼" × 10". . . . . *12 – 15*
Platter, rectangular, 15¾" × 11¾". . . . . *15 – 18*
Relish, square, rattan handle, 7⅛". . . . . *15 – 18*
Saucer, round, 5¾". . . . . *1 – 2*
Saucer, square, 5¾". . . . . *1 – 2*
Sugar . . . . *8 – 10*
Teapot . . . . *20 – 25*

PASTORAL   (ca. 1954)

This pattern was made for Quaker Oats by both TS&T and Homer Laughlin.

Cup . . . . *$4 – $6*
Dish, 5¾". . . . . *2 – 3*
Plate, 6½". . . . . *1 – 2*
Saucer . . . . *1 – 2*

PEBBLEFORD

A decoration on the Versatile shape. Designed by John Gilkes. A plain round coupe shape. The cheese dish is square with a wedge-shaped lid. There are two styles of coffee pot, one narrower at the top, measuring 3" and 4" respectively. The 4" lid also fits the teapot. There are two styles of sugar. One has a bottom with lug handles to match the lid, the other does not.

The glaze has a speckled effect. Known colors include: Burnt Orange, Granite gray, Honey (beige), Mint Green, Pink, Sand (melon/pumpkin), Teal, Turquoise, Sunburst yellow and Marble White. I have also seen an unnamed green and a cup with a black outside and a Sunburst interior. Because some colors were dropped and new ones added during production, every piece may not have been made in every color.

Bowl, lug, soup, w/lid . . . . *$8 – $10*
Bowl, soup, coupe . . . . *10 – 12*
Bowl, vegetable, divided . . . . *15 – 18*
Bowl, vegetable, oval. . . . . *10 – 12*
Bowl, vegetable, round . . . . *15 – 18*
Butter, ¼-pound . . . . *20 – 25*
Casserole . . . . *20 – 25*

1. DINNER
2. SALAD
3. BREAD & BUTTER
4. FRUIT
5. LUG SOUP
6. LUG SOUP COVER
7. COUPE SOUP
8. CUP
9. SAUCER
10. VEGETABLE, ROUND
11. VEGETABLE, OVAL
12. PLATTER, 11"
13. PLATTER, 13"
14. HANDLED COVERED SUGAR
15. UNHANDLED COVERED SUGAR
16. GRAVY
17. PICKLE
19. & 20. SHAKERS
21. COFFEE POT
22. CHOP PLATE/BUFFET TRAY
23. CASSEROLE
24. CASSEROLE COVER

Pebbleford

Cheese dish	*ND*
Coffee pot	*$35 – $40*
Creamer	*4 – 6*
Cup	*4 – 6*
Dish	*2 – 3*
Gravy	*12 – 15*
Gravy liner	*6 – 8*
Jug, water	*15 – 18*
Plate, 6"*	*1 – 2*
Plate, 8"*	*4 – 5*
Plate, 10"	*10 – 12*
Plate, chop, 14"*	*15 – 20*

Platter, 11" .... *$10 – $12*
Platter, 13" .... *12 – 15*
Saucer .... *1 – 2*
Shaker, pair.. *8 – 10*
Sugar w/handle.. *8 – 10*
Sugar w/o handle .... *8 – 10*
Teapot .... *25 – 30*

PLYMOUTH   (mid 1937)

A beaded edge around the rims and hollowware bodies identifies this shape.
Made in ivory and pink bodies.

   Plymouth was available in plain ivory, as well as many decals, including
Adobe (southwestern dwellings), Holland Mills (windmill and tulips), Hyde
Park Tulips (a row of tulips), Mexican Fantasy (seven different decals with re-
lated Mexican subjects), and Pine Cone (tones of brown and green).

Casserole... *$20 – $25*
Coaster, lug, 4¹/₄" .... *8 – 12*
Creamer .... *4 – 6*
Cup .... *4 – 6*
Plate, 7¹/₄" .... *4 – 5*
Plate, 9¹/₄" .... *7 – 9*
Plate, chop, lug, 11¹/₄"... *10 – 12*
Plate, chop, lug, 12¹/₄"... *12 – 15*
Saucer .... *1 – 2*
Shaker, pair.. *8 – 10*
Sugar .... *8 – 10*
Teapot, 2-cup.. *20 – 25*
Teapot, 6-cup.. *25 – 30*

*Plymouth: Tall
shakers
(Petitpoint),
Mexican Fantasy
chop plate and
cup (two of seven
variations in this
pattern), and
teapot
(Petitpoint).*

VISTOSA   (1938)

Green, blue, yellow, and red. Eggcups have turned up in matte white, and some decal-decorated pieces have been found.

Bowl, lug, soup, 6¹/₂" .... *$25 – $30*
Bowl, salad, footed. .... *125 – 150*
Bowl, soup, 7¹/₂". .... *15 – 18*
Bowl, vegetable, round, 8¹/₂" .... *90 – 100*
Creamer .... *10 – 12*
Cup .... *10 – 12*
Cup, AD. .... *12 – 15*
Dish, 5" .... *10 – 12*
Eggcup. .... *25 – 30*
Gravy boat .... *125 – 150*
Jug, ball .... *50 – 60*
Plate, 6" .... *3 – 4*
Plate, 7". .... *5 – 7*
Plate, 9" .... *8 – 10*
Plate, 10" .... *12 – 15*

Vistosa: Shakers, plate, and gravy. Very few pieces of decaled Vistosa have been seen.

Vistosa

Plate, chop, 11" .... *$20 – $25*
Plate, chop, 14" .... *30 – 35*
Saucer .... *3 – 5*
Saucer, AD .... *5 – 7*
Shaker, each .... *8 – 10*
Sugar .... *15 – 18*
Teapot .... *100 – 125*

VOGUE (1934–1941>)

Designed by J. P. Thorley. A swirl is engraved into the rim of the flatware and the body of the hollowware. The handles and finials have an embossed flower.

Generally decal-decorated. Also, look for the underglaze "Dots" series: Spiral Dot just on the narrow spirals, Polka Dot all over the rims and hollowware bodies, and Border Dot just around the edges. All came in either blue, pink, or green.

In the 1940s, Montgomery Ward's catalogs show a service of "Rainbow" that consists of a Luray jug and shakers and several items in the Vogue shape, all of these in Luray colors. /L in the listing below indicates pieces of Vogue that were used in this line. There was also a glass with colored bands around the base.

Bowl, lug, soup . . . . *$8 – $10*
Bowl, soup, 8"* . . . . *10 – 12*
Bowl, 36s . . . . *7 – 10*
Butter dish . . . . *20 – 25*
Casserole, no handles . . . . *20 – 25*
Casserole, footed, handled . . . . *20 – 25*
Creamer /L . . . . *4 – 6*
Cup /L . . . . *4 – 6*
Cup, cream soup . . . . *12 – 16*
Dish, 5¹⁄₂"* . . . . *2 – 3*
Dish, 6¹⁄₄"* . . . . *3 – 4*
Eggcup . . . . *10 – 12*
Gravy . . . . *12 – 15*
Gravy faststand   /L . . . . *12 – 15*
Gravy liner . . . . *6 – 8*
Plate, 6¹⁄₄" . . . . *1 – 2*
Plate, 7¹⁄₄" . . . . *4 – 5*
Plate, 9¹⁄₄" . . . . *7 – 9*
Plate, 10" . . . . *10 – 12*
Plate, square, 7³⁄₄" . . . . *4 – 5*

Vogue: Cup (silver stamping), bread & butter (Stagecoach), dinner plate
(Cabin in the Woods), dinner plate (cross-stitch Southern Belle), teapot
(Orange Poppies), and dinner plate (Spiral Dot). The stagecoach (and
other forms of transportation) and the cabin in the woods are two of many
monochrome designs. I have seen these in blue, black, and burgundy; I
would expect other colors.

Platter, 11"* .... *$10 – $12*
Platter, 13"* .... *12 – 15*
Platter, 15"* .... *15 – 18*
Saucer   /L.. *1 – 2*
Saucer, cream soup .... *6 – 8*
Sugar   /L.. *8 – 10*
Teapot   /L.. *30 – 35*

C. C. THOMPSON POTTERY COMPANY

East Liverpool, Ohio

CHAPTER AT A GLANCE

CHATHAM
HANOVER
OLD LIVERPOOL

SEVILLE
STAFFORD

One of the longer-lived East Liverpool potteries, Thompson was founded in 1868. Built close to the Ohio River, it survived several floods in its early decades. With the removal of Harker to Chester, West Virginia, Thompson was the last pottery left on the river road in East Liverpool. Many others in that city had been razed to make way for gas stations and mercantile establishments. Thompson ceased operations in September 1938.

MARKS   Two basic backstamps were used on most of Thompson's pottery. The earlier stamp is the star with the pottery's initials around it. The later, introduced ca. 1932, is the crossed T. Both usually had the shape name in block letters beneath it, though sometimes they did not.

CHATHAM   (1932)

Periodic embossing on the rim of the flatware and around the shoulder of the hollowware.

Bowl, oval, 9"	$10 – $12
Casserole	20 – 25
Creamer	4 – 6
Cup	4 – 6
Dish, 5½"*	2 – 3
Plate, 6¼"	1 – 2
Plate, 9½"	7 – 9
Plate, 10"	10 – 12

Hanover: Soup bowl (green).

Platter, 11"* .... *$10 – $12*
Saucer .... *1 – 2*
Sugar .... *8 – 10*

HANOVER   (1931)

An octagonal shape with alternating panels of embossed latticework. It was made in a white body as well as Creme, Jade, and Sunshine Pink.

Bowl, oval, 9"* .... *$10 – $12*
Bowl, soup, 8½" .... *10 – 12*
Casserole .... *20 – 25*
Creamer .... *4 – 6*
Cup .... *4 – 6*
Dish, 5½"* .... *2 – 3*
Plate, 6"* .... *1 – 2*
Plate, 9"* .... *7 – 9*
Platter, 11"* .... *10 – 12*
Saucer .... *1 – 2*
Sugar .... *8 – 10*

OLD LIVERPOOL   (1935)

Fancy embossing around the rim of the flatware and the body of the hollowware.

MARK   One of the few Thompson shapes to have its own backstamp. Since it reads "1868 Thompson's Old Liverpool Ware," some people assume that 1868 is the date of manufacture. Not.

Old Liverpool: Plate and creamer.

Bowl, oval, 9"* . . . . *$10 – $12*
Casserole . . . . *20 – 25*
Creamer . . . . *4 – 6*
Cup . . . . *4 – 6*
Dish, 5¹/₂"* . . . . *2 – 3*
Plate, 6"* . . . . *1 – 2*
Plate, 9¹/₂"* . . . . *7 – 9*
Plate, 10¹/₄" . . . . *10 – 12*
Plate, square, 7³/₄" . . . . *6 – 7*
Platter, oval, 11¹/₂" . . . . *10 – 12*
Saucer . . . . *1 – 2*
Sugar . . . . *8 – 10*
Teapot . . . . *25 – 30*

SEVILLE   (1932)

A square shape with an embossed decoration around the rim of the flatware and the shoulder of the hollowware.

Seville: Plate (Hollyhocks at Fence).

Bowl, oval, 9"* .... *$10 – $12*
Casserole .... *20 – 25*
Creamer .... *4 – 6*
Cup .... *4 – 6*
Dish, 5½"* .... *2 – 3*
Plate, 6"* .... *1 – 2*
Plate, 7" .... *4 – 5*
Plate, 9" .... *7 – 9*
Platter, 11"* .... *10 – 12*
Saucer .... *1 – 2*
Sugar .... *8 – 10*

STAFFORD   (1926)

The flatware is round with octagonal wells, and the hollowware is octagonal. There is a thin band of embossed ribs around the outside of the flatware and around the shoulder of the hollowware.

Stafford was made in Pearl White, which may make it Thompson's first shape in an ivory body.

Bowl, oval, 9"* .... *$10 – $12*
Bowl, round, 9" .... *15 – 18*
Casserole .... *20 – 25*
Creamer .... *4 – 6*
Cup .... *4 – 6*
Dish, 5½"* .... *2 – 3*
Plate, 6"* .... *1 – 2*
Plate, 9¼" .... *7 – 9*
Plate, grill, octagonal, 10" .... *10 – 12*
Platter, 11" .... *10 – 12*
Saucer .... *1 – 2*
Sugar .... *8 – 10*
Teapot .... *20 – 25*

Stafford: Plate and teapot.

TREASURE CRAFT

Compton, California

CHAPTER AT A GLANCE

COOKIE JARS
  Country Critters
  Disney

Pet Shop
Rose Petal Place

Al Levin began the company in 1946 as a jobber, buying from local potteries and selling to retail outlets. In 1948 manufacturing began, primarily wall planters and 32-ounce jumbo mugs. Cookie jars were added in the early fifties.

Woodstain, a non-fired finish, was first used on the Barrel line in the early to mid-fifties and was discontinued in the mid-eighties. The woodstain is rubbed onto the bisque and then lacquered. The colored details were done in one of two ways. Either they were glazed in the greenware and hardened in the bisque firing (the woodstain did not adhere to these details), or color enamel was used (cold paint).

The design has been done by Al Levin who works closely with modelers to craft the finished pieces. Don Winton of the Twin Wintons became associated with the company around 1975 to 1980 and is still doing work for them. In fact, Treasure Craft bought the cookie jar molds from the Twin Wintons, and Don has helped modify several for Treasure Craft. Treasure Craft was acquired by Pfaltzgraff in 1993.

Pottery Craft was a company started in 1972. Treasure Craft of Hawaii made Hawaiian souvenirs for thirty years. It closed in 1989.

See Roerig in Bibliography.

COOKIE JARS

Adobe House	$35 – $45
Angel	65 – 75
Apple	45 – 50
Balloon, Hot Air, "Cookie Balloon"	40 – 50
Balls	
Baseball	35 – 45
Basketball	35 – 45
Bowling Ball	35 – 45
Eightball	35 – 45
Gold Ball	35 – 45
Soccer Ball	35 – 45
Tennis Ball	35 – 45

Bandito. . . . . *$65 – $75*
Barn w/owl finial & hen in hayloft, "Cookie Barn" . . . . *35 – 45*
Baseball Boy . . . . *35 – 45*
Bear, Panda, w/baby. . . . . *40 – 50*
Bear, standing on hands (Circus Bear). . . . . *40 – 50*
Bear w/visored cap and bow tie. . . . . *35 – 45*
Cactus. . . . . *40 – 50*
Canister, brown w/orange apples . . . . *20 – 25*
Castle . . . . *40 – 50*
Cat in dress w/flower basket . . . . *40 – 45*
Cat on pillow, "Cookies". . . . . *35 – 45*
Cat w/fish bowl, fish finial. . . . . *50 – 60*
Chef in toque w/spoon, "Cookie Chef" . . . . *35 – 45*
Coffee Pot, "Cookies" . . . . *25 – 35*
Cook Books . . . . *65 – 75*
Covered Wagon, Stained. . . . . *65 – 75*
   Bank . . . . *25 – 35*
Cowboy Pig w/Rabbit [DW]. . . . . *40 – 45*
Coyote . . . . *45 – 55*
Crock, wood grain w/embossed girl on fence & butterfly finial . . . . *20 – 25*
Dinosaur (Cookiesaurus). . . . . *80 – 90*
Dog w/barrel around neck, "Cookies". . . . . *35 – 45*
   Bank. . . . . *20 – 30*
Dog w/cap and neckerchief . . . . *40 – 50*
Duck. . . . . *35 – 45*
Decoy . . . . *40 – 45*
Elephant in sailor clothes. "U.S.N.". . . . . *40 – 45*
Famous Amos bag. . . . . *65 – 75*
   Bank. . . . . *30 – 40*
Fish, Tropical . . . . *35 – 45*
Football Player (Football Boy) . . . . *100 – 125*
Girl w/bunny in apron pocket, Black (Spice) . . . . *50 – 60*
Girl w/bunny in apron pocket (Sugar). . . . . *50 – 60*
Goose w/bow around neck. . . . . *40 – 45*
Grandfather Clock . . . . *25 – 30*
Grandma w/bowl of cookies. . . . . *40 – 50*
Gumball Machine . . . . *40 – 50*
Hen. . . . . *40 – 50*
Hobo w/cigar stub and sack. . . . . *35 – 45*
House, Gingerbread . . . . *35 – 45*
House, Victorian. . . . . *30 – 35*
   Bank. . . . . *25 – 35*
House w/pillared porch, "Cookieville" . . . . *30 – 35*
Ice Cream Cone. . . . . *30 – 40*
Ice Wagon w/"Home" finial, "ICE Co. Estab. 1902". . . . . *50 – 60*
   Bank. . . . . *25 – 35*
Jukebox, "Wurlitzer". . . . . *100 – 125*
Katrina. . . . . *500 +*

Lamb . . . . *$40 – $50*
    Bank . . . . *20 – 30*
Milk can . . . . *35 – 45*
Monk w/scroll, "Thou Shalt Not Steal (Cookies)" [DW] . . . . *35 – 45*
    Bank . . . . *20 – 30*
Monkey w/bow tie, "Cookies" . . . . *35 – 45*
    Bank . . . . *20 – 30*
Mouse w/airplane in hand . . . . *35 – 45*
Mushroom House . . . . *40 – 50*
Noah's Ark w/two owls finial [DW]. . . . . *35 – 45*
    Bank . . . . *20 – 30*
Owl w/apron, "Cookies" . . . . *30 – 40*
Pig Chef . . . . *35 – 45*
Pig w/cap and sack, "Cookies" . . . . *35 – 45*
Puppy w/cap and scarf . . . . *35 – 45*
Rabbit w/baseball bat . . . . *30 – 40*
    Bank . . . . *20 – 30*
Radio, Old Fashioned. . . . . *30 – 35*
Rocking Horse w/flower finial . . . . *35 – 45*
Slot Machine, "Jack Pot". . . . . *40 – 50*
Snow White (decal) . . . . *100 – 125*
Stagecoach . . . . *90 – 100*
    Bank . . . . *25 – 35*
Stove, pot-bellied . . . . *35 – 45*
    Bank . . . . *20 – 30*
Tiki . . . . *50 – 60*
    Shaker, pair . . . . *20 – 25*
Toucan . . . . *50 – 60*
Trolley w/kids, "Cookie Trolley" . . . . *35 – 45*
Truck, Pick-Up
    Brown. . . . . *50 – 60*
    Red . . . . *300 – 350*
TV (Nickelodeon). . . . . *300 +*
Van . . . . *50 – 60*

Country Critters All have straw hats with red band.

Cat . . . . *$40 – $50*
Dog. . . . . *40 – 50*
Pig . . . . *40 – 50*
Rabbit . . . . *40 – 50*

Disney

Bear w/guitar and hat (Big Al) (The Jungle Book). . . . . *$100 – $125*
    Bank. . . . . *30 – 40*
Bulldog Cafe (The Rocketeer) . . . . *125 – 150*
Genie (Aladdin). . . . . *50 – 60*
Jack's Tomb (The Nightmare Before Christmas) . . . . *60 – 70*
Mickey Mouse. . . . . *60 – 70*

Mickey Mouse (3-D). . . . . *$90 – $100*
   Shaker, pair . . . . *30 – 35*
Minnie Mouse . . . . *60 – 70*
Mrs. Potts (Beauty & the Beast) . . . . *50 – 60*
Pinocchio . . . . *80 – 90*
Roly Dalmatian (101 Dalmatians) . . . . *45 – 55*
Simba (The Lion King) . . . . *60 – 70*
Winnie the Pooh . . . . *60 – 70*

SNOW WHITE & THE SEVEN DWARFS

Dopey . . . . *$60 – $70*
Snow White . . . . *60 – 70*
Spoon Rest (Grumpy) . . . . *15 – 20*
Teapot (Doc) . . . . *50 – 60*
Utensil Holder (Happy) . . . . *35 – 40*

Pet Shop All have a blue-and-white checked bandanna around the neck.

Cat . . . . *$40 – $50*
Dog . . . . *40 – 50*
Monkey . . . . *40 – 50*
Rabbit . . . . *40 – 50*

Rose Petal Place

Caterpillar Coach (P.D.) . . . . *$375 – $425*
Football w/coach . . . . *225 – 250*
Hedgehog (Tumbles) . . . . *350 – 375*
Snail (Seymour) . . . . *325 – 350*
Tree w/book, bird finial (Elmer) . . . . *500 – 550*
Watering Can . . . . *150 – 175*

Rose Petal Place: Tree w/book cookie jar, bird finial (Elmer).

TWIN WINTON

Pasadena, El Monte, and
San Juan Capistrano, California

CHAPTER AT A GLANCE

COOKIE JARS   HILLBILLY
COWBOY

The Twin Wintons (Don Winton was the designer and modeler; his twin brother Ross was the mold man and business manager) began in business in 1936 in partnership with Helen Burke; they were 16 and still in high school. They made small, Disney-like figures that Burke hand-decorated and sold. They went on their own in 1939, suspended work in 1943 to join the military, and reopened in 1946, at which time older brother Bruce joined them as business manager.

Production of the Hillbilly line began in 1947. In 1951, limited production of cookie jars began with the introduction of the wood finish. In 1952, Don and Ross sold their interest to Bruce and began working as freelancers for Bruce and others. In 1953, Bruce moved to El Monte and in 1964 to the old Brad Keeler plant in San Juan Capistrano. Solid colors were added in 1970, and a special Collectors' Series was brought out in 1974. Gold Seal items were made just before the company closed in 1975.

Over the years, besides working for themselves, they have done cookie jars for Brush, Disney, and Treasure Craft among others. Ross died in 1980. One of the more prolific designers in the U.S. pottery industry, Don is still active and in early 1994 began actively designing again for his revived company.

See Chipman and see Roerig in Bibliography.

COLORS Most Twin Winton pieces will be found in the brown (color varies) wood finish, with detail in black and usually one to three other colors, such as blue, green, pink, white, or yellow.

The **solid colors** introduced in 1970 include avocado, gray, orange, pineapple, and red. Most of these do not have color accents. The **Collectors' Series** jars are generally ivory with orange and turquoise decoration and small touches of black, brown, and yellow. **Gold Seal** jars are high-glazed and are marked with a little gold label.

COOKIE JARS

Go-withs, such as shakers, are not always a miniature of the jar. The Tepee has the sitting Indian shakers, and the Clock has mouse shakers that match the finial.

PRICING Unless described otherwise, all prices are for jars with brown wood finish. The popular Collectors' Series and Gold Seal are priced separately. Solid-color jars are worth slightly less than those with the wood finish; many collectors find these less attractive as they don't have the accent colors.

Apple, house w/worm. . . . . *$100 – $125*
Barn, "Cookie Barn" . . . . *35 – 45*
    Collectors' Series. . . . . *150 – 175*
    Canister, "Flour Stable"   /CM . . . . *30 – 35*
    Canister, "Sugar Dairy"   /CM . . . . *25 – 30*
    Canister, "Coffee Coop"   /CM. . . . . *20 – 25*
    Canister, "Tea Sty"   /CM . . . . *15 – 20*
    [Above canisters in descending size]
    Shakers. . . . . *35 – 45*
Barrel w/"Flour/Sugar" sacks, mouse finial,
    "(Grandma's face, embossed) Cookies" . . . . *60 – 70*
    Shakers. . . . . *25 – 35*
Barrel w/sacks, "Grandma's Cookies" . . . . *60 – 70*
Bear w/badge. . . . . *65 – 75*
    Shakers. . . . . *25 – 35*
Bear w/Forest Ranger hat, sitting (Ranger Bear) . . . . *35 – 45*
    Collectors' Series. . . . . *125 – 150*
    Bank. . . . . *35 – 45*
    Napkin holder . . . . *55 – 65*
    Planter . . . . *30 – 35*
    Shakers. . . . . *35 – 45*
    Spoon rest . . . . *25 – 35*
    Wall pocket . . . . *40 – 50*
Bear in sheriff's outfit. . . . . *35 – 45*
    Collectors' Series. . . . . *175 – 250*
    Shakers. . . . . *40 – 50*
Bucket, "Ye Olde Cookie Bucket". . . . . *30 – 35*
    Canister, "Ye Olde Flour Bucket". . . . . *25 – 30*
    Canister, "Ye Olde Sugar Bucket" . . . . *20 – 25*
    Canister, "Ye Olde Coffee Bucket". . . . . *15 – 20*
    Canister, "Ye Olde Tea Bucket" . . . . *12 – 15*
    Canister, "Ye Olde Salt Bucket" . . . . *10 – 12*
    [Above canisters in descending size]
    Shakers. . . . . *15 – 20*
Buddha (see Hotei)
Bull, sitting, floral wreath (Ferdinand/Happy Bull)   /95 . . . . *75 – 95*
    Bank. . . . . *40 – 50*
    Shakers. . . . . *60 – 70*
Butler . . . . *200 – 225*
    Shakers. . . . . *50 – 60*
Cable car "Cookie Car". . . . . *65 – 75*
Castle, with turrets . . . . *200 – 250*
Cat, Persian Kitten . . . . *80 – 90*
    Ashtray. . . . . *35 – 45*
    Bank. . . . . *35 – 45*

Spoon holder . . . . *$25 – $35*
Chef w/bowl of cookies . . . . *200 +*
Child in Shoe . . . . *35 – 45*
   Bank . . . . *40 – 50*
Chipmunk w/sack of acorns . . . . *65 – 75*
   Shakers . . . . *35 – 45*
Churn w/cat . . . . *65 – 75*
   Shakers . . . . *25 – 35*
Clock, mouse finial, "Cookie Time" . . . . *40 – 50*
   Shakers, Mouse . . . . *35 – 45*
Clock w/2 bare feet, "Cookie Time" . . . . *ND*
Coach, pumpkin . . . . *100 – 125*
Coffee grinder . . . . *150 – 175*
Cop, Keystone style, saluting . . . . *100 – 125*
     Collectors' Series . . . . *125 – 150*
   Bank . . . . *40 – 50*
   Shakers . . . . *35 – 45*
Cow w/white spots, bell around neck   /69 . . . . *65 – 75*
   Creamer . . . . *35 – 45*
   Napkin holder . . . . *35 – 45*
   Shakers . . . . *50 – 60*
   Spoon rest . . . . *25 – 35*
Deer with tree trunk (Bambi) . . . . *75 – 85*
   Napkin holder . . . . *30 – 40*
   Planter . . . . *35 – 45*
Dinosaur . . . . *450 +*
   Shakers . . . . *200 +*
Dog in basket . . . . *50 – 60*
Dog on drum . . . . *200 – 250*
Dog w/bow . . . . *100 – 125*
   Wall pocket, head only . . . . *40 – 50*
Dog catcher, "Cookie Catcher" . . . . *65 – 75*
Donkey w/hat and jacket . . . . *65 – 75*
     Collectors' Series . . . . *200 – 225*
   Shakers . . . . *35 – 45*
Donkey and cart . . . . *200 – 225*
Duck (Rubber Ducky) . . . . *100 – 125*
   Shakers . . . . *35 – 45*
Duck w/mixing bowl . . . . *125 – 150*
Dutch Girl . . . . *65 – 75*
   Bank . . . . *50 – 60*
   Napkin holder . . . . *35 – 45*
   Shakers . . . . *50 – 60*
   Spoon rest . . . . *25 – 35*
Elephant w/white sailor hat, sitting (Sailor Elephant)   /86/R . . . . *35 – 45*
     Collectors' Series . . . . *150 – 175*
   Bank, regular . . . . *75 – 85*
   Bank, dime (shaker w/slot) . . . . *85 – 95*
   Candy jar . . . . *40 – 50*

Napkin . . . . *$25 – $35*
Planter . . . . *30 – 40*
Shakers. . . . . *35 – 40*
Spoon rest . . . . *25 – 35*
Talking picture . . . . *100 – 125*
Wall pocket . . . . *80 – 90*
Elf Bakery Tree Stump, "Bakery" . . . . *50 – 60*
  Gold Seal . . . . *50 – 60*
Elf on stump w/cookie   /R . . . . *60 – 75*
  Bank . . . . *45 – 55*
  Candy jar. . . . . *25 – 35*
  Spoon rest . . . . *25 – 35*
Fire engine, "FD". . . . . *100 – 125*
Fox in pirate outfit w/sword and eye patch (Pirate Fox). . . . . *65 – 75*
  Collectors Series . . . . *175 – 200*
  Bank . . . . *50 – 60*
Frog, licking lips . . . . *200 – 225*
  Shakers. . . . . *50 – 60*
Gorilla in derby hat and tie (Magilla Gorilla) . . . . *325 +*
Grandma w/bowl of cookies. . . . . *150 – 175*
Grandma w/spoon. . . . . *125 – 150*
Guard in shelter, "Cookie Guard" . . . . *85 – 95*
Head, modern . . . . *250 +*
Hen on nest . . . . *50 – 60*
  Shakers. . . . . *25 – 35*
Horse, sitting, wearing hat (Dobbin) . . . . *85 – 95*
  Bank . . . . *40 – 50*
  Napkin holder . . . . *35 – 45*
  Shakers. . . . . *35 – 45*
Hotei (Buddha). . . . . *80 – 90*
  Bank . . . . *65 – 75*
  Napkin holder . . . . *35 – 45*
  Shakers. . . . . *50 – 60*
  Spoon rest . . . . *25 – 35*
House, 2-story . . . . *225 – 250*
  Shakers. . . . . *50 – 60*
Howard Johnson's Restaurant . . . . *1500 +*
Jack in Box . . . . *350 +*
  Shakers. . . . . *200 – 250*
Kangaroo . . . . *250 – 275*
  Shakers. . . . . *150 – 175*
King w/pipe and bowl (Ole King Cole) . . . . *200 – 225*
Kitten in basket . . . . *50 – 60*
Lamb, "For Good Little Lambs *Only*"   /R . . . . *40 – 50*
  Collectors' Series. . . . . *125 – 150*
  Gold Seal . . . . *50 – 60*
  Bank . . . . *35 – 45*
  Napkin holder . . . . *25 – 35*

Shakers. . . . . *$35 – $45*
Spoon rest . . . . *25 – 35*
Lighthouse . . . . *200 +*
Lion, wearing crown. . . . . *80 – 90*
Shakers. . . . . *40 – 50*
Monk, "Thou Shall Not Steal!" (Friar Tuck). . . . . *35 – 45*
Gold Seal . . . . *50 – 60*
Bank. . . . . *35 – 45*
Shakers. . . . . *35 – 45*
Mother Goose   /R . . . . *125 – 150*
Collectors' Series. . . . . *200 – 225*
Shakers, pair . . . . *35 – 45*
Mouse wearing sailor suit (Sailor Mouse) . . . . *35 – 45*
Shakers, pair . . . . *25 – 30*
Noah's Ark   /R . . . . *50 – 60*
Nut w/squirrel finial, "Cookie Nut" . . . . *50 – 55*
Bank . . . . *35 – 45*
Owl w/glasses and mortarboard . . . . *35 – 45*
Collectors' Series. . . . . *125 – 150*
Shakers, pair . . . . *25 – 35*
Spoon rest . . . . *25 – 35*
Pig (Porky) . . . . *65 – 75*
Bank. . . . . *35 – 45*
Napkin holder . . . . *35 – 45*
Spoon rest . . . . *25 – 35*
Poodle behind "Cookie Counter" . . . . *100 – 125*
Napkin holder . . . . *40 – 50*
Shakers. . . . . *40 – 50*
Spoon rest . . . . *25 – 35*
Pot w/handle, footed, "Pot O' Cookies" . . . . *25 – 35*
Candy jar, "Pot O' Candy" . . . . *25 – 35*
Shakers, pair . . . . *20 – 25*
Rabbit in cowboy outfit w/gun belt (Gunfighter Rabbit). . . . . *85 – 95*
Shakers, pair . . . . *35 – 45*
Raccoon wearing sweater. . . . . *50 – 60*
Shakers, pair . . . . *35 – 45*
TV Lamp . . . . *150 – 175*
Raggedy Andy on drum, Collectors' Series   /R . . . . *175 – 200*
Raggedy Ann, Collectors' Series   /R . . . . *175 – 200*
Rocking Horse, Collectors' Series . . . . *250 +*
Rooster. . . . . *75 – 95*
Collectors' Series. . . . . *200 – 225*
Shakers, pair . . . . *30 – 40*
Spoon rest . . . . *25 – 35*
Sack, "Cookie Sack" . . . . *35 – 45*
Safe, money bag finial, "Cookie Safe". . . . . *125 – 150*
Shack, "Cookie Shack" . . . . *30 – 40*
Gold Seal . . . . *40 – 50*

Candy jar, "Candy House" .... *$50 – $60*
Napkin holder .... *25 – 35*
Snail .... *250 +*
Squirrel w/cookie .... *40 – 50*
    Planter .... *35 – 45*
    Shakers... *40 – 50*
    Spoon rest .... *25 – 35*
Stove, old-fashioned... *100 – 125*
Stove, pot-bellied .... *65 – 75*
    Shakers... *25 – 35*
Teddy Bear w/ ribbon tie .... *50 – 60*
    Bank... *35 – 45*
    Shakers... *35 – 45*
Tepee, "Cookie Chief"... *200 – 250*
    Shakers, sitting Indians .... *35 – 45*
Train, w/face, "97"   /89 .... *75 – 80*
Tug Boat .... *100 – 125*
Turtle w/top hat, sitting .... *100 – 125*
    Candy jar.. *40 – 50*
    Spoon rest .... *25 – 35*
Walrus w/clown hat .... *200 – 225*
Wheelbarrow... *150 – 175*

COWBOY

Ashtray, cowboy... *$40 – $50*
Coaster, embossed steer head .... *20 – 25*
Shakers, saddle, pair .... *35 – 45*

HILLBILLY (1947)

Based on the Paul Webb comic strip, which was also the basis for Imperial Porcelain's Hillbilly line. (Paul Webb's "Blue Ridge Mountain Boys" were popular cartoon comic strips in the 1930s and 1940s. They were used in advertising and appeared in movies.)

The lamp will be found with different shades and with or without a wooden base.

One of the fun things about this line is the variation in decoration. For instance, the Hillbillies on the handles of the mugs usually have blue pants, but there is a great variation in their hair color (black, blond, brown, and white) and their shirts (striped, solid, flowered).

Ashtray, "Clem" .... *$45 – $55*
Bank, Hillbilly in barrel, "Mountain Dew 100 Proof"   /CM .... *75 – 85*
Bowl, Bathing Hillbilly .... *40 – 50*
Bowl, pretzel, half-barrel...................................... *30 – 40*
Cigarette holder with match holder, Outhouse and barrel........ *65 – 75*
Cup, "Ma" .... *35 – 45*
Cup, "Pa"... *35 – 45*
Cup, Punch .... *8 – 10*

Dino the Dinosaur cookie jar with matching salt and pepper shakers.

Ice bucket, "Ice"

   Bottoms Up . . . . *$125 – $150*

   Hillbilly bathing . . . . *200 – 225*

   Hillbilly w/jug . . . . *125 – 150*

   Hillbilly w/suspenders . . . . *125 – 150*

Jar/Canister, Outhouse . . . . *325 +*

Jug . . . . *50 – 65*

Mug

   Fully glazed . . . . *15 – 20*

   Partly glazed . . . . *15 – 20*

Mug, Tankard . . . . *30 – 40*

Pouring Spout . . . . *25 – 35*

   Fence-shape holder for above, "Twin Winton Corral" . . . . *ND*

Shakers, man in barrel, pair . . . . *20 – 30*

Table lamp, Hillbilly on barrel, "Moonshine, 100 proof" . . . . *175 +*

UHL POTTERY COMPANY

Huntingburg, Indiana

CHAPTER AT A GLANCE

ASHTRAYS	KITCHENWARE
Advertising	LIQUOR BOTTLES / JUGS
BEVERAGE ITEMS	MINIATURES
DINNERWARE	MISCELLANY
FIGURES / ANIMALS	VASES

The Uhl Pottery Company (pronounced "ool" not "yule") was founded by August Uhl, who came to America from Germany in 1846, and his brother Louis, who joined him in 1849. They established the A. and L. Uhl Pottery in Evansville. The business prospered, but the poor clay in the area sent them in search of better-quality clay, which they found and had shipped from Huntingburg.

In 1879, Louis bought out his brother August and brought in his son George. The firm name was changed to Louis Uhl & Son. A few years later, after more family ownership changes, the name became the Uhl Pottery Company.

Louis Uhl died in 1908, after which it was decided to move the plant closer to the clay deposits in Huntingburg. The business office remained in Evansville until 1934.

In 1940, the United Brick and Clay Workers Union became the bargaining agent for the employees. There were sporadic strikes until 1944, when a six-month strike pushed Louis C. Uhl, grandson of the founder, to decide to close the pottery. Rising costs and Japanese imports were other important factors in his decision.

In 1945 the plant was leased to the Vogue Pottery, which continued to manufacture some Uhl items until 1947, when it closed. In 1948, Louisville Pottery leased the plant, and they too made items from some of the Uhl molds. They closed near the end of 1950. The plant lay idle while the family attempted to sell the property. Finally, in 1957, it was bought by the Huntingburg Furniture Company. The company was officially dissolved in 1959.

MARKS The most common mark is a backstamp of a circle with the words "UHL POTTERY COMPANY, HUNTINGBURG, IND." Note that all the words are in capital letters. A fake mark with the same words has surfaced recently on woodgrain pitchers that are not Uhl. This mark has "UHL" in capital letters and the remaining words in upper- and lowercase letters.

NOTE When items were made in specific colors, those colors are noted with the item in the listing. When various colors are indicated, they include

Black, Blue, Brown, Green, Peach, Pink, Purple, Tan (also called Brindle), and Yellow.

PRICING   Brown and tan are at the low end of the range. Black, Green, Peach, and Yellow are just below the middle of the range. Blue is at the top of the range, with Pink and Purple just below.

ASHTRAYS

These will be found in assorted colors.

Acorn	$260 – $425
Modern	55 – 115
Pig	155 – 240
Round	35 – 65
Round /140	50 – 100
Round w/dog raising leg	225 – 275
Round w/dog and hydrant	330 – 450
Round w/donkey	800 – 1200
Round w/elephant	800 – 1200
Round w/raised acorn in center	260 – 345

Advertising

Cannelton Sewer Pipe, brown	$110
Meier Winery	150 – 260
Shell Gas, tan and yellow	150

BEVERAGE ITEMS

The **Grape** pieces are in Blue or Dark. For the **Rustic Barrel** pieces, the quarter-gallon jug is glazed in assorted colors, the hundred-ounce jug in Brindle, and the steins in Brindle or Tan. The other pieces are in Ivory or Tan.

Barrel pitcher, 3-quart	$60 – $150
w/lid	120 – 250
Barrel pitcher, brown, 100-ounce	70
Barrel pitcher, Rustic, 1-quart	45 – 70
Barrel stein, tan, 12-ounce	17
Barrel stein, tan, 14-ounce	17
Barrel stein, tan, 16-ounce	17
Barrel stein, tan, 18-ounce	17
Barrel stein, tan, 20-ounce	20
Barrel stein, Rustic, 8-ounce	25 – 60
Barrel stein, Rustic, 10-ounce	25 – 60
Bellied pitcher, blue sponge, 1/4-gallon	340
Bellied pitcher, blue sponge, 1/2-gallon	380
Bellied pitcher, blue sponge, 1-gallon	430
Flagon pitcher, 5-pint	60 – 95
Flagon stein, 8-ounce	25 – 45
Flagon stein, 10-ounce	25 – 45
Flagon stein, 12-ounce	25 – 45

Flagon stein, 14-ounce .... *$25 – $45*
Flagon stein, 16-ounce .... *25 – 45*
Grape pitcher, 1-quart .... *80 – 225*
Grape pitcher, 2-quart .... *65 – 165*
Grape pitcher, 3-quart .... *70 – 175*
Grape pitcher, squat, 2-quart .... *75 – 175*
Grape stein, 12-ounce... *50 – 120*
Grape stein, 16-ounce... *50 – 120*
Lincoln pitcher, blue, ½-pint *220*
Lincoln pitcher, blue, 1-pint...................................... *290*
Lincoln pitcher, blue, 1-quart..................................... *375*
Lincoln pitcher, blue, 2-quart..................................... *500*
Lincoln pitcher, blue, 3-quart..................................... *630*
Liquor Bottle .... *45 – 70*
   Cup .... *70 – 110*
   Tray.. *75 – 125*
Rustic Keg w/spigot, brown, 1-pint *60*
Rustic Keg w/spigot, brown, 3-pint *55*
Rustic Keg w/spigot, brown, 1-gallon *125*
   Cup, 1½-ounce .... *75 – 100*
   Cup, 2-ounce .... *75 – 100*
   Oak stand *10*

DINNERWARE

Most of the dinnerware came in Jet Black, Light Blue, Periwinkle Blue, Blue Green, and Pink, usually with white inside. The coffee pots also came in Brindle or Yellow. Every piece did not come in every color.

Bowl, chili, 12-ounce.. *$20 – $35*
Bowl, chili, 16-ounce.. *20 – 35*
Bowl, luncheon, 7".. *25 – 40*
Bowl, luncheon, 8".. *25 – 40*
Bowl, salad, 7".. *55 – 80*
Bowl, salad, 9".. *60 – 90*
Bowl, salad, 11"... *70 – 110*
Bowl, soup, 6" .... *20 – 35*
Casserole, 3-pint   /529 .... *35 – 65*
Casserole, 5-pint   /528 .... *40 – 70*
Casserole, stick handle, small .... *25 – 50*
Casserole, stick handle, medium................................. *40 – 70*
Casserole, stick handle, large .... *50 – 80*
Coffee pot, 6-cup
   w/aluminum drip .... *225 – 430*
   w/ceramic drip .... *300 – 530*
Creamer .... *50 – 75*
Cup .... *25 – 50*
Custard, 5-ounce... *20 – 30*
Custard, 7-ounce... *20 – 30*

Dish, cereal, 4"... *$50 – $80*
Dish, porridge, 5"... *20 – 40*
Mug, coffee, 8-ounce.. *30 – 60*
Plate, 6".. *25 – 65*
Plate, 8".. *30 – 70*
Plate, 10"... *35 – 80*
Plate, chop, 14"... *80 – 125*
Plate, grill, 9"... *50 – 90*
Ramekin, 8-ounce.. *30 – 40*
Saucer.. *15 – 30*
Sugar... *50 – 85*
Teapot, 2-cup   /131 .... *140 – 295*
Teapot, 4-cup   /132 .... *135 – 250*
Teapot, 8-cup   /143 .... *125 – 240*
Teapot, side handle .... *225 – 350*

FIGURES / ANIMALS

The dog has its right rear leg raised. This is the only version that Uhl made. A squatting dog, attributed to Uhl, was made by Morton.
    These animals are decorated in natural colors unless otherwise indicated.

Dog, leg raised
    Blue *$325*
    Brown *250*
Frog, green, 3½"... *170*
Frog, green, 6".. *265*
Frog, green, 9".. *430*
Frog, green, 13"... *900*
Turtle, 3½"
    Brindle... *140*
    Brown *210*
Turtle, green, 6" *275*
Turtle, green, 9" *450*
Turtle, green, 13" *650*

KITCHENWARE

Many of these items were glazed Blue, Green, or Pink with white inside, unless otherwise indicated.

Bean pot, brown *$40*
Bowl, batter, 8" .... *50 – 85*
Bowl, batter, 10" .... *60 – 100*
Bowl, mixing, blue, 4".. *175*
Bowl, mixing, blue, 5" *70*
Bowl, mixing, blue, 6" *50*
Bowl, mixing, blue, 7" *50*
Bowl, mixing, blue, 8" *55*
Bowl, mixing, blue, 9" *55*

Bowl, mixing, blue, 10" *$60*
Bowl, mixing, blue, 11" *65*
Bowl, mixing, blue, 12" *80*
Bowl, mixing, basket, 6"   /6 . . . . *45 – 80*
Bowl, mixing, basket, 7³/₄"   /8 . . . . *50 – 95*
Bowl, mixing, basket, 9¹/₂"   /10 . . . . *60 – 105*
Butter jar, bailed, w/lid, blue, 2-pound *100*
Cookie jar, bean pot shape, 1-gallon   /522 . . . . *75 – 235*
Cookie jar, white w/blue band, 1-gallon. *325*
Cookie jar, white w/blue band, 2-gallon. *325*
Drip/Grease jar . . . . *50 – 90*
Jar, bread, white w/blue bands, 5-gallon. *450*
Jar, flour, white w/blue bands, 7-gallon *500*
Jar, cake, white w/blue bands, 10" *375*
Jar, clamp, 10-ounce. . . . . *35 – 70*
Jar, egg-beater, white w/blue bands, 1-quart *165*
Jar, Handy/Utility, ¹/₂-pint. . . . . *15 – 35*
Jar, Handy/Utility, 1-pint . . . . *20 – 45*
Jar, Handy/Utility, 1-quart . . . . *25 – 50*
Jar, orange, 10-ounce . . . . *65 – 120*
Jar, squat, 10-ounce. . . . . *40 – 75*
Jug, ball, ice lip, 5-pint . . . . *60 – 100*
Jug, Polar, 2-quart . . . . *275 – 500*
Jug, refrigerator, ball, 4-pint . . . . *60 – 100*
Jug, syrup, 1-pint . . . . *90 – 155*
Keg, 10-ounce . . . . *30 – 70*
Roaster, self-basting, 11" . . . . *100 – 185*
Salt box . . . . *75 – 235*
Shaker, range, pair . . . . *60 – 120*

LIQUOR BOTTLES / JUGS

The **Bellied** jugs are Black. The **Canteen** jugs are Blue, Brown, Ivory, or Rose. The **Creme de Coffee** and **Creme de Prunella** are Brown and Ivory. The **Creme de Mint** is ivory and green. The **Curacao** jugs are Russet. The **Egyptian** jugs are assorted colors.

Acorn, brown and tan, 10-ounce. *$60*
Bellied, ¹/₂-pint. . . . . *30 – 60*
Bellied, 1-pint . . . . *35 – 80*
Bellied, 1-quart . . . . *45 – 100*
Bellied, 2-quart . . . . *50 – 110*
Canteen, ¹/₂-pint. . . . . *35 – 80*
Canteen, 1-pint . . . . *45 – 100*
Creme de Coffee, 25-ounce . . . . *25 – 50*
Creme de Mint, 25-ounce. . . . . *35 – 65*
Creme de Prunella, 8-ounce. . . . . *25 – 50*
Creme de Prunella, 25-ounce. . . . . *35 – 75*
Curacao/Demijohn, no handle, 12-ounce . . . . *15 – 30*
    w/handle . . . . *20 – 35*

ACORN

BELLIED

CANTEEN

CREME DE COFFEE

CREME DE MINT

CREME DE PRUNELLA

EGYPTIAN

SHOULDER

Liquor Jugs

Curacao/Demijohn, no handle, 16-ounce	*$15 – $30*
w/handle	*20 – 35*
Curacao/Demijohn, squat, no handle, 25³/₈-ounce	*15 – 30*
w/handle	*20 – 25*
Curacao/Demijohn, tail, no handle, 25³/₈-ounce	*15 – 30*
w/handle	*20 – 35*
Curacao/Demijohn, no handle, 32-ounce	*25 – 40*
w/handle	*30 – 45*
Egyptian, 8-ounce	*30 – 50*
Egyptian, 12-ounce	*30 – 50*
Egyptian, 16-ounce	*35 – 55*
Egyptian, 25-ounce	*45 – 75*
w/ball stopper	*70 – 115*

MINIATURES

Most of the miniatures came in assorted colors.

PRICING Paper labels do not add anything appreciable to these prices. While some people collect these for the labels, others soak them off—to the chagrin of the first group.

Bud vase	/22	*$50 – $85*
Bud vase	/23	*50 – 85*

BARREL-SHAPED
PITCHER

BASEBALL JUG

BELLIED PITCHER

DUTCH SHOE

FOOTBALL JUG

GLOBE COOKIE JAR

GRECIAN JUG

MILITARY BOOT

RING JUG

SALAD BOWL

SQUARE JUG

TWO-HANDLED
JUG

#21 PITCHER
VASE

#22 BUD VASE

#23 BUD
VASE

#24 BUD VASE

#25 MATCH
HOLDER

#28 PITCHER
VASE

#29 PITCHER
VASE

#30 BUD VASE

#522 COOKIE JAR

Miniatures

Bud vase /24 .... $125 – $190
Bud vase /30 .... 105 – 160
Cookie jar /522 .... 90 – 200
Creamer, 1-ounce .... 200 – 300
Flowerpot, ribbed, w/saucer .... 85 – 180
Globe cookie jar .... 80 – 175
Jug, Acorn, brown, 4-ounce /3 175
Jug, Barrel-shaped .... 55 – 120
Jug, Baseball, white, 2-ounce /12 70
Jug, Bellied, 2½-ounce /4 .... 35 – 70
Jug, Canteen, 2-ounce /7 .... 25 – 60
Jug, Canteen, 4-ounce .... 30 – 65
Jug, Cat .... 65 – 155
Jug, Demijohn, 2-ounce /5 .... 35 – 60
Jug, Egyptian, 3-ounce .... 35 – 60
Jug, Elephant .... 45 – 90
Jug, Football, brown, 3-ounce /13 45
Jug, Globe, 2-ounce /1 .... 25 – 60
Jug, Grecian, 2½-ounce .... 25 – 60
Jug, Horse .... 125 – 195
Jug, Octagon, handled .... 35 – 80
Jug, Prunella, 2-ounce /9 .... 30 – 75
Jug, Prunella, 4-ounce .... 35 – 80
Jug, Ring, 1-ounce /14 .... 125 – 295
Jug, Shoulder, 2½-ounce /2 .... 25 – 60
Jug, Square, 2-ounce /11 .... 25 – 60
Jug, 2-handled, 2-ounce /20 .... 25 – 60
Match Holder /25 .... 125 – 205
Pitcher/Vase /28 .... 65 – 105
Pitcher/Vase /29 .... 70 – 120
Pitcher/Vase /21 .... 65 – 110
Salad bowl .... 125 – 210
Shoe, Baby .... 50 – 105
Shoe, Cowboy Boot .... 85 – 110
Shoe, Dutch, #2 .... 35 – 65
Shoe, Dutch, #3 .... 40 – 70
Shoe, Dutch, #6 .... 45 – 75
Shoe, Military Boot .... 45 – 75
Shoe, Slipper .... 40 – 65
Stein, 3-ounce .... 85 – 160

MISCELLANY

The Lamb planter is facing forward. It is the only version that Uhl made.
These pieces came in assorted colors unless otherwise noted.

Bank, Bellied jug .... $200 – $300
Bank, pig, 3 different sizes
    Pointed ears .... 400 – 700

Round ears .... *$125 – $175*
Cuspidor, Blue Stipple/Dark, 6" *100*
Cuspidor, Embossed, Blue Tint/Dark, 7" *100*
Cuspidor, Hotel, Blue, 7" *130*
Dog Feeder, 4½"   /128 .... *35 – 80*
Dog Feeder, 5"   /129 .... *70 – 125*
Dog Feeder, 7"   /130 .... *80 – 140*
Dog Feeder   /144 .... *55 – 95*
Dog Feeder, 6½"   /146 .... *75 – 130*
Dog Feeder, 7½"   /145 .... *80 – 135*
Pitcher, Hall Boy, Blue Tint/White, 5-pint *260*
Planter, Donkey .... *275 – 385*
Planter, Elephant, 4" .... *100 – 180*
Planter, Lamb .... *75 – 160*
Planter, Rabbit .... *90 – 150*
Plaque, Lincoln, Brindle *650*
Polar jar, blue tint, 2-gallon *450*
Polar jar, blue tint, 4-gallon *575*
Polar jar, blue tint, 6-gallon *625*
Polar jar, blue tint, 8-gallon *675*

#106–107 BUD VASE

#112 BUD VASE

#113-115 CUT
FLOWER VASE

#117 CUT
FLOWER VASE

#516 BUD VASE

THIEVES JAR

Vases

Polar jar, blue tint, 10-gallon *$725*
Polar Sand jar, 14¹/₂" high, ivory lined w/green *350*
Tobacco jar, 1-pound /532 . . . . *150 – 360*
Wren house, Green/Terra Cotta /525 . . . . *310*

VASES

The vases came in assorted colors unless otherwise noted.

Bud, 4¹/₂" /107 . . . . *$40 – $75*
Bud, 5" /112. . . . . *40 – 75*
Bud, 7" /106. . . . . *45 – 85*
Bud, 8" /516. . . . . *60 – 100*
Cut flower, 5" /116 . . . . *35 – 70*
Cut flower, 8" /113 . . . . *35 – 70*
Cut flower, 8" /123 . . . . *40 – 80*
Cut flower, 10" /114 . . . . *40 – 80*
Cut flower, 10" /117 . . . . *45 – 95*
Cut flower, 12" /115 . . . . *50 – 100*
Cut flower, Grecian, Brindle/Brushed Green, 15" /526 . . . . *100*
Orange Blossom, 4" /118 . . . . *60 – 110*
Thieves jar, 3". . . . . *150 – 235*
Thieves jar, 5". . . . . *140 – 220*
Thieves jar, 7". . . . . *110 – 190*
Thieves jar, 9". . . . . *145 – 210*
Venetian, 4". . . . . *60 – 100*

UNIVERSAL POTTERIES, INC.

Cambridge, Ohio

CHAPTER AT A GLANCE

In mid 1932, the Atlas-Globe China company was reorganized and became the Oxford Pottery Company. It was reorganized again in early 1934 and took the name Universal Potteries. It continued to manufacture semivitreous dinnerware, kitchenware, and specialty ware, including some of Atlas-Globe's more popular shapes and patterns. Universal ceased producing these wares in 1954 and turned to tile manufacturing.

Its most famous shape is Ballerina; Upico, Mount Vernon and much of its kitchenware will be easily found as well. It is best known for its Cattail decal which will be found on many pieces.

MARKS Universal used only one general backstamp, the company name encircling the union mark. Due to this mark, many people call this pottery Universal-Cambridge.

DINNERWARE

BALLERINA

Like other popular dinnerware, items were added and dropped over the years. Consequently, if you collect a specific decoration, you may not find all the items listed below in your color or decals. The platters were called Utility Trays.

Both solid colors and decals were used. Known colors are Burgundy, Charcoal, Chartreuse, Dove Gray, Forest Green, Jade Green, Jonquil Yellow, Periwinkle Blue, Pink, and Sierra Rust. There are at least two dozen decals. Most easily found are Moss Rose and Thistle.

860

PRICING   Solid colors are at the high end of the range.

Dinnerware   The tid-bit tray is made up of the 7³/₈" and 10" plates.

Bowl, salad, individual, 7³/₄" . . . . *$10 – $12*
Bowl, soup, coupe, 7³/₄" . . . . *10 – 12*
Bowl, 36s . . . . *7 – 10*
Bowl, vegetable, oval, 9¹/₄" . . . . *10 – 12*
Bowl, vegetable, round, 7³/₄" . . . . *10 – 12*
Bowl, vegetable, round, 9¹/₈" . . . . *15 – 18*
Butter, ¹/₄-pound . . . . *20 – 25*
Casserole, 8¹/₄" . . . . *20 – 25*
Casserole, 10³/₈" . . . . *20 – 25*
Casserole, French, open, 14-ounce . . . . *12 – 15*
Coaster . . . . *8 – 12*
Coffee server, 64-ounce . . . . *35 – 40*
Coffee server, 36-ounce, AD . . . . *30 – 40*
Creamer . . . . *4 – 6*
Cup . . . . *4 – 6*
Cup, AD . . . . *10 – 12*
Cup, cream soup, lug, 6⁷/₈" . . . . *12 – 16*
Dish, 5¹/₄" . . . . *2 – 3*
Dish, 6" . . . . *3 – 4*
Eggcup . . . . *10 – 12*
Gravy . . . . *12 – 15*
Gravy liner/pickle . . . . *6 – 8*
Jug, ice lip, 54-ounce . . . . *20 – 25*
Mug, 10-ounce . . . . *12 – 15*
Plate, 6¹/₄" . . . . *1 – 2*
Plate, 7³/₈" . . . . *4 – 5*
Plate, 9¹/₈" . . . . *7 – 9*
Plate, 10" . . . . *10 – 12*
Plate, square, 7¹/₄" . . . . *5 – 6*
Platter, round, lug, 10¹/₄" . . . . *10 – 12*
Platter, round, lug, 11¹/₂" . . . . *10 – 12*
Platter, round, 13¹/₄" . . . . *12 – 15*
Saucer . . . . *1 – 2*
Saucer, AD . . . . *3 – 5*
Shaker, pair . . . . *8 – 10*
Sugar . . . . *8 – 10*
Teapot, 6-cup . . . . *25 – 30*

Ballerina

Tidbit tray, 2-tier .... $10 – $15
Tumbler, 10-ounce .... 15 – 20

Kitchenware (1954)

Bowl, mixing, 6½" .... $8 – $10
Bowl, mixing, 7½" .... 10 – 12
Bowl, mixing, 8½" .... 10 – 12

Bowl, salad bowl, 9" . . . . *$15 – $18*
Custard, 5-ounce. . . . . *4 – 6*
Drip jar . . . . *12 – 15*
Jug, open, 1-quart . . . . *12 – 15*
Jug, ice lip, 3-quart . . . . *18 – 20*
Leftover, round, 4" . . . . *6 – 10*
Leftover, round, 5" . . . . *10 – 15*
Leftover, round, 6" . . . . *15 – 20*
Pie baker, 10" . . . . *10 – 12*
Shaker, range, pair . . . . *15 – 20*
Utensil, salad server, left . . . . *15 – 20*
Utensil, salad server, right . . . . *15 – 20*

SPECIAL PRICE LIST

BITTERSWEET (1949)

This decoration was an exclusive for the Jewel Tea Company. "Clusters of bright scarlet bittersweet berries" on "rambling vines."

Bowl, mixing, 1-quart. . . . . *$10 – $12*
Bowl, mixing, 2-quart. . . . . *12 – 15*
Bowl, mixing, 3-quart. . . . . *15 – 20*
Bowl, salad, round, 64-ounce, 9½". . . . . *18 – 20*
Bowl, soup, 7¾" . . . . *12 – 15*
Bowl, vegetable, round, 8½" . . . . *18 – 20*
Casserole, 5-pint (Pedestal) . . . . *25 – 30*
Creamer (Camwood). . . . . *6 – 8*
Cup . . . . *6 – 8*
Dish, lug, 6" . . . . *5 – 6*
Drip, 1-pint (Pedestal) . . . . *15 – 18*
Jug (Pedestal). . . . . *20 – 25*
Plate, 7⅛" . . . . *5 – 6*
Plate, 9" . . . . *8 – 10*
Platter, oval, 13½". . . . . *15 – 18*
Platter, oval, lug, 13¼" (Camwood) . . . . *15 – 18*
Saucer. . . . . *2 – 3*
Shaker, pair . . . . *10 – 12*
Shaker, range (Pedestal), pair . . . . *20 – 25*
Stack set, round, 4-piece . . . . *40 – 50*
Sugar (Camwood) . . . . *10 – 15*

CAMWOOD (1932–1934)

Camwood was introduced in 1932 as the Oxford Pottery Company's Concord shape. It was retained and renamed when the company reorganized in 1934.

Most Camwood is decal-decorated, but I have seen it in colors associated with other shapes, both Ballerina Jade Green and Jonquil Yellow (curiously, both had the Camwood Ivory mark) and Oxford purple. Common decals are: "Anemone," Calico Fruit, Cattail, Cottage Garden, "Nove Rose," Orchid, and Poppy.

Bowl, salad bowl, 9"	$15 – $18
Bowl, soup, 8"	10 – 12
Bowl, soup, embossed lug, 6"	8 – 10
Bowl, 36s	7 – 10
Bowl, vegetable, round, 8⅞"	12 – 15
Bowl, vegetable, round, 9⅝"	12 – 15
Butter dish	20 – 25
Casserole, embossed lug handle, 9½"	20 – 25
Creamer	4 – 6
Cup, tea	4 – 6
Cup, coffee	5 – 7
Dish, 5¼"	2 – 3
Dish, 6"	3 – 4
Gravy	12 – 15
Gravy liner/pickle	6 – 8
Plate, 6⅛"	1 – 2
Plate, 7"	4 – 5
Plate, 8"	5 – 6
Plate, 9⅛"	7 – 9
Plate, 9¾"	10 – 12
Plate, grill, 9¾"	12 – 15
Plate, square, 7¼"	5 – 6
Platter, oblong, lug, 13½"	12 – 15
Platter, oval, 7⅛"	6 – 8
Platter, oval, 11½"	10 – 12
Platter, round, lug, 11"	12 – 15
Saucer	1 – 2
Sugar	8 – 10
Teapot	25 – 30

SPECIAL PRICE LIST

CATTAIL

The vast majority of Cattail is trimmed with a red line, but there is also a variation with both red and black lines around the rim. Although this list contains all the Cattail that I know of, I'm sure many more pieces exist. For more Cattail, see Index.

America

Bean pot, 2 handles	*$30 – $35*
Bowl, low, 4¼"	*6 – 8*
Bowl, low, 6¼"	*8 – 10*
Bowl, low, sunken knob lid, 7¼"	*20 – 25*
Bowl, low, sunken knob lid, 2-quart, 8¼"	*25 – 30*
Bowl, high, round, 6¼"	*8 – 10*
Bowl, high, round, 7¼"	*10 – 12*

[The above have lids with a flat center]

Bowl, high, straight side, 4¼"	*6 – 8*
Bowl, high, straight side, 5¼"	*8 – 10*
Bowl, high, straight side, 6¼"	*10 – 12*

[The above have smooth, almost flat lids]

Casserole, 1¾-quart, 8¼" diameter, tab handles	*25 – 30*
Cookie jar	*40 – 50*
Custard, 3½"	*6 – 8*
Drip (same as small leftover)	*10 – 12*
Gravy	*15 – 18*
Jug, 1-quart, 6" high	*20 – 25*
Jug, ice lip, 2-quart, 5⅞" high	*25 – 30*
Leftover, 4" diameter	*10 – 12*
Leftover, 5" diameter	*15 – 18*
Leftover, 6" diameter	*20 – 25*
Shaker, pair	*15 – 20*

Ballerina

Cream	*$6 – $8*
Cup	*6 – 8*
Gravy	*15 – 18*
Plate, 10"	*12 – 15*
Saucer	*2 – 3*
Sugar	*10 – 12*

Camwood

Bowl, footed, 9½"	*$18 – $20*
Bowl, round, 9"	*18 – 20*
Bowl, soup, 8"	*12 – 15*
Bowl, soup, embossed lug, 6"	*10 – 12*
Cream	*6 – 8*
Dish, 5¼"	*3 – 4*
Gravy	*15 – 18*
Gravy liner/pickle	*8 – 10*
Plate, 6"	*2 – 3*
Plate, 8"	*6 – 7*
Plate, 9¾"	*8 – 10*
Plate, grill	*12 – 15*

Plate, square, 7¼". . . . . *$6 – $7*
Platter, oval, 11½". . . . . *12 – 15*
Platter, round, tab, 11". . . . . *12 – 15*
Shaker, pair . . . . *10 – 12*
Sugar . . . . *10 – 12*

Empress

Platter, oval, 13½". . . . . *$15 – $18*

Kitchenware   The fork and spoon priced below are the elusive decaled short ones, not the long ones with just a red line.

Butter, 1-pound . . . . *$30 – $35*
Cookie jar, barrel. . . . . *50 – 55*
Jug, ball, ceramic-tipped stopper . . . . *30 – 35*
Jug, canteen, regular. . . . . *30 – 35*
Jug, canteen, wide . . . . *30 – 35*
Pie baker, 8½". . . . . *12 – 15*
Pie baker, 10" . . . . *15 – 18*
Tumbler, tall, 4½". . . . . *20 – 25*
Utensil, pie server. . . . . *15 – 20*
Utensil, fork. . . . . *30+*
Utensil, spoon . . . . *25+*

Laurella

Creamer. . . . . *$6 – $8*
Shaker, pair . . . . *10 – 12*
Sugar . . . . *10 – 12*

Mount Vernon

Bowl, soup, 7¾". . . . . *$12 – $15*
Creamer. . . . . *6 – 8*
Custard . . . . *6 – 8*
Dish, 5⅛". . . . . *3 – 4*
Plate, 6¼". . . . . *2 – 3*
Plate, 9" . . . . *10 – 12*
Plate, chop . . . . *15 – 20*
Plate, square, 10" . . . . *12 – 15*
Plate, oval, 13½". . . . . *15 – 18*
Shaker, pair . . . . *10 – 12*
Sugar . . . . *10 – 12*
Teapot . . . . *40 – 45*

KITCHENWARE

Bowl, mixing, 6". . . . . *$8 – $10*
Bowl, mixing, 7". . . . . *10 – 12*
Bowl, mixing, 8". . . . . *12 – 15*
Bowl, mixing, 9". . . . . *15 – 20*
Jug, batter. . . . . *35 – 40*
Jug, syrup. . . . . *30 – 35*

Netherlands

Bowl, soup, 7³/₄"	$12 – $15
Creamer	6 – 8
Cup	6 – 8
Dish, 5⁵/₈"	3 – 4
Plate, 6"	2 – 3
Saucer	2 – 3
Sugar	10 – 12

Oxford   (Old Style)

Butter, 1-pound	$65 – $75
Teapot	35 – 40

Oxford   (Restyled)

Teapot, 6-cup	$35 – $40

Upico

Butter, ¹/₄-pound	$40 – $45
Butter, 1-pound	65 – 75
Casserole, tab handle, 7¹/₂"	25 – 30
Creamer	6 – 8
Cup	6 – 8
Jug, batter, chrome top	60 – 65
Jug, batter, round	35 – 40
Jug, syrup, chrome top	40 – 45
Jug, syrup, round	30 – 35
Plate, 9¹/₄"	10 – 12
Saucer	2 – 3
Shaker, pair	15 – 20
Sugar	10 – 12
Teapot	35 – 40
Tray, batter set	18 – 20

CHILDREN'S WARE

Divided dish, all pottery	$30 – $35
Divided dish /Upico, all pottery	30 – 35
Feeding dish, metal bottom	20 – 25
Mug	15 – 20

LAURELLA   (1948)

Embossed laurel leaves around the rim and edges.

Decorated in solid pastel colors of Cocotan, Jade (green), Jonquil (yellow), and Periwinkle (blue).

Bowl, salad, 9" .... *$15 – $18*
Bowl, soup, 8" .... *10 – 12*
Creamer .... *4 – 6*
Cup .... *4 – 6*
Dish, 5⅝" .... *2 – 3*
Plate, 6½" .... *1 – 2*
Plate, 9"* .... *7 – 9*
Plate, cake, lug, 11" .... *10 – 12*
Platter, 11"* .... *10 – 12*
Saucer .... *1 – 2*
Shaker, pair .... *8 – 10*
Sugar .... *8 – 10*

"LEAF"

I see very little of this shape, and by the nature of the few pieces that have
come to my attention, I suspect this is a small luncheon or tea set. Solid pastel
colors: Gray, green, flesh pink, and yellow. I include it so that it won't be confused with Steubenville's Woodfield.

Cup .... *$4 – $6*
Plate, party .... *6 – 8*
Shaker, pair .... *8 – 10*

MOUNT VERNON   (mid 1934)

Dinnerware added in 1935. This shape is a restyling of Atlas-Globe's Broadway shape. In most dinnerware lines, the creamer and sugar are easier to find
than the teapot. In this line, the teapot is easy to find; the creamer and sugar
very difficult.

Usually decal-decorated; common decals found are Cattail, Cottage Garden,
Orchid, and Poppy.

A bowl set has turned up in Oxford colors of (smallest to largest) red, yellow, green, and blue, as well as a green shaker.

Mt. Vernon: Plate, creamer, sugar, shaker (green), and teapot (Iris).

Dinnerware

Bowl, soup, 7³/₄"	$10 – $12
Casserole, pierced lug handle, 9¹/₂"	20 – 25
Creamer	10 – 12
Cup	4 – 6
Dish, 5¹/₈"	2 – 3
Plate, 9"	7 – 9
Plate, chop, 11¹/₄"	12 – 15
Plate, round, 6¹/₂"	2 – 3
Plate, square, 10"	10 – 12
Platter, oval, 13¹/₂"	12 – 15
Saucer	1 – 2
Shaker, pair	8 – 10
Sugar	15 – 20
Teapot	30 – 35

Kitchenware   The drip coffee is the teapot with a handled china drip; the drip is *not* in the Mount Vernon shape.

Baker, round, 5"	$4 – $6
Baker, round 5³/₄"	6 – 8
Bowl, mixing, 5¹/₄"	6 – 8
Bowl, mixing, 6¹/₄"	8 – 10
Bowl, mixing, 7¹/₂"	10 – 12
Bowl, mixing, 9"	12 – 15
Casserole, 7¹/₂"	20 – 25
Custard	4 – 6
Dish, shirred egg, lug, 6"	8 – 10
Drip coffee	ND
Jug, batter	25 – 30
Jug, syrup	20 – 25

Leftover, round, 4¹/₈"... *$6 – $10*
Leftover, round, 5¹/₈".. *10 – 15*
Leftover, round, 6¹/₈".. *15 – 20*

NETHERLANDS   (1932/1934)

This is Atlas-Globe's Old Holland shape which they brought out in 1932. Universal retained the name for a while and then changed it to Netherlands.

Netherlands was made with both square and round flatware. It is an embossed design showing both windmills and people.

Decal decorations include an Early American monochrome scene and Poppy, as well as many florals.

Bowl, soup, 7³/₄"... *$10 – $12*
Bowl, vegetable, round 8¹/₂".. *15 – 18*
Bowl, vegetable, rectangular, 9¹/₄"................................... *10 – 12*
Creamer .... *4 – 6*
Cup .... *4 – 6*
Dish, 5⁵/₈"... *2 – 3*
Plate, 6" .... *1 – 2*
Plate, 9" .... *7 – 9*

Netherlands:
Creamer, plate,
and Cattail sugar.

Plate, 10" .... *$10 – $12*
Platter, oval, 11¼" .... *10 – 12*
Platter, rectangular, 13" .... *12 – 15*
Platter, oblong, lug, 12" .... *12 – 15*
Saucer .... *1 – 2*
Sugar .... *8 – 10*

RODEO

An embossed rope design just in from the edge of the flatware and the rim of hollowware. I have seen solid colors of gray, green, turquoise, and yellow. Decals: Hopalong Cassidy and Poppy.

Bowl, soup, 9" .... *$10 – $12*
Creamer .... *4 – 6*
Cup .... *4 – 6*
Plate, 6¼" .... *1 – 2*
Plate, 9¼" .... *7 – 9*
   Hopalong Cassidy .... *35 – 40*
Platter, lug, 11" .... *10 – 12*
Saucer .... *1 – 2*
Sugar .... *8 – 10*

UPICO   (1937)

Designed by Walter Karl Titze. The name apparently stands for *U*niversal *Pot*teries *I*nc., *C*ambridge, *O*hio. This is one of the most extensive of Universal's shapes, including both dinnerware and kitchenware. The easy-to-find pieces are pitchers, leftovers, casseroles, and plates. Hard-to-find pieces are the teapot, Tom and Jerry bowl and mugs, and child's dish (see Child's Ware).

Decorations include solid colors, decals, and combinations of both. The solid colors were put on the lower, banded portions of the hollowware and the rims of the flatware. The easiest color to find is Eleanor blue. Red, Midnight Black, and Sunlight Yellow are scarce. Gold (this may be the official name for yellow) and Orange Sunset are mentioned in the trade papers but I have not seen them. Look for the "patriotic" rectangular canteen jug with the red china-tipped stopper, white upper body, and blue lower body. The tilt-top jug was used in the brown Snowflower line.

The most common decal found is Circus, almost always with Eleanor blue except on the flatware. Many other decals will be found including "Anemone," Cattail, and Chrysanthemum. Look for the salad set with six square plates, each with a different decal representing a type of salad: Fruit, vegetable, chicken, crab, lobster, and shrimp.

Upico: Circus shaker, small ball jug, "Red Rose" creamer, teapot, and "Red Rose" sugar.

PRICING　Prices are for decal-decorated or Eleanor blue pieces. Add 50% for red, black or yellow pieces.

Dinnerware

Bean pot, individual . . . . *$6 – $8*
Bowl, nested, 5¹/₈" . . . . *6 – 8*
Bowl, nested, 8³/₄" . . . . *12 – 15*
Bowl, salad, 9¹/₄" . . . . *15 – 18*
Casserole, lugged bottom, 8¹/₂" . . . . *20 – 25*
Creamer . . . . *4 – 6*
Cup . . . . *4 – 6*
Custard . . . . *4 – 6*
Gravy boat . . . . *12 – 15*
Plate, 6¹/₄" . . . . *1 – 2*
Plate, 8¹/₈" . . . . *5 – 6*
Plate, 9¹/₄" . . . . *7 – 9*
Plate, 10¹/₄" . . . . *10 – 12*
Plate, square, 7¹/₄" . . . . *7 – 9*
Saucer . . . . *1 – 2*
Sugar . . . . *8 – 10*
Teapot . . . . *40 – 45*
Tumbler, small . . . . *4 – 6*

Kitchenware　The 10¹/₂" mixing bowl was used for the Tom and Jerry bowl. The 11¹/₂" lug tray holds the four-piece, chrome-topped batter set (1940):

two jugs, tray, and silver-topped shaker (for sugar). The shaker is an unusual addition; I have never seen one in other butter sets.

Bean pot, 2 handles .... *$15 – $20*
Bowl, mixing, 5¼" .... *6 – 8*
Bowl, mixing, 6½" .... *8 – 10*
Bowl, mixing, 7½" .... *10 – 12*
Bowl, mixing, 9" .... *12 – 15*
Bowl, mixing, 10½" .... *15 – 20*
　　Tom and Jerry .... *25 – 30*
Butter, ¼-pound .... *20 – 25*
Butter, 1-pound .... *20 – 25*
Casserole, tab lid, 7½" .... *20 – 25*
Jug, ball .... *15 – 18*
Jug, ball, individual .... *12 – 15*
Jug, canteen, rectangular, cork tip .... *25 – 30*
Jug, rectangular, batter, flat lid .... *25 – 30*
Jug, rectangular, syrup, flat lid .... *20 – 25*
Jug, rectangular, water .... *25 – 30*
Jug, round, batter .... *35 – 40*
Jug, round, syrup .... *30 – 35*
Jug, round, batter, chrome top .... *40 – 45*
Jug, round, syrup, chrome top .... *35 – 40*
Jug, round, tilt-top, 3-pint, 8½" .... *30 – 35*
Leftover, rectangular, pinch knob, 7¼" .... *15 – 20*
Leftover, rectangular, tab finial, 7¾" .... *15 – 20*
Leftover, round, 4¾" .... *6 – 10*
Leftover, round 5½" (plain lid) .... *10 – 15*
Mug .... *12 – 15*
　　Tom and Jerry .... *15 – 18*
Shaker, pair .... *10 – 12*
Tray, round, lug, 11½" .... *12 – 15*

KITCHENWARE

Universal has a very extensive kitchenware line if you include all the pieces in America, "Pedestal," and Oxford, plus the miscellaneous pieces, as well as the kitchenware that matches the dinnerware in the Ballerina, Mt. Vernon, and Upico shapes.

AMERICA　(mid 1934)

I found this shape name in an old ad picturing the cookie jar and the bean pot. The cookie jar also appears in an old Sears catalog, along with a number of other pieces that seem to be of the same shape.

Bean pot, lug handle .... *$15 – $20*
Bean pot, open handle .... *15 – 20*
Bowl, low, 4¼" .... *6 – 8*

Kitchenware: America and Barrel: Cattail America bean pot (open handles), Cattail America cookie jar, Hollyhock America bean pot (tab handles), and Cattail barrel cookie jar.

Bowl, low, 6¼" .... $8 – $10
Bowl, low, sunken knob lid, 7¼" .... 15 – 20
Bowl, low, sunken knob lid, 2-quart, 8¼" .... 20 – 25
Bowl, high, round, 6¼" .... 6 – 10
Bowl, high, round, 7¼" .... 10 – 15
  [The above have lids with a flat center]
Bowl, high, straight side, 4¼" .... 6 – 10
Bowl, high, straight side, 5¼" .... 6 – 10
Bowl, high, straight side, 6¼" .... 8 – 10
  [The above have smooth, almost flat lids]
Casserole, 1¾" quart, 8¼" diameter, tab handles .... 20 – 25
Cookie jar .... 30 – 35
Custard, 3½" .... 4 – 6
Drip (same as small leftover) .... 6 – 10
Jug, 1-quart, 6" high .... 15 – 20
Jug, ice lip, 2-quart, 5⅞" high .... 20 – 25
Leftover, round, 4" diameter .... 6 – 10
Leftover, round, 5" diameter .... 10 – 15
Leftover, round, 6" diameter .... 15 – 20
Shaker, pair .... 15 – 20

MISCELLANY

The cake server comes in one size only. The original fork and spoon were short and came with a variety of decal decorations. These are not easy to find. It would seem that they were replaced at least as early as mid-1936 with the long fork and spoon which will be found either with generic red lines, blue or brown with white handles, or in Carnival solid colors.

Kitchenware: Canteen Jugs. Chrysanthemum tall canteen jug, Old Curiosity shop regular canteen jug, Calico Fruit tilt-top canteen jug, and Cattail wide canteen jug.

The ball jug with the ceramic-tipped cork seems to be the jug that was sold with the tumblers. I have never seen a large canteen jug with a decoration other than Chrysanthemum. The reamer sat on top of the barrel jug.

Decals you will find include Cattail, Dinette, Kitchen Bouquet, Orchid, "Stendahl Poppy," and "Stendahl Wheat."

Bowl, salad, 9¼"	$15 – $18
Cake plate	10 – 12
Cookie jar, barrel	30 – 35
Jug, ball	15 – 18
Jug, ball, ceramic-tipped stopper	20 – 25
Jug, barrel	25 – 30
Jug, canteen	20 – 25
Jug, canteen, tall	20 – 25
Jug, canteen, tilt-top	20 – 25

Kitchenware: "Stendahl Poppy" Puffin tilt-top jug, Texas under Six Flags stoppered ball jug, and "Rose Bouquet" Puffin jug.

Jug, canteen, wide . . . . *$20 – $25*
Jug, "Puffin" . . . . *25 – 30*
Jug, "Puffin," tilt-top . . . . *25 – 30*
Leftover, crimped base, rectangular, 5" × 8" . . . . *10 – 15*
Leftover, crimped base, rectangular, 6¹/₂" × 9³/₄" . . . . *15 – 20*
Mug . . . . *12 – 15*
Pie baker, 8¹/₂" . . . . *10 – 12*
Pie baker, 10" . . . . *10 – 12*
Reamer . . . . *ND*
Tumbler, short, 2¹/₄" × 2¹/₂" wide . . . . *6 – 8*
Tumbler, tall, 4¹/₂" . . . . *20 – 25*
Utensil, cake server . . . . *12 – 15*
Utensil, fork, long
    Red lines . . . . *20 – 25*
    Solid colors . . . . *25 – 30*
Utensil, fork, short . . . . *25 – 30*
Utensil, spoon, long
    Red lines . . . . *15 – 20*
    Solid colors . . . . *20 – 25*
Utensil, spoon, short . . . . *20 – 25*

COUPE   Decorated in solid color of Chinese Red or various decals. The Chinese Red seems more common.

Bowl, 9¹/₂" . . . . *$15 – $18*
Jug, batter . . . . *25 – 30*
Jug, syrup . . . . *20 – 25*
Shaker, range, pair . . . . *15 – 20*

OXFORD   (Oldstyle)

A kitchenware line with a rippled shape. The leftover bottoms are the same bowl as the mixing bowls, with the addition of lids. In Sears' catalog, the Upico tilt-top jug and the 10" fork and spoon were part of the set.

It was decorated in both solid colors and decals. Solid colors include dark blue (marine), brown, Chinese Red, turquoise (called Aqua-blue in the Sears catalog), and yellow. The brown was sometimes decorated with the incised Snowflower pattern in white.

Decals include Cattail and Circus with Eleanor blue bottoms.

Bowl, nesting, 3³/₈" (custard) . . . . *$4 – $6*
Bowl, nesting, 16-ounce, 5" . . . . *8 – 10*
Bowl, nesting, 28-ounce, 6" . . . . *10 – 12*
Bowl, nesting, 42-ounce, 7" . . . . *12 – 15*
Bowl, nesting, 66-ounce, 8¹/₄" . . . . *15 – 20*
Bowl, salad, 4¹/₂-pint, 9¹/₄" . . . . *15 – 18*
Casserole, 4¹/₂-pint, 8" . . . . *20 – 25*
Drip/Jam jar, 16-ounce . . . . *12 – 15*
Jug, 2-pint, 6" . . . . *15 – 20*
Leftover, round, 12-ounce, 4" . . . . *6 – 10*

Oxford/Old Style (Clockwise from top): *Circus six-cup teapot, four-cup teapot, two-cup teapot, Snowflower small bowl, shaker, and mug.*

Leftover, round, 16-ounce, 5" . . . . *$10 – $15*
Leftover, round, 28-ounce, 6" . . . . *15 – 20*
Mug, handled . . . . *12 – 15*
Shaker, range, pair, 4½" . . . . *15 – 20*
Teapot, 2-cup . . . . *20 – 25*
Teapot, 4-cup . . . . *20 – 25*
Teapot, 6-cup . . . . *20 – 25*

OXFORD   (Redesigned / 1939)

The ripple shape was dropped. The line seems to be an amalgam of old and new shapes. Can be found in solid Carnival colors of red, green, blue, yellow, and purple as well as decals.

Bean pot, individual . . . . *$5 – $7*
Bowl, mixing, four sizes . . . . *ND*
Bowl, salad bowl . . . . *15 – 18*
Butter, 1-pound . . . . *20 – 25*
Casserole . . . . *20 – 25*
Casserole, French, open . . . . *15 – 20*
Custard . . . . *4 – 6*
Jug, ball . . . . *15 – 18*
Jug, canteen, rectangular . . . . *20 – 25*
Pie baker . . . . *10 – 12*
Shaker, range, pair . . . . *15 – 20*
Teapot, 2-cup . . . . *20 – 25*

Oxford/Restyled: Shaker, Cattail teapot, and small mixing bowl.

Teapot, 4-cup. . . . . *$20 – $25*
Teapot, 6-cup. . . . . *20 – 25*

"PEDESTAL"

Only five pieces of this kitchenware shape have been seen, most often with the Bittersweet decal. It may have been made specifically for this decal, although pieces will also be found in Chinese Red.

    PRICING   Values below are for Chinese Red. Other decorations, except Bittersweet prices above, will be 20% less.

Casserole, 5-pint . . . . *$20 – $25*
Drip, 1-pint . . . . *15 - 18*
Jug, tilt-top. . . . . *25 – 30*
Shaker, range, pair . . . . *15 – 20*
Stack set . . . . *40 – 45*

VAN BRIGGLE POTTERY

Colorado Springs, Colorado

Founded in 1901 by Artus Van Briggle, who had worked as a decorator at Rookwood, and his wife Anne. Artus moved to Colorado for his health but died in 1904. His widow continued the business for eight years and then it passed into other hands. Still in operation. See Traveler's Directory.

Artus Van Briggle is known for his dead matte glaze, which he worked for several years to perfect, and for his use of modeling and colored glazes, as opposed to hand painting, to achieve his effects. Pre-1921 pieces are the most desirable to collectors.

See Evans, see Kovel, see Nelson and see Sasicki in Bibliography. See Traveler's Directory.

MARKS   The common elements of a Van Briggle mark are the conjoint A and the name "Van Briggle." Pieces were dated through 1920. For a detailed chronology see Nelson in the Bibliography.

PRICING   Each entry is followed by the shape number (reference Nelson in Bibliography). Prices are chronological, with the date or period included in each listing.

Bookends, Owl and moon, teens period, pair, 6"
  Light blue *$175*
  Yellow brown *325*
Bowl, plain design, 4" diameter   /#41
  Cobalt, 1903 . . . . *475*
  Turquoise, marked "Original"/1940s *25*
Bowl, stylized leaves, 6" diameter   /#22
  Curdled green, 1907–1912 . . . . *375*
  Maroon, 1916 . . . . *125*
Bowl, Pine Cone and branches, 10" diameter   /#762
  Pink, 1907–1912 . . . . *850*
  Turquoise, 1970s (75th Anniversary) *275*
Conch Shell   /1940s
  Turquoise, 8" *35*
  Maroon, 12" *75*
Jug, "Firewater" w/stopper, 7"   /#12
  Green, 1902 . . . . *3500*
  Curdled brown, 1907–1912 . . . . *2250*
Lamp, Damsel at Damascus, 12"
  Maroon, 1940s *275*
  Turquoise, 1940s *225*
Mug, leaves, 5½"   /#108B
  Light green, 1903 . . . . *675*

Dark blue, 1906 .... *$450*
Paperweight, Rabbit 2½"
  Turquoise, teens *75*
  Maroon, teens *110*
Plaque, Indian Head, 2½" × 4"
  Maroon & dark blue, fine mold, teens................................. *275*
  Turquoise, 1920s.. *75*
  Turquoise, 1970s.. *35*
Plate, goose heads, 6"   /#20
  Black, 1902 .... *1200*
  Yellow, 1906 .... *500*
  Turquoise, 1907–1912 .... *275*
Tile, 1907–1912, 6"
  Landscape, four colors, marked "VBP Co."............................. *475*
  Art Nouveau floral design, rose, green, yellow and blue, unmarked *275*
Vase, Violets & leaves, 4½"   /#645
  White w/green buds, 1907–1912...................................... *375*
  Light and dark green, 1915.. *150*
  Light and dark blue, 1920s (USA) *35*
  Dark brown w/green, 1930s... *45*
Vase, stylized flowers, 5½"   /#833
  Light blue stippled glaze w/pink flowers, 1907–1912 .... *875*
  Curdled green, 1917.. *375*
  Maroon & dark blue, poor mold, 1920s *25*
  High glaze orange, 1920s *275*
  Light brown & green *35*
  Blue & turquoise, 1940s.. *20*
Vase, flowers, 6"   /#132
  Light green w/red flowers *1250*
  Bronzed, 1907–1912.. *1500*
Vase, floral design, 8"
  Turquoise matt, 1960s *25*
  Moonglo matt white, 1970s *25*
  High glaze brown w/green drip, marked "Anna Van" *20*
  Black matt, 1980s.. *35*
  Cobalt blue, 1986 .... *25*
  Tawny yellow, 1989 .... *20*
Vase, Despondency, 14"   /#9
  Mustard, 1902... *25000*
  Yellow, 1907–1912 .... *7500*
  Dark Maroon, 1917 .... *850*
  Brown w/green, 1930s *450*
  Turquoise & Blue, 1970s *125*
Vase, plain w/two handles, 10½"   /#240
  Black matt, 1904.. *950*
  Medium green, 1906... *675*
  Dark maroon, 1920s... *175*
Vase, Three-Headed Indian, 12"
  Brown, 1915 .... *1500*

Maroon, 1920s *$250*

Turquoise, 1990s. *125*

Vase, closed Yucca, 17"   /#157

Green, 1903. . . . . *2500*

Yellow w/red flowers, 1903 . . . . *4500*

Maroon, 1904 . . . . *1800*

Blue w/green leaves, white flowers, 1907–1912 . . . . *3000*

Vase, Poppy pods, 4"   /#21

Charcoal green, 1902. . . . . *1000*

Olive Green, 1904 (experimental marks) *850*

Turquoise, 1920s. *40*

VERNON POTTERIES, LTD. / VERNON KILNS

Vernon (Los Angeles), California

CHAPTER AT A GLANCE

DINNERWARE
ANYTIME
  Heavenly Days
  Imperial
  Tickled Pink
CHATELAINE
  Solid / Multicolors
MELINDA
  Melinda /
    Native California (Solid Colors)
  Fruitdale
  Hawaii
  May Flower
  Monterey
MONTECITO
  Coronado (Solid Colors)
  Early / Modern California
    (Solid Colors)
  Brown-Eyed Susan
  Coastline
  Frontier Days / Winchester '73
  Plaid / Variations
SAN MARINO
  Casual California
  California Shadows
  California Originals (California
    Heritage)
ULTRA
  Ultra California (Solid Colors)

Moby Dick
Our America
Salamina
Walt Disney
FIGURES
DISNEY
  Vases and Bowls
MISCELLANY
MOVIE STARS
SOUVENIR / SPECIALTY ITEMS
GENERAL
  Airplanes
  Business
  Cities
  Events
  Foreign
  Other
  People
  Railroad
  States
  World War II
SETS
  Bits of America
  Cocktail Hour
  French Opera
  Historic Baltimore
  Music Masters

In 1931 Fay Bennison bought the Poxon China Company and renamed it Vernon Kilns. At first Vernon used Poxon molds but soon developed its own distinctive dinnerware shapes. Specialties and some art ware were also produced, all in an earthenware body. In 1958 the pottery was sold to Metlox (which see), which continued to produce a few lines in their Vernonware division.

Vernon has the largest variety of collectible lines of any California pottery: its specialty ware depicting cities, states, famous people, and more; its bright and pastel-colored dinnerware; its lines by famous designers such as Rockwell

Kent (Salamina, Moby Dick, and Our America) and Don Blanding (fish and floral lines); and Walt Disney figurines and dinnerware.

See Chipman and see Nelson in Bibliography. See Clubs/Newsletters.

MARKS   Vernon used a wide variety of marks, most specific to the lines they appear on.

DINNERWARE

At first, I found Vernon's dinnerware patterns a little difficult to comprehend due to its practice of using the same design in different colors and giving each variation a separate name. It all became clear to me thanks to Maxine Nelson's excellent book (see Bibliography). She is also to be credited with devising some of the shape names used by collectors (Vernon seems not to have named a number of its shapes).

ANYTIME   (ca.1955)

Designed by Elliott House. There are several patterns on this shape, but Heavenly Days and Tickled Pink (the same design but in different colors, continued by Metlox after it bought Vernon) are the most popular because of their 1950s geometric look, and Imperial is hard to find.

The pepper shaker is shorter than the salt shaker. The tidbits have metal or wooden handles.

Heavenly Days   Small squares and crosses in aqua, pink, and mocha-charcoal. Solid turquoise cups, serving pieces (casserole has patterned lid), and shakers and turquoise lids on coffee pot and sugar.

PRICING   See Tickled Pink.

Imperial   Abstract sgraffito pattern on black glaze.

PRICING   Use high end of Tickled Pink.

Tickled Pink   Small squares and crosses in pink and charcoal. Solid-pink cups, serving pieces (casserole has patterned lid) and shakers, and pink lids on coffee pot and sugar.

PRICING   Both Heavenly Days and Tickled Pink are approximately the same value, Tickled Pink being a little higher.

Bowl, chowder, 6"	$7 – $10
Bowl, soup, coupe	12 – 15
Bowl, vegetable, round, 7½"	10 – 12
Bowl, vegetable, round, 9"	12 – 14
Bowl, vegetable, divided, 9"	15 – 20
Butter, ¼-pound	22 – 35
Butter pat, 2½"	15 – 18
Coffee pot, 8-cup	35 – 45
Creamer	7 – 12
Cup	7 – 8
Dish, fruit, 5½"	3 – 6
Gravy	15 – 18

Jug, 1-pint	$15 – $18
Jug, 1-quart	20 – 25
Jug, 2-quart, 10" tall	25 – 30
Mug, 12-ounce	12 – 18
Plate, 6"	4 – 6
Plate, 7½"	5 – 8
Plate, 10"	8 – 10
Plate, chop, 13"	18 – 25
Plate, party, 12" × 8"	35 – 40
Platter, 9½"	9 – 12
Platter, 11"	15 – 18
Platter, 13½"	15 – 22
Relish, ring handle, oval, 6"	15 – 18
Relish, 3-part	22
Saucer	2 – 4
Shaker, wood top, each	6 – 10
Sugar	12 – 15
Teapot	30 – 45
Tidbit, 2-tier	15 – 18
Tidbit, 3-tier	18 – 25
Tumbler, 14-ounce	12 – 20

CHATELAINE (ca. 1953)

Designed by Sharon Merrill. Solid colors of Bronze (chocolate brown) and Topaz (warm beige) and decorated colors of Platinum (ivory with reddish-brown and yellow leaf accents) and Jade (soft green with lighter green and Topaz leaf accents).

PRICING Use the lower half of the range for Bronze and Topaz; use the upper half for the decorated colors, as these are more popular, especially the Jade.

Bowl, chowder, 6"	$12 – $18
Bowl, salad, 12"	45 – 70
Bowl, serving, 9"	25 – 45
Creamer	30 – 40
Cup, coffee, flat base	14 – 22
Cup, tea, pedestal	15 – 25
Plate, 6½"	10 – 14
Plate, 7½"	12 – 18
Plate, 2 corners decorated, 10½"	15 – 25
Plate, 4 corners decorated, 10½"	18 – 35
Plate, chop, 14"	45 – 65
Platter, 16"	55 – 80
Saucer, coffee	6
Saucer, tea	6
Shaker, pair	25 – 40
Sugar	35 – 50
Teapot	200 +

MELINDA   (1942)

Designed by Royal Hickman. There is an embossed rope effect around the flatware and on the bases of the hollowware. Handles have an embossed leaf at the top, and finials resemble flowers.

Bowl, chowder, lug, 6" .... *$10 – $15*
Bowl, petal, 10" .... *40 – 45*
Bowl, salad, 12¹/₂" .... *45 – 65*
Bowl, serving, oval, 10" .... *18 – 25*
Bowl, serving, round, 9" .... *15 – 25*
Bowl, soup, rimmed, 8" .... *12 – 18*
Butter, ¹/₄-pound .... *30 – 45*
Casserole, 8" .... *35 – 65*
Casserole, individual, 4³/₄" .... *25 – 35*
Coffee pot, 8-cup .... *35 – 65*
Creamer, both sizes .... *10 – 15*
Cup .... *10 – 20*
Cup, AD .... *12 – 23*
Dish, fruit, 5¹/₂" .... *5 – 8*
Eggcup .... *15 – 20*
Gravy .... *20 – 35*
Jam jar .... *55 – 65*
Jug, 1¹/₂-pint .... *20 – 30*
Jug, 2-quart .... *30 – 40*
Plate, 6¹/₂" .... *5 – 8*
Plate, 7¹/₂" .... *7 – 12*
Plate, 9¹/₂" .... *9 – 15*
Plate, 10¹/₂" .... *12 – 18*
Plate, chop, 12" .... *15 – 30*
Plate, chop, 14" .... *30 – 50*
Plate, square, 8¹/₂" .... *20 – 30*
Platter, 12" .... *15 – 25*
Platter, 14" .... *20 – 35*
Platter, 16" .... *35 – 60*
Relish, single, leaf shape, 12" .... *20 – 25*
Relish, 2-part, leaf shape, 11" .... *25 – 35*
Relish, 4-part, leaf shape, 14" .... *35 – 60*
Saucer .... *2 – 5*
Saucer, AD .... *3 – 5*
Shaker, pair .... *12 – 24*
Sugar .... *12 – 20*
Teapot, 6-cup .... *45 – 65*
Tidbit, 2-tier .... *20 – 30*
Tidbit, 3-tier .... *25 – 40*

Melinda / Native California, Solid Colors
Melinda, the shape, came in two color lines. One is called Melinda. It has high-glaze colors of aqua and white. Price this at the high end of the range. The other is Native California. It has matte colors of aqua, blue, green, ivory, pink, and yellow. Price this at the low end of the range.

Fruitdale   Fruits and flowers.
  PRICING   Use the middle of the range.

Hawaii   A lotus flower maroon print with hand painting. This is the same design as Lei Lani on the Melinda shape.
  PRICING   Two times the high end of the range.

May Flower   Transfer print of a large spray of flowers with hand painting.
  PRICING   Use the low end of the range.

Monterey   Blue and red bands emphasize the shape.
  PRICING   Use the middle of the range.

MONTECITO

The original Montecito was an angular shape that was restyled at least twice, per Bill Stern, and given a rounded look. Pieces restyled include cup, 1-pint bowl, large salad bowl, cream, sugar, gravy, casserole, teapot, coffee server, tankard (replaced by the 1-quart bulb-bottomed jug), 14" chop plate, butter, AD cup, AD creamer, and AD sugar. The early AD sugar was open.

Montecito was decorated in solid colors and hand-painted patterns. The desirable hand-painted patterns are by Gale Turnbull and include Brown-Eyed Susan, Coastline, Native American, and a wide variety of Plaids. Also highly desirable is Paul Davidson's Frontier Days/Winchester '73 and the patterns designed by Harry Bird.

NOTE   Please remember that pieces were added and dropped from the line, and all patterns were not produced over the life of the line. This means that you will not find every piece in every pattern. To help in understanding this, /* follows early pieces and /** follows late pieces in the listings.

Coronado, Solid Colors   This is a variation on the Montecito shape. It has what Maxine Nelson calls a "cubist band" around the rims of the flatware and tumbler and around the shoulder of the hollowware. A variant cup with the band around the bottom was shown in Vernon Views. This is not an extensive line.

The following solid colors have been reported: Blue, brown, Green, light blue, light green, Orange, pale blue-gray, peach, pink, turquoise, and Yellow.

Bowl, soup	*$12 – $15*
Carafe, wooden handle	*30*
Creamer	*10 – 12*
Cup	*8 – 10*
Dish, dessert, 5½"	*5 – 6*
Plate, 6½"	*4 – 5*
Plate, 10½"	*8 – 12*
Platter	*15 – 18*
Saucer	*2 – 3*
Sugar	*10 – 12*
Tumbler	*15 – 20*

Early / Modern California, Solid Colors   The candle holder listed below is a Jane Bennison design. It is not part of the Montecito shape but comes in many of the solid colors. The 7½" soup bowl and the 7½" vegetable bowl are almost identical except that the latter is a little deeper.

Montecito was decorated in three solid color lines. There were the strong **Early California** colors of brown, dark blue (cobalt), green, ivory (white), maroon, orange, pink, turquoise, and yellow (blue and peach have also been reported) and the soft, pastel **Modern California** colors of Azure (blue), Mist (gray), Orchid, Pistachio (green), Sand (beige), and Straw (pale yellow).

In addition, Bill Stern informs me that there was a solid-color Montecito line that predates the above two. Colors confirmed in this line so far include Ivory (white) and yellow (darker than Early California yellow).

NOTE The list below is as complete as I could currently make it of known Montecito pieces. Pieces confirmed as having been made in solid colors are priced; unpriced items were only used in decaled or hand-painted lines.

PRICING Ivory (white), maroon, and Sand are at the upper end of the range.

Ashtray, round, 4¾" /* .... $12 – $15
Ashtray, round, 5" /*. .... 15 – 18
Ashtray, square, 3" /* .... 8 – 12
Ashtray, square, 4" /**
Bowl, 1-pint. .... 18 – 20
Bowl, chowder, lug, open, 6". .... 12 – 15
  w/lid .... 15 – 24
Bowl, mixing, 5" .... 15 – 20
Bowl, mixing, 6" .... 19 – 25
Bowl, mixing, 7" .... 22 – 30
Bowl, mixing, 8" .... 25 – 35
Bowl, mixing, 9" .... 30 – 40
Bowl, salad, 10½" /**
Bowl, serving, angular, 13" .... 40 – 60
Bowl, soup, 8½". .... 12 – 15
Bowl, vegetable, oval, 10". .... 18 – 22
Bowl, vegetable, round, 7½"
Bowl, vegetable, round, 8½"
Bowl, vegetable, round, 9". .... 18 – 22
  w/ridged lid .... 35 – 40
Butter, ¼-pound .... 35 – 45
Candle holder 50
Carafe, w/stopper, w/Bakelite handle.............................. 30 – 35
  w/ceramic handle .... ND
  w/wooden handle .... 30 – 35
Casserole, 8" .... 30 – 45
Casserole, individual, 4" /**
Chicken pie server, stick handle, 4" /** .... ND
Coaster/Cup warmer, 4½". .... 18 – 22
Coffee pot, AD .... 60 – 65
Compote, 9½" /* .... 45 – 65
Creamer, AD. .... 15 – 18
Creamer, covered .... 15 – 22
Creamer, open. .... 10 – 18

Cup . . . . *$10 – $12*
Cup, AD. . . . . *15 – 22*
Custard, 3"   /**
Dish, 5¹/₂". . . . . *5 – 8*
Eggcup. . . . . *15 – 20*
Gravy boat . . . . *18 – 25*
Gravy faststand . . . . *20 – 30*
Jam jar, 5"   /* . . . . *55 – 65*
Jug, bulb bottom, 1-pint . . . . *20 – 22*
Jug, bulb bottom, 1-quart . . . . *30 – 35*
Jug, disk   /*. . . . . *45 – 75*
Jug, tankard, 1¹/₂-quart. . . . . *50 – 65*
Lapel pin   /**
Muffin cover/tray . . . . *50 – 75*
Mug, clip handle, 8-ounce   /* . . . . *18 – 22*
Mug, handle, 8-ounce . . . . *20 – 25*
Plate, 6¹/₂" . . . . *5 – 8*
Plate, 7¹/₂" . . . . *8 – 12*
Plate, 8¹/₂" . . . . *8 – 12*
Plate, 9¹/₂" . . . . *9 – 14*
Plate, 10¹/₂" . . . . *12 – 18*
Plate, chop, 12" . . . . *15 – 30*
Plate, chop, 14" . . . . *20 – 50*
Plate, chop, 17" . . . . *35 – 75*
Plate, grill, 11"   /*. . . . . *18 – 22*
Plate, grill, 13¹/₂" × 10¹/₂" . . . . *35 – 45*
Platter, 9" . . . . *12 – 14*
Platter, 10¹/₂". . . . . *15 – 20*
Platter, 12" . . . . *17 – 25*
Platter, 14" . . . . *22 – 40*
Platter, 16" . . . . *35 – 60*
Saucer . . . . *2 – 3*
Saucer, AD . . . . *3 – 4*
Shaker, each . . . . *7 – 10*
Sugar. . . . . *12 – 18*
Sugar, AD . . . . *15 – 20*
Teapot, 6-cup   /* . . . . *35 – 65*
Tumbler, all styles . . . . *18 – 25*

Brown-Eyed Susan   A few items will be found in the Ultra shape. A beverage set consisted of one 2-quart jug and six 14-ounce tumblers.

Bowl, 1-pint *$25*
Bowl, chowder, lug, 6" *35*
Bowl, salad, 10¹/₂" *85*
Bowl, soup *18*
Bowl, vegetable, divided *25*
Bowl, vegetable, round, 9". *15*
Butter, ¹/₄-pound *50*

Butter pat, 2½" *$30*
Casserole, individual, 4" *35*
Casserole, 8" *50*
Chicken pie server, stick handle, 4" *35*
Coaster, 4" *30*
Coffee server/Carafe w/stopper, 10-cup *45*
Creamer *15*
Cup *7*
Cup, AD. *22*
Cup, jumbo *40*
Custard, 3" *40*
Dish, fruit *6*
Dish, salad, 5½" *6*
Eggcup, double *28*
Flowerpot, 3" *35*
Flowerpot, 4" *40*
Flowerpot, 5" *45*
Gravy *20*
Jug, 1-pint *40*
Jug, 1-quart *45*
Jug, 2-quart *40*
Jug, syrup, metal top *55*
Lapel pin *30*
Mug, 9-ounce *25*
Pepper mill, wood and ceramic *75*
Plate, 6½" *6*
Plate, 7½" *8*
Plate, 9½" *10*
Plate, 10½" *13*
Plate, chop, 12" *25*
Plate, chop, 14" *35*
Platter, 9½" *12*
Platter, 12" *20*
Platter, 14" *30*
Sauce boat *25*
Saucer *5*
Saucer, AD *18*
Saucer, jumbo *18*
Saucer, flowerpot, 3" *15*
Saucer, flowerpot, 4" *15*
Saucer, flowerpot, 5" *15*
Shaker, pair *12*
Shaker, large, pair *35*
Spoon holder *65*
Sugar *15*
Teapot *65*
Tidbit, 2-tier *25*
Tidbit, 3-tier *28*
Tumbler, 14-ounce *30*

MATCHING GLASSWARE

Sherbet, stemmed, 3¹/₂" high
Tumbler, 10-ounce, 5¹/₂" high
Tumbler, frosted, 10-ounce, 4¹/₂" high

Coastline

Designed by Gale Turnbull. Hand-painted maps done in black and blue with red highlights on ivory background.

Ashtray/Louisiana	*$20 – $22*
Bowl, serving, 13"	*75 – 85*
Coaster, 4"	*35*
Coffee server/carafe, w/stopper	*65 – 70*
Creamer	*20 – 25*
Cup/Southern California	*25 – 30*
Jug, small	*35 – 45*
Plate, 6¹/₂" /New England	*12*
Plate, 7¹/₂" /Maine	*20*
Plate, 7¹/₂" /New York	*20*
Plate, 9¹/₂" /Southern California	*25*
Plate, 10¹/₂" /Northern California	*35*
Plate, 10¹/₂" /Central California	*35*
Plate, 10¹/₂" /Southern California	*35*
Plate, chop, 12" /Lake Michigan	*45 – 50*
Plate or oval platter, 14" /Gulf of Mexico	*45 – 65*
Saucer /Southern California	*10*
Sugar /Florida, Gulf Coast	*25 – 30*
Teapot	*90 – 100*

Frontier Days / Winchester '73   (1950)

This is a print and paint pattern designed by Paul Davidson. It was tied in promotionally with Universal Pictures' *Winchester '73*, which starred James Stewart and Shelley Winters. A disagreement with the Winchester Arms Corporation over continued use of the name resulted in the change of name to Frontier Days in 1953. There is hard-to-find barware by Heisey with a matching Winchester '73 etching.

Every piece has a different scene, which is listed after the slash in each entry when known. Some Winchester '73 will be found on shapes other than Montecito. These are listed here and noted with the shape name in parentheses.

Napkin rings have been reported.

NOTE   Winchester '73 was advertised as having a soft green background. However, it is found with an ivory background, and Frontier Days has the green background. (See the Ultra piece below for an exception.)

PRICING   Two to four times values for Early/Modern California. The following list is known items.

Ashtray   /Cowboy on fence
Bowl, 1-pint
Bowl, chowder, lug, open, 6"   /Prospector and burro
Bowl, mixing, 5"

Bowl, mixing, 6"
Bowl, mixing, 7"   /Bronco busting
Bowl, mixing, 8"   /Cowboy campfire
Bowl, mixing, 9"   /Wild horses
Bowl, salad, individual, 5¹/₂"
Bowl, salad, 10¹/₂"   /Train, stagecoach, and bucking horse
Bowl, soup, rimmed, 8¹/₂"   /Stagecoach holdup
Bowl, vegetable, oval, 10"
Bowl, vegetable, oval, divided   /Prospector and burro
Bowl, vegetable, round, 9"   /Shoot-up
Butter, ¹/₂-pound   /Stagecoach
Casserole, 8"   /Lassoing a calf
Chicken pie server, stick handle, 4"   /Indian head and saddle
Coaster/Ashtray, 4"   /Prospector and burro
Coffee server w/stopper, 10-cup   /Train
Creamer
Cup   /Buffalo hunt
Cup, AD
Cup, jumbo
Dish, fruit, 5¹/₂"   /Indian lighting fire
Eggcup   /Bucking bronco
Gravy   /Cavalry charge
Jug, big bottom, 1-pint   /Roping and branding calves
Jug, big botton, 1-quart
Jug, streamline, 2-quart   /Prospectors and mules
Mug, 9-ounce   /Indian on horseback
Pepper mill, wood and ceramic   /Indian and cowboy smoking peace pipe
Plate, 6¹/₂"   /Roping horses
Plate, 7¹/₂"   /Roping a steer
Plate, 9¹/₂"   /Wagon train
Plate, 10¹/₂"   /Campfire and chuckwagon
Plate, chop, 12"   /Bucking bronco
Plate, chop, 14" (Montecito/Ultra)   /Rifle divides well. Top: Wagon train.
   Bottom: Indians chasing stagecoach.
Plate, chop, 14" (Melinda)   /Cowboy on bucking horse
Platter, 10"   /Cowboy wrestling steer
Platter, 12"
Platter, 14"   /Bank robbery
Platter, 16"
Saucer   /Buffalo hunt
Saucer, AD
Saucer, jumbo
Shaker   /Card game
Shaker, salt, large, wood and ceramic   /Indian and cowboy smoking peace pipe
Sugar   /Cowboy, horse and steer heads
Teapot, 8-cup
Tidbit, two-tier
Tumbler, 14-ounce   /Branding cattle

Plaids / Variations

Some of these were designed by Gale Turnbull. Calico, Gingham, Homespun, Organdie, Tam O'Shanter, and Tweed are the most common of the Plaids. The others appear to be early designs of which little was produced; they are not easily found and are not included in the pricing. All items were *not* made in all colors. Organdie is the most common of the Plaids; do not overpay.

PRICING   Prices below are for Gingham, Homespun, Organdie, and Tam O'Shanter. Add 25% for Calico and Tweed.

Ashtray/Coaster, round, 4".. $28
Bowl, 1-pint 20
Bowl, chowder, lug, open, 6"... 11
    w/lid 30
Bowl, mixing, 5" 26
Bowl, mixing, 6" 29
Bowl, mixing, 7" 32
Bowl, mixing, 8" 35
Bowl, mixing, 9" 38
Bowl, salad, 10½" 75
Bowl, vegetable, divided 25
Bowl, vegetable, oval, 10" 25
Bowl, vegetable, round 7½".. 20
Bowl, vegetable, round or oval, 9".................................... 15
Butter, ¼-pound 45
Butter pat 28
Candle holder 50
Carafe, w/stopper 40
Casserole, 8" 45
Casserole, individual, 4" 35
Chicken pie server, stick handle, 4"................................. 30
Compote, 9½"... 75
Creamer, covered 15
Creamer, open... 12
Cup 6
Cup, AD... 25
Cup, Jumbo 35
Cup, Colossal... 150
Custard, 3" 40
Dish, 5½".. 5
Eggcup.. 25
Flowerpot, 3" 30
Flowerpot, 4" 35
Flowerpot, 5" 40
Gravyboat... 18
Jug, ¼-pint... 25
Jug, ½-pint... 30
Jug, 1-pint 35
Jug, 1-quart 40

Jug, 2-quart *$35*
Jug, bulb bottom, 1-pint *25*
Jug, bulb bottom, 1-quart *35*
Jug, disk. *195*
Jug, syrup. *75*
Lapel pin *28*
Muffin cover/tray *150*
Mug, clip handle, 8-ounce. *28*
Mug, 9-ounce. *23*
Pepper mill *65*
Plate, 6$^1/_2$" *5*
Plate, 7$^1/_2$" *7*
Plate, 9$^1/_2$" *9*
Plate, 10$^1/_2$" *12*
Plate, chop, 12" *20*
Plate, chop, 13" *24*
Plate, chop, 14" *30*
Plate, chop, 17" *55*
Platter, 8$^1/_2$" *15*
Platter, 9$^1/_2$" *10*
Platter, 10$^1/_2$" *12*
Platter, 12" *18*
Platter, 14" *25*
Platter, 16" *35*
Saucer *5*
Saucer, AD *15*
Saucer, Jumbo. *15*
Saucer, Colossal *50*
Saucer, flowerpot, 3". *15*
Saucer, flowerpot, 4". *15*
Saucer, flowerpot, 5". *15*
Server, center handle, 6". *22*
Server, 2-tier *22*
Server, 3-tier *25*
Shaker, pair. *10*
Shaker, large, pair. *30*
Spoon holder. *55*
Sugar *12*
Syrup, metal lid. *75*
Teapot, 8-cup. *55*
Tumbler, all styles *25*

THE PLAIDS

Calico: Pink and blue
Coronation/Organdie (T-508): Gray and rose

Gingham: Green and yellow w/green border
Homespun: Green, rust, and yellow w/rust border
Organdie: Brown and yellow
Organdie (T-511): Brown and yellow, with more detail than the above
Organdie (T-512): Deep rose and green
Organdie (T-513): Yellow and green
Tam O'Shanter: Rust, chartreuse, and green w/green border
Tweed: Gray and yellow
(T-515): Gray and forest green
(T-604): Rust brown and medium blue w/blue border

SAN MARINO (1947)

Decorated in solid colors and decals.

Casual California   Acacia Yellow, Dawn Pink, Dusk Gray, Lime Green, Mahogany Brown, Mocha Brown, Pine Green, Snowhite, and Turquoise Blue.

California Shadows   Drip glaze color of Antique Gray and Cocoa Brown.

California Originals (California Heritage)   Drip glaze colors of *Almond Yellow* ("a golden vital hue ... crisp, sun-browned almond shells"), *Raisin Purple* ("the regal purple of rare, deep amethysts"), *Redwood Brown* ("a rich-grained brown with the timeless beauty of the giant redwood forests") and *Vineyard Green* ("the soft green of growing things ... sunlight on a vineyard in springtime").

   PRICING   The values below are for patterns as well as solid colors.

Ashtray, 5"	$12 – $15
Bowl, chowder, 6"	9 – 12
Bowl, coupe soup, 8½"	10 – 14
Bowl, divided, 10"	15 – 20
Bowl, mixing, 5"	12 – 15
Bowl, mixing, 6"	15 – 22
Bowl, mixing, 7"	20 – 28
Bowl, mixing, 8"	25 – 32
Bowl, mixing, 9"	28 – 35
Bowl, salad, 10½"	30 – 45
Bowl, salad, individual, 5"	10 – 15
Bowl, serving, round, 7½"	10 – 14
Bowl, serving, round, 9"	12 – 18
Butter, ¼-pound	25 – 40
Butter pat, 2½"	12 – 18
Casserole, 8"	25 – 35
Casserole, individual, 4"	13 – 18
Casserole, individual, stick handle, 4"	15 – 20
Coaster, 4"	10 – 15

Coffee server w/stopper, 10-cup .... *$25 – $30*
Creamer .... *7 – 12*
Cup .... *6 – 10*
Cup, colossal .... *95 – 125*
Cup, jumbo .... *15 – 25*
Custard, 3" .... *18 – 22*
Dish, fruit, 5¹/₂" .... *4 – 7*
Eggcup, double .... *13 – 18*
Flowerpot, 3" .... *23 – 32*
Flowerpot, 4" .... *30 – 35*
Flowerpot, 5" .... *33 – 40*
Gravy .... *15 – 20*
Jug, ¹/₄-pint .... *12 – 15*
Jug, ¹/₂-pint .... *12 – 15*
Jug, 1-pint .... *18 – 22*
Jug, 1-quart .... *20 – 25*
Jug, 2-quart .... *25 – 35*
Jug, syrup .... *40 – 45*
Mug, 9-ounce .... *15 – 20*
Pepper mill, wood encased, 4¹/₂" .... *30 – 45*
Plate, chop, 13" .... *15 – 30*
Plate, 6" .... *4 – 7*
Plate, 7¹/₂" .... *5 – 10*
Plate, 10" .... *10 – 15*
Platter, 9¹/₂" .... *10 – 15*
Platter, 11" .... *11 – 16*
Platter, 13¹/₂" .... *15 – 24*
Salt cellar, wood encased, 4¹/₂" .... *20 – 30*
Saucer .... *2 – 3*
Saucer, colossal .... *25 – 30*
Saucer, jumbo .... *5 – 7*
Shaker, gourd, pair .... *15 – 20*
Spoon holder .... *20 – 25*

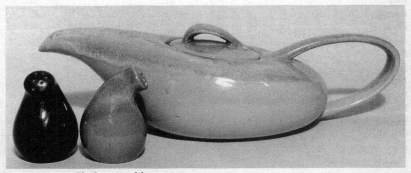

San Marino: Shakers and long teapot.

Sugar	$10 – $15
Teapot, 11" long	30 – 45
Teapot, 14½" long	50 – 65
Tumbler, 14-ounce	15 – 22

ULTRA (1937)

Decorated in solid colors, hand-painted designs, and transfer prints.

The most desirable transfer prints are Moby Dick, Our America, Salamina, and Walt Disney. Also popular are the hand-painted designs of Gale Turnbull and the tropical designs of Don Blanding.

Ultra California, Solid Colors
The solid colors are "half tones" of Astor (blue), Buttercup (yellow), Carnation (pink), Gardenia (ivory), Ice green, and Maroon.

PRICING The values listed here can also be used for the patterns, with Turnbull designs at the high end. Double solid-color prices for Blanding designs such as Hawaiian Flowers/Lei Lani, etc. See below for Walt Disney and Kent.

Bowl, 1-pint, 5"	$15 – $20
Bowl, chowder, lug, 7½"	10 – 18
w/lid	25 – 30
Bowl, round, low, 8"	15 – 20
Bowl, salad, 11"	45 – 50
Bowl, vegetable, round, deep, 8"	12 – 22
Bowl, vegetable, round, 9"	15 – 30
Butter, ¼-pound	35 – 50
Casserole, 8"	35 – 55
Coffee pot, AD	60 – 70
Coffee pot	45 – 80
Compote /Montecito	ND
Creamer, AD	12 – 20
Creamer, low	12 – 18
Creamer, tall	12 – 18
Cup	10 – 15
Cup, AD	18 – 25
Cup, jumbo	30 – 35
Dish, 5½"	6 – 12
Dish, 6"	10 – 15
Eggcup, single	15 – 20
Jam jar	55 – 65
Muffin cover	35 – 65
Mug, 8-ounce	18 – 30
Pickle, round, lug, 6"	20 – 30
Pitcher, 1-pint	18 – 32
w/lid	35 – 50
Pitcher, 2-quart	35 – 60
w/lid	50 – 75
Pitcher, disk /Montecito	35 – 75

Plate, 6½" .... *$5 – $10*
Plate, 7½" .... *7 – 12*
Plate, 8½" .... *8 – 15*
Plate, 9½" .... *10 – 20*
Plate, 10½" .... *12 – 24*
Plate, chop, 12" .... *20 – 50*
Plate, chop, 14" .... *35 – 75*
Plate, chop, 17" .... *45 – 95*
Sauce boat .... *18 – 35*
Saucer *3*
Saucer, AD *4*
Saucer, jumbo *6*
Shaker, pair .... *15 – 25*
Sugar, AD .... *20 – 30*
Sugar, low .... *15 – 25*
Sugar, tall .... *15 – 25*
Teapot, 6-cup .... *40 – 70*
Tumbler, 13-ounce .... *18 – 35*
Tureenette, 7" .... *60 – 85*

Moby Dick   (1939)   Designed by Rockwell Kent. Based on his illustrations of the novel, there are one-color scenes in Dark Blue, Light Orange, Maroon, and Walnut Brown. Dark Blue and Maroon are the common colors; Light Orange is rare.

The 6½", 8½", and 10½" plates in blue with touches of hand coloring on the sails and waves will be found with Farberware chrome frames that are 6" wide. These could be used as serving plates or hung on the wall. As well, the 6" dish was made into a 12" serving bowl with the addition of a chrome frame.

PRICING   In 1938 a 20-piece starter set cost $7.95. Price this at 2½ times solid-color Ultra values. The list below is of known pieces.

Bowl, 1-pint	**Cup**, jumbo	**Plate**, 9½"
Bowl, chowder, w/lid, 6"	**Dish**, fruit, 5½"	**Plate**, 10½"
Bowl, salad, 11"	**Dish**, cereal, 6"	**Plate**, chop, 12"
Bowl, soup, coupe, 7¼"	**Eggcup**, single	**Plate**, chop, 14"
Bowl, vegetable, round, 8"	**Gravy**	**Plate**, chop, 17"
Bowl, vegetable, round, 9"	**Jam jar**, notched lid	**Saucer**
Butter, ¼-pound	**Jug**, w/lid, 1-pint	**Saucer**, AD
Candle holders, square	**Jug**, w/lid, 2-quart	**Saucer**, jumbo
Casserole, 8"	**Muffin cover**	**Shaker**
Coffee pot, 2-cup, AD	**Mug**, 8-ounce	**Sugar**
Coffee pot, 6-cup	**Pickle dish**, round, 6"	**Sugar**, individual
Creamer, open	**Plate**, 6½"	**Teapot**, 6-cup
Creamer, individual, open	**Plate**, 7½"	**Tumbler**, 13-ounce
Cup	**Plate**, 8½"	**Tureenette**, notched lid, 7"
Cup, AD		

Our America   (1940)   Designed by Rockwell Kent. There are over thirty-one color scenes from around the United States done in Dark Blue, Green, Maroon, or Walnut Brown. Walnut Brown is the most common color, Green the scarcest. The 17" chop plate also comes in a hand-tinted version.

PRICING Price this at 2½ times solid-color Ultra values. The list below is of known pieces.

Bowl, 1-pint /Gulf: Sailfishing
Bowl, chowder /Gulf: Florida coconut palms
Bowl, salad, 11" /Pacific: Big trees, dam, and lake
Bowl, soup, 7½" /Southern: Mansion w/cotton pickers
Butter dish /Mississippi River: Steamboat
Casserole /Great Lakes: Steamers and yachts
Coffee pot, 10-cup /Pacific: Building suspension bridge
Coffee pot, AD /Southern: Riding to hounds in Virginia
Creamer /Gulf: Florida houseboaters
Creamer, AD /Gulf: Florida Everglades
Cup /Mississippi River: Wharves at New Orleans
Cup, AD /New England: Newport yacht racing
Cup, jumbo /New England: Vermont maple sugaring
Dish, fruit, 5½" /Gulf: Florida coconut palms
Eggcup /New England: College campus
Gravy /Plains: Smelters in mining country
Jam jar, notched lid /Plains: Texas oil derricks
Jug, 1-pint /Pacific: Steamers on Columbia River
Jug, 2-quart /Middle Atlantic: Building skyscrapers
Muffin cover /New England: Fishing fleet puts out to sea
Mug /Southern: Blue Grass country and Sport of Kings
Pickle dish /New England: Newport yacht racing
Plate, 6½" /Mississippi River: Stern wheeler
Plate, 7½" /Southern: Mansion w/cotton pickers
Plate, 8½" /New England: Fishing banks
Plate, 9½" /Great Lakes: Chicago seen from river
Plate, 10½" /Middle Atlantic: New York City
Plate, chop, 12" /Middle West: Cattle and grain
Plate, chop, 14" /Pacific: Big trees, dam, and lake
Plate, chop, 17¼" /Map of the USA
Saucer /Mississippi River: New Orleans wharves
Saucer, AD /New England: Newport yacht racing
Saucer, jumbo /New England: Vermont maple sugaring
Shaker /Mississippi River: Flat boats
Sugar /Mississippi River: Sugar cane fields
Sugar, AD /Mississippi River: Gulf shrimp fishermen
Teapot /Plains: Indians of high mesa herding sheep
Tumbler, 13-ounce /Great Lakes: Speedboats
Tureenette /Pacific: Northwest lumbering

OUR AMERICA REGIONS

In devising his drawings, Rockwell Kent divided the United States into eight regions. They are

1. New England States: Connecticut, Maine, Massachusetts, New Hampshire, Rhode Island, and Vermont.

2. Middle Atlantic States: Delaware, Maryland, New York, New Jersey, and Pennsylvania.

3. Southern Colonial States: Georgia, No. Carolina, So. Carolina, Virginia, and West Virginia.

4. Mississippi River States: Arkansas, Kentucky, Louisiana, Mississippi, Missouri, and Tennessee.

5. Great Lakes States: Illinois, Indiana, Michigan, Minnesota, Ohio, and Wisconsin.

6. Plains and Mountain States: Arizona, Colorado, Idaho, Iowa, Kansas, Montana, Nebraska, Nevada, New Mexico, No. Dakota, Oklahoma, So. Dakota, Texas, Utah, and Wyoming.

7. Gulf States: Alabama and Florida.

8. Pacific States: California, Oregon, and Washington.

Salamina   (1939)   Designed by Rockwell Kent, Salamina is a print and paint design in bright colors based on the drawings in Kent's book of the same name.

PRICING   In 1940, a 20-piece starter set cost $10.75. Price these at five to seven times solid-color Ultra values. The list below is of known pieces.

Bowl, 1-pint
Bowl, chowder, w/lid
Bowl, salad, 11"

Bowl, soup, coupe, 7¼"
Bowl, vegetable, round, 8"
Bowl, vegetable, round, 9"

*Salamina: 12" chop plate,
hand-tinted decal decoration.*

Butter
Casserole, 8"
Coffee pot, 2-cup, AD
Coffee pot, 6-cup
Creamer, open
Creamer, individual, open
Cup
Cup, AD
Cup, jumbo
Dish, fruit, 5¹/₂"
Dish, cereal, 6"
Eggcup, single
Gravy
Jam jar, notched lid
Jug, disk
Jug, w/lid, 1-pint
Jug, w/lid, 2-quart
Muffin cover
Mug, 8-ounce

Pickle dish, round, 6"
Plate, 6¹/₂"
Plate, 7¹/₂"
Plate, 8¹/₂"
Plate, 9¹/₂"
Plate, 10¹/₂"
Plate, chop, 12"
Plate, chop, 14"
Plate, chop, 17"
Saucer
Saucer, AD
Saucer, jumbo
Shaker
Sugar
Sugar, individual
Teapot, 6-cup
Tumbler, 13-ounce
Tureenette, notched lid, 7"

Walt Disney   (1940)   Designs based on the movie *Fantasia*. Floral prints (some with nymphs) in colors of blue, brown, or maroon. Some are plain; some have been hand tinted.

Found primarily on the Ultra shape. Pieces on other shapes are noted in the listings. There are no clear records as to which pieces were made in this line.

PRICING   This is a difficult line to price as so very little of it turns up. Figure some seven to eight times the solid-color Ultra prices. The list following is of known pieces.

Bowl, mixing, set
Coffee server, Bakelite handle   /Montecito
Creamer
Creamer w/lid   /Montecito
Cup
Muffin cover
Mug
Pickle dish
Plate, 6¹/₂"
Plate, 8¹/₂"

Plate, 10¹/₂"
Plate, chop, 14"
Plate, chop, 17"
Saucer
Shaker
Shaker   /Montecito
Sugar
Sugar   /Montecito
Teapot, 6-cup

WALT DISNEY VARIATIONS

All of these designs are floral, and some have nymphs as well. The hollowware has allover patterns; the flatware is either allover or rim-decorated.

Autumn Ballet   Maroon print with hand painting
Dewdrop Fairies   Blue print, rim-decorated

Enchantment   Blue print with hand painting, rim-decorated
Fairyland   Blue print with hand painting
Fantasia   Brown print with hand painting
Flower Ballet   Maroon print with hand painting, rim-decorated
Milkweed Dance   Blue print or Maroon print
Nutcracker   Brown print with hand painting, rim-decorated

FIGURES

DISNEY   (1941)

Available for 1½ years. Figurines 1 through 36 are from *Fantasia*, 37 from *The Reluctant Dragon*, and 38 through 42 from *Dumbo*. Some of these were later produced by the American Pottery. See also "Dinnerware/Fantasia."

   PRICING   These figurines will bring higher prices at auction.

1	/Satyr, 4½"	$200 – $350
2	/Satyr, 4½"	200 – 350
3	/Satyr, piping, 4½"	200 – 350
4	/Satyr, 4½"	200 – 350
5	/Satyr, 4½"	200 – 350
6	/Satyr, 4½"	200 – 350
7	/Sprite, hands clasped, 4½"	200 – 350
8	/Sprite, reclining, 3"	200 – 350
9	/Sprite, 4½"	200 – 350
10	/Winged Sprite, 4½"	200 – 350
11	/Sprite, arms folded, 4½"	200 – 350
12	/Sprite, 4½"	200 – 350
13	/Unicorn, black w/yellow horn	250 – 400
14	/Unicorn, sitting, 5"	300 – 450
15	/Unicorn, rearing, 6"	300 – 500
16	/Donkey Unicorn, reclining, 5½"	500 – 650
17	/Centaurette, sitting, 5½"	600 – 750
18	/Centaurette, posing, 7½"	750 – 900
19	/Pegasus, baby, black, 4½"	250 – 400
20	/Pegasus, white, head turned, 5"	300 – 400
21	/Pegasus, white, 5½"	300 – 400
22	/Centaurette, arms around head, 7½" (8½"?)	800 – 950
23	/Nubian Centaurette, w/flowers in arms, 8"	900 – 1100
24	/Nubian Centaurette, left hand at throat, 7½"	900 – 1000
25	/Elephant, 5"	400 – 550
26	/Elephant, trunk raised	400 – 550
27	/Elephant, dancing, trunk up, 5½"	400 – 550
28	/Ostrich Ballerina, on point, 6"	800 – 1200
29	/Ostrich Ballerina, bowing, 8"	800 – 1200
30	/Ostrich, 9"	800 – 1200
31	/Centaur, bunch of grapes in each arm, 10"	900 – 1200

32	/Hippo in Tutu, arms out, 5½"	$400 – $500
33	/Hippo, holding tutu	400 – 500
34	/Hippo, hands on hips, 5"	400 – 500
35/36	/Hop Low Mushroom, shakers, pair, 3½"	95 – 125
37	/Baby Weems, sitting, 6"	350
38	/Timothy Mouse, 6"	200
39	/Mr. Crow	1000 – 1200
40	/Dumbo, falling on his ear, 5"	150 – 200
41	/Dumbo, sitting, 5"	150 – 200
42	/Mr. Stork, pointing left wing, 8¾"	1200 – 1500

Vases and Bowls

These were available either in solid colors (pink, blue, turquoise, and white) or hand painted.

	Solid	Hand Painted
120/Bowl, Mushroom		$150 – $200
121/Bowl, Goldfish	$600 – $700	400
122/Bowl, Winged Nymph	200 – 350	350
123/Vase, Winged Nymph, 7"		250 – 350
124/Bowl, Satyr	250 – 400	400
125/Bowl, Sprite		250 – 400
126/Vase, Goddess, 10½"	500 – 700	700
127/Vase, Winged Pegasus	600 – 1200	1200

MISCELLANY

Bird, 7½", tail forms tray	$150
Bust, Lady, palm flat (Jane Bennison)	500 +
Godey Lady, 10"	175

MOVIE STARS

The actor's name is followed by the year of release, name of the movie, and character played, when known. As these were probably promotional pieces, the year of release gives you a pretty good idea of the period in which these were made.

PRICING It is a seller's market on these very-hard-to-find figures. Size does not seem to have an effect on price; they are all expensive.

Wallace Beery, 7½" (1936, *Message to Garcia*)	$700 +
Wallace Beery, 17½" (1934, *Viva Villa!* Pancho Villa)	700 +
Madeleine Carroll (1940, *Northwest Mounted Police*)	700 +
Gary Cooper, 16½" (1940, *Northwest Mounted Police*, Dusty Rivers)	700 +
Bette Davis	700 +
Preston Foster, 11½" (1940, *Northwest Mounted Police*, Sgt. Bret)	700 +
Paulette Goddard (1940, *Northwest Mounted Police*, Louvette)	700 +
Walter Hampden (1940, *Northwest Mounted Police*, Chief Big Bear)	700 +
Dorothy Lamour, 10" (1947, *Road to Rio*?)	700 +
Victor McLaughlin, 17" (*The Quiet Man*?)	700 +
Lynn Overman, 8½" (1940, *Northwest Mounted Police*, Tod McDuff)	700 +
Robert Preston (1940, *Northwest Mounted Police*, Ronnie Logan)	700 +

Anne Shirley	*$700 +*
Evelyn Venable, 11"	*700 +*

SOUVENIR / SPECIALTY ITEMS

Vernon made hundreds of plates commemorating locations, organizations, and events. Many of the plates were stock items; others were special orders. The majority were made on 10½" plates, though 8½" and 12½" plates will also be found. Shapes used were Melinda, Montecito, San Fernando, and Ultra (both regular and modified). Sometimes ashtrays, cups, saucers, and other matching pieces were made as well.

All plates were one-color transfer prints on ivory, with blue, brown, and maroon being the usual colors (various shades of blue and maroon will be found; these two colors are more common than brown) and a few done in purple or green (these do not seem to be appreciably more valuable). In 1953, hand-painted (hand-tinted) items were introduced. These were the transfer prints with color filled in by hand, variously called "print and paint" or "print and fill."

While efforts are being made to track down all these pieces, there is no complete list. I do not have room to list all the known ones, so I am including what I hope is a representative sampling. Some are of particular interest; others are common ones for which you should not overpay.

GENERAL

Except for the plates lumped together in "Other," these lists reflect some of the categories set up by Bess Christensen, which are standard for collectors.

Airplanes

Boeing	*$45 – $60*
Consolidated Aircraft	*45 – 60*
Curtiss-Wright	*45 – 60*
Douglas, First Around the World	*45 – 60*
Douglas, Long Beach, CA	*45 – 60*
In the Air—It's Convair (Consolidated Vultee)	*45 – 60*
Lockheed Aircraft	*45 – 60*
Martin Aircraft	*45 – 60*
North American Aviation	*45 – 60*
Vultee Get 'em into the Blue	*45 – 60*

Business

Cliftons of Los Angeles	*$15 – $25*
Dorchester, Mass./Walter Baker Anniversary	
1st Edition	*35 – 50*
2nd Edition	*35 – 50*
Farmer's Market, LA map	*15 – 25*
Farmer's Market, LA people	*15 – 25*
Pritzlaff Hardware, Milwaukee, 100th Anniversary	*15 – 25*
Trader Vic's	*15 – 25*
Webbs City, Inc. (drugstore), St. Petersburg, FL	*15 – 25*

Cities   There are many city plates known; some may have been stock items.

  PRICING   In general, prices range from $12 to $30. The plentiful, one-color plates go for $12 to $18. Multicolor (hand-tinted) plates are $18 to $30, high price for rare plates only. There is a Philadelphia plate in black, the only plate found so far in black; value: $20 to $35.

Chicago, designed by Orpha Klinker	*$15 – $25*
Chicago, Marshall Fields	*15 – 25*
Colorful San Francisco	*15 – 25*
Detroit: Home of the General Motors	*15 – 25*
Hollywood	*20 – 25*
Los Angeles	*15 – 25*
New York	*15 – 25*
Omaha	*15 – 25*
Our National Capitol	*15 – 25*
Philadelphia	*15 – 25*
San Antonio	*15 – 25*
San Francisco Cable Car	*15 – 25*
Vallejo, CA., Home of Mare Island	*15 – 25*

Events

Chicago Fair, atomic symbol	*$15 – $25*
Chicago Fair, Sederling	*15 – 25*
Chicago Railroad Fair, Consolidated Concessions	*25 – 35*
Chicago Railroad Fair, Marshall Fields	*25 – 35*
Easter Fires of Fredericksburg, Texas, 1949	*25 – 35*
Republican National Convention, 1956, 12³/₄"	*50 – 60*

Foreign   The Jose Martí is hand painted, the rest are monochrome.

Caracas, Venezuela	*$25 – $40*
El Paso/Juarez	*25 – 40*
Great Northwest (Canada?), 14"	*25 – 40*
Jose Martí, in Spanish	*25 – 40*
Philippines	*25 – 40*
Venezuela, Colombia, Ecuador	*25 – 40*

Other

Alaska, Crippled Children's Association	
Cup/Saucer	*$20 – $30*
Plate	*15 – 25*
Black Hills Passion Play, Last Supper	*15 – 25*
Christmas Tree, 10¹/₂"	*20 – 30*
El Camino Real, 14"	*35 – 45*
In My Merry Oldsmobile	*25 – 35*
My Own Mother Goose	*25 – 35*
Noah's Ark, 9¹/₂"	*40 – 60*
Presidents, 3 designs	*15 – 25*

Santa Claus, 10¹/₂" .... $25 – $35
    Cup/ Saucer .... 20 – 30
The Statue of Liberty, 2 designs .... 20 – 30

People   MacArthur is the most common of all of these; do not overpay. Some will be found on the Melinda shape with a red and blue border; these are worth a little more.

Jefferson Davis .... $15 – $25
Eisenhower and Nixon .... 60 – 75
Generalissimo and Mme. Chiang Kai-shek .... 35 – 40
Robert E. Lee .... 15 – 25
Abraham Lincoln, 2 designs .... 15 – 25
General Douglas MacArthur, 2 designs .... 15 – 20
Will Rogers .... 15 – 25
FDR, WW II .... 35 – 40
FDR, 3 other designs .... 15 – 25
Theodore Roosevelt .... 15 – 25
Mark Twain .... 15 – 25
Woodrow Wilson, 2 designs .... 15 – 25

Railroad   Trains turn up with other illustrations on a number of plates. The ones listed here are "pure" railroad plates. See also Event plates.

The "Emma Sweeney," 10¹/₂" .... $25 – $35
The Galloping Goose, 10¹/₂" .... 25 – 35
San Bernardino, w/Streamliner border, 10¹/₂" .... 25 – 35
The San Juan, 10¹/₂" .... 25 – 35
Virginia & Truckee RR, 8¹/₂" .... 25 – 35

States   There are two types of state plate. One is the State Picture plate, which shows scenes and buildings from around each state, generally with the state capitol in the center and the state flower around the border; and the other is the State Map plate, which shows a map of the state with pictures of various locations in place geographically.

    PRICING   In general, prices range from $12 to $30. The plentiful, one-color plates go for $12 to $18. Multicolor (hand-tinted) plates are $18 to $30, high price for rare plates only.

World War II   The backstamp on the Pearl Harbor plate does not mention the Vernon Kilns name. It is not an uncommon plate; do not overpay.

Army Air Corps Song .... $35 – $40
Marine Corps Hymn .... 35 – 40
Navy Oath of Allegiance .... 35 – 40
Remember Pearl Harbor .... 15 – 25
US Naval Air Gunner's School, Purcell, OK .... 15 – 25
US Naval Air Station, Alameda, CA .... 15 – 25
US Naval Air Station, Pensacola, FL .... 15 – 25

SETS

These plates are all 8¹/₂".

Bits of America   There are eight lines, all done in multicolor (though a brown "Old New England: Tapping for Sugar" has been found). Note: (1) No chop plate for Old Northwest; (2) California Mission and Old Northwest plates are scarcer than the others.

Bits of the Middle West
   Plate, 8½" *$45*
   Plate, chop, 12¼" *90*
Bits of Old England
   Plate, 8½" *25*
   Plate, chop, 12¼" *40*
Bits of Old New England
   Plate, 8½" *30*
   Plate, chop, 12¼" *55*
Bits of the Old Northwest
   Plate, 8½" *50*
Bits of the Old South
   Plate, 8½" *20*
   Plate, chop, 12¼" *40*
Bits of the Old Southwest
   Plate, 8½" *40*
   Plate, chop, 12¼" *80*
Bits of the Old West
   Plate, 8½" *45*
   Plate, chop, 12¼" *90*
California Missions
   Plate, 8½"
      Northern Missions *35*
      Southern Missions *25*
   Plate, chop, 12¼" *45*

Cocktail Hour   Monochrome brown prints on the Ultra shape.

Bacardi .... *$45 – $50*
The Bronx .... *45 – 50*
Hot Toddy .... *45 – 50*
Manhattan .... *45 – 50*
Old-Fashioned .... *45 – 50*
Pink Lady .... *45 – 50*
Singapore Sling .... *45 – 50*
Whiskey Sour .... *45 – 50*

French Opera   These hand-tinted plates were reproductions of eight nineteenth-century French plates that came in a series of twelve. Do not confuse these with very similar plates produced for an importer and marked "PV." Fortunately, the Vernon plates are always marked.

1. Le Pre Aux Clercs .... *$20 – $25*
3. Barbiere de Seville
   Plate, 8½" .... *20 – 25*
   Plate, chop, 14" .... *30 – 40*

5. **Guillaume Tell** .... *$20 – $25*
6. **Les Dragons de Villars**. .... *20 – 25*
7. **La Dame Blanche** .... *20 – 25*
9. **Lucie de Lammermoor** .... *20 – 25*
10. **La Musette de Portici**. .... *20 – 25*
12. **Faust** .... *20 – 25*

Historic Baltimore   Monochrome maroon or blue (scarcer) made for Hutzler Brothers.

1. **Carroll Mansion "Homewood"**. .... *$40 – $45*
2. **Baltimore Harbor**. .... *40 – 45*
3. **University of Maryland School of Medicine** .... *40 – 45*
4. **Johns Hopkins Hospital**. .... *40 – 45*
5. **Fort McHenry**. .... *40 – 45*
6. **Court House and Battle Monument** .... *40 – 45*
7. **Washington Monument**. .... *40 – 45*
8. **Old Shot Tower** .... *40 – 45*

Music Masters   (1943)   Monochrome brown prints on ivory 8½" Ultra plates.

Beethoven .... *$20 – $25*
Chopin. .... *20 – 25*
Grieg .... *20 – 25*
Liszt .... *20 – 25*
Mendelssohn. .... *20 – 25*
Paderewski .... *20 – 25*
Schubert .... *20 – 25*
Tschaikowsky .... *20 – 25*

WAHPETON POTTERY COMPANY (ROSEMEADE)

Wahpeton, North Dakota

CHAPTER AT A GLANCE

ASHTRAYS
FIGURINES
  Animals
  Other
KITCHENWARE / FIGURAL
MISCELLANY
PLANTERS

SHAKERS
  Animals
  Plants
  Other
VASES
  Notched Birds

The Wahpeton Pottery Company was begun in 1940 by Robert J. Hughes (president) and Laura A. Taylor (secretary, treasurer, and designer), who were married in 1943. They decided to call their product Rosemeade. Initially, the pottery was made on the premises (in a shed) of the Globe-Gazette Printing Company, Hughes's other business, but increasing demand sparked a move to new premises in 1944.

Howard Lewis, a ceramic engineer who had worked at Niloak (which see), was hired in 1944 as plant manager. He formulated all the glazes and, from his background at Niloak, introduced the swirl pieces, which are very hard to find.

Laura Taylor Hughes died in 1959, and the pottery ceased production in 1961, though the salesroom was kept open until 1964.

The most collectible Rosemeade items are the shakers, figures, ashtrays, and other pieces, all in animal shapes, reflecting Laura Taylor's interest in wildlife. These are glazed in solid colors or hand painted in natural colors, these latter being the most popular.

Note that I have used the name Buffalo in my listings; these are also referred to as Bison. Irene Harms's research has turned up the fact that Donkeys are correctly called Mules, and Flickertails are correctly called Prairie Dogs; I have used that terminology.

See Harms in Bibliography. See Clubs/Newsletters.

MARKS Pieces will be found backstamped in black or blue and/or with a paper label. Marks are reproduced from the book *Beautiful Rosemeade*, courtesy of Irene J. Harms. The rose, green, and gold paper label features the Wild Rose, North Dakota's state flower.

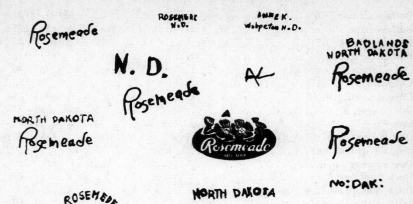

ASHTRAYS

Of the state shapes, 28 states are known.

Animals, large	$100 – $125
Animals, small	50 – 75
Minnesota shape (Minnesota Centennial)	50 – 75
Oval, Tepee	50 – 75
Pony, large	125 – 150
Rectangular, Fenn's Walnut Crush	85 – 100
Rectangular, horse head	70 – 85
Round, cowboy	50 – 75
State shape	20 – 40
Teddy Bear, "Teddy Roosevelt Memorial Park"	75 – 100
United States shape	175 – 200
Viking ship	100 – 125

FIGURINES

Animals

Alligator, 7³/₄" long	$200 – $250
Bear, souvenir, 3¹/₈"	75 – 90
Bear	35 – 50
Bear cubs	25 – 30
Bear cubs, miniature	25 – 30
Bird, Parakeet	75 – 90
Bird, Goldfinch, miniature	25 – 40
Bird, Roadrunner	75 – 90
Buffalo, small, 2¹/₂"	50 – 75

Buffalo, medium, 3³/₄" .... $100 – $125
Buffalo, large, 5³/₄" .... 150 – 175
Buffalo (ND Clay), 3³/₄" .... 150 – 175
Buffalo (white clay), 4" .... 150 – 175
Cat, miniature .... 25 – 40
Chicken .... 40 – 50
Coyote, howling, 4¹/₂" .... 100 – 125
Doe, leaping, 6" .... 50 – 75
Doe, 7¹/₂" .... 50 – 75
Dog, Pointer .... 125 – 150
Dog, sitting, miniature .... 125 – 150
Dog, standing, miniature .... 125 – 150
Duck, miniature .... 30 – 45
Duck, Mallard Drake, 6" .... 175 – 200
Duck, Mallard Hen .... 50 – 60
Elephant, miniature .... 20 – 25
Elephant, trunk up .... 150 – 175
Fighting cocks, head up/head down .... 100 – 125
Fighting cocks, head up/head down, ruffs open .... 100 – 125
Fish .... 100 – 110
Fish, Bluegill, miniature .... 100 – 110
Fish, Rainbow trout, miniature .... 100 – 110
Fish, Seahorse, 8" .... 100 – 110
Fox, miniature, 1¹/₂" .... 75 – 90
Fox, Red .... 100 – 125
Goose, miniature, 2" .... 50 – 75
Gopher, large, 4" .... 75 – 90
Hippopotamus .... 75 – 100
Horse, head in .... 75 – 100
Horse, head out, 5¹/₂" .... 75 – 100
Horse, standing, 6¹/₂" .... 75 – 100
Horse, large, 9¹/₄" .... 200 – 225
Koala .... 225 – 250
Lamb .... 100 – 125

*Horse, head out;
horse, large; and
horse, standing.*

Mice, miniature (2 different poses) .... *$15 – $20*
Monkey, Hear/See/Speak No Evil, miniature, 2" .... *150 – 200*
Mountain Goat, small, 2" .... *50 – 75*
Mountain Goat, medium .... *150 – 175*
Mule, 3³/₄" .... *100 – 125*
Mule, 4¹/₄" .... *100 – 125*
Mule, 5" .... *100 – 125*
Mule on base .... *100 – 125*
Panda .... *300 – 325*
Penguin, mother and baby, miniature .... *20 – 30*
Penguin .... *75 – 100*
Pheasant, miniature .... *50 – 75*
Pheasant .... *40 – 60*
Pheasant, cock, tail down, 9" long .... *200 – 275*
Pheasant, cock, tail down, 10¹/₂" long .... *225 – 250*
Pheasant, cock, tail down, 12¹/₂" long .... *250 – 275*
Pheasant, hen, tail down, 11" long .... *200 – 225*
Pigeon, strutting .... *50 – 75*
Pony .... *100 – 125*
Prairie Dog (Flickertail), miniature .... *25 – 30*
Rabbit, 3" .... *25 – 35*
Raccoon, miniature .... *25 – 30*
Rooster, large .... *100 – 125*
Seal, mamma, papa, and baby, miniature .... *30 – 40*
Skunk, miniature .... *20 – 25*
Walrus .... *300 – 325*
Wolfhound, 6¹/₂" .... *75 – 100*
Zebra .... *75 – 100*

Other

Indian "God of Peace," 8¹/₄" .... *$75 – $100*
ND capitol building .... *300 – 350*
Sailboat, large .... *100 – 125*
Sailboat, small .... *50 – 75*

KITCHENWARE / FIGURAL

Hen, chicken (casserole) .... *$200 – $225*
Mallard
   Casserole, hen .... *175 – 200*
   Creamer, drake .... *70 – 90*
   Dish .... *75 – 100*
   Sugar, hen .... *70 – 90*
Pick Holders (Hors d'Oeuvres)
   Fish .... *50 – 75*
   Pheasant .... *50 – 75*
   Rooster .... *35 – 50*
Tidbit tray
   Pheasant .... *50 – 75*

Strutting Cock	*$50 – $75*
Turkey	
Covered dish	*75 – 90*
Covered dish w/spoon notch	*75 – 90*
Creamer	*50 – 75*
Pick holders (Hors d'Oeuvres)	*75 – 90*
Spoon rest	*100 – 125*
Sugar	*50 – 75*
Tidbit tray	*75 – 100*

MISCELLANY

Ball jug	*$25 – $30*
Bank, Bear	*300 – 350*
Bank, Buffalo (white clay)	*175 – 200*
Bank, Buffalo (ND clay)	*175 – 200*
Bank, Elephant	*125 – 150*
Bank, Fish	*300 – 350*
Bank, Hippo	*300 – 350*
Bank, Log Cabin	*275 – 300*
Bank, Panda	*300 – 350*
Bank, Pony	*325 – 375*
Bank, Rhinoceros	*300 – 350*
Bell, Elephant	*75 – 100*
Bell, Flamingo	*90 – 100*
Bell, Peacock	*100 – 125*
Bell, Tulips (3)	*75 – 100*
Bookend, Bear, 4"	*200 – 225*
Bookend, Buffalo, 5³⁄₄"	*175 – 200*
Bookend, Wolfhound	*75 – 100*
Bowl, Viking ship, small	*50 – 75*
Bowl, Viking ship, medium	*100 – 150*
Bowl, Viking ship, large	*150 – 200*
Candle holder, Bird	*20 – 25*
Candle holder, Egyptian	*75 – 100*
Candle holder, Heart shape	*35 – 50*
Candle holder, Prairie Rose	*50 – 75*
Cigarette box, embossed horse	*75 – 100*
Cotton holder, Rabbit	*60 – 75*
Flower holder/frog, Fawn	*30 – 45*
Flower holder/frog, Fish	*40 – 50*
Flower holder/frog, Heron, 6³⁄₄"	*30 – 45*
Flower holder/frog, Pheasant	*40 – 50*
Flower holder/frog, Squirrel	*30 – 45*
Incense burner, Elephant	*75 – 100*
Incense burner, Log Cabin	*75 – 100*
Incense burner, Tepee	*75 – 100*
Jam jar, barrel shape	*50 – 75*
Jardiniere, Egyptian, 5"	*60 – 75*

Mug, Game Bird decals . . . . *$50 – $65*
Mug, Indian Head . . . . *75 – 90*
Mug, Theodore Roosevelt's head . . . . *75 – 100*
Mustache cup . . . . *75 – 90*
Paperweight, round (Minnesota Centennial) . . . . *40 – 50*
Paperweight, round (Theodore Roosevelt) . . . . *75 – 90*
Paperweight, square (Theodore Roosevelt) . . . . *75 – 90*
Peace Garden ashtray . . . . *50 – 75*
Peace Garden shakers . . . . *50 – 60*
Peace Garden souvenir, 4¹/₂" . . . . *75 – 100*
Pin, Bear . . . . *40 – 60*
Pin, Blackbird . . . . *40 – 60*
Pin, Fish . . . . *40 – 60*
Pin, Heart . . . . *30 – 40*
Pin, Horse head . . . . *40 – 60*
Pin, Meadowlark . . . . *40 – 60*
Pin, Prairie Rose . . . . *30 – 40*
Pin, Rabbit . . . . *40 – 60*
Pin, Squirrel . . . . *40 – 60*
Plaque, Coyote . . . . *100 – 125*
Plaque, Dove . . . . *100 – 125*
Plaque, Gopher . . . . *75 – 100*
Plaque, Fish (10 different), 3¹/₂" to 6" . . . . *100 – 125*
Plaque, Horse head, small . . . . *50 – 75*
Plaque, Horse head, large . . . . *75 – 100*
Plaque, Mallard Drake, 5¹/₄" . . . . *100 – 125*
Plaque, Mallard Drake, 6¹/₂" . . . . *100 – 125*
Plaque, Mallard Drake, 7¹/₂" . . . . *100 – 125*
Plaque, Mallard Hen, 7¹/₂" . . . . *100 – 125*
Plaque, Meadowlark . . . . *75 – 100*
Plaque, Mountain goat mother and baby, 4¹/₂" . . . . *250 – 275*
Plaque, Pheasant cock, 7¹/₂" . . . . *100 – 125*
Plaque, Pheasant hen, 7" . . . . *100 – 125*
Plaque, Sea gull (3 different poses), 6¹/₂" . . . . *275 – 300*
Plate (Mouse) . . . . *50 – 75*
Plate (Theodore Roosevelt) . . . . *100 – 125*
Snack set w/cup . . . . *40 – 60*
Snack set w/mug . . . . *40 – 60*
Souvenir, Shrine of Democracy, Mt. Rushmore, 3¹/₂" × 5¹/₂" long . . . . *250 – 275*
Spoon rest, Bat . . . . *75 – 100*
Spoon rest, Cactus . . . . *30 – 40*
Spoon rest, Cocker spaniel . . . . *75 – 100*
Spoon rest, Elephant . . . . *50 – 75*
Spoon rest, Fish . . . . *50 – 75*
Spoon rest, Ladyslipper . . . . *30 – 40*
Spoon rest, Money bag . . . . *75 – 100*
Spoon rest, Spoon (Minnesota Centennial) . . . . *25 – 40*
Spoon rest, Pansy . . . . *30 – 40*

Spoon rest, Pheasant . . . . *$30 – $50*
Spoon rest, Pig . . . . *75 – 100*
Spoon rest, Poppy . . . . *30 – 40*
Spoon rest, Prairie Rose . . . . *30 – 50*
Spoon rest, Squirrel . . . . *75 – 90*
Spoon rest, Sunflower . . . . *30 – 40*
Spoon rest, Tulip . . . . *30 – 40*
TV lamp, Rooster, 15" . . . . *500 – 550*
TV lamp, Dog, running, 6" . . . . *300 – 325*
TV lamp, Fawn . . . . *300 – 350*
TV lamp, Horse, 9¼" . . . . *300 – 325*
TV lamp, Panther, 7" . . . . *350 – 400*
TV lamp, Pheasant, 9½" . . . . *300 – 350*
TV lamp, Stag, leaping, 11" . . . . *300 – 350*
Wall pocket, Dove . . . . *100 – 125*
Wall pocket, Egyptian . . . . *50 – 75*
Wall pocket, Moon and Maid . . . . *50 – 75*
Wall pocket/string holder, Kitten, 7" . . . . *100 – 125*

PLANTERS

Basket, small . . . . *$20 – $25*
Basket, large . . . . *30 – 35*
Bird, 6½" . . . . *20 – 25*
Doe, 8" . . . . *45 – 50*
Dove (2 different poses), 5½" . . . . *100 – 125*
Elephant, 4¾" . . . . *75 – 90*
Grapes . . . . *30 – 35*
Kangaroo, 5" . . . . *60 – 75*
Koala, 5" . . . . *125 – 150*
Lamb, sitting . . . . *75 – 100*
Lamb, standing, 5" . . . . *75 – 100*
Mule, 5" . . . . *125 – 150*
Pheasant, 9¼" long . . . . *100 – 125*
Pony, 5¼" . . . . *75 – 90*
Squirrel, 4½" . . . . *25 – 40*
Watering can . . . . *40 – 50*
Wooden shoe . . . . *25 – 30*

SHAKERS

See Miscellany for matching items.

Animals

Badgers, 2¾" long . . . . *$75 – $80*
Bird, Bluebird . . . . *40 – 50*
Bird, Bobwhite quail . . . . *35 – 40*
Bird, Chickadee . . . . *40 – 50*
Bird, Dove . . . . *65 – 75*

Bird, Finch. . . . . *$40 – $50*
Bird, Flamingo. . . . . *60 – 70*
Bird, Jay hawk. . . . . *75 – 100*
Bird, Parakeet on perch . . . . *50 – 60*
Bird, Parrot . . . . *45 – 50*
Bird, Pelican, small . . . . *45 – 50*
Bird, Pelican, large . . . . *45 – 50*
Bird, Pigeon, strutting . . . . *60 – 70*
Bird, Roadrunner, 4¹/₂" long . . . . *75 – 80*
Bird, Robin . . . . *40 – 50*
Bird, Swan. . . . . *60 – 75*
Bird, Western Quail w/real top feathers . . . . *35 – 40*
Bison . . . . *70 – 75*
Cat, small. . . . . *35 – 40*
Cat, large . . . . *45 – 50*
Cat, "Rosemede" . . . . *35 – 40*
Cattle . . . . *50 – 60*
Chicken . . . . *20 – 25*
Chicken, large . . . . *35 – 40*
Chicken, roosting . . . . *70 – 75*
Coyote, howling. . . . . *75 – 100*
Coyote, pup . . . . *75 – 100*
Deer, leaping . . . . *70 – 75*
Deer, sitting . . . . *70 – 75*
Dog, heads
    Bloodhound. . . . . *25 – 30*
    Boston Terrier . . . . *25 – 30*
    Chow-Chow . . . . *25 – 30*
    Cocker Spaniel . . . . *125 – 150*
    Dalmatian . . . . *25 – 30*
    English Bull Dog. . . . . *25 – 30*
    English Setter . . . . *25 – 30*
    English Toy Terrier . . . . *25 – 30*
    Greyhound . . . . *25 – 30*
    Mexican Chihuahua. . . . . *100 – 125*
    Pekingese. . . . . *60 – 75*
    Scottish Terrier . . . . *25 – 30*
    Wire-Haired Fox Terrier. . . . . *25 – 30*
Dog, Pointer . . . . *175 – 200*
Elephant . . . . *45 – 50*
Fighting cock . . . . *50 – 60*
Fish, 4" to 5" long
    Bass, small-mouth . . . . *150 – 175*
    Bass, large-mouth . . . . *150 – 175*
    Bluegill. . . . . *150 – 175*
    Brown trout . . . . *150 – 175*
    Bullhead . . . . *175 – 200*
    Catfish . . . . *175 – 200*

Crappie .... *$150 – $175*
Muskellunge (Muskie) .... *150 – 175*
Northerns .... *150 – 175*
Rainbow trout .... *150 – 175*
Rainbow trout, upright .... *100 – 150*
Salmon .... *150 – 175*
Walleye .... *150 – 175*
Gopher, small .... *35 – 40*
Gopher, large .... *40 – 45*
Horse, head .... *45 – 50*
Horse, sitting and standing .... *20 – 25*
Kangaroo, w/babies in pouch .... *60 – 70*
Kangaroo .... *45 – 50*
Kitten, 2¼" .... *20 – 25*
Mice, 1¼" to 1¾" .... *20 – 25*
Mountain goat, 2" .... *60 – 70*
Mule, head .... *45 – 50*
Ox, head .... *40 – 50*
Pheasant, lively cocks, large, w/tail up .... *85 – 90*
Pheasant w/tail up .... *20 – 25*
Pheasant, Golden .... *75 – 80*
Pheasant, miniature .... *85 – 95*
Pheasant, large, w/tail down .... *40 – 50*
Pheasant, crouching .... *60 – 75*
Pig .... *50 – 60*
Prairie Dog (Flickertail) .... *25 – 30*
Puma (mountain lion), 4¼" long .... *125 – 150*
Rabbit, small .... *60 – 70*
Rabbit, large, 3" .... *75 – 80*
Raccoon .... *40 – 50*
Rooster, strutting .... *50 – 60*
Rooster and hen w/chick, large .... *70 – 75*
Skunk, small, ¾" .... *30 – 35*
Skunk, medium, 1½" .... *25 – 30*
Skunk, large, 2¾" .... *20 – 25*
Turkey, miniature .... *75 – 80*
Turkey .... *40 – 50*

Plants

Brussels sprout, 1½" .... *$25 – $30*
Cactus, Barrel .... *30 – 35*
Cactus, Devils Finger .... *30 – 35*
Cactus, Pin Cushion .... *30 – 35*
Cactus, Sand Dollar .... *30 – 35*
Corn, small, w/tray .... *50 – 60*
Corn, tall .... *75 – 85*
Cucumber, 1½" .... *25 – 30*
Pepper, 1¾" .... *25 – 30*

Potato, small . . . . *$45 – $50*
Potato, large. . . . . *50 – 60*
Prairie Rose . . . . *25 – 30*
Tulip . . . . *35 – 40*
Wheat . . . . *45 – 50*

Other

Boxing gloves . . . . *$100 – $125*
Canopic jars (set of four) . . . . *150 – 175*
Indian Head . . . . *60 – 70*
Paul Bunyan and Babe (blue ox), heads . . . . *50 – 60*
Sailboat . . . . *80 – 90*
Shapes . . . . *30 – 40*
Square . . . . *20 – 25*
Tulsa Bank, first . . . . *70 – 75*
Viking ship . . . . *80 – 90*
Windmill . . . . *50 – 60*

VASES

Bird on tree, 6½" . . . . *$30 – $35*
Doe, sitting. . . . . *20 – 25*
Egyptian, 5½" to 8". . . . . *50 – 75*
Fawn . . . . *25 – 30*
Koala on tree, 8¼" . . . . *200 – 250*
Lovebird, 6" . . . . *30 – 45*
Maid w/horn, 7¼". . . . . *100 – 125*
Mermaid . . . . *100 – 125*
Peacock, 7½". . . . . *100 – 125*
Rooster . . . . *125 – 150*
Swan, 5". . . . . *30 – 40*

Notched Birds to Perch on Vases

Bluebird. . . . . *$35 – $50*
Chickadee . . . . *35 – 50*
Goldfinch. . . . . *35 – 50*
Robin . . . . *35 – 50*

WALLACE CHINA COMPANY, LTD.

Huntington Park, California

The company was formed in 1931 for the production of vitrified hotel ware. It was purchased by Shenango China of New Castle, Pennsylvania, in 1959 and operated as a wholly owned subsidiary. During an outside audit in 1963, it was discovered that the inventory had been figured incorrectly for a number of years. This resulted in a serious loss of inventory, and Wallace was liquidated in 1964.

Westward Ho is the most popularly collected line.

See Chipman in Bibliography.

MARKS   This is the mark commonly found on Westward Ho.

WESTWARD HO   (1945)

Designed by Till Goodan. The M. C. Wentz Company, giftware wholesalers, bought two of Goodan's Western paintings to be used as background at a Los Angeles gift show. They generated so much interest that the artist was approached to do this line of "barbecue" ware. Wallace, a hotel ware manufacturer, was chosen to produce the line. Wentz had these on display at their Westward Ho Ranch House in Pasadena.

There are four underglaze patterns: Boots and Saddle (ranch brand borders with boots and saddle design in the center in saddle brown on buckskin background), Longhorn (a continuous cattle drive around the rim with a Longhorn head in the center in brown on a white background, *not* designed by Goodan), Pioneer Trails (covered wagon borders with center designs depicting early history of the West), and Rodeo (ranch brand borders with center designs depicting rodeo events in saddle brown on a buckskin background with two-color handwork). All the brands are authentic, representing real ranches.

The **mixing bowls** were also listed as individual salads. A three-piece child's set, called a **Little Buckaroo Chuck Set**, was added in 1949. It consisted of the cup (called a mug), 9" plate, and individual soup/salad which was called a cereal for this set. All had a "Ride 'Em Cowboy" motif.

Goodan also designed matching glassware which was made by Libbey. Also, look for a tablecloth and napkins, and paper cocktail napkins in an alternating dark and light squares pattern with brands.

TEXAS SOUVENIR   Some pieces had an alternate decoration: the addition of the word "Texas" over the well decoration, and "The Lone Star State" under it. It was put on the ashtray, the four plates, and the tall shakers. It was called Texas Souvenir.

PRICING   Boots and Saddle, Longhorn and Pioneer Trails are at the low end of the range, and Rodeo is at the high end.

Ashtray, Boots and Saddle, 5½" .... *$45 – $55*
Ashtray, Pioneer Trails, 5½" .... *45 – 55*
   Kit Carson... *45 – 55*
   Sam Houston.. *45 – 55*
   Will Rogers... *45 – 55*
   Mark Twain.. *45 – 55*
Bowl, mixing, 6" *50*
Bowl, mixing, 7" *75*
Bowl, mixing, 9" *100*
Bowl, mixing, 10" *125*
Bowl, mixing, 12" *150*
Bowl, salad, 13" × 5" deep .... *400 – 500*
Bowl, soup/individual salad, 5¾" .... *55 – 65*
Bowl, soup, rim, 8"* .... *150 – 175*
Bowl, vegetable, round, 8".. *175 – 225*
Bowl, vegetable, round, 9⅛".. *175 – 225*
Bowl, vegetable, oval, 12"... *175 – 200*
Child's bowl .... *125 – 150*
Child's mug... *125 – 150*
Child's plate .... *125 – 150*
Creamer, footed .... *75 – 95*
Creamer, small, 5 ounce... *85 – 115*
Cup, 7½-ounce .... *35 – 45*

Westward-Ho ashtray.

Cup, AD. . . . . *$40 – $50*

Cup, jumbo, 11-ounce . . . . *65 – 75*

Cup, stack, 6¾-ounce . . . . *25 – 35*

Custard . . . . *35 – 55*

Dish, fruit, 5" . . . . *50 – 60*

Dish, 6½" . . . . *35 – 40*

Jug, disk, 72-ounce . . . . *300 – 400*

Napkin ring . . . . *50 – 60*

Plate, 7" . . . . *45 – 60*

Plate, 9" . . . . *115 – 125*

Plate, 10¾" . . . . *75 – 95*

Plate, chop, 13" . . . . *175 – 200*

Platter, oval, 15½" . . . . *175 – 200*

Saucer . . . . *10 – 15*

Saucer, AD *10*

Saucer, jumbo . . . . *10 – 15*

Saucer, stack . . . . *5 – 7*

Shaker, large, 5¼", each . . . . *125 – 150*

Shaker, small, 3½", each . . . . *60 – 80*

Sugar/Ramekin, footed, 4½" . . . . *125 – 150*

Sugar, small, open, 5" . . . . *55 – 75*

WATT POTTERY COMPANY

Crooksville, Ohio

The Watt Pottery was founded in 1922 by William J. Watt and his sons Thomas, Marion, and Harry. The sons had been working for the Ransbottom Brothers Pottery. Watt bought the old Globe Pottery from Zane Burley and began production of stoneware, mainly jars, jugs, and mixing bowls. In 1935, they began production of oven-safe kitchenware, although the most collectible lines were not brought out until the 1950s. A fire destroyed the plant on October 4, 1965. It was not rebuilt.

Watt made a wide variety of kitchenware and little dinnerware, which is why it is so highly valued. Its hand-painted underglaze ware is the most collectible, especially with advertising on it.

See Morris and see Thompson in Bibliography. See Clubs/Newsletters.

MARKS   Shape numbers were impressed on most pieces. "Watt Ware" or "Watt Oven Ware" impressed in a circle will also be found. Impressed "Watt" in script is an early mark.

HAND-PAINTED DINNERWARE / KITCHENWARE

TERMINOLOGY   Watt changed the name of items from catalog to catalog; for example, bean pots became cookie jars. I have tried to make these names as accurate as possible. Note the following: if a bowl had a lip to hold a lid, it is called a casserole. If it didn't, it is called a baker. Sometimes bakers had lids; in these cases, I have listed them as baker w/lid.

DINNERWARE   The **Chip 'n Dip** set is a metal stand with a #120 bowl on top and an #119 bowl below. The **#62 creamer** is the same shape as the

#15, #16, and #17 jugs. The **ice bucket** is the #59 cookie jar but with a flat lid rather than a domed one. The **#115 pitcher** is also called a carafe or coffee server.

KITCHENWARE   The **#5 to #9 bowls** came in three styles: lipped, lipped with a shoulder, and horizontally ribbed with a smooth panel around the top. **Bowls #600 to #604** are ribbed around the bottom and smooth around the top. There are two different shapes for the **#72 canister**: one is straight-sided, 9½" high, and one has a pinched waist, 7¼" high. The **drip jar** was sold separately and as a range set with the hourglass shakers.

PRICING   Stamped advertising pieces are desirable to some collectors but not all. Those who like them will pay a little more. Add 10% to prices for bowls, pitchers, and shakers; add 10% to 15% to cookie jars and covered casseroles. For salesmen's samples ("Your advertising in this space") add 25%. For covered casseroles, the lid is worth *two-thirds* of the total price.

AMERICAN RED BUD   (Also called Bleeding Heart or Teardrop)

Pendant red buds, green leaves, and brown stems.

Dinnerware

Bean cup, individual, no lid, 3½" /75	*$15 – $20*
Bowl, salad, 9½" /73	*125 – 150*
Casserole, individual, French handle, 8" /18.	*225 – 275*
Casserole, oval, 1½-quart, 10" /86	*800 – 900*
Creamer /62	*175 – 225*
Dish, cereal/salad, 5½" /74	*30 – 40*

American Red Bud: The back of this postcard reads: "Because we have sincerely missed you . . . the valuable gift pictured on the other side is yours free . . . just for re-opening or adding to your account. Brandt Jewelers, Racine, WI."

Jug, 1-pint, 5½"   /15 . . . . *$50 – $60*
Jug, 2-pint, 6½"   /16 . . . . *100 – 150*
Jug, square, 5-pint, 8"   /69 . . . . *475 – 525*
Shaker, barrel, each   /45   /46 . . . . *125 – 150*

Kitchenware

Baker, square, 8" . . . . *$800 – $900*
Bean pot, 2 handles, 6½" high   /76 . . . . *75 – 90*
Bowl, deep, 2-pint, 6½"   /63 . . . . *40 – 65*
Bowl, deep, 4-pint, 7½"   /64 . . . . *40 – 65*
Bowl, deep, 6-pint, 8½"   /65 . . . . *40 – 65*
Bowl, mixing, lipped, 5"   /5 . . . . *40 – 50*
Bowl, mixing, lipped, 6"   /6 . . . . *40 – 50*
Bowl, mixing, lipped, 7"   /7 . . . . *40 – 50*
Bowl, mixing, lipped, 8"   /8 . . . . *40 – 50*
Bowl, mixing, lipped, 9"   /9 . . . . *40 – 50*
Bowl, ribbed, 4"   /04 . . . . *35 – 40*
Bowl, ribbed, 5"   /05 . . . . *35 – 40*
Bowl, ribbed, 6"   /06 . . . . *35 – 40*
Bowl, ribbed, 7"   /07 . . . . *35 – 40*
Cheese crock, 8" high   /80 . . . . *250 – 350*

APPLE   (Also Red Apple) (1952)

This most popular of Watt's decorations comes in several variations. The ones you will see most often are a solid-red apple with a twig and two or three leaves. The variations are: Double Apple (two apples with twig and leaves), Open Apple (apple is outlined, revealing core, with stem and two leaves), and Reduced Decoration Apple (apple looks like a heart with two leaves, no twig).

PRICING   For Double Apple and Open Apple, add 300% for the #62 creamer; add 100% for all other pieces.

Dinnerware

Baker, 1½-quart, open, 8"   /67 . . . . *$50 – $70*
  w/lid . . . . *125 – 150*

Apple: Teapots /506 and /112.

Baker, open, 8½" /96 . . . . *$45 – $50*
  w/lid . . . . *100 – 125*
Bean cup, individual, no lid, 3½" /75 . . . . *300 – 400*
Bowl, cereal/salad/individual popcorn, 6½" /52 . . . . *40 – 50*
Bowl, flat soup/individual spaghetti, 8" /44
  Inside band . . . . *400 – 450*
  Outside band . . . . *150 – 175*
Bowl, salad, 9½" /73 . . . . *75 – 85*
Bowl, salad, footed, 11" /106 . . . . *450 – 550*
Bowl, salad/spaghetti, 11½" /55 . . . . *100 – 125*
Bowl, spaghetti, 13" /39 . . . . *100 – 150*
Casserole, individual, tab, 5" /18 . . . . *175 – 250*
Casserole, individual, French handle, 8" /18 . . . . *225 – 275*
Casserole, individual, stick handle, 7½" /18 . . . . *175 – 250*
Casserole, 8½" /3 /19 . . . . *175 – 225*
Casserole/Covered Salad, 9½" /73 . . . . *180 – 225*
Cheese crock, 8" high /80 . . . . *900 – 1200*
Chip 'n Dip . . . . *300 – 350*
Coffee pot, w/lid, 9¾" /115 . . . . *3000 +*
Creamer, 4¼" /62 . . . . *90 – 120*
Creamer, cutout finger hole . . . . *ND*
Cruet, china-tipped cork, embossed "O" /"V", set /126 . . . . *2000 +*
Dish, cereal/salad, 5½" /74 . . . . *35 – 40*
Dish, cereal, 6" /94 . . . . *35 – 40*
Drip jar, 5½" /01 . . . . *275 – 325*
Ice bucket, flat lid, 7¼" high /59 . . . . *225 – 325*
Jug, 1-pint, 5½" /15 . . . . *65 – 85*
Jug, 2-pint, 6½" /16 . . . . *90 – 120*
Jug, 5-pint, 8" /17 . . . . *225 – 275*
Jug, ice lip, 5-pint, 8" /17 . . . . *200 – 225*
Jug, square, 5-pint, 8" /69 . . . . *400 – 500*
Mug, barrel /501 . . . . *300 – 350*
Mug, coffee /121 . . . . *175 – 225*
Mug, cutout finger hole /701 . . . . *400 – 500*
Mug, low /61 . . . . *ND*
Pie baker, 9" /33 . . . . *90 – 135*
Plate, 9½" . . . . *450 – 550*
Plate, 10" /101 . . . . *500 – 600*
Plate, grill, 10½" . . . . *800 – 900*
Platter, round, 12" /49 . . . . *300 – 400*
Platter, round, 15" /31 . . . . *300 – 400*
Shaker, barrel, each /45 /46 . . . . *225 – 250*
Shaker, hourglass, "S"/"P" holes on top, each /117 /118 . . . . *100 – 135*
Shaker, hourglass, embossed "S"/"P," each /117 /118 . . . . *110 – 150*
Sugar, cutout finger hole . . . . *ND*
Sugar, open /98 . . . . *150 – 200*
  w/lid . . . . *325 – 400*
Teapot, 5¾" /505 . . . . *3000 +*

Teapot, straight side, 6" /112 . . . . *$2000 +*
Tumbler, slant-sided, 4½" /56 . . . . *ND*

Kitchenware

Baking dish, rectangular, lug, 10" × 5¼" /85 . . . . *$1200 – $1600*
Bean pot, 2 handles, 6½" high /76 . . . . *175 – 225*
Bowl, deep, 2-pint, 6½" /63 . . . . *80 – 90*
Bowl, deep, 4-pint, 7½" /64 . . . . *80 – 90*
Bowl, deep, 6-pint, 8½" /65 . . . . *80 – 90*
Bowl, mixing, lipped, 5" /5 . . . . *40 – 60*
Bowl, mixing, lipped, 6" /6 . . . . *40 – 60*
Bowl, mixing, lipped, 7" /7 . . . . *40 – 60*
Bowl, mixing, lipped, 8" /8 . . . . *40 – 60*
Bowl, mixing, lipped, 9" /9 . . . . *40 – 60*
Bowl, mixing, ribbed, 5" /5 . . . . *50 – 65*
Bowl, mixing, ribbed, 6" /6 . . . . *50 – 65*
Bowl, mixing, ribbed, 7" /7 . . . . *50 – 65*
Bowl, mixing, ribbed, 8" /8 . . . . *50 – 65*
Bowl, ribbed, 4" /04 . . . . *50 – 60*
Bowl, ribbed, 5" /05 . . . . *30 – 50*
  w/lid . . . . *125 – 130*
Bowl, ribbed, 6" /06 . . . . *30 – 50*
Bowl, ribbed, 7" /07 . . . . *30 – 50*
Bowl, ribbed, 4¾" /602 . . . . *125 – 150*
Bowl, ribbed, 5¾" /603 . . . . *125 – 150*
Bowl, ribbed, 6¾" /604 . . . . *125 – 150*
Bowl, ribbed, 7¾" /600 . . . . *75 – 90*
  w/lid . . . . *125 – 150*
Bowl, ribbed, 8¾" /601 . . . . *75 – 90*
  w/lid . . . . *125 – 150*
Canister, 7" high, "Coffee" /82 . . . . *450 – 550*
Canister, 7" high, "Tea" /82 . . . . *450 – 550*
Canister, 8" high, "Flour" /81 . . . . *450 – 550*
Canister, 8" high, "Sugar" /81 . . . . *450 – 550*
Canister, 9½" high /72 . . . . *500 – 625*
Canister, dome top, 10¾" high /91 . . . . *900 – 1200*
Cookie jar, 7½" high /21 . . . . *275 – 375*
Cookie jar, 8¼" high /503 . . . . *425 – 500*
Fondue, stick handle . . . . *ND*
Lazy Susan . . . . *ND*
Warmer, electric (for casserole) . . . . *600 – 800*

AUTUMN FOLIAGE (1959)

Brown leaves and stems.

Dinnerware

Baker, open (cereal/salad), 6" /94 . . . . *$30 – $40*
Baker w/lid, 8½" /96 . . . . *100 – 120*

Autumn Foliage: Covered baker /110.

Bowl, salad, 9½"　/73 . . . . *$80 – $100*
Bowl, salad, 11"　/106 . . . . *80 – 90*
Bowl, spaghetti, 13"　/39 . . . . *125 – 150*
Carafe, ribbon handle, open, 9½"　/115 . . . . *150 – 250*
Casserole, 2-quart, 8"　/110 . . . . *125 – 150*
Creamer　/62 . . . . *175 – 225*
Cruet, Oil/Vinegar, china-tipped cork, set　/126 . . . . *350 – 500*
Fondue, stick handle, 9"　/506 . . . . *250 – 300*
Ice bucket, flat lid, 7¼" high　/59 . . . . *225 – 275*
Jug, 1-pint, 5½"　/15 . . . . *60 – 70*
Jug, 2-pint, 6½"　/16 . . . . *85 – 100*
Jug, 5-pint, 8"　/17 . . . . *175 – 225*
Mug, barrel　/501 . . . . *125 – 175*
Mug, coffee　/121 . . . . *175 – 225*
Pie baker, 9"　/33 . . . . *135 – 160*
Platter, round, 15"　/31 . . . . *125 – 150*
Shaker, hourglass, embossed "S"/"P," each　/117　/118 . . . . *90 – 120*
Shaker, hourglass, "S"/"P" holes on top, each . . . . *90 – 120*
Sugar, open　/98 . . . . *125 – 175*
　w/lid . . . . *300 – 325*
Teapot　/505 . . . . *2000 +*

Kitchenware

Bean pot, 2 handles, 6½" high　/76 . . . . *$125 – $160*
Bowl, deep, 2-pint, 6½"　/63 . . . . *40 – 50*
Bowl, deep, 4-pint, 7½"　/64 . . . . *40 – 50*
Bowl, deep, 6-pint, 8½"　/65 . . . . *40 – 50*
Bowl, low, banded, 6½-ounce　/04 . . . . *30 – 40*
Bowl, mixing, ribbed, 5"　/5 . . . . *30 – 45*
Bowl, mixing, ribbed, 6"　/6 . . . . *30 – 45*
Bowl, mixing, ribbed, 7"　/7 . . . . *30 – 45*
Bowl, mixing, ribbed, 8"　/8 . . . . *30 – 45*
Bowl, mixing, ribbed, 9"　/9 . . . . *30 – 45*

Bowl, ribbed, 4³/₄"   /602 .... $40 – $50
Bowl, ribbed, 5³/₄"   /603 .... 40 – 50
Bowl, ribbed, 6³/₄"   /604 .... 40 – 50
Bowl, ribbed, 7³/₄"   /600 .... 30 – 40
Bowl, ribbed, 8³/₄"   /601 .... 30 – 40
Drip jar, 5¹/₂"   /01 .... 200 – 225

CHERRY

This decoration consists of three red cherries and a red flower with green leaves and brown stem. Smaller pieces will have two cherries only; this is not a variation but an accommodation to the smaller size.

Dinnerware   Only one barrel pepper shaker has been found so far.

Bowl, berry, 5¹/₂"   /4 .... $25 – $35
Bowl, cereal/salad/individual popcorn, 6¹/₂"   /52 .... 25 – 35
Bowl, spaghetti, 13"   /39 .... 110 – 135
Casserole, 9"   /3   /19 .... 135 – 150
Dish, cereal/salad, 5³/₄"   /23 .... 25 – 35
Jug, 1-pint, 5¹/₂"   /15 .... 125 – 150
Jug, 2-pint. 6¹/₂"   /16 .... 100 – 135
Jug, 5-pint, 8"   /17 .... 200 – 250
Platter, round, 15"   /31 .... 120 – 140
Shaker, barrel, salt   /45 .... 90 – 110
Shaker, barrel, pepper   /46 .... ND

Cherry: Platter /49 and spaghetti bowl /39.

Kitchenware

Bowl, mixing, lipped w/shoulder, 5"　/5 .... $40 – $50
Bowl, mixing, lipped w/shoulder, 6"　/6 .... 40 – 50
Bowl, mixing, lipped w/shoulder, 7"　/7 .... 40 – 50
Bowl, mixing, lipped w/shoulder, 8"　/8 .... 40 – 50
Bowl, mixing, lipped w/shoulder, 9"　/9 .... 40 – 50
Cookie jar, 7¹/₂" high　/21 .... 225 – 275

DUTCH TULIP　(1956)

A Pennsylvania Dutch–style decoration with blue tulip and red and green leaves.

Dinnerware

Baker, 1-quart, open, 7"　/66 .... $85 – $100
　w/lid .... 225 – 250
Baker, 1¹/₂-quart, open, 8"　/67 .... 85 – 100
　w/lid .... 225 – 250
Baker, 5"　/68 .... 100 – 125
Bowl, spaghetti, 13"　/39 .... 400 – 450
Casserole, individual, French handle, 8"　/18 .... 250 – 350
Creamer　/62 .... 225 – 300
Jug, 1-pint, 5¹/₂"　/15 .... 130 – 175
Jug, 2-pint, 6¹/₂"　/16 .... 150 – 200
Jug, square, 5-pint, 8"　/69 .... 500 – 625
Plate, grill, 10¹/₂" .... 800 – 900

Kitchenware

Bean pot, 2 handles, 6¹/₂" high　/76 .... $275 – $350
Bowl, deep, 2-pint, 6¹/₂"　/63 .... 90 – 110

Dutch Tulip:
Canisters /81 and
/82.

Bowl, deep, 4-pint, 7½" /64 .... $90 – $110
Bowl, deep, 6-pint, 8½" /65 .... 90 – 110
Bowl, ribbed, w/lid, 5" /05 .... 200 – 225
Canister, 7" high, "Coffee" /82 .... 500 – 600
Canister, 7" high, "Tea" /82 .... 500 – 600
Canister, 8" high, "Flour" /81 .... 500 – 600
Canister, 8" high, "Sugar" /81 .... 500 – 600
Cheese crock, 8" high /80 .... 500 – 900

EAGLE

Maroon eagle with wings spread and three stars above head.

Dinnerware

Dish, cereal/salad, 5½" /74 .... $100 – $125
Jug, ice lip, 5-pint, 8" /17 .... 375 – 450

Kitchenware

Bowl, mixing, lipped w/shoulder, 10" /10 .... $135 – $175
Bowl, mixing, lipped w/shoulder, 12" /12 .... 135 – 175
Bowl, mixing, ribbed, 5" /5 .... 135 – 175
Bowl, mixing, ribbed, 6" /6 .... 135 – 175
Bowl, mixing, ribbed, 7" /7 .... 135 – 175
Bowl, mixing, ribbed, 8" /8 .... 135 – 175
Bowl, mixing, ribbed, 9" /9 .... 135 – 175
Canister, 7¼" high /72 .... 700 – 900

MORNING GLORY (ca. 1958)

Morning Glory differs from other hand-painted Watt lines in that the pattern is
embossed: flowers, leaves, and lattice. The red flowers and green leaves are
on either an ivory or yellow background. A variation is an ivory flower and

Eagle: Pitcher /17.

lattice on brown. This was achieved by first glazing the piece in ivory, then glazing it in brown and wiping off the glaze from the high points of the pattern before firing.

Some of these shape numbers differ from Watt's standard numbering system. Where the number differs, I have indicated the standard number in parentheses.

PRICING   There is little difference in price for the red and green on ivory or yellow background. The ivory on brown has been seen so far only on the cookie jar; see below.

Dinnerware

Casserole, 2-quart, 8½"   /94. . . . . $300 – $375
Creamer,   /97 (62) . . . . 350 – 650
Jug, ice lip, 5-pint, 8"   /96 (17). . . . . 250 – 300
Sugar, open   /98 . . . . 200 – 275

Kitchenware

Bowl, mixing, 5"   /5 . . . . $90 – $100
Bowl, mixing, 6"   /6 . . . . 90 – 100
Bowl, mixing, 7"   /7 . . . . 90 – 100
Bowl, mixing, 8"   /8 . . . . 90 – 100
Bowl, mixing, 9"   /9 . . . . 90 – 100

IVORY ON BROWN

Cookie jar, 11" high   /95 . . . . $400 – $500

RIO ROSE   (Pansy) (ca. 1949)

The official name for this pattern is Rio Rose; some collectors call it Pansy. Of the several variations, the two most readily found are Cut-leaf (red flower with yellow center and veined leaves) and Solid Leaf (leaves do not have veining). A white cross is sometimes found in the center of the flower; this is called

Rio Rose: Canister /72.

Cross-hatch. Pieces with green and red bands are called Bull's-eye by collectors; this can be additionally decorated with red swirls.

PRICING   Prices below are for Cut-leaf, Solid Leaf, and Bull's-eye. Double prices for Cross-hatch.

Dinnerware

Bowl, 15" *$125*
Bowl, flat soup/individual spaghetti, 8"   /44. . . . . *20 – 35*
Bowl, spaghetti, 11"   /24. . . . . *60 – 80*
Bowl, spaghetti, 13"   /39. . . . . *75 – 90*
Casserole, individual, stick handle, 7½"   /18. . . . . *100 – 125*
Casserole, 7½"   /2   /48 . . . . *50 – 70*
Casserole, 8¾" . . . . *50 – 70*
Casserole, 9"   /3   /19 . . . . *60 – 80*
Casserole, 4 handles, 9½" . . . . *75 – 100*
Creamer . . . . *100 – 125*
Cup . . . . *65 – 85*
Dish, cereal/salad, 5½"   /74 . . . . *25 – 35*
Jug, old style, 7" high . . . . *150 – 200*
Jug, 1-pint, 5½"   /15 . . . . *125 – 200*
Jug, 2-pint, 6½"   /16 . . . . *100 – 125*
Jug, 5-pint, 8"   /17 . . . . *165 – 200*
Plate, 7½" . . . . *30 – 45*
Plate, 8½" . . . . *30 – 45*
Plate, party, 11¾" . . . . *60 – 80*
Platter, 12"   /49 . . . . *50 – 60*
Platter, round, 15"   /31. . . . . *90 – 100*
Saucer . . . . *15 – 25*
Sugar . . . . *110 – 150*

Kitchenware

Bowl, mixing, lipped, 5"   /5 . . . . *$25 – $50*
Bowl, mixing, lipped, 6"   /6 . . . . *25 – 50*
Bowl, mixing, lipped, 7"   /7 . . . . *25 – 50*
Bowl, mixing, lipped, 8"   /8 . . . . *25 – 50*
Bowl, mixing, lipped, 9"   /9 . . . . *25 – 50*
Cookie jar, 7½" high. . . . . *150 – 175*
Dutch oven, 10½"   /20 . . . . *75 – 125*
Pie baker, 9" . . . . *125 – 150*

ROOSTER   (1955)

A black, green, and red rooster standing in green grass.

Dinnerware

Baker, 1-quart, 7"   /66 . . . . *$85 – $100*
Baker, 1½-quart, open, 8"   /67. . . . . *90 – 120*
    w/lid. . . . . *150 – 225*
Baker, 5"   /68 . . . . *100 – 125*

Rooster: Ice bucket /59 and bean pot /76.

Bowl, salad, 9½"   /73 . . . . *$300 – $350*
Bowl, spaghetti, 13"   /39. . . . . *325 – 375*
Casserole, individual, French-handle, 8"   /18 . . . . *175 – 225*
Creamer   /62 . . . .*175 – 225*
Ice bucket, flat lid, 7¼"   /59. . . . . *250 – 350*
Jug, 1-pint, 5½"   /15. . . . . *110 – 130*
Jug, 2-pint, 6½"   /16. . . . . *125 – 150*
Jug, square, 5-pint, 8"   /69 . . . . *450 – 550*
Shaker, barrel, each   /45   /46. . . . . *200 – 225*
Shaker, hourglass, "S"/"P" holes on top, each   /117   /118 . . . . *135 – 190*
Sugar, open   /98 . . . . *175 – 225*
   w/lid. . . . . *450 – 500*

Kitchenware

Baking dish, rectangular, lug, 10" × 5¼". . . . . *$800 – $1000*
Bean pot, 2 handles, 6½" high   /76 . . . . *300 – 375*
Bowl, deep, 2-pint, 6½"   /63. . . . . *90 – 120*
Bowl, deep, 4-pint, 7½"   /64. . . . . *90 – 120*
Bowl, deep, 6-pint, 8½"   /65. . . . . *90 – 120*
Bowl, mixing, ribbed, 5"   /5 . . . . *75 – 90*
Bowl, mixing, ribbed, 6"   /6 . . . . *75 – 90*
Bowl, mixing, ribbed, 7"   /7 . . . . *75 – 90*
Bowl, mixing, ribbed, 8"   /8 . . . . *75 – 90*
Bowl, mixing, ribbed, 9"   /9 . . . . *75 – 90*
Bowl, ribbed, w/lid, 5"   /05. . . . . *175 – 225*
Canister, 7" high, "Coffee"   /82. . . . . *450 – 550*
Canister, 7" high, "Tea"   /82. . . . . *450 – 550*
Canister, 8" high, "Flour"   /81. . . . . *450 – 550*
Canister, 8" high, "Sugar"   /81 . . . . *450 – 550*

STARFLOWER (1951)

There are two basic variations for this decoration that are generally found: five red petals and a red bud, which was made from ca. 1951 to 1958, and four petals, no bud, which was made from 1959 to 1961.

Harder-to-find variations are Moonflower (1950, pale pink or white flowers on black or green background), Silhouette (1953, chartreuse flower on brown sprayed background), and Special Starflower (white flowers on blue, green, or red background), which is found primarily on the #39 Spaghetti bowl.

PRICING Prices are for four- and five-petal Starflower and for Silhouette. For Special Starflower, add 50%. Moonflower is almost a separate shape as most of the pieces it appears on are similar to the Rio Rose line, not Starflower. Use Rio Rose prices for Moonflower.

Dinnerware

Bean cup, individual, no lid, 3½"   /75 . . . . $35 – $45
Bowl, salad, 9½"   /73. . . . . 90 – 120
Bowl, spaghetti, 13"   /39 . . . . 125 – 175
Bowl, cereal/salad/individual popcorn, 6½"   /52. . . . . 40 – 50
Bowl, 7½"   /53. . . . . 40 – 50
Bowl, 8½"   /54. . . . . 40 – 50
Bowl   /55 . . . . 90 – 120
Casserole, individual, tab, 5"   /18. . . . . 120 – 160
Casserole, individual, stick handle, 7½"   /18 . . . . 120 – 140
Casserole, open, 8½"   /54 . . . . 40 – 50
     w/lid . . . . 120 – 130
Creamer   /62. . . . . 150 – 225
Dish, berry, 5¾" . . . . 30 – 40
Dish, cereal/salad, 5½"   /74. . . . . 30 – 40
Ice Bucket, flat lid, 7¼" high   /59 . . . . 135 – 175
Jug, 1-pint, 5½"   /15
     Four-petal . . . . 150 – 190
     Five-petal . . . . 65 – 85

Starflower (five-petal): Jugs /17, /16, /15 and creamer /62.

Jug, 2-pint, 6½" /16 .... $80 – $90
Jug, 5-pint, 8" /17.. 160 – 190
Jug, ice lip, 5-pint, 8" /17.................................. 160 – 190
Jug, square, 5-pint, 8" /69 .... 500 +
Mug, barrel /501.. 80 – 90
Mug, coffee /121... ND
Platter, round, 15" /31 .... 150 – 200
Shaker, hourglass, embossed "S"/"P," each, /117 /118............. 150 – 200
Shaker, barrel /45 /46.. 85 – 100
Tumbler, slant-sided, 4½" /56................................. 325 – 400
Tumbler, round bottom, 4" /56 .... 325 – 400

Kitchenware

Baker w/lid, 8½" /96.. $100 – $125
Bean pot, 2 handles, 6½" high /76 .... 110 – 140
Bowl, mixing, lipped w/shoulder, 5" /5........................ 35 – 40
Bowl, mixing, lipped w/shoulder, 6" /6........................ 35 – 40
Bowl, mixing, lipped w/shoulder, 7" /7........................ 35 – 40
Bowl, mixing, lipped w/shoulder, 8" /8........................ 35 – 40
Bowl, mixing, lipped w/shoulder, 9" /9........................ 35 – 40
Bowl, deep, 2-pint, 6½" /63.................................. 45 – 60
Bowl, deep, 4-pint, 7½" /64.................................. 45 – 60
Bowl, deep, 6-pint, 8½" /65.................................. 45 – 60
Bowl, ribbed, 4" /04.. 40 – 50
Bowl, ribbed, 5" /05.. 40 – 50
Bowl, ribbed, 6" /06.. 40 – 50
Bowl, ribbed, 7" /07.. 40 – 50
Cookie jar, 7½" high /21.................................... 200 – 250
Drip jar, 4½" /47.. 325 – 425
Drip jar, 5½" /01.. 300 – 350
Pie baker, 9" /33 .... 150 – 175

TULIP (ca. 1963)

A red tulip and a blue tulip with green leaves.

Dinnerware

Bowl, salad, 9½" /73 .... $250 – $300
Creamer /62 .... 225 – 300
Jug, 1-pint, 5½" /15... 500 – 600
Jug, 2-pint, 6½" /16... 150 – 200
Jug, ice lip, 5-pint, 8" /17 .... 225 – 300

Kitchenware

Bowl, deep, 2-pint, 6½" /63.................................. $90 – $100
Bowl, deep, 4-pint, 7½" /64.................................. 90 – 100
Bowl, deep, 6-pint, 8½" /65.................................. 90 – 100
Bowl, ribbed, 4¾" /602...................................... 150 – 275

Bowl, ribbed, 5³/₄"　/603 . . . . *$150 – $275*
Bowl, ribbed, 6³/₄"　/604 . . . . *150 – 275*
Bowl, ribbed, 7³/₄"　/600 . . . . *120 – 140*
Bowl, ribbed, 8³/₄"　/601 . . . . *120 – 140*
Cookie jar, 8¹/₄" high　/503 . . . . *375 – 450*

MISCELLANY

The dog and kitty dishes were made in various colors, including brown, copper, green, turquoise, and yellow. About 90% of the iced-tea kegs are found without bases; add $25 for bases. For these kegs, brown is at the low end of the range; aqua, green, and ivory toward the upper end.

Bowl, chili, Mexican man, 5³/₄"　/603 . . . . *$10 – $15*
Cookie barrel, woodgrain　/617W . . . . *85 – 125*
Cookie jar, Happy/Sad Face　/34 . . . . *150 – 250*
Cookie jar, Policeman, 11" . . . . *1500 – 1800*
"Dog" dish, 6" . . . . *40 – 65*
"Dog" dish, 7" . . . . *40 – 65*
"Goodies" jar (ice bucket)　/59 . . . . *300 – 400*
"Goodies" jar (canister)　/72 . . . . *300 – 400*
"Goodies" jar (bean pot)　/76 . . . . *200 – 275*
Iced Tea Keg w/faucet, 2-gallon　/400–2
　　"Iced Tea" . . . . *65 – 125*
　　w/embossed advertising . . . . *120 – 175*
Jardiniere, quilted, green/white, 6¹/₂" . . . . *35 – 75*
Jardiniere, quilted, green/white, 7¹/₂" . . . . *35 – 75*
Jardiniere, quilted, green/white, 8¹/₄" . . . . *35 – 75*
Jardiniere, quilted, green/white, 10¹/₂" . . . . *35 – 75*
Jardiniere, quilted, green/white, 13" . . . . *35 – 75*
"Kitty" dish, 5" . . . . *40 – 65*
"Kitty" dish, 6" . . . . *40 – 65*
"Kitty" dish, 7" . . . . *40 – 65*
Lemonade Keg w/faucet　/401 . . . . *100 – 150*
Mink dish, "Purina Mink Chow," 9" . . . . *50 – 75*

WELLSVILLE POTTERY COMPANY

Wellsville, Ohio

In 1902 the old Pioneer Pottery was purchased by a group headed by Monroe Patterson. Wellsville manufactured semivitreous dinnerware and toilet sets and specialty items. In 1933 they began manufacturing vitrified china hotel ware. In 1959 the Sterling China Company, also in Wellsville, took control of the Wellsville Pottery, hoping to keep it operating by providing money and technical support. After ten years, Sterling closed the pottery in 1969.

KITCHENWARE

Wellsville's vitrified kitchenware is somewhat lighter than one would expect. I would date these to the late 1920s and early 1930s. In addition to the items listed below, there is a 6" baking dish (shape unknown).

Known overglaze decal decorations are "Geranium" and B108, a vining floral. Underglaze decoration G101 is lines of either Black, Green, Golden brown, or Maroon.

MARKS "Bake Rite" was a general backstamp used on some of the kitchenware.

DESOTO

A vertical flute shape.

Baker, 1-pint . . . . *$10 – $12*
Casserole, baking, 7" . . . . *15 – 20*

VITRIFIED KITCHENWARE

3 pc. Rnd. Ref. Set

Decoration B108

Baking Casserole   Covd. Ref. Jug
Decoration G101

Custard

12s Mixing Bowl   Baking Casserole   Pie Plate

Kitchenware

Casserole, baking, 8".. *$20 – $25*
Custard .... *4 – 6*
Jug, round, w/lid, 1-pint .... *10 – 15*
Jug, round, w/lid, 2-pint .... *15 – 20*
Jug, round, w/lid, 4-pint .... *25 – 30*
Plate, casserole undertray, 8⁷/₈" .... *7 – 9*
Refrigerator set, round, 3-piece .... *30 – 35*

GENERAL LINE

The mixing bowls are footed, with a paneled shape.

Bowl, mixing, 2¹/₂-pint, 7" .... *$6 – $8*
Bowl, mixing, 4-pint, 8³/₄" .... *8 – 10*
Bowl, mixing, 6-pint, 9³/₄" .... *10 – 12*
Bowl, mixing, 8-pint, 10³/₄" .... *12 – 15*
Bowl, mixing, 10-pint, 12" .... *15 – 20*
Pie baker, 9" .... *10 – 12*
Pie baker, 9³/₄" .... *10 – 12*

WISECARVER ORIGINALS

Roseville, Ohio

Because of his artistic background, Rick Wisecarver was encouraged to paint on pottery vases in his mother's ceramic shop. This led to experimentation with clays and glazes, and in 1983 Wisecarver began producing his line of "Classic Cookie Jars." He is still creating today.

As a Wisecarver display plaque states: "Hand Painted Quality Not Quantity." Wisecarver sculpts all of his designs and hand paints each one. He usually produces between 200 and 300 jars in any one design.

Wisecarver is best known for his Black Americana jars and his Indian jars. He added fairy tales to his repertoire in 1992. For a retail catalog, write to Wisecarver's Pottery, 42 Maple Street, Roseville, Ohio 43777.

See Roerig in Bibliography.

MARKS Every jar will have some variation of "Wihoa's Original Cookie Classic by Rick Wisecarver, Roseville, Ohio" with dates, other numbers, and his partner's name, R. Sims, incised on the bottom. Wihoa's is made up of the first two letters of his last name, the first two of his mother's maiden name, Hoadley, the *a* for his cousin Ault, and the *s* for his partner. All jars except the Old Cookstove Mammy contain his signature.

COOKIE JARS

The Angel and the Santa came in both black and white versions. Some jars come with matching shakers included in the price. These are indicated below. Jars currently in production are identified with a /C in the list below. Some jars had short runs; when known, approximate production figures are given in parentheses.

Blacks

Angel /C	*$150*
Banjo Man w/woman singing along (200)	*225 – 250*
Bust, man, black/gray hair (Pappy)	*225 – 250*
Shakers, pair	*50*
Bust, woman, black/gray hair (Mammy)	*225 – 250*
Shaker	*50*
Choir Lady and Preacher /C	*165*
Colonial Mammy, hands on hips	*250 – 300*
Shakers, Colonial Home/Mammy w/girl, pair (50)	*50*
Cookie Jar Mammy, "Cookie"	*225 – 250*
Cookstove Mammy, Old, stirring food (50)	*300 – 350*
Cookstove Mammy, New, holding bread /C	*165 – 175*
Haywagon, w/black children /C	*225*

Mammy w/cookie jar .... *$225 – $250*
Milk Churn Mammy w/child .... *225 – 250*
Miss America w/roses *250*
Mixing Bowl Mammy *225*
Morning Aggravation w/cat and stove *225*
Mrs. Claus .... *400 +*
Pickers (three), on horse-drawn cart .... *500 +*
   Shakers, 2 mammies sorting cotton, pair .... *50 – 75*
Quilting Mammy, w/gray hair /C .... *150 – 165*
Santa and Mrs. Claus, double jar (Christmas Day) /C *185*
Santa w/tree and bag of toys .... *400 +*
Saturday Bath, Mammy w/2 kids in washtub .... *175 – 200*
Sunday Dinner, Mammy w/knife chasing chickens, w/chicken shakers /C *165*
Woman w/apron full of vegetables (Young Mammy) .... *250 – 300*

Indians

Bust, "Geronimo" *$225*
Canoe /C *175*
Chief (5 or 6) .... *300 +*
Chief, Harvest, w/fruits and vegetables, 15" /C *185*
Chief, seated, leaning on one arm *225*
Maiden, Harvest, w/fruits and vegetables, 14" /C *185*
Maiden, on rocks by running water *225*
Teepee w/man, woman, and child .... *250 – 300*

Nursery Stories Black-faced Red Riding Hoods were special gifts; they were not production items. Hansel and Gretel is five pieces: the jar is the house, the sugar is a stove, the creamer is a witch, and Hansel and Gretel are shakers.

Beauty and the Beast (not Disney) /C *$175*
Hansel and Gretel, 5 pieces /C *225*
Little Red Riding Hood w/wolf in Grandma's clothes, #1 .... *600 – 700*
Little Red Riding Hood, wolf in bed, w/Red Riding Hood
and basket shakers, #2 /C *165*
Little Red Riding Hood, hugging grandma, #3 /C *185*
Rumpelstiltskin w/princess and spinning wheel /C *225*
Snow White, globe shape /C *300*

Others The Angel and the two Santa jars are white versions of jars listed in the Blacks section above.

Angel /C *$150*
Covered Bridge (50) .... *250 – 300*
Cow and Calf, bird finial
   Black-and-white Holsteins *100*
   Brown (Jer-see I and Jer-see IV) *100*
Ducks in Flight .... *175 – 200*
Hill Folk, man, woman, pig, and dog *225*
Kittens, 3, w/basket (20) .... *200 – 250*
Mill w/waterfall (10) .... *300 +*

Nativity, globe shape, Angel finial   /C *$225*
Pig, mother w/baby, w/piggy shakers................................... *200*
Raccoons, family w/tree stump *125*
Santa w/tree and bag of toys .... *500* +
Santa and Mrs. Claus, double jar (Christmas Day)   /C.................... *250*
Swan
  Natural.. *150*
   w/quilted cape *150*
Witch (Witchy Flo) *225*

W. I. TYCER POTTERY COMPANY

Zanesville, Ohio

In 1919 (or 1921, information varies), Warren Ivy Tycer bought the F. S. Lowry Pottery Company and renamed it. He produced baking dishes and kitchenware (Cook-Rite was a later trade name) as well as solid-color dinnerware. He retired in 1956, selling the company to Dave Thomas, who, with his partners, renamed it Tycer Pottery Inc. They owned it for three years and sold it to Melick Pottery.

MARKS The owners' pride in making a genuine stoneware body, as opposed to potteries that used a semivitreous body and just called it stoneware, is reflected in the mark.

TYCER POTTERY, INC
ROSEVILLE, OHIO
True American Stoneware

LONGHORN

This is a short, informal line of what is called barbecue ware.

Beanpot	$25 – $30
Bowl, soup, 5"	12 – 15
Bowl, salad	20 – 25
Coffee pot	45 – 50
Creamer	8 – 10

Longhorn: Bowl, mug, and coffee pot.

Mug	*$20 – $25*
Plate, 10"	*15 – 18*
Sugar	*12 – 15*

DRIP

Ed Rubel and Fred Press developed the Tycer drip glaze.

Bean pot	*$15 – $20*
Bean pot, individual	*6 – 8*
Bowl, salad	*15 – 18*
Bowl, soup, 5"	*8 – 10*
Casserole, French	*20 – 25*
Coffee pot	*35 – 40*
Creamer	*4 – 6*
Cup	*4 – 6*
Mug	*4 – 6*
Plate, 10"	*10 – 12*
Plate, party	*12 – 15*
Saucer	*1 – 2*
Shakers, pair	*8 – 10*
Sugar	*8 – 10*
Teapot	*25 – 30*

APPENDIX

BLUEBIRD

I have not been able to discover when the Bluebird decal first became popular. Possibly it was the 1910s. Certainly by the 1920s almost every dinnerware manufacturer in the United States was decorating with this decal. Below is a list of potteries known or reported to have made Bluebird. It is certainly not complete but will give you an idea of what you can look for.

Note that, despite the word "China" in the names of many of these companies, *all* put the Bluebird decal on semiporcelain bodies, not china. This explains why much of what you will find is crazed, stained, or imperfect in other ways.

Albright China Co.	Homer Laughlin
Bennett Bros. Pottery	Limoges China
Carrollton China Co.	D. E. McNicol
Cleveland China Co.	Mt. Clemens/Round
Colonial China Co.	Potters Co-Operative
Crown Pottery/Round	Salem China
Dresden Pottery Co.	Saxon China
French China Company	Sebring Pottery
W. S. George Pottery Co.	Southern Potteries/Ransom
Harker Pottery Co.	Steubenville Pottery
Hopewell China	C. C. Thompson Pottery
Illinois China Co.	Wellsville/Round
E. M. Knowles	West End Pottery
Knowles, Taylor & Knowles	H. R. Wyllie

Shapes

Generally, the shapes you will find reflect the dinnerware styles of the 1920s. Much of it will be plain round or octagonal. Remember that plain round lines usually had oval platters and serving pieces and that octagonal lines had twelve-sided platters and, often, hexagonal serving pieces. And there are many variations within these parameters.

Any one of these potteries could have put the decal on a variety of shapes. If you are buying by mail, don't assume that the shape of the piece you are getting will be the same as something you have, just because the manufacturer is the same.

The most important point is that, unless you are lucky enough to stumble upon a complete set (which is not very likely), you must be prepared to mix and match to assemble a service.

Variations

The basic Bluebird decal has the birds and pale pink flowers with pale green leaves. This is the most often found version. The most common trim is a thin blue line. You will also find pieces (1) untrimmed, (2) with a gold line, or (3) with gold and blue lines.

Other decals with bluebirds will be found. There is a version that incorporates a yellow, bracket-like device. Another is the large dark bluebird found on canister and cruet sets, as well as other pieces. I have seen these in old Brush Pottery catalogs and on pieces marked "Knowles, Taylor, Knowles," among others. Also, bluebirds will be found in other decals, often with flowers. Birds and flowers were a popular decal combination. While the prices below are appropriate for many of these decals, they are not the province of this appendix.

Pricing

I have deliberately not put dimensions or capacities in this list, except for general differentiation, as measurements will vary between companies. Prices are "generic" for each item.

Bone dish. . . . . *$12 – $15*
Bowl, salad. . . . . *15 – 18*
Bowl, soup . . . . *10 – 12*
Bowl, 36s . . . . *7 – 10*
Bowl, vegetable, oval. . . . . *10 – 12*
Butter dish . . . . *20 – 25*
Butter pat . . . . *4 – 6*
Casserole . . . . *20 – 25*
Creamer . . . . *4 – 6*
Cup . . . . *4 – 6*
Cup, cream soup . . . . *12 – 16*
Dish, 5¼" . . . . *2 – 3*
Gravy. . . . . *12 – 15*
Gravy liner/pickle . . . . *6 – 8*
Jug, small. . . . . *15 – 20*

Bluebird: Butter (unmarked), plate (D. E. McNicol), cream soup (unmarked), and jug (unmarked).

Jug, large . . . . *$20 – $25*
Mug . . . . *12 – 15*
Plate, B & B . . . . *1 – 2*
Plate, dinner . . . . *10 – 12*
Plate, salad . . . . *8 – 9*
Platter, 11½" . . . . *10 – 12*
Platter, 13½" . . . . *12 – 15*
Platter, 15½" . . . . *15 – 18*
Saucer . . . . *1 – 2*
Sugar . . . . *8 – 10*
Teapot, 2-cup . . . . *25 – 30*
Teapot, 6-cup . . . . *30 – 35*

REPRODUCTIONS

Here's the irony. If we had not collected pottery to the point of pushing many items into the realm of the highly desirable, then no one would have thought it worth reproducing them.

First, reproductions of all sorts have been around longer than any of us. Some, such as fine furniture reproductions, have a value of their own. Reproductions can't be eliminated; other approaches are necessary.

Second, I believe manufacturers have a right to make repros, just as I have a right *not* to buy them. However, they must be clearly marked as repros. This does not mean a paper label which can easily be removed. An underglaze stamped mark is required at the very least; though this can be sanded off, evidence of its removal would be there. I used to think that an impressed mark was best of all, but I'm told these are being filled in.

Third, I believe stores have a right to sell repros, as long as they are clear about it, and I believe collectors have a right to buy repros if they so choose. It is not my kind of collecting, but I am not here to tell people what to collect.

So where does that leave us?

I believe we have several options, all of which can help to varying degrees. The names of certain reproducers are known. We can refuse to sell rare items to them, so these can't be used for making the repros. And we must spread the word about these reproducers to prevent others from being duped by them. If someone is infringing a copyright, and you feel a legal challenge might be effective, contact the person or company whose rights are being violated and let them know what is happening.

Next are the dealers and auctioneers who handle these repros. Remember that the vast majority of these people are honest. Their reputations are important to them, and they do not wish to unknowingly pass along improper merchandise. And they can be victimized by these repros as much as collectors can. If we don't help educate them, we cannot point a finger.

After you've told the seller that something is a repro, they may remove it from sale or mark it as a repro. Either approach is fine. After all, they have money invested in these items and shouldn't be penalized. Ideally, they might post a sign telling their customers that they do not handle reproductions. This would help in the general educational effort, and it is education that is needed.

If the dealer does not respond positively and continues to be duplicitous, then stronger measures are called for. Report them to the Better Business Bureau, pass out leaflets, organize a picket, and invite the media. They deserve whatever you throw at them.

The newsletters can help by spreading the word. Perhaps a periodic listing of repros and how to identify them such as *The Daze* does.

Will all this help? Hopefully, but we can always refine our approach. Remember, this is a situation we will have to live with all our lives. We must try to manage it or it will manage us.

A Final Note: If a dealer has so many hard-to-find pieces, or pieces with perfect gold in the case of Shawnee or Little Red Riding Hood, that it seems too good to be true, it probably *is* too good to be true. And if a reproduction is intended to fool the buyer into thinking it is original, then let us call it what it really is: FORGERY.

Camark

The wistful kitten aquaria has been available through mail-order catalogs for several years. It is lighter and not as large as the original.

Cookie Jars

Cookie jar reproductions (and forgeries) are so extensive that I have marked as much as I can in the individual chapters, either in the text or with an "/R" after the particular listing. Some jars have been made into Ceramic Molds, which are sold to hobbyists through hobby shops. These are marked "/CM."

Kay Finch

In his book *Collector's Encyclopedia of California Pottery*, Jack Chipman states that some Finch designs can be found as molds-for-hobbyists. These should be easily distinguishable from the originals by their decoration.

Gonder

Pirate and Sheriff cookie jars.

Morton

According to Burdell Hall, author of *Morton Potteries*, two pie birds, the Bird and the Duckling, are being reproduced. Also, the Teddy Bear bank and planter, items I don't list. The new pieces are smaller and lighter than the originals.

Pennsbury

I have been informed that someone had molds for the Hen and Rooster and was decorating them in any color desired. This was some years ago and may have been discontinued.

The Barbershop beer mugs are being reproduced. They have white bottoms and are unmarked.

Also I am told there is a Japanese version of the "Washington Crossing the Delaware" 5-inch round plaque.

Shawnee (by Pam Curran, Publisher, *Exclusively Shawnee*)

There are two areas causing concern to Shawnee collectors.

CORN-KING DINNERWARE There are two different reproductions being made. One is being reproduced in the same size and the same markings (the word "Shawnee). The only way to differentiate between authentic and reproduced versions is that the new pieces vary slightly in color; the yellow of the kernels is the same but the leaves are a sort of variegated brown/green.

The other is easier to identify. First, the bottom is flat and unglazed, and the kernels line up horizontally and vertically. Shawnee bottoms were glazed and the kernels were staggered. The most glaring difference is that the cups, creamers, and sugars have handles that are open at the bottom, not closed as the traditional pieces.

REFIRING OF OLD PIECES Old cookie jars, pitchers, teapots, and more are being refired with new gold trim and decals where there had been none before. Unscrupulous dealers have been adding these to the plain older pieces since products with gold trim and decals command a higher price on the market.

You can recognize these pieces from the following characteristics:

1. Gold *sometimes* appears pitted and uneven.
2. Black dots *may* appear on the surface of the glaze.

Close attention must be paid before buying to all gold-trimmed Shawnee because the size and detail and bottom marks on the refired pieces are not only *like* the original, they *are* the original. It is just the gold trim and decal that are more recent.

There are also new pieces being made by the McCoy Pottery of Tennessee. These are the Smiley Pig cookie jar (marked "USA") and the Muggsy shakers (marked "McCoy"). These pieces also differ in color from the originals.

While it is the new collector who must be made aware of these problems in collecting, it is worth everyone's while to consider getting a guarantee from the seller that the purchased piece is genuine, and that they will honor returns. If not, walk away from high-ticket purchases until you feel more comfortable in your field of collecting.

Stangl Pottery (by Harvey Duke, Author of *Stangl Pottery*)

The problem for Stangl collectors is the hundreds, if not thousands, of Stangl molds still in existence. Briefly, Wheaton Industries bought the Stangl Pottery upon the death of Martin Stangl in 1972, and continued production for six years with little success. In 1978 it sold Stangl to the Pfaltzgraff Pottery of York, Pennsylvania, but retained many of Stangl's molds.

In 1991, Wheaton began very limited production of some Stangl lines, with both traditional and "new" decorations. Fortunately, thanks to a lack of business acumen, manufacturing was short-lived.

These pieces are fairly easily identified by a crudeness of execution and lack of production values (bubbles on the glaze surface and other flaws). The following items were made:

FLOWERPOTS Dolphins, Town and Country, Tulips, and new florals have been used. There is no problem identifying the patterns that were never made by Stangl. As to the Town and Country, see my comments below.

KIDDIE WARE Pink and Blue Carousel and Dolphins of the traditional patterns were used. These new patterns are on a white body and are not carved.

TOWN AND COUNTRY/BLUE Pitcher and bowl, dealer sign, and flowerpots. The blue color varies among pieces, but doesn't match the original. The black line is crudely applied. To the experienced eye, the sponge pattern is not authentic.

WIG STANDS (New "faces" such as cowboys and beatniks) The mark most often used on the new items was a script "Stangl" in an oval. This is almost identical to the old mark. Sometimes the words "Millville, NJ" were in the new mark and this helps with identification, since the old mark often had "Trenton, NJ," which is where Stangl was made. Unfortunately, many people are not aware of this, so the addition of Millville doesn't always help. It is telling that Wheaton had been asked to mark them more clearly as new items and did not do so.

Wallace

The Rodeo pattern in Westward Ho! and El Rancho both with and without the well decoration have been reproduced. I am told these are marked in such a way as to tell they are new.

Buy the books, learn as much as you can. The more that you know, the less you can be fooled.

GLOSSARY

The purpose of this glossary is to give you simple definitions and explanations of pottery terms and processes. Many glossaries assume a certain level of knowledge; I have tried to assume nothing and to define every term, no matter how basic, especially with the novice collector in mind.

For those who wish to understand the process of manufacture, start with the entry *Designer*.

Acid Etching   Some ware has acid-etched decoration. After a piece has been glazed, certain parts are masked off (using wax, rubber, or other materials), and the piece is dipped in acid. This removes the glaze from the unmasked portion. The mask is then removed and the gilding applied. The effect of the decoration is in the contrast of the gilding over the bisque versus the gilding over the glazed portions.

AD   ("After Dinner," same as Demitasse) A small-size coffee set, traditionally including coffee pot, creamer, sugar, cups, and saucers, for after-dinner coffee, usually referred to as AD by the potteries. These pieces and sets were also used as children's dishes (see Appendixes) and as parts of Breakfast Sets.

Applied Decoration   (also called Sprig) A molded piece of clay applied by hand to a piece of greenware with slip. Sprigs can be used as decoration (flowers and leaves, for example) or to customize a piece for a particular customer (name or logo of a business or organization).

Art Glaze   A temperature-sensitive glaze that needs to be fired at lower temperatures than those for regular glazes so that the proper color is maintained.

Art Pottery   Ornamental ware either hand decorated by an artist or glazed with a special controlled effect. In the strictest sense, pottery made and decorated by hand. See also *Production Ware*.

Art Ware   See *Production Ware*.

B & B   See *Bread and Butter Plate*.

Baker   Industry terminology for the open, oval serving dish, usually called a vegetable dish.

Banding   (also Band) Similar to lining but the gold, silver, or color applied is wider than a line. See also *Liner*.

Batter Jug   See *Batter Set*.

Batter Set   (also called Waffle Set) Consists of a batter jug, syrup and undertray. This came into use at the time the electric waffle maker was invented, which allowed waffles to be made at the table instead of on the stove.

Beater Bowl   Cylindrical bowl into which fits a beater/mixer. See next entry.

Beater Bowl Pitcher   Same as above but with a handle and spout.

Beehive Kiln   See *Kiln*.

Belleek China   Delicate, pale-cream-colored, highly translucent porcelain with iridescent glaze. Sometimes called "eggshell china" because of its extreme thinness. First developed in Ireland.

Bennington Ware   See *Rockingham*.

Beverage Server   Appearing in the 1940s and 1950s, this multiple-use piece replaced coffee pots, teapots, and jugs to some extent. Handled with a pouring spout and, usually, a lid, it could be used covered (to keep the heat in) for coffee, tea, and other hot beverages, as well as for cold beverages (without a lid if preferred) such as juice, milk, punch and the like.

Bisque Firing   This is the first firing, or baking. The greenware is subjected to high heat, which removes the remaining moisture and hardens the body into its final shape. For the next step, see *Bisque Ware*.

Bisque Ware   (also Biscuit Ware) Clay ware that has been hardened through a first firing. Bisque Ware can be left undecorated (see *Parian* for one example). For the next step, see *Glaze, Overglaze Decoration*, and *Underglaze Decoration*.

Blank   A piece of ware that has yet to be decorated.

Body   The physical composition of a piece of pottery or porcelain, as opposed to its glaze or composition. Keep in mind that the color of a piece of ware can be in the body or on it. See *Engobe* and *Glaze*.

Bone China   A form of porcelain that contains bone ash, made from calcined cattle bones, for added translucency and whiteness.

Bottle Kiln   See *Kiln*.

Bouillon Cup and Saucer   See *Cups*.

Bread and Butter Plate   (also called B & B) A 6" to 6½" plate used to hold bread or rolls and butter. May also be used as the plates in a cake set.

Breakfast Set   Service for one consisted of an AD coffee pot, sugar and creamer, a regular-size cup and saucer, covered muffin, eggcup, cereal dish, and breakfast plate. Service for two was also made with two cups, saucers, eggcups, dishes, and plates.

Bright Gold   See *Gold*.

Burnished Gold   See *Gold*.

Cable   An institutional-ware shape brought over from France, where it may have originated, in the 1880s. It is a plain round shape distinguished by a cable/rope-like decoration around the handles or in the finials of hollowware pieces.

Cactus Planters   These figural planters are designed so that the cactus completes the planter image. Usually they are animals with their bottoms up so that the cactus grows into a long tail, or a house with the cactus as the smoke coming out of the chimney.

Cake Set   A set consisting of a large cake plate, cake server, and, usually, six smaller plates, generally 6" or 7".

Casserole   A round or oval covered dish. Some china companies designed the lids to alternate as pie bakers. See also *Dutch Casserole* and *French Casserole*.

Casting   Slip is poured into plaster molds. The plaster draws moisture out of the clay so that the ware can be handled when it is unmolded. For next step, see *Finishing*.

Casual China   True porcelain dinnerware that is thicker, heavier, and more durable than fine china but not translucent. Generally intended to be less formal than a traditional set of porcelain.

CC Ware   (Cream-Colored Ware) A cheap grade of pottery, similar to white granite but with a creamier body, hence the name. The two differ in color, density, and quality of glaze.

Celadon   A French name for a Chinese color. The color originated during the

Sung dynasty (960–1279) and was originally brighter than current celadons; the Chinese compared it to fresh onion sprouts. It was one of a number of bright colors on Chinese porcelain.

An eighteenth-century novel, *Astree*, featured a main character named the Bergen Celadon, who dressed in beautifully colored silks. Somehow, this led to all the Chinese colors being called celadons and later just the green. For unknown reasons, the color changed into a grayish sea green along the way.

Ceramics   In its original and true meaning, ceramics means the art of making any article of clay. Americans use the word to cover all of the silicate industries where the burning process is essential in manufacture.

Cereal Dish   (also called Oatmeal) A shallow dish, usually 6½" in diameter, intended for cereal.

China   Another name for porcelain, so used because true porcelain was first made in China. Today china has become a generic term for almost anything that is used for dinnerware. See *Porcelain*.

Chocolate Pot   See *Pots*.

Chop Plate   Large round or square serving plate, usually 12" or more in diameter.

Clay   There are different kinds of clay, and other minerals are added to impart desired qualities to the finished product. Clay and these other materials are mixed with water to make slip (see *Casting*). Then impurities are removed, the water is pressed out, the clay is dried, and the air is expelled. Now the clay is ready to be shaped. For the next step, see *Forming*.

Cocotte   A round or oval casserole intended especially for cooking individual portions.

Coffee Cup   See *Cups*.

Coffee Pot   See *Pots*.

Coin Gold   See *Gold*.

Cold Paint   Oil paint that is applied over the glaze for decorative purposes after the final firing. As it is not protected by the glaze, it is susceptible to chipping and wear.

Compote   (also, incorrectly, Comport, though it will be found so spelled in many old catalogs) A dish on a stem, in various sizes, for serving candy, nuts, or fruit.

Console Set   A round or oval bowl with two matching candle holders, intended as a decorative element for dining table or side table.

Cooking Ware   See *Ovenware*.

Coupe   A contemporary shape that does not have a rim (shoulder), is flat across the diameter, and rolls up slightly at the edge. Generally refers to flatware and soup bowls.

Coupe Soup   A shallow, flat round bowl without handles or rim, 7" or 8" in diameter.

Cover Plate   See *Service or Cover Plate*.

Cozy Set   A three-piece set consisting of two slender, rectangular pots that sit side-by-side on a tray. One pot, with a long spout, is for tea; the other, with a short spout, is for hot water, used to dilute the tea. Originating in England, these sets were made in the United States by a number of manufacturers. The largest maker was Hall China, which produced three lines, called Twin-Tee, Tea-for-Two, and Tea-for-Four.

Crackle   (also Craquelle) A decorative effect. The surface of the ware shows a network of tiny cracks that resembles crazing. Dedham Pottery is a good example.

Crazing   Minute cracks in the glaze caused by the uneven contraction of glaze and body. The body and glaze are formulated so that contraction should occur at an even rate. Crazed pieces are discarded at the factory. However, exposure to heat and/or moisture can cause crazing at a later time.

Cream-colored Ware   See *CC Ware*.

Cream Soup Cup and Saucer   See *Cups*.

Creamer   A small open bowl, with handle and spout for pouring milk or cream. On rare occasion, a creamer was designed to have a lid.

Crockery   Earthenware.

Cruet   A small bottle for holding oil, vinegar, or other condiments on the table. Ceramic cruets seem to have made their first appearance in the work of Ben Seibel, Eva Zeisel, and others in the late 1940s and 1950s.

Cups   I have grouped these under one heading so that you can appreciate the variety of cups.

   AD (Demitasse)   A small cup and saucer. See *AD*.

   Bouillon cup and saucer   A two-handled cup, similar to a teacup, used for serving clear soups. It is not as low as a cream soup cup.

   Coffee cup   Larger than a teacup and used for coffee. It can be mug shaped and does not always come with a saucer.

   Cream soup cup and saucer   A low two-handled cup used for serving bisques and cream soups. Can have regular or lug handles. Often comes with a saucer that is slightly larger than the tea saucer.

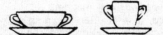

Bouillon/cream soup: This drawing shows the differences between the cream soup cup and saucer on the left and the bouillon cup and saucer on the right.

   Jumbo cup and saucer   A specialty item. Oversize coffee cup, sometimes with the word "Mom/Mother" or "Dad/Father" on it.

   St. Denis cup and saucer   A particular style of large cup and saucer used by a number of potteries.

Decal   (also Decalcomania) 1. A transfer decoration, sometimes one or two colors, sometimes multicolored, which is printed on special emulsion-coated paper and then coated with plastic film. When ready to use, the plastic is peeled off with the decoration adhering to it and applied to the ware. In firing, the plastic burns away, and the printed decoration "melts" into the glaze.

St. Denis cup: Hall China's Taverne pattern.

This is the last step. The word "decal" is used as both the singular and plural.

2. Paper decals were available for sale during the 1930s. One could moisten the back and affix it to any object, from shower doors to cribs to kitchen items. You will find pieces of ware with these decals. Some collectors remove them, as they were not applied by the manufacturer; other collectors leave them, as they reflect the period when the ware was made. They do not increase the value of a piece.

Decorating Kiln   See *Glost Kiln.*

Decoration   See *Glaze, Overglaze Decoration,* and *Underglaze Decoration.*

Decorator   Usually refers to the person who applies lines, bands, decals, or decorative highlights.

Demitasse   From the French for "half cup." Also refers to the strong black coffee served in this cup. See *AD.*

Designer   The person who does the original sketch for a piece of pottery. It is usually based on his/her conception but can be based on someone else's ideas. An art or design background is not sufficient for pottery design. A pottery designer must have an accurate understanding of how pottery is made; otherwise the piece may be too expensive or impossible to manufacture. See *Modeler.*

Dinner Plate   Eight- to ten-inch plate used for the main course.

Dinnerware   (Tableware) Refers to the items used at the table during a meal. Usually broken down into two categories: Flatware and Hollowware.

Dipping   That process of covering a bisque body with a glaze by immersion in the liquid, either by hand or by machine.

Dish   In modern usage, dish is often a synonym for plate. Traditionally, it refers to an open container, shallow and concave, for holding or serving food.

Drip Jar   A covered container, intended to be kept on or near the stove, for storing bacon drippings and other cooking fat for further use. Sometimes found marked with the word "Drips" or, rarely, "Lard." See *Range Set.*

Dutch Casserole   Round, straight-sided casserole with hollow lug handles for easy portability.

Earthenware   Opaque ware, somewhat porous, with a clear, transparent glaze. Coarse earthenware is not fired to as hard a state as fine earthenware. When earthenware is made of refined clays and fired at a high temperature to a hard state but is still somewhat porous, it is referred to as fine earthenware in England and semivitreous ware in the United States.

Eggcup   Single eggcup: Small, like a custard cup, no handle. Double eggcup: An hourglass-shaped double cup of two sizes.

Embossing   (also called Relief) A raised decoration produced in the mold. See *Applied Decoration.*

Encrustation   A decoration of gold or platinum that is applied in liquid form and then fired.

Engobe   (also called Slip Coating) A white or colored slip used as an intermediate layer between the body and the glaze. Sometimes a white engobe is used over colored clays so that the ware appears to be made of white clay. See *Slip.*

Engraving   A decoration that has been carved, cut, or etched into the body of a piece of ware. Intaglio is another name for this process of beneath-the-surface design. The term "incised" will also be used. See also *Sgraffito.*

Epergne   A decorative centerpiece that may be compartmented or branched, for fruit, flowers, or whatever your imagination conceives.

Faststand Gravy Boat A gravy boat, often with two spouts and no handle, that is attached to a plate.

Fine China Thin, translucent china that, despite its delicacy, is quite strong. It is made of top-quality clays fired at high temperatures that fuse into a hard, nonporous body.

Finial The knob on top of a lid. Especially used when the knob is fanciful or figural.

Finishing Smoothing out of mold seams or rough spots with a sponge or similar article after removal from the molds. For the next step, see *Greenware*.

Firing Process of heat treatment of ceramic products for the purpose of securing resistance and permanency of product (hardening, strengthening). Also called burning. See *Bisque Firing, Glost Firing*, and *Decoration Firing*.

Flatware Dinnerware, such as plates and platters, that is flat or near-flat. See also *Hollowware*.

Foot

Forming The making of a piece of clay into an object, no matter what process is used. See *Casting, Jiggering*, and *Throwing*. For the next step see *Greenware*.

French Casserole A round casserole with a stick handle. Large French casseroles may have a lug handle opposite the stick handle for easier handling.

Frog A flat-bottomed, perforated object, usually round or oval, made to hold stems in a flower arrangement. Frogs can have a figural component. Used primarily with bowls.

Fruit Dish (also called Sauce dish) A small, shallow bowl used for fruits or sauces.

Gadroon (also called Gadroon Edge, Egg and Dart) An in-the-mold decoration, usually found on the edge or rim of a dinnerware item, that resembles alternating ovals and lines.

Gilding The application of precious metals such as gold and platinum (which resembles silver).

Gadroon edge: Salem's Heirloom above Steubenville's Olivia. Heirloom is closer to the classic egg and dart design but Olivia is more representative of what you will find.

Glaze A mixture of mineral substances, either transparent or colored, that will melt and harden on the surface of the clay body during the glost-firing process. It is used as a covering for ceramic wares in order to (1) make a porous body nonporous, (2) secure greater permanency, and (3) beautify an object. Literally, a glass. This can be the last step in the manufacturing process (see *Glost Firing*), or the next-to-last step if an overglaze decoration is to be applied. See *Decal, Overglaze*.

Glost Firing Firing that matures the glaze, which after cooling produces a hard, glass-like surface. This firing is not as hot as the bisque firing nor as long.

Glost Kiln Oven for firing glazed pieces. Decal-decorated pieces can also be fired here.

Gold

   1. Acid-Gold: The design is acid-etched into the body of the ware, then painted with liquid gold that is fired on and burnished.

   2. Bright Gold: A liquid gold paint decoration that comes out bright and requires no polishing (burnishing) after being fired.

   3. Burnished Gold (also Coin Gold): A more expensive decoration than bright gold, this is dull after being fired and must be rubbed up (burnished). See also *Encrustation*.

Gravy or Sauce Boat A low, oval bowl with handle and spout.

Greenware After the piece has been finished, it is allowed to dry further. At this stage it can be handled, but care must be taken. For next step, see *Bisque Firing*. (For an exception to this process, see *Once Fired*.)

Grill Plate A dinner-size plate divided into three or more sections.

Ground-lay An underglaze dinnerware decoration usually in the form of wide borders of dark colors. The process consists of dusting the powdered color onto an oil coating.

Hand Painting Can refer to work ranging from that of the artist who painted Indian Head Rookwood vases to the artisans who decorated ware from a sample set in front of them. A clear glaze is usually applied over this work.

High Foot See *Foot*.

Hollowware Dinnerware serving pieces such as bowls, casseroles, pitchers, creamers, and sugars. See also *Flatware*.

Hotelware See *Restaurant Ware*.

Impressed Marked or stamped with pressure. This can be done by hand or in the mold.

Incised See *Engraving*.

Institutional Ware This refers to items, usually china, made for airlines, businesses, churches, clubs, hotels, railroads, restaurants, schools, and steamships, often with the name and/or logo of that institution in the design and/or the backstamp. While much of it is dinnerware, you will also find ashtrays, candle holders, jugs, spittoons, and more.

Intaglio See *Engraving*.

Ironstone See *White Granite*.

Jardiniere A decorated flowerpot intended to hold a plain terra-cotta flowerpot.

Jiggering The process used for making plates and other fairly flat items. The clay is placed on a form that represents the top of the piece, pressed down, and spun. A template representing the outline of the underside of the piece is placed against the clay and finishes the shaping. See *Greenware*.

Jug Industry term for a pitcher. There were many kinds. Refrigerator jugs were usually flat-sided and designed to take up as little space as possible in the refrigerator. The popular Ball Jug was first introduced by Hall China in 1938.

Jumbo Cup and Saucer See *Cups.*

Kiln An ovenlike structure for the firing (baking) of a greenware, glazes, and decorations. These are not fired together, as each requires different firing temperatures.

Early commercial kilns were shaped like beehives or bottles and were named according to their shape. In the 1920s, tunnel kilns were developed, in which ware is fired by being carried through on flat cars that move very slowly. Modern kilns move ware through on a conveyor system in a matter of hours.

Kitchenware Items that are used in the kitchen (canisters, batter sets, and range sets), refrigerator (water jugs, leftovers), or oven (casseroles, bean pots). See also *Ovenware.*

Lead Glaze A shiny glaze containing lead oxide.

Liner
1. (also Stand, Underplate, or Undertray) The following items were sometimes sold as sets with a liner: gravy boats (the plate does double duty as a pickle plate), batter sets, casseroles, and tureens.
2. A person who applies *Lining, Banding*, or a *Stroke* to a piece of ware.

Lining
1. (also Line) A decorative process. A thin line or lines of gold, silver, or color applied to the ware by hand or machine. Can be found around a rim, foot, spout, lid, and knob among other places.
2. The interior color of a piece of hollowware. If a bowl is blue on the outside and ivory on the inside, you can say, "It is a blue bowl lined with ivory." See also *Liner.*

Lug Handle A tab-like handle that is often parallel to the tabletop. Sometimes it has a cutout; this is called "pierced."

Lug Soup (also Onion Soup or Purée Bowl) Similar to a cream soup but slightly larger and with *Lug handles*. Also called onion soup or purée bowl.

Luncheon Plate (also called Breakfast Plate) Seven- or eight-inch plate used for main course at breakfast or luncheon.

Luster A glaze, metallic in nature, that gives ware an iridescent effect.

Marriage A covered piece that has a mismatched lid and bottom. (see "Tips.")

Matte Glaze (also Mat or Matt) A flat, nonreflective finish, sometimes with a rough texture. Typical of art pottery of the Arts and Crafts movement, its development is attributed to William Grueby.

Model See *Modeler.*

Modeler After a piece has been designed, the modeler (who can also be the designer) "sculpts" the piece in plaster. This will be a little larger than the finished piece is intended to be so as to allow for shrinkage between greenware and bisque. See *Molds.*

Molds From the model, the block mold is made. A few samples might be made from the block mold. This is then used to make the case, and the case is used to make the production molds, from which all the ware is made. Because many production molds are used in the manufacturing process and because these molds wear down, a manufacturer will go back to the case many times to make new production molds. See *Clay.*

Nove Rose: This is a Paden City version of this decoration. Some potteries called it Dresden.

Nappy Round, uncovered vegetable or salad dish usually 8" or 9" in diameter.

Novelties A class of merchandise that included banks, bookends, bowls, cookie jars, figures, planters, shakers, and vases, many of them figural. Much of this merchandise was made for the chain stores.

Nove Rose I do not know the "story" behind this decal decoration, but many potteries had some version of it. It is a bouquet of flowers with a large rose in the center and a tulip extending out from the mass.

Ohio Jug A round, flat-bottomed jug that is wider at the base than at the top. Handle and finial treatment will vary; a few will be paneled.

Once Fired Some ware is produced by glazing greenware and firing only once.

Open Stock Dinnerware that can be bought by the individual piece or small group, as opposed to being available only in complete, predetermined sets. There is an implied promise that open-stock patterns will be available indefinitely.

Orange bowl: Made by Sebring, this has a tiny floral decal and a gold interior.

Orange Bowl   A bowl, often footed, with a deeply scalloped rim, for holding oranges. Dates from the late nineteenth and early twentieth centuries, when many tabletop pieces were made for specific purposes.

Ovenware   Ware that can withstand the heat of an oven without being damaged and then can be used to serve the food that has been cooked in it. Usually categorized with *Kitchenware.*

Overglaze Decoration   When colors or decorations are applied to the ware after the glost firing and then fired, they are called overglaze. A wide range of colors may be used because the heat in the decorating kiln need not be as high to "harden the colors" (i.e., to fuse them onto the glaze) as the heat needed to harden the glaze. The colors are apt to be brighter and sharper.

You can identify overglaze by running your finger over the ware from the background to the decoration. If you feel a change in texture, it is overglaze. See *Decals, Print and Paint*, and *Underglaze Decoration.*

Parian   Unglazed porcelain (bisque ware) intended to resemble marble.

Party Plate   (also called Snack Plate or Tea and Toast) A luncheon-size plate with a cup ring near the rim. Usually round, but other shapes such as oblong and crescent were made. Used to hold a teacup and tea sandwiches, cookies, or cake.

Pâté-sur-Pâté   (French) The successive application of semifluid clay to build up a design in slight relief. First employed in China during the eighteenth century.

Pickle Dish   Small platter, usually around 9" in length, used for pickles or condiments or as an underplate for the gravy.

Pierced   See *Lug Handle.*

Pitcher   See *Jug.*

Plaque   A flat slab or disk that is decorated and intended for mounting on a wall.

Platter   Oval serving tray varying from 8" to 20" in length. Some rectangular or square dinnerware lines will have similarly shaped platters. Large round serving pieces are called chop plates.

Porcelain   A clear, translucent ware with a body that is nonporous, nonabsorbent, or "vitrified." To be a true porcelain, a piece of ware should show the shadow of your hand when held before light. If artificial color has been introduced into the body, the translucency is reduced. When a piece of porcelain is struck, there is a clear, bell-like tone.

Pots: This drawing shows the basic pot shapes which most *potteries followed* most *of the time, but you will find exceptions.* L to R: *Teapot, coffee pot, and chocolate pot.*

Pots   I have seen a definition of a *teapot* as covered bowl, usually round and rather flat, with handle and spout for serving tea. Certainly, there is more variety to teapot shapes than that definition would suggest.

A *coffee pot* is similar to a teapot but larger and often taller, sometimes with a shorter spout.

A *chocolate pot* is a taller, slimmer, often more elegant version of a coffee pot.

Pottery (1) (also called Earthenware) Opaque, nonvitrified ware (see *Porcelain*); (2) the factory where ware is made, regardless of whether it is pottery or porcelain.

Premium A piece of china given away as part of a promotion. Promotions took many different forms; you could get a dish when you bought a box of soap, gasoline, furniture, or other items. You could buy dishes with coupons from local route salesmen. And of course, there was dish night at the movies.

Print and Paint (also Print and Fill, Filling-in) The outline of a design is printed on bisque ware or glazed ware, filled in with one or more colors by hand, and then fired. A clear glaze is then applied. This is the last step.

Production Ware (also Art Ware) Art pottery that has been decorated by an artisan rather than an artist. Also refers to non–art pottery.

Ramekin A small, flat-bottomed dish with fairly vertical sides and a very narrow rim, usually accompanied by a plate. Used for serving individual portions of food. These are most common in restaurant lines.

Range Set A three-piece set, consisting of a *Drip Jar* and two *Range Shakers*, usually kept on the stove (range). Some range sets and stoves were specifically designed so that the sets fit a niche on the stove.

Range Shaker A large shaker, intended for cooking use as opposed to table use. See *Range Set*.

Reamer Industry term for a juicer. Of the few dinnerware companies that made reamers, most were intended to sit atop a juice pitcher. Other potteries made them as novelties.

Redware Earthenware made from a clay with a high amount of ferrous oxide. This gives the body its red color. Usually has a lead glaze.

Refrigerator Jug See *Jug*.

Relief See *Embossing*.

Restaurant Ware (also Hotel Ware, Institutional Ware) Thick, vitrified china dinnerware. Because it has to stand up to heavy use, it will not have the delicacy of china made for the home.

Rim (also shoulder) The lip of a traditionally shaped plate or bowl. It can be narrow or wide, plain or embossed, depending on the design. See also *Coupe*.

R.K. (or R.K. selects) See *Run of Kiln*.

Rockingham Yellow ware with a brown glaze that is usually mottled but can be almost solid. Sometimes called Bennington ware because a goodly amount of Rockingham was made in the potteries of Bennington, Vermont. Rockingham was also produced in large quantities at potteries in East Liverpool, Ohio, as well as at other potteries. Rock, as it is casually referred to, was in continuous production into the twentieth century and was later revived by some companies in a style that has little relation to the original—a creamy foam with brown undertones edging a brown glaze.

Rolled Edge A restaurant ware term, referring to a thickening on the outer rim of a plate to give it extra durability as well as making it easier to grip.

Run of Kiln A grading term. It indicates dinnerware that appears perfect after manufacture but may not be completely perfect on close inspection. See *Selects*.

Salad Set A set consisting of a large salad bowl, serving fork and spoon, and, usually, six salad plates.

Salt Glaze   Salt is thrown into the kiln during the glost firing, where it vaporizes and combines with the silica in the body of the ware, producing a shiny glaze.

Sauce Dish   See *Fruit Dish.*

Saucer   Besides teacups, saucers were used for other styles of cups. See *Cup.*

Screen Printing   The use of stencil-like screens to apply color to ware.

Seconds   (second grade) Ware with imperfections from the manufacturing process that do not affect its usefulness. Depending upon the extent of the imperfections, they could be sent either to a reclaim department, to an outlet shop for sale, or to an outside decorator.

Selects   Near-perfect dinnerware, as indicated in the process of selection that follows manufacture, in which imperfect pieces are either sent to a reclaim department, sold as seconds, or discarded. See *Run of Kiln.*

Semiporcelain   Resembling porcelain but having little or no translucency and more porosity. It is made from more refined raw materials but is not vitrified. This is a trade name or designation that is a misnomer. Being semiporcelain is like being semipregnant.

Semivitreous   (also Semivitrified) An alternative term for semiporcelain.

Service or Cover Plate   A plate an inch or so larger than a dinner plate, used at formal events to hold the container for the first course. Can be ornately decorated.

Sgrafitto   A decoration achieved by scratching through a surface of slip or glaze to the body beneath, which color, often different from the slip, then shows through. Sometimes a sgrafitto design was filled in with color.

Shelf-sitter   A novelty item, usually a figurine, that is designed to sit on the edge of a shelf or on an accessory such as a bench, with part of the piece hanging over the side.

Shirred Egg Dish   A low, flat dish with almost straight sides. Shirred eggs are shelled eggs that are baked in a mold or shirred egg dish.

Shoulder   See *Rim.*

Slip   A mixture of clay, water, and other materials that aid flow, resulting in a mixture with a cream-like consistency. It can be used in manufacture (see *Casting*) and in decoration (see *Engobe* and *Slip Trailing*). It can also be applied with a brush.

Slip Coating   See *Engobe.*

Slip Decoration   See *Engobe* and *Slip Trailing.*

Slip Trailing   Slip is applied to the greenware through a tube or nozzle, much like icing is applied to a cake.

Snack Plate   See *Party Plate.*

Shirred egg dish: Universal's Mt. Vernon shape.

Specialty Ware   A term used by dinnerware manufacturers that applied to other lines they made: card plates, children's sets, jardinieres, jumbo cups, salad sets, spittoons, tea sets, and much more.

Sponge Ware   Color is applied with a sponge or rag in a random or precise pattern.

Sprig   See *Applied Decoration.*

Squeeze-bag Technique   See *Slip Trailing.*

Stamping   Rubber or sponge stamps with handles (like the ones you might use for the return address on an envelope) were used for backstamps (see "Background on Marks") and decorations.

St. Denis   See *Cups.*

Stick-handled Casserole   See *French Casserole.*

Stock Decal   A decal that is not owned exclusively by one particular pottery but can be bought from the decal manufacturer by any number of potteries.

Stoneware   This ware is made from clays that have some impurities in them so that they burn to a dark color. Will stand a relatively high temperature and burn to a dense hard body, as hard and nonporous as china but lacking the light color, delicacy, and translucency. Usually covered with a salt or lead glaze.

Stroke   A decorative mark or short line made with a brush and usually applied to handles and spouts. These differ from lines in that they are freehand, rather than following the outline of a rim or spout. See also *Liner.*

Syrup Jug/Pitcher   See *Batter Set.*

Tab Handle   See *Lug Handle.*

Tableware   See *Dinnerware.*

Tankard   A tall drinking cup with a handle.

Tea and Toast   See *Party Plate.*

Terra Cotta   From the Italian meaning "cooked earth." A hard, semifired, absorbent clay used for both decorative and construction products. Colors can range from grayish to dark reddish orange, light to medium reddish brown, or strong brown to brownish or deep orange.

Texture Glaze   A colored glaze in which dripping, running, eruption, or some other controlled disturbance is introduced to heighten the decorative effect.

Throwing   Forming of a piece of ware by hand on a potter's wheel. See *Greenware.*

Toby Jug   A jug in the shape of a prosperous-looking man, or his head only, wearing a three-cornered hat, one corner of which serves as the pouring spout.

Toiletware   Toilet sets were used on (usually) marble-topped wash stands before the advent of indoor plumbing, though they were made well into the twentieth century. They consisted of some or all of the following: a brush vase (toothbrush holder) or covered brush box, chamber pot (bedroom vessel for body wastes), combinet (lidded pail, combination chamber pot and slop jar), covered soap dish or soap slab (slab could be either square, rectangular or oval, some had ribs for drainage, some could be hung on a wall), ewer and basin (pitcher and bowl) for washing, jarette (jar with lid and two handles), mouth ewer, mug, and slop jar (large pail used to receive waste water from wash basin and contents of chamber pot). Most dinnerware manufacturers also made toiletware.

Tom and Jerry   A hot punch made from rum, a beaten egg, milk or water, sugar and spices. I assume that Tom and Jerry bowls and mugs, made especially for this drink, date to the repeal of Prohibition, when there was a surge in the production of beer mugs and related items. The name comes from two main characters, Tom and Jerry Hawthorn, in the novel *Life in London* (1821) by Pierce Egan.

Transfer Printing   A design is etched onto a copper or steel plate, which prints it onto a piece of film that is then applied to the body in the bisque stage. A sponge is used to remove the paper, leaving behind a colored image. The colors are mixed with oil before being applied. The ware is usually then fired in a low-temperature kiln to burn off the oil and harden the color before the glaze is applied. The range of colors is limited since many colors change or fade out completely if subjected to great heat.

Translucent   A good deal of light can pass through the article. This is possible when firing has been intense enough to cause vitrification. (See *Vitrified*.)

Tunnel Kiln   See *Kiln*.

Underglaze Decoration   If designs and colors are put on the bisque before it is glazed, the decoration is known as underglaze. After the application of the decoration, a clear glaze is applied, and the ware is fired a second time. Because of the high temperatures needed to harden the glaze, underglaze decoration colors tend not to be too bright. (See *Hand Painting, Overglaze Decoration, Print and Paint, Transfer Printing*.)

Underplate   See *Liner*.

Utility Ware   Usually used in reference to stoneware (can mean earthenware as well). Refers to bowls, crocks, churns, jugs, and toilet items.

Variety Store Items   Many potteries manufactured items only for variety stores and five-and-dimes such as Woolworth. These items included ashtrays, bowls, figurines, planters, vases, and wall pockets.

Verge   The point at which the rim and well meet.

Vitrified   Glass-like. Nonporous ware that has been fired at a higher temperature than earthenware and contains silica, which makes a body nonabsorbent.

Waffle Set   See *Batter Set*.

Wall Pocket   Flat-backed vase with hole for hanging on a wall. Can be used without flowers as a decorative object.

Ware   The product of a pottery. It can describe the product at any stage of manufacture (greenware, bisque ware, decorated ware) or the output of a pottery as a whole ("The ware produced at Lenox was exceptionally fine"). It is used in both the singular and the plural.

Well   The major surface of a plate or bowl that is surrounded by the rim.

White Granite   (also White Ironstone, Pearl China, Pearl White, Pearl Granite, Porcelain Granite, Graniteware, Flintware, and Opaque China) Commercial names intended to inspire confidence in the strength of the ware, which was harder and stronger than earthenware. Ground stone was used in the body. Color varies from creamy white to bluish or grayish white.

White Ware   Pottery or porcelain with a white body, so called to distinguish it from red ware and yellow ware. See *White Granite*.

Yellow Ware   Body color varies in hue from ecru to mustard. Made from a naturally occurring clay. See *Rockingham*.

BIBLIOGRAPHY

CHAPTER AT A GLANCE

BOOKS / PERIODICALS
  Coming Attractions
BOOKS
  Bibliographies

Marks Books
Booksellers
Out-of-Print Books
PERIODICALS

BOOKS / PERIODICALS

A complete bibliography in the field of pottery and porcelain would take up a large volume of its own. The books I've listed either are related to the potteries covered herein, are of general interest to pottery collectors, or are worth reading even though they fall outside the purview of this book. Some I have used in preparing this book. Some books are so poorly done or inaccurate that I have omitted them. I have listed some out-of-print titles because they are worth looking for. I have tried to keep abreast of those books that have gone out of print, but I may have missed some.

In the case of books on specific potteries, these books are recommended. Some are excellent, others leave something to be desired in terms of accuracy of information or reliability of pricing. However, if you intend to buy or sell by mail, most dealers and collectors use these books as references.

A number of titles listed here are catalogs of museum exhibitions. I recommend them because, even though they don't have prices and vary in terms of how many pieces are pictured, they are well researched and give an excellent overview of a designer or pottery, which can only enhance your collecting.

Where possible, I have listed price and ordering information. "Prices" means that prices are printed in the book. "W/price guide" means a separate booklet is included. "Photos throughout" means black-and-white photos.

COMING ATTRACTIONS I have been told that the following books are in the works, meaning anything from being written to manuscript at a publisher. When a publisher/approximate time of publication is known, these are included.

American Bisque by Joyce Roerig (Collector Books).
Bauer by Mitch Tuchman (Chronicle Books).
Brastoff (Collector Books).
Buffalo Blue Willow by Phillip Sullivan
Cowan Pottery by Mark Bassett and Victoria Naumann
Florence Pottery by Douglas Foland.
Little Red Riding Hood by Joyce Roerig (Collector Books).
Metlox Pottery by Carl Gibbs (Collector Books, Spring '95).
Morton Pottery by Doris and Burdell Hall (L-W, Spring '95)
Oklahoma Potteries by Phyllis and Tom Bess (Schiffer, Spring '95).

Red Wing Art Pottery by Ray Reiss (Privately published: Ray Reiss, 2144 No. Leavitt, Chicago, IL 60647/Spring, '95).

Royal Copley by Joe Devine (Collector Books).

Shawnee Pottery by Pam Curran (Schiffer, Spring '95).

Twin Winton by Bev and Jim Mangus (Collector Books).

BOOKS

Altman, Seymour and Violet, *The Book of Buffalo Pottery*. Bonanza Books, division of Crown Publishers, 201 East 50th Street, New York, NY 10022. 1969. Hardcover, 8½" × 11", 192 pages. No prices. Color section, black-and-white photos throughout.

Anderson, Ross and Barbara Perry, *Diversions of Keramos: American Clay Sculpture, 1925–1950*. Everson Museum of Art, 401 Harrison Street, Syracuse, NY 13202. 1983. 118 pages. No prices. Color section, photos throughout. Catalog of the exhibit. Includes Waylande Gregory, Vally Wieselthier, Viktor Schreckengost, Thelma Winter, Edris Eckhardt, Russell Barnett Aitken, Walter Sinz and Carl Walters.

Barber, William Atlee, *The Pottery and Porcelain of the United States/Marks of American Potters*. The first and still one of the most important histories of American pottery and porcelain. [Out of Print] Order from: Arts & Crafts Quarterly Library.

Bess, Phyllis and Tom, *Frankoma Treasures*. Phyllis and Tom Bess, 14535 East 13th Street, Tulsa, OK 74108. $15.95 plus $1.50 P&H. W/Price Guide. Color section, photos throughout.

Blasberg, Robert W., *Fulper Art Pottery: An Aesthetic Appreciation 1909–1929*. Jordan-Volpe Gallery, 475 West Broadway, New York, NY 10012. 1979. Softcover, 8½" × 11", 88 pages. No prices. Color section, black and white throughout. This book was also the gallery exhibit catalog. [Out of Print]

Blasberg, Robert W., *George E. Ohr and His Biloxi Art Pottery*. J. W. Carpenter, RD 1, Box 274, Port Jervis, NY 12771. 1973. 40 pages. No prices. Photos throughout. [Out of Print]

Blasberg, Robert W., *The Unknown Ohr*. Peaceable Press, PO Box 1362, Milford, PA 18337. 1986. Softcover, 8½" × 11", 84 pages. $35. Order from: Arts & Crafts Quarterly Library. A sequel to the monograph listed above.

Bougie, Stanley J. and David A. Newkirk, *Red Wing Dinnerware*. Hearthside Books, 2246 95th Street NW, Maple Lake, MN 55358. 1980. $9.95 plus $1.50 P&H. Color section, photos throughout; catalog reprints. Price Guide: $2.50 plus .50 P&H. Dinnerware Update: $3.50 plus .75 P&H.

Bray, Hazel V., *The Potter's Art in California: 1885 to 1955*. Oakland Museum Store, 1000 Oak Street, Oakland, CA 94607. $9.95 plus $2.75 P&H (CA residents add .65 tax). No prices. Color section, photos throughout. Art potters and studio potters. Museum exhibit catalog.

Burke, Barbara Loveless Gick-, *Collector's Guide to Hull Pottery: The Dinnerware Lines*. Collector Books. Order from: Barbara Burke, 4213 Sandhurst Drive, Orlando, FL 32813. $16.95 plus $2.00 P&H. 1993. Softcover, 8½" × 11", 168 pages. W/prices. Color throughout; catalog reprints.

Buxton, Virginia Hillway, *Roseville Pottery, For Love . . . or Money*. Tymbre Hill Publishing Company. W/price indicator. Color throughout; catalog reprints. [Out of Print]

Carey, Larry and Sylvia Tompkins, *Salt and Pepper Over 1,001 Shakers*. Schiffer Publishing. 1994. $19.95 plus $2.95 P&H. You can get an auto-graphed copy for $22 which includes P&H, a $1 savings, by ordering from Larry Carey, PO Box 329, Merchanicsburg, PA 17055. Paper cover, 8½" × 11", 112 pages. Prices. Color throughout.

Carlton, Carol and Jim, *Collector's Encyclopedia of Colorado Pottery*. Collec-tor Books. 1994. $19.95 plus $2.00 P&H. Hardcover, 8½" × 11", 168 pages. Color throughout.

Ceramic Circle of Charlotte, *The Pottery of Walter Stephen*. Journal of Studies of the Ceramic Circle of Charlotte, Charlotte, NC, Volume III, 1978. Reprint: 1988. $10. Paper cover, 7" × 8½", 28 pages. Order from: Arts & Crafts Quarterly Library.

Chipman, Jack and Judy Stangler, *The Complete Collector's Guide to Bauer Pottery*. Jack Chipman, PO Box 1079, Venice, CA 90291. $14.95 plus $1 P&H. Color section; photos throughout, catalog reprints. Thorough and well researched. [Out of Print]

Chipman, Jack and Judy Stangler, *Bauer Pottery Price Guide and Supplement*. Jack Chipman, see address above. $5.95 plus .50 P&H [Out of Print]

Chipman, Jack, *California Pottery*. 1992. Order from Jack Chipman, see ad-dress above. $24.95 plus $3.50 P&H (California residents add $2.35 sales tax). Hardcover, 8½" × 11", 168 pages. Prices. Large color section. Excel-lent. Required reading for California pottery collectors.

Cincinnati Art Galleries, *Rookwood*. Cincinnati Art Galleries, 635 Main Street, Cincinnati, OH 45202. 513-381-2128. $45 plus $3 P&H. A catalog of the largest auction of Rookwood ever (over 1,200 items). *Every item pictured in color.*

Clark, Garth and Margie Hughto, *A Century of Ceramics in the United States: 1878–1978*. Abbeville Press, 488 Madison Avenue, New York, NY 10022. $75 plus $2 P&H. Color section; photos throughout. A good twentieth-century historical overview. This is a revised and updated edition of *A Cen-tury of Ceramics in the United States: 1878–1978*, which is now out of print.

Cooper-Hewitt Museum, *American Art Pottery*. Distributed by University of Washington Press, Seattle, WA. 1987. Paper cover, 8½" × 11", 144 pages. No prices. $24.95. Order from Arts & Crafts Quarterly Library.

Crawford, Jean, *Jugtown Pottery: History and Design*. John F. Blair. 1964. Hardcover, 144 pages. No prices. Color section; photos throughout. Worth searching out. [Out of Print]

Dale, Ron, *George Ohr: The Mad Biloxi Potter*. 1983. 24 pages. No prices. Color section. Exhibit catalog. [Out of Print]

Dale, Sharon, *Frederick Hurten Rhead: An English Potter in America*. Erie Art Museum, 411 State Street, Erie, PA 16501. $25 plus $2 P&H. No prices. Color section, photos throughout. If you have any interest in pottery design or designers, buy this book.

Darling, Sharon, *Teco: Art Pottery of the Prairie School*. Erie Art Museum, 411 State Street, Erie, PA 16501. $34.95 plus $2 P&H. 1989.

DePasquale, Dan and Gail, *Red Wing Collectibles*. $9.95 ppd.

DePasquale, *Red Wing Stoneware*. $9.95 ppd. DePasquale, 404 Ridgeway, Norfolk, NE 68701.

Derwich, Jenny B. and Dr. Mary Latos, *Dictionary Guide to American Pottery and Porcelain (19th & 20th Century)*. Jenstan, PO Box 674, Franklin, MI 48025. 1984. Softcover, 8½" × 11". $30 (includes P&H). No prices. Color section, no other photos. Encyclopedic listing of hundreds of potteries.

Dickota Pottery Catalog. Roger Sannes, 16 City Center Mall, Grand Forks, ND 58201. $5 (includes postage). No prices. Xerox of undated catalog.

Dietz, Ulysses G., *The Newark Museum Collection of American Art Pottery.* The Newark Museum, 40 Washington Street, Newark, NJ 07101. 1984. Softcover, 128 pages, 8½" × 11".

Dubiel, Jay and Bruce Johnson, *Dedham Pottery Catalog: 1938.* Dedham Foloio, PO Box 826, Halifax, VA 24558. $9.95 plus $1 P&H. No prices. Photos throughout. A reprint of the only known catalog with a preface by Marilee Meyer. Essential.

Duke, Harvey, *Hall China, A Guide for Collectors.* ELO Books, PO Box 020627, Brooklyn, NY 11202. $14.95 plus $1.50 P&H. Color throughout.

Duke, Harvey, *Hall 2.* ELO Books, PO Box 020627, Brooklyn, NY 11202. $14.95 plus $1.50 P&H. Color section, photos throughout. With its companion, the best reviewed books on Hall China.

Duke, Harvey, *Hall Price Guide Update.* ELO Books, Box 020627, Brooklyn, NY 11202. $7.50 plus $1 P&H. Current prices for all items in the above two books.

Duke, Harvey, *Stangl Pottery.* Wallace-Homestead. $19.95 plus $2.50 P&H. Order from Buttzville Center, Box 106, Buttzville, NJ 07829. 1993. Prices. Paper cover, 7" × 10", 160 pages. Color section, photos throughout; catalog reprints.

Easley, Shirley, *Jewel T. Reprints.* Shirley Easley, 120 West Dowell Road, McHenry, IL 60050. With prices. $14.95 plus $2 P&H. Highlights from Jewel Tea catalogs featuring Autumn Leaf and other dinnerware.

Eidelberg, Martin, *Eva Zeinsel: Designer for Industry.* University of Chicago Press, 11030 So. Langley Avenue, Chicago, IL 60628. No prices. Color and black-and-white photos throughout. Exhibit catalog.

Eidelberg, Martin, Editor, *From Our Native Clay: Art Pottery from the Collections of The American Ceramic Arts Society.* Turn of the Century Editions, 250 West Broadway, New York, NY 10013. 1987. Hard cover, 9" × 12", 112 pages. Order from Arts & Crafts Quarterly Library. Issued in conjunction with an exhibit at Christies.

Enge, Delleen, *Franciscan: Embossed Handpainted.* Delleen Enge, 154 East El Roblar Drive, Suite 10, Ojai, CA 93023. $19.95 plus $2 P&H. Paper cover, 8½" × 11", 96 pages. Colors; catalog reprints.

Evans, Paul, *Art Pottery of the United States.* Feingold & Lewis Publishing, 1088 Madison Avenue, New York, NY 10028. $45 plus $2 P&H. No prices. Color section; photos throughout. The classic updated.

Everson Museum of Art, *American Heroes Portrayed in Ceramics.* Everson Museum of Art, 401 Harrison Street, Syracuse, NY 13202. 1976. 24 pages. No prices. Photos throughout. Exhibit catalog.

Everson Museum of Art, *Grueby.* Everson Museum of Art, 401 Harrison Street, Syracuse, NY 13202. No prices. Four color photos, some black-and-white. Catalog of the museum exhibit. [Out of Print]

Everson Museum of Art, *Onondaga Pottery.* Everson Museum of Art, 401 Harrison Street, Syracuse, NY 13202. No prices. Photos throughout. 1973. 8 pages. Catalog of the exhibit. Early stoneware potteries of Onondaga County, NY.

Fogleman, Marv, *Franciscan Price Guide.*

Fogleman, Marv, *Metlox Price Guide* These guides are $12 *each* (postage paid). Order from: Marv's Memories, 1914 W. Carriage Drive, Santa

Ana, CA 92704. 1994 (they will be kept updated). Paper cover, 5½" × 8½", 16 pages.

Frelinghuysen, Alice Cooney, *American Porcelain: 1770–1920*. Metropolitan Museum of Art, 5th Avenue at 82nd Street, New York, NY 10028. $40. No prices. Color and black-and-white throughout. No prices. Catalog of the exhibit. A wealth of information.

Garmon, Lee and Doris Frizzell, *Collecting Royal Haeger*. Collector Books. $19.95 plus $2 P&H. W/prices. Large color section, black-and-white photos throughout; catalog reprints.

Gaston, Mary Frank, *American Belleek*. Mary Frank Gaston, PO Box 32, Bryan, TX 77806. $19.95 plus $1 P&H. W/prices. Color throughout.

Gates, William C., Jr., *The City of Hills and Kilns: Life and Work in East Liverpool, Ohio*. The East Liverpool Historical Society, East Liverpool, Ohio 43920. Fascinating history of a pottery town. [Out of Print]

Gates, William C., Jr. and Dale Ormered *The East Liverpool Pottery District*. Society for Historical Archaeology. East Liverpool Museum of Ceramics, 400 East Fifth Street, East Liverpool, OH 43920. $20 plus $3 P&H. Histories of the potteries and over 2,000 marks illustrated with chronological information for this important pottery center.

Gifford, David Edwin, *Niloak: A Reference and Value Guide*. 1993. Hardcover, 8½" × 11", 256 pages. Order from: David Edwin Gifford, PO Box 7617, Little Rock, AR 72217. $19.95 plus $2 P&H. W/prices. Color throughout; catalog reprints.

Hall, Burdell and Doris, *Morton's Potteries: 99 Years*. 1983. B and B Antiques, 210 West Sassafras Drive, Morton, IL 61550. $10 plus $1.50 P&H. Updated price guide (1992), $3 post-paid. Color section; black-and-white photos throughout.

Harms, Irene, *Beautiful Rosemeade*. Irene J. Harms, 2316 West 18th Street, Sioux Falls, SD 57104. $19 plus $1 P&H. 1986. W/prices. Color throughout; advertising reprints.

Heaivilin, Annise Doring, *Grandma's Tea Leaf Ironstone*. Wallace-Homestead Book Company, One Chilton Way, Radnor, PA 19089. $19.95. Price guide is free with book, $2.95 if ordered separately. Primarily English, but has a good amount of info about United States Tea Leaf production.

Hennessey, William J., *Russel Wright: American Designer*. MIT Press, 55 Hayward Street, Cambridge, MA 02142. $15 plus $2.50 P&H. No prices. Color section, black-and-white photos throughout. Catalog of the traveling museum exhibit.

Henzke, Lucille, *American Art Pottery*. Thomas Nelson Inc., New York, NY. Color section, photos throughout; catalog reprints. No prices. The first important study. [Out of Print]

Henzke, Lucille, *Art Pottery of America*. $45. Order from: Arts & Crafts Quarterly Library. No prices. Color section, photos throughout: catalog reprints. Both books are much more than just pretty pictures.

Henzke, Lucille, *Pennsbury Pottery*. Schiffer Publishing. 1990. $24.95. Paper cover, 8½" × 11", 128 pages.

Hibel, DeFalco and Rago, *The Fulper Book*. Hard cover: $55, paper cover: $25. Order from: Arts & Crafts Quarterly Library.

Holthaus, Tim and Jim Petzold, *A Collector's Inventory and Price Guide for Ceramic Arts Studio*. Ceramic Arts Studio Collectors Association, PO Box

46, Madison, WI 53701. $10. Soft cover, 8½" × 11". W/prices. No photos. Updated yearly.

Hoopes, Ron, *The Collector's Guide and History of Gonder Pottery*. L-W Book Sales, PO Box 69, Gas City, IN 46933. $12.95 plus $2 P&H. 1992. Softcover, 5½" × 8½", 132 pages. Prices. Color throughout; catalog reprints.

Hull, Joan Gray, *Hull, the Heavenly Pottery*. $19.95 plus $1.05 P&H. Third Edition, 1993. Paper cover, 5½" × 8½", 128 pages. Prices. Color throughout.

Hull, Joan Gray, *Hull Shirt Pocket Price List*. $7.95 plus $1.05 P&H. 1994. Paper cover, 3½" × 5½", 52 pages. Order both books from: Joan Gray Hull, 1376 Nevada SW, Huron, SD 57350.

Huxford, Sharon and Bob, *Fiesta*. W/prices. Color throughout.

Huxford, Sharon and Bob, *McCoy Pottery*. W/prices. Color throughout.

Huxford, Sharon and Bob, *Roseville Pottery, First Series*.

Huxford, Sharon and Bob, *Roseville Pottery, Second Series*. W/price guide. Color throughout, also black-and-white photos and catalog reprints.

Huxford, Sharon and Bob, *Weller Pottery*. W/price guide. Color throughout; catalog reprints. Each of the above titles is $19.95 plus $1.50 P&H. Collector Books.

Jasper, Joanne, *The Collector's Encyclopedia of Homer Laughlin China*. Collector Books. 1993. $24.95 plus $2. Hardcover, 8½" × 11", 208 pages. Prices. Color throughout; catalog reprints.

Kovel, Ralph and Terry, *Kovels' American Art Pottery: The Collector's Guide to Makers, Marks and Factory Histories*. Crown Publishers, Inc., 201 East 50th Street, New York, NY 10022. 1993. $60 plus P&H. Hardcover, 9" × 12", 336 pages. No prices. Color and black-and-white throughout. Thorough overview.

Laumbach, Sabra Olson, *Harrington Figurines*. Order from: Sabra Olson Laumbach, c/o Antiques Minnesota Inc., 1516 East Lake Street, Minneapolis, MN 55407. 1985. $19.95 plus $2 P&H. Hardcover, 8½" × 11", 72 pages. Prices. Color throughout.

Lehner, Lois, *Lehner's Encyclopedia of U. S. Marks on Pottery, Porcelain and Clay*. Collector Books. $24.95 plus $2 P&H. Covers over 1,500 potteries and 8,000 marks. Truly encyclopedic.

Lehner, Lois, *Complete Book of American Kitchen and Dinnerware*. Wallace-Homestead. 240 pages, black-and-white photos throughout, 125 photos. No prices. [Out of Print]

Levin, Elaine, *The History of American Ceramics: 1607 to the Present* (From Pipkins and Bean Pots to Contemporary Forms). 352 pages, 352 illustrations (252 color, 100 black-and-white), Harry Abrams, 1988. $65 plus shipping.

Luckin, Richard, *Dining on Rails*. RK Publishing, 621 Cascade Court, Golden, CO 80403-1581. 1994. Softcover, 8½" × 11". $49.95 plus $5.50 P&H. No prices. Lavish black-and-white photos throughout. First edition is out of print. This is the expanded third edition, which includes everything from the first two editions and much new material.

Luckin, Richard, *Teapot Treasury (and Related Items)*. RK Publishing, 621 Cascade Court, Golden, CO 80403–1581. $24.95 postpaid. No prices. Lots of black-and-white photos throughout.

Mangus, Jim and Bev, *Shawnee Pottery: An Identification and Value Guide*. Collector Books. Order from The Manguses, 5147 Broadway NE, Louisville,

OH 44641. $24.95 plus $2 P&H. 1994. Hardcover, 8¹/₂" × 11", 256 pages. Prices. Color throughout.

Martin, Jim and Bette Cooper, *Monmouth-Western Stoneware*. Wallace-Homestead Book Company, Radnor, PA. No prices. Color section, black-and-white photos throughout; catalog reprints. [Out of Print]

McCurdy, F. Earl and Jane A McCurdy, *A Collector's Guide and History of Uhl Pottery*. W/price guide. Color section, black-and-white photos throughout. [Out of Print]

McDonald, Ann Gilbert, *All About Weller: A History & Collector's Guide to Weller Pottery*. Antique Publications, PO Box 553, Marietta, OH 45750. $24.95. Price guide: $2.50. Add $2.50 P&H. Color section, photos throughout; catalog reprints. The most authoritative book on Weller.

McIntyre, Douglas W., *The Official Guide to Railroad Dining Car China*. Golden Spike Enterprises, PO Box 422, Williamsville, NY 14221. $39.95 + $3.50 P&H (UPS) + 8% sales tax for NYS residents. 1990. Softcover, 8¹/₂" × 11", 204 pages. Forty-page color section, black-and-white photos throughout.

Meugniot, Elinor, *Old Sleepy Eye*. The Homestead Press, PO Box 50415, Tulsa, OK 74150. 1979. W/price guide. Color section, photos throughout. [Out of Print]

Michigan State University & Ars Ceramica, Ltd., *Highlights of Pewabic Pottery*. Ars Ceramica, Ltd., PO Box 7500, Ann Arbor, MI 48107. 1977. 32 pages. No prices. Color and black-and-white throughout. Adapted from "Pewabic Pottery: An Official History" by Bleicher, Hu and Uren. [Out of Print]

Montgomery, Susan, *The Ceramics of William H. Grueby*. 1993. Hardcover: $55, paper cover: $40. 160 pages. Color section; photos throughout. Order from: Arts & Crafts Quarterly Library.

Morris, Sue and Dave, *Watt Pottery: An Identification and Value Guide*. Collector Books. $22 includes P&H (Iowa residents add sales tax). 1992. Hardcover, 8¹/₂" × 11", 160 pages. Prices. Color throughout.

Morris, Sue, *Purinton Pottery*. Collector Books. 1994. $27.95 includes P&H (Iowa residents add sales tax). Hardcover, 8¹/₂" × 11", 272 pages. Prices. Color throughout. Order both titles from: Susan Morris, PO Box 708–DZ, Mason City, IA 50402.

Nelson, Marion John, *Art Pottery of the Midwest*. University Art Museum, University of Minnesota, Minneapolis, MN. 1988. Paper cover, 10" × 8", 120 pages. No prices. Color section; photos throughout. This is the catalog of the exhibition.

Nelson, Maxine Feek, *Versatile Vernon Kilns, Book II*. [Out of Print]

Nelson, Maxine Feek, *Versatile Vernon Kilns, Book III*. Maxine Feek Nelson, 873 Marigold Court, Carlsbad, CA 92008. 1994. $24.95 plus $2 P&H. Hardcover, 8¹/₂" × 11", 256 pages. Prices. Color throughout; catalog reprints. Great depth of information.

Nelson, Scott, *A Collector's Guide to Van Briggle Pottery*. Scott Nelson, PO Box 5327, Rockville, MD 20851. $30 for book, $3 for price guide, $2 P&H. Color section, photos throughout. Thorough mark/dating section. Meticulous research.

Newbound, Betty, *Blue Ridge Dinnerware*. Collector Books. $14.95 plus $2 P&H. Prices. Color throughout.

Perry, Barbara, Ed., *American Ceramics: The Collection of Everson Museum of Art*. Rizzoli International. $75 (hardcover), $35 (softcover).

Pfaltzgraff, *Pfaltzgraff: America's Potter*. The Pfaltzgraff Company, PO Box 2026, York, PA 17405–2026. $19.95 plus shipping. Color section, photos throughout. No prices. Thorough mark/dating section. Catalog of the York Historical Society exhibit.

Pickel, Susan E., *From Kiln to Kitchen: American Ceramic Design in Tableware*. Illinois State Museum. 1980. 16 pages. No prices. Photos throughout. Catalog of the exhibit.

Poesch, Jessie, *Newcomb Pottery: An Enterprise for Southern Women*. Schiffer Publishing. $14.95 plus P&H. No prices. Color and black-and-white throughout. Includes catalog of the museum exhibit, extensive mark/dating and signature section.

Reed, Cleota, *Henry Chapman Mercer and the Moravian Pottery and Tile Works*. University of Pennsylvania Press. $59.95. Hard cover, 256 pages. Color and black-and-white. Order from: Arts & Crafts Quarterly Library.

Roberts, Brenda, *Hull Pottery*. Color and black-and-white throughout; catalog reprints.

Roberts, Brenda, *The Ultimate Encyclopedia of Hull Pottery*. $41.95 plus $4 P&H. Ultimate is the correct word.

Roberts, Brenda, *Companion*. $24.95 plus $3 P&H. Brenda Roberts, Route 2, Highway 65 So., Marshall, MO 65340.

Roerig, Fred and Joyce, *The Collector's Encyclopedia of Cookie Jars*. 1991. $24.95 plus $2 P&H. Hardcover, 8¹/₂" × 11", 312 pages. W/updated prices. Color throughout.

Roerig, Fred and Joyce, *The Collector's Encyclopedia of Cookie Jars, Book II* 1994. $24.95 plus $2 P&H. Hardcover 8¹/₂" × 11", 400 pages, W/prices. Color throughout. No duplications from the first book. Order both from: The Roerigs, Route 2, Box 504, Walterboro, SC 29488. The two best books on cookie jars.

Roller, Gayle, Kathleen Rose and Joan Berkwitz, *The Hagen-Renaker Handbook*. Self-published, Gayle Roller, PO Box 1866, San Marcos, CA 92079. 1989. $40 (includes P&H; CA residents add state tax). Paper cover, 8¹/₂" × 11", 80 pages. No prices. Large color section; large black-and-white section. Reprints from catalog sheets throughout.

Rosenthal, Lee, *Catalina: Tile of the Magic Isle*. Tile Heritage, $15. Paper cover, 96 pages. Color photos. Order from: Arts & Crafts Quarterly Library.

Sanford, Martha and Steve, *The Guide to Brush-McCoy Pottery*. Self-published, Martha and Steve Sanford, 230 Harrison Avenue, Campbell, CA 95008. 1992. $40 plus $3 P&H (CA residents add 8.25% sales tax). Hardcover, 9" × 12", 144 pages. W/price guide. Lavish color throughout; includes many catalog reprints in color.

Sasicki, Richard & Josie Fania, *The Collector's Encyclopedia of Van Briggle Art Pottery*. Collector Books. $24.95 plus $2 P&H. 1993. Hardcover, 8¹/₂" × 11", 144 pages. Prices. Color throughout; catalog reprints.

Schneider, Robert, *Coors Rosebud Pottery*. Self-published, Robert Schneider, 3808 Carr Place No., Seattle, WA 98103. $12.95 plus $1 P&H. Prices. Color throughout; catalog reprints.

Spargo, John, *Early American Pottery and China*. Charles E. Tuttle Company, PO Box 410, 28 So. Main Street, Rutland, VT 05701. $12.50 plus $2 P&H.

Teftt, Gary and Bonnie, *Red Wing Potters & Their Wares*. Locust Enterprises, W174 N9422 Devonwood Road, Menomonee Falls, WI 53051. $24.95 ppd. (hardcover) or $18.95 ppd. (softcover). Add $1.50 for price guide ($2.10

ppd. if ordered separately). Color section, photos throughout; catalog reprints.

Thompson, Dennis and Bryce Watt, *Watt Pottery: A Collector's Reference with Price Guide*. Order from: Dennis Thompson, Box 26067, Fairview Park, OH 44126. 1994. $39.95 plus $2.95 P&H. Hardcover, 8½" × 11", 240 pages. Prices. Color throughout; catalog reprints.

Vanderbilt, Duane, *The Collector's Guide to Shawnee Pottery*. Collector Books. Order from Vanderbilt, 4040 Westover Drive, Indianapolis, IN 46268. 1992. $19.95 plus $2 P&H. Hardcover, 8½"× 11", 160 pages. Prices. Color throughout; catalog reprints.

Viehl, Lyndon C., *The Clay Giants: The Stoneware of Red Wing, Goodhue County, Minnesota, Book 3*. Wallace-Homestead Book Company, One Chilton Way, Radnor, PA 19089. $24.95. Price guide is free with book, $2.95 if ordered separately. P&H is $2 for the first book and $.50 each additional book. No color, copious photos throughout; catalog reprints.

Webb, Frances Finch, *Kay Finch Ceramics*. Frances Finch Webb, 1589 Gretel Lane, Mountain View, CA 94040. 1992. 12.95 plus $2 P&H. Paper cover, 8½" × 11", 40 pages. No prices. Black-and-white catalog reprints throughout.

Weiss, Peg, Editor, *Adelaide Alsop Robineau: Glory in Porcelain*. Syracuse University Press. 1981. 252 pages. Order from: Everson Museum of Art, 401 Harrison Street, Syracuse, NY 13202. No prices. Color section, photos throughout.

Wolfe, Leslie and Marjorie, *Royal Copley*. Collector Books.

Wolfe, Leslie and Marjorie, *More About Royal Copley*. Collector Books. $14.95/each book. Paper cover, 6" × 9", 128 pages. Color throughout.

Bibliographies

Each of these books has its separate strengths; the Weidner is more extensive, but the Strong is annotated.

Strong, Susan R., *History of American Ceramics: An Annotated Bibliography*. The Scarecrow Press, 52 Liberty Street, Box 4167, Metuchen, NJ. 1983. Hardcover, 208 pages. $19.50 plus $2.50 P&H. No prices. No photos.

Weidner, Ruth Irwin, *American Ceramics Before 1930*. Greenwood Press, Congressional Information Service, Inc., 88 Post Road West, Westport, CT 06881. $36.95 plus $3 P&H. No prices. No photos.

Marks Books

The three titles I have listed are by Barber, Gates and Lehner (see above). For a discussion of these titles, see *Marks* in the "How to Use This Book" section.

Booksellers

There are many good booksellers that carry titles of interest to pottery collectors. I list two.

Arts & Crafts Quarterly, 9 So. Main Street, Lambertville, NJ 08530. 609-397-4104. Arts & Crafts Quarterly Library carries some titles that are available nowhere else. These are noted in the listings above.

L-W Book Sales. 1-800-777-6450. L-W Book Sales sells its own publications plus most titles from other publishers. If you buy six or more, mix or match, they will give you the wholesale discount price which is often a good savings.

Out-of-Print Books

I have included certain out-of-print titles in the above listing because I believe they are worth having if they can be found. This can be a catch-as-catch-can process. Some book dealers occasionally have one or two. The catalog below can be a good source.

Keramos, PO Box 7500, Ann Arbor, MI 48107. Free catalog. Specialists in books on ceramics, Oriental art and fine arts; current and out-of-print.

PERIODICALS

For the following newspapers, a good idea would be to request a sample issue and current subscription rates. Also see Clubs/Newsletters for a more extensive listing of specialized publications.

The Antique Trader, PO Box 1050, Dubuque, IA 52001
The Daze, 10271 State, Otisville, MI 48463.

CLUBS / NEWSLETTERS / CONVENTIONS / CALENDAR

Almost all clubs publish newsletters, and subscribing to a newsletter is like being in a club. And many clubs and newsletters sponsor annual conventions. I suggest sending a large self-addressed stamped envelope for information or three dollars for a sample newsletter; quality varies greatly, so you should judge for yourself.

Most of the newsletters are quality publications with articles by competent researchers. However, a few have been known to publish articles with inaccurate information. The more you know, the more you can assess the accuracy of what you read.

I have revised the way in which I list these resources. I am not breaking them down into "club" or "newsletter" lists because of overlap.

The word "club" indicates that there is a board of directors, and the possibility of local activities. This is followed in the entry by newsletter and/or annual convention information. An annual convention does not necessarily imply a club; many wonderful and successful conventions are run by newsletter publishers or individuals.

These resources are followed by a list of annual conventions and shows in a chronological format. All listings are subject to change; always call to get the latest information, especially before traveling.

Abingdon Pottery Collectors Mrs. Elaine Westover, RR 1, Abingdon, IL 61410. Club: newsletter and convention.

American Art Pottery Association Jean Oberkirsch, Secretary/Treasurer, 125 East Rose, St. Louis, MO 63119. Club: bimonthy Journal of the American Art Pottery Association and annual convention.

Arts & Crafts Quarterly 9 So. Main Street, Lambertville, NJ 08530. Pottery as well as other Arts & Crafts products.

Bauer News Ceased publication.

Blue and White Pottery Club 224 12 Street NW, Center Point, IA 52405. Newsletter.

Blue Ridge Club Phyllis Ledford, Rte 3, Box 161, Erwin, TN 37650. Annual show and sale.

Blue Ridge Newsletter Norma Lilly, 144 Highland Drive, Rte 5, Box 62, Blountville, TN 37617.

Camark Collectors Newsletter In formation at time of publication. Linda Lane, 1529 Kempton Court, Longmont, CO 80501.

Ceramic Arts Studio Collector Ceramic Arts Studio Collectors Association, PO Box 46, Madison, WI 53701. Bimonthly newsletter.

Cookie Jarrin' Joyce and Fred Roerig, Rte 2, Box 504, Walterboro, SC 29488. Bimontly newsletter.

The Copley Connection Ceased publication.

Cowan Pottery Journal Cowan Pottery Museum of Rocky River Library, 1600 Hampton Road, Rocky River, OH 44116. Twice a year; $3 donation per issue.

Dedham Pottery Collectors Society Newsletter c/o Jim Kaufman, 248 Highland Street, Dedham, MA 02026. Quarterly newsletter.

Franciscan Collectors Club, USA 8412 Fifth Avenue NE, Seattle, WA 98115. Quarterly newsletter. FAX: 206.362.5520, E-Mail: gmcb1@aol. com.

Frankoma Collectors Bob Hase, 244 Fox Lane, Belvidere, IL 61008. Club. Bimonthly newsletter; annual convention.

Friends of Terra Cotta c/o Susan Tunick, 34 Gramercy Park, New York, NY 10003.

The Glass Menagerie c/o Susan Candelaria, 5440 El Arbol Drive, Carlsbad, CA 92008. Despite its name, this bimontly newsletter is devoted to model animals, with a strong emphasis on Hagen-Renaker and Breyer.

Gonder Collector Ron Hoopes, PO Box 4263, North Myrtle Beach, SC 29597. Quarterly. Annual meeting.

Hagen-Renaker See The Glass Menagerie.

Hall China Encore Kim Boss, 317 No. Pleasant Street, Oberlin, OH 44074.

Head Hunters Maddy Gordon, PO Box 83-H, Scarsdale, NY 10583. For collectors of head vases. Quarterly newsletter; annual convention.

Hull Pottery Association c/o Lowell Thomsen, 4 Hilltop Road, Council Bluffs, IA 51503.

Hull Pottery Newsletter Dan and Kimberly Pfaff, 466 Foreston Place, Webster Grove, MO 63119.

International Willow Collectors c/o Barbara Stevens, 86 No. Portwine Road, Roselle, IL 60172. Annual convention.

Laughlin Eagle Richard G. Racheter, 1270 63rd Terrace So., St. Petersburg, FL 33705. Bimonthly newsletter.

Mid-America Reamer Collectors Ray Maxwell, 222 Cooper Avenue, Elgin, IL 60120.

Minnesota Art Pottery Association Gordon Hoppe, 10120 32nd Avenue No., Plymouth, MN 55441. Art pottery enthusiasts who meet informally from September to June.

National Autumn Leaf Collector's Society Beverly Robbins, 7346 Shamrock Drive, Indianapolis, IN 46217. Club. Bimonthly newsletter; annual and local conventions.

National Reamer Collectors' Association Larry Branstad, 405 Benson Road No., Frederic, WI 54837. Annual convention. Pottery and glass reamers.

The N(elson) M(cCoy) Express c/o Jean Bushnell, 3081 Rock Creek Drive, Broomfield, CO 80020. Monthly newsletter.

North Dakota Pottery Collectors Society Todd A. Hanson, 506 Third Street NW, Mandan, ND 58554. Club. Quarterly newsletter and convention.

Novelty Salt & Pepper Shakers Club Irene Thornburg, 581 Joy Road, Battle Creek, MI 49017. Club: newsletter and convention. Many regional chapters.

Ohio Willow Society c/o Marge LaLonde, 4820 Center Road, Rte 83, Avon, OH 44011.

Old Sleepy Eye Collectors Club of America, Inc. Box 12, Monmouth, IL 61462. Newsletter.

Piebirds Unlimited   c/o Lilian M. Cole, 14 Harmony School Road, Fleming-ton, NJ 08822. Newsletter.

The Porcelier Paper   Shirley Hall, 21 Tamarac Swamp Road, Wallingford, CT 06492. Bimonthly newsletter.

Pottery Lover's Newsletter   Pat Sallaz, 4969 Hudson Drive, Stow, OH 44224. Quarterly; specifically about the annual Pottery Lovers Reunion festival in Zanesville and Roseville, OH in July.

Purinton Pastimes   Lori Hinterleiter and Jim Schulte, 20401 Ivybridge Court, Gaithersburg, MD 20879. Quarterly newsletter; annual convention.

Red Wing Collectors Society   c/o Ken and Deedee Gorgan, PO Box 124, Neosho, WI 53059. Club: bimontly newsletter and convention. Local chapters.

Shawnee Pottery Collectors   PO Box 713, New Smyrna Beach, FL 32170-0713. Newsletter ten times/year (*Exclusively Shawnee*); annual convention.

Southwest Art Pottery Association   Jack Kilgore, Rosebud Antiques, 345 Main Street, Rosebud, TX 76570. Art pottery enthusiasts who meet informally from September to May.

Stangl/Fulper Collectors Club   PO Box 64, Changewater, NJ 07831. Club; quarterly newsletter and annual meeting. Spring auction, Fall show and sale.

Tile Heritage Foundation   PO Box 1850, Healdsburg, CA 95448. 707-431-8452. For preservation, research and restoration of ceramic surfaces. A non-profit corporation. Newsletter; annual meeting.

Uhl Collector's Society   Tom and Donna Uebelhor, 233 E. Timberlin Lane, Huntingburg, IN 47542. Club. Bimonthly newsletter; annual convention.

Vernon Views   PO Box 945, Scottsdale, AZ 85252. Quarterly newsletter for Vernon Kilns collectors.

Watt Collectors Association   PO Box 184, Galesburg, IL 61402. Club. Quarterly newsletter (*Watt's News*); annual convention.

Watt Pottery Collectors USA   Box 26067, Fairview Park, OH 44126. Quarterly newsletter (*Spoutings*); annual convention.

White Ironstone Club   Ernie Dieringer, WICA Inc., Box 536, Redding Ridge, CT 06896.

Willow Society of North Texas   PO Box 13382, Arlington, TX 76094. Bimonthly meetings.

The Willow Word   PO Box 13382, Arlington, TX 76094. Bimonthly newsletter.

Wisconsin Pottery Association   PO Box 1171, Madison, WI 53701. Pottery enthusiasts who meet informally once a month.

CHRONOLOGICAL CALENDAR

One of the nice things about club involvement is the growth of regional chapters that sponsor their own activities. Please check with the national clubs that can give you more information about these events.

This listing is general and is based on conventions held in 1994. Most conventions take place around the same weekend of the same month every year, but of course are subject to change.

April

Midwest Hull Pottery Collectors
Tile Heritage Foundation, PO Box 1850, Healdsburg, CA 95448
American Art Pottery Association

May

Stangl/Fulper Collectors Club/Auction. Bob Perzel: 908-782-9631
Watt Pottery Convention

June

East Liverpool Collectors' Convention, East Liverpool, OH
Blue Willow Collectors
North Dakota Pottery Collectors
National Autumn Leaf Collectors Club
Uhl Collectors Society

July

Red Wing Collectors Society
Novelty Salt and Pepper Shaker Collectors
Hull Collectors Convention, Crooksville, OH
Watt Fest
Pottery Lovers Reunion, Zanesville, OH
McCoy Lovers Reunion
Reamer Collectors

August

Abingdon Collectors Club

September

Ohio Autumn Leaf Show

October

All-American All-Pottery Show and Sale, Flemington, NJ. Bob Perzel:
   908-782-9631
APEC (American Pottery, Earthenware and China), Springfield, IL. Norman
   and Barbara Haas: 517-639-8537
E.S.C.A.P.A.D.E. (*E*astern *S*tates *C*hina, *A*merican *P*ottery *A*nd *D*innerware
   *E*xhibition), Laurence Harbor, NJ. Joe Miklos: 908-738-5677

TRAVELER'S DIRECTORY

There are three kinds of places you can visit to enhance your collecting experience. Whether you are traveling or lucky enough to live nearby, check them out.

FACTORY Seeing pottery being made will broaden your understanding of the processes involved and the nature of items in your collection.

FACTORY OUTLET It's always useful to see what new production is being done, especially where questions of reissues and reproductions are concerned. And they are wonderful places to pick up souvenirs and gifts for friends.

MUSEUM No book, however good, can substitute for seeing pottery in person. And you can also get a sense of the scope of a pottery's output from seeing good collections. And who knows, you may find something new to collect.

Hours, days, and phone numbers are subject to change. Always call ahead before making definite plans. Also, if you are visiting a museum, check to make sure that what you want to see is on display. Some exhibits are rotated, while others are permanent. Factory tours are free. For group tours, write and see what special arrangements need to be made.

ARKANSAS

Little Rock

The Old State House, 300 West Markham, 72201. 501-324-9685. An agency of the Department of Arkansas Heritage. Camark collection.

CALIFORNIA

Oakland

The Oakland Museum, 1000 Oak Street, 94607. 415-273-3005. Open Wednesday to Sunday. Art Department has 400-piece collection, 50 to 60 items on display at one time, Arts and Crafts and Studio Potters featured. No commercial pottery. History Department, 415-273-3842, has separate display of commercial pottery.

COLORADO

Colorado Springs

Van Briggle Pottery, 600 So. 21st Street, 80901. 719-633-4080. Factory tour/gift shop. Extensive collection of early pieces, copies of originals. Closed Sunday.

ILLINOIS

Chicago

Chicago Historical Society, Art Institute of Chicago, Clark Street at North Avenue, Chicago, IL 60614-6099. 312-642-4600. Over 25 pieces of Teco (the largest institutional collection).

Dundee

Haeger Potteries, 7 Maiden Lane, 60118. 312-426-3441. Plant tour: 5 days. Outlet shop (in plant): 7 days. Includes museum display of Haeger pieces.

Knoxville

Knox County Historical Museum, Main Street (on the Square). The museum does not have regular hours except during the Scenic Drive. To see the collection, phone City Hall (309-289-2814; they will put you in touch with an appropriate person) or Harriet Goff (309-289-4605) to make arrangements. Over 300 pieces of Abingdon, the largest museum collection.

Lemont

Cookie Jar Museum, 111 Stephen Street, 60439. 312-257-5012. Southwest of Chicago on Rte 171. From I-55, take Lemont Road (Exit 271) and drive south into town. Owner: Lucille Brumberek. Open 7 days. On display is the owner's personal collection of over 2,000 cookie jars.

MICHIGAN

Detroit

Pewabic Pottery, 10125 East Jefferson, 48214. 313-823-0954. Historic and contemporary ceramics, drawings, and writings. Provides guided tours and organized educational programs.

MINNESOTA

Red Wing

Goodhue County Historical Society, 1166 Oak Street, 55066. 612-388-6024. Red Wing collection: good stoneware, some art pottery, and some dinnerware.

St. Paul

Minnesota History Center, 345 Kellogg Boulevard West, 55102. 612-296-0150. Developing a Red Wing collection.

NEW JERSEY

Millville

Wheaton Village. Largest collection of Stangl in the country.

Newark

The Newark Museum, 49 Washington Street, PO Box 540, 07101. 201-596-6550. A strong art pottery collection.

Trenton

New Jersey State Museum. Fulper collection.

NEW YORK

Syracuse

Everson Museum of Art, 401 Harrison Street, 13202. 315-474-6064. A collection of 3,500 pieces on permanent display in the Ceramics Gallery; approximately 1,300–1,500 pieces are American, ranging from early red ware and stoneware to the present. No commercial pieces; emphasis is on design. Strong collection of Robineau.

NORTH DAKOTA

Wahpeton

Richland County Historical Society, Museum and Rosemeade collection donated by Robert J. Hughes.

OHIO

Cincinnati

Cincinnati Art Museum, Eden Park. 513-721-5204. Excellent collection of Rookwood.

Cleveland   [See Rocky River, OH]

Cleveland Museum of Art, University Circle. 216-421-7340. A small but select collection of American pieces, including Tucker, Bennett, American Faience, Rookwood, Weller, Ohr, and twentieth-century Cleveland studio potters.

Western Reserve Historical Society, 10825 East Boulevard, 44106. 216-721-5722. Ohio art pottery including Rookwood, Roseville, Weller, Owens, and Ohr, as well as Cleveland School potters including Winter, Gregory, and Schreckengost. Some pottery displayed in period domestic settings.

Columbus

Ohio Historical Society, Interstate 71 and 17th Avenue. 614-466-4663. The Ceramics Gallery has an overview of Ohio pottery, with changing exhibits of over 100 pieces.

Crooksville

Ohio Ceramic Center, State Rte 93, 43731. (Mail: Box 200) 614-697-7021. Collection: Development of pottery from 1750 to modern. Includes exhibits on how clay is prepared, formed, glazed, and fired. [Al and Nancy Dennis: 614-697-7969 (home)]

East Liverpool   [See Newell, WV]

Hall China Company, 2356 Elizabeth Avenue. 216-385-2900. Monday to Friday, 9 AM to 1 PM.
   There is a fascinating self-guided plant tour. Little has changed in the way Hall makes its china, and you see clearly the care, skill, and patience that gives Hall its famous quality.

Hall Closet. Outside access; in the Hall factory. Monday through Saturday, 9 AM to 5 PM.
   Hall's retail shop where seconds are sold. Most of what is available here is from current production runs. There's something new almost every day. You'll get a good idea of the colors Hall is presently producing.

Museum of Ceramics, 25 Fifth Avenue. 216-386-6001. March through October, Tuesday to Saturday, 9:30 AM to 5 PM and Sunday 12 to 5 PM. [Mark Twiford]
   A warm, friendly museum that will awe you with the beauty and range of the ware made in the East Liverpool area from the 1850s to the 1930s. A highlight is the excellent Lotus Ware collection, much of which is on permanent display.

Norwich

National Road Museum, 8850 East Pike, 43767. 614-872-3143. Closed December to February.
   Over 250 pieces of Roseville and Weller on permanent display.

Rocky River   [Just west of Cleveland]

Cowan Pottery Museum, Rocky River Public Library, 1600 Hampton Road, 44116. 216-333-7610. Seven days; closed Sundays during the summer.
   From 800 to 1,000 pieces make this the largest public collection of Cowan in the country, understandable as his studio was in Rocky River. The collection has everything from production art wares to rare pieces such as Schreckengost's punch bowl and Gregory's King and Queen decanters. As well as group tours, there are group programs, either on site or at your location.

Roseville

The Robinson-Ransbottom Pottery Company, Ransbottom Road, 43777. Factory tour/outlet store (614-697-7735), 5 days. Store closed January and February.

Westerville

American Ceramic Society, 757 Brooksedge Plaza Drive, 43081–6136. 614-890-4700. Small museum.

Zanesville

Zanesville Art Center, 620 Military Road, 43701. 614-452-0741. Permanent displays and special exhibits of pottery made in Zanesville.

OKLAHOMA

Sapulpa

Frankoma Potteries, 2400 Frankoma Road, 74006. 918-224-5511. Plant tour: 6 days. Outlet shop: 7 days.

PENNSYLVANIA

Doylestown

Fonthill Museum, East Court Street, 18901. 215-348-9461. "A National Historic Landmark, [this] unusual concrete edifice boasts a tower and more than 40 different rooms." Formerly Mercer's home, Fonthill displays tens of thousands of tiles from his extensive world-wide collections, and from his factory, as well as 1,000 of his 4,000 print collection. Guided tours: 7 days.

Moravian Pottery & Tile Works, Swamp Road (Rte 313), 18901. 215-345-6722. "A National Historic Landmark operating as a living history museum producing tiles in a manner nearly identical to that employed in 1900." Self-guided tours, gift shop: 7 days.

York

The Industrial Museum of York, 217 West Princess, 17403. 717-852-7007. A collection of Pfaltzgraff pottery.

WEST VIRGINIA

Newell   (across the river from East Liverpool, Ohio)

Homer Laughlin China Company, 304-387-1300. Plant tours, outlet shop and museum.

REPLACEMENT SERVICES

These services are an excellent source for both those who don't shop flea markets, malls, or antique stores looking for a particular piece or pieces they need, and for those who do but have been having a hard time finding what they want. Essentially, these services have done all the leg work for you, saving you time and travel expenses.

All of these services will keep your wants on file and notify you when they have something you are looking for. Replacements keeps the names of the patterns you are looking for and sends you lists of everything available in that pattern. The other services will register patterns as well, but will also search for specific items.

GENERAL

Replacements, Ltd., PO Box 26029, Greensboro, NC 27420. 800-562-4462. The largest matching/replacement service in the United States. Carries all the popular patterns and many obscure ones.

PFALTZGRAFF POTTERY

David Ziegler, PO Box 105, Spring Grove, PA 17362. Carries most dinnerware lines, and deals in other Pfaltzgraff items as well, such as art pottery and stonework.

STANGL POTTERY

Popkorn, 4 Mine Street, Flemington, NJ 08822. 908-782-9631. Carries most dinnerware lines, as well as art pottery, birds and other items.

REPAIR SERVICES

For many collectors, repair of pieces is a viable option. Whether a piece is chipped, cracked, or has something missing, a good restorer can work magic. I have not had any of my own pieces repaired, but I have seen some impressive work.

One of the problems one could encounter when getting something repaired is poor quality of work. I cannot evaluate every restorer, or even a few. Nor would I wish to. What I have decided to do is list what restorers I could find, and make a few suggestions for you to keep in mind when evaluating them.

1. A good repairer will ask you some questions about your piece of pottery to determine if it falls into their area of expertise. For example, someone may work with solid glazes, but not do the handwork necessary to restore a decaled or hand-painted piece.

2. A good repairer will tell you that they want to look at your piece first, then let you know if they think they can do the work. Run, don't walk, from anyone who makes guarantees about a repair sight unseen.

3. Make sure you have a written estimate. The final cost may exceed the estimate, but the allowable percentage, usually ten percent, should be covered in the letter with the estimate. The letter should also include a time frame for the completion of the work and what course will be followed if the work is not done within the settled-upon time or a reasonable period (spell this out) afterward.

4. Ask for references. It is best to use someone in your area so you can inspect their work (ideally a friend will recommend someone they have used), but this may not be possible. A telephone call may have to do.

5. Ask how long they have been in business. I'd like to think that a shoddy worker would not survive long. True, someone may just be starting out, but you may not feel comfortable dealing with someone new to the business.

Don't worry if you do not live close to one of these restorers, as most do business via the mails.

Arizona
Shirley Vickers, PO Box 688, Pine, AZ 85544. 602-476-3703 or 817-571-4605.

Arkansas
David Brown, River's Daughter Restoration, Rte 4, Box 400L, Fayetteville, AR 72703. 501-361-2003 (days). 501-444-7210 (evenings). Specializes in matte Hull Pottery repairs.

California
Mark J. Dorian, 101 West Olive, Fresno, CA 93728.

Idaho

Sue Thiessan, 25115 Cemetary Road, Middleton, ID 83644. 208-585-3243. Specializes in Hagen-Renaker.

Illinois

Broken Art Restoration, William and Michelle Marhoefer, 1841 West Chicago Avenue, Chicago, IL 60622. 312-226-8200. Brochure. Specializes in art pottery.

Mississippi

Tice Goodson, Rte 5, Box 985, Batesville, MS 38606. 800-221-9177 or 601-563-1718. Specializes in Majolica, Roseville, Weller, Hull, Rookwood, Stone, and China.

New Jersey

Antique Restorations, Tom and Judy Aiello, 1313 Mt. Holly Road, Rte 541, Burlington Township, NJ 08016. 609-387-2587.

North Carolina

Richard Beggs, 9553 White Tail Trail, Kernersville, NC 27284.

Ohio

Old World Restorations, Inc., 347 Stanley Avenue, Cincinnati, OH 45226. 513-321-1911. Specializing in art pottery and porcelain. Brochure.

Wiebold, Inc., 413 Terrace Place, Terrace Park (Cincinnati), OH 45174. 513-831-2541. Fax: 513-831-2815. Specializing in art pottery, porcelain, and ceramics. Brochure.

Texas

David Brdecko, 115 West Virginia, McKinney, TX 75069. 214-542-3739 or 214-584-8085. Cleaning and restoration of china, pottery, and porcelain.

Virginia

John and Donna Nichols, PO Box 178, Bell Haven, VA 23306. 804-442-5964. Specializes in Boehm, Franklin, and Ispanky.

AFTERWORD / INVITATION

Some books that I have read over the years are what I think of as "heart pounders." The excitement of reading them, the sense of discovery, has felt like being on a roller coaster, turning pages and finding thrills everywhere. I hope this book has been that for you.

This is an important book to me, reflecting my love of pottery; it is a very personal book as well. While I have tried to cover every collectible pottery, I have included some that may be obscure but nonetheless are favorites of mine. I include some potteries because I have information that hasn't been published elsewhere, and I know there are people out there who will be happy to see it. I hope that some potteries will become more popular with collectors because I have covered them.

But there is still a ways to go. When I first started this project, I listed over 250 potteries that could be included. I've only done about ninety so far. So write and let me know what you would like to see covered, particularly if you have some information or expertise that will allow us, you and me, to construct a useful chapter. Perhaps you're a dealer who deals extensively in a particular pottery and knows it well. Or you're a collector with a substantial collection and an intelligent eye. Or you are doing research with the intent of writing a book. Remember, if I don't cover a pottery, it's not because I don't value that pottery, it's because I don't have enough research to feel I can do a good job myself, and/or I haven't found a suitable consultant.

Finally, I want to thank everyone who wrote and told me how happy they were with the book, how useful they found it. An author is not like a stage performer who gets immediate feedback on the quality of his/her work, so your letters are very important to me. Thanks.

Write me:

Harvey Duke
115 Montague Street
Brooklyn, NY 11201

ABOUT THE AUTHOR

HARVEY DUKE has worked in the publishing industry, as production manager and designer, for the past 25 years, handling adult and juvenile hardcover books, magazines, and paperbacks.

Extracurricular activities include many years working Off-Off-Broadway at LaMama Experimental Theater Club and the legendary Cafe Cino. He has devoted much of his time to volunteer hotlines, and particularly to training volunteers in crisis-intervention and listening skills.

He bought his first piece of pottery in 1965 and now has between four and five thousand pieces. It is considered the most representative collection of American pottery, private or public, in the country, with an emphasis on Ohio/West Virginia potteries and their output from the mid-twenties to the second World War.

Mr. Duke lectures, does appraisals, researches, and writes in the field of American pottery. His most recent book is *Stangl Pottery*. He has published the two definitive books on Hall China, as well as the seventh and eighth editions of *The Official Price Guide to Pottery and Porcelain*, a Better Homes and Gardens Book Club selection. He has written numerous articles, and consulted on the *Time-Life Encyclopedia of Collectibles* and Warman's *Americana and Collectibles*.